The Fontana Biographical
Companion to Modern Thought

Alan Bullock is Founding Master of St Catherine's College, Oxford, a Fellow of the British Academy, and former Vice-Chancellor of the University of Oxford. He has been Chairman of the Trustees of the Tate Gallery, of the Schools Council and of two official inquiries – on literacy and on industrial democracy. Among his books on twentieth-century history are *Hitler: a Study in Tyranny* and, most recently, a three-volume biography of Ernest Bevin; and he is joint editor of the Oxford History of Modern Europe.

R. B. Woodings is Senior Lecturer in Publishing at Oxford Polytechnic. Previously he taught at the University of East Anglia and worked for ten years as a senior editor with various London publishers.

The Fontana Biographical Companion to Modern Thought

Edited by
ALAN BULLOCK
and
R. B. WOODINGS
with the assistance of
John Cumming

Fontana Paperbacks

Fontana Paperbacks
8 Grafton Street, London W1X 3LA
First published 1983

Copyright © Alan Bullock, R. B. Woodings
and John Cumming 1983

A hardback edition is published by
William Collins Sons & Co. Ltd

Computer set in 8 on 8.5 point Times by
Aylesbury Keyboarding, Aylesbury, Buckinghamshire

Made and printed in Great Britain by
the University Press, Oxford

Preface

When Oliver Stallybrass joined me in editing *The Fontana Dictionary of Modern Thought*, we had reluctantly to accept that it was impossible, for reasons of space, to include biographical entries. We resolved, therefore, if the *Dictionary* proved sufficiently successful, to undertake the preparation of a further volume, self-contained but complementary to the *Dictionary* and following the same design, which would provide the biographical information, often difficult to obtain, which anyone may need in exploring the world of modern thought.

The reception of the *Dictionary of Modern Thought* was such as to encourage us to go ahead, and we began the preliminary work together. At that point, before we could start to invite contributions, the tragic death of Oliver Stallybrass robbed me of a much-prized collaborator as well as friend. The last letter I received from him urged me not to abandon the idea which we had developed together, and I have been fortunate to find in Bob Woodings a colleague who has not only grasped but extended our conception of the enterprise and shared the work of editing with me.

We should not have been able to complete our task without the help of many other people. We owe our particular thanks to Susan Burton, who, experienced through the *Dictionary*, assumed responsibility for editorial organization and administration, and for liaising between contributors and editors; and to the editorial team of Camilla Darell, Heather Dayus and Lucinda McNeile. Without Andrew Best, of Curtis Brown, neither the *Companion* nor the *Dictionary* would ever have appeared, and at every stage we have been encouraged and supported by Simon King and Helen Fraser of Fontana. The proposal to include a classified index, invaluable advice on how to design it, and its final compilation we owe to Derek Langridge. The task of proofreading has been undertaken by Anne Rieley. Our keyboarder, Margaret Davis of Aylesbury Keyboarding, has excelled in speed and accuracy. To all these, and to John Cumming who acted as joint editor in the earlier stages of putting the book together, we offer our gratitude. Finally, I wish to express my own thanks to Mrs Betty Willbery and Mrs Pam Thomas for typing and keeping track of so many drafts in Oxford.

More than 300 authors have written the entries, and without their willingness to contribute and to bear with the editors' insistent requests there would have been no book at all. To all of them, too, we wish to express our thanks and in particular to those whose willingness to help with advice on planning the entries went far beyond anything we could have expected: Daniel Bell, N. B. Chapman, Margaret Gowing, D. R. Newth, Harry Rosenberg, E. B. Smith, Donald Watt and John Willett. In addition we are most grateful for the patience of all those whom we bothered in the search after assistance or information, whether friends, colleagues or contributors.

ALCB

Introduction

When we first started planning this *Companion*, we had in mind the same need which we tried to meet in the *Fontana Dictionary* – the need which anyone, however well qualified, encounters who is tempted to explore outside his or her own field of interest and inevitably comes up against the barrier of unfamiliar names, esoteric terms and unexplained allusions. In an age of specialization as complete as ours, this is a handicap from which no one is exempt. Few people could identify more than a proportion of the names which appear in this volume; for most people it would hardly be more than a few hundred out of a total of nearly 2000.

Yet everyone will say at once, in regard to his or her own field of knowledge, that no one can begin to read about physics without feeling the need to pin down, for example, who were Kamerlingh Onnes, Max Planck, Niels Bohr, Heisenberg, Rutherford, Schrödinger, and what are the different contributions they have made; or, to take a handful of names from philosophy, who were Heidegger, Carnap, Wittgenstein, John Austin, Frege, Karl Popper, Whitehead; which of them belong to the same generation, and which of the movements of modern thought they have been associated with. Even in a good reference library it is surprisingly difficult to obtain satisfactory answers to such questions for those figures who have made their mark in the last twenty or thirty years or in the less publicized fields of knowledge. And few people have a good reference library close to where they are reading. We have therefore set out to provide such information, within a single volume, for a selection of names drawn from across the whole range of twentieth-century thought, with numerous cross-references and with carefully selected reading lists for those who want to pursue their inquiries further.

Begun very shortly after the publication of the *Dictionary*, this *Companion* adopts many of the same procedures and approaches. The editors identified the subject areas for inclusion and then sought advice as to the choice of actual entries from specialists, some of whom subsequently served as contributors themselves or recommended others. The end result of the editorial process was some 300 contributors delivering some 2000 entries. But our aim has been to produce something more than a *Who's Who*. The factual information is intended as the frame for the essential considerations: what has the particular person done that makes him or her important; why has that person to be included among the 1945 names eventually selected; what is the present evaluation of his or her work? In inviting contributors to answer such questions, we have made it clear that they should feel free to express an informed opinion of their own, with which the editors may not necessarily agree. We have made no attempt to homogenize the style of the different entries, accepting that some contributors will write more discursively or briefly than others and allowing them, within the limits of space, to express themselves naturally.

By 'modern' is meant the period from 1900 to the present. In practice this excludes almost all who died before the turn of the century or who did not produce at least some of their significant work after that date. The exceptions are a small number of outstanding figures (such as Marx, Babbage, Kierkegaard, Boole) who by dates belong securely to the nineteenth century but whose achievements were only made available, or adequately recognized, in this century as key contributions to modern thought.

In this context 'modern thought' is that body of knowledge and concepts, assumptions and relationships, originally defined by writers, philosophers, natural scientists, social scientists, artists, etc., which is broadly recognized as belonging uniquely to this century and which has progressively become available as part of a common culture and intellectual context, to be encountered and handled in everyday experience. This may be through a particular scientific discovery – the expression of a new physical concept; a particular way of understanding human behaviour – the application of psychological insight; a way of reading colours and shapes – the influence of a particular artist.

Outside the rare originators and individuals of inspired genius, the creators of modern thought are not available as a self-defined list. Instead their selection – just as the editorial weighting of particular subject areas and of the balance between specialist interests within them – has to be made as a series of necessary but contradictory judgements. From what perspective is the choice to be made – from the angle of today (i.e. from the standpoint of the knowledge now possessed) or from that of history (i.e. admitting that a subject's contemporary relevance may be slight, but at the time his or her contribution was critical)? Is the selection to be of men and women who were primarily of importance within their particular subject area, or of those who enjoy a more general influence or reputation? Is the choice to be of established, intellectually approved figures, or should the outsider, the overlooked, the played-down be picked out? Is a contemporary to be excluded because of uncertainty about the later assessment of his achievement? The issues are complex, and subject to continuing debate in which we hope our readers will participate. As we have discussed and argued out particular claims between ourselves and with advisers and contributors, the decisive factor which has emerged has been the degree to which an individual working in a particular field has modified that field's very definition and subsequent development, and remains a presence to be reckoned with by later workers.

We have taken modern thought to embrace a very wide range of subject areas, and the entries reflect that. The scope extends to literature, music and the visual arts, as well as to philosophy, religion, mathematics, psychology and the full range of the humanities, the natural sciences and the social sciences. Particular attention has been paid to those subjects or areas of interest that have either come into prominence or been developed in the twentieth century, whether cinema and photography, communications and computer studies, jazz and popular music, feminism and the counter-cultures. For practical reasons and because we have European and American readers principally in mind, we have limited the entries, with relatively few exceptions, to the western cultural scene.

The majority of names fall within categories whose inclusion no one will question. There are three groups of entries, however, which take us on to more debatable ground. Few politicians have been original thinkers or significant writers – who would remember the polemical pamphlets of Lenin or the thoughts of Chairman Mao if it were not for their roles in the world of action? On the other hand, no one seeking to penetrate modern political and social thought, not to mention much of its imaginative literature and art (the work of Camus and Pasternak, and Picasso's *Guernica*, to take only three examples) can get far without asking who was Hitler, who was Stalin – or Gandhi, or Roosevelt – and what did they do to have such an impact not only on the events, but on the minds and imaginations of the twentieth century. We believe these are questions to which a *Biographical Companion to Modern Thought* ought to provide answers, and so we have extended its scope to include not only thinkers and writers but also the most important of those whose activities created the problems with which many of the former have been preoccupied. Similar considerations justify the inclusion of a handful of representative figures from the practical worlds of the inventor, the technologist and the businessman, who have also played a major part in transforming the context of modern thought.

Some politicians – Che Guevara, for example, or John F. Kennedy – enjoy a symbolic existence as representatives of a distinctive standpoint or style of action. Such 'symbolic existence' is even more relevant to the performer, whether of the stage, screen or concert hall, some of whom (Casals, for example, Charlie Chaplin, Marilyn Monroe) have already become legends. We came to the conclusion, after much debate, that a selective group of these too had to be included because it was their skills that gave expressive form to the particular arts in which they worked, a classic expression in fact which defined possibilities and provided interpretations that have become indelibly part of the particular medium and thereby of modern consciousness. But such achievements in expressive form must equally embrace those remarkable figures whose work has redefined the lifestyles and the stock of aspirations available – whether, for example, in fashions of dress, in new genres of popular writing, or in definitive vogues in interior design.

We hope that this volume will enable the reader to pursue his interests through its pages in his or her own particular way, at the same time becoming aware of certain general themes that interweave through the pattern of modern thought. As examples we cite the role of Commonwealth countries as a source of talent often subsequently developed in the UK and USA; the interrelations between particular scientific ideas and the literary or artistic expression of related concepts; the sequence of development in the emergence of new concepts; the coincidence of dates; and (a feature we have particularly noted) the extraordinary contribution of the scientists, writers and artists driven out of Germany, Austria, Hungary, Poland and Russia by totalitarian persecution before and after the Second World War.

Reading and editing these entries, we have been made acutely aware of just how much detail and information is included, information which, as we learned to our cost in trying to confirm some fact or reference, is not available elsewhere in such thoroughness or across such a consistent range. But even more, as the contributors delivered their copy we realized something that had not been planned; that this is a 'companion' in the other sense, a book that is there to browse in and be read for sheer pleasure. Where else, for example, could one encounter in neighbouring pages the explorer of children's thinking (Piaget), the biologist who developed the oral contraceptive (Pincus), the inventor of the brassière (Poiret), and the creator of Peter Rabbit (Potter)?

According to Thomas Carlyle, 'History is the essence of innumerable biographies.' At the end of editing this *Biographical Companion* we feel that we are justified in adding, 'And so is modern thought.' We are left with the conviction that anyone who has the patience to turn the pages that follow will find it hard to maintain that the twentieth century has fallen short of the creative energy and genius of earlier ages.

ALCB
RBW

Editors' Note

To ensure that basic information is readily identifiable, the following conventions have been adopted throughout.

Subject's name. This takes the form of surname followed by all personal names, irrespective of which is the 'known' name. If the subject's name is a pseudonym or has been changed for any reason, that name is followed by either 'ps. of ...' or '*né*' or '*née*'. Any consistently adopted nickname is added in brackets. Details of titles, honours and decorations have been omitted in headings and entries, not out of disrespect but because otherwise, in such a book, such documentation would have taken up a disproportionate amount of space. The exceptions are the Nobel prizes, recorded in the entries, and those very few instances where inherited titles provided the name by which an individual was known throughout his life.

Details of birth and death. Place and country are recorded in their historically correct form. If the name of either has changed subsequently, that name will be followed by [now ...]; if the country or the current form given in square brackets is the same for birth and death, that name is not repeated. To identify the geographical location more precisely, the appropriate county or state is also given according to current (1983) usage, for all places in the UK, the USA, Western Europe and the Commonwealth and selectively elsewhere. County and state locations, however, are not provided for any national capitals, nor in those cases where they are virtually the same as the name of city or town. In the case of Germany, [now East Germany] is added where applicable, whereas places in West Germany are identified by the state name. Any omission in the information regarding dates of birth and death means that such is not available.

Subject's category. This is given as nationality and specialism. Any changes in nationality are recorded unless they occurred when the subject was a minor. In classifying the specialism the contributor has been allowed space only to enter the subject's primary vocation. This description forms the basis for the classified index.

Subject's publications. All titles are cited in the language of the first edition, with the place and date of publication and, where required, with the details of the published English translation (the translator's name is provided only for literary and philosophical works). If more than one translation has been published, the date and place of the first are given, but the full entry is left for the latest and/or most adequate. If no translation exists, the title is translated literally within square brackets. Later editions of any publication are indicated simply by a date and a superscript number, e.g. London, 1953, ^{2}1972. For pamphlets or periodical publication, a date alone is provided. For plays and films the accompanying dates refer respectively to first performance and release.

Cross-references. Whenever reference is made to a person who is the subject of a separate entry, that person's surname is picked out in small capitals; if the surname is shared, initials are added.

Bibliographies. These are restricted to critical studies relating to the subject's life or work; details of the subject's own publications are given in the entry itself. With few exceptions these suggestions for further reading are limited to two titles.

Science bibliographies. Many of the scientific entries may seem sparse in their provision of further reading suggestions. Partly this is because there are not many studies, still fewer biographies, devoted to the life-work of individual scientists. More important, further information is only available from a small number of basic reference sources, and it seemed more sensible to list these in one place than to have the same references recurring through a large number of entries.

In the majority of cases further information will be found in *Dictionary of Scientific Biography* (ed. C. C. Gillispie, 16 vols, NY, 1970–80).

Further information on American scientists is available in *Biographical Memoirs of the National Academy of Sciences*.

For British scientists the memoirs published by the Royal Society are of great value: *Obituary Notices of Fellows of the Royal Society of London* (from 1932 to 1954) and *Biographical Memoirs of Fellows of the Royal Society of London* (from 1955). For those British scientists who died before 1932, the Royal Society Year Book can be consulted.

Contributors. Each entry bears its author's initials, and these are identified in the List of Contributors.

Classified index. The index classifies the nearly 2000 names into some 60 subject categories. But given the extensive range of the *Biographical Companion* and the limitations of space, it has not been possible to include separately all the descriptive categories applied in the individual entries nor to allow any figure more than a single entry in the index. But the addition of cross-references between some of the classifications and notes on the scope of particular subject areas should aid a reader's search for further information about the book and the entries that it includes.

List of Contributors

ABMcM	Arnold McMillin, Professor of Russian, University of Liverpool.
ADB	A. D. Best, Senior Lecturer, Department of German, University of Hull.
ADHC	Antony Hippisley Coxe, author of *A Seat at the Circus*.
ADT	Doug Thompson, Lecturer in Italian Studies, University of Hull.
ADVB	Alberto Vizoso, formerly member of the Medical Research Council.
AG	Andrew Gamble, Reader in Political Theory and Institutions, University of Sheffield.
AGPW	A. G. Prys Williams, Lecturer in Social Statistics, University College of Swansea.
AH	A. Hallam, Lapworth Professor of Geology, University of Birmingham.
AHF	Albert Friedlander, Dean and Lecturer, Leo Baeck College, London.
AIO	Anthony Ogus, Professor of Law, University of Newcastle upon Tyne.
AJH	Sir Alan Harris, Professor of Concrete Structures and Technology, Hydraulics and Transport, Imperial College of Science and Technology, London.
AJK	Adam Kuper, Professor of African Anthropology, University of Leiden.
AJM	A. J. Meech, Lecturer in Drama, University of Hull.
AJP	Alan Parkin, Lecturer in Experimental Psychology, University of Sussex.
AJS	Antony Smith, Deputy Editor, *British Medical Journal*.
ALCB	Alan, Lord Bullock, FBA, Founding Master of St Catherine's College, Oxford, and former Vice-Chancellor, University of Oxford.
AM	Arthur Marwick, Professor of History, The Open University.
AMC	Andrew Colman, Lecturer in Psychology, University of Leicester.
AMS	Ann Shukman, writer.
ANRN	Alastair Niven, Director-General, Africa Centre, London, and Honorary Lecturer, School of Oriental and African Studies, University of London.
AO	Adrian Oldfield, Lecturer, Department of Sociological and Political Studies, University of Salford.
AP	A. J. Pollard, Senior Lecturer in Education, Oxford Polytechnic.
APJ	A. P. Jessop, Lecturer in Genetics, University of Glasgow.
AQ	Anthony, Lord Quinton, FBA, President of Trinity College, Oxford.
AS	Alistair Stead, Lecturer in English Literature, University of Leeds.
ATKC	A. T. K. Crozier, Lecturer in English, University of Sussex.
AW	Alan Windsor, Lecturer in the History of Art, University of Reading.
BAF	Brian Farrell, formerly Reader in Mental Philosophy, University of Oxford, and Fellow of Corpus Christi College, Oxford.
BB	Bernard Bergonzi, Professor of English and Comparative Literary Studies, University of Warwick.
BC	Barbara Cartlidge, Director of Electrum Gallery, London.
BDB	Brian D. Brown, Senior Lecturer in Sociology of Education and leader of the Television Research Unit, Faculty of Education, Oxford Polytechnic.
BEJ	Barrie Juniper, University Lecturer in Botany, University of Oxford, and Fellow of St Catherine's College, Oxford.
BF	Brian Firth, Principal Lecturer in English, St Mary's College, Strawberry Hill, London.
BH	Barbara Heldt, Professor of Russian, University of British Columbia.

LIST OF CONTRIBUTORS

BJ	Betty Joseph, member of the British Psychoanalytical Society.
BM	Brendan Murphy, Statutory Lecturer in Architecture, University College, Dublin.
BMGR	Bernard M. G. Reardon, formerly Head of Department of Religious Studies, University of Newcastle upon Tyne.
BRC	Bernard Crick, Professor of Politics, Birkbeck College, University of London.
BS	Bernard Sharratt, Lecturer in English and American Literature, University of Kent.
BSB	B. S. Benedikz, Sub-Librarian Special Collections, University of Birmingham.
BWC	Barry Cunliffe, FBA, Professor of European Archaeology, University of Oxford, and Fellow of Keble College, Oxford.
BWFP	Brian Powell, Lecturer in Japanese Studies, University of Oxford, and Fellow of St Antony's College, Oxford.
CA	Chimen Abramsky, Professor Emeritus, University College London, co-author of *Karl Marx and the Labour Movement* and other works.
CAB	Charlotte Benton, art historian; teaching at the Architectural Association.
CAL	C. A. Longhurst, Senior Lecturer in Spanish, University of Leeds.
CDG	Christine Gray, Fellow in Law, St Hilda's College, Oxford.
CF	Charles Ford, freelance writer and lecturer.
CH	Christopher Headington, composer, pianist, writer and broadcaster.
CHP	Charles Peake, Professor of English Language and Literature, Queen Mary College, University of London.
CMH	Christopher Hutton, Fellow of the YIVO Institute for Jewish Research, New York, USA.
CR	Caroline Richmond, Publications Editor, Public Health Laboratory Service.
CS	Corbet Stewart, Lecturer in German, Queen Mary College, University of London.
CTJ	Colin Jones, University Lecturer in Developmental Physiology, Nuffield Institute for Medical Research, and Fellow and Tutor in Medical Studies, St Catherine's College, Oxford.
CW	Charles Webster, Director, Wellcome Unit for the History of Medicine, and Fellow of Corpus Christi College, Oxford.
DAD	David Dougill, Dance Critic, *Sunday Times*.
DBe	Daniel Bell, Professor of Sociology, University of Harvard, USA.
DBr	Denis Brass, Professor Extraordinary in the University of Coimbra, Portugal.
DC	David Carroll, Professor of English Literature, University of Lancaster.
DCr	Derek Crabtree, Master of Keynes College, University of Kent.
DCW	D. C. Watt, Stevenson Professor of International History in the University of London, London School of Economics and Political Science.
DD	Dick Davis, writer.
DEB	D. E. Blackwell, Professor of Astronomy, University of Oxford, and Fellow of New College, Oxford.
DEJ	D. E. Jenkinson, Principal Lecturer in German, Goldsmiths' College, University of London.
DGL	Daniel Limon, Lecturer in Modern Languages and European History, University of East Anglia.
DH	David Holloway, Lecturer in Politics, University of Edinburgh.
DHE	D. H. Everett, FRS, Emeritus Professor of Physical Chemistry, University of Bristol.
DHK	Dermot Killingley, Senior Lecturer in Religious Studies, University of Newcastle upon Tyne.

DHP	D. H. Perkins, FRS, Professor of Elementary Particle Physics, University of Oxford, and Fellow of St Catherine's College, Oxford.
DHR	D. H. Roy, Director of Drama, University of Hull.
DJD	D. J. Deletant, Lecturer in Romanian Language and Literature, School of Slavonic and East European Studies, University of London.
DJL	David Lodge, Professor of Modern English Literature, University of Birmingham.
DJM	David J. Mabberley, Tutor in Plant Sciences, and Fellow of Wadham College, Oxford.
DKP	D. K. Peacock, Lecturer in Drama, University of Hull.
DLE	David L. Edwards, Provost of Southwark.
DM	David Macey, translator.
DMHP	David Pennington, Financial Statistics Division, Bank of England.
DMJ	Dale M. Johnson, Senior Lecturer in Mathematics, Hatfield Polytechnic.
DMM	Denis MacEoin, Lecturer in Islamic Studies, University of Newcastle upon Tyne.
DMOC	David Cohen, Editor, *Psychology News*.
DMW	David Walker, QC, FBA, Regius Professor of Law, University of Glasgow.
DOM	Debora O. MacKenzie, freelance writer on science.
DP	Dilys Powell, Film Critic of *Punch*, Critic of films on television for *Sunday Times*.
DRic	David Richards, Lecturer in English, University of Birmingham.
DRid	David Ridgway, Lecturer in Archaeology, University of Edinburgh.
DRN	D. R. Newth, formerly Regius Professor of Zoology, University of Glasgow.
DS	Deyan Sudjic, Architecture Correspondent, *Sunday Times*.
DTC	David Corker, Lecturer in English and American Studies, University of East Anglia.
DTM	David McLellan, Professor of Political Theory, University of Kent.
DWL	Derek Langridge, Principal Lecturer, School of Librarianship and Information Studies, Polytechnic of North London.
EBS	Brian Smith, Lecturer in Physical Chemistry, University of Oxford, and Fellow of St Catherine's College, Oxford.
ECH	Celia Hawkesworth, Lecturer in Serbo-Croat Language and Literature, School of Slavonic and East European Studies, University of London.
EFi	Emilie Fitzgibbon, Tutor in English, University College, Cork.
EFo	Eckart Förster, Lecturer in Philosophy, Balliol College, Oxford.
EFT	E. F. Timms, Lecturer in German, University of Cambridge, and Fellow of Gonville and Caius College, Cambridge.
EH	Eric Homberger, Lecturer in English and American Studies, University of East Anglia.
EHR	E. H. Robertson, Baptist minister, author, broadcaster and editor of the Bonhoeffer papers.
EJH	John Harris, author and historian.
EJK	Edmund King, Emeritus Professor of Education in the University of London.
EK	Eileen Kane, Lecturer in the History of Art, University College, Dublin.
EL	E. Lampert, Professor of Russian Studies, Keele University.
EMT	Edward M. Thomas, Senior Lecturer, University College of Wales, Aberystwyth.
ERL	E. R. Laithwaite, Professor of Heavy Electrical Engineering, Imperial College of Science and Technology, London.
EV	Eric Vickers, Senior Lecturer, School of Librarianship and Information Studies, Polytechnic of North London.

LIST OF CONTRIBUTORS

FHMcC	F. H. McClintock, Professor of Criminology, University of Edinburgh.
FJJ	F. J. Jones, Professor of Italian Studies, University College, Cardiff.
FK	Fergus Kerr, Lecturer in Theology, Blackfriars, Oxford.
FPW	Frank Whitford, Lecturer in the History of Art, Homerton College, Cambridge.
FW	F. White, Curator of the Forest Herbarium and Fielding-Druce Herbarium, University of Oxford.
GA	Gerhard Adler, psychotherapist, author, lecturer and editor.
GAH	G. Ainsworth Harrison, Professor of Biological Anthropology, University of Oxford, and Fellow of Linacre College, Oxford.
GDW	Glenn Wilson, Senior Lecturer in Psychology, Institute of Psychiatry, University of London.
GFC	G. F. Cushing, Professor of Hungarian Language and Literature, School of Slavonic and East European Studies, University of London.
GHC	G. H. Claridge, Lecturer in English and American Literature, University of Kent.
GHD	Gareth Davies, freelance journalist specializing in environmental subjects.
GIH	Gordon Heald, Joint Managing Director, Gallup Poll, London.
GJ	Gregory James, Lecturer in Applied Linguistics, University of Exeter.
GL	G. Leaf, formerly Grieve Lecturer in Biochemistry, University of Glasgow.
GM	George Melly, jazz singer and writer, lecturer and writer on surrealism.
GNS	G. N. Stanton, Professor of New Testament Studies, King's College, London.
GRS	Geoffrey Sampson, Reader in Linguistics, University of Lancaster.
GS	G. Singh, Professor of Italian Language and Literature, The Queen's University of Belfast.
GSS	G. S. Smith, Research Fellow, University of Liverpool.
GT	Geoffrey Turner, Senior Lecturer in Theology, Trinity and All Saints College, Leeds.
HJB	Hector Blackhurst, Assistant Librarian, John Rylands University Library of Manchester.
HMR	H. M. Rosenberg, Reader in Physics, University of Oxford, and Fellow of St Catherine's College, Oxford.
IC	Ian Campbell, Reader in English Literature, University of Edinburgh.
IG-G	I. Grattan-Guinness, Reader in Mathematics, Middlesex Polytechnic.
IH	Ian Hamnett, Reader in Anthropology, University of Bristol.
IJ	Ian Jeffrey, Senior Lecturer in the History of Art, Goldsmiths' College, University of London.
IV	I. Vasiljev, National Committee of Automatic Control of the USSR.
IW	Ian Wallace, Lecturer in German, University of Dundee.
JAC	John A. Clarke, Research Student in English, University College London.
JAG	Jeffrey Gray, Lecturer in Psychology, University of Oxford, and Fellow of University College, Oxford.
JAS	John Sutherland, Reader in English, University College London.
JAW	John Wightman, Lecturer in Law, University of Kent.
JB	John Baldwin, Director of the Institute of Judicial Administration, University of Birmingham.
JC	Joseph Connolly, writer and bookseller.
JCM	J. C. Miller, Research Officer, Department of Astrophysics, University of Oxford.
JCr	Joyce Crick, Lecturer in German, University College London.
JCu	John Cumming, writer and editor.
JE	John Elsom, author, dramatist and theatre historian.
JEEH	Jane Havell, freelance writer and editor.

JEHW   J. E. Hall Williams, Reader in Criminology, London School of Economics and Political Science.

JGo   J. Gooch, Senior Lecturer in History, University of Lancaster, and Editor, *Journal of Strategic Studies*.

JGr   John Griffiths, writer.

JHC   John Collins, Research Student, Department of German, University of Liverpool.

JHG   John Goldthorpe, Official Fellow, Nuffield College, Oxford.

JIS   Jeffrey Somers, Research Director, Fine Books Oriental Ltd.

JJC   John Chilton, writer and musician, leader of the 'Feetwarmers'.

JJG   Jeremy Gray, Lecturer in Mathematics, The Open University.

JL   John Lade, writer, broadcaster and former Head of Gramophone Programmes, BBC.

JLahr   John Lahr, writer and critic.

JM   Janet Morgan, writer, biographer of Agatha Christie.

JMA   Jean Aitchison, Senior Lecturer in Linguistics, London School of Economics and Political Science.

JMacI   John MacInnes, Senior Lecturer, School of Scottish Studies, University of Edinburgh.

JMFR   Jessica Rutherford, Keeper of Decorative Arts, Royal Pavilion, Art Gallery and Museums, Brighton.

JMM   Juliet McLean, Divisional Co-ordinator of Schools and Children's Library Services, Hertfordshire Library Service.

JMT   J. M. Thomas, FRS, Head of the Department of Physical Chemistry, and Professorial Fellow, King's College, Cambridge.

JMW   J. M. Walton, Senior Lecturer in Drama, University of Hull.

JPG   John Gillett, Film Research Officer, British Film Institute.

JPP   Philip Payne, Lecturer in German Studies, University of Lancaster.

JPW   John P. White, Head of English Department, St Mary's College of Education, Newcastle upon Tyne.

JPWh   John White, Reader in Education, University of London.

JRP   J. R. Pole, Rhodes Professor of American History and Institutions, University of Oxford, and Fellow of St Catherine's College, Oxford.

JRT   John Torrance, Lecturer in Politics, University of Oxford, and Fellow of Hertford College, Oxford.

JSh   John Shorter, Emeritus Reader in Chemistry, University of Hull.

JSo   Jacob Sonntag, Editor, *Jewish Quarterly*.

JSR   J. S. Rowlinson, FRS, Dr Lee's Professor of Chemistry, University of Oxford, and Fellow of Exeter College, Oxford.

JW   John Worthen, Lecturer in English, University College of Swansea.

JWB   Joanne Brogden, Professor and Head of the Fashion School, Royal College of Art, London.

JWLB   Sir James Beament, FRS, Drapers Professor of Agriculture, University of Cambridge.

JWMcF   James McFarlane, Professor of European Literature, University of East Anglia.

JWMW   John Willett, co-Editor, UK and US editions of Brecht's plays, poetry and prose; former Assistant Editor, *Times Literary Supplement*.

JWNW   J. W. N. Watkins, Professor of Philosophy, London School of Economics and Political Science.

KB   Kenneth Buthlay, Senior Lecturer in Scottish Literature, University of Glasgow.

KC   Keith Carabine, Lecturer in English and American Literature, University of Kent.

KEDH   Desirée Hirst, Lecturer in English, University College of Swansea.

KF   Kay Flavell, Research Fellow, Department of German, University of Liverpool.

LIST OF CONTRIBUTORS

KGM	K. G. Mathieson, School of English and American Studies, University of East Anglia.
KKS	Kirsti Simonsuuri, Docent, Senior Research Fellow, University of Helsinki, Finland.
KMcL	Kathleen McLaughlin, translator.
KRS	Kenneth Seddon, Lecturer in Experimental Chemistry, University of Sussex.
LJC	L. J. Cooke, writer and lecturer in film studies.
LJH	Linda Hurcombe, writer and teacher of literature.
LJJ	Ludmilla Jordanova, Lecturer in History, University of Essex.
LL	Leo Labedz, Editor of *Survey*.
LMC	Laurie Clements, Lecturer in Sociology, Trent Polytechnic.
LPS	Leon Schlamm, Lecturer in Theology, University of Kent.
MA	Michael Anderson, Professor of Drama, University College of North Wales, Bangor.
MB	Michael Billington, Drama Critic of the *Guardian*; presenter of various BBC radio arts programmes.
MDCG	Michael Gilsenan, Reader in Anthropology, University College London.
MGB	Michael Butler, Senior Lecturer in German, University of Birmingham.
MH-B	Mark Haworth-Booth, Assistant Keeper of Photographs, Victoria and Albert Museum, London.
MI	Mary Ingham, author of *Now We Are Thirty*.
MJA	Michael Alexander, Senior Lecturer in English, University of Stirling.
MJS	M. J. Shallis, Staff Tutor in Physical Sciences, Department of External Studies, University of Oxford.
MJW	M. J. Whelan, Reader in the Physical Examination of Materials, Department of Metallurgy and Science of Materials, University of Oxford, and Fellow of Linacre College, Oxford.
MMG	Margaret Gowing, FBA, Professor of the History of Science, University of Oxford, and Fellow of Linacre College, Oxford.
MOC	Marion O'Connor, Lecturer in English, University of Kent.
MOJN	Michael Newman, art historian and critic.
MRAT	Maryon Tysoe, Psychology Correspondent, *New Society*.
MS	Michael Sullivan, Fellow of St Catherine's College, Oxford, and Christensen Professor of Chinese Art, Stanford University, California, USA.
MT	Malcolm Todd, Professor of Archaeology, University of Exeter.
MWE	Michael Eysenck, Reader in Psychology, University of London.
MWS	Martin Swales, Professor of German, University College London.
NAJH	Nick Hern, Drama Editor of Methuen London.
NBC	N. B. Chapman, Emeritus Professor of Chemistry, University of Hull.
NHK	N. H. Keeble, Lecturer in English, University of Stirling.
NJJ	N. J. Johnson, Senior Lecturer in Law, Oxford Polytechnic.
NP	Neil Philip, freelance writer.
NT	Nina Taylor, translator, and postgraduate student at School of Slavonic and East European Studies, University of London.
NW	Newton Watson, Bartlett Professor of Architecture, University of London.
OS	the late Oliver Stallybrass, Editor, Abinger edition of E. M. Forster; joint Editor, *The Fontana Dictionary of Modern Thought*.
PAC	Peter Coe, Lecturer in Architecture, University of Bristol.
PAH	Peter Hebblethwaite, freelance writer specializing in Vatican affairs.
PAS	Penny Sparke, Tutor in Cultural History, Royal College of Art, London.
PB	Peter Banks, Professor of Biochemistry, University of Sheffield.
PC	Pietro Corsi, Senior Research Officer, University of Pisa, Italy.
PEB	Peter Bryant, Watts Professor of Psychology, University of Oxford, and Fellow of Wolfson College, Oxford.

PEH	P. E. Hodgson, Lecturer in Nuclear Physics, University of Oxford, and Fellow of Corpus Christi College, Oxford.
PF	Peter Fuller, art critic and author.
PFL	Paul Lakeland, Assistant Professor of Religious Studies, Fairfield University, Connecticut, USA.
PG	Paul Griffiths, Music Critic of *The Times*.
PH	Peter Haggett, Professor of Urban and Regional Geography, University of Bristol.
PHB	Peter Butter, Regius Professor of English, University of Glasgow.
PJB	P. J. Branscombe, Professor of Austrian Studies, University of St Andrews.
PJH	P. J. Harris, Principal Lecturer in Law, Sheffield Polytechnic.
PJM	Patrick J. Meade, formerly Deputy Director-General, Meteorological Office, Bracknell.
PL	Peter Lund, writer; formerly Senior Lecturer in Education, Huddersfield Polytechnic.
PLC	Peter Caracciolo, Lecturer in English Literature, Royal Holloway College, University of London.
PLFH	Paul Heelas, Lecturer in the Anthropology of Religion, University of Lancaster.
PM	Patricia Monaghan, Lecturer in Zoology, University of Glasgow.
PMcD	Patricia McDermott, Lecturer in Spanish, University of Leeds.
PMD	Phyllis Deane, FBA, Professor of Economic History, University of Cambridge, and Fellow of Newnham College, Cambridge.
PMO	Peter Oppenheimer, Student of Christ Church, Oxford.
PMWT	P. M. W. Thody, Professor of French Literature, University of Leeds.
PNQ	Peter Quartermaine, Lecturer in English, University of Exeter.
PP	Patrick Parrinder, Reader in English, University of Reading.
PR	Philip Roberts, Senior Lecturer in English Literature, University of Sheffield.
PS	Paul Sturges, Lecturer in Library and Information Studies, Loughborough University.
PSF	P. S. Fisher, Lecturer in Physics, University of Oxford, and Fellow of Trinity College, Oxford.
PSR	Philip Rawson, Dean, School of Art and Design, Goldsmiths' College, University of London.
RAH	Anthony Hyman, author of *Charles Babbage, Pioneer of the Computer*, etc.
RAN	Robert Nowell, journalist and author.
RAP	R. A. Pearson, Senior Lecturer in Social Policy, Sheffield City Polytechnic.
RB	Raymond Boston, Director of Studies, Centre for Journalism Studies, University College, Cardiff.
RBH	Roger Hardy, Lecturer in English and American Literature, University of Kent.
RBJG	Reg Gadney, Senior Tutor, Royal College of Art, London.
RBP	Robert B. Pynsent, Lecturer in Czech and Slovak Language and Literature, University of London.
RBW	R. B. Woodings, Senior Lecturer in Publishing, Oxford Polytechnic.
RC	Robert Cheesmond, Lecturer in Drama, University of Hull.
RDG	Ronald Gray, Fellow of Emmanuel College, Cambridge.
REA	Ronald Alley, Keeper of the Modern Collection, Tate Gallery, London.
RFB	R. F. Barrow, Reader in Physical Chemistry, University of Oxford, and Fellow of Exeter College, Oxford.
RH	Robin Hallett, writer on African affairs.
RHR	R. H. Robins, Professor of General Linguistics, University of London.
RHV	Ruth Hurst Vose, author; formerly Assistant Curator, Pilkington Glass Museum, Merseyside.

LIST OF CONTRIBUTORS

RIT	R. I. Tricker, Director of The Corporate Policy Group, Nuffield College, Oxford, and Professorial Fellow, Oxford Centre for Management Studies.
RJB	Robert Bailey, Senior Lecturer in Education, Oxford Polytechnic.
RJC	R. J. Cashmore, Lecturer in Physics, University of Oxford, and Fellow of Balliol College, Oxford.
RJH	R. J. Harrison, Lecturer in Archaeology, University of Bristol.
RJJ	R. J. Johnston, Professor of Geography, University of Sheffield.
RJS	Richard Sherwood, Lecturer in Russian, University College of Wales, Aberystwyth.
RM	Robert Morgan, Lecturer in Theology, University of Oxford, and Fellow of Linacre College, Oxford.
RMB	Roderick Beaton, Lecturer in Modern Greek Language and Literature, King's College, London.
RNH	Roger Hausheer, Lecturer in German Studies, University of Bradford, and Research Student in German Thought, Wolfson College, Oxford.
RPA	Roy Armes, Reader in Film and Television, Middlesex Polytechnic.
RP-M	Robert Pring-Mill, Fellow of St Catherine's College, Oxford.
RPMi	R. P. Minney, Lecturer in Religious Education, University of Durham.
RPS	R. P. Sheldon, Senior Lecturer in Polymer Science, University of Bradford.
RR	Robert Reiner, Lecturer in Sociology, University of Bristol.
RRS	Ron Stewart, Lecturer in Educational Psychology, University of Liverpool.
RRStr	Roger Straughan, Lecturer in Education, University of Reading.
RS	Roger Sharrock, Emeritus Professor of English Language and Literature in the University of London.
RSm	Roger Smith, Lecturer in the History of Science, University of Lancaster.
RSS	Robert Short, Senior Lecturer, School of Modern Languages and European History, University of East Anglia.
RTa	Roberto Tarzariol, teacher of English, Turin; formerly Italian Language Assistant, University of Hull.
RTay	Richard Taylor, Lecturer in Politics and Russian Studies, University College of Swansea.
RTi	Roger Tippett, Lecturer in Zoology, University of Glasgow.
RWL	Rex W. Last, Professor of Modern Languages, University of Dundee.
SAJ	Stephanie Jordan, Dance Critic of the *New Statesman*; Head of Dance, Crewe and Alsager College of Higher Education.
SB	Steven Boldy, Assistant Professor of Spanish, Tulane University, New Orleans, USA.
SBJ	S. Beynon John, Reader in French, University of Sussex.
SC	Shirley Chew, Lecturer in English, University of Leeds.
SCW	Sarah Woodcock, Research Assistant, Theatre Museum, Victoria and Albert Museum, London.
SED	Susan Dowell, writer and teacher.
SH	Stephen Heath, Fellow of Jesus College, Cambridge.
SJN	S. J. Newman, Lecturer in English, University of Liverpool.
SLN	Stephen Nugent, Lecturer in Anthropology, Goldsmiths' College, and University College London.
SOBT	Sarah O'Brien Twohig, freelance lecturer in art.
SPC	Sue Compton, freelance writer; author of *The World Backwards: Russian Futurist Books, 1912–16.*
SRC	S. R. Charsley, Lecturer in Sociology, University of Glasgow.
ST	Simon Trussler, Drama Department, Goldsmiths' College, University of London.
SWB	Simon Blackburn, Fellow and Lecturer in Philosophy, Pembroke College, Oxford.

TC	Tom Colverson, book designer, formerly Senior Lecturer in Book Design and Production, Oxford Polytechnic.
TE	Terry Eagleton, writer; author of *Walter Benjamin* and *The Rape of Clarissa*, and Fellow of Wadham College, Oxford.
TEC	Thomas Chatburn, Chairman, Musical Studies, Oxford Polytechnic.
TFC	Tom Clarke, Lecturer in Sociology, Trent Polytechnic.
TG	Terry Gifford, Head of English, Yewlands Comprehensive School, Sheffield.
TGH	T. G. Halsall, Lecturer in Organic Chemistry, University of Oxford, and Fellow of Linacre College, Oxford.
TLSS	T. L. S. Sprigge, Professor of Logic and Metaphysics, University of Edinburgh.
TON	Tom O'Neill, Senior Lecturer in Italian, and Fellow of Trinity College, Dublin.
TPM	Terence Morris, Professor of Social Institutions, University of London.
TT	Ted Tapper, Lecturer in Politics, University of Sussex.
TWF	T. W. Freeman, Emeritus Professor of Geography, University of Manchester.
TWM	Tony Mitchell, freelance writer and translator.
UPB	Peter Burke, Fellow of Emmanuel College, Cambridge.
VAMc	V. A. McClelland, Professor of Educational Studies, University of Hull.
VC	Vernon Coleman, author.
VP	Valentina Polukhina, Lecturer in Russian, University of Keele.
WBS	W. B. Smith, Senior Lecturer in French, Newcastle upon Tyne Polytechnic.
WFB	W. F. Bynum, Assistant Director (Research), Wellcome Institute for the History of Medicine, London.
WGR	W. Graham Richards, Lecturer in Chemistry, University of Oxford, and Fellow of Brasenose College, Oxford.
WJ	Waldemar Januszczak, Art Critic of the *Guardian*.
WLT	W. L. Twining, Quain Professor of Jurisprudence, University College London.
WP	Sir William Paton, FRS, Professor of Pharmacology, University of Oxford, and Fellow of Balliol College, Oxford.
WSD	Steven Dodd, Lecturer in Applied Linguistics, Language centre, University of Exeter.
WTD	W. T. Davies, Emeritus Fellow of St Cross College, Oxford, formerly Lecturer in Nuclear Physics, University of Oxford.
WvdW	Wilfried van der Will, Lecturer in German, University of Birmingham.
ZW	Zena Waloff, entomologist (retired), formerly Centre for Overseas Pest Research.

A

Aalto, Hugo Alvar Henrik (b. Kuortane, Finland, 3.2.1898; d. Helsinki, 11.5.1976). Finnish architect and furniture designer. The leading architect of his country and one of the major proponents of the modern movement in architecture, Aalto studied at the Helsinki Technical University (1916–21) under Lindgren. He went to the USA in 1938 and was a professor at MIT and at the Cambridge Mass. College of Architecture (1940–6). After WW2 he worked again in Finland and carried out projects principally in Denmark, West Germany, France, Sweden, the USA and Iraq. Aalto changed his style in the late 1920s from an unremarkable neoclassicism to a humane modernism which allowed each project individual treatment and did not subordinate a building to an architectural ideology, whether overriding formal precision or a modular determination of individual spatial needs. His respect for materials and their combinations (especially timber and brick) and their appropriateness to environment was coupled with a genius for producing an impression of movement in buildings (and furniture) that nevertheless satisfied the demand for clarity typical of the age. A number of his important projects were produced in the spirit of the social planning movement that revolutionized Finnish and other Scandinavian architecture before WW2 and reached its height in the 1950s. The Viipuri library (1927–35), the Paimio convalescent home (1929–33), the MIT students' dormitory (1947) with its S-curve and projecting staircases varying the treatment of individual units, the Säynatsälo town hall and centre (1951) with its timber ceilings contrasted with brick walls, the Helsinki House of Culture (1955–8), and the Finlandia concert hall at Helsinki (1971) are examples of his strong, increasingly expressive management of functional building. His Maison Carré near Paris (1956–8) uses an exciting diagonal roof and dynamically curved ceilings that reiterate in a suitably domestic form the bravura of the almost inwards-falling, superbly undulating wall of his Finnish pavilion for the New York World's Fair (1939). The Maison Carré was furnished by Aalto with bentwood furniture; this carried forward his versatile use of the bent plywood introduced in 1932. With K. Fleig he edited his *Collected Works* (2 vols, Zürich, 1963–71). JGr

F. Gutheim, *Alvar Aalto* (NY, 1960).

Abel, Wilhelm (b. Bütow, Germany [now Bytòw, Poland], 25.8.1904). German economic historian, who held the chair at Göttingen from 1949 to 1972. His first and most important book *Agrarkrisen und Agrarkonjunktur* (Berlin & Hamburg, 1935, ²1966; *Agricultural Fluctuations in Europe*, London, 1980) is concerned with the agrarian history of Europe from the 13c to the 20c, seen in terms of alternating phases of expansion and contraction, essentially in response to population trends. Abel has also published a study of deserted villages in the later Middle Ages, *Die Wüstungen des ausgehenden Mittelalters* (Jena, 1943, ²1955); a general history of German agriculture and rural life, *Geschichte der deutschen Landwirtschaft* [History of the German rural economy] (Stuttgart, 1962); and an essay on poverty and famine in preindustrial Europe, *Massenarmut und Hungerkrisen im vorindustriellen Europa* [Mass poverty and subsistence crises in preindustrial Europe] (Hamburg, 1974), which emphasizes the extent of poverty before the Industrial Revolution. A pioneering agrarian historian whose concern with cycles, crises and long-term trends antedates the published work of Postan, BRAUDEL and LE ROY LADURIE, Abel has been too little appreciated in the English-speaking world. UPB

Abercrombie, Michael (b. Ryton, Glos., UK, 16.8.1912; d. Cambridge, 28.5.1979). British cell biologist. A son of the poet Lascelles Abercrombie, he trained as a zoologist at Oxford (1931–4) and was then initiated into a research career at the Strangeways Research Laboratory, Cambridge. Although at first an experimental embryologist, his most important and influential work was in cell population dynamics and in cell behaviour. His major discovery, that in certain circumstances a moving animal cell in tissue culture is halted merely by touching another cell, was followed by the important corollary that certain cancer cells are not so affected. Since the ability of cancer cells to invade normal tissues is often crucial to their malignancy, this opened an approach to their biology of great theoretical interest and with clear implications for medicine. Abercrombie worked in succession in the anatomy department (1947–62) and as Jodrell professor of zoology (1962–70) at University College London, and from 1970 until his death as director of the Strangeways Laboratory. He not only introduced quantitative rigour into the study of parts of cell biology, but was also a significant popularizer of science as cofounder and coeditor of *Penguin New Biology* and as a contributor to it.   DRN

Abramovitch, Shalom Jacob, see MENDELE, MOCHER SEFORIM.

Achebe, Chinua, *né* Albert Chinualumgu (b. Ogidi, Nigeria, 16.11.1930). Nigerian novelist and critic. Educated as one of its first graduates at University College, Ibadan, and later at the universities of London and Leeds, Achebe has done much to awaken the world to the new cultural independence of Africa. Ironically this influence has been partly due to his own moderation (though his commitment to Africa and to its culture is clear) and to the subtlety with which he has charted the effects of that clash of cultures which began with the 19c missionaries and traders in Africa. *Things Fall Apart* (London, 1958) remains a classic study of this clash, but Achebe shows clearly that (for him) the tribal culture of Africa also contained fatal flaws upon which the incoming imperialists exerted previously unknown pressure. This even-handed appraisal of African life and politics, together with his firm belief that the English language was a valuable tool to be seized and

applied for African ends, has earned him criticism from some African quarters. His own position is finely expressed in *Morning Yet on Creation Day* (London, 1975), a collection of essays and lectures which makes clear the practical link he sees between the writer and the world of politics. The recipient of numerous awards, Achebe has devoted most of his time since 1972 to teaching at the University of Nigeria, where he is professor of English.   PNQ

D. Carroll, *Chinua Achebe* (London, 1980).

Acheson, Dean Gooderham (b. Middletown, Conn., USA, 11.4.1893; d. Sandy Spring, Md, 12.10.1971). US under-secretary of state (1941–7); secretary of state under TRUMAN (1949–53). The most balanced and mature of Democratic secretaries of state in the 20c, his New England patrician upbringing made him the target of – and enabled him to endure – the right-wing populist and anti-intellectualist denunciations of the era of MCCARTHY. No ardent ROOSEVELTian, his war years were spent in economic warfare against Germany and Japan. He accompanied G. C. MARSHALL on his mediatory mission in China in 1946. His name is particularly associated with (1) the American proposals of March 1946 for international control of commerce in fusionable materials and reactors; (2) the '15 weeks' revolution in foreign policy in 1947 which produced the Truman doctrine and the Marshall plan; (3) the application of KENNAN's doctrines of containment of the USSR, and the creation of NATO; and (4) the seeming exclusion in 1949 of Korea from the American-defended periphery in Asia which preceded the outbreak of the Korean War. He served as one of the more 'hawkish' of KENNEDY's senior advisers from 1961 to 1962. Acheson published his political memoirs as *Present at the Creation* (NY, 1969).   DCW

Adamov, Arthur (b. Kislovodsk, Russia, 23.8.1908; d. Paris, France, 15.3.1970). Russian dramatist who settled in France in 1924. The nature of the disabling neuroses which marked him from infancy can be traced in his confessional texts: *L'Aveu* [The confession] (Paris, 1946), *L'Homme et l'enfant* [Man and child] (Paris, 1968), *Je ... Ils ... [I ... they ...]* (Paris, 1969). Though painful and often moving, these examples of perverse eroticism, sexual degradation and neurotic anxiety speak more of the clinic than of common human experience; but they provide vital keys to Adamov's theatre. The influence of STRINDBERG and ARTAUD is evident in his early plays which constitute a kind of psychodrama, projecting the traumas of his inner life in nightmarish stage images of terror, persecution and humiliation: *La Grande et la petite manoeuvre* [The great and small manoeuvre] (1950), *La Parodie* [The parody] (1950), *L'Invasion* (1950; tr. R. Doan, *The Invasion*, Philadelphia, 1968), *Le Sens de la marche* [The way to go] (1953), *Tous contre tous* [All against all] (1953), *Le Professeur Taranne* (1953; tr. P. Meyer, *Professor Taranne* in *Two Plays*, London, 1962). The influence of BRECHT is discernible in the political plays Adamov wrote after 1954. In these he aimed to find a theatrical form capable of linking the sickness of individual and society, as argued in his theoretical essays *Ici et maintenant* [Here and now] (Paris, 1964). The result is either a form of political allegory exposing the inhumanity of capitalism, as in *Le Ping-Pong* (1955; tr. D. Prouse, *Ping pong* in *Two Plays*, London, 1962) and *Paolo Paoli* (1957; tr. G. Brereton, London, 1960), or the MARXIST propaganda of his play about the Paris Commune *Le Printemps '71* [Spring '71] (1960), or the uneven, but haunting fusion of neurotic dream-play and political satire: *La Politique des restes* [The politics of rubbish] (1963), *Sainte Europe* [Holy Europe] (1966), *M. le Modéré* [Mr Moderate] (1968), *Off Limits* (1969), *Si l'été revenait* [If summer came again] (1970).   SBJ

M. Esslin, *The Theatre of the Absurd* (NY, ²1969); J. H. Reilly, *Arthur Adamov* (NY, 1974).

Adenauer, Konrad (b. Cologne, N. Rhine-Westphalia, Germany, 5.1.1876; d. Rhöndorf, West Germany, 19.4.1967). First chancellor of the German Federal Republic (1949–63); also foreign minister (1951–5) and chairman of the leading Federal party, the Christian Democrats. Burgomaster of Cologne (1917–33, 1945), dismissed and twice imprisoned under HITLER. His policy of choosing power for the West German state through reconciliation with Germany's former enemies in the West, and of building up the West German economy and armed forces within a West European framework (the Coal and Steel Community, the European Defence Community, the North Atlantic Treaty and the West European Union organizations, the European Atomic Community, the European Economic Community) was originally intended to bring about the absorption of the (East) German Democratic Republic, whose legitimacy he adamantly refused to recognize, into Federal Germany, following the anticipated surrender of the Soviets to superior Western power. From 1958 onwards, his fear that Germany might become the victim of Anglo–American–Soviet rapprochement (and especially his disappointment at the moderation shown by KENNEDY after the Cuban missile crisis of 1961) led him to support DE GAULLE's policy of European union under French leadership, a policy regretted by his countrymen and reversed by his successors.   DCW

T. Prittie, *Adenauer: a Study in Fortitude* (London, 1972).

Adler, Lawrence (Larry) (b. Baltimore, Md, USA, 10.12.1914). American musician. When only 13, Adler won a contest for playing Beethoven's Minuet in G on an instrument which, for years, he insisted on calling the harmonica. Presumably he chose this, instead of mouth organ, because it sounded less reminiscent of the kerbside busker, even though it was musicologically incorrect. Gradually in music halls and concert halls throughout the world Adler astonished audiences with his virtuosity, and, in time, many distinguished composers including Malcolm Arnold, HINDEMITH, Milhaud and VAUGHAN WILLIAMS composed works specially for him. Adler has won for the mouth organ a musical status it never previously enjoyed.   JL

Adorno, Theodor Wiesengrund (b. Frankfurt a. M., Hesse, Germany, 11.9.1903; d. Zermatt im Wallis, Valais, Switzerland, 7.8.1969). German philosopher, social theorist and music critic. Adorno studied music, philosophy and sociology at Frankfurt and in 1925 was a student of BERG in Vienna. In 1930 he became an associate of the Institut für Sozialforschung at Frankfurt. In 1934 he was driven to emigrate to the USA where he taught at the institute in exile in New York (The New School for Social Research), returning with it to Frankfurt in 1960. Adorno is generally regarded as the most brilliant and versatile, but also the most perversely obscure, of the first generation of the Frankfurt school. His most important work was less in philosophy than in musicology and the sociology of art, music and mass culture, e.g. *Die Philosophie der neuen Musik* [The philosophy of the new music] (Frankfurt, 1949). The fullest and most general statement of Adorno's thought is his *Negative Dialektik* (Frankfurt, 1966; tr. E. B. Ashton, *Negative Dialectics*, NY, 1973), possibly the most rebarbative philosophical work ever written in German. Its central purpose is to dissolve all conceptual distinctions before they can harden into straitjackets arresting the free movement and deforming the true nature of reality. Adorno argues that all philosophers hitherto have committed the cardinal error of seeking an absolute starting-point in metaphysics and epistemology – some ultimate 'stuff' or 'identity' in terms of which everything else can be analysed. Not only is this impossible because there is no such 'primacy'; it is above all dangerous, because it tends to encourage totalitarian, oppressive and levelling forms of thought that 'reify' the human subject, turning it into some kind of manipulable object. For Adorno, MARXism, with its dissolution of theory in the 'primacy of practice', is no exception to this rule. Not even existentialism, with its elevation of the individual subject to the status of absolute reality insulated from external influences, escapes this judgement, for in thus ignoring repressive social bonds it leaves them as they are and tacitly accepts them. Consciously or not, all systems of thought express and help perpetuate one or another form of 'reifying' domination. The most serious modern offender is empirical science which, ignoring qualitative differences, equates rationality with quantifiability, and becomes a willing servant of the market which reduces everything to the 'identity' of a saleable commodity. Adorno was convinced that philosophy, i.e. critical theory, can do nothing else at this stage of historical development but systematically negate all theories as spurious embodiments of the ultimate 'identity'. This 'negative dialectics' – a quasi-Hegelian dialectical logic which may seem to many a denial of all logic – is an endless process in which fluid concepts are constantly reformed to fit the object; and in this way the unattainable goal of integration of subject and object, word and thing, is asymptotically approached, while a lapse into the 'reifying' tendencies of the false search for 'primacy' is avoided.

In conjunction with HORKHEIMER, Adorno wrote *Die Dialektik der Aufklärung* (Amsterdam, 1947; tr. J. Cumming, *Dialectic of Enlightenment*, NY, 1972), an historical account of how reason, initially an Enlightenment weapon against myth, religion and interested error, has turned against itself in modern technocratic societies and become self-destructive. The establishment of the institute in the USA after the rise of Nazism led to important cooperative studies of a more empirical nature on anti-Semitism and mass culture, and to the collective work published by T. W. Adorno *et al.*, *The Authoritarian Personality* (NY, 1950).   RNH

M. Jay, *The Dialectical Imagination* (London, 1973); G. Rose, *The Melancholy Science* (London, 1979).

Adrian, Edgar Douglas (b. London, UK, 30.11.1889; d. Cambridge, 4.8.1977). British physiologist. Adrian was awarded the 1932 Nobel prize for physiology and medicine (with SHERRINGTON) for work on the neuron (nerve cell). He was among the first to record reliably the electrical activity of single sensory endings and single motor fibres, and is a founder of modern electrophysiology. He made many of the first measurements of the various neural responses which produce sensation, developing the frequency theory of coding basic to modern sensory physiology. After 1934 Adrian switched to the more complex territory of the brain, working on the patterns of electrical activity – sometimes called 'brainwaves' – produced by the firing of thousands of neurons which are revealed by the electroencephalogram (EEG). These investigations advanced modern understanding of epilepsy and the ability to localize cerebral damage. Elected president of the Royal Society in 1950, he spent almost all of his career at Cambridge, graduating in natural sciences (1911) and medicine (1915), lecturing on the nervous system (1929–35), serving as professor of physiology (1935–51) and master of Trinity College (1951–65). During WW1 he studied servicemen suffering from nerve injuries. A summary of his work is to be found in *The Mechanism of Nervous Action* (Philadelphia, 1959). His influence at the famous Physiological Laboratory in Cambridge helped make it in many ways the birthplace of modern neurophysiology.   DOM

Ady, Endre (b. Érmindszent, Austria-Hungary [now Hungary], 22.11.1877; d. Budapest, 27.1.1919). Hungarian poet. The most controversial figure in 20c Hungarian literature, he startled critics with *Új versek* [New poems] (Budapest, 1906) and subsequent volumes of verse. His poetry displays a mixture of eroticism, radical politics, patriotic despair, Messianic prophecy, Calvinist theology and love of money. Strict forms are matched with a cavalier treatment of language and symbolism. Literary opinion was divided into two camps, those who hailed him as the genius of the new age, and those who regarded him as traitorous and unintelligible. His association with the Budapest journal *Nyugat* [West] from 1908 to 1919 kept him in the public eye. In both poetry and prose he advocated modernity and castigated Hungary as a backward-looking land without culture. During WW1, by which time his language had been refined and simplified, he protested vigorously against the inhumanity of war. His themes were few; his virtuoso technique

reveals itself in his metrical range; his language spans from slang to the high romantic. His journalism, couched in the same language, reveals similar social and political concerns. Ady was unique; he founded no school, but became the yardstick by which modern Hungarian writing was measured. An English collection of his essays is *The Explosive Country* (tr. G. F. Cushing, Budapest, 1977).   GFC
J. Reményi, *Hungarian Writers and Literature* (New Brunswick, NJ, 1964).

Afghānī (Asadābādī), Jamāl al-dīn (b. Asadābād, Persia [now Iran], 1839; d. Istanbul, Ottoman Empire [now Turkey] 9.3.1897). Iranian Muslim reformer and apologist, proponent of 'pan-Islamism'. Afghānī is considered one of the most influential figures in the development of the modern Muslim response to western colonialism and secularism. His aim of reviving and uniting Islam against western influences has gained relevance recently. He spent his early life in Afghanistan, where he was briefly involved in politics until 1869. In later years he travelled to India, Egypt, Turkey, Iran, England, France and Russia, constantly engaging in political debate and becoming a source of controversy. In Cairo (1871–9) he had a profound influence on a young generation of religious and political reformers, including MUHAMMAD ᶜABDUH and Saᶜd Zaghlūl. In India (1879–82) he began his main work, later published in Arabic as *Al-radd ᶜalā 'l-dahriyyīn* [Refutation of the materialists] (Beirut, 1886). In Paris (1883–6) he edited with ᶜAbduh the shortlived but influential journal *Al-ᶜurwa al-wuthqā* [The firm cord]. During the second of two stays in Iran (1889–91) he became a leading opponent of Nāṣir al-Dīn Shāh; he instigated the Tobacco Rebellion of 1891, and it was one of his followers who assassinated Nāsir al-Dīn in 1896. He went to Istanbul in 1893 at the request of Sultan ᶜAbdal-Ḥamīd, but his hopes of the latter came to nothing well before his death.   DMM
E. Kedourie, *Afghani and ᶜAbduh* (London, 1966); N. Keddie, *Sayyid Jamāl ad-Dīn 'al-Afghānī': a Political Biography* (Berkeley, Calif., 1972).

Agnelli, Giovanni (b. Villar Perosa, Piedmont, Italy, 13.8.1866; d. Turin, Piedmont, 16.12.1945). Italian industrialist. FIAT (Fabbrica Italiana Automobili Torino S.p.A.), which was to become Italy's largest private business, was founded by Agnelli at the turn of the century. He also established a ball-bearing industry in Italy. In 1923 he became a senator and was a major force in mobilizing Italy's industry during WW2. In addition to being one of Italy's foremost industrialists, he is also remembered for his philanthropic work.

RIT

Agnon, Shmuel Yosef, *né* Czaczkes (b. Buczacz, Galicia, Austria-Hungary [now Buchach, USSR], 17.7.1888; d. Jerusalem, Israel, 17.2.1970). The foremost Hebrew novelist of modern times. He settled in Palestine in 1907, and made his first appearance as a story writer there in 1908, although he published poems as early as 1903. From 1913 to 1924 he lived in Germany, and from 1924 to his death in Jerusalem. He published many stories and some long novels, the majority of which depict the declining Jewish life of the Hasidim in the little towns of Galicia, the rebellion of younger elements in the Jewish communities to start a pioneering life in Palestine-Israel. From the beginning his stories made a profound impact on the Russian-Polish Jewish intelligentsia in Palestine and, later, on the German Jewish writers and thinkers BUBER and SCHOLEM who translated some of his stories into German. His stories and novels are distinguished by their unique style – a veritable mosaic of classic and rabbinic Hebrew, and Yiddish revived in a spoken Hebrew – but particularly noticeable was the immense power of story telling with a double-edged irony mocking both the religious Jews-Hasidim – by whom he was fascinated, and the frailties in human nature. His two outstanding novels are *Hakhnasat Kallah* (Jerusalem, 1919; tr. I. M. Lask, *The Bridal Canopy*, NY, 1937) and *Temol Shilshom* [Yesterday and the day before] (Jerusalem, 1945). In the first, a picaresque novel, he describes in lively humour the ups and downs of a Hasidic family, its poverty and fantasy life at the turn of the century; basically, it is an allegory on the decline and futility of Jewish religious life in the whole of Poland. In the second he presents the building up of Palestine-Israel amid the background of persecution of Jews and its culmination in the Holocaust. His novels are the cornerstone of modern Hebrew prose. His works were published in eight volumes, and two posthumous novels *Shirah* (Jerusalem, 1972) and *In the Shop of Mr Lublin* (Jerusalem, 1975) appeared later. He is the only Hebrew novelist to receive a Nobel prize (1966).

CA

A. J. Band, *Agnon: Nostalgia and Nightmare* (Berkeley, Calif., 1968); G. Scholem, *From Berlin to Jerusalem* (Philadelphia, 1980).

Ahad-Ha'Am, ps. of Asher Hirsch Ginsberg (b. Skvira, Ukraine, Russia, 18.8.1856; d. Tel Aviv, Palestine [now Israel], 2.1.1927). Zionist thinker, essayist and editor. Born into a religious Hasidic family and privately tutored in Jewish matters, he was self-taught in secular education and broke with traditional behaviour at the age of 22. He mastered Russian, German, French, English and Latin, and was the only Hebrew writer to come under the influence of John Stuart Mill rather than German or Russian thinkers. He began writing in 1889 with a bitter criticism of the early Zionist movement, signing himself Ahad-Ha'Am [One of the People], the nickname which he chose for all his later writings. He pointed out the unpreparedness of the Zionist movement to settle Jews in Palestine, and in later essays advocated the setting up in Palestine of a spiritual centre 'to save Judaism rather than rescue Jews', which he believed Palestine could not achieve. Judaism meant for him the national idea, the eternal ethical values in the Jewish religion embodied in the Hebrew language but emasculated in the religious observances. He was the first Zionist thinker to be profoundly aware of the Arab issue. When HERZL became the Zionist leader (1897–1904), Ahad-Ha'Am was his severest critic for neglecting the spiritual side of the movement, for being ignorant of Jewish history and traditions. He rejected Herzl's catastrophic theory that the Jews face extinction, yet he denied the possibility of a full Jewish life in the diaspora. In 1897 he founded the most prestigious Hebrew literary monthly *Ha'Shilo'ach*, which he edited until 1904 and in which he published many of his essays. His style was precise, modelled on English and French, rejecting the old Hebrew rhetoric. He wrote a series of brilliant essays on the historiography of Jews: 'Moses' (1904), 'The priests and prophets', 'The rule of reason', on Maimonides (1904), and many others. His impact on the Jewish intellectuals in Russia was immense. From 1904 to 1920 he lived in London where, isolated from the mass of Jews, he yet had an influential circle round him, including Chaim WEIZMANN and Sir Leon Simon. His essays were collected in *Al Parashat Derachim* [At the cross-roads] (4 vols, Tel Aviv, 1922), and his letters appeared in six volumes (*Iggarot*, Tel Aviv, 1923–5). His impact on modern Hebrew literature, particularly on BIALIK, has been decisive. A selection of his writings is in *Ahad Ha'Am: Essays, Letters, Memoirs* (tr. L. Simon, London, 1946). CA

N. Bentwich, *Ahad Ha'Am and his Philosophy* (London, 1927); L. Simon, *Ahad Ha'Am, Asher Ginsberg: a Biography* (London, 1960); J. Fraenkel, *Dubnow, Herzl and Ahad Ha'Am* (London, 1963).

Akhmatova, Anna Andreevna, ps. of Anna Gorenko (b. nr Odessa, Russia, 23.6.1889; d. Domodedovo, nr Moscow, USSR, 5.3.1966). Russian poet. The first Russian woman to acquire the reputation of a great 20c poet. She began to write poetry when 11. In 1910 she married the poet Gumilev; with MANDEL'SHTAM they initiated the Acmeist movement, which stood for clarity and concreteness in opposition to symbolist diffuseness and mysticism. Akhmatova's collection *Vecner* [Evening] (St Petersburg, 1912) shows her characteristically concise and evocative manner. The next four collections (*Chetki* [Rosary], St Petersburg, 1914; *Belaia Staia* [White flock], Petrograd, 1917; *Podorozhnik* [Plantain], Petrograd, 1921; and *Anno Domini MCMXXI*, Petrograd, 1921) won her a considerable reputation

as the 'Sappho of the New Era'. This poetry combines intimacy with detachment, lyricism with drama, and has a religious undertone. Famous artists (e.g. MODIGLIANI) painted her portrait, but the attention subsided when Gumilev was executed in 1921 for 'military conspiracy against the revolution'. From 1923 to 1940 and from 1946 to 1956 she was ostracized, ceased to appear in print, and earned her living by translations. In a series of short poems, *Rekviiem*, written 1935–40 (Munich, 1963; tr. D. M. Thomas, *'Requiem' and 'Poem Without a Hero'*, London, 1976), she identified herself with 'writhed innocent Russia'. Her son spent 14 years in STALIN's labour camps and her third husband died there. She became increasingly preoccupied with bearing witness to 'the true 20c'. In 1940 a collection of 20 new poems *Iz snesti knig* [Selection from six books] was published. In 1941 she experienced the siege of Leningrad. Evacuated to Tashkent, she wrote her most 'avant-garde' poem *'Putem vseyia zemlei'* (tr. D. M. Thomas, *Way of All the Earth*, London, 1979), and continued to write *Poema bez geroya* [Poem without a hero] (1940–62), her most powerful lyrical work, which is about time and the fate of a poet in 'this cruel age', faced with being either Russia's voice or its silence. In 1946 she was attacked by ZHDANOV for 'the pernicious spirit of her poetry', and expelled from the writers' union.

After 1956 and the rehabilitation of her son, Akhmatova's poetry was published again in the literary resurgence after Stalin's death. The collection *Stikhotvoreniya* [Poems] (Moscow, 1958) was followed by *Stikhotvoreniya: 1909–1960*. Her late lyrics confirm Mandel'shtam's view that 'Akhmatova has brought into Russian poetry all the complexity and richness of the 19c Russian novel'. She was awarded the Italian Literary Prize and a DLitt at Oxford. From being the 'silence' of Russia, she had become its voice and conscience. Her complete poetry is available as *Sochineniya* [Collected works] (2 vols, NY, 1967–8). Among English versions see *Selected Poems* (tr. W. Arndt, London, 1976). VP

S. Driver, *Anna Akhmatova* (London, 1972); A. Haight, *Anna Akhmatova: a Poetic Pilgrimage* (London, 1976).

Albee, Edward Franklin (b. Washington, DC, USA, 12.3.1928). American dramatist. He began writing for the theatre only as he neared the age of 30, and whose early works seemed to declare him an American exponent of the European 'theatre of the absurd'. Thus his first short play *The Zoo Story* (1959) is a park-bench two-hander about the impossibility of communication, and *The American Dream* (1961) is a family conversation-piece employing a collage of clichés in the manner of IONESCO. Albee's first full-length play *Who's Afraid of Virginia Woolf?* (1962) struck a more recognizably American vein, its apparently naturalistic confrontation between two academic couples merging into the sadomasochistic fantasy which sustains one of their relationships. The theme of interfamilial guilt and responsibility recurred in *A Delicate Balance* (1966), which struck its own balance between symbolism and naturalism, whereas the metaphysical *Tiny Alice* (1964) toyed less successfully with its Russian-doll version of reality. *All Over* (1971) blended a multiple stream-of-consciousness with a sharply focused sense of mortality, again within the domestic framework which, together with Albee's sense of the necessity for self-recognition and mutual responsiveness, have been among the few unifying elements in his formally and thematically diverse output. The individuality of his tone of voice – manifest most notably in a wit that can be caustic or oblique as appropriate – is the most distinctive in the American theatre since Arthur MILLER.

ST

C. W. E. Bigsby, *Albee* (Edinburgh, 1969); M. E. Rutenberg, *Edward Albee: Playwright in Protest* (NY, 1969).

Albers, Josef (b. Bottrop, N. Rhine-Westphalia, Germany, 19.3.1888; naturalized American citizen, 1939; d. New Haven, Conn., USA, 25.3.1976). German/American painter, designer and graphic artist. His early work, mostly graphic, was influenced by cubism and expressionism. In 1920 he became a student at the Bauhaus and taught there from 1923 to 1933. He organized the glass workshop, designed furniture (including the first laminated-wood chair intended for mass production), and contributed to the preliminary course for which he was entirely responsible after MOHOLY-NAGY's departure in 1928. In 1933 he emigrated to the USA, where he introduced Bauhaus ideas and ideals. With Moholy-Nagy, Albers shifted the emphasis at the Bauhaus from its early intuitive, improvisational (handcraft) bias to a more impersonal, functional (technological) approach, based on geometric principles. His investigations into the properties of different materials, though chiefly concerned with economy of means as a principle of construction, eventually led him to study the psychology of form and optical illusions, insisting that the simpler the artistic means, the more intense the effect. Albers explored the shifting perceptual relationship between the surface reality and the illusionistic depth suggested by the juxtaposition of colour forms. These ideas culminated in the series of paintings and lithographs called *Homage to the Square*, begun in 1949, in which he reduced his formal language to three or four superimposed squares of flat, unmodulated colours placed on the surface in mathematical proportions. In *The Interaction of Color* (New Haven, 1963) he states that colour is the chief medium of pictorial language and explores the notion that colour suggests movement. Albers claimed that by means of his mathematically calculated proportions he had created a new form of 'spiritual' content in art.

SOBT

E. Gomringer, *Josef Albers* (Starnberg, 1968).

Alberti, Rafael (b. Puerto de Santa María, Cadiz, Spain, 16.12.1902). Spanish poet and politician. His Andalusian childhood by the sea and its contrast with Madrid (to which his family moved in 1917) underlies the deft lyrics of his first book *Marinero en tierra* [Sailor ashore] (Madrid, 1924), more deeply influenced by folksong than those of any poet since Lope de Vega. Alberti's major prepolitical collections are *Cal y canto* [Lime and song; but the punning title is also an idiom meaning 'sturdily built'] (Madrid, 1929), an important contribution to the Gongorine revival of the generation of 1927, and the intricate, self-tortured *Sobre los ángeles* (Madrid, 1929; tr. G. Connell, *Concerning the Angels*, London, 1967) – pronably his greatest work – which completed 'the closed cycle of my irremediable contribution to bourgeois poetry'. Alberti became a communist in 1931, putting poetry at the service of his politics in, for example, *Un fantasma recorre Europa* [A spectre is haunting Europe] (Madrid, 1933), and writing old-style ballads (*romances*) for the Republican militiamen during the Spanish civil war. From the end of the civil war until FRANCO's death (1975) Alberti lived in exile, chiefly in Argentina and Italy, writing both political and 'artistic' poetry; the latter includes a notable sequence on painters and painting, *A la pintura* [On painting] (Buenos Aires, 1945). His 'committed' verse was collected as *El poeta en la calle: poesía civil 1931–1965* (Paris, 1966; for English versions, see tr. L. Mallan, *Selected Poems*, NY, 1944, and tr. B. Belitt, *Selected Poems*, Berkeley, 1966). An early autobiography *La arboleda perdida* (Mexico City, 1942; tr. G. Berns, *Lost Grove*, Berkeley, 1977) sheds much personal light on the intellectuals of the generation of 1927. Alberti was elected to the Spanish Cortes as a communist in 1978.

RP-M

C. B. Morris, *A Generation of Spanish Poets (1920–1936)* (London, 1969); R. C. Manteiga, *The Poetry of Rafael Alberti: a Visual Approach* (London, 1979).

Aleixandre, Vicente (b. Seville, Spain, 28.4.1898). Spanish poet. One of the few members of the 1927 generation to remain in Spain after the civil war, Aleixandre became the doyen of Spanish contemporary poetry. A neoromantic proclaiming love as universal principle, Aleixandre's philosophy (a combination of pantheism and humanism) and poetic evolution (from an individualist to a collective poetic) are typical of his generation. Like all Spanish surrealist poets rejecting the concept of automatic writing, he explored the natural world and the subconscious through startling dream images, nowhere more so than in his early masterpiece *La destrucción o el amor* [Destruction or love] (Madrid, 1935). His poetry is dominated by creation myths, culminating in *Sombra del paraíso* [Shadows of paradise] (Madrid, 1944), a nostalgic evocation of the lost Eden. The change of focus and style in Aleixandre's postwar verse gave a lead to the new generation of social poets. *Historia del corazón* [The heart's story] (Madrid, 1954) examined man in society and preached human solidarity. He now celebrated the supremacy of ethics over aesthetics and of poetry as communication with the common man. As a consequence his own poetry became simpler and more readily intelligible, although technically as masterly as ever. Aleixandre received the Nobel prize for literature in 1977, an acknowledgement not only of the extraordinary achievement of Spanish lyric poetry in the 20c but of renascent Spanish democracy.   PMcD

K. Schwartz, *Vicente Aleixandre* (NY, 1970).

Aleksandrov, Pavel Sergeevich (b. Bogorodska, Russia, 7.5.1896; d. Moscow, USSR, 16.11.1982). Russian mathematician who contributed primarily to the development of topology, a modern form of geometry. While a student at the University of Moscow, he became interested in abstract set theory, as founded by CANTOR. In the early 1920s he vigorously developed set-theoretic topology with his friend P. S. Uryson. They developed the theory of general topological spaces and compact topological spaces, initiated by FRÉCHET and F. Hausdorff. After Uryson died in an accident in 1924, Aleksandrov turned increasingly towards investigating combinatorial or algebraic topology, as founded by POINCARÉ. He thus created a homological theory of dimension. With the Swiss mathematician H. Hopf he planned a three-volume comprehensive treatise on topology. Only the first volume *Topologie I* (Berlin, 1935) was published, but this has been highly influential. A founder of the Moscow school of topology, he trained many Russian mathematicians in research and wrote extensively, both research works and student textbooks. DMJ

Allende (Gossens), Salvador (b. Valparaiso, Chile, 26.7.1908; d. Santiago, 11.9.1973). Chilean left-wing political leader. Allende was born into an upper-middle-class family and graduated from medical school in 1932. In 1933 he took part in founding Chile's Socialist party, serving (1939–42) as minister of health in the radical coalition of President Aguirre Cerda. After three unsuccessful attempts at election to the presidency (1952, 1958, 1964) he succeeded as the candidate of Popular Unity, a bloc of socialists, communists, radicals and some dissident Christian democrats. He failed to secure a popular majority but came first in a three-cornered contest. Confirmed in office by Congress, he was inaugurated as Chile's first MARXist president on 3.11.1970.

Allende's programme was the restructuring of Chilean society on socialist lines. He nationalized several industries; secured the right to appropriate the nation's mineral resources; handed over large estates to peasant cooperatives; and supported the industrial workers' claims to large wage increases. Abroad, Allende established friendly relations with two communist governments, in China and Cuba. Relations with the USA became strained as a result of the threat to the large American investments in Chile. Some US-owned copper mines were expropriated without compensation and US business interests retaliated by an embargo on the sale of the copper and by cutting off foreign loans. In turn Allende established closer relations with the USSR. After two years in office, his regime was faced with a runaway inflation and mounting resistance from the middle class. A military coup, which the left claim was supported by the Americans, overthrew his government on 11.9.1973. Allende's death was reported to have been by his own hand. He was succeeded by a repressive right-wing military junta which reversed the changes he had introduced. The Allende regime continues to excite controversy over the question whether its overthrow was due to its own contradictions and failures or shows the readiness of the propertied classes and the multinational companies to go to any lengths to defend their privileges. ALCB

Althusser, Louis (b. Birmandreïs, Algiers, France [now Algeria], 16.10.1918). French philosopher. Althusser was educated at Algiers, Marseilles and Lyons, and at the Ecole Normale Supérieure. He spent five years in concentration camps during WW2. In 1948 he was appointed to teach at the ENS and joined the French Communist party. In 1981 he was committed to a mental hospital after strangling his wife.

Althusser's first major articles were published in the early 1960s in *La Pensée* and *La Nouvelle Critique* and collected in *Pour Marx* (Paris, 1965; tr. B. Brewster, *For Marx*, London, 1969). They sought to establish the Marxian canon as 'historical materialism', with a theory of history which freed the 'scientific' MARX not only from some STALINist distortions but from the Feuerbachian and especially the Hegelian traits reassigned to him by neo-Marxist theory. For Althusser, Marxism was neither a world-view nor a 'philosophy' nor an ideology, but the revolutionary science of history conceived as class struggle. Less comprehensibly, it was philosophy as the 'practice of the production of concepts', or the 'theory of theoretical practice'. Althusser's representation of Marxism was indebted to French antipositivist epistemology (BACHELARD and FOUCAULT) for the notion of the *coupure épistémologique* or 'epistemological break'. According to Althusser, the 'humanist' and utopian early Marx was discarded by Marx himself and cannot be traced consistently in the later works. The year of the break was 1845, two years after Marx's critique of Hegel's *Philosophy of Right*. From 1857 Marx was a fully fledged Marxist, seeing the authentic subjects of production, of history, not as real men but as productive forces and relations, their contradictions and structure.

In *Lire le Capitale* (with E. Balibar, Paris, 1965; tr. B. Brewster, *Reading Capital*, London, 1969) Althusser was confessedly influenced by Bachelard when he elicited the fundamental structure or 'objective internal reference system of ... [the] particular themes' of *Capital*: the 'Marx of the gaps' – not what Marx appeared to say, but the problems he posed implicitly behind the answers which he proposed explicitly. Psychoanalysis (Foucault in particular) enabled Althusser to produce not only this version of the 'significant lapse' of FREUDian theory but the notion of complex effect or 'overdetermination' in social formations: the economic, political and ideological elements of a social structure or ensemble help to determine and are determined by that structure; the relationship is reciprocal but complex and uneven. In *Lénine et la philosophie* (Paris, 1968; tr. B. Brewster, *Lenin and Philosophy*, London, 1971) and in several 'autocritical essays' he elaborated his idea of philosophy as the theoretical expression of politics, and tried to reconcile with class struggle his hitherto 'theoreticist' approximation of philosophy to 'science'.

Althusser's theories have been influential in many spheres (e.g. in aesthetics: Macherey), but above all in the recent Marxist study of capitalism and class function (Poulantzas, Bettelheim). A major objection to them is the absence of criteria for the verification of his science as science, apart from its authentication by an elite or an individual engaged in the class struggle not in practice but in the 'theory of practice'.

JCu

N.. Poulantzas, *Political Power and Social Classes* (London, 1973); A. Callinicos, *Althusser's Marxism* (London, 1976).

Amado, Jorge (b. Pirangi, Bahía, Brazil, 10.8.1912). Brazilian novelist. A bestseller in Latin America, and one of the four representative writers of the Brazilian north-east, Amado was born on his father's plantation, fled school and became a reporter. In 1931 he studied law in Rio de Janeiro, simultaneously publishing his first novel *O país do carnaval* [Carnival country] (Rio de Janeiro, 1931). With *Cacau* [Cocoa] (Rio de Janeiro, 1933) and *Suor* [Sweat] (Rio de Janeiro, 1934) he declared his political alignment with movements of the left. After the suppression of communism in Brazil, he was imprisoned, then

lived abroad in Buenos Aires, France, Eastern Europe and the USSR. His narratives are concerned with the social and political problems of the Brazilian north-east: abandoned, delinquent children; the misery of dock-workers and urban blacks; periodical drought; the roving *cangaçeiros* (outlaws); the exploited rural labourer and the exploiting plantation-owner. His work portrays the poetry and folklore of his region, especially the importations from Africa. He is an honorary voodoo priest (*paido-santo*). His later novels – *Gabriela, Cravo e Canela* (São Paulo, 1958; tr. J. L. Taylor & W. C. Grossman, *Gabriela, Clove and Cinnamon*, NY, 1962), *Os velhos marinheiros* (Lisbon, 1961; tr. H. de Onis, *Home to the Sailor*, NY, 1964), *Os pastores da noite* (São Paulo, 1966; tr. H. de Onis, *Shepherds of the Night*, NY, 1967) and *Dona Flor e seus dois maridos* (São Paulo, 1966; tr. H. de Onis, *Dona Flor and Her Two Husbands*, NY, 1969) – show the novelist proper taking over from the writer with a thesis.

DBr

F. P. Ellison, *Brazil's New Novel* (Berkeley, Calif., 1954).

Amin, Idi Dada (b. Koboko, West Nile, Uganda, 1925). President of Uganda from 1971 to 1979. The most publicized African head of state of the 1970s, at once tyrant and buffoon, Amin was responsible for strengthening notions of African 'barbarism' and 'savagery' in the minds of many non-Africans. A Muslim of little formal education, from the remote north-west of Uganda, he rose through the ranks of the King's African Rifles to become President Obote's most trusted army officer and hatchet man. Ousting Obote in a coup in 1971, Amin built up his own power with ruthless adroitness, purged the army of Obote's fellow-tribesmen, murdered key members of the Ugandan bourgeoisie, expelled the Asian minority, recruited mercenaries from the southern Sudan, and took arms from the USSR and money from Libya. He was a consummate self-dramatizer; his ribald and irreverent attitude to the British won him considerable populist support in black Africa: he was elected chairman of the Organization of African Unity in 1975. But the brutality of his actions discredited him completely with many Ugandans and with his neighbour, President NYERERE of Tanzania. In 1979 the Tanzanian army, provoked by an abortive Ugandan attack on Tanzanian territory, invaded Uganda and forced Amin to seek refuge in Libya. RH

D. Martin, *General Amin* (London, 1978).

Andenaes, Johannes (b. Innvik, Norway, 7.9.1912). Norwegian criminologist. Andenaes has had a distinguished academic career in the University of Oslo, as successively professor of criminal law and criminology, dean of the law faculty and latterly rector of the university. His contribution to the Norwegian academic community and to Norwegian legal studies in particular has been immense. He has also served on many governmental committees on penal law, criminal procedure and penal reform. But his eminence as a scholar is derived from his outstanding contribution to criminal law. Through his writing on specific aspects of Norwegian criminal theory he has greatly contributed to the wider perspectives of criminal law and criminal justice studies in the western industrial societies. His international reputation was recognized in the publication of his *The General Part of the Criminal Law of Norway* in 1965 as the first volume in the American Criminal Law project. As a scholar in criminal law and criminology Andenaes is best known for his numerous writings on the general preventative effects of criminal law, a subject which until recently was almost completely neglected in criminological and sociolegal studies, although it had for long occupied a central position in the philosophy of criminal law, in penal legislation and in the sentencing policies of the courts. FHMcC

Anderson, Sherwood (b. Camden, Ohio, USA, 13.9.1876; d. Colon, Panama, 8.3.1941). American novelist and short-story writer. Anderson's mythic version of his own life – that in middle age he repudiated a business career and became an artist – embodies the recurrent themes of his writing: the maiming by commercial values of an innocent America of pastoral fulfilment, and the frustrated search by Americans for meaning and value in a disorderly modern civilization. His use of midwestern subject matter has much in common with that of DREISER, but the demands of large-scale narrative eluded or coarsened his talent. *Winesburg, Ohio* (NY, 1919), a series of sketches of small-town life as seen through the eyes of an adolescent, persuasively conveys compassion for lives of damaged and incoherent expectation. With its command of the expressive uses of the observer's imperfect comprehension, and symbolic interpretation of detail, accommodated to an adequate extended form, the book is deservedly thought to be Anderson's finest work. These qualities, which were to influence HEMINGWAY and FAULKNER, are strongly marked also in the collections of stories *The Triumph of the Egg* (NY, 1921) and *Horses and Men* (NY, 1923), and in the memoirs *A Story Teller's Story* (NY, 1924) and *Tar: a Midwest Childhood* (NY, 1926). ATKC

J. Schevill, *Sherwood Anderson: his Life and Work* (Denver, 1951).

Andrić, Ivo (b. Travnik, Bosnia, Austria-Hungary [now Yugoslavia], 9.10.1892; d. Belgrade, 13.3.1975). Serbian novelist and short-story writer. Educated in Sarajevo, Vienna, Cracow and Graz, Andrić was involved in the Young Bosnia movement responsible for the assassination of Archduke Franz Ferdinand in 1914. After WW1 he involved himself in the literary life of Zagreb before joining the diplomatic service. Based in Belgrade he was posted to several European capitals, ending his career as ambassador in Berlin in 1939. Between the wars Andrić published several collections of short stories and some essays, and in 1945 the three novels for which he is best known abroad: *Travnička hronika* (Belgrade, 1945; tr. K. Johnstone, *Bosnian Story*, London, 1958), *Na Drini ćuprija* (Belgrade, 1945; tr. L. Edwards, *The Bridge on the Drina*, London, 1959) and *Gospodjica* (Belgrade, 1945; tr. J. Hitrec, *The Woman from Sarajevo*, London, 1965). After WW2 he published several more volumes of stories and the novella *Prokleta avlija* (Belgrade, 1954; tr. K. Johnstone, *Devil's*

Yard, London, 1962), widely considered his masterpiece. In 1961 he was awarded the Nobel prize for literature. Several new works were published after his death including a collection of reflections *Znakovi pored puta* [Signs by the roadside] (Belgrade, 1977). The attitude to life that emerges from this intellectual diary, as from all Andrić's writing, is one that grew out of his particular experience of life between East and West: an essentially stoical outlook, an awareness of the vanity, as well as the vital importance, of the search to transcend the absurd through art. ECH

Andrzejewski, Jerzy (b. Warsaw, Russian Poland [now Poland], 19.8.1909; d. Warsaw, 20.4.1983). Polish novelist and short-story writer. His first full-length novel *Ład serca* [Harmony of the heart] (Warsaw, 1938) won him the title of Catholic writer and moralist. But it was *Popiół i diament* (Warsaw, 1948; tr. D. Welsh, *Ashes and Diamonds*, London, 1962) and its subsequent screen adaptation (1958) by WAJDA that brought him international fame. MIŁOSZ's pen-portrait of Andrzejewski in *The Captive Mind* (1953) is tendentious to a fault; and Andrzejewski soon outlived the political and journalistic commitments of his socialist realist phase. Since the publication of *Ciemności kryją ziemię* (Warsaw, 1957; tr. K. Syrop, *The Inquisitors*, London, 1960) his novels invariably provoke intense controversy – and frequent misrepresentation – in the literary press: and indeed his infinite intricacies and ambiguities of style and thought elude simplistic interpretation. His fiction investigates the problems of totalitarianism and the corruption of power (see *Apelacja*, Paris, 1968; tr. C. Wieniewska, *The Appeal*, London, 1971). Another constant theme is the dilemma facing the creative artist (*Idzie skacząc po górach*, Warsaw, 1963; tr. C. Wieniewska, *He Cometh Leaping upon the Mountains*, London, 1965; *Już prawie nic* [End of the road], Warsaw, 1976; *Miazga* [Pulp], Warsaw, 1979). Although Andrzejewski does not profess himself an innovator, he is widely recognized as Poland's outstanding master of prose prosody; while spiritually he belongs with Dostoevsky, BERNANOS, CÉLINE and CONRAD. NT

Anokhin, Pyotr Kuz'mich (b. St Petersburg [now Leningrad], Russia, 26.1.1898; d. Moscow, USSR, 6.3.1974). Soviet psychologist. Anokhin graduated from the Leningrad Medical Institute in 1926 and worked in PAVLOV's laboratory from 1922 to 1930. Professor at the Gorki Medical Institute from 1930, he was subsequently director of the Physiology Institute (1946–9) and then, from 1950, director of the Neurophysiological Laboratory under the USSR Academy of Medical Sciences. In 1935 Anokhin made a major discovery in behavioural physiology: all responses are followed by afferent impulses which comprise information on the response process (return afferentation). This observation was influential in the development of the notion of feedback in cybernetics. He worked out a theory of functional organic systems whose principles are used in technology, automatic control – or cybernetics – biology and medicine. He also developed the principle of compensating disrupted functions applied in Soviet medicine. IV

Anouilh, Jean (b. Bordeaux, Gironde, France, 23.6.1910). French dramatist who has combined boulevard popularity with a bitterly ironic view of life in a career devoted almost exclusively to the theatre. Loneliness, lack of communication between intimates, the corruption of innocence and the pathos of old age are his constant themes. But it is his supreme technical adroitness, often exemplified in the 'play-within-a-play' format, that animates his work. Strongly influenced by GIRAUDOUX, he began his career as secretary to the director Louis Jouvet, wrote his first play at 19 and has since regularly produced work which he categorizes as dark, rosy, sparkling or grating. His richest period coincided with France's own era of insecurity; and indeed his work has often reflected national divisions; *Antigone* (1944; tr. L. Galantière, London, 1951) was a rewrite of Sophocles in which Creon became identified with the German occupiers and Antigone with the indomitable rebel; *Pauvre Bitos* (1956; tr. L. Hill,

Poor Bitos, London, 1964) was initially taken as a slander on the resistance. Even so, Anouilh's plays are more about private pain than political events: even a historical play like *Becket* (1959; tr. L. Hill, London, 1961) is less about recorded fact than about the cold priest's inability to return Henry II's love. The lasting impression one carries away from his work is horror at the contrast between what life could be and what it actually is: a horror rendered with dazzling dramatic skill. MB

J. Harvey, *Anouilh, a Study in Theatrics* (NY, 1964); P. Thody, *Anouilh* (London, 1968).

Antal, Frederick (b. Budapest, Austria-Hungary [now Hungary], 21.12.1887; naturalized British citizen, 1946; d. London, UK, 4.4.1954). Hungarian/British art historian. After studying in Vienna under Max Dvorak he worked in Budapest, Florence and Vienna (1914–22). In 1922 he settled in Berlin where he remained until he emigrated to the UK in 1933. Proceeding from Dvorak's interpretation of art history as *Geistesgeschichte*, or cultural history, Antal rejected as historically invalid the purely formal analysis of style prevalent in the 1920s and 1930s. Given that each style is a specific combination of subject matter and form, Antal thought that the theme offered the primary introduction to the worldview or philosophy reflected in a specific work; only when this had been grasped was it possible to discern the complex relationship between the formal elements and the social or philosophical outlook. In regard to the coexistence of different styles in the same period, Antal stressed the need to study the economic, social and political conditions of various social sectors of any period to enable the art historian to reconstruct their philosophies and thus penetrate to their art. His major works include: *Florentine Painting and its Social Background,* written 1932–8 (London, 1948); *Fuseli Studies* (London, 1956); *Hogarth and his Place in European Art* (London, 1962); *Classicism and Romanticism* (London, 1966). SOBT

Antonioni, Michelangelo (b. Ferrara, Emilia-Romagna, Italy, 29.9.1912).

Italian film director whose work is rooted in the French cinema of the 1930s (he was at one time assistant to Carné) and in Italian neorealism of the 1940s. Antonioni began his directing career with works such as *Cronaca di un amore* [Chronicle of a love, 1950], *Le Amiche* (*The Girlfriends*, 1955) and *Il grido* (*The Cry*, 1957), which draw on earlier developments: they have all the pessimism of neorealist cinema and the plots are circular, allowing the characters no development. But the causes of the anguish are no longer merely socially defined, and emphasis shifts from outward social pressures to inner frustrations and violence. This psychological realism reached its height with the 'trilogy' formed by *L'Avventura* [The adventure, 1960], *La Notte* [The night, 1961] and *L'Eclisse* (*The Eclipse*, 1962). Subsequently Antonioni has worked in colour and with a new awareness of moral ambiguity: *Deserto rosso* (*Red Desert*, 1964), *Blow-Up* (England: 1966), *Zabriskie Point* (USA: 1969) and *Profession: Reporter* (*The Passenger*, USA: 1975). For all their undoubted qualities, these films took him away from his Italian roots and placed him in a world of fashionable international chic. His attempts at renewal through a documentary on China (*Chung Kuo*, 1972), an Italian television drama (*Il mistero di Oberwald*, after COCTEAU, 1980) and a new feature *Identificazione di una donna* [Identification of a woman, 1982] achieved only limited impact. Michelangelo Antonioni's early 1960s work has, however, a continued validity, alongside the contemporaneous work of the rather younger film makers associated with the French 'New Wave'. Antonioni proved to a new generation the validity of the cinema as a medium for psychological fiction independent of the schematization of character and onward-rushing melodramatic plot typical of the Hollywood movie. While the popular success of a film like *Blow-Up* is in some ways surprising, Antonioni's profound impact on film sensibility since the 1960s is no more than a true reflection of his willingness to follow the guidings of his talent and his conception of a new form of cinematic narration. RPA

P. Leprohon, *Michelangelo Antonioni* (NY, 1963); I. Cameron & R. Wood, *Antonioni* (London, 1968).

Apollinaire, Guillaume, ps. of Wilhelm Apollinaris de Kostrowitzky (b. Rome, Italy, 26.8.1880; d. Paris, France, 9.11.1918). French poet of illegitimate birth and mixed Polish and Italian ancestry, Wilhelm de Kostrowitzky travelled in Germany before settling in Paris and signing his first poems as Guillaume Apollinaire in 1903. He mixed with a circle of artists and writers which included PICASSO, DERAIN and JARRY, and became the lover of the painter Marie Laurencin. He edited a number of reviews, published satirical and semi-pornographic texts, and proclaimed that the writing of Sade would dominate the 20c. In 1913 the publication of *Alcools* (Paris; tr. A. Hyde Greet, Berkeley, 1964) confirmed his reputation as a major, highly original poet, combining the traditional poetic themes of love and the poet's happiness with an evocation of the modern city which is one of his links with Baudelaire and ELIOT. In December 1914 Apollinaire joined the French army, was commissioned in 1915, wounded in 1916 and died in 1918. The publication of *Calligrammes* (Paris, 1918; tr. O. Barnard in *Selected Poems*, London, 1965) marked a new development in his work, with an intenser eroticism and an even more original verbal and typographical style. It contained some of the finest poems in French about WW1. His surrealist play *Les Mamelles de Tiresias* (Paris, 1917; tr. L. Simpson, *The Breasts of Tiresias*, NY, 1961) combines his own sexual obsessions with a satirical, highly amusing exploitation of Greek legend and an ironic preoccupation with the low birthrate in 19c–20c France. His stature has continued to grow since his death, as the precursor of surrealism and as a modernist poet whose work transcends aesthetic experimentalism to speak directly of the human condition. PMWT

M. Davies, *Apollinaire* (Edinburgh, 1964); C. Tournadre (ed.), *Les Critiques de notre temps et Apollinaire* (Paris, 1971).

Appel, Karel (b. Amsterdam, The Netherlands, 25.4.1925). Dutch painter who was one of the leading neo-expressionists of postwar Europe. He had his first one-man exhibition in 1946, and in 1948 was one of the founders of the Dutch Experimental group which merged with the Cobra group, formed in Paris during the same year. The aim of the latter was to express unconscious forces through violent gesture painting and imagery related to primitive art and Nordic folklore. In 1949 Appel's mural for the cafeteria of the city hall, Amsterdam, was whitewashed after a public outcry, and in the following year he moved to Paris where he began to achieve an international reputation. He is best known for his paintings using thick impasto and intense colour, often straight from the tube, to depict imagery reminiscent of child and psychotic art; they combine a sense of humour with aggressiveness and fear. During the later 1960s he began to make sculpture, and by the early 1970s his paintings had become calmer, characterized by flat areas of colour within defined borders. MOJN

C. Hugo, *Karel Appel, Painter* (London, 1963); Wildenstein Gallery, *Appel* (London, 1975).

Appia, Adolfe François (b. Geneva, Switzerland, 1.9.1862; d. Nyon, Vaud, 29.2.1928). Swiss theatre designer and theorist. Influenced by classical Greek theatre and French symbolism, Appia devoted himself in 1888 to reforming the techniques of stage presentation, in particular of Wagner's 'Tondramen', which he regarded as the only possible theatre for the future. He proposed an end to realistic settings, fixed lighting, footlights and painted shadows, in favour of projected lighting on three-dimensional, abstract scenery placed on a multilevel stage. The actors, in simple costumes, were to be 'depersonalized' through the music, both in their movement (away from clichéd poses) and in their voices towards the supreme illusion of the tone poet. His major theoretical work *La Musique et la mise-en-scène* was written between 1892 and 1897 and first published as *Die Musik und die Inscenierung* (Munich, 1899; *Music and* *the Art of the Theatre*, Miami, 1962). Rejected at first, he staged scenes from *Carmen* and *Manfred* privately in Paris in 1903, then *Orpheus and Euridice* in Hellerau in 1912–13, *Tristan and Isolde* at La Scala, Milan, in 1923, and finally *Das Rheingold, Die Walküre* and *Prometheus* in Basle in 1924–5. His influence on the 20c theatre, particularly of his theories of 'active light' and 'living space', is to be seen in the productions of Wieland WAGNER after WW2. AJM

Appleton, Edward Victor (b. Bradford, W. Yorks., UK, 6.9.1892; d. Edinburgh, Lothian, 21.4.1965). British physicist. Appleton was the pioneer investigator of the region high in the atmosphere (above about 70 km) called the ionosphere. Here the ultra-violet rays from the sun are strong enough to remove electrons from the gas molecules so that the atmosphere becomes a tenuous region of freely moving positive and negative charged particles. The existence of the ionosphere had already been suggested, but Appleton first established its existence experimentally. This he did by showing that it could reflect radio waves from a distant transmitter. He demonstrated that the reflecting layer became less effective towards dawn but that there was a higher layer present from which reflections could still be obtained. He called the lower of these layers the *E* layer and the upper the *F* layer (this latter is sometimes referred to as the Appleton layer). For this work he was awarded a Nobel prize for physics in 1947. The improved radio reception of distant stations at night and the fading of signals are two ionospheric effects with which everyone is familiar; Appleton's work laid the foundations for understanding not only these phenomena, but the general principles of long-distance radio propagation. HMR

Arafat, Yasser (b. Gaza, Palestine [now Israel], 1929). Palestinian Arab political leader who trained as an engineer in Cairo, was president of the League of Palestinian Students (1952–6), and became chairman of the Palestinian Liberation Organization in the aftermath of the 1969 Arab–Israeli war. This was at a time when the generalized feelings of Arab nationalism were beginning to yield to more specific feelings of Palestinianism, under the spur of repeated Arab defeats at Israel's hands and a consequent battle between Egypt, Jordan and Syria to control Palestinian activities in their own interests. Challenged after 1970 by the extremists of the 'rejectionist' front backed by Iraq to reject anything but total war against Israel, Arafat parleyed his precarious hold on the PLO's variegated groupings into a position where the PLO increasingly came to enjoy, especially at international conferences and UN gatherings, a status analogous to that of a wartime government in exile. The 1978 Egyptian–Israeli peace treaty, however, faced him with the dilemma of whether to accept the establishment of a Palestinian self-governing entity on the West Bank and recognize the state of Israel, or see all that he had gained lost through insistence on the PLO's aim, incorporated in its constitution, of destroying the state of Israel. Before he was called on to decide, Arafat's position was changed again by Begin's continued colonization of the West Bank in breach of the understanding with Egypt and the Israelis' 1982 invasion of Lebanon. The PLO's armed forces were destroyed or dispersed but the political advantage to be derived from the widespread condemnation and disillusionment with Israel, particularly in the USA, may yet more than compensate Arafat for the PLO's military defeat. DCW

Aragon, Louis (b. Paris, France, 3.10.1897; d. Paris, 24.12.1982). French poet, novelist, essayist and journalist. With prodigiously diverse literary gifts and an output of over 60 books spanning a writing career of six and a half decades, Aragon has been described by Gaëton Picon as 'one of the most dazzling comets ever to have crossed our literary sky'. In 1919 Aragon, BRETON and Philippe Soupault founded the review *Littérature* which became the principal mouthpiece of Paris dadaism and subsequently of the nascent surrealist movement. His verve, his seductive facility with words, first shown in his poems *Feu de joie* [Fire of joy] (Paris, 1920), the passion and insolent invective of his revolt against his bourgeois inheritance, his physical courage (he received the Croix de Guerre in both wars), ensured him a role second only to that of Breton in the elaboration of surrealism in the 1920s. Always a conscious virtuoso of style, Aragon seldom resorted to surrealist methods of automatic writing. In *Le Paysan de Paris* (Paris, 1926; tr. S. Watson-Taylor, *Paris Peasant*, London, 1971), his attention was already focused on the real world, in this case some innocuous corners of Paris wherein he intuited a latent surreality. Aragon as a surrealist combined the pursuit of the marvellous concealed within the modern everyday world with the uninhibited exaltation of the potential of language to change life. In 1932, after falling in love with the Russian-born novelist Elsa Triolet, and bowled over by the achievements of the USSR, Aragon broke with surrealism. Henceforth he devotedly served the Communist party and in 1937 was appointed editor of the new party newspaper *Ce Soir*. He became the leading advocate of socialist realism, which he saw as the best means of merging literary work with the onward movement of humanity at large, beyond the individualism of writers. In his monumental cycle of novels entitled *Le Monde Réel* [The real world] (5 vols, Paris, 1934–51), Aragon sought to interweave the individual destinies of his characters, his sense of place and eye for the telling detail with the broader lines of the MARXist interpretation of history. But as the series progressed it became more prosaic and straightforwardly propagandist. During the occupation, Aragon was active in the intellectual resistance and founded the National Committee of Writers. As prolific as ever after WW2 – whether in poems, fiction, in art criticism, history and journalism (founder-editor of *Les Lettres Françaises* in 1953) – Aragon in his own lifetime became a monument in the French classical literary tradition. Latterly, as if to counter the growing opinion that he might after all be only an elegant *précieux* who lost his true path, he asserted his freedom to criticize Soviet policy and was at pains to prove the consistency of his evolution from surrealism to communism.   RSS

C. Savage, *Malraux, Sartre and Aragon as Political Novelists* (Gainesville, 1964); L. F. Becker, *Louis Aragon* (NY, 1971).

Arber, Werner (b. Gränichen, Aargau, Switzerland, 3.6.1929). Swiss molecular biologist. After study in Zürich and Geneva (1953–7), Arber like many Swiss scientists did some research in the USA (at the universities of Southern California, 1958–9, and Berkeley, 1970–1). He shared in the earliest use of bacteriophage viruses as a model for studying genes when S. Luria observed that virus genes can be modified by the particular strain of bacteria they attack. Back in Geneva as professor of microbiology at the University of Basle from 1971, Arber, with Daisy Dussoix, showed that this was due to the bacterium's ability to cut DNA (genes) at specific chemical junctions. The bacterium, by a chemical modification, protected the cutting of such junctions in its own genes. Thus the enzyme responsible had to work only on that particular chemical structure, so as not to run rampant in the rest of the bacterial genome. Aside from their usefulness to virus-beleaguered bacteria, such 'site-specific DNA endonucleases' were quickly realized to be of tremendous use to science. Cutting DNA in specific places permits sequencing and eventual understanding of the structure and function of genes. Arber shared the 1978 Nobel prize for physiology and medicine with others who participated in the explosion of results which followed his observation. More than anything else endonucleases make possible the modern study of genes and their manipulation in genetic engineering.   DOM

Arbus, Diane, ps. of Diane Nemerov (b. New York, USA, 14.3.1923; d. New York, 26.7.1971). American photographer. A student (1955–7) of the photographer Lisette Model who taught at the New School for Social Research in New York, she began to publish her photographs in such magazines as *Harper's Bazaar* and *Esquire* in the early 1960s. Supported by Guggenheim fellowships in 1963 and 1966 she undertook documentary projects on American rites, manners and customs. She explained herself thus in her application to the Guggenheim Foundation: 'I want simply to save them, for what is ceremonious and curious and commonplace will be legendary.' In 1967 a group of her pictures appeared in the show 'New Documents' at New York's Museum of Modern Art. In the late 1960s she taught photography courses at Parson's School of Design, Rhode Island School of Design, and Cooper Union. In 1971 she committed suicide. A major retrospective of her work at the Museum of Modern Art in 1972 was the most widely discussed and influential exhibition of the decade.

Arbus was mainly a portraitist, and many of her subjects were exhibitionists and picturesque outsiders: transvestites, hermaphrodites, dwarfs, tattooed men. These outsiders, and other more commonplace people, face her camera awkwardly; they know something of what is expected of them, but are rarely capable of realizing that 'something'. Arbus's principal subject was the gap between stereotype and actuality, between how we imagine ourselves and how we look. She also contradicted dominant pictorial stereotypes: her women can look as formidable as warriors and her transvestite men have a fashion-plate elegance. In part her work can be illuminated by reference to that of Lisette Model, also greatly interested in the jolting physicality of her subjects; but Arbus's thoroughly ironic treatment of the principal stereotypes of American culture is without precedent.   IJ

diane arbus (Aperture History of Photography) (NY, 1972).

Archipenko, Alexander (b. Kiev, Russia, 30.5.1887; naturalized American citizen, 1928; d. New York, USA, 25.2.1964). Russian/American sculptor. Archipenko studied at Kiev and Moscow before moving to Paris (1908) where he studied Egyptian, African and other primitive arts. Introduced to cubism by LÉGER, he began in 1912 to treat the surface as a series of interlocking convex and concave forms, leaving the central space of the head and body empty (e.g. *Walking*, 1912). For the first time in modern sculpture a hole was no longer a void,

but an autonomous, structured shape. In 1912 he began to assemble figures from various materials such as wood, metal, cardboard and glass (e.g. *Medrano II*, 1912), which pre-empt dada. After exhibitions in Hagen, Berlin and New York (all 1913) his absorption of space into sculpture was widely influential (e.g. LIPCHITZ, PICASSO and later Henry MOORE). From 1912 he attempted a synthesis of painting and sculpture (e.g. *Bather*, 1915) in which wood and metal elements project from the illusionistic background as extensions of the same form. In 1921 Archipenko broke with cubism and moved to Berlin where he embraced constructivism. In 1923 he emigrated to the USA where he invented 'Archipentura', an attempt to fuse painting, sculpture and time in a moving picture. In 1935-6 he taught at Washington University and in 1937 at the New Bauhaus. In 1937 he opened his own school in Chicago, and in 1939 a sculpture school in New York. From 1946 he made 'light modulators', or interior-lit Plexiglass sculptures.   SOBT

A. Archipenko *et al.*, *Alexander Archipenko, Fifty Creative Years, 1908–1958* (NY, 1960); D. Karshaw, *Archipenko*, exh. cat. (Los Angeles, 1969).

Arden, John (b. Barnsley, S. Yorks., UK, 26.10.1930). British dramatist. Initially the author of a set of tough, ambiguous, verse-filled fables that ransacked the past for parallels with contemporary events, he has latterly devoted himself to an attempt to found an ideal community theatre. His reputation rests principally on his own early plays in which, more Brechtian than BRECHT, he offers a painful, often confusing moral choice. In *Live Like Pigs* (1958) sympathy is divided equally between an anarchic tribe of vagabonds and a lower-middle-class council estate family. In *Serjeant Musgrave's Dance* (1959), set in a strike-bound northern town in the 1880s, the ferocious scourge of colonial warfare turns out to be a religious maniac. In *The Workhouse Donkey* (1962), the first postwar British play to put a community on stage, the pendulum of sympathy swings between a Rabelaisian councillor and an incorruptible chief constable. Partly because of this moral complexity, Arden never broke through to the large popular audience he was seeking with these plays. Since 1967 he has written overtly committed community shows with his wife Margaretta D'Arcy. Their one excursion into large-scale, London-subsidized theatre, *The Island of the Mighty* (1972), was presented by the Royal Shakespeare Company in a form the authors objected to. The Ardens live in Ireland and devote much energy to disinterring that country's history; in *The Non-Stop Connolly Show* (Dublin, 1975) they produced a 24-hour show about a revolutionary hero. But Arden has returned to his earlier ironic complexity in a morally and verbally rich radio play *The Pearl* (1978) and in a major first novel *Silence Among the Weapons* (London, 1982) dealing with the factions inside the Roman Republic during the first century BC. MB

A. Hunt, *Arden: a Study of His Plays* (London, 1974).

Arendt, Hannah (b. Hanover, Lower Saxony, Germany, 14.10.1906; naturalized American citizen, 1950; d. New York, USA, 4.12.1975). German/American political philosopher. After studying with HUSSERL and particularly JASPERS, under whose guidance she wrote a dissertation on the concept of love in St Augustine, Arendt moved to Paris in 1933 with the advent of HITLER and engaged in Jewish social work. She escaped to the USA in 1941 and held posts in Jewish organizations and in publishing until her first academic appointment in Chicago in 1963. From 1967 until her death she was a notable figure at the New School in New York City. Her first significant publication was *The Origins of Totalitarianism* (NY, 1951) in which the likeness to each other and the historical novelty of the ideological terror-systems of Nazism and Soviet communism were asserted. *The Human Condition* (NY, 1958) explored the related ideas of labour, work and action in a spirit of etymological improvisation. Her *On Revolution* (NY, 1963) compared the French and American revolutions to the disadvantage of the former, but did not consider the large differences between the kinds of revolution involved. Her *New Yorker* article of 1961, 'Eichmann in Jerusalem' (also as *Eichmann in Jerusalem: Report on the Banality of Evil*, NY, 1961), excited controversy, more for its suggestion of the complicity of the European Jews in their own annihilation than for its picture of Eichmann as a mechanized bureaucrat and not an evil but responsible monster. Her posthumous and unfinished *The Life of the Mind* (NY, 1978) adopted a grandly systematic posture which its elusive content did little to sustain. AQ

M. Canovan, *The Political Theory of Hannah Arendt* (NY, 1974).

Argand, Emile (b. Geneva, Switzerland, 6.1.1879; d. Neuchâtel, 14.9.1940). Swiss geologist. Probably the greatest of a group of outstanding Swiss and French geologists who unravelled the complex structure of the Alps early this century, Argand studied at Lausanne under Maurice Lugeon, and eventually became professor of geology at Neuchâtel, where he spent the rest of his life. A man of many gifts who could have been a successful architect, linguist, writer or businessman, his ability to think in three dimensions, and capacity for visual recall stood him in great stead in his Alpine research. The nappe structure in the Helvetic Alps had been worked out by Lugeon and others; Argand's contribution was to recognize nappes (sheets of rock which have moved sideways over neighbouring strata) in the far more difficult terrain of the Pennine Alps, where there were few stratigraphic markers. He was the first to use the inversion of metamorphic zones in structural explanation, recognizing huge cylindrical structures with axial culminations and depressions. He developed his theory of embryotectonics, whereby ancient ridges and troughs guided the subsequent growth of fold mountains, an idea which, though no longer accepted, stimulated later Alpine research. Argand produced a valuable synthesis of Eurasian tectonics in which he espoused the new ideas on continental mobilism put forward by WEGENER when such notions were decidedly heretical. AH

Arghezi, Tudor, ps. of Ion Theodorescu (b. Bucharest, Romania, 23.5.1880; d. Bucharest, 14.7.1967). Romanian poet, pamphleteer, essayist and novelist. After the publication of his first poems in 1896 his career briefly followed a religious path with his initiation as a monk in 1899. Returning to Romania after several years abroad (1904–10), he acquired a name as a fiery polemicist and achieved notoriety as a pacifist following Romania's entry into WW1 in 1916. In 1918 he was imprisoned for a year for contributing to a newspaper which was published under the German occupation. The volume *Cuvinte potrivite* [Fitting words] (Bucharest, 1927), which reflects the anguish of a spirit in search of God and the poet's association with the land and the peasant, brought him a controversial press because of its prosodic innovation and abrasive metaphor but nevertheless represents his major poetical achievement. His life as a monk provided the inspiration for the novel *Icoane de lemn* [Wooden icons] (Bucharest, 1930), while a second novel *Poarta neagră* [The black gate] (Bucharest, 1930) and the volume of poems *Flori de mucegai* [Mildew flowers] (Bucharest, 1931) are based on his life in prison. His literary output continued until 1943 when a pamphlet attacking the German ambassador to Romania led to his internment. A brief period of activity after WW2 was followed by silence (1948–54) and his subsequent re-emergence with two cycles of poetry in harmony with the cultural dictates of the period: *1907* (Bucharest, 1955) and *Cîntare omului* [Hymn to mankind] (Bucharest, 1956). The result was his official elevation to the status of a classic, a poet laureate of the People's Republic. A volume of his work has been translated into English as *Selected Poems of Tudor Arghezi* (tr. M. Impey & B. Swann, Princeton, 1976).   DJD

Ariès, Philippe (b. Blois, Loir-et-Cher, France, 21.7.1914). French historian. Self-styled 'weekend historian' who has spent his conventional working life as an information officer on tropical agriculture. His interest in the links between historical demography, in the style of HENRY, and the history of 'mentalities', in the tradition of Marc BLOCH and FEBVRE, goes back to his *Histoire des populations françaises et de leurs attitudes devant la vie* [History of the French population and their attitudes to life] (Paris, 1948). He became widely known as a result of *L'Enfant et la vie familiale sous l'ancien régime* (Paris, 1960; *Centuries of Childhood*, London, 1962), concerned with the awareness of childhood, a notion which, according to Ariès, did not exist in the Middle Ages but, together with the 'child-centred family', developed in the course of the 17c and 18c in France and elsewhere. *L'Homme devant la mort* (Paris, 1977; abridged tr. *Western Attitudes toward Death*, Baltimore, 1974) deals with the decline of the traditional familiarity with death and the rise of a view of death as unnameable and shameful. Ariès makes great use of pictures and literary texts as sources. His approach and his urbane but acute critique of modernity are highly intuitive and personal. Although many of his specific conclusions have been challenged by recent research, his book on the sense of childhood virtually brought that subject to the attention of historians.   UPB

Armstrong, Daniel Louis (Satchmo) (b. New Orleans, La, USA, c. 4.7.1900; d. Corona, NY, 6.7.1971). American jazz trumpeter, vocalist and composer. The first great jazz soloist, whose rhythmic phrasing, note selection and sense of form revolutionized early jazz improvisation. He moved to Chicago in 1922. His amazing sense of timing is discernible on his first recordings (with King Oliver's band, 1923). In New York he joined the most famous Negro band of that era, led by pianist Fletcher Henderson. Armstrong returned to Chicago in 1925 and began a series of recordings with his own small band; his improvised solos were still being copied 50 years later. On several recordings he sang in a totally original style: in *Heebie Jeebies* (1926) his vocal contains a series of wordless improvisations – this practice became known as 'scat' singing. In 1928, before a decade of big band work, he recorded *West End Blues* (pianist: Earl Hines). The daring musical interplay between Armstrong and Hines inspired younger jazz musicians to experiment. During this period, Armstrong's technique and control in the upper register pioneered high-note jazz trumpet playing. Throughout the 1930s Armstrong was often accompanied by his own big band, which struggled to maintain accompaniment worthy of his artistry. In 1947, he reverted to small band work, and led a highly mobile sextet, 'The All Stars', whose extensive international tours gave Armstrong the nickname 'Ambassador Satch'. For his own account of his achievement, see *My Life in New Orleans* (London, 1955).   JJC

M. Jones & J. Chilton, *Louis. The Louis Armstrong Story* (London, 1975).

Arnon, Daniel Israel (b. Warsaw, Russian Poland [now Poland], 14.11.1910). American plant biochemist, whose discoveries have formed contemporary knowledge on the path of energy in photosynthesis. He has spent his entire professional career on the faculty of the University of California, after emigrating to the USA in his early youth. Before Arnon's work, the overall aspect of photosynthesis was well established, the using of the energy of sunlight for the conversion of CO_2 and water into carbohydrates and oxygen. Arnon's innovation was to chart the conversion of solar energy into chemical energy prior to CO_2 assimilation. His key discovery of photosynthetic phosphorylation (photophosphorylation) demonstrated the ability of the photosynthetic membrane system of chloroplasts to use the electromagnetic energy of sunlight to generate adenosine triphosphate (ATP). This discovery unveiled a new major process of ATP formation in nature that, on an evolutionary scale, preceded ATP formation in respiration by mitochondria. Arnon and his co-workers discovered two types of photophosphorylation: the cyclic type in which ATP is the sole product of energy conversion and the noncyclic type in which the formation of ATP is accompanied by the liberation of oxygen and formation of a strong reductant, reduced ferredoxin, present in all photosynthetic cells. To interpret his findings, Arnon formulated the then novel and now accepted concepts of light-induced cyclic and noncyclic electron flow. Later, Arnon demonstrated that chloroplasts can assimilate CO_2 outside the cell, a capacity once attributed to chloroplasts without adequate evidence and later denied them because of what seemed to be evidence to the contrary.

Arnon's other major accomplishments include the isolation, crystallization and partial characterization of chloroplast ferredoxin as the most electronegative soluble protein electron carrier that plays a key role in the bioenergetics of photosynthesis. His work on other ferredoxins led Arnon and his associates to the discovery of a new carbon fixation cycle in photosynthetic bacteria (the reductive carboxylic acid cycle). Throughout his career these discoveries have been milestones that displaced from textbooks earlier concepts of photosynthesis. This innovative bent continues in Arnon's current research in which he proposes a novel mechanism for noncyclic phosphorylation, at variance with the widely accepted so-called Z scheme.   BEJ

Aron, Raymond (b. Paris, France, 14.3.1905). French sociologist and publicist. Professor of sociology at the Sorbonne (1955–68) and one of the most influential of French political commentators (in *Le Figaro*), Aron's influence has derived from his independence and his courage in challenging intellectual fashions. In his earlier years he was a close associate of SARTRE, but in *L'Opium des intellectuels* (Paris, 1955; *The Opium of the Intellectuals*, London, 1957) he attacked Sartre and the MARXists for their unquestioning support of the USSR. At the same time he became a leading critic of DE GAULLE and a strong supporter of the Western alliance under American leadership. He subsequently wrote the best reply to revisionist criticism of American foreign policy in *République impériale* (Paris, 1973; *The Imperial Republic: the US and the World 1945–73*, Englewood Cliffs, 1974). He was equally opposed to colonialism and showed courage in advocating French withdrawal from Algeria in advance of the Algerian revolution (*L'Algérie et la République* [Algeria and the republic], Paris, 1958).

Aron's writings on sociology are as free from jargon as his journalism: *Dix-huit leçons sur la société industrielle* (Paris, 1961; *Eighteen Lectures on Industrial Society*, London, 1967) was followed by two further comparative studies of Western and Soviet society, *La Lutte de classes* [The class struggle] (Paris, 1964) and *Démocratie et totalitarisme* (Paris, 1966; *Democracy and Totalitarianism*, London, 1968), and these in turn by *Progress and Disillusion: the Dialectics of Modern Society* (London, 1968). In the same year he resigned his chair at the Sorbonne in protest at the pusillanimous behaviour of his colleagues in face of the student revolt which he analysed in *La Révolution introuvable* (Paris, 1968; *The Elusive Revolution. Anatomy of a Student Revolt*, London, 1969). ALCB

Aron's interest in strategic studies produced *Paix et guerre entre les nations* (Paris, 1962; *Peace and War*, London, 1966) in which he noted the implications of the transition from a balance of power to a balance of terror. He developed his ideas with *Penser la guerre: Clausewitz* [Thinking about war: Clausewitz] (Paris, 1976), arguing that nuclear weapons confirmed the supremacy of the political will over the military instrument. JGo

R. Dahrendorf, 'The achievements of Raymond Aron', *Encounter* (May 1980).

Arp, Jean/Hans (b. Strassburg, Alsace, Germany [now Strasbourg, France], 16.9.1887; d. Basle, Switzerland, 7.6.1966). German/French painter, sculptor and poet. After training in Strassburg, Weimar and Paris, Arp spent 1908–11 in Switzerland reading philosophy and painting experimental abstract landscapes. He became interested not in the surface details of natural forms but in their underlying organic structure and rhythms, and especially in the simplified human body and its organic shapes – a sum of tensions between line and plane. In 1911 he visited Munich and took part in the second *Blaue Reiter* exhibition (February 1912). After a period in Cologne in 1914, where he met ERNST, he spent some months in Paris, where he met APOLLINAIRE, PICASSO and MODI-

GLIANI. Evading military service (he was legally a German citizen) he spent WW1 in Zürich where he participated (1916–19) in Ball's Cabaret Voltaire, reciting his dada poems. He also made collages and reliefs of superimposed pieces of plywood (e.g. *Forest*, 1916) in which natural shapes are simplified as overlapping organic forms painted in bright colours and silhouetted against the background plane, thus creating a symbolic language to express natural principles of growth and continuous transformation. These reliefs and his abstract collages of textiles and paper were intentionally impersonal: to ensure this he had the reliefs sawn by a carpenter, and the collage pieces cut by machine. In 1916 he began to make collages in which the pieces were arranged arbitrarily. In 1919–20 he worked with Ernst at Cologne, helping to edit the dada journal *Die Schammade*, and published two volumes of poetry, *Die Wolkenpumpe* [The cloud-pump] (Hanover, 1920) and *Der Vogel Selbdritt* [The bird self-third] (Berlin, 1920), the latter illustrated. Welcomed to Paris in 1922 by BRETON and the surrealists, he became a central figure in the movement. From this time on his poetry and visual work were characterized by playful whimsy. He settled in Paris (1926–40). In 1930 he turned to freestanding sculpture in plaster, marble, stone, wood and bronze which he called 'concretions', i.e. 'the natural process of condensation ... or solidification of mass'. In 1931 he and his wife Sophie were cofounders of the Abstraction–Création group. During the 1930s and 1940s he occasionally made collages of torn paper to express the contemporary mood of destruction. He spent the years 1942–5 in exile in Switzerland after which he returned to Paris, where he remained for the rest of his life. For Arp art was a 'fruit that grows in a man, like a fruit on a plant'. The final shape of his sculpture underwent many transformations until he felt there was nothing more to change and so he gave it a name. The most enigmatic and suggestive of his forms are those which fuse elements of the human torso with vestigial botanical shapes (e.g. *Growth*, 1938; *Torso Gerbe*, 1958; *Torso Fruit*, 1960). SOBT

J. T. Soby, *Arp* (NY, 1958).

Arrabal, Fernando (b. Melilla, Spanish Morocco [now Morocco], 11.8.1932). Spanish dramatist who, in protest against the FRANCO regime, went into self-imposed exile in Paris in 1955. Stylistically his theatre displays a tension between its language of adoption (French) and a sensibility and imagination that are intensely Spanish, finding expression in baroque imagery and highly ritualized scenes of violence, eroticism and sacrilege which have frequently outraged critics and audiences alike. Brief and schematic in form, unreal or dreamlike in atmosphere, often linking the themes of civil war and dictatorship with private obsessions, Arrabal's plays of the 1950s shock and disturb through their constantly recurring victims and executioners, and casual deployment of horror: the father's corpse trussed to a pole like a hunter's trophy in *Les Deux bourreaux* (1958; tr. B. Wright, *The Two Executioners* in *Four Plays*, London, 1962), the parodic crucifixion of the musician Emanou in the junkyard of *Le Cimetière des voitures* (1958; tr. B. Wright, *The Car Cemetery* in *Four Plays*). Aesthetic principles already present in Arrabal's plays of the 1950s are used more systematically to animate his so-called 'panic theatre' of the 1960s which orchestrates elements of confusion, humour, terror, chance and euphoria in a surrealistic union of opposites. The most complex example is *L'Architecte et l'Empereur d'Assyrie* (1967; tr. J. Benedetti & J. Calder, *The Architect and the Emperor of Assyria*, London, 1970) with its chess motif, roleplaying and profane parody of transubstantiation. In its latest phase Arrabal's theatre becomes more explicitly political, as in *Et ils passèrent des menottes aux fleurs* (1969; tr. C. Marowitz, *And They Put Handcuffs on the Flowers*, London, 1973).   SBJ

G. Orenstein, *The Theater of the Marvelous* (NY, 1975); P. L. Podol, *Fernando Arrabal* (NY, 1978).

Arrhenius, Svante August (b. Vik, Uppsala, Sweden, 19.2.1859; d. Stockholm, 2.10.1927). Swedish chemist, and one of the founders of physical chemistry,

Arrhenius's doctoral dissertation (1884) contained a new idea, the electrolytic theory of dissociation. Couched in relatively imprecise terms, it was rejected by the University of Uppsala, although enthusiastically supported by van't HOFF, Wilhelm OSTWALD, and other leading scientists. This stated that salts, upon dissolution in water, separate into mobile oppositely charged ions, even in the absence of an applied electric field. Arrhenius went on to rationalize in terms of his theory many seemingly puzzling properties pertaining to the behaviour of solutions, e.g. the hydrolysis of salts, acids and bases; the solubility of salts and its variation within temperature; the constancy of the observed heat of neutralization of strong acids and strong bases. But his theory's greatest triumph was that it offered a logical explanation for the factor 'i' in the famous van't Hoff equation (1885) for osmotic pressure π ($\pi v = iRT$). This factor, he demonstrated, could be equated to the number of ions in solution. In 1889, following his penetrating analysis of the rate of inversion of cane sugar, Arrhenius considered the influence of temperature upon the velocity of chemical reaction. Taking as a point of departure a thermodynamic equation of van't Hoff, he arrived at the equation which expresses the rate constant 'k' of a reaction as $A \exp(-E_a/RT)$ where R is the gas constant and T the absolute temperature. Arrhenius rightly argued that an equation of this form indicates that molecules (or ions) must acquire a certain critical energy, E_a, now designated the activation energy, before they can react. This equation, named after him, remains one of the cornerstones of chemical kinetics. In later life Arrhenius devoted much time applying physicochemical principles as a means of understanding geological, astronomical, meteorological and immunological phenomena. But his most important and influential texts were in mainstream physical and theoretical chemistry. In 1903 Arrhenius became the first Swede to be awarded a Nobel prize, and in 1905 he became director of the department of physical chemistry of the Nobel Institute in Stockholm (a post created for him).   JMT

Arrow, Kenneth Joseph (b. New York, USA, 23.8.1921). American economist. Educated at City College, New York, and at Columbia University, he saw service in WW2 before beginning his academic career. He has held posts at the universities of Chicago, Stanford and Harvard, and since 1979 has been professor of economics and operations research at Stanford. In 1972 he shared the Nobel prize for economics with HICKS. His main achievements in economic theory span three interconnected fields. First, the theory of social choice (i.e. the problem of aggregating the preference orderings of individuals into a single combined preference ordering for society as a whole). In *Social Choice and Individual Values* (NY, 1951) Arrow showed that such aggregation cannot in general be accomplished and that – ruling out dictatorship – the nearest one can get to it is the PARETO social choice mechanism, with the Pareto optimum as its central focus. Secondly, together with G. Debreu and others, Arrow has helped to develop mathematical analyses and proofs of the existence, stability, uniqueness and optimality of WALRASian general equilibrium. This highly technical work has also shed light on the stringent requirements regarding coverage of future transactions and consequent restriction of uncertainty which a market system must satisfy in order to guarantee full and efficient use of resources. The economics of information, uncertainty, risk-bearing and insurance has been Arrow's third field of inquiry (see *Aspects of the Theory of Risk-Bearing*, NY, 1965, and *Essays in the Theory of Risk-Bearing*, NY, 1971). A central finding here is that in the presence of uncertainty the efficient use of resources depends partly on relationships or controls extraneous to the price mechanism, such as family ties, moral principles or investigative procedures to ensure compliance with the terms of an insurance contract. Arrow has also contributed extensively to the theory and technique of mathematical programming and inventory control, and to the theory of public expenditure and fiscal policy.

PMO

A. K. Sen, *Collective Choice and Economic Welfare* (NY, 1970).

Artaud, Antonin Marie Joseph (b. Marseilles, Bouches-du-Rhône, France, 4.9.1896; d. Ivry, nr Paris, 4.3.1948). French actor, stage producer and theorist of the theatre. *Le Théâtre et son double* (Paris, 1938; tr. M. C. Richards, *The Theater and its Double*, NY, 1958) marked a radical departure in theatrical thinking. Presented as a collection of essays, the book rejected established conventions and theatrical forms, such as reliance on texts, psychological analysis and plot. Artaud's concept of a theatre of cruelty is in fact a huge assault on accepted values and at the same time a redefinition of the role of drama; constantly he argued for a return to a primitive rite, a ceremony concerned with elemental human needs and emotions. Rational language is dismissed in favour of purely irrational assemblages of sounds, a preverbal language producing an unperverted pantomime in which stylized movements and gestures communicate ideas. Sounds, lights, colours, rhythms hypnotize the audience which is now 'trapped', surrounded by the stage and submitted to pure theatricality. Increasingly implicated in the action as its assurance is undermined, the audience is made to feel itself one with the destiny within and enveloping it. With Artaud the theatre recovers its familiarity with the cosmic. His views were endorsed by the majority of avant-garde playwrights and producers.

It is somehow paradoxical though that Artaud should be remembered mainly for *Le Théâtre et son double*, for his ultimate aim was to use drama to destroy drama; the theatre of cruelty had as its goal not only the abolition of the very idea of theatre as 'representation' but also the fusion of art and life. Artaud's motive for joining the surrealist movement in October 1924 was precisely to protest against the artificial values imposed by a rationalist culture and a repressive social order. After being a leading figure in the surrealist group (in January 1925 he became director of the Surrealist Research Bureau), he was expelled in June 1928 after his production of STRINDBERG's *Dream Play* at the Théâtre de l'Avenue. Artaud later accused the surrealists of conservatism and set out in 'La grande nuit ou le bluff surréaliste' [The long night or the surrealist bluff] (in *Chez l'auteur*, Paris, 1927) his deep disappointment with a group who initially wanted to change man and the world and ended up joining the French Communist party and busying themselves with wage settlements. Artaud was to be satisfied with nothing less than a complete restructuring of society, that society which made madness the only healthy alternative. Throughout his life he suffered physically and mentally, what he called his 'mental erosion', and after the late 1930s he spent the rest of his life in four mental hospitals. Even so he still carried on writing (*Collected Works*, 4 vols, London, 1968–74; tr. H. Weaver, *Selected Writings*, ed. S. Sontag, NY, 1976). The recent tendency has been to present Artaud as one of a long line of '*poètes maudits*'; however, the extreme way he incarnated his ideas rather than merely expressing them puts him beyond the reach of any convenient categorization. DGL

A. Virmaux, *Antonin Artaud et le thé-âtre* (Paris, 1970); M. Esslin, *Artaud* (London, 1976).

Artin, Emil (b. Vienna, Austria-Hungary [now Austria], 3.3.1898; d. Hamburg, West Germany, 20.12.1962). Austrian mathematician. The analogies Artin detected between algebraic and analytic number theory have inspired much subsequent work, including the resolution of conjectures later made by André WEIL partly on the basis of Artin's work. In his Leipzig thesis (1921) Artin studied quadratic extensions of the field of rational functions in one variable over a finite field, introduced a zeta function and proposed a hypothesis for it analogous to the Riemann hypothesis in the complex case. He established the hypothesis in various cases: in 1934 Hasse gave a more general proof, and in 1948 Weil gave a complete proof. In 1923, when he was a lecturer at the University of Hamburg, before holding the chair in mathematics (1926–37), Artin introduced his L-series, which generalize Dirichlet's, and using them produced his important general reciprocity theorem, a cornerstone of Abelian classfield theory. Artin had considerable influence on the development of abstract algebra and on the applications of group theory to topology. He spent the period 1937–58 in the USA, from 1946 at Princeton University, where his influence is considerable. He returned to the University of Hamburg in 1958. Artin was an extremely talented amateur musician, playing the flute, clavichord and harpsichord. JJG

S. Lang & J. T. Tate (eds), *The Collected Papers of Emil Artin* (Reading, Mass., 1965).

Astaire, Frederick Austerlitz (Fred) (b. Omaha, Nebr., USA, 10.5.1899). American dancer, choreographer and film actor. He was a stage performer until he was 34, when he began the creation of a new style of film dancing: he took tap and ballroom and turned them into an art which belongs to the cinema. His father had come from Vienna, hence the name Austerlitz. His sister Adele showed natural talent, and in 1904 both children were placed in a New York dancing school. As child prodigies they danced in vaudeville; always together, they became a famous team in musical comedy in both New York and London. In 1932 Adele married and retired. Astaire was a success on his own; but in 1933 he left the stage and began film playing. He found the ideal partner in Ginger Rogers; his work with her established a type of musical comedy which depended mainly on its dancing. His modest but subtle manner of singing was liked by the composers – GERSHWIN, Cole PORTER, Irving Berlin, Jerome Kern. By the end of the 1960s he had abandoned dancing and was playing dramatic roles, as in *The Towering Inferno* (1975). His fame rests on his choreography, his dazzling technique and the supreme elegance he brought to his best films: *Top Hat* (1935), *Swing Time* (1936), *Shall We Dance?* (1937), *Yolanda and the Thief* (1945), *The Barkleys of Broadway* (1948). DP

M. Freeland, *Fred Astaire* (London, 1976).

Asturias, Miguel Ángel (b. Guatemala City, Guatemala, 19.10.1899; d. Paris, France, 9.6.1974). Guatemalan novelist. Awarded the Nobel prize for literature in 1967, he established his reputation as a stylist with *Leyendas de Guatemala* [Guatemalan legends] (Madrid, 1930), an imaginative re-creation of his country's Mayan heritage, and as the leading Spanish-American novelist of his generation with *El Señor Presidente* (Mexico City, 1946; tr. F. Partridge, *The President*, London, 1963), the first major 20c novel on the theme of Latin American dictatorship. This avoided the realist trap of documentary fiction thanks to the imaginative use of French experimental techniques, and had a decisive influence on the following generation (i.e. CORTÁZAR, GARCÍA MÁRQUEZ, VARGAS LLOSA, FUENTES). His copious production is distinguished by its stylistic and structural experimentation, by its grounding in the regional folk heritage (most notably in *Hombres de maíz*, Buenos Aires, 1949; tr. G. Martin, *Men of Maize*, NY, 1975), and by its strong social concern – especially in the 'Banana Trilogy': *Viento fuerte* (Buenos Aires, 1950; tr. D. Flakoll & C. Alegría, *The Cyclone*, London, 1967), *El papa verde* (Buenos Aires, 1954; tr. G. Rabassa, *The Green Pope*, NY, 1975), and *Los ojos de los enterrados* (Buenos Aires, 1960; tr. G. Rabassa, *The Eyes of the Interred*, NY, 1973). His two best later novels are *El alhajadito* (Buenos Aires, 1961; tr. M. Shuttleworth, *The Bejeweled Boy*, NY, 1971) and *Mulata de Tal* (Buenos Aires, 1963; tr. G. Rabasso, *Mulata*, NY, 1967). His poetry is interesting chiefly for the light it sheds on his prose. He went into voluntary exile after the American-inspired Guatemalan coup of 1954, until a later government named him its ambassador in Paris – a post he held from 1966 until his death.   RP-M

L. Harss & B. Dohmann, *Into the Mainstream: Conversations with Latin-American Writers* (NY, 1967); R. Callam, *Miguel Ángel Asturias* (NY, 1972).

Atatürk, Mustafa Kemal (b. Salonika, Greece, 19.5.1881; d. Istanbul, Turkey, 10.11.1938). President of the Turkish Republic (1923–38) and architect of modern Turkey. Cadet and member of the 1908 Turkish military revolutionary elite, successful military commander in the wars against Italy in Libya (1911), against Bulgaria (1912–13) and against the Anglo–French landings at Gallipoli (1915). Although not a member of the Young Turk leadership, Atatürk raised a nationalist revolution in Anatolia against the Allied puppet government set up on the Turkish surrender in 1918 and against Allied plans to dismember Asiatic Turkey, allying his provisional revolutionary government with the Soviet Union, defeating the Greek army in Anatolia and successfully confronting – while avoiding war – British forces at Chanak in 1922. His Bismarckian realism in external affairs, which took Turkey steadily away from the Soviet attachment into ever closer relations with the UK and with Turkey's Balkan neighbours in Europe, including Greece, with whom an exchange of populations was arranged, went with the most ruthless imposition of westernization on the Turkish peoples. It involved abolishing the Caliphate, secularizing the state, especially as regards the system of law of religious charity, of male and female dress and education, adopting Western-style surnames, substituting the Latin for the Arabic alphabet, introducing state-owned industry and control of the financial and economic systems. The abiding strength of Islam among the largely peasant mass of the Turkish people necessitated the maintenance of an elitist dictatorship which the officer class and their opposite numbers in the bureaucratic and professional classes united to support.   DCW

J. P. D. Kinross, *Atatürk: the Rebirth of a Nation* (London, 1964).

Atget, Jean-Eugène-Auguste (b. Libourne, Gironde, France, 12.2.1857; d. Paris, 4.8.1927). French photographer. Atget was a prolific recorder of Parisian architecture and statuary. An actor working in suburban theatres around Paris, he began to take photographs in the early 1890s. In 1899 he sold 100 pictures of Old Paris to the Bibliothèque Historique de la Ville de Paris. By this time he had begun to systematize his collection which he intended as a guide to the older part of the city. He continued to document Paris until the end of his life. In 1910 he produced two picture series *Paris Interiors* and *The*

Horse-drawn Cart in Paris, followed by *Street Scenes* in 1912 and *Fortifications* in 1913. After WW1 he photographed in the parks at Versailles, Saint-Cloud and Sceaux. Altogether he seems to have taken around 8000 pictures, and many of his glass negatives still survive in public collections in Paris and New York. He sold picture sets to museums, libraries and artists. Looked on as an artisan in his lifetime, his reputation began to rise in the late 1920s. Documentary photographers, as well as constructivist and surrealist artists, came to admire his work which was quickly exhibited and published. His stock has continued to rise ever since. For his fame is not simply that of a documentarist. His subject was culture in its broadest sense, evolving and decaying. He examined primary materials and culture's ways of designating those materials. The sites he chose to photograph were inscribed and marked by pictograms and symbols, by embossed shields and wrought-iron manikins. In the royal parks he took pictures of classical statuary, of gods and goddesses returning to nature, as they were before the stories were written. In Paris he recorded lumber yards and flea-markets, terminal sites in the making of the city. His influence has been wide ranging, with his most notable disciple the American photographer Walker EVANS.   IJ

H. G. Puttnies, *Atget* (Cologne, 1980).

Atiyah, Michael Francis (b. London, UK, 22.4.1929). British mathematician. A student of W. D. V. Hodge at Cambridge, Atiyah has made crucial contributions to the study of algebraic geometry by topological means, and then in the late 1950s with Hirzebruch he developed a tool, K-theory, which he has since put to great use in the theory of elliptic partial differential equations. His work in this area represents a major advance in the study of a topic which, at its simplest, includes the steady-state equation for heat distribution. His studies provide a topological meaning for terms previously defined analytically, a considerable conceptual gain. More recently he has investigated a geometric theory of instantons of interest to particle physicists. An enthusiastic collabora-

tor with others, and a forceful popularizer of and propagandizer for mathematics, especially geometry, he exerts a beneficial influence on many branches of the subject and at many levels. He was awarded a Fields medal in 1966. Savilian professor of mathematics at Oxford (1963–9), he held the chair in mathematics at the Institute of Advanced Studies, Princeton (1969–72), before returning to St Catherine's College, Oxford, in 1973 as Royal Society research professor.   JJG

Atwood, Margaret Eleanor (b. Ottawa, Ont., Canada, 18.11.1939). Canadian poet and novelist. In her native Canada she enjoys a high reputation as a poet who explores the pioneering psyche of her country. Of her many collections of poetry *The Journals of Susanna Moodie* (Toronto, 1970) is probably the most admired, transforming Mrs Moodie's journal of the mid-19c into a metaphor for establishing cultural identity and questioning sexual stereotypes. Atwood's novel *Surfacing* (Toronto, 1972) has extended her reputation as an advocate of feminist radicalism, perhaps obscuring the deeply anti-American (and hence pro-Canadian) tone of the book. More recently she has written *Lady Oracle* (Toronto, 1976) and *Life Before Man* (Toronto, 1979). She is a writer who appears to reject conventions of literary form but who nevertheless has a powerful ability to evoke landscape and myth. By yoking together her sense of how Canada emerged from the wilderness with her questioning of where the nation currently stands, Atwood has greatly helped the maturation of a Canadian literary personality.   ANRN

S. Grace, *Violent Duality: a Study of Margaret Atwood* (Montreal, 1980).

Auden, Wystan Hugh (b. York, UK, 21.2.1907; naturalized American citizen, 1946; d. Vienna, Austria, 29.9.1973). British/American poet. When 15 Auden decided to become a poet. He read natural sciences, changed to English at Oxford (1925–8) and published some poems in a limited edition printed by Stephen Spender (1928). In the 1930s, when not abroad, he worked as a schoolmaster. He wrote collaborative travel books (with MACNEICE: *Letters from Iceland*, London, 1937; with ISHERWOOD, about China: *Journey to a War*, London, 1939), worked as a librettist with BRITTEN on, e.g. documentary films (such as *Night Mail*, produced by GRIERSON's GPO Film Unit) and on the operetta *Paul Bunyan*, and later with Chester Kallmann (e.g. on STRAVINSKY's *The Rake's Progress* and on Mozart's *The Magic Flute*). In 1936, though a homosexual, he married Thomas MANN's daughter Erika to give her the British citizenship needed to escape Nazi persecution. From 1939 he lived in New York, returned to Anglicanism, and in later years alternated between living in the USA and in Austria. He published much criticism, especially reviews (e.g. *The Dyer's Hand*, NY, 1962), and was a notable anthologist (e.g. *The Poet's Tongue*, with J. Garrett, 2 vols, London, 1935; *Poets of the English Language*, with N. H. Pearson, 5 vols, NY, 1950), translator (e.g. of BRECHT's *The Caucasian Chalk Circle*, with J. & T. Stern, and – in collaboration – of Goethe, Hammarskjöld, and the *Elder Edda*) and preface-writer. He was guest professor at many US colleges from 1940, and was professor of poetry at Oxford from 1956 to 1961.

Auden's early poetry, from *Poems* (London, 1930, ²1933) to *Look, Stranger!* (London, 1936), excited partly by its confusion of impulse: mimicry of archaic forms; contemporary mannerisms; leftist politics; and post-FREUDian psychology. Much of his verse (and the BRECHTian plays, written with Isherwood: *The Dog beneath the Skin*, London, 1935; *The Ascent of F6*, London, 1936; *On the Frontier*, London, 1938) encouraged readers to identify him with the left and with an idiosyncratic Englishness. The sense of betrayal when he went to the USA in 1939 no doubt increased British coolness to his immediately subsequent verse. Nevertheless, the view that *For the Time Being* (NY, 1944) and its companion *The Sea and the Mirror* were poetical reflections rather than poems, and that *New Year Letter* (London, 1941) had shown a fatal descent into slickness, had a dangerous degree of truth. The volumes from *Nones* (NY, 1951) up to *Epistle to a*

Godson (NY, 1972) were greeted with recognition of old dexterity and criticism of diminishing seriousness. The earlier poetry, with its mixture of specific detail and massive generalization, its contemporary relevance and its mythical overtones, has certainly a resonance that the later verse lacks. Nevertheless, it is fair to say that Auden suffered largely because he *was* the outstanding poet of his generation, who had foisted on him the status of a leader, and then the shame of a lost one. The suggestion, fuelled by the cavalier self-editing of *Collected Shorter Poems, 1927–1957* (London, 1966), that he was trying to bury his old self affected much later criticism, and comparison of the pre- and postwar poet became obsessive. His bibliography is complicated. The *Collected Poems* were edited by E. Mendelson (NY, 1976) and the work in verse and prose of 1927–39 was edited, also by Mendelson, in *The English Auden* (NY, 1977). BF

E. Mendelson, *Early Auden* (London, 1981); H. Carpenter, *W. H. Auden* (London, 1981).

Auerbach, Erich (b. Berlin, Germany, 9.11.1892; naturalized American citizen, 1953; d. New Haven Conn., USA, 13.10.1957). German/American literary theorist and historian. Auerbach's greatest and most influential work *Mimesis: Dargestellte Wirklichkeit in der abendländischen Literatur* (Bern, 1946; tr. W. R. Trask, *Mimesis: Representation of Reality in Western Literature*, Princeton, 1953) is one of the most successful exercises in truly comparative literature. More than just a general history of realism, it is concerned with men's changing conceptions of reality as they are reflected in literary works. With an incomparable sense of the concrete and particular, and starting from specific texts ranging from Homer to PROUST, Auerbach applies a method which involves philology, interpretation, close stylistic analysis, and, branching out into history and sociology, arrives at what he calls 'inner' history or *Geistesgeschichte*. The last entails a study of man's general attitude to the world at a given place and time, and unearths the conscious and unconscious epistemology that underlies it. Though himself free of all speculative ambition, Auerbach's belief in the concrete truth of the unique and the particular reveals the influence of Hegel and of German romanticism. Indeed, his belief that values, literary or otherwise, can only be viewed as historical products induces scepticism of all absolute standards, and leads ultimately to a form of relativism.

RNH

Auerbach, Frank (b. Berlin, Germany, 29.4.1931). British painter. Sent to England before he was eight, he moved to London in 1947 and began to attend BOMBERG's drawing classes at the Borough Polytechnic. Bomberg's teaching had a profound effect on Auerbach's subsequent attitudes and techniques. After studying at St Martin's and the Royal College of Art, Auerbach began exhibiting regularly in 1959. He painted portraits of his family and friends; nudes from the model; and scenes in and around London. He worked in a thick impasto, employing extraordinary quantities of paint, but combined this with a delicate drawing style. His work has often been likened to that of KOSSOFF, who studied with him under Bomberg, although in fact Auerbach's handling is often much freer and more abstracted, and his use of colour more vivid. Auerbach's painting was always admired within a small circle of collectors, but it was only with the withering of American hegemony over the visual arts that he began to receive his due. Today he is widely admired by a new generation of younger, expressionist painters.

PF

Frank Auerbach, Arts Council exh. cat. (London, 1978).

Auger, Pierre Victor (b. Paris, France, 14.5.1899). French physicist, who studied the Auger effect, which occurs when a material is bombarded with X-rays. By a rather complicated process these X-rays can transfer some of their energy to electrons which orbit the atoms, thereby enabling them to be expelled from the material. It has been found that the energy of these electrons, instead of being related to the energy of the bombarding X-rays, is characteristic of the atoms from which they have been removed. A study of these Auger electrons enables us to investigate the energy which binds electrons to atoms; it is particularly useful for studying the properties of electrons close to the surface of a crystal. Auger's other research has been concerned with cosmic rays and with neutrons. During WW2 he was head of the physics division of the Anglo–Canadian research project on atomic energy; after 1945 he played a very important part in the development of French and European scientific policy. From 1948 to 1959 he was director of the natural sciences department of UNESCO and in 1960 he became director-general of the European Space Research Organization (ESRO; now ESA).

HMR

Austin, John Langshaw (b. Lancaster, UK, 26.3.1911; d. Oxford, 8.2.1960). British philosopher. Austin was educated at Oxford, and spent his life teaching there, becoming professor of moral philosophy in 1952. He published only a handful of articles in his lifetime, collected with other items in *Philosophical Papers* (Oxford, 1961), but the force of his mind and the freshness and clarity of his spoken utterance made him the unquestioned leader of 'Oxford philosophy' in its 15 years of highest activity and repute, from the end of WW2 until his death. Austin held, with WITTGENSTEIN and Gilbert RYLE, that perplexing collisions between philosophical theses and everyday beliefs are caused by misunderstanding of common language. But he applied this with a degree of scholarly and lexicographical intransigence that went far beyond anything they envisaged. Its chief fruits were a witty, many-sided attack on the view that all we really perceive is our own ideas or sensations, in his *Sense and Sensibilia* (Oxford, 1962); and a distinction between 'performative' and 'constative' utterances (those in which something is done, like promising or baptizing, and those in which information is communicated) developed in his *How to Do Things with Words* (Oxford, 1962). He also discussed illuminatingly, if often inconclusively, truth, pretence and the array of excuses at our disposal for the disclaiming of responsibility. The ghosts Austin sought to exorcize have largely refused to vanish and he has left no real following, only a fine example of scrupulous thoroughness of inquiry. AQ

K. T. Fann (ed.), *Symposium on J. L. Austin* (London, 1969); I. Berlin *et al.*, *Essays on J. L. Austin* (Oxford, 1973).

Avery, Oswald Theodore (b. Halifax, NS, Canada, 21.10.1877; d. Nashville, Tenn., USA, 20.2.1955). American bacteriologist. Avery greatly extended our knowledge of the relations between bacteria and the hosts which they infect. Particularly interested in pneumococci, he showed that the serological characteristics of different strains are determined by the chemical nature of the polysaccharides in their capsules and that both characteristics are inherent to a particular strain. He was therefore sceptical of a claim by Griffith (1928) that, through certain laboratory manipulations, pneumococci could be made to change their serological specificity, and that in particular a nonvirulent, unencapsulated or 'rough' strain could be transformed into a 'smooth', encapsulated form that was virulent. When such a transformation was achieved in Avery's own laboratory, using a cell-free extract of the smooth strain, he had to accept the claim, and proceeded, in collaboration with C. M. MacLeod and M. McCarty, to purify the transforming principle and show that it consisted of deoxyribonucleic acid (DNA). This provided the first evidence that DNA is the genetic material of the chromosomes. The implications of this discovery were so contrary to current biological thought that acceptance was slow. Once its truth was accepted, however, it revolutionized genetical thinking and provided a foundation for the dramatic growth of the new discipline of molecular biology. GL

Ayer, Alfred Jules (b. London, UK, 29.10.1910). British philosopher. Graduating from Oxford, where he had been a pupil of G. RYLE, in 1932, Ayer taught there until joining the army in 1940. During this period he attended sessions of the Vienna circle and published his concise, brilliant, combative *Language, Truth and Logic* (London, 1936) in which the doctrines of SCHLICK, CARNAP and their associates were expounded to an English-speaking readership in a way that stressed their affinity with the native empiricist tradition running from Locke and Hume to Mill, Bertrand RUSSELL and G. E. MOORE. Like the Viennese logical positivists, Ayer asserted that for an utterance to be meaningful it must be verifiable either by sense experience or by scrutiny of the conventions governing the use of its terms. Utterances that were neither empirical nor analytic (true in virtue of their meaning) he branded as not literally significant and therefore as at best expressions of feeling. This account of moral and religious affirmations evoked some angry criticism. Ayer applied his conception of philosophy as the analysis of language to numerous philosophical problems in this first book, and to a favourite British problem, that of perception, in his next work *The Foundations of Empirical Knowledge* (London, 1940). In it he worked out a modernized version of John Stuart Mill's phenomenalist account of material things as 'permanent possibilities of sensation'. He was offered, in 1946, the chair of philosophy at University College London, and soon brought the department there to a leading position in both reputation and performance. In *The Problem of Knowledge* (London, 1956) he treated a range of epistemological problems in the less vehement spirit intimated by the preface to the second edition (1946) of his original book. In 1959 he returned to Oxford as Wykeham professor of logic and remained there until his retirement in 1977. He published essay collections in 1954, 1963 and 1969, and two critical volumes on previous philosophers (*The Origins of Pragmatism*, London, 1968, and *Russell and Moore*, London, 1971). *The Central Questions of Philosophy* (London, 1972) expounds views recognizably affiliated to his bold affirmations of 1936, but with greater recognition of the point and complexity of opposed points of view. A lucid, compact and forceful stylist and an indefatigably dextrous arguer, Ayer consciously follows, and sometimes improves upon, Russell, as also in his libertarian stance on moral and political issues. AQ

Azikiwe, Nnamdi (Zik) (b. Zungeru, Northern Nigeria [now Nigeria], 16.11.1904). Nigerian politician. Regarded by some Nigerians as the father of Nigerian nationalism, Azikiwe has been active in Nigerian politics for more than 40 years. The first Ibo to achieve a reputation in modern Nigerian politics, he was one of the first Nigerians to study in the USA. In the mid-1930s he made a name first in Accra, then in Lagos, as a hard-hitting journalist whose paper the *West African Pilot* was very popular among clerks and teachers. In 1944 he was one of the founders of Nigeria's first truly national party, the National Council of Nigeria and the Cameroons. Azikiwe's reputation as a radical nationalist was at its height in the late 1940s. In the 1950s, when he became premier of Eastern Nigeria, many Nigerians felt that he was too closely associated with the Ibo people; his reputation was also affected by financial scandals. He became first president of an independent Nigeria but the bitter divisions of Nigerian politics made his position as constitutional head of state an unhappy one. During the civil war he first sided with Biafra, then made his peace with the federal government. In 1979 he emerged from retirement to contest (unsuccessfully) the presidential election as leader of the newly formed Nigerian People's party. He has published *Zik: a Selection of Speeches* (London, 1961) and an autobiography *My Odyssey* (London, 1967). RH

Azorín, ps. of José Martínez Ruíz (b. Monóvar, Alicante, Spain, 8.6.1893; d. Madrid, 2.3.1967). Spanish essayist, novelist and critic. More noted for his style than for his substance, he achieved success with *El alma castellana (1600–1800)* [The Castilian soul] (Madrid, 1900). His pseudonym appeared as a character's name in two early novels (*La voluntad* [The will], Barcelona, 1902; *Antonio Azorín*, Madrid, 1903). Best known for his lyrical evocation of Spain's landscape, past and 'soul', in such discursive works as *Las confesiones de un pequeño filósofo* [Confessions of a small philosopher] (Madrid, 1904) – still under his real name – *La ruta de Don Quijote* [The route of Don Quixote] (Madrid, 1905), and *Una hora de España* (Madrid, 1924; tr. A. Raleigh, *An Hour of Spain between 1560 and 1590*, London, 1930). To the same period belongs his brief novel *Don Juan* (Madrid, 1922; tr. C. A. Phillips, London, 1922). Azorín shared the self-searching and Spain-probing of the other members of the 'generation of 1898' (a term he probably coined, in *Clásicos y modernos* [Classics and moderns], Madrid, 1913). His stress on the historical significance of 'little things' rather than major 'events' parallels UNAMUNO's concept of *intrahistoria*, foreshadowing modern social history, but in the absence of supporting scholarship his recreation of the 'little things' in, e.g. *Una hora de España*, is merely an imaginative exercise. As a stylist, he preached the virtues of a transparent prose whose art lies in concealing art, and though his own studied simplicity now feels dated, the best peninsular Spanish literary prose of the 1920s, 1930s and 1940s owes much of its expressiveness to his example. RP-M

E. I. Fox, *Azorín as a Literary Critic* (NY, 1962); K. Glenn, *The Novelistic Technique of Azorín (José Martínez Ruíz)* (Madrid, 1973).

B

Baade, Wilhelm Heinrich Walter (b. Schröttinghausen, N. Rhine-Westphalia, Germany, 24.3.1893; d. Bad Salzuflen, West Germany, 25.6.1960). German astronomer, and one of the outstanding deductive users of the large telescopes of the first decades of this century. He studied at Münster, and at Göttingen (PhD, 1919). His astronomical career began at the Hamburg Observatory, Bergerdorf, where he discovered the asteroid Icarus which approaches very close to the sun and the earth. After a fellowship at the Mt Wilson Observatory, he accepted a permanent post there in 1931, and used the 60-in and 100-in telescopes to study globular clusters and supernovae. With Minkowski he distinguished two kinds of supernova: type I (intrinsically very bright at maximum light) and type II (not so bright at maximum). Classified as an alien during WW2, Baade was allowed to continue his work with the 100-in telescope. With additional time, little competition for use of the telescope and an unusually dark sky (from the partial blackout of the area), he made an extremely careful photographic study of the inner regions of the M31 galaxy (the Andromeda nebula). He was the first to resolve this galaxy into its individual stars, but only in *red* light. His classical paper on this topic (*Astrophysical Journal*, 100 [1944], 137) states: ' ... the plate ... shows the hitherto amorphous nebulosity disintegrated into a dense sheet of extremely faint stars, all close to the limit of the plate.' This was one piece of evidence that led to his classification of stars into two types: population I (young, with a HERTZSPRUNG–RUSSELL diagram appropriate to the solar neighbourhood) and population II (old, with a Hertzsprung–Russell diagram appropriate to globular clusters), a classification of the greatest importance in the theory of stellar evolution. Baade also studied the M31 galaxy with the 100-in telescope. Its apparent stellar content was not as expected, and he correctly deduced that this galaxy, and all others, is about twice as distant as had been supposed. Baade continued to make observations with the 100-in and 200-in telescopes until his retirement in 1958, but published relatively little of his work after 1944, although he passed much material on to other astronomers. DEB

W. Baade, *Evolution of Stars and Galaxies*, ed. C. Payne-Gaposchkin (Cambridge, Mass., 1963).

Babbage, Charles (b. London, UK, 26.12.1791; d. London, 18.10.1871). British computer pioneer, born a century too soon. While they were undergraduates at Cambridge, Babbage, John Herschel and others founded the Analytical Society to introduce continental notation in calculus to England. From their work developed the modern school of English mathematics. Babbage's own early work was in the theory of functions and modern algebra, of which he was one of the main pioneers. Between 1822 and 1833 he developed a Difference Engine to form and print mathematical tables for navigation, etc. In 1830 he wrote *On the Decline of Science* and led a campaign to turn the Royal Society into a professional body. This the campaign failed to do, but it did result in the foundation of the British Association for the Advancement of Science. In 1832 he published *On the Economy of Machinery and Manufactures* (London), which placed the factory at the centre of political economy and exerted a strong influence on John Stuart Mill and MARX. Babbage twice stood for the newly reformed Parliament and in 1833 published *A Word to the Wise*, advocating life peerages. In 1837 he published *The Ninth Bridgewater Treatise*, which presented the deity as computer programmer. From 1834 to 1848 he developed many plans for 'analytical engines', which were versatile programmable mechanical calculators with a decimal number representation, and between 1848 and 1856 he considered the question of how to construct such. Technically it was practicable but it proved impossible to raise the necessary finance. In 1856 he returned to the analytical engines as a hobby for his old age. Babbage's engines incorporate an extraordinary range of ideas utilized in modern computing, including: program control, microprogramming, a range of peripherals, separate store and mill, multiprocessing, and even array processing. RAH

A. Hyman, *Charles Babbage: Pioneer of the Computer* (Oxford, 1982).

Babbit, Milton Byron (b. Philadelphia, Pa, USA, 10.5.1916). American composer whose creative and theoretical extension of SCHOENBERG and WEBERN's serialism has had a notable influence on musical thought since WW2. In his elaborately structured works he uses serial methods to determine not only pitches but rhythmic aspects, tone-colour and formal shaping. Among his compositions are four string quartets, piano works, songs and electronic pieces in which he has used the RCA synthesizer's capacity for prescribing sounds in detail. His rigorous technique has gained him the reputation of an abstract, mathematical constructor, though the expressive force of such works as *Philomel* (1963) for soprano and tape suggests otherwise. PG

Babcock, Horace Welcome (b. Pasadena, Calif., USA, 13.9.1912). American astronomer. Babcock's two most significant contributions to optical astronomy were his pioneering work on detecting magnetic fields in distant stars and his invention and development of the magnetograph. At Mt Wilson Observatory, of which he was director from 1964 to 1978, Babcock embarked on his major work on magnetic stars, detecting the presence or absence of a stellar magnetic field by means of the ZEEMAN effect, whereby spectral lines are split into separate components in the presence of a magnetic field. Observations for this effect are exceedingly difficult as the Zeeman splitting is very small and easily masked by other properties of a star that broadens its spectral lines. However, in 1947 Babcock announced his first detection of a magnetic field in the star 78 Virginis and has since provided

an enormous amount of information about stellar magnetic effects. In his 1958 catalogue he listed over 150 magnetic stars from more than 300 he had studied. These magnetic stars form a class of their own; their magnetic fields are about a thousand times as strong as that of the sun and they nearly all coincide with stars which display unusual and variable spectral characteristics. In the 1950s Babcock turned to more detailed studies of solar magnetism, and designed and built the first of several magnetographs which have become major instruments in solar physics at Mt Wilson and elsewhere. In 1961, as a result of detailed study of the behaviour of the sun's magnetic field, he proposed an explanation of the 22-year sunspot and magnetic cycle. According to Babcock's theory the lines of magnetic flux passing through the material of the sun from pole to pole became twisted and knotted due to the differential rotation of the sun. This knotting of the magnetic field causes outbreaks of magnetic flux from the surface of the sun, made visible in the cooler temperatures of the sunspots. This concept proved highly stimulating to subsequent solar physics. MJS

Babel', Isaak Emmanuilovich (b. Odessa, Russia, 13.7.1894; d. Siberia, USSR, 17.3.1941). Russian short-story writer and dramatist who, with his finely constructed, subtle and ambiguous accounts of events during the Soviet–Polish war of 1921 and of life in the ghettoes of prerevolutionary Odessa, brought a new sophistication to Russian prose. Son of a tradesman, he joined the army, going over to the Bolsheviks in 1917, serving with the *Cheka* and, later, Budyonny's cavalry. Babel's first published work was *El'ya Isaakovich and Margarita Prokof'evna*, which appeared in a Petrograd journal in 1916, but he made his name with the collection *Konarmiya* (Moscow, 1926; tr. N. Helstein, *Red Cavalry*, NY, 1929). This episodic, yet thematically unified and indeed epic account of the experiences of a Jewish officer assigned to a regiment of traditionally anti-Semitic Cossacks is rich in irony and ambiguity: basically a pacifist, the narrator prays for 'the simplest of abilities – the ability to kill a man'; alienated from the Polish Jews around him, he is sensually attracted both by Poland's Catholic churches and by his glamorous but dangerous companions, whose respect he attempts to win with acts of bathetic brutality; a bespectacled cavalry officer, he can barely ride, and comes nearest to fighting in a quarrel with a fellow officer. Examples of such irony abound. Like Maupassant, Babel' often surprises the reader with twists in the plot of his highly concise stories, but he is also consciously manipulating the reader's sensibility to reach something akin to JOYCEan epiphany. Babel' is a master craftsman, and his exquisite yet garish, refined yet brutal miniatures require the close attention demanded by lyric poetry. The swashbuckling *Odesskie rasskazy* [Odessa stories] (Moscow, 1931) use broader strokes and more open humour to depict the Jewish underworld on the eve of revolution. Among the best of his uncollected stories are some subtle, quasi-autobiographical depictions of a boy's attainment of sexual and spiritual maturity during violent pogroms. Babel's plays are less distinguished: among them *Zakat* [Sunset] (Moscow, 1928) is set in prerevolutionary Odessa, and *Mariya* (Moscow, 1933 –5) portrays survivors from an earlier age in a hostile, new environment. Babel' himself was forced to adopt 'the genre of silence' and disappeared in the purges of the 1930s. He was rehabilitated in 1957. Translations of his stories were published in *Isaak Babel: Collected Stories* (tr. W. Morrison, London, 1957).

ABMcM

P. Carden, *Isaac Babel* (Cornell, 1972); J. E. Falen, *Isaac Babel* (Knoxville, 1974).

Babits, Mihály (b. Szekszárd, Austria-Hungary [now Hungary], 26.11.1883; d. Budapest, 4.8.1941). Hungarian poet, novelist, essayist and editor. The most erudite writer in modern Hungarian literature, he combined a love of classical learning and European – particularly English – culture with a deep appreciation of contemporary philosophy and psychology. He broke with Hungarian tradition in striving towards an objective lyric idiom, far removed

from the passion of ADY and the nationalism of many of his contemporaries. A lonely figure, he was compelled in the increasing gloom of the European scene in the 1930s to react to the political situation; the result is the remarkable personal confession of faith *Jónás könyve* [Book of Jonah] (Budapest, 1938). His novels are experimental, often exploring psychological problems, as in *A gólyakalifa* (Budapest, 1913; tr. E. Rácz, *The Nightmare*, Budapest, 1966). As editor of *Nyugat* [West] from 1929 until his death, he exercised a profound influence on a generation of young writers; his essays on literary and philosophical subjects are models that they followed. His translations show his catholicity of taste, ranging from medieval Latin hymns to Dante and erotic verse; his knowledge of the European scene is clearly observed in his highly personal evocation of European literature *Az európai irodalom története* [History of European literature] (Budapest, 1936). GFC

J. Reményi, *Hungarian Writers and Literature* (New Brunswick, NJ, 1964).

Bachelard, Gaston (b. Bar-sur-Aube, Aube, France, 27.6.1884; d. Paris, 16.10.1962). French philosopher. Bachelard's ideas have influenced the work of French intellectuals in the history of science, psychoanalysis, epistemology and the New Criticism. He emphasized that the development of modern science defied the requirements of empiricist or positivist epistemologies, and that the abstract nature of modern calculus deeply changed the nature of physical experience and theory (the concept of 'epistemological obstacle'). Scientific advance had come to be seen as the progressive conquest of mathematical abstraction, as opposed to the 'colourful' obstacle represented by the 'concrete and real, immediate and natural' experience of nature. Bachelard argued that a true psychoanalysis of knowledge was required, in order to free the understanding from the fascination of the concrete. However, Bachelard did not reject the role of images and the study of intellectual and emotional *rêveries* and his theory of the transposition in the poet's unconscious of the four primary elements became indispensable complements to his epistemology (see, e.g. *La Psychoanalyse du feu*, Paris, 1937, *The Psychoanalysis of Fire*, London, 1964; *La Flamme d'une chandelle*, Paris, 1961, *On Poetic Imagination and Reverie*, Indianapolis, 1971). His friendship with ELUARD and many Parisian literary figures reinforced his literary interests. His study of Lautréamont's poetical imagery (*Lautréamont*, Paris, 1939) is still regarded as a model of philosophical and psychoanalytical literary criticism. In the history of science, his researches betrayed excessive theoretical preoccupation; his example has dominated much recent French production in the history of science. PC

Bacon, Francis (b. Dublin, Ireland, UK [now Irish Republic], 28.10.1909). British figure painter. Born of English parents, Bacon spent two years as a youth in Berlin and Paris, then settled in London about 1929 and made a brief attempt to establish himself as an interior decorator and furniture designer. He soon turned to painting, at which he was self-taught, but rarely exhibited until after WW2 and destroyed all but a few of his early works. His *Three Studies for Figures at the Base of a Crucifixion* (1944), a triptych of violently distorted polyp-like surrealistic figures against an orange background, marks the culmination of his early style. From then on, however, he began to represent the human figure more directly, and has become one of the most influential figure painters of the postwar period. At first the figures were presented in a violent and shocking way, and with startling combinations of imagery such as a screaming figure crouching under an umbrella or heads dissolving into curtains and accompanied by tassels or safety pins. The imagery was drawn from widely different sources such as medical photographs, film-stills (notably the famous close-up of a wounded nurse screaming, from EISENSTEIN's film *The Battleship Potemkin*), MUYBRIDGE's photographs of humans and animals in movement, and Velasquez's portrait of Pope Innocent X. Bacon's figure paintings combined the immediacy of contemporary news photographs with a grandeur of presentation and rich, sensuous handling of paint reminiscent of 16c and early 17c Venetian and Spanish painting. Since the mid-1950s his work has become more straightforward, though the imagery and distortions are still sometimes strange and disturbing. He has based most of his subsequent paintings on friends, working usually from memory rather than directly from the model. His most characteristic theme is a single figure, usually male, seated or standing in an enclosed, windowless interior, as though isolated and trapped in his or her private hell. REA

R. Alley & J. Rothenstein, *Francis Bacon* (London, 1964); D. Sylvester, *Interviews with Francis Bacon, 1962–1979* (London, ²1980).

Baeck, Leo (b. Lissa, Prussia, Germany [now Leseno, Poland], 23.5.1873; d. London, UK, 2.11.1956). German Jewish religious leader and theologian, who became the paradigm of German Jewry during the Holocaust. His first major work *Das Wesen des Judentums* (Berlin, 1905; tr. I. Howe, *The Essence of Judaism*, NY, 1948) combined neo-Kantianism with ancient rabbinic patterns of ethical rigorism, stressing the ongoing dynamic development of human response to divine imperatives and presenting a rational modern faith built upon 19c philosophy. Subsequently Baeck moved into new areas – mysticism, New Testament studies, dialogue – leading to a renewal of the sense of mystery within Judaism. His last work, written in the concentration camp (*Dieses Volk: jüdische Existenz*, Frankfurt, 1955; tr. A. H. Friedlander, *This People Israel: the Meaning of Jewish Existence*, NY, 1966), in its development from essence to existence, recapitulates Jewish life in the 20c. Elected head of the German Jewish community in 1933, Baeck was the centre of a spiritual resistance to the Nazis which did not end when he himself entered the concentration camp. He taught, guided and comforted the inmates, but has been sharply criticized for neither resisting physically, nor warning about the death camps. Scholars have confirmed his heroic role and basic integrity, which also established him as a leader in postwar Jewry, a voice of dialogue and reconciliation.

AHF

A. H. Friedlander, *Leo Baeck: Teacher of Theresienstadt* (NY, 1968); L. Baker, *Days of Sorrow and Pain: Leo Baeck and the Berlin Jews* (NY, 1978).

Bahā' Allāh (Bahā'u'llāh), Mīrzā Ḥusayn ʿAlī Nūrī (b. Tehran, Persia [now Iran], 12.11.1817; d. Acre, Palestine, Ottoman Empire [now Israel], 29.5.1892). Iranian founder of Baha'ism, a development of Babism (a 19c messianic movement within Shīʿī Islam in Persia), now a widespread religion. The son of a government minister, he early developed an interest in religious matters and was an early Bābī convert in 1844. Babism was militarily defeated and its founder executed in 1850. In 1852 a Bābī attempt on the life of Nāṣer al-Dīn Shāh led to the exile of members of the sect, including Bahā' Allāh, to Baghdad. Here he emerged as *de facto* leader of the movement. By the 1860s he had begun to develop a new form of Babism, playing down the esotericism and fanaticism of the original movement, emphasizing political quietism and stressing independence from Islam in a new revelation centred in himself. Later exiles took him to Istanbul (1863), Adrianople (1863–8) and Palestine (1868–92). During his last years he led a secluded life in a mansion near Acre where he developed his claim to be a 'divine Manifestation' and the 'promised one' of all religions. He wrote extensively, combining western liberal ideas with traditional concepts from Islam and Christianity, emphasizing world unity and peace. Alone of modern Islamic movements, Baha'ism has succeeded in establishing itself as a religion independent of Islam.

DMM

H. M. Balyuzi, *Bahā'u'llāh* (Oxford, 1980).

Baird, John Logie (b. Helensburgh, Strath., UK, 13.8.1888; d. Bexhill-on-Sea, E. Sussex, 14.6.1946). British pioneer of television. Baird tried his hand at many business ventures – selling marmalade, French soap, Australian honey. He then decided to develop the transmission of visual images and, in 1925, succeeded in transmitting an image of the head of a ventriloquist's doll. In 1926 he televised moving objects and in 1928 demonstrated colour television. His system was essentially mechanical and he suffered a great disappointment when, in 1936, the BBC adopted an electrical method.

RIT

Balanchine, George, *né* Georgi Melitonovitch Balantchivadze (b. St Petersburg [now Leningrad], Russia, 22.1.1904; naturalized American citizen; d. New York, USA, 30.4.1983). Russian/American dancer and choreographer, one of the most prolific and important creators of 20c ballets. A student of both the Imperial Ballet School and the Conservatory of Music, he experimented early in choreography which in its style and choice of music antagonized the ballet establishment. While on tour in Europe, he was engaged by DIAGHILEV in 1924 and soon became the principal choreographer of the nomadic Ballets Russes, his creations including *Le Chant du rossignol* (STRAVINSKY, 1925), *Barabau* (Rieti, 1925), *La Chatte* (Sauguet, 1927), *Le Bal* (Rieti, 1929), and his two most important works which survive from the Diaghilev repertory *Apollo* (Stravinsky, 1928) and *Prodigal Son* (PROKOFIEV, 1929). Balanchine's subsequent career has been synonymous with the creation of the national ballet of the USA. With Lincoln Kirstein he founded the School of American Ballet in New York (1934), and a troupe of dancers who eventually (1948) became New York City Ballet, one of the greatest ballet companies in the West. His first 'American' ballet was *Serenade* (Tchaikovsky, 1934), which remains a masterpiece and (like *Apollo*) a statement of Balanchine's new neoclassicism. This both preserves and transforms the classical ballet of his Russian training, and is expressed in his massive output of ballets. His choice of composers has ranged from Bach to IVES; but pre-eminent has been his collaboration with Stravinsky, producing work in which music and dance are instinctively interwoven: *Agon* (1957), *Monumentum pro Gesualdo* (1960), *Movements for Piano and Orchestra* (1963), *Rubies* (1967) and (following Stravinsky's death) *Symphony in Three Movements*, *Violin Concerto* and *Duo Con-*

certante (all 1972) are fine examples.
DAD
B. Taper, *Balanchine* (NY, 1963); L. Kirstein, *The New York City Ballet* (NY, 1973).

Baldwin, James Arthur (b. New York, USA, 2.8.1924). American novelist and essayist. A native of Harlem, Baldwin's uneasy relations with his stepfather, his problems over sexual identity and his experience of racism in his first job in Newark, drove him in 1948 into a 10-year exile in Europe, where he fulfilled his early literary ambitions. *Go Tell It on the Mountain* (NY, 1953) and *Notes of a Native Son* (Boston, 1955) clearly enunciated the weight of black anger and the burden of white guilt under which American society laboured. Consistently fusing autobiographical material with social concerns, Baldwin pursued the same issue of civil rights through the next two decades, notably in *The Fire Next Time* (NY, 1963). His work is characterized by a recurring search for some form of redemptive love which would ease both the social and personal burdens he acutely felt. His belief, however, in any such possibility eroded with the failure of the civil rights movement and the assassination of Martin Luther KING, and a later work like *No Name in the Street* (NY, 1972) bitterly and despairingly begins to acknowledge that violence may be the only route to racial justice. KGM
F. Eckman, *The Furious Passage of James Baldwin* (NY, 1966).

Balfour, Arthur James (b. Whittingehame, Lothian, UK, 25.7.1848; d. Woking, Surrey, 19.3.1930). Leader of the British Conservative party (1902–11); prime minister (1902–5); foreign secretary (1916–19). Aristocratic (nephew of Lord Salisbury), actively interested in metaphysics, profoundly pessimistic in his conservatism, he is most closely associated with four major elements in British history in the 20c: (1) the passing of the leadership of the Conservative party from the aristocratic large-scale landowners to the industrialist classes under the impact of the Liberal governments of 1905–15; (2) the Balfour Declaration of 2.11.1917 promising a 'national home' for Jews in the then Ottoman provinces of Palestine, provided safeguards could be secured for 'non-Jewish' communities; (3) the post-1920 Anglo–American settlements over war debts (1922) and rivalry in naval armaments and the Far East (Washington Conference and Treaties 1921–2); (4) the attempt to shape the relationship between Britain and the increasingly independent Dominions into a community by functionalist-administrative means, especially in the fields of defence and foreign policy, notably at the Imperial conferences of 1921, 1923 and 1926 at which Balfour evolved a formula, largely incorporated into the 1931 Statute of Westminster, to cover the Dominions' insistence on control of their own external relations within a supposedly united Commonwealth. DCW
B. E. C. Dugdale, *Arthur James Balfour* (2 vols, London, 1936).

Balla, Giacomo (b. Turin, Piedmont, Italy, 18.8.1871; d. Rome, 5.3.1958). Italian futurist painter. Based almost entirely in Rome from 1895, apart from seven months in Paris (1900); there he acquired the divisionist colour techniques of neoimpressionism and used them to give heightened realism to works with an implied social comment, often evoking the pathos of poverty, unemployment or harsh proletarian life. He passed on his colour theory to BOCCIONI and Severini, who developed its abstract potential to express the sense of the movement and speed of modern urban life which became the chief tenet of futurism. Balla's own work became more concerned with the abstract investigation of light (e.g. *Street Light – Study of Light*, 1909). Although he was one of the signatories of the *Initial Manifesto of Futurism* (11.2.1910) and the *Technical Manifesto of Futurist Painting* (11.4.1910), Balla did not violently reject the art of the past as demanded by MARINETTI and Boccioni; nor did he participate in any of the futurist 'happenings' staged round Europe, but concentrated on depicting movement with an increasingly precise divisionist technique. In works such as *Dynamism of a Dog on a Leash* and *Rhythm of the Violinist* (both 1912) he rendered the sequence of a movement 'simultaneously' in an analytical manner reminiscent of Marey's chrono-photographic studies of human and animal locomotion. Later in 1912, his analyses of motion turned from the solid object to light activated by rhythm. He experimented with non-objective patterns of prismatic colour in order to depict differing structures of light in his series of *Iridescent Interpenetrations* (begun 1912). He went on to produce a series of variations on birds in flight, and on speeding cars in near-abstract forms where car wheels are suggested by a series of expanding spirals and forward motion by a succession of diagonals. In 1914 he tried to convey a sense of infinite space and the movement of light through the cosmos as in *Mercury Passing before the Sun as Seen through a Telescope*. His sweeping rhythmic patterns soon gave way to mechanical, decorative forms. In the mid-1930s Balla reverted to impressionistic figurative painting and returned to abstraction only a few years before his death. SOBT

Giacomo Balla, exh. cat., Galleria d'Arte Moderna (Turin, 1963).

Balthus, ps. of Balthasar Klossowski de Rola (b. Paris, France, 29.2.1908). French painter. Son of the Polish painter and art historian Erich Klossowski, and of the painter Elisabeth Dorothée Spiro (her friend was the German poet RILKE who spent prolonged periods in Balthus's Swiss home during the father's absence). DERAIN, BONNARD and Rilke encouraged the young painter. Balthus spent his childhood in Switzerland and in 1924 moved to Paris where he taught himself to paint. Though called up in WW2, Balthus was discharged unfit for service in 1943. In 1961 MALRAUX arranged his appointment as director of the Académie de France at the Villa Medici in Rome, and until his appointment ended in 1978 Balthus often travelled in the East from his Roman base. *The Street*, exhibited at his first one-man show (1934), typifies his treatment of streetscapes and interiors 'realistically' yet with a sense of anguish and menace. Most of his later interiors have been concerned with early adolescence in girls, in which the primary object of the representation is a tension between gawkiness and burgeoning sexuality (e.g. *Nude in Profile*, 1973–7; *Getting Up*, 1975–8). From the 1950s onwards, the solemnity of Balthus's paintings has been reduced by movement from a dull to a bright palette, by the use more of tempera than of oils, and by areas of colourful patterning in the Japanese as well as the Sienese manner which are contrasted with the soft erotic line of the girls' bodies (e.g. *The Cat in the Mirror*, 1977 –80, and *Reclining Nude*, 1980). Balthus's achievement has been to combine and adapt traditional representational approaches, with suggestions of 20c themes such as the cult of youth, the child as sexual being, and the complex nature of sexuality.   JGr

Balthus, exh. cat., Musée des Arts Décoratifs (Paris, 1966); *Balthus*, exh. cat., Venice Biennale (Venice, 1980).

Banda, Hastings Kamuzu (b. Kasunga District, Nyasaland [now Malawi], 14.5.1906). President of Malawi. One of the most profoundly conservative leaders of black Africa, in the late 1950s Banda seemed one of the most militant opponents of British colonialism. Absent from his native Nyasaland for nearly 40 years, when he studied medicine in the USA and practised in Britain and Ghana, Banda was invited back by the young radicals of the Nyasaland African Congress to play the role of a political messiah. His militancy landed him in gaol but also helped to shatter the central African Federation and to bring independence to Nyasaland (renamed Malawi) in 1964. Banda then removed his radical supporters from office and created a highly autocratic regime. He established cordial relations with South Africa in the 1970s and avoided involvement in the guerrilla wars in neighbouring Mozambique and Zimbabwe, thus keeping his country an oasis of stability and moderate prosperity in a troubled region. The exact nature of his standing among his people will only become apparent when he has left the political scene.   RH

P. Short, *Banda* (London, 1974).

Bandera, Stepan (b. Uhryniw-Stany, Galicia, Austria-Hungary [now USSR], 1.1.1909; d. Munich, Bavaria, West Germany, 15.10.1959). Leader of the Ukrainian nationalist minority in interwar Poland, he founded the Organization of Ukrainian Nationalists in 1936. With the German invasion of Russia in 1941 he was associated with the brief declaration of an independent Ukrainian state only to see it suppressed by the Germans. In 1942 he founded and led the Ukrainian People's Army (UPA), an organization of guerrillas which fought Germans and Russians indiscriminately; he escaped with elements of the UPA via Poland and Czechoslovakia in 1947–8 into the American-occupied zones of Austria and Germany. He was assassinated by a Soviet agent in Munich in 1959, the most considerable, though by no means the only Ukrainian nationalist figure to die in this way.   DCW

Banting, Frederick Grant (b. Alliston, Ont., Canada, 14.11.1891; d. nr Musgrave Harbour, Nfld, 21.2.1941). Canadian physiologist. After medical service during WW1, Banting combined part-time physiological research with general practice in London, Ontario. Becoming interested in the internal secretion of the pancreas, he moved to Toronto, where J. J. R. Macleod, professor of physiology, encouraged him. Together with the physiologist C. H. Best and the biochemist J. B. Collip, Banting devised methods for extracting the pancreatic substance (insulin) in sufficient quantity and purity to treat diabetes. The first clinical trials, in January 1922, were successful and commercial production was soon possible. The group's rapid success had been a joint effort, and Banting and Macleod shared their 1923 Nobel prize money with Best and Collip. Banting spent the rest of his life as director of the Banting–Best department of medical research at the University of Toronto, working on problems relating to cancer, silicosis and heart disease. He died in an air crash while pursuing wartime scientific duties.   WFB

L. G. Stevenson, *Sir Frederick Banting* (Toronto, ²1947).

Barbu, Ion, ps. of Dan Barbilian (b. Cîmpulung Muscel, Romania, 19.3.1895; d. Bucharest, 11.8.1961). Romanian poet and mathematician. An unusual example of a person with two vocations, Barbu became professor of algebra at Bucharest University in 1942. He made his debut as a poet in 1918, his early verse being generally in the Parnassian mould. Between 1920 and 1925 his compositions are distinguished by their Turkish atmosphere, the poet offering brilliant cameos of Balkan life. After 1925 he applied a mathematical vision of the world to his verse which became cryptic and hermetic. His collected verse appeared in the volume *Joc secund* [Second play] (Bucharest, 1930) upon which Barbu's reputation rests, for subsequently he devoted himself entirely to mathematics. Although the sum of his work is small, its density makes him a major Romanian writer. Barbu's preoccupation with the analogies between poetry and mathematics produced a verse characterized by mathematical metaphor, by the symmetrical regularity of stanzas, and yet where striking sonority and musicality prevail. To the geometry of his form Barbu added a vast range of analogies, associations of ideas and references to facts or persons which are sometimes the product of his imagination, thus transforming his verse into a cryptic message, one made more private by the use of incongruous expressions and scientific terms with the value of metonymies.   DJD

A. Cioranescu, *Ion Barbu* (NY, 1981).

Bardeen, John (b. Madison, Wis., USA, 23.5.1908). American physicist. Bardeen is a theoretical physicist whose most important work has been concerned with the theory of solids, and especially those properties of solids in which the behaviour of electrons plays a crucial role. At Bell Telephone laboratories he was involved in work on the physics of surfaces and showed that the properties of a contact between a metal and a semiconductor were controlled by the rather unusual behaviour of electrons when very close to the surface of a solid. This work was crucial to the invention (with W. H. Brattain) of the point-contact transistor (1948). For this and for all the development work on semiconducting devices they and SHOCKLEY were awarded the Nobel prize for physics in 1956. Bardeen's other major achievement was in the successful development of the theory of superconductivity, for which he was awarded a second Nobel prize in 1972, with L. N. Cooper and J. R. Schrieffer. The phenomenon of superconductivity (the complete vanishing of the electrical resistance of certain metals at very low temperatures) had been a mystery since its first discovery in 1911 (KAMERLINGH ONNES), because it implied that the electrons were able to move through the body of a metal without any hindrance. Bardeen and colleagues proposed a mechanism whereby at low temperatures the electrons are able to pair together; they showed that this would lead to superconductivity. Subsequent experiments have demonstrated the existence of these electron pairs and the detailed consequences of the theory have been confirmed. HMR

Bar-Hillel, Yehoshua (b. Vienna, Austria-Hungary [now Austria], 8.9.1915; d. Jerusalem, Israel, 25.9.1975). Austrian/Israeli logician, philosopher and theoretical linguist. From 1961 he was professor of logic and the philosophy of science at the Hebrew University, Jerusalem. He received his doctorate at the Hebrew University in 1947, then spent three years at Chicago University under CARNAP, followed by a further three years at MIT (1950–3). Carnap's influence was decisive, confirming him in a rejection of nonrigorous approaches to philosophy. His career spanned a wide range of formal, applied and philosophical perspectives on language. He participated in the machine translation (MT) and cybernetics boom of the early 1950s, but turned increasingly to algebraic and mathematical linguistics and, under CHOMSKY's influence, to the application of logic to the study of natural language. A major contribution was to foster mutual awareness between linguists and logicians. He made technical contributions to formal syntax, and his work is characterized by an insistence on methodological consistency. In the late 1960s and early 1970s he encouraged the growth of pragmatics (a branch of linguistics concerned with relevance to speaker and context). The collection of essays *Language and Information* (Cambridge, Mass., 1964) deals especially with information theory and mathematical linguistics, and *Aspects of Language* (Jerusalem, 1970) shows his later interest in general issues in the philosophy of language and methodology of linguistics. He was a prominent figure in Israeli academic life. CMH

A. Kasher (ed.), *Language in Focus: Foundations, Methods and Systems: Essays in Memory of Yehoshua Bar-Hillel* (Dordrecht, 1976).

Barnard, Christiaan Neethling (b. Beaufort West, Cape Province, South Africa, 8.11.1922). South African surgeon. Barnard studied at the University of Cape Town and qualified as a doctor in 1946. After working at the city hospital in Cape Town he became resident surgeon at the Groote Schuur Hospital in Cape Town (1953–6), where he identified the cause of a rare congenital problem. After completing his studies in America he returned to the Groote Schuur Hospital and Cape Town University as a specialist in cardiothoracic surgery and a lecturer and director of surgical research. He introduced open heart surgery to South Africa and did original work on artificial heart valves. In 1967 Barnard and a team of 20 surgeons replaced the heart of a South African called Louis Washkansky with the heart taken from a fatally injured accident victim. Washkansky lived only 18 days after the transplant operation but the procedure led the way for a number of other surgeons around the world to perform heart transplant operations. Barnard is sometimes thought of as one of the men in the forefront of high-technology medicine. His work subsequently led to much discussion and argument about the role of doctors in modern society. VC

P. Hawthorne, *The Transplanted Heart* (Johannesburg, 1968).

Baroja y Nessi, Pío (b. San Sebastian, Guipúzcoa, Spain, 28.12.1872; d. Madrid, 30.10.1956). Spanish novelist. A prolific if uneven writer (he published

66 novels) he did not become a full-time novelist until he was 30. Earlier he had studied medicine, obtaining his MD in 1893, and his earliest novels developed from his strong interest in psychology and mental disease. In the trilogy *La lucha por la vida* (Madrid, 1904; tr. I. Goldberg, *The Quest*, NY, 1922, *Weeds*, NY, 1923, and *Red Dawn*, NY, 1924) he turned his attention to the Madrid underworld, and this was followed by several adventure novels of which good examples are *La feria de los discretos* (Madrid, 1905; tr. J. S. Fasset Jr, *The City of the Discreet*, NY, 1917) and *Las inquietudes de Shanti Andía* (Madrid, 1911; tr. A. Kerrigan, *The Restlessness of Shanti Andía*, Ann Arbor, 1959). *César o nada* (Madrid, 1910; tr. L. How, *Caesar or Nothing*, NY, 1919), a novel which combines a study of personality with an analysis of politics in rural Spain, and *El árbol de la ciencia* (Madrid, 1911; tr. A. F. G. Bell, *The Tree of Knowledge*, NY, 1928), a philosophical novel which dramatizes the collapse of confidence in scientific rationalism at the turn of the century, are arguably Baroja's two most significant works. After 1912 he devoted himself predominantly to the historical novel with a series of 22 volumes *Memorias de un hombre de acción* [Memoirs of a man of action] (Madrid, 1913–34) which captures in a vivid and unconventional manner the fury of factional wars in 19c Spain.

Baroja's work stands out for its vivid impressionism, its breadth of vision and its anguished exploration of the social and spiritual problems of modern man. It is full of the paradoxes, ironies and insights that characterize the work of such European novelists as CONRAD, D. H. LAWRENCE and Thomas MANN. Of the modern Spanish novelists he is the one who most clearly exemplifies the problematic transition from 19c realism to 20c modernism. His technique varies from the deliberately indifferent to the complex and cryptic and his topics range from the crudely realistic to the aesthetically sophisticated and the deeply philosophical. Although his blunt denunciations of many aspects of Spanish life earned him the hostility of the Establishment and of the church, official recognition came eventually when he was elected to the Royal Spanish Academy in 1934, and he would almost certainly have been awarded the Nobel prize in the 1950s had it not been for his anti-Semitic views. Baroja has been a major and acknowledged influence on the younger generation of Spanish novelists who began their careers after the civil war as well as on such writers as HEMINGWAY and DOS PASSOS.   CAL

B. P. Patt, *Pío Baroja* (NY, 1971); C. A. Longhurst, *Pío Baroja: 'El mundo es ansí'* (London, 1977).

Baron, Hans (b. Berlin, Germany, 22.6.1900; naturalized American citizen). German/American historian. Baron's lifelong preoccupation has been the relationship between political and cultural history in the early modern period, more especially the 'civic spirit' of the 15c and 16c. At first he worked more or less simultaneously on the Renaissance and the Reformation, with *Calvins Staatsanschauung* [Calvin's conception of the state] (Berlin, 1924), balanced by an edition of the Florentine humanist Leonardo Bruni (Berlin, 1928), and studies of the awakening of historical thought in Quattrocento humanism, and of 'Religion and politics in the German imperial cities' (*English Historical Review*, 52 [1937], 405–27, 614–33). After exile to the USA in 1938 Baron more or less confined himself to Renaissance Italy, especially republican Florence. Most of his leading ideas found expression in his major work *The Crisis of the Early Italian Renaissance* (2 vols, Princeton, 1955, [2]1966). Baron's identification with the 'civic humanism' of early 15c Florence may have made him a little uncritical of the republic, but his example has stimulated important work on the later history of civic humanism, such as D. Weinstein on Savonarola, W. Bouwsma on Sarpi, and J. Pocock's studies of the civic tradition in Britain and America.
    UPB

A. Molho & J. A. Tedeschi (eds), *Renaissance Studies in Honor of Hans Baron* (Florence, 1971).

Barraqué, Jean (b. Paris, France, 17.1.1928; d. Paris, 17.8.1973). French composer. A pupil of MESSIAEN who shared many of the concerns of his older colleague BOULEZ. However, his first published compositions, the Piano Sonata (1952) and *Séquence* (1955), show an uncommon willingness to tackle large-scale forms with the disintegrated means of advanced serialism and display his romantic temperament, evident in the Beethovenian breadth of the sonata and in the lyricism of *Séquence*, where poems by NIETZSCHE are set for soprano, piano and other instruments. After this work Barraqué began a vast system of musical commentaries on BROCH's *The Death of Virgil* (1945), but he completed only three parts: ... *au delà du hasard* [Beyond chance] for women's voices and instrumental groups (1959), *Chant après chant* [Song after song] for soprano, piano and percussion (1966) and *Le temps restitué* [Time restored] for voices and orchestra (1969). With the Concerto for clarinet, vibraphone and orchestra (1968), these are among the small body of musical masterpieces produced since WW2. PG

A. Hodeir, *Since Debussy* (NY, 1961).

Barrault, Jean-Louis (b. Le Vésinet, Seine-et-Oise, France, 8.9.1910). French actor, theatre director and manager. In the early 1930s he studied at the Atelier where he became interested in mime, exploited in his first production *Autour d'une mère* (1935). After acting and directing at the Comédie-Française during WW2, in 1946 he and Madeleine Renaud formed their own company at the Marigny. Here his full originality emerged. With an eclectic range of productions he kept alive the spirit of the 'art' theatre of the interwar Cartel, in particular experimenting with 'total theatre' which marshals all elements of theatrical presentation and all the actor's physical resources of expression, an approach akin to ARTAUD's 'theatre of cruelty' though without his metaphysical pretensions (see *Réflexions sur le théâtre*, Paris, 1949; tr. B. Wall, *Reflections on the Theatre*, London, 1951, and *Nouvelles Réflexions sur le théâtre*, Paris, 1959; tr. J. Chiari, *The Theatre of Jean-Louis Barrault*, London, 1961). In 1959 he took over the Odéon-Théâtre de France, which he opened to plays by IONESCO,

BECKETT, GENET and other avant-garde writers, as well as reviving CLAUDEL whose works he has rescued from presumed unstageability. Dismissed in 1968 for alleged complicity in the student occupation of the building, he has continued running his independent company successively in a wrestling stadium, a disused railway station and a skating rink. Seeing performance as essentially an act of communion, at once sensual and spiritual, he has rendered himself unfashionable with the politically committed and the young; but he answers charges of commercialism by observing that 'authenticity is commercial, not calculation' (see *Souvenirs pour demain*, Paris, 1972; tr. J. Griffin, *Memories for Tomorrow*, London, 1974). DHR

Barrès, Maurice (b. Charmes-sur-Moselle, Vosges, France, 19.8.1862; d. Paris, 3.12.1923). French politician and novelist. Educated at the *lycée* and then the law faculty in Nancy, Barrès entered the Parisian literary world as a journalist, rapidly becoming known as the 'prince of youth' because of the individualism and heroism enshrined in the novels of the *Culte de moi* [The cult of the ego] series: *Sous l'oeil des barbares* [Under barbarian eyes] (Paris, 1888), *Un Homme libre* [A free man] (Paris, 1889) and *Le Jardin de Bérénice* [The garden of Bérénice] (Paris, 1891). He began his political career as deputy for Nancy and subsequently represented a Paris constituency from 1906. A supporter of Boulanger and a spokesman for the Nationalists during the Dreyfus affair, he was a founder member of the anti-Semitic *Ligue de la Patrie Française* in 1889. The three volumes of the so-called *Roman de l'Energie nationale* [The novel of national energy] – *Les Déracinés* [The uprooted] (Paris, 1897), *L'Appel au soldat* [The call to the soldier] (Paris, 1900) and *Leurs Figures* [Their faces] (Paris, 1902) – were a major influence on Charles Maurras and the ideologues of *Action Française*. Like all Barrès's works they are dominated by a strong anti-German feeling born largely of the author's attachment to his native Lorraine, lost to Prussia after the humiliating defeat of 1871, and by the opposition between *pays légal* (the formal institutions of the republic) and *pays réel* (the true nation, exemplified by the old provinces of France as opposed to the rootless cosmopolitanism of Paris). In his WW1 journalism these themes combine with a cult of the nation's heroic dead to produce an almost mystical patriotism that has had a lasting effect on French nationalism. Elected to the Académie Française in 1906, Barrès was given a full state funeral in Notre Dame.   DM

Barth, Fredrik (b. Leipzig, Germany [now East Germany], 22.2.1928). Norwegian social anthropologist. He received his anthropological training in the USA and in the UK (Cambridge), and played a central part in the modifying of the structural-functional paradigm in British anthropology in the 1950s and 1960s, as well as promoting the development of models as a strategy of explanation. He is best known for his association with the Pathans of Swat in Pakistan: *Political Leadership among Swat Pathans* (London, 1959); *Features of Person and Society in Swat* (London, 1981). His 1959 monograph, though much challenged, remains the classic example of a transactional analysis of political relations in terms of individual choice and competitive strategy. Here, and subsequently in *Models of Social Organization* (London, 1966), he experimented with the explanation of variable and changing social forms by means of models which could generate them. The range of his many other field studies, often brief but always intellectually fertile, e.g. in relation to ethnic boundaries and ecologic niches in the Middle East, is also notable. As professor successively at Bergen and Oslo, he has been instrumental in building up Norwegian anthropology and including within it a concern with applying anthropological ideas in the study of the home society: *The Role of the Entrepreneur in Social Change in Northern Norway* (ed. Barth, Bergen, 1963).   SRC

Barth, Karl (b. Basle, Switzerland, 10.5.1886; d. Basle, 9.12.1968). Swiss theologian. Barth studied in Berlin and Marburg before becoming an assistant pastor in Geneva in 1909 and the pastor of the Swiss village of Safenwil (1911–21). By education he had become a liberal optimist in theology and a socialist in politics. Yet his experience of preaching the Christian gospel to villagers, his reading in existentialist literature about human weakness, and above all his disillusionment when in 1914 many of his former German teachers backed the Kaiser, compelled him to work out a more distinctive and a tougher message. He attempted to deduce all his doctrines from the Bible, without going so far as fundamentalism in rejecting the Higher Criticism of the text. In a commentary on St Paul's Epistle to the Romans (*Das Römerbrief*, Bern, 1919, [6]1928; *The Epistle to the Romans*, London, 1933) he attacked Protestant liberalism's belief that man could reach religious understanding by his own reason and develop nobly by his own will. When recalled to the academic world as a professor at Göttingen (1921), Münster (1925) and Bonn (1930), he elaborated a system of 'dogmatics' in lectures and books marked by a confidence in the transcendence of majestic 'otherness', and in the graciousness of the God revealed in Jesus Christ. He extolled Christ as the 'Risen Lord' and as the one Saviour, and (unlike other Calvinists) maintained that God had predestined all to heaven. The church to him was the community of the faithful. He took the lead in drawing up the Barmen Declaration (1934) against the pseudoreligious claims of Nazism. The influence of the neo-orthodoxy to which he gave eloquent expression helped many Protestants to regard the Bible as the Word of God powerfully confronting the calamities of the 1930s and 1940s. He returned to Basle as a professor in 1935. It was after 1945 that his patriarchal prestige among Protestant preachers rose to its peak. The influence of his teaching declined because it was thought not to be sufficiently in dialogue with modern agnosticism. Barth also angered many in the West by his refusal to advise his many disciples in Eastern Europe to treat communism as he had treated Nazism. But many Roman Catholics (e.g. KÜNG) took a respectful interest in his systematic theology, and Barth certainly threw out some intellectual bridges to the West and the East by his increasing emphasis on the gracious 'humanity' of God. His *Kirchliche Dogmatik* (Zürich, 1932–67; *Church Dogmatics*, Edinburgh, 1936–69) had exceeded 9000 pages in print by his death but was left incomplete. Even readers who found the arguments difficult to swallow admired the zest of this colossal work and the learning packed into its many extended footnotes. Barth addressed the 20c with a confidence rare among theologians.   DLE

H. Hartwell, *The Theology of Karl Barth* (London, 1964); E. Busch, *Karl Barth: his Life from Letters and Autobiographical Texts* (London, 1976).

Barthes, Roland (b. Cherbourg, Manche, France, 12.11.1915; d. Paris, 26.3.1980). French writer and critic of wide-ranging influence. Barthes's first book *Le Degré zéro de l'écriture* (Paris, 1953; tr. A. Lavers & C. Smith, *Writing Degree Zero*, London, 1972) looked at the historical conditions of literary language and posed the difficulty of a modern practice of writing: committed to language the writer is at once caught up in particular discursive orders, the socially instituted forms of writing, a set of signs – a myth – of 'literature'; hence the search for an unmarked language, before the closure of myth, a writing degree zero. The analysis of literature was complemented in *Mythologies* (Paris, 1957; tr. A. Lavers, London, 1972) by an analysis of the general regime of signs in contemporary culture: everyday life is produced in relations of meaning that Barthes showed to be those of a process of naturalization, specific ideological values being thus proposed as universal. This account of myth today involved Barthes in the development of semiology, the science 'studying the life of signs at the heart of social life' envisaged at the beginning of the 20c by the linguist SAUSSURE. In 1962 Barthes became a director of studies at the Ecole Pratique des Hautes Etudes in Paris, with responsibility for a seminar devoted to the 'sociology of signs, symbols and representations'. *Eléments de sémiologie* (in *Communications* no. 4, Paris, 1964; tr. A. Lavers & C. Smith, *Elements of Semiology*, London, 1967)

set out the terms and principles of semiology and Barthes made a number of semiological analyses of cultural facts, notably fashion in *Système de la Mode* [System of fashion] (Paris, 1967). Barthes championed BRECHT in France and was influential in the reception of ROBBE-GRILLET and the '*nouveau roman*'. *Sur Racine* (Paris, 1963; tr. R. Howard, *On Racine*, NY, 1964) and *Essais critiques* (Paris, 1964; tr. R. Howard, *Critical Essays*, Evanston, Ill., 1972) challenged traditional assumptions of literary studies (the status of the author, the treatment of language and the conception of the interpretation of texts, the idea of history) and Barthes was identified and attacked as the main representative of a new criticism, '*la nouvelle critique*'. His reply was made in *Critique et vérité* [Criticism and truth] (Paris, 1966). In *S/Z* (Paris, 1970; tr. R. Miller, NY, 1974) he gave a phrase-by-phrase analysis of a Balzac story and initiated an examination of the experience of reading, of the relations of the reader as subject to the movements of language in texts. Subsequent works returned to questions posed from points of subjective response or intensity: *Le Plaisir du texte* (Paris, 1973; tr. R. Miller, *The Pleasure of the Text*, NY, 1975) considered implications of pleasure in texts; *Roland Barthes par Roland Barthes* (Paris, 1975; tr. R. Howard, *Roland Barthes by Roland Barthes*, NY, 1977) was an autobiographical novel of the writer's 'I', unravelling the masks and personae and resistances of the ego; while the bestselling *Fragments d'un discours amoureux* (Paris, 1977; tr. R. Howard, *A Lover's Discourse: Fragments*, NY, 1978) explored – half analysis, half simulation – the figures of the discourse of love. In 1976 Barthes was appointed to the chair of 'literary semiology' at the Collège de France. His last book was *La Chambre claire* (Paris, 1980; tr. R. Howard, *Camera Lucida*, NY, 1982), a reflection on the levels of meaning of the photograph.

Barthes's work was immensely varied in its range and enormously influential for literary studies, semiotics and modern critical thought. Towards the end of his life Barthes was increasingly recognized for what he truly was: a great modern writer.   SH

A. Lavers, *Roland Barthes: Structuralism and After* (London, 1982).

Bartlett, Frederic Charles (b. Stow-on-the-Wold, Glos., UK, 20.10.1886; d. Cambridge, 30.9.1969). A founding father of British experimental psychology. After an attack of pleurisy in childhood, Bartlett was educated at home. This may partly explain the nature of his psychological thinking, which was never straitjacketed by notions of academic orthodoxy. He graduated as an external student of London University in 1910 with first-class honours in philosophy. He joined the new laboratory of experimental psychology at Cambridge, first as a student, then as a member of staff. In 1922 he was made director of the laboratory and in 1931 was appointed as first professor of experimental psychology at Cambridge University, where he remained until his retirement in 1952. His contribution to scholarship lay in his application of original experimental techniques to the performance of individuals. In his valuable account of the workings of memory *Remembering* (Cambridge, 1932) he presented evidence for the view that a set of constructive processes are involved: the individual implicitly edits, transforms and selectively recalls experiences in a way that departs significantly from the 'objective' view of the same events. The tradition of memory research established by Bartlett now dominates the contemporary scene, by contrast with the earlier German work on rote learning. A large part of his influence is attributable to his brilliance as a teacher and to his charismatic leadership style which left its mark on the generation of research students who worked with him at Cambridge.   RRS

Bartlett, Maurice Stevenson (b. Scrooby, Notts., UK, 18.6.1910). British statistician, with ICI from 1934 to 1938 and since then holding academic posts in mathematics and statistics at Cambridge (1937–47), Manchester (1947–60), London (1960–7) and Oxford (1967–75) where he is now emeritus professor of biomathematics. Starting from the problem of establishing the basic virulence of epidemics, Bartlett built up a general methodology of inference for 'point-processes'. He saw, as had many others, that it is relatively easy to model the course of an epidemic in a known population, if the underlying infectivity is known. It is very difficult, however, to infer the basic virulence from the number of actual cases since the same disease may be either exploding or dying out. By taking as his data the time intervals between cases, Bartlett succeeded in applying reliable statistical analysis (see *An Introduction to Stochastic Processes*, Cambridge, 1955, [3]1978).   AGPW

Bartlett, Neil (b. Newcastle-upon-Tyne, Tyne & Wear, UK, 15.9.1932). British chemist, who currently holds a chair at Berkeley. Bartlett discovered the first chemical compound of xenon, although the element had been known for over 60 years. Xenon, and indeed all the other noble (or 'inert') gases discovered by RAMSAY, had for over half a century been considered completely unreactive. Although a number of theoreticians (including PAULING) had suggested that xenon should form many fluorides and oxides, all attempts to induce reactions of the noble gases had failed. Bartlett's experiments, designed upon careful thermodynamic arguments, were successful, and the work was published early in 1962 (*Proc. Chem. Soc.*, 218). Within a year, with the psychological barrier of the word 'inert' removed, a further seven compounds of xenon (and compounds of krypton and radon) had been identified: many more are now known.   KRS

Bartlett, Paul Doughty (b. Ann Arbor, Mich., USA, 14.8.1907). American organic chemist. Bartlett's early education was at Amherst College and at Harvard University. The main part of his career has been at Harvard, as Ewing professor from 1948 to 1975 (now emeritus) and latterly at Texas Christian University as Robert A. Welch professor. Bartlett's research interests have been extremely wide: they include stereochemistry, the mechanism and kinetics of organic reactions, especially the Walden inversion, polymerization, and molecular rearrangements. To each of these topics, all of major importance to organic chemical thought, Bartlett has brought his own kind of elegant and penetrating method of experimental investigation. He has also studied free-radical reactions, cyclo-additions, organic reactions of sulphur, photo-oxidation reactions of organic lithium compounds, alkylation of alkenes, and highly branched organic compounds. Some of these reactions share with those mentioned earlier considerable importance in chemical thought; some are more esoteric and speculative. Bartlett has also paid special attention to the structural details of reactive intermediates in organic reactions, including unstable carbocations (and hydride transfer to them from hydrocarbons) and triplet radical-pairs. The results have shed great light on critical aspects of reaction mechanisms. He is also notable for the study of reactions at bridgeheads, cage effects and concerted decompositions of peroxyesters.   NBC

Bartók, Béla Viktor János (b. Nagyszentmiklós, Austria-Hungary [now Sînnicolaul-Mare, Romania], 25.3.1881; d. New York, USA, 26.9.1945). Hungarian musician; not only an outstanding composer but an excellent pianist and an assiduous student of folk music. His ethnological research, his reverence for past composers (especially Beethoven and Bach), and his awareness of the musical present, including DEBUSSY, Richard STRAUSS and SCHOENBERG, strongly influenced his exceptionally individual and coherent musical style. During the decade before WW1 Bartók spent much time collecting and arranging folksongs, often in collaboration with his friend Zoltán Kodály. They also tried to revitalize Hungarian musical life and to create a genuinely Hungarian musical style with such works as Bartók's First String Quartet (1910) and his sole opera *A kékszakállú herceg vára* (*Duke Bluebeard's Castle*, 1918). Bartók reacted to his experience of Schoenberg with his two sonatas for violin and piano (1922, 1923) and to that of STRAVINSKY with his ballet *A Csodálatos mandarin* (*The Miraculous*

Mandarin, composed 1918–19, produced 1926 – it was its sordid scenario that delayed its first stage performance). These influences were quickly absorbed. The orchestral *Dance Suite* (1923) was Bartók's first great popular success.

He was now an international figure, touring Europe and the USA as a concert pianist, but he continued his work on folk music. One of his main tasks was to classify variants of a melody; this intensive work may have contributed to his far-reaching variation technique, shown, for example, in the Third String Quartet (1929). It is reflected too in the symmetrical forms and rigorous workings of other works of this period, including the Fourth and Fifth Quartets (1929 & 1935), the first two piano concertos (1927 & 1933) and the *Music for Strings, Percussion and Celesta* (1937). The works of the 1930s were clearer in harmony than the Third Quartet. After emigrating to the USA in 1940 Bartók continued this relaxation in works which include the ebullient Concerto for Orchestra (1944) and the Third Piano Concerto (1945).   PG

H. Stevens, *The Life and Music of Béla Bartók* (NY, 1953, [2]1964); E. Lendvai, *Béla Bartók: an Analysis of his Music* (London, 1971).

Barton, Derek Harold Richard (b. Gravesend, Kent, UK, 8.9.1918). British organic chemist. Barton's early work was in the field of natural products. At first he studied terpene and steroid chemistry, with special reference to limonin (from the seeds of citrus fruits) and aldosterone (one of the adrenal cortical hormones). Problems in the field of steroid structures led him in 1950 to create the system of ideas known as conformational analysis. If open-chain molecules are considered from the standpoint of rotation of one part of the molecule with respect to the other about a particular single bond, an infinite number of geometrical orientations is possible. Some, however, correspond to energy maxima, some to energy minima: these latter are called 'preferred conformations' ('conformation' is a term first used in 1929 by HAWORTH). This system of ideas is of special relevance to cyclic compounds, leading, for example, to the concept of the boat and chair conformations of six-membered alicyclic rings, to that of equatorial and axial bonds and substituents in cyclohexanes, and to the prediction, since widely verified, of differences in chemical behaviour between equatorial and axial substituents. Conformational analysis brightly illuminates the structure and reactivity of steroids, terpenes, carbohydrates and many other groups of compounds; it has had a tremendous impact on organic chemistry, biochemistry and medicinal chemistry. Barton was awarded a Nobel prize for this work in 1969, jointly with HASSEL.   NBC

Basie, William (Count) (b. Red Bank, NJ, USA, 21.8.1904). American jazz pianist and leader of an internationally successful big band for over 40 years. Basie began as an orthodox piano stylist, whose powerful and accurate left-hand work typified the Harlem 'stride' school. In Kansas City, Missouri, from the late 1920s he developed a highly individual style of piano-playing, which juxtaposed sparse single-note playing by the right hand with sturdy, emphatic chording by the left hand. After forming a band in Kansas City, he moved with it to New York in 1936. By 1938, the band's soloists included trumpeters Buck Clayton and Harry Edison, trombonist Dicky Wells, tenor saxophonists YOUNG and Hershel Evans; its greatest asset was its rhythm section, which consisted of Basie on piano, Freddie Greene on guitar, Walter Page on string-bass, and Jo Jones on drums. Vocalists Jimmy Rushing and Billie Holliday, and later Helen Humes, widened the band's appeal, but it was the unmistakable sound of the rhythm section on recordings such as *One o'Clock Jump* (1937) and *Jumping at the Woodside* (1938) that held the public's attention.   JJC
S. Dance, *The World of Count Basie* (NY, 1979).

Bataille, Georges (b. Billom, Puy-de-Dôme, France, 10.9.1897; d. Paris, 10.7.1962). French writer officially excommunicated from the surrealist movement by BRETON in 1929; his work continued to have strong surrealistic affinities and echoes. He was violently

opposed to any attempts at rational thought and to all forms of morality; was fascinated by the possibilities, offered by evil and eroticism, of escaping from the human condition (*La Littérature et le mal*, Paris, 1949, tr. A. Hamilton, *Literature and Evil*, London, 1973; *L'Erotisme*, Paris, 1958, tr. M. Dalwood, *Eroticism*, London, 1962); rejected all traditional literature and considered that the ultimate aim of all intellectual, artistic or religious activity should be the annihilation of the rational individual in a violent, transcendental act of communion. Bataille was especially interested in writers and historical figures who, like Sade, NIETZSCHE and Gilles de Rais, had exalted the power and potentialities of evil. He also played an important part in the general intellectual and literary life of France as the founder (1946) of the influential review *Critique*. His long editorship was marked by a greater sanity of comment and assessment than his own personal views might suggest. Since the early 1960s, his work has been widely admired by the present French avant-garde – BARTHES, Lucette Finas, KRISTEVA and Philippe Sollers have all written enthusiastically about his work. The publication of his complete works, in ten volumes, began in Paris in 1970.
                                        PMWT
Hommages à Georges Bataille, special issue of *Critique*, nos 195–6 (Paris, 1963); P. Sollers (ed.), *Vers une révolution culturelle: Artaud, Bataille* (Paris, 1973).

Bateson, Gregory (b. Grantchester, Cambs., UK, 9.5.1904; naturalized American citizen; d. San Francisco, Calif., USA, 4.7.1980). British/American anthropologist and cyberneticist, but above all a thinker about ideas in their contexts and interrelations, striving to develop 'a science which does not yet exist as an organized body of theory or knowledge'. He later called this study of the relation between context, meaning and learning *Steps to an Ecology of Mind* (London, 1972), the title of his collected essays. These showed the progress of an unconventional career that had begun in *Naven* (Cambridge, 1936) with a multilayered examination of ritual among the Iatmul, a New Guinea people. Its theoretical focus was on opposition, entropy and control in social systems. *Balinese Character: a Photographic Analysis* (NY, 1942), written with his first wife Margaret MEAD, crossed into that realm of culture and personality which social anthropology has always ignored. His studies branched out into evolution, epistemology and forms of communication in humans and animals from schizophrenics to dolphins. Enormously wide ranging and stimulating, his work is sometimes more suggestive than rigorously developed (see *Mind and Nature: a Necessary Unity*, NY, 1979). But for inspiring a sense of the opening up of intellectual space it is a vital legacy. MDCG

J. Blockman (ed.), *About Bateson* (London, 1978).

Bateson, William (b. Whitby, N. Yorks., UK, 8.8.1861; d. Merton, Surrey, 8.2.1926). British geneticist. Educated at Rugby School and St John's College, Cambridge, where he was for many years a fellow, he was finally appointed professor of biology at Cambridge in 1908. Subsequently he became the first director of the John Innes Horticultural Institute. From an early interest in natural history Bateson developed an awareness of the problems relating to the kind of variation that might be the raw material of evolution. At that time most biologists assumed that evolutionary change involved only characters subject to continuous variation (i.e. variation that does not fall into discrete classes), since these include characters that are obvious components of Darwinian fitness. Gradually Bateson became convinced, from extensive observations of organisms in the wild and under domestication, of the importance of characters subject to discontinuous variation (i.e. variation that falls into discrete classes). In *Materials for the Study of Variation* (London, 1894) he emphasized the widespread occurrence of such variation. Then realizing the suitability of discrete variants for investigating the mechanism of heredity, Bateson used these in experimental hybridizations with plants and with poultry, unaware of MENDEL's earlier deductions from similar crosses with

peas. When in 1900 he read Mendel's classic paper 'Experiments with plant hybrids' (1866) he at once appreciated its significance, and spent the next 10 years promulgating what he termed 'Mendelism' (see *Mendel's Principles of Heredity*, Cambridge, 1902). By referring to his own data and that of other hybridizers, interpretable by Mendel's explanations, he was able to answer the criticism that general principles could not be deduced from Mendel's own experiments. Among his 'Mendelian' interpretations were those of A. E. GARROD's data on human inborn errors of metabolism; Bateson realized that deleterious recessive alleles could persist in the human population, only detectable in the offspring of two carriers. From his own experimental crosses he made the important deduction that the effect of a gene on the phenotype depends on the other genes in the organism. Data obtained by himself and R. C. Punnett provided the first evidence that genes may show linked segregation ('Experimental studies in the physiology of heredity', 1905). Subsequently T. H. MORGAN's group at Columbia University demonstrated that linkage is a consequence of genes being on chromosomes, though it took 12 years before Bateson, who had interpreted his own data differently, was convinced by the 'chromosome theory'. From 1910 Bateson built up the John Innes Institute as a centre of experimental plant breeding and genetics. His own contribution to genetics became somewhat less. Nevertheless, his earlier influence earned him the title of the 'real founder of genetics'.

APJ

B. Bateson, *William Bateson FRS: Naturalist* (London, 1928); L. C. Dunn, *A Short History of Genetics* (London, 1965).

Baxter, James Keir (b. Dunedin, Otago, New Zealand, 29.6.1926; d. Auckland, 22.10.1972). New Zealand poet. Educated at Quaker schools in New Zealand and in the UK, he studied at Otago University, Dunedin, and Victoria University, Wellington. Always a deeply committed writer, Baxter established his reputation at 18 with *Beyond the Palisade: Poems* (Christchurch, 1944). A great 'character', Baxter became a Catholic in 1958, a decision reflected in the fine collection *In Fires of No Return* (London, 1958). *Howrah Bridge and Other Poems* (Oxford, 1961) collected earlier pieces, but also charted his reactions to a visit to India. His outstanding work is *Pig Island Letters* (Oxford, 1966) in which Baxter's wit and scholarship found a natural focus in poems exploring the inner landscape of his native islands. His continual spiritual drive expressed itself in later years in the establishment of communes and shelters for young people and society's rejects. It was his own life of hard work and material deprivation which produced the *Jerusalem Sonnets* (Wellington, 1970), *Jerusalem Daybook* (Wellington, 1971) and *Autumn Testament* (Wellington, 1972), an imaginative combination of prose and poetry which both reflected and furthered what he saw as the inextricable link between his writing and his practical religious service. As man and poet Baxter's example is as rare as it is important; *Collected Poems* (Wellington, 1979) documents at least the poetry.   PNQ

Baylis, Lilian Mary (b. London, UK, 9.5.1874; d. London, 25.11.1937). British theatrical manager and founder of the Old Vic and Sadler's Wells companies. Her father was a keen amateur musician and Lilian, the eldest of nine children, received some musical education. In 1890 William Baylis transformed his family's hobby into its profession by starting a concert party, The Gypsy Revellers, which played with indifferent success in England and South Africa. In 1897, after a serious illness, Lilian returned from Johannesburg to London to help her maternal aunt with the management of the Royal Victoria Coffee and Music Hall near Waterloo, a philanthropic institution offering teetotal entertainment. In 1912 Baylis took over the organization and by 1914 had instituted a policy of presenting a regular Shakespearean season, interspersed with opera. The conditions at the Old Vic were appalling, but through energy, zeal and an uncanny knack of selecting the right people, Baylis created the finest Shakespearean company of the interwar years. Harcourt Williams and Tyrone Guthrie were among her directors, GIELGUD, the Thorndikes and OLIVIER in her casts. When it proved impossible to maintain a skeletal opera company and a Shakespearean company in the same building, Baylis undertook the task of raising the funds to acquire and renovate Sadler's Wells in Islington, then a run-down theatre, which became the home for Sadler's Wells opera and ballet. An intensely religious woman, she had only a limited knowledge of the arts which she did so much to further; but her life was devoted to her theatres. She was appointed a Companion of Honour in 1929 and was only the second woman outside the university to be awarded an honorary MA at Oxford in 1924.   JE

A. Dent, *A Theatre for Everybody* (London, 1945); R. Findlater, *Lilian Baylis: the Lady of the Old Vic* (London, 1975).

Bazin, André (b. Angers, Maine-et-Loire, France, 18.4.1918; d. Paris, 11.11.1958). French film theorist. One of the cinema's most important and influential thinkers, Bazin published no full-scale treatment of film theory. But his views, scattered through articles and subsequently collected in the volumes *Qu'est-ce que le cinéma* (4 vols, Paris, 1958–62; sel. ed. *What is Cinema?*, 2 vols, Berkeley, Calif., 1967–71), helped shape the ideas of the whole French New Wave cinema: TRUFFAUT, GODARD and Rivette were all personally influenced by him. While he contributed much to the revaluation of Hollywood cinema and to Jean RENOIR's status as a major film maker (see *Jean Renoir*, Paris, 1971; London, 1974), Bazin's principal impact was in the establishment of a realist aesthetics of cinema, rooted in his own Catholicism and flexible enough to embrace both WELLES's *Citizen Kane* and the Italian neorealists.   RPA

D. Andrew, *André Bazin* (NY, 1978).

Beadle, George Wells (b. Wahoo, Nebr., USA, 22.10.1903). American molecular biologist. Work with Ephrussi in Paris on genetics of eye colour in *Drosophila* gave Beadle the first hint of a relationship between genes and the biosynthesis of enzymes. So he sought firmer evidence using a simpler organism – the bread mould *Neurospora crassa*. In collaboration with TATUM he showed that, after irradiation of spores, he could isolate mutants which had lost the ability to synthesize one or other of the nutrients required for growth. Investigation of the biochemical and genetic characteristics of these mutants led him to conclude that 'one gene controls the synthesis of one enzyme'. In the light of later knowledge it is more correct to say that one functional unit of DNA controls the synthesis of one peptide chain, but the fundamental concept remains unchallenged, providing the basis for many of the modern developments in genetics and for the new science of molecular biology. Beadle's techniques for selecting 'auxotrophic' mutants also made possible production of organisms uniquely suited to investigation of particular genetical problems and have proved invaluable for elucidating the metabolic pathways by which essential metabolites, such as amino acids and vitamins, are synthesized in the living cell.   GL

Beard, Charles Austin (b. Knightstown, Ind., USA, 27.11.1874; d. New Haven, Conn., 1.9.1948). American historian and political scientist. Beard did more than any other individual to introduce to the American academic mind, and through it to the public, an idea which it already knew: that economic and material conditions and motives exert powerful influence over politics. Before Beard wrote his celebrated work *An Economic Interpretation of the Constitution of the United States* (NY, 1913), a curious dichotomy had existed between values and facts. Americans never attributed to the founders of the republic the kind of interest in material things which nearly all Americans recognized as the stuff of political life. The irreverence of *An Economic Interpretation* caused an initial shock, but its tone was completely congruent with the social criticism of the Progressive era and it soon acquired influence far beyond its merits. Its flawed scholarship and tendentious use of records were not exposed to serious examination until the 1950s. Beard

was never a MARXist, and thought he had found an adequate explanatory principle for American politics in James Madison's tenth essay in *The Federalist* – which Beard made famous. Faction and interest were seen as normal in politics, with unequal distribution of property as the chief cause of discontent. In *The Rise of American Civilization* (NY, 1927), written with his wife Mary R. Beard, he achieved a powerful synthesis of general history in which the economic theme was prominent. A genuine progressive in many ways, Beard courageously opposed American participation in WW1, and as a result lost his professorship at Columbia University. When Franklin ROOSEVELT warned Americans of the dangers of war in the late 1930s, Beard thought he had detected the earlier symptoms again and accused Roosevelt of dragging the country into war. His prolonged and bitter opposition to the war lost Beard much of his earlier influence over his profession.   JRP

R. Hofstadter, *The Progressive Historians* (NY, 1968).

Beatles, The. British rock group consisting of John Lennon (b. Liverpool, Mers., UK, 9.10.1940; d. New York, USA, 19.12.80), Paul McCartney (b. Liverpool, Mers., UK, 18.6.1942), George Harrison (b. Liverpool, Mers., UK, 25.2.1943) and Ringo Starr, ps. of Richard Starkey (b. Liverpool, Mers., UK, 7.7.1940). The Beatles' success was one of the social phenomena of the 1960s; their music seemed to chart the course of the changing decade and express the feelings of their generation the world over. They would not have achieved their immense popularity without two such creative musicians as John Lennon and Paul McCartney: many of the Beatles' songs were signed by them. But it soon became clear that McCartney's special talent was for lyrical melody, as in such numbers as 'Yesterday', whereas Lennon's music was more aggressive, socially concerned and influenced by American rock music. The collaboration was unstable and the group split up in 1970. Before that, in the album *Revolver* and still more in its successor *Sgt Pepper's Lonely Hearts Club*

Band the Beatles' electronic effects and musical sophistication seemed appropriate to their new topics: the search for peace, love and enlightenment through drugs or Indian mysticism, and a wide range from satire to sympathy with the old and the dispossessed. The Beatles' distinctive use of a great number of moods, themes and musical styles is unequalled in popular music. PG

W. Mellers, *Twilight of the Gods: the Beatles in Retrospect* (London, 1977); P. Norman, *Shout! The Story of the Beatles* (London, 1981).

Beaton, Cecil Walter Hardy (b. London, UK, 14.1.1904; d. Broadchalke, Wilts., 18.1.1980). British photographer. Educated at Harrow School and at Cambridge, Beaton began to take pictures for illustrated society magazines from 1925 onwards. His first major exhibition was at the Cooling Galleries in 1927. He represented Britain at the famous Stuttgart '*Film und Foto*' exhibition in 1929, and in 1930 he published his *Book of Beauty* (London), a portrait gallery of contemporary beauties assembled to a Victorian model. During the 1930s he was a fashion photographer and portraitist for such Condé Nast publications as *Vogue* and *Vanity Fair*. During WW2 he was an official photographer in blitzed London, and in India, Burma and China; some of his most stylish pictures date from this period of war service. Beaton's subjects are coolly, even dispassionately, presented. They reveal little of themselves, preferring to appear in this or that guise or role. In this respect his pictures differ from those of his European contemporaries (e.g. Henri CARTIER-BRESSON), who imply that their subjects can be known, their inner natures uncovered. Beaton's suggestion is of a wholly theatrical and social world, one in which appearance matters above all. His most outstanding successor is an American portraitist, Irving Penn, who acknowledges that Beaton's was a formative influence in the 1940s.

IJ

D. Mellor, *Modern British Photography*, Arts Council exh. cat. (London, 1980).

Beauvoir, Simone de (b. Paris, France, 9.1.1908). French novelist and feminist. Famous for her lifelong association with SARTRE, whom she met at the Sorbonne in 1929, de Beauvoir achieved independent recognition through her study of women and their social position, *Le Deuxième sexe* (2 vols, Paris, 1949; tr. H. M. Parshley, *The Second Sex*, London, 1953). This applied the Hegelian concept of self and other to rationalize male domination of women and through a complex literary and historical analysis, coloured by personal anecdotes, de Beauvoir explored the feminine predicament. Whereas a man can freely integrate his sexual and personal drives, she argued, a woman's sexuality and biological processes compete with and deplete her individual identity and freedom. Thus hobbled, women perpetuate male domination by accepting dependence in marriage. De Beauvoir insisted that while such inauthentic choices exist, women should eschew marriage and motherhood, a principle by which she still abides. Although latterly accused of extolling the 'masculine' to the detriment of the 'feminine', *Le Deuxième sexe* remains her greatest achievement, and a seminal feminist work. MI

Her autobiographical writings (*Mémoires d'une jeune fille rangée*, Paris, 1958, tr. J. Kirkup, *Memoirs of a Dutiful Daughter*, London, 1959; *La Force de l'âge*, Paris, 1960, tr. P. Green, *The Prime of Life*; *La Force des choses*, Paris, 1963, tr. R. Howard, *The Force of Circumstance*, London, 1965; *Tout compte fait*, Paris, 1972, tr. P. O'Brian, *All Said and Done*, London, 1974) are invaluable, not only as an intimate account of the author's relationship with Sartre (now completed by the moving and often harrowing account of his last years in *La Cérémonie des adieux* [The farewell ceremony], Paris, 1981), but also for their classic picture of a middle-class girlhood and as a record of some 40 years of Parisian intellectual life. Her novels, of which the most successful is *Les Mandarins* (Paris, 1954; tr. L. M. Friedmann, *The Mandarins*, London, 1957), the winner of the Prix Goncourt, are perhaps less attractive although their documentary interest remains considerable. They also exemplify many of the themes of *Le Deuxième sexe*, notably the problems caused by a woman's over-identification with her lover's interests and ambitions. Her later essays take the form of a prolonged meditation on old age (as in *La Vieillesse*, Paris, 1970; tr. P. O'Brian, *Old Age*, London, 1972, a bitter indictment of society's indifference to the old) and death (as in *Une Mort très douce*, Paris, 1964; tr. P. O'Brian, *A Very Easy Death*, London, 1972, a moving account of her mother's death from cancer). DM

A. Whitmarsh, *Simone de Beauvoir and the Limits of Commitment* (Cambridge, 1981).

Beaverbrook, William Max Aitken (b. Maple, Ont., Canada, 25.5.1879; d. Leatherhead, Surrey, UK, 9.6.1964). Canadian-born British newspaper magnate, political champion of the unity of the British Empire and imperial protectionism, and unsuccessful populist challenger of the elitist leadership of the Conservative party under Baldwin (1929–30) and CHURCHILL (1942), he served as chancellor of the Duchy of Lancaster and minister of information in LLOYD GEORGE's coalition cabinet in 1918, and as minister of aircraft production (1940–1), minister of supply (1941–2) and Lord Privy Seal (1943–5) in Churchill's wartime cabinet. A man of enormous energy, a brilliant journalist and newspaper owner (*Daily Express*, *Sunday Express*, *Evening Standard*), he used his press as an instrument of policy; its masthead – the sign of the crusader in chains – was significant of his general lack of success in British politics save as a destructive and disruptive force, his vision of imperial unity finding favour neither in his native Canada nor in the long run in his adopted Britain. The main beneficiaries of his methods of propaganda were a series of brilliant figures on the radical wing of the Labour party, including Michael Foot, leader of the Labour party since 1979. DCW

A. J. P. Taylor, *Beaverbrook* (London, 1972).

Beazley, John Davidson (b. Glasgow, Strath., UK, 13.9.1885; d. Oxford, 6.5.1970). British classical archaeologist. Tutor at Christ Church, Oxford, from 1908 and Lincoln professor of classical archaeology at Oxford from 1925, Beazley devoted himself to the study of Attic vases, a field already established by German scholars such as Adolf Furtwängler and Paul Hartwig. He evolved a method, partly inspired by Giovanni Morelli's work on Italian Renaissance paintings, by which he could discover, identify and organize the various schools, styles, masters and pupils in Attic red-figure vases. Vase-painting is specially important for Greek art history since virtually all other examples of Greek painting have been lost; the vases have an artistic quality of their own and are also significant as sources to Greek mythology. Beazley published seminal articles in the *Journal of Hellenic Studies* from 1910, giving an account of the artists and their stylistic relations, establishing provenance and assessing artistic merit. His books *Attic Red-figure Vase-painters* (Oxford, 1942, ²1963) and *Attic Black-figure Vase-painters* (Oxford, 1956) set the study of Greek art on a completely new foundation. KKS

Bechet, Sidney Joseph (b. New Orleans, La, USA, 14.5.1897; d. Paris, France, 14.5.1959). American jazz saxophonist, clarinetist and composer. Bechet's work was never universally acclaimed because some listeners found his heavy vibrato too distracting; nevertheless, many musicians learnt from his highly rhythmical phrasing, and rhapsodic improvisations on ballads. He spent much of his career in Europe. During his first English tour (1919) he became a pioneer of specialization on the soprano saxophone and the first jazz musician to receive serious critical praise: the Swiss conductor Ernest Ansermet called him an 'artist of genius'. During the 1930s, Bechet toured the USA in a big band led by Noble Sissle. In 1938, with revived interest in traditional jazz, Bechet left Sissle and thereafter worked only in small bands. Though not a trained musician, Bechet had a great flair for composing strong melodies ('Petite Fleur', 'The Fish Seller', 'The Onions'), but his music for a ballet, *La Nuit est une sorcière* [The night is a witch] (1953), is disappointing.

His autobiography was published as *Treat It Gentle* (London, 1960).   JJC

M. Williams, *Jazz Masters of New Orleans* (NY, 1967).

Becker, Carl Lotus (b. Blackhawk Co., Iowa, USA, 7.9.1873; d. Ithaca, NY, 10.4.1945). American historian. Becker's principal appointment was at Cornell, where he was professor of history from 1917 to 1941. His field of study was the late 18c and his outstanding book *The Heavenly City of the Eighteenth-Century Philosophers* (New Haven, 1932), a study of the relationship between Christianity and the secularized beliefs of the Enlightenment. Becker was best known, however, for his challenge to the orthodox assumption of the time that history could be a scientific, value-free study. Expressing scepticism about the so-called 'facts' of history, he wrote that these 'do not exist for any historian until he creates them, and into every fact that he creates some part of his own individual experience must enter'. Becker argued that each age had its own distinctive 'climate of opinion' which determined its picture of the past, and in *Everyman his own Historian* (NY, 1935), an expanded version of his presidential address to the American Historical Association, he wrote: 'The past is a kind of screen upon which each generation projects its vision of the future.' Becker, however, drew back from the conclusions less subtle minds might draw from his relativism, affirming his belief in the value of the *search* for objective historical knowledge, and adding that it was a fallacy to suppose 'that because truth is in some sense relative it cannot be distinguished from error'.

ALCB

B. T. Wilkins, *Carl Becker* (Cambridge, Mass., 1961).

Beckett, Samuel Barclay (b. Dublin, Ireland, UK [now Irish Republic], 13.4.1906). Irish dramatist and novelist. Beckett's rasping comicality and his obsession with language can be related to JOYCE, to whom he was amanuensis during the writing of *Finnegans Wake* – though Beckett explores a more sombre territory than Joyce. Since 1932 he has lived in France, and has written more in

French than English. He received the 1969 Nobel prize for literature. His work of the 1940s and 1950s stands in shadowy rather than systematic alliance with French existentialist writing but the ground was laid in his monograph on *Proust* (London, 1931), where he writes of 'the only world that has reality and significance, the world of our own latent consciousness' and denominates suffering as 'the main condition of the artistic experience'. The first novel *Murphy* (London, 1938) was followed by *Watt* (Paris, 1953; written earlier) and the trilogy comprising *Molloy* (Paris, 1951; tr. P. Bowles & S. Beckett, Paris, 1955), *Malone meurt* (Paris, 1951; tr. S. Beckett, *Malone Dies*, NY, 1956) and *L'Innommable* (Paris, 1953; tr. S. Beckett, *The Unnamable*, NY, 1958). *Watt* has high humour; *The Unnamable* reaches a climax of anguished solipsism where the narrator, up to his neck in a jar by a shambles, elaborates without stop upon 'the inability to speak, the inability to be silent, and solitude'.

Beckett's novels, for all their pained vitality, are a lesser product: he is primarily a dramatist. In *En attendant Godot* (Paris, 1952; tr. S. Beckett, *Waiting for Godot*, London, 1956) Estragon and Vladimir, seedy dropouts, maintain a music-hall duologue against a background of nearly unalleviated despair, filling the boredom until Godot comes. Godot does not come; but the bourgeois tyrant Pozzo visits them, with his slave Lucky on the end of a rope. At the play's dead centre Lucky 'thinks' in a rampant monologue, of which the meaning is that we die – a meaning too heavy for Estragon and Vladimir to bear: they need to hope that time will continue, even though they end each act with the intention of hanging themselves. *Fin de partie* (Paris, 1957; tr. S. Beckett, *Endgame*, London, 1958) also presents men in mutual dependence at tether's end: Hamm and Clov (Hammer and Nail) occupy a room with Nagg and Nell, who are in dustbins. Worlds fade; outside is ocean and – 'zero'. 'You're on earth,' says Hamm from his wheelchair, 'there's no cure for that!' In more than a dozen other plays for stage and radio little except language appears to happen – although Beckett is a master of gesture and stage-property. In his two mimes and a film called *Film* (produced in New York in 1964) despairing action supersedes words.

If Beckett's motifs depress, his modes stimulate. The work lives in a continual audience-consciousness (his art, as distinct from its propositional features, is far from solipsistic) and acts through a disciplined syntactic structure; it is comic in its wry savaging of existence; and – most important – it breathes with the imaginative vigour of poetry. Its covert theme is precisely the yearning of the artist to fashion a communicative object. In his more memorable productions Beckett is a greatly original tragic genius.   JPW

M. J. Friedman (ed.), *Samuel Beckett Now* (Chicago, 1970); A. Alvarez, *Beckett* (London, 1973).

Beckmann, Max (b. Leipzig, Germany [now East Germany], 12.2.1884; d. New York, USA, 27.12.1950). German painter and graphic artist. After training at the Weimar Academy (1900–3) Beckmann settled in Berlin, and won acclaim at the Sezession with his perceptive portraits (e.g. *Countess von Hagen*, 1908) and his grandiose human melodramas (e.g. *Resurrection*, 1908; *The Sinking of the Titanic*, 1912). In contrast, the agonized distortions of the *Great Death Scene* (1906, painted to exorcize the shock of his mother's death shortly after his marriage to Minna Tube) reveal his debt to MUNCH and German expressionism. The experience of WW1 profoundly changed his art, as is shown by numerous tortured drawings and etchings. Discharged from the army for health reasons (1915), he settled in Frankfurt and began a series of expressionistically distorted paintings and graphic works (e.g. *Hell*, 1919; *Kermesse*, 1921) reflecting the disillusionment and misery around him, moral self-doubt and the attenuated spirituality of German Gothic painting (e.g. *The Descent from the Cross*, 1917; *The Dream*, 1921), with its staccato rhythms and dense allegories. *The Night* (1918–19) is a scene of anonymous nocturnal torture, physical and mental, symbolizing the horror of war and the senseless bloodshed after the Spartacist revolt (Berlin,

January 1919). Henceforth, Beckmann assumed the role of the artist-seer, combining expressionist intensity and distortion with an often enigmatic blend of symbols (drawn from the Bible, the Kabbala, the Greek myths, the medieval mystics, and literature) to record the uncertainty and anguish of contemporary Germany. In numerous self-portraits he charted the progress of the Weimar republic and the Third Reich on his own body and face (e.g. *Self-Portrait with Horn*, 1938). He portrayed himself as acrobat, clown or king in emphatic references to the moral imperative of the individual to maintain spiritual freedom (e.g. *Acrobat on Trapeze*, 1940; *Carnival [Pierette and Clown]*, 1925). He developed the allegory of life as a theatrical pageant in nine triptychs painted between 1932 and his death (e.g. *Departure*, 1932–3; *The Actors*, 1942).

From 1925 to 1933 he was a professor at the Städtisches Institut in Frankfurt, spending the winters of 1929 to 1932 in Paris. Inspired by MATISSE, he began to introduce more glowing colours, sensuous textures and soft arabesques into his works, especially the many portraits of his second wife Quappi and nudes (e.g. *Odysseus and Calypso*, 1943). In 1933 he was dismissed from his teaching post by the Nazis and moved to Berlin. When some of his works were included in the Degenerate Art Exhibition (1937) he emigrated to Holland, where he spent WW2 in isolation. He went to the USA in 1947, taught at Washington University, St Louis (1947–9), and spent the last two years of his life in New York.   SOBT

E. Göpel, *Max Beckmann* (Munich, 1977).

Bednár, Alfonz (b. Rosenau, Slovakia, Austria-Hungary [now Rožňova Neporadz, Czechoslovakia], 13.10.1914). Slovak novelist, who began as a translator of English literature. He has always remained outside literary cliques and trends; he manifests assiduous forthrightness and love of humanity; thus he has been spared persecution. The main subject of his works is human violence, mental and physical. He neither praises nor condemns it, merely states it. His first novel *Sklený vrch* [Glass mountain] (Bratislava, 1954) marks the beginning of the thaw in Slovak literature. Through a convincingly female narrator we learn of inefficiency and corruption in socialist building programmes, of the ambiguity of some Communists' role in the WW2 Slovak uprising, and the cruelty of the postwar expulsion of Hungarians. The collection of *novelle* reappraising the uprising, *Hodiny a minúty* [The hours and the minutes] (Bratislava, 1956, ³1964), is even more polemical. Here Bednár sees little difference between Nazi and STALINist terror, except that the Stalinists have more to hide. His concern is with the political imposition of lies. The humorous side of his love of humanity and his scepticism come to the fore in *Za hrst' drobných* [Just a handful] (Bratislava, 1970) where the canine narrator observes three generations of human beings' absurd behaviour.   RBP

Beecham, Thomas (b. St Helens, Mers., UK, 29.4.1879; d. London, 8.3.1961). British conductor. Son of the manufacturing chemist and patron of music and ballet, Beecham made his mark with the opera seasons he conducted in London between 1909 and 1919, at which he introduced many new works, including R. STRAUSS's *Salome, Elektra, Der Rosenkavalier* and *Ariadne*. He was also active in the concert halls, notably as an advocate of DELIUS, on whom he wrote a study *Frederick Delius* (London, 1959). In 1928 he became conductor of the London Symphony Orchestra; in 1932 he left to found his own, the London Philharmonic. In 1944 he established yet another orchestra, the Royal Philharmonic, with which he made many recordings. These testify to the spirit and grace of his Haydn and Mozart, the clear details of his Berlioz and Liszt, the elegance of his Delius, and the panache of his 'lollipops' – the lighter pieces in his repertory. He was a musician of great wit and charm, and, if a tenth of the stories that survive about him are not apocryphal, a master of repartee. He wrote an autobiography *A Mingled Chime* (London, 1944).   PG

N. Cardus, *Sir Thomas Beecham* (London, 1961); H. Procter-Gregg, *Beecham Remembered* (London, 1976).

Begin, Menachem (b. Brest Litovsk, Russian Poland [now Brest, USSR], 16.8.1913). Israeli politician, terrorist and prime minister. Born in Tsarist Poland, he spent his youth under Polish rule as a prominent member of the Polish Jewish Youth movement. Arrested by the Russians after the Nazi –Soviet partition of Poland in 1939 and interned in a Siberian concentration camp, he reached Palestine only in 1942, immediately joining and rising to command the extremist Irgun Zvai Leumi terrorist organization. On Israeli independence he was elected to the Knesset for the Herut party. Minister without portfolio (1967–70), he formed and became joint chairman of the Likud party in 1973, winning the 1977 general election and becoming prime minister. Long known as an advocate of Israeli expansion to the frontiers of biblical Israel, and an uncompromising opponent of a settlement with Israel's Arab enemies, fear of a possible US–Soviet agreement on a Middle Eastern settlement led him in November 1977 to welcome the Egyptian President SADAT's dramatic visit to Israel, and to negotiate and sign an Israeli–Egyptian treaty of peace. To Egypt's requirement that some degree of self-government be conceded for the Palestinian Arabs of the West Bank territories captured by Israel in 1967, Begin paid only token attention. The extension of Israeli settlements into strategic positions within the West Bank made clear his intention to establish long-term Israeli domination of the area. Begin's invasion of the Lebanon in 1982 to destroy the Palestinians' base for raids on Israel, and the loss of life and widespread destruction which this inflicted, escalated into the most serious crisis since Israel's foundation. Under unprecedented pressure from the US government, Begin was forced to break off the war, but not before criticism of his policy had bitterly divided the Israelis themselves and for the first time called in question the support from the USA on which Israel had depended.   DCW

Behrens, Peter (b. Hamburg, Germany, 14.4.1868; d. Berlin, 27.2.1940). German architect and designer. After studying as a painter in Hamburg, Karlsruhe and Düsseldorf, Behrens moved to Munich, where he became a founder member of the 1893 Sezession, the first formal, organized secession from a German academy. He was drawn into the practice of applied art, following a successful career of about 10 years as a painter and graphic artist. As a result of his achievements in this field he was invited (1899) to join the famous Artists' Colony in Darmstadt under the patronage of the Grand Duke Ernst Ludwig. There he designed his first house (for himself and his young family) which was furnished down to the smallest details according to his own designs. At Darmstadt he contributed to the development of the modern theatre, inspired by his friendship with the poets Richard Dehmel and Otto Erich Hartleben, and he designed his first typefaces. Over the period 1900–14 Behrens's work changed in style from art nouveau to a form of free neoclassicism. This reflected general tendencies in Europe during that period, and he played a leading role in effecting these changes. Then and subsequently he designed, as a self-taught architect, a great range of buildings, from embassies to churches, from factories to luxurious villas. His prolific output as a designer ranged from cutlery to suspension bridges.

As a teacher Behrens made an important contribution to art education in Germany, as director of the School of Applied Art in Düsseldorf (1903–7) and in Austria where he ran a *Meisterschule* for postgraduates of architecture at the Vienna Academy (1922–36). A founder member of the German *Werkbund* (the association of artists, architects, designers, economists and industrialists), Behrens epitomized its ideals in the period 1907–14, when he was artistic adviser to the giant electrical combine AEG. As adviser he progressed from designing posters and brochures to the creation of all manner of electrical appliances, from arc lamps to locomotives, great factory buildings and housing estates for the employees. It was during this period that severally GROPIUS, Adolf Meyer, MIES VAN DER ROHE and LE CORBUSIER worked in his office.

Behrens was close to the centre of the major industrial and social developments in Germany during the Wilhelminian empire, the Weimar republic and the Third Reich, and his many writings and articles are important reflections of the changing artistic and spiritual aspirations. Despite his liberal range of association with major Jewish industrialists, with socialists, liberals and foreigners of all kinds, he conformed with the Nazi regime sufficiently in his last years to hold a post at the Berlin Academy until his death, and to design an AEG headquarters for HITLER and Speer's projected North–South axis in Berlin.   AW

S. Anderson, *Peter Behrens and the New Architecture of Germany, 1900–1917* (Ann Arbor, 1978); A. Windsor, *Peter Behrens: Architect and Designer* (London, 1981).

Beiderbecke, Leon Bismarck (Bix) (b. Davenport, Iowa, USA, 10.3.1903; d. New York, 6.8.1931). American jazz cornetist, pianist and composer. A self-taught musician whose lyrical style of improvising and exquisite cornet tone made him one of the most original musicians of the 1920s. His first inspiration came via the recordings of the Original Dixieland Jazz Band (and its cornetist Dominic LaRocca), and by 1924 he was recording with The Wolverines. Two years later he played in a band led by saxophonist Frank Trumbauer (another influential figure of the era) – their recording of 'Singing the Blues' (1927) was a jazz landmark; both men also worked together in Jean Goldkette's Band. Beiderbecke eventually graduated into the leading dance orchestra of the era (led by Paul Whiteman), but alcoholism cut short his career and he died prematurely.

Beiderbecke's keen interest in the works of DEBUSSY and Eastwood Lane is apparent in his compositions for piano, but his more substantial contributions to jazz were as a brass player. Many of the bell-like phrases he conceived on cornet are still slavishly copied, but at the time they were unique in concept, revealing a startlingly new approach to jazz improvisation that was elegant and ingenious. His tragic life style retains a strong fascination and has been the subject of films and several books.   JJC

R. M. Sudhalter & P. R. Evans, *Bix: Man and Legend* (NY, 1974).

Béjart, Maurice (b. Marseilles, Bouches-du-Rhône, France, 1.1.1927). French dancer, choreographer and ballet director, best known for spectacular productions using dance as a vehicle for carrying a broad political or spiritual message. In the 1940s and 1950s Béjart danced professionally before directing and choreographing for various short-lived companies of his own. Following his most successful ballet *Le Sacre du printemps* (1959), he was invited to Brussels to direct the Ballet du XXième siècle, with which company he has largely worked ever since. In 1970 he founded MUDRA in Brussels, a centre for research into total theatre. Béjart's ballets, many of them set to large orchestral scores, are eclectic stylistically and culturally, embracing classical, contemporary, jazz and acrobatic idioms, ranging from Persian and Indian themes to commentaries on Wagner and NIJINSKY. Though Béjart has created some pure dance works, his dramatic pieces are better known. Even so abundant theatricality often fails to camouflage lack of choreographic skill. His company has proved especially successful with new, young audiences in Europe and the USA where it has performed in stadia, public squares and circuses as well as conventional theatres. Critical reaction to Béjart's work remains very mixed. SAJ

Béjart by Béjart (NY, 1980).

Bell, Alexander Graham (b. Edinburgh, Lothian, UK, 3.6.1847; naturalized American citizen, 1882; d. Cape Breton Island, NS, Canada, 2.8.1922). British/American inventor of the telephone. Educated in Edinburgh and London, Bell worked with his father on the physiology of speech. His family emigrated to Canada in 1870. He gave lectures on speech and deafness in the USA and became a professor at Boston University. Concurrently, he worked on a system of multiple telegraphy, using 'sympathetic vibrations'. While developing this 'harmonic telegraph', Bell discovered that an iron reed, vibrating near an electromagnetic coil, could transform mechanical energy into an undulating electric current. Within hours of the discovery, he produced the first working model of the telephone for which he was granted the original patent in March 1876. His prospectus to investors set out a vision of local, national and international telephone systems, interconnected to comprehend the entire world. This was the origin of the American Telephone and Telegraph Company, the world's largest corporation. Most telecommunications inventions have been based on the telephone research and development which Bell initiated.

RIT

R. V. Bruce, *Alexander Graham Bell and the Conquest of Solitude* (Boston, 1973).

Bell, Daniel (b. New York, USA, 10.5.1919). American sociologist. Bell combined journalism with social history until 1958, when he left *Fortune* magazine to teach at Columbia University. Since 1969 he has been professor of sociology at Harvard. His work in political sociology and social forecasting (he edited the report *Toward the Year 2000*, Boston, Mass, 1968) expresses a preoccupation with long-term trends in contemporary history. *The End of Ideology* (Glencoe, Ill., 1960) popularized the idea that the welfare state and mixed economy had brought pluralistic consensus politics to the West, removing ideological conflict to the international arena and developing countries. Study of MCCARTHYism led to *The Radical Right* (NY, 1963) where right-extremism was analysed as a response of minorities unadjusted to the new consensus. Although the revival of ideology in domestic politics in the late 1960s prompted criticism of Bell's thesis, in *The Coming of Post-Industrial Society* (NY, 1973) he persuasively re-emphasized the growing social and political importance of technical knowledge and decision-making, forecasting greater power for scientific elites and hence dilemmas for democracy. *The Cultural Contradictions of Capitalism* (NY, 1976) depicts the new technology at odds with an increasingly hedonistic popular culture. Bell has since published a collection of essays (*Sociological Journeys, 1960–80*, London, 1980), two of which, originally written in 1977 – 'The return of the sacred, the argument on the future of religion' and 'Beyond modernism, beyond self' – carry further his discussion of cultural trends in post-industrial society. JRT

Belloc, Joseph Pierre René Hilaire (b. St Cloud, Seine, France, 27.7.1870; naturalized British citizen, 1903; d. Guildford, Surrey, UK, 16.7.1953). French/British writer and Catholic controversialist. The son of a French barrister and an English mother, he was educated under Newman at the Oratory School, Birmingham, and Balliol College, Oxford, but did military service in the French army. With CHESTERTON ('Chester–Belloc') he attacked secularism and capitalist plutocracy and defended traditional Catholic values and a polity based on the rights of small private property owners which he called distributism (*The Servile State*, London, 1912). Although harking back to an idealized Middle Ages, he was where France was concerned a passionate republican (*Robespierre*, London, 1901; *Marie Antoinette*, London, 1909) and his early prose, plain but strong and eloquent, expresses a melancholy feeling for mortality as well as a zest for the good things of physical life (*The Path to Rome*, London, 1902). A lover of France, Sussex and the sea, his best work lies in his histories where he presents a vision of the civilizing fact of Catholic Christendom against the abstract thinking which would deny man's dependence upon his historical inheritance. RS

R. Haynes, *Hilaire Belloc* (London, 1953); R. Speaight, *Hilaire Belloc* (London, 1956).

Bellow, Saul (b. Lachine, Quebec, Canada, 10.7.1915). American novelist. The son of Russian-Jewish emigrants, Bellow grew up in Montreal; but then moved with his parents to Chicago where he was educated, taking his BA in anthropology and sociology from Northwestern University in 1937. Since his decision to abandon university teaching and devote himself to literature, Bellow has produced a body of fiction which has made him the most celebrated novelist of his generation. He seems less interested in 'telling stories' than in the ethical dilemmas raised by contemporary life. In the 19c Bellow would have been a moralist, a sage. In our time, the intellectual and novelist often assume equivalent roles. In his later books Bellow has increasingly set himself against contemporary values. His books have mirrored the preoccupations of the educated classes in the USA, from the existential introspection of *Dangling Man* (NY, 1944) to the bold verbal energy of *The Adventures of Augie March* (NY, 1953). *Henderson the Rain King* (NY, 1959) did much to establish his reputation, although with its elaborate allegorical structure and setting in a mythological Africa, it is hardly characteristic of Bellow's urban landscape. *Herzog* (NY, 1964) is his greatest novel in the power of its characterization, and the range of its sympathies plumbed. The novels which followed – *Mr Sammler's Planet* (NY, 1970), *Humboldt's Gift* (NY, 1975) and *The Dean's Daughter* (NY, 1982) – confirmed his position without enhancing it. *Humboldt's Gift* won him the Nobel prize for literature (1976), but the previous novel was felt to betray a lack of sympathy for the aspirations of American blacks. It is part of the irony of our times that a humanist like Bellow should find himself so alienated from much of American life. The values he has endorsed have often been domestic: affection, kindness, a philosophic sympathy which he sees as embattled. The sources of the threat are egotism, a belief in unbridled self-assertion, selfishness, and the society which feeds and sustains the desire for instantaneous gratification. Bellow's America is a violent society, but in his eyes it is more seriously threatened by immaturity and a consequent inability to establish stable personal relations than by its absurd immensity. EH

J. J. Clayton, *Saul Bellow in Defense of Man* (NY, 1968); M. Bradbury, *Saul Bellow* (London, 1982).

Bely, Andrey, ps. of Boris Nikolayevich Bugaev (b. Moscow, Russia, 26.10.1880; d. Moscow, USSR, 8.1.1934). Russian poet, novelist and critic, who made his literary debut as a younger spokesman of the revival of literary culture in early 20c Russia. Brought up in an educated milieu (his father was dean of the faculty of science at Moscow), Bely was one of the most cultivated and talented men of his remarkable generation. He was endowed with magical charm and a quick-witted, provocative, protean and somewhat egomaniacal mind. He was all accelerating ideas and wayward judgement; the speed and manner with which he changed intellectual and political allegiances evoked scorn and praise. His early work, startlingly called *Simfoniia* [Symphonies in prose] (Moscow, 1902–8), as well as much of his poetry (*Zoloto v lazuri* [Gold in azure], Moscow, 1904; *Kubok metelei* [The cup of blizzards], Moscow, 1908; *Pepel* [Ashes], Moscow, 1909; and *Urna* [The urn], Moscow, 1909) were designed as musical compositions to produce a motley of auditory effects and having, as he put it himself, 'a musical sense, a satirical sense, and, besides, a philosophical-symbolical sense'. Some of it was contrived and obscure, but invariably displayed a dazzling virtuosity. An admirer of the idealist and mystical philosopher Soloviev, a fickle follower of Merezhkovsky (initiator of the Russian symbolist movement), an enemy-friend of BLOK, a populist, revolutionary and champion of the futurists, he became, in 1913, Russia's leading STEINERite anthroposophist. But after returning to Russia in 1923 from emigration, finished as a MARXist. Bely's first novel was *Serabryaniy golub* [The silver dove] (Moscow, 1909) about a Rasputinizing mystical Russian sect. The prose goes back to Gogol in its mixture of the actual and the fantastic and irrational. Even more irrational was the next novel *Petersburg* (Moscow, 1913; tr. R. Maguire & J. Malmstadt, Indiana, 1978) – a variation on the familiar Russian themes of 'fathers and sons' and 'East–West'. The chief character is a revolutionary intellectual, or rather a terrifying Dostoevskyan Petersburg figure, haunting him like a phantom of his own afflicted mind. Bely became even more experimental after the revolution – in his autobiographical *Kotik Letaev* (Moscow, 1915–18, 1922), where would-be PROUSTian and JOYCEan 'formalist' devices express a humorously realist view of life. Much simpler and marvellously suggestive are his *Iz vospominanii o Bloke* [Recollections of Alexander Blok] (Moscow, 1922), which provides a penetrating account of Russian symbolism, and three additional 'Recollections' (*Na rubezhe dvukh stolety* [On the threshold of the centuries], *Nachalo veka* [Beginning of the century], *Mezhdu dvukh revoliutsiy* [Between two revolutions], Moscow, 1931–4), a tetralogy which recreates in unforgettable and, at times, comic images social and cultural life in Russia before, during and after the revolution. Bely also wrote a great deal of literary criticism, which is wild, complex and brilliant. The collected verse is *Stikhotvorenya i poemy* (Moscow, 1966).

EL

S. Cioran, *The Apocalyptic Symbolism of Andrej Belyj* (The Hague, 1973); K. Mochulskij, *Andrey Belyi: his Life and Work* (Ann Arbor, 1977).

Benes, Eduard (b. Kozlány, Bohemia, Austria-Hungary [now Czechoslovakia], 28.5.1884; d. Sezimova Usti, 3.9.1948). Successively Czechoslovak foreign secretary (1918–35), prime minister (1921–2) and president (1935–8, 1945–8), and head of the provisional Czech government in exile (1941–5). Highly educated and of great integrity, he had a somewhat weak and colourless personality, and owed his advancement to his position as deputy to MASARYK, the first president of Czechoslovakia, at a time when most Czech political figures disowned him. As foreign secretary he saw the role of his country as committed to the League of Nations and against any revision of the treaties of Versailles, St Germain and Trianon, into which the charter of the League had been incorporated; this led him to make his country a close ally of France, earning him the hostility and suspicions of Britain. He did not share Masaryk's antipathy towards Russia, and both as president and as head of the Czech provisional government in exile he tried to make his country the bridge between the West and Soviet Russia, arousing the suspicions of the former while not abating in any way the antagonism towards the ideals of western bourgeois society of the latter, sacrificing in the interim all hopes of rapprochement with Czechoslovakia's neighbouring states, Poland and Austria. He was maladroit and weak in domestic politics and his regime was no match for Nazi German exploitation of Czech–German and Czech–Slovak antagonisms in 1935–8, nor for Anglo–French diplomacy which culminated in the Munich agreement of September 1938, nor for the machinations of the Czech Communist party in 1945–8, and the Soviet-sponsored coup of February 1948 which led to his resignation of the presidency and to his death.   DCW

Ben-Gurion, David, *né* Gruen (b. Plonsk, Russian Poland [now Poland], 16.10.1886; d. Tel Aviv, Israel, 1.12.1973). First prime minister (1948–53, 1955–63) and architect of Israel. Hebraicizing his name to Ben-Gurion in 1910, he emigrated to Palestine with the second *Aliyah* in 1916. He became secretary-general of the Jewish Labour Federation (1926–33), leader of the Mapai party (1930–63), and chairman of the Jewish Agency (1935–48). This last appointment represented a major shift in the leadership of the Zionist movement from its international creators, HERZL and WEIZMANN, towards the Jewish settlers in Palestine, the Yishuv, away from Zionist diplomacy towards political and military organization, the promotion of Jewish immigration, legal and illegal, and the fight against the efforts of the mandatory power, Britain, to freeze the Arab–Jewish relationship in Palestine to roughly its 1939 ratio. As prime minister, Ben-Gurion's policy towards the Arab population of Palestine and towards Israel's Arab neighbours answered their refusal to accept the establishment of Israel with equal intransigence. His second term as premier was marked by the initiation of punitive action against the bases in the Egyptian-occupied Gaza strip and in Jordan from which Arab fedayeen raided into Israel, an action which drove Egypt's Colonel NASSER into buying arms from the USSR and ended in the Suez war. In 1965, two years after retirement, he returned to politics to lead a breakaway group of old Mapai members critical of the less 'hawkish' line followed by his successor as premier, Golda Meir. His role in the creation of Israel and in its early industrial and agricultural development was thus eclipsed by his embodiment of Israel's intransigence towards the Arab states of the Middle East.   DCW

M. Bar-Zohar, *The Armed Prophet: a Biography of Ben-Gurion* (London, 1967).

Benjamin, Walter (b. Berlin, Germany, 15.7.1892; d. Port Bou, Pyrénées-Orientales, France, 26.9.1940). German writer and one of the most intriguing and original MARXist cultural theorists of the 20c. Born into a middle-class Jewish family, as a student Benjamin came under the influence of Jewish messianic and Kabbalistic ideas, and produced a brilliant esoteric thesis on 17c German baroque drama *Ursprung des deutschen Trauerspiels* (Berlin, 1928; tr. J. Osborne, *The Origin of German Tragic Drama*, London, 1978), which failed to win him an academic post. He made a precarious living in Berlin as a literary journalist, and partly under the influence of Ernst BLOCH and LUKÁCS, turned towards Marxism. In the late 1920s he became a close friend of BRECHT, championing his revolutionary 'epic theatre'. Driven from Germany in 1933 by the rise of Nazism, Benjamin settled in Paris, where he had close associations with the surrealists and embarked on a mammoth study of Charles Baudelaire and 19c Paris, now published in part as *Charles Baudelaire: a Lyric Poet in the Era of High Capitalism* (tr. H. Zohn, London, 1973). When the Nazis invaded France, Benjamin fled to the Spanish frontier, where on being denied entry he committed suicide.

Benjamin's writings are a curious mixture of esoteric, sometimes mystical Jewish thought, artistic modernism and unorthodox Marxism. He united an apocalyptic vision of history with a concern for the material, productive basis of art, expressed in his key essays 'The author as producer' (1934) in *Versuche über Brecht* (Frankfurt, 1966; tr. A. Bostock, *Understanding Brecht*, London, 1966) and 'The work of art in the age of mechanical reproduction' (1936) in *Illuminationeh* (Frankfurt, 1961; ed. ARENDT, tr. H. Zohn, *Illuminations*, NY, 1968). Fascinated by tradition yet a radical spokesman for the new techno-logical media, steeped in high German philosophy but a champion of the prole-tariat, Benjamin was in turn philologist, literary critic, political commentator and philosopher of history. His extraordina-rily rich and suggestive work, a hybrid of metaphysics and materialism, is per-haps best exemplified in the selections of his essays published as *Illuminations* and *Einbahnstrasse* (Berlin, 1928; tr. E. Jephcott & K. Shorter, *One-Way Street*, London, 1979). TE

R. Wolin, *Walter Benjamin: an Aes-thetic of Redemption* (NY, 1982).

Benn, Gottfried (b. Mansfeld, Germany [now East Germany], 2.5.1886; d. West Berlin, 7.7.1956). German poet and essayist. Benn studied philology and the-ology before turning to medicine (Berlin 1905–12). He was a military doctor in WW1 and WW2, and from 1917 to 1935 ran a practice specializing in skin and venereal diseases. One of the most important precursors of contemporary German verse, he had an immense influ-ence on the literary generations immedi-ately before and after the Third Reich. His work was banned by the Nazis as degenerate, and later by the Allies because of his initial support for HITLER. His poetry offers an introverted nihilism: an existentialist philosophy which sees artistic expression as the only purposeful action. In his early poems Benn used his medical experience and terminology to portray a morbid conception of humanity as another spe-cies of disease-ridden animal. The title of his first collection of poems *Morgue* [Morgue] (Berlin, 1912) indicates this preoccupation. As an escape from the ugliness of reality, Benn posited an ele-mental world of dream, myth and drugs, represented poetically by the theme of 'the South': the classical world and the warm blue sea (see *Die Gesammelten Schriften* [The collected works], Berlin, 1922). In his later verse, he drew on various technical jargons, often stressing their poetic potential by means of unu-sual rhyme schemes, as in *Statische Gedichte* [Static poems] (Zürich, 1948), and forsaking normal syntax, so that his thoughts became a flood of nouns, with *ich* [I] as the fixed point and link between the idea and the world. JHC

E. B. Ashton (ed.), *Primal Vision: Selected Poetry and Prose of Gottfried Benn* (NY, 1961); T. Koch, *Gottfried Benn* (Munich, ²1970).

Bennett, Enoch Arnold (b. Hanley, Staffs., UK, 27.5.1867; d. London, 27.3.1931). British novelist. A desire to escape provincialism and moral narrow-ness led the young Bennett, typically, to London. As his success grew, his jour-nalism, fiction, and writing for the stage and cinema earned him a substantial income. Although his immense output can overshadow the merit of his best work, there is some connection between his profuseness and the scale on which his realism operates, as there is between his upbringing in the industrial and Methodist community of the North Staf-fordshire Potteries and the many contra-dictions in his career. His lifelong admi-ration for the up-to-date and convenient is apparent in the novels of luxury hotel life *The Grand Babylon Hotel* (London, 1902) and *Imperial Hotel* (London, 1930). At the same time, influenced by the realism of Zola and its English equivalent in the work of George Moore, he found his best material in the regional life of the Potteries. *Anna of the Five Towns* (London, 1902), *The Old Wives' Tale* (London, 1908) and the *Clayhanger* trilogy (London, 1910–1916) trace the patterns of individual lives with exhaustive specificity and detach-ment, paying particular attention to the lives of women. His examination of the ways in which conflict is experienced between social values and individual transgressive impulse recognizes loss and deprivation without conceding the notion of personal failure. ATKC

M. Drabble, *Arnold Bennett* (London, 1974).

Benveniste, Emile (b. Aleppo, Syria, Ottoman Empire [now Syria], 27.5.1902; d. Versailles, Yvelines, France, 3.10.1976). French linguist. Emile

Benveniste obtained his first degree at the Sorbonne in 1919. A student of comparative grammar and Iranian languages under Antoine Meillet, he received the qualification of *agrégation* in 1922, and the diploma of the Ecole des Hautes Etudes in Paris, with a dissertation on the grammar of Sogdian, in 1923. In 1927, after military service, he replaced Meillet as director of studies in the comparative grammar of Indo-European languages at the Ecole des Haute Etudes and was professor of comparative grammar at the Collège de France from 1937 until 1969, when ill health compelled him to retire prematurely. Although later in his career he became more theoretically oriented, he remained a comparativist, a historian of the language and culture of the Indo-Europeans. His doctoral thesis *Les Infinitifs avestiques* [Infinitives in Avestan] (Paris, 1935) was iconoclastic in its treatment of accepted theories of word formation in Indo-European, and his reconstructions of the social and institutional systems of the Indo-Europeans via linguistic phenomena, notably vocabulary, are his major contribution to our understanding of the origins of western culture: *Origines de la formation des noms en indo-européen* [Origins of the formation of nouns in Indo-European] (Paris, 1935), *Noms d'agent et noms d'action en indo-européen* [Nouns of agent and nouns of action in Indo-European] (Paris, 1948), *Le Vocabulaire des institutions indo-européennes* (Paris, 1969; tr. E. Palmer, *Indo-European Language and Society*, London, 1973). His research covered all the Indo-European languages, both ancient and modern, but the greater proportion of his published work is devoted to aspects of Iranian languages.　　GJ

Benz, Karl Friedrich (b. Karlsruhe, Baden-Württemberg, Germany, 25.11.1844; d. Ladenburg, Baden-Württemberg, 4.4.1929). German pioneer of the internal combustion engine. In 1885, at the same time as DAIMLER, he built a tricycle with a four-stroke petrol engine. In 1893 he incorporated the engine into a four-wheeled vehicle. He created the Benz Motor Company, which was to merge with the Daimler Company, and subsequently with the Mercedes Company, and was the first man to sell a standard model car; he sold hundreds before 1900. He was an early pioneer of the racing car.　　RIT

Benzer, Seymour (b. New York, USA, 15.10.1921). American biologist. Originally trained as a physicist at Purdue University, Benzer was captivated by SCHRÖDINGER's *What is Life?* (1944) and attracted to the study of bacterial viruses (phage). Subsequently he distinguished himself by answering the question 'what is a gene?' By refining the techniques of recombination ('crossing over') analysis, he was able to map in detail the structure of a particular locus (rII) of the chromosome of the phage T4 approaching the molecular limit (i.e. the individual nucleotide pair). Thereby he gave a new reality and precision to the geneticist's conception of the gene as the functional unit of heredity, also relating this conception firmly to the chemical view of the chromosome as two complementary strands of a linear polymer of nucleotide units. More recently Benzer has directed his attention to higher levels of biological organization, attempting to determine how, and how far, behaviour is genetically determined. He has successfully used techniques of genetic analysis, especially mosaic mapping, to trace the development of organ systems, particularly the nervous system in the fruit fly *Drosophila melanogaster*.　　GL

Berdyaev, Nikolas Aleksandrovich (b. Kiev, Ukraine, Russia, 19.3.1874; d. Paris, France, 23.3.1948). Russian religious philosopher. Born an aristocrat, his early revolutionary sympathies and vocation for philosophy fused in a passion for freedom that was the fountainhead of all his writing and thinking. An ardent student of MARX, he welcomed the 1917 revolution and was awarded with a professorship at Moscow. But his spiritual ideals led to political conflict and he was exiled in 1922. He settled in Berlin where he founded an academy of the philosophy of religion which he later transferred to France. Always aware of the church's authoritarian tendencies, he nevertheless abandoned his early scepticism and found his way back to the Orthodox church in 1905. Even so Berdyaev described himself as a 'believing free-thinker', and his 'spiritual Christianity' shunned doctrinal and liturgical formulation. He was also profoundly critical of clericalism and ecclesiastical collusion with political power structures. As a consequence his individualism has exposed him to charges of gnosticism and elitism. Berdyaev rejected traditional doctrines of the Creation and the Fall. For him freedom and evil belong together, like darkness and light, originating before creation in the world of nonbeing. Freedom, as the meaning and goal of human life, is rooted in God himself and the Christian revelation is the means of man's struggle with the brutalizing limitations of the material world. His central ideas are formulated in *O naznachemi cheloveka* (Paris, 1931; tr. N. Duddington, *The Destiny of Man*, London, 1937) and *Smysl Istorii* (Berlin, 1923; tr. G. Reavey, *The Meaning of History*, London, 1936), while *Samopoznaniye: Opyt Filosofskoy avtobiograf* (Paris, 1949; tr. K. Lampert, *Dream and Reality*, London, 1950) is 'an essay in autobiography'.   SED

D. A. Lowrie, *Rebellious Prophet: a Life of Nicolai Berdyaev* (London, 1960).

Berenson, Bernard (b. Vilna, Lithuania, Russia [now Lithuania, USSR], 26.6.1865; d. Florence, Tuscany, Italy, 6.10.1959). American connoisseur and historian of art. From a poor immigrant family, Berenson progressed to Harvard where he studied languages and literature. A visit to Italy and the influence of Giovanni Morelli transferred his allegiance to art history. He concentrated upon developing the skills of connoisseurship which opened up his two great careers – as artistic adviser to the Gardner Collection and Lord Duveen, and as the compiler of catalogues of Italian Renaissance artists. Berenson's achievement was to establish the consensus of authorship out of the chaos of 19c attribution, and his 'Lists' published from the 1920s onwards are still definitive. Philosophically Berenson was concerned with aesthetic experience, understood in terms of 'ideated sensation', an empathy dependent upon the spectator's perception of 'tactile values'. He never completed his great work on the decline of classical art. His excellent diaries – *The Passionate Sightseer* (London, 1960) – reveal a complex and cynical aesthete whose personal influence upon a generation of Anglo-American art historians should not be underestimated.   CF

E. Samuels, *Bernard Berenson: the Making of a Connoisseur* (Harvard, 1979); M. Secrest, *Being Bernard Berenson: a Biography* (London, 1979).

Berg, Alban Maria Johannes (b. Vienna, Austria-Hungary [now Austria], 9.2.1885; d. Vienna, 24.12.1935). Austrian composer. Born into a bourgeois family, Berg began composing songs in his youth. In 1904, at the same time as WEBERN, he became a pupil of SCHOENBERG, who introduced him to sustained instrumental composition. His op.1, the single-movement Piano Sonata (1908), reflects the crisis in tonality rather as does Schoenberg's contemporary First Quartet, but the work also shows Berg's enthusiasm for DEBUSSY and, especially, MAHLER. Under the influence of Schoenberg and Mahler, Berg developed a style in which tonality and atonality are fused, in which the old system is viewed with nostalgia as irrevocably lost. His intensely expressive works have been more popular than those of any other atonal composer. Mahler's direct impact is most obvious in the Three Orchestral Pieces (composed 1914–15, performed 1930), which were followed by *Wozzeck* (1925), the first atonal opera. Based on Büchner's fragmentary drama, *Wozzeck* is the story of a humble, simple batman at the mercy of neurotically obsessed superior officers and of his own inadequacies; in it Berg showed his delight in musical symbolism, his sympathy with the suffering anti-hero and his ability to invent musical ideas which define character or atmosphere.

While searching for a second libretto he completed two major instrumental works: the Chamber Concerto for piano, violin and wind band (1927) and the *Lyric Suite* for string quartet (1927). The former, intended to celebrate the fellowship of Schoenberg, Berg and Webern, is filled with musical ciphers and private

references, and yet sounds like a free, romantic outpouring. There is a similar paradox in the *Lyric Suite*, which, though composed of alternating serial and nonserial movements in traditional forms, has a secret thread of allusions to a love affair running through it. Berg's second opera *Lulu* (1937), based on two plays by WEDEKIND, concerns an untamed woman who holds together by her attractive power the other characters in the plot; Berg charts her rise and fall in an immense musical palindrome containing many cross-references. Work on the opera was interrupted by the valedictory Violin Concerto (1936); Berg died with the final act still unfinished. It was completed by Friedrich Cerha for the first performance of the integral version in 1979.   PG
   W. Reich, *Alban Berg* (London, 1965); M. Carner, *Alban Berg* (London, 1975).

Berger, John Peter (b. Stoke Newington, London, UK, 5.11.1926). British essayist, art critic and novelist. Berger trained as a painter, but soon turned to art criticism. In a controversial column in the *New Statesman*, contributed during the 1950s, he supported socialist realism and opposed the new abstract art emanating from the USA. His writing was, however, rarely merely tendentious. His views changed radically as he endeavoured to relate art to every aspect of individual and social potentiality. Through his book on PICASSO (*Success and Failure of Picasso*, London, 1965), he established himself as the most original British writer on art since WW2; and *Ways of Seeing* (London, 1973) demonstrated how influential was his distinctive approach to painting. Many recent works have been produced in collaboration with Jean Mohr: these reflect the broadening of Berger's interests and his concern with the experience of those – exiles, immigrants and peasants – whose values are not those of the dominant culture. *A Painter of Our Time* (London, 1958) and *G* (London, 1972) demonstrate Berger's stature as a novelist.   PF
   P. Fuller, *Seeing Berger* (London, 1980).

Berger, Peter Ludwig (b. Vienna, Austria, 17.3.1929; naturalized American citizen). Austrian/American sociologist. Berger's distinctiveness consists in his approach to the sociology of knowledge and the attention he gives to the phenomenon of religion. His writings have concentrated on the examination of everyday ways of knowing and thinking in particular social contexts (with LUCKMANN, *The Social Construction of Reality*, NY, 1966). In these contexts he sees religion functioning as the ultimate legitimator of society's institutional arrangements. Berger is a leading figure in American sociology and a considerable influence in the academic study of religion. Although espousing 'methodological atheism', his evident sympathy for religious values has led to illuminating work on many aspects of the contemporary phenomenon of religion, notably on alienation, on secularization as it affects religion's role in society, and on religious pluralism.   PFL

Bergman, Ingmar (b. Uppsala, Sweden, 14.7.1918). Swedish film director. The son of a Lutheran clergyman, Bergman worked in the theatre before turning to the cinema in the mid-1940s, first as writer and then as director. His early works, such as his script *Hets* (*Frenzy*, 1944) and his first feature *Kris* (*Crisis*, 1946), are full of youthful despair and revolt. This period, which culminated in *Sommarlek* (*Summer Interlude*, 1951), is also marked by the presence of the spiritual and existentialist concerns of contemporary Swedish literature. It was in the 1950s that Bergman began to achieve an international reputation; that decade culminated in two masterly works, the symbolic tale of death and the knight *Det Sjunde Inseglet* (*The Seventh Seal*, 1956) and the complexly told study of contemporary old age *Smultronstället* (*Wild Strawberries*, 1957). The early 1960s were marked by a striking if desolate trilogy – *Såsom i en Spegel* (*Through a Glass Darkly*), *Nattvardsgästerna* (*Winter Light*) and *Tystnaden* (*The Silence*) – which in turn was followed by a return to the theatre. A fresh series of studies of the problems and anguish of human communication, from *Persona* (1966) to *Viskningar och Rop* (*Cries and*

Whispers, 1972), formed the culmination of that stage of his film career. Although Bergman subsequently worked away from the mainstream of Swedish cinema – directing television series and two German-made features – his career is one of the most significant in European cinema. A master of the introspective style, in which personal obsessions and the crises of creativity are indissolubly mingled, Bergman has produced some of modern cinema's most searing studies of human identity as well as some of its most complex and ambiguous narratives. RPA

R. Wood, *Ingmar Bergman* (London, 1969); S. M. Kaminsky (ed.), *Ingmar Bergman, Essays in Criticism* (NY, 1975).

Bergson, Henri Louis (b. Paris, France, 18.10.1859; d. Paris, 4.1.1941). French philosopher. Bergson was the son of a prosperous Polish Jewish musician and an English mother. He studied at the Ecole Normale Supérieure from 1877 to 1881 and spent the following 16 years as a philosophy teacher in a succession of *lycées*. In 1891 he married a cousin of the novelist PROUST. In 1900, after three years teaching at the Ecole Normale Supérieure, he was made professor at the Collège de France where he lectured until 1914. He was awarded the Nobel prize for literature in 1928. Bergson's most original idea was expounded in his first significant work *Essai sur les données immédiates de conscience* (Paris, 1889; tr. F. L. Pogson, *Time and Free Will: an Essay on the Immediate Data of Consciousness*, London, 1910). This is the distinction between duration, or time as it is experienced, wholly fluid and continuous, and the mechanized clock time of scientific thinking, which we misrepresent, in a way that is nevertheless practically convenient, as if it were divisible into straightforwardly measurable parts. For Bergson the real world is the Heraclitean flux that is actually experienced; the mechanical world described by science is a convenient fiction. Thus the real world is one of continuous becoming or process, a position in which Bergson anticipated WHITEHEAD and other later metaphysicians. It is not a deterministic sys-

tem and its prime material is not inert but is informed with *élan vital* or living energy. In *Matière et mémoire* (Paris, 1896; tr. N. M. Paul & W. S. Palmer, *Matter and Memory*, London, 1911) he drew on studies of aphasia, a condition in which the expression of thought is impossible but not thought itself, to argue for the mind's independence of its material embodiment. In *L'Evolution créatrice* (Paris, 1907; tr. A. Mitchell, *Creative Evolution*, London, 1911) he rejected the prevailing mechanistic account of the phenomena of evolution. In the years up to WW1 Bergson was the object of a fashionable cult and his lectures were attended by large crowds. Of more lasting importance was the influence he exerted on the one hand, through his connection by marriage, on Proust, and on the other on the revolutionary social philosopher SOREL, who saw science, not as a revelation of the true structure of the world, but as a blueprint for the imposition of the human will on an amorphous nature. In his *Introduction à la métaphysique* (Paris, 1903; tr. T. E. Hulme, *An Introduction to Metaphysics*, London, 1912) Bergson applied his contrast between dynamic reality and static appearance to the activities of the mind, seeing intuition, the direct apprehension of process, as the discoverer of truth, where intellect, the analytic faculty, is only the servant of the will. Finally in his *Les deux sources de la morale et de la religion* (Paris, 1932; tr. R. A. Audra & C. Brereton, *The Two Sources of Morality and Religion*, London, 1935) he opposed static custom, the armature of the closed society, to the creative, innovatory spirit of saints and heroes, swimming against the current. Although not a practising Jew, Bergson refused the Vichy government's offers to excuse him from the scope of their anti-Semitic laws as an act of solidarity with his oppressed people. AQ

T. Hanna (ed.), *The Bergsonian Heritage* (NY, 1962).

Beria, Lavrenty Pavlovich (b. Merkheuli, Georgia, Russia, 29.3.1899; d. Moscow, USSR, 23.12.1953). Head of the Soviet security organization under STALIN (1938–53). Beria, like Stalin, came from

Georgia, a fact which assisted his rise to power. After the Bolshevik revolution he became head of the security police in Georgia (OGPU) and in 1931 leader of the Transcaucasian republics, responsible for their integration into the USSR. In 1938 Stalin brought him to Moscow and put him in charge of the Commissariat for Internal Security (the NKVD). In addition to his responsibility for the operation of the security forces in a police state, like his opposite number in Nazi Germany, HIMMLER, he administered a vast network of labour camps and played an important role in armaments production. A deputy prime minister from 1941 and a member of the Politburo from 1946, Beria was more closely identified than any other figure with the repressive regime on which Stalin's dictatorship was based. He survived Stalin by only a few months; he was arrested in July 1953 on trumped-up charges of 'criminal antiparty and antistate activities', and executed before the end of the year. Together with Himmler, Beria personifies the 20c police state with all its inhuman apparatus of spying, arbitrary arrest, imprisonment without trial, torture, forced confession and forced labour, experiences which millions of Soviet citizens endured under his direction.   ALCB

Berio, Luciano (b. Oneglia, Liguria, Italy, 24.10.1925). Italian composer. Born into a family of composers, he began by emulating STRAVINSKY's neoclassicism but, under the guidance of Dallapiccola, moved into the graceful serial manner of his *Chamber Music* for soprano and trio (1952). The development of his style was influenced by his contacts with STOCKHAUSEN, BOULEZ and other members of the avant-garde, and he began to produce such complex scores as *Tempi concertati* for four solo instruments and ensemble (1959). All his works of the 1950s have two prominent characteristics: a liking for supple gestures (specially notable in his series of solo instrumental *Sequenze*, from 1958) and the influence of contemporary linguistics. In his vocal works he has tended to create a fluid continuity between verbal sound and instrumental tone, linguistic sense and musical mean-

ing. The central movement of his *Sinfonia* (1969), which weaves a tapestry of textual and musical quotations around the scherzo from MAHLER's Second Symphony, is the most extreme instance of those allusive, dream-like passages in much of Berio's music with voices. His *Opera* (1970) looks back to the origins of the genre in developing metaphors of disintegration, both musical and political.   PG

Berlin, Isaiah (b. Riga, Latvia [now Latvia, USSR], 6.6.1909). British philosopher and historian of ideas. Berlin is one of the most formidable defenders of philosophical liberalism in the 20c and since the death of LOVEJOY has emerged as the most distinguished practitioner of the history of ideas. Sceptical of the search of logical positivists for a timeless, logically perfect language whose structure would exactly mirror that of reality, and guided by his sense of the infinite variety of other ages and cultures, Berlin took up COLLINGWOOD's idea that the thought of a period or an individual is organized by 'constellations of absolute presuppositions'. Thus philosophical investigation – the unearthing, analysis and evaluation of the basic concepts and categories which order the experience of men – took on an historical dimension. Berlin discerns a great mutation of ideas in the West which began in the 1730s and remains active in our own time. The doctrines of the major initiators of this process are examined in *Vico and Herder* (London, 1976) and in the essays on Machiavelli, Montesquieu and Hamann in *Against the Current: Essays in the History of Ideas* (London, 1979). These thinkers helped to undermine the millennial foundations of western thought: the doctrines that all reality, and all the branches of our knowledge of it, form a rational whole; that this can in principle be discovered once and for all by all men; and that ultimate harmony reigns between human ends. In various ways they replaced this traditional monism with a radical pluralism both in the realms of ethical, political and aesthetic values, and in the sphere of human knowledge. From this deep transformation there sprang a dissident family of exceedingly ill-assorted siblings: irrationalism, voluntarism, relativism, nationalism, fascism, but also populism, romanticism, existentialism, and, above all, some of the central values of liberalism. The latter are defended by Berlin most explicitly in *Four Essays on Liberty* (Oxford, 1969), where historical determinism is subjected to devastating criticism, and an impassioned plea is made for 'negative' as opposed to 'positive' liberty: liberty is in essence the casting off of chains and a function of the number of doors open to the individual. Berlin argues that all those doctrines which define liberty as self-realization and then, on *a priori* or dogmatic grounds, prescribe what this is, end up by defending liberty's opposite. To the perennial human problems (he claims) there are no final answers. Given universal observance of only a handful of principles which enter into our very definition of what it is to be human, Berlin allows a door to open on to an expanding universe of possible moral systems. The philosophical justification of this radical pluralism, and the related questions of ethical and cultural relativism, remain to be fully discussed by Berlin.   RNH

Bernal, John Desmond (b. Nenagh, Munster, Ireland, UK [now Irish Republic], 10.5.1901; d. London, UK, 15.9.1971). British X-ray crystallographer and writer on science and society. He studied crystal structure and developed a powerful graphical method of indexing crystal planes based on the concept of the reciprocal lattice. This was widely used for analysing X-ray diffraction photographs. Analyses of water in collaboration with W. H. Fowler indicated that it retains a hydrogen-bonded structure similar to that of ice. With D. HODGKIN he studied liquid crystals and contributed to the understanding of the mesomorphic state. He also analysed sterols and proteins, and was a member of the group that took the first X-ray diffraction photographs of haemoglobin, chymotrypsin and insulin. During WW2 he worked on civil defence, particularly on protection against bomb damage, and was adviser to the chief of Combined Operations. Subsequently he

became professor of physics at Birkbeck College, London, and continued scientific work on the structure of liquids and the origin of life. A convinced MARXist, he wrote extensively on the social function of science and the organization of scientific research. His thesis that science should be planned and directed met strong opposition. His books include *The Social Function of Science* (London, 1939), *The Physical Basis of Life* (London, 1951), *Science and Industry in the Nineteenth Century* (London, 1953), *The Science of Science* (London, 1964) and *World without War* (London, 1968).   PEH

M. Goldsmith, *Sage: a Life of J. D. Bernal* (London, 1980).

Bernanos, Georges (b. Paris, France, 20.2.1888; d. Neuilly, Paris, 5.7.1948). French novelist and pamphleteer. Unlike many French writers of his time, Bernanos was a man of the right, an ardent supporter of the French monarchy. His equally fervent Catholicism entered into conflict with his royalist beliefs when the *Action Française* was condemned by the Vatican in 1926, and in 1932 he broke off all contact with the movement. He violently attacked the French middle class in *La Grande Peur des bien-pensants* [The terror of the well-wishers] (Paris, 1931) and, by denouncing FRANCO's rebellion against the Spanish republic in *Les Grands Cimetières sous la lune* (Paris, 1938; tr. P. Morris, *The Diary of My Times*, London, 1938), again showed that his attachment to monarchism by no means entailed endorsement of all forms of conservatism. Bernanos's novels show a similarly uncompromising attitude towards the need to maintain spiritual values. This is especially true of his most famous *Journal d'un curé de campagne* (Paris, 1936; tr. P. Morris, *Diary of a Country Priest*, London, 1937). This study of the efforts made by an enthusiastic but youthful and inexperienced priest to introduce a tragic and extreme version of Christianity into an ugly and indifferent parish in northern France was made into a successful film by BRESSON in 1950, and led Bernanos to be described by Robert Speaight as 'the greatest Christian novelist since Dostoevsky'. Like GREENE,

MAURIAC and WAUGH, Bernanos represents a style of Catholic writing which leaves edification to the preacher and dwells quite fully on sin.   PMWT

A. Béguin, *Bernanos par lui-même* (Paris, 1954); W. Bush, *Georges Bernanos* (NY, 1969).

Bernstein, Basil Bernard (b. London, UK, 1.11.1924). British sociologist of education whose papers in scattered academic journals in the late 1950s and 1960s were widely influential among educationalists before they were published in book form in 1971 (*Class, Codes and Control*: vol. 1 *Theoretical Studies in the Sociology of Language*, London). By that date a new discipline, the sociology of education, had become fully established within teacher training and a generation of teachers and administrators had been deeply influenced by Bernstein's ideas. Centrally he has been concerned with the classic sociological problems of social reproduction: how a given social structure becomes part of individual personality. His distinctive contribution has been to draw attention to the role played by language in socialization and to the interacting relationship between social class and the distinctive language forms available to and used by different social groups in that process. It was while working as a teacher (1955–60) of day-release students at the City Day College, London, that Bernstein came to realize that social success was to be equated with greater facility of self-expression, as with middle-class children, and social disadvantage with restricted verbal facility, as with working-class children. Educationalists and planners eagerly welcomed his suggestion that working-class language forms were, comparatively, deficient as justification for various compensatory educational programmes, just as they saw his inference of a correlation between social class and language independent of intelligence as a major contribution to the attack on inequality. Meanwhile in 1963 Bernstein established a sociological research unit at the University of London to substantiate his assertions while his critics levelled their charges: from the left, that he devalued working-class language and encouraged programmes of compensatory education which were bound to fail; from the right, that his views were socially divisive and provoked egalitarian innovations. Severe though the criticisms of his early work, and especially its methodology, may have been, the contribution made by Bernstein's intuitive insights has been substantial and has opened the way for others to follow. His own recent work has focused on the way knowledge is organized and presented through the structure of the school and the formal and informal curriculum.   BDB

Bernstein, Eduard (b. Berlin, Germany, 6.1.1850; d. Berlin, 18.12.1932). German social democratic leader and theorist. Expelled from Germany as a result of Bismarck's antisocialist laws, he emigrated to Switzerland and with MARX's consent became editor of the Zürich edition of *Der Sozialdemokrat*, the rallying point of the underground Socialist party. When Bismarck secured his expulsion from Switzerland, he continued publication of the periodical from London, where he became a friend of Engels and of the leaders of the Fabian Society. In 1899 he published *Die Voraussetzungen des Sozialismus und die Aufgaben der Sozialdemokratie* (Berlin; *Evolutionary Socialism*, London, 1909).

Bernstein returned to Germany in 1901 and became the theoretician of the revisionist school of socialism which rejected Marx's prediction of the approaching collapse of capitalism, the class war and the achievement of socialism by revolution. Bernstein saw socialism not as a revolt against capitalism but as an extension of liberalism, and argued that such reforms as factory legislation and the legalization of trade unions had altered the course of history which Marx had foreseen as ending in a violent confrontation between labour and capital. For Bernstein democratic reforms opened up the prospect of improving the lot of the working class by peaceful means. These views brought Bernstein into conflict with the dogmatic Marxism of KAUTSKY and divided the Social Democratic party of which Bernstein had been elected a deputy in 1902. After WW1 he opposed those who wanted to turn the political revolution of November 1918 into a social revolution. He believed the establishment of the German parliamentary republic opened the way to indefinite progress, and served as secretary of state for economy and finance in 1919. The German Social Democratic party had become the popular reformist movement for which he had worked and he inspired much of its programme; but he lived to see the democratic regime in which he believed undermined by the disloyalty of the conservatives and the extremisms of communism and Nazism.

ALCB

P. Gay, *The Dilemma of Democratic Socialism: Eduard Bernstein's Challenge to Marx* (NY, 1952).

Berry, Brian Joe Lobley (b. Sedgely, Staffs., UK, 16.2.1934; naturalized American citizen, 1965). British/American geographer and urbanist. After graduating in geography from University College London, Berry joined the group working with William Garrison at the University of Washington, Seattle, in the mid-1950s. They made many contributions to the introduction of economic modelling of spatial organization and the use of quantitative methods in geography: Berry's seminal work was on central place theory, summarized in his later text on *The Geography of Market Centers and Retail Distribution* (Englewood Cliffs, 1967). Subsequently at the University of Chicago he ranged widely through human geography, emphasizing multivariate statistical analysis. Through a prodigious output of research papers and books such as *The Human Consequences of Urbanization* (London, 1973), Berry became one of the most influential human geographers in the world during the 1960s and early 1970s. He has been involved in much practical, contract research, being responsible, for example, for the conception and design of a new spatial framework (the Daily Urban System) for the presentation and analysis of census data. A general interest in applied social science led to joint appointments at Chicago; he moved to posts in planning and related fields at Harvard, and then to dean of urban studies at Carnegie-Mellon.　　RJJ

Berryman, John (b. McAlester, Okla, USA, 25.9.1914; d. Minneapolis, Minn., 7.1.1972). American poet. Berryman belonged to the generation of poets and critics who emerged in the 1940s. The New Criticism was to exercise continuing influence on Berryman, as it did on his contemporaries Randall Jarrell and LOWELL. Educated at Columbia University and in the UK at Cambridge, Berryman spent most of his career teaching in US universities. His critical essays, collected in the posthumous *The Freedom of the Poet* (NY, 1976), suggest that although Berryman lacked Jarrell's distinctive wit and combative verve, he was more truly learned and scholarly than any other American poet of his generation. As a poet he utterly lacked the feel for poetic structure in the larger sense. His characteristic form, the verse sequence, shows Berryman throwing syntax into violent opposition to the formal structure of each poem in the sequence. The effect, especially on *The Dream Songs* (published in various volumes between 1964 and 1977), was fragmented, jagged and incoherent, though capable of forcefulness and moments of intensity. His verse undoubtedly gives a powerful feeling of modernity, but in retrospect this is more a consequence of the mannerism of his style and temperament than any profundity of reflection concerning the alienated state of modern man.　　EH

J. Conarroe, *Berryman: an Introduction to the Poetry* (NY, 1977); J. Haffenden, *The Life of John Berryman* (London, 1982).

Bertoia, Harry (b. San Marino, Friuli-Venezia Giulia, Italy, 10.3.1915; naturalized American citizen, 1946; d. Barto, Pa, USA, 6.11.1978). Italian/American sculptor and designer. Bertoia emigrated to the USA with his family in 1930. He studied at the Detroit Society of Arts and Crafts and at the Cranbrook Academy of Art, Bloomfield Hills, Michigan, where he taught from 1937 to 1941 and established a metalwork division in 1939. In 1943 he went to California to work with EAMES. From 1950 he worked for Knoll Associated in New York, and designed the wire shell chair known as the 'Bertoia chair', which is adjusted by the sitter's movement. This and other furniture designs were adapted to the demands of the newly fashionable domestic and business open-plan settings. Bertoia was interested in integrated sculptural and architectural environments; he produced decorative flow-welded metal screens combining abstract forms and abstracted natural shapes and using brass, bronze, nickel-silver alloys and steel to offer versatile interplays of voids and solids.   JGr

J. K. Nelson, *Harry Bertoia, Sculptor* (NY, 1970).

Besant, Annie, *née* Wood (b. London, UK, 1.10.1847; d. Adyar, Tamil Nadu, India, 20.9.1933). British Theosophist. Escaping from an unhappy marriage, she became a radical and then a socialist; in 1899 she joined the Theosophical Society, rejecting materialism along with her former Christianity. From 1893 she lived in India, and from 1907 until her death was president of the Theosophical Society. A prodigious traveller, orator and pamphleteer, her work in India included education (founding in 1898 what later became Benares Hindu University), journalism, social reform, Scouting and the Home Rule movement. In 1917 she became president of the Indian National Congress (the fifth and last European, and the first woman), but her political influence was soon eclipsed by M. GANDHI's noncooperation campaign. She viewed her political and Theosophical activities as parts of one movement for world brotherhood under occult guidance. The number of outstanding people who broke with Theosophy – especially Rudolf STEINER, who founded Anthroposophy, and J. Krishnamurti, whom she had promoted as the future world teacher – shows her capacity both to attract and to antagonize.   DHK

A. H. Nethercot, *The First Five Lives of Annie Besant* (London, 1961); *The Last Four Lives of Annie Besant* (London, 1963).

Bethe, Hans Albrecht (b. Strassburg, Alsace, Germany [now France], 2.7.1906; naturalized American citizen). German/American physicist. Bethe was a student of SOMMERFELD in Munich, with whom he studied theoretical phys-

ics. He left Germany in 1933 and after a short stay in England settled in the USA. Bethe made very important contributions to the quantum theory of atoms and to solid state theory, but his outstanding work has centred on the theory of atomic nuclei and nuclear interactions. In particular he has studied the types of nuclear reaction which might occur in the extremely hot regions of the interior of stars in order to account for the observed rate of stellar energy production. His extensive survey of all possible processes indicated that only two of these were likely to play an appreciable role as a source of stellar energy. Both processes involve the fusion of hydrogen nuclei (protons) which after several intermediate stages eventually form a helium nucleus. Suggestions on these lines had been made earlier but Bethe's detailed calculations showed which processes were the most important and probable. He was awarded a Nobel prize for physics in 1967. He was also the first scientist to explain the LAMB shift, thereby laying the foundation for the theory of quantum electrodynamics (FEYNMANN). HMR

Betjeman, John (b. London, UK, 28.8.1906). British poet. Betjeman was educated at Marlborough School and Magdalen College, Oxford. His journalism, television appearances and campaigning enthusiasm for historic, and especially Victorian architecture, have made him a public figure. He was, as a poet, read with pleasure for many years without being taken seriously by academic critics. To some extent, the demand by a number of younger poets for a return to traditional forms and clarity of expression in verse (LARKIN is the significant name here) brought him a more sympathetic attention. He was knighted in 1969, and became poet laureate in 1972. His poetry, which can hardly be said to have developed between *Continual Dew* (London, 1937) and *A Few Late Chrysanthemums* (London, 1954), appeals by its nostalgic Englishness, its social, architectural and topographical precision, and its blend of mild satire and mild pathos. It is difficult to separate the English tenderness for Betjeman from its tenderness for the subjects he espouses. His *Collected Poems* (London, 1958) were most recently revised in 1979. Perhaps the best introduction to Betjeman is his own autobiographical poem *Summoned By Bells* (London, 1960). BF

J. Press, *John Betjeman* (London, 1974).

Beuys, Joseph (b. Cleves, N. Rhine-Westphalia, Germany, 1921). German artist and much celebrated figure within avant-garde art movements of the 1960s and 1970s – especially 'Arte Povera'. He studied at Düsseldorf and was appointed professor of sculpture there in 1961, a post from which he was 'summarily dismissed' in 1971. His early work consisted of 'sculptures' made out of junk and other unworked materials. He developed enduring obsessions with the symbolic associations of felt, fat, dead hares, bricks and rust brown. He came to hold that speech was a form of invisible sculpture, and engaged in quasi-pedagogic and quasi-political activities. Beuys's many vociferous proponents maintain that he is demonstrating that the whole process of living itself can be regarded as a creative act. In reality, however, Beuys may be little more than an adroit poseur who has successfully exploited the decadence of late modernist vanguardism to his own advantage. PF

C. Tisdal, *Joseph Beuys* (London, 1977).

Bevan, Aneurin (Nye) (b. Tredegar, Gwent, UK, 15.11.1897; d. Chesham, Bucks., 6.7.1960). British minister of health (1945–51); minister of labour (1951); leader of the radical left of the Labour party and unsuccessful challenger of GAITSKELL for the leadership of the Labour party (1951–7); and deputy leader of the party (1959–60). Bevan, Welsh-born son of a miner, spokesman for South Wales miners and MP for Ebbw Vale (1929–60), is most closely associated (1) with the noncommunist radical wing of the Labour party and its journal *Tribune*; (2) with continuous and seemingly hostile criticism of CHURCHILL's government from the parliamentary back benches (1941–5); (3) with the establishment, despite the bitter

initial opposition of the bulk of the British medical profession, of the British National Health Service in 1948 with enormous benefit to the standards of public and national health; (4) with the leadership and subsequent desertion over the issue of nuclear weapons of the radical wing of the Labour party. His confession of faith *In Place of Fear* (London, 1952), an emotional defence of democratic socialism, made a great stir at the time of publication but is now largely forgotten. DCW

M. Foot, *Aneurin Bevan* (2 vols, London, 1962–73).

Beveridge, William Henry (b. Rangpur, Bengal, India, 5.3.1879; d. Oxford, UK, 16.3.1963). British academic economist, first director of the London School of Economics (1919–37), and one of the founders of the British Welfare State. His name is unshakeably associated with the Beveridge Report of December 1942, produced by an interdepartmental committee of senior British civil servants under his chairmanship, on 'Social Insurance and the Allied Services', proposing a system of social security for all citizens 'from the cradle to the grave'. Beveridge set out the arguments in support of his recommendations (much influenced by KEYNES's economics) in *Full Employment in a Free Society* (London, 1944). The Beveridge Report had an impact hardly equalled by any other official report. Its publication created a sensation even in wartime and set in motion, first, the initial steps taken by the wartime coalition government towards welfare legislation covering the whole population; then much of the social insurance and welfare elements in the Labour government's (1945 –50) legislation; and finally the conversion to the Welfare State of the Conservative party of the 1950s and 1960s under the guidance of Butler. DCW

J. Harris, *William Beveridge* (London, 1977).

Bevin, Ernest (b. Winsford, Som., UK, 9.3.1881; d. London, 14.4.1951). British trade union leader and foreign secretary. Farm labourer, carter, assistant secretary of the Dockers' Union (1911); creator of the British Transport and General

Workers' Union, for long the largest trades union in the world; minister of labour (1940–5); foreign secretary (1945–51). A social patriot in the tradition of Robert Blatchford, he saw the interests of Britain as being identical with those of the working classes from which he came, and fought bitterly and resolutely against their enemies, whether money-pinching employers, communists (whom he saw as an alien and divisive force weakening to the unity and, therefore, to the strength of the Labour movement) or Britain's German and other enemies abroad. During the 1930s he was a severe critic of the pacifist idealism in the Labour movement and in favour of resistance to HITLER and MUSSOLINI. A member of CHURCHILL's War cabinet, he was responsible for the high degree of mobilization of British manpower during WW2. As foreign secretary in the Attlee government after WW2, his vision of a Europe united in its common heritage against Soviet communism made him the main mover behind the European realization of the MARSHALL plan, the creation of the Western Union (Brussels Treaty) in March 1948 and of NATO in April 1949. His vision of Europe was merged into a larger view of a North Atlantic community and of a multiracial Commonwealth, united by the Colombo Plan (1950), in the initiation of which he played a major part. In the Middle East he failed in his attempt to negotiate a new treaty with Egypt or to find a settlement in Palestine after WW2 which would be acceptable to both Jews and Arabs. In face of the Zionist drive to create a Jewish state he acted to surrender the British mandate to the UN and so relieve Britain of a responsibility it could no longer discharge.   DCW

A. Bullock, *Life and Times of Ernest Bevin* (3 vols, London, 1960–83).

Bialik, Hayyim Nahman (b. Zhitomir, Ukraine, Russia, 11.1.1873; d. Vienna, Austria, 4.7.1934). Hebrew poet, short-story writer, essayist and translator. Bialik is the foremost Hebrew national poet of modern times. He studied in the famous Lithuanian Talmudic Academy ('Yeshivah') of Volozhin, which made a lasting impression on him. His poetry's major themes are Jewish national revival and the increasing sufferings of the Jews in the Russian empire. He also wrote short, deeply lyrical poems about his feelings for nature, for his beloved girl and the tragic loneliness in the world of the poet himself. In 1894 he immortalized his stay in Volozhin with a major epic poem on the eternal Talmudic student 'Hamatmid', in which he portrays the rapidly vanishing life of traditional orthodox Jewish past. In 1903, after the pogrom against Jews in Kishinev, he wrote his most famous long poem *'be-'Ir heharega'* [In the city of slaughter], in which he castigated bitterly, in prophetic language, the Russian society and Tsarist state for killing Jews, and sarcastically criticized Jewish passivity against anti-Semitic hooligans. After that his poems became more personal, intensely lyrical and fewer in output. He shows an exceptional mastery of every layer of the Hebrew language. His poetry is romantic-realistic and was deeply influenced by Spanish Hebrew medieval poetry as well as by Pushkin and Lermontov. In stories he is a realist, describing Jewish life in the little Ukrainian towns in relation to the surrounding people. A superb essayist on literature and medieval Hebrew poetry, in which he pioneered research, he also translated Cervantes's *Don Quixote* and Schiller's *Wilhelm Tell*. His works, published in four volumes, have been reprinted many times: *Kol Kitvei* (Tel Aviv, 1924).   CA

I. Efros, *Hayyim Nahman Bialik* (NY, 1940); S. Halkin, *Trends in Modern Hebrew Literature* (NY, 1950).

Biko, Stephen Bantu (b. King Williams Town, Eastern Cape, South Africa, 18.12.1946; d. Pretoria, Transvaal, 12.9.1977). South African nationalist leader. Steve Biko's death at the hands of the South African security police transformed a relatively unknown young black radical leader into a figure of international significance: martyr, hero and spokesman for a whole generation of young black South Africans. In 1968, when black South African political activity was at its lowest ebb, Biko, then a medical student, helped to found the South African Students' Organization and later the Black People's Convention. The most articulate exponent of 'black consciousness' (see his *I Write as I Please*, London, 1978), Biko aimed to infuse the black community with a new-found pride in themselves and so encourage them to unite and throw off 'the shackles of servitude'. Banned and therefore silenced in 1973, Biko had already achieved 'an almost messianic status' among black students; his brutal death extended and consolidated his reputation.   RH

D. Woods, *Steve Biko* (London, 1978).

Binet, Alfred (b. Nice, Alpes-Maritimes, France, 8.7.1857; d. Paris, 18.10.1911). French psychologist. After obtaining a doctorate in science from the University of Paris, he, together with Henri Beaunis, established the first French psychological laboratory at the Sorbonne in 1889. He was its director from 1894 until his death. He was initially interested in hypnotism, abnormal psychology and suggestibility, but his fame rests on his subsequent work on intelligence. In 1904 the French minister of public instruction set up a committee to consider the education of retarded children in Paris, and as a consequence Binet and Simon constructed the first proper intelligence test (with T. Simon, 'Methodes nouvelles pour le diagnostic du niveau intellectuel des anormaux' [New methods for diagnosing the intellectual level of abnormal people] in *L'Année psychologique*, Paris, 1905, 191–244). While the original test was simply designed to identify retardation, it was revised in 1908 to permit a more general assessment of intelligence. The test was further revised in 1911, and the notion of 'mental age' was introduced, thus allowing for a measurement of IQ. Binet made two separate major contributions to psychology: he was the first person to use cognitively demanding items in an intelligence test, a practice that is still followed; and he was the first to attempt the precise quantitative assessment of intelligence.   MWE

Binford, Louis Robert (b. Norfolk, Va, USA, 21.11.1929). American archaeologist. One of the foremost exponents of the so-called 'New Archaeology' which became fashionable in the USA and the UK in the 1960s and 1970s. In harmony with the work of Walter Taylor (1948), who saw the supreme goal of archaeology as the establishment of general laws of human behaviour, Binford argued that since the archaeological record had been moulded by the cultural systems at work the proper study of that record would allow the interacting subsystems to be defined within any given social group ('Archaeology as anthropology', *American Antiquity*, 28, 1962, 217–25; 'Archaeological systematics and the study of cultural process', *American Antiquity*, 31, 1965, 203–10). To provide suitable experimental data to test his beliefs, he engaged in a detailed study of the residual remains left by contemporary societies whose social structures can be observed, e.g. Eskimo camps. His papers, particularly 'Archaeological perspectives' in S. R. & L. R. Binford (eds), *New Perspectives in Archaeology* (Chicago, 1968), have been influential in America, Britain and Scandinavia. The focus of much of his recent work has been upon the archaeology of hunter-gatherer societies, from the Mousterian assemblages of Palaeolithic France to the Australian aborigines and the Nunamiut Eskimo (*Nunamiut Ethnoarchaeology*, NY, 1978). His *An Archaeological Perspective* (NY, 1972) is a volume of collected papers with autobiographical connecting passages, and his edited volume *For Theory Building in Archaeology* (NY, 1977) emphasizes his concern that archaeology should develop on a sound theoretical basis. This is developed further in his *Bones: Ancient Men and Modern Myths* (NY, 1981), which also draws upon his ethnoarchaeological experience.   BWC

Bishop, Elizabeth (b. Worcester, Mass., USA, 8.2.1911; d. Boston, Mass., 6.10.1979). American poet. Brought up and educated in New England, she spent much of her adult life travelling, particularly in the tropics. After 1951 she lived for many years in Petropolis, Brazil. Her first book *North and South* (Boston, 1945) opens with 'The Map', a poem that identifies her major theme – the experiences of the rootless, inquisitive but finally uncomprehending traveller. The emphasis is confirmed in *Questions of Travel* (NY, 1965) and *Geography III* (London, 1977). Her poetry is structured by tensions between scepticism and romanticism, the fastidious and the fantastic, an ascetic rationalism and a luxuriantly witty imagination. Such polarities seem elaborations of her own divided biography: partly rooted in New England, partly *décraciné* and tropical. The recipient of numerous literary awards, her *oeuvre* is small; though for many years she was thought of as a minor writer, she is now seen as one of the most considerable poets of her generation.   DD

Bjerknes, Vilhelm Firman Koren (b. Oslo, Norway, 14.3.1862; d. Oslo, 9.4.1951). Norwegian meteorologist. One of the pioneers who created the science of dynamical meteorology, he founded and inspired the Bergen school of 'frontal' meteorology. Through his circulation theorem he made original contributions of major importance in hydrodynamics and the construction of contour charts of isobaric surfaces. Some of his early research was in the field of electromagnetic waves and his studies of electrical resonance belong to the classical papers on radio science. His outstanding achievement was to build a bridge between classical hydrodynamics and classical thermodynamics which brought the atmosphere and the oceans within the scope of those two disciplines and opened up the field of applications for the quantitative treatment of motion on various scales in the atmosphere and oceans. He was thus led to formulate the idea that depressions originate as waves on a sloping surface of discontinuity. This suggestion inspired many empirical investigations and resulted in his collaborators – T. Bergeron, H. Solberg, and his son J. Bjerknes – discovering major features of the structure of cyclones and of the polar front. As professor of geophysics at Leipzig University (1912–17) and then as professor of theoretical meteorology at the Geophysical Institute in Bergen he exerted a lasting influence upon meteorologists throughout the world.   PJM

Bjerrum, Niels Janniksen (b. Copenhagen, Denmark, 11.3.1879; d. Copenhagen, 25.9.1958). Danish physical chemist. Bjerrum provided the first convincing evidence for the complete dissociation of strong electrolytes, developed both the thermodynamics and experimental techniques for the measurement of the electromotive force of electrochemical cells, and contributed to the development of the DEBYE–HÜCKEL theory of electrolyte solutions. His earliest work was on the complex ions of chromium; his novel application of a range of physicochemical techniques set the pattern for all subsequent research on complexes, and provided much of the evidence on which, in 1909, he based his arguments for the complete dissociation of strong electrolytes. As early as 1916 he showed that the assumption of complete dissociation, together with the effect of ionic interactions calculated on the basis of Milner's (1912–13) theory, accounted for the observed properties of, e.g. potassium chloride solutions. After publication of the Debye–Hückel theory in 1923, Bjerrum showed (in 1926) that certain shortcomings of this theory could be overcome by allowing for the effects of 'ion pairing'.

In 1910 Bjerrum worked with NERNST and was the first to apply quantum theory to correlate the heat capacity of diatomic gases with the vibration frequency of the atoms. His work on the acid-base properties of soils, and his introduction of the idea that in certain pH ranges proteins exist as 'zwitter-ions', led up to the monumental work (with Unmack) on the electrochemical determination of acid-base equilibria. In 1914 Bjerrum became professor of chemistry in the Royal Veterinary and Agricultural College at Copenhagen, and remained there until his retirement in 1949. In that year *Selected Papers of Niels Bjerrum* (Copenhagen) were published.   DHE

Blackett, Patrick Maynard Stuart (b. London, UK, 18.11.1897; d. London, 13.7.1974). British physicist. A naval officer cadet at 12, Blackett saw action in WW1. After it, he studied and did research in physics, chiefly under RUTHERFORD at Cambridge but also at Göttingen. He combined to a rare degree theoretical, experimental and technological skills and practised them with outstanding success in four main fields: nuclear physics; the development of cloud chambers; the study of cosmic rays; geomagnetism. He headed highly productive physics departments at Birkbeck College (1933–7), Manchester University (1937–53) and Imperial College (1953–65). He received the Nobel prize for physics in 1948 and was president of the Royal Society (1965–70). Blackett was a member of the strife-ridden pre-WW2 TIZARD committee on air defence. In WW2 he did important work for all three services, most notably in operational research. A member of the Maud Committee which led to the atomic bomb, he strongly opposed postwar Anglo–American atomic policy (see his *Military and Political Consequences of Atomic Energy*, London, 1948). Greatly alarmed at Britain's technological backwardness, and politically left-wing, he played a key role in the National Research and Development Corporation and in the Ministry of Technology of the 1964 Labour government. Deep concern for the underdeveloped world led to intimate association with India.   MMG

Blaga, Lucian (b. Lancrăm, Romania, 9.5.1895; d. Cluj, 6.5.1961). Romanian poet, dramatist and philosopher. He studied theology and took his doctorate at Vienna with the thesis '*Kultur und Erkenntnis*' [Culture and knowledge] in 1922. From 1937 he held the chair of the philosophy of culture at Cluj University, after having been made a member of the Romanian Academy in 1936. His poetry is almost exclusively philosophic and often expressed in symbols and myths. His obsession with 'light' as a natural agent of the universe and its mysterious character is the theme of *Poemele luminii* [The poems of light] (Sibiu, 1919). For Blaga man lives in the aspiration of the revelation of mysteries and his existence is the genetic transition towards death: *Ȋn marea trecere* [In the great transition] (Cluj, 1924). As a playwright he adapted national myths in *Zamolxe* (1921), *Mesterul Manole* [Master Manole] (1927) as well as uni-

versal ones in *Arca lui Noe* [Noah's ark] (1944). His principal work on the philosophy of culture *Trilogia culturii* [The trilogy of culture] (Bucharest, 1944) formulates the concept of the 'stylistic matrix' the impression of which is given by the unconscious to everything created by man. Dismissed from his chair in 1948 for ideological reasons, he spent the years until his death as an archivist, at the same time composing doom-laden poems. The beauty of his profound yet simple verse, the originality of his dramas, as well as his acute observations on what he called the styles of various cultures, make him a unique figure among Romanian intellects.   DJD

Blalock, Alfred (b. Culloden, Ga, USA, 5.4.1899; d. Baltimore, Md, 15.9.1964). American surgeon. Educated at the universities of Georgia and Johns Hopkins, Blalock spent the first half of his career at Vanderbilt University Hospital in Tennessee, becoming professor of surgery before returning to Johns Hopkins as professor and surgeon-in-chief. Brilliant and prolific, he was one of the first American surgeons to have a background in experimental research, acquired under W. S. Halsted at Johns Hopkins. His most notable achievements were his work on the dangers of surgical shock and the successful surgical treatment of pulmonary stenosis, known also as Fallot's tetralogy. His operation of systemic-pulmonary anastomosis inspired the development of cardiac surgery. He received worldwide acclaim and was the recipient of many honorary degrees, fellowships and medals. Outside the field of heart surgery, he undertook work on hypertension, the lymphatic system, the value of thymectomy for thymic tumours and myasthenia gravis: his first paper was on the surgery of the biliary tract. He himself was dogged by ill health throughout his life, and he died three months after retiring.   CR

Blau, Peter Michael (b. Vienna, Austria-Hungary [now Austria], 7.2.1918; naturalized American citizen, 1943). American sociologist. Educated in sociology, Blau graduated from Elmhurst in 1942 and received his doctorate from Columbia in 1952. He has taught at Cornell and Chicago universities, and since 1970 has been Quetelet professor of sociology at Columbia University. Blau's major academic achievements have been in the area of organizational studies. With W. Scott he wrote *Formal Organizations* (San Francisco, 1962) which developed the '*cui bono*' classification of organizational activity. This enabled them to distinguish a fourfold typology of organization each associated with particular organizational problems. Whilst improving upon monolithic theories of organization, the classification remains firmly within a functionalist framework and fails to confront the realities of power and organizational control. In his empirical studies Blau questioned the implication in M. WEBER's work that rationality is monopolized at the apex of any organization, thereby providing also a critique of F. W. TAYLOR and the scientific management school. He demonstrated that systematic infringement of rules could improve efficiency and suggested that decentralized control structures should be encouraged to increase participation in decision-making. This was a considerable influence on theorists of human relations oriented towards work group-participation. Finally in *Exchange and Power in Social Life* (NY, 1964) Blau pioneered the model of exchange theory, a microsociological development of Weber's theory of power.   TFC/LMC

Bliss, Henry Evelyn (b. New York, USA, 29.1.1870; d. Plainfield, NJ, 9.8.1955). American librarian. The antithesis of Melville DEWEY, Bliss was a thinker rather than a man of action, a specialist in classification rather than a man of many parts. He explored his subject in *The Organization of Knowledge and the System of the Sciences* (NY, 1929) and *The Organization of Knowledge in Libraries and the Subject Approach to Books* (NY, 1933) before producing *A Bibliographic Classification* (NY, 1940–53). In 1876 Dewey had been concerned mainly with the practical aspects of converting libraries to a system in which readers could find books for themselves. With this objective achieved, Bliss was able to concentrate on the intrinsic, intellectual quality of his classification, though he also

made innovations in notation. The influence of Comte on his thought was unfortunate, but even so his careful analysis of disciplines and their relationships is without equal in other bibliographic classifications. His scheme is used in the University of London and many other academic libraries. A complete revision by J. Mills, now in progress, will ensure that, unlike Dewey's *Decimal Classification*, it does remain a fitting memorial to its originator.   DWL

J. Mills, 'Bibliographic classification' in *Encyclopaedia of Library and Information Science* (33 vols, NY, 1968–81); D. J. Campbell, 'A short biography of Henry Evelyn Bliss' in *Bliss Bibliographic Classification: Introduction and Auxiliary Schedules* (London, 1977).

Blixen, Karen, also wrote as Isak Dinesen (b. Rungsted, Denmark, 17.10.1885; d. Rungsted, 7.9.1962). Danish novelist and short-story writer, and founder member of the Danish Academy (1960), who nevertheless belongs as much to English literature as to Danish. At the age of 28 and newly married, she left Denmark with her husband to run a 6000-acre farm in Kenya, where she lived for 17 years before returning to Denmark in 1931. This period of her life was later movingly recorded in *Out of Africa* (London, 1937). Her real literary debut (discounting a number of slighter pieces written earlier under the pen name of Osceola) came three years later with the publication in English, under the name Isak Dinesen, of *Seven Gothic Tales* (London, 1934) – elaborate tales of fantasy, set in an atmosphere of decadence and material self-indulgence startlingly at odds with the usual stern social commitment of 1930s fiction. Subsequent collections of stories testify to a mind which could now be aristocratic and sophisticated, now melodramatic and sentimental; they include *Winter's Tales* (London, 1942), *Last Tales* (London, 1957), *Anecdotes of Destiny* (London, 1958), *Shadows on the Grass* (London, 1960) and *Ehrengard* (London, 1963). *The Angelic Avengers* (London, 1946), a novel ascribed on the title-page to 'Pierre Andrézel', was only very much later acknowledged by her as her own work but dismissed as 'an illegitimate child'. JWMcF

R. Langbaum, *The Gayety of Vision* (London, 1964); D. Hannah, *'Isak Dinesen' and Karen Blixen* (London, 1971).

Bloch, Ernst (b. Ludwigshafen, Rhineland-Palatinate, Germany, 8.7.1875; d. Tübingen, Baden-Württemberg, West Germany, 4.8.1977). German philosopher. Bloch's philosophy, set out in its most fascinating complexity in *Das Prinzip Hoffnung* [The principle of hope] (Berlin, 1949, ²1959), is pervaded by a single thought: that mankind's sociohistoric existence, embedded in the vast cosmic time of natural history, is but a beginning in the elaboration of the humanity of man. Man's labour, the historical and ontological manifestation of his being, is the lever for the transformation of the given into the hoped-for realization of utopia. The son of a Bavarian railway manager, Bloch's florid, late romantic imagination was developed in stark contrast to the drab redbrick environment of industrial Ludwigshafen. His first major work was on the spirit of utopian thought (*Geist der Utopie* [Spirit of utopia], Munich, 1918) in poetry, art, myth and, above all, music as pointers to a not-yet which promised future fulfilment. It was also a forceful piece of rebellious expressionist prose against the martial patriotism of the Europeans. In pursuit of his messianic socialism Bloch dedicated his next study to *Thomas Münzer* (Munich, 1921), the 16c rebel theologian. Like his close friend BENJAMIN, Bloch emigrated from HITLER's Germany. In *Erbschaft dieser Zeit* [The heritage of this age] (Zürich, 1935) he collected some of the most penetrating critical observations on the politics and culture of the 1920s. In 1948 he was given a chair in philosophy at the University of Leipzig. After falling into disgrace in East Germany he accepted a professorship at Tübingen (1961), where he wrote *Tübinger Einleitung in die Philosophie* (Frankfurt, 1963; tr. J. Cumming, *A Philosophy of the Future*, NY, 1970). His influence is strong among unorthodox MARXists and theologians. WvdW

C. E. Braasten, 'Toward a theology of hope', *Theology Today*, 24 (1967), 206–26; D. Gross, 'Marxism and Utopia: Ernst Bloch' in *Towards a New Marxism* (eds B. Grahl & P. Piccone, St Louis, 1973).

Bloch, Felix (b. Zürich, Switzerland, 23.10.1905; naturalized American citizen). Swiss/American physicist. Bloch studied first at the Federal Institute of Technology in Zürich and in 1927 under HEISENBERG at Leipzig. He left Germany in 1933 and went in 1934 to Stanford where, apart from a period during WW2, he has remained. In 1954–5 he took leave to become director of CERN, Geneva. Bloch has contributed to many areas in the physics of solids, particularly those relating to their electrical and magnetic properties. An early success was to use the new ideas of wave mechanics to show that the electrons in a metal can move freely between the ions (or atoms) in the material without being deflected by them, if the ions are arranged in a perfectly regular pattern; he thus showed that the electrical resistance of a metal is due to imperfections in the arrangement of its constituent atoms, and was able to derive the theory of the behaviour of the electrical resistance of a metal. Bloch solved several problems concerned with the properties of ferromagnetic material (such as iron). These materials are divided into small regions called domains in each of which the magnetism points in a different direction. Bloch showed which factors influenced the formation of the boundaries or 'walls' between these domains and calculated their thickness. He introduced the model of 'spin waves' in magnetic materials, which has proved extremely valuable in understanding how magnetic properties deteriorate when the temperature of the material is raised. Bloch then turned his attention to the magnetic properties of atomic nuclei. In 1939 he measured the magnetic moment of the neutron (with L. Alvarez) and after WW2, with W. W. Hansen and M. E. Packhard, he developed the technique of nuclear magnetic resonance (nmr). This involves measuring the absorption of radio waves by the nucleus of an atom.

It can only occur if the atom is in a magnetic field of just the right value for the particular atom under investigation. Nmr is now widely used as an analytical tool in chemistry and biochemistry. Bloch was awarded the Nobel prize for physics in 1952. HMR

Bloch, Konrad Emil (b. Neisse, Germany [now Nysa, Poland], 21.1.1912; naturalized American citizen, 1944). German/American biological chemist. Bloch's early education was at the Technische Hochschule in Munich, and, after emigration in 1936 to the USA, at Columbia University. He has held chairs at Columbia, Chicago, and Harvard where, in 1954, he became the first professor of biochemistry. His research has been concerned with the structure, function and biosynthesis of lipids (see CORNFORTH). Bloch and his collaborators worked separately from but contemporaneously with LYNEN on the biosynthesis in humans of cholesterol, which is involved in cardiovascular disease (arterio-sclerosis). Cholesterol, necessary for the life of human cells, is the biological precursor of the adrenal cortical hormones and of the sex hormones. Bloch discovered this last fact. He and his colleagues have also shown that the hydrocarbon squalene (30 carbon atoms) is a biological precursor of lanosterol and thence of cholesterol: squalene is converted in a novel type of reaction into a steroid. Both Bloch and Lynen contributed to our knowledge of the biosynthesis of squalene from acetate, and they were jointly awarded the Nobel prize for physiology and medicine in 1964. NBC

Bloch, Marc (b. Lyons, Rhône, France, 6.7.1886; d. nr Trévoux, Finistère, 16.6.1944). French historian. While professor at Strasbourg University (1919–36), he met FEBVRE with whom he founded in 1929 the journal *Annales d'histoire économique et sociale*, one of the most influential journals in modern historical studies. Among Bloch's most important books are *Les Rois thaumaturges* (Paris, 1924; *The Royal Touch*, London, 1973), which deals with the history of the belief in the power of French and English monarchs to cure the 'king's evil'; *Les Caractères originaux de l'histoire rurale français* (Oslo, 1931; *French Rural History: an Essay on its Basic Characteristics*, London, 1966), a pioneering contribution to peasant studies and an exemplary study of long-term developments; and *La Société féodale* (2 vols, Paris, 1939–40; *Feudal Society*, London, 1961), which discusses the genesis and development of European feudalism from the social and cultural as well as from the political and military point of view. Some of Bloch's articles, collected as *Mélanges historiques* (Paris, 1966; sel. *Land and Work in Medieval Europe*, London, 1967; further sel. *Slavery and Serfdom in the Middle Ages*, Berkeley, Calif., 1975), have had an influence out of proportion to their length. They include discussions of the 'natural economy' of the Middle Ages, of technical change as a problem of collective psychology, and of the uses of comparative history. Bloch's approach to history was more revolutionary than his calm and sober presentation suggests. Without neglecting political or economic history, he insisted that they were parts of a whole which included social history and the history of 'collective mentalities'. Like DURKHEIM and PIRENNE, both of whom he much admired, Bloch studied historical problems in a comparative framework. His unfinished *Apologie pour l'histoire, ou métier d'historien* (Paris, 1949; *The Historian's Craft*, Manchester, 1954) gives some idea of his approach to history. Few books show more vividly what the study of the past can contribute to the understanding of the present than Bloch's reflections, written in 1940, on the French army's failure to resist German invasion: *L'étrange défaite* (Paris, 1946; *Strange Defeat*, London, 1949). UPB

Blok, Aleksandr Aleksandrovich (b. St Petersburg [now Leningrad], Russia, 16.11.1880; d. Moscow, USSR, 7.8.1921). Russian poet, probably the most important after Pushkin. His father was a sardonic scholar and a professor of law, his mother a possessive and highly cultivated woman, daughter of the rector of the University of St Petersburg. The parents divorced when Blok was a small child. He began his creative life at the turn of the century, a period marked by part-mystical, part-decadent trends and by an awakening of poetic imagination. He came under the influence of Soloviev and his vision of Sophia (Divine Wisdom) – the shadowy 'She', 'The Beautiful Lady' of Blok's early verse, *Stikhi o prekrasnoi Dame* [Verses about the beautiful lady] (Petersburg, 1898–1904) and, in other manifestations, the muse of missing superiority of his later work. He did not reject it even when realistic moods began to dominate his poetry, as when he parodied it in, for example, the poetic drama *Balaganchik* [The puppet show] (Petersburg, 1906). In the *Kniga vtoraya* [Second book of verse] (Moscow, 1904–8) the Beautiful Lady gives way to a succession of spectres and illusions which relieved Blok's growing sense of loss and despair. This was superseded by quasi-messianic preoccupation with Russia's historical and revolutionary fate (most of *The Third Book of Verse*, Petersburg, 1921), coinciding with a break away from the imaginative world of aesthetes and decadents. Much of his poetry can be explained biographically. The early verse comprises some of the most magical love poems in world literature. They reflect his relation with Liubov' Mendeleeva whom he wooed as the incarnation of divine Sophia and eventually married (it turned out a most unhappy marriage). There is nothing in Russian poetry, or even in French and German symbolism, comparable to Blok's musical alchemy of words. He was haunted by the sound of events, objects, attitudes, and the faintest signs which showed where the sickness of the world lay and the drama of a new one was enacted. His later more toughminded and mocking verse expressed a conjunction of the visionary and a critical sense of particular situations. Faced with the reaction and stagnation in post-1905 Russia, he experienced a longing for a 'storm' which would 'purge the old world'. Unlike many of his fellow-writers, he not only accepted the 1917 revolution but saw it as a manifestation of the spirit of music. The experience culminated in his greatest poem *Dvenadtsat'* (Petrograd, 1918; tr. J. Stallworthy & P. France, *The Twelve and Other Poems*, London, 1975), conceived as a kind of apocryphal, all but blasphemous gospel of 12 Red Army soldiers, marching like a haughty host, driven by blizzards and forcing their way, with Jesus Christ at the head, through icy streets, between the blank houses of hungry Petrograd in the first winter of Bolshevik Russia. Their procession was to Blok mankind processing through the 20c, redeemed or redeemable through suffering and blood. Thereafter he had hardly anything more to say, and became the spent prophet and genius of the Russian revolution. His ideas were naive and confused but his hearing and clairvoyance were infallible and produced a state of mind in which poems wrote themselves. For the collected works see *Sobranie sochineniy* (8 vols, Moscow, 1960–3), and for English versions *Selected Poems of Aleksandr Blok* (tr. & ed. J. Woodward, London, 1968).   EL

S. Hackel, *The Poet and the Revolution: Alexandr Blok's 'The Twelve'* (London, 1975); A. Pyman, *The Life of Aleksandr Blok*, 2 vols (Oxford, 1979–80).

Blondel, Maurice Edouard (b. Dijon, Côte-d'Or, France, 2.11.1861; d. Aix-en-Provence, Bouches-du-Rhône, France, 4.6.1949). French Catholic philosopher. A graduate of the Sorbonne, Blondel eventually became professor of philosophy at Aix-en-Provence, from where he retired in 1927. He believed that his philosophy was developed independently of faith, but at the same time could open out into a readiness to welcome faith. This became known as 'the method of immanence': the analysis of any human activity reveals, he tried to show, that there is in the person a desire for the supernatural which is inaccessible to mere human effort. One can only wait on grace. 'Action', in his sense, always points beyond itself. There were polemics about his work after 1907 when Pius X condemned 'religious immanentism' in his encyclical *Pascendi*. Blondel did not feel that this was aimed at him, but others did. Echoes of these battles are found, e.g. in *Lettre sur les exigences de la pensée contemporaine en matière d'apologétique* [Letter on apologetics] (Paris, 1896) and *Histoire et* *dogma* (Paris, 1904; *History and Dogma*, London, 1964). Unlikely ever to be a popular writer, Blondel nevertheless influenced many theologians – including JOHN PAUL II – by enabling them to explain how revelation satisfied the deepest hunger of the human heart. Thus he solved the problem of 'relevance'. PAH

J. J. McNeill, *The Blondelian Synthesis* (Leiden, 1966); J. M. Somerville, *Total Commitment* (Washington, 1968).

Bloomfield, Leonard (b. Chicago, Ill., USA, 1.4.1887; d. New Haven, Conn., 18.4.1949). The most important American linguist in the first half of the 20c. Brought up in Chicago and Wisconsin, he went to Harvard in 1903 where his main academic interest was in German. After graduating, he moved to the University of Wisconsin, where a meeting with the Germanicist Eduard Prokosch convinced him that he 'should always work in linguistics'. He taught German and linguistics at various American universities, and at the time of his death was professor of linguistics at Yale. Bloomfield's early work consisted of relatively detailed studies of small areas within Indo-European philology, but his interests widened as he increasingly worked on American-Indian languages and linguistics. Bloomfield considered that the linguist's main concern was 'the difficult and peculiar technique of deriving the structural system and the lexicon from the record of actual speech utterance', and he tried to lay down foolproof methods or 'discovery procedures' for doing this. These are expounded in his book *Language* (NY, 1933), which provides a rigid theoretical and methodological framework for the descriptive analysis of language. This book has been called 'a work without equal as an exposition and synthesis of linguistic science', and remained unsurpassed as a basic textbook for over 20 years. He was interested in the form rather than the meaning of utterances, claiming that 'the signals can be analysed, but not the things signalled about'. He utilized meaning only in the preliminary stages of linguistic analysis, in order to discover which utterances were treated as 'the same' by speakers, and which as

'different'. In Bloomfield's opinion the description of a language should begin with an analysis of the phonology (sound system) which should identify each phoneme (phonological unit) and state which combinations of phonemes occur. The linguist should then move on to the level of morphology (word segments), where an analysis should identify morphemes described as sequences of phonemes, and state which combinations of morphemes occur. Morphemes in turn would form the basis of the description of the next level up, and so on. JMA

Blum, Léon (b. Paris, France, 9.4.1872; d. Jouy-en-Josas, Yvelines, 30.3.1950). French socialist leader, intellectual, prime minister of the Popular Front government in France in 1936–7 and briefly in 1938, and again prime minister in 1946–7. Blum stood for democratic socialist reform within a capitalist system, with legislation designed to strengthen the working classes against their employers, in wage and contract negotiations, hours worked, holidays with pay, etc. His socialism sprang more from a desire for fraternity and social justice than from any ideological convictions, and his reform programme, while dividing France deeply at the time when German rearmament and the German and Italian drive for hegemony in Europe were making significant progress, failed to command the support of the radical section of his government. His position was further weakened by the outbreak of the Spanish civil war, which he feared might spread to France, and the polarization of French politics which accompanied this made his parliamentary failure inevitable. Blum defended himself with courage when placed on trial by the Vichy government (see *Léon Blum before his judges at the Supreme Court of* RIOM, *11–12 March 1942*, tr. C. Home, London, 1943). But his career epitomized French socialism as a political force in most of the 20c: intellectually outstanding, founded on sentiment and principle rather than interest and ideology, unable either to produce a united working-class movement or to compete successfully with the Communists for the working-class vote. Only when MITTERRAND turned the tables on the Communists in 1981 and formed a government in which the Socialists were again the leading party was the prospect of an effective Popular Front programme reopened.   DCW

J. B. Joll, *Intellectuals in Politics* (London, 1960); J. Colton, *Léon Blum, Humanist in Politics* (London, 1974).

Blumenberg, Hans (b. Lübeck, Schleswig-Holstein, Germany, 13.7.1920). German historian of ideas. His major work *Die Legitimität der Neuzeit* [The legitimacy of the modern era] (Frankfurt, 1966, [2]1977) represents a refreshing large-scale rebuttal of the central thesis of those historians of ideas who, like LÖWITH, claim that the ruling categories of thought of the modern epoch are no more than secularized versions of theological notions. He shows that the modern work ethic is not, *pace* M. WEBER, genetically connected with puritanical asceticism, nor the future realm of freedom promised by the *Communist Manifesto* (1848) with Jewish messianism, nor Descartes's search for absolute philosophical certainty with the search for the absolute certainty of religious salvation, nor the idea of the equality of all men before the law with the belief in the equality of all men before God. The dignity and independence of the modern world are devalued if its major distinctive characteristics are presented as an illegitimate transformation of theological ideas, as a kind of Christian heresy. In the name of a just understanding and proper evaluation of the *Neuzeit*, Blumenberg affirms, the autonomy of 'humane self-assertion' must be firmly established against 'theologischer Absolutismus'. Here Blumenberg's bold, original and complex studies, particularly on the fate of the concept of *curiositas* – its innocent acceptance by the Greeks, its virulent rejection by Christianity and its rehabilitation in the modern era – are of vital importance.   RNH

Boas, Franz (b. Minden, N. Rhine-Westphalia, Germany, 9.7.1858; naturalized American citizen, 1892; d. New York, USA, 22.12.1942). German/American anthropologist primarily responsible for the professionalization of the discipline in the USA. Trained initially as a geographer (doctorate, Kiel 1881), Boas shifted his interests to ethnology as the result of contacts with Eskimos in the course of Arctic expeditions. Work in British Columbia – especially among the Kwakiutl – led him to devote himself entirely to anthropology and also to emigrate to the USA. Work as an editor at *Science* and as a museum curator was followed by appointments at Clark University and later at Columbia (professorship, 1899) where he remained until his retirement in 1936. Boas's work spanned the four cognate fields which have come to form the basis of US anthropological training (ethnology, physical anthropology, linguistics, archaeology). While sharing with British social anthropology an emphasis on detailed field research, Boas differed in that his approach was largely inductive and he rejected nomothetic approaches in favour of the ideographic. There is a Boasian 'school' of anthropology only in a weak sense. His theoretical position, broadly referred to as historical particularism and cultural relativism, was set against what he saw as the mistaken assumptions of the dominant explanatory frameworks of his day, Tylorian evolutionism, geographical determinism and racial determinism. For Boas, culture was a more or less autonomous realm which could not be explained in terms of other factors, and his emphasis on the variety of different cultures militated against the formulation of a clear theoretical line (see *Race, Language, and Culture*, NY, 1940). While not rejecting the possibility of discovering general laws within cultures, Boas argued that the complexity of cultural phenomena was such that generalities were inevitably overwhelmed by detail. Boas's insistence on the importance of gathering as much ethnographic detail as possible was informed not only by his view of what the science of anthropology should be, but also by his belief that materials of dying cultures should be recorded before they became extinct. This latter belief was part of a general view of the role of anthropology as necessarily located in a political nexus (see *The Mind of Primitive Man*, NY, 1911). Boas's position as the major figure in American anthropology is due not only to his contributions to ethnology, linguistics, physical anthropology, and a view of anthropology as engaged in serious human issues, but also to his having guided the first generation of American anthropologists.   SLN

Boccioni, Umberto (b. Reggio di Calabria, Calabria, Italy, 19.10.1882; d. Sorte, nr Verona, Veneto, 17.8.1916). Italian futurist painter and theorist. His early works combine social protest with *fin-de-siècle* melancholy. The turning-point in his stylistic development was the instruction he received from BALLA in the divisionist colour theories of neo-impressionism (1900), reinforced by his own visit to Paris (1902–4). In 1907, while working as a commercial artist in Milan, he met MARINETTI, and in the winter of 1909–10, stimulated by Marinetti's *Foundation and Manifesto of Futurism* (February 1909), began to adapt his divisionist technique in response to Marinetti's demand for a new art based on speed, the dynamic element of modern life. He dissolved forms in a blaze of divisionist colours (i.e. light), creating a dramatic interaction between space and solid; he also began to distort forms and space to increase the excitement of movement. In *The City Rises* (1909–10), his first major futurist work, he tried to synthesize 'labour, light and movement' and evoke the growth of the modern industrial city, symbolized by a huge cart-horse straining along a forceful diagonal across the centre of the composition and dragging along his driver and several labourers. The divisionist technique no longer relates to the perceptual world but is distorted to convey a sense of movement and vitality; this Boccioni called 'dynamic abstraction'. Together with Carrà, Russolo and Balla he signed the futurist manifestos of February and April 1911. In *The Noise of the Street Penetrates the House* (1911) he continued his experiments with simultaneous images, opening out forms in a series of angular facets to echo the physical and psychological penetration of noise into the life of the individual. Cubism, after a visit to Paris in October 1911, showed Boccioni how to create a complex spatial composition without losing clarity.

In *Materia* (1912) he adapted the cubist faceting of objects and space to integrate external appearance with inner animation. This concept was further exemplified in paintings such as *Elasticity* (1912), *Dynamism of a Soccer Player* (1913), and in sculptures such as *Development of a Bottle in Space* (1912) and *Unique Forms of Continuity in Space* (1913). In his *Technical Manifesto of Futurist Sculpture* (1910) he asked for enclosed sculpture to be abolished, and for plastic forms to be opened out to enclose the space around them.   SOBT

G. Ballo, *Umberto Boccioni. La Vita e l'Opera* (Milan, 1964).

Bodenstein, Ernst August Max (b. Magdeburg, Germany [now East Germany], 15.7.1871; d. Berlin, 3.9.1942). German physical chemist, distinguished for his pioneering work in chemical kinetics. He studied under Victor Meyer at Heidelberg and NERNST at Göttingen. For several years he collaborated with OSTWALD in Leipzig. He was professor of physical chemistry at Hanover (1908–23), and at Berlin (1923–42). Bodenstein may be called the father of classical gas kinetics. He devoted most of his research to the investigation of the reactions between hydrogen and the halogens. For the iodine system his results indicated an almost 'pure' bimolecular reaction (much more recently shown to be an oversimplification), whereas those for the bromine system and particularly for the chlorine system were much more complex. Their interpretation involved developing the concept of radical chain reactions and the steady state principle for intermediate products. These and related studies laid the foundations for the work of HINSHELWOOD, SEMENOV and many more recent researchers. In his early collaboration with Ostwald, Bodenstein had done important work in the kinetics of heterogeneous reactions and the mode of action of catalysts. He returned to this area in his Berlin years and helped to lay the foundations of a part of chemistry which is of great scientific and technical importance today.

JSh

Bohr, Aage Niels (b. Copenhagen, Denmark, 19.6.1922). Danish physicist. The son of Niels BOHR, he was educated at Copenhagen University. Around 1950 two models of the nucleus existed, the liquid-drop model and the shell model, each giving an excellent description of some of the properties of the nucleus. The challenge was to obtain a description which incorporated the best features of both approaches. Bohr and the US physicists Mottelson (b. 1926) and Rainwater (b. 1917) provided such a model, the collective model of the nucleus. In this, groups of nucleons (protons and neutrons), instead of just one nucleon (as in the shell model), could move in orbits within the nucleus, distorting its surface in a way similar to that envisaged in the liquid-drop model. Hence Bohr synthesized the main ideas of nuclear physics, leading to a concept of the nucleus which has remained intact until the present day. Bohr received the Nobel prize in 1975 together with Mottelson and Rainwater.

RJC

Bohr, Niels Henrik David (b. Copenhagen, Denmark, 7.9.1885; d. Copenhagen, 18.11.1962). Danish theoretical physicist who made fundamental contributions to atomic and nuclear theory and to the epistemology of science. His early work was devoted to hydrodynamics and the electron theory of metals where the difficulties of a classical description convinced him of the need for a radically new theory of atomic phenomena. He moved to Manchester to work with RUTHERFORD and deduced some of the implications of the nuclear atom, in particular the relation between atomic number and the number of electrons, the displacement laws of radioactive elements and the rate of energy loss of charged particles passing through matter. Back in Copenhagen, he worked out in 1912 his quantum theory of atomic structure, with the electrons moving round the nucleus in discrete orbits, like planets round the sun. These electrons can jump from one orbit to another, leading to the emission of light of a frequency corresponding to the energy difference between the initial and final orbits. This accounted for the series of lines in the spectrum of hydrogen, and gave an expression for Rydberg's con-

stant in terms of known quantities. The theory won immediate acceptance, although its conceptual difficulties were not removed until the development of quantum mechanics. In this work he was helped by his correspondence principle which says that in the limit of large energies the quantum theory must give the same results as the classical theory. Many physicists came to Copenhagen to work on the quantum theory and an Institute of Theoretical Physics was founded, with Bohr as director. The renewed interest in spectroscopy produced many new results analysed by extensions of Bohr's theory. For his work on atomic theory Bohr was awarded the Nobel prize in 1922. In subsequent years he explored the philosophical implications of HEISENBERG's uncertainty principle and from the implied mutual exclusion of pairs of measurements derived the concept of complementarity. He realized that in such situations it is necessary to include in the analysis the description of the experimental arrangement, and stressed that the complementary phenomena belong to aspects of our experience that are mutually exclusive but indispensable for a full account of experience. He maintained that a statistical form of causality is the only possible link between quantal phenomena, and that the statistical description of quantum mechanics gives an exhaustive account of all observable aspects of phenomena.

In the 1930s Bohr turned to nuclear physics and studied the results of FERMI on the capture of slow neutrons by nuclei. He was able to account for many features of the reaction by the compound nucleus model, based on an analogy between the nucleus and a drop of liquid. He used the model to explain nuclear fission, and showed that only the rare isotope uranium 235 is fissile by slow neutrons, so that separation of the isotopes is necessary to produce a nuclear explosion. This model of the nucleus was later developed into the collective model, which explains many features of deformed nuclei. During WW2 he was for a time at Los Alamos and participated in the development of the atomic bomb. In 1950 he wrote a letter to the UN pleading for an open world as a precondition for peace. He wrote and lectured extensively on his philosophical views, applying the concept of complementarity to a wide range of human problems. He saw in this concept a rational method of avoiding the exclusion of any fruitful line of thought. These ideas are developed in his books *Atomic Theory and the Description of Nature* (Cambridge, 1934), *Atomic Physics and Human Knowledge* (NY, 1958) and *Essays, 1958–1962: on Atomic Physics and Human Knowledge* (NY, 1963). His *Collected Works* are being edited by L. Rosenfeld *et al.* (3 vols to date, Amsterdam, 1976–). PEH

S. Rozental (ed.), *Niels Bohr, his Life and Work* (Amsterdam, 1967).

Böll, Heinrich (b. Cologne, N. Rhine-Westphalia, Germany, 21.12.1917). German novelist, awarded the Nobel prize for literature in 1972. Through his novels, short stories and essays he has become the leading chronicler and critic of West German society since WW2. The wartime experiences of his generation of disillusioned conscripts are reflected in his early writings, particularly in collections of short stories like *Wanderer, kommst du nach Spa* (Cologne, 1950; tr. M. Savill, *Traveller, If You Come to Spa*, London, 1956). The stresses of living in postwar Germany during the period of economic recovery are portrayed in several short novels such as *Und sagte kein einziges Wort* (Cologne, 1953; tr. L. Vennewitz, *And Never Said a Word*, London, 1978). Böll's more ambitious later novels relate the malaise underlying the German 'economic miracle' to a failure to accept responsibility for the disasters of WW1 and of Nazism: *Billiard um halb zehn* (Cologne, 1959; tr. P. Bowles, *Billiards at Half Past Nine*, London, 1961), *Ansichten eines Clowns* (Cologne, 1963; tr. L. Vennewitz, *The Clown*, London, 1965), and *Gruppenbild mit Dame* (Cologne, 1971; tr. L. Vennewitz, *Group Portrait with Lady*, London, 1973). A strong sense of the ethical responsibilities of authorship, linked to his Catholic faith, underlies Böll's critical attitude towards social institutions, including the church itself, the state bureaucracy, the army and the press. His writings espouse the rights of the individual against the repressive tendencies of society, and he has never shrunk from controversy. Right-wing critics, particularly in the popular press, have accused him of sympathizing with social dissidents and even condoning the aims of terrorists. Böll's reply has included a vivid fictional picture of the way the press distorts the truth and infringes the privacy of individuals in *Die verlorene Ehre der Katharina Blum* (Cologne, 1974; tr. L. Vennewitz, *The Lost Honour of Katharina Blum*, London, 1975, and also very effectively filmed). Böll writes in a plain and accessible style, and his books have been translated into many languages. His writings are not formally as inventive as those of his contemporary GRASS, and occasionally his novels become overelaborate, but he writes with a satirical verve and a sharpness of social observation which are perhaps most effective in his short stories. In his essays he sees it as his function as a writer to act as the social conscience of his age. His recent writings give prominence to the dangers of escalating nuclear armaments and the creeping powers of the state security system. EFT

R. H. Thomas & W. van der Will, *The German Novel and the Affluent Society* (Manchester, 1968); E. Macpherson, *Heinrich Böll: a Student's Guide* (London, 1972).

Boltzmann, Ludwig Eduard (b. Vienna, Austria-Hungary [now Austria], 20.2.1844; d. Duino, Friuli-Venezia Giulia, Italy, 5.9.1906). Austrian physicist. Boltzmann, one of the great classical (i.e. prequantum) theoretical physicists, is best known for his contributions to the development of statistical mechanics. He showed that in order to calculate the behaviour of systems containing a large number of atoms it was not necessary to know how each atom would behave, which would have been impossible: instead it could be predicted on the basis of *probability*. He extended Maxwell's work and derived a simple expression which enables us to calculate what fraction of the atoms in an assembly at a particular temperature will have energies within a specified range. He showed that the entropy of a system could be calculated very simply from a knowledge of the number of different possible arrangements of atoms in their energy states. He also contributed to the theories of radiation and electromagnetism. His work came under strong attack from the logical positivists in Vienna, who held that one's understanding should only be based on what could be obtained by direct sensory perception and opposed atomistic theories since at that time direct evidence for the existence of atoms had yet to be obtained. Boltzmann was prone to depression and this opposition could have contributed to his suicide. **HMR**

Bomberg, David (b. Birmingham, W. Mids, UK, 5.12.1890; d. London, 19.8.1957). British painter and draughtsman. He studied at the Slade School of Art from 1911 to 1913 and subsequently exhibited with the vorticists. Although he painted some impressive pictures in this style (e.g. *The Mud Bath*, 1912–13, and *In the Hold*, 1913–14), Bomberg became increasingly disillusioned with the direction the modernist movement in art was taking. The topographical landscapes he painted in Palestine and Petra in the 1920s reveal the depth of his crisis of vision. Gradually, when painting in Spain, he came to see that CÉZANNE had been misunderstood, and his achievement distorted within modernism. Bomberg rejected drawing based on eye and hand alone, and advocated a quest for what he called 'the spirit in the mass'. This emphasis on imaginative intelligence in the artist's approach to drawing and response to nature rendered him intensely unfashionable. Although his work was largely neglected, he gathered a group of devoted students around him at the Borough Polytechnic in London between 1945 and 1953. During the 1970s, however, a crisis of confidence in the value of the successive modernist fashions in art led to a growing recognition of the stature and relevance of Bomberg's achievement, especially that of his later years. **PF**

W. Lipke, *David Bomberg* (London, 1967).

Bond, Edward (b. London, UK, 18.7.1934). British dramatist, author of, since 1962, 13 full-length plays, five short plays, two libretti (for HENZE), four play translations, a book of poems (*Theatre Poems and Songs*, London, 1978), a number of film scripts (including ANTONIONI's *Blow-Up*, 1966, and Roeg's *Walkabout*, 1970) and an important collection of theoretical writings (*The Activists' Papers*, London, 1980). *Saved* (1965), which brought him to prominence, was the subject of a court case in 1966 on the grounds of its blasphemy and violence; *Early Morning* (1968) was the last play to be banned in its entirety by the censor; and *Narrow Road to the Deep North* (1968) was subject to a demand for cuts. In 1968 Bond was given the George Devine award for the first two plays and the John Whiting award for the third.

Bond's plays address themselves to crucial issues of contemporary society, while employing a variety of historical and present-day locations. In plays such as *Lear* (1971) and its companion piece *The Sea* (1973) he explores both the problems of political violence and the strength of individuals to solve their difficulties. A subsequent trilogy (*Bingo*, 1973; *The Fool*, 1975; and *The Woman*, 1978) debated the position of the artist in modern society and the necessity for organized revolutionary action. In *The Bundle* (1978) Bond for the first time explored a successful socialist revolution. *The Worlds* (1978) dealt specifically, in a contemporary setting, with guerrilla warfare against a multinational corporation. His two most recent works are *Restoration* (1981), a musical play, and *Summer* (1982). **PR**

M. Hay & P. Roberts, *Edward Bond: a Companion to the Plays* (London, 1978); and *Bond: a Study of his Plays* (London, 1980).

Bondi, Herman (b. Vienna, Austria, 1.11.1919; naturalized British citizen, 1947). Austrian/British mathematician and cosmologist. Bondi has been professor of mathematics at King's College, London, since 1954. In 1948, while still working in Cambridge, he was the joint author with HOYLE and Thomas Gold of the 'steady-state' theory of the universe. This postulated that the observed expansion of the universe was compensated by a continuous creation of matter throughout space at a rate that was too low to be directly observable (see *Cosmology*, Cambridge, 1952, ²1960). Since it required neither an initial moment of creation nor a limit to the extension of space, such a theory had obvious attractions. More recently it has lost ground to the alternative 'big-bang' hypothesis both because of the evidence from radio astronomy that the distribution of galaxies is evolving rather than remaining in a steady state and because of the discovery of cosmic background radiation.

ALCB

Bonhoeffer, Dietrich (b. Breslau, Silesia, Germany [now Wročlav, Poland], 4.2.1906; d. Flossenbürg, Bavaria, 9.4.1945). German theologian. Bonhoeffer grew up surrounded by academics, and studied theology at Tübingen and Berlin universities. During travels in the late 1920s and early 1930s to Barcelona as pastor of the Confessing church, to New York's Union Theological Seminary as a graduate student, and as pastor in London, Bonhoeffer's interest in associating theology with politics became clear. In 1931 he took up a position as professor of systematic theology at the University of Berlin. Active in protests against the Nazi regime from the earliest days of its rise to power in 1933, he particularly criticized its anti-Semitism. In 1935 he was appointed head of the new seminary for the Confessing church at Finkenwalde, which continued undercover even after the Gestapo closure in autumn 1937. There Bonhoeffer experimented with practices of prayer, private confession, common discipline and celibacy. The experience was recorded and described in *Gemeinsames Leben* (Munich, 1939; tr. J. W. Doberstein, *Life Together*, London, 1954). From this period also came *Nachfolge* (Munich, 1937; tr. R. H. Fuller, *The Cost of Discipleship*, London, 1948), a study of the Sermon on the Mount and attacking 'cheap grace', i.e. unlimited forgiveness, believing it to be a cover for moral laxity. At this time he described his views on international relations as 'conditional pacifism', then

unique in German theological circles; he remained a vigorous ecumenist despite growing nationalism in Germany. Events in the late 1930s led inevitably to increased political involvement and Bonhoeffer's brother-in-law introduced him to the group seeking HITLER's overthrow. Bonhoeffer went to the USA in 1939 and considered taking refuge there; but he returned to Germany after only two weeks to 'share in the trials of this time with my people'. Forbidden to publish or to speak publicly, he continued to work underground for the church. In April 1943 he was arrested by the Gestapo, imprisoned first in Berlin and then Buchenwald. Subsequent discovery of documents linking Bonhoeffer with the unsuccessful attempt to kill Hitler on 20 July 1944 led to his hanging, shortly before the liberation of the region by the American army.

Unfinished manuscripts of a volume on Christian ethics on which Bonhoeffer worked intermittently from 1940 to 1943 were published posthumously as *Ethik* (ed. E. Bethge, Munich, 1949; tr. N. H. Smith, *Ethics*, London, 1953, ²1964). Here Bonhoeffer rejected the dualistic separation of church and world, sacred and profane, and called for a unitive earthly ethic based on Christology in which work, family life and institutions are to be seen as mandates from God rather than orders of creation. In his prison writings (*Widerstund und Ergebung*, ed. E. Bethge, Munich, 1951; tr. R. H. Fuller, *Letters and Papers from Prison*, London, 1953, ²1964), Bonhoeffer welcomed the coming together of Christianity and secular humanism. He believed that the church ought to affirm 'mankind come of age', and to encourage a 'stripping off of the traditional emphases on the world to come' and personal salvation in order to reconnect with its Jewish roots. The creation of a 'religionless Christianity' would, he thought, preserve Christian values without necessitating the traditional ideas of a supernatural God. It would be difficult to overestimate the importance of these ideas on later reformist and critical movements within the church: in the challenges of John ROBINSON's 'honest to God' debate; in the 'death of God' controversy of the

1960s; in the discussions surrounding *The Myth of God Incarnate* (ed. J. Hick, 1977) and in D. Cupitt's *Taking Leave of God* (1980); and less directly on theologies of hope and liberation and on feminist theology.   LJH

E. Bethge, *Dietrich Bonhoeffer* (Munich, 1967; tr. T. Mosbacher *et al.*, London, 1970); R. Gregor Smith (ed.), *World Come of Age* (London, 1967).

Bonnard, Pierre (b. Fontenay-aux-Roses, Seine, France, 13.10.1867; d. Le Cannet, Alpes-Maritimes, 23.1.1947). French painter, designer and graphic artist. While studying at the Académie Julian in 1888 he met Denis, Sérusier and VUILLARD with whom he founded the Nabis group in 1889. However, in the 1890s Bonnard was less interested in the literary and theoretical aspirations of symbolism than in the creation of richly patterned yet subtle colour harmonies, for which he was dubbed 'le Nabi Japonard'. He aimed to fuse the sparkling surface quality of impressionism with the flat, decorative compositional design he admired in Japanese art. From 1891 to 1905 he concentrated on graphics and design. In 1893 he helped design the stage-set for the first French production of IBSEN's *Rosmersholm*. His lithographs, e.g. the poster for *La Revue Blanche* (1894), are reminiscent of Lautrec's incisive, simplified designs, but integrate image and text more subtly. His many book illustrations, e.g. for Vollard's edition of Verlaine's *Parallèlement* (1900), demonstrate his versatility in interpreting complex literary expression. From c. 1905 he devoted himself largely to painting, stimulated by the sensuous colour harmonies of the late MONET. Although superficially similar to impressionism in theme (landscapes, townscapes, interiors), colour and texture, Bonnard's work remained faithful to the symbolist notion that every human thought or sensation had a corresponding plastic and decorative form, and an equivalent aesthetic. He tried to express this in intimate scenes of domestic life (girls seated at laden dining-room tables, women standing or seated reflectively in cool interiors, and nudes in the bath). His precise observation of light, rendered by bright colour harmonies (mostly primaries and secondaries) is combined with a strong surface design, conveying a sense of simple yet detached intimacy.   SOBT

J. & H. Dauberville, *Bonnard: Catalogue raisonné de l'oeuvre peint* (2 vols, Paris, 1965); A. Vaillan, *Pierre Bonnard* (London, 1966).

Boole, George (b. Lincoln, UK, 2.11.1815; d. Ballintemple, Munster, Ireland, UK [now Irish Republic], 8.12.1864). British mathematician and logician. Boole learned his early lessons in mathematics from his father, an amateur mathematician and optical instrument maker. Thereafter he was self-taught. He became a school teacher at 16. In 1847 he published a pamphlet *The Mathematical Analysis of Logic* (Cambridge) which bridged the gap previously separating mathematics from formal logic. This development was crucial in advancing the potential powers of the analytical engines of BABBAGE, and later the 20c digital computers. Boole became a protégé of the English mathematician Augustus de Morgan, and with his support was elected to the chair of mathematics at Queen's College, Cork, in spite of his lack of formal qualifications. In 1854 he published his mature work on mathematical logic *An Investigation into the Laws of Thought, on which are Founded the Mathematical Theories of Logic and Probabilities* (London). In 1859 he published his *Treatise on Differential Equations* (Cambridge) and in 1860 his *Treatise on the Calculus of Finite Differences* (Cambridge). The development of Boolean algebra was fundamental to mathematical logic, and is the basic logical tool in designing modern computers. William Stanley Jevons built a 'logical piano' for implementing Boolean algebra in the 1860s. His *Collected Logical Works* (London) were published in 1916.   RAH

C. & R. Eames, *A Computer Perspective* (Harvard, 1973); R. A. Hyman, *Charles Babbage: Pioneer of the Computer* (Oxford, 1982).

Borel, Emile Félix-Edouard-Justin (b. St Affrique, Aveyron, France, 7.1.1871; d. Paris, 3.2.1956). French mathematician, who also filled various administrative positions in education, especially at the Ecole Normale Supérieure in Paris. His mathematical activity at first centred on problems in mathematical analysis, especially the growing use then being made of the set theory of CANTOR. One of Borel's theorems of that time is now normally called 'the Heine–Borel theorem'. He also systematized the study of nonconvergent infinite series, and obtained many results for functions of a complex variable. An important aspect of these achievements was to individuate the concept of a 'measure' as a generalization of the intuitive ideas of length, breadth and volume. In the 1900s he noticed that the properties of a measure were also satisfied by probability, and worked extensively on that subject from then on. He was also a founder of game theory. Borel took an interest in the philosophy of mathematics. He put forward a form of 'constructivism', which asserts that only processes which actually indicate the method of construction are valid in mathematics. In addition to his research and administrative duties, Borel was extremely active as a popularizer and textbook writer in mathematics. He edited, and contributed to, an important series of mathematical monographs for the house of Gauthier-Villars. His writings are collected in *Oeuvres* (4 vols, Paris, 1972). With his wife, the novelist Camille Marbo, he launched in 1906 the general periodical *La Revue du mois*, which ran for 14 years. His public positions included minister of the navy (1925) and founder-director of the Institut Henri Poincaré from 1928 until his death. IG-G

Borges, Jorge Luis (b. Buenos Aires, Argentina, 24.8.1899). Argentine short-story writer, essayist and poet. Like most Argentine intellectuals of his generation, Borges was profoundly influenced by European culture, but in his case the usual French influence was outweighed by that of English literature (from Old English to CHESTERTON) and thinkers, such as Berkeley. Residence in Europe during and after WW1 brought him in contact with numerous intellectual trends, and he was identified with Spanish *ultraismo* before his return to Buenos Aires in 1921. He also brought a romantic passion to the atmospheric recreation of Buenos Aires in the poems of *Fervor de Buenos Aires* [Buenos Aires fervour] (Buenos Aires, 1923) and *Cuaderno de San Martín* [San Martín sketchbook] (Buenos Aires, 1929), and this romanticism interweaves with a zest for philosophical enigmas and for puzzle-building in the numerous collections of short stories for which he is best known. These are always intricately patterned, generally fantastic, and sometimes highly disturbing: see especially *Ficciones* (Buenos Aires, 1941; tr. A. Kerrigan, London, 1962); *El Aleph* (Buenos Aires, 1949; tr. N. T. di Giovanni with Borges, *The Aleph and Other Stories, 1933–1969*, NY, 1970); *El informe de Brodie* (Buenos Aires, 1970; tr. N. T. di Giovanni with Borges, *Dr Brodie's Report*, NY, 1972). One favourite motif is that of the labyrinth, and *Labyrinths: Selected Stories and Other Writings* (ed. D. A. Yates & J. E. Irby, tr. by various hands, NY, 1962, augmented 1964) includes tales from four collections. Borges is also a notable (if overintellectual) poet, much given to revising his texts from one edition to the next, so that the versions in the first collected *Poemas, 1922–1943* (Buenos Aires, 1943) go through several intermediate stages on their way to *Obra poética 1923 –1967* (Buenos Aires, 1967, the basis for *Selected Poems 1923–1967*, tr. M. T. di Giovanni *et al.*, NY, 1972) – itself revised again in *Obra poética 1923–1976* (Buenos Aires, 1979). One important volume contains both poems and stories: *El hacedor* (Buenos Aires, 1960; selected prose tr. M. Boyer, selected verse tr. H. Morland, *Dreamtigers*, Austin, 1964). The poetry collection *El oro de los tigres* (Buenos Aires, 1972) gives its title to *The Gold of the Tigers* (selected later poems, tr. A. Reid, NY, 1977). Borges has always been nonpolitical as a writer, which makes him anathema to the Latin American left on the 'he who is not with me is against me' principle; his alleged right-wing stance has also probably stood between him and the Nobel prize, for which he has frequently been nominated. RP-M

J. Sturrock, *Paper Tigers: the Ideal Fictions of Jorge Luis Borges* (Oxford,

1977); G. R. McMurray, *Jorge Luis Borges* (NY, 1980).

Born, Max (b. Breslau, Silesia, Germany [now Wročlav, Poland], 11.12.1882; d. Bad Pyrmont, Lower Saxony, West Germany, 5.1.1970). German physicist. Born, whose father was professor of embryology at Breslau University, was educated at the universities of Breslau, Heidelberg, Zürich and Göttingen. His early work, which formed the basis of a lifelong interest, was concerned with the elastic properties of solids. Jointly with von Kármón he developed his quantum theory of the specific heats of crystalline solids. He was director of the physical institute at Göttingen University from 1921 until 1933 when he was expelled by the Nazis. During this time his interests shifted to quantum mechanics and his department attracted a dazzling group of young scientists, among them PAULI, HEISENBERG and Jordan. He showed how the abstract symbolic methods of Heisenberg could be replaced by matrix algebra and he published the classic paper on the subject with Heisenberg and Jordan. Many of the results of his work are summarized in the relationship between the noncommuting operators p and q representing pairs of conjugate physical quantities, the most notable being components of momentum and position along a common axis $qp - pq = ih/2\pi$ where $i = \sqrt{-1}$ and h is PLANCK's constant. Shortly after this he gave, for the first time, the now accepted interpretation of the wave function introduced into quantum mechanics by SCHRÖDINGER. He treated the square modules of the wave function as a measure of the probability density and vindicated this interpretation with his quantum mechanical theory of atomic scattering. The great importance of this work was recognized by the award of the Nobel prize for physics in 1954.

In 1936 he accepted the chair of natural philosophy at Edinburgh and remained there until his retirement in 1953. Here he continued his work on crystalline materials and made important contributions to the theory of liquids. He was a notably successful writer of textbooks, the best known in English being *Principles of Optics* (with Wolf, London, 1959), *Atomic Physics* (London, 1935) and *Dynamical Theory of Crystal Lattices* (with Huang, Oxford, 1954). During the 1950s and 1960s he was active in alerting the public to the dangers of nuclear warfare, and his statement jointly with HAHN and Heisenberg was one of the formative influences in the development of the Pugwash movement. PSF

Bornkamm, Günther (b. Görlitz, Germany [now East Germany], 8.10.1905). German New Testament scholar. Bornkamm lost his position at Königsberg in 1936 on account of his activities in the Confessing church against HITLER. He became professor at Göttingen in 1947, and at Heidelberg in 1949 until his retirement in 1971. A pupil of BULTMANN, he pioneered the redaction criticism of the gospels, especially Matthew; participated in the demythologizing debate of the 1940s and 1950s; and became with his bestseller *Jesus von Nazareth* (Stuttgart, 1956; tr. I. & F. McLuskey, *Jesus of Nazareth*, London, 1960) one of the standard-bearers of the so-called 'new quest of the historical Jesus' undertaken by scholars who presupposed the historical methods and sceptical conclusions of the form critics (i.e. those who attempt to discern the form taken by a story or teaching in order to make it more easily memorable, or more impressive, as it was passed on in oral tradition). His *Paulus* (Stuttgart, 1969; tr. D. M. G. Stalker, *Paul*, London, 1971) was similarly successful in communicating the best of German theological scholarship to a wider readership, but its Lutheran flavour limited its appeal in England. Bornkamm also had a remarkable record as a doctoral supervisor, with many influential monographs issuing from his pupils. RM

Bosch, Carl (b. Cologne, N. Rhine-Westphalia, Germany, 27.8.1874; d. Heidelberg, Baden-Württemberg, 26.4.1940). German developer of chemical fertilizer. Agriculture and the use of land were revolutionized by the use of synthetic nitrogen as a fertilizer. HABER, who discovered the process, was awarded the Nobel prize in 1919; Bosch developed it commercially and, by 1930, was selling 2.5 million tons per annum through BASF, the German chemical company (later I. G. Farben) of which Bosch became president. In 1931 Bosch himself shared the Nobel prize for chemistry with Friedrich Bergius for devising chemical high-pressure methods.   RIT

Bosch Gimpera, Pedro (b. Barcelona, Spain, 22.3.1891; naturalized Mexican citizen, 1942; d. Mexico City, Mexico, 9.10.1974). Spanish/Mexican archaeologist and ancient historian who through his excavations brought the ancient Iberian peoples from a legendary twilight to a concrete reality. In 1916 he helped found the Spanish government excavations service, and in the next 20 years he established and directed the Archaeological Museum in Barcelona, then, in 1930, the Seminario de Prehistoria. He was an active field archaeologist and did pioneering work in Aragón on the Iberian town of Calaceite in 1914, and between 1932 and 1936 at the Graeco-Roman city of Ampurias. Bosch's writings tackled grand themes on an impressive scale, successfully marrying archaeological and textual records to show how the native peoples of ancient Spain were transformed by contact with Punic, Carthaginian, Greek and Roman civilizations: *Los pueblos primitivos de España* [The primitive peoples of Spain] (2 vols, Madrid, 1925). His wider linguistic interests led him to write on Indo-European archaeology and European prehistory: *El poblamiento Indoeuropea* [The Indo-Europeans] (Mexico City, 1963). From 1933 to 1939 he was rector of Barcelona University and councillor of justice to the Generalitat de Catalunya. At the fall of the Republican government in 1939 he left Spain, never to return. His exile began in Oxford, and by 1941 he was in Mexico. Although he remained active until his death, it was his work in 1915–39 that made a lasting impact.   RJH

Boucherot, Paul-Marie-Joachim (b. Paris, France, 3.10.1869; d. Ardentes, Indre, 7.8.1943). French engineer. Boucherot was responsible for one of the most important aspects of electric motor design. Until 1905 the induction motor

(invented by TESLA) could not be made in large sizes or started up without one or other of a number of expensive attachments. Boucherot's 'double-cage' rotor made direct-on-line starting possible and helped the development of induction motors until they dominated the world of electric drives. He pioneered constant current networks and developed diverse alternators, including high-frequency and self-excited machines. He first used capacitors in long-line transmission systems to obtain constant voltages and the magnetic saturation of steel to produce harmonic frequencies. His enthusiasm for alternating current networks did for France what FERRANTI did for Britain.   ERL

Boulez, Pierre (b. Montbrison, Loire, France, 26.3.1925). French composer and conductor who believes that a new musical language has to be constructed on the basis of major musical innovations; he requires each new work to make a technical or aesthetic contribution to that language. He is rigorously self-critical and tends to withdraw works or revise and extend them over long periods; his output is small. His first compositions, which include two piano sonatas (1946 and 1950), are intellectually controlled and lyrically or violently expressive. His consistently personal style nevertheless displays its roots in SCHOENBERG, WEBERN and STRAVINSKY, and in the music of his teacher MESSIAEN. In the first book of *Structures* for two pianos (1952), however, he obliterated all traces of the past by using a 'total serial' technique to organize each musical aspect – pitches, durations, intensities and attacks – according to serial rules. Even within *Structures* this severity became flexible, and in *Le Marteau sans maître* [The hammer unmastered] (1955) he produced a fast-moving masterpiece in which the contralto was joined by a sextet owing as much to African and Asian as to European models in its emphasis on percussion. Boulez's next innovation was to allow chance into his music, following the work of CAGE but with strict limitations. His Third Piano Sonata (1957) leaves matters of tempo, loudness and even the ordering of segments to the performer's choice, and his *Pli selon pli* [Fold by fold] for soprano and orchestra (1962) is similarly open to interpretation. It is also a portrait of Mallarmé, whose aesthetics are central to its planning and whose imagery is translated into the glacial sounds of pitched percussion instruments (harps, bells, xylophones, etc.). These are also important in the orchestral *Eclat/multiples* (begun 1965), one of several later 'works in progress'. As a conductor Boulez has been noted for the clarity and rhythmic precision he has brought to 20c works and for his adventurous programmes. Since the mid-1970s he has conducted less, in order to concentrate on his direction of the Institut de Recherche et Coordination Acoustique/Musique which encourages collaboration between musicians and scientists to develop new instruments, electronic media and compositional methods.   PG

P. Boulez, *Conversations with Celestin Deliège* (London, 1977); P. Griffiths, *Boulez* (London, 1978).

Bourbaki, Nicolas. Collective *nom de plume* under which a group of (mostly) French mathematicians publishes an encyclopedic treatise on advanced mathematics called *Eléments de mathématiques*. It was launched in the early 1930s by mathematicians such as H. Cartan, J. Dieudonné and André WEIL, who had found themselves, as students in the 1920s, taught by much older men, the intermediate generation having been killed during WW1. They wanted to create a *published* record of mathematics, which would be immune from the perils of mass carnage in the future. Retirement from the group at 50 is compulsory, in order to prevent Bourbakist mathematics from becoming *passé*. Nevertheless, the modern generation of young French mathematicians is mostly unsympathetic to Bourbaki's rather arid and formal style, in which great emphasis is laid on set theory and abstract algebra, and theories and proofs are formalized to a high degree of sophistication. The *Eléments* began appearing in earnest after WW2, but have become less frequent in recent years.   IG-G

Bourdieu, Pierre (b. Dengvin, Basses-Pyrénées, France, 1.8.1930). French sociologist and educationalist. A student at the Ecole Normale Supérieure, he attained *agrégé* in philosophy. In 1959–60 he lectured at the faculty of letters in Algeria, in 1960–2 at the University of Paris and in 1962–4 at the University of Lille. Bourdieu then became director of studies at the Ecole des Hautes Etudes and director of the Centre for European Sociology, Paris, where with a group of colleagues he embarked on pioneering extensive collective research on problems concerned with the maintenance of a system of power by means of the transmission of a dominant culture. With Jean-Claude Passeron he wrote *La Reproduction* (Paris, 1970; *Reproduction in Education, Society and Culture*, London, 1977), which by a precise examination of the French educational system rigorously tested the proposition that if a power succeeds in imposing meanings that are accepted as legitimate, then power relations are concealed, and symbolic power is added to economic and political power. Thus pedagogic action imposes a symbolic violence which contributes to the reproduction of the power of the dominant formation. A disturbing correspondence is implied between the school system's monopoly of legitimate symbolic violence and the state's monopoly of the legitimate use of physical violence. The method of testing theoretical propositions by empirical verification employed here is developed in *Esquisse d'une théorie de la pratique, précédé de trois études d'ethnologie kabyle* (Geneva, 1972; *Outline of a Theory of Practice*, Cambridge, 1972, with additional chapters). In the effort to overcome the disabling division between piecemeal empirical inquiry and self-sufficient theoretical speculation, Bourdieu launched the journal *Actes de la Recherche en Sciences Sociales*, devoted to deconsecrating the mechanisms by which cultural production helps sustain the dominant structure of society.   TFC/LMC

Bovet, Daniel (b. Neuchâtel, Switzerland, 23.3.1907). Swiss pharmacologist. After gaining a doctorate in zoology and comparative anatomy at the University of Geneva, Bovet joined the Institut Pasteur in Paris, eventually becoming director of the laboratory of therapeutic chemistry. In 1947 he moved to Italy and since 1971 has been professor of psychobiology in Rome. He was awarded the Nobel prize for medicine in 1957. Bovet's three principal contributions have been in medicinal chemistry. In Paris, with three colleagues, he showed that 'prontosil rubrum', discovered by DOMAGK, owed its antibacterial action to the release in the body of sulfanilamide, the precursor of the large sulphonamide family. Second, the discovery that certain thymoxy compounds could antagonize histamine paved the way for the modern antihistamines. The third contribution, in Rome, came after the usefulness of the South American arrow poison curare had been shown for relaxing muscles at surgical operations and during electroconvulsive therapy, and after Harold King at DALE's laboratory had discovered the structure of a major alkaloid, d-tubocurarine. Bovet and his colleagues showed that curare-like activity was retained when the molecule was much simplified, and discovered the first clinically useful synthetic curare, gallamine. Following the introduction of the yet simpler decamethonium by Paton & Zaimis and Ing & Barlow, with its different type of action, Bovet and others synthesized the now widely used succinylcholine, active by a similar mechanism, but with a much briefer action due to its susceptibility to cholinesterase in the blood. Bovet has also worked on nicotine, on drugs for treating Parkinson's disease, and on psychoactive substances. His research is marked by biological imagination combined with chemical intuition.   WP

Bowen, Norman Levi (b. Kingston, Ont., Canada, 21.6.1887; d. Washington, DC, USA, 11.9.1956). Canadian petrologist. Bowen pioneered the use of physical chemistry for understanding the genesis of metamorphic and, more especially, igneous rocks. His and his successors' outstanding experimental work at the geophysical laboratory of the Carnegie Institution in Washington, where he spent most of his working life, made it a place of pilgrimage for researchers in

experimental petrology. His work on the reaction principle in petrogenesis has been called the most important contribution to petrology of this century. Besides other fundamental contributions he did much work in mineralogy which has been widely applied in ceramics, glass and metallurgical industries. Much of his best work is summarized in his classic *The Evolution of Igneous Rocks* (Princeton, 1928).   AH

Bowers, Fredson Thayer (b. New Haven, Conn., USA, 25.4.1905). American bibliographer. After graduating from Brown and Harvard universities, Bowers joined the University of Virginia, becoming Linden Kent professor of English in 1968. Since its inception in 1948 he has been editor of *Studies in Bibliography*, organ of the University of Virginia Bibliographical Society. Building on the work of his predecessors, such as A. W. Pollard and W. W. Greg, Bowers codified the practice of bibliography in *Principles of Bibliographic Description* (Princeton, 1949, ²1962) and developed the concept, notably in *Textual and Literary Criticism* (Cambridge, 1958) and *Bibliography and Textual Criticism* (Oxford, 1964). His achievement was to establish analytical bibliography as an independent discipline for the distinguishing and ordering of editions and their exact description, based on minute knowledge of the techniques of book production and consequent textual transmission. These principles he put to use in critical editions of English 17c and American authors and in establishing definitive standards in textual criticism and editing.   EV

Bowlby, John (b. London, UK, 26.2.1907). British psychoanalyst who has used theories drawn from animal studies to explain some aspects of child development. Bowlby trained as an analyst and in 1946 published his first famous study (*Forty-four Juvenile Thieves*, London) – of 44 juvenile thieves who had in common that, at a very young age, they had experienced prolonged separation from their mothers. This research coincided with the dramatic discovery by the Harlows in America that infant monkeys reared away from their mothers became depressed, often socially isolated and unable to mate. Bowlby, given his own results and this monkey research, pressed ahead with work on 'maternal deprivation'. In a series of books for the World Health Organization he argued that the young child needs prolonged attention and affection from its mother: that is how it learns to love. Bowlby's work inspired a series of dramatic films which showed the anger and depression of children in hospital without their mothers. The 'maternal deprivation' hypothesis has had considerable social impact. Hospitals, for example, now routinely admit mothers with their sick children. Many feminists, on the other hand, have attacked Bowlby for chaining women to their children and inspiring maternal guilt. Even so, in his attempt to link psychoanalysis with ethology and fairly rigorous studies of animal behaviour Bowlby showed much imagination. More recently he has gone on to study how children react to bereavement, and has suggested that these reactions resemble the ways in which children react to the absence of the mother. Bowlby's approach has been recognized as giving analytic ideas a breath of fresh air. He may, however, have overstated his essential hypothesis; there need not be only one way for children to learn to love.   DMOC

Bowman, Isaiah (b. Waterloo, Ont., Canada, 26.12.1878; d. Baltimore, Md, USA, 6.1.1950). American geographer. A Harvard graduate who studied under W. M. Davis and was director of the American Geographical Society (1915–35) and president of Johns Hopkins University (1935–48), Bowman is probably best known for *The New World* (NY, 1921); one of the most influential books on political geography, it described the reshaped world emerging from the boundary changes of WW1. Bowman based his analysis of the world's tension areas on experience as leader of the American team accompanying Woodrow WILSON to the Versailles Peace Conference of 1919. Bowman's government service continued with Franklin ROOSEVELT in WW2; he was adviser to the US delegation at Dumbarton Oaks

(1944) and to the UN conference at San Francisco (1945). His role as a government adviser and geopolitical analyst represents only a minor part of his work. Three other significant areas can be distinguished. First, his contribution to the understanding of the regional geography of South America based on extensive field research before WW1 and summarized in two monographs *The Andes of Southern Peru* (NY, 1916) and *Desert Trails of Atacama* (NY, 1924). Second, as director of the American Geographical Society he launched in 1920 the project for mapping the whole of Latin America at the scale of 1:1,000,000. When completed in 1945 the 107-sheet mapping programme had cost over $400,000 but had already resolved boundary disputes in poorly demarcated areas. Third, in the mid-1920s Bowman initiated another AGS programme for a study of the world's pioneer settlement fringes and wrote a key volume on the theme, *The Pioneer Fringe* (NY, 1931). As a university president Bowman found little time for field research but he continued his geographical work and in *Geography in Relation to the Social Sciences* (NY, 1934) gave a measured view of the discipline's problems and potential. His last major task for the US government was to draw up feasibility plans for resettling refugees of WW2 in western pioneer fringe areas.   PH

Box, George Edward Pelham (b. Gravesend, Kent, UK, 18.10.1919). British statistician. Employed at ICI from 1948 to 1956, he has since then pursued an academic career in the USA. In statistics, modelling of mechanisms in the light of data is commonly a process that uses, and potentially rejects, all existing theory. This is tiresome for outside users and impossible for computers. Box has a reputation for finding areas in which, and procedures by which, this modelling can be made highly systematic: especially (with G. M. Jenkins) in the forecasting of time-series, where his techniques (partly for lack of alternatives) have been very widely adopted (see *Time-Series Analysis, Forecasting, and Control,* NY, 1970). He also produced (with G. Tiao) an analytical system for scientific experiments using subjective probabilities. AGPW

Bragg, William Henry (b. Westward, Cumbria, UK, 2.7.1862; d. London, 15.3.1942). British pioneer of X-ray crystallography. As professor in Adelaide he studied radioactivity and showed that the alpha-particles from radium may be divided into a few groups, each with a different range. He studied X-rays and interpreted his results in terms of a corpuscular model. He continued this work in England and tried to understand the pattern of spots observed by LAUE when X-rays passed through a crystal. His son William Lawrence BRAGG realized that they could be explained by diffraction of the X-rays from the planes of the crystal lattice: the angles of the diffracted beams are related to the wavelength of the X-rays and the spacing between the crystal planes. Furthermore, measurements of the direction and intensities of the diffracted beams provide vital information on crystal structure. Bragg used these ideas to design an X-ray spectrometer which he used to study the spectral nature of X-rays, and, together with his son, to determine the structures of sulphur, quartz and diamond. For this work they were jointly awarded a Nobel prize in 1915. During WW1 Bragg worked for the Admiralty on the detection of underwater sounds, and developed the hydrophone for antisubmarine warfare. After the war he continued his X-ray analyses of crystal structure, subsequently, as director of the Royal Institution, concentrating on organic compounds. He excelled as a lecturer, and had a special gift of explaining science in a simple way. As president of the Royal Society (1935–40) he served on science advisory committees, broadcast frequently on scientific subjects and thus became a widely respected national figure. PEH

G. M. Caroe, *William Henry Bragg* (Cambridge, 1978).

Bragg, William Lawrence (b. Adelaide, S. Australia, Australia, 30.4.1890; d. Waldringford, Suffolk, UK, 1.7.1971). British physicist who first explained the diffraction of X-rays by crystals in terms of reflections from crystal planes and thus laid the foundations of X-ray crystallography. In his early years he was strongly influenced by his father William Henry BRAGG, who was engaged in pioneer studies of X-rays. Together they studied the corpuscular and wave theories, and the scattering of X-rays by crystals observed by LAUE. Bragg realized that this can easily be explained by reflections from layers of atoms in the crystal, and applied optical diffraction theory to obtain the relation between the wavelength of the X-rays, the distance between the crystal planes and the angle of reflection (now known as Bragg's law). Bragg was also the first to see that X-ray diffraction could be used for crystal-structure analysis and he first applied it to determine the structures of the alkali halides. For this work Bragg was awarded the Nobel prize in 1915 jointly with his father. During WW1 Bragg developed the methods of sound-ranging of enemy guns. Subsequently at Manchester he put X-ray analysis on a quantitative basis and showed how the intensities of the reflected X-rays could be used to determine the electron distribution in the atoms. He determined the structures of increasingly complicated molecules, including the silicates and other minerals and alloys.

In 1938 Bragg succeeded RUTHERFORD at Cambridge and encouraged new areas of research, including radio astronomy, metal physics and molecular biology. The X-ray analysis of complicated molecules culminated in the determination of the structures of proteins and DNA. He moved to the Royal Institution in 1954 and established a new research group to continue the analysis of proteins. As a physicist, Bragg excelled in the three-dimensional visualization of complex molecules and the determination of their structure by optical methods. His work essentially founded the sciences of mineralogy, metallurgy and molecular biophysics, and he summarized it in his books on the *History of X-ray Analysis* (London, 1967) and *The Development of X-ray Analysis* (eds D. C. Phillips & H. Lipson, London, 1975). PEH

Brancusi, Constantin (b. Pestiani Goj, Romania, 21.2.1876; naturalized French citizen, 1957; d. Paris, France, 16.3.1957). Romanian/French sculptor. In 1904, after six years' study in Romania, Brancusi went to Paris and enrolled at the Ecole des Beaux-Arts. In 1907 he worked briefly with RODIN before establishing his own studio. His early style fused peasant wood-carving with academic naturalism. By 1908 Brancusi began to reject Rodin's rhetoric and heavily modelled surfaces. He was convinced that reality was beneath the surface and could be revealed only by direct carving. His belief that the forms which emerged from this confrontation with the mass (of stone, marble, wood, etc.) accorded with organic growth in nature (e.g. *The Kiss*, 1907–8) was very influential in modern sculpture (e.g. ARP, Henry MOORE). Brancusi's search for the 'essentially real' led him to simplify forms as much as possible; for example, the gradual reduction of the naturalistic head of the *Sleeping Muse* (1906) to a stylized ovoid shape with a hint of human features (*New Born*, 1915), culminating in *The Beginning of the World* (1924), a translucent marble egg poised in perfect equilibrium on a shining disk placed on a rough-hewn wooden base. This he called 'absolute equity'. Over the years Brancusi refined a relatively small number of themes (head, egg, bird, fish, full-length figure), though he insisted that his forms were never abstract but embodied an organic concept. In spite of his declared respect for the intrinsic nature of a material, he often gave his works polished surfaces that denied their mass, and made polished bronze versions of his major themes (e.g. *Maiastra*, 1912; *Bird in Space*, 1941). Brancusi was the first to explore the potential of the base in shaping reactions to a sculpture. His bases are integral parts of the works, and are often roughly carved in contrast to the sophistication of the form above, symbolizing the creation of life out of chaos.   SOBT

C. Giedion-Welcker (ed.), *Constantin Brancusi* (London, 1959); S. Geist, *Brancusi* (NY, 1968).

Brandeis, Louis Dembitz (b. Louisville, Ky, USA, 13.11.1856; d. Washington, DC, 5.10.1941). American lawyer and associate justice of the US Supreme Court. As attorney he regularly represented consumers and labour unions and sought to have the Supreme Court uphold statutes fixing minimum wages and maximum hours of work. He devised the 'Brandeis brief', that is, the introduction of economic and sociological data to support his legal arguments. He influenced the passing of the Clayton Anti-Trust Act and the Federal Trade Commission Act, 1914, which strengthened the government's antitrust powers. As associate justice of the Supreme Court (1916–39) he opposed economic monopolies, supported freedom of ideas and political expression, and the rights of the states within the Federal Union. He was the first Jew to sit on the Supreme Court, and Brandeis University, Waltham, Mass. (1948) was named for him.   DMW

A. T. Mason, *Brandeis: a Free Man's Life* (NY, 1946); A. M. Bickel, *The Unpublished Opinions of Mr Justice Brandeis: the Supreme Court at Work* (NY, 1957).

Brandes, Georg (b. Copenhagen, Denmark, 4.2.1842; d. Copenhagen, 19.2.1927). Danish literary critic and scholar. As a young man he made an explosive impact on Danish and Scandinavian cultural life in 1871 with the first of his public lectures on *Hovedstrómninger i det 19de Aarhundredes Litteratur* (6 vols, Copenhagen, 1872–87; tr. W. Archer, *Main Currents in Nineteenth Century Literature*, London, 1901–5) before going on to establish himself as one of Europe's foremost literary critics. This inaugurated a new spirit of fearless inquiry in Scandinavian – and subsequently in European – literature: the so-called 'modern breakthrough' by which writers were exhorted to 'subject problems to debate'. IBSEN and Björnson in Norway and STRINDBERG in Sweden were decisively influenced by him; and naturalism, as a European literary movement, owed much of its vigour to his ideas. In 1888, in a further series of public lectures in Copenhagen, Brandes 'discovered' NIETZSCHE for

Europe and for the 20c; and in consequence his own ideological outlook shifted towards what he called Nietzschean 'aristocratic radicalism'. Brandes's later career was largely devoted to writing biographies of a more popular kind: of Shakespeare (1895–6), Goethe (1915), Voltaire (1916), Caesar (1918) and Michelangelo (1921).   JWMcF

R. Wellek, *A History of Modern Criticism*, iv (New Haven, 1965); B. Nolin, *Georg Brandes* (Boston, Mass., 1976).

Brando, Marlon (b. Omaha, Nebr., USA, 3.4.1924). American film actor. Son of a midwest salesman and a woman with frustrated stage ambitions, he grew up a rebellious individualist. He was an adherent of the 'method', an acting style based on self-immolation in the character performed. He was parodied for his mumbling diction, though he showed he could discard it as with Mark Antony in *Julius Caesar* (1951). His Broadway performance in *A Streetcar Named Desire* (1947) stunned New York and led to a long series of cinema roles, beginning with *The Men* (1950) and including *A Streetcar Named Desire* (1952). Brando revolutionized film acting, substituting naturalism for formality and influencing a generation of players, among them DEAN. After *On the Waterfront* (1954) he played one or two faintly masochistic parts, *The Fugitive Kind* (1962) and *One-Eyed Jacks* (1961), which he directed. At a disadvantage under the direction of CHAPLIN in *A Countess from Hong Kong* (1967), he returned to command in *The Godfather* (1972) and in Bertolucci's sexually explicit *Last Tango in Paris* (1973); later he played a secondary but significant role in *Apocalypse Now* (1979) and supplied a remote paternal sketch in *Superman* (1978). He has been a defender of the blacks and a champion of the American Indians. He was married, briefly and stormily, to the actress Anna Kashfi.   DP

B. Thomas, *Brando: Portrait of the Rebel as an Artist* (London, 1973).

Brandt, William (Bill) (b. London, UK, 2.5.1904). British photographer. Brandt trained in the Paris studio of Man Ray in 1929 and was there exposed to surrealist ideas in the movement's magazines and in the films of BUÑUEL and DALI. He became a leading photojournalist in the 1930s and published his first book *The English at Home* (London) in 1936. His second *A Night in London* (London) followed in 1938 when Brandt had his first exhibition in the gallery of Arts et Métiers in Paris. His photographs appeared in *Weekly Illustrated, Picture Post* and *Lilliput*. He photographed underground shelters for the Ministry of Information in 1940. During the next two decades he worked on assignment for *Harper's Bazaar* and on a personal project which was first published as *Perspective of Nudes* (London, 1961). His major collection of photographs *Shadow of Light* was published in 1966 (London, [2]1976). In 1975 Brandt selected the exhibition 'The Land: 20th-century Landscape Photographs' for the Victoria and Albert Museum. Brandt has worked at the highest level of achievement in reportage, portraiture, landscape and the nude. In all these fields he has introduced new methods of composition of striking originality. The clarity of the formal structure of his photographs is allied to a preference for strong effects of chiaroscuro. His first book scrutinized English society with uncanny precision and made contrasts between different social strata, including pointed comparisons of wealthy households in Mayfair and Kensington and slum conditions in the East End. His series of nudes is among the most imaginative sets of photographs in the history of the medium. His only extended statement on photography is the introduction to *Camera in London* (London, 1948).   MH-B

Brandt, Willy, ps. of Karl Herbert Frahm (b. Lübeck, Schleswig-Holstein, Germany, 18.12.1913). Chancellor of the German Federal Republic (1969–74). Mayor of Berlin (1957–66); chairman of the German Social Democratic party (1964–6); foreign minister of West Germany (1966–9). He fled from the Nazis to Norway, taking out Norwegian citizenship, and from 1940 worked as Norwegian courier through to neutral Sweden, returning to Germany in 1945. Brandt is associated principally with (1) the maintenance of morale of West Berlin during the second Berlin crisis (1958–63), against Soviet and East German pressure; (2) abandonment by the West German Socialist party of MARXism at Bad Godesberg (1959) in favour of social democratic reformism; (3) leadership in West German *Ostpolitik* (1966–72), in reconciliation with Poland, treaty with the USSR in 1972, direct approaches to the East German government; (4) the Brandt Report (1979), produced by an international commission, focusing attention on North–South relationships and the need in long-term interests of world peace greatly to increase industrial aid and linkages between heavily industrialized states of the northern hemisphere and the rest of the world.   DCW

Braque, Georges (b. Argenteuil, Val-d'Oise, France, 13.5.1882; d. Paris, 31.8.1963). French painter. Although apprenticed to his family's trade of painter-decorator, Braque went to Paris to study art. He joined the fauve movement in 1905 and painted brightly coloured landscapes, then became increasingly interested in simplification and structure, partly under the influence of CÉZANNE. After meeting PICASSO late in 1907 and seeing his *Demoiselles d'Avignon*, he embarked on a more radical style, working from memory with block-like shapes superimposed in relief on the background and painted in a range of restrained greens, ochres and greys. His landscapes painted at L'Estaque in the summer of 1908 prompted the remark from the critic Louis Vauxcelles that Braque reduced 'everything, sites, figures and houses to geometric outlines, to *cubes*', and led to the use of the word 'cubism' to denote this new style. However, he soon began to combine different viewpoints and break up the objects into facets which he integrated with the background.

In 1909 he became a close friend of Picasso who had been developing independently along similar lines, and for the next five years they worked in very close collaboration: cubism was their joint creation. Whereas Picasso was as much interested in the human figure as in still life, Braque concentrated mainly on still-life themes, such as musical instruments. Nevertheless their styles were so similar that many of their pictures could easily be confused, except that Braque's tended to be slightly more sensuous in their handling of paint and colour. Together they were responsible for pioneering the development from analytical into synthetic cubism, including the invention of collage. Among the innovations for which Braque was personally responsible were the introduction of passages of imitation marbling or wood-graining, variations of texture made by mixing paint with sand, and the incorporation of letters or words, all practices related to his early training as a house-painter.

From 1914 to 1917 Braque's career, unlike Picasso's, was interrupted by war service. When he was able to resume painting he found himself working in isolation. His work gradually became softer and more naturalistic, blending traditional qualities and a postcubist idiom in a series of magisterial still lifes and semiclassical nudes of bathers or women holding baskets of flowers, executed in greens, browns, creamy whites and greys, with succulent variations of texture. Between about 1930 and 1940 he painted a number of still lifes of a more linear kind, with areas of contrasting patterns and bold colours, combining recognizable forms with rhythmical abstract shapes. His tendency to take in more of the surrounding space (including some pictures with a genre subject such as the flattened silhouette of a painter seated at an easel or a woman playing a piano) culminated in a series of large 'Studios' painted from 1948 onwards, in which an accumulation of still-life objects creates a highly complex, ambiguous and mysterious space.
                                                    REA
J. Golding, *Cubism 1909–1914* (London, 1959); E. Mullins, *Braque* (London, 1968).

Brassai, ps. of Gyula Halász (b. Brasso, Transylvania, Austria-Hungary [now Braşov, Romania], 9.9.1899; naturalized French citizen, 1948). Hungarian/French photographer. Brassai studied art in Budapest and Berlin, before moving to Paris in the mid-1920s. He was encouraged to take up photography by a friend, the Hungarian photographer KERTÉSZ. In particular Kertész introduced him to the techniques of nighttime photography and in 1933 Brassai's *Paris de Nuit* (*Camera in Paris*, London, 1949) was published, a collection of 60 photographs with an introduction by the writer Paul Morand. *Paris de Nuit* is part of a genre of city-books popular in the early 1930s. As with Kertész, Brassai's subject was privacy; his book is that of a discreet noctambulist, at home in the dark passages of Paris. Many of his photographs of prostitutes, transvestites, brothel interiors were unpublishable at the time and only appeared in *The Secret Paris of the '30s* (London, 1976). He continued to be active as a photoreporter, publishing in *Vu* magazine in the 1930s. With CARTIER-BRESSON, Robert Doisneau, Willy Ronis, Nora Dumas and Roger Schall, Brassai is one of those photographers who, in the 1940s, established a picture of France as a largely rural utopia, peopled by characteristic peasants and tradesmen.   IJ

Brassai (NY, 1968).

Brathwaite, Edward Kamau (b. Bridgetown, Barbados, 11.5.1930). West Indian poet. He has successfully combined an influential administrative and, later, academic career with the writing of poetry and criticism. Regarded as one of the Caribbean's outstanding writers, he lived in Ghana from 1955 to 1962 and, by watching its transition from the colonial Gold Coast to an independent nation, he absorbed a feeling for African history which he defined in *The Arrivants* (Oxford, 1973). This is a trilogy of epic poems – *Rights of Passage* (Oxford, 1967), *Masks* (Oxford, 1968) and *Islands* (Oxford, 1969) – shifting between the West Indies and West Africa in a semi-allegorical arrangement of movements which evoke the diaspora of the black man. His shorter poems are collected together in *Other Exiles* (Oxford, 1975). In *Mother Poem* (Oxford, 1977) he explores the personality of his native Barbados in a complex epic which, by uniting European and African imagery and assonance, makes an aural commentary upon the interfusion of the two cultures. Brathwaite is also a noted historian of the West Indies, especially of slave and Creole society.   ANRN

G. Rohlehr, *Pathfinder: Black Awakening in 'The Arrivants' of Edward Kamau Brathwaite* (Tunapuna, Trinidad, 1981).

Braudel, Fernand Paul (b. Lunéville, Lorraine, France, 24.8.1902). French historian. From 1923 to 1933 Braudel taught history in Algerian schools, and from 1935 to 1938 at the University of São Paulo. WW2, most of which he spent in a prison camp near Lübeck, gave him the leisure to write his masterpiece *La Méditerranée et le monde méditerranéen à l'époque de Philippe II* (Paris, 1949, ²1966; *The Mediterranean and the Mediterranean World in the Age of Philip II*, 2 vols, London, 1972–3). This work caused a sensation by its displacement of attention from the personality of the king and the history of political and military events not only to economic and social trends, but to the slowly moving history of the relationship between man and his environment, the mountains and plains, land-routes and sea-routes of the Mediterranean region. It is also remarkable for its 'global' approach, placing the history of the sea within that of a 'Greater Mediterranean' region stretching from the Atlantic to the Sahara. A highly original and independent follower of FEBVRE, Braudel has less time for the history of 'mentalities' and a greater interest in material culture, as is shown by his second major work *Civilisation matérielle et capitalisme* (vol. 1, Paris, 1967; *Capitalism and Material Life*, London, 1973; vols 1–3 published as *Civilisation matérielle, économie et capitalisme*, Paris, 1979; 2. *The Wheels of Commerce*, London, 1982. A sketch of vols 2–3 is contained in *Afterthoughts on Material Civilization and Capitalism*, Baltimore, 1977). For Braudel, 'material civilization' includes population, food, clothes, housing, money and towns; he focuses on Europe in the period 1400–1800 but is much concerned to relate long-term trends in the West to trends in other parts of the globe. No living European historian is less ethnocentric than Braudel, and no one this century has done more to change the way in which history is written. From 1956 to 1972 he occupied the influential position of president of the VIth Section of the Ecole des Hautes Etudes.   UPB

Special issues on Braudel of the *Journal of Modern History*, 44 (1972) and *Review*, 2 (1978).

Braun, Wernher von (b. Wirsitz, Germany [now Wyrzysk, Poland], 23.3.1912; naturalized American citizen, 1955; d. Alexandria, Va, USA, 16.6.1977). German/American inventor of rockets. Having pioneered the development of the V2 rocket used by Germany to bomb the UK in WW2, he moved to the USA after the war to contribute to the space programme. He was involved in designing the rockets that put the first US satellite, Explorer I, into orbit in 1958, and also the Saturn rocket for the Apollo lunar missions.   RIT

Brecht, Berthold [Bertolt] Eugen Friedrich (b. Augsburg, Bavaria, Germany, 10.2.1898; d. East Berlin, 14.8.1956). German poet and dramatist. A great natural poet, Brecht consciously applied himself above all to the theatre, for which he wrote and directed plays, worked out a coherent system of theoretical principles, and trained and inspired one of the world's outstanding companies. His impact was felt in many spheres, partly because those principles apply far outside the theatre, partly because of the strong political backbone to his work, which gives it a worldwide appeal to radicals. A rare mixture of single- and open-mindedness, he owed his peculiar force as an artist to his readiness to seem inconsistent, to amend or scrap his own work, to engage other people's talents and energies, and never to take it easy. He was the least bohemian of geniuses: ruthlessly self-critical yet always productive.

As a schoolboy and as a drop-out medical student in Bavaria he mainly wrote songs and poems, and at first hesitated between the theatre and the silent film. Then with his play *Trommeln in der Nacht* (1922; *Drums in the Night*) he won the Kleist prize, a national reputation as a successor to the expressionists, and a whole-time job as a *Dramaturg*. He moved to Berlin in 1924 and was already recognized by critics and fellow-professionals when, almost by accident, he scored his great popular success in 1928 with the *Dreigroschenoper* (*The Threepenny Opera*), a free adaptation of Gay's *The Beggar's Opera* with songs by WEILL. This highly original, if also plagiaristic hotchpotch was played all over the Continent and was followed by the opera *Mahagonny* (1930) and other works with Weill, embodying a quite new approach to musical theatre.

In the crisis year of 1929 Brecht aligned himself with the Communist party, and for the next eight years his work tried to follow its line, above all in its fight with the Nazis. This was the period of his austerely didactic '*Lehrstücke*', his political poems and songs with EISLER, and his topical, almost naturalistic antifascist plays and sketches. Exiled in Scandinavia, he became the poet of what he termed 'the dark times' of the later 1930s. Detaching himself c. 1937 from short-term tactics, and critical of the 'socialist realism' prescribed by the party, he wrote his biggest plays, from *Galileo* (1938) to *Arturo Ui* (1941), as well as the long 'Svendborg Poems' and many of his major theoretical essays. Most of the time he was cut off from the German-language theatre.

The war made him move to the USA, where he settled in California in 1941 and tried vainly to establish himself as a film writer; his chief work from this period was his play *Der Kaukasische Kreidekreis* (written 1944, performed professionally 1954; *The Caucasian Chalk Circle*). He returned to Europe in 1947 and wrote the 'Short Organum' (in *Brecht on Theatre*, tr. & ed. J. Willett, London, 1964) to summarize his theoretical ideas such as *episches Theater*, *Gestik* and *Verfremdungseffekt* ['epic theatre', the 'gest' and the 'alienation effect']. From 1949 till his death in 1956 he lived in East Berlin, where he staged his Thirty Years War play *Mutter Courage* (written 1939, performed 1941; *Mother Courage*), and helped found the Berliner Ensemble, whose productions made him world-famous. Since then the full range of his work has only gradually been appreciated, and it remains rich in surprises and new ideas – particularly for those countries where it is not yet regarded as politically or academically 'established'. Permeated as it is with English and American influences which stretch from the Elizabethans to KIPLING, WALEY and the modern crime novel, it lies curiously close to the English tradition and had a formative effect on AUDEN.

A collected German edition of Brecht's work has recently been made available: *Gesammelte Werke, Texte für Film, Arbeitsjournal, Tagebücher 1920–1922, Briefe, Gedichte: aller der Nachlass* (Frankfurt, 1967–82). Collected editions of Brecht's *Plays, Poetry and Prose* in English translation, (eds R. Mannheim & J. Willett) are in course of publication (from 1970) in London and New York.   JWMW

J. Willett, *The Theatre of Bertolt Brecht* (London, 1959); K. Völker, *Brecht Chronicle* (NY, 1976).

Bresson, Robert (b. Bromont-Lamothe, Puy-de-Dôme, France, 25.9.1909). French film director. With only a dozen films in some 40 years' activity, Bresson is one of the cinema's most austere artists. His first films, made during the German occupation, were stylized pieces which still retained theatrical elements. But from the early 1950s onwards he pared down his style, drawing inspiration from such writers as BERNANOS and Dostoevsky but rethinking each subject in purely filmic terms (see *Notes on the Cinematograph*, London, 1977). In the four films from *Le Journal d'un Curé de Campagne* [Diary of a country priest, 1951] to *Procès de Jeanne d'Arc* [Trial of Joan of Arc, 1962] he created a remarkable gallery of characters on their way to sainthood. Subsequently his vision darkened and in the later films the characteristic heroine – *Mouchette* (1967) or *Une Femme Douce* [A gentle woman, 1969] – is a passive and defeated victim. Bresson's version of *Lancelot du Lac* (1974) likewise empties the Arthurian legend of all its glamour and glory and gives us instead a bleak and remorseless picture of Lancelot and Guinevere's failure to achieve divine grace. Taken as a whole, Bresson's films display a unique coherence, constituting the cinema's profoundest investigation into the ways of the flesh and the workings of the soul in a life lived under the oppressive shadow of sin and death. RPA

I. Cameron (ed.), *The Films of Robert Bresson* (London, 1969).

Breton, André (b. Tinchebray, Orne, France, 18.2.1896; d. Paris, 28.9.1966). French surrealist writer. Believing, as a result of WW1, that the values of western civilization, its particular belief in progress and perfectibility, lay in ruins, Breton and his friends, ARAGON, Soupault, ELUARD and Peret, welcomed dada's attack on standards, but became disillusioned with its negative aspects. In 1924 Breton's first *Manifeste du surréalisme* (tr. R. Seaver & H. R. Lane, *Manifestoes of Surrealism*, Ann Arbor, 1969) offered his alternative. It defined surrealism as 'pure psychic automatism by which it is intended to express, either verbally or in writing, the prime function of thought. Thought dictated in the absence of all control exerted by reason, and outside all aesthetic or moral preoccupations.' Despite Breton's admiration for CHIRICO and ERNST, there was originally no intention of being a visual or literary school. Poetry and painting were considered as tools for understanding and releasing our true nature and desires, never as aesthetic ends. Surrealism's original method, later modified, was a recourse to automatic writing without conscious control. The first authentic surrealist work is *Les Champs magnétiques* [The magnetic fields] (Paris, 1924) by Breton and Soupault. At the same time the surrealists took over from the dadaists the concept of 'scandal for scandal's sake'. One of their first actions was to publish a pamphlet attacking the recently dead and revered writer Anatole France. It was called *A corpse* (1924). Breton soon emerged as the leader of the group, editing, after its first few numbers, *La Révolution Surréaliste* (1924–9).

The success of the surrealist painters weakened the serious impact of the movement by allowing the public to equate surrealism with a mere manner; Breton insisted on the *meaning* of surrealism (see *Surrealism and Painting*, tr. S. W. Taylor, London, 1972). The effort required to live the surrealist life, however, while invigorating, could prove dangerous: a supposition supported by the high rate of suicides among its adherents. Breton's fragment of autobiography *Nadja* (Paris, 1928), an account of his meetings with a strange psychic girl with whom he fell in love and who eventually went mad, is a marvellous description of that world of 'the certainty of chance', the cornerstone of surrealism as a way of life. The paradox of Breton is that, within a movement totally devoted to love and freedom, he exerted his will with such rigour as to earn the title 'The Surrealist Pope'; yet without him it is doubtful if the movement would have existed at all.

Breton's return to Paris, after spending WW2 in the USA, was tragic. SARTRE's existentialism had filled the intellectual vacuum, and surrealism appeared to be both irrelevant and old hat. Breton's death in 1966 seemed no more than the final full stop at the end of a closed story, but with the contemporary failure of rational materialism, the surrealist struggle to achieve 'the whole man' has acquired a new relevance (see A. Breton *et al.*, *Le Surréalisme au service de la Révolution*, Paris, ²1977). GM

J. H. Mathews, *André Breton* (London, 1967); A. E. Balakian, *André Breton: the Magus of Surrealism* (NY, 1971).

Breuer, Marcel Lajos (b. Pécs, Austria-Hungary [now Hungary], 21.5.1902; naturalized American citizen, 1944; d. New York, USA, 1.7.1981). Hungarian/American architect and designer. Breuer studied at the Bauhaus from 1920 to 1925 when GROPIUS appointed him as form master in charge of the carpentry and joinery workshop. In the same year he designed the first tubular-steel chair to complement the impersonal style, flexibility and spaciousness of Bauhaus architecture, and revolutionized furniture design. In 1928 Breuer moved to Berlin, then from 1931 to 1935 travelled extensively in Europe and North Africa, prior to spending two years in London in partnership with F. R. S. Yorke. In 1937 he emigrated to the USA where he joined Gropius in the faculty of architecture at Harvard until 1946. Gropius and Breuer were also in partnership from 1937 to 1941 in an independent practice that Breuer had established. His first commissions were for private houses in New England (e.g. House II, New Canaan, Conn., 1951) characterized by the skilful use of natural materials to blend with the surroundings (rubble, field stone, weathered wood). In 1953 he collaborated with Bernhard Zehrfuss and the engineer NERVI on the design for the UNESCO secretariat in Paris. Working with Nervi, who was chiefly responsible for the complex eight-storey Y-shaped building, influenced his ideas about the use of concrete and engineering principles. The change was clear in his first public US commission, the Abbey Church of St John (at the Benedictine College, Collegeville, Minn., 1953–63) for which he conceived a dramatic pylon-shaped concrete bell tower detached from the main body of the church. Bolder still is the dramatically cantilevered concrete mass of the lecture hall he designed for New York University (1961), with a rough texture relieved only by a few windows. He developed the motif of windows set within deep, heavy concrete frames in his huge double Y-plan for the IBM-France Research Centre (La Grande Var, 1962). The mass of his design for the Whitney Museum of American Art in New York (1966) is severe yet dramatically sculptural, consisting of a top-heavy series of three massive, almost windowless concrete tiers overhanging the street aggressively; the effect is intensified by using the same heavy, dark granite and roughly textured concrete inside and outside. The 'brutalism' of these later works had a considerable influence on architecture in the 1970s (e.g. The National Theatre, London). SOBT

P. Blake, *Marcel Breuer, Architect and Designer* (NY, 1949); G. C. Argan, *Marcel Breuer* (London, 1955).

Breuil, Henri (b. Mortain, Manche, France, 28.2.1877; d. L'Isle Adam, Seine-et-Oise, 14.8.1961). French archaeologist. His interests were first aroused by visiting excavations in the Dordogne in 1897. Thereafter his scholarly life was devoted to the study of the material culture and art of the Palaeolithic period principally in France and Spain and to some extent Central and East Europe, with less successful excursions into African prehistory. In an important early paper 'Les Subdivisions du Paléolithique supérieur et leur Signification' [The subdivisions of the upper Palaeolithic and their importance] published in *Comptes Rendus* of the *Congrès International d'Anthropologie et d'Archéologie préhistoriques* (Geneva, 1912, ²1937), he laid the classificatory basis which dominated European Palaeolithic studies for the next half century and still retains importance. He was instrumental in bringing Palaeolithic art to the attention of the public by authenticating hitherto uncertain attributions, and in publishing most of the major sites largely through the auspices of the Institut de Paléontologie Humaine, culminating in his famous general survey *Quatre cent siècles d'art pariétal* [Four hundred centuries of cave art] (Montignac, 1952). He also published numerous articles on aspects of the French and European Lower Palaeolithic and studied both Pleistocene geology and human palaeontology in this connection.   BWC

A. H. Brodrick, *The Abbé Breuil, Prehistorian* (London, 1963).

Brezhnev, Leonid Ilyich (b. Kamenskoye [since 1936 renamed Dneprodzerzhinsk], Ukraine, Russia, 19.12.1906; d. Moscow, USSR, 10.11.1982). Head of the Soviet government (1964–82). The son of a steelmaker, Brezhnev rose to prominence as a protégé of KRUSHCHEV, first in the Ukraine, later (in the 1950s) on the national scene. Elected to the Central Committee of the CPSU in 1952; placed in charge of Krushchev's 'Virgin Lands' agricultural drive; full member of the Politburo, 1957. He joined in ousting Krushchev from power (October 1964) and succeeded him as general secretary of the CPSU's Central Committee, a post which he held from 1964 to his death, combining it with the chairmanship of the Praesidium of the Supreme Soviet (i.e. head of state) from 1977. Under Brezhnev, a more pedestrian but more predictable leader than either STALIN or Krushchev, the USSR enjoyed a longer period of stability and consolidation than at any time since the Bolshevik revolution. His collegial style of leadership meant that he neither attempted to usurp the policy-making powers of his Politburo colleagues nor, on the other hand, had difficulty in defeating possible challenges to his position.

The so-called 'Brezhnev doctrine', the right and duty to intervene wherever socialism was threatened in another 'socialist state', was invoked to justify the Russian invasion of Czechoslovakia in 1968, but was common ground among the Soviet leaders. He is more accurately identified with the policy of détente with the West which he launched at the beginning of the 1970s following Soviet achievement of strategic parity with the USA. Its initial success in the regularization of relations with West Germany (August 1970) was followed by an improvement in Soviet–US relations, beginning with President NIXON's visit to Russia (May 1972) and reaching a peak in the Helsinki Agreement of 1975. There were strict limits, however, to détente in Soviet eyes. It did not extend to liberalization of the East European regimes or to halting the build-up of Russian military power. It did not exclude the forceful extension of Soviet influence in the nonaligned areas of Africa and Asia, nor keeping up the propaganda offensive against the West as vigorously as ever. Disillusionment with détente was followed by a sharp deterioration in US–Soviet relations in Brezhnev's final years: Soviet intervention in Afghanistan; REAGAN's election; Soviet pressure on Poland. It may still appear, however, that the limited détente pursued by Brezhnev in the earlier 1970s represents the nearest practicable approach to a stabilization of East –West relations.   ALCB

Březina, Otokar (b. Počátky, Bohemia, Austria-Hungary [now Czechoslovakia], 13.9.1868; d. Jaroměřice, 25.3.1929). Czech poet and conversationalist. The son of a country cobbler, Březina was something of a recluse, whose unusual mind is not as evident in his verse as in his conversations and correspondence. His five collections of verse (1895–1901) develop from Decadent individualism to a grandiose conception of a humanity united in brotherhood, from pessimism to optimism. He tries to embrace the whole of human experience in hymnic poems whose meaning is often given more by the acoustic than the semantic value of words. The way he blends the materialist with the metaphysical in these poems gives them an oriental atmosphere. Selections of his poems are included in *An Anthology of Czechoslovakian Literature* (ed. & tr. P. Selver, London, 1929) and *Czech Poetry: a Bilingual Anthology* (vol. 1, ed. A. French, Ann Arbor, 1973). After his essays-cum-prose-poems *Hudba pramenů* [The music of sources] (Prague, 1903) he did not publish another book. Having refused a professorship at Brno University (1921), he retired from elementary schoolmastering in 1925. Prague University gave him an honorary doctorate in 1929. RBP

Bridgman, Percy Williams (b. Cambridge, Mass., USA, 21.4.1882; d. Randolph, NH, 20.8.1961). American physicist and philosopher of science. A skilful experimentalist, Bridgman developed an ingenious pressure seal by which the high pressure inside the pressure vessel automatically tightens the packing so that the pressure attained is limited only by the strength of the vessel itself. By this means he attained pressures up to about 400,000 atm, far higher than ever before. He also developed a series of instruments to measure the mechanical, electrical and thermal properties of materials at these high pressures, and applied them to determine the characteristics of a large range of substances. Much of this work is described in *The Physics of High Pressure* (London, 1931) and in very many papers. He discovered many new phenomena such as refining by zone melting and polymorphism at high pressures; these led to increased understanding of the processes in the earth's interior. The obligation to give advanced courses in electrodynamics forced him to examine the logical structure of physics, and turned his attention to the philosophy of science. To avoid the imprecisions of ordinary speech he identified the meaning of a concept in terms of the set of operations used to measure it. If no such operations exist, the concept has no meaning. These ideas, known as operationalism, are

developed in *The Logic of Modern Physics* (NY, 1927). In subsequent works on *The Nature of Physical Theory* (Princeton, 1936), *The Nature of Thermodynamics* (Cambridge, Mass., 1941) and *A Sophisticate's Primer of Relativity* (London, 1963) he extended and deepened his critical examination of the concepts and theories of physics. His radical empiricism weakened his interest in the reality behind phenomena, so that he seldom sought to understand the properties of matter at high pressure in terms of atomic structure. He considered the difference between laboratory physics and the cosmology of general relativity to be the difference between science and nonscience. PEH

Britten, Edward Benjamin (b. Lowestoft, Suffolk, UK, 22.11.1913; d. Aldeburgh, Suffolk, 4.2.1976). British composer. Britten was already well known by the mid-1930s as an *enfant terrible*, emulating the harmonic piquancy of STRAVINSKY and displaying an extraordinarily agile technique. His opera *Peter Grimes* (1945) established him as a proven composer. Based on a poem by Crabbe, it was the first English opera to enter the international repertory and was followed by many others, including *Billy Budd* (1951), *The Turn of the Screw* (1954), *A Midsummer Night's Dream* (1960), and *Death in Venice* (1973). There was also a trilogy of dramatic 'parables' for performance in church (1964–8). Several of these stage works had their first performances at the Aldeburgh Festival, which Britten, together with his companion Peter Pears, founded in 1948. Each year he produced at least one new work for the festival, often writing for local performers or for celebrated musicians who were his friends. No one benefited more from his skill than Pears, for whom he wrote all the leading tenor roles in his operas as well as numerous other works. Britten also wrote music for particular occasions, whether a big choral work to mark the consecration of Coventry cathedral (*War Requiem,* 1961) or *The Young Person's Guide to the Orchestra* (1946). PG

A. Gishford (ed.), *Tribute to Benjamin Britten on his Fiftieth Birthday* (London,

1963); P. Evans, *The Music of Benjamin Britten* (London, 1979).

Broch, Hermann (b. Vienna, Austria-Hungary [now Austria], 1.11.1886; naturalized American citizen; d. New Haven, Conn., USA, 30.5.1951). Austrian/American novelist. After working for many years in the family textile firm, he devoted himself from the age of 40 to intellectual pursuits first in Austria and after 1938 in exile in the USA. His reputation rests on a number of formally inventive and intellectually ambitious novels. The disintegration of cultural values in Germany in the period between 1880 and 1920 forms the subject of the trilogy *Die Schlafwandler* (Zürich, 1931–2; tr. W. & E. Muir, *The Sleepwalkers*, London, 1932). Its theme is underscored by a formal development from narrative realism to a plurality of narrative perspectives. This experimental tendency is taken a stage further by the interior monologue technique of *Der Tod des Vergil* (NY, 1945; tr. J. S. Untermeyer, *The Death of Vergil*, London, 1945). The dilemma of the artist in a period of historical crisis, explored through the lyrical reflections of the Vergil figure, is also the subject of a number of Broch's critical essays. The ethical vacuum which characterized public life in the final decades of the Hapsburg empire is analysed in the essay 'Hofmannsthal und seine Zeit' [Hofmannsthal and his age] (1951). And his interest in the collective psychological sources of Nazism is expressed in the posthumously published essays on *Massenpsychologie* [Psychology of the masses] (Zürich, 1959) and in the novel *Der Versucher* [The tempter] (Zürich, 1953). Broch's attempts to reconcile the scientific worldview with a mystical conception of experience is at times reminiscent of his Austrian contemporary MUSIL.   EFT

T. Ziolkowski, *Hermann Broch* (NY, 1964).

Brodie, Bernard (b. Chicago, Ill., USA, 20.5.1910; d. Los Angeles, Calif., 24.11.1978). American strategist. Brodie was one of a triad of strategic theorists at the US RAND Corporation in the late 1950s and early 1960s, along with

SCHELLING and WOHLSTETTER. His early work was on naval history, but in *Strategy in the Missile Age* (Princeton, 1959) he turned to command of the air as the central strategic issue in the nuclear age. Conceiving first strike as impractical and immoral, he suggested that deterrence could be best assured when the Strategic Air Command had defences adequate enough to enable it to survive an enemy strike and then retaliate. As missiles became relatively invulnerable, command of the air would be denied to either side; thus the possession by both Russia and the USA of invulnerable retaliatory forces would make for a stable central balance. In these circumstances Brodie foresaw the civilian population becoming the prime strategic target and requiring active and passive defences. *Escalation and the Nuclear Option* (Princeton, 1966) challenged the concept of the 'firebreak', or high nuclear threshold, as likely to allow or even encourage heavy conventional engagements before the contestants resorted to nuclear weapons. Brodie suggested instead that tactical nuclear weapons might possess a deterrent value and that their use might slow down or halt escalation.   JGo

M. H. Halperin, *Limited War in the Nuclear Age* (London, 1963).

Brodsky, Iosif Aleksandrovich (Joseph) (b. Leningrad, USSR, 24.5.1940; naturalized American citizen, 1977). Russian/American poet, generally recognized as the most important to emerge from the USSR since WW2; also essayist and critic. From a modest Jewish background, he survived the Leningrad blockade, became a factory worker at 15, then had various jobs, some involving travel to remote parts of the USSR. He educated himself through voracious reading. Active as a poet since the late 1950s, he led a brilliant renaissance of Leningrad poetry under the spiritual aegis of AKHMATOVA. Brodsky was arrested for 'parasitism' in 1964, and released from exile in the far north after protests from senior Soviet writers and Western literary figures. He became an involuntary exile from the USSR in June 1972, since when he has been based in the USA, eventually settling in

New York. He has taught at several universities, and continues to gain recognition in the USA and international literary circles, publishing in English as well as Russian (though remaining almost completely unpublished in the USSR). The last poems written in Russia were collected in *Konets prekrasnoi epokhi* [The end of a beautiful era] (Ann Arbor, 1977); since living in the West he has written *Chast' rechi* (Ann Arbor, 1977; tr. various hands, *A Part of Speech*, Oxford, 1980) and *Uraniya* [Urania] (Ann Arbor, 1983). *Selected Poems* (tr. & ed. G. L. Kline, with a foreword by AUDEN, Harmondsworth, 1973) is another collection in English. Brodsky has demonstrated in his poetry astonishing technical virtuosity, pulling off the most daunting formal feats with nonchalant skill. He has written some of the best elegiac love poetry in the Russian language, but his forte is discursive, meditative soliloquy. His tone is dry, ironic and disenchanted; he has brought the atmosphere of anglophone modernism (ELIOT, STEVENS, Auden) and the nervous intellectual brio of the English metaphysicals into modern Russian poetry, a radical departure from the central tradition. He is increasingly concerned with culturological problems, haunted by a BECKETT-like awareness of being overcome by wintry desolation against which human speech must be pitted as a token of survival. The plenitude of his talent, and the mythopoeic progress of his life, make him the pivotal figure in contemporary Russian poetry. He published an autobiography *Less Than One* (NY) in 1981.   GSS

de Broglie, Louis Victor Pierre Raymond (b. Dieppe, Haute-Garonne, France, 15.8.1892). French theoretical physicist. Louis, prince de Broglie, became seventh duke on the death of his brother Maurice, himself a physicist of distinction, in 1960. His first degree was in history (1910) but he graduated subsequently in science (1913). After WW1 service he specialized in theoretical physics, particularly in the study of radiation and quanta. His research work began in his brother's private laboratory, and was continued at the university in Paris, where, from 1932, he was professor of theoretical physics. He was also for many years the permanent secretary of the Academy of Sciences. In the early 1920s there was an unresolved contradiction between the wave and particulate nature of matter and energy. PLANCK had shown that energy was not indefinitely divisible but was radiated in quanta. BOHR had used this hypothesis to explain the energies adopted by the electrons in atomic hydrogen. De Broglie brought these ideas together and so laid the foundation of wave mechanics (one of the forms in which quantum mechanics can be expressed) when he proposed in his doctoral dissertation (1924) that each particle of mass m and velocity v (and so of momentum p = mv) had associated with it a wave of length $\lambda = h/p$, where h is Planck's constant. This hypothesis was confirmed experimentally within the next few years when DAVISSON and GERMER in the USA, and G. P. THOMSON in the UK, showed that electrons could form diffraction patterns. The waves are now generally called de Broglie waves. He received the Nobel prize for physics in 1929, and Davisson and Thomson in 1937.   JSR

Brønsted, Johannes Nicolaus (b. Varde, Jutland, Denmark, 22.2.1879; d. Copenhagen, 17.12.1947). Danish physical chemist. Brønsted's main contributions to science were his researches on electrolyte solutions, his general definition of acids and bases, his recognition of general acid-base catalysis and his thermodynamic studies. His career closely paralleled that of his classmate BJERRUM. After graduating in engineering at the polytechnic in Copenhagen, he changed to chemistry, and in 1908 secured the new chair of physical chemistry at the university, a post he held until his death. His early experimental and theoretical studies of affinity were of importance comparable with those of G. LEWIS and NERNST, while work on dilute electrolyte solutions provided the first striking confirmation of the theory of DEBYE and HÜCKEL. At higher concentrations the properties of electrolytes depend on the ionic strength, and are correlated through Brønsted's principle of specific ionic interaction. Studies of the effects of salt concentration on the rates of reactions involving ions led to the concepts of primary and secondary salt effects which are explicable in terms essentially similar to the transition state theory of EYRING and POLANYI. Brønsted gave an extended definition of acids and bases as substances which can, respectively, donate or accept protons (see also T. M. LOWRY). It led on to his experimental demonstration of general acid-base catalysis, and to the correlation between catalytic power and acidic or basic strength (the Brønsted relation). Later he reformulated the basic principles of thermodynamics in terms of 'energetics'. Although these ideas were controversial in the form in which Brønsted originally presented them, their value is becoming increasingly appreciated. His important publications include *Lærebog i fysisk Kemi* (Copenhagen, 1936; *Physical Chemistry*, London, 1937) and *Principer og Problemer i Energetiken* (Copenhagen, 1946; *Principles and Problems in Energetics*, NY, 1955). DHE

Brook, Peter Stephen Paul (b. London, UK, 21.3.1925). British stage and film director whose inventive productions and iconoclastic approach have done much to change the course of British theatre. Of Russian descent, Brook first attracted attention as an Oxford undergraduate, directing under the difficult circumstances of the little theatres in London during WW2; and in 1945 Sir Barry Jackson entrusted him with major productions at the Shakespeare Memorial Theatre at Stratford. He was noted in the early 1950s for his elegant productions in the West End of plays by ANOUILH and Roussin, but his true power as a director emerged with an outstanding Stratford production of *Titus Andronicus* with OLIVIER, for which he also designed the sets and composed the *musique concrète*. This success eventually paved the way for the demanding mixture of shock tactics, derived from the ideas of ARTAUD, and cool analysis which characterized his productions with the Royal Shakespeare Company in the 1960s, such as the *Marat/Sade* (1964) and *US* (1966). His work always has shown the capacity to absorb many influences: 'Any theory that restricts the theatre is a wrong theory.' Any empty space for Brook can become a theatre, even a mountainside or a clearing in a desert village. With a grant from the Ford Foundation he established an International Centre for Theatre Research in Paris in 1971, whose chief rule was to have no rules. He took his small company around Africa playing mime plays to remote tribes, which culminated in two productions seen in London, *The Iks* (1975) and *The Conference of Birds* (1976). Among his many films are *King Lear* (1962), *Lord of the Flies* (1963) and *Tell Me Lies* (1966). JE

J. C. Trewin, *Peter Brook* (London, 1971); J. Heilpern, *The Conference of Birds* (London, 1977).

Brouwer, Luitzen Egbertus Jan (b. Overschie, S. Holland, The Netherlands, 27.7.1881; d. Blaricum, N. Holland, 2.12.1966). Dutch mathematician. Brouwer's chief mathematical interests were twofold. One was a philosophical standpoint about mathematics, in which he permitted only methods of reasoning which led by direct construction from step to step. He called this view 'intuitionism', since he considered that 'intuitionist mathematics is an essentially languageless activity of the mind having its origin in the perception of a move of time'. Brouwer's position was controversial for several reasons. Firstly, it was very radical; for example, it entailed the rejection of the law of excluded middle. Secondly, his assertion of the primacy of time in mathematical thought was philosophically contentious (one could say, naive). Thirdly, he brought into mathematics elements of mysticism (on which he published a book) by allowing a role for languagelessness (akin to states of mystical ecstasy). Finally, his technical reconstruction of mathematics was full of difficult definitions and obscure procedures. Nevertheless, his criticism of established mathematical procedures deepened mathematicians' awareness of philosophical problems in their subject and has led to the development of similar, and less cryptically phrased, positions. Brouwer's second interest lay in topology, where he not only proved various important theorems but also exposed the naivety of the ordinary conception of dimension. His work here involved important applications of the set theory of CANTOR. His writings are published as *Collected Works* (2 vols, Amsterdam, 1975–6). IG-G

Brown, Herbert Charles (b. London, UK, 22.5.1912; naturalized American citizen, 1936). British/American organic chemist, distinguished for contributions to physical organic chemistry and synthetic organic chemistry. The Brown family emigrated to Chicago in 1914. Brown obtained a PhD at Chicago under H. I. Schlesinger. After working for a year with KHARASCH on free radical chemistry, he became assistant to Schlesinger. Their work together was on boron compounds and this profoundly influenced Brown's later researches at Purdue where he was professor from 1947 to 1978. His work in physical organic chemistry has been on three main topics, which overlap to some extent: he has made detailed studies of the role of steric effects in influencing reactivity in various processes; he has pioneered the extension of the HAMMETT equation to electrophilic aromatic substitution and the development of the reactivity-selectivity principle; and he has tried to establish the structures of the carbonium ions, which are intermediates in many organic reactions. The last involved a prolonged controversy with the late Saul Winstein on so-called 'classical' *v.* 'non-classical' structures, Brown being the protagonist of the former. Brown's contribution to synthetic organic chemistry is his discovery of a facile preparation of organoboranes and the exploitation of their innumerable reactions, which provide convenient routes for obtaining many different types of organic compound (see *Boranes in Organic Chemistry*, Ithaca, NY, 1972). He is author or coauthor of more than 700 publications, and was awarded the Nobel prize for chemistry, shared with WITTIG, in 1979. JSh

H. C. Brown (with P. von R. Schleyer), *The Nonclassical Ion Problem* (NY, 1977).

Brown, Norman Oliver (b. El Oro, Mexico, 25.9.1913). American cultural critic. During his academic career Brown has been professor of classics at Wesleyan University; of classics and comparative literature at the University of Rochester; and of humanities at the University of California at Santa Cruz. Following work on Greek myth, Brown published *Life against Death: the Psychoanalytical Meaning of History* (Middletown, 1959). This caused an intellectual sensation. With a brilliant sweep Brown re-examined FREUDian psychoanalysis, 'reclaiming [the] id territory' of unconscious, sometimes destructive forces (bodily erotism and death instinct) to render it applicable to history and culture. Thereby he simultaneously challenged the rational optimism of neo-Freudianism, liberal progressivism and modern Protestantism, arguing that they perpetuated sublimation and negation; only psychoanalysis offered hope for a 'resurrection of the body', which in the 1960s, though not expressed in political categories, confirmed the association of political and sexual liberation. Brown followed up this profound cultural critique with *Love's Body* (NY, 1966) and *Closing Time* (NY, 1973), more aphoristic explorations – religious, poetic, psychoanalytic – of the symbolical life of the body. RSm

Brown, Robert Hanbury (b. Aruvankadu, Nilgiri, India, 31.8.1916). British astronomer. On graduation Hanbury Brown worked in the UK and the USA on radar and continued this work during WW2. In 1949 he joined LOVELL's group at Jodrell Bank as a research student. At this stage in radio astronomy the number of discrete radio sources was rapidly increasing, but in general their positions were not known with sufficient accuracy to enable optical identifications to be made. Brown established that the Andromeda nebula (M31) and several other galaxies are radio sources, but because of the long wavelength of radio waves their resolution was inadequate to show the true size of most sources in the radio region. While he was still a student, Brown and Richard Twiss devised a new interferometer, the 'intensity interferometer', with a much better spatial resolution than a simple radio telescope. Brown and Twiss planned to use their interferometer in the optical region to measure the angular diameters of stars. In 1920 Michelson had been able to measure the diameters of a few nearby giant stars; smaller angular diameters than these, however, could not be measured because of the blurring effect of the earth's atmosphere. The new interferometer was used to obtain the angular diameters of 32 stars with good accuracy, the limits of its capability. Brown, who moved to Sydney University in 1964, has now turned his attention to the construction of a greatly improved Michelson interferometer in order to pursue the measurement of angular diameters (see Brown's own account in *The Intensity Interferometer*, London, 1974).   DEB

Brubeck, David Warren (b. Concord, Calif., USA, 6.12.1920). American pianist, composer, and leader of a jazz quartet whose recordings sold in vast quantities. In the late 1940s, after studying with Milhaud and SCHOENBERG, Brubeck formed experimental groups, the largest of which, an octet, began recording in 1948. His later quartet (using piano, alto-saxophone, string-bass and drums), achieved worldwide fame. The group's musical star was alto-saxophonist Paul Desmond, whose improvisations were supremely graceful and highly imaginative (he also composed the quartet's biggest recording success, *Take Five*, 1959). The quartet's main appeal was one of novelty: the leader's compositional forms and time-signatures were unusual in jazz. Brubeck's use of advanced harmonies was fluent, and no one disputed his originality, but the drawback for jazz listeners was that his piano playing seemed both unrhythmic and lacking in expression. Hence his music always invited controversy. Besides writing for his own groups, Brubeck composed several extended works that were occasionally performed by American symphony orchestras. The quartet with Paul Desmond disbanded in 1967, and a new four-piece group was formed, with baritone-saxophonist Gerry Mulligan, but broke up in the early 1970s. For the rest of the decade Brubeck worked mostly with a small group that featured his sons Chris, Daniel and David Darius.   JJC

Bruner, Jerome Seymour (b. New York, USA, 1.10.1915). American psychologist who has made important contributions to research on cognitive development and to curriculum design in schools. He is the leading advocate of the value of the phenomenological tradition in psychology and has attacked the radical behaviourism of SKINNER as having deflected psychology from a proper regard for the main problems of humanity. After early training in Harvard's postgraduate psychology school, he carried out a series of studies of coin perception in children from contrasting socioeconomic backgrounds. The results, which showed that children from poorer homes overestimated coin size, were startling. This work, and a classic investigation of concept attainment strategies (*A Study of Thinking*, NY, 1957), helped to shape cognitive psychology by showing that it was possible to combine a concern for internal mental states such as values and hypotheses with scrupulous experimental methods. After the publication of *The Process of Education* (Harvard, 1960) his reputation as a curriculum innovator grew. In a number of works published in the 1960s he stressed the centrality of teaching for underlying cognitive structure, and the usefulness of the 'spiral curriculum' through which a learner successively re-enters the same domain of knowledge at increasingly deep levels. A landmark in curriculum development is his humanities programme *Man: a Course of Study* (MACOS), described in *Toward a Theory of Instruction* (NY, 1966). Bruner has also pioneered techniques for investigating infant perception, and after his appointment as Watts professor of experimental psychology at the University of Oxford in 1971 he conducted an evaluation of systems of preschool child care. Since returning to Harvard in 1979 he has worked on a new theory of language acquisition.   RRS

Brunhes, Jean (b. Toulouse, Haute-Garonne, France, 25.10.1869; d. Paris, 24.8.1932). French geographer. A pupil of VIDAL DE LA BLACHE, Brunhes pioneered French systematic (as against regional) human geography; he published very widely, however, including work in physical geography, prior to his appointment to the Collège de France in 1912. Brunhes's work emphasized the study of human material artifacts, the theme developed in his *La Géographie humaine* [Human geography] (Paris, 1910). These were studied in the context of the physical environment, which constrained but did not determine decision-making; the concepts which he emphasized in his general geography were *milieu, civilisation, genre de vie* and *circulation* whereas his social geography focused on *travail* and *organisation sociale* (but with little attention to sociological investigations). His main works included *La Géographie de l'histoire* [Historical geography] (with C. Vallaux, Paris, 1921) and *Géographie humaine de la France* [Human geography of France] (vol. 1, with P. Girardin, Paris, 1920; vol. 2, with P. Diffontaines, Paris, 1926).

RJJ

A. Buttimer, *Society and Milieu in the French Geographic Tradition* (Chicago, 1971).

Buber, Martin (b. Vienna, Austria-Hungary [now Austria], 8.2.1878; d. Jerusalem, Israel, 13.6.1965). Austrian/Israeli religious philosopher. His unique contribution to 20c western thought is twofold: he made some of the richest cultural and religious experience available to Gentile culture and Christian theology (Buber, in fact, is more widely read and drawn upon by Christianity than by Jewry); and in the development of his 'I-Thou' spirituality he profoundly influenced subsequent theology and ethics. Buber studied philosophy and the history of art at the universities of Vienna and Berlin, receiving his PhD from Berlin in 1904. In 1898 he had joined the Zionist movement and in 1901 he became editor of the Zionist journal *Die Welt* and subsequently a leader of those Zionists who sought cultural renaissance as opposed to a purely political movement, a position he maintained throughout his life. In 1902 he helped found the Judischer Verlag, a German-Jewish publishing house, and in 1916 the periodical

Der Jude, which became an influential organ of German-speaking Jewry. In 1926 he started a periodical *Die Kreatur* with Protestant and Catholic collaborators during the period (1923–33) that he was teaching Jewish philosophy of religion and, later, the history of religions at the University of Frankfurt. At the same time he was working, with Franz Rosenzweig, on the translation of the Hebrew Bible into German. In 1938 he left Germany for Palestine, where he became professor of social philosophy at the Hebrew University in Jerusalem.

Buber's earliest essays, published in 1900, witness to his deepening immersion in Hasidism (the Jewish mystical tradition enshrined in the postbiblical Kabbala, which had developed in 18c Europe). What particularly attracted Buber was its view that God is to be found in everything and everything in God, and that the created world is to be redeemed rather than escaped. Buber's accounts of Hasidic values are found in *Die Chassidischen Bücher, Gesamtausgabe* (Hellerau, 1928; tr. L. Cohen, *Jewish Mysticism and the Legends of Baalschem*, London, 1931) and *Hasidism* (NY, 1948).

With the publication of *Ich und Du* (Leipzig, 1923; tr. R. G. Smith, *I and Thou*, Edinburgh, 1937) Buber's dialogic philosophy reached its maturity, absorbing many of his earlier ideas. Two primary human attitudes and relations are here defined: I-Thou and I-It. The former is essentially holistic, expressed through mutuality and recognition; I-It describes the objective and functional dimension of human behaviour. The 'It' is named and defined, the 'Thou' is addressed. For Buber, God is the eternal Thou encountered in everyday life and within the soul: 'Every particular Thou is a glimpse through to the eternal Thou.' Buber's views have been widely influential, especially on European Catholics such as MARITAIN and MARCEL, and in the implications of 'I-Thou' for human relations on psychotherapy and educational theory. SED

M. S. Friedman, *Martin Buber: the Life of Dialogue* (London, 1955); P. A. Schlipp & M. Friedman, *The Philosophy of Martin Buber* (La Salle, Ill., 1967).

Büchner, Eduard (b. Munich, Bavaria, Germany, 20.5.1860; d. Focsani, Romania, 24.8.1917). German biochemist. Descendant of an old Bavarian family of scholars, Büchner settled, in 1897, one of the most famous scientific controversies of the 19c, begun by Pasteur and von Liebig, concerning alcoholic fermentation. Büchner demonstrated that the causative agent was a soluble chemical component of yeast cells and not the whole cell itself, by experimentally conducting 'cell-free' fermentation using yeast extracts in solution. Büchner called the active principle 'zymase', and was awarded the 1907 Nobel prize in chemistry for its discovery. Originally labelled 'ferments' after the system where they were first observed – and they are still named that in German – such principles are now called enzymes, and are known to be proteins. The catalytic activity and specificity of enzymes underlie virtually all chemical transformations basic to the living state. Büchner held professorships in chemistry at Tübingen (1896–8), Berlin (1898–1909), Breslau (1909–11) and Würzburg (1911 –17) and was killed on active service in WW1. DOM

Bukharin, Nikolai Ivanovich (b. Moscow, Russia, 9.10.1888; d. Moscow, USSR, 14.3.1938). Russian revolutionary who joined the Russian Social Democratic party in 1906 and in 1908 took charge of the Moscow Bolshevik organization. Arrested in 1910, he escaped abroad. From 1912 he was close to LENIN who criticized him (in 1914) on the national and peasant question, but borrowed from his writings arguments on the economic theory of imperialism and on state capitalism. Bukharin's first book (written in 1914) was a critique of the Austrian school of marginal economics which he denounced as an expression of the interests of the parasitic bourgeoisie. He believed in the disappearance of the state after the revolution, a view also expressed by Lenin in *State and Revolution* (1917), but later was criticized by him for this 'semi-anarchist' position. Returning to Russia after the February revolution of 1917, he supported Lenin's 'April Theses' and became a member of the Central Committee of the Bolshevik party. After the October revolution, he became the editor of *Pravda* (a post he held until 1929), and as the leader of the 'Left Communists' in 1918 criticized Lenin on the question of the Brest Litovsk treaty negotiations, advocating revolutionary war instead. He supported Lenin's policy of 'War Communism', and in his books *Azbuka kommunizma* (with E. Preobrazhensky, Moscow, 1918; *The ABC of Communism*, London, 1924) and *Ekonomika perekhodnovo perioda* (Moscow, 1920; *The Economics of the Transformation Period*, NY, 1971) he propagated the idea that the state should take over all the functions of the market and that the socialist economy should be organized on the basis of militarization of labour and compulsory requisition of agricultural produce.

Bukharin soon abandoned these positions, became a supporter of the New Economic Policy and eventually a leader of the 'Rightist' wing of the party. He sided with STALIN against TROTSKY and opposed the Left opposition's idea of 'super-industrialization' which he considered unrealistic and dangerous since it provoked the hostility of the peasantry. He turned against Stalin when the latter adopted this policy in 1928. Together with Rykov and Tomsky, Bukharin then constituted the Right opposition, trying in vain to prevent the policy (inaugurated in 1929) of collectivization and to stop the subsequent 'industrialization at breakneck speed', which was accompanied by a policy of coercion and terror. As a result Bukharin and his followers were purged from all their posts. Bukharin himself remained a member of the Central Committee (though not of the Politburo) and – after further penance – he even became the editor of *Izvestiya* in 1934. He was the chairman of the commission which produced the draft of the 1936 'Stalinist Constitution', but soon after its official proclamation was arrested (in February 1937) and shot. He became a model for Rubashov, the hero of KOESTLER's novel *Darkness at Noon* (1940). In spite of the efforts of his son and the support of some western Communist parties, he has not been officially rehabilitated in the USSR. LL

S. F. Cohen, *Bukharin and the Bolshevik Revolution: a Political Biography 1888–1938* (NY, 1973).

Bulgakov, Mikhail Afanas'evich (b. Kiev, Russia, 15.5.1891; d. Moscow, USSR, 10.3.1940). Russian novelist and dramatist. Bulgakov died virtually forgotten; today he is not only internationally respected but very fashionable in the USSR. The eldest son of a professor of divinity at Kiev Theological Academy, he studied medicine at Kiev University and briefly practised as a country doctor (1916–18). In 1919 he abandoned medicine and went to the Caucasus where he wrote stories for newspapers and plays for local theatres. In 1921 he settled in Moscow and for the next three years worked as a journalist. In 1925 two parts of his novel *Belaya gvardiya* (Moscow, 1925; tr. M. Glenny, *The White Guard*, NY, 1971) were published; at the request of the Moscow Art Theatre he dramatized it as *Dni Turbinych* [The days of the Turbins] (1926). The play brought the author overnight success and became 'a new *Seagull* for the new generation', although it received hundreds of hostile reviews for the sympathetic portrayal of White officers. He dedicated his next few years to MAT as dramatist, director and actor. His new plays, and especially *Beg* [The flight] (1928), were harshly criticized, and from 1929 all of his plays were banned. Deprived of all means of support, he appealed to the Soviet government, and as a result of STALIN's personal intervention he was invited to join the staff of MAT. *Dni Turbinych* was hastily resurrected and proved very popular. His next play *Mol'ere* [Molière] (written 1930) was an obvious parallel to Bulgakov's own treatment by the censorship. The rehearsals lasted four years (during which time – 1932–6 – Bulgakov wrote his brilliant biography of Molière, *Molodaya Gvardiya* [The young guard], not published until 1962) and after seven nights' run the play was banned. With the other new plays neither published nor staged, this was the end of his love-hate relationship with MAT, which he described in *Tetralnyi roman* (Moscow, 1965; written 1936–7; tr. M. Glenny, *Black Show, a*

Theatrical Novel, NY, 1967) as his revenge on STANISLAVSKY for the failure of *Mol'ere*. From 1928 to 1940 he was working on his masterpiece – which exists in eight versions – *Master i Margarita* (Moscow, 1966; tr. M. Glenny, *The Master and Margarita*, NY, 1967), although by 1938 he was incurably ill and in 1939 blindness forced him to dictate further changes to his wife. This extraordinary novel about a novel asserts Bulgakov's belief that art is the only way of travelling through time. It combines many-levelled irony, uncontrolled fantasy with subtle psychological observation and paradoxical contrasts. Examining a series of philosophical and religious problems, it interconnects two epicentres of events – the intrusion of the devil into the life of modern Moscow and the crucifixion of Christ – in an elaborate system of imagery, parallel events and universal themes. In this novel Bulgakov found the form most appropriate to his talent.

VP

E. Mahlow, *Bulgakov's 'The Master and Margarita': the Text as Cipher* (NY, 1975); A. C. Wright, *M. Bulgakov: Life and Interpretations* (London, 1978).

Bultmann, Rudolf Karl (b. Oldenburg, Lower Saxony, Germany, 20.8.1884; d. Marburg, Hesse, West Germany, 30.7.1976). German Lutheran theologian, professor of New Testament studies at Marburg (1921–51), then emeritus professor. As a pioneer of form criticism (i.e. an analysis principally of the first three gospels which identifies different types of literary unit), Bultmann held that the gospels were a patchwork of traditional elements united by the evangelist (*Die Geschichte der synoptischen Tradition*, Göttingen, 1921; tr. J. Marsh, *History of the Synoptic Tradition*, Oxford, 1963). These units represent the beliefs of the church at the time the gospels were composed, rather than the original teaching of Jesus. The gospels, then, are a form of preaching (*kerygma*) presented in the framework of historical narrative. Bultmann expressed his scepticism about what we can know of Jesus of Nazareth in an early work *Jesus* (Berlin, 1926; tr. L. P. Smith & E. H. Lantero, *Jesus and the Word*, NY, 1934).

He later claimed that all we need to know about Jesus was that he lived and preached; Bultmann never revised the substance of his early ideas.

Influenced by the early HEIDEGGER, who was a colleague at Marburg in the 1920s, Bultmann saw man as a questioning being in search of self-understanding and affirmed that only the New Testament provides authentic answers to questions about the basis of human existence. Like BARTH, he never attempted to substantiate this positivistic claim on behalf of 'the Word of God'. Bultmann developed a kerygmatic theology in which the historicality of the earthly Jesus is largely bypassed, while attention is focused on the existential significance of the preached Christ for the hearer, who must respond in the ever-present moment with faith (characterized as 'decision'). Similarly, traditional Christian assertions about the future are seen as primitive mythological statements about present existence. In his 'existential interpretation of the New Testament', Bultmann recognized that not all the early *kerygma* directly concerns present existence. We find there a primitive religious world of miracles, resurrection, heaven, hell and so on. Such ideas are labelled 'myth', and Bultmann is best known for his notion of *Entmythologisierung*, or 'demythologizing programme' ('Neues Testament und Mythologie' in *Kerygma und Mythos*, Hamburg, 1948; tr. R. H. Fuller, 'New Testament and Mythology' in *Kerygma and Myth*, ed. H.-W. Bartsch, London, 1953). These 'myths' which seem not to concern human existence must not be discounted but interpreted existentially.

Bultmann's major works include *Theologie des Neuen Testaments* (3 vols, Tübingen, 1948–53; tr. K. Grobel, *Theology of the New Testament*, 2 vols, NY, 1951–5) and his collected articles *Glauben und Verstehen* (4 vols, Tübingen, 1933–65; vol. 1, tr. L. P. Smith, *Faith and Understanding*, London, 1969; vol. 2, tr. J. C. G. Greig, *Essays Philosophical and Theological*, London, 1955). A dominating influence in the 1950s and 1960s, Bultmann is now regarded more critically, as excessively individualistic, nonpolitical and nonhistorical. His influ-

ence in theology has receded with the fading fortunes of existentialism generally.   GT

W. Schmithals, *An Introduction to the Theology of Rudolf Bultmann*, tr. J. Bowden (London, 1968); R. C. Roberts, *Rudolf Bultmann's Theology* (Michigan, 1976).

Bunin, Ivan Alekseyevich (b. Voronezh, Russia, 10.10.1870; d. Paris, France, 8.11.1953). Russian poet, short-story writer and novelist, last important representative of 19c Russian literature. Although he lived and wrote until the middle of the 20c (the last 35 years as an émigré), Bunin's work is in the 'classical' tradition of Turgenev, Goncharov and Leo TOLSTOY. He was born into a family of country gentry and this milieu provided the context for most of his characteristic writings. Ironically, he joined originally the GORKY group of proletarian and revolutionary writers, associated with the Znanie publishing house, but politics as such never entered into his subject matter. His mood remained apolitical even when he took an anti-Bolshevik position in 1917 and left the USSR in 1918, or when he arranged, shortly before his death, to have his works published in the USSR and all his papers transferred to Moscow. In 1933 he won the Nobel prize for literature after a years-long campaign he conducted on his own behalf. He began his literary career as a poet in a nonmodernist mode, and his prose, especially his early prose *Antonovskie yabloki* [Antonov apples] (Moscow, 1900), is 'lyrical'. The lyricism is controlled and somewhat frigid. Balance, sense of proportion, even immobility, and an attachment to the visible world of things are characteristic features of his work as a whole. Behind it there peers a fastidious romantic, who sees too much to justify either facile optimism or furious pessimism. However, Bunin's early short novel *Derevnya* (Moscow, 1910; tr. I. F. Hapgood, *The Village*, London, 1923) is one of the gloomiest books about the Russian countryside and the poverty-stricken, savage life of the Russian peasantry. Hardly less gloomy, and of greater artistic merit, is *Sukhodol* [Dry valley] (Moscow, 1912), in which the author gives a picture of disintegrating manor life from the point of view of a female servant. Russia, mainly rural Russia, is Bunin's pervasive theme, although a number of stories deal with distant lands and one, *Gospodin iz San Franzisko* (Moscow, 1916; tr. D. H. LAWRENCE *et al.*, *The Gentleman from San Francisco*, London, 1922), the best known abroad of his works and an undoubted masterpiece, is a satire on western bourgeois civilization. Without being 'tendentious', it is imbued with sarcasm against the power of money. Bunin's postrevolutionary work is entirely subsumed by Russian themes. *Mitina lyubov'* (Moscow, 1925; tr. M. Boyd, *Mitya's Love*, London, 1926), an ageless love story, and especially the autobiographical *Zhizn' Arsenieva* [The life of Arseniev] (2 vols, Moscow, 1930) and its sequel *Lika* (Moscow, 1939) are exercises, typical of the older generation of Russian émigré writers, in 'the art of embalming'. But Bunin did the 'embalming' with extraordinary artistic skill and restraint. His judgement of his own work was: 'I think I was a good craftsman.' EL

O. Mikhailov, *Ivan Alekseevich Bunin* (Moscow, 1967); J. Woodward, *Ivan Bunin: a Study of His Fiction* (North Carolina, 1980).

Bunshaft, Gordon (b. Buffalo, NY, USA, 9.5.1909). American architect. Bunshaft was for 30 years the design force behind Skidmore Owings & Merrill, one of the largest and most prolific architectural practices in the USA. A tough-minded and forceful modernist, he was largely responsible for the adoption by corporate America of the minimalist aesthetics of steel and glass high-rise slabs. He took the elements of MIES VAN DER ROHE's work and turned them into a more commercially acceptable form. Bunshaft's Lever House in New York (1952), a slender glass slab rising out of a lower block at right angles to it and set back across a plaza from the street, became the model for countless imitations, with disastrous results for the skylines of cities all over the world. In later years Bunshaft adopted a more massively monumental approach, using mar-

ble for his Yale University library (1958) and masonry for the Hirshhorn Museum in Washington (1974). Neither enjoyed the critical acclaim of Lever House. Bunshaft's presence was a major factor in the success of Skidmore Owings & Merrill, a firm which is responsible for the design of the Sears Roebuck Tower in Chicago (1974), the world's tallest building. DS

Buñuel, Luis (b. Calanda, Ternel, Spain, 22.2.1900). Spanish surrealist film maker who made his name in Paris – initially through collaboration with DALI – in the late 1920s. *Un Chien Andalou* [An Andalusian dog] (1928) and *L'Age d'Or* [The golden age] (1930) are among the rare avant-garde works of the period to retain the power to shock, while *Las Hurdas* (*Land Without Bread*, 1932) has lost none of its documentary power. Buñuel re-emerged as a world-class director in Mexico, where he settled in 1946, with a series of brutally realistic social studies, from *Los Olvidados* (*The Young and the Damned*, 1950) to *Nazarin* (1959). The characteristic works of his maturity, following his subsequent return to Europe, are the more relaxed studies of the contradictions of bourgeois behaviour told with a delightful refusal to follow the rules of conventional bourgeois cinema typified by *Belle de Jour* (1967), *Tristana* (1970) and *Le Charme discret de la Bourgeoisie* (*The Discreet Charm of the Bourgeoisie*, 1972).

Although most of Buñuel's career has been spent in exile from his native Spain, his work has a total consistency of purpose. Proving himself a master of the art of involving an audience in a fictional narrative, he has also retained into his 70s a fascination with every aspect of film language. All his major films are explorations of some aspect of this: the cut in *Un Chien Andalou*, the realism of the image in *Los Olvidados*, the interplay of reality and imagination in *Belle de Jour* and, most extreme of all, perhaps, the very concept of the unified fictional character in *Cet obscur Objet du Désir* (*That Obscure Object of Desire*, 1977) made at the age of 77, where the heroine is played by two actresses. RPA

F. Aranda, *Luis Buñuel: a Critical Biography* (London, 1975); J. Mellen, *The World of Luis Buñuel* (NY, 1978).

Burke, Kenneth Duya (b. Pittsburgh, Pa, USA, 5.5.1897). American literary critic and philosopher. After short periods of study at Ohio State and Columbia universities, Burke joined the postwar avant-garde of American writers in Greenwich Village, New York, in 1918. There he began eight years of association with the influential journal the *Dial*, most notably as a music critic. After the demise of the *Dial* in 1929, Burke devoted himself almost entirely to literary criticism and critical theory, developing a critical position noted for its iconoclasm, philosophical rigour and intellectual range. Neither a New Critic nor a formalist his work is characterized both by a careful attentiveness to textual and semantic features and a concern with scheme and argument in a work of art. *Counter-Statement* (NY, 1931) established Burke's interest in the rhetorical analysis of literary works and their status as modes of revelation. *The Philosophy of Literary Form* (Baton Rouge, 1941) argues Burke's concept of works of literature as forms of symbolic action, ritual strategies that enable authors to deal with the 'dramatic situations' about which they write. *Language as Symbolic Action* (Berkeley, 1966) brings together a number of important essays on drama, poetry and mythology which indicate the vitality and intellectual breadth of Burke's thinking.   GHC

S. E. Hyman, *The Armed Vision* (NY, 1948); A. P. Frank, *Kenneth Burke* (NY, 1969).

Burnet, Frank Macfarlane (b. Traralgon, Victoria, Australia, 3.9.1899). Australian medical scientist. Burnet trained in medicine in Melbourne and most of his research career has been spent there, at the Walter and Eliza Hall Institute for Medical Research of which he became director in 1944. Distinguished work on the immunology of typhoid fever and of influenza (summarized in his *The Natural History of Infectious Disease*, Cambridge, 1953) brought him an international reputation. His greatest influence, however, followed his theoretical and practical work on the ways in which animals, including man, differentiate between cells or cell-products which are 'self' (and which they are well advised to tolerate) and those which are 'not self' (which they may attack with immunological weapons). Since one individual's 'self' is another's 'not self' the problem is not a simple one. It is of obvious importance to medicine in the practice of organ or tissue transplantation, but it also has implications for so-called autoimmune diseases and for the natural control of cancers. Burnet's views received support from the experiments of MEDAWAR and his colleagues and he shared a Nobel prize with Medawar in 1960. Among his books *The Clonal Selection Theory of Acquired Immunity* (Cambridge, 1959) was, perhaps, the most influential, but he has also written on the wider issues of biomedical science, e.g. in *Genes, Dreams and Realities* (Aylesbury, 1971).
                                              DRN

Burroughs, William Seward (b. St Louis, Mo., USA, 5.2.1914). American novelist. While Allen GINSBERG's *Howl* (1956) and KEROUAC's *On the Road* (1957) were establishing the myth of the Beat generation, the myth within the myth, the *éminence grise* and the guru of the Beats was Burroughs. The publication of *The Naked Lunch* in Paris in 1959 confirmed Burroughs's cult status. As with JOYCE and Henry MILLER, changes in social and cultural *mores* made commercial publication in America a possibility. Drug addiction, graphically described in *Junkie* (NY, 1953), gave his imaginative world shape and meaning. Physical violence, homosexuality and paranoia fill out the space which remained. The novels of Henry Miller, so notorious in their day, seem sweet and humane beside Burroughs's sick aggressions. The disjointed and surrealistic techniques employed in his books are admired by some critics, who look to Burroughs as a wise prophetic sage.   EH

M. B. Goodman, *Burroughs* (NY, 1975).

Burt, Cyril Lodowic (b. Stratford-on-Avon, Warwicks., UK, 3.3.1883; d. London, 10.10.1971). British psychologist. After receiving a DSc from Oxford University in 1906, he served as a clinical psychologist in the first official British child guidance clinic, and was an educational psychologist to the London County Council between 1913 and 1932. His last academic position was professor of psychology at University College, London, from 1931 to 1950. His academic interests were diverse, and included the inheritance of intelligence, mental testing, statistical techniques, as well as the problems of special groups such as delinquents, neurotics, the gifted and the subnormal. The unifying theme running through these topics is Burt's consuming interest in individual differences, and his belief that the study of individuality was fundamental to the development of general psychology. His first important book was *The Young Delinquent* (London, 1925), in which he argued that delinquency is caused mainly by environmental factors such as overcrowding, broken homes and lack of recreational facilities. In the 1930s Burt was one of those who developed factor analysis, a statistical technique which is still used in the description of the structure of intelligence and personality. His work in this area led him to write an influential work *The Factors of the Mind* (London, 1940). In spite of his major contributions to differential psychology, his reputation has been somewhat tarnished by the revelation that some of his findings on the importance of heredity in intelligence were fraudulent. Ironically, his conclusions are supported by the evidence of other researchers.　MWE

Busoni, Ferruccio Benvenuto (b. Empoli, Tuscany, Italy, 1.4.1866; d. Berlin, Germany, 27.7.1924). Italian composer and pianist. He studied in his mother's country, Austria, and from 1894 lived mainly in Berlin, though he continued to travel widely as a piano recitalist. He also conducted concerts of new music including his own. As a composer Busoni aimed first at a synthesis of past and present musical techniques which he summed up in the phrase 'young classicism'; to this period of his life belongs the Piano Concerto (1904), a five-movement work lasting over an hour and with a choral finale for male voices.

With his seven *Elegies* (1907) for piano solo he passed what he himself saw as a turning point and ventured into new realms that departed from the traditional key system, for example in his Sonatina No. 2 (1912) for piano. By this time he had also published his *Entwurf einer neuen Asthetik der Tonkunst* (Trieste, 1907; *Sketch of a New Aesthetic of Music*, in *Three Classics in the Aesthetic of Music*, NY, 1962) in which he imagined the use of third-of-a-tone intervals and other such innovations; however, these radical ideas did not find realization in his compositions. He was concerned also with the relationship between music and drama, and his unfinished opera *Doktor Faust* (completed by his pupil Jarnach), on which he was working until his death, is perhaps his masterpiece. Too intellectual to achieve incontestable greatness, Busoni has nonetheless his place in this century's music.　CH

Butenandt, Adolf Frederick Johann (b. Bremerhaven, Lower Saxony, Germany, 24.3.1903). German organic chemist. Butenandt studied chemistry at Marburg University and at Göttingen under WINDAUS. From 1936 to 1960 he was professor in Berlin and director of the Max Planck Institute for Biochemistry, Berlin-Dahlem (later in Tübingen, then in Munich). Butenandt's main work was in the field of the chemistry of steroidal sex hormones. In 1929 he isolated pure crystalline oestrone (almost simultaneously with E. A. Doisy in the USA), confirmed Marrian's discovery of oestriol (1930) in 1931, and obtained pure crystalline androsterone, from which, in 1939, he prepared testosterone (also so prepared independently by RUŽIČKA). Testosterone had been isolated from testes in 1935. Progesterone was also isolated pure from corpus luteum by Butenandt in 1934, and in addition he studied widely the chemical constitutions and interrelationships of sex hormones. In a little over a decade the main architecture of sex-hormone chemistry had been established. This work on sex hormones formed the basis from which a large-scale production of the drug cortisone was developed. Butenandt has received many honours and distinctions including the Nobel prize for chemistry (jointly with L. Ružička) in 1939.   NBC

Butor, Michel Marie François (b. Mons-en-Baroeul, Nord, France, 14.9.1920). French novelist and essayist. Frequently associated with ROBBE-GRILLET, Butor adopts a highly original and experimental attitude to novel writing. His best novel *La Modification* (Paris, 1957; tr. J. Stewart, *Second Thoughts*, London, 1958) is told throughout in the second person plural. The narrator talks to himself during a train journey from Paris to Rome before eventually deciding that he will not, after all, leave his wife for his mistress. Instead, he elects to write a book that will become *La Modification*. Like the other French *nouveaux romanciers* of the 1950s, Butor is very interested in physical objects, the most banal of which he considers can be made poetic by being inserted into a sufficiently rigorous structure. In 1965 he wrote a splendid description of the unbanal Niagara Falls, *6,810,000 litres d'eau par seconde, étude stéréophonique* [A stereophonic study] (Paris, 1965). This was originally commissioned by Radio Stuttgart and produced to inaugurate the Maison de la Culture at Grenoble. Butor has published four volumes of criticism (*Répertoire* [Repertory],

Paris, 1960–74) dealing with a wide variety of writers and artists.   PMWT

G. Gaillard, *Butor* (Paris, 1968); M. A. Grant, *Michel Butor: 'l'Emploi du Temps'* (London, 1973).

Buzzati, Dino (b. Belluno, Veneto, Italy, 16.10.1906; d. Milan, Lombardy, 28.1.1972). Italian novelist. A journalist with the *Corriere della Sera*, Buzzati became well known with the publication of his best novel *Il deserto dei Tartari* (Milan, 1940; tr. S. C. Hood, *The Tartar Steppe*, NY, 1965), which is at once realistic and allegorical and which has led critics to regard him as an 'Italian KAFKA'. Buzzati's other novels – *Il grande ritratto* (Milan, 1960; tr. H. Reed, *Larger Than Life*, London, 1962), a science fiction novel; *Un amore* (Milan, 1963; tr. J. Green, *A Love Affair*, London, 1965) and *Poema a fumetti* [Cartoon poems] (Milan, 1969) – are attempts at experimenting with new narrative forms and techniques as well as with new themes. Buzzati is also the author of a book of short stories *Sessanta racconti* (Milan, 1958; tr. J. Landry & C. Jolly, *Catastrophe: the Strange Stories of Dino Buzzati*, London, 1965) for which he was awarded the Strega prize for literature in 1958.   GS

C

Cabral, Amilcar (b. Bafata, Portuguese Guinea [now Guiné-Bissau], 12.9.1924; d. Conakry, 20.1.1973). The revolutionary leader of Guiné-Bissau, Cabral established an international reputation as a practitioner and theoretician of revolution. Trained as an agronomist at Lisbon University, he entered the colonial service and laid the foundations of his intimate knowledge of his country by organizing its first agricultural census. In 1956 he was one of the founders of the PAIGC (African Independence party of Guiné-Bissau and Cape Verde). Finding that peaceful demonstrations were useless in the face of Portuguese repression, party militants led by Cabral planned a guerrilla war which began in 1964. In 1973 Cabral was assassinated in a plot instigated by the Portuguese; shortly afterwards the PAIGC, by now in control of two-thirds of their country's territory, proclaimed its independence. The strength of Cabral's revolutionary theory was its rigorous practicality. He defined the 'national liberation struggle' as the process whereby a people 'regained their historical personality' which had been distorted by colonialism; but it was essential for the struggle to bring 'real improvements in the conditions of life' of ordinary people. Each people would have to work out its own formula for the struggle: in Guiné-Bissau leadership would be provided by the 'revolutionary petty-bourgeoisie' whose members must be prepared 'to commit suicide as a class' by identifying themselves completely with the peasant masses. The revolutionary party would become the state; it would also 'be the people'. The successful outcome of the guerrilla war was practical vindication of Cabral's ideas.   RH

A. Cabral, *Return to the Source: Selected Speeches* (NY, 1973).

Cabral de Melo Neto, João (b. Recife, Brazil, 9.1.1920). Brazilian poet. Brazilian writers in the 1940s to 1960s were influenced by the movement of modernism, initiated by the famous week of modern art in São Paulo in 1922, to turn away from the Europe of 1914–18 to make fresh contacts in the postwar climate; above all, to seek a national conscience and literature. João Neto came in the wake of this movement. He studied in Rio and entered the diplomatic service. He lived abroad, especially in Spain, and the collection *Paisagens e figuras* [Landscapes and figures] (Rio de Janeiro, 1954) captures the spirit of many places. He accepts the discipline of metre and rhyme which structures *Morte e vida severina* [Death and life of Severino] (1955), the haunting nativity play set in his own region of Pernambuco with its social problems.
                    DBr

Cage, John (b. Los Angeles, Calif., USA, 15.9.1912). American composer. Cage was one of SCHOENBERG's first American pupils but he was more influenced by COWELL's experimental approach. In 1938 he invented the 'prepared piano', a piano converted into a noise instrument by the insertion of objects between the strings; in 1939 he produced the first example of live electronic music, his *Imaginary Landscape no. 1*, with two players operating gramophones. All his later music has been similarly independent of the European tradition. At first he used systematic rhythmic procedures more akin to eastern styles (particularly Balinese gamelan playing) than to western music. Then, under the influence of Zen Buddhism, he came to place greatest value on the purposeless, the directionless and even the silent: his notorious *4′ 33″* (1952) requires the player to give a soundless performance for that duration. During the next few years his many works gave the performers considerable freedom; his scores sometimes consisted of highly ambiguous graphic designs. The minimal material of *Variations IV* (1963), for instance, can be interpreted with any performed or recorded sounds whatever, while other works of the

CAJAL

period embrace not only a sonic clutter but elements of theatre. Cage's works and ideas have had enormous influence in Europe and America since the mid-1950s. Most of his important writings are in *Silence* (Middletown, 1961), *A Year from Monday* (Middletown, 1967) and *M* (Middletown, 1973). PG

R. Kostelanetz (ed.), *John Cage* (London, 1971); M. Nyman, *Experimental Music* (London, 1974).

Cajal, Santiago Ramon y (b. Petilla de Aragon, Navarra, Spain, 1.5.1852; d. Madrid, 17.10.1934). Spanish histologist. After taking his degree in medicine at Zaragoza University in 1873, Cajal joined the Spanish army as a medical officer, serving in Cuba during the Spanish-American war. By 1884 he was professor of anatomy at Valencia University, moving to the University of Barcelona in 1887. To illustrate his work Cajal mastered lithography and he was probably the first person in Spain to combine text with photographic illustrations. In his pathological research he was able to display the structure of individual cells and the contact of dendrites with adjacent cells by modifying a hitherto unreliable method of staining. This new staining technique also provided for long-distance tracing of axons to other parts of the brain or junction with other nerve bundles. Conscious of his isolation Cajal used his savings to attend a meeting of the Anatomical Society in Berlin in 1889. Although his paper, delivered in French, aroused little comment his histological preparations attracted great interest and in 1894 he was invited to give the Royal Society's Cronian lecture. From 1892 he held the chair of histology at Madrid University, and in 1906 he received the Nobel prize for medicine, shared with Camilo Golgi. Extensive studies of the brain, cerebellum, ganglia and spinal cord had led Cajal to formulate the neuronal theory which underlies modern neurophysiology. Based on the individuality of the nerve cell, this concept replaced the older view of a reticular system of nerve channels through which impulses were distributed. The results of Cajal's monumental work were published in *Histologie du système nerveux de l'homme et des vertébrées* [Histology of the human and vertebrate nervous system] (2 vols, Madrid, 1952) in a French translation illustrated by some 1000 of the author's drawings. Between 1905 and 1913 he made an intensive study of Wallerian degeneration and regeneration of nervous tissue: *Degeneration and Regeneration of the Nervous System* (Oxford, 1928). He also wrote an autobiography *Recuerdos de mi vida* (Madrid, 1917; *Recollections of My Life*, Philadelphia, 1937). ADVB

H. Williams, *Don Quixote of the Microscope* (London, 1954).

Calder, Alexander (b. Philadelphia, Pa, USA, 22.7.1898; d. New York, 11.11.1976). American sculptor. Calder trained as an engineer before enrolling at the Art Students' League school in New York in 1923, where he produced humorous drawings, drawings of animals, and paintings. His first sculptures, wood carvings, date from 1926, shortly before he went to France. He spent most of the next seven years in Paris. Many leading abstract artists came to his studio to see performances of his miniature puppet-circus, using figures and animals he had made from wire and string. These led to his first wire sculptures: portraits, animals and figurative groups (e.g. *Romulus and Remus*, 1928). After meeting MONDRIAN (1930), he began to make nonobjective constructions, described later by ARP as 'stabiles'. Curious to see the effect of Mondrian's static rectangles set in motion, he used his engineering knowledge to make (from 1932) manual and motorized 'mobiles' – as they were dubbed by DUCHAMP. These were geometric elements of varying shapes, sizes and colours (mostly black and primary colours), linked to a main axis yet free to move independently, thus creating a constantly shifting pattern of solids in space. Calder later made wind-driven mobiles which permitted a more arbitrary, natural movement. He spent the next 20 years developing the potential of stabiles and mobiles in works that combined verve with weightlessness and delicacy (e.g. *Little Spider*, c. 1940). From the late 1930s his shapes reveal the influence of MIRÓ's abstract-organic forms (e.g. *Mobile*, 1963). The scale increased as many of his later works were intended for outdoor sites. In the 1950s and 1960s he made numerous stabiles, many opposed to the weightless whimsicality of the mobiles, and at times even threatening (e.g. *Three Arches*, 1963). Calder's inspiration was essentially biomorphic, even in the colossal stabiles and mobiles commissioned for state and commercial institutions in the 1970s, the largest of which, *Teodelapio*, a 60-ft-high stabile, was installed at a road junction in Spoleto, Italy, in 1962.   SOBT

H. H. Arnason & P. E. Guerrero, *Calder* (Princeton, 1966).

Callas, Maria, *née* Calogeropoulou (b. New York, USA, 2.12.1923; naturalized Greek citizen, 1966; d. Paris, France, 16.9.1977). American/Greek soprano. Among operatic singers she stands as the very epitome of the *diva* or *prima donna*. Her parents were Greek, and despite her American birth her studies and early career were all in Europe. Her debut, at the Athens Opera in 1941, was in the title role of PUCCINI's *Tosca*, an opera which she later recorded and in which she achieved many triumphs. It is tempting to identify her with that role, of a beautiful and temperamental singer living for love and for her art, but that would be to limit her range, which included Wagnerian roles like Isolde and Brünnhilde and the title roles of Cherubini's *Medea* and Donizetti's *Lucia di Lammermoor*. Indeed Callas encompassed both the Wagnerian and the Italian coloratura repertory. Critics often claimed that her voice, judged purely as a beautiful instrument, was not flawless; but her musical insight and stage presence were inimitable and made her a household name. She is one of the very few singers of whom one would use the word genius.   CH

J. Ardoin & G. Fitzgerald, *Callas* (NY, 1974).

Calvin, Melvin (b. St Paul, Minn., USA, 8.4.1911). American chemist. Unusually for a modern scientist, Calvin has made important contributions to all branches of chemistry, including biochemistry. In 1961 he was awarded the Nobel prize for elucidating the chemical pathways of photosynthesis (the processes by which plants use the carbon in carbon-dioxide to manufacture substances necessary for their growth). He fed radioactive carbon-dioxide to plants for very short periods of time and by sophisticated analytical techniques, including the newly developed chromatography, identified the compounds in which it was first incorporated. He showed that photosynthesis involved a cycle of chemical reactions in which a phosphorylated organic acid, phosphoglyceric acid, played a key role. In 1957, with J. A. Bassham, he described these results in *Path of Carbon in Photosynthesis* (NY). More recently he investigated those plants which produce materials from which petroleum-like products can be extracted. The economics of the plantations he established suggested that such plants could make an important contribution to the world's energy requirements. He has also investigated the traces of organic matter in ancient rocks and has discussed the results in terms of chemical evolution and, more widely, the origin of life in his book *Chemical Evolution* (Oxford, 1961). Calvin was educated at the Michigan College of Mining and Technology, and received a doctorate from Minnesota in 1935 for researches in physical chemistry. After a year at the University of Manchester with POLYANI, he joined the faculty of chemistry at Berkeley in 1937. Since 1960, as director of the Laboratory of Chemical Biodynamics, he has been associated with its wide range of research activities, including those into neurophysiology and carcinogenesis. EBS

Calvino, Italo (b. Santiago de Las Vegas, Cuba, 15.10.1923). Italian writer. An original blend of seriousness and humour, profundity and crystal-clear readability gives Calvino's fiction a unique position in contemporary Italian literature. His main achievement lies in the forced coexistence of opposites, resulting in a precarious yet fascinating balance between apparently irreconcilable extremes which runs consistently through his career, from the crude realities of guerrilla war seen through the myth-creating eyes of a child-partisan, through the geometric precision of his allegorical characters in wild historical fantasies (*I nostri antenati*, Turin, 1960; tr. A. Colquhoun, *Our Ancestors*, London, 1980), to the marriage of cosmology and comic fantasies. More recently, after the use of the tarot cards for a structuralist game (*Il castello dei destini incrociati*, Turin, 1973; tr. W. Weaver, *The Castle of Crossed Destinies*, NY, 1976) and Marco Polo's two-sided accounts of imaginary cities to a rationalizing Kubla Khan (*Le Citte invisibili*, Turin, 1972; tr. W. Weaver, *Invisible Cities*, NY, 1974), with the adventures of a reader who can never complete the novels he begins (*Se una notte d'inverno un viaggiatore*, Turin, 1979; tr. W. Weaver, *If on a Winter's Night a Traveller*, London, 1981), literature in the computer age is shown as opposed and equal to the archetypal model of the *Arabian Nights*.   RTa

Camara, Helder Pessoa (b. Fortaleza, Ceará, Brazil, 7.2.1909). Brazilian theologian and Roman Catholic archbishop of Olinda and Recife, Brazil, since 1964. Much influenced by M. GANDHI, Camara recommends the 'violence of the pacifist' in an attempt to change economic and political structures in underdeveloped countries. Violent and oppressive governments must be subjected to 'liberating moral pressure' in the pursuit of justice, for violence must be eschewed. Ultimately 'justice is the condition of peace' and this demands the removal of 'internal colonialism' where a nation's wealth is controlled by a small minority. Camara organized the Brazilian Conference of Bishops in the 1950s and was the first vice-president of the Latin American Bishops' Conference (CELAM). Under his influence there has been a radical realignment of the Latin American Catholic churches in favour of a vigorous defence of the poor, despite fierce conservative opposition. His ideas, simple and unelaborated, are to be found in a series of lectures, chiefly *Terra Mondo Defraudato* (Turin, 1968; *Church and Colonialism*, London, 1969) and *Spirale de Violence* (Brussels, 1970; *Spiral of Violence*, London, 1971). 'Liberation theology', a peculiarly Latin American phenomenon, has followed in

his wake. Camara has received several peace prizes, but was denied a Nobel prize in 1970 after opposition from the Brazilian and US governments.   GT

J. de Broucker, *The Violence of a Peacemaker* (NY, 1970).

Cambridge Group. The Cambridge Group for the History of Population and Social Structure was founded in 1964 by Thomas Peter Ruffell Laslett (b. Bedford, 18.12.1915) while he was finishing a book on English society before industrialization, *The World We have Lost* (London, 1965), and by his former pupil Edward Anthony Wrigley (b. Manchester, 17.8.1931), who had written his thesis on *Industrial Growth and Population Change* (Cambridge, 1961). An interim account was drawn up in E. A. Wrigley (ed.), *An Introduction to English Historical Demography* (London, 1966). The Group's original work consisted of the private research of its founders: Wrigley, on family limitation and mortality in the Devonshire village of Colyton; and Laslett, on household composition and other social features of Clayworth in Nottinghamshire. It was enormously expanded almost at once by the unpaid assistance of volunteers exploiting local parish registers for aggregative information. Grants from the Gulbenkian Foundation and the Social Science Research Council provided for research assistance, and in 1974 the Group became an independent unit of the SSRC of London. From the first there was close collaboration with HENRY and other demographers working on these lines in France and elsewhere. In 1969 an international conference was held on household size and structure, published as P. Laslett & R. Wall (eds), *Household and Family in Past Time* (Cambridge, 1972). The Group's third director Roger Schofield (b. Leeds, Yorks., 26.8.1937), who joined in 1966, has specialized in the development of methods of analysis in historical demography and has also been concerned with the measurement of literacy.   UPB

Campana, Dino (b. Marradi, Tuscany, Italy, 20.8.1885; d. Scandicci, nr Florence, Tuscany, 1.3.1932). Italian poet who studied chemistry and pharmacy intermittently between 1906 and 1913 at Bologna and Florence between bouts of madness, and in the same period travelled widely over Europe and the Americas, gaining for himself the reputation of an Italian Rimbaud. He published his one volume of poetry *Canti orfici* (Marradi, 1914; tr. I. L. Salomon, *Orphic Songs*, NY, 1968) as a private venture and hawked copies around the cafés of Florence and Bologna. He also contributed to various avant-garde periodicals like *La Voce* or *La riviera ligure*. He had a somewhat agitated love affair with the poetess Sibilla Aleramo in 1916–17, but in 1918 was permanently confined to the asylum of Castel Pulci where he eventually died. His *Canti orfici* is a highly fragmented collection which has been expanded in successive editions by further verse and prose fragments drawn from his notebooks. Nowhere does he define his orphism clearly but his lyrical practice does adumbrate a new form of orphic insight, a cumulative aesthetico-historical perspective of mankind's cultural development. The dynamic plasticity of his imagery thus contrasts with the largely static visions of ancient orphism. In particular he uses colour and word-music to attain a form of dynamic recession from reality to myth; often the various stages of such recessions are colour-punctuated. He was influenced by the avant-garde painters of his day, especially the fauvistes and the orphic painting of DELAUNAY, in whom colour also predominates over form. Campana's own influence has been mainly an Italian phenomenon and was considerable on the hermetic movement between the two world wars.　FJJ

Maura del Serra, *L'immagine aperta* (Florence, 1973); F. J. Jones, *La poesia italiana contemporanea* (Florence, 1975).

Campbell, Royston Dunnachie (Roy) (b. Durban, Natal, South Africa, 2.10.1901; d. Lisbon, Portugal, 23.4.1957). South African poet whose 15 principal collections of poetry established him as a prominent writer on the fringes of English political and religious debate in the 1930s. Campbell went to Oxford in 1918, but after a year gave up the idea of an academic career, turning instead

to the pursuit of a literary life in London in the company of ELIOT, the Sitwells and Wyndham LEWIS. His first long poem *The Flaming Terrapin* (London, 1924) made an immediate impact, using the story of Noah's ark as an allegory for the world after WW1. His return to South Africa in 1926 was not successful and back in London he vented his rage in *The Wayzgoose* (London, 1928). In the 1930s he was at his most prolific, publishing 10 books of poetry, the best known of which, *Flowering Rifle* (London, 1939), was his own version of his military contribution to FRANCO's cause in the Spanish civil war. Converted to Roman Catholicism he translated Spanish plays and religious poems, and led a picaresque life as, at different times, secret service agent, lecturer, bullfighter and broadcaster. Though a distinguished modern poet, his work is not notably African. He is remembered as much for his place in the literary company he frequented as for the individuality of his writing. His poems have been reassembled as *Collected Poems* (3 vols, London, 1949–60).　ANRN

P. Alexander, *Roy Campbell: a Critical Biography* (Oxford, 1982).

Camus, Albert (b. Mondovi, French Algeria [now Algeria], 7.11.1913; d. Petit-Villeblevin, Yonne, France, 4.1.1960). French writer. In 1942 and 1943, the publication in Paris of *L'Etranger* (tr. S. Gilbert, *The Outsider*, London, 1946) and of *Le Mythe de Sisyphe* (tr. J. O'Brien, *The Myth of Sisyphus*, London, 1955) brought immediate fame to Camus. His evocation of a totally absurd world in which a man might be executed for not having wept at his mother's funeral exactly fitted the mood of occupied France after the defeat of 1940, while his pagan insistence on the intensity of conscious delights stemming from the recognition of the beauty as well as of the absurdity of life provided a fascinating antidote to despair. The Liberation of 1944 revealed him as having been active in the resistance movement. His editorials in *Combat* expressed the revolutionary fervour of liberated France, but gave way to a more sober assessment of the limits of political action in *La Peste* (Paris, 1947; tr. S. Gilbert, *The Plague*, London, 1948). This transposition of the experience of occupation and resistance into an outbreak of plague in Oran was also, as Camus himself said, his most anti-Christian work, insisting as it did on the incompatibility between the physical suffering of the innocent and the existence of an all-powerful, all-merciful God. Camus's twin rejection of communism and Christianity was expressed in more philosophical terms in *L'Homme révolté* (Paris, 1951; tr. A. Bower, *The Rebel*, London, 1953), whose publication led in 1952 to a violent public quarrel with SARTRE, who considered an alliance with the French Communist party essential for a genuine revolutionary. Camus's denunciation of left-wing totalitarianism was closely linked with his opposition to the death penalty, and led him to collaborate in 1957 with KOESTLER in a joint volume denouncing it. Camus's essay *Réflexions sur la guillotine* (Paris, 1957) was translated by J. O'Brien in *Resistance, Rebellion and Death* (London, 1961). *La Chute* (Paris, 1956; tr. J. O'Brien, *The Fall*, London, 1957) revealed a more anguished, self-doubting Camus than the humanist of *L'Homme révolté*, and led some critics to predict a conversion to Christianity. In 1957 Camus was awarded the Nobel prize for literature, no small achievement for a man whose father was an itinerant agricultural labourer killed in WW1 and whose mother was an illiterate charwoman. Camus's strong attachment to his native Algeria led him to differ violently from other French literary intellectuals in refusing to support the demand of the Arab Front de Libération Nationale for a totally independent Algeria, and pleading the cause of the European Algerians. He was killed in a car accident, with a railway ticket in his pocket.

PMWT

R. Quilliot, *La Mer et les prisons* (Paris, 1956); J. Cruickshank, *Albert Camus and the Literature of Revolt* (London, 1960); H. R. Lottman, *Albert Camus* (NY, 1980).

Canetti, Elias (b. Rutschuk, Bulgaria, 25.7.1905; naturalized British citizen, 1952). Bulgarian/British novelist and essayist. Although writing in German, he is descended from a Sephardic Jewish community, originating in Spain, and his imagination was shaped by the ethnic pluralism of the Austro-Hungarian empire. His early experiences are memorably described in the autobiographical volumes *Die gerettete Zunge* (Munich, 1977; *The Tongue Set Free*, NY, 1980) and *Die Fackel im Ohr* (Munich, 1980; *The Torch in My Ear*, NY, 1982). Since 1938 he has spent many years living in England and in Switzerland. His reputation rests principally on the novel *Die Blendung* (Vienna, 1935; tr. C. V. Wedgewood, *Auto da Fé*, London, 1946). This claustrophobic study of the relationship between an isolated Viennese intellectual and his threatening environment has been taken as an allegory of the failure of central European intellectuals to achieve effective social integration. The sense of foreboding which pervades the novel is given more explicit form in the political reflections Canetti wrote in exile under the title *Masse und Macht* (Hamburg, 1960; tr. C. Stewart, *Crowds and Power*, London, 1962, [2]1973). This ambitious attempt at a psychology of mass behaviour identifies the fundamental human impulse as a ruthless instinct for survival, linking modern politics to the evidence of history, anthropology and psychoanalysis. As a counterweight to these baleful themes Canetti's notebooks and essays testify to his faith in the ethical capacity of the human mind, linked to the responsible use of language. His models are provided by the existential seriousness of KAFKA and the ethical commitment of KRAUS. The implications of this conception of language are explored in *Das Gewissen der Worte* (Munich, 1975; tr. J. Neugroschel, *The Conscience of Words*, NY, 1979). It was perhaps not simply an individual author, but a whole tradition of discourse about the connections between language and morality, that was honoured by the award of the Nobel prize for literature to Canetti in 1981.

EFT

D. Barnouw, *Elias Canetti* (Stuttgart, 1979).

Cankar, Ivan (b. Vrhnik, nr Laibach, Slovenia, Austria-Hungary [now

Ljubljana, Yugoslavia], 10.5.1876; d. Ljubljana, 11.12.1918). Slovene novelist, dramatist and short-story writer. The small community of Slovene speakers, which now makes up the Yugoslav Republic of Slovenia, succeeded in maintaining its language and a literary tradition under Hapsburg rule. Cankar began to write with a group of modernist poets in Ljubljana at the turn of the century, moving to Vienna in 1896 where he wrote the majority of his works. Returning to Ljubljana in 1909, he was interned during WW1 but survived to see the collapse of Austria-Hungary in 1918. Well read in French, Russian and German literature, Cankar introduced a new note into Slovene literature. A prolific dramatist and short-story writer, he is best known for two novellas: *Hiša Marije Pomočnice* [The house of Our Lady of Sorrows] (Ljubljana, 1904) and *Hlapec Jernej in njegova pravica* (Ljubljana, 1907; tr. S. Yeras & H. C. Sewell Grant, *The Bailiff Yerney and His Rights*, London, 1930). Both works are typical in their combination of concern for the unfortunate, their sharp satire and delicate lyricism: characteristics of Cankar's writing which have greatly enriched Slovene literature.

ECH

Cannon, Walter Bradford (b. Prairie du Chien, Wis., USA, 19.10.1871; d. Franklin, NH, 1.10.1945). American physiologist. Cannon spent most of his working life at Harvard University, as an undergraduate, medical student and, from 1906 to 1942, as George Higginson professor of physiology. His earliest work, begun as a medical student, used the recently discovered X-rays to investigate physiological features of eating and digestion, including swallowing, and gastric and small-intestine peristalsis. Cannon's *Mechanical Factors of Digestion* (NY, 1911) summarized this work, which was followed by an examination of the effect of strong emotions such as pain, fear and rage on the automatic nervous system: the so-called 'fight or flight' reactions. Related problems of traumatic shock following blood loss occupied him during the latter part of WW1. The physiological response to shock and to pain increases the output of adrenaline (epinephrine) by the adrenal glands, and Cannon and others showed in the 1920s that stimulation of various peripheral nerves releases a substance, subsequently shown by LOEWI and Cannon's long-time friend DALE to be adrenaline and involved in the transmission of nerve impulses. In addition to his work on chemical transmission of nerve impulses, Cannon continued his searching inquiries into the functions of the autonomic nervous system, many of which are concerned with the maintenance of constant ranges of salt, sugar, oxygen and temperature within the living body. Cannon coined the term 'homeostasis' to describe this capacity of organisms to maintain physiological equilibrium and summarized homeostatic mechanisms in his classic monograph *The Wisdom of the Body* (NY, 1932). With his Harvard colleague L. J. Henderson, he used the concepts of equilibrium and homeostasis to explain social organization. This inevitably drew him into international politics, where he was particularly concerned with the status of scientists in the USSR and with the preservation of the Spanish republic against FRANCO. His autobiography *The Way of an Investigator* (NY, 1945) was published in the year of his death. WFB

C. McC. Brooks *et al.* (eds), *The Life and Contributions of Walter Bradford Cannon* (NY, 1975).

Cantimori, Delio (b. Russi, nr Ravenna, Emilia-Romagna, Italy, 30.8.1904; d. Florence, Tuscany, 13.9.1966). Italian historian. Studied and taught at the Scuola Normale di Pisa. Although he also wrote about Italian humanists, utopians and Jacobins, and modern German thought, Cantimori's importance as a historian rests squarely on his studies of Italian heretics, notably *Eretici italiani del '500* [Italian heretics of the 16c] (Florence, 1939) and *Prospettive di storia ereticale del '500* [Perspectives on the history of heretics since AD 500] (Bari, 1960), in which he showed the importance of the Italian tradition of dissent and its development from Italian humanism. These studies, concerned for the most part with Italians outside Italy, were the work of an Italian who was also at home in central

Europe. Like FEBVRE's, Cantimori's studies of the 16c, especially the later ones, suggested that ecclesiastical history ought to be seen as part of a wider cultural and social history. He was particularly interested in the 'Nicodemites' who tried to conceal their unorthodox beliefs behind an outward conformity, and in the methodological problems involved in writing their history. (A 'Hegelian and semi-MARXist' intellectual in fascist Italy, Cantimori was something of a Nicodemite himself.) His awareness of problems of method was one of Cantimori's great strengths, illustrated by his studies of Burckhardt, CHABOD, Febvre, HUIZINGA and other historians (reprinted in his *Studi di storia* [Studies in history], Turin, 1959, and again in *Storici e storia* [Historians and history], Turin, 1971). UPB

Cantor, Georg Ferdinand Ludwig Philipp (b. St Petersburg [now Leningrad], Russia, 3.3.1845; naturalized German citizen; d. Halle, Germany, 6.1.1918). Russian/German mathematician. Educated at Zürich, Berlin and Göttingen universities and appointed to the University of Halle in 1869, Cantor was responsible for the development of modern set theory, the system to which all modern mathematics is referred. His first achievements were in the traditional field of trigonometric series, whence he was led to consideration of the different kinds of sets of numbers that can appear in mathematics. He gradually showed that 19c ideas on the connection between the dimension of a set and the number of its elements were dangerously fallacious. For instance, the plane, the real continuum, and the Cantor ternary set all have the same number of elements, although the first covers two dimensions; the second, one; and the third, nothing. All of them are uncountable using the natural numbers, and Cantor, while inventing many concepts in point-set topology (closure, denseness) which have been essential to successful theories of dimension, concentrated on enumeration. He used the concept of the one-to-one mapping as his equivalence relation, and developed the ordinal numbers as the equivalence classes when these mappings are order-preserving. Thus if the natural numbers (1, 2, 3, ...) are the first ordinal, the set (2, 3, 4, ... ; 1) is the second, since the numbers 2, 3, ... 'absorb' all the numbers in the first set. Cardinal numbers are obtained from ordinal numbers by relaxing the restriction; both the sets cited have the same cardinality. Cantor showed that the set of all sequences of elements from a set of given cardinality has a higher cardinality than the parent set, but could not prove his hypothesis that there is no cardinal number between that of the natural numbers and the cardinality of the continuum. This continuum hypothesis has been proved, after great labour, to be optional. Cantor assumed that all sets could be well-ordered, that is, arranged so that every subset has a least element within itself; this postulate, which is equivalent to the axiom of choice, provoked great dissension among mathematicians then as now. It is logically independent of the other axioms needed for formalizations of set theory; most pure mathematicians find it useful; but no one has the least conception of what a well-ordering of the real continuum would look like. AGPW/JCu

H. W. Dauben, *Georg Cantor* (Cambridge, Mass., 1979).

Capa, Robert (b. Budapest, Austria-Hungary [now Hungary], 22.10.1913; d. Thai-Binh, Vietnam, 25.5.1954). Hungarian photographer. Capa established a new style in photojournalism in the 1930s, a style which flourished through to the era of protest in the late 1960s. Capa's predecessors in European photojournalism (e.g. EISENSTAEDT) had been expository documentarists, patient informants. Capa, by contrast, was a witness who reported from the thick of the action, especially from the front line in Spain during the civil war (1936–8). In 1930 many Europeans had envisaged themselves building for better times, and photojournalism reflected this concern; with the onset of war in Ethiopia, Spain and China present troubles demanded immediate responses. Capa's reports on the fighting in Spain in 1936 made his reputation and he remained the world's foremost war-photographer until his death in Indochina. Trained in Berlin in

1931, he moved, as did many other photographers, to Paris in 1933. He worked in Spain until 1938, and then covered the Japanese invasion of China. He reported on WW2 in Europe for *Life* magazine, and from 1948 recorded the foundation of Israel. In 1947, along with CARTIER-BRESSON, George Rodger and David Seymour, he founded the cooperative photographic agency Magnum. There are no pictorial precedents for Capa's photographs. Previous photojournalists had been careful picture-makers. His, by contrast, is action-photography: 'If your pictures aren't good enough, you aren't close enough.' After WW2 his photographs were admired as embodiments of human vivacity, expressions of the ability to survive recent horrors (see *Images of War*, NY, 1964). He stressed communication through feeling and experience, and such American successors as Leonard Freed and Dan Weiner took his example to heart.   IJ

Čapek, Karel (b. Malé Svatoňovice, Bohemia, Austria-Hungary [now Czechoslovakia], 9.1.1890; d. Prague, 25.12.1938). Czech writer. A version of JAMESian pragmatism prescribed his attitudes. His pacifism, his fear of man's destruction of himself by science and his interest in the 'ordinary man' reflected and supported the period's mental atmosphere. In his best-known play *RUR* [Rossum's Universal Robots] (Prague, 1920; tr. P. Selver, *R.U.R.*, London, 1923) the robots, having destroyed mankind, gain souls and we have a new Adam and Eve. Such optimistic endings are typical of Čapek's writing until the last two years of his life. Among his most important works are *Trapné providky* (Prague, 1921; tr. F. P. Marchant *et al.*, *Money and Other Stories*, London, 1929), *Apokryfy* (Prague, 1932; tr. D. Round, *Apocryphal Stories*, London, 1949) and *Obyčejný život* (Prague, 1934; tr. M. & R. Weatherall, *An Ordinary Life*, London, 1936). Every man consists of many men; happiness comes when that man whose life is work dominates. Čapek's is a comfortable philosophy.   RBP

W. E. Harkins, *Karel Čapek* (NY, 1962); A Matuška, *Karel Čapek: Man against Destruction* (London, 1964).

Capra, Frank (b. Palermo, Sicily, Italy, 19.5.1897). American film director. Capra emigrated to the USA in 1903 and became known in Hollywood by writing and directing Harry Langdon's best films in the early to mid-1920s. But it was not until Harry Cohn signed him for Columbia Pictures that Capra's name (and the success of Columbia as one of the 'big five' studios) became established. In 1931 he directed *Platinum Blonde*, one of Jean Harlow's best films, but he is best known for his sentimental comedies – *It Happened One Night* (1934), *Mr Deeds Goes to Town* (1936), *You Can't Take It With You* (1938), each of which won Capra an Academy award – and for his 'political' films – *Mr Smith Goes to Washington* (1939) and *Meet John Doe* (1941). Capra's films of the 1930s reflected his idealistic faith in Franklin D. ROOSEVELT's New Deal programme, the recurrent theme being that of the common man as hero, whose essential 'goodness' would see honesty and justice triumph over greed and deceit, no matter what the odds. The formula received an enthusiastic reception from critics and the public during the bleak years of the depression, but after WW2 Capra found it difficult to adjust to the demands of a new audience and a different political climate. His postwar films failed to achieve the success that his entertaining, yet socially pertinent, movies of the 1930s had and it is these films which constitute his major contribution to the history of American cinema.   LJC

Cardenal, Ernesto (b. Granada, Nicaragua, 20.1.1925). Nicaraguan poet. The leading Spanish-American 'committed' poet since NERUDA; Roman Catholic priest; and ideologue of Nicaragua's Sandinista revolution. A student activist, his religious conversion (1956) took him into the Trappist novitiate under MERTON, but he completed his training in a Colombian seminary. His Trappist stay produced *Vida en el amor* (Buenos Aires, 1970; tr. K. Reinhardt, *To Live is* *to Love*, NY, 1972), a mystical treatise influenced by TEILHARD DE CHARDIN; while 25 updated *Salmos* from the seminary reflect Colombian progressive Catholic feeling (Medellín, 1964; tr. various hands, *Psalms*, London, 1981), highlighting the sociopolitical implications of the biblical originals. After ordination, Cardenal established his Solentiname commune (1966) on an island in Lake Nicaragua, preaching Mertonian nonviolence. After Merton's death, however, a stay in Cuba (see *En Cuba*, Buenos Aires, 1972; tr. D. D. Walsh, *In Cuba*, NY, 1974) led to Cardenal's 'second conversion': his resultant utopian conception of 'Communism or God's kingdom on earth' (fusing 'liberation theology', the 'communism' of the early church, and Cuba's vision of New Man) informs the dialogues of *El Evangelio en Solentiname* (Salamanca, 1975 & 1977; tr. D. D. Walsh, *The Gospel in Solentiname*, NY, 1976–80). Nonviolence was abandoned, and when Solentiname was destroyed after its members attacked a nearby garrison (1977), Cardenal declared his membership of the FSLN (Sandinista National Liberation Front). After Somoza's fall (1979), Cardenal became minister of culture in the 'Government of Reconstruction'. Abroad, his influence has so far been greater as a poet, popularizing techniques he learnt from Ezra POUND: epigrammatic irony, the incorporation of prose source-material, dialectical cross-cutting, an imagist stress on direct statement (*exteriorismo*). These already show in *Hora O*, composed 1954–6 (Mexico City, 1960; tr. D. D. Walsh in *Zero Hour and Other Documentary Poems*, NY, 1980). His most important collection *Homenaje a los indios americanos* (León, Nicaragua, 1969; tr. M. & C. Altschul, *Homage to the American Indians*, Baltimore, 1973) uses selective evocations of advanced pre-Spanish and primitive Amerindian (including redskin) cultures as an oblique critique of modern capitalist society. For wide-ranging selections, see *Marilyn Monroe and Other Poems* (1948–70), tr. R. Pring-Mill (London, 1975), and *Apocalypse and Other Poems* (1950–74), tr. T. Merton *et al.* (NY, 1977).   RP-M

Carder, Frederick (b. Wordsley, Staffs., UK, 18.9.1863; naturalized American citizen; d. Corning, NY, USA, 10.12.1963). British/American glassmaker. Frederick Carder's active career extended over three-quarters of a century during which he designed and made glass using an astonishing range of techniques including numerous innovations of his own. Son of a potter, he worked first in the pottery business, studying art at the Stourbridge School of Arts and receiving a technical training at nearby Dudley. He joined the glassmaking firm of Stevens & Williams, Brierley Hill, as a designer at the age of 17 and produced cameo glass of the highest quality. He studied coloured glass in England and on the Continent and in 1903 was invited to set up the Steuben Glass Works at Corning, New York, by the cut glass firm of T. G. Hawkes & Co., where he spent the rest of his working life. Although a superb technician and accomplished artist, Carder did not develop a distinct personal style in glassware. He is most remembered for his mastery of a huge variety of glass techniques and, above all, for his wonderful use of colour. RHV

P. V. Gardner, *The Glass of Frederick Carder* (NY, 1971).

Cardozo, Benjamin Nathan (b. New York, USA, 24.5.1870; d. Port Chester, NY, 9.7.1938). American lawyer, judge of New York Court of Appeals (1914–26) and chief judge (1926–32), and associate justice of the US Supreme Court (1932–8). As a judge, Cardozo was a noted liberal and supported the social welfare elements of F. D. ROOSEVELT's New Deal legislation. He also favoured the progressive and law-creative function of the courts under the common law system, holding that courts must be involved with public policy and seek to modernize legal principles accordingly. The pieces collected in M. E. Hall's edition of *Selected Writings of Benjamin Nathan Cardozo* (NY, 1947) powerfully state the ethical justifications for many principles of law, disclose liberal sympathies, and reveal the methods of the judicial process.   DMW

B. H. Levy, *Cardozo and the Frontiers of Legal Thinking* (NY, 1938); G. S.

Hellman, *Benjamin N. Cardozo: American Judge* (NY, 1940).

Carlson, Chester (b. Seattle, Wash., USA, 8.2.1906; d. New York, 19.9.1968). American inventor of xerography. In his youth Carlson worked for a printer and acquired a printing press. He graduated in physics at the California Institute of Technology and then worked for the Bell Telephone laboratories. He moved to the electronics firm of P. M. Mallory, took a law degree, and ran their patent department. He then settled down in his spare time to look systematically for a cheap method of document reproduction, and developed a dry method using electrostatic images. He employed an assistant and on 22.10.1938 first successfully formed a dry image. In 1944 the Battelle Memorial Institute took over development work, and invited the Haloid Co., later Xerox, to develop a practical xerographic printer. Xerography has made document reproduction cheap and ubiquitous. In its latest form, with computer-generated information controlling a laser for writing on selenium-coated drums, the xerographic printer has become a versatile and powerful printing system. RAH

Carnap, Rudolf (b. Ronsdorf, N. Rhine-Westphalia, Germany, 18.5.1891; naturalized American citizen, 1941; d. Santa Monica, Calif., USA, 14.9.1970). German/American philosopher. Between 1910 and 1914 Carnap studied physics and mathematics at Freiburg and Jena (where he was a pupil of FREGE). After war service he achieved his doctorate in 1921 with a thesis on different concepts of space that foreshadowed his later style and interests. In 1926 he was invited to Vienna by SCHLICK and two years later published his lucid, complicated, ingenious *Der logische Aufbau der Welt* (Berlin, 1928; ²1961; tr. R. A. George, *The Logical Structure of the World*, London, 1967) in which the whole system of concepts required to express scientific knowledge is defined in terms of concepts applicable to immediate experience. This was an unprecedentedly thorough fulfilment of a longstanding promise by empiricist philosophers. In 1930 he and REICHENBACH inaugurated *Erkenntnis*, the official periodical of logical positivism whose brilliant career ended with WW2. Influential shorter works of this period argued for the elimination of the 'pseudo-problems' of metaphysics by showing how their assertions were meaningless not only in the light of the verification principle but also through the thesis that the only necessary truths are those whose truth depends on the conventions that give meaning to the terms that express them. In 1931 Carnap moved to the German University of Prague and published *Der logische Syntax der Sprache* (Vienna, 1934; tr. A. Smeaton, *The Logical Syntax of Language*, London, 1937) which argued that soluble philosophical problems really concern the logic of scientific language, something that Carnap believed was best carried on through the study of artificial language-models. After his move to Chicago in 1935 this line of thought was further developed in a series of 'studies in semantics' (including *Meaning and Necessity*, Chicago, 1947) under the influence of TARSKI. The main work of his later years was on probability. In *The Logical Foundations of Probability* (Chicago, 1950, ²1962) he presented with enormous detail and thoroughness a modern version of the classical theory which assumes that probabilities can be calculated in advance of experience. Carnap was an admirably open and reasonable philosopher, almost too ready to suppose that philosophical disagreement could be removed by the congenial work of formalizing the opposing viewpoints. His work is still alive through its influence on QUINE and N. GOODMAN. AQ

P. A. Schilpp (ed.), *The Philosophy of Rudolf Carnap* (La Salle, Ill., 1963).

Carothers, Wallace Hume (b. Burlington, Iowa, USA, 27.4.1896; d. Philadelphia, Pa, 29.4.1937). American industrial chemist. Carothers studied and taught at the universities of Illinois and South Dakota and at Harvard. He was later selected to lead the organic chemical section in the research department at Wilmington, Delaware, of the chemical firm E. I. du Pont de Nemours. Carothers's objective was to prepare high-molecular-weight organic compounds and to examine their properties with a view to developing novel, commercially valuable materials. He produced the first successful synthetic rubber, neoprene (or polychloroprene, i.e. poly-2-chlorobuta-1,3-diene), notable for its resistance to oil degradation. This process required the unstable vinylacetylene, then little known, as an intermediate, preparation of which Carothers successfully developed. He then turned from polymerization (a self-addition process) to the more versatile polycondensation (often with elimination of water), first to form polyesters from diols and dicarboxylic acids. The products appeared unpromising (they were later developed further by Whinfield and Dickson to give the now well-known polyester fibres), so Carothers turned to polyamides, prepared from dibasic acids and diamines. The product from the 6-carbon-atom containing adipic acid (butane-1,4-dicarboxylic acid) and hexamethylenediamine is Nylon 66. This rapidly achieved commercial success and is now used worldwide in the textile industry. NBC

Carpentier, Alejo (b. Havana, Cuba, 26.12.1904; d. Paris, France, 24.4.1980). Cuban novelist, musicologist, journalist and cultural representative: the major Cuban writer of the 20c. Born of a French architect father and Russian mother, after imprisonment in 1927 for opposition to MACHADO he lived in France until 1939, devoted to musical pursuits and closely associated with the surrealist movement. On a visit to Haiti in 1943, he discovered in the Caribbean a reality which he considered more fantastic than the inventions of the avant-garde, and referred to as the '*lo real maravilloso*' ('marvellous real'), in the prologue to *El reino de este mundo* (Lima, 1948; tr. H. de Onis, *The Kingdom of this World*, NY, 1957). Here, and in *El siglo de las luces* (Mexico City, 1962; tr. H. de Onís, *Explosion in a Cathedral*, London, 1963), the coexistence of different cultures in the Caribbean world around the time of the French revolution is recreated in a baroque, contrapuntal, stylistically rich vision. His rather archetypal overview of

history is brought alive by a keen sense of irony, tragedy and farce. In *Los pasos perdidos* (Mexico City, 1953; tr. H. de Onís, *The Lost Steps*, London, 1956) he brilliantly uses this same structure to gloss the tension between the persistent Latin American quest for utopia and lost origins, and the rationalistic heritage of Europe. After living from 1945 to 1959 in Venezuela he returned to Cuba, whose revolution he served in many official cultural roles, in Cuba and at the Paris embassy, but especially in the undiminished quality of his novels, e.g. *El recurso del método* (Mexico City, 1974; tr. H. Partridge, *Reasons of State*, London, 1976), one of the most intelligent of the many Latin American novels denouncing dictatorship. SB

Carr, Edward Hallett (b. London, UK, 28.6.1892; d. Cambridge, 5.11.1982). British historian. After graduating from Cambridge, he entered the Foreign Office in 1916 and served in various capacities, including in the legation at Riga (1925–9), until his resignation in 1936. Professor of international politics at University College of Wales (1936–40), he was a fellow of Trinity College, Cambridge, from 1955 until his death. After various abrupt changes of opinion, from his hostile study *Karl Marx: a Study in Fanaticism* (London, 1934) to the essentially 'vulgar Marxist' *The Twenty Years' Crisis, 1919–1939* (London, 1939), through his well-researched, but dismissive studies of *Michael Bakunin* (London, 1937) and Alexander Herzen in *The Romantic Exiles* (London, 1933), Carr settled to produce his massive *A History of Soviet Russia: the Bolshevik Revolution, 1917–1923* (3 vols, London, 1950–3), *The Interregnum, 1923–1924* (London, 1954), *Socialism in One Country, 1924–1926* (3 vols, London, 1958–64), *Foundations of a Planned Economy, 1926–1929* (3 vols, London, 1969–78). Upon this highly controversial work his reputation as an historian rests: despite its enormous wealth of scrupulously researched, and skilfully marshalled and presented, historical information, its crude ideological foundations, as well as the explicit theoretical statements of *What is History?* (London, 1961), have come in for sustained criticism. According to Carr, the historian is a socially conditioned and historically determined observer who cannot possibly see the past with objective detachment; hence the old liberal historians' view of historical objectivity as meting out even-handed justice to all sides is immature and sentimental. And since history is the March of Progress determined by laws, true objectivity consists in discovering and describing men and movements who press forward along the iron rails leading into the future. But by Carr's own refusal to look fairly at the full complexity of human situations, and through his belief that the successful exercise of power is all, his historical outlook is distorting and deeply unjust. This is admirably summed up by Leonard Woolf in his review of the first volume of *A History*: 'Professor Carr's vision makes it impossible to see these events except through the eyes of Lenin and the Bolshevik party, for theirs is the kingdom, the power, and the glory, and nothing else counts.' RNH

Carson, Rachel Louise (b. Springdale, Pa, USA, 27.5.1907; d. Silver Springs, Md, 14.4.1964). American naturalist and writer. In *Silent Spring* (Boston, Mass., 1962) she was one of the first to direct public and governmental attention to the damage done to the environment, and ultimately to people, by the widespread and indiscriminate use of pesticides and insecticides in agriculture. Her claims that controls on the use of chemicals, and research into their effects, were inadequate were taken seriously at the highest level. Such was the public concern she aroused that after a call by President KENNEDY's science advisory committee, far tougher controls on toxic agricultural chemicals were enacted in the USA. The book influenced government thinking and action in other countries too. Carson had earlier established her credentials as a conservationist by recording the delicate and complex ecology of the sea: her trilogy of *Under the Sea Wind* (NY, 1941), *The Sea around Us* (NY, 1951) and *The Edge of the Sea* (NY, 1955) drew on her expertise as a marine biologist in the US Bureau of Fisheries. Her talent was to combine a precise scientific insight with a compelling and descriptive prose style which ensured a wide audience for the message of conservation at a time when it was not as widely grasped as it became by the 1970s. GHD

Cartan, Élie (b. Dolomieu, Isère, France, 9.4.1869; d. Paris, 6.5.1951). French mathematician. Cartan was decisive in extending the theory of analysis on differentiable manifolds, now perhaps the central domain of mathematics. Cartan's thesis (1894) greatly clarified and sometimes corrected work of Killing and M. Lie, classifying simple, real and complex Lie algebras. Later he studied their representations and in 1913 discovered the spinor groups, of use in quantum mechanics. After 1925, influenced by WEYL, he studied the global theory of compact Lie groups and outlined their homology theory. He studied systems of differential equations in great generality, and he prefigured the theory of infinite Lie pseudo-groups. His work on differential geometry was decisive in its development to conceptual generality; in particular the concept of fibre bundle is implicit in it, and his theory of connections (analogues of directional derivatives on manifolds) which he discussed in correspondence with EINSTEIN is fundamental in general relativity as presently formulated. Cartan was professor of mathematics at Paris University from 1912 to 1940. Until 1930, however, he was somewhat isolated by virtue of the profound novelty of his interests, and also because of the weak state of French mathematics following WW1 in which several young French specialists had been killed. His work was edited as *Oeuvres complètes* (6 vols, Paris, 1952–5). JJG

Carter, Elliott Cook, Jr (b. New York, USA, 11.12.1908). American composer whose early works, such as *Holiday Overture* (1944), are in a typically American post-STRAVINSKY style. With the Piano Sonata (1946), however, there began a process of growth which reached fruition in the First String Quartet (1951). Carter extended his harmonic range into dissonance, introduced a new rhythmic flexibility and began to create forms which are conversations of musical characters, defined by their harmonic natures. He discarded the neoclassical inheritance; his new language was tough, elegant and complex. Since developing this style Carter has worked slowly and concentrated on instrumental music; his output includes two further quartets (1959 and 1973) and various orchestral compositions (see also his *Collected Writings*, NY, 1977). PG

Cartier-Bresson, Henri (b. Chanteloup, Seine-et-Marne, France, 22.8.1908). French photographer. Cartier-Bresson studied painting with André Lhote in Paris (1927–8) and took up photography in 1931. His first works were shown at the Julien Levy Gallery, New York, in 1932 and his first reportage published in *Vu* (Paris) the same year. His style was formed during periods of work in Spain in 1932 and 1933 and synthesizes elements derived from late cubist painting, CHIRICO, the Leica 'snapshots' of KERTESZ and the dynamic photography of movement by Martin Munkasci. Cartier-Bresson developed an aesthetic which combines maximum complexity with maximum clarity of design and a sense of narrative pointedness for which he coined the phrase 'the decisive moment'. The influence of Cartier-Bresson's photographs and formulations, first published in *Images à la Sauvette* [The decisive moment] (Paris, 1952), has been worldwide. He worked as assistant to Jean RENOIR on three films, including *La règle du jeu* (1939), and himself directed *Victoire de la vie* [Victory of life] (1937), on hospitals in Republican Spain, and codirected *Le Retour* [The return] (1944–5). He shared with Jean Renoir both a sense of the visual repertoire drawn from the traditions of great painting and a sharp observation of the conditions and philosophical dilemmas of contemporary life. They worked together on the Front Populaire film *La vie est à nous* (*The People of France*, 1936). Cartier-Bresson was active in setting up the Magnum cooperative photographic agency in 1947. From 1948 to 1950 he worked in India, Pakistan, China (during the last six months of the Kuomintang and the first six months of the People's Republic) and in Indonesia.

In 1954 he became the first photographer from the West to be allowed to photograph in the USSR since WW2. *People of Moscow* was published in 1955, as was also his second major collection *The Europeans*. In recent years he has concentrated on drawing but still photographs. MH-B

Henri Cartier-Bresson: Photographs (NY, 1980).

Caruso, Enrico (b. Naples, Campania, Italy, 27.2.1873; d. Naples, 2.8.1921). Italian operatic tenor. Born of poor parents, he became the leading male opera singer of his day and perhaps of the whole 20c. Oddly enough it was not so much in his native Naples that he made his reputation – indeed, after a dubious reception in 1901 he never sang there again – nor even in Italy as a whole, but rather in London (where he sang the Duke of Mantua in Verdi's *Rigoletto* in 1902 at Covent Garden) and in the other operatic capitals of Europe. He also regularly sang at the Metropolitan Opera in New York between 1902 and 1920, where for the American operatic public he was a major star. During these years he made many gramophone records, and the huge sums he earned from them show the extent to which he became a household name even among music-lovers who never attended an operatic performance. Vocally, Caruso had a baritone-like quality as well as a tenor's heroic character and range. He sang in both Italian and French opera. His 'life story' was filmed in 1951 as *The Great Caruso*, with Mario Lanza in the title role. CH

Cary, Arthur Joyce Lunel (b. Londonderry, Ireland [now Northern Ireland], UK, 7.12.1888; d. Oxford, 29.3.1957). British novelist. Cary's family lost their property through the Irish Land Acts of the 1880s and went as exiles to London. As a child, therefore, he discovered 'the fundamental injustice and instability of things'. His later experiences, which encompassed the bohemian world of art, the Balkan War (1912–13) and the Nigerian political service, helped to underscore this view. So did the political, social and aesthetic movements and revolutions of the first

half of the 20c. From *Aissa Saved*
(London, 1932) onwards, his central
concern was to render a comprehensive
idea of the world which would explain
its dynamism and its tragedy. This
rested upon a rejection of the Victorian
concept of freedom as 'absence of
restraint' and redefining it as 'creation
in the act'. *Mister Johnson* (London,
1939) is the best of his African novels
while the two trilogies of the 1940s and
1950s show him at his most inventive
and complex. The self-revealing narratives, multiple perspectives and historical
sweep of *Herself Surprised* (London,
1941), *To be a Pilgrim* (London, 1942)
and *The Horse's Mouth* (London, 1944),
for example, answer entirely to their
author's principle that a novel should
combine fullness of life with strict unity
of form.   SC
A. Wright, *Joyce Cary: a Preface to
his Novels* (London, 1958); B. Fisher,
Joyce Cary: the Writer and his Theme
(Gerrards Cross, 1980).

Casals, Pablo Carlos Salvador (b. Ven-
drell, Tarragona, Spain, 29.12.1876; d.
Rio Piedras, Puerto Rico, 22.10.1973).
Spanish cellist. Casals was a man of
immutable integrity and a musician of
immense expressive power. He would
not appear in HITLER's Germany and
he accepted voluntary exile from
FRANCO's Spain, living first in Prades in
the French Pyrenees, where he organized
annual Bach festivals from 1950 to
1968, and then in Puerto Rico. His
musicianship was evident in his dedicated conducting and composition: his
works include church music, cello pieces
and a peace oratorio *El pessebre* [The
crib], by which he set great store. However, he will be remembered above all
as a cellist. His recordings, especially
those of the Bach suites (which he
brought back into the repertory) and the
Dvořák concerto, reveal his capacity to
assert his control over big, expressive
phrases in a manner that no other cellist
of the century has equalled. Yet he was
also capable of extraordinary delicacy
and, in the important trio he formed
with the violinist Jacques Thibaud and
the pianist Alfred Cortot, of intimate
response to the playing of others. He
published *The Memoirs of Pablo Casals*

(NY, 1959) and *Joys and Sorrows* (NY,
1970).   PG
H. L. Kirk, *Pablo Casals: a Biography*
(London, 1974); D. Bloom, *Casals and
the Art of Interpretation* (London, 1977).

Cassirer, Ernst (b. Breslau, Germany
[now Wrocław, Poland], 28.7.1874; naturalized Swedish citizen; d. New York,
USA, 13.4.1945). German/Swedish philosopher and historian of ideas. A late
product of the classic tradition of German philosophical idealism, Cassirer
became professor at Hamburg in 1919.
He left Germany when HITLER came to
power and taught at Oxford and Göteborg before moving to the USA in 1941.
Cassirer developed Kant's thought in
two main ways: he transformed the
static critique of reason, according to
which the fundamental concepts and
categories by means of which we organize experience are universal and immutable, into a dynamic critique, according
to which they are not permanently fixed
but open to constant development; and
he broke free of one-sided fixation on
the epistemological primacy of scientific
knowledge, extending his critique to
embrace as the equals of natural science
all forms of creative human activity,
including language, myth, religion and
history, folklore, magic and astrology. In
an attempt to introduce systematic unity
into these seemingly disparate realms,
Cassirer developed his theory of 'symbolization' or 'symbolic representation':
Philosophie der symbolischen Formen (3
vols, Berlin, 1923–31; tr. R. Manheim,
Philosophy of Symbolic Forms, 3 vols,
New Haven, 1953–7). Man is above all
a symbolizing animal. He seeks to interpret and understand himself and his
world, and the symbols and systems of
symbols he devises are constitutive of
that world. On this view there is no
reality-in-itself prior to the imposition
by our minds upon it of our spontaneously generated symbolic patterns. All
forms of intellectual activity are seen as
being creative, more akin to the activity
of the artist who invents than to that of
the investigator who discovers. Philosophical investigation thus becomes in
large part identical with historical
research into the ideal forms and categories of the human mind from its early

beginnings. Cassirer himself in studies of ancient science, and on the philosophy of almost all periods of western civilization, displayed a rare capacity for entering into the peculiar moral and mental worlds of other ages and thinkers, and threw fresh light particularly on the Renaissance and the European Enlightenment. *An Essay on Man* (New Haven, 1944) and *The Myth of the State* (New Haven, 1946) contain in their clearest and most compendious and developed form his central ideas on the philosophy of culture. RNH

P. A. Schilpp (ed.), *The Philosophy of Ernst Cassirer* (NY, 1949).

Castro, Fidel (b. nr Birán, Cuba, 13.8.1926). Cuban revolutionary leader and since 1959 head of the Cuban government. The background to Castro's career is the political and economic domination of Cuba by the USA from the latter part of the 19c. He was born the son of a Spanish immigrant labourer, who made himself the owner of a large sugar plantation by hard work, and a Cuban Creole mother. He took part in two attempts to overthrow the Trujillo government in the early 1950s. Released from prison in 1955, he gathered a group of revolutionary fighters (including GUEVARA) in Mexico and after a disastrous landing in Cuba escaped with no more than 11 companions to the mountains of the Sierra Maestra where he spent the next two years building up a guerrilla army. Although this did not number more than 1000 *Fidelistas*, by August 1958 Castro felt confident enough to take on the government forces and by 1.1.1959 he was master of the country.

Castro's programme was vague but based on the support of the poor peasants, the urban workers, the nonwhite population and the young. Its immediate objectives were land reform and the nationalization of US-owned property. The US government retorted by imposing a trade embargo, breaking off diplomatic relations and supporting an unsuccessful invasion by Cuban exiles (Bay of Pigs, April 1961). Castro turned to the USSR as an alternative trading partner and source of funds, a move which divided his own movement, led to the emigration of many Cubans and involved the country in the 1962 missiles confrontation between the USA and the USSR. In more than 20 years since he took power, Castro's radical reforms have not solved Cuba's economic or social problems. Cuba remains dependent upon the USSR for its economic viability as well as its security. But it can be argued that Castro's revolution, despite brutal repression of any opposition, has produced a more equal society. Abroad he has appealed with success to the Third World by his defiance of 'American imperialism', and by his identification with the nonaligned movement.

Castro's magnetic personality, his record as a guerrilla fighter who refused to let himself be turned into a bureaucrat, made him the idol of the student left and of Third World revolutionaries who saw in him the romantic hero of 20c revolution. The glamour has faded, but Castro remains the master of Cuba and of the revolution he made. ALCB

H. L. Matthews, *Castro: a Political Biography* (London, 1969); H. Thomas, *Cuba; or the Pursuit of Freedom* (London, 1971).

Castro, José Maria Ferreira de (b. Salgueiros, Oliveira de Azemeis, Portugal, 24.5.1898). Portuguese novelist. Orphaned at eight years, he emigrated aged 12 to Belém do Pará, Brazil. He worked hard on the 'Paradise' rubber plantation on the Madeira river, returning to Belém after four years. Destitute, he found work on the ships and as a bill-sticker. He published his first novel *Criminoso por ambição* [Criminal by ambition] (Rio de Janeiro), written at the age of 14, in 1916. Castro returned to Portugal in 1919 and edited the satirical *O Diabo* [The devil]. The objectivity captured in the novel *Emigrantes* (Lisbon, 1928; tr. D. Ball, *Emigrants*, NY, 1962) was carried further in his greatest achievement, the autobiographical novel *A selva* (Lisbon, 1930; tr. C. Duff, *Jungle*, London, 1934), perhaps the best-known Portuguese work of the 20c. The hero of *A selva* is a political refugee in Brazil, working on an Amazon rubber plantation. The grandeur and luxurance of the tropical forest stand in contrast to the inhuman conditions of slavery on the plantation. Later novels include *Terra fria* [Cold lands] (Lisbon, 1934), *A tempestade* [The tempest] (Lisbon, 1940) and *A missão* (Lisbon, 1954; tr. A. Stevens, *The Mission*, London, 1963). DBr

J. Brasil, *Ferreira de Castro: a Obra e o Homem* (Lisbon, 1961).

Cather, Willa (b. Back Creek Valley, Va, USA, 7.12.1873; d. New York, 24.4.1947). American novelist. Beginning her career as a journalist, Cather gradually turned to short stories, and then to novels. Her primary subject was life on the Nebraska plains, which she had experienced as a child. Her novels, written years after she had left the plains, have been praised for the delicacy of her sense of place and descriptions of nature. *O Pioneers!* (NY, 1913) and *My Àntonia* (NY, 1918), her strongest novels, are notable for the portrayal of Scandinavian emigrants struggling to survive on the plains of the Midwest, and for the sympathetic portrayals of pioneer women. Never a bestselling writer, Cather won a Pulitzer prize in 1923. Her reputation has grown since her death, as shown by the reprinting of, for example, *Death Comes for the Archbishop* (NY, 1927). EH

P. L. Gerber, *Cather* (NY, 1975).

Caudwell, Christopher, ps. of Christopher St John Sprigg (b. Putney, London, UK, 20.10.1907; d. Madrid, Spain, 12.2.1937). British literary theorist. Caudwell made his living as a journalist and professional writer, joined the Communist party and produced a novel (*This My Hand*, London, 1936), poetry, and a series of MARXist cultural essays published as *Studies in a Dying Culture* (London, 1938). His major work, however, was *Illusion and Reality* (London, 1937), in which he tried to create a complete Marxist aesthetics, examining the origin, nature and development of poetry in its historical context. A further work *Romance and Realism* (Princeton, 1970), a Marxist interpretation of English literature, was posthumously published, after Caudwell was killed fighting with the International Brigade in defence of Madrid. His work, though often eclectic, reductive and overgeneralized, represents the most sustained and serious Marxist criticism to emerge from Britain in the 1930s. TE

Cavafy (Kavafis), Konstantinos Petrou (b. Alexandria, Egypt, 29.4.1863; d. Alexandria, 29.4.1933). Greek poet. Born of Greek parents in Alexandria, Cavafy spent his early life in England and Constantinople before returning to Alexandria for good at the age of 23. He began to write (in English and French as well as in Greek) at an early age but it was not until the mid-1890s that he wrote the first poems that he decided to publish, and his mature style was not developed until he was about 50. The poems published in his lifetime were collected after his death in *Poiemata 1896–1933* [Poems] (Athens, 1933), translated, together with a selection from *Anekdota poiemata 1882–1923* [Unpublished poems] (Athens, 1968), as *Collected Poems* (tr. E. Keeley & P. Sherrard, London, 1975).

Although he visited Greece only rarely and seems rather to have disliked what he saw, Cavafy has become universally recognized as the foremost Greek poet of the first part of the 20c. His style, which is spare, ironic and shuns pretension, and his clear-sighted presentation of his themes, chiefly drawn from Greek history or from homosexual experiences in contemporary Alexandria, represent a major innovation after Greek and European romantic poetry of the 19c. Unique features of Cavafy's poetry which have defied imitators are the poet's sense of the past and of time (even recent experiences are already the victims of time when presented in a poem by Cavafy) and his genius for ironic subtlety, which permits the dramatic presentation of conflicting points of view, leaving it to the reader to pass judgement. RMB

R. Liddell, *Cavafy: a Critical Biography* (London, 1974); E. Keeley, *Cavafy's Alexandria* (London, 1977).

Ceausescu, Nicolae (b. Scornicesti, Romania, 26.1.1918). General secretary of the Romanian Communist party since 1965; president of Romania since 1967. Determinedly nationalist leader of

Romania, he has maintained a frequently marked degree of independence from Soviet leadership in his conduct of Romanian foreign policy (though remaining within the Soviet-led system of alliances and economic cooperation) at the cost to his country of an unrelentingly repressive regime, based on a STALINesque 'cult of personality'.   DCW

Cela, Camilo José (b. nr La Coruña, Spain, 11.5.1916). Spanish novelist and essayist. Of the postcivil war novelists Cela was the first to come on the scene and has remained the best known in Spain and internationally. Since 1942 he has published 10 novels, the most acclaimed being *La familia de Pascual Duarte* (Madrid, 1942; tr. A. Kerrigan, *The Family of Pascual Duarte*, Boston, Mass., 1964) and *La colmena* (Buenos Aires, 1951; tr. J. M. Cohen, *The Hive*, NY, 1953). In *La familia de Pascual Duarte* Cela employs techniques drawn from the Renaissance Spanish picaresque novel to give a first-person account of the life of a murderer awaiting execution. The brilliant depiction of primitive violence caused a literary sensation in a Spain that had just lived through terrible carnage and it instituted a vogue for *tremendismo*, the uncompromising description of violence and horror. *La colmena*, generally considered Cela's masterpiece, captures three days in the life of Madrid four years after the civil war. With close on 200 characters and a dislocated chronology, the novel is structurally complex, but Cela has used cinematic technique to great advantage, and the work vividly portrays the poverty, degradation and hypocritical pretence of well-being of postwar Spanish society. *La colmena* inaugurated a new novelistic style known as *objetivismo*, a kind of documentary realism based on a camera and taperecorder narrative technique meant to eliminate the author's voice. Consistently an experimental novelist, his work of the 1940s and 1950s has met with greater critical acclaim than his more recent novels, which have been attacked as unduly whimsical.   CAL

D. W. Foster, *Forms of the Novel in the Work of C. J. Cela* (Columbia, Miss., 1967); D. W. McPheeters, *Camilo José Cela* (NY, 1969).

Celan, Paul, ps. of Paul Antschel (b. Czernovitz, Bukowina, Romania [now Chernovtsy, Ukraine, USSR], 23.11.1920; d. Paris, France, 1.5.1970). Romanian poet, widely regarded as the most important poet writing in German since WW2. Celan is a difficult and complex artist whose work has roots both in the poetic tradition of European symbolism and in the religious tradition of Jewish mysticism. The son of German-Jewish parents, he experienced Nazi persecution at first hand when in 1939 German troops overran his homeland and his parents were deported to a death-camp. Himself confined for a time in a Romanian labour-camp, he lived after WW2 for two years in Bucharest, moved briefly to Vienna and then in 1948 to Paris, which became his home until his suicide (by drowning) in 1970.

Throughout his work Celan was deeply preoccupied with the point where language cedes to silence: either the silence of death and nothingness or the silence which threatens to ensue upon the failure of language. His earlier poetry, especially that contained in *Mohn und Gedächtnis* [Poppy and memory] (Stuttgart, 1952), surrealistic in imagery and of obsessive rhythmic intensity, gives place in his third and fourth collections *Sprachgitter* [Language-grille] (Frankfurt, 1959) and *Die Niemandsrose* [The no one's rose] (Frankfurt, 1964) to a poetry of great linguistic circumspection, slow-moving, tentative and often fragmentary: poetry, as he himself put it, *'am Rande des Verstummens'* [on the verge of falling silent]. In the five volumes of his later years, three of them published posthumously, this fragmentary and reticent quality predominates. Combined with a strong tendency towards allusiveness, both cultural and personal, it led to a degree of difficulty which some critics have considered excessive.

Yet Celan's best work is, despite its difficulties, intensely communicative and extremely moving. Devoid of easy certainties, and relentlessly self-scrutinizing, his poems are, as he said, *'Daseinsentwürfe'*, sketches of, or towards, existence: of what can be salvaged and shaped after human destructiveness has reached its most catastrophic excesses. His poetry is collected in *Paul Celan: Gedichte* [Poems] (2 vols, Frankfurt, 1976); a selection in English is *Paul Celan: Poems* (tr. M. Hamburger, Manchester, 1980). CS

Céline, Louis-Ferdinand, ps. of Louis-Ferdinand Destouches (b. Courbevoie, Seine, France, 27.5.1894; d. Meudon, Seine-et-Oise, 1.7.1961). French novelist. Decorated and badly wounded in WW1, Destouches qualified as a doctor in 1924 and worked in Africa and the USA for the Rockefeller Foundation and the League of Nations before setting up in practice in the Clichy district of Paris. He adopted the pseudonym Céline (his grandmother's Christian name) on publishing his controversial first novel *Voyage au bout de la nuit* (Paris, 1932; tr. J. H. P. Marks, *Journey to the End of Night*, NY, 1960) which won the Prix Renaudot. Based in part upon Céline's own experiences, the novel combines a deep pessimism with a grotesque black humour in its account of the nightmarish adventures of its hero as he moves from the battlefields of Europe to Africa, America and back to working-class Paris. The revolutionary style, often seen as a spontaneous transposition of spoken French, is in fact the sophisticated product of endless revisions. Although Céline was never a member of any political party, the rabid anti-Semitism of his pamphlet *Bagatelles pour un massacre* [Baubles for a massacre] (Paris, 1937) added a political dimension to a controversial reputation which was further compromised by his notorious contributions to the wartime collaborationist press. Fearing assassination at the hands of the Resistance, Céline left Paris in 1944, fleeing to Germany and finally to Denmark where he was interned. Céline's exile lasted until 1951, when he returned to live in solitude at Meudon. His final trilogy (*D'un château l'autre*, Paris, 1957; tr. R. Manheim, *Castle to Castle*, NY, 1963, and the posthumously published *Nord*, Paris, 1963; tr. R. Manheim, *North*, NY, 1972, and *Rigodon*, Paris, 1969; tr. R. Manheim, *Rigadoon*, NY, 1974) gives a harrowing account of his travels across a devastated Europe, the despair being relieved only by the blackest of humour. Vilified for his anti-Semitism and virtually ignored until after his death, Céline has been widely acclaimed for his liberation of the French novel from its traditional syntax and vocabulary. In the USA he was hailed as a forebear by Henry MILLER and the Beat poets – but they failed to equal either his bitterness or his corrosive humour. DM

E. Ostrovsky, *Céline and his Vision* (NY, 1967); P. H. McCarthy, *Céline* (London, 1975).

Cernuda, Luis (b. Seville, Spain, 21.9.1902; d. Mexico City, Mexico, 5.11.1963). Spanish poet. A member of the poetic generation of 1927, he always remained an outsider, spiritually nonconformist and sexually deviant, his mental exile in prewar Spain being compounded after the civil war by physical exile in the UK, USA and Mexico. His life was governed by the twin imperatives of love and poetry. The conquest of self and self-expression is a major theme running through his collected work *La Realidad y el Deseo* [Reality and desire] (Madrid, 1936, ²1940, ³1958, ⁴1964), the final version comprising 11 separate collections of verse. The total organic poem is a spiritual and artistic autobiography in which 'reality' and 'desire' are the poles of the conflict at the root of his life and work. Surrealism provided the stimulus for an open confrontation with his homosexuality in verse and *Un río, un amor* [One river, one love] (Madrid, 1936), *Los placeres prohibidos* [Forbidden pleasures] (Madrid, 1931) and *Donde habite el olvido* [Where oblivion dwells] (Madrid, 1934) are rare sequences of forbidden love which found its apotheosis in the record of a late Mexican love affair *Poemas para un cuerpo* [Poems for a body] (Málaga, 1957). The Latin temper of his prewar verse was modified in exile by contact with Anglo-Saxon culture to produce the more meditative and objective, less rhetorical verse of his mature masterpieces *Las nubes* [Clouds] (Mexico City, 1940) and *Como quien espera el alba* [Like one awaiting dawn] (Buenos Aires, 1947). Cernuda refused to commit his verse to any political ideology, but his radical sympathies were obvious when he dealt with contemporary Spanish reality. Inevitably his work was ostracized by the right in postwar Spain, but some of the most significant contemporary Spanish poets have taken his independent ethical, aesthetic and vocational integrity as a poetic guide.

PMcD

P. Silver, 'Et in Arcadia Ego': a Study of the Poetry of Luis Cernuda (London, 1965); D. Harris, Luis Cernuda: a Study of the Poetry (London, 1973).

Césaire, Aimé (b. Basse-Pointe, French Martinique, 25.6.1913). West Indian poet and dramatist. Deeply influenced by the Senegalese poet SENGHOR, whom he met while studying in a Parisian lycée, his first book Cahier d'un retour au pays natal (Paris, 1947; tr. E. Snyder, Return to My Native Land, Paris, 1968) is an exuberant collection of verse and prose-poems, expressing his delight in the rediscovery of his African roots. His poetry displays a linguistic luxuriance evoking scenes of tropical life. The proliferation of adjectives creates a network of surrealist images whose rhythm conjures up the irresistible magic of African drums. The most striking factor in Césaire's work is perhaps the impermeability of text to western reading processes; the language is French, but constantly distorted, transgressed and based on non-European values. In Cadastre (Paris, 1961; tr. E. Snyder & S. Lipson, Cadastre: Poems, NY, 1973) there is a violent reaction against modes of thought imposed on Negroes by French colonialism; objects are described as having magic powers, which must be, like language, decolonized. Césaire's evolution takes two directions, ultimately merging: surrealism and greater commitment. Les armes miraculeuses [The miraculous weapons] (Paris, 1946) can be read as a surrealist protest against the abuses of colonialism, its linguistic games drawing attention to the misery of an oppressed people and the destruction of its culture. The same is equally the case in the political plays: La tragédie du roi Christophe [The tragedy of King Christopher] (Paris, 1963) and Les chiens se taisent

[Dogs hold their noise] (Paris, 1964). His most recent works Une Saison au Congo (1963; tr. R. Manheim, A Season in Congo, NY, 1969) and Discours sur le colonialisme (Paris, 1955; tr. J. Pinkham, Discourse on Colonialism, NY, 1972) accentuate the virulence of his political commitment.

DGL

Cézanne, Paul (b. Aix-en-Provence, Bouches-du-Rhône, France, 6.1.1839; d. Aix-en-Provence, 22.10.1906). French painter. Although Cézanne only lived for a few years into the 20c, he has had a profound influence on 20c art. He moved to Paris in 1861 to become a painter and worked from the models at the Académie Suisse, but without taking any formal instruction. His early paintings were dark in tone and heavily, sometimes violently executed, and brooding and turbulent in feeling. Camille Pissarro encouraged him to lighten his palette and he exhibited with the impressionists in 1874 and 1877, but soon resolved to try to go beyond impressionism and make of it something 'solid and enduring, like the art of museums'. Working from about 1882 onwards mainly in and around Aix, in isolation, he painted landscapes, still lifes and occasional portraits and figure compositions in which he tried various ways of resolving the forms before him, the subject of his intense scrutiny, into a monumental, timeless, pictorial unity, relating the forms to one another and to the background and working towards a dense saturation of colour. Motifs such as the Montagne Ste Victoire near Aix, or arrangements of oranges, plates and patterned tablecloths on a table were tackled over and over again, with a flattening and compression of space. Though he painted some figure compositions on the theme of bathers in a landscape, including several which are very monumental and quite large in scale, he showed that it was possible to make a profound pictorial statement with a painting of the simplest, most humble objects, and that the relationships of forms and colours one to another could become a rich and inexhaustible field of study for the painter. His works executed after 1900 are among his greatest. In these last years he was approached by various younger artists and attempted, in conversation and in letters, to articulate some of the basic ideas and intuitions behind his work. His widespread influence was particularly crucial to the creation of cubism, which was deeply indebted to his development of a shallow picture space, a shifting viewpoint and fractured forms. Cézanne attached great importance to his sensations in front of nature and probably would have disapproved of the more abstract developments which followed very soon after his death. Cézanne's *Letters* were collected by J. Rewalt (tr. M. Kay, Oxford, 1976). REA

W. Rubin (ed.), *Cézanne: the Late Work* (NY, 1977); L. Venturi, *Paul Cézanne* (NY, 1978).

Chabod, Federico (b. Aosta, Piedmont, Italy, 23.2.1901; d. Rome, 14.7.1960). Italian historian. Chabod began by writing on the history of political thought, notably *Del 'Principe' di Niccolò Machiavelli* (Milan, 1926; tr. in his *Machiavelli and the Renaissance*, London, 1958). While retaining his interest in the history of ideas, and publishing important studies on the political thought of Giovanni Botero and Paolo Sarpi, Chabod turned to archive-based political and religious history at the local level, producing *Lo Stato di Milano nell' impero di Carlo V* [The state of Milan in the reign of Charles V] (Rome, 1934), and *Per la storia religiosa dello Stato di Milano* [Religious history of the state of Milan] (Bologna, 1938). Without giving up his study of the early modern period, he accepted an invitation to write a history of Italian foreign policy since unification. He published no more than the introductory volume *Storia della politica estera italiana: le premesse* [History of Italian foreign policy: the preconditions] (Bari, 1951), which was of great importance as an early example of a 'new diplomatic history', since Chabod tried, as in his studies of Charles V and his officials, to see political history as part of a larger whole, to describe the 'material and moral basis' of foreign policy. The author of a history of the idea of Europe, Chabod was a good European as well as a patriotic Savoyard. His achievement was to make

a successful synthesis of traditional political narrative history with German *Geistesgeschichte* in the style of MEINECKE and French social history in the style of FEBVRE.   UPB

Chadwick, James (b. Bollington, Macclesfield, Ches., UK, 20.10.1891; d. Cambridge, 24.7.1974). British physicist. He was taught by RUTHERFORD at Manchester University and as a research student there and in Berlin (he was interned in WW1) he met many outstanding contemporary scientists. He went with Rutherford in 1919 to Cambridge and they collaborated closely for 16 years, concentrating on the experimental study of the atomic nucleus. Chadwick organized research at the Cavendish Laboratory and played a crucial part in its great achievements. His discovery of the neutron in 1932, for which he received a Nobel prize in 1935, launched a new era in nuclear physics. He was a brilliant experimenter who speculated with great imagination but would accept no speculations until they had been verified by experiment. He became professor of physics at Liverpool University in 1935 and built its moribund physics department into a leading world centre of experimental physics. It possessed the first British cyclotron. During WW2 Chadwick was the key person in Britain's atomic project. He coordinated the work of the Maud Committee, which showed how and why a bomb was possible, and largely drafted their remarkable 1941 report which pushed the floundering American project off the ground. When Anglo–American atomic cooperation was renewed in 1943 (after a long breakdown) and British scientists joined the US project, Chadwick was their leader; retiring and sensitive by nature, he was a superb diplomat who made Anglo–American collaboration work smoothly. He returned to the UK after the war, exhausted physically, mentally and spiritually. He spent much of his time advising on Britain's atomic project and nuclear physics programmes. In 1948 Chadwick became master of his former Cambridge college, Gonville and Caius: an unhappy end to his career, the more so as he lost contact with physics. He resigned (early) in 1958.

MMG

M. Gowing, *Britain and Atomic Energy, 1939–45* (London, 1964); N. Feather, 'Chadwick's neutron', *Contemporary Physics,* 6 (1974), 565–72.

Chagall, Marc (b. Vitebsk, Russia, 7.7.1887). Russian painter. Chagall is an isolated figure in 20c art, stylistically and in subject-matter. His mature style is an eclectic blend of Russian folk art, Gauguinesque self-conscious primitivism, a highly selective interpretation of cubist fragmentation of objects and space, and orphist creation of space with colour planes. Once formed (c. 1915), it remained essentially unchanged. The theme which has preoccupied him throughout his life is a subjective evocation of his childhood memories in a deeply religious Hasidic community in provincial Russia. The figures which constitute the main elements of his work – rabbis, musicians, acrobats, pedlars, animals – stem from the people and religious festivals which were the highpoints of the year in this remote area (e.g. *Return from the Synagogue*, 1925; *The Blue Violinist*, 1947). Although he rejected institutionalized religion, Chagall retains a fundamental Hasidic belief in God's immanence. Nowhere in the world is God's presence more apparent than in the loving union of two human beings – a theme to which he has returned repeatedly (e.g. *Over the City*, 1917; *The Bridal Pair before the Eiffel Tower*, 1938). Chagall's approach to his chosen themes is never naturalistic or rational. Employing a method of composition analogous to the experiments of surrealist poets, he has sought to create visual metaphors for the deepest yet simplest emotions and beliefs. His figures defy spatial logic as they float above cities or landscapes, or in the blue void of the universe (like ethereal, disembodied Blakean angels), adopting daring acrobatic poses, perched on top of each other, or upside down (e.g. *Double Portrait with Wineglass*, 1917). The sense of dream in his works is heightened by the rich, antinaturalistic colours, especially saturated reds, blues and greens. In this and in the conscious distortion of size and scale, Chagall is far closer to expressionism than to surrealism. This tendency to expressionistic pathos is also found in the biblical scenes he began to include in his works from the mid-1920s (e.g. 105 etchings for Vollard, 1930; the *Message Biblique* series of paintings, 1955–66; and the Jerusalem stained-glass cycle of *The Twelve Tribes*, 1961). In later years he has carried out many public commissions for stained-glass windows and murals (e.g. the Paris Opera, 1964; the Metropolitan Opera, NY, 1966) in which he has raised the delicate whimsicality of his painting to a monumental scale.

SOBT

J. Cassou, *Chagall* (London, 1965); S. Alexander, *Marc Chagall: a Biography* (London, 1977).

Chain, Ernst Boris (b. Berlin, Germany, 19.6.1906; naturalized British citizen; d. Co. Mayo, Irish Republic, 12.8.1979). German/British biochemist. Chain studied physiology and chemistry at the University of Berlin, leaving Nazi Germany in 1933. After two years with F. G. HOPKINS in Cambridge, he joined FLOREY's staff in Oxford (1935), where he worked on the biochemistry of lysozyme and, from 1938, the antibacterial substance (penicillin) produced by the *Penicillium* mould. He and Florey shared the 1945 Nobel prize with FLEMING, but Chain, who felt that the British authorities had neglected the mass-production of penicillin, became in 1948 the scientific director of the International Research Centre for Chemical Microbiology in Rome. In 1961 he returned to London as professor of biochemistry at Imperial College. His later work was devoted to carbohydrate metabolism in animals and the biochemical synthesis of useful substances, including new forms of penicillin.

WFB

Chaliapin, Fyodor Ivanovich (b. Kazan, Russia, 13.2.1873; d. Paris, France, 12.4.1938). Russian bass singer, who during an international career of some 35 years established himself as the leading singer-actor of his day. His background was unusual in that he came from a poor family and learned his operatic craft in small provincial companies before receiving formal training in singing, taking both bass and baritone roles as required. It was in Moscow, where he joined the Bolshoi Opera in 1899, that he developed his celebrated interpretation of the title role in Mussorgsky's *Boris Godunov*, bringing to the character of the noble but guilt-tortured tsar a power, dignity and insight that seem together to have defined the role for succeeding singers. However, despite his success in this and other Russian operas, Chaliapin widened his repertory considerably after he left Russia in 1921. He was naturally suited to such a role as that of King Philip II in Verdi's *Don Carlos*, but perhaps less expected was his gift for comedy as Don Basilio in Rossini's *Barber of Seville* and Leporello in Mozart's *Don Giovanni*, while he created the role of *Don Quichotte* in Massenet's opera of this title (1910). Like CALLAS, he brought dramatic insight and force, as well as vocal skill, to the operatic stage. His autobiography was *Stranitsy iz Moyey Zhizni* (Leningrad, 1926; *Pages from My Life*, London, 1927). CH

Chamberlain, Arthur Neville (b. Birmingham, W. Mids, UK, 18.3.1869; d. Heckfield, Hants., 9.11.1940). British Conservative minister of health (1924–9); chancellor of the exchequer (1931–7); prime minister (1937–40). Son of Joseph Chamberlain and irrevocably associated in the public mind with the policy of appeasement which was practised towards Nazi Germany, fascist Italy and imperial Japan, and which involved unrequited concessions usually at the expense, not of British interests, but of those of the expansionist power's most immediate target, in the confidence that such expansionism was fired by legitimate grievances and would disappear once those grievances were allayed. Although he was certainly inspired by the hope of avoiding WW2, he tried to regulate European conflicts without involving either the USA or the USSR, fearing the irremediable cost to British interests such involvement would incur. But his true motives in abandoning sanctions against Italy after the conquest of Ethiopia (1936), in failing to act on the German occupation and annexation of Austria and in avoiding a European war by the sacrifice of Czechoslovakia's western frontiers by the Munich agreement of September 1938, appear to have been a consciousness of Britain's financial and military weakness and a desire to postpone confrontation with Germany by so managing the crises into which the expansionists manoeuvred Britain as to avoid conflict at least until such time as the British rearmament programme (in which he played a major part) had produced an appearance of strength adequate to deter the aggressors from further unilateral action and to enable a final settlement of their major claims to be negotiated. His dominance of Parliament and his contempt for the lack of realism, as he saw it, of those who disagreed with or opposed his policy do much to account for the ignominy which overtook him once his policy had failed, war had broken out and the full degree of British military weakness and ineptitude had been disclosed by the German success in Norway. In domestic politics he was a very considerable social reformer, both as minister of health and as chancellor of the exchequer when his policies, while failing completely to deal with the problems of long-term structural unemployment in Wales, Scotland and northern England, made possible a massive housing construction programme and the development of new industries in light engineering, radio, electronics, etc., in the Midlands and south-east England.

DCW

K. Feiling, *The Life of Neville Chamberlain* (London, 1946, [2]1970); H. Montgomery Hyde, *Neville Chamberlain* (London, 1976).

Chandler, Raymond (b. Chicago, Ill., USA, 23.7.1888; d. La Jolla, Calif., 26.3.1959). American detective-story writer who rivals D. HAMMETT as the finest exponent of the hardboiled tradition. His aim and achievement was to create within the crime formula works of literary significance and merit. Plot mattered less to Chandler than style, character and acid social comment. For all the superficial cynicism of his narrator-hero Philip Marlowe's wisecracks, Chandler is a romantic rather than realist, presenting the private-eye as the ultimate knight-errant. Chandler had a classical English public-school education at Dulwich College. He came to writing late in life, publishing his first short story in 1933, and his first novel *The Big Sleep* (NY) in 1939. This was instantly acclaimed, as were *Farewell, My Lovely* (NY, 1940), *The High Window* (NY, 1942), *The Lady in the Lake* (NY, 1943), *The Little Sister* (Boston, Mass., 1949) and *The Long Goodbye* (Boston, Mass., 1953), all of which have been filmed. Chandler also wrote successful screenplays for *Double Indemnity* (1944), *The Blue Dahlia* (1946) and *Strangers on a Train* (1951), though he found his Hollywood career intensely frustrating.   RR

F. MacShane, *The Life of Raymond Chandler* (NY, 1976); J. Speir, *Raymond Chandler* (NY, 1981).

Chanel, Gabrielle (Coco) (b. Saumur, Maine-et-Loire, France, 20.8.1883; d. Paris, 2.1.1971). French couturière. Chanel was abandoned by her widowed father and raised in an austere convent orphanage at Aubazine. In 1903 she was apprenticed to a provincial hatmaker and haberdasher in the cavalry garrison town of Moulins, where through her first protector she met Arthur 'Boy' Capel. With his backing in 1910 she set up as hat designer at 21 Rue Cambon, Paris, the street she made famous. From 1914 onwards Chanel fashioned, in contrast to prevailing style, a new simplicity with soft, unfettered clothes and ideas frequently taken from masculine attire, such as seamen's knitwear, Breton smocks and pyjamas. The 'little black dress' was another unique Chanel contribution to fashion, and she was also directly responsible for making suntan, hitherto denoting low birth, chic and desirable for wealthy women. 1920 saw the famous scent Chanel No. 5 launched in a then revolutionary cube-shaped bottle. The first to be designer-named, it made her a multimillion fortune. Having friends who were brilliant painters and musicians, she costumed avant-garde theatre productions: COCTEAU's *Antigone* (1922), *Orphèe* (1926), and *Oedipus Rex* (1937); and, much celebrated in 1924, DIAGHILEV's *Le Train bleu*. Chanel closed her workrooms in 1939, then

reopened in 1954. Her second career was as influential as her first. The Chanel tweed suit became the most widely copied status symbol throughout the world for another 15 years, as did the Chanel shoe, handbag and mock jewels.
JWB

Chaplin, Charles Spencer (b. London, UK, 16.4.1889; d. Vaud, Vevey, Switzerland, 25.12.1977). British film actor and director. More than any other figure in the cinema, Chaplin was responsible for turning a popular entertainment into an art. After an impoverished London childhood, he went with a music-hall troupe to the USA, where in 1913 he began film work, immediately selecting the tramp's outfit which was to be world-famous. He made many brilliant short comedies (e.g. *The Immigrant*, 1917; *Easy Street*, 1917; *Shoulder Arms*, 1918). With *The Kid* (1921) he began his great series of irreverent feature films. In 1923 he directed a serious drama *A Woman of Paris*, marked by the subtlety of its acting; then back to comedy with *The Gold Rush* (1925), *The Circus* (1928) and his masterpiece *City Lights* (1931). Despite the date, he was still silent in his films. *Modern Times* (1936), satirizing factory life, betrayed socialist views. In *The Great Dictator* (1940), parodying HITLER, he capitulated to speech and delivered a sentimental harangue about freedom. Seven years later with *Monsieur Verdoux* (1947) he finally abandoned his tramp character and emerged as pacifist and would-be social philosopher, positions which, combined with an unfortunate paternity suit, exposed him to vituperation in the USA (he had never renounced his British nationality). After *Limelight* (1957) he worked on *A King in New York* (1957) in the UK, where also he directed the unsuccessful *A Countess From Hong Kong* (1966). His genius had encompassed acting, writing, directing and producing, and composing music for his films; *My Autobiography* (London, 1964) showed considerable writing gifts. But his achievement shone most brightly in such small passages of incomparable invention as the short *The Pawnshop* (1916) and the roll-dance in *The Gold Rush*. He was four times married, finally to O'NEILL's daughter Oona, with whom he lived happily in Switzerland until his death.　　　　　　　DP

T. Huff, *Charlie Chaplin* (London, 1952).

Chapman, Sydney (b. Eccles, Lancs., UK, 29.1.1888; d. Boulder, Colo., USA, 16.6.1970). British geophysicist. Chapman's work covered a very wide range and gave him a great influence upon the scientific world. He had a profound insight into scientific problems and during a long and active life he made outstanding contributions in the kinetic theory of gases, in ionospheric physics and aeronomy, in geomagnetism and aurorae, in solar and plasma physics, and in meteorology. He predicted the phenomenon of thermal diffusion and led the way in applying the theory to problems of viscosity, diffusion and heat conduction in ionized gases. He transformed the science of geomagnetism into an organic whole and gave it a new vitality. His name is also associated with outstanding theoretical work on lunar and solar tides, on the ionizing effects of solar ultra-violet radiation in the ionosphere (Chapman layer) and on the formation of ozone in the atmosphere.

After graduating in mathematics at Cambridge in 1910, Chapman held professorships at Manchester (1919–24), Imperial College, London (1924–46), and Oxford (1946–53). In 1954 he moved to the USA to carry out research at the High Altitude Observatory at Boulder, Colorado, and to be the advisory director of the Geophysical Institute in the University of Alaska. In all these posts he attracted not only young research students but also distinguished scientists to work with him. He became a legend in his lifetime, and in books and in several hundred scientific papers he left a vast store of scientific works and a host of ideas which continue to provide a powerful stimulus to research. Among his books are *The Mathematical Theory of Non-Uniform Gases* (with T. G. Cowling, Cambridge, 1939), *Geomagnetism* (with J. Bartels, Oxford, 1940) and *Atmospheric Tides* (with R. S. Lindzen, Dordrecht, 1970).　　PJM

Char, René (b. L'Isle-sur-la-Sorgue, Vaucluse, France, 14.6.1907). French poet who began his poetic career in the surrealist movement - one of his first collections of poems *Artine* (Paris, 1930) was decorated by DALI. However, after writing the best of his early work *Le Marteau sans Maître* [The hammer without a master] (Paris, 1934), he quietly moved away from the surrealists, though without rejecting the influence of Rimbaud or the close collaboration of ELUARD. He became increasingly concerned with politics, and in 1943 was promoted captain in the resistance movement. He described some of his experiences in his best-known work *Feuillets d'Hypnos* (Paris, 1946; tr. J. Matthews, *Leaves of Hypnos*, Rome, 1954), but remained essentially a poet of nature and the private life. His poetic style is vivid, elliptical and occasionally obscure. He specializes in prose poems and aphorisms, celebrating the communion of man with nature in a way that led CAMUS to qualify him, speaking of *Fureur et mystère* [Fury and mystery] (Paris, 1948), as 'our greatest living poet'. He writes vividly, especially in *La Parole en archipel* [The word in archipelago] (Paris, 1962), of the beauty of the Vaucluse region in the south of France, and links his erotic imagery with a consuming ethical concern unusual in contemporary French poetry.　　PMWT

P. Guerre, *René Char* (Paris, 1961); J. R. Lawler, *René Char: the Myth and the Poem* (Princeton, 1978).

Chargaff, Erwin (b. Czernowitz, Bohemia, Austria-Hungary [now Cernovice, Czechoslovakia], 11.8.1905; naturalized American citizen). Czech/American biochemist. Although initially interested in the biochemistry of lipids, Chargaff is best known for his work on nucleic acids (see *Essays on Nucleic Acids*, Amsterdam, 1963). He demolished the 'tetranucleotide hypothesis' by demonstrating that there are many different nucleic acids varying, according to origin, in their molecular proportions of purine and pyrimidine bases. He further showed that, although a single organism contains many different ribonucleic acids, its deoxyribonucleic acid (DNA) is of constant composition characteristic of the organism and its species. Although over the whole range of species examined the composition of DNA varied widely, Chargaff was able to discern regularities which he systematized in what became known as the 'Chargaff rules'. The most important turned out to be that 'the molar ratios adenine:thymine and guanine:cytosine are always close to one'. This provided an essential clue for the element of complementariness in the 'double helix' structure proposed for DNA by J. D. WATSON and CRICK and thus for our present understanding of the molecular basis of heredity. GL

Charney, Jule Gregory (b. San Francisco, Calif., USA, 1.1.1917; d. Boston, Mass., 16.6.1981). American meteorologist. In the enormous increase in meteorological research during and after WW2 Charney quickly came to the forefront in the field of dynamic meteorology. After graduating in mathematics, he embarked on research into the formation of mid-latitude depressions, a problem engaging the attention of many of the leading meteorologists of the day. He chose baroclinic instability as the subject of his doctoral thesis and produced theoretical results which were a complete departure from earlier studies of cyclogenesis. His paper 'The dynamics of long waves in a baroclinic westerly current' (1947) is one of the most remarkable papers in meteorological literature. Two years later, in collaboration with J. VON NEUMANN and R. Fjortoft, Charney made major original advances in numerical weather prediction. Two crucial elements were his development of the quasi-geostrophic system of prediction equations, which bypassed problems which had previously proved intractable, and his development, with A. Eliassen, of the concept of the 'equivalent-barotropic level'. Charney made notable contributions to other important problems, including the inertial theory of the Gulf Stream, the application of conditional instability theory to hurricane formation, and the large-scale vertical propagation of energy in the atmosphere. During the 1960s and 1970s Charney played a leading role in the formulation and experimental design of the Global Atmospheric Research Programme and the 1978–9 Global Weather experiment. PJM

Charnley, John (b. Bury, Lancs., UK, 29.8.1912; d. Manchester, 5.8.1982). British surgeon. Working in Manchester, he designed and introduced treatment with the artificial hip joint made of metal and plastic. Tens of thousands of patients crippled by arthritis have been restored to mobility by insertion of one or two Charnley prosthetic hip joints. Although he was by no means the first surgeon to design an artificial joint to replace one damaged by arthritis, other surgeons had instinctively based their design on the healthy joint, whereas Charnley's engineering approach produced a ball-and-socket joint with the small metal ball (much smaller than the bony head of the femur) fitting into a cup made of special low-friction plastic. Charnley was convinced from his own research in the 1950s that the chief cause of failure of the early artificial joints had been their lack of adequate lubrication. The low-friction plastic proved to be the answer. Charnley also pioneered a meticulous germ-free technique for the operation of joint replacement. He showed that the risks of deep infection occurring inside the hip after the operation could be reduced almost to zero if the surgery was carried out in a totally enclosed chamber containing only the surgeon, his assistant, and the lower half of the patient with a continuous flow of sterile air through the chamber during the operation. AJS

Chekhov, Anton Pavlovich (b. Taganrog, Russia, 29.1.1860; d. Badenweiler, Baden-Württemberg, Germany, 15.7.1904). Russian writer. Chekhov began a dual career in medicine and writing as soon as he left the provinces for Moscow in 1879. While in medical school he wrote short comic pieces to support his mother, sister and brothers. Although these light sketches, first published in Moscow humour magazines, are generally discounted in terms of literary merit, they made Chekhov into a skilled practitioner of the art of the short story, ultimately influencing writers in that genre in most other countries. By 1886 he had established himself as a major writer, although never entirely abandoning medicine. In Chekhov's mature stories tragic events occur in a minor key, as part of everyday life. Misunderstandings and nonevents dominate his plots rather than narrated definite occurrences, so the concept of 'plot' changes as well. Often the events of the story are filtered through the consciousness of a single character estranged from 'normal' family life. Chekhov is best known for his portrayals of life in the Russian small town or in the provincial minds of vulgar city dwellers. Every detail counts in his stories: a long grey fence or a cockroach in the soup have a value not only symbolic but realistic. These two modes blend in Chekhov, who lived in an age of generally dichotomized stylistic schools: naturalism and symbolism. In some later, longer stories he shows the social disruption that industrialization has brought to the countryside. In this sense some of his works point towards revolution; but Chekhov is always against easy political stances. When his characters speak of a bright future, their words, seen in context, are full of self-delusion and imply a new form of entrapment. Later Chekhov's association with the theatre came to dominate his life and work. He married the actress Olga Knipper, after a long bachelorhood. His earlier one-act plays gave way to the four major dramas still in the international repertoire: *Chaika* (1896; *The Seagull*, London, 1912, tr. R. Hingley, London, 1967), *Dyadya Vanya* (1897; *Uncle Vanya*, NY, 1922, tr. R. Hingley, London, 1964), *Tri sestry* (1901; *The Three Sisters*, NY, 1922, tr. R. Hingley, London, 1964) and *Vishnëvyi sad* (1904; *The Cherry Orchard*, London, 1912, tr. R. Hingley, London, 1964). The direction of STANISLAVSKY and the interpretation of his Moscow Art Theatre helped to create the impact of the early performances. These were marked by a new naturalism: realistic sets and sound effects, and what became known as 'method' acting. But the plays fare equally well if their nonrealistic, subjective aspects are stressed, i.e. those of perception, memory and self-consciousness. The character interactions are the-

atrically revolutionary. The length of pauses in which actors communicate by not speaking may be crucial. No one character ever stands as Chekhov's surrogate. His plays, like his stories, reflect a multitude of possible viewpoints, a modernistic perception of reality.   BH

Letters of Anton Chekhov, tr. M. Heim and intro. S. Karlinsky (NY, 1973); R. Hingley, *A New Life of Anton Chekhov* (London, 1976).

Cherwell, Lord, see LINDEMANN, FREDERICK ALEXANDER.

Chesterton, Gilbert Keith (b. London, UK, 29.5.1874; d. Beaconsfield, Bucks., 14.6.1936). British essayist, critic, novelist and poet. Essentially a journalist, first in print and latterly as a brilliant radio broadcaster, he developed a unique manner of playful-serious argument in which by paradox and parallelism he exposed the conventional thinking behind the liberal and agnostic assumptions of his time to reveal the mystery and beauty of life. A Catholic convert, he joined with his friend BELLOC in attacking the secular evolutionism of WELLS and G. B. SHAW, but he was always a more urbane controversialist than Belloc. He had a sympathy for the strange and grotesque as vehicles for insight, and here his talent as a visual artist was displayed (he illustrated much of Belloc's work). Thus he proved a discerning critic of Browning (*Robert Browning*, London, 1903) and Dickens (*Dickens*, London, 1906). He will best be remembered for his fantastic modern romances like *The Napoleon of Notting Hill* (London, 1904) and for his tales of a clerical detective (*Father Brown Stories*, London, 1933).   RS

M. Ward, *Gilbert Keith Chesterton* (London, 1944); J. Sullivan (ed.), *G. K. Chesterton: a Centenary Appraisal* (London, 1974).

Chiang Kai-Shek (b. Fenghua, Chekiang, China, 31.10.1887; d. Taipeh, Taiwan, 5.4.1975). Chinese general, chairman of the Chinese Revolutionary Nationalist party, the Kuomintang (1928–75), and president of China (1928–49) and, later, of the Chinese Nationalist Government of Taiwan (1950–75). Viewed by the non-Chinese world as the embodiment of the new postrevolutionary China, he enjoyed much prestige and during WW2 was advanced by F. D. ROOSEVELT as one of the 'Big Four' statesmen who would win the war and decide the peace. The military record of the Chinese armies under his command in 1944 –5, however, did much to disillusion the American leadership, and his concentration on winning the civil war with the Chinese Communists (which had begun in 1927, four years before the Japanese attack in Manchuria and 10 before the Sino–Japanese war), rather than on fighting the Japanese, lost him much support both within and outside China. His failure and the collapse of organized resistance to the Chinese Communists in 1948–9 resulted from his inability to promote and maintain ability in the government of China, and from the consequent corruption and mismanagement of his government.   DCW

Child, Charles Manning (b. Ypsilanti, Mich., USA, 2.2.1869; d. Palo Alto, Calif., 19.12.1954). American developmental biologist. Child graduated from Wesleyan University in 1892 and went to Leipzig for research training, taking his PhD there in 1895. On his return to the USA he joined the University of Chicago. Child sought to bring the phenomena of embryonic development and of regeneration into a single system of analysis. In both cases an apparently undifferentiated population of cells proceeds in time, and in an orderly fashion, to form a heterogeneous cell population in which subpopulations with different properties and functions occur. Child's explanation of the ways in which cell behaviour could be controlled by the topological relations, or the position, of the cell in the organism was at one time unfashionable, but has in recent years proved profitable. He saw in gradients of metabolic activity the coordinates in terms of which the position of each cell could be uniquely specified and its behaviour determined. His most influential works were *Individuality in Organisms* (Chicago, 1915) and *Patterns and Problems of Development* (Chicago, 1941).   DRN

Childe, Vere Gordon (b. Sydney, N.S. Wales, Australia, 14.4.1892; d. Mount Victoria, N.S. Wales, 19.10.1957). Australian archaeologist and prehistorian. Lived and worked most of his life in the UK as Abercromby professor of prehistoric archaeology at Edinburgh (1927–46) and director of the Institute of Archaeology in the University of London (1946–57). His significance lies in his encyclopedic knowledge of European and Near Eastern prehistory, his adherence to his own peculiar brand of MARXist philosophy and his ability to synthesize on a scale never before achieved (and possibly never to be managed again). Three factors, his early political training in Australia as secretary to the Labour premier of New South Wales, months spent wandering through the sites and museums of Eastern Europe in the unstable years following WW1 and his growing awareness of the German concept of culture, provided the basis for his future prolific works. His concern was, in his own words, to distil 'from archaeological remains a preliterate substitute for the conventional politicomilitary history with cultures, instead of statesmen, as actors, and migrations in place of battles'. This broad theme, presented against a generalized Marxist model, runs throughout his published works and is best displayed in his first major book *The Dawn of European Civilization* (London, 1925, ²1957). A year later, in *The Aryans: a Study of Indo-European Origins* (London, 1926), he examined the relationship between archaeology and comparative philology, extending his field of vision still further in *The Most Ancient East* (London, 1928). The next year saw the publication of the archaeological data upon which *The Dawn* was based (*The Danube in Prehistory*, Oxford, 1929). His impressive body of work was completed with *The Bronze Age* (Cambridge, 1930) in which he developed the theme that regular trade, and with it the emergence of craftsmen elites, was a major turning point in cultural evolution since it marked the first significant step towards the social division of labour. In the next decade (1930–40) his theoretical thinking evolved still further with the introduction, in *New Light on the*

Most Ancient East (London, 1934), of the concept of Neolithic and urban 'revolutions' – the prehistoric precursors of the Industrial Revolution. Subsequent works, of which there were many, further explored these approaches and are best presented in his more popular books: *Man Makes Himself* (London, 1936), *What Happened in History* (London, 1942), *Social Evolution* (London, 1951) and *The Prehistory of European Society* (London, 1958). Although his mild diffusionism is no longer widely accepted and the revolution brought about by radiocarbon dating has significantly altered our understanding of Old World archaeology, it can fairly be claimed that Childe was the most influential thinker to have emerged in the field of European prehistory in the 20c.   BWC

B. G. Trigger, *Gordon Childe: Revolutionary Archaeology* (London, 1980); S. Green, *Prehistorian: a Biography of V. G. Childe* (London, 1981).

Chirico, Giorgio de (b. Volos, Greece, 10.7.1888; d. Rome, Italy, 20.11.1978). Italian painter, whose early work was a crucial influence on the dada and surrealist movements. Born of Italian parents, he studied painting first in Athens and then in Munich where he was influenced by the paintings of Böcklin. After spending two years in Italy, he moved in 1911 to Paris where he began a series of pictures which were dreamlike evocations of Italian piazzas, with long shadows, colonnades, statues, and trains puffing smoke in the background. The introduction into some of them of strange still-life objects such as eggs, artichokes or bunches of bananas led on to paintings in which still life was the main theme, but often with a glimpse of some architectural setting in the background. The peculiarity and originality of these paintings rested largely in their juxtaposition of apparently unrelated objects such as gloves, arrows, draughtsmen's tools, maps, biscuits painted in a *trompe l'oeil* manner and so on; mostly commonplace objects wrenched out of their normal context and juxtaposed so as to suggest some mysterious ritual symbolism or perhaps a FREUDian sexual interpretation. Their haunting,

unreal quality was also heightened by abrupt shifts of perspective and by a tendency to cut off vistas abruptly, so that the spatial structure becomes impossible to read in any coherent, logical way. Various other paintings of the same period included mannequin figures like tailors' dummies or robots, but without eyes or mouth. All these works – to which he gave titles such as *The Enigma of Fatality* or *The Dream of the Poet* – have an intensely dreamlike, hallucinatory character.

Chirico continued to develop this style, known as 'metaphysical painting' (*pittura metafisica*), for several years after his return to Italy in 1915, then in 1919 began a study of the old masters and their techniques which led to a decisive reorientation in his work. Although he continued to repeat some of the metaphysical themes from time to time right up to the end of his life (though usually in a heavier, more classical way), he began to make many paintings of still life, nudes, gladiators, horses by the sea or self-portraits influenced by Auguste RENOIR, Delacroix and the baroque, and claimed to be the sole great exponent of the true traditions at a time of decadence in painting. The surrealists, who greatly admired his early paintings, quarrelled with him violently over his change of style and pointed to a deterioration and loss of inspiration in his later works. His autobiography was published as *Memorie della mia vita* (Rome, 1945; *The Memoirs of G. de C.*, London, 1971).   REA

J. T. Soby, *Giorgio de Chirico* (NY, 1955).

Chomsky, Avram Noam (b. Philadelphia, Pa, USA, 7.12.1928). American linguist, philosopher and political activist. Chomsky's father William was an expert on medieval Hebrew grammar; as an undergraduate at the University of Pennsylvania Noam Chomsky was attracted to the study of formal linguistics partly through sharing the radical political orientation of the linguistics teacher Zellig Harris. Since 1955 Chomsky has taught at MIT. His publications turned grammar, previously an esoteric subject, into a central concern of modern philosophy and psychology. Among the most important of Chomsky's many books on linguistics are *Syntactic Structures* ('s-Gravenhage, 1957), *Cartesian Linguistics* (NY, 1966), and *Reflections on Language* (London, 1976). Chomsky argues that the speed and accuracy with which children master the grammatical structure of their mother tongue, and the degree of grammatical similarity between the languages of the world, show that grammar is not learned from scratch but innate. Opposing the Lockean view of mind as a blank slate inscribed by experience, Chomsky urges that our mental attributes, like our physiology, must be largely determined by our genes: grammatical constructions 'grow' in the mind rather as teeth grow in the mouth. Grammar offers unusually clear examples of this principle, but it applies generally; for instance Chomsky argues that new scientific theories and new movements in the arts are drawn from an innately fixed stock which might be (may, indeed, already be) exhausted. Chomsky thus recasts the rationalism of Plato and Descartes in terms of modern biology.

Politically, Chomsky advocates a syndicalist combination of anarchism and socialism; but his political influence has been associated less with theory than with specific issues. He was a leader of resistance to the American war in Vietnam. Chomsky marshals copious evidence indicting the US military-industrial complex of installing and supporting barbaric regimes in Latin American and other client states; he argues that since WW2 the USA has consistently been the chief promoter of administrative torture and massacre in the Third World, and that for commercial reasons the American media conspire to conceal this as effectively as a state censorship (see, with E. S. Herman, *The Political Economy of Human Rights*, 2 vols, Nottingham, 1979).

Several commentators, beginning with his teacher Harris, have detected relationships between the academic and political sides of Chomsky's thought; and Chomsky has sometimes made such links explicit, for instance in arguing that Lockean empiricist philosophy paved the way for imperialism. Recently, however, Chomsky has insisted on a rigid separation between the two aspects of his work.

Chomsky's influence in academic and political life was greatest about 1970. His appeal to American youth was blunted once the danger of being drafted to fight in Vietnam passed; and he forfeited authority as a political commentator by a series of actions widely regarded as ill-judged (repeated polemics minimizing the Khmer Rouge atrocities in Cambodia; endorsement of a book – which Chomsky admitted he had not read – that denied the historical reality of the Jewish Holocaust). Linguistics, too, has begun to shift its attention away from Chomsky's concerns, partly because his emphasis on formal grammatical structure is felt to distort the nature of real-life speech. But Chomsky remains a major influence even on the work of many linguists who would not call themselves Chomskyans.   GRS

J. Lyons, *Chomsky* (London, ²1977); G. R. Sampson, *Liberty and Language* (Oxford, 1979).

Chorley, Richard John (b. Minehead, Som., UK, 4.9.1927). British geographer who has made the leading contribution to the introduction of quantitative methods and systems analysis into physical geography in the last two decades. An Oxford graduate, Chorley went to the USA in 1951 to work under A. N. Strahler at Columbia University, then the leading centre in quantitative geomorphology, and subsequently lectured at Brown University. His return to England and appointment to Cambridge in 1958 saw the beginning of a flood of books and papers (sometimes coauthored) exploring the implications of mathematical and systems models of the world's physical environment. Among his major works are *Models in Geography* (London, 1967), *Physical Geography* (London, 1971) and *Environmental Systems* (London, 1978). He is also principal author of the multivolume *History of the Study of Landforms* (London, 1964–), which critically examines the growth of geomorphology as a scientific discipline.   PH

Chou En-Lai (b. Huaian, Kiangsu, China, 5.3.1898; d. Peking, 8.1.1976).

Prime minister of the People's Republic of China (1949–76) and foreign minister (1949–58), he was educated in Tientsin and Paris. After joining the Chinese Communist party (in 1924) he became principal adviser to MAO TSE-TUNG, first on urban affairs and then on relations with the noncommunist world, acting from 1941 to 1945 as Mao's representative in Chungking. The close relationship he established with Mao in these early days was to preserve him through the changes and intrigues which surrounded the Cultural Revolution of the mid-1960s, despite his deserved reputation as an advocate of amicable relations both in diplomatic and economic terms with the principal capitalist states including the USA. He played a major part in the Geneva South East Asian Conference (1954), in the Bandung Conference (1955) and the enunciation of the Panch Shila (the Five Principles of noninterference and peaceful coexistence), as in the US–Chinese détente of 1972–3, his orientation being essentially towards the development of China's strength and status as a major world power rather than as the central embodiment of MARXist revolutionary orthodoxy.   DCW

Christaller, Walter (b. Berneck, Baden-Württemberg, Germany, 21.4.1893; d. Königstein, East Germany, 9.3.1969). German geographer who laid the foundations of a rational theory for human settlements. His doctoral thesis at Erlangen, *Die Zentralen Orte in Süddeutschland* (Jena, 1933; tr. C. W. Baskin, *Central Places of Southern Germany*, Englewood Cliffs, 1966), was based on a critical analysis of the size and function of the villages, towns and cities of Bavaria in terms of his three optimizing principles of market, traffic and administrative organization. The intricate, crystal-like lattices which Christaller saw holding the settlement fabric together provided new insights into the way the human population organizes itself to exploit the natural resources and locational attributes of a region. Christaller's ideas owed something to the German settlement geographer Robert Gradmann, and to his teacher, the loca-

tional theorist Alfred Weber. Christaller was, however, something of the 'odd man out' amongst the German geographers of his generation. His thesis attracted little attention at the time it was published and he did not hold a university post. It was not until the 1950s that his ideas were widely introduced in the English-speaking world. In the latter part of his life, Christaller developed a complementary 'theory of the periphery' to explain the apparently anomalous structure of settlements in peripheral locations.   PH

Christie, Agatha Clarissa Mary, *née* Miller (b. Torquay, Devon, UK, 16.9.1890; d. Wallingford, Oxon., 12.1.1976). British detective-story writer. The youngest daughter of an American businessman, she was educated at home and in Paris, but abandoned a musical career because of extreme shyness. In 1914 she married Archibald Christie, an RFC officer, and herself became a VAD and then a qualified dispenser. Her first detective story *The Mysterious Affair at Styles* was published in 1920 by John Lane, who also published her next six books. In 1926, the year of her 'disappearance' (after 11 days she was discovered in a Harrogate hotel), William Collins published *The Murder of Roger Ackroyd*, whose ingenuity firmly established her reputation. Her marriage was dissolved in 1927; in 1930 she married the archaeologist Max (later Sir Max) Mallowan. In all, Agatha Christie published 65 detective stories, a dozen plays (including the record-breaking *The Mousetrap*, 1952), 16 volumes of short stories and two of poems, a children's book *Star over Bethlehem* (London, 1965), and, as Mary Westmacott, six novels. To date 21 works have been filmed. Her *Autobiography* (London, 1977) was published after her death. By the early 1960s UNESCO figures showed that more copies of her books were purchased, worldwide, than those of any other author writing in English, and her annual paperback sales exceed 1.5 million copies. Miss Marple and Hercule Poirot, two of her creations, are known in the remotest parts of the world for their detective skill.   JM

Churchill, Winston Leonard Spencer (b. Woodstock, Oxon., UK, 30.11.1874; d. London, 24.1.1965). British prime minister and war leader. President of the board of trade (1908–10); home secretary (1910–11); first lord of the admiralty (1911–16); minister of munitions (1917–18); minister for war and air (1919–20); colonial secretary (1921–2); chancellor of the exchequer (1924–9); first lord of the admiralty (1939–40); prime minister and minister of defence (1940–5); prime minister (1951–5). He is irrevocably associated with the leadership he provided for Britain in WW2, both for his oratorical role, as the ultimate moral inspiration for British refusal to yield to German victories (1940–1), and for his dominance, as prime minister and minister of defence, of the central direction of the war in the UK. He will also be remembered for his role as home secretary in 1911 in using troops against strikers in South Wales, and as chancellor of the exchequer for the part he played in defeating the General Strike of 1926 as an opponent of organized labour when the latter came into direct conflict with the principle of public order and government. Churchill's career was anything but orthodox, as is illustrated by his support of the Zionist movement in Palestine (1921–2), his opposition to the Government of India Bill (1931–3), his attempts to alert British opinion to the threat of German rearmament (1933–9), his impassioned and ill-advised loyalty to Edward VIII during the Abdication Crisis (1936), his attempt during the 1945 election campaign to brand Labour as a totalitarian party, his warning of the dangers of Russian expansionism in his speech at Fulton, Missouri (1946), his role as initial inspiration of the European movement which resulted in the formation in 1949 of the Council of Europe, his long and ultimately fruitless efforts to bring an end to the first phase of the Cold War by a summit conference between himself, Eisenhower and STALIN (1952–5), and the assiduity with which he pursued his vision of a world led by a partnership of the 'English-speaking peoples' – his version of the pan-Anglo-Saxonism he had imbibed in his imperialist youth. His oratorical skill was matched by his literary ability as an historian. If Churchill had died in 1940, he would have been regarded as a brilliant failure, but the five years of his war leadership (1940–5) secured him a place in British history unequalled save perhaps by the 18c statesman Chatham.

DCW

V. Bonham-Carter, *Winston Churchill as I Knew Him* (London, 1965); R. Churchill & M. Gilbert, *Winston S. Churchill* (vol. 1 –, London, 1966–); H. M. Pelling, *Winston Churchill* (London, 1974).

Clark, Alfred Joseph (b. Glastonbury, Som., UK, 19.8.1885; d. Edinburgh, Lothian, 30.7.1941). British pharmacologist. Clark trained at Cambridge and St Bartholomew's Hospital, and qualified in medicine in 1909. He then turned to pharmacology, and was appointed in 1920 to the chair at University College London, moving to Edinburgh in 1926. In WW2 he rejoined the army (he had won the Military Cross in WW1) and was among those evacuated from Dunkirk.

Clark's outstanding contribution is expressed in two books *The Mode of Action of Drugs on Cells* (London, 1933) and *General Pharmacology* (London, 1937). In these he sought to discover the general laws of drug action. EHRLICH's work had been based on substances which entered into a firm, irreversible, identifiable chemical combination with the tissues. But this left a vast range of drugs, such as the alkaloids and anaesthetics, whose action was reversible, often brief, and of which no distinct chemical account could then be given. Clark, partly through his own work, partly by very extensive and thoughtful review, showed that there were consistent patterns in the relation between dose of drug and response; and between drug action on the one hand, and the reaction of substrate with enzyme, gas adsorption on metals, and the combination of carbon monoxide with haemoglobin on the other. His own work on the action of acetylcholine on the heart showed that there must be specific receptors on the cell membrane, since the amount of acetylcholine required for action would cover less than 0.1 per cent of the cell surface. By being able to bring out the analogies between drug action and other well-defined physicochemical systems, he was able to substantiate the conception of the drug receptor, even though the beginning of its isolation and definition had to wait for 40 years of technological advance. A man of great intellectual honesty, Clark objected to the exploitation of the public, and his work on patent medicines paved the way for much-needed reform. WP

Clark, Andrew Hill (b. Fairford, Man., Canada, 29.4.1911; d. Madison, Wis., USA, 21.5.1975). Canadian geographer who made distinctive contributions to regional historical geography. His special research focused on the settlement structures and land-use patterns created by migrants from the shores of the North Sea when colonizing mid-latitude maritime areas overseas; and on the ways in which institutions brought from the Old World survived, or failed to survive, the transoceanic implant. The main regional focus of his work was the maritime provinces of Canada, where his own grandparents had settled and his family roots ran deep. *Three Centuries and the Island* (Toronto, 1959), a study of Prince Edward Island, and *Arcadia* (Madison, 1968), a study of French settlement in Nova Scotia, summarize many years of research in that area. An early opportunity to work in New Zealand allowed him to pursue the same theme in *The Invasion of New Zealand by People, Plants, and Animals* (New Brunswick, NJ, 1949), a classic study of geographical changes in the South Island. Although Canadian by birth and research focus, Clark spent most of his academic life in the USA. SAUER, under whom he did his doctoral work at Berkeley, and the Canadian economic historian Harold Innis were both major influences on his thinking. Clark set his own studies in a precise methodological framework and created a distinctive graduate school of historical geography at Madison where he held a chair in the University of Wisconsin from 1951 to his death. PH

Clark, John Grahame Douglas (b. Shortlands, Kent, UK, 28.7.1907). British archaeologist and prehistorian. His formative years in pre-WW2 Cambridge in an intellectual atmosphere which saw the rapid development of environmental studies (including pollen analysis and varve dating – techniques being exploited by prehistorians in Scandinavia) provided the inspiration for his first major works *The Mesolithic Age in Britain* (Cambridge, 1932) and *The Mesolithic Settlement of Northern Europe* (Cambridge, 1936). The theme there explored, the relationship of man the hunter-gatherer to his environment, was further developed by his major excavation of Starr Carr in Yorkshire (*Starr Carr*, Cambridge, 1954; reconsidered in *Starr Carr; a Case Study in Bioarchaeology*, Reading, Mass., 1972) and returned to later in *The Earlier Stone Age Settlement of Scandinavia* (Cambridge, 1975). His primary research in the Mesolithic period formed the springboard for a wide-ranging examination of the economic factors influencing the evolution of society in prehistoric Europe, culminating in the publication of *Prehistoric Europe: the Economic Basis* (London, 1952). While adeptly using the techniques of typological study and excavation, Clark's primary concern has been to explore the nature of human society as a factor in the dynamic relationship between man and the natural environment. His more recent work *World Prehistory – an Outline* (Cambridge, 1961; subtitled 'In New Perspective', Cambridge, 1977) shows the distillation of his thinking to encompass the world. From 1952 to 1974 he was Disney professor of archaeology at Cambridge. BWC

Clarke, Arthur Charles (b. Minehead, Som., UK, 16.12.1917). British novelist and prophet of space flight whose article on 'Extra-terrestrial relays' (1945) originated the communications satellite. Clarke joined the fledgling British Interplanetary Society at 17, becoming its chairman while completing his BSc at King's College, London, in the late 1940s. *The Exploration of Space* (London, 1951) was the first of a series of books expounding his technical knowledge and enthusiasm for the 'space age' to a wide public. At the same time he established himself – together with the Americans Isaac Asimov, Ray Bradbury and Robert Heinlein – in the front rank of postwar science-fiction writers. His novels include *Childhood's End* (NY, 1953), *The City and the Stars* (London, 1956) and *Rendezvous with Rama* (London, 1973). With Stanley Kubrick he wrote the script for *2001: a Space Odyssey* (1968), perhaps the most imaginative of all science-fiction films. Clarke's visions of the future alternate between rational projections couched in rough-and-ready prose, and a more mystical mode reminiscent of STAPLEDON. He portrays man's encounter with alien intelligence as the chief turning point in a future which is cosmic and evolutionary rather than mundane and catastrophic. His numerous awards include a UNESCO Kalinga prize (1962). Since 1956 he has been resident in Sri Lanka.   PP

J. D. Olander & N. H. Greenberg (eds), *Arthur C. Clarke* (NY, 1976).

Clarke, David Leonard (b. Bromleigh, Kent, UK, 3.11.1937; d. Cambridge, 27.6.1976). British archaeologist whose short working life was spent in the department of archaeology and anthropology at Cambridge University. His principal contribution lay in the field of archaeological theory. Aware of the rapid development of techniques and theory in kindred disciplines, in particular the social sciences – techniques such as computer simulations, analytical and inductive statistics, locational analysis, systems theory, etc. – Clarke set out, in parallel with US workers like BINFORD, to create a central synthesizing theory for archaeology. In his first major work *Analytical Archaeology* (London, 1968) he presented his considered views which were further developed in several substantial papers, two of which appeared in a volume which he edited: *Models in Archaeology* (London, 1972). His work and that of his US contemporaries has been influential in the development of the 'New Archaeology' – a reaction against the more intuitive reasoning hitherto adopted by archaeologists. BWC

Clarke, Fred (b. Oxford, UK, 2.8.1880; d. London, 7.1.1952). British educator. Educated privately and at Oxford University, Clarke showed early brilliance as a teacher. He was professor of education at University College, Southampton (1906–11), then head of the faculty of education at South Africa College, later the University of Cape Town (1911–29). There he did much for harmony with Afrikaans speakers, becoming fluent in the language and building links with Stellenbosch. In 1929 he moved to McGill University in Montreal, again working for intercommunity cooperation and university extension programmes – notably at Antigonish, Nova Scotia. From there he moved to the London University Institute of Education as adviser to overseas students (1935–6) and then as professor of education and director (1936–45). He was consulted by R. A. Butler on the preparation of the Education Act of 1944, and became chairman of the new Central Advisory Council established by it. He was a prolific writer, emphasizing that education and culture are inseparable from society and from a working life. In this and in other ways Clarke fostered the DURKHEIM view of education. *Essays in the Politics of Education* (London, 1923), *Education and Social Change* (London, 1940) and *Freedom in the Educative Society* (London, 1948) highlight his message. Both as a scholar and as a superb teacher he strongly served the postwar expansion of education in Britain and the Commonwealth.   EJK

Claudel, Paul (b. Villeneuve-sur-Fère-en-Tardenois, Aisne, France, 6.8.1868; d. Paris, 23.2.1955). French poet and dramatist who escaped from what he regarded as the life-denying doctrines of late 19c scientific determinism by reading the poetry of Rimbaud. A bronze plate set in the floor of the Cathedral of Notre Dame in Paris commemorates the instant of his conversion to Christianity on Christmas Day 1886. He had a distinguished career in the French consular and diplomatic service, ensuring French food supplies from South America during WW1, travelling widely in the Far East, and representing France as ambassador in Washington in the 1920s.

Although Claudel's career in the theatre began in 1912 with the first performance of his medieval drama *L'Annonce faite à Marie* (Paris, 1910; tr. W. Fowlie, *The Tidings Brought to Mary*, Chicago, 1960), a legend of which he wrote several versions, it was not until BARRAULT's production of *Le Soulier de Satin* (Paris, 1924; tr. J. O'Connor, *The Satin Slipper; or the Worst is Not the Surest*, London, 1931) at the Comédie-Française in 1943 that he attracted really large audiences. This story of passionate, albeit unconsummated love in 16c Europe and South America is told in Claudel's characteristically high-flown language, with his insistence upon the underlying providence which God uses to make everything in the universe meaningful. Like *Partage de Midi* (Paris, 1906; tr. W. Fowlie, *Break of Noon*, Chicago, 1960), part of which was produced by ARTAUD in 1928, and again imposed on a larger public by Barrault in 1948, it is a very long play. The Anglo-Saxon spectator has to fight hard to allow his scepticism to be overwhelmed by Claudel's use of long, rhythmical, highly poetic, symbolist free-verse. Claudel's other plays included *Jeanne au Bucher* [Joan of Arc at the stake], first produced in 1939 with music by Honneger. His highly conservative religious and political opinions, together with his unreserved support for the French military offensives of 1917, were pardoned by AUDEN in 1939 in 'In Memory of W. B. Yeats' on the ground that Claudel wrote well. The letters he exchanged with GIDE (Paris, 1949; tr. J. Russell, *The Correspondence 1889–1926 between Paul Claudel and André Gide*, London, 1952) are a splendid example of the failure of a belligerent believer to convert a subtle agnostic. PMWT

A. Alter, *Claudel* (Paris, 1968); R. Griffiths (ed.), *Claudel: a Reappraisal* (London, 1968).

Cleaver, Leroy Eldridge (b. Little Rock, Ark., USA, 3.18.1935). American radical writer. Brought up in Los Angeles' black slums, Cleaver was in penal institutions from the age of 12. While in prison (1957–66) for rape, he read extensively in classical and contemporary MARXist texts, as well as FANON and the American Negro novelist Richard Wright, and wrote the essays collected as *Soul on Ice* (NY, 1968), a book which immediately gained international recognition. In these essays he analysed varied facets of racism in American society, not least the tensions and induced self-hatred of blacks, particularly as evidenced in sexual matters, with a clarity and self-awareness which give them lasting value. Freed on parole he became a leading force in the Black Panther movement and a major figure in redirecting blacks from Martin Luther KING's ideal of assimilation to more radical aims. He later left the USA and took no further direct part in American politics but remains one of the cult figures of the decade of radicalism. DCr

Clemenceau, Georges (b. Mouilleron-en-Pareds, Vendée, France, 28.9.1841; d. Paris, 24.11.1929). French minister for home affairs (1906); prime minister (1906–9 and 1917–20). Patriot, Anglophile, member of the Radical party, notorious for his caustic wit and ruthless repression of strikes in France, he became during the war years (1914–17), first the most outspoken critic of French military incompetence and governmental defeatism, and then, as prime minister, the indomitable embodiment of French resistance in face of the massive German advances of spring 1918. A realist, he accepted that French inability to cope with Germany on her own necessitated a unified supreme command of the Allied forces in France and close cooperation with France's British ally. Towards President WILSON he remained a sceptic while recognizing American power; his willingness to accept less from the peace settlement with Germany than the permanent occupation of the Rhine bridgeheads and the separation of the Rhineland, and to sacrifice French ambitions in the Near East to a settlement in Europe exposed him to attack from the ultra-patriotic right. The failure of the Treaty of Versailles to secure ratification in the US Senate destroyed the Anglo–American treaty guaranteeing France's eastern frontiers and led to his parliamentary defeat and eclipse at the hands of those who believed that France should, and could, rely on her own strength alone. DCW

D. R. Watson, *Georges Clemenceau: a Political Biography* (London, 1974).

Cockcroft, John Douglas (b. Todmorden, W. Yorks., UK, 27.5.1897; d. Cambridge, 18.9.1967). British physicist. Educated at the universities of Manchester and Cambridge, in 1922 he joined RUTHERFORD's group at the Cavendish Laboratory. With E. T. S. Walton he developed a simple voltage-doubling system for producing high voltages. By this means they accelerated protons to energies sufficient to induce the disintegration of lithium into two alpha particles. This was the first time a nuclear reaction had been induced by particles accelerated to high energies in the laboratory. It owed its success to Cockcroft's realization that protons could be induced to enter a nucleus by the newly predicted process of quantum mechanical tunnelling even though they lacked the energy to overcome entirely the electrostatic repulsion of the lithium nucleus. For this work he was awarded the 1951 Nobel prize for physics jointly with Walton. He was Jackson professor of natural philosophy at Cambridge from 1939 to 1946 and the founder-director of the Atomic Energy Research Establishment at Harwell from 1946 until 1958. In 1959 he assumed the mastership of the newly created Churchill College, Cambridge, a post he held until his death. PSF

Cockerell, Christopher Sidney (b. Cambridge, UK, 4.6.1910). British radio engineer, and inventor of hovercraft. After graduating from Cambridge, Cockerell went into industry, working at the Marconi Company from 1935 to 1950. He then started building small boats and began to consider the old problem of reducing water resistance. He investigated methods of raising a craft on a cushion of air, both theoretically and experimentally. Towards the end of 1954 a critical experiment, with an industrial drier powering two tins suspended over a pair of kitchen scales, gave encouraging results. The following year a model craft worked successfully, both on land and water, and Cockerell applied for his first British patent. In 1958 Hovercraft Development Ltd was established with Cockerell as technical director. A manned experimental craft, the SRN1, built by Saunders Roe, was completed on 28.5.1959, and the hovercraft is now a well-established means of transport.

RAH

Cocteau, Jean (b. Maisons-Laffitte, Paris, France, 5.7.1855; d. Milly-la-Forêt, nr Paris, 11.10.1963). French writer, artist and film maker. Cocteau combined an apparent versatility as poet, painter, novelist, film maker, playwright, critic and essayist with a genuine uniqueness of preoccupation: himself. He was also much concerned with what he considered to be the Poet's role. This runs through his best-known films – *Le Sang d'un Poète* (1932; tr. L. Pons, *The Blood of a Poet*, Oxford, 1936), *Orphée* (1950) and *Le Testament d'Orphée* (1960) – in which he stresses the importance of unconscious inspiration. He was much influenced by FREUD; as is shown by his heavily psychoanalytical adaptation of the Oedipus legend in *La Machine infernale* (Paris, 1934; tr. C. Wildman, *The Infernal Machine*, London, 1936). He explored the Jocasta complex in a play *Les Parents terribles* (Paris, 1938; tr. C. Frank, *Intimate Relations*, London, 1962) and the complexities of an intense brother–sister relationship in a novel *Les Enfants terribles* (Paris, 1929; tr. R. Lehmann, *Children of the Game*, London, 1955), later made into a film by J. P. Melville (1950). He made little secret of his homosexuality and launched both the boy-wonder novelist Radiguet and the actor Jean Marais. He enjoyed painting, and decorated a number of buildings in the south of France in his own, peculiarly rounded and unchanging style. In 1955 he made literary history by being elected a member of the Académie Française without making the traditional visits to established members. PMWT

Cocteau par lui-même (Paris, 1957); F. Steegmuller, *Cocteau: a Biography* (London, 1970).

Cohen, Albert Kircidel (b. Boston, Mass., USA, 15.6.1918). American sociologist employed at the universities of Indiana and of Connecticut. He is mainly known and cited for his contribution to understanding the nature of gang delinquency. He is the leading theorist in the 'subcultural tradition' and his work continues to be influential in the development of criminological theory. He argued that the group delinquency of adolescents could be best understood in terms of a rejection of dominant social values (academic attainment, deferred gratification, cleanliness and the like) and the adoption of their opposites. Cohen viewed destructive violence and vandalism as an attempt by adolescents to demonstrate to others as well as to themselves their contempt for the values they had rejected. Although not without its critics, Cohen's theory has stimulated a great deal of research on group delinquency and schools, particularly in the USA. His book *Delinquent Boys: the Culture of the Gang* (Glencoe, Ill., 1955) remains a central criminological text. JB

Cole, George Douglas Howard (b. Cambridge, UK, 25.9.1889; d. London, 14.1.1959). British political scientist. Leading theorist of the British Labour movement who wrote voluminously on Labour history, economics and political and social theory which he also taught at Oxford. He was prominent in the Guild Socialist movement (1913–24), stressing in such books as *Self-Government in Industry* (London, 1917) the dangers of an omnipotent state, while advocating the overthrow of capitalism. He held that industry should be reorganized into self-governing national guilds which should also contribute to the legislative process. He later moved to a more orthodox Labour view set out in *The Next Ten Years in British Social and Economic Policy* (London, 1929), seeing public ownership under parliamentary control as the basis for democratic socialism. However, he retained a lifelong sympathy for experiments in industrial democracy. Cole's work is marked by a powerful advocacy of the need to carry the gains of liberalism into any future socialist society and to maximize democracy at work and in the community. AO

M. I. Cole, *The Life of G. D. H. Cole* (London, 1971); A. Wright, *G. D. H. Cole and Democratic Socialism* (Oxford, 1979).

Coleman, Ornette (b. Fort Worth, Tex., USA, 19.3.1930). American jazz saxophonist, violinist, trumpeter and composer. Probably the most controversial figure in jazz history, Coleman achieved his position in the forefront of the music's avant-garde movement by exploring the improvisational possibilities that exist outside of set time metres and conventional harmonies. In 1958 his first recordings (with trumpeter Don Cherry) caused a sensation. On live appearances the music was openly derided, but after several eminent jazz players had praised the energy and potential of the new approach it gained a devoted following.

Coleman, largely self-taught, played alto-saxophone in conventional rhythm-and-blues groups and dance bands during adolescence, but even then he determinedly chose to improvise solos that were not based on the harmonies that his accompanists provided. These revolutionary experiments provided the basis for what Coleman saw as a 'free' approach to jazz improvising. Coleman's ideas have inspired many musicians who felt that their improvisational capabilities were being restricted by accompaniment that was both preplanned harmonically and shackled rhythmically to a set number of beats per bar.

Since the 1960s Coleman has also recorded on violin, trumpet and tenor-saxophone, and he has composed extended works which have occasionally been played by large orchestras. But his own public performances are rare; he chooses to concentrate on composing and teaching. JJC

A. B. Spellman, *Four Lives in the Bebop Business* (NY, 1966).

Colette, Sidonie Gabrielle (b. Saint-Sauveur-en-Puisaye, Yonne, France, 28.1.1873; d. Paris, 3.8.1954). French novelist. Colette ended her long life as something of an institution, becoming in 1945 the president of the Académie Goncourt and receiving the signal honour of a state funeral. Her beginnings were less immediately respectable, for this child of impeccably middle-class provincial parents began her career as neglected wife and exploited ghost-writer for Henri Gauthiers-Villars, nicknamed

'Willy'. Her *Claudine à l'école* (Paris, 1900; tr. A. White, *Claudine at School*, London, 1956) was an instant success, thanks to a mixture of her native talent and the slightly salacious details of adolescent sexuality which her husband persuaded her to add. She left Willy in 1906, had a spell on the Halls, and, from 1920 onwards, was a well-loved figure in the French literary world as one of the most sensitive of French novelists. She was very fond of animals, writing of them with sympathy in *Dialogues des Bêtes* [Dialogues of animals] (Paris, 1904) and *La Paix chez les Bêtes* (Paris, 1916; tr. E. McLeod, *Creatures Great and Small*, London, 1951) and taking as the subject for one of her best novels *La Chatte* (Paris, 1933; tr. A. White, *The Cat*, London, 1953) the sexual jealousy which a young wife feels for her husband's pet cat. Her study of adolescent sexuality *Le Blé en Herbe* (Paris, 1923; tr. R. Senhouse, *Ripening Seed*, London, 1955) was made into an excellent film by Autant-Lara in 1954.

PMWT

M. Davies, *Madame Colette: a Provincial in Paris* (London, 1953); A. A. Ketchum, *Colette ou la naissance du jour* (Paris, 1968).

Collingwood, Robin George (b. Cartmel Fell, Lancs., UK, 22.2.1889; d. Coniston, Cumbria, 9.1.1943). British philosopher and historian. The son of a painter and archaeologist who was the secretary and then the biographer of Ruskin, Collingwood was educated at Rugby and at University College, Oxford. He came to philosophy at a time when the Hegelian idealism, dominant in Oxford since the 1870s and very attractive to him, was retreating in the face of a determined realist assault. As philosophy tutor at Pembroke College from 1912 to 1935 and then professor of metaphysics until retirement in 1941, he was in a lonely intellectual position. His first book *Religion and Philosophy* (London, 1916) treated religion from a Hegelian point of view, intellectualizing away its more embarrassingly superstitious-looking elements. *Speculum Mentis* (Oxford, 1924), his first major book, is an ordered survey of the five major forms of human experience – art, religion, science, history, philosophy – showing the influence of CROCE but so far still clearly distinguishing philosophy from history. His *Essay on Philosophical Method* (Oxford, 1933) assigns a particular style of thought to philosophy, a dialectical one in which ideas are seen as making up an overlapping sequence, and not as exclusively separated from each other. But by 1940 and his *Essay on Metaphysics* (Oxford) he was arguing that metaphysics, at any rate, was an irreducibly historical discipline, one concerned to extricate and exhibit the unquestioned 'absolute presuppositions' of its epoch (see also his vivid *Autobiography*, London, 1939). Philosophy, so conceived, becomes intellectual history. His earlier, very Crocean *Principles of Art* (Oxford, 1938) had no historic emphasis. The nature of art is considered as a timeless problem. Its solution is that art is the expressive activity of the imagination without which the intuitions of the senses cannot be brought to consciousness. Two posthumous works *The Idea of Nature* (Oxford, 1945) and *The Idea of History* (Oxford, 1946) are, however, devised as reflections on the concepts of nature and history prevailing at different stages in the history of thought. Collingwood's historical work proper was on Roman Britain on whose archaeology he was an acknowledged, if recognizedly speculative, authority. He was a masterly prose writer and a man of extremely broad learning.

AQ

A. Donagan, *The Later Philosophy of R. G. Collingwood* (Oxford, 1962); L. Rubinoff, *Collingwood and the Reform of Metaphysics* (Toronto, 1970).

Coltrane, John William (b. Hamlet, NC, USA, 23.6.1926; d. New York, 17.7.1967). American jazz saxophonist and composer and the most influential jazz musician of the 1960s, who brought new harmonic, rhythmic and tonal concepts into improvisation. His solos linked Eastern modes with highly complex harmonies, and his sense of timing showed the possibilities of implying more than one time-signature simultaneously. During his teens, 'Trane' was a disciple of PARKER's alto-saxophone playing; later, he developed an individual tenor-saxophone style encouraged by trumpeter Miles Davis (one of the first jazzmen to explore the possibilities of modal music). Coltrane's prodigious technique and stamina allowed him energetically and inventively to improvise for an hour or more on one theme. His control in the upper register was astounding, no less so when he began doubling on soprano saxophone. His method of improvising influenced not only fellow saxophonists but young jazz instrumentalists of many kinds into the 1970s, alongside the more avant-garde work of alto-saxophonist COLEMAN. JJC

C. O. Simpkins, *Coltrane: a Biography* (NY, 1975); B. Cole, *John Coltrane* (NY, 1976).

Compton, Arthur Holly (b. Wooster, Ohio, USA, 10.9.1892; d. Berkeley, Calif., 15.3.1962). American physicist. His early work on the scattering and absorption of X-rays led to the concept of the Compton wavelength $\lambda = h/mc$ of electrons. He studied the effect of magnetization on the intensity of the X-rays reflected from magnetic crystals and showed that the magnetic orientation of the electron due to its spin is the cause of ferromagnetism. Later he showed that scattered X-rays undergo a change of wavelength related to their energy and scattering angle, a phenomenon now known as the Compton effect. The change in wavelength is just what would be expected for a classical collision between a particle of energy $h\nu$ and momentum $h\nu/c$ with a free electron, thus providing strong support for EINSTEIN's attribution of energy and linear momentum to photons. Compton showed that this holds for each individual collision so that the BOHR–KRAMERS–Slater statistical theory is untenable. He was awarded the Nobel prize in 1927 for his work on the Compton effect. Subsequently he showed that X-rays can be reflected by noncrystalline materials and diffracted by ruled gratings. In the early 1930s he showed that the intensity of cosmic radiation varies over the earth's surface, so that at least some of the primary particles are charged. During WW2 he was influential in starting and directing the atomic energy project, as described in his *Atomic Quest* (Oxford, 1954). After the war he became chancellor of Washington University, where he proved a tower of strength in troubled years. PEH

M. Johnston (ed.), *The Cosmos of Arthur Holly Compton* (NY, 1967).

Compton-Burnett, Ivy (b. Pinner, London, UK, 5.6.1884; d. London, 27.8.1969). British novelist. Educated mainly at home, then at Royal Holloway College, London, where she read classics. Her first novel *Dolores* (London, 1911) was an early indication of her talent but she wrote nothing further until *Pastors and Masters* (London, 1925). In this her unique style appeared already fully matured. She wrote 18 further novels, all similar in theme and range, dealing essentially with violent emotional and family tensions. Her work, English in subject matter but deriving much of its patterning from Greek melodrama, is distinguished by bare, witty, mannered dialogue, highly theatrical in effect. Her uncompromising treatment of eccentricity, hypocrisy and crime and her mastery of domestic comedy have assured her a special place in English 20c writing, although her readership has always been limited. JEEH

A Conversation (with M. Jourdain, London, 1945); E. Sprigge, *The Life of Ivy Compton-Burnett* (London, 1973).

Conant, James Bryant (b. Dorchester, Mass., USA, 26.3.1893; d. Hanover, NH, 11.2.1978). American educator and chemist. After receiving his doctorate in chemistry from Harvard University, Conant worked for the Chemical Warfare Service during WW1. Later he returned to Harvard, becoming its president in 1933, and writing a number of influential books about American education, including *Education in a Divided World* (Cambridge, Mass., 1945), *The American High School Today* (NY, 1959) and *The Education of American Teachers* (NY, 1963). Conant's most concrete influence was upon the development of American scientific policy, as demonstrated in his successful advocacy of the National Science Foundation. On a more general level he reinforced the demand that schooling should be used as an instrument of national purpose. Schools had to stretch the capacities of the most talented while cementing that common citizenship required by American democracy. Such ideas found a ready audience within the context of the Cold War and then the post-Sputnik period.   TT

T. Grissom, 'Education and the Cold War', in C. J. Karier *et al.* (eds), *Roots of Crisis: American Education in the Twentieth Century* (Chicago, 1973).

Conrad, Joseph, *né* Józef Teodor Konrad Nalecz Korzeniowski (b. Berdyczew, Ukraine, Russia, 3.12.1857; naturalized British citizen, 1884; d. Bishopsbourne, Kent, UK, 3.8.1924). Polish/British novelist. Conrad's father, a leading Polish patriot, was exiled to Vologda, Russia, for his part in the Warsaw uprising of 1863. Orphaned at 11, Conrad insisted on going to sea. After several years in Marseilles where he attempted suicide, he began his career (1880) in the English merchant service. He travelled extensively in the East which provides the exotic settings of his most popular works such as *The Nigger of the 'Narcissus'* (London, 1898), 'Youth' (in *Youth and Two Other Stories*, Edinburgh, 1902), *Lord Jim* (London, 1900), *Typhoon* (London, 1902). He gained his Master's certificate in 1886, and in 1890 he visited the Belgian Congo, later basing 'Heart of Darkness' (in *Youth and Two Other Stories*), one of the key texts of literary modernism, on the experience. His career as a seaman ended in January 1894 and a year later he published his first novel *Almayer's Folly* (begun in 1889; London, 1895). Central to Conrad's best fiction is a clash between irreconcilable value systems and beliefs; between his conviction that 'the temporal world rests on a very few simple ideas ... notably ... the idea of Fidelity' (*Some Reminiscences*, London, 1912) and his haunting sense that 'Faith is a myth' and man is alienated; between the invincibility of human fellowship and the sanctified but terrible loneliness of the individual mind. Conrad conceived his fiction in terms of a planned sequence of effects upon the reader which led to 'an intimacy between author and reader that is ... unique in modern fiction' (Watt). Expressive of intimacy is Conrad's crea-

tion of Marlow the narrator of 'Youth', 'Heart of Darkness', *Lord Jim* and *Chance* (London, 1913) who enables Conrad both to dramatize his fiction and to bring home 'to the minds and bosoms of the readers' the universal applications of his stories. Conrad's intricate mastery of time shifts, of switches in perspective and of an ironic method which works, in his own words, for both 'pity and scorn', involves the reader in the fiction and demands that he both reconstruct and reinterpret the action. Conrad's most panoramic and expansive novel – and undoubtedly the best political novel in the English language – is *Nostromo* (London, 1904), set in an invented South American country called Costaguana. *The Secret Agent* (London, 1907) is a subtle study of anarchists and spies in Edwardian London. *Under Western Eyes* (London, 1911), perhaps his most personal novel, is the story of a Russian student who is sucked inadvertently into the revolutionary politics of his generation. Upon its completion in the early months of 1910, Conrad suffered a severe mental breakdown. Subsequently, apart from *Chance*, *Victory* (London, 1915) and *The Shadow-Line* (London, 1917), his career declined. In 1906 Henry JAMES declared of Conrad 'No one has *known* – for intellectual use – the things you know, and you have, as the artist of the whole matter, an authority that no one has approached.' Of the many subsequent writers influenced by Conrad the most prominent are ELIOT, FAULKNER, Scott FITZGERALD and GREENE.   KC

F. R. Karl, *Joseph Conrad: the Three Lives* (London, 1979); I. Watt, *Conrad in the Nineteenth Century* (London, 1980).

Coomaraswamy, Ananda Kentish (b. Colombo, Ceylon [now Sri Lanka], 22.8.1877; d. Needham, Mass., USA, 9.9.1947). Sri Lankan art historian whose most significant contribution was to portray traditional (especially Indian) art as a form of knowledge with the power to effect transformation of being. Trained in London as a geologist (DSc, 1905), Coomaraswamy's return to Ceylon resulted in another kind of appreciation of the past: he decided that traditional Ceylonese culture had been corroded by western influence and that it deserved a spokesman. Regarding post-Renaissance art as impoverished, his role was to become that of a pioneer, even prophet, treating traditional cultures as a way of entering abandoned lands of the spirit. Founding the first subdepartment of Indian art in an American museum (1917), the remainder of his life in Boston was not simply spent helping transform the history of art into a scholarly pursuit. He increasingly saw art as a form of rhetoric, as an 'effective expression of metaphysical theses' (see *Figures of Speech or Figures of Thought*, London, 1946). Profoundly influenced by Plato, Guenon and other metaphysicians and mystics, Coomaraswamy placed art in the context of what he took to be the *philosophia perennis*: a traditional work of art is not aesthetic but is inspirational, bringing to life man's forgotten homeland. His greatest contribution was to emphasize the communicative aspect of culture. What many have been critical of was his ever greater tendency to be mystical – 'understanding involves belief'; as he also wrote, 'I have not remained untouched by the religious philosophies I have studied and to which I was led by way of the history of art.' It is true that his interpretations were sometimes too religiously magisterial, informed by what he took the truth to be.   PLFH

R. Lipsey (ed.), *Coomaraswamy: Selected Papers* (2 vols, Princeton, 1977); R. Lipsey, *Coomaraswamy: his Life and Work* (Princeton, 1977).

Copeau, Jacques (b. Paris, France, 4.2.1879; d. Beaune, Côte-d'Or, 20.10.1949). French theatre critic, director and actor. In articles for the *Nouvelle Revue Française* before WW1 he condemned the current state of theatre for its lack of seriousness, its predilection for naturalism or meretricious spectacle and its subservience to the 'star system', advocating instead the rediscovery of 'pure theatre' staged on a 'bare platform'. In 1913 he opened his own Théâtre du Vieux-Colombier where, using experience gained during two wartime seasons in New York, he evolved a radically simplified stage. This dispensed with front curtain, conventional scenery and wing space in favour of an open, fixed structure incorporating numerous steps and levels to encourage three-dimensional action and adaptable to the intrinsic style and rhythms of individual plays. In 1924, tiring of the struggle for independence in the face of commercial odds and conscious of his failure to attract a broad-based audience, he founded in Burgundy a community theatre collective, nicknamed the 'Copiaus', which improvised touring shows for village audiences. After 1929 he alternated criticism with occasional large-scale, open-air productions and subsequently directed plays at the Comédie-Française, of which he was briefly administrator in 1940. Copeau's creation of a simple, adaptable stage, his interpretation of the director as dutiful servant to the literary text rather than showman, his emphasis on actors working as an ensemble and as artists rather than as slaves to an 'industrialized' profession, and his ultimate search for a truly popular form of theatre, discussed in his *Le Théâtre populaire* [The popular theatre] (Paris, 1941), exercised a profound influence on his collaborators, several of whom became leading actor-directors.   DHR

F. Anders, *Jacques Copeau et le Cartel des Quatre* (Paris, 1959); C. Borgal, *Jacques Copeau* (Paris, 1960).

Coper, Hans (b. Chemnitz, Saxony, Germany [now Karl-Marx-Stadt, East Germany], 8.4.1920; naturalized British citizen, 1958; d. Frome, Som., UK, 16.6.1981). German/British studio potter. Trained as an engineer, and attracted to painting and sculpture, he was introduced to ceramics in 1946 when he joined RIE in her studio, after leaving Germany. He evolved a personal style which has been very influential in modern ceramics, partly through his close connection with the Royal College of Art in London. His wares present tightly controlled, continuous, smoothed contours, which generate perfectly inflected surfaces, and relate to his early training as an engineer. The pot body is usually buff to brown; and all the mottling and irregularity is kept below the strictly cut surface. He was attached to extremely clear articulation of distinct single forms into one piece, in a way which could be called 'modernist'. The great virtue of Coper's forms lies in the metaphorical reference of their single shapes, especially to the closing calyces of flowers. For many years he evolved a 'tulip vase' constructed of a curved single volume container with a cut-off converging lip, resting on a simple foot, the relative proportions subtly adjusted. These were often flattened from front to back, thus offering deliberate faces and profiles. Many of his shapes were evolved from types originating in ancient western Asia, an important departure in terms of modern ceramic practice. His works have been imitated on both sides of the Atlantic.   PSR

M. Rose, *Artist Potters in England* (London, ²1970).

Copland, Aaron (b. New York, USA, 14.11.1900). American composer. His Jewish background was musically rich and subsequent study in Paris matured his musical skills. On returning to the USA in 1924 he taught, wrote reviews and essays, and promoted concerts of new music; later he was to write, for example *Our New Music* (NY, 1941, enlarged ²1968 as *The New Music 1900–1960*). After his Organ Symphony (1925) he was accepted as a 'serious' American composer whose stated aim was to write in a style 'that would immediately be recognized as American in character' and yet 'left popular music far behind'. However, he never became obscure, writing ballets like *Billy the Kid* (1938), *Rodeo* (1942), with its 'Saturday Night Waltz' and 'Hoedown', and *Appalachian Spring* (1944), which makes use of the Shaker song 'Simple Gifts'. Latin American music inspired the brilliantly uninhibited orchestral *El Salón México* (1936). Copland also found an authentically 'American' style for his film scores including *Of Mice and Men* (1939) and *The Red Pony* (1948). It is through such works, rather than his concert music, that he has been most influential. His style, owing something to STRAVINSKY, jazz and folk music, is characteristically 'clean' in sound and athletic in rhythm, though occasionally slow and trancelike: it set a tone for American art music of its generation. Copland's fellow-American Leonard Bernstein has called him 'the best we have'.   CH

J. F. Smith, *Aaron Copland: his Work and Contribution to American Music* (NY, 1955).

Corbusier, see LE CORBUSIER.

Corey, Elias James (b. Methven, Mass., USA, 12.7.1928). American organic chemist. A graduate of MIT, Corey had professional experience with A. D. Little Co., Inc., and has held a chair at the University of Illinois and then at Harvard (1968). Corey's outstanding research has been in the field of stereochemistry, and in structural, synthetic, and theoretical organic chemistry. He has accomplished numerous total syntheses of complex natural products, especially in the field of the prostaglandins (a group of fatty compounds with an extraordinary range and level of biological activity), and in the field of macrolide antibiotics and in that of insect juvenile hormones. In addition he has developed numerous novel synthetic reactions and versatile reagents, and a tremendous range of synthetically valuable functional-group transformations. A pioneer in the use of computer analysis in the design of complex syntheses, his contributions to the technique, art and logic of organic synthesis have been of outstanding value.   NBC

Corner, Edred John Henry (b. London, UK, 12.1.1906). British botanist. Introduced to the writings of the highly original Oxford botanist A. H. Church while at Rugby School, Corner found the botany taught at Cambridge dull and pedestrian. Having met Church and embarked on a classic study of fungi, he was appointed assistant director of the Botanical Gardens, Singapore, a post he held from 1929 to 1945. Church's revolutionary ideas inspired Corner to broaden his studies and to question the received orthodoxy of botany based on the study of temperate floras. The result was the formulation of his Durian theory (1949), the only comprehensive theory of the origin and development of the tropical plant world. Subsequently he has been able to embrace all plant life in melding Church's ideas with his own equally original ones in his highly influential *Life of Plants* (London, 1964), with further extensions of his thesis in *The Natural History of Palms* (London, 1966) and *The Seeds of Dicotyledons* (Cambridge, 1976). His ideas on coevolution of animals and plants and of 'transference of function' embedded in the Durian theory are today's orthodoxy. A controversial generalist in all matters, Corner was responsible for publicizing the fate of tropical vegetation as early as the 1940s when he worked in South America as well as in the Far East. His dedication to science and scholarship led to his controversial cooperation with the Japanese occupation forces in Singapore (1942–5) when he was interned in the Botanical Gardens, but his zeal saved the libraries, collections and records for the modern state of Singapore (*The Marquis: a tale of Syonan-to*, Kuala Lumpur, 1981). Since WW2 he has worked at Cambridge, where he was professor of tropical botany. DJM

D. J. Mabberley & Chang Kiaw Lan (eds), *Tropical Botany. Essays presented to E. J. H. Corner* (Singapore, 1977); D. J. Mabberley (ed.), *Revolutionary Botany* (Oxford, 1981).

Cornforth, John Warcup (b. Sydney, N.S. Wales, Australia, 7.9.1917). Australian organic chemist. Cornforth graduated in chemistry at the University of Sydney and then did research on Australian plants, some of which he collected himself. Thereafter he joined Sir Robert ROBINSON in Oxford for research on the synthesis of steroids and on the structure of the most important of the antibiotics, penicillin, at that time a new drug of exciting potential, since massively realized. In 1946 Cornforth joined the staff of the British Medical Research Council and continued his work on the synthesis of steroids. He achieved the first synthesis of nonaromatic steroids in 1951. About this time he developed an interest in the biosynthesis of steroids (in collaboration with the biochemist G. Popják) and this interest widened to that of biosynthesis in general. Biosynthesis deals with the processes whereby living organisms assemble simple starting molecules into biologically important products of complex structure. Isotopic labelling with radioactive carbon is an indispensable technique in such investigations, and integration of chemistry and biochemistry is essential. The stereochemistry of enzyme-catalysed reactions has also been imaginatively investigated, especially by the introduction of artificial asymmetry into symmetric compounds by labelling them with hydrogen isotopes. This led to the important novel concept of the chiral methyl group. Cornforth has also achieved important syntheses in the heterocyclic field, e.g. of oxazole, a fundamental five-membered ring compound with both oxygen and nitrogen as heteroatoms. He was awarded the Nobel prize jointly with PRELOG in 1975. NBC

Cortázar, Julio (b. Brussels, Belgium, 26.8.1914). Argentine novelist and short-story writer. A great innovator, though he owes many gimmicks to the French. Along with VARGAS LLOSA and GARCÍA MÁRQUEZ, responsible for 'el Boom' in Spanish-American fiction. He was merely a minor poet until he moved to Paris in the year he published his first collection of stories *Bestiario* [Bestiary] (Buenos Aires, 1951), followed by *Final del juego* [End of the game] (Mexico City, 1956) and *Las armas secretas* [Secret weapons] (Buenos Aires, 1959); these first three collections are all represented in tr. P. Blackburn, *End of the Game and Other Stories* (NY, 1967). Their combination of apparent reality with patent fantasy continued in the tales of *Historias de cronopios y famas* (Buenos Aires, 1962; tr. P. Blackburn, *Cronopios and Famas*, NY, 1969), preparing the way for his best-known work, the novel *Rayuela* (Buenos Aires, 1963; tr. G. Rabassa, *Hopscotch*, NY, 1966), described by Harss as a 'therapeutic work' offering 'a course of treatment against the empty dialectics of Western civilization'; less charitable readers find its own dialectic empty and its double-ordering of chapters frustrating, but its interpolation of nonliterary texts, its linguistic gamesmanship, and its intermittent crudities have all proved influential. A later collection of stories, perhaps his best, is *Todos los fuegos el fuego* (Buenos Aires, 1966; tr. J. S. Levine, *All Fires* *the Fire, and Other Stories*, NY, 1973); while two more recent novels, *62: modelo para armar* (Buenos Aires, 1968; tr. G. Rabassa, *62: a Model Kit*, NY, 1972), and the intricately textured and structured *Libro de Manuel* [The book of Manuel] (Buenos Aires, 1973) continue to delight and dazzle his admirers. RP-M

E. Picon Garfield, *Julio Cortázar* (NY, 1975); J. Alazraki & I. Ivask (eds), *The Final Island: the Fiction of Julio Cortázar* (Norman, Okla, 1978).

Cortesão, Jaime Zuzarte (b. Ançã, Beira Litoral, Portugal, 29.4.1884; d. Lisbon, 14.8.1960). Portuguese historian, poet and dramatist. An ardent republican, Cortesão was associated with various literary movements, seeking a national renewal, between 1890 and 1914. After graduating in medicine in 1910, he published a volume of short horror stories and a collection of poetry. He championed the Allied cause in WW1 and served in the trenches as a volunteer medical officer, describing his experiences in *Memórias da Grande Guerra* [Memoirs of the Great War] (Oporto, 1919), unique in Portuguese letters. From 1919 to 1927 he was director of the National Library, Lisbon, a period that launched his many monographs on the history of Portuguese expansion. In his elegantly written historical works he explores the ideas of democracy and Franciscanism in the origins and development of Portugal: *História da colonização Brasileira* [The history of Brazilian colonization] (Lisbon, 1922), *História de Portugal* [History of Portugal], with Damião Peres (8 vols, Oporto, 1928–37), *Alexandre de Gusmão e o Tratado de Madrid* [Alexandre de Gusmão and the treaty of Madrid] (2 vols, Rio de Janeiro, 1940). Between 1927 and 1957 Cortesão was intermittently in exile in France and Spain (where he worked in the archives) and, from 1940, in Brazil. His historical publications, fundamental for the study of Portuguese and Brazilian history, are included in his collected works, which to date comprise 23 volumes (Lisbon, 1964–). DBr

O. Lopes, *Jaime Cortesão: a Obra e o Homem* (Lisbon, 1963).

Cotton, Frank Albert (b. Philadelphia, Pa, USA, 9.4.1930). American chemist. Cotton is perhaps best known for his pioneering work upon complexes containing multiple metal–metal bonds. He obtained his doctorate at Harvard in 1955, and was appointed to MIT. In 1973 he became professor of chemistry at Texas A & M University. Cotton's early work followed in the field established by HIEBER, of metal carbonyl complexes. Adopting Berry's ideas of pseudorotation, Cotton made tremendous progress in the understanding of molecular fluxionality (i.e. the processes which allow a molecule to change its configuration) and in correlating structures found in the solid state with those found in solution. He contends that, whenever practicable, a molecule of special interest should always be studied by crystallographic techniques of structural determination, and that chemists should not rely on the 'sporting methods' of spectroscopy. Applying this principle to a wide range of inorganic systems led to his discovery of a very important category of complexes – those containing discrete multiple metal-metal bonds – in the mid-1960s. Since then, Cotton and his research group have used their synthetic skills to show that this was not a unique phenomenon shown by a few extraordinary compounds, but a hitherto unrecognized general phenomenon exhibited by many elements in the periodic table, and found in many known compounds. Cotton is the author of *Chemical Applications of Group Theory* (NY, ²1971), and coauthor (with G. WILKINSON) of the standard textbooks on *Basic Inorganic Chemistry* (NY, 1976) and *Advanced Inorganic Chemistry* (NY, 1980). KRS

Coulson, Alfred Charles (b. Dudley, W. Mids, UK, 13.12.1910; d. Oxford, 7.1.1974). British theoretical chemist, physicist and mathematician. He held chairs in theoretical physics in London, and in applied mathematics and, later, theoretical chemistry at Oxford. He also published significant work in meteorology and in biology. His main contribution to science was in molecular orbital theory. Chemists write chemical structures in the form of diagrams with lines which represent 'bonds' between atoms. Although it had been appreciated that some bonds could not be either single or double, Coulson introduced a quantitative definition of fractional bond orders based on quantum mechanical calculations. These simple calculations permit the prediction of bond length from a knowledge of the molecular formula. For a particular class of very important hydrocarbon molecules which includes benzene, he produced some important generalizations which greatly simplify the understanding of their properties. These contributions and the reconciliation of molecular orbital theory and valence bond theory are covered in his *Valence* (Oxford, 1961). Coulson's work on isolated molecules was extended to the array of atoms which make up a solid. In particular his interest in graphite and in the structure and properties of diamond continued for many years. He showed for the first time why irradiated diamonds appear blue. Although much of his work predated electronic computers, some of the methods he devised for performing integrals are now of great importance in computer-based molecular orbital calculations and still provide the standard techniques. Coulson was also an intuitive thinker who published many books and articles on religion, including *Science and Christian Belief* (London, 1958). WGR

Courant, Richard (b. Lublinitz, Silesia, Germany [now Poland], 8.1.1888; naturalized American citizen, 1940; d. New Rochelle, NY, USA, 27.1.1972). German/American mathematician, also important in the development of the mathematics profession. Educated at Göttingen, he worked in differential equations and their applications to physical problems. *Methoden der mathematischen Physik* (2 vols, Berlin, 1931; *Methods of Mathematical Physics*, NY, 1953), written by him but to which he added HILBERT's name, turned out to be a timely primer of mathematical techniques for quantum mechanics. During the 1920s he also inaugurated a Mathematical Institute in Göttingen, and launched important journals and a research monograph series (the 'Yellow Books') with Springer-Verlag. As a Jew, Courant was suspended from his appointment in 1931. An uncertain period ended with an offer in 1934 from New York University, where he spent the rest of his career. He built up its research programme substantially, culminating in the founding of the Courant Institute of Mathematical Studies in 1965. During his New York career he also published another volume of *Methods of Mathematical Physics* (NY, 1937), research monographs on specific topics (including shock waves), and a popular book called *What is Mathematics?* (with H. Robbins, Oxford, 1941). IG-G

C. Reid, *Courant in Göttingen and New York* (NY, 1976).

Coward, Noël Pierce (b. Teddington, London, UK, 16.12.1896; d. Blue Harbour, Jamaica, 26.3.1973). British dramatist, actor and composer, who first appeared on the stage in 1911, wrote his earliest play in 1918 and the last of a canon of 50 in 1966, and was knighted in 1970. While his rapid graduation from hard-edged cynicism in his first major success *The Vortex* (1924) to the sentimental if well-orchestrated jingoism of the musical *Cavalcade* (1931) testified to the ease with which the English Establishment absorbed its latest rebel, such a shift between elitism and populism continued to characterize his work, and on occasion gave it an unexpected depth of social insight. Coward gave closest definition, however, to the world of the 1920s, when London society remained sufficiently self-confident to be titillated by the 'shocking' behaviour of the characters eponymously defined in *Fallen Angels* (1925) and *Easy Virtue* (1925). The bohemianism became more self-conscious in such later 'society' comedies as *Private Lives* (1930), *Design for Living* (1933), *Present Laughter* (1943) and *Relative Values* (1951), while the social conscience worn on the shirtcuffs of *This Happy Breed* (1942) and *Peace in Our Time* (1947) seems more out-of-character than it should in the light of Coward's actual wartime work with British Intelligence. To this he brought the same professionalism which distinguished the assured lyrical movement and the clipped, precise artic-

161

ulation of his own songs, which helped to sustain wartime morale no less surely than they had earlier pinned down the brittle lifestyle of the 'bright young things'. Most notably when playing opposite Gertrude Lawrence, his acting, too, achieved a wry, throwaway intensity well suited to the oxymoronic exchanges of his dialogue. Arguably, his plays now revive better the further they edge towards the situation comedy of *Hay Fever* (1925) or *Blithe Spirit* (1941), and away from the 'mannered' presentation of social and sexual mores more enduringly captured in the reluctant *tristesse* of his lyrics. Only in the fantasticated, posthumously staged *Semi-Monde* (1977) and the aptly titled *A Song at Twilight* (1966) was he able to explore his own homosexuality in other than veiled theatrical terms.   ST

R. Mander & J. Mitchenson, *Theatrical Companion to Coward* (London, 1957); S. Morley, *A Talent to Amuse: a Biography of Coward* (London, 1969); J. Lahr, *Coward: the Playwright* (London, 1982).

Cowell, Henry Dixon (b. Memlo Park, Calif., USA, 11.3.1897; d. Shady, NY, 10.12.1965). American pianist and composer. Of Irish extraction, Cowell studied at the University of California and at the New York Institute of Applied Music. A Guggenheim fellowship enabled further study in Berlin. Although Cowell's early works were conventional, he founded a number of organizations to promote contemporary music. Later he developed new compositional techniques, many of which influenced and have been carried to the extreme by CAGE. Cowell originated the term 'tone cluster' which signified large numbers of notes to be played on the piano either with the fist, whole hand or with the horizontal forearm. Certain of his works call for the piano strings to be plucked or strummed as in 'Aeolian Harp' (1933); 'The Banshee', a slightly earlier piece, has to be played entirely on the strings while an assistant holds down the damper pedal. In 1933 Cowell edited and contributed to a symposium *American Composers on American Music* (Stanford, Calif.).   JL

B. Saylor, *The Writings of Henry Cowell: a Descriptive Bibliography* (NY, 1977).

Cowley, John Maxwell (b. Peterborough, S. Australia, Australia, 18.2.1923). Australian physicist. He studied at the University of Adelaide (BSc 1945) and MIT (PhD 1957), and became professor of physics at Melbourne in 1962. Eight years later he moved to Arizona State University to take up the Galvin chair in physics. Cowley is one of the world's leading electron microscopists, having pioneered the use of electron beams to study the structure of materials. He has developed both theory and practice of image reconstruction to the point where microscopic visualization of single atoms is sometimes possible. Biological work, in particular, stands to benefit from advances in this area, as molecular researchers start trying to locate in the cell the reactions they have studied in the test tube. Cowley's texts (for example, *Diffraction Physics*, Oxford, 1975) are considered basic and definitive reading for electron microscopists.   DOM

Cox, Harvey Gallagher (b. Phoenixville, Pa, USA, 19.5.1929). American theologian. Cox came to prominence with and remains best known for *The Secular City* (NY, 1965), an analysis of the phenomena of secularization and urbanization, and a proposal for a theology of the Christian church to meet the needs of the new situation. Conceived originally as a study guide for college students, Cox's book was an immediate bestseller. In some respects it represented a reappearance of the American Protestant tradition of the social gospel; in others it was the popularization of the theological legacy of BONHOEFFER. Bonhoeffer had written of 'a world come of age', and Cox applied this to a radical and political theology of the USA in the 1960s. In finding a biblical warrant for secularization, Cox also contributed to an evangelical Protestant basis for a political theology. Cox's subsequent publications have remained in the same vein of popular theology, dealing especially with the theology of fantasy – *Feast of Fools* (Cambridge, Mass., 1969) – and with the dialogue between Eastern and Western currents in spirituality – *Turning East* (NY, 1977) – but none has struck the imagination of the moment quite like *The Secular City*. PFL

Craig, Edward Henry Gordon (b. Stevenage, Herts., UK, 16.1.1872; d. Vence, Alpes-Maritimes, France, 29.7.1966). British theatre designer, director and theorist. Son of Ellen Terry and of architect Edward William Godwin, Craig arguably had a greater influence on the development of 20c theatre than any other Englishman. Such a claim is based less on his achievements as a practitioner than on a series of writings and design ideas, most notably *The Art of the Theatre* (London, 1905; with other essays as *On the Art of the Theatre*, 1911), *Towards a New Theatre* (London, 1913) and many articles under pseudonyms in the *Mask* which he founded and edited, with breaks, between 1908 and 1929. It was here that he first propounded his belief in the 'noble artificiality' of the theatre, and in the need for the dominance of the director, and of a new kind of actor trained to the austerity and selflessness of the marionette. His most influential and far-reaching ideas were in stage design. Advocating the use of massive screens and flights of steps whose mood could be altered by light, he matched the independent work of APPIA, and eventually went far beyond it. Often accused, though unjustly, of being impractical, Craig had spent 10 years as an actor, often with Irving, 15 as designer and director of plays and operas. Much of his work was done in collaboration, notably with STANISLAVSKY, with whom he produced *Hamlet* at the Moscow Art Theatre in 1912. He was unwilling ever to compromise, however, and spent most of his last 50 years abroad in semiretirement. JMW

Crane, Harold Hart (b. Garretsville, Ohio, USA, 21.7.1899; d. at sea, 27.4.1932). American poet. Crane was a child of the 1920s, celebrating the ambiguous promise of American life: 'This was the Promised Land, and still it is/To the persuasive suburban land agent/In bootleg roadhouses where the gin fizz/Bubbles ... ' (*The Bridge*). In his most ambitious poem *The Bridge* (Paris, 1930) Crane sought through symbol and image to capture the texture and meaning of modern American life. His choice of symbols, particularly the Brooklyn Bridge, was influenced by the romantic and symbolist belief in the creative powers of the imagination. The sense of space and time in the poem – the European heritage, the early explorers, natives and emerging myths – gave Crane a unique complexity and resonance. He argued that the function of poetry lay in 'the articulation of the contemporary human consciousness *sub specie aeternitatis*'. Like ELIOT, Crane saw in the 'superior logic' of metaphor, rather than in discursive narrative, the basis for a modern poetry; but he rejected Eliot's remoteness from, and dislike of, contemporary life. He argued that 'unless poetry can absorb the machine, i.e. *acclimatize* it as naturally and casually as trees, cattle, galleons, castles and all other human associations of the past, then poetry has failed of its full contemporary function'. Crane's *Collected Poems* appeared posthumously in 1933 (NY; ed. B. Wever, ²1966). EH

J. Unterecker, *Voyager* (NY, 1969).

Crawford, Osbert Guy Stanhope (b. Breech Candy, Bombay, India, 28.10.1886; d. Nursling, Hants., UK, 29.11.1957). British archaeologist. The development of British archaeology owes much to Crawford, notably in the fields of air photography and cartography. During service in France in WW1 he was impressed by the potential value of aerial survey for the discovery and mapping of ancient sites and landscapes. Opportunity for developing the technique in Britain came after 1920 when he was appointed archaeology officer of the Ordnance Survey, a post which he held until 1946. Major publications arising from his work in the air and on the ground include *The Long Barrows of the Cotswolds* (Gloucester, 1925), *Wessex from the Air* (with A. Keiller, Oxford, 1928) and *The Topography of Roman Scotland North of the Antonine Wall* (Cambridge, 1949). Under his guidance the Ordnance Survey also began to issue period maps, beginning in 1924 with the *Map of Roman Britain*, and these quickly established themselves as a major repository of information. Crawford was also involved from the beginning with the *Tabula Imperii Romani*, a series of maps which would cover the entire Roman Empire. His own fieldwork, including much important work in the Sudan and air photography, continued alongside his official cartography, as did his outstanding editorship of the journal *Antiquity*, which he founded in 1927 and edited until his death, making it the most influential, popular archaeological journal in Europe. MT

Cressey, Donald Ray (b. Fergus Falls, Minn., USA, 27.4.1919). American criminologist and sociologist. Student and later collaborator with Edwin SUTHERLAND in the publication of later editions of the latter's basic textbook of the discipline *Principles of Criminology* (NY, ⁵1955, ¹⁰1978). Cressey himself conducted a pioneering study of trust violation (*Other People's Money*, Glencoe, Ill., 1953, ²1961), establishing for the first time the syndrome of that variety of 'white collar' crime that has subsequently been extensively verified. Later studies by Cressey have included a reappraisal of Sutherland's theory of differential association and an investigation of the problems of organized crime and the Mafia (*Theft of a Nation*, NY, 1969).
TPM

Crick, Francis Harry Compton (b. Northampton, UK, 8.6.1916). British molecular biologist. Crick graduated in physics from University College London in 1937. He worked as a scientist for the British admiralty during WW2; then turned to the study of biology, joining the Medical Research Council Unit at Cambridge under PERUTZ in 1949. In 1962 he received the Nobel prize for medicine with J. D. WATSON and WILKINS. In 1951 Crick and Watson began a collaboration which resulted in the elucidation of the molecular structure of DNA. DNA was known at that time to be the genetic material, but chemical analyses had yielded little insight into the nature of the properties that suited it for this role. Following their construction of models that were compatible with the X-ray diffraction data obtained

by FRANKLIN in Wilkins's laboratory at University College London, Crick and Watson proposed that the DNA molecule had a double-helical structure, with complementary pairing of component bases, a proposal which revolutionized approaches to the study of genetic structure and function. Crick and Watson realized that each strand could act as a template during DNA replication, and they suggested a mechanism for mutation. Their model also gave strong support to the idea of Dounce and GAMOW that the sequence of nucleotides might determine the sequence of amino acids in proteins. In the years following, Crick was concerned with the problem of how the gene is expressed, in particular with the genetic code and how this is read. Since moving to the Salk Institute for Biological Studies at San Diego, California, he has been exploring some of the wider biological implications of current findings in molecular genetics. APJ

J. D. Watson, *The Double Helix: a Personal Account of the Discovery of the Structure of DNA* (London, 1968).

Croce, Benedetto (b. Percasseroli, Abruzzi, Italy, 25.2.1866; d. Naples, Campania, 20.11.1952). Italian philosopher and historian. Born into a landowning family, Croce spent most of his life as a private scholar in Naples, particularly after the death of his parents in an earthquake in 1883. For the next 20 years he gave himself wholly to study, above all in the historical and literary fields he never abandoned. His concern with art (especially literature) and history (in particular his studies in MARX's historical materialism) led him to begin the development of his 'Philosophy of Spirit', whose best-known first part came out in 1902: *Estetica* (Bari; tr. D. Ainslie, *Aesthetic as Science of Expression and General Linguistic*, London, 1909). Succeeding volumes were *Logica* (Bari, 1905; tr. D. Ainslie, *Logic as the Science of the Pure Concept*, London, 1917), *Filosofia della pratica* (Bari, 1909; tr. D. Ainslie, *Philosophy of the Practical*, London, 1913) and *Teoria e storia della storiografia* (Bari, 1917; tr. D. Ainslie, *Theory and History of Historiography*, London, 1921). In 1903 he founded the periodical *La Critica* for the preliminary publication of his ideas, contributing to it voluminously for the next 41 years. For Croce there are two kinds of theoretical or cognitive activity: one conceptual, studied by logic, the other intuitive, studied in aesthetics. Intuition is direct experience which we bring to consciousness by giving it expression. Art is simply the most developed form of this expression, and its point and value lie within the experience itself; entertainment and instruction are alien to it. Croce also rejects the idea of artistic genres. In his logic Croce distinguishes the genuine, dialectically related concepts that figure in the historical apprehension of the activities of spirit from the pseudoconcepts of the natural sciences, which are only practical instruments. He ruled out metaphysics and religion almost as firmly as the logical positivists did, but in the interests not of science, but of history which, as the rational study of the development of spirit, is what Croce believed philosophy in the end amounts to. Croce draws a parallel distinction between two kinds of practice: economic, aimed at singular ends, and ethical, with a universal purpose. After WW1 Croce became involved in public life, as senator and then minister of education in the collapsing parliamentary system and, after 1925 and the evident decision of MUSSOLINI to rule in a purely dictatorial way, as leader of the intellectual opposition to fascism. During the fascist years Croce wrote important histories of Naples, of Italy since 1871 and of 19c Europe, in part as vehicles for his criticism of the regime. At his death he was the unchallenged presiding figure in the intellectual life of Italy. AQ

C. Sprigge, *Croce, Man and Thinker* (London, 1952).

Crosby, Harry Lillis (Bing) (b. Tacoma, Wash., USA, 2.5.1904; d. Madrid, Spain, 14.10.1977). American popular singer and screen actor. From about 1931 he was a highly successful radio singer and his name became synonymous with the word 'crooner' (i.e. the kind of soft, intimate vocal style which radio microphones made possible). Songs like 'Where the Blue of the Night Meets the Gold of the Day' and 'White

Christmas' (from the film *Holiday Inn*, 1942) seem to sum up an art in which a gentle warmth escapes sentimentality by virtue of evident intelligence and a touch of humour. Crosby's agreeable appearance and acting talent, together with his sense of timing, allowed him to appear on equal comic terms with Bob Hope in the seven 'Road' films, beginning with *Road to Singapore* (1940) and ending with *Road to Hong Kong* (1962). He also played semiserious roles such as the singing priest Father O'Malley in *Going My Way* (1944), for which he won an Academy award, and its sequel *The Bells of St Mary's* in the following year. 'Bing' – the 'old groaner' – was among the most loved of show business figures. He was taken ill and died while playing golf, and that he enjoyed life until the last seems to symbolize his art. He described his career in *Call Me Lucky* (with P. Martin, NY, 1953). CH

Crosland, Anthony (b. London, UK, 29.8.1918; d. Oxford, 19.2.1977). Cabinet minister in the British Labour governments of 1964–6, 1966–70, 1974 and 1974–7, who became the ideologue of the social democrat wing of the Labour party with the publication of *The Future of Socialism* (London, 1957), and inspired the unsuccessful attempt in 1959–60 to eliminate Clause 4 (the advocacy of wholesale nationalization) from the party's constitution. His assumption that post-1945 capitalism reformed on KEYNESian lines had solved the twin problems of economic stability and progress under a regime of full employment led to the conclusion that socialism should chiefly concern itself with the division on egalitarian lines of the inexorable fruits of that solution. In this process, however, he and his followers abandoned the long-standing Fabian socialist concern with the efficient functioning of government at a time when bureaucratic growth and increasing state intervention were effectively destroying the ability of Britain's mixed economy to fulfil their basic assumptions. This robbed Crosland's generation of Labour middle-class university-educated 'meritocrats' of the chance to recognize, or develop answers to, the new challenges to that social democracy for which he and his contemporaries had fought during WW2 and which the Labour governments of 1945–51 had sought to establish.   DCW

Cudlipp, Hugh (b. Cardiff, S. Glam., UK, 28.8.1913). The pacemaker in British tabloid journalism (1935–68). Cudlipp secured his first London appointment on the *Sunday Chronicle* at 19. He quickly became known nationally for his flamboyant boldness 'at slinging type, writing bright headlines and chopping pictures in the right place'. When the *Daily Mirror* was redesigned as an American-style tabloid under new management, Cudlipp felt immediately drawn to it 'as to an open challenge'. At the age of 22 he became its features editor, rapidly helping to give it an original character with an overall formula for success based on sex, crime and rabble-rousing 'factory-floor' politics. The circulation of the paper at this point was around 750,000. After three years under Cudlipp's influence, it passed the two million mark and after WW2, when he returned to the *Daily Mirror* as editorial director (1952–63), he increased its circulation beyond five million, without deviating from his original formula and flamboyance. For Cudlipp's own account see *Publish and Be Damned: the Story of the Daily Mirror* (London, 1953) and his autobiography *Walking on the Water* (London, 1976).
          RB

Cummings, Edward Estlin (b. Cambridge, Mass., USA, 14.10.1894; d. Silver Lake, NH, 3.9.1962). American poet. Cummings's father had been the first lecturer in sociology at Harvard, and later became a Unitarian minister. When Cummings went to Harvard (where he became a close friend of DOS PASSOS) he rebelled against the proprieties of his parents' world. He became an aesthete, began to dress unconventionally, and dedicated himself to painting and literature. He appeared along with Dos Passos in *Eight Harvard Poets* (NY, 1917). After the USA declared war on Germany, Cummings volunteered to join the Norton-Harjes Ambulance Service. Indiscreet comments in the letters of a friend led to Cummings's arrest and incarceration in a French concentration camp at La Ferté-Macé. This experience produced his first book, the autobiographical prose work *The Enormous Room* (NY, 1922). On his return to America he published several volumes of poetry: *Tulips and Chimneys* (NY, 1923) and *XLI Poems* (NY, 1925) which established him as a clever experimental poet and a rebellious spirit. Following APOLLINAIRE, he enthusiastically altered punctuation and spelling, and by disturbing the spatial relationships of the verse line and stanza went far towards eliminating the idea of rhythm. Cummings's successes are genuine, but even his best poems are sometimes marred by playfulness for its own sake. In his writing he celebrated a hedonistic anarchism which, as he grew older, came to sound more like a cranky New England conservatism. Among his later books, *Eimi* (NY, 1933) describes a brief, disillusioned visit to the Soviet Union. His *i: six nonlectures* (Cambridge, Mass., 1953) give an account of his early years.   EH

M. Cowley, *A Second Flowering* (London, 1973); R. S. Kennedy, *Dreams in the Mirror* (NY, 1980).

Curie, Jean F. Joliot, see JOLIOT-CURIE, IRENE.

Curie, Marie, *née* Sklodowska (b. Warsaw, Russian Poland [now Poland], 7.11.1867; d. Haute-Savoie, France, 4.7.1934). Polish/French physicist and radiochemist, and **Curie, Pierre** (b. Paris, France, 15.5.1859; d. Paris, 19.4.1906). French physicist. In association with her husband, Mme Curie played a leading role in the early development of radiochemistry and became the greatest woman in science of her time. She was a pioneer in the handling, separation and analysis of radioactive substances and thus laid the foundation of the science of radiochemistry.

Marie Sklodowska left Poland in 1891 to study at the Sorbonne in Paris. In 1895 she married Pierre Curie. He was already a distinguished physicist, who had established that ferromagnets lose their magnetism above a certain temperature (the Curie temperature) and had made significant contributions to the theory of magnetism (Curie–Weiss law).

Marie gave up her early work on the magnetic properties of steel to devote herself unstintingly to the study of radioactivity which had been discovered by Becquerel in 1896. In attempting to identify the origin of the radioactivity of natural uranium ore (pitchblende) she applied the techniques of analytical chemistry to identify the components of the mineral, using radioactivity to monitor the components thus separated. In this way two previously unknown radioactive elements, namely polonium and radium, were identified (1898) and their salts purified. The magnificence of this achievement, under laboratory conditions which would be condemned today, is brought out by the fact that one tonne of pitchblende contains no more than 200 milligrams of radium and only a fraction of a milligram of polonium – quantities far too small to have been detected by any conventional chemical means. The magnitude of this task established Mme Curie as a heroic world figure. The scientific impact of the discovery of radium, and with it the birth of radiochemistry, was one of the most important events in the history of science, leading as it has to the rapid evolution of atomic and nuclear physics. In 1904 the Curies, jointly with Becquerel, received the Nobel prize in physics. After the tragic death of Pierre Curie, Mme Curie continued her study of the radioactive elements and in 1911 became the first person to be awarded a second Nobel prize, this time in chemistry. She became director of the Radium Institute. Her death through anaemia was almost certainly hastened by exposure over most of her working life to ionizing radiation.   DHE

E. Curie, *Madame Curie* (Paris, 1938; abridged tr., Cambridge, 1943); E. Cotton, *Les Curies* (Paris, 1963).

Curie, Pierre, see CURIE, MARIE.

Curtius, Ernst Robert (b. Thann, Alsace, Germany [now France], 14.4.1886; d. Rome, Italy, 19.4.1956). German historian of literature and of ideas. In his approach to literature and philology – mainly Romance, medieval Latin and English – Curtius transcended traditional disciplinary boundaries, paying equal attention to aesthetic, historical, philosophical and philological questions. His studies in European literature from the Middle Ages to the 20c acquire their unity from Curtius's humanist conviction, shored up by vast learning, that all later western literature may fruitfully be conceived as a continuation of the achievements of antiquity. This is best shown by his influential *Europäischen Literatur und Lateinisches Mittelalter* (Bern, 1948; tr. W. R. Trask, *European Literature and the Latin Middle Ages*, London, 1953). Ranging from Homer to ELIOT and VALÉRY, classical works and their influence, primary and secondary, on subsequent individual writers, literary movements and schools are traced with a great wealth and sharpness of detail and a vivid awareness of specific historical context. In the manner of Aby WARBURG and of his own teacher Gustav Gröber, Curtius identifies basic *topoi* – symbols, images, figures – generated by antiquity, and pursues their course as they recur in modified forms in the works of succeeding centuries. His strengths as a critic, and his cosmopolitan humanism, are best seen in his *Kritische Essays zur Europäischen Literatur* [Critical essays on European literature] (Bern, 1950).   RNH

Cushing, Harvey Williams (b. Cleveland, Ohio, USA, 8.4.1869; d. New Haven, Conn., 7.10.1939). American neurophysiologist and neurosurgeon. Son of a doctor, Cushing was an undergraduate at Yale and a medical student at Harvard. He then devoted himself to surgery, eventually specializing in the still new field of neurosurgery, where he developed better techniques for the diagnosis, localization and surgical removal of brain tumours. A skilled surgical technician, Cushing also spent much time in experimental work on problems relating to the cerebral spinal fluid, surgical shock, anaesthesia and sepsis. Military service in WW1 also confronted him with the surgical aspects of head wounds. Tumours of the pituitary gland (hypophysis) stimulated his interest in endocrinology, to which he made significant contributions including the description of one form of hyperpituitarism, now called Cushing's disease. Cushing was also an avid bibliophile, medical historian and bibliographer whose library (with those of two book-collecting friends, J. F. Fulton and Arnold Klebs) was presented to Yale University. He had returned to Yale in 1933 after his surgical career at the Johns Hopkins Hospital, Baltimore, and, from 1912, as Moseley professor of surgery at Harvard and surgeon-in-chief of the Peter Bent Brigham Hospital. WFB

J. F. Fulton, *Harvey Cushing: a Biography* (Springfield, 1946); E. H. Thomson, *Harvey Cushing: Surgeon, Author, Artist* (NY, 1950, ²1981).

Cushny, Arthur Robertson (b. Speymouth, Grampian, UK, 6.3.1866; d. Edinburgh, Lothian, 25.2.1926). British pharmacologist. After training in medicine in Aberdeen, Cushny studied physiology with H. Kronecker in Bern and then joined Schmiedeberg, the leading pharmacologist of the day, in Strassburg. After 12 years in Michigan, USA, he returned to Britain in 1905, first to University College London, and then in 1918 to Edinburgh.

Cushny's principal scientific work included: the first direct studies of the action of the cardiac drug digitalis on the heart, where he both discovered its strengthening effect on muscle contraction and, from other work, predicted the existence of auricular fibrillation in man 10 years before this could be verified electrocardiographically; the development of a modern theory of the kidney, reviving an approach suggested earlier by Carl Ludwig, which replaced 'vitalist' conceptions of secretion by a mechanism of passive filtration of the water and solutes in the blood followed by differential diffusive reabsorption in the kidney tubules; the demonstration, following Pasteur's chemical work on crystals, that certain drugs (including adrenaline) which, because of an asymmetric carbon atom in their structure, can exist in two mirror-image forms otherwise identical in physical and chemical properties, are more active biologically in one form than the other – which meant that the structures in the body on which the drugs act must therefore also be asymmetrical. Cushny also wrote the first authoritative English textbook on *Experimental Pharmacology* (London, 1900) which helped to lay an experiment-based foundation for the therapeutic revolution of the 1930s. WP

Cvijić, Jovan (b. Loznica, Serbia [now Yugoslavia], 12.10.1865; d. Belgrade, 10.1.1926). Serb geographer, at first a medical student in Belgrade but from 1884 a geographer eagerly studying his homeland on fieldwork tours. From 1889 to 1893 he was a research student in Vienna, where he gained his doctorate for *Das Karstphänomen* [The phenomena of Karsts] (Vienna, 1893), a study of the limestone country of Serbia, on which he wrote much more later and acquired world renown. In 1893 he became professor of geography at the Belgrade High School (later University), and all his remaining years were given to study of the physical and human geography of the Balkan peninsula. In 1915 he moved to Neuchâtel and then to Paris, where he was welcomed at the Sorbonne and wrote his regional study, *La Péninsule balkanique et les pays slaves du Sud* [The Balkan peninsula and the south Slav lands] (Paris, 1918). This work was a significant contribution to the formation of Yugoslavia at the treaty of Versailles in 1919. Much respected for his work and his personal qualities at the Paris Peace Conference, he then returned to Belgrade and continued his studies in physical geography, many of which were gathered together in his *Morphologie terrestre* [Morphology of the earth] (2 vols, Paris, 1924–6).

TWF

T. W. Freeman, *The Geographer's Craft* (Manchester, 1967).

D

Daimler, Gottlieb Wilhelm (b. Schorndorf, Baden-Württemberg, Germany, 17.3.1834; d. Bad Cannstatt, Baden-Württemberg, 6.3.1900). German pioneer of the internal combustion engine. In 1885 he developed a three-wheel 'horseless carriage' using a petrol engine, and in the following year built a four-wheeled car. In 1890 he founded the Daimler Motor Company. Over the same period, though they were ignorant of each other's work, BENZ was also developing the internal combustion engine. They never met, but their companies were merged in the 1920s. RIT

Dale, Henry Hallet (b. London, UK, 9.6.1875; d. Cambridge, 23.7.1968). British physiologist and pharmacologist. Dale began his studies under EHRLICH and the physiologist STARLING, and became director of the Wellcome Physiological Laboratory at the age of 29. His work on the action of ergot extracts which inhibit the sympathetic nervous system led to the discovery that the body produces its own 'autopharmacologically' active substances. Among the consequences of this initial insight were his later discovery of 'sympathomimetic' amines and of posterior pituitary substances which were to be of much therapeutic importance, and of the role of histamine release in anaphylaxis. Dale is best known, however, for establishing, with LOEWI, that acetylcholine is the chemical 'transmitter' which carries nerve signals to muscles, for which discovery they shared the 1936 Nobel prize for physiology and medicine. Dale's further experiments, of outstanding clarity and precision, became the basis for much modern understanding of neurotransmitter physiology and pharmacology. He also helped bring about international standardization of biological substances, chaired the wartime Scientific Advisory Committee, was president of the Royal Society and the able administrator of the Wellcome Trust for medical research until retirement at 85. He described much of his work in *Adventures in Physiology* (London, 1953). DOM

Daley, William (b. Hastings-on-Hudson, NY, USA, 7.3.1925). American studio potter. Daley studied at Massachusetts College of Art, Boston, and at Columbia University Teachers College, and has taught at schools in Iowa, New York and New Mexico. In 1966 he became head of the ceramics department of the Philadelphia College of Art. Daley is an exceptionally influential practitioner and teacher whose own work is outstandingly original. His technique is to build his works in clay inverted over a hump. They can be very large, and are usually intended to be floor pieces. A visit to Pueblo sites in New Mexico inspired him to follow not only the example of south-western ceramics, but also the structural imagery of the dwelling sites. Inside his large bowls he creates patterns of cells and levels which reflect the interaction of positive and negative spaces. For such work he favours a straightforward open-bodied red-firing clay. He uses sharp edges, clear and definite shapes, and sharply defined cut channels which give his work a resemblance to architectural complexes that have grown by controlled accretion. His work is not easy to imitate, and the implications of his original ceramic thought are only now being fully explored by the rising generation of ceramists. PSR

Dali, Salvador (b. Figueras, Gerona, Spain, 11.5.1904). Spanish painter, poet, novelist, sculptor; designer of furniture, jewellery and textiles. After a turbulent childhood and adolescence, he joined the surrealists in 1929. The precision of his technique and his simulated but convincing use of paranoia produced universally fascinating images, while his extravagant behaviour and views attracted publicity. The most directly FREUDian of the surrealist masters, he painted double and even treble images and drew out concealed and frequently sexual meaning from such unlikely sources as Millet's *Angelus*. The Dalinian plain, littered with crutches, lobsters, soft watches, elongated buttocks and melting structures of ambiguous meaning, all casting long shadows and frequently swarming with jewel-like ants, is, for many, the essence of visual surrealism. He contributed essays to surrealist publications, many on the rehabilitation of such then-despised artifacts as art nouveau architecture or the painting of certain 19c academics. The most important statement of his aims and methods is contained in a pamphlet, *La Conquête de l'Irrationel* (Paris, 1935; tr. D. Gascoyne, *The Conquest of the Irrational*, NY, 1935). He wrote an autobiography: *The Secret Life of Salvador Dali* (NY, 1961). He painted his best work between 1929 and 1939.

Dali's increasing rapacity and a suspect obsession with HITLER resulted in his expulsion from the surrealist movement in the mid-1930s. For a time he was invited to contribute to exhibitions but his commercialism and opportunism led to a complete rupture; he compounded the offence by his reconciliation with the Catholic church and acceptance of a medal from FRANCO. Aided and abetted by his wife Gala, originally married to ELUARD, he has since exploited himself outrageously. Yet he remains an enigma. It is uncertain how much of his utterance is self-mockery; certainly his rather perverse intelligence remains intact. As an artist, however, he was of interest only while he remained within the surrealist movement.   GM

J. T. Soby, *Salvador Dali: Paintings, Drawings, Prints* (NY, 1941); R. Descharnes, *Salvador Dali* (NY, 1969).

D'Annunzio, Gabriele (b. Pescara, Abruzzi e Molise, Italy, 12.3.1863; d. Gardone, Lombardy, 1.3.1938). Italian poet, novelist and dramatist. Controversy has always surrounded D'Annunzio as writer or politician, but as MONTALE wrote, 'D'Annunzio experimented with all the linguistic and prosodic possibilities of our time ... Not to have learnt from him would be a very bad sign.' Yet Montale as well as UNGARETTI and Saba reacted against

him, just as D'Annunzio had reacted against the poetic tradition represented by Carducci and Pascoli. D'Annunzio's metrical and linguistic innovations altered expression and reflected a new sensibility. A prolific writer (in French and in Italian), his first book of poems *Primo Vere* [Spring] came out in 1879 (Chieti) and his last *Teneo te, Africa* in 1936 (Milan). In between he published several important books of fiction, poetry and drama. His most important book of lyrics *Alcyone* (Milan, 1904) – the third of the four books (*Maia*, Milan, 1903; *Elettra*, Milan, 1904; *Merope*, Milan, 1918) in the cycle of poems called *Laudi del cielo del mare della terra degli eroi* [Praises of the skies, the sea, the earth and the heroes] – offers a synthesis between his naturalistic creed and rhythmic mastery and control. Among his plays the most important are *Francesca da Rimini* (Milan, 1902), *La figlia di Iorio* (Milan, 1904; tr. C. Porter, *The Daughter of Iorio*, London, 1907) and *La città morta* (Milan, 1898; tr. A. Symons, *The Dead City*, London, 1900); and among his novels *Il piacere* (Milan, 1889; tr. G. Harding, *The Child of Pleasure*, NY, 1898), which epitomizes D'Annunzio's sensual aestheticism; *Il fuoco* (Milan, 1900; tr. K. Vivaria, *The Flame of Life*, London, 1900); *Forse che sì forse che no* [Perhaps yes, perhaps no] (Milan, 1910); and *Notturno* [Nocturne] (Milan, 1921). Love and beauty, politics and war and, behind them all, a crudely nationalistic sort of patriotism are *leitmotifs* of D'Annunzio's work and the guiding principles of his life. This patriotism led him to celebrate the war in Libya, fight in WW1, and with volunteers besiege the port of Fiume in September 1919 and hold it for a year. In 1924 the Italian government conferred upon him the title 'Principe di Montenevoso'; in 1937 he was nominated president of the Accademia d'Italia.   GS

H. James, *Essays on the Novel* (London, 1957); A. Rhodes, *D'Annunzio: the Poet as Superman* (NY, 1960).

Darby, Henry Clifford (b. Resolven, W. Glam., UK, 7.2.1909). British historical geographer. At Cambridge in the 1930s Darby worked on the Fenland in medieval times and developed an approach to historical geography which emphasized the reconstruction of past geographies based on particular archival sources. This 'cross-sectional approach' was the focus of a volume he edited, *A Historical Geography of England before AD 1800* (Cambridge, 1936). It was the basis of Darby's major project and contribution to historical geography, on the geography of England as displayed by the Domesday Book: this produced seven volumes – five regional surveys (edited and coauthored by Darby, 1952–1967), a gazetteer (1975) and a general survey *Domesday England* (Cambridge, 1977). After WW2 Darby stimulated much work on historical geography at the three departments in which he held chairs consecutively: Liverpool, University College London, and Cambridge. His methodological writings were less inflexible than the early cross-sectional approach suggested, and he encouraged experiment in the development of narrative studies of change, as in *A New Historical Geography of England* (Cambridge, 1973).　　RJJ

Darlington, Cyril Dean (b. Chorley, Lancs., UK, 19.12.1903; d. Oxford, 26.3.1981). British geneticist and botanist. A graduate in agriculture of Wye College, University of London, he was destined for a farming career in Australia. But he came across Morgan's *The Physical Basis of Heredity* (1919) during his course, and under its stimulus persuaded William BATESON at the John Innes Horticultural Institute to make him a temporary research fellow in 1923. He became head of the cytology department, working on the structure, mechanics and divisions of chromosomes. He surmised later that he was one of perhaps five people in the UK who believed in the integral role of chromosomes in heredity. But in a mere nine years a series of papers on meiosis, chiasmata and chromosome pairing in diploids and polyploids was synthesized in *Recent Advances in Cytology* (London, 1932, ²1937). The worldwide impact of this little book converted the chaos of contemporary cell studies into a cohesive discipline. A few years later in *The Evolution of Genetic Systems* (Cam-

bridge, 1939, ²1958) he integrated cytology with population and evolutionary genetics in a way that has influenced all subsequent thinking in these subjects. In 1939 he became the institute's director, still producing seminal papers on cytoplasmic inheritance, plasmagenes, viruses and variegated plants. Indeed, one of his greatest contributions may ultimately be seen to be his influence on the breaking down of the intellectual barriers between heredity and infection. Throughout the early postwar period he hammered away at the absurdities and cruelties of the LYSENKOist regime in the USSR, a tyranny which murdered many of his friends. In 1953 he was appointed Sherardian professor of botany at Oxford. He turned his attention increasingly to the role of genetic variations in human affairs, publishing in 1964 *The Genetics of Man* (London) and in 1969 the controversial *The Evolution of Man and Society* (London).　　APJ/BEJ

Dart, Raymond (b. Brisbane, Queensland, Australia, 4.2.1893). Australian anatomist and palaeoanthropologist who made important finds of fossils in South Africa representing early stages in the evolutionary origin of man. Dart graduated from the universities of Brisbane and Sydney and after holding a number of posts and fellowships in the UK and the USA, was appointed to the chair of anatomy at Witwatersrand University, Johannesburg, in 1923, retiring in 1958. In 1925 Dart reported on the remains of an incomplete infant skull and endocranial caste found at Taungs in Botswana. He referred this to a new genus and species *Australopithecus africanus* which, although the overall appearance was apelike, Dart considered was ancestral to man, mainly on the basis of tooth structure. Few accepted this judgement at the time, but following a series of further discoveries in former limestone caves in the Transvaal, by Dart, J. T. Robinson and, particularly, Robert Broom, and extensive study by W. E. Le Gros Clark, few now dispute that the australopithecines represent an early stage in the evolutionary differentiation of man. These fossils demonstrate that one of the first features to be evolved was terrestrial bipedalism. Only later came the substantial brain expansion and jaw reduction which characterize modern man. The significance of bipedalism was that it completely emancipated the arms and hands from support and locomotor function. Whether the South African australopithecines actually made tools is uncertain but Dart considers there is evidence for the fashioning of bones, teeth and horn – the osteodontokeratic culture.   GAH

Davis, Stuart (b. Philadelphia, Pa, USA, 7.12.1894; d. New York, 24.6.1964). American painter. After training under Robert Henri, leader of the 'Ashcan school' of early 20c realists (1910–13), Davis came into contact with European art from impressionism to cubism at the Armory show in New York (1913), at which he showed five of his own watercolours. He later described this exhibition as the greatest single influence on him. Works such as *The President* (1917) show his response to Van Gogh's expressive colours, combined with the flattened planes of cubism. In c. 1920 Davis began to paint imitation collages of cigarette-package labels (e.g. *Lucky Strike*, 1921). In his first abstract works (the *Egg Beater* series, 1927 – a still life of an electric fan, rubber gloves and an egg beater, and his sole theme for a year) objects were reduced to a rhythmic abstract pattern of solid planes and lines. In the 1930s he used abstract rhythms to evoke the tempo, flashing neon lights and jazzy sounds of American, especially New York, life – recurrent motifs being gas stations, neon signs and advertisement hoardings. He took part in the Federal Art projects (1935–40), producing four major murals, including an abstract stylization of musical and electronic symbols for radio station WNYC (1939). In the 1940s, influenced by MATISSE, his colours became even brighter, interacting with the sharply defined shapes in a syncopated rhythm (e.g. *Hot Still-scape for six colours*, 1940). The dynamic relationship between line and plane continued in the 1950s (e.g. *Visa*, 1951, where arbitrarily selected words in illogical combinations are distributed rhythmically across the

surface, resembling a brilliant signboard).   SOBT

J. Lane, *Stuart Davis: Art and Art Theory* (NY, 1978).

Davis, William Morris (b. Philadelphia, Pa, USA, 12.2.1850; d. Pasadena, Calif., 5.2.1934). American geographer. Arguably the most influential physical geographer of his generation, and the one whose work did most to shape modern geomorphology, Davis published over 600 papers and books and travelled widely in North America and the other continents. His voluminous writings include *The Rivers and Valleys of Pennsylvania* (Washington, 1889), *Physical Geography* (Boston, Mass., 1898), *Geographical Essays* (Boston, Mass., 1909), and *The Coral Reef Problem* (NY, 1928). He spent most of his academic life in Harvard, continuing very active work after his retirement in 1912. He saw the evolution of landforms (the earth's surface terrain) as a function of three factors: geological structure, erosional and depositional processes, and temporal stage. He laid special stress on the importance of the third element, time, and argued that three distinct phases – youth, maturity and old age – could be recognized in it. Together these formed a life cycle of landforms, later known as the Davisian cycle. He later modified the cycle by incorporating climatic changes and structural interruptions. Although Davis's ideas have been challenged, notably by emphasizing the much greater mobility of the earth's crust, his contribution to our understanding of the evolution of the earth's surface remains a major one. Although a geologist by early training, Davis saw the need for a separate and coherent geographical science and played a leading part in the early organization of geographical studies in the USA, most notably the founding of the Association of American Geographers (1905).   PH

R. J. Chorley *et al.* (eds), *The Life and Works of William Morris Davis* (NY, 1973).

Davisson, Clinton Joseph (b. Bloomington, Ill., USA, 22.10.1881; d. Charlottesville, Va, 1.2.1958). American physicist who in collaboration with GERMER discovered the diffraction of electrons by the crystal lattice of nickel, thus showing their wave nature. Davisson worked at the Bell Telephone laboratories on thermionics and on the emission of secondary electrons from metals bombarded by electrons. With C. H. Kunsman he found that the angular distribution of the secondary electrons shows peaks. In April 1925 a target was accidentally oxidized, and he found that even after cleaning by prolonged heating the angular distribution of the secondary electrons had completely changed and strongly depended on the crystal orientation. He correctly attributed this to recrystallization due to heating, which made many small crystals coalesce to a few large ones. He and Germer obtained further results which they realized could be explained by de BROGLIE's hypothesis that electrons have a wave nature. These matter waves are diffracted by the single crystals, and the angles of maximum emission can be connected with the energy of the electrons and the properties of the crystal. He was awarded the Nobel prize for physics, with G. P. THOMSON, in 1937.   PEH

Dean, James Byron (b. Marion, Ind., USA, 8.2.1931; d. Paso Robles, Calif., 30.9.1955). American film actor. Dean appeared in only three main roles before his death, aged 24, in a road accident, and only one of his films, *East of Eden* (1955), appeared in his lifetime. Dean's performance in this adaptation of STEINBECK's novel, and the characters he portrayed in *Giant* (1956) and *Rebel Without a Cause* (1955) appear almost interchangeable with the vulnerability, frustration and anger of his own emergent personality. The violent circumstances of his death driving a Spyder Porsche to a car race were greatly publicized. His death, as much as his short life, provided a general focus for the anxiety of western teenagers before a clearer expression was offered by Beat writers such as KEROUAC and the popular culture surrounding rock and roll.
   RBJG

Debussy, Achille-Claude (b. St-Germain-en-Laye, nr Paris, Yvelines, France, 22.8.1862; d. Paris, 25.3.1918). French

composer. Often termed 'impressionist' by analogy with the works of MONET in particular, Debussy's music had closer links with the symbolist poets. One of his first important works, the orchestral *Prélude à l'après-midi d'un faune* [The afternoon of a faun] (1894), was suggested by Mallarmé's eclogue; his single opera *Pelléas et Mélisande* (1902) was based on the play by Maeterlinck; and his many songs include settings of verse by Verlaine, Mallarmé and Louÿs. Like these writers, his concern was not with the outside world but with interior feelings and impressions; he paid little heed to musical conventions. He developed a harmonic style in which logical development was abandoned in favour of suggestion, allusion and ellipsis. His music introduces a variety of chords in which the sense of tonality is weak, and there is no firm anchorage to his harmonic progressions. Such vague and ambiguous material could not readily be contained in standard musical forms. Debussy rarely tried to adapt his music to earlier modes but developed new forms of musical evolution and free association. This new approach to form, which later influenced BOULEZ and others, is particularly remarkable in some of the later works, including the ballet *Jeux* [Games] (1913) and several of the twelve *Etudes* for piano (1916).

Debussy's fluid harmony and shaping were matched by his mobile rhythms and variety of colour, an essential element (as in most subsequent 20c music) and not decoration. His orchestral works – including the three *Nocturnes* (1901), the symphonic sketches *La mer* [The sea] (1905) and the three *Images* (1913) – depend very much on skilled orchestration. Even his piano pieces, especially the two books of *Préludes* (1911 & 1913), rely on nuances of timbre.   PG

E. Lockspeiser, *Debussy: his Life and Mind* (2 vols, London, ²1965); R. Nichols, *Debussy* (London, 1972).

Debye, Peter Joseph Wilhelm (b. Maastricht, Limburg, The Netherlands, 24.3.1884; naturalized American citizen, 1946; d. Ithaca, NY, USA, 2.11.1966). Dutch/American physicist and physical chemist. Debye's work illustrates the essential unity of the physical sciences:

it ranged from early researches on the quantization of electron energies in atoms to his final work on the size and shape of polymer molecules. He was one of the few scientists ever to be awarded two Nobel prizes. Debye studied at the Technische Hochschule in Aachen under SOMMERFELD and moved with him to Munich (1906). There he developed his interest in the interaction of radiation with matter which was to be the main theme of his subsequent work. In 1911 he succeeded EINSTEIN as professor of theoretical physics at Zürich where he extended and improved Einstein's theory of the heat capacity of crystalline solids, the properties of a solid being dependent on the 'Debye characteristic temperature'. He also commenced work on molecular electric dipole moments (now measured in 'Debyes') and their evaluation from experimental measurements. At Utrecht he developed his theory of the frequency dependence of dielectric constants and, within a few months of LAUE's discovery of X-ray diffraction (1912), had worked out a theoretical treatment of the influence of lattice vibrations on the intensity of X-ray reflections. He moved to Göttingen in 1914 and, in collaboration with Scherrer, developed the technique of X-ray powder diffraction which bears their names. He also contributed to the theory of 'VAN DER WAALS forces' between molecules in terms of dipole-induced dipole effects.

Debye returned to Zürich in 1920 where his theory of the scattering of X-rays by electrons (COMPTON effect) was arrived at independently and simultaneously with Compton's own theory. For this work they shared the Nobel prize in physics (1927). To this period also belongs the development with HÜCKEL of the theory of strong electrolytes (Debye–Hückel equation), and their electrical conductivity. These theories stimulated a vigorous worldwide study of electrolyte solutions which has formed one of the main streams of physical chemistry in the past 50 years. Other highly important contributions from this period were in cooling by adiabatic demagnetization and in the X-ray diffraction of liquids and single molecules. After Debye moved to Leipzig in

1927, this latter topic led to his second Nobel prize, in chemistry (1936). He became director of the Kaiser Wilhelm (later the Max Planck) Institute in Berlin in 1934, but left in the early months of 1940 to become chairman of the chemistry department at Cornell University, where he worked for the rest of his life. In this last phase of his career his main interest was in polymer chemistry and in light scattering by solutions. DHE

Déchelette, Joseph (b. Roanne, Loire, France, 8.1.1862; d. L'Aisne, 8.10.1914). French archaeologist. His early interest in Iron Age and Roman archaeology led him to translate the work of Pič on the Bohemian oppidum of Stradonice and to write an account of the excavations of the oppidum of Bibracte (Mont Beuvray). But he is best known as a systematizer producing order out of the archaeological chaos of the times. His early work on Les Vases céramique ornés de la Gaule romaine [Gallo-Roman decorated ceramic vases] (2 vols, Paris, 1904) is still a classic but is overshadowed by the magisterial volumes of his great Manuel d'Archéologie: vol. 1, Préhistorique, was published in parts in 1908; vol. 2, Celtique et Gallo-romaine, was completed after Déchelette's death by Albert Grenier and appeared in parts in Paris between 1910 and 1915 [Manual of prehistoric, Celtic and Gallo-Roman archaeology]. Its value is shown by its republication in 1971 (5 vols, Farnborough). BWC

De Forrest, Lee (b. Council Bluffs, Iowa, USA, 26.8.1873; d. Hollywood, Calif., 30.6.1961). American inventor. De Forrest was educated at Yale and did research there on radio waves. Searching for improved signal detectors, he introduced a third electrode into Fleming's diode and patented the idea of the triode valve in 1906. The amplifying valve, which was developed from De Forrest's idea, was fundamental to electronics and was without rival until the invention of the transistor. RAH

De Gasperi, Alcide (b. Pieve Tesino, Trentino-Alto Adige, Italy, 3.4.1881; d. Sella di Valsugana, 19.8.1954). Secretary-general, Italian People's party (1919–

25); leader of the Italian Christian Democrat party, and prime minister of Italy (1945–53). Following 20 years of fascism, De Gasperi represented the first attempt to translate the voting strength of Catholicism into an organized and progressive political party in Italy. This attempt fractured on the continuing feudal city-state nature of Italian political life at the constituency level. De Gasperi therefore translated the idealist element in Italian Christian democracy into an early and wholehearted support of European integration at the military level through NATO, where Italy was France's natural partner against the UK and the USA, and at the political level through the Council of Europe, and the European Coal and Steel Community. De Gasperi's Christian Democrat party took a resolutely anticommunist line, strengthened by the challenge to Italian national sentiments from Yugoslav claims, backed by the USSR, on Trieste. This, taken with the strength of the Italian-American vote in both American political parties, assured De Gasperi general American economic aid.   DCW

Delaunay, Robert (b. Paris, France, 12.4.1885; d. Montpellier, Hérault, 25.10.1941). French painter. Delaunay trained as a decorator and became a painter in 1904. He was influenced at first by the Pont Aven school (1904, in Brittany) and the fauves (e.g. *Landscape with Setting Sun*, 1906). His 1909 series of interiors of the Gothic church at *St Séverin* showed an interest in CÉZANNE's shifting perspectives and changing relationships of objects in space, rendered in grey-green cubist harmonies. The *Eiffel Tower* series (1910–11) marked a transition to a fully cubist fragmentation of forms in space, used to express the dynamism of the city. The tower, symbol of the modern city, is seen simultaneously from above and below in a series of fragmented facets, and spatial continuity is interrupted by abrupt changes in perspective, giving the surface a sense of movement, but in a unified, balanced composition. In the *Fenêtres Simultanées* series (1910–13) he experimented with Chevreul's law of simultaneous colour contrast to create chromatic harmonies, contrasts and discords which could suggest light and movement, while retaining scarcely discernible representational motifs. In the *Discs* series (1912–13) he temporarily abandoned 'all images of reality that come to corrupt colour', using wheel-shaped colour gradations, harmonies and discords to suggest light, movement and space (e.g. *Simultaneous Contrasts: Sun and Moon*, 1913). APOLLINAIRE described this transformation of the optical experience into colour rhythms as 'orphism'. The optical perception of space created by colour fused with an impression of moving bodies or objects remained Delaunay's concern (e.g. the second *Eiffel Tower* series, 1921; *Les Coureurs*, the footballer series, 1913–24; and the vast murals for the Palais de l'Aéronautique and the Palais des Chemins de Fer at the 1937 Paris World Fair).   SOBT

Robert Delaunay, exh. cat., Orangerie des Tuileries (Paris, 1976).

Delbrück, Max (b. Berlin, Germany, 4.9.1906; naturalized American citizen, 1945; d. Pasadena, Calif., USA, 9.3.1981). German/American molecular biologist. Gunter Stent, prominent chronicler of molecular biology, notes that Delbrück's importance in the field is 'hard to explain to strangers, since he made none of the breakthrough discoveries'. Rather, he set standards of experiment and analysis which did as much to establish molecular biology as the actual discoveries. Educated at Tübingen, Copenhagen and Göttingen, he began as a physicist, working with Niels BOHR when the implications of modern physics for biology were being considered. Delbrück went to Thomas MORGAN's genetics department at the California Institute of Technology precisely to look for a complementarity relation, such as that exemplified by HEISENBERG uncertainty in genes. This search proved unfounded, but in the course of it Delbrück and colleagues laid the foundations of phage and bacterial genetics, and discovered genetic recombination in viruses, all results leading to much fruitful work in many laboratories. For helping establish the 'informational school' of molecular biology, Delbrück shared the 1969 Nobel prize in physiology and medicine. As professor of biology (1947–77) and then as professor emeritus (1977–81) at Cal. Tech., Delbrück continued to search for the paradox which would reveal complementarity, in light transduction by fungus as a model for sensory processes – but without success.   DOM

Delius, Frederick Fritz Theodore Albert (b. Bradford, W. Yorks., UK, 29.1.1862; d. Grez-sur-Loing, Seine-et-Marne, France, 10.6.1934). British composer of German parentage. As a young man he travelled in Europe for his father's wool business and then settled briefly in Florida as an orange-grower. But in 1886 his passionate interest in music took him to study at Leipzig where he met the Norwegian composer Grieg, whose influence as a musical 'nature poet' was to remain strong. In 1889 he settled in France, first in Paris and then with his painter wife Jelka in the peaceful village of Grez-sur-Loing, near Fontainebleau. In his final decade, incapacitated by blindness and paralysis, he was helped by the young Yorkshireman Eric Fenby who acted as an amanuensis for his last compositions. Delius like MAHLER was a late-romantic poet of nostalgia, even world-weariness, affected profoundly by the beauty and inevitable transience of nature. This mood is strongest in such works as the opera *A Village Romeo and Juliet* (1901) and the vocal-orchestral *Sea Drift* (1904). Less poignant but equally evocative are such orchestral pieces as *Paris: the Song of a Great City* (1899) and *Brigg Fair: an English Rhapsody* (1907) as well as the ecstatic choral *Song of the High Hills* (1911). Delius's music is never intellectual, but sensuous and vibrant; not to everyone's taste, its flavour is unique.   CH

A. Hutchings, *Delius* (London, 1948); A. Jefferson, *Delius* (London, 1972).

Deller, Alfred George (b. Margate, Kent, UK, 31.5.1912; d. Bologna, Emilia-Romagna, Italy, 16.7.1979). British countertenor. In 1940 Deller joined Canterbury cathedral choir where TIPPETT heard him sing and arranged for him to make his concert debut at Morley College, London. This was to lead to a full-time career as one of the world's

foremost countertenors. 'There is nothing remarkable about being able to sing high,' he is reported to have said, 'a lot of men can sing higher than I can. What matters is what one does with the voice'; and that was the secret of Deller's artistry. He specialized in the music of Dowland and Purcell, appearing not only as a soloist but with his own consort. He founded the Stour Festival in Kent and an Academy of English Music at Sénanque, Provence. A number of composers wrote specially for him including BRITTEN (Oberon in *A Midsummer Night's Dream*). Deller made many recordings, mainly of English music.   JL

De Mille, Cecil Blount (b. Ashfield, Mass., USA, 12.8.1881; d. Hollywood, Calif., 21.1.1959). American film director. In 1913 Cecil B. De Mille formed the Lasky Feature Play Company with Jess Lasky and Sam Goldfish (later Goldwyn). In the same year he directed *The Squaw Man* (with Oscar Apfel) in the frontier village of Hollywood – the beginnings of the world's greatest movie centre are often dated from this moment. At six reels long, *The Squaw Man* was the first feature-length film to be made in Hollywood and its commercial and critical success helped establish De Mille as a director to be reckoned with. By 1917 the Lasky Company had been incorporated into Paramount, one of the five big Hollywood studios, and De Mille was at the centre of Paramount's success, not only directing and producing many films himself but supervising the company's entire output. His movies are an exemplification of traditional storytelling, entertaining narratives spiced with a liberal sprinkling of sex and violence but counterbalanced by a redeeming Victorian moralism. This 'sin and redemption' formula achieved its greatest commercial success in his spectacular Biblical epics: *The Ten Commandments* (1923, remade 1956), *The King of Kings* (1927), *Samson and Delilah* (1949). The mammoth scope of these and his other historical epics are visual testaments to the enormity of his contribution to the establishment of Hollywood as the world's foremost film centre. His own version of his life is in *Autobiography* (NY, 1959). LJC

Deng Xiao Ping (b. Sinkiang Province, China, 22.8.1904). Chinese Communist leader. Deng was among the early Chinese Communists trained in France and the USSR. He rose quickly in the party hierarchy after his transfer to Peking from the south-west in 1952, becoming a member of the Politburo Standing Committee in 1956 as well as general secretary of the Chinese Communist party. Purged during the Cultural Revolution as a leading 'revisionist', he was rehabilitated in 1973, and in 1976 was ranked number three in the Chinese hierarchy after MAO and CHOU EN-LAI. On the latter's death in 1976 Deng was expected to succeed him as premier but was ousted by the 'Gang of Four' and subjected to 10 months of public vilification before making a second comeback (1977) when the 'Gang of Four' was overthrown. Reinstated as vice-premier and vice-chairman of the Chinese Communist Party Central Council, he was seen as the driving force behind the new course, replacing with a pragmatic approach the radicalism which had turned China upside down in Mao's last 10 years, giving priority to the modernization of China and the establishment of friendly relations with the USA and the rest of the non-Soviet world. He retired as vice-premier in September 1980; but not before he had secured the promotion of leaders sharing his views to the key positions in the state. He retained his position as vice-chairman of the party. When the 12th Party Congress was held in September 1982 to adopt a new constitution (the fourth since 1949) Deng at 78 appeared as powerful as ever, the leading figure in the Politburo's six-man standing committee that runs China, and the congress endorsed the line he had advocated since 1977. ALCB

Denning, Alfred Thompson (b. Whitchurch, Hants., UK, 23.1.1899). British judge. He studied mathematics, then law at Oxford. In 1923 he was called to the Bar, in 1938 he became a KC, and in 1944 he was appointed a High Court judge. He worked his way up the judicial hierarchy until in 1957 he was appointed to the House of Lords. In 1962 he chose to return to the Court of Appeal as Master of the Rolls in order to exercise a greater influence on the development of the law. His much-publicized determination to do justice in all cases, his stand as the protector of the individual, the clear, simple and colourful language in which his judgements are written have captured the imagination of the general public. His recent books on the law and his approach to it have been bestsellers. But for the legal profession and for academics he is a controversial figure. His rejection of the constraints of precedent has been criticized as a perversion of the judicial function, a usurpation of the role of the legislature. Among the best known of his contributions to the development of the law are his protection of deserted wives' property rights, his redressing of the balance between unequal parties in contract, and his commitment to judicial review of the legality of administrative action. Lord Denning's *The Family Story* was published in London in 1981. CDG

P. Robson & P. Watchman, *Justice, Lord Denning and the Constitution* (Farnborough, 1981).

Derain, André (b. Chatou, nr Paris, France, 10.6.1880; d. Garches, Seine-et-Oise, 8.9.1954). French painter, sculptor and designer. Together with MATISSE, whom he met while studying at the Académie Carrière (1898–9) and VLAMINCK, with whom he shared a studio and formed the Ecole de Chatou (1900), Derain developed the bright, antinaturalistic colours of the symbolists and neoimpressionists to create a highly subjective and expressive interpretation of the perceptual world. The distorted forms and colours of the works they exhibited at the 1905 Salon d'Automne prompted the critic Louis Vauxcelles to describe them as 'fauves', or wild beasts. The series of landscapes Derain painted at Collioure with Matisse (1905) are still divisionist in technique, with hasty dabs of bright colours offset against the white ground to suggest space and light. In a series of views of London and the Thames (1905–6; e.g. *The Pool of*

London, 1906), large patches of contrasting colours are carefully juxtaposed and modulated to create an illusion of volume, space and atmosphere, and a decorative surface pattern. In c. 1908 he renounced brilliant colours for a muted palette. Using elements drawn from CÉZANNE, cubism and various old masters (the French and Italian primitives, Caravaggio, Rubens and Poussin), he created still lifes, landscapes (*The Bagpiper*, 1911; *The Church at Vers*, 1912) and figure compositions (*Two Sisters*, 1914; *The Italian Model*, 1921–2) in which he sought to re-establish a harmonious balance between form and design, solid volumes and classical simplicity, which in his view had been lost to modern art. Between 1914 and 1918 he designed stage sets for the Ballets Russes, including one for DIAGHILEV's *Boutique Fantastique* (1919). After 1920 his classicism became more pronounced (e.g. *Pierrot and Harlequin*, 1924), and he ignored all subsequent developments in modern art.   SOBT

G. Diehl, *André Derain* (Paris, 1964).

Derrida, Jacques (b. El Biar, Algiers, French Algeria [now Algeria], 15.7.1930). French philosopher. Derrida studied at the Ecole Normale Supérieure in Paris. He taught at the Sorbonne from 1960 to 1964, and at the ENS (from 1965). His work is a continuation of ideas developed by NIETZSCHE, HUSSERL, HEIDEGGER and SAUSSURE. In his concern for a more exact definition of how the human mind works, he also invites readers to look more carefully at the idea of the unconscious in FREUD. He argues (in *La Voix et le phénomène*, Paris, 1967; tr. D. Allison, *Speech and Writing*, Evanston, Ill., 1973; and in *De la Grammatologie*, Paris, 1967; tr. G. Chaknovorty, *Of Grammatology*, Baltimore, 1976) that philosophers have gone wrong in trying to make sense of experience by looking for essential truth lying with the 'essence of things'. What they should do is look at language itself, but without seeing individual words as having a meaning because of the link which they are alleged to have with the objects, concepts or activities they designate. Instead they should follow out the full implications of Saussure's remark that language contains only differences and that meaning is created by the distinction between the sounds of, e.g. 'pin' and 'pen'. Such distinctions are not random but form part of a system. The task of the philosopher is to examine how language works both by the differences within it and by the chain of expectations which the writer or speaker sets up and which require the listener to defer the moment when she or he decides what a particular sentence may or may not mean. The importance of both these ideas is indicated by the fact that Derrida frequently puns on the similarity of sound between *différence* (difference) and *différance* (the act of deferring) in his best-known work *L'Ecriture et la différence* (Paris, 1967; tr. A. Bass, *Writing and Difference*, Chicago, 1978). This book also contains a sustained critique of Rousseau's essay on the origin of language. As against Rousseau's view that we should look primarily at speech, Derrida puts the case for writing as primordial. His ideas are very difficult to understand in the form he gives them, but he is very widely discussed in advanced intellectual circles in the USA and France, among the practitioners of 'deconstruction'.

PMWT

D. C. Wood, 'An introduction to Derrida', *Radical Philosophy*, 21 (Spring 1979); G. A. Hartmann, *Saving the Text: Literature, Derrida, Philosophy* (Baltimore, 1981).

De Sica, Vittorio (b. Sora, Latium, Italy, 7.7.1901; d. Paris, France, 3.11.1974). Italian film director. De Sica had an extremely long and commercially successful career in the cinema, making his debut as an actor in 1922 and directing his last film in the year of his death. But his key contribution to film history is contained in the eight years from *I Bambini ci Guardano* (*The Children Are Watching Us*, 1943) to *Umberto D* (1951), a period which takes in *Sciuscia* (*Shoeshine*, 1946), *Ladri di Biciclette* (*Bicycle Thieves*, 1948) and *Miracolo a Milano* (*Miracle in Milan*, 1950). Before this, De Sica had made a first reputation as a matinée idol and after it he resumed a commercial career first as a star and then as a director, often with

Sophia Loren, with whom he worked regularly from *L'Oro di Napoli* (*Gold of Naples*, 1954) to *Il Viaggio* (*The Voyage*, 1974). The key films of De Sica's career were made in collaboration with his inseparable companion, the scriptwriter ZAVATTINI, and display all the characteristic features of the Italian neorealist movement which the two of them helped to create: open-ended plots, non-professional actors, real locations and subjects chosen from the margins of contemporary society. The roots of this style, for De Sica, lie not in any sort of social or political analysis, but in the perennial comedy of the 'little man', and his films form part of that humanist tradition of cinema that stems from CHAPLIN, Mark Donskoi and FLAHERTY. His best films achieve a unique distillation of the poetry of real life, underlying which is a profound sense of human solitude. RPA

P. Leprohon, *Vittorio De Sica* (Paris, 1966).

De Valéra, Eamonn (b. New York, USA, 14.10.1882; d. Dublin, Irish Republic, 29.8.1975). Irish nationalist leader. President of Sinn Féin (1917–26); leader of the Fianna Fail party (1926–73); prime minister of the Irish Free State, then of Eire (1932–48), and of the Republic of Ireland (1951–9); president of the Republic (1959–73). Unrepentant opponent of all links between the Irish state and Great Britain, battalion commander of the Irish volunteers in the 1916 'Easter Rising', condemned to death by the British but escaped execution because of his American citizenship (he was born of a Spanish father and an Irish mother), an armed opponent of the Irish settlement (1922–3), he only accepted the elected parliament in 1926. In 1937 he was responsible for the new constitution creating the sovereign state of Eire, which remained neutral from 1939 to 1945 despite its nominal membership of the Commonwealth, offering to enter the war only if Ulster were ceded to Eire by the British government. His nationalism spilt over into the enforcing of a revival of Irish Gaelic, then almost totally moribund, and its elevation to the official language of the Irish state. De Valéra's nationalism was politically founded on his courtship of the most extreme aspects of Irish Catholicism which in its hatred of Protestantism, and in its sexual puritanism and literary censorship, accentuated the divisions between Eire and Ulster. At the same time his doctrinaire hostility to almost all manifestations of modern industrialism perpetuated the colonialist dependence of the economy of Eire on that of Britain as a market for Irish dairy and other liquid products and for the employment of the Irish people. DCW

D. Gwynn, *De Valera* (London, 1933); Lord Longford & T. P. O'Neill, *Eamon De Valera* (London, 1970).

Dewey, John (b. Burlington, Vt, USA, 20.10.1859; d. New York, 1.6.1952). American philosopher and educational theorist. The son of a grocer, Dewey was raised in a small New England industrial town. In 1875 he went to the University of Vermont and, on graduation, spent three years as a high school teacher, an exposure to the practice of education important for his later work as an educational theorist. In 1882 he began graduate work at Johns Hopkins University where he was attracted by the biological doctrines of T. H. Huxley and by the philosophy of Hegel. These very distinct influences combined to inspire in him a conviction of the organic interrelatedness of things which he never gave up and which expressed itself as a fixed resolve to oppose all dualisms – of matter and mind, experience and necessity, fact and value. In 1884 he joined the University of Michigan and, while teaching there, published several works on psychology. Ten years later he moved to Chicago University, and established an experimental school where he tested and applied the theory of learning by doing set out in *The School and Society* (Chicago, 1899) and elsewhere. Dewey's rejection of the authoritarian teaching of passive pupils rested on his refutation of what he called the spectator theory of knowledge: the view, as old as Plato, that knowledge is something received as a gift from an outside source, and not an acquisition won by constructive effort on the part of the knower. For Dewey the knower is an active experimenter, provoked by some obstacle into the work of inquiry. However, his conception of the knowledge in which that inquiry terminates as a matter of satisfactory adjustment between the knower and his circumstances does not sufficiently distinguish between adjusting the knower's beliefs to the facts and changing his circumstances to accord with his wishes. Dewey's place in the pragmatist succession is established by his view that knowledge is a matter of success or satisfaction and by his proposal to replace the notion of truth with that of 'warranted assertibility'. In 1904 he moved to Columbia University where he remained until his formal retirement in 1930. The important periodical *Journal of Philosophy* was started at Columbia largely as a means for the presentation and discussion of Dewey's ideas. In large volumes of woolly and cumbrous prose he applied his principle that the mind is an instrument of men's practical purposes over a wide range: logic, metaphysics, art, ethics and social problems. In the 1930s he was a prominent public figure, campaigning against militarism and in favour of civil liberties; he presided over an inquiry into lies told about TROTSKY at the Moscow trials and in 1940 he was active in defence of Bertrand RUSSELL against absurd legal harassment in New York. AQ

As an educationist, Dewey argued that home and social life should be the omega point of the educative process. Knowledge is power in that it not only enables man to cope with his environment and ultimately dominate it but also makes possible processes of experimentation and readjustment in a lifelong process commencing at birth and ending only with death. For Dewey the school essentially copes with a child's interests and aptitudes and not with future needs or altruistic aims. Subject delimitations within the school curriculum were anathema to him. The cultivated interests of the child make teaching topic-centred, not subject-based, and Dewey gives no recognition to a hierarchy of values among subjects. He fails to give due allowance to the conceptual framework of education, ignores man's need to subscribe to ideals towards which he can strive and against which he can measure progress, accepting society as it is. His morality is relative and situational. Dewey's advocacy of activity methods elevates teachers into a new form of sacerdotal class, controlling and guiding child development. The most serious criticism, however, is that Dewey based his educational programme upon personal inspiration and shrewd hunches rather than upon rigorous scientific analysis of the evidence. VAMc

P. A. Schilpp (ed.) *The Philosophy of John Dewey* (NY, 1939); R. J. Bernstein, *John Dewey* (NY, 1966).

Dewey, Melville Louis Kossuth (b. Adams Center, NY, USA, 10.12.1851; d. Lake Placid, Fla, 26.12.1931). American librarian. The first biography of Dewey (1932) bears the subtitle 'Seer: Doer: Inspirer'. That is just: Dewey was a quintessential American, idealistic and pragmatic. He was the most influential pioneer of modern librarianship whose achievement was the development of an effective profession. He founded the American Library Association, the Library Bureau (dealing with methods), the *Library Journal* and the first library school. He was an advocate of lifelong education for all and a champion of women's rights. He is best known for his *Decimal Classification* (NY, 1876, [19]1979), still the most widely used scheme in libraries throughout the world. Its original popularity was due to timely appearance and important technical innovations; its long life must be attributed to the difficulties of change and professional inertia. Despite editorial attempts at improvement it is now inappropriate in structure, inadequate in detail and incompetent in method. Dewey deserves a better memorial. DWL

G. Dawe, *Melvil Dewey* (NY, 1932); F. Rider, *Melvil Dewey* (Chicago, 1944).

Diaghilev, Sergei Pavlovich (b. Selistchev Barracks, Novgorod, Russia, 17.3.1872; d. Venice, Veneto, Italy, 19.8.1929). Russian impresario and founder and director of the itinerant Ballets Russes, which for 20 years (1909–29) exercised a profound influence on cultural life in Europe. With associates including Alexandre Benois and Leon Bakst, he published an important art periodical *Mir Iskusstva* [The world of art] in St Petersburg (1898–1904) and mounted a massive exhibition of historical portraits (1905). Having revealed Russia to herself, he then revealed Russia to the West – first in Paris, with an exhibition of Russian painting (1906), concerts of Russian music (1907), and the first production outside Russia of Mussorgsky's *Boris Godunov* with CHALIAPIN (1908). Finally, in ballet, he found an art form which could combine the disciplines of choreography, drama, painting and music: and his taste, fondness for experiment and patronage of artists in these fields produced many 20c masterpieces. Between 1909 and 1913 new and exotic ballets by FOKINE, with Benois and Bakst as designers, were followed by controversial modern works by NIJINSKY. STRAVINSKY's *The Firebird* (1910), *Petrushka* (1911) and *The Rite of Spring* (1913) and RAVEL's *Daphnis and Chloë* (1911) must rank among the most important musical scores commissioned by Diaghilev. In later years his enormous achievement may be measured by the range of artists he employed (and often 'discovered'): in choreography MASSINE, Bronislava Nijinska, BALANCHINE; in music Stravinsky, PROKOFIEV, SATIE, Poulenc, Auric, Milhaud; in design Goncharova, LARIONOV, PICASSO, DERAIN, MATISSE, GRIS, BRAQUE, UTRILLO, Tchelitchev; and dancers too numerous to mention, who, after Diaghilev's death and the disbanding of his company, founded ballet schools and companies throughout the West.   DAD

B. Kochno, *Diaghilev and the Ballets Russes* (NY, 1970); R. Buckle, *Diaghilev* (London, 1979).

Dibelius, Martin (b. Dresden, Saxony, Germany [now East Germany], 14.9.1883; d. Heidelberg, Baden-Württemberg, West Germany, 11.11.1947). German New Testament scholar in Berlin from 1910 and in Heidelberg from 1915. Influenced by the history of religions school, especially by Gunkel, he became a pioneer of form criticism with *Die Formgeschichte des Evangeliums* (Tübingen, 1919; *From Tradition to Gospel*, London, 1934). (Form criticism is

the attempt to discern the form taken by a story or teaching in order to make it more easily memorable, or more impressive, as it was passed on in oral tradition.) His other most influential work was on Acts, where he pioneered the same methods: *Aufsätze zur Apostelgeschichte* (Göttingen, 1951; *Studies in the Acts of the Apostles*, London, 1956). In his commentaries on several New Testament epistles, notably James, he clarified the forms of their ethical admonitions, especially the so-called 'household codes'. Dibelius also wrote more popular works, some of which were widely read in English, e.g. his posthumous *Paulus* (ed. W. G. Kümmel, Berlin, 1951; *Paul*, London, 1953), and *Jesus* (Göschen, 1939; London, 1963).
RM

Dicey, Albert Venn (b. nr Lutterworth, Leics., UK, 4.2.1835; d. Oxford, 7.4.1922). British lawyer who had a decisive influence on the study of constitutional law and the conflict of laws. He practised at the Bar from 1861 until 1882 when, on the strength of two relatively minor works, he was appointed Vinerian professor of English law at Oxford. He held this post until his resignation in 1909. The publication of *Law of the Constitution* (London, 1885) established him as the leading constitutional lawyer of his day. From his examination of practice he derived fundamental constitutional principles: the sovereignty of Parliament, the rule of law and the conventions of the constitution. These concepts remain indispensable to an understanding of constitutional law, and his book, the leading 19c textbook, remains a classic. However, his great work was *Conflict of Laws* (London, 1896), still in print in a new edition. His influence on this subject, then relatively new, was, and still is, enormous: he set out in systematic form rules and principles derived from the case-law. It is for these legal works rather than for the political writings against Home Rule for Ireland – to which he devoted the greater part of his energy – that he is best known today.
CDG

R. S. Rait, *Memorials of Albert Venn Dicey* (London, 1925); R. A. Cosgrove,

The Rule of Law: Albert Venn Dicey, Victorian Jurist (London, 1980).

Diels, Otto Paul Hermann (b. Hamburg, Germany, 23.1.1876; d. Kiel, Schleswig-Holstein, West Germany, 7.3.1954). German organic chemist. Diels first studied chemistry under Emil FISCHER at Berlin University and became titular professor there in 1906. In 1916 he took up the chair at Kiel and held it until he retired in 1948. His first major discovery (1906) was that of carbon suboxide (C_3O_2), prepared by removal of the elements of water from malonic acid, a conceptually simple process. He was also a pioneer in steroid chemistry, primarily by utilizing dehydrogenation with selenium (replacing the related and previously used sulphur) to convert steroids into aromatic hydrocarbons. Knowledge of the structure of one of these ('Diels hydrocarbon') was vital to the determination of the carbon skeleton of steroids. Diels also studied the reactions of azo-dicarboxylic esters and this eventually led him, with Kurt Alder his research assistant, to the discovery of the vastly important reaction which bears their names. This is the addition of a conjugated diene to any one of a wide range of unsaturated compounds, mainly those containing an electron-depleted ethylenic linkage, to give a product having a six-membered ring. This versatile and often facile reaction is of immense importance in synthetic organic chemistry. Diels and Alder were jointly awarded the Nobel prize for chemistry in 1950.   NBC

Diesel, Rudolph (b. Paris, France, 18.3.1858; d. at sea, 29.4.1913). French inventor and industrialist. In a paper 'The theory and construction of an economical heat engine' (1889) he proposed a more efficient engine than the petrol engine, in which no carburettor or ignition system would be required since spontaneous ignition would occur as the fresh-air mixture was compressed. KRUPP backed the project and the engine bearing Diesel's name was created. Diesel was a proverbial success for 15 years, as inventor and captain of industry. He combined his inventive talent with the social skills of the modern executive, being competent, widely travelled, and fluent in various languages. When he vanished without trace from a cross-Channel steamer, he was found to be heading for bankruptcy.   RIT

Dietrich, Marie Magdalena (Marlene) (b. Berlin, Germany, 2.12.1901; naturalized American citizen, 1939). American film actress. Too different from GARBO to be called her challenger, though that was the intended role, Dietrich shared the eminence; if Garbo had the bloom of the pearl, Dietrich was cut diamond. Josef von Sternberg, who directed her in Germany in the erotic *The Blue Angel* (1930) and brought her to Hollywood, is credited with forming her as a star. Her most typical work was done with him: *Morocco* (1930), *Dishonoured* (1931), *Shanghai Express* (1932) and *The Scarlet Empress* (1934). By the mid-1930s, when director and star parted, her image as the cool flawless beauty was set; she could discard her carefully calculated sheen in the western *Destry Rides Again* (1939), but she remained the symbol of glamour. She made 30 or so films in the USA (and a few in the UK and France), among them *Desire* (1936), *Seven Sinners* (1940), *A Foreign Affair* (1948), *Witness for the Prosecution* (1957) and *Judgment at Nuremberg* (1961). She began her career in Germany in the theatre; finally she returned to the stage, narrating and singing in her magical dusky voice. She married a film producer, Rudolph Sieber; they separated but never divorced.   DP

C. Higham, *Marlene* (NY, 1977).

Dilthey, Wilhelm (b. Biebrich, Hesse, Germany, 19.11.1833; d. Seis, South Tyrol, Austria [now Bolzano, Italy], 1.10.1911). German philosopher and social scientist. Dilthey is probably the key figure in the 'idealist' tradition in modern social thought; he radically extended some aspects of Kant's philosophy into the methodology of the social sciences. He made a radical separation between the natural sciences (*Naturwissenschaften*), which could explain physical events by subsuming them under causal laws, and the cultural sciences (*Geisteswissenschaften*) which could only understand (*verstehen*) events in terms of intentions and meanings that individuals attached to them (*Der Aufbau der geschichtlichen Welt in den Geisteswissenschaften*) [The construction of the historical world in the cultural sciences] (Leipzig, 1910–27). He accepted Kant's argument that what we know is shaped by the categories of mind which, as prisms, select and organize our sense-experiences but, as against Kant's idea that these categories are intrinsic properties of mind, Dilthey argued that such categories are themselves changing products of history and culture. He thus introduced a radical relativism into social thought by the argument – today known as historicism – that knowledge is time-bound and context-laden. Though originally a student of the great German historian Leopold von Ranke, Dilthey came to the conclusion, opposite to Ranke's, that we can never know what the past was actually like, but that all we can do is to ask what questions individuals in the past were responding to. In that respect, Dilthey influenced such diverse figures as COLLINGWOOD and ORTEGA Y GASSET in their historical relativism. His interest in 'understanding' led him to emphasize the psychological elements in history and to feel that biography was the best mode of reading history, and so believe that since interpretations of texts change radically over time, a theory of hermeneutics, or working rules for the interpretations of texts, was a necessary dimension of historical writing. His interest in the philosophy of culture and in hermeneutics led him to write *Das Leben Schleiermachers* [The life of Schleiermachers] (Berlin, 1870), a great biography of the German theologian who had made such hermeneutically systematic biblical criticism a philosophical discipline. Never a systematic thinker, Dilthey ranged over dozens of different fields, but crucial to his thought was the idea of *Weltanschauungen* (worldviews) which he felt could be developed into a typology that might embrace the various ways of looking at man's relation to the world: those of naturalism, or an impersonal order of nature; freedom, which sees man as a free agent; and objective idealism, which sees the world as an organic whole: *Weltanschauung und Analyse des Menschen seit Renaissance und Reformation* [Philosophy and analysis of man since the Renaissance and Reformation] (Leipzig, 1921). This move to typologies may have represented Dilthey's own belief that however much one posits an idea of historical relativism, philosophers need some logical net outside history to make worldviews intelligible.

DBe

M. Ermarth, *Wilhelm Dilthey: the Critique of Historical Reason* (NY, 1978); H. P. Rickman, *Wilhelm Dilthey: Pioneer of the Human Studies* (NY, 1979).

Dinesen, Isak, see BLIXEN, KAREN.

Dior, Christian (b. Granville, Manche, France, 21.1.1905; d. Montecatini, Tuscany, Italy, 24.10.1957). French couturier, who in 1947 revolutionized the shape of women's clothes. Son of a prosperous Normandy industrialist ruined by the 1929 crisis, Dior worked in a small art gallery in Paris. Illness forced him to leave, and the sale of a now famous painting by DUFY – he had purchased from Poiret *Le Plan de Paris* – sufficed to keep him. Having designed for Agnès, Robert Piguet and Lucien Lelong between 1935 and 1944, Dior was approached by Marcel Boussac, the cotton magnate, to set up a couture house. The establishment opened in 1947 with the famous collection known as the New Look, a style of clothing in total contrast to the skimpy, short, square-shouldered clothes of the war years. Dior's designs were sumptuously feminine with emphasized full bosoms, tiny waists and rounded hips together with sloping shoulders. Skirt lengths were dramatically just above the ankle. Despite UK and USA government strictures against extravagant use of cloth, the style was universally adopted within a year. By continuing to invent new shapes and cut in clothes twice a year, Dior attracted all the foreign buyers and the company grew swiftly. By the time of his death, the house of Dior had expanded to include underwear, stockings, all accessories, cosmetics, scent and furs in its business.

JWB

Dirac, Paul Adrien Maurice (b. Bristol, Avon, UK, 8.9.1902). British physicist.

Dirac showed his brilliance while still a research student at Cambridge. The new quantum mechanics was being developed and he evolved a new mathematics, equivalent to the formulations of HEISENBERG, SCHRÖDINGER and others, but extremely elegant in form. It could be used for determining the energies of electrons in their charge clouds around the atomic nucleus. One problem of quantum mechanics was that its equations did not satisfy EINSTEIN's theory of relativity, and one of Dirac's great achievements was to formulate these equations so that they were 'relativistically invariant', i.e. so that they had the same mathematical form, independent of the motion of the observer. The solution (1928) to these equations was surprising because it yielded information about the electron which hitherto had had to be assumed without theoretical justification. This was that the electron had an intrinsic 'spin' (GOUDSMID, PAULI) and that the magnetic moment associated with this spin was double that to be expected from a classical spinning charge. The solution also suggested the possibility of the existence of a short-lived particle with the same mass as the electron but with a positive charge and which could be annihilated by combining with an ordinary electron. This prediction of the 'positron', as it came to be called, was later confirmed by experiment. For his contribution to the development of quantum mechanics, Dirac was awarded the Nobel prize for physics in 1933.

Dirac predicted the existence of a negatively charged proton – the antiproton – which was discovered later. He also applied his relativistic quantum theory to a successful solution of the problem of the radiation emitted when X-rays strike an atom (the COMPTON effect) which the standard theory did not describe correctly. In yet another field, independently of FERMI, he determined the statistics which govern the energy distribution of an assembly of a large number of electrons (the Fermi–Dirac statistics). This development is crucial to understanding the electrical behaviour of metals and semiconductors. From 1932 to 1968 Dirac was Lucasian professor of mathematics at Cambridge.

HMR

Disney, Walter Elias (Walt) (b. Chicago, Ill., USA, 5.12.1901; d. Los Angeles, Calif., 15.12.1966). American film maker and entertainment entrepreneur who created Mickey Mouse. Disney's animated figure of Mickey Mouse first appeared in *Plain Crazy* (1928), but it was the third animated film cartoon *Steamboat Bill* (1928) which established him as perhaps the most famous of all animated cartoon characters. Drawn by Disney's partner Ub Iwerks, its voice was Disney's, a confection of worried *falsetto*, troubled 'hey-hey-hey' and gulping innocence. Banal stories of fidelity to sweetheart and loved-one, likeability derived from coy mischief, and exceptional liveliness of draughtsmanship in both black and white and, later, colour ensured his abiding popularity. Mickey and Minnie Mouse also appeared throughout the 1930s on the packaging of manufactured goods such as handkerchiefs, ice-cream cones, toy electric trains and wristwatches, all of which increased their hold upon the popular imagination. *Snow White and the Seven Dwarfs* (1937) was Disney's first full-length film, followed by *Pinocchio* (1940), *Fantasia* (1940) and *Bambi* (1942). Disney also created Donald Duck in 1931 and Goofy and Pluto in successive years. After WW2 Disney's films, often more memorable for dismissing the conventions of suggested sex or explicit violence rather than for what they actually showed, dominated the world of children's entertainment. Among these were *The Living Desert* (1953), *Davy Crockett* (1955), *Swiss Family Robinson* (1960), and *Mary Poppins* (1964). Supported by the vast financial success derived from his films, Disney used his studio technicians and planners to open Disneyland in Anaheim, California, and in 1971 a second larger showground in Orlando, Florida, which contains a bizarre display of animated American presidents, the first of its kind. RBJG

C. Finch, *The Art of Walt Disney* (London, 1975); B. Thomas, *Walt Disney: an American Original* (NY, 1976).

Dix, Otto (b. Gera, Germany [now East Germany], 2.12.1891; d. Singen, Baden-Württemberg, West Germany, 25.7.1969). German artist. As a highly unflattering portraitist and uninhibited social commentator, Dix was a leader of the Dresden Sezession which helped produce the *Neue Sachlichkeit* of the mid-1920s and he had a strong influence on German communist painting before 1933 and after the mid-1950s. After his first expressionist drawings of the western front, he veered to a fiercely antimilitarist dadaism after 1918, using collage and brutal caricature before going over to an increasingly traditional technique. His 1920s portraits, his verist paintings of bars and whores, and his terrifyingly reconstructed battlefield landscapes were all painted with an old-masterly skill which gradually eased out the earlier sharpness of vision, particularly after his return to Dresden as an academy professor in 1927. While he remained in Germany under HITLER, this never endeared him to the Nazis, who could not forgive his 'deeply wounding' attacks on the army in such works as the cycle of etchings *Der Krieg* (*War*, 1924) and so treated him as a 'degenerate artist'.   JWMW

F. Loeffler, *Otto Dix* (Dresden, 1967).

Djilas, Milovan (b. Polja, Kolašin, Montenegro [now Yugoslavia], 12.6.1911). Former Yugoslav revolutionary leader and critic of communism. Graduating as a lawyer from Belgrade University in 1933, Djilas was arrested and imprisoned for political activities. Meeting TITO in 1937, he became a member of the Yugoslav Communist party's Central Committee in 1938 and of its Politburo in 1940. A leader of the partisan resistance to the Germans in WW2, he became one of the principal members of Tito's cabinet after the war, and took a strong line in the Yugoslav Communists' assertion of their independence of the USSR. In January 1953 Djilas was appointed one of the country's four vice-presidents and in December was chosen president of the Federal People's Assembly. Increasing political and personal disagreement with the leadership, however, led to his expulsion from all his posts and resignation from the party in April 1954.

Djilas no longer felt able to keep silent about the effect that the corruption and compromises of power had had upon the Communist movement. Imprisoned (December 1956) for publishing an article in the USA praising the Hungarian rising of 1956, he smuggled out of prison a manuscript published in the West as *The New Class* (London, 1957) in which he expressed his disillusionment with communism in practice as the creation of an entrenched oligarchy separated from and enjoying both political and economic privileges over the working classes which it claims to represent.

Released in 1961, Djilas was imprisoned again in 1962 for publishing in the West *Conversations with Stalin* (London, 1962), a revelation of the cynical and arbitrary way in which STALIN treated his collaborators and allies. After 1966, when he was released, Djilas was allowed to visit the USA and to return to Belgrade. He extended his analysis of communist societies further in *The Unperfect Society: Beyond the New Class* (London, 1969). He has remained an uncompromising critic of the regime he helped to create (see his *Memoirs of a Revolutionary*, London, 1973), spending the last 25 years of his life in political and social isolation – nine of them in gaol – under Tito's rule.   ALCB

Dobzhansky, Theodosius (b. Nemirov, Russia, 25.1.1900; naturalized American citizen; d. Davis, Calif., USA, 18.12.1975). Russian/American evolutionary biologist who provided the empirical evidence for the integration of Darwinian evolutionary theory with the laws of inheritance established by MENDEL. Dobzhansky graduated from the University of Kiev in 1921, migrated to the USA in 1927 to work with T. H. MORGAN and subsequently held posts in genetics at Cal Tech, Columbia, Rockefeller and Davis, California, universities. He pioneered the genetic study of populations both in field studies and laboratory experiments, mainly using variety within different species of the fruit fly *Drosophila* as his scientific material. He demonstrated unambiguously the action of natural selection in wild populations and showed it to be the critical evolutionary force. But he was also concerned in elucidating the role of gene and chromosome mutation, drift (or chance) and movement in determining the genetic structure of populations. Dobzhansky was one of the few general biologists who became deeply involved in understanding the nature of human variety and evolution. He developed sophisticated models of the interrelationships between hereditary and environmental influences in human development and wrote extensively about the phenomenon of race in man. He provided the now classical definition of races as Mendelian populations which differ in gene frequencies. His major books are *Genetics and the Origin of Species* (NY, 1937), *Mankind Evolving* (New Haven, 1962) and *Genetics of the Evolutionary Process* (NY, 1970). GAH

M. H. Hecht & W. C. Steere (eds), *Essays in Evolution and Genetics in Honour of Theodosius Dobzhansky* (NY, 1970).

Dodd, Charles Harold (b. Wrexham, Clwyd, UK, 7.4.1884; d. Oxford, 22.9.1973). Doyen of British New Testament scholars. Lecturer (from 1915) and professor (from 1918) at Mansfield College, Oxford; Rylands professor at Manchester (from 1930); and Norris-Hulse professor at Cambridge (1935-49), where his seminar became the dovecote of English biblical scholarship. His life was his work, his most influential book being *The Parables of the Kingdom* (London, 1935), which sought to answer Albert SCHWEITZER's account of Jesus as an apocalyptic fanatic with the 'realized eschatology' thesis that Jesus claimed the kingdom of God as already present in his ministry. Dodd also attempted to identify a unified early Christian *kerygma*, or preaching, in *The Apostolic Preaching and its Developments* (London, 1936). But his best work was on John, and *The Interpretation of the Fourth Gospel* (Cambridge, 1953) remains a classic. His permanent concern with the historicity of the Gospels is apparent in *Historical Tradition in the Fourth Gospel* (Cambridge, 1963), and a late popular work on *The Founder of Christianity* (London, 1971). Dodd's Pauline interpretation, including the *Moffatt Commentary on Romans* (London, 1932) was less successful, but equally influential. It left its mark on the New Testament (1961) part of the New English Bible, a project which Dodd directed from 1949 to 1970. Several more popular works have maintained a wide appeal, combining theological sanity, critical acumen and a felicitous style. RM

F. W. Dillistone, *C. H. Dodd, Interpreter of the New Testament* (London, 1977).

Dodds, Edward Charles (b. Liverpool, Mers., UK, 13.10.1899; d. London, 16.12.1973). British biochemist. Appointed professor of biochemistry at University College London, at the age of 26, he built up a strong department with close clinical associations. His own research was concerned with endocrinology (with F. Dickens, *The Chemical and Physiological Properties of Internal Secretions*, Oxford, 1925) and his most important discovery was that certain synthetic chemicals mimic the action of the female sex hormone, oestrone. In particular 4,4-dihydroxystilbene or stilboestrol is some three times more active than the natural hormone and has found much use as a drug for treatment of hormonal disorders in women. Dodds's public recognition (knighthood 1954, presidency of Royal College of Surgeons 1962-6) followed on his success in promoting the more effective use of biochemical techniques for the solution of medical problems. His *Recent Advances in Medicine* (London, 1924), written with G. E. Beaumont, ran to 13 editions. GL

Dodds, Eric Robertson (b. Banbridge, Down, Ireland [now Northern Ireland], UK, 26.7.1893; d. Old Marston, Oxon., 8.4.1979). British classical philologist and regius professor of Greek at Oxford (1936-60) where, as Gilbert Murray's successor, he similarly exercised a vital influence on the course of Greek studies. Educated at Campbell College, Belfast, and University College, Oxford, his first scholarly publication, the edition of Proclus' *Elements of Theology* (Oxford, 1933), was thorough and exemplary, as were his two later editions, of Euripides' *Bacchae* (Oxford, 1944, [2]1960) and of Plato's *Gorgias* (Oxford, 1959). Dodds's many-faceted contributions to scholarship express both a personal and a social need; the themes that dominate his work are the tension between rationalism and mysticism, and the factors contributing to the collapse of rational elements in culture. His influential study of the impact of oriental mystery cults on Greek religious life, *The Greeks and the Irrational* (Berkeley, 1951), is at the same time an investigation of the interpretations of a particular type of human experience which has unique cultural significance. Throughout his life Dodds championed the need for continued teaching of the classics, which he saw as the key to the understanding of European literature and historical development. KKS

Doderer, Heimito von (b. Weidlingau, nr Vienna, Austria-Hungary [now Austria], 5.9.1896; d. Vienna, 23.12.1966). Austrian novelist. With *Die Strudlhofstiege* [The Strudlhof steps] (Munich, 1951) and *Die Dämonen* (Munich, 1956; tr. R. & C. Winston, *The Demons*, NY, 1961) Doderer established himself as the foremost Austrian novelist of the immediate postwar years. Both novels are set in Vienna and trace the lives of a large number of characters over the period from 1910 to 1935. Common to both works is one theme: the characters find themselves unable to accept the complex fortuitousness of modern life and take refuge in a private world (Doderer calls it a 'second reality'), which promises order and security. Gradually, however, they are educated into an acceptance of the everyday world as it is. In formal terms, the novels enact this theme: they capture the profuse randomness of life in Vienna while at the same time allowing the reader (like the characters) to find sense and meaning in that disorder. In its political ramifications (as an attempted unmasking of ideology) Doderer's theme is less than persuasive. But his novels –he wrote 11 altogether – do give a suggestive and unsentimental portrait of Vienna before and after WW2. The major works represent an intriguing marriage of modern formal and narrative techniques with an unashamedly old-fashioned educative purpose. MWS

M. Bachem, *Heimito von Doderer* (Boston, Mass., 1981).

Doesburg, Theo van, ps. of Christian Emil Marie Küpper (b. Utrecht, The Netherlands, 30.8.1883; d. Davos, Graubünden, Switzerland, 7.3.1931). Dutch artist. In neutral Holland during WW1 Doesburg joined with MONDRIAN and others to start the arts review *De Stijl*, which preached a blend of abstraction and machine aesthetic. Applying Mondrian's pictorial concept of *nieuwe beelding* [neoplasticism] to design and architecture, the 'style' in question was akin to the new contructivism further east. With the reopening of international communications, Doesburg widened its basis, settling temporarily in Weimar where he helped inspire a more technological attitude in the Bauhaus. In 1923 his architectural projects with Cornelis van Eesteren were shown in Paris. Overshadowed by Mondrian as a painter and by OUD and RIETVELD as an architect, he teamed up with SCHWITTERS that year in a belated effort to launch dada in Holland via his short-lived new review *Mécano* and his 'I. K. Bonset' poems. In 1929 he moved to Paris, where he was active in the Abstraction-Création group. *De Stijl* still appeared sporadically up to his death, its penultimate number being devoted to his subsequently demolished masterpiece, the decorations of the Café de l'Aubette at Strasbourg on which he collaborated with his friends the ARPs (1926–8). His *Principles of Neo-Plastic Art* was published in English translation in London in 1969. JWMW

H. L. C. Jaffé, *De Stijl* (London, 1970).

Dolmetsch, Arnold (b. Le Mans, Sarthe, France, 24.2.1858; naturalized British citizen, 1931; d. Haslemere, Surrey, UK, 28.2.1940). French/British musicologist, instrument-maker and performer. Dolmetsch came of a long line of musicians, studied violin in Brussels with Vieuxtemps and then transferred to the Royal College of Music in London. In 1885 he began to teach violin at Dulwich College, where he also evolved his enlightened principles of authentic performance using contemporary instruments, an interest intensified by his discovery in the British Museum of some early music for viols. After working first in the USA for Chickering, where he made some of his best keyboard instruments as well as lutes and viols, and then in Paris for Gaveau, he resettled in England at Haslemere. He remained there until his death, founding with members of his talented family the Haslemere Festival, which continues to encourage and develop an increased appreciation and understanding of early music. His invaluable *The Interpretation of the Music of the Seventeenth and Eighteenth Centuries* was published in London in 1915.   JL

M. Dolmetsch, *Personal Recollections of Arnold Dolmetsch* (London, 1958); M. Campbell, *Dolmetsch: the Man and his Work* (London, 1975).

Domagk, Gerhard (b. Lagow, Germany [now Poland], 30.10.1895; d. Burberg, N. Rhine-Westphalia, West Germany, 24.4.1964). German chemist and pathologist. Domagk began training in medicine at Kiel before WW1, during which he became impressed by the then helplessness of medicine against infections such as typhus, typhoid and cholera. From 1927 until 1960 he worked in the research laboratories of I. G. Farbenindustrie in Wuppertal, becoming head of a department of pathological anatomy and bacteriology.

Domagk's great contribution, the discovery of the antibacterial action of 'prontosil rubrum', sprang from work with dyes, in the tradition of EHRLICH, the drug itself being intended as a leather dye. His only daughter was one of the first to be treated with it. Domagk had had the wisdom to use an animal model for his work, namely mice infected by an organism from a patient who had died from streptococcal septicaemia. Tested *in vitro*, the drug was inactive; it was, therefore, one of the first drugs discovered which are activated in the body. A French team (which included BOVET) showed that this was due to the release of sulfanilamide, the start of an immense range of drugs made famous by the M & B 693 used in treating CHURCHILL's pneumonia. Until this time, it was suspected that only higher organisms (protozoa such as malaria or syphilis) could be attacked by chemotherapy. Sulfanila-

mide possesses a rather simple chemical structure, and this, together with the later proof that it owed its action to a similarity to and competition with an essential bacterial metabolite, was an immense stimulus to pharmaceutical industrial research. Domagk later did work leading to drugs (thiosemicarbazones) effective in tuberculosis treatment, and to a new class of antiseptic. He was awarded the Nobel prize in 1939, but was forced by the Nazis to refuse it.   WP

Donnan, Frederick George (b. Colombo, Ceylon [now Sri Lanka], 5.9.1870; d. Canterbury, Kent, UK, 16.12.1956). British chemist. Donnan studied first at Belfast, but learnt his physical chemistry from his years in Germany with OSTWALD and VAN'T HOFF. On his return to the UK he became one of those responsible for introducing the new German work in physical chemistry, which he did first at Liverpool and, from 1913, at University College London. Colloid chemistry was his field of research, where he is remembered for his classic paper of 1911, 'The theory of membrane equilibrium in the presence of a nondialysable electrolyte', in which he gave a thermodynamic analysis of the equilibrium across a membrane between solutions of electrolytes when one of the ions is too large to pass through the pores in the membrane (e.g. a protein). The theory has applications in technical fields (leather and gelatin) but since about 1922 its principal importance has been its use for interpreting the equilibrium across the membranes of living cells.   JSR

Dos Passos, John (b. Chicago, Ill., USA, 14.1.1896; d. Baltimore, Md, 28.9.1970). American novelist. Dos Passos's first two novels came directly out of his experience during WW1, and revealed the pressure of what Edmund WILSON described as 'adolescent resentments'. The US army is portrayed as a relentless 'machine' against which young men struggled in vain; the war itself hardly figures in the experience of Dos Passos's characters: the army is the real enemy. He was the first American writer to capture the disillusionment with WW1, and

Three Soldiers (NY, 1923) was an important addition to US war literature. Dos Passos's commitment to the Sacco and Vanzetti appeal in 1927 accelerated a radicalization which closely involved him in left-wing politics. His criticism of American life, first expressed in *Manhattan Transfer* (NY, 1925), culminated in the *U.S.A.* trilogy: *The 42nd Parallel* (NY, 1930), *Nineteen Nineteen* (NY, 1932) and *The Big Money* (NY, 1936). The scope and ambition of *U.S.A.* firmly established Dos Passos as a major novelist. Unlike Upton Sinclair and DREISER, Dos Passos broke with the traditions of naturalistic social fiction and employed a dazzling series of technical innovations, such as literary 'montage', which affirm his place in modernist writing.   EH

J. P. Diggins, *Up from Communism* (NY, 1975); T. Ludington, *John Dos Passos: a Twentieth-century Odyssey* (NY, 1981).

Douglas, Clifford Hugh (Major) (b. Stockport, Ches., UK, 20.1.1879; d. Dundee, Tayside, 29.9.1952). British economist who began a career in engineering and management but then devoted his life to expounding the theory known as Social Credit. This was based on the agreement that the fundamental economic problem of modern societies is the chronic deficiency of purchasing power. Douglas proposed to cure this by controlling prices and creating 'social credit' in a number of different ways, by paying discounts to retailers, subsidies to producers and 'dividends' to citizens. Douglas first published his ideas in 1919 in A. R. Orage's periodical *The New Age* and then in a book *Economic Democracy* (London, 1920, ³1930). They attracted considerable attention in the 1920s, but the only attempt to apply them was in Canada. A Social Credit party was founded by William Aberhart in 1935. This dominated Alberta's provincial governments from 1935 to 1971, British Columbia's from 1952 to 1972, and held a number of seats in the Federal Parliament. The party, however, virtually abandoned Douglas's principles in the late 1930s, and these have little following anywhere today.   ALCB

Douglas, Keith Castellain (b. Tunbridge Wells, Kent, UK, 24.1.1920; d. St Pierre, Calvados, France, 9.6.1944). British poet. Douglas emerged from the undergraduate literary coteries of Oxford University to become one of WW2's major poets. Leaving Oxford in 1941 for the Sherwood Rangers Yeomanry, he quickly distinguished himself as a tank commander in the North African campaign. Douglas's cavalier-like enjoyment of action and his fascination with foreign places are reflected in his prose account of that campaign, *Alamein to Zem Zem* (London, 1946). His poetry (*Complete Poems*, ed. D. Graham, Oxford, 1979), written throughout five years' service, expresses more the dehumanizing brutality and boredom of modern warfare. Douglas's finest poems, such as 'Dead Men' and 'How to Kill', combine the poet's sensitivity to suffering with the professional response of an intelligent soldier. Judging that the role of the WW2 poets was neither to warn nor awaken, Douglas felt unable to claim any prophetic purpose, and aimed instead to comprehend fighting experience with lucidity and objectivity. Cynicism, bordering sometimes on nihilism, characterizes some late poems. Douglas was killed during the D-day landings.

JAC

D. Graham, *Keith Douglas 1920– 1944: a Biography* (London, 1974).

Douhet, Giulio (b. Caserta, Campania, Italy, 30.5.1869; d. Rome, 15.2.1930). Italian general and the first modern theorist of air warfare. Douhet's stormy career – which included a spell in prison in 1916 for criticizing the higher direction of the war – ended with his promotion to general in 1921, and his resignation shortly afterwards. In the same year he published *Il dominio dell' aria* (Rome, 1921; *The Command of the Air*, NY, 1942) setting out his belief that command of the air could be won in the early stages of a future war by attacking an enemy's air force and the ground installations and services supplying it, and that subsequent unrestricted aerial bombardment of urban centres would quickly produce a breakdown in social structure and an irresistible pressure for peace. His ideas, which neglected the possibilities of aerial defence, were immensely influential in the period between the wars in Europe and the USA.   JGo

E. M. Earle (ed.), *Makers of Modern Strategy* (Princeton, 1943, ²1971).

Dovzhenko, Aleksandr Petrovich (b. Vyunishche, Ukraine, Russia, 11.9.1894; d. Moscow, USSR, 26.11.1956). Russian film director. After brief careers as a civil servant, diplomat and magazine illustrator, Dovzhenko threw himself into film-making at the age of 32. Two years later he made his first important film *Zvenigora* (1928), an extraordinarily lyrical and somewhat oblique evocation of the Ukrainian countryside. His next film *Arsenal* (1929), a vivid illustration of the October revolution in the Ukraine, brought him wider recognition. But his silent masterpiece was *Zemlya* (*Earth*, 1930), which was Dovzhenko's film about collectivization. The absence of a clear political line and the film's concentration on Ukrainian folklore and lyrical shots of nature (apples, raindrops, etc.) brought official denunciations alleging 'counter-revolutionary defeatism'; but a jury of film critics at the 1957 Brussels World Fair voted *Zemlya* the best film of all time. It is a film deeply imbued with a sense of nature, culture and history. Dovzhenko's first sound film was *Ivan* (1932), which portrayed the reactions of a young peasant employed on the construction of the Dnieper Dam. Like *Zemlya*, *Ivan* is a study in cultural transition. In 1935 Dovzhenko made *Aerograd* in the Soviet Far East. Both this film and *Shchors* (1939), set in the civil war after the revolution, were intended as warnings to possible enemies. *Shchors*, unlike the earlier films, is fast-moving and dynamic, but still characterized by a deep sense of Ukrainian history and culture. It is that sense, and its lyrical expression, that distinguish all Dovzhenko's works. A selection of his writings has been translated as *The Poet as Film-maker* (ed. M. Carynnyk, London, 1973).   RTay

Dreiser, Herman Theodore (b. Terre Haute, Ind., USA, 27.8.1871; d. Los Angeles, Calif., 28.12.1945). American novelist. Dreiser spent a restless childhood in the American Midwest. His parents were pious, repressive and poor. He worked at various jobs before turning to journalism. His fiction at its best has the feel of life observed with a journalist's eye for telling detail. Dreiser's most memorable characters live within the orbit of the vulgar materialism of turn-of-the-century America. At the same time, Dreiser's unease at the hedonism of the age made him sensitive to the contradictions and tragic inner conflicts of American life. His first novel *Sister Carrie* (NY, 1900) was virtually suppressed after publication, and Dreiser's realism was often too strong for contemporary taste. His most ambitious book *An American Tragedy* (NY, 1926) was based on a murder committed in upper New York State in 1906. The dilemma of Dreiser's protagonist, Clyde Griffiths, who is caught up and destroyed by ambitions which he cannot fully realize, embodied the essence of Dreiser's naturalistic view of human nature and society. A realist, Dreiser was something of an artistic anachronism at the end of his life, when the modernism of Henry JAMES and JOYCE were in the ascendant. His best work has survived more due to his grasp of America, and the ambiguity of its ideals, than to his craft as a writer or powers as a stylist. There is an undoubted intensity in his work, but in *An American Tragedy* it is the product of situation, not of action; the book is essentially a tragedy of entrapment, which owes its power to the remorseless unfolding of an initial premise. It is perhaps the worst written of the great American novels, but the criticism of America which it offers is powerful and, for many readers, persuasive.   EH

W. A. Swanberg, *Dreiser* (NY, 1965); E. Moers, *Two Dreisers* (NY, 1969).

Dreyer, Carl Theodor (b. Copenhagen, Denmark, 3.2.1889; d. Copenhagen, 19.3.1968). Danish film maker. The paradoxical impulses and fluctuating rhythms behind Dreyer's career are as subtle and mysterious as those contained in his films themselves. He wrote his first script in 1912 and moved over to directing in 1919, making nine films in all before the advent of sound in the late 1920s. At this stage Dreyer was an uneven, eclectic director, working in a number of European countries (Germany, Sweden, Norway and France, as well as his native Denmark), exploring cinematic technique, and ranging in style from bucolic comedy to studies of sainthood. In the last four decades of his life he made only five films, one of which he subsequently disowned because of the concessions forced upon him by the producer. His four sound masterpieces come at virtually 10-year intervals: *Vampyr* in 1932, *Vredens Dag* (*Day of Wrath*) in 1943, *Ordet* (*The Word*) in 1954 and *Gertrud* in 1964. At the time of his death he was planning a life of Jesus, the script of which has been published.

Virtually all Dreyer's films – with the exception of his silent masterpiece *La Passion de Jeanne d'Arc* (*The Passion of Joan of Arc*, 1927), which is based on court records of the trial – are adapted from novels and plays. It is clear that Dreyer did not see himself as a writer-director and was interested less in the text itself than in its visual realization. Even his sound films – including *Gertrud*, made as late as the 1960s – are to be understood as visual statements. Any reading of them in mere literary terms fails to uncover their essential beauty, for it is in the visuals themselves that we find the core of Dreyer's vision; not a search for beautiful images but a probing of the interaction of the real and the fantastic. Dreyer, who can depict the everyday world in its utmost solidity with the simplest of brush-strokes, is essentially a poet of the mystical experience, so that his work abounds in vampires and witches, scenes of martyrdom and resurrection. Though rooted firmly in the past (*Gertrud* is based on a play written in 1906), Dreyer's work has the timelessness of the true classic.   RPA

T. Milne, *The Cinema of Carl Dreyer* (London, 1971); D. Skoller (ed.), *Dreyer in Double Reflection* (NY, 1973).

Driesch, Hans Adolf Eduard (b. Bad Kreuznach, Rhineland-Palatinate, Germany, 28.10.1867; d. Leipzig [now East Germany], 17.4.1941). German developmental biologist and philosopher. A founder of experimental embryology, he began his career at the Marine Biological Station in Naples (1891–1900) as a proponent of a mechanistic view of development. By compressing embryos and changing the location of the first few nuclei resulting from cleavage, he provided evidence that the same genetic material enters all cells, thereby helping disprove Roux's theory of differential gene partition. He showed that the size of regenerating hydroids is controlled by the size of the regenerating piece, and that when sea urchin embryos are cut in half along the 'animal-vegetal' axis they form two complete embryos, establishing respectively the important concepts of morphyllaxis and regulation. He introduced the ideas of cell fate as dependent on its position in the embryo, of positional information and of patterning, which remain central to developmental biology. His perception of the difficulties in explaining such events as regulation in any physical terms then available, however, led him to abandon mechanism for vitalism, postulating Aristotle's 'entelechy' as the purposive intelligence which governs development. In 1908 he delivered the Gifford lectures *The Science and Philosophy of the Organism* (Aberdeen) and then took up a new career in academic philosophy, becoming professor of systematic philosophy at Cologne in 1919 and then, in 1921, at Leipzig. Towards the end of his life he became a prominent member of the British Society for Parapsychology. Paradoxically it was the experimental tradition Driesch helped found which finally discredited such philosophic ideas. He may be the last prominent vitalist of modern biology.   DOM

Drieu La Rochelle, Pierre (b. Paris, France, 13.1.1893; d. Paris, 15.3.1945). French novelist, poet, essayist and political journalist of the interwar and occupation years. Deeply marked by an unhappy childhood and by his front-line experiences in WW1, Drieu enjoyed precocious literary success with his war poems *Fond de cantine* [Bottom of the canteen] (Paris, 1920). Recurring themes in his novels thereafter – *La Comédie de Charleroi* [The comedy of Charleroi]

(Paris, 1934), *Rêveuse Bourgeoisie* [A dreamy bourgeoisie] (Paris, 1937), *Gilles* (Paris, 1939) – are the excitement, virility, loyalty and authority of combat-life, seen as unique in permitting full expression of the self and its natural impulses, contrasted with the decadence, mediocrity, hypocrisy and compromise of civilian France in post-1919 peacetime. Drieu dabbled successively in a variety of incompatible movements – surrealism, *Action Française* and Gaston Bergery's *Front Commun* – before proclaiming himself a fascist in 1934. Two years later he was one of the leading intellectuals in Jacques Doriot's Parti Populaire Français. Drieu collaborated energetically with the Nazis and became editor of the prestigious literary monthly *Nouvelle Revue Française*. The success of his third attempt at suicide, a decision movingly justified in his *Récit secret* [Secret account] (Paris, 1951), probably saved him from a liberation firing squad. It is too simple to label Drieu as the typical fascist intellectual. He constantly struggled to reconcile contradictory ideas: nationalism and European federalism, socialism and aristocracy; the heroic and the meditative ideals, the demands of the intelligence and of the body. His exposure of decadence carries much greater conviction than his celebration of a more vigorous alternative. As an extended confession his novels offer a panoramic, if highly tendentious, survey of interwar France. Drieu's sincerity and lucidity and alertness to the currents of the modern world, his refusal to be duped by expedient rationalizations, or to separate what he was from what he wrote, were matched by fatal weaknesses of character, by indecisiveness and oscillating allegiances. Together they made him one of the most acidly critical witnesses and representative figures of his age, but they also defeated his ambition to stand beside MALRAUX, GIDE, MAURIAC and BRETON as one of his generation's 'directors of conscience'.   RSS

F. Field, *Three French Writers and the First World War* (Cambridge, 1975); R. Soucy, *Fascist Intellectual: Drieu La Rochelle* (Berkeley, 1979).

Drucker, Peter Ferdinand (b. Vienna, Austria-Hungary [now Austria], 19.11.1909; naturalized American citizen). Austrian/American contributor to the study of business management. He qualified as a lawyer and worked on the editorial staff of the *Frankfurter General-Anzeiger* until the rise of the Nazis. In 1937 he moved to New York and became a newspaper correspondent, economic adviser and consultant to companies. In 1950 he became professor of management at New York University and, since then, has influenced management thinking through his writing. Believing that the emergence of the large-scale organization in the first half of this century may be one of the most important changes in man's social history, he has focused on the management of such organizations. In *Concept of the Corporation* (NY, 1946) he described the development of General Motors under SLOAN. His main emphasis has been on managerial effectiveness; his influential work has involved management objectives, performance and measurement. 'Management by objectives' enables the individual to be integrated with organizational purpose as motivation and commitment are increased. Organizational goals are reached by having 'common people achieve uncommon performance' (see *The Practice of Management*, London, 1953; *Managing for Results*, London, 1964; *The Effective Executive*, London, 1966).   RIT

Dubček, Alexander (b. Uhrovec, Czechoslovakia, 27.11.1921). Czechoslovak Communist leader. Dubček took part in the Slovak resistance to the Germans during WW2, culminating in the Slovak national rising in the winter of 1944–5. In the 10 years after the war he rose steadily in the Communist party bureaucracy, serving as a deputy in the National Assembly (1951–5). He spent the years 1955–8 studying at the Soviet party's political college in Moscow, returning to become a member of the central committees of both the Slovak and the Czechoslovak CPs, and in 1962 a full member of the Central Committee's praesidium. In May 1963 he succeeded to the post of first secretary of the Communist party in Slovakia.

In October 1967 a Central Committee meeting was held in Prague at which Dubček rallied a reformist group, as well as Slovak nationalists, against the leadership of Antonin Novotný and replaced him as first secretary of the Czechoslovak CP in January 1968. On 9 April a programme was published under the title of 'Czechoslovakia's Road to Socialism', promising a series of liberal reforms to humanize communist rule by introducing basic civil freedoms, an independent judiciary and other democratic practices. The programme was supported by leading economists who recognized that the policy of economic decentralization, already accepted and giving some degree of initiative to individual enterprises, would fail unless accompanied by political changes. The Russian leadership, however, alarmed at a challenge which might spread to other countries in Eastern Europe, insisted on a meeting with the Czechoslovak leaders at Cierna (Slovakia) from 29 July to 2 August. Their efforts to persuade Dubček to abandon his new course, or alternatively to find Czechoslovak Communists prepared to oust him, failed, and the Red Army occupied the country on the night of 20–21 August. Dubček and five other leaders were seized and taken to Moscow where they were forced to make major concessions. On his return to Prague Dubček urged the nation to cooperate but the momentum of the reform movement had been killed and he was no longer in a position to resist Soviet pressure. In 1969 he and his supporters were forced out of office. Dubček disappeared from history, but the memory of 'the Prague Spring', with its slogan of 'Socialism with a human face', has contributed to the discrediting of Soviet communism as incapable of any other response to reform than repression. ALCB

Dubuffet, Jean-Philippe-Arthur (b. Le Havre, Seine-Maritime, France, 31.7.1901). French painter. Dubuffet studied briefly at the Académie Julian (1918) but did not become a full-time painter until 1942. His first works, exhibited in 1944, had a childlike quality reminiscent of KLEE, with shapes and forms emerging from textured surfaces worked with the palette knife. In the later 1940s he developed more expressive surfaces of plaster, glue, putty and asphalt applied thickly and kneaded to give an impasto effect. In these surfaces he 'intuitively' discerned heads, masks and figures on which he scribbled 'spontaneously', creating images recalling the art of children and of the insane (which – like Klee – he had studied). This production of images from the material itself he called *l'art brut*: 'true' or 'honest' art in contrast to that produced following classical or 'rational' canons. Travels in the Sahara (1947–9) and the desert landscape moulded by the elements inspired desert images of sand, putty and glue. In 1950 he began the *Woman's Body* series in which nudes swollen like fertility symbols are vigorously incised in the thick, swirling impasto. In the 1951 *Earth and Land* and *Radiant Worlds* series he worked the ground to resemble geological formations and fossil shapes, peopled by tiny, childlike figures. In 1956 he cut a prepared canvas into small shapes (stars, circles, etc.) which he placed arbitrarily on the surface in mosaic-like patterns (e.g. *Grass runs; Stone jump*, 1956). In the *Paris Circus* series (1961–2) he used this method to produce phantasmagoric images of the modern city (e.g. *Business Prospers*, 1961). SOBT

P. Selz, *The Works of Jean Dubuffet* (NY, 1962).

Duby, Georges (b. Paris, France, 7.10.1919). French historian. Duby has been professor at Aix-en-Provence (1951 –70) and, since 1970, at the Collège de France. He made his reputation with a regional study in rural history *La Société aux 11e et 12e siècles dans la région mâconnaise* [Eleventh- and twelfth-century society in the Mâcon region] (Paris, 1953). He extended this approach to Western Europe in *Economie rurale et la vie des campagnes en occident* (Paris, 1962; *Rural Economy and Country Life in the Medieval West*, London, 1968). His *Guerriers et paysans* (Paris, 1973; *The Early Growth of the European Economy*, London, 1974) is a bold attempt at building a model of economic growth for Europe between the 7c and 12c, emphasizing the profits of war and the conspicuous consumption of the aristocracy. Duby's interest in typologies can also be seen in his *Medieval Marriage: Two Models from Twelfth-century France* (Baltimore, 1978) and *Les Trois Ordres* (Paris, 1978; *The Three Orders*, Chicago, 1980), concerned as they are with the history of a medieval image of society, that of the 'three estates' who respectively pray, fight and work. Duby's interests have steadily widened and now embrace most of the major problems in medieval society and culture, the arts included, notably in *Le Temps des cathédrales* (Paris, 1976; *The Age of the Cathedrals: Art and Society, 980–1420*, London, 1981). His essays have been collected in English in *The Chivalrous Society* (London, 1978). The most distinguished living French medievalist, Duby's blend of caution and imagination, and his interest in the social sciences as well as his concern for rural history, make him the true heir of Marc BLOCH. UPB

Duchamp, Marcel (b. Blainville, Seine-Maritime, France, 28.7.1887; d. Neuilly, Paris, 2.10.1968). French painter and art theorist. Brother of Jacques Villon and Duchamp-Villon (they agreed to use different surnames c. 1901), Duchamp's first mature work *Nude Descending a Staircase* (1911–12, 2nd version) caused immense controversy when shown at the 1912 Section d'Or exhibition and again at the 1913 Armory Show in New York. In this work, cubist-derived fragmentation is combined with successive phases of movement recorded in chronophotographic fashion so that the human figure becomes a kinetic mechanism. In *King and Queen, surrounded by swift nudes* (1912) the human figure is reduced to a menacing, robot-like chessman (hence the title). The man-machine analogy here has sinister overtones, indicating Duchamp's rejection of the futurists' adulation of the machine and their disregard of its possible consequences for mankind. In *Passage of the Virgin to Bride* and *The Bride* (both 1912) the female reproductive system is a bizarre mechanical assemblage of pipes, distilling equipment and compression chambers, introducing irony to temper the gloomy implications of the mechanized

(human) object. In 1914 Duchamp decided it was no longer valid to make an artistic equivalent of an object: any common object, isolated at random from its normal context (e.g. a bottle rack, spade, urinal), placed in an incongruous setting and furnished with an ironical title and signature, could be identified as a work of art; the only possible meaning of a work of art consisted in the spectator's consciousness of it, in a *cervellité* or mental fact. These ready-mades or *objets trouvés* were the first examples of a new mode of the artistic interpretation of reality, by which everyday objects become vehicles for ideas (e.g. *In advance of the Broken Arm*, 1915–45 – a shining new snow-shovel leaning against a wall). After moving to New York in 1915, Duchamp worked intermittently on a large composition in oil, wire and lead foil on two glass panels, entitled *The Bride Stripped Bare by her Bachelors, Even* (abandoned unfinished in 1923 as an anti-art gesture). *The Bride* is a harsh comment on erotic attraction and sexual frustration in modern times: all biological elements are replaced by mechanical devices, symbolizing the annihilation of human values. His ideas influenced the dada movement in Europe and in the USA, but Duchamp refused to accept its espousal of the irrational. His concern was solely to 'show man the limited place of his reason'. In 1920 he renounced artistic activity, apart from the occasional 'assisted' ready-made, in which different elements have been combined by the artist; he devoted himself to chess, which he described as 'a mechanistic sculpture with exciting possibilities'. SOBT

R. Lebel, *Duchamp* (NY, 1959); R. Hamilton, *Almost Complete Works of Marcel Duchamp*, exh. cat. (London, 1966).

Dufy, Raoul (b. Le Havre, Seine-Maritime, France, 3.6.1877; d. Forcalquier, Basses-Alpes, 23.3.1953). French painter. Dufy's training in Le Havre and Paris (1900) was followed by an intensive study of Van Gogh's use of colour (1901). In 1905, after seeing MATISSE's *Luxe, Calme et Volupté*, he adopted fauvist colour techniques. His fauvism was emphatic yet light-hearted, using expressive colours and distortions to create a decorative effect (e.g. *Placards at Trouville*, 1906). In 1908 he visited l'Estaque with BRAQUE, a friend from Le Havre. He tried to work in the cubist manner, but could never reconcile his love of sensuous colours with the rigorous emphasis on structure favoured by Braque. In 1918 he developed a fauve style of his own, characterized by whimsical naivety, delicate surface patterns and sketchily applied colour washes (e.g. *Avenue of the Bois de Boulogne*, 1930). His love of arabesque patterns is possibly related to his textile and tapestry designs for the fashion designer POIRET, whom he met in 1911. In his best works (e.g. *Indian Model in the Studio at L'Impasse Guelma*, 1930) the light, sinuous outlines and warm, intimate colours create a happy and elegant atmosphere. He most often depicted scenes from gambling casinos, racetracks and regattas frequented by the world of fashion. From c. 1947 he simplified this style by limiting himself to a virtually monochrome colour scheme (e.g. *Homage to Bach*, 1950).   SOBT

R. Cogniat, *Raoul Dufy* (NY, 1962).

Duhem, Pierre Maurice Marie (b. Paris, France, 10.6.1861; d. Cabrespine, Aude, 14.9.1916). French physicist, historian and philosopher of science. Duhem's early work was on the application of the concept of thermodynamic potential to problems in physics and chemistry. At that time mechanical models were proving inadequate, so he tried to develop a continuum theory in the form of a generalized thermodynamics that would account for all physics. Many of his ideas were in advance of his time and are still relevant today. In his philosophical writings he steered between the naive realism of the mechanists and the positivism of MACH and Comte. The principal task of a scientific theory is *Sauver les phénomènes* (Paris, 1908; *To Save the Phenomena: an Essay on the Idea of Physical Theory from Plato to Galileo*, Chicago, 1969), that is, to represent in mathematical terms the experimental laws as simply and exactly as possible, but this methodological positivism is balanced by an insistence on the

need for common sense to provide assurance about external reality. Duhem believed that the human mind can grasp the inner nature of the physical world, and that as physics progresses it approaches asymptotically the only true theory.

His studies of the basic problems of physical theory led him to write *L'Evolution de la mécanique* [The evolution of mechanics] (Paris, 1903) and *Les Origines de la statique* [The origins of statics] (Paris, 1905–6). In the course of these partly historical investigations he uncovered unsuspected aspects of medieval science. Indeed, with the publication of his *Etudes sur Léonard de Vince* [Studies on Leonardo da Vinci] (3 vols, Paris, 1906–13) and his monumental *Système du monde* [The structure of the world] (10 vols, Paris, 1913–59) he destroyed the myth of medieval scientific backwardness. He brought to light the Parisian school, in particular the work of Jean Buridan, Albert of Saxony and Nicole Oresme, and showed how their work on mechanics was known to Leonardo and subsequently led in the 17c to the development of such basic notions of Galilean and Newtonian physics as impetus (momentum) and inertia. In spite of his 40 volumes and about 400 papers making signal advances in theoretical physics and in the history and philosophy of science, Duhem received little recognition in his lifetime, partly because some of his early work disproved the maximum work principle, a favourite theorem of Berthelot, an influential chemist and minister of education who saw to it that Duhem was never elected to a chair at Paris, and partly because of Duhem's conservative political views and deep Catholic faith, which were not congenial to the liberal and militantly anticlerical atmosphere of the Third Republic.   PEH

Dulles, John Foster (b. Washington, DC, USA, 25.1.1888; d. Washington, 24.5.1959). US secretary of state (1953–9). Lawyer, previously chief US spokesman on reparations at Paris Peace Conference (1919), took part in San Francisco Conference (1945) and in drafting preamble to United Nations Charter, and served as US delegate to United

Nations General Assembly (1946, 1947, 1950). As secretary of state to Eisenhower, Dulles advocated departure from the TRUMAN administration's policy of 'containment' of the USSR, in favour of 'rolling back' the frontiers of Soviet influence. Soviet threats of force were to be inhibited by a deterrent strategy based on 'massive retaliation' with nuclear weapons. In crises, he preferred not to signal his intentions to his opponents, relying on a policy of 'brinkmanship', i.e. a threat of escalation into open war. A simple and devout Christian, his attitude to the complexities of the external world was equally simple, not to say fundamentalist. He did not believe in the existence of, let alone the possibility of, major disagreement or conflict between the USSR and China. Neutrality and 'neutralism' were to him hypocritical. If a state was not prepared to ally itself with the USA on all issues against the communist powers, then it was to be treated as an enemy. Hostility to communism rather than possession of a democratic system of government was the yardstick by which he approved would-be allies, friends or partners. Lasting agreement with communism was, he believed, impossible in view of what he saw as the communist attitude to keeping one's word. Attempts to reach agreement were in his view synonymous with appeasement. To his innate hostility to communism he added an equal hostility to British and European systems of colonial rule, believing that the USA recognizably retained the aura of anticolonialism which had attached itself to their foundation, and that the resistance of colonial peoples to communist domination would become the dominating force in their foreign policy, making them automatic allies of the USA against the Soviet bloc once the colonial power had withdrawn.   DCW

L. L. Gerson, *John Foster Dulles* (NY, 1967); T. Hooper, *The Devil and John Foster Dulles* (Boston, 1973).

Duncan, Isadora, *née* Dora Angela Duncan (b. San Francisco, Calif., USA, 26.5.1877; d. Nice, Alpes-Maritimes, France, 14.9.1927). American dancer, pioneer of a new 'free' dance style. Duncan rebelled against what she con-

sidered to be the contorted and inexpressive stage dancing of the early 20c. Her aim was to express in movement the essence of life, not character or situation. She was among the first to dance to the music of the great classical composers, and to reject constricting contemporary stage dress. Much of her inspiration came from Greek art – she performed barefoot in Greek-inspired draperies and considered her art a revival of the dances of ancient Greece. For her, all movement originated from the solar plexus, and in this, and in yielding to the force of gravity in her dances (as opposed to classical ballet which seeks to defy gravity), she developed two principles that have been absorbed into the mainstream of modern dance. A rebel against formal dance training, she left no specific influence upon technique; her attempts to found a school in Germany (1904) and later in Moscow (1921) ultimately failed for there was no definable technique to be taught and her dances, though carefully prepared, did not survive her death, for they depended upon a strong improvisational element which could not be transmitted. Most of her career was spent in Europe and Russia, although in America, where she was rejected and scorned as a performer, she is now hailed as a pioneer of modern dance. Her work revealed the expressive potential of movement, and the body's capacity to evoke emotion as potently as poetry or music.   SCW

I. Duncan, *The Technique of Isadora Duncan* (NY, 1937); V. Seroff, *The Real Isadora* (NY, 1971).

Duncan, Robert Edward (b. Oakland, Calif., USA, 7.1.1919). American poet. Duncan is the most ambitious of the projectivist poets associated with OLSON and Black Mountain College, and the one who has displayed the strongest dedication to his poetic vocation. Since the 1940s he has been a leading member of the San Francisco circle, working with such poets as Kenneth Rexroth, Robert Creeley and Denise Levertov. His poems are large-scale works, discursive reveries on interrelated and ramifying themes. His earlier work (*Heavenly City, Earthly City*, Berkeley, 1947; *The Opening of the Field*, NY, 1960; and

Roots and Branches, NY, 1964) is largely concerned with a mystical, neopagan religion and creativity; later volumes (e.g. *Bending the Bow*, NY, 1968) have added to these themes a political concern (antiwar, antimonopoly capitalism). He has called himself 'an artist of abundancies' who does not 'seek a synthesis but a mêlée'. The structure of his poems is, to use his own phrase, 'an increment of associations'. His technique is fundamentally imagist; of the two major American imagists – Ezra POUND and William Carlos WILLIAMS – his mentor is clearly Pound. The flow of associated images is frequently interrupted by didactic and hortatory passages (a practice deriving from that of Pound in the *Cantos*); these didactic interludes are usually the least successful parts of Duncan's poetry and often obscure his undeniable talent for moments of discrete imagist evocation. Duncan has also written plays and prose; much of the latter enlarges on the themes of his verse.   DD

Duras, Marguerite, ps. of Marguerite Donnadieu (b. Giadinh, Indochina [now Vietnam], 4.4.1914). French novelist. Duras spent her formative years in Indochina and the suffering, pain and degradation of the teeming masses of the Far East engendered in her a hatred of colonialism and a sense of alienation which was to become one of the mainsprings of her work. She was an active member of the French resistance and a member of the French Communist party from 1944 until her expulsion in 1955. Her earlier works, which include *Un Barrage contre le Pacifique* (Paris, 1950; tr. A. White, *A Sea of Troubles*, London, 1953) and *Moderato Cantabile* (Paris, 1958; tr. R. Seaver, NY, 1960), have a neorealist tone; the settings are well defined and to some extent their content is autobiographical, although the novelist preserves a sense of detachment from the fates of her characters. Her collaboration with RESNAIS, which produced the film *Hiroshima mon amour* (1960), marks a turning-point in her career. Hereafter, her work becomes much more experimental (*Dix heures et demie du soir en été* (Paris, 1960; tr. R. Seaver, *Ten Thirty on a Summer Night*,

London, 1962); while narrative thread, characters and context remain recognizable, they are already being significantly eroded. Since the mid-1960s, her work has gone yet further down this path: the settings are indeterminate, speech is elliptical and linear narrative has totally disappeared. The result is that the text is now only distantly related to what convention would recognize as a novel.
                                              WBS

A. Cismaru, *Marguerite Duras* (NY, 1971).

Durkheim, Emile (b. Epinal, Lorraine, France, 15.4.1858; d. Paris, 15.11.1917). French sociologist. Durkheim, along with M. WEBER, is a founding father of modern sociology. Oddly enough, though they were contemporaries, Durkheim scarcely referred to Weber's work, nor Weber openly to Durkheim; Weber was editor of the *Archiv für Sozialwissenschaft* and Durkheim the editor of *L'Année Sociologique*, the two major sociological journals of the time, yet in neither of the journals is there any contrasting discussion of the other's work. In part, this is because the two derived from very different intellectual traditions – Weber from German historical thinking, Durkheim from French rationalism – and, in consequence, their approaches and styles of work differed radically. Where Weber grounded his theoretical propositions in specific historical situations, Durkheim sought to develop 'elementary forms' or pure types as the building-blocks of a theory of society. In his studies of religion, Durkheim began with a specific definition and sought for an explanation of religion in terms of a basic attachment, namely totemism as an elementary form, whereas, in his, Weber eschewed formal definitions and built his propositions from a study of the great historic religions such as those of India and China, and Judaism and Christianity. The heart of Durkheim's sociology is a rejection of the individualist basis of society – the idea, characteristic of English utilitarian thought, from Hobbes through Bentham, that the individual and his self-interest comprise the unit of society and that the community is an artificial entity or a fiction. For Durkheim, the society was prior to the individual and, methodologically, the social could not be reduced to the psychological. All else flowed from these two theorems. The first of these propositions was laid out in *De la division du travail social* (Paris, 1893, ²1902; *The Division of Labor in Society*, NY, 1933), in which Durkheim attacked the notion that society was simply a 'contract' between individuals for, as he argued, the norms which govern contracts are embedded in a broader context of moral understandings or social solidarity. In that book, Durkheim also moved away from the historical view of the development of society to posit two basic types of solidarity which he called 'mechanical' and 'organic'. In the first, akin to traditional or 'primitive' societies, there was little division of labour and men were subject to common norms. In the second, functions became specialized, the family was replaced by the occupational milieu as the locus of attachment, and the norms governing behaviour were specific to the roles played by individuals. For that very reason, modern society posed a problem of what Durkheim, in the preface to the second edition, called *anomie*, or behaviour that was not governed by norms. Along with the idea of alienation, anomie has become one of the stock terms, if not clichés, of modern sociology.

The second theorem, about the irreducibility of the social, is exemplified by Durkheim's classic work, *Le Suicide* (Paris, 1897; *Suicide*, London, 1952), in which he distinguished between three kinds of suicide, which he called egoistic, altruistic and anomic after the different kinds of cultural causes. The *rates* of suicide in the first derive from the different degrees of attachment or integration of an individual to a group; in the second (as in Japan) from the sense of failure *to* the group; and in the third because of a lack *of* a group, or restraints upon an individual's conduct. Durkheim's method is best understood by his analysis of the first type. He began by arguing that psychological interpretations could not explain the *variations* in suicide rates, such as the higher rates of suicide among unmarried than married persons, or the higher rates among Protestants than Catholics.

It was, he argued, the degree of social cohesion – the bonds of marriage or the injunctions of the faith – which alone could account for these variations. In these respects, one can see the source of Durkheim's statement that society is essentially a moral order bound by shared sentiments, and that the crucial problem for sociological analysis is the kind and degree of social integration in a society and the sources of disorder.

Towards the end of his life, Durkheim planned two works, one on the religious foundations of society, the other on moral universalism, which, in form, would parallel his earlier distinctions between mechanical and organic solidarity. He wrote only one work, *Les Formes élémentaires de la vie religieuse* (Paris, 1912; *The Elementary Forms of Religious Life*, London, 1915); the failure to publish the other has resulted in a significant distortion of Durkheim's work by most writers who have not known of this intention. In the *Elementary Forms*, Durkheim put forth two arguments. One was that the religious bond was simply the symbolic representation of the social bond, expressed through ritual. The other was the distinction between the sacred and the profane: religion could best be defined not by considerations of the supernatural or by magic or personal or mystic experiences but by the ability of societies to maintain this distinction. This has led many writers to assume that Durkheim saw religion and society only in terms of this reductive *conscience collective*, or collective consciousness. Yet in the second work, Durkheim planned to write of the role of moral education and citizenship as promoting emergent universal values that men could give allegiance to in a common humanity. Perhaps WW1, in which Durkheim lost a son and where half the 1913 class of the famed Ecole Normale, the school of the French intellectual elite, was killed, destroyed that faith as well. He published a major work on the rules of sociological methodology: *Les Règles de la méthode sociologique* (Paris, 1895; *The Rules of Sociological Method*, Chicago, 1938).   DBe

S. Lukes, *Emile Durkheim* (London, 1973).

Durrell, Lawrence George (b. Julundur, Punjab, India, 27.2.1912). British novelist and poet. Durrell describes himself as 'Irish mother, English father ... lusty Mutiny stock ... one of the world's expatriates'. His work, ranging from the pullulating private world of *The Black Book* (Paris, 1938), through the lyrics – *Collected Poems 1931–1974* (London, 1980) – which in tone and technique have affinities with the work of AUDEN and GRAVES, to the HUXLEYan comedy of *Nunquam* (London, 1970), attempts to reconcile imaginative insight into British technology and Puritanism with a Mediterranean temperament: confident, exotic and humane. His most celebrated achievement is *The Alexandria Quartet* (London, 1962, consisting of *Justine*, London, 1957; *Balthazar*, London, 1958; *Mountolive*, London, 1958; *Clea*, London, 1960). Formally experimental, 'a four-decker novel based on the relativity proposition', it is distinguished by its poetic sense of place, sensuously intelligent exploration of love, conjunction of public and private lives, and keenly imagined scenes and characters. Experience of the diplomatic corps lends comic and sinister effect to these novels and to *Tunc* (London, 1968), and is the inspiration of his humorous books *Esprit de Corps* (London, 1957), *Stiff Upper Lip* (London, 1958) and *Sauve qui Peut* (London, 1966). The travel books *Prospero's Cell* (London, 1945), *Reflections on a Marine Venus* (London, 1953) and *Bitter Lemons* (London, 1957) display Durrell's acute eye for unofficial people and politics. He is currently engaged on a 'quincunx' of novels, which so far include *Monsieur* (London, 1974), *Livia* (London, 1978) and *Constance, or Solitary Practices* (London, 1982). SJN

H. T. Moore (ed.), *The World of Lawrence Durrell* (Carbondale, 1962); G. S. Fraser, *Lawrence Durrell: a Study* (London, 1968).

Dürrenmatt, Friedrich (b. Konolfingen, Bern, Switzerland, 5.1.1921). Swiss dramatist, novelist and essayist. A Protestant minister's son, he studied desultorily in Zürich and Bern, preferring to devote his time to drawing, painting and writing. With Max FRISCH he achieved prominence in postwar Switzerland and Germany with a series of controversial plays which helped to fill the cultural vacuum left by the Nazis. International recognition came with the parable plays *Der Besuch der alten Dame* (Zürich, 1956; adapted and tr. M. Valency, *The Visit*, NY, 1958) and *Die Physiker* (Zürich, 1962; tr. J. Kirkup, *The Physicists*, London, 1963). His subsequent dramatic work largely failed to appeal to the politicized German theatre of the late 1960s and 1970s. Since the mid-1970s he has concentrated on prose experiments, combining political/philosophical essays with fiction. The most important examples form a loose 'trilogy': *Der Mitmacher. Ein Komplex* [The conniver: a complex (of questions)] (Zürich, 1976); *Zusammenhänge. Essay über Israel* [Connections: essay on Israel] (Zürich, 1976); and the first instalment of an autobiographical account of his imaginative writing and its sources, *Stoffe I–III* [Materials I–III] (Zürich, 1981). The dominant image in Dürrenmatt's writing is the labyrinth. The rebellious individual is depicted struggling for freedom and justice in an increasingly opaque and menacing environment. Despite their scepticism and frequently macabre cynicism, Dürrenmatt's comic inventions possess an irreducible core of humanism. Grotesque distortions and aggressive mockery paradoxically assert the need to return to the battered ideals of the Enlightenment. His recent work demonstrates an extraordinary grasp of science, theology and philosophy, revealing a 'new', more speculative and challenging Dürrenmatt. Numerous literary prizes and international honours attest to a protean phenomenon in contemporary German literature. MGB

T. Tiusanen, *Dürrenmatt: a Study in Plays, Prose, Theory* (Princeton, 1977); K. Whitton, *The Theatre of Friedrich Dürrenmatt* (London, 1980).

Du Vigneaud, Vincent (b. Chicago, Ill., USA, 18.5.1901; d. Scarsdale, NY, 11.12.1978). American bio-organic chemist. Du Vigneaud studied chemistry at the University of Illinois under C. S. Marvel. Following postdoctoral work at Johns Hopkins University, at Edinburgh (with Barger), and University College Hospital (with Harington), he moved via Illinois University and George Washington University to become professor and head of the biochemistry department in Cornell Medical School (1938). Du Vigneaud's early work centred on the chemistry of insulin, in particular the proof that the sulphur-containing compound cystine was one of its component amino-acids. During the course of this work the biologically important tripeptide glutathione was synthesized. He then took up the study of two structurally similar polypeptide hormones of the posterior lobe of the pituitary gland, viz. oxytocin, which stimulates uterine contraction and milk ejection, and vasopressin which raises blood pressure and regulates kidney function. Not only were the structures of these hormones determined but also in 1953 oxytocin was synthesized and the product was shown to be identical with the natural product. This was the first synthesis of a polypeptide hormone: it demonstrated beyond doubt that peptides of great physiological importance can be synthesized rationally. Du Vigneaud has also studied intermediary metabolism, transmethylation, trans-sulphurization, biotin and penicillin. Throughout all this work the connecting thread has been, in du Vigneaud's own words, 'a trail of sulphur research'. He received the Nobel prize for chemistry in 1955. NBC

Dylan, Bob, ps. of Robert Allen Zimmerman (b. Duluth, Minn., USA,

24.5.1941). American minstrel and songwriter. Having taught himself the guitar (plus piano and harmonica) he formed a rock band in 1955 and also began writing. By the early 1960s his informal semisinging style to basic guitar chords had attracted attention and he soon was a popular performer and recording artist. The gently rebellious mood of his lyrics and his tunes was entirely in line with the feelings of his generation as adumbrated in e.g. the film *Rebel without a Cause* (1955) that showed the inarticulate unease of American middle-class teenagers; this group were to experiment, aided by drugs, with 'flower power' and various other manifestations of disillusionment. Dylan's 'Blowin' in the Wind' (1962) and 'The Times They are a-Changin'' (1964) have rightly been called 'anthems for the protest and civil rights movements'. On the other hand his 'Mr Tambourine Man' (1965) has been said to embody the 'dreamy intensity ... of the drugged state and its justification in the face of all reason'. More recently he has repudiated his earlier political commitment and has disconcerted some of his fans by adopting a more religious stance. Dylan's music is simple, his lyrics having more skill and subtlety; nevertheless his songs have power and passion and, for many, have spoken eloquently of their moods and ideals. CH

C. McGregor (ed.), *Bob Dylan: a Retrospective* (London, 1972).

E

Eames, Charles (b. St Louis, Mo., USA, 17.6.1907; d. St Louis, 21.8.1978). American architect and designer. After a brief period of formal study, Eames practised as an architect until 1937, and then spent three years as head of the department of experimental design at Cranbrook Academy, Michigan. In 1940 he won an important design prize (with SAARINEN) for a chair. From 1944 he practised as a designer in California with his wife Ray Eames. In his designs for furniture, toys, showrooms and exhibitions, and in the presentation of documentary films, he was as much concerned with the communication of ideas through visual images as with the design and making of artefacts. This work is characterized by a concern for visual aesthetics, the disciplined use of materials, technical skill, attention to detail and rich colours. Although startling when they first appeared, his designs have been quickly and widely assimilated into contemporary culture. Most widely known for his chairs, mostly made of moulded plywood or moulded plastic, his lounge chair with ottoman (1956) is one of the most famous of 20c chairs. Eames is not noted for his buildings, with the exception of his own house in California which, built in 1949 from commercially available, factory-made components, had considerable impact. The significance of his work lies in the new forms and in the new attitudes to the design of everyday objects which he brought to a very wide audience.   BM

R. Caplan, *Connections: the Work of Charles and Ray Eames* (Los Angeles, 1976).

Eastman, George (b. Waterville, NY, USA, 12.7.1854; d. Rochester, NY, 14.3.1932). American inventor of roll-film photography. In 1884 he formed the Eastman Dry Plate and Film Company and patented the roll photographic film, using a paper roll. In 1889 he replaced the paper roll with celluloid, and in 1924 improved it further by using cellulose acetate. Eastman developed a camera to use the roll film, and marketed it under the trade name Kodak with the slogan, 'You press the button: we do the rest.' His work contributed to the development of amateur photography and enabled EDISON to develop the moving film camera.   RIT

Eccles, John Carew (b. Melbourne, Victoria, Australia, 27.1.1903). British neurobiologist. He took his first degree in medicine at Melbourne University in 1925, and then as a postgraduate went to Magdalen College, Oxford, where he subsequently became a fellow (1934–7). Eccles became professor of physiology at Dunedin, New Zealand (1944–51), and at Canberra, Australia (1951–66), then finally professor of neurobiology at Buffalo, New York (1968–75). Following up the idea first proposed by SHERRINGTON in 1934, Eccles showed that nerve impulses in preganglionic fibres passed to postganglionic fibres, with a short delay, indicating that some chemical neurotransmission mechanism may be involved. His life's work has concentrated upon the mechanism of neurotransmission throughout the nervous system for which he developed techniques for intracellular recording from fine neurones. For this he received the Nobel prize for medicine in 1963. This work has been summarized in a number of books, notably *The Physiology of Nerve Cells* (Baltimore, 1957) and *The Physiology of Synapses* (Heidelberg, 1964). More recently Eccles has become involved with some of the more philosophical aspects of brain function (see *Facing Reality*, London, 1970).   CTJ

Eddington, Arthur Stanley (b. Kendal, Cumbria, UK, 28.12.1882; d. Cambridge, 22.11.1944). British astrophysicist. After a distinguished undergraduate career at Cambridge, Eddington spent seven years as chief assistant at Greenwich Observatory from 1906. His interests soon turned to the interpretation of observational data, more especially those connected with the movements of stars and star streaming. These studies led to his first book *Stellar Movements and the Structure of the Universe* (London, 1914). On his appointment as Plumian professor of astronomy at Cambridge in 1913, Eddington started his classical work on the structure of stars, in which he pointed out the importance of the transfer of energy by radiation through a star, and saw that, in spite of its high density, matter in the interior of a star behaves as a perfect gas. This work led to a natural explanation of the relation between the masses of stars and their luminosities (the total rate at which they emit energy). Although he was not aware of the detailed nature of energy generation in stars (he supposed it to be 'subatomic' and that the star 'burns away its mass'), many of these related ideas have formed the basis of subsequent work. His researches led to another major book *The Internal Constitution of the Stars* (Cambridge, 1926), which remains a classical work in modern astronomy. In 1917 Eddington was one of the first in the UK to hear of and to appreciate the theory of general relativity which was developed by EINSTEIN during WW1. The theory predicted that light rays passing close to the sun would be deflected. The deflection should be measurable at a time of total solar eclipse when the sky is so darkened that stars can be seen and photographed close to the sun. In 1919 Eddington led an expedition from Greenwich to observe the solar eclipse at Principe in order to test this prediction, the measurement to be made being the very small change in the normal position of a star when it is close to the solar limb. The expedition was successful, as was a second one, to Brazil from Greenwich; both provided confirmatory evidence for Einstein's theory.

Eddington's later years were spent in work on his 'fundamental theory', in which he tried to derive the numerical values of constants of nature (discussed in his posthumous *Fundamental Theory*, Cambridge, 1946). He also wrote several philosophical and semipopular books renowned for their clear expositions (e.g. *The Expanding Universe*, Cambridge, 1935).   DEB

A. V. Douglas, *The Life of Arthur Stanley Eddington* (London, 1956).

Eden, Robert Anthony (b. Windlestone, Durham, UK, 12.6.1897; d. Alvediston, Wilts., 14.1.1977). British minister for League of Nations affairs (1934–5); foreign secretary (1935–8); Dominions secretary (1939–40); secretary of war (1940–1); foreign secretary (1941–5, 1951–5); prime minister (1955–7). Associated in the public mind with opposition to the policy of 'appeasement' practised by the Conservative government (1933–9) headed by Baldwin and CHAMBERLAIN, he resigned office in 1938, but returned under CHURCHILL to serve as foreign secretary in the wartime coalition. When he finally succeeded Churchill as leader of the Conservative party and prime minister in 1955, he was driven out of office by the disaster which overtook Britain in the Suez crisis (1956). Eden's reputation for opposing appeasement, in which he himself came to believe, to his own downfall, rested more on his opposition to the appeasement of fascist Italy than of Nazi Germany, and the 'lessons of the 1930s' to which he made frequent appeal in 1956, rested more on contemporary mythology than on accurate recollection of the past. He has indeed been greatly criticized for the lengths to which he was prepared to go in 1944–5 to secure Soviet participation in the postwar settlement. Highly skilled in the arts of negotiation, his greatest triumph was probably the Geneva Conference on South East Asia (1954) which averted the escalation of the French war with the Vietminh revolutionaries into a US–Chinese war, at the expense of alienating DULLES. In the Suez operation he equated NASSER with HITLER, and the nationalization of the Suez Canal with the reoccupation of the Rhineland; he acted against American advice, against the advice of all but a handful of his foreign policy advisers, against the opposition of most of the Commonwealth, with the bulk of his cabinet kept in ignorance of the degree of his prior agreement with Israel and France and in the face of the declared hostility of the Labour opposition, and, so many believed, in contradiction to Britain's obligations under the charter of the UN.

The Suez episode ended Eden's career and exposed to the world the vulnerability and powerlessness of Britain's post-war position. Eden's own account of his career is given in *The Eden Memoirs* (3 vols, London, 1960–5). DCW

Edgeworth, Francis Ysidro (b. Edgeworthstown, Longford, Ireland, UK [now Irish Republic], 8.2.1845; d. Oxford, UK, 13.2.1926). Irish/British economist of mixed Irish, Spanish and Huguenot descent. Educated by tutors at the family home, then at Trinity College, Dublin, and at Magdalen Hall and Balliol College, Oxford, where he obtained a first class in classics. He was called to the Bar in 1877, but subsequently became a lecturer in logic and then Tooke professor of political economy at King's College, London. In 1891 he was elected Drummond professor of political economy at Oxford, and a fellow of All Souls, where he remained for the rest of his life (retiring from the chair in 1922). His most celebrated publication was the quaintly titled *Mathematical Psychics* (London, 1881). His *Papers Relating to Political Economy* (3 vols, London) appeared in 1925.

Edgeworth made important contributions to mathematical economics and statistics, notably on general equilibrium theory, probability, correlation and index numbers. His main achievement – not adequately appreciated until the development of game theory and related topics after 1944 – was to pioneer an approach to general equilibrium based not (like WALRAS's scheme) on an explicit economy-wide price mechanism but on direct cooperation between individual agents in the absence of prices. This approach has subsequently been shown to yield an optimum effectively identical with the competitive optimum of Walras and PARETO. In his obituary of Edgeworth in the *Economic Journal* (of which Edgeworth was editor or joint editor from its first issue in March 1891 until his death) KEYNES drew a memorable contrast between Edgeworth and his contemporary (and Keynes's teacher) Alfred MARSHALL: 'To judge from his published works, Edgeworth reached economics, as Marshall had before him, through mathematics and ethics. But

here the resemblance ceases. Marshall's interest was intellectual and moral, Edgeworth's intellectual and aesthetic. Edgeworth wished to establish *theorems* of intellectual and aesthetic interest, Marshall to establish *maxims* of practical and moral importance. In respect of technical training and of lightness and security of touch, Marshall was much his superior in the mathematical field – Marshall had been Second Wrangler, Edgeworth had graduated in *Litteris Humanioribus*. Yet Edgeworth, clumsy and awkward though he often was in his handling of the mathematical instrument, was in originality, in accomplishment, and in the bias of his natural interest considerably the greater mathematician.' PMO

J. M. Keynes, 'F. Y. Edgeworth' in *Essays in Biography* (London, 1933); J. S. Chipman, 'The nature and meaning of equilibrium in economic theory' in D. Martindale (ed.), *Functionalism in the Social Sciences* (American Academy of Political and Social Science, 1965), rep. H. Townsend (ed.), *Price Theory* (Harmondsworth, 1971).

Edison, Thomas Alva (b. Milan, Ohio, USA, 11.2.1847; d. West Orange, NJ, 18.10.1931). American inventor whose work was fundamental to the development of the telephone, wireless telegraphy, electric light, the phonograph and the motion picture projector, each of which has changed life expectations and patterns of thought. His primary motivation was to make invention profitable.

Edison was educated at home by his mother. His father thought he was stupid; after three months his school teacher found him uneducable. At 12 he began working on the railroad, selling newspapers and candy on trains. Instead of a wage he worked for profit and was able to hire two assistants. He bought a second-hand news-press and printed his own newspaper, *en route*, in the baggage car of the train. When he became a telegraph operator (1862–8), deafness enabled him to concentrate on the telegraph's clicks and he became a first-class operator. He developed a way of boosting the current to transmit messages over longer distances, and built a device for recording messages on paper tape. The Western Union Telegraph Company commissioned him to develop the telegraphic stock ticker. With the proceeds he set up as a fulltime inventor and manufacturer. He took out 38 patents in 1872 and 25 in 1873. He designed a transmitter which improved the quality of A. G. BELL's telephone system. He invented the electric-lamp bulb (1878–9). He developed the aerial mast and the microphone, and the electric lamp became the basis of the valve; all these were fundamental to MARCONI's work on wireless. He invented the phonograph in 1877, which remained a novelty for 10 years until Bell patented an improved wax-coated cylinder. Edison, in competition, produced a solid wax cylinder, a floating stylus and an electro-plated master record from which copies could be pressed. Then he set out 'to devise an instrument which would do for the eye what the phonograph does for the ear'. EASTMAN's development of the celluloid film roll enabled Edison to design the kinetoscope, the forerunner of the moving film projector. In the 1890s he foresaw the possibilities of the motor car, but concluded that electricity would be more reliable than petrol. He developed a battery which was useful in telegraphy and submarines. But one of his engineers, Henry FORD, left him to develop the petrol-driven car. Edison was not the lonely, idiosyncratic inventor of the popular image; nor was he an academic interested in knowledge for its own sake. He was commercially orientated. He led a team of engineers and scientists, and created an industrial research laboratory at Menlo Park, New Jersey, the first such complex in the world. Apart from his own inventions, Edison set the direction for future research and development.   RIT

W. H. Meadowcroft, *Edison: his Life and Inventions*, (2 vols, NY, 1929); M. Josephson, *Edison: a Biography* (NY, 1959).

Ehrenburg, Iliya Grigorievich (b. Kiev, Russia, 27.1.1891; d. Moscow, USSR, 1.9.1969). Russian writer, who began his career as a symbolist poet but soon turned to fiction, journalism and, later, literary criticism and autobiography. At 16 he became involved in revolutionary activities, was arrested and escaped to France. From 1909 to 1917 he stayed in Paris, where he was associated with modernist artistic circles. Life in France imbued him with a love-hate attachment to France and to the West in general. After many vicissitudes inside and outside postrevolutionary Russia, he finally (in 1924) returned to the USSR and was identified with early experimental trends. By 1932 he had discarded these and embarked on new ones, by joining the school of socialist realism. His will to accept the new ideal of life proved as sincere as his (relative) inability to do so. He was a brilliant journalist rather than novelist, and an outstanding war correspondent during WW2. Among his most interesting novels is *Neobychainy pokhozhdeniya Khuilis Khurenito* (Paris, 1921; tr. A. Bostock & A. Kapp, *Julio Jurenito*, London, 1958) – a modernized *Candide* – which vividly satirizes contemporary civilization. The subsequent work, fictional and journalistic, continued to portray in an animated and ironic, if more restrained, manner the moods of STALINist and post-Stalinist Russia. *Den' vtoroi* [The second day] (Moscow, 1933) evoked the conflicting emotions generated by rapid industrialization; *Voina* (Moscow, 1943; tr. G. Shelley, *Russia at War*, London, 1943), a collection of articles, describes the horrors of the German invasion and the experiences of the Soviet people during WW2; *Burya* (Moscow, 1948; tr. E. Hartley & T. Glurbina, *The Storm*, London, 1949), a sequel to *Padenie Parizha* (Moscow, 1942; tr. G. Shelley, *The Fall of Paris*, London, 1962), a forceful attack on the West, reflects international tensions, leading to the Cold War; *Ottepel'* (Moscow, 1954; tr. M. Harari, *The Thaw*, London, 1965) marks the symptoms at the beginning of cultural de-Stalinization. Thereafter, even when criticized for ideological errors, Ehrenburg hit back with vigour, which pleased the young intelligentsia who tended to look on him as their spokesman. At the same time he received a number of the highest state awards for literature. His crowning work is a long autobiography *Liudi, gody, zhizn'* (tr. M. Harari *et al.*, *Men, Years,*

Life (London, 1962–6), combining an account of personal survival in an upside-down world with clever, epigrammatic, at times poignant but seldom profound portraits of Russian and foreign writers and artists, friends and enemies alike. Ehrenburg's popularity has diminished, but he remains a prominent and, in an ambivalent way, typical figure in the development of Soviet letters. EL

G. Belaya & L. Lazarev (eds), *Vospominaniya ob Iliye Ehrenburge* (Moscow, 1975).

Ehrenfest, Paul (b. Vienna, Austria-Hungary [now Austria], 18.1.1880; d. Amsterdam, The Netherlands, 25.9.1933). Austrian theoretical physicist who specialized mainly in statistical mechanics. Stimulated by working with BOLTZMANN, and by a period in Göttingen, he studied PLANCK's theory of black-body radiation and its relation to the foundations of statistical mechanics. He tackled the basic problem of reconciling the reversibility of classical mechanics with the irreversibility of the events of ordinary experience, showing that this is due to the extreme improbability of processes in which order spontaneously increases. He clarified many of the basic assumptions of statistical mechanics, and showed that it is logically necessary for the energy to have only certain discrete allowed values. In an analysis of the motion of a wave packet, he showed that its position and momentum obey the same equations of motion as a classical particle (Ehrenfest's theorem). His genius lay not in creation or in calculation but in criticism. He strove to understand the essence of a theory and to express it as clearly as possible. He knew what the problems were, he sharpened up the issues and asked the right questions. He was never satisfied with his work and always felt insecure and inadequate. This, together with the persecution of the Jews by the Nazis, led him to take his own life. PEH

M. J. Klein, *Paul Ehrenfest: the Making of a Theoretical Physicist* (Amsterdam, 1970).

Ehrlich, Paul (b. Strehlen, Silesia, Germany [now Strzelin, Poland], 14.3.1854; d. Bad Homburg, Hesse, Germany, 20.8.1915). German pharmacologist. After graduating in medicine and after a period as medical assistant at the Charité Hospital in Berlin, Ehrlich joined KOCH in his new Institute for Infectious Diseases. In 1896 an institute for serum research and serum control was created in Berlin, under his direction. Later the Georg Speyer House was built nearby, and from 1906 until his death Ehrlich directed both institutes. Among many distinctions, he won the Nobel prize in 1908.

At the time Ehrlich began work, the new aniline dyes were being discovered, and a cousin, Carl Weigert, had introduced them into microscopic technique. Ehrlich began his work in Weigert's laboratory by studying their capacity for selective staining; and one can trace almost all his later work back to the specific interaction between chemical substances and particular biological structures that dyes reveal, whose full significance he was the first to see. An early discovery was the so-called 'mast cell', a large cell with distinctive granules taking up basic dyes, now known to be rich in histamine and to mediate many allergic reactions. A year later he defined the 'eosinophil' cells that occur in blood, now known to be particularly involved in resistance to parasitic infections. Extending his work to bacteria, he was the first to stain tubercle bacilli. The same insight led him to recognize the 'blood-brain barrier', through which only drugs with sufficient fat solubility (lipotropism) can penetrate. Further discoveries were that the dye methylene blue selectively stained nervous tissue *in vivo*; and that other dyes, which bleach on removal of oxygen, allowed the study of the varying oxygen demand of different tissues.

In 1888 tubercle bacilli were found in his sputum. He was cured and developed an interest in immunity. He demonstrated that antibodies were transmitted in maternal milk to provide 'passive' immunity to a newborn animal. His chemical skill enabled him to produce a preparation of diphtheria antitoxin (recently discovered by von Behring) sufficiently concentrated for its first clinical use. Its success led to the necessity of a standardization of toxin and antitoxin, which Ehrlich solved by preparing a dried, evacuated reference sample of antitoxin as an international standard, with which the toxin was titrated. This was the beginning of the now extensive international scheme of biological standards. His observation that toxin might lose its pathogenicity but not its capacity to generate antibodies led to the use of so-called 'toxoids' in immunization, and, more deeply, to a distinction between combining power (illustrated by the 'lock-and-key' simile) and activity of a toxin, with the complementary postulate of 'haptophore' and 'toxophore' chemical groups. His 'side-chain theory' envisaged that a toxin which could combine with but not kill a cell would give rise to a proliferation of the cellular binding sites involved, by analogy with the proliferative regeneration described by his cousin Weigert; these, shed into the blood, constituted the immune antibodies.

As the failure of 'immunotherapy' against diseases such as trypanosomiasis, malaria and syphilis became apparent, Ehrlich turned again to 'chemotherapy', the use of chemicals, not for histology but as specially constructed 'magic bullets', designed to find, bind to, and act on the parasite. A range of phenols proved to be inhibited by serum and too toxic. The dye 'trypan red' was found effective against trypanosomes, but 'drug resistance' developed – the first description of this phenomenon. The discovery of the spirochaetes of syphilis prompted his arsenical research, during which he formulated the idea of a 'therapeutic index' for a drug (ratio of curative to tolerated dose). Compound No. 606 proved effective in human syphilis and, as 'Salvarsan', revolutionized its treatment. Adverse reactions, however, led to much harassing controversy, until the safer No. 914, 'Neosalvarsan', appeared. A forceful personality, often engaged in controversy yet inspiring great loyalty, smoking more than 25 cigars a day but drinking only mineral water, Ehrlich dominated the first phase of the chemotherapeutic revolution which ended with his death and

was not resumed until 20 years later with the discovery by DOMAGK of the antibacterial action of the dye prontosil rubrum. *The Collected Papers of Paul Erlich* have been edited by F. Himmelweit (vols 1–3, London, 1956). WP

M. Marquadt, *Paul Erlich* (London, 1949).

Eigen, Manfred (b. Bochum, N. Rhine-Westphalia, Germany, 9.5.1927). German biophysical chemist. The discipline itself is barely 30 years old, but Eigen's place in it is assured by his development of two techniques whereby chemical reactions in solution, of such rapidity as previously to be inaccessible to experimental study, can now be the subject of rate measurements. The first of these, the temperature-jump technique, involves the setting up of transient chemical effects by rapid thermal pulses, thereby disturbing equilibrium in such a way as to set in train consequences amenable to detailed spectrometric study. Reactions complete in a millisecond can thus be studied. The second technique involves the use of ultrasonic waves for studying the rates of the extremely rapid reactions of ions in aqueous solution. For this work, jointly with NORRISH and G. PORTER, Eigen was awarded the Nobel prize in 1967. In recent years he has broken new ground by publishing work on hypercycles, 'a principle of natural self-organization allowing an integration and coherent evolution of sets of functionally coupled self-replicative entities'. Hypercycles are amenable to a unified mathematical treatment. Since 1964 he has been director of the Max-Planck Institute for Biophysical Chemistry in Göttingen. NBC

Einstein, Albert (b. Ulm, Baden-Württemberg, Germany, 14.3.1879; naturalized Swiss citizen, 1900; naturalized American citizen, 1940; d. Princeton, NJ, USA, 18.4.1955). German/Swiss/American theoretical physicist who radically revised our concepts of space and time and whose work, together with that of PLANCK on quantum theory, laid the foundations of modern physics. In 1906 he published three papers, each making a great creative advance, on the theory of relativity, the photoelectric effect and the Brownian motion. All his efforts were directed towards finding simple, general and unifying principles describing the objective nature of the world. He tried to imagine what a light wave would look like to an observer travelling along with it, and realized that the description was inconsistent with Maxwell's equations, known to describe the electromagnetic field to high accuracy. He found that the inconsistency would be removed by using the transformation equations from one moving system to another, as already found by H. A. LORENTZ in his studies of the theory of electrons. This transformation differs from the Galilean transformation associated with the Newtonian concepts of space and time, and Einstein realized that it must be replaced by the Lorentz transformation not only for electromagnetic phenomena but for all transformations from one moving system to another. It implies that very high velocities do not add arithmetically and that no velocity can exceed that of light, and it automatically ensures that the velocity of light is the same in all reference-frames. The consequences of this revolutionary theory were soon confirmed experimentally, removing a whole series of anomalies in the old ether theory (see *Relativity, the Special and the General Theory: a Popular Exposition*, London, 1920; and, with L. Infeld, *The Evolution of Physics*, Cambridge, 1938). It also implies the equivalence of mass and energy that is verified to high accuracy in nuclear reactions and in the atomic bomb.

Einstein's work on the photoelectric effect was more readily accepted than the radical concepts of relativity theory, and for this work he was awarded the Nobel prize in 1922. Early measurements had shown that the energy of electrons ejected from metallic surfaces by light depends on the frequency but not on the intensity of the light. This is inexplicable classically, but Einstein showed that it is immediately explicable if light is composed of discrete quanta of energy $h\nu$, where h is Planck's constant and ν the frequency. Einstein also showed that this idea accounts for anomalies in fluorescence and photo-ion-

ization. This work goes far beyond Planck's original suggestion, and in the following years Einstein applied it to other phenomena, in particular the quantum theory of specific heats. In another series of investigations, Einstein showed that the mean fluctuation of the energy of a system about its average value is related to BOLTZMANN's constant, and hence to Avogadro's number, implying that the measurement of such fluctuations would provide a way of determining the number of atoms in a given weight of any substance. A familiar example of fluctuations is provided by the irregular motion of small particles suspended in a liquid. Einstein developed a theory of these motions and showed how they could be analysed to give Avogadro's number. This provided a direct and convincing demonstration of the reality of molecular motions (see PERRIN).

Einstein's work was soon recognized. In 1916 he extended his theory of relativity to include accelerated motions, and explained gravitation as the influence of massive bodies on the surrounding space-time. This theory successfully accounted for the discrepancy between the observed rate of advance of the perihelion of the planet Mercury and the value calculated from Newtonian mechanics, and for the bending of starlight by the sun's gravitational field observed during the solar eclipse of 1919. In his later years Einstein worked continuously on the unification of quantum theory and gravitation, but without success.

Although he was initially influenced by MACH, his scientific creativity forced him to repudiate sensationalism, and thereafter he firmly believed in a realist interpretation of science. He regarded quantum mechanics as essentially a statistical theory applicable to an ensemble of systems and not to each individual event. He refused to accept the Copenhagen interpretation of quantum mechanics, with its attribution of an essential indeterminacy to atomic processes, summing up his belief with the aphorism, 'God does not play dice.' He devised many conceptual experiments to show the logical inconsistency of quantum mechanics, but these were refuted by N. BOHR. Einstein's attitude to quantum mechanics led to his becoming increasingly isolated from most physicists, although Planck, SCHRÖDINGER and LAUE shared his convictions, and today an increasing number of physicists believe that he was right (see P. A. Schlipp, ed., *Albert Einstein: Philosopher-Scientist*, Evanston, Ill., 1951).

In his later years Einstein played an influential role in international affairs, signing the letter to President ROOSEVELT urging the development of atomic weapons, and a manifesto with Bertrand RUSSELL on the dangers of the arms race, and warmly supporting Zionist causes (see *The World As I See It*, NY, 1934; *Out of My Later Years*, NY, 1950; and *Ideas and Opinions*, NY, 1954). Throughout his life he remained a simple kindly man, impervious to ambition and power. With his wildly flowing hair, his absorption in profound theories and his general air of absent-minded benevolence, he became for many the archetypal scientist. In the magnitude of his creative achievement and the profundity of his revolutionary worldview he made the greatest contribution to science since Isaac Newton.

PEH

A. I. Miller, *Albert Einstein's Special Theory of Relativity* (London, 1981); A. Pais, *'Subtle is the Lord': the Science and the Life of Albert Einstein* (Oxford, 1982).

Eisenstaedt, Alfred (b. Dirschau, Prussia, Germany [now East Germany], 6.12.1898; naturalized American citizen, 1943). German/American photographer. Brought up in Berlin, Eisenstaedt became a freelance photographer in the 1920s while working as a salesman. In 1927 he sold his first picture to *Weltspiegel*. He became a professional photographer in 1929 and his first assignment, for *Die Funkstunde* – a Berlin radio weekly – was to cover the award of the Nobel prize for literature to Thomas MANN, 9.12.1929. In 1931 he became a reporter for Pacific and Atlantic Photos, later taken over by Associated Press, and in 1935 left Germany for the USA where he became a principal photographer for *Life* magazine, first published in November 1936. Eisenstaedt worked on *Life* for 40 years and had over 2000 assignments for the magazine, which used his photographs on over 90 front covers.

Eisenstaedt belongs to a generation of enterprising photojournalists who came to the fore in Germany during the late 1920s, and who worked for an expanding illustrated press, headed by the *Berliner Illustrierte Zeitung* and the *Münchner Illustrierte Presse* (see *Eisenstaedt: Germany*, NY, 1981). German photographers, and their associates from Eastern Europe, developed investigative photojournalism, took their audiences behind the scenes and revealed practical details of industrial labour, the conduct of wars and the making of celebrities. They explained in pictures, and worked as though for an audience with strictly practical interests. Eisenstaedt was partly responsible for establishing this as a dominant photographic mode in the USA. Felix Man, Kurt Hubschmann and Tim Gidal, who all worked for *Picture Post* from 1938, performed the same service in Britain. For his own account, see *Witness to Our Time* (NY, 1966).

IJ

Eisenstein, Sergei Mikhailovich (b. Riga, Latvia, Russia [now Latvia, USSR], 23.1.1898; d. Moscow, USSR, 10.2.1948). Russian film maker. Eisenstein belongs to the same generation as HITCHCOCK and John FORD, but because he died at the tragically early age of 50 he seems in some ways to belong to an older generation. Despite the fact that he completed only seven feature films in a directing career that stretched from 1924 to 1944, his importance as a film maker and a theorist remains undiminished. A bourgeois who joined the revolution, an engineer fascinated by art, an intellectual committed to making films for the masses, a life-long MARXist obsessed with religious and sexual imagery, a materialist afraid of black cats, Fridays and walking under ladders, Eisenstein was a sum of contradictions. He once described himself as the 'son of D. W. GRIFFITH and the Russian Revolution', and as a teenager he plunged into the artistic turmoil of post-1917 Soviet Russia. Working first in the theatre, he developed his desire not to tell stories and create psychologically convincing characters, but to treat on film the great themes and ideas of contemporary society.

Stachka (*Strike*, 1924), his first film, is a strikingly mature work which draws on both the spirit of revolt of the time and the bubbling inventiveness of post-revolution Soviet theatre. Eisenstein continued his celebration of the recent past in *Bronenosets Potyomkin* (*The Battleship Potemkin*, 1925), his most polished and unified work, which had enormous influence on film makers throughout the world in the 1920s. In *Oktyabr'* (*October*, 1927) the tendency towards highly elaborate editing patterns and rhythms ('intellectual *montage*') is taken to extremes, producing a work of extreme interest for the scholar but one which would have communicated only with difficulty with its intended peasant audience. *Staroye i Novoye* (*The General Line*, 1929), on the collectivization of agriculture, is a deliberately simpler work and reveals more fully than any of his other films his very real sense of humour.

The 1930s were a period of intense frustration for Eisenstein. He came to the West to explore the possibilities of sound, but projects in Hollywood and Mexico came to nothing. Returning to the USSR he began *Bezhin lug* (*Bezhin Meadow*) in 1935, but the film was abandoned and he was forced to recant publicly. At last, in 1938, he completed his first sound film, *Alesandr Nevsky* (1938), a patriotic piece which celebrates an ancient Russian triumph over the Teutonic knights, only to have its release coincide with the Molotov–Ribbentrop Agreements. Only two parts of his projected trilogy on *Ivan Grosny* (*Ivan the Terrible*, 1944–6) were completed in the Alma Ata Studios in Central Asia, and again Eisenstein had trouble with the authorities. Part II was banned for 12 years and the material shot for the projected Part III destroyed.

Eisenstein's life, latterly marked by ill-health, was a constant battle with producers, whether Soviet bureaucrats, Hollywood moguls or good-intentioned amateurs (like the novelist Upton Sinclair who financed and then abandoned *Que Viva Mexico!*). Much of his theoretical writing is a product of his teaching and his frustration at not being able to direct. His writings teem with references, quotations and original ideas and are as complex and contradictory as himself. But the subtle thinking that he brought to bear on the problems of film language, of editing or *montage*, relation of image and sound or of film work and audience still has relevance for today. Still unsurpassed in 30 years, the importance of his writings is clearer now than ever before: *The Film Sense* (tr. NY, 1942), *Film Form* (tr. NY, 1949), *Notes of a Film Director* (tr. London, 1959) and *Film Essays* (tr., London, 1968).

RPA

M. Seton, *Sergei M. Eisenstein* (NY, 1960); Y. Barna, *Eisenstein* (London, 1973).

Eisler, Hanns (b. Leipzig, Germany [now East Germany], 6.7.1898; d. East Berlin, 6.9.1962). German composer. Eisler, third and youngest of SCHOENBERG's outstanding Viennese disciples prior to 1925, was led astray from the narrow dodecaphonic path by the MARXism acquired from his politician brother and sister – Gerhart Eisler and Ruth Fischer – and went on to establish a new form of socialist music. Moving to Berlin that year, he wrote simple yet musically sophisticated songs and marches for communist choirs and agit-prop shows. Then in 1929 began a life-long collaboration with BRECHT: their products range from the militantly didactic *Die Massnahme* [The measures taken] (1930) and *Die Mutter* [The mother] (1932) to the 'Hollywood Elegies' *Lieder* cycle (1942) with its Schoenbergian echoes; altogether his Brecht settings run into the hundreds. He was also a pioneer of film music, on which he wrote a book with ADORNO (*Composing for the Film*, NY, 1947). In the 1930s he headed a short-lived International Music Bureau in Moscow before emigrating to the USA in 1938. Thanks to his sister's subsequent denunciation of her brothers, he was heard by the Un-American Affairs Committee in 1947 and deported, settling first in Vienna, then, from 1950, in East Berlin. Artistically, intellectually and politically he was always close to Brecht, but lacked the latter's obstinacy and stamina. A striking melodist with unusual sensitivity to verbal sounds, rhythms and meanings, a master of small instrumental combinations, Eisler wrote few big-scale works and ultimately seemed torn between his radically original social approach and the Schoenbergian disciplines in which he had been trained. A German edition of his work is currently being edited (*Gesammelte Werke*, Leipzig, 1973–), and the greater part of his work is being issued on 42 gramophone records (1978–) by VEB Deutsche Schallplatte, East Berlin. JWMW

A. Betz, *Hanns Eisler: Political Musician*, tr. W. Hopkins (Cambridge, 1982).

Elgar, Edward William (b. Lower Broadheath, nr Worcester, Here. & Worcs., UK, 2.6.1857; d. Worcester, 23.2.1934). British composer. During the 19c British music was at its lowest ebb; the star of Sterndale Bennett shone too dimly to prevent Britain being dubbed '*Das Land ohne Musik*' [The land without music], a jibe that was slow to die. Elgar was undoubtedly the first important English composer since Purcell, though he was not to make a significant impact till 1899 when Hans Richter conducted the first performance of the *Enigma Variations* in London. Of even greater consequence was the first German performance of *The Dream of Gerontius* in Düsseldorf conducted by Julius Buths in December 1901. This was only some 14 months after the rather tepid reception of the work at its première in Birmingham under Richter (another German!). Some weeks after *Gerontius*, Buths introduced the *Enigma*, again in Düsseldorf. At last two major works by an English composer had been well received on the Continent and in the next few years *Gerontius* would be heard in Paris and New York.

Until the turn of the century Elgar had received only modest recognition in his own country. Apart from the success of the *Enigma*, *Froissart* was a disappointment at the Three Choirs Festival, but Manns helped by introducing the 'Imperial March' at the Crystal Palace in 1897. Three years later the composer conducted *Sea Pictures*, his first work to

be featured at a Royal Philharmonic concert (the soloist was Clara Butt). A number of works followed which were to ensure Elgar's continuing high reputation not only in the UK but internationally. These include the two symphonies (1908 and 1911), the Cello Concerto (1919) and the symphonic study *Falstaff* (1913). Elgar was later to become the first considerable British composer to conduct his own works for the gramophone. Several recordings, including the young MENUHIN's performance of the Violin Concerto, are still obtainable. JL

J. N. Moore, *Elgar: a Life in Pictures* (London, 1972); M. Kennedy, *Portrait of Elgar* (London, ²1982).

Eliade, Mircea (b. Bucharest, Romania, 9.3.1907). Romanian author and historian of religions. After graduating in philosophy at Bucharest in 1928, he took his doctorate at the University of Calcutta in 1933 with the thesis 'The Comparative History of Yoga Techniques'. In the same year he was appointed associate professor in the faculty of letters at Bucharest University. He was Romanian cultural attaché in London (1940) and in Lisbon (1941–4), then did not return to Romania after WW2 but held posts at various European universities before becoming in 1957 professor of the history of religions at Chicago. In Eliade's fiction – which is better known in France than in the English-speaking world – the sacred and the mythical often manifest themselves in everyday life as ordinary people are initiated into religious experience: *Domnişoara Christine* [Miss Christina] (Bucharest, 1936), *Nuntă în cer* [Marriage in heaven] (Bucharest, 1938), *La Forêt interdite* [The forbidden forest] (Paris, 1954) and *La Ţigănci* [At the gypsies'] (Bucharest, 1969). Eliade's extensive research into the history of religions has led to such basic works as *Traité d'histoire des religions* (Paris, 1949; *Patterns of Comparative Religion*, NY, 1958), *Le Chamanisme et les techniques archaïques de l'extase* (Paris, 1951; *Shamanism: Archaic Techniques of Ecstasy*, NY, 1964), *From Primitives to Zen* (NY, 1967) and *Occultism, Witchcraft and Cultural Fashions* (Chicago,

1976). *Le Mythe de l'éternel retour* (Paris, 1949; *The Myth of the Eternal Return*, NY, 1954) examines the fundamental conceptions of primitive societies which disregard the notion of exact historical time in their aspiration for a return to the time of their mythical origins. *Mythes, rêves et mystères* (Paris, 1957; *Myths, Dreams and Mysteries*, London, 1960) discusses the relationship between the unconscious, as manifested in dreams and the imagination, and the structures of religions, while *De Zalmoxis à Gengis-Khan* (Paris, 1970; tr. W. R. Trask, *Zalmoxis: the Vanishing God*, Chicago, 1972) is a collection of essays on the religious origins of the ethnic name of the Dacians, the cult of Zalmoxis, and the cosmogonic myth in Romanian folklore. The development of a methodology for the study of the history of religions is exemplified in *Histoires des croyances et des idées religieuses* [Histories of religious beliefs and ideas] (3 vols, Paris, 1976–81), the synthesis of Eliade's life's work as a scholar.   DJD

G. R. Slater, *The Role of Myth in Religion: a Study of Mircea Eliade's Phenomenology of Religion* (Toronto, 1973).

Eliot, Thomas Stearns (b. St Louis, Mo., USA, 26.9.1888; naturalized British citizen, 1927; d. London, UK, 4.1.1965). American/British poet and critic. Generally, but not unanimously, regarded as a great poet; the claim has been resisted by literary conservatives, usually English, who dislike the revolutionary aspects of his art, and by literary radicals, usually American, who dislike his commitment to tradition, impersonality and the mind of Europe, and who find his aloof, austere personality antipathetic.

Eliot's first important poem was 'The Love Song of J. Alfred Prufrock' (written 1910–11, published 1915). This 'truly 20c poem' (Ezra POUND) explored an unstable consciousness tormented by the problem of identity in an unsympathetic social context, using an innovatory and difficult if memorable technique of juxtaposition, contrast and bizarre images. The same can be said of *The Waste Land* (London, 1922), which remains a central text of modernism.

Soon after publication *The Waste Land* was regarded as a typical product of the 1920s, a jazzy expression of postwar disillusionment, and a poetic statement of severance from religious faith. Later critics emphasized its anthropological elements and its indebtedness to Jessie Weston and FRAZER. Others saw it as a lament for 20c civilization, contrasted with earlier and finer ages. Recent criticism reads the poem as profoundly personal, even autobiographical, dwelling on the sexual aspiration and suffering that seems to underlie it; or Eliot's search for religious faith; or a combination of both. It is characteristic of Eliot's poetry that with the passing of time it reveals itself in quite new and unexpected lights.

In 1927 Eliot, who had lived in England since 1915, became a British subject and formally joined the Church of England. His progress in ˹ ᶦ˙ᵇ, which for him was a constant ᵤstruggle, was marked poetically by *Ash Wednesday* (London, 1930), and by *Four Quartets* (published separately between 1936 and 1942, combined in one volume, London, 1944). Taking a broad view, *The Waste Land* and *Four Quartets* are the dominant works in Eliot's sparse poetic output. Some readers prefer *The Waste Land* for its involvement with urban life, the startling juxtapositions, and particular images of things and places. Others are drawn to the more reflective *Quartets*, which explore in a manner analogous to chamber music questions of time and incarnation. Paradoxically, Eliot is a poet of negation and elusiveness, often seeming to withdraw from life, but celebrating these negations and withdrawals in rich yet precise language.

Eliot was an immensely influential critic, directing attention to literary works and periods that had influenced his own art: Dante, the English metaphysical poets, the Jacobean dramatists, and the French symbolists. In the 1930s he published two important poetic dramas, *Murder in the Cathedral* (London, 1935) and *The Family Reunion* (London, 1939). His later plays, written in the 1950s, are less interesting.   BB

H. Kenner, *The Invisible Poet* (London, 1960); B. Bergonzi, *T. S. Eliot* (NY, 1972).

Ellington, Edward Kennedy (Duke) (b. Washington, DC, USA, 29.4.1899; d. New York, 24.5.1974). American jazz composer and bandleader. Duke Ellington's orchestra began its first important residency at the Cotton Club, New York, in December 1927. Required to accompany exotic cabaret acts, Ellington began experimenting in his arrangements with what he called his 'jungle effects'. When the sounds of 'growling' trumpets and trombones, sinuous clarinets and eerie percussion were recorded, the originality of the orchestrations was immediately grasped internationally by music critics and record buyers. The sounds were, in effect, trimmings for Ellington's masterly and highly original compositions, which include 'Creole Love Call' (1928), 'Mood Indigo' (1934), 'Solitude' (1934) and 'Don't Get Around Much Anymore' (1940). As a jazz arranger his great gift was in balancing orchestration and improvisation; always allowing soloists space for their extemporizations. He was also a skilful bandleader, able to develop originality in musicians who had formerly been orthodox players. All of these attributes tended to overshadow Ellington's remarkable piano playing which, though never technically brilliant, revealed a highly individual way of voicing chords and phrasing melody. His output was enhanced by a long period of collaboration (1939–71) with pianist-composer Billy Strayhorn. Frequently Ellington's worldwide tours with his orchestra inspired extended compositions such as *The Far East Suite* (1964) and *Toga Brava Suite* (1971). During the latter part of his life he also composed several religious works including *In the Beginning God* (1965). For his own account of his music, see *Music is My Mistress* (NY, 1973).   JJC

S. Dance, *The World of Duke Ellington* (NY, 1970).

Ellis, Henry Havelock (b. Croydon, Surrey, UK, 2.2.1859; d. Washbrook, Suffolk, 8.7.1939). British doctor and author. Ellis started his medical studies at St Thomas's Hospital, London, in 1881 after having travelled to Australia and having worked as a teacher for four years. Brought up in a strict Victorian, asexual atmosphere, he admits in his autobiography – *My Life* (Boston, Mass., 1939) – that by the time he had reached 16 he still had not seen or heard anything that would have shocked a modest Victorian schoolgirl. None of his four sisters ever married and Ellis himself was still a virgin when he married at the age of 32. Despite (or perhaps because of) this austere upbringing Ellis is remembered for his studies of human sexual behaviour. His major work was *Studies in the Psychology of Sex* (7 vols, NY, 1897–1928). This work, like much of FREUD's, owes a good deal to Ellis's own experiences and feelings. Until 1935 his work was legally available only to members of the medical profession: it was considered unsuitable for public consumption. Modern writers on sexual topics may have succeeded in exploring this subject more exhaustively, but Ellis undoubtedly led the way.   VC

P. Grosskurth, *Havelock Ellis: a Biography* (London, 1980).

Elton, Charles Sutherland (b. London, UK, 29.3.1900). British ecologist. Elton was educated at Oxford, a university with which he retained connections throughout his working life. After graduation he was appointed research fellow, and accompanied a number of university expeditions to Spitzbergen and other arctic regions. In 1932 he was appointed director of the Bureau of Animal Populations at Oxford, and in 1936 university reader in zoology. He held both these posts until retirement in 1967. The publication of Elton's *Animal Ecology* (London, 1927) was one of the most influential events in the study of ecology in Britain. His approach to the structure of animal communities pointed the direction for ecological research for the following decades, and such terms as 'food chain' and 'pyramid of numbers' came into common use. It was Elton who first used the term 'niche', which he defined in functional terms within the structure of a community. Among Elton's influential studies, the most important include: *Animal Ecology and Evolution* (London, 1930), *Ecology of Animals* (London, 1933), *The Ecology of Invaders* (London, 1950), and *The Pat-*

tern of Animal Communities (London, 1966).   RTi

Eluard, Paul, ps. of Eugène-Emile-Paul Grindel (b. Saint Denis, Paris, France, 14.12.1896; d. Paris, 18.11.1952). French poet who adopted his maternal grandmother's name of Eluard when signing his second collection of poems *Le devoir et l'inquiétude* [Duty and concern] (Paris, 1920), written while he was serving in an ambulance unit during WW1. He ran away from home, went round the world, and, in the 1920s, played an active part in the attempt of the surrealist movement to destroy all established cultural, social and moral values. In 1926 he published one of his best-known collections of poems *Capitale de la douleur* [Capital of grief] (Paris, 1926). In 1930 he collaborated with BRETON in writing *L'Immaculée conception* [Immaculate conception] (Paris, 1930), an attempt to transpose into poetry the widest possible variety of states of mental disturbance. *Donner à voir* [Showing what is] (Paris, 1939) is also highly original and well in keeping with the aims of the surrealist movement in its mingling of prose poems, quotations from writers and philosophers such as NIETZSCHE, Sade, Blake, Novalis and Lautréamont, with lengthy reflections on art. In 1942 *Poésie et Vérité* [Poetry and truth] expressed Eluard's opposition to the German occupation of France. It rapidly became one of the best-known collections of resistance poetry, and it was dropped by parachute to encourage the Maquis fighters in their struggle. *Au rendez-vous allemand* [The German meeting] (Paris, 1943) continued in the same vein, and Eluard remained an active member of the French Communist party after the war, attending many international conferences. The last collection published in his lifetime, *Poèmes pour tous* [Poems for everyone] (Paris, 1952), brought together poems written between 1917 and 1952, showing the strength and continuity of Eluard's political commitment. The posthumous *Poésie ininterrompue* (Paris, 1953; tr. L. Alexander, *Uninterrupted Poetry*, London, 1977) contained poems in his more satisfying erotic and sensuous vein.   PMWT

M. Carrouges, *Eluard et Claudel* (Paris, 1945); W. Fowlie, *Mid-Century French Poets* (NY, 1955).

Empson, William (b. Yokefleet, Howden, Humb., UK, 27.9.1906). British literary critic and poet. A prodigiously talented undergraduate, Empson studied mathematics at Cambridge before transferring in his final year to the English faculty where he came under the influence of RICHARDS. From him he inherited the view that poetry had its own ontological status and that it is best interpreted through detailed semantic analysis; but Empson was more systematic than his mentor and a more gifted close reader of poetry. His brilliant first book *Seven Types of Ambiguity* (London, 1930) offered the argument that the greatness of a poem might inhere in its multiplicities of meanings, meanings which may not be intentionally present. Empson argued that the ambiguities involved in poetic statements establish the very tension in poetry that makes for its dramatic richness. His second book *Some Versions of Pastoral* (London, 1935) shows a greater concern with structural and generic considerations and is openly MARXist in some of its analyses. With *The Structure of Complex Words* (London, 1951) he returned to semantic matters but the book is notable for its interest in the psychology of the author. Empson's poetry (see *Poems*, London, 1935, and *The Gathering Storm*, London, 1940) is witty, intellectual and obscure, and is highly regarded by postwar English poets such as Kingsley Amis, Thom Gunn and John Wain. He retired from the chair of English literature at the University of Sheffield in 1971.   GHC

R. Gill (ed.), *William Empson: the Man and his Work* (London, 1974).

Ensor, James Sydney (b. Ostend, W. Flanders, Belgium, 13.4.1860; d. Ostend, 19.11.1949). Belgian painter, etcher and draughtsman. After studying in Brussels (1877–80) he spent the rest of his life at Ostend where his mother ran a souvenir shop selling the sea shells, chinoiserie, fans, toys and carnival masks which comprise the basis iconography of his paintings. In the early 1880s he painted landscapes, still lifes and interior scenes with figures in a style influenced by Courbet and Manet (e.g. *Russian Music*, 1882), which earned him recognition at the Brussels and Paris salons in 1881 and 1882. This success was short-lived; from 1883, when he began painting haunting, often grotesque, visionary pictures of masks, skeletons and ghosts (e.g. *Skeleton Examining Chinoiseries*, 1885), his works were rejected for exhibition and subjected to violent criticism. Using what he called the 'suffering, scandalized, insolent, cruel and malicious masks' of the Lenten carnival as a disguise, he expressed his obsessional belief in the fundamental evil of life. Distorted masks covering reality with a layer of fantasy mingle with skeletal images of death, especially after his father's death in 1887 (e.g. *Masks Confronting Death*, 1888). His largest and best-known work *Entry of Christ into Brussels* (1888) employs carnival imagery to create a scene of a workers' demonstration mocking Christ. The two thematic preoccupations of his work from then on are identification with the persecuted Christ (e.g. *Self-portrait with Masks*, 1899), and attacks on the social order and on social hypocrisy (e.g. *Intrigue*, 1890). All these works are characterized by grotesque figural distortions, heightened by garish colour combinations and a harsh, expressionistic surface texture, and the virtual suppression of any illusion of space behind the figures, thus transforming them into hallucinatory images of fear. Spatial distortion and bright colours are used in the later still lifes (e.g. *The Ray*, 1892) to create a proto-surreal effect. In c. 1900 his work lost its hallucinatory quality and he was often reduced to making copies of earlier works. The fame he had so desired came in the form of a barony conferred in 1929, when his creative power had almost ebbed.   SOBT

P. Haesarts, *James Ensor* (Brussels, 1957).

Epstein, Jacob (b. New York, USA, 10.11.1880; naturalized British citizen, 1907; d. London, UK, 19.8.1959). American/British sculptor. His parents were Polish Jews, and he came to London in 1905. Two years later he secured his first public commission: to carve 18 figures for the British Medical Association building in the Strand. These provoked the first bout of that controversy which dogged him for much of his working life. In 1911 he made the memorial for Oscar Wilde at the Père Lachaise Cemetery in Paris; when in France, he met PICASSO, BRANCUSI and MODIGLIANI. On his return to the UK he became involved with the vorticists, and exhibited his notorious *Rock Drill* with the London Group in 1913; this showed a man metamorphosing into a machine. Epstein's association with vanguardism was short lived. He soon began to carve religious subjects expressed through a confident mastery of the human figure. However, he eschewed western sculptural conventions and drew on his sympathy for the art of 'primitive' cultures. Works like his *Risen Christ* (completed in 1919) continued to cause public outcry. In 1928 he made *Night and Day* for the London Transport Underground headquarters building. Other major sculptures included *Ecce Homo* (1935), *Consummatum Est* (1937), *Adam* (1939) and *Jacob and the Angel* (1942). Some of Epstein's works were acquired by a showman and exhibited in fairs and seaside resorts alongside freaks and wax-works. Despite further scandals over *Lucifer* (1946), he began to gain greater popular acceptance after WW2. In the 1950s he received a spate of public commissions, including *Social Consciousness* for Philadelphia; *Christ in Majesty* for Llandaff cathedral; and *St Michael and the Devil* for Coventry cathedral. Simultaneously his reputation among sculptors and critics fell; Epstein was commonly described as the last 'romantic'. He was seen as belonging to the tradition of RODIN, and was felt to have little relevance to the reductive excesses which were the concern of many late modernist sculptors. Today, however, his true stature is becoming more readily discernible: he was one of the most versatile, original and imaginative sculptors of the 20c. As a maker of expressive, modelled, portrait heads he has probably never been surpassed. He published *Epstein: an Autobiography* (London) in 1955.   PF

R. Buckle, *Jacob Epstein, Sculptor* (London, 1963).

Ernst, Max (b. Bruhl, N. Rhine-Westphalia, Germany, 2.4.1891; naturalized French citizen, 1958; d. Seillans, Var, France, 1.4.1976). German/French painter. Originally intending to study philosophy and psychology, a meeting with the painter August Macke in 1911 persuaded him to become an artist, initially expressionist in manner although always with certain poetic and illogical elements. In 1914 he met the sculptor and poet ARP who remained a friend and sometimes collaborator. After serving in WW1, Ernst, in his own words, was 'resuscitated on 11 November 1918 as a young man aspiring to become a magician, to find the myth of his time'. Inspired by the Italian Metaphysical painter CHIRICO, he painted several large pictures combining mechanical elements, nude women and a disturbing eroticism. He turned collage to poetic ends and used 'frottage' (the rubbing of textures through paper or on to paint) to provoke hallucinatory images involving forests, cities, birds, vegetation and monsters. He called the use of these and other mechanical means 'inspiration to order'. Ernst is almost unique among surrealist painters in that his work swings between the magic illusionism deriving from de Chirico and automatism, or the exploitation of chance. Active in the German dada movement, he arrived in Paris in time to be present at the birth of BRETON's surrealism. He took little part or interest in its political activities but remained in often uneasy association with the group until 1954 when a rift was brought about by his acceptance of first prize at the Venice Biennale.

Primarily a painter, Ernst also made sculpture and created a series of books, among them *Histoire naturelle* [A natural story] (Paris, 1926) with plates of frottage drawings and a preface by Arp, and several 'collage novels' including *Une Semaine de bonté* [A week of goodness] (Paris, 1935). His many writings are generously represented in *Beyond Painting and Other Writings by the Artist and His Friends* (NY, 1948). Ernst's inventive work throughout the 1920s

and 1930s caused Breton to call him 'the most magnificently haunted mind in Europe'. His reaction to the approach of the HITLERian war was a series of increasingly complex images of tragic and prophetic anxiety. Interned in France as an alien, Ernst escaped and, after astounding adventures, found refuge in the USA. Several times married, there he met his last wife, the young painter Dorothea Tanning. In his later years his art lost much of its tension and meaning, becoming somewhat decorative and even whimsical. As a whole, his work places him among the great masters of the 20c; it might be said that his early ambition 'to find the myth of his time' was triumphantly realized. GM

J. Russell, *Max Ernst: Life and Work* (London, 1967).

Esenin, Sergey Aleksandrovich (b. Konstantinovo, Ryazan, Russia, 3.10.1895; d. Leningrad, USSR, 27.12.1925). Russian poet. Known in the West mainly as an exotic supporting character in the Isadora DUNCAN saga, Esenin ranks in popularity with Pushkin and MAYAKOVSKY among ordinary Russian readers. Son of a peasant and himself a former shepherd, he arrived in Petrograd in 1915 and, with a bundle of lyrics, presented himself to BLOK, under whose patronage he joined a group of peasant poets, including Nikolai Kliuev. Later he became the leader of the short-lived imagist movement, which to some extent continued the symbolist trend, but advocated 'broken strings of striking images' as essential to poetry. The manner is evident in Esenin's *Pugachev* (Petrograd, 1922) – about the 18c peasant rebel – which, though designed as a narrative poem, represents a succession of disjointed and partly contrived images. It was prompted by a search for new poetic devices, but was also symptomatic of a certain dissociation of sensibility. Esenin had a brief, hectic and haunted life, ending in suicide. Much of it was spent in alcoholic orgies, by comparison with which the escapades of Dylan THOMAS are mere antics. At first he was just out to shock, believing that 'scandal, especially a beautiful scandal, is always a help to talent'. In fact, his talent was enormous, and the outrageous exhibitionism, the cultivated posture of a 'hooligan poet', surrounded his melodious and tender poetic gift with an aura of excitement. Esenin dramatized, sometimes melodramatized, his peasant origins, but his celebration of the dignity of rural life – 'derevyannaya [wooden] Rus' – struck a genuine lyrical note. He opposed it to urban decadence, of which he himself became a major victim by turning himself into a 'peasant dandy'. Like Blok and Mayakovsky, he welcomed the October revolution. But he scarcely understood its nature. He daubed blasphemous couplets on the walls of convents, but his poetry is steeped in the imagery of the Orthodox church. In a way, his was a 'holy' hooliganism. His poem Ispoved' Khuligana (Moscow, 1924; tr. G. Thurley, The Confession of a Hooligan, London, 1973) combines the spirit of aggressive moral dissolution with self-immolation and a search for love, purity and humanity. By 1923 his misery, loneliness and self-estrangement ('I am a stranger to myself') were almost paranoid. They were accompanied by extreme chauvinism (fortified by a depressing visit to the West with Isadora Duncan, his wife at the time) and a longing for a new kind of revolution. Before dying he wrote his remarkable suicide poem 'Do svidania drug moi' [Goodbye my friend] in the blood from his slashed wrist, but he died a day later by hanging. Some believe that Esenin's suicide was a revolt against the realities of Soviet life. The belief cannot be sustained, except perhaps in terms of his own paranoia about them. Though 'Eseninism' was strongly condemned by the Soviet authorities, Esenin was never impelled 'to step on the throat of his song', as Mayakovsky was to say. An edition of his collected works appeared soon after his suicide and a smaller one even in 1948, at the height of STALINism. English translations of his poetry are available in Selected Poems (tr. J. Davies, Bakewell, 1979).   EL

G. McVay, Esenin: a Life (Ann Arbor, 1976); G. McVay, Isadora and Esenin (Ann Arbor, 1980).

Evans, Arthur John (b. Nash Mills, Herts., UK, 8.7.1851; d. Yolbury,

Oxon., 11.7.1941). British archaeologist, best known for his excavations at Knossos in Crete which began in 1889 and were published as The Palace of Minos at Knossos in four volumes (London, 1921–36). In 1904 Evans proposed the name Minoan for the Bronze Age civilization which he had discovered (published in corrected form as Essai de classification des époques de la civilisation Minoenne, London, 1906). He defined nine Minoan periods which, following a study of contemporary material from the Cyclades in 1907, he was able to equate with his Early, Middle and Late Cycladic periods. The hieroglyphs and linear scripts from Knossos were published in Scripta Minoa (Oxford, 1909).
                                        BWC

Evans, Walker (b. St Louis, Mo., USA, 3.11.1903; d. New Haven, Conn., 10.4.1975). American photographer. In 1938 the Museum of Modern Art, New York, published an illustrated catalogue of Evans's work, American Photographs, which remains one of photography's principal art-works. Like ATGET before him, Evans concerned himself with society and culture, examining vernacular building in the south and east of the USA and photographing the interiors of barbers' shops, stores and country cabins. In this respect he was unusual, for American photographers looked in the main to nature or took self as their subject. Evans himself spent some time in Paris in 1926, and had begun to photograph by his return to the USA in 1927. In 1930 three of his pictures were used to illustrate an edition of CRANE's The Bridge. From 1935 to 1938 he worked for the Farm Security Administration, and it was during this period that he took some of his best-known pictures, which were collected in Let Us Now Praise Famous Men (NY, 1941), on which he collaborated with the writer James Agee. After 1945 he became an associate editor with Fortune magazine, until 1965 when he joined the faculty at Yale. His cool, analytical style has been widely imitated, but no other photographer has had quite such a fastidious eye.   IJ

Walker Evans, intro. J. Szarkowski (NY, 1971).

Evans-Pritchard, Edward Evan (b. Crowborough, Sussex, UK, 21.9.1902; d. Oxford, 11.9.1973). British anthropologist. He was educated at Winchester, at Oxford, and at the London School of Economics, where he was one of the first of the pioneering generation of ethnographers trained by MALINOWSKI. Between 1926 and 1939 he made six expeditions to the Southern Sudan, most notably to the Azande and the Nuer peoples. His first book *Witchcraft, Oracles and Magic among the Azande* (Oxford, 1937) is perhaps his masterpiece, though he is best known for the trilogy of Nuer studies: *The Nuer: a Description of the Modes of Livelihood and Political Institutions of the Nilotic People* (Oxford, 1940), *Kinship and Marriage among the Nuer* (Oxford, 1951) and *Nuer Religion* (Oxford, 1956). These ethnographic studies were exceptionally powerful representations of tribal cultures. Their impact was in part a tribute to the quality of the observations, but perhaps equally significant was the manner in which they appeared to give life to anthropological models of how tribal peoples thought, and how tribal society was ordered. They were read – and presumably written – as 'type cases', implicitly demonstrating the truth of orthodox anthropological theories. The first Azande monograph illustrated theories of the 'rationality' of apparently mystical ways of thought. Azande beliefs about witches, magic and oracles made sense when the connections between the ideas were set out, and the context described. Similarly, the famous study of the 'ordered anarchy' of the Nuer was a vivid realization of well-established but highly speculative anthropological theories of how stateless societies might be ordered on the principles of 'blood and soil'.

In 1946 Evans-Pritchard succeeded RADCLIFFE-BROWN as professor of social anthropology at Oxford. He now turned more explicitly to theoretical matters; but, paradoxically, while his great ethnographies were expressions of orthodox theoretical models, he now, as a theoretician, argued against these broadly DURKHEIMian ideas (associated in Britain particularly with Radcliffe-Brown). Social anthropology was not, could not be, 'scientific'; it was an art, a study similar to history. (He was an influential figure in the modern rapprochement between anthropology and history.) Strict comparison of social institutions was impossible, the search for laws of human social behaviour doomed to failure. Evans-Pritchard's theoretical reversal (perhaps related to his conversion to Catholicism in 1944) has, retrospectively, raised a number of questions about the direction of his earlier work. Yet whatever the disagreements on these matters, and although the models incorporated in his early monographs are now unfashionable, his ethnographies are greatly admired and remain profoundly influential. His best monographs on African tribal life are wonderfully literate, penetrating and evocative; they are among the classics of anthropology. AJK

Evtushenko, Evgeny, see YEVTUSHENKO, YEVGENY.

Eyring, Henry (b. Colonia Juarez, Chihuahua, Mexico, 20.2.1901; naturalized American citizen, 1935; d. Salt Lake City, Utah, USA, 26.12.1981). American physical chemist, distinguished for contributions to the application of quantum mechanics to chemistry, the theory of reaction rates, and the theory of liquids. He trained as a mining engineer in Arizona but transferred to chemistry for his PhD at Berkeley (1927). Eyring's interest in chemical kinetics was aroused by association with Daniels at the University of Wisconsin (1927–9) and POLANYI in Berlin (1929–30). He was on the chemistry faculty at Princeton (1931–46), and at the University of Utah (1946–67). He has been very active in retirement. With Polanyi, Eyring pioneered the calculation of potential energy surfaces for simple reactions by means of quantum mechanics. He thus began his work on the 'activated-complex' theory of chemical kinetics, to which he made signal contributions for many years. He wrote *The Theory of Rate Processes* (with S. Glasstone & K. J. Laidler, NY, 1941). After the discovery of deuterium by UREY, Eyring worked extensively on the rates of isotopic reactions. Later he became interested in biological problems, notably bioluminescence, and wrote *The Kinetic Basis of Molecular Biology* (with F. H. Johnson & M. J. Pollissar, NY, 1954) and *The Theory of Rate Processes in Biology and Medicine* (with F. H. Johnson & B. Stover, NY, 1974). Among his other activities Eyring has helped to develop (with T. Ree & N. Hirai) the 'significant structure' theory of liquids. His general interest in quantum mechanics led to *Quantum Chemistry* (with J. Walter & G. E. Kimball, NY, 1944). JSh

Eysenck, Hans Jürgen (b. Berlin, Germany, 4.3.1916; naturalized British citizen). German/British behavioural psychologist. Eysenck left Germany for political reasons during the Nazi rise to power. After studying psychology under Spearman and BURT in London, he was given the opportunity to set up a new University of London psychology department at the Maudsley Hospital. From the beginning his emphasis was on laboratory and questionnaire studies of human personality and abnormal behaviour; he made considerable use of the statistical technique of factor analysis pioneered by his mentors. His scepticism about FREUDian-style theories and therapy made him world-famous, particularly when in 1952 he published a journal article which argued that no satisfactory evidence supported the efficacy of psychotherapy, and that the 'cures' claimed in the past might just as well be due to placebo effects or spontaneous remission. A few years later he coined the term 'behaviour therapy' for methods of psychotherapy based on laboratory findings with respect to the principles of learning, and tested for effectiveness by controlled experimental trials. These new behavioural approaches to therapy, of which Eysenck continues to be a major proponent, differ from traditional methods in that concern is with practical efforts to change behaviour that the patient regards as undesirable, rather than with interpretation of symptoms in terms of unconscious motives and childhood experiences. Eysenck is also well known for his claim that intelligence, personality and even social behaviours such as criminality and political attitudes are considerably influenced by genetic and constitutional factors. His evidence comes from a variety of sources including twin studies, adoption studies, drug experiments and animal breeding studies, for which highly sophisticated techniques of analysis have been developed over the years. He has written some 700 journal articles and more than 30 books, including *Uses and Abuses of Psychology* (London, 1953), *The Biological Basis of Personality* (London, 1967), *Psychology is About People* (London, 1972), *The Measurement of Intelligence* (London, 1973) and *You and Neurosis* (London, 1977). GDW

F

Falla, Manuel de (b. Cadiz, Spain, 23.11.1876; d. Alta Gracia, Argentina, 14.11.1946). Spanish composer. After spending the years 1907–14 in Paris, where he was in friendly contact with DEBUSSY and RAVEL, he made his reputation with such works as *Noches en los jardines de España* [Nights in the gardens of Spain] for piano and orchestra and the 'ballet with songs' *El amor brujo* [Love the sorcerer], both of which date from 1915. In such pieces as these, and the ballet *El sombrero de tres picos* [The three-cornered hat] (1919), he drew on his resources of folk-like material (the music often suggests guitar or castanets in typical Spanish dance rhythms and melodic shapes) together with an orchestral technique learned partly from Debussy. (After Debussy's death he composed a guitar *Homenaje* [Homage] in his memory, and Falla once confessed that without his experience in France he could have achieved nothing.) His puppet opera after Cervantes, *El retablo de maese Pedro* [Master Peter's puppet show] (1922), was written for a wealthy French patron at whose house it was first staged; and in 1926 he wrote a chamber Harpsichord Concerto in which he alluded to the styles of older Spanish music. But after this he composed little, partly through ill-health. From 1939 he lived in Argentina, working intermittently on an oratorio *Atlántida* that remained unfinished at his death. Had he completed it, we might have a different idea of his stature; as it is, he sums up, more than any other composer, Spanish nationalist musical style.   CH

Fanon, Frantz (b. Port-de-France, French Martinique, 20.7.1925; d. Washington, DC, USA, 6.12.1961). French psychiatrist and revolutionary writer. Fanon studied medicine and psychiatry in France after serving in WW2. Eclectic in his psychiatry, in *Peau noir, masques blancs* (Paris, 1952; *Black Skin, White Masks*, NY, 1967) he analysed the impact of white colonialism on blacks, in studies which, influenced by SARTRE's existentialism as well as by psychoanalysis, showed the deforming effect on both peoples. Experience as head of a psychiatric hospital in Algeria (1953–6) strengthened his commitment to Algerian revolution. Subsequent writings dealt with its progress, and *Les Damnés de la terre* (Paris, 1961; *The Wretched of the Earth*, NY, 1964) extended the analysis to the need for revolution in the Third World, with the peasantry as its vehicle. Imperialism being rooted in violence, violence must characterize its overthrow, and comes to have a cleansing, cathartic effect for Fanon. Briefly ambassador of the provisional Algerian government to Ghana, he died of leukaemia in the USA, where his writings, with their stress on the conflict between the races, exercised a profound influence on new black leaders of the 1960s, as on radicals generally in the 1970s.   DCr

D. Caute, *Fanon* (London, 1970); I. L. Gendzier, *Frantz Fanon* (London, 1973).

Faulkner, William (b. New Albany, Miss., USA, 25.10.1897; d. Oxford, Miss., 6.6.1962). American novelist. Faulkner survived a long period of neglect to receive the Nobel prize for literature (1950), and the common recognition of his achievement. His strongly felt identification with his home in the American South, and his absorption and mastery of the techniques of European modernism (such as the stream-of-consciousness narrative technique) give him a distinctive place in American letters. He neither belongs unambiguously to a regional literature of local colour and realism, nor is his technical originality and courageousness sufficiently understood to place him with the PROUSTs, KAFKAs and JOYCEs of the modernist novel. In a series of novels from *The Sound and the Fury* (NY, 1929) to *The Reivers* (NY, 1962), Faulkner wrote a fictional history of Yoknapatawpha County, Mississippi. Behind his stories of the South there is the disastrous defeat in the Civil War, and the attitudes (towards blacks, women, Yankees, and abstract concepts such as 'honour' and the gentleman's code of behaviour) which the burden of Southern history locked into place. The intermingling of family histories and sexual tension in Faulkner's Yoknapatawpha novels has led some critics to dwell upon their dark, violent aspects, and to speak of Faulkner as a writer of American Gothic. It is true that he remained preoccupied with the literal and symbolic violation of nature, and the failure of human ideals (the Southern code of honour) before avarice and prejudice. But the rediscovery of his work, following the publication of an anthology *The Portable Faulkner* edited by Malcolm Cowley in 1946, came when a darker vision of America was increasingly acceptable. Economic depression and war drove some of the optimism out of American literature. In *The Sound and the Fury* and *Light in August* (NY, 1932) Americans found an image of themselves which raised a not unfamiliar violence and racial tension to the level of a tragedy of the decline of a place and a way of life.   EH

F. J. Hoffman & O. W. Vickery (eds), *William Faulkner: Three Decades of Criticism* (East Lansing, 1960); M. Cowley, *The Faulkner-Cowley File: Letters and Memories, 1944–62* (London, 1966); J. Blotner, *Faulkner: a Biography* (2 vols, NY, 1974).

Fayol, Henri (b. Constantinople, Ottoman Empire [now Turkey], 29.7.1841; d. Paris, France, 11.1925). French contributor to management studies. His entire working life was spent with the Conambault mining group; he was managing director from 1888 until 1918. Two years before retirement he published *Administration industrielle et générale – prévoyance, organisation, commandement, coordination, contrôle* (1916, Paris, 1925; *General and Industrial Management*, London, 1949). This offered the first analysis of the management function – to plan, organize, command, coordinate and control, which he separated from the other functions in an enterprise – technical, commercial,

financial, security and accounting. He also deduced 14 principles, including the need to divide work and specialize (see F. W. TAYLOR), to have authority commensurate with responsibility, to have unity of command (one man: one boss), and to have equity ('a combination of kindliness and justice').   RIT

Febvre, Lucien (b. Nancy, Meurthe-et-Moselle, France, 22.7.1878; d. Saint-Amour, Jura, 20.9.1956). French historian. His thesis on *Philippe II et la Franche-Comté* (Paris, 1911) established him as a leading historian, and revealed his interest in economic and social change as well as in religious and political developments. After WW1 he became professor at the University of Strasbourg, where he met Marc BLOCH, with whom he founded, in 1929, *Annales d'histoire économique et sociale*, a journal planned to encourage a new kind of history – problem-oriented, 'total' and interdisciplinary. *La Terre et l'évolution humaine* (Paris, 1922; *A Geographical Introduction to History*, London, 1925) had already shown Febvre's interest in historical geography; his later work, concentrated on the history of religious ideas in 16c France, drew to some extent on social psychology. His most influential study is probably *Le Problème de l'incroyance au 16e siècle: la religion de Rabelais* [The problem of unbelief in the 16c: the religion of Rabelais] (Paris, 1942), one of the first books to be concerned with the history of 'collective mentalities'. Febvre put a great deal of himself into scattered essays and reviews, now collected into *Combats pour l'histoire* [Combats for history] (Paris, 1953); *Au coeur religieux du 16e siècle* [At the religious heart of the 16c] (Paris, 1957); and *Pour une histoire à part entière* [A new kind of history] (Paris, 1962). Selections from these volumes have been published as *A New Kind of History* (London, 1973). This new kind of history he also encouraged officially as president of the VIth section of the Ecole Pratique des Hautes Etudes, a post in which he was succeeded by his 'favourite son' BRAUDEL. Less well known, at least in the English-speaking world, than his friend and colleague Bloch, Febvre played an even greater part in the creation of the so-called 'Annales school'.   UPB

H. S. Hughes, *The Obstructed Path* (NY, 1969).

Fellini, Federico (b. Rimini, Emilia-Romagna, Italy, 20.1.1920). Italian film director who began his career as a writer with ROSSELLINI during the neorealist era and whose early films, the best of which are *I Vitelloni* [The young and the passionate, 1953] and the Chaplinesque *La Strada* (1955), were rooted in an essentially realistic approach. With *La Dolce Vita* (1959) he became world-famous as a director and since that date virtually his only subject has been himself as film maker and creator of spectacle. Though this theme is realized through a series of alter egos, the key thread from *Otto e Mezzo* (8½, 1963) to *La Città delle Donne* (*City of the Women*, 1980) is the actor Marcello Mastroianni. Always it is Fellini himself who is set against the ostensible subject matter, a technique reflected in such titles as *Fellini Satyricon* (1970), *Fellini Roma* (1973) and *Il Casanova di Fellini* (*Casanova*, 1977). Fellini's imagery is rooted in a studio-produced notion of spectacle and the depiction of characters, especially women, is exuberant, grotesque and startling. Yet we never lose ourselves in the maze of dazzling images or doubt our sense of distinction between the real and the imagined, for we are carried along by the flow of the action contrived by Fellini the master storyteller, who mixes dream, nostalgia, sentiment and satire with a comforting certainty. Far from being one of the tortured self-analysts of modern existential cinema, Fellini is totally autobiographical and unproblematic: like those Renaissance painters who filled innumerable walls and ceilings with barely disguised portraits of their mistresses, friends and patrons.   RPA

E. Murray, *Fellini the Artist* (NY, 1976); P. Bondanella, *Federico Fellini: Essays in Criticism* (NY, 1978).

Felsenstein, Walter (b. Vienna, Austria-Hungary [now Austria], 30.5.1901). Austrian theatre director. Educated in Graz, Felsenstein worked from 1923 to 1932 as an actor in Lübeck, Mannheim, Basle and Freiburg im Breisgau. From 1932 to 1947 he was employed as a theatre and opera director in Cologne and Berlin, with guest appointments at Metz, Strasbourg and the Salzburg Festival. Since 1947 he has won acclaim as the leading exponent of '*Musiktheater*' at the Komische Oper in East Berlin. Adding often sharp satire of contemporary society to the classics, he encourages his singers to abandon the conventions of operatic singing in favour of more realistic performances which transcend the barriers between spoken and sung drama. He has adapted or retranslated many classics including *Carmen* in 1949, and *La Traviata* in 1955.   AJM

Fenollosa, Ernest Francisco (b. Salem, Mass., USA, 18.2.1853; d. London, UK, 21.9.1908). American writer and interpreter of Japanese culture to the West. In 1879 he was appointed lecturer at the Imperial University, Tokyo, arriving when the tide of indiscriminate westernization that followed the Meiji Restoration was at its height. He became an admirer of Japanese art, expressed his concern at the neglect by the Japanese of their own heritage and thus helped turn the tide against western art and bring about the birth of the New Nihonga (Japanese painting) movement. In 1890 he left for Boston where he helped to form the great oriental collection in the Museum of Fine Arts. His chief pupil and collaborator in Japan, Okakura Kakuzō (1862–1913), later succeeded him as curator. At the request of Fenollosa's widow, Ezra POUND edited his papers, notably 'The Chinese written character as a medium for poetry', an essay which deeply influenced Pound's own development, and was included in *Instigations of Ezra Pound* (NY, 1920). Fenollosa's *Epochs of Chinese and Japanese Art* (2 vols, NY, 1911), although pioneering, suffers from the narrow viewpoint of a conservative of the Kanō lineage of academic painters, into which Fenollosa was adopted. He is little read today, but in his time his influence, both in Japan and in the West, was considerable.   MS

L. Chisholm, *Fenollosa, the Far East, and American Culture* (New Haven, 1963).

Fermi, Enrico (b. Rome, Italy, 29.9.1901; naturalized American citizen; d. Chicago, Ill., USA, 29.11.1954). Italian/American physicist. At home in theory and experiment and a born teacher, he made fundamental contributions to statistical mechanics, electromagnetic theory and atomic and nuclear physics. Fermi studied at Pisa, at Göttingen with BORN and at Leiden with EHRENFEST. As a young man he read extensively in mathematics and then applied the new quantum mechanics to atomic problems, in particular ionic spectra, the Raman effect, molecular vibrations, hyperfine structure and the magnetic moments of nuclei. He studied the properties of gases composed of indistinguishable particles obeying the PAULI exclusion principle; DIRAC obtained the same results by another method and their theory is known as Fermi–Dirac statistics. Fermi calculated the stopping power of matter for charged particles, worked on radiation theory, and developed a theory of beta decay.

In Rome in the 1930s Fermi gathered an enthusiastic band of physicists (Rasetti, Amaldi, Segrè and Persico), who read about RUTHERFORD's work in Cambridge and decided to make experiments on artificial radioactivity. Using a radium-beryllium source, they irradiated a large number of elements with neutrons, and amassed data on the cross-sections of the reactions. They noticed the great increase in the reaction rates in the presence of paraffin, and thus discovered slow neutrons, later so important for nuclear reactors. For this work Fermi was awarded the Nobel prize in 1938. Rejecting fascism he emigrated to the USA and worked at Columbia with Anderson, Zinn and SZILARD on the problem of producing a chain reaction in uranium. Later this work was moved to Chicago. Fermi supervised the building of the pile of graphite and uranium, and on 2.12.1942 it went critical for the first time. This reactor was the prototype of the reactors that produced plutonium for the atomic bomb and of all nuclear power reactors. Work on the atomic bomb was concentrated in Los Alamos where Fermi was in charge of a division responsible for tackling problems that did not fit into the work of other divisions. After WW2 he returned to Chicago, where he used the new accelerators to explore nuclear reactions at high energies. He studied the interaction of neutrons with solids using the high flux from the Argonne reactor, and developed the strong interaction model for multiple pion production, and a theory of the origin of the cosmic radiation.

All Fermi's work was characterized by directness and simplicity. He rapidly identified the essential features of any problem, however complicated, and estimated their magnitude using his pocket slide rule. In this way he obtained results in a few hours in situations where a full calculation would have taken months. His *Collected Papers* (ed. E. Segrè, Chicago) were published in 1962.   PEH

L. Fermi, *Atoms in the Family* (Chicago, 1954); E. Segrè, *Enrico Fermi, Physicist* (Chicago, 1970).

Ferranti, Sebastian Ziani de (b. Liverpool, Mers., UK, 9.4.1864; d. Zürich, Switzerland, 13.1.1930). British electrical engineer. Ferranti's abilities were evident at a very early age: he was superintending plant installation while still a boy. He made his first dynamo at 17 and sold it in the Euston Road for £5; by 19 he was buying back his own patents. In 1889 he demonstrated before representatives of the Board of Trade that supreme quality of an engineer – faith in his own convictions – by driving a spike into a sheathed underground cable to show its safety. Following TESLA's invention of the induction motor in 1888, Ferranti was convinced that any national electricity facility should be an ac system. Even EDISON expressed his disapproval. Yet, despite a split with his company directors, he won his 'battle of the systems'. He was the first engineer to use strip steel for the lamination of transformer cores, replacing the earlier, less effective bundles of iron wire. He laid the foundations of the British Grid – still the largest electrical distribution network in the world.   ERL

W. L. Randell, *S. Z. de Ferranti* (London, 1943).

Feynman, Richard Phillips (b. New York, USA, 11.5.1918). American physicist, educated at MIT and Princeton University. Feynman's early work was concerned with processes of quantum electrodynamics. He laid the groundwork for modern quantum electrodynamics and developed a very elegant graphical approach – the Feynman diagrams. This method was so successful and widely applicable that all modern theories of interactions can be couched in the same framework. This interest in electromagnetic phenomena led naturally to the description (with GELL-MANN) of weak interactions in terms of currents. More recently Feynman was initially responsible for the development of the quark parton model of elementary particles. This idea, based on experiment, is that the proton (and other particles) is made up of parts, the partons, which are point-like and can be associated with the quarks. More than any other person, Feynman has shaped the mathematical way in which particle physics is discussed today. However, his work has always been characterized by a deep physical insight. He received a Nobel prize in 1965.   RJC

de Finetti, Bruno (b. Innsbruck, Tyrol, Austria-Hungary [now Austria], 13.6.1906). Italian statistical theorist, working at the University of Rome. He developed subjective probabilities, given not only to events but to hypotheses, when the calculus of probabilities becomes a normative theory for testing ideas against evidence. Ideas are to be arranged so that all relevant hypotheses can be listed and do not interact, with their probabilities mutually comparable and consistent; there is then an unequivocal rule for adjusting their probabilities to take account of new evidence. Spurred by the parallel thinking of L. J. Savage and the mediation of D. V. Lindley, this has developed over 50 years into a substantial alternative theory of statistics which sometimes reinterprets and sometimes replaces classical methods.   AGPW

Firbank, Arthur Annesley Ronald (b. London, UK, 17.1.1886; d. Rome, Italy, 21.5.1926). British novelist. Firbank grafts modernist materials, notably jazz, social anthropology and psychoanalysis, upon the disdainful manners of high comedy to produce elliptical structures which, despite their frivolity and 'brilliant and vicious' style, seem calculated to mock the cultivated readers they most attract. Described by Edmund WILSON as 'extremely intellectual', they also reveal a poetic dimension formed by psychological and historical tensions. Firbank's grandfather was a miner who became a railway magnate, and this ancestry seems to have fought psychologically with his sense of style to impact brutal images against an elegant carapace. Historically, the novels are private refractions of public violence: in an early work Firbank prophetically depicts himself as an 'irregular-looking bird' which *'means we are about to have a war'*. In its mixture of the dainty and the momentous, Firbank's art has special affinities with the poetry of Marvell. The final impression is of evanescent lives engraved in steel. His first published book was of the stories *Odette d'Antrevernes and a Study in Temperament* (London, 1905). His first novel *Vainglory* (London, 1915) was followed most notably by *Valmouth* (London, 1919) and *Prancing Nigger* (NY, 1924). These and his posthumously published novels are collected in *The Complete Firbank* (London, 1973), with other writings available in *Memoirs and Critiques* (London, 1977).   SJN

B. Brophy, *Prancing Novelist* (London, 1973).

Firth, John Rupert (b. Keighley, W. Yorks., UK, 17.6.1890; d. Lindfield, W. Sussex, 14.12.1960). British linguist who held the first chair of general linguistics in the UK, and is regarded as the founder of the 'London school' of linguistics. Originally a historian, he graduated from Leeds University with first-class honours in 1911, and then spent a number of years in India, where he eventually became professor of English at the University of the Punjab at Lahore. He returned to London in 1928, and developed a close friendship with the anthropologist MALINOWSKI, whose ideas influenced him considerably. In 1944 he was appointed to the newly established chair of general linguistics at London, a post he held until his retirement. Throughout his life Firth maintained an independent viewpoint, remaining outside the mainstream of contemporary (American) linguistics. He wrote two popularizing books *Speech* (London, 1930) and *The Tongues of Men* (London, 1937), though his main ideas occur in articles, which tended to be programmatic and obscure. The most important of these are published in *Papers in Linguistics 1934–51* (London, 1957) and *Selected Papers of J. R. Firth: 1952–9* (London, 1968). He concerned himself above all with semantics, where he propounded a theory of meaning involving the 'context of situation', and phonology (sound patterns) in which he developed a type of analysis known as 'prosodic phonology'. In the former, Firth took over and elaborated Malinowski's theory of context of situation, which stated that an utterance could be understood only in the context of the total speech event, which included the actions, surroundings and personal history of the participants, as well as the utterance itself. Firth introduced the notion of a 'typical' context of situation, claiming that 'conversation is much more of a roughly prescribed ritual than most people think.' Since any individual plays only a limited number of social roles in his life, the number of typical contexts of situation which he will encounter will be finite, and will largely determine what the speaker will say. In phonology, Firth suggested that as well as dividing speech up into consonant and vowel segments, it was necessary to consider 'prosodies', i.e. those properties of speech longer than a single segment, such as stress, intonation and nasalization. He maintained that this type of analysis should be done *ad hoc* for each language, and specifically denied the possibility of phonological universals. His work on phonology has been more influential than his work on meaning, and has formed the basis of a number of studies by former students.   JMA

D. T. Langendoen, *The London School of Linguistics* (Cambridge, Mass., 1968); T. F. Mitchell, *Principles of Firthian Linguistics* (London, 1975).

Fischer, Ernst Otto (b. Solln, Munich, Bavaria, Germany, 10.11.1918). German chemist. Fischer's outstanding contribution has been in the field of synthetic organometallic chemistry. He studied metal carbonyl complexes under HIEBER, receiving his PhD in 1952. In 1957 he took a chair at Munich, and in 1964 (on Hieber's retirement) he inherited his ex-supervisor's position as professor of inorganic chemistry at Munich Technical University. In independent work parallel to that of WILKINSON Fischer laid the foundations of modern organometallic chemistry; for their pioneering work in 1952 (*Z. Naturforsch.Teil B*, 7 [1952], 377) they jointly received the Nobel prize for chemistry 21 years later. From this early work on the so-called 'sandwich compounds', Fischer's studies in organometallic chemistry (a field which fostered a large number of commercially important catalysts) led him to discover and develop the fields of carbene and carbyne chemistry, and he is today one of the world's foremost synthetic inorganic chemists.   KRS

Fischer, Fritz (b. Ludwigstadt, Bavaria, Germany, 5.3.1908). German historian. Professor at Hamburg (1948–73), he started a bitter controversy in Germany with the publication in 1961 of *Griff nach der Weltmacht* (*Germany's Aims in the First World War*, London, 1967). Making use for the first time of the recently opened German archives for 1914–18, Fischer asserted that the German government had been committed to a programme of major territorial annexations from the beginning of WW1 and that this was no more than the logical extension of a driving purpose to secure for Germany the position of a world power which had preceded the outbreak of war and had been the decisive factor in bringing it about. Fischer's thesis was strongly attacked by other German historians: apart from detailed criticisms of his handling of the evidence, a far-reaching debate was opened on the question whether, despite important differences, there had not been a strong element of continuity between HITLER's will to world power and the policy pursued by imperial Germany not only during WW1 but in the years before. In 1969 Fischer published a second book *Krieg der Illusionen* (*War of Illusions*, London, 1975). In this, far from retreating from his earlier views, Fischer reinforced them with a detailed examination of Germany's foreign policy in the years 1911–14 and its connection with the German domestic situation. 'The aim', he wrote, 'was to consolidate the position of the ruling classes with a successful imperialist foreign policy, indeed it was hoped a war would resolve the growing social tensions.' Historians outside Germany were neither surprised nor shocked by Fischer's thesis. Although generally critical of the portrait he drew of Bethmann-Hollweg as too harsh, they were impressed by the amount of new material he had unearthed. Inside Germany his greatest service was not just to reopen the controversy about WW1 but to bring into the open the question, which had sooner or later to be faced, of the relationship between the Nazi period and earlier German history as far back as Bismarck. Fischer's was not the final word, and the process of revision has continued and been extended since he wrote; but it was Fischer who opened the way for it, and the controversy he stirred up marks a watershed in German historiography. ALCB

Fischer, Hans (b. Hoechst-am-Main, Hessen, Germany, 27.7.1881; d. Munich, Bavaria, West Germany, 31.3.1945). German organic chemist. Hans Fischer studied chemistry and medicine simultaneously, first at Lausanne and then at Marburg. After working in the second medical clinic at Munich and the first Berlin chemical institute (under H. E. FISCHER) he returned to Munich and became lecturer in internal medicine in 1912, and then in 1913 lecturer in physiology. In 1916 he succeeded WINDAUS as professor of medical chemistry at Innsbruck. From 1921 until his death he held the chair of organic chemistry at the Technische Hochschule in Munich, as successor to WIELAND. Fischer's scientific work was almost exclusively concerned with the degradation, structure and synthesis of the pigments of blood (haemin), of bile (e.g. bilirubin, formed biologically from blood pigment), and of green leaves (chlorophyll), all of which belong to the porphyrin series and which are sometimes referred to as tetrapyrrolic compounds. (Haemin also contains iron, chlorophyll magnesium.) This inevitably involved extensive studies of the technically difficult chemistry of pyrrole derivatives. An important success was the synthesis of bilirubin as well as that of haemin. Fischer received the Nobel prize for chemistry in 1930.

NBC

Fischer, Hermann Emil (b. Euskirchen, N. Rhine-Westphalia, Germany, 9.10.1852; d. Berlin, 15.7.1919). German organic chemist. Possibly the greatest organic chemist of all time, Fischer studied under Kekulé in Bonn, and then under von Baeyer in Strassburg and Munich. He held chairs in Erlangen (1882), Würzburg (1885) and Berlin (1892 until his death). His early discovery of phenylhydrazine (he suffered poisoning from it) led to important discoveries in carbohydrate chemistry. With his cousin Otto Fischer in Munich he also worked on triphenylmethane dyes; later he himself worked on the Walden inversion (1911). Fischer laid secure foundations in knowledge of four major groups of organic compounds: heterocyclic nitrogen compounds related to uric acid, which he named purines (he synthesized purine itself in 1898), and which play a vital role in nucleic acid chemistry (Fischer was the first to synthesize a nucleotide); carbohydrates, including the determination of the stereochemical configuration of the 16 aldohexoses, of which glucose is the most important member, which he also synthesized; polypeptides and proteins, mainly by devising a brilliant, workable synthesis (very laborious by modern standards and now superseded) of polypeptides, including, in 1907, one containing 18 amino-acids; depsides and tannins (condensation products of hydroxybenzoic acids). He also devised the classic Fischer synthesis of indole derivatives (important heterocyclic compounds) which is still the method of choice for many indole derivatives. More than any other man, Fischer placed the growing science of biochemistry on a sound organic chemical basis. He received the Nobel prize in 1902.

NBC

K. Hoesch, *Emil Fischer, sein Leben und sein Werk* (Berlin, 1921).

Fisher, Irving (b. Saugerties, NY, USA, 27.2.1867; d. New Haven, Conn., 29.4.1947). American economist. Fisher studied mathematics at Yale and was appointed assistant professor in that subject. His PhD thesis was on *Mathematical Investigations in the Theory of Value and Prices* (New Haven, 1892) and in 1895 he was appointed professor of political economy; he remained at Yale throughout his career. An immensely fertile theorist, Fisher enunciated ideas in many areas of economics and economic statistics, some of which are now seldom remembered even though they anticipated or helped to initiate later developments. This applies, for instance, to his early formulation of the theory of indifference curves; to his pioneer work on distributed lags; and to his recognition in the 1920s of what later became known as wage-push inflation.

His major influential contributions, on the other hand, lay in three main areas. First, in the theory and practical application of index numbers, on which he published a substantial treatise in 1922 (*The Making of Index Numbers*, Boston, Mass.). Second, in the theory of capital and interest: see *The Nature of Capital and Income* (NY, 1906), which also contained an economic theory of accounting, and *The Rate of Interest* (NY, 1907; revised as *The Theory of Interest*, ²1930). Until Fisher's work, interest had been regarded essentially as a return, like wages or rent, to a specific factor of production (in this case capital). Fisher, basing himself on the approach of the Austrian school, notably Böhm-Bawerk, brought out the fact that the essence of interest was time; and that interest was therefore not a return to an individual factor of production but a discounting or compounding mechanism applicable in principle to any type of income flow. In other words, interest is the price of goods today relative to goods tomorrow. Fisher also examined the impact of price expectations upon the rate of interest, thereby elaborating the important distinction between the 'nominal' (i.e. money) rate and the 'real' rate, the latter being the nominal rate *minus* the expected rate of increase, or *plus* the expected rate of decrease, of prices. As for capital, this term was applicable to anything capable of generating a flow of income and therefore subject to valuation by capitalizing the income flow in question at some relevant rate of interest. Like Wicksell, Fisher, with his notion of 'rate of return over cost' thus anticipated KEYNES's concept of the marginal efficiency of capital.

Third, Fisher's *The Purchasing Power of Money* (with H. G. Brown, New Haven, 1911, ²1913), while covering a wide range including the nature of bank credit and the monetary theory of business cycles, is celebrated chiefly for establishing the 'equation of exchange', $MV = PT$, which is the basic framework for the quantity theory of money. The equation, which in the first instance is actually an identity, says that the flow of money round the economy (i.e. the quantity of money M multiplied by its velocity of circulation V) equals the value of transactions financed by this flow (P being the price level and T the volume of transactions). PMO

W. Fellner *et al.*, *Ten Economic Studies in the Tradition of Irving Fisher* (NY, 1967); M. Blaug, *Economic Theory in Retrospect* (London, ³1978).

Fisher, Ronald Aylmer (b. London, UK, 17.2.1890; d. Adelaide, S. Australia, Australia, 29.7.1962). British statistician and geneticist. Fisher worked at the Agricultural Research Station at Rothamstead (1919–33) before becoming professor of eugenics in London, and, later, of genetics at Cambridge. He first came to notice by his derivation of the sampling distribution of the correlation coefficient given independence. He later added distributions for the non-independent case, for partial and multiple correlations, and for means of small samples, mean deviations, variance ratios and higher-order moments. His work on estimation and inference was based on the likelihood function, expressing the variation, over the possible values of the underlying parameters, of the probability of the data actually observed. His principle of maximum likelihood estimation was to choose those values that maximized that probability. He developed analytical means to this end, especially the concept of a sufficient statistic for a parameter, which is a suitable quantity summarizing all the information in a sample that has any bearing on that parameter. If data, coming from several sources, are all drawn from one population, the variation of the group means will reflect the population variance, and so will the variation within the groups. If not, there will be a discrepancy which can be assessed by a variance ratio test. This technique of the analysis of variance was made ubiquitous by Fisher, with simultaneous assessments of many potential sources of variation being made by way of orthogonal components. In studying responses of, say, fruit trees to fertilizers, few of those variables that might obscure the truth can be controlled, and those left are too numerous to be accounted for numerically. Fisher realized that if each experiment has the layout of the trees, together with the assignment of fertilizers, chosen at random from among all viable designs, then the chance of a persistent fortuitous result can be virtually eliminated. This principle of randomization (sometimes misinterpreted as an imperative that can override ethics) started the modern science of experimental design (see his book *The Design of Experiments*, London, 1938).　AGPW

Fisher had always been interested in biology and he made significant contributions towards the solving of two central problems in genetics: the hereditary determination of continuous variation, and the relationship between Darwin's theory of natural selection and MENDEL's principles of heredity. Many biometricians had maintained that the theory of blending inheritance was more applicable to continuous variation than was the theory of particulate inheritance. But the possibility that continuous variation could be the result of many genes affecting the same character had been advanced by a number of people (including W. Weinberg, who anticipated Fisher in his approach). By analysing correlations between human relatives, Fisher clearly showed not only that these correlations could be interpreted according to Mendelian inheritance, but that Mendelian inheritance must lead to the observed correlations (see 'The correlation between relatives on the supposition of Mendelian inheritance', 1918). The theory of blending inheritance had been advocated earlier by Darwin, but led to difficulties in that it predicts a reduction in the genetic variation on which natural selection acts. That Mendelian heredity provides an answer to the problem of the origin of genetic variation was not fully appreciated until Fisher pointed out that it conserves this, and furthermore that mutations do not themselves direct the course of evolution (see *The Genetical Theory of Natural Selection*, Oxford, 1930). The development by Fisher of his fundamental theorem of natural selection is one of the cornerstones of population and evolutionary genetics.　APJ

Fitzgerald, Ella (b. Newport News, Va, USA, 25.4.1918). American jazz singer and composer. Though Fitzgerald does not possess the majesty of Bessie SMITH's voice or the improvisational skills of Billie Holiday, her peerless vocal technique has gained her an enormous, lasting following. She entered the musical profession via an amateur talent show in New York (where she was raised); subsequently bandleader Chick Webb was persuaded to add her to his personnel in 1935. In 1938 Fitzgerald enjoyed widespread success with a recording of her own tune 'A Tisket, A Tasket'. After Webb's death in 1939 Fitzgerald took over the leadership of the band for two years before concentrating on a highly successful solo career. In the late 1940s she began a long and productive business association with impresario Norman Granz and was encouraged to record a number of tributes to American composers, including GERSHWIN, Cole PORTER and ELLINGTON, which established her as a vocal artiste of considerable flexibility and expressiveness. Although some jazz fans disapprove of Fitzgerald's smoothness of delivery, her consistently superb singing confirms that she is an outstanding vocalist, whose work dominates both sides of the borders between jazz and popular song.   JJC

Fitzgerald, Francis Scott Key (b. St Paul, Minn., USA, 24.9.1896; d. Hollywood, Calif., 21.12.1940). American novelist. The close relationship between Fitzgerald's life and his recurrent fable of the idealistic hero's defeat in love is given a powerful twist since both were made in the image of the times. In *The Crack-Up* (NY, 1945), a posthumous collection of memoirs and letters, he assessed the cost of having lived beyond his material and spiritual resources, a self-analysis which also re-enacts the movement of the American economy from boom to slump. For Fitzgerald worldly desires (he knew none other) carry a price-tag marked with self-loss, while style and wealth exist in dangerous symbiosis. If his midwestern background explains his sense of style as something enjoyed by others, writing and wealth were the instruments to attain unrealized desires. His first novel *This Side of Paradise* (NY, 1920), a sentimental study of youthful disillusion, had a popular success which made him enough money to retrieve and marry the girl who had jilted him because he was not rich. Their life of discordant hedonism, alternating between the USA and Europe, culminated in his wife's mental breakdown in 1930. During the 1930s Fitzgerald's reputation and confidence were at a low ebb, his subject matter of wealth and pleasure irrelevant to the social concerns of the day. But in the three years before his death he was a well-paid Hollywood scriptwriter. His best novels, *The Great Gatsby* (NY, 1925), *Tender is the Night* (NY, 1934) and the unfinished *The Last Tycoon* (NY, 1941), deal with the compromise and destruction of talent by established wealth. *The Great Gatsby* achieves a genuinely complex picture of the moral confusion of its age: Gatsby is equally talented at moneymaking and idealistic love, and his covert gangsterism is no less a comment on the economic morality of American society and on his unconscious superiority to the vulgar pleasure-seeking of the rich and their hangers-on. In the end Fitzgerald forgoes the irony and judgement of this double view for nostalgia. Despite Fitzgerald's ability to evoke the sensuous qualities of moments of awareness, it is hard not to think that everything he wrote was a mythic rehearsal of his own sense of exclusion.   ATKC

A. Turnbull, *Scott Fitzgerald* (London, 1962).

Flagstad, Kirsten (b. Hamar, Hedmark, Norway, 12.7.1895; d. Oslo, 7.12.1962). Norwegian soprano. Her career was at first confined to Scandinavia, but after a performance as Isolde in Wagner's *Tristan und Isolde* (Oslo 1932) she was invited to appear at the centre of Wagnerian culture, Bayreuth, in Germany. This was the beginning of her international career and between 1935 and 1937 she was acclaimed at the Metropolitan Opera, New York, and in London's Covent Garden in such Wagnerian roles as Isolde, Brünnhilde (in the *Ring* cycle) and Senta (in *The Flying Dutchman*). After the outbreak of WW2 she went to German-occupied Norway to be with her husband and for a while this clouded her reputation in the postwar years. But further London performances from 1948 restored her glory as the greatest Wagner soprano of her generation, and she also sang (in English) a memorable Dido in Purcell's *Dido and Aeneas* (London 1951–2). Flagstad's voice was powerful yet pure and is preserved in a number of recordings.   CH

Flaherty, Robert (b. Iron Mountain, Mich., USA, 16.2.1894; d. Dunnerston, Vt, 23.7.1951). American documentary film maker. Born the son of a mining engineer, Flaherty had little formal education but from an early age worked as prospector and explorer. He was also a superbly gifted storyteller and all his film making – beginning with *Nanook of the North* (1922), an Eskimo tale, and *Moana* (1926), set in the Samoan Islands – grows out of his own sense of discovery and the need to communicate this. Always apart from the entertainment world of Hollywood in both method and ambition, Flaherty was less successful in his attempts to work with regular feature directors, such as W. S. Van Dyke on *White Shadows of the*

South Seas (1928) and MURNAU on *Tabu* (1931). A difficult and demanding man, he had an immense impact on the documentary movement, especially in Britain, but was unable to work successfully with GRIERSON when he went to England in the early 1930s. During the last 20 years of his life, indeed, he was able to complete only two films, *Man of Aran* (1934) and *Louisiana Story* (1948), but these are among his best. Flaherty's methods – unique in his day – have become an inspiration to subsequent documentary film makers. Rejecting a trite and pre-scripted fictionalized narrative, he insisted that the story of his films had to grow out of the lives of his characters, even if this meant living for two or three years among them. Uninterested in literal truth (in both *Moana* and *Man of Aran* he restaged practices which had been abandoned for decades), Flaherty nonetheless produced a series of films which stand as perhaps the cinema's greatest and most authentic tales of man's struggle against nature.   RPA

A. Marshall, *The Innocent Eye* (London, 1963); F. H. Flaherty, *The Odyssey of a Film Maker* (NY, 1972).

Fleming, Alexander (b. Lochfield, Strath., UK, 6.8.1881; d. London, 11.3.1955). British bacteriologist. According to a now well-established legend, Fleming had been working in his laboratory at St Mary's Hospital in London in 1928 when he noticed that a culture dish containing *staphylococcus* bacteria had been contaminated by something which had stopped the growth of the bacteria. Fleming was a good enough scientist to take note of the unexpected. He made careful records and the following year published details of his observations in the *British Journal of Experimental Pathology*. He called the substance which had inhibited the growth of his bacteria 'penicillin'. Tests showed that the penicillin was safe for human use and Fleming forecast that one day it would prove to be useful. It was not until a team of scientists in Oxford discovered how to manufacture penicillin in a stable form that the drug's potential was realized. Their research coincided with the outbreak of WW2, and the military significance of the drug meant that it was manufactured in large quantities. Fleming shared the 1945 Nobel prize for physiology and medicine with CHAIN and FLOREY, whose work had helped turn his observation into one of the most important medical breakthroughs of the 20c. Penicillin and similar drugs which were introduced subsequently helped doctors to deal effectively with infectious diseases previously regarded as life-threatening.   VC

L. J. Ludovici, *Fleming: Discoverer of Penicillin* (London, 1952); J. Malkin, *Sir Alexander Fleming: Man of Penicillin* (London, 1981).

Fleure, Herbert John (b. Guernsey, Channel Islands, UK, 6.6.1877; d. Cheam, Surrey, 1.7.1969). British geographer. Fleure was too delicate to go to school, but went to the University College of Wales, Aberystwyth, graduating in zoology in 1901. After a research period in Zürich he returned to Aberystwyth where he became professor of zoology (1910) and from 1917 professor of geography and anthropology. In 1918 he became honorary secretary of the Geographical Association and through this growing organization he worked tirelessly for geography teaching in schools and colleges. A flourishing honours school of geography developed in Aberystwyth, marked by Fleure's broad approach reflecting his wide experience of the natural sciences, the then prevalent interest in Darwinian theories, and new research on racial characteristics, based partly on population movements from prehistoric times and on social attributes of communities. Bilingual in French and English, he was an admirer of VIDAL DE LA BLACHE and the French school of geography. With an archaeologist, H. J. E. Peake, he published a study of European prehistory *Corridors of Time* (10 vols, Oxford, 1927–56). From 1930 to 1944 he was professor of geography at Manchester University, and in his retirement years in London he continued to write stimulating papers and to work on medical geography, an interest of many years' standing.   TWF

Flöckinger, Gerda (b. Innsbruck, Tyrol, Austria, 8.12.1927; naturalized British citizen, 1946). Austrian/British jeweller. After arriving in the UK as a refugee in 1938, she studied fine art at St Martin's School of Art, London (1945–50), and jewellery and enamelling at the Central School of Arts and Crafts, London (until 1954). Her work has been widely exhibited at British and international exhibitions, including at the Victoria and Albert Museum, London (1971), where she was the first woman and jeweller to have a one-man show. It is also represented in many public collections such as the Goldsmiths' Hall and the Victoria and Albert Museum. She created the course for modern jewellery at Hornsey College of Art, which she taught from 1962 to 1968. Flöckinger's early work was already notable but by the mid-1960s she had developed a unique and original style that broke away from traditional structure and used jewellery as an art-form. She evolved new techniques which included controlled fusion, with gold and silver, to obtain fine textures, broken surfaces and fluid lines. Many of her pieces incorporate opals, topaz or amethyst, cut and polished by herself, as well as tiny diamonds and baroque pearls. Her overall concepts are a subtle blend of abstract form and Eastern splendour, with a distant echo of the flowing elements in art nouveau.   BC

B. Beaumont-Nesbitt, 'Gerda Flöckinger's jewellery', *Connoisseur* (Sept., 1973); A. Ward, J. Cherry, C. Gere & B. Cartlidge, *The Ring from Antiquity to the Twentieth Century* (London, 1981).

Florey, Howard Walter (b. Adelaide, S. Australia, Australia, 24.9.1898; d. Oxford, UK, 21.2.1968). British medical scientist. After education and medical qualification in Australia, Florey went to Oxford as a Rhodes scholar in 1922, where SHERRINGTON fired his interest in medical research. Junior posts at the London Hospital and the University of Cambridge were followed by his appointment as professor of pathology at Sheffield (1932) and professor in the Sir William Dunn school of pathology at Oxford (1935). In 1962 he became provost of the Queen's College, Oxford, by which time he was also president of the Royal Society. Florey's approach to pathology was physiological, and his early work tackled many problems, including the secretion of mucus, the treatment of tetanus, and the action of lysozyme (naturally occurring enzymes which attack the cell walls of many bacteria). Lysozyme led him to *Penicillium*, a mould whose antibiotic properties had been noted by FLEMING in 1929. Between 1938 and 1943 Florey's team at Oxford, including CHAIN, N. G. Heatley and others, studied penicillin, produced it in large enough quantities to conduct clinical trials, and demonstrated its efficacy in a variety of serious bacterial infections. Commercial production permitted widescale use of penicillin by the end of WW2. Fleming, Florey and Chain shared the Nobel prize in 1945 for their work on penicillin; although Fleming courted, and received, more massive popular acclaim, Florey was the greater scientist. After the war Florey continued work on antibiotics, including cephalasporin and tetracycline, and on the pathology of atherosclerosis, as well as directing fundamental research on many physiological, pathological and immunological problems. He combined a fertile scientific imagination with the patience and technical ability to submit his ideas to experimental investigation.
                                                     WFB

G. Macfarlane, *Howard Florey: the Making of a Great Scientist* (Oxford, 1979).

Flory, Paul John (b. Sterling, Ill., USA, 19.5.1910). American chemist. Polymers or macromolecules occur naturally (e.g. rubber, cellulose, proteins, etc.) and new ones were first synthesized systematically in the 1930s. We owe to the organic chemist STAUDINGER our understanding that they are normal molecules of unusually large size, held together by conventional bonds, and not a mysterious form of matter held together by unknown 'secondary forces', as had earlier been supposed. It was, however, primarily Flory's work which brought them within the framework of conventional physical chemistry by showing that the standard disciplines of thermodynamics, statistical mechanics and chemical kinetics suffice for a quantitative understanding of their physical and chemical properties, of the properties of their solutions, and of the reactions that govern their formation and degradation. One example is the equation (discovered also independently by M. Huggins) which serves as the norm for describing the thermodynamic properties of polymer solutions. It is now known by their two names. Flory started his work in 1934 when he joined CAROTHERS (the discoverer of nylon) at Du Pont, and has pursued it ever since in a career divided between industry and universities. Its fruits are summarized in his *Principles of Polymer Chemistry* (Ithaca, NY, 1953), and *Statistical Mechanics of Chain Molecules* (NY, 1969). He was awarded the Nobel prize for chemistry in 1974.   JSR

Fo, Dario (b. San Giano, Lombardy, Italy, 24.3.1926). Italian dramatist, actor, director and songwriter. After writing and performing in satirical revues in Milan in the early 1950s, Fo married the actress Franca Rame who became the principal female lead and collaborator in much of his subsequent work, which began with satirical farces and continued under the influence of BRECHT's music theatre, MAYAKOVSKY and the ideas of GRAMSCI. Fo has developed an improvisational form of satirical, agitprop farce derived from the stories and playlets performed by the medieval *giullari* [strolling players]; incisive, controversial and popular pieces which represent a working-class and peasant alternative to the more 'official' form of the Commedia dell'Arte. His style of acting is distinctively physical, grotesque, comical and mime-based, and he performs much of his work in a mixture of dialect and improvised language similar to scat-song in jazz, and derived from the 'grammelot' of the French *jongleurs*, the most important example of this being his *Mistero Buffo* [Comical mystery plays] (Milan, 1967). The Fos abandoned the official Italian theatre circuit in 1968 and set up their own alternative outlet, presenting plays on contemporary issues such as police interrogation, militant housewives, feminism and terrorism. Notable among these plays is *Morte accidentale di un anarchico* (Milan, 1970; tr. G. Hanna, adapted G. Richards, *Accidental Death of an Anarchist*, London, 1979).   TWM

Foch, Ferdinand (b. Tarbes, Hautes-Pyrénées, France, 2.10.1851; d. Paris, 20.3.1929). French general and strategist. Greatly affected by the military and political events of the Franco–Prussian war (1870–1), Foch showed early intellectual promise at the Ecole Supérieure de Guerre, from which he graduated fourth in his year in 1887, and to which he returned as an instructor in 1895, and again as commandant 13 years later. After important roles in the battles of the Marne (1914) and the Somme (1916), he became generalissimo of Allied forces in the west in March 1918. He was elected a member of the French Academy in 1920. Foch was the most influential proponent of the *offensive à outrance* school which saw battle as the central act of war and the attack as eminently possible despite the marked improvement in rifles and machine-guns which seemed to make movement on the battlefield almost impossible. For him, the solution lay in moral determination and will-power, and in *Principes de la Guerre* (Paris, 1903; *The Principles of War*, London, 1918) and *De la Conduite de la Guerre* [On the conduct of war] (Paris, 1905), he put forward views which differed little from the more unrestrained portions of Clausewitz. Though claiming to believe in fixed principles, such as the economy of force and the need to preserve freedom of action, he emphasized that strategy was a question of will and commonsense. To morale Foch gave central importance: 'a battle won is a battle in which one will not confess oneself beaten'. Preparation, mass and impulse, he claimed, could produce tactical success; since more attackers than defenders could be massed at a given point, their superior firepower would overcome the advantages of fixed defences. 1914 proved him wrong.   JGo

J. Marshall-Cornwall, *Foch as Military Commander* (London, 1972).

Focillon, Henri-Joseph (b. Dijon, Côte-d'Or, France, 7.9.1881; d. New Haven,

Conn., USA, 3.3.1943). French art historian. The son of an engraver, Focillon grew up among artists (including Claude MONET and RODIN). After a doctoral thesis on G. B. Piranesi (Paris, 1918), he studied 16c and 17c graphic art and 19c painting. He also wrote on Buddhist art and on Hokusai. At Lyons he was both a professor at the university and director of the municipal museums and galleries. However, Focillon is best known for his work on the Middle Ages, notably *L'Art des sculpteurs romans* [The art of the romanesque sculptors] (Paris, 1931), and *Art d'Occident* (Paris, 1938; *The Art of the West in the Middle Ages*, London, 1963). Acutely aware of the importance of technique in the history of art, Focillon was also much concerned (as in *L'An mil*, Paris, 1952; *The Year 1000*, NY, 1969) with the way in which art expresses the worldviews or dominant attitudes in particular periods. His interest in generalizing about recurrent features in art history comes out most clearly in his *Vie des formes* (Paris, 1934; *The Life of Forms in Art*, New Haven, 1942), which discusses the evolution of styles through three phases – the experimental, the classical and the baroque – and the coexistence, at any point in time, of the advanced, the contemporary and the retarded, and the interaction between them. It has been said of Focillon that 'few experts have escaped with more sovereign ease from the bonds of specialization'.   UPB

Fokine, Michel, *né* Mikhail Mikhailovich (b. St Petersburg [now Leningrad], Russia, 25.4.1880; naturalized American citizen; d. New York, USA, 22.8.1942). Russian/American dancer, teacher and choreographer. One of the earliest choreographers to reveal the expressive potential of classical ballet. Fokine believed that a ballet should be a fusion of dance, design and music, in which the demands of the subject and its period should dictate the style of the choreography, music and design; the choreography, not formal mime, should transmit meaning; the *corps de ballet* should be integrated into the action. These ideas found no favour in the Imperial Russian Ballet in St Petersburg, where Fokine was dancer and teacher,

but he found a champion in DIAGHILEV, who determined to take the Russian Ballet and Fokine's works to Europe. The first Ballets Russes season in Paris in 1909 consisted entirely of ballets choreographed by Fokine, including *Les Sylphides* (revised 1908) and the *Polovtsian Dances* from *Prince Igor* (1909). They established the one-act ballet as the dominant form for 20c ballet; restored the male dancer, in NIJINSKY and Adolph Bolm, to public favour; and raised ballet in Europe to art status. For later Ballets Russes seasons in the West, Fokine created his masterpieces: *Carnaval* (1910), *Sheherazade* (1910), *L'Oiseau de feu* (*The Firebird*, 1910), *Le Spectre de la Rose* (1911) and *Petrushka* (1911). By 1914 he had severed his connection with Diaghilev and for the rest of his life he worked with various companies in Russia, Europe and the USA. Few of his works from this period survive, but his ballets for the Diaghilev Ballets Russes formed the backbone of its repertory throughout its existence, and have since proved its and Fokine's most enduring legacy. His autobiography was published as *Memoirs of a Ballet Master* (London, 1961).   SCW

C. W. Beaumont, *Michael Fokine and his Ballets* (London, 1935).

Follett, Mary Parker (b. Boston, Mass., USA, 3.9.1868; d. Boston, Mass., 18.12.1933). American contributor to management studies. She was one of the first people to apply the social sciences to management, providing new insights into relationships in organizations. A political and social philosopher, she wrote *The New State* (London, 1920) and *Creative Experience* (London, 1924). In 1924 she began to write and advise on industrial organization, arguing that integration and coordination were necessary to resolve conflict. Cooperation was vital: a leader must create a sense of group power rather than exercise a dominant, personal power based on hierarchical authority. Participation in decisions increased motivation. People in organizations needed lateral contacts and communication as well as instructions in a vertical chain of command. Her thinking influenced ROWNTREE, for whom she lectured in 1926 and 1928.

She retired to London in 1929. Her great contribution was to add a sense of human dynamics to previously static ideas on organizational structures. RIT

Fonteyn, Margot, ps. of Margaret Peggy Hookham (b. Reigate, Surrey, UK, 18.5.1919). British ballet dancer whose career has run parallel with the creation of a native ballet tradition in England, and who achieved her international reputation as the leading ballerina of the Sadler's Wells Ballet – later the Royal Ballet – for some 30 years. Nurtured by the company's founder Ninette de Valois, Fonteyn took on the ballerina roles in the great classics while still in her teens (as successor to Alicia Markova from 1935) – notably Odette-Odile in *Swan Lake* and Aurora in *The Sleeping Beauty*; in these and many other works her partner was Robert Helpmann. Frederick Ashton, the choreographic architect of the company's style and creator of the lyrical English school of classicism, found his muse in her artistry, musicality and dramatic expressiveness. Ashton ballets indelibly associated with Fonteyn include *Apparitions* (1936), *A Wedding Bouquet* (1937), *Symphonic Variations* (1946), *Cinderella* (1948), *Ondine* (1958) and *Marguerite and Armand* (1963). Fonteyn led the company on its first triumphant visit to New York in 1949, and later – as guest-ballerina with the Royal Ballet – to the USSR in 1961. From 1962 her career took on fresh impetus in a famous partnership with the young Russian dancer NUREYEV, especially in *Giselle, Swan Lake, Marguerite and Armand* and Kenneth MacMillan's *Romeo and Juliet* (1965). Fonteyn has been president of the Royal Academy of Dancing since 1954. She has published an *Autobiography* (London, 1975); and in 1979 she devised and presented a series of television programmes, 'The Magic of Dance', which brought the history and variety of theatrical dancing to a massive new audience. DAD
K. Money, *Fonteyn: the Making of a Legend* (London, 1973).

Ford, Ford Madox, *né* Ford Hermann Hueffer (b. Merton, Surrey, UK, 17.12.1873; d. Deauville, Calvados, France, 26.6.1939). British novelist, critic and literary editor. Writing as Ford Madox Hueffer, he first came to wide notice as CONRAD's collaborator in *The Inheritors* (London, 1901) and *Romance* (London, 1903). At least five of his novels will last: *The Good Soldier: a Tale of Passion* (London, 1915; Ford's original and preferred title was *The Saddest Story*) and *Parades End*, the Tietjens tetralogy: *Some Do Not* (London, 1924), *No More Parades* (London, 1925), *A Man Could Stand Up* (London, 1926) and *Last Post* (London, 1928). *The Good Soldier* – Ford's 46th book – is a study of the explosive forces lurking beneath the blandest exterior; brilliantly employing a passive, bemused narrator who does not fully appreciate the implications of what he tells. The Tietjens books deal with WW1, in which Ford was badly gassed. Read as a whole, William Carlos WILLIAMS called them 'the English prose masterpiece of their time'. Ford's fictional technique is impressionistic, depending on the subtle manipulation of time; his style is based on his study of the French novelists, notably Flaubert. His poetry is of minor importance; his various entertaining memoirs (selected and introduced by Michael Killigrew as *Your Mirror to My Times*, NY, 1971) are, on his own admission, 'full of inaccuracies as to facts'. Facts were of no account: 'accuracy as to impressions is absolute'. Ford was founder editor of the *English Review* (London, 1908–9), which provided a testing ground for the imagists and vorticists, and of *Transatlantic Review* (Paris, 1924), which published JOYCE and Gertrude STEIN and gave HEMINGWAY his first major platform. Ford's last work was *The March of Literature from Confucius to Modern Times* (London, 1939), 'the book of an old man mad about writing'. NP
A.M. Mizener, *The Saddest Story: a Biography of Ford Madox Ford* (NY, 1971); F. MacShane, *Ford Madox Ford: the Critical Heritage* (London, 1972).

Ford, Henry (b. Detroit, Mich., USA, 30.7.1863; d. Greenfield, Ill., 7.4.1947). American automobile manufacturer and innovator. By developing the assembly line for building cars, he pioneered mass production, achieving levels of output unheard of in the days of craftsman-built vehicles. At the same time he contributed to the high-wage, high-consumption society. By aggressive marketing (increasing volume and decreasing unit cost brought significant price reductions) he provided motoring for millions. Over 15 million model-T Fords were sold between 1908 and 1927. But mass production and mass consumption also led to deskilled workers and changing expectations. The Ford Motor Company was formed in 1903. Although Ford had no formal title in the company, he dominated its management. Henry's grandson, Henry Ford II, is still at the head of the Ford Company.   RIT

A. Nevins, F. E. Hill *et al., Ford: the Times, the Man, the Company* (NY, 1954); *Ford: Expansion and Challenge 1915–33* (NY, 1957); *Ford: Decline and Rebirth 1933–62* (NY, 1963).

Ford, John, *né* Sean Aloysius O'Feeney/O'Fearna (b. Cape Elizabeth, Maine, USA, 1.2.1895; d. Palm Desert, Calif., 31.8.1973). American film director. Ford's 50-year career makes him one of the longest serving and most prolific Hollywood directors. Most notable as a director of westerns featuring WAYNE, his *oeuvre* included many other genres, giving emphasis to his expertise as a craftsman and storyteller in the classic Hollywood tradition. He served his apprenticeship directing about 30 westerns featuring Harry Carey between 1917 and 1921. During the 1920s and 1930s he developed his craft in a number of other genres but returned to the western to make one of the all-time classics with *Stagecoach* in 1939. This and subsequent films like *Young Mr Lincoln* (1939), *The Grapes of Wrath* (1940) and *How Green Was My Valley* (1941) confirmed his status as one of America's greatest directors. Although he worked in other forms after WW2 his reputation as a (perhaps *the*) master practitioner of the western was confirmed with such films as *My Darling Clementine* (1946), *Fort Apache* (1948), *Rio Grande* (1950), *The Searchers* (1956) and *The Man Who Shot Liberty Valance* (1962). From his first short western film in 1917 to *Cheyenne Autumn* in 1964,

Ford succeeded in making his name (and also that of Wayne) synonymous with the Hollywood western. By his own admission he was obsessed with the folklore of the West, but his romanticized vision of a West dominated by masculine values and majestic landscapes where 'good' and 'evil' were polarized into the inevitable and eternal opposition between 'civilized' white Americans and 'uncivilized' red Indians has led to a decline in critical appreciation among the more politically sensitive critics of the 1960s and 1970s. Ford's reactionary politics, however, cannot diminish his considerable achievement. Sheer longevity and persistence helped to fashion a consistent visual style which was both economical and majestic. While his political attitude may now be considered objectionable, the professional manner in which his films are constructed leaves much to be admired.
                                                                          LJC

A. Sarris, *The John Ford Movie Mystery* (London, 1976).

Forster, Edward Morgan (b. London, UK, 1.1.1879; d. Coventry, Warwicks., 8.6.1970). British novelist. Forster's early career as a novelist and story-writer was followed by a long period of growing repute as a sage exponent, notably in essays and broadcasts (selections: *Abinger Harvest*, London, 1936; *Two Cheers for Democracy*, London, 1951), of values implicit in the fiction. To label these as humanist and liberal is to simplify, since Forster's mistrust of institutional religion was accompanied by respect for mysticism, his liberalism by the acknowledgement of weaknesses in the liberal position and temperament, his famous belief in personal relationships by awareness that 'psychology has ... shattered the idea of a "Person"'. His novels, often ironic in manner, subtle and perceptive within their limited range of character and incident, full of leitmotifs and occasionally obtrusive symbols, are concerned with a clash of cultures embodying different values (*Where Angels Fear to Tread*, London, 1905; *A Passage to India*, London, 1924), with the struggle between opposed forces for the soul of a central character (*The Longest Journey*, London,

1907; *A Room with a View*, London, 1908), or with the attempt to reconcile such forces ('Only connect'; *Howards End*, London, 1910). His reputation has perhaps not been helped by the posthumous publication of an inferior homosexual novel (*Maurice*, London, 1971) and of homosexual short stories laced with violence; but *A Passage to India*, at least, has a permanent value far transcending the probability that it hastened the British departure from India. The definitive Abinger edition of Forster's complete writings is currently being published, the first 11 volumes under the editorship of O. Stallybrass (London, 1975–80).   OS

J. Colmer, *E. M. Forster: the Personal Voice* (London, 1975); P. N. Furbank, *E. M. Forster: a Life* (2 vols, London, 1977–8).

Fortuny, Mariano (b. Granada, Spain, 11.5.1871; d. Venice, Veneto, Italy, 3.5.1949). Spanish designer of scenery and stage lighting. He is notable chiefly as the inventor, in 1902, of a system of diffused lighting based on the principle of reflecting light from a 'sky-dome' (the forerunner of the modern cyclorama) in order to imitate the softness of natural light; this was done in conjunction with direct spotlighting where necessary. Sufficient illumination was achieved only by exceedingly high power output, and the system is now obsolete. The cyclorama, most usually with the overhead, or 'sky', section, has become a standard theatrical appointment.   RC

Foucault, Michel (b. Poitiers, Vienne, France, 15.10.1926). French philosopher. Foucault studied under ALTHUSSER at the Ecole Normale Supérieure and then taught at Clermont-Ferrand and Paris. In 1970 he was appointed to a chair in the 'history of systems of thought' at the Collège de France. *Histoire de la folie* (Paris, 1961; tr. R. Howard, *Madness and Civilization*, London, 1971) initiated, by means of an idiosyncratic history of social attitudes to madness since the early modern period, a continuing interest in the way in which various classes of social deviant are categorized and repressed: the insane, the sick, the criminal. In seeing these exclusions as questionable Foucault is expressing a relativistic conception of the prevailing assumptions about what is to count as knowledge and as acceptable discourse. The historical variety of these 'épistèmes' is examined in *Les Mots et les choses* (Paris, 1966; tr. A. Sheridan, *The Order of Things*, London, 1970) and in *L'Archéologie du savoir* (Paris, 1969; tr. A. M. Sheridan-Smith, *The Archaeology of Knowledge*, London, 1972). Foucault is a 'Nietzschean subverter' of conventional assumptions who takes seriously the implication of his type of relativism: that he cannot pretend to think from a position outside the variety he describes. His idea that the approved knowledge of a period is a leading device for the exercise of power over those it brands as deviant carries some tremulous hint of emancipating the oppressed.   AQ

A. Sheridan, *The Will to Truth* (London, 1980).

Franco (y Bahamonde), Francisco (b. El Ferrol, La Coruña, Galicia, Spain, 4.12.1892; d. Madrid, 20.11.1975). Chief of the Spanish General Staff (1935–6); governor of the Canary Isles (1935); head of the military junta (with the title of *Generalissimo*) at the head of the Spanish army rebellion which opened the Spanish civil war; proclaimed head of state of Spain (1936); declared head of state (*Caudillo*) for life (1947–75). An old-style military dictator, Franco used the Spanish Fascist party, the Falange, the only political party permitted to function, as his tool rather than his identification mark, very much limiting and restraining its freedom of action from 1947 onwards. His system of rule being essentially authoritarian, his policy was *immobiliste* on all points until his very last years when in 1969 he nominated Prince JUAN CARLOS, grandson of King Alfonso XIII of Spain (who had abdicated in 1931), as his successor. Under his rule, which lasted for 40 years, Spain recovered from the civil war, remaining Catholic, dominated by the central Castilian government (to the point of suppression of the Catalan and Basque autonomist movements), and bureaucratic and nationalist, rather than fascist. Demands in 1945–6 pressed by the Russians, that the Allied coalition which had defeated the Germans should overthrow Franco's regime for its ostensibly benevolent, if formally neutral, attitude to Germany and Italy during WW2, strengthened rather than weakened its popular support in Spain. That support rested on a universal unwillingness to face a repetition of the Spanish civil war with its enormous death toll and can be justified retrospectively by the fact that the transition to democracy under Franco's successor, King Juan Carlos, has been made peacefully. DCW

Frank, Robert (b. Zürich, Switzerland, 9.11.1924; naturalized American citizen). Swiss/American photographer. Frank is the author of *Les Américains* (Paris, 1958), the most influential photo-book of recent decades. His survey of America was carried out in 1955–7, partly with the aid of a Guggenheim award. In 1959 the book was published as *The Americans* (Grove Press, NY). It met with a hostile reception in the USA, as idiosyncratic and ironic. Frank's view of the USA was melancholic. Although drawn to honoured sites and traditional folk events, he chose to work the edges of the crowd; the results often show Americans as alienated and bored. This picture was in sharp contrast to that of the 'human-interest' photographers who, since the 1930s, have envisaged mankind optimistically, striving and overcoming. Frank also made use of 'available light', which resulted in high contrast between deep shadows and vivid lights. His survey is less an objective study than an interpretation, a moralized landscape touched here and there by signs of salvation. At the same time an American photographer, William Klein, was at work on similarly subjective accounts of New York and Rome. These two photographers familiarized their audiences with a new sort of subjective documentary style, and had many followers in the late 1960s and 1970s. Frank's last photographic book was *Lines of My Hand* (NY, 1972); by then he had turned from photography to film-making.

Though often looked on as an American artist, Frank was trained in Switzerland, and his work may be likened to that of the Swiss Gotthard Schuh,

whose sombre variants on 'human-interest' norms had already appeared in the late 1930s. His photography can also be compared to that of Bill BRANDT, whose markedly personal documentary surveys of Britain had appeared in the 1930s. IJ

Franklin, Rosalind Elsie (b. London, UK, 25.7.1920; d. London, 16.4.1958). British biophysicist. After taking a degree in physical chemistry at Cambridge (1941), Franklin worked from 1947 to 1950 in Paris where she used X-ray diffraction to study the structure of coal and graphite. A desire to return to England, however, brought her in 1951 to the new biophysical laboratory at King's College, London, and the X-ray crystallographic study of the structure of DNA, the genetic material. Lack of clarity over responsibility for the project between herself and her colleague WILKINS plus, it has been suggested, claustrophobia in her basement laboratory, led to unhappiness and misunderstandings with some co-workers. Nonetheless she produced some of the best diffraction images of DNA available at the time. These were among the most compelling data that led to James WATSON and CRICK's Nobel prize-winning model of the DNA double helix, published in 1953, a prize which Franklin's early death prevented her from sharing. After her DNA work, she went on to study virus structure, refining the crystallographic techniques and showing that virus particles are hollow. Although knowing she was fatally ill, she continued her experimental work until her death. DOM

A. Klug, 'Rosalind Franklin and the discovery of the structure of DNA', *Nature*, 219 (1968), 808–44.

Fraser, Thomas Richard (b. Calcutta, W. Bengal, India, 4.1.1841; d. Edinburgh, Lothian, UK, 4.1.1920). British pharmacologist. Fraser qualified in medicine at Edinburgh University in 1862, and returned there in 1877, to the chair of Materia Medica, which he held for 41 years, combining it with the chair of clinical medicine. Fraser first worked on the active principle of the Calabar bean (an African ordeal poison) which he named eserine and recommended for treatment of glaucoma. In a study of the antidotal action against it of atropine, he drew 'isobols' – contours of equal physiological effect – for various combinations of the drugs and various times, an approach many decades ahead of its time. With a chemist Alexander Crum Brown, he showed that chemical conversion of a range of alkaloids of varying action to their corresponding quaternary salts reduced or abolished their original effect, replacing it by a uniform curare-like action. This was the first great generalization on the relation between chemical constitution and pharmacological action, one of the first pointers to chemical transmission at the nerve-muscle junction by the quaternary compound acetylcholine, and the first systematic collaboration by a pharmacologist and a chemist. In later work, returning to naturally occurring poisons, he showed that the African arrow poison made from *Strophanthus* contained a glycoside acting like digitalis on the heart, isolated it, and introduced it into clinical practice (where it is still used when brevity of action is desired) – a unique triple achievement. He also prepared a serum against a snake venom.   WP

Frazer, James George (b. Glasgow, Strath., UK, 1.1.1854; d. Cambridge, 7.5.1941). British anthropologist. Frazer began his career as a classicist. His interest in social anthropology was aroused by reading E. B. Tylor's *Primitive Culture* (1871) and encouraged by his friend W. Robertson-Smith, a pioneer in the sociological study of religion. A number of early articles in journals of folklore and anthropology were followed by the publication of the first edition of *The Golden Bough* (2 vols, London, 1890). This, his most famous work, was twice revised and expanded, the final, third edition appearing in 12 volumes (London, 1911–15). While revising *The Golden Bough* he also published *Psyche's Task* (London, 1909) and *Totemism and Exogamy* (London, 1910). Later anthropological works included *The Belief in Immortality and the Worship of the Dead* (London, 1913–24) and *Folklore in the Old Testament* (London, 1918). He also

wrote on classical and literary topics. Frazer's anthropology was psychological and evolutionary: he saw in man's continuing attempts to understand his relationship to the social and material environment an explanation of the origin and development of customs, beliefs and institutions. Early man, he argued, believed it was possible to manipulate his environment by magical practices. The failures of magic led man to believe in a world of spirits and gods who controlled his destiny but who could be influenced in his favour. The stage of magic was thus followed by the stage of religion. Religion itself was eventually superseded by science. Customs deriving from earlier periods persisted as survivals into later ages where they were frequently reinterpreted according to the dominant mode of thought. This scheme added little to earlier 19c evolutionary theories, and even when first published was somewhat old-fashioned. Today it is part of the history rather than the current orientation of anthropology. Frazer's methods of argument relied heavily on the extensive illustration of the beliefs and customs he described. His books are consequently a storehouse of ethnographic information, albeit of variable quality, from all over the world and many periods of human history. His comparisons between nonliterate peoples and the societies of ancient Greece and Rome influenced the thinking of classical scholars such as Jane Harrison and F. M. Cornford, and his ideas and vivid descriptions stimulated a number of 20c writers, including D. H. LAWRENCE and ELIOT. The foundation of his popular reputation, always greater than that accorded him in professional anthropology, must be sought partly in the exotic subject matter of his books and partly in his command of an ornate and graceful prose style.   HJB

E. R. Leach, 'Frazer and Malinowski: on the "founding fathers"', in *Encounter* (November, 1965), 24–36; J. B. Vickery, *The Literary Impact of The Golden Bough* (Princeton, 1973).

Fréchet, Maurice-René (b. Maligny, Yonne, France, 10.9.1878; d. Paris, 4.6.1973). French mathematician who helped found the theory of abstract spaces and set-theoretical or general topology and contributed to the development of functional and abstract analysis. When studying mathematics at the University of Paris he was encouraged to examine the emerging field of functional analysis, a generalization of classical analysis, by his thesis supervisor HADAMARD. The result was his important and influential doctoral thesis 'Sur quelque points du Calcul fonctionnel' [Some aspects of functional calculus] of 1906, in which he initiated the study of various abstract spaces from a set-theoretical viewpoint. The most important type of space was the (E) class or metric space as Hausdorff later called it. He also isolated the concept of compactness as an abstract notion and investigated various function spaces and functionals. He then applied the results to branches of analysis. Around 1909–10 he created an interesting topological theory of dimension. His early work on abstract spaces influenced many mathematicians who were developing analysis from an abstract viewpoint. His work was generalized by F. Hausdorff in the general theory of topological spaces given in Hausdorff's *Fundamentals of Quantity Theory* (1914). Up to 1928 Fréchet continued to investigate many types of abstract spaces and many parts of abstract analysis; he summarized his work in his most important book *Les Espaces abstraits* [Abstract spaces] (Paris, 1928). After that time he turned to the study of probability theory. The kind of abstract mathematics which Fréchet helped to develop has been very much in vogue during the 20c.   DMJ

Frege, Gottlob (b. Wismar, Germany [now East Germany], 8.11.1848; d. Bad Kleinen, 26.7.1925). German philosopher and mathematician. The son of a Protestant clergyman, Frege spent his whole professional career at the University of Jena. He carried on his work in isolation and comparative obscurity, although in the first decade of the century his importance was recognized by HUSSERL, who creditably acknowledged the authority of a fierce review of his first book (*Philosophie der Arithmetik*, 1891) by Frege, and by Bertrand RUSSELL, who devoted an appendix in *The*

Principles of Mathematics (1903) to Frege's ideas, having arrived himself at a position much like Frege's, although less rigorously thought out. And some 40 years after the end of his main productive period, Frege was mentioned admiringly in WITTGENSTEIN's *Tractatus* (1922). At a time when pure mathematics was becoming ever more abstract and remote from intuition, Frege saw the need for a thorough investigation, to be conducted with the greatest possible degree of logical rigour, both of the foundations of the discipline and of its subsequent development. The first step in this project was his working out of a new formal notation for logic in *Begriffschrift* (Halle, 1879; tr. T. W. Bynum in *Conceptual Notation and Related Articles*, Oxford, 1972). But Frege's choice of a complex idiographic notation contributed to his consequent neglect by its lack of perspicuity. In his *Die Grundlagen der Arithmetik* (Breslau, 1884; tr. J. L. Austin, *The Foundations of Arithmetic*, Oxford, 1950, ²1953) he argued for the 'logistic' thesis (independently arrived at by Russell some 20 years later) that mathematics is really a direct continuation of, or deduction from, an enriched formal logic. Crucial to the thesis is his definition of number in terms of classes or sets. The importance of this definition was undermined by Russell's discovery, communicated to Frege in a letter in June 1902, of the paradox that the class of classes that are not members of themselves both is and is not a member of itself. Frege replied, without irony, 'arithmetic totters'. He had already worked out the derivation via classes or sets in detail in his *Die Grundgesetze der Arithmetik* (2 vols, Jena, 1893–1903; tr. M. Furth, *The Basic Laws of Arithmetic*, Berkeley, Calif., 1964). The logic from which Frege began the derivation had as a vital constituent predicate logic or quantification theory, an incomparably more powerful and comprehensive account of the relations between statements about all, some or none of the things of a given kind than is to be found in Aristotle's theory of the syllogism which plays only a small, elementary part in Frege's system. Frege went on, in a series of essays still profoundly influential in their own right and not simply as the initiators of later developments, to transform the philosophical understanding of the basic notions of logic, most importantly in 'Über Sinn und Bedeutung' [On sense and reference] (1892; tr. P. Geech & M. Black in *Translations from the Philosophical Writings of Gottlob Frege*, Oxford, ²1960) in which the distinction between meaning proper and reference, often previously recognized in principle, was examined with unprecedented thoroughness and penetration. Here, as in his other writings, Frege was a tireless and lethal critic of 'psychologism', the point of view which takes human thought processes to be the subject matter of logic and mathematics. He maintained that these exact disciplines concerned a third realm, distinct from both mind and physical nature, composed of timeless Platonic essences. Logicians today recognize Frege as the only exponent of their science to rank with Aristotle. His work remains unmatched for its combination of constructive fertility, rigour of execution and breadth of scope.   AQ

M. Dummett, *Frege, the Philosophy of Language* (London, 1973).

Freire, Paulo (b. Recife, Brazil, 1921). Brazilian educator. Freire began his work in Brazil as secretary of education and general coordinator on the National Plan of Adult Literacy. Forced into exile after the military coup of 1964, he worked in Chile at the university and as consultant to UNESCO's Institute of Research and Training in Agrarian Reform. Later he became visiting professor at the Harvard Center for Studies in Education and Development. From 1974 to 1981 he was consultant to the office of education of the World Council of Churches in Geneva. Since returning to Brazil in 1981 he has been professor of education in the Catholic University of São Paulo. Freire is known mainly for his controversial teaching programmes, in which he involved peasant illiterates. He used pictures and drawings to help participants conceptualize community problems and visualize their perceptions both of themselves and of their relations to the programme's organizers. Among the books in which

he outlines his ideas are *Educação como Practica da Liberdade* (Rio de Janeiro, 1967; *Education: the Practice of Freedom*, London, 1976) and *Cultural Action for Freedom* (Boston, Mass., 1970).   PL

D. E. Collins, *Paulo Freire: his Life and Thought* (Ramsey, NJ, 1977).

Freud, Sigmund (b. Freiburg, Moravia, Austria-Hungary [now Přibor, Czechoslovakia], 6.5.1856; d. London, UK, 23.9.1939). Austrian founder of psychoanalysis. He trained in medicine at the University of Vienna, and went on to specialize in neurology. He cooperated with Joseph Breuer in the use of a cathartic method with hysterical disorders (*Studien über Hysterie*, Leipzig and Vienna, 1895; in *Selected Papers on Hysteria and Other Psychoneuroses*, NY, 1909, *Standard Edition*, II, London, 1955), which method he developed after a few years into what is known as 'free association'. He described his procedure as 'psycho-analysis', and went on to apply it to himself in a 'self-analysis'. The chief immediate results were his book *Die Traumdeutung* (Leipzig and Vienna, 1900; *The Interpretation of Dreams*, London, 1913, *Standard Edition*, IV, London, 1953), in which he also offered his first psychological model of mental functioning; and his *Drei Abhandlungen zur Sexual theorie* (Vienna, 1905; *Three Contributions to the Sexual Theory*, NY, 1910, *Standard Edition*, VII, London, 1953), in which he produced his theory of infantile sexuality and libidinal development.

By 1914–15 Freud had developed his theory further to cover and explain the distinction between conscious and unconscious functioning, by means, in particular, of the concept of repression (see especially his papers on repression and the unconscious in the *Internationale Zeitschrift für Psychoanalyse*, 1915; *Repression*, London, 1925, and *The Unconscious*, London, 1925, *Standard Edition*, XIV, London, 1957); as well as the nature of neurotic disorder (*Vorlesungen zur einführung in die Psychoanalyse*, Leipzig and Vienna, 1916–17; *A General Introduction to Psychoanalysis*, NY, 1920, *Standard Edition*, XV, London, 1963). By the beginning of the 1920s the work of Freud had contributed greatly 'to establish' the category of 'the neuroses' in contemporary psychiatry.

Having revised his first instinct theory so as to encompass the contrast between the Life and Death instincts (*Jenseits des Lustprinzips*, Leipzig, Vienna and Zürich, 1920; *Beyond the Pleasure Principle*, London, 1922, *Standard Edition*, XVIII, London, 1955), Freud went on to develop his earlier views by stressing the role of the ego and the super-ego (*Das Ich und das Es*, Vienna, 1923; *The Ego and the Id*, London, 1927, *Standard Edition*, XIX, London, 1961), and to apply his ideas to account for various things. For example, religious belief (*Die Zukunft einer Illusion*, Leipzig, Vienna and Zürich, 1927; *The Future of an Illusion*, London, 1928, *Standard Edition*, XXI, London, 1961), and social discontents (*Das Unbehagen in der Kultur*, Leipzig, Vienna and Zürich, 1930; *Civilization and its Discontents*, London, 1930, *Standard Edition*, XXI, London, 1961). Throughout his life as a psychoanalyst, Freud, and those stimulated by him, produced a range of concepts, which were new for the most part, to describe and explain human reactivity – such as regression, identification, displacement, sublimation, projection.

Freud was active in the politics that led to the founding of psychoanalytic journals, and of the International Association of Psychoanalysis in 1910. Freud soon lost his early associates Alfred Adler and JUNG, but the association remained to give rise to societies in other countries. With HITLER's seizure of power, psychoanalytic work came to an end in Germany, and Freud's books were burnt in Berlin. In the 1930s also Freud's views were declared in the USSR to be contrary to the philosophy of MARXism-LENINism, and it became impossible to practise there as an analyst.

In 1923 Freud had his first operation for cancer of the upper jaw; and from then on he lived a life that required regular medical attention, and that was full of pain and great suffering. After the Nazis invaded Austria, he was persuaded to leave Vienna, and he reached London in June 1938. Although his condition had become inoperable, he continued writing up to his death.

What makes Freud important in the West is the great controversial role he plays in our culture. His work has affected almost every department of it, and in the popular mind he has revolutionized our view of human nature. His method of treatment led to the use of psychotherapy, and greatly extended our sensitivity about human relations in general, and between doctor and patient in particular. His influence on psychiatry, and related disciplines, has been continuous; and his ideas remain a source of heuristic interest in psychology. But it is difficult to point to any of Freud's allegedly 'important discoveries' which has not escaped serious challenge in one way or another; and there is at present no consensus about them. Freud's view of human nature may turn out in the end to be an interesting and important mistake, rather like Aristotle's physics, or phlogiston theory, or mesmerism. On the other hand, it may turn out to contain a prescient core of important truth. This whole question is one that the future of science will have to settle, and it will probably be a long time before the value of Freud's achievement is ultimately determined. Freud's writings have been translated into English in the *Standard Edition of the Complete Psychological Works of Sigmund Freud* (ed. J. Strachey, 24 vols, London, 1953–74).

BAF

E. Jones, *Sigmund Freud: Life and Work* (3 vols, London, 1953–7); B. A. Farrell, *The Standing of Psychoanalysis* (Oxford, 1981).

Freyre, Gilberto de Mello (b. Recife, Brazil, 15.3.1900). Brazilian social historian, sociologist and/or social anthropologist (see *Comeo e porque sou e não sou sociologo* [How and why I am and am not a sociologist] Brasilia, 1968). Freyre and his literary friends were involved in the regionalist movement which centred on Recife in the 1920s; he has always approached the social history of Brazil through that of his native North-east, as in the trilogy for which he is best known: *Casa grande e senzala* (Rio, 1933; *The Masters and the Slaves*, NY, 1946), on the 'Big House' as the expression of a slave-holding, patriarchal, plantation society; *Sobrados e mucambos* (Rio, 1936; *The Mansions and the Shanties*, NY, 1963), on the decline of patriarchalism in the late 18c and early 19c; and *Ordem e progresso* (Rio, 1959; *Order and Progress*, NY, 1970), which deals with the period of the republic and is partly based on recollections solicited from about 1000 representative Brazilians born in this period. A major theme in Freyre's work is the ethnically hybrid nature of Brazilian society, the importance of the negro in the sexual and family life of the Brazilian, and the capacity of Brazilian civilization to assimilate different races and cultures. His work has been criticized for its celebratory tone and its identification of the history of the North-east with that of the country as a whole. He remains one of the pioneering social historians of the century as well as a gifted literary artist. UPB

Freyssinet, Eugène (b. Objat, Corrèze, France, 13.7.1879; d. St Martin Vesubie, Alpes-Maritimes, 7.6.1962). French civil engineer. Famous first as a designer and constructor in reinforced concrete (bridges – Le Veurdre, Allier, 1905, to Plougastel, Finistère, 1928; shell roofs, culminating in the airship hangars at Orly, Paris, 1926; concrete sea-going ships, 1916; concreting techniques – vibration, compression, steam-curing); then as the innovator of prestressed concrete. When first tried at Le Veurdre bridge, creep of concrete seemed to render the idea impracticable, but later research at Plougastel bridge proved its soundness. Failing to convince his associates, Freyssinet left his contracting firm in 1928 and devoted his fortune to its development. The first application, mass-produced pylons (1931), a brilliant technical success, failed commercially; desperate, he undertook a bold project for arresting the subsidence of the Gare Maritime at Le Havre (1934) whose success launched prestressed concrete worldwide. He continued to produce major works in the material until his death. AJH

Fried, Erich (b. Vienna, Austria, 6.5.1921). Austrian poet and political campaigner. Brought up in Vienna, Fried fled to England after his parents had been interned in 1938. After a variety of jobs, Fried became a freelance writer in 1946, since when he has been based in London. Among his many translations, those of Shakespeare stand out because of their freshness, linguistic virtuosity and rare insight into the complexities of the English original. His main reputation, however, rests on his own poetry, which is unique in the way it combines both 'public' and 'private' writing, and employs a wide range of techniques, from the orthodox lyrical via poems based on word-play to overtly experimental verse. Among the antiwar poems of *Und Vietnam und* [And Vietnam and] (Berlin, 1966), and the incisive questioning of the Jews in *Höre, o Israel!* [Hear, O Israel!] (Berlin, 1974), all posing a keen intellectual challenge to the reader, are verses exploring personal relationships and private experience with a genuine lyrical power and conviction, as can be witnessed in his latest collection *Zur Zeit und zur Unzeit* [In season and out of season] (Berlin, 1981). Fried may be open to criticism for his overenthusiastic espousal of extreme political causes, but his work represents a serious challenge to political orthodoxy and to an unthinking approach to personal life and relationships. RWL
R. Last, 'Erich Fried: poetry and politics', in A. Best & H. Wolfschütz (eds), *Modern Austrian Writing* (London, 1980).

Friedan, Betty (b. Peoria, Ill., USA, 4.2.1921). American feminist. When Betty Friedan gave up her journalistic career in the late 1940s to get married and start a family, she was achieving the then twin heights of feminine ambition. However, the malaise she began to suffer was confirmed by interviews with other American housewives; Friedan defined it as the reality of mindless, unhealthily child-centred, lonely drudgery behind the romantic myth of domestic contentment for which most women sacrificed any chance of personal fulfilment. Friedan called this idealization of the female role 'the feminine mystique', a conspiracy to discourage women from competing with men. The nationwide response to her book *The Feminine Mystique* (NY, 1963) encouraged her to cofound the National Organization for Women in 1966, advocating equal role-sharing between the sexes. Its first president, she was rapidly overtaken by younger, more radical elements in the women's liberation movement. Her second book *It Changed My Life* (NY, 1976) was a reflective journal of her years campaigning throughout the USA. Hailed as the 'mother' of the modern women's movement, she has continued to maintain her reformist stance, and her third book *The Second Stage* (NY, 1982) foresees its fulfilment, through men's liberation.　　　　MI

Friedman, Milton (b. New York, USA, 31.7.1912). American economist, and the most influential figure in economic analysis and policy since KEYNES. Friedman studied at Rutgers, Chicago and Columbia universities. From 1935 onwards he held various research posts in the US government service and in the academic world. In 1948 he was appointed professor of economics at the University of Chicago, and in 1976 he became senior research fellow at the Hoover Institute of Stanford University. In that same year he was awarded a Nobel prize for economics.

Friedman's influence is bound up with his unswerving ideological commitment to *laissez-faire* liberalism. It stems not from any pioneering advances in theory, but from consistent and wide-ranging efforts, backed by empirical and historical research and by formidable propagandistic and debating skill, to reorientate the mainstream of post-Keynesian macroeconomics and rehabilitate key features of pre-Keynesian thinking. This means in particular the so-called classical dichotomy, which in the modern context asserts that government monetary and fiscal policies have no lasting influence on aggregate output and employment, but are, on the contrary, the exclusive determinants of the price level (and of the share of national output which the government takes up). Monetarism is the label nowadays applied to these views. In line with the classical tradition Friedman maintains

that correct insight into the working of the economic system requires long-run models, the long run being, however, of somewhat indeterminate length. Government efforts to stabilize the system in the short run are doomed to frustration because of erratic timelags in the operation of monetary and fiscal policies. Friedman's view has been that governments should orientate fiscal and monetary policy to the attainment of a steady and preannounced proportional rate of growth of the money supply, and refrain from formulating any policy targets for output and employment (see *A Program for Monetary Stability*, NY, 1959). A further element in his scheme of thought is that the market system itself has a much greater degree of natural stability than appears in Keynesian economics. Of importance here is *A Theory of the Consumption Function* (NY, 1957) in which Friedman argued that consumers' expenditure depended not merely on their current income but on their longer-term income expectations, called by him 'permanent income'; this made it relatively immune to short-run fluctuations in the economic climate.

Friedman's largest single work in the area of money is his *Monetary History of the United States 1857–1960* (with A. J. Schwartz, NY, 1963), which was followed by the same authors' *Monetary Statistics of the United States* (NY, 1970) and *Monetary Trends in the United States and the United Kingdom: their Relation to Income Prices and Interest Rates, 1867–1975* (Chicago, 1982). Some of Friedman's most influential contributions on money and stabilization policy may be found in his collections of papers, notably *Essays in Positive Economics* (NY, 1953) and *The Optimum Quantity of Money and Other Essays* (NY, 1969). The former contains his celebrated essay on 'The Methodology of Positive Economics', in which he sets forth the view that an economic theory is to be judged not by the realism of its assumptions but by its ability to predict the facts; and that simple theorems which predict 'much from little' are preferable to more elaborate but ambiguous structures. Friedman's impact on economic thinking was enhanced as a result of the mounting inflation problem afflicting western countries from the late 1960s onwards, and the failure of governments in these circumstances either to curb rising prices or to restore full employment. PMO

Friedrich, Carl Joachim (b. Leipzig, Saxony, Germany [now East Germany], 5.6.1901; naturalized American citizen). German/American political scientist. After studying medicine in Germany and Austria he turned to social sciences at Heidelberg. He settled at Harvard, where he had done postdoctoral work in 1927, later becoming Easton professor of government, and retiring in 1971. During the period 1955–66 he was concurrently professor at Heidelberg. His work was dominated by two great, related interests – limited government and its antithesis, totalitarianism, on which he wrote *Totalitarianism, Dictatorship and Autocracy* (with Z. K. Brzezinski, NY, 1961). *Constitutional Government and Politics* (NY, 1937) was important in stressing the political factors necessary for the success of constitutionalism, as well as analysing its legal aspects; and his later writings emphasize the significance of a religious underpinning for political ideals. Totalitarianism he saw as a distinctly 20c form of government, dependent on contemporary technology, not least in communications, for the diffusion of the controlling ideology. Friedrich's commitment to constitutional government found outlet in work with the American government of occupied Germany and in his contribution to the constitution drafting of the Federal German Republic and of the European Community. His writings impress by their range of knowledge across history, philosophy, law and politics. DCr

Frisch, Karl von (b. Vienna, Austria-Hungary [now Austria], 20.11.1886). Austrian ethologist. Von Frisch was educated at Munich and Vienna universities. His early scientific work was concerned with sudden colour changes in fish, and he became involved in a violent controversy with the then director of the Munich eye clinic over the capacity of invertebrate animals and fish to perceive colour. He moved from university to university, eventually settling at

Munich, from which he retired in 1958. Von Frisch is best known for his brilliant work on bees, demonstrating the way in which they use elaborate dances to inform each other of the quantity and direction of food. Although recently challenged, his conclusions were confirmed in 1975. Von Frisch is regarded as being one of the founders of ethology, to which he contributed much by coupling observations in the field with experimental techniques. He is the author of numerous scientific papers and several books, notably: *Aus dem Leben der Bienen* (Vienna, 1927; *The Dancing Bees: an Account of the Life and Senses of the Honey Bee*, London, 1954); *Tanzsprache und Orientierung der Bienen* (Berlin, 1965; *The Dance Language and Orientation of Bees*, Cambridge, Mass., 1967). He shared the Nobel prize for medicine in 1973 with fellow ethologists Konrad LORENZ and N. TINBERGEN for outstanding work on the 'organization and elicitation of individual and social behaviour patterns'. PM

W. H. Thorpe, *The Origins and Rise of Ethology* (London, 1979).

Frisch, Max (b. Zürich, Switzerland, 15.5.1911). Swiss novelist and dramatist. His father's death forced him to break off his literary studies and train as an architect in Zürich. He served in the army periodically during WW2, and from 1942 to 1954 ran his own architectural practice alongside his writing. The critical success of his second novel *Stiller* (Frankfurt, 1954; tr. M. Bullock, *I'm Not Stiller*, London, 1958) and the collapse of his first marriage led to the decision to write full-time. Despite the major significance of his novels *Stiller*, *Homo Faber* (Frankfurt, 1957; tr. M. Bullock, *Homo Faber*, London, 1959) and *Mein Name sei Gantenbein* (Frankfurt, 1964; tr. M. Bullock, *A Wilderness of Mirrors*, London, 1965), his international fame rests primarily on two parable plays *Biedermann und die Brandstifter* (Zürich, 1958; tr. M. Bullock, *The Fireraisers*, London, 1961) and *Andorra* (Zürich, 1961; tr. M. Bullock, London, 1962). Influenced technically by WILDER and BRECHT, his plays attack the private and public face of bourgeois hypocrisy. His narrative fiction focuses on existential questions of guilt and identity, exploring ideological distortions of language and personal relationships, especially marriage. Two important diaries *Tagebuch 1946–1949* (Frankfurt, 1950; tr. G. Skelton, *Sketchbook 1946–1949*, NY, 1977) and *Tagebuch 1966–1971* (Frankfurt, 1972; tr. G. Skelton, *Sketchbook 1966–1971*, NY, 1974) represent a unique combination of literary workshop and sociopolitical commentary. Frisch's recent work in theatre and narrative fiction is on a smaller scale and shows a move towards greater abstraction, while retaining his individual brand of sceptical humanism. Many literary prizes and honours underline an achievement of European stature.   MGB

M. Butler, *The Novels of Max Frisch* (London, 1976); M. Pender, *Max Frisch: his Work and its Swiss Background* (Stuttgart, 1979).

Frisch, Otto Robert (b. Vienna, Austria-Hungary [now Austria], 1.10.1904; naturalized British citizen; d. Cambridge, UK, 10.10.1979). Austrian/British physicist. Frisch spent most of his research career as an experimental nuclear physicist. He is best known for his part in the events which led up to the atom bomb project. As a young man he worked in Hamburg with STERN, who was exploiting the technique of molecular beams, and he collaborated in an important experiment in which the magnetic moment of the proton was measured. In 1933 he left Germany for a short stay in London with BLACKETT and from 1934 to 1939 he worked with Niels BOHR in Copenhagen. Towards the end of this period (December 1938) he went to see his aunt Lise MEITNER in Sweden on 'the most momentous visit of my whole life'. Meitner had just received a letter from HAHN in Berlin which described the results of some experiments with STRASSMANN in which the element barium seemed to have been produced when uranium was bombarded with neutrons. Frisch and Meitner realized that this must be because the uranium nucleus had split in two; in their subsequent paper to *Nature* they called this process 'nuclear fission'. Shortly afterwards, on his return to Copenhagen, Frisch confirmed this hypothesis by experiment.

In 1939 Frisch came to England. In Birmingham he and PEIERLS calculated that if the light isotope of uranium, ^{235}U, could be separated from natural uranium, then only a pound or two of this material would be needed for a super-bomb. They submitted a report to the government and this was really decisive in initiating the development of the atomic bomb. For the rest of WW2 Frisch was engaged on this project, first in Liverpool and then in Los Alamos, New Mexico. In 1946 he returned to England to become head of the nuclear physics division at Harwell and in 1948 was appointed Jacksonian professor of natural philosophy at Cambridge where one of his interests was the design of 'Sweepnik', a machine for automatically measuring the tracks of nuclear particles. For his own recollections, see *What Little I Remember* (Cambridge, 1979).

  HMR

Frisch, Ragnar Anton Kittil (b. Oslo, Norway, 3.3.1895; d. Oslo, 31.1.1973). Norwegian econometrician. It was Frisch himself who invented the term econometrics for the application of mathematical and statistical methods to economic problems which he, and others such as Jan TINBERGEN, pioneered. During his long tenure of the Oslo University chair, created specially for him in 1931, he exercised an extraordinary influence on both the teaching of economics in Norway and the management of the Norwegian economy. The models and techniques used by successive Norwegian governments after 1945 were almost entirely due to him and his pupils. His high standing in economics the world over matched his reputation in Norway. Nevertheless he published relatively little, many of his papers circulating in duplicated form; the collection *Economic Planning Studies* (Dordrecht, 1976), however, contains some of his better known contributions. He was frequently called upon to advise foreign governments and in his later years paid particular attention to the problems of underdeveloped countries. He was founder of the Econometric Society in 1931, editor of its journal *Econometrica*

(1933–55), and received, jointly with Tinbergen, the first Nobel prize in economics (1969).   PS

Fromm, Erich (b. Frankfurt, Hesse, Germany, 23.3.1900; naturalized American citizen, 1934; d. Muralto, Ticino, Switzerland, 18.3.1980). German/American psychoanalyst. After training in Germany, he fled from the Nazis and settled in the USA. In his first book *Escape from Freedom* (NY, 1941) he argued that human beings only developed a sense of their own individuality at the time of the Renaissance. Up to that time, people felt – and thought – that they were part of a crowd. Authority, therefore, was easy to accept. Fromm believed that human beings were not mature enough to cope with this individual freedom. The Nazis, he argued, succeeded because so many people longed to revert to collective responsibility. However, Fromm's popular success rests largely on two later works *The Art of Loving* (NY, 1956) and *To Have or to Be* (NY, 1976), in which he urged readers to abandon the lure of materialism for meaningful love.   DMOC

Frost, Robert Lee (b. San Francisco, Calif., USA, 26.3.1874; d. Boston, Mass., 29.1.1963). American poet. Although born and partly raised in San Francisco, most of Frost's life was spent in New England, and his poetry is closely identified with the inhabitants and depleted rural landscapes of New Hampshire and Vermont. After attending Harvard he worked as a farmer and as a schoolteacher. But in 1912 he took his family to England, where he published his first books *A Boy's Will* and *North of Boston* (London, 1913 & 1914); he also befriended and encouraged the poetic ambitions of Edward THOMAS. Frost returned to the USA in 1915 to enjoy ever-increasing adulation, culminating in 1961 in the invitation to read his poetry at the Inauguration of President KENNEDY. Undoubtedly certain aspects of his work sustain myths deeply inscribed in the American psyche; the critical question, on which opinion is divided, is whether these aspects are fundamental to his work. His early books, published at an age by which many poets have concluded their careers, were praised by his fellow expatriate Ezra POUND for their directness of language and colloquial rendering of speech. In retrospect such qualities seem less those of a modern poet than of one preoccupied with the dramatization of point of view. Arguably his work developed little after his initial success, and he was content to present nature as a mysterious, unsympathetic force against which men and women must struggle, in an almost metaphysical contest, to maintain their being. Boundaries and limits of many sorts symbolize the wilful, arbitrary character of this self-assertion, and Frost decries moral choice in a world in which sheer persistence is the rule of life. In his best poems, however, Frost is less concerned with the wit and wisdom of this cross-grained self-sufficiency than with the experience of loneliness.   ATKC
R. A. Brower, *The Poetry of Robert Frost* (NY, 1963).

Frutiger, Adrian (b. Unterseen, Bern, Switzerland, 24.3.1928). Swiss calligrapher, typeface designer, typographer. He was apprenticed in Schlaeffli's Interlaken printing office, where he also learned wood engraving (1944–8), before studying calligraphy and letter design at Zürich School of Fine Arts (1948–51). In 1952 he became a typeface designer, and in 1958 a director, of Deberny & Peignot, Paris. In 1956 he also joined the board of the Paris publisher Hermann. In 1960 he started his own studio and began to teach at the Estienne School and at the School of Decorative Arts. He has designed many distinguished typefaces, including Phoebus, Président, Méridien, Ondine, Opéra, Serifa and (the first *new* Monophoto face) Apollo, and also redesigned several classical faces for Lumitype (Photon) filmsetting. In 1945 he began to design a fully comprehensive lineale typefamily: 21 variants, each size in several weights, each weight in several widths, intended for Lumitype; subsequently adapted for Monophoto, Monotype, ATF and – simplified – for typewriter. Since 1961 this Univers family has rivalled the 1930s popularity of GILL Sanserif. In 1961 the European Computer Manufacturers' Association commissioned from him a new machine-readable serifless alphabet printable by all conventional processes, by computer print-out, serigraphy and typewriter: OCR-B is acceptable wherever the roman alphabet is used. And in 1967 the Indian National Institute of Design, Ahmedabad, invited him to study, in India, the fundamental shapes of Devanagari script and to recommend simplifications which would further spread literacy: he collaborated with Mahendra Patel to design the typeface called Monotype Devanagari.   TC

Fry, Roger Elliot (b. London, UK, 14.12.1866; d. London, 9.9.1934). British painter and writer on art. After a Quaker childhood and taking a double first in natural sciences at Cambridge, Fry turned to painting as a career. Visits to Italy and the influence of Giovanni Morelli interested him in Renaissance art and connoisseurship. His edition of Reynolds's *Discourses* (London, 1905) made his name. He cofounded the *Burlington Magazine*, and was appointed director of the Metropolitan Museum in New York in 1905. In 1906 Fry saw his first CÉZANNE and was converted to modern French painting. Returning to London in 1910, he organized the celebrated 'Post-Impressionist' show at the Grafton Galleries. In 1913 he formed the Omega workshops to encourage young designers and artists, all much influenced by contemporary continental art. His academic theory found re-expression in the new aesthetic, much being made of the structure ('plastic sequences') and 'purity' of a work of art – he abhorred 'finish' or decoration. Collections of his criticism – *Vision and Design* (London, 1920) and *Transformations* (London, 1926) – were immensely influential, as was the monograph *Cézanne* (London, 1927). Fry's paintings from the very start bear the imprint of his successive enthusiasms, though perhaps too earnestly to reproduce much of their charm.   CF

D. A. Laing, *Roger Fry: an Annotated Bibliography of his Published Writings* (NY, 1979); F. Spalding, *Roger Fry* (London, 1980).

Frye, Herman Northrop (b. Sherbrooke, Quebec, Canada, 14.7.1912). Canadian literary critic. Frye studied at Toronto and Oxford universities, and was ordained into the United Church ministry in 1936. He has spent his academic life at Victoria College, University of Toronto, as lecturer in English (from 1939), as professor (from 1952) and, since 1959, as principal. From his first book *Fearful Symmetry: a Study of William Blake* (Princeton, 1947) – a pioneering and widely influential reinterpretation of the poet – he has demonstrated a passionate concern for understanding the form and structure of literature, especially in its mythic dimension. *Fearful Symmetry* advances his interest in traditional generic classifications and mythological universals, and he has explored these central concerns in Shakespeare (*A Natural Perspective: the Development of Shakespearean Comedy and Romance*, NY, 1965; and *Fools of Time: Studies in Shakespearean Tragedy*, Toronto, 1967); in Milton (*The Return of Eden: Five Studies in Milton's Epics*, Toronto, 1965); and most recently in the Bible (*The Great Code*, London, 1982). Frye's most important work, and the one that stakes his claim as one of the most important of postwar theoretical critics, is *Anatomy of Criticism* (Princeton, 1957). In a 'Polemical Introduction' he indicates that literature is not a 'subject' but an 'object' of study: teachers teach criticism; literature cannot be taught. He argues for system in the critical process; this entails a taxonomy of literary modes and symbols, a consideration of myths, and a theory of genres. The clearest approach to Frye's theories is through the later 'Criticism, Visible and Invisible' in *The Stubborn Structure* (London, 1970), where his neo-Aristotelianism appears in the assertion that 'values' are not teachable, that 'the structure and imagery of literature are central considerations of criticism', and that 'the end of criticism ... is not an aesthetic but an ethical and participating end'. Frye leaves unanswered questions; but in his critical relativism and his clear and forceful deployment of wide learning and deep sensitivity he has made a strong bridge between scholarship and criticism. In *The Bush Gar-*

den: Essays on the Canadian Imagination (Toronto, 1971) he focused his talents upon his home ground to produce a work of seminal importance in Canadian studies. JPW/PQ

M. Krieger (ed.), *Northrop Frye in Modern Criticism* (Columbia, 1966).

Fuentes, Carlos (b. Mexico City, Mexico, 11.11.1928). Mexican novelist, short-story writer, dramatist and essayist. Son of a Mexican diplomat, his youth and education were markedly cosmopolitan (Rio, Washington, Buenos Aires, Geneva), and his early career was in diplomacy and international law. A brilliant and prolific novelist, he helped to conquer for Mexican letters the techniques and subtlety of the contemporary Western novel, while cultivating, as another element in the baroque texture of his prose, a vividly colloquial Mexican idiom. A frantic eroticism, an immensely wide range of cultural and historical reference, an interest in the fantastic, and a constant, critical preoccupation with the action and stagnation of the Mexican revolution constitute further dimensions. Three landmarks in his development are: *La muerte de Artemio Cruz* (Mexico City, 1962; tr. S. Hileman, *The Death of Artemio Cruz*, London, 1964), the death-bed memories of a typical revolutionary officer turned agent of international capitalism; *Cambio de piel* (Mexico City, 1967; tr. S. Hileman, *A Change of Skin*, London, 1968), a complex and enigmatic incursion, mainly through the psyche of a failed writer, into a maze of cultural, artistic, psychological and political questions; and the vast masterpiece *Terra Nostra* (Mexico City, 1975; tr. M. Sayers Peden, London, 1977), a combinatory game with strands of European and Spanish Renaissance thought, Hapsburg kings and Aztec mythology, projected towards the present and future of Latin America.
SB

Fugard, Athol (b. Middleburg, Cape Province, South Africa, 11.6.1932). South African dramatist whose work has become increasingly one of the main outlets internationally for the expression of opposition to apartheid. It was with his third full-length play *The Blood Knot* (1961), a graphic examination of some of the tensions and absurdities of race laws which can denote one brother black and the other white, that he achieved wide recognition. In 1965 he founded the Serpent Players in Port Elizabeth and in 1972 the Space experimental theatre that evolved from improvisation, a process reaching its culmination in *Sizwe Bansi is Dead* (1972), which he wrote with two black South African actors John Kani and Winston Ntshona. Almost all Fugard's work explores the racial dichotomies of his country. He has also written filmscripts and one novel *Tsotsi* (Johannesburg, 1980). His work effectively documents the sterility and viciousness of South Africa's race laws while making a significant contribution to the techniques of modern drama. ANRN

D. Walder, *Selected Plays of Athol Fugard* (Harlow, 1981); S. Gray (ed.), *Athol Fugard* (Johannesburg, 1982).

Fukui, Kenichi (b. nr Kyoto, Japan, 4.10.1918). Japanese physical chemist. Fukui and HOFFMANN won the Nobel prize for chemistry in 1981 for their theories about the course of chemical reactions. The chemistry of a molecule is determined by the spatial distribution of its electrons and by how tightly these electrons are bound to the molecule at particular locations. Fukui's method of frontier orbitals concentrates on the electrons which are the least tightly held by the molecule. If a reactant is involved in donating electrons to form new chemical bonds, then the electrons involved are most likely to be these loosely bound ones and the bond will be created where they are located. Conversely the chemistry of the electron-accepting partner will be dominated by the ease with which extra electrons can be accommodated in the various parts of the molecule. Fukui's ideas were developed and exploited before the era when chemists were blessed with large computers, but the range of their applicability is now very general and frontier orbital theory is widely used in giving a rationale to the chemistry of carbon compounds (i.e. organic chemistry). WGR

Fuller, John Frederick Charles (b. Chichester, W. Sussex, UK, 1.9.1878; d. Falmouth, Cornwall, 10.2.1966). A British army officer, much involved in tank operations during WW1, Fuller became – along with LIDDELL HART – one of the earliest and most influential theorists of mechanized warfare. His military career effectively ended in 1927, due to his own touchiness, but his ideas were expounded in 45 books and numerous articles. An idea and an actuality combined to serve as the foundation of his thought. Evolution, he believed, made possible the prediction of future events, and dictated that armies must adapt to changes in their environment to remain fit for war; mechanization had decisively changed that environment and would permit mobility on the battlefield. Fuller believed the new instruments should be used to demoralize rather than to destroy the enemy, and in his second and third volumes of *Lectures on Field Service Regulations* (London, 1931–3) he put forward his theory of 'strategic paralysis': battle must be sought, not avoided, and the tank – used in combination with mechanized infantry – employed to penetrate behind the enemy's front line once he had been 'fixed' by an initial attack. His lectures were adopted for study by the German, Soviet and Czechoslovak armies. Fuller underestimated the impact of air power on the battlefield, and the capacity of industrialized powers to create mechanized armies of vast size, thereby making rapid decisions harder and not easier to achieve.   JGo

A. J. Trythall, *'Boney' Fuller: the Intellectual General* (London, 1977); B. H. Reid, 'J. F. C. Fuller's theory of mechanized warfare', *Journal of Strategic Studies*, I (1978).

Fuller, Richard Buckminster (b. Milton, Mass., USA, 12.7.1895). American inventor and philosopher. Fuller is a maverick figure, a generalist in an increasingly specialized era (see *Critical Path*, London, 1983). He has achieved greatest recognition for his contribution to architecture; yet he produced not architecture, but huge engineering structures. The best known of these are the geodesic domes based on the three-dimensional structural principles that he developed to achieve maximum spans with a minimum of material. There are now more than 100,000 around the world. The most spectacular of them was the huge structure that he built for the Montreal Exposition of 1967. He became a guru to generations of architectural students because of his unquenchable optimism and his belief in technology as a tool for improving the quality of life. Many of his schemes remained simply dreams, but have been no less influential for that. He had the rugged individualism of the frontier pioneers, his philosophy crudely but effectively expressed by a verse that he composed while teaching at Yale: 'Roam home to a dome, / Where Georgian and Gothic once stood, / Now chemical bonds alone guard our blondes, / And even the plumbing looks good.' After WW1 Fuller spent several years working in industry before in 1927 producing his first important design, the Dymaxion house ('dynamic plus maximum efficiency'), which was meant to be a high-technology response to the chronic housing shortage of the depression. Unlike the skin-deep functionalism of European architects in the 1920s who produced houses that looked like machine-made objects but were actually built by laborious handcraft, the Dymaxion house was to be a prototype for mass-producing cheap houses just like Model T Fords: production-line houses equipped with all the basic services and equipment built-in and ready to be connected up to the mains. Nothing came of the scheme directly, but the philosophy behind it – the need to turn building from a craft into a matter of prefabricating factory-made components – can be traced in the system-building of the 1960s. Later, Fuller's ideas for lightweight structures were to have more commercial applications. 'How much does your building weigh?' he was fond of asking.   DS

Furtwängler, Wilhelm (b. Berlin, Germany, 25.1.1886; d. Baden-Baden, Baden-Württemberg, West Germany, 30.11.1954). German conductor. Together with TOSCANINI, sometimes regarded as his antipole, one of the first conductors to gain a wide audience through recordings; his performances of Wagner operas and Beethoven symphonies remain outstanding documents. Furtwängler's style involved a very considered drawing-out of expressive nuances. His rhythm was wayward only in the interests of emotional profundity and formal integrity. A close relationship between conductor and orchestra was probably a prerequisite of this style

and Furtwängler did most of his best work with the Berlin Philharmonic, which he directed from 1922 until his death. He produced three symphonies and various other compositions, and several volumes of essays, including *Gespräche über Musik* (ed. W. Abendroth, Zürich, 1948; *Concerning Music*, London, 1953).   PG

C. Riess, *Furtwängler* (London, 1955).

G

Gabo, Naum, ps. of Naum Neemia Pevsner (b. Briansk, Russia, 5.8.1890; naturalized American citizen, 1952; d. Waterbury, Conn., USA, 23.8.1977). Russian/American constructivist sculptor, brother of the sculptor Antoine Pevsner. Originally a student of natural science and engineering in Munich, he began to make sculptures in 1915 adopting a method of open, stereometric construction used for mathematical models; he also changed his name to Naum Gabo. His first sculptures were in the form of the human figure but from 1917 he adopted a completely abstract style. In 1920 he issued a 'realistic manifesto' in Moscow, which was also signed by his brother, setting out the principles of constructivism, including the possibilities of kinetic sculpture which he demonstrated in a simple form in his *Kinetic Sculpture (Standing Wave)* of 1919–20, a vibrating metal rod which in motion suggested a wave form. This, however, remained an isolated work, and the majority of his sculptures from about 1920 onwards were constructions made out of the new material of transparent colourless plastic, including a number of small models for projects which he hoped some day to be able to carry out on a much larger scale. Among them were various projects for columns and monuments, which were intended to be a fusion between abstract sculpture and architecture.

In 1923 he left Russia and settled in Berlin, where he remained until 1932 when he moved to Paris. From 1935 to 1946 he lived in England, in close touch with Ben NICHOLSON and HEPWORTH, then emigrated to the USA where he spent the rest of his life. Whereas his brother soon changed to making welded-metal sculpture, Gabo continued to work mainly with plastic, constructing completely abstract sculptures of extraordinary delicacy and transparency, including rhythmical spherical or rectilinear forms strung with nylon threads which are open to the light and the surrounding space. With the exception of a few stone carvings, his sculptures have very little mass but consist of planes articulated in space in a manner which sometimes suggests three-dimensional geometry. In the last 25 years of his life he was able for the first time to carry out some of his projects on a large scale, including a monumental standing construction of 1955–7 sited outside the Bijenkorf department store in Rotterdam. REA

H. Read & L. Martin, *Gabo: Constructions, Sculpture, Paintings, Drawings, Engravings* (London, 1957).

Gabor, Dennis (b. Budapest, Austria-Hungary [now Hungary], 5.6.1900; naturalized British citizen; d. London, UK, 9.2.1979). Hungarian/British electrical engineer, who won the Nobel prize for physics in 1971 for his invention of holography. This is a technique which Gabor developed in 1947–8 while seeking to improve the electron microscope. It made possible the recording of a three-dimensional photographic image without a lens. The image itself, a hologram, appears as an unrecognizable pattern of stripes and holes until illuminated by coherent light. Gabor's proposal was of limited practical interest until the development of lasers in the early 1960s made possible the widespread application of holography in medicine, mapmaking, communications and computer technology. Gabor fled to the UK as a refugee from Nazi Germany in 1933 and worked in industry. His invention of holography was followed by a move to Imperial College, London, where he became professor of applied electron physics in 1958. His other work included research on high speed oscilloscopes, communication theory, physical optics and television. In 1970 he produced a list of 137 innovations to be expected in the next 50 years: *Innovations: Scientific, Technological & Social* (Oxford, 1970). ALCB

Gadafi, Muammar, see QUADDAFI, MUAMMAR AL-.

Gadamer, Hans-Georg (b. Marburg, Hesse, Germany, 11.2.1900). German philosopher. A pupil and lifelong friend of HEIDEGGER, Gadamer began his teaching career at Marburg and Leipzig where, after the collapse of Nazi Germany, he became rector of the university and was actively involved in its restoration under Russian occupation. In 1947 he was appointed to a chair at Frankfurt and, two years later, to a chair at Heidelberg which he held until his retirement in 1968. Gadamer's most distinctive contribution to philosophy is his theory of philosophical hermeneutics which attemps to elucidate the fundamental conditions that underlie the phenomenon of understanding in all its modes. In his major work *Wahrheit und Methode* (Tübingen, 1960; tr. G. Bardon & W. G.-Doepel, *Truth and Method*, London, 1975), Gadamer represents understanding not so much as a methodical act of reconstruction of a text, event or work of art, but as an entering into a process of constant mediation of past and present. To the interpreter's own participation in history, his historically determined pre-understanding of what is to be interpreted, is attributed a constitutive role in the process of understanding. By reflecting on such pre-understanding, and the totality of our relations with the world which is manifested in it, Gadamer attempts to bring to light experiences of truth which fall outside the scope of any methodical knowledge or scientific specialization. This conception of hermeneutics has proved to be of major importance to philosophy and several related subjects. In addition, Gadamer has published a number of influential works on the history of philosophy, aesthetics and the philosophy of history.   EFo

Gadda, Carlo Emilio (b. Milan, Lombardy, Italy, 14.11.1893; d. Rome, 21.5.1973). Italian novelist and essayist, best known for his two incomplete detective stories *Quel pasticciaccio brutto della Via Merulana* (Milan, 1957; tr. W. Weaver, *That Awful Mess on Via Merulana*, London, 1966) and *La cognizione del dolore* (Turin, 1963; tr. W. Weaver, *Acquainted with Grief*, London, 1969), both of which had first appeared in instalments, respectively in 1946–7 and 1938–41, in the Florentine literary review *Letteratura*. Gadda, arguably the most complex of modern Italian prose writers, explores the dramatically 'baroque' nature of the real world with an anguish for its manifest injustices that clearly derives from his fellow Lombard, the 19c novelist Alessandro Manzoni, but he does so with a literary style and linguistic complexity that is almost unique in Italian literature. Gadda makes great use of a wide-ranging literary pastiche in both novels, and linguistically, especially in the *Pasticciaccio*, he employs within the body of a highly organized and literary prose an incredible number of dialects (Roman, Venetian and Neapolitan, among others). Gadda, who translated CONRAD's *The Secret Agent*, was awarded in 1963 both the Prix International de Littérature and the Formentor prize.   TON

O. Ragusa, *Narrative and Drama* (The Hague, 1976).

Gaddum, John Henry (b. Hale, Ches., UK, 31.3.1900; d. Cambridge, 30.6.1965). British pharmacologist. After a brief period at the Wellcome laboratories, Gaddum joined DALE during the 'anni mirabiles' when the Hampstead laboratory was establishing the chemical transmission of nerve effects. He held the chair in Edinburgh for 16 years and from 1958 until his death the directorship of the Agricultural Research Council's Institute of Animal Physiology near Cambridge. Gaddum had a flair for devising delicate specific biological tests for natural substances in the body, present in minute concentrations, at a time when chemical methods were far too insensitive to detect them. He proved the release of acetylcholine in autonomic ganglia and of adrenaline by sympathetic nerves; showed the presence of 5-hydroxytryptamine (5HT) in brain and of histamine in blood; discovered (with the American von Euler) Substance P; and studied the properties of the kinins. Almost all his observations have proved to have deep physiological significance. He also investigated the drug receptor and established the classical laws of drug antagonism at a time when the concept of specific drug-receptor interaction was unfashionable; discovered the antagonism by LSD of 5HT, being one of the first to try to explain mental disturbance by a specific chemical interference; and wrote an undergraduate textbook *Pharmacology* (Oxford, 1940) of outstanding economy, precision and charm. His wholehearted commitment to pharmacology was vital to its growth as an independent discipline. WP

Gagné, Robert Mills (b. North Andover, Mass., USA, 21.8.1916). American behavioural psychologist whose approach to the process of instruction has had a marked influence on developments in the school curriculum, particularly in the sciences. His early interest in learning processes turned towards the application of task analysis when, in the late 1940s, he became director of research at Lakeland Air Force Base, Texas. In 1966 he became a professor at the University of California, Berkeley, and professor of educational research at Florida State University in 1969. His key work is *The Conditions of Learning* (NY, 1955, [3]1977). It offers a comprehensive framework within which any learning task can be placed, analysed for its structure and sequence, and then related to the type of psychological processes involved. Its attraction lies in its total approach to effective learning through the teacher managing the environment. His focus on the hierarchical structure of most school subjects, requiring a breakdown into prerequisite skills which are then graded step by step, and on the importance of concept learning, has had considerable heuristic value in education. His approach has close affinities with the 'aims and objectives' movement associated with B.S Bloom and with SKINNER's approach to the curriculum through programmed learning. RRS

Gaitskell, Hugh Todd Naylor (b. London, UK, 9.4.1906; d. London, 18.1.1963). British politician; Labour chancellor of the exchequer (1950–1); leader of the Labour party in opposition (1955–63); regarded after his premature death in 1963 by many of the middle-class generation which voted Labour from 1945 onwards and supported the meritocratic aspects of the Welfare State, as Labour's 'lost leader'. Gaitskell's support in the Labour party rested ironically enough on the votes of the largest trade unions with whose aid he overcame his unpopularity with Labour activists for introducing charges for the National Health Service, and stood off challenges to his leadership from BEVAN and Harold Wilson, making himself the party mouthpiece for the new emphasis on egalitarianism for which CROSLAND was the ideologue. This repudiation of his own upper-middle-class intellectual background (education at Winchester and Oxford), combined with some determined political infighting at the constituency party level by the Campaign for Democratic Socialism, enabled him to survive defeat at the 1959 general election and, at the hands of the left-dominated Campaign for Nuclear Disarmament, at the party conferences in 1959 and 1960, though many of his supporters were dismayed by his subsequent alliance with the left to oppose Britain's first attempt to join the European Economic Community in 1962.

Gaitskell is to be seen as a representative of the middle-class Fabian tradition in the Labour party, with its emphasis on social and economic planning and efficiency in government, and his reputation for intellectual integrity made him the beneficiary of that tradition of party loyalty for which the Labour party was once so distinguished. DCW

P. Williams, *Hugh Gaitskell* (London, 1979).

Gajdusek, Carlton (b. Yonkers, NY, USA, 9.9.1923). American paediatrician and neurologist who determined the cause of the disease kuru and in so doing discovered a new type of slow virus, the so-called unconventional virus, with distinctive physical and biological properties, and a very long incubation period. Gajdusek majored in physics in the University of Rochester, attended Harvard Medical School and worked as a postdoctoral student at Caltech with PAULING and Kirkwood. From the Boston Children's Hospital and later the National Institute of Health at Bethesda, he became involved in studying diseases of children in traditional societies and was introduced to kuru in Papua New Guinea. This disease is largely confined to the Foré people in the Highlands. It is a progressive degenerative disease of the brain and accounted for many deaths among these people, particularly children and adult women. It tended to have a familial distribution and for some time was thought to have a genetic basis. Gajdusek demonstrated that it could be transmitted to other primates, particularly the chimpanzee, and was an infectious disease. Apparently among the Foré it used to be transmitted by ritualistic cannibalism in which the brains of dead relatives are eaten by women and children. The discovery provides a fine example of a contribution from anthropology to epidemiology. Gajdusek has continued working on other slow viruses, particularly those causing the Creutzfeldt–Jakob disease which bears a similarity to kuru, but is widely distributed throughout human populations, though always rare. For this work Gajdusek was awarded a Nobel prize in 1976.   GAH

Galbraith, John Kenneth (b. Iona Station, Ont., Canada, 15.10.1908). American economist; the Harvard professor (1949–75) who was, until the rise of FRIEDMAN, perhaps the living economist best known to the general public. He is a brilliant popularizer, as much at home in his spectacular BBC TV series 'The Age of Uncertainty' (1977) as on the lecture stand. His published work is witty and persuasive and directed at both a professional and general readership. In a series of bestselling books he has developed his own critique of 20c society. *American Capitalism* (Boston, Mass., 1952) replaced conventional explanations of the workings of the market with the concept of 'countervailing forces'. *The Affluent Society* (Boston, Mass., 1958) introduced a new term into the popular idiom – 'private affluence versus public squalor' – contrasting the aggressive spending of the great corporations with the decline in public services and the continuing plight of the poor. In *The New Industrial State* (Boston, Mass., 1967) he pursued his examination of the intimate connections between big business and government in terms of the rising influence of the 'technostructure'. *Economics and the Public Purpose* (Boston, Mass., 1973) presents his views in even more polemical form, arguing that it is necessary to prise the corporations and the state apart so that social inequalities can be tackled effectively. Fellow economists tend to be dismissive of his scientific contribution and decry his unorthodox faith in planning and the management of market forces. Nevertheless they honoured him with the presidency of the American Economic Association (1972). He was an unofficial adviser to President KENNEDY, who appointed him as US ambassador to India (1961–3), and remains to this day a major intellectual force in the Democratic party.   PS

M. E. Sharpe, *John Kenneth Galbraith and the Lower Economics* (White Plains, NY, 1973).

Gallup, George Horace (b. Jefferson, Iowa, USA, 18.11.1901). American opinion pollster and social researcher. Gallup received his PhD in psychology from the University of Iowa (1928), then taught at Iowa, Drake, Northwestern and Columbia universities. He was the pioneer of scientific polling techniques as a method of assessing public opinion by means of sample surveys. In October 1935, after three years of experimental work, sponsored weekly reports on the state of public opinion on national issues in the USA started appearing in newspapers, and they have continued each week ever since. He demonstrated that by interviewing a comparatively small, but genuinely representative, sample of respondents across even a large nation – typically 1500 in the USA and 1000 in European countries – an accurate snapshot of the attitudes and opinions of the national population could be taken. The technique transformed election forecasting and widened the concept of democratic accountability by making governments increasingly sensitive to the weight of public opinion. In 1976 Gallup initiated one of the world's largest sample surveys when a global survey on the quality of life was conducted in more than 60 countries covering two-thirds of the world's population. His book *The Sophisticated Poll Watcher's Guide* (Princeton, 1976) summarized 40 years' practical experience. Gallup's procedures are currently used throughout the western world (British Gallup, the oldest affiliated company, was established in 1937), and his name has become the generic word for opinion polling.   GIH

Galsworthy, John (b. Coombe, Surrey, UK, 14.8.1867; d. London, 31.1.1933). British novelist and dramatist. Encouraged to write by his wife Ada, whose unhappy first marriage inspired much of his fiction, he made a double reputation in 1906 with *The Silver Box*, prototype of several realistic well-made thesis plays dispassionately anatomizing social injustices, and *The Man of Property*, first and finest novel in the popular trilogy the 'Forsyte Saga'. Foremost among his satires on his own upper-middle-class society, the novel boasts a memorable villain-hero in Soames Forsyte, the epitome of Forsyte possessiveness. A grimly ironical counterpoint of divided classes characterizes *Strife* (London, 1909), his impressive tragedy of labour against capital, and *Fraternity* (London, 1909), his best non-Forsyte novel. A tireless campaigner, he reformed prison administration through his play *Justice* (London, 1910). His postwar fiction betrayed more extensively the flatness and sentimentality afflicting even the work of his Edwardian heyday. He was awarded the Nobel prize for literature in 1932.   AS

R. D. Barker, *The Man of Principle* (London, 1963); C. Dupré, *John Galsworthy* (London, 1976).

Galton, Francis (b. Birmingham, W. Mids, UK, 16.2.1822; d. Haslemere, Surrey, 17.1.1911). British psychologist and polymath. He was a cousin of Charles Darwin. Despite a severe mental breakdown in the early 1840s, he graduated from Cambridge University and then travelled widely, becoming interested in many scientific disciplines including psychology, meteorology and geography. He is mainly known for his numerous contributions to psychology, but he received a Gold medal from the Royal Geographical Society for exploring the then unknown area of central South West Africa, and establishing the existence of anticyclones. His first major work was *Hereditary Genius* (London, 1869), in which he argued that mental characteristics are inherited in the same way as physical characteristics, supporting this thesis by the fact that eminence runs in families. This line of thought led in 1876 to the very first behavioural study of twins in an endeavour to distinguish between genetic and environmental influences; the twin-study approach is still of vital importance in this area. He made a major contribution to psychometrics and statistics in 1877 when he proposed a measure of correlation that was subsequently elaborated by his student Karl PEARSON. In 1882 he set up the world's first mental test centre in London, at which various physical, reaction-time and sensory measurements were taken. *Inquiries into Human Faculty and its Development* (London, 1883) presented a gallimaufry of findings and ideas concerned *inter alia* with the inefficacy of prayer, the Australian marriage system and arithmetic by smell. In that book, he initiated research into individual differences in imagery, and used word associations to reveal the impact of childhood experiences on adult thinking. He had a somewhat dilettante approach, but succeeded in founding the study and measurement of individual differences.   MWE

D. W. Forrest, *Francis Galton: the Life and Work of a Victorian Genius* (London, 1974).

Gamow, George Antony (b. Odessa, Russia, 4.3.1904; naturalized American citizen, 1934; d. Boulder, Colo, USA, 19.8.1968). Russian/American astrophysicist. Gamow's name is perhaps most closely associated with the 'big bang' theory of the origin of the universe, of which he was a strong advocate, but he worked in nuclear physics as well as in astronomy and is one of a handful of scientists who made a distinctive mark on 20c science. He was educated in the USSR. He studied nuclear physics in Göttingen, Germany, in 1928 and spent some time in Cambridge at the Cavendish Laboratory in 1929, where RUTH-ERFORD asked him to calculate the energy required to split the atom, with the result that Rutherford went ahead with his famous experiment. Gamow's calculations on the probability of nuclear reactions also enabled astronomers to confirm that nuclear fusion was the primary energy source in stars. Gamow left Russia in 1933, was appointed professor of physics at George Washington University, USA, in 1934 and in 1956 became professor of physics at the University of Colorado. In the late 1930s he used his wide knowledge of nuclear physics in stellar evolution studies and in work concerning the mass-luminosity relationship for stars. By 1939 he was advocating the theory of the expansion of the universe, based on his understanding of the observational data. He was also concerned with the energy source in red giant stars and continued to sort out the role played by neutrinos in the supernova explosion of stars. By 1948 Gamow had coined the term 'big bang' for the cosmological model that described the universe beginning in a highly dense, compact fireball, whose explosive expansion we still witness through the recession of the distant galaxies. Work with Ralph Alpher on the synthesis of chemical elements in the early stages of the universe led to the famous paper by Alpher, BETHE and Gamow (Hans Bethe's name was borrowed for the joke) which was published on 1.4.1948. That theory was the best of its day. Gamow's work on big-bang cosmology led him to predict the cosmic abundance of the element helium and the presence of low temperature cosmic background radiation. This latter prediction was brilliantly confirmed observationally by PENZIAS and Wilson in 1965. Showing his diversity in thinking, Gamow was the first to suggest, in 1954, a coding scheme for the genetic code which was later acknowledged as a key stepping-stone for molecular biologists. Author of 30 books popularizing science, Gamow had great success in explaining difficult concepts to the public. *The Creation of the Universe* (NY, 1952), *One Two Three ... Infinity* (NY, 1955) and *Thirty Years that Shook Phys-*ics (NY, 1965) were celebrated works, as were his series of books featuring Mr Tompkins (who explained physics to the reader).   MJS

Gance, Abel (b. Paris, France, 25.10.1889; d. Paris, 10.11.1981). French film director. One of the most dynamic and ambitious figures ever to work in the French – or indeed world – cinema, Gance launched himself on a career as poet and dramatist which culminated in the writing of an (unproduced) play for Sarah Bernhardt in 1913. But already, at 19, he had begun to finance his career by writing filmscripts and had turned to direction – in a characteristic desire to control his work – some two years later. He learned his craft by turning out a large number of films and among his prolific output during these early years two films stand out: *La Folie du Docteur Tube* [The madness of Dr Tube, 1915], a fascinating example of the use of distorting lenses and subjective camerawork, and *J'Accuse* (*I Accuse*, 1919), a passionate antiwar parable.

Gance's greatest successes came in the 1920s, first with the symbolic melodrama *La Roue* [The wheel, 1923] – the life of a railway engineer turned into a psychological epic with music by Honegger – and then – after considering such subjects as the fall of Jericho, the life of Christ and the end of the world – with an epic biography of *Napoléon* (1927). Gance continued as a film director throughout the 1930s, making sound versions of some of his earlier successes and favouring, in addition, melodramatic stories about great historical figures, such as *Lucrèce Borgia* (*Lucrezia Borgia*, 1935) and *Un Grand Amour de Beethoven* (*The Life and Loves of Beethoven*, 1936). However, he now lacked the control he had once had over his work and though he was active into the 1960s – with *Austerlitz* (1960) and *Cyrano et D'Artagnan* (1963) – his chosen mode of colour spectacle achieved only limited success.

Surviving into his 90s, Abel Gance saw his true status as one of the major successors to GRIFFITH finally and universally recognized. Kevin Brownlow's persistent advocacy of his work, which culminated in the restoration of a virtually complete, three-screen print of his epic masterpiece *Napoléon*, has revealed the true splendours of this work to a new generation of filmgoers. In many ways the late silent era when Gance was at his peak is one of the most difficult periods of all film history: our view of it is hampered by inadequate prints, incompleteness of material, the lack of proper musical accompaniment, and alien rhythms and often melodramatic acting style. The viewings of *Napoléon* arranged by Brownlow confirm that the emotional and melodramatic excesses of Gance's masterpiece are far outweighed by its technical ingenuity and bravura cutting style. RPA

R. Jeanne & C. Ford, *Abel Gance* (Paris, 1963); K. Brownlow, *The Parade's Gone By* (London, 1968).

Gandhi, Indira, *née* Priyadarshini (b. Allahabad, Uttar Pradesh, India, 19.11.1917). Indian minister of broadcasting and information (1964–6); prime minister (1966–77, 1979–). Daughter of NEHRU; no relation to the Mahatma GANDHI. After having been condemned for electoral malpractice by the Indian High Court and barred from office for six years in 1975, Mrs Gandhi succeeded in translating her personal charisma and very considerable gains in the 1971 elections into what appeared to be an unconstitutional dictatorship based on a tacit alliance with the Indian Communist party, the arrest of political opponents under the Maintenance of Internal Security Act, and the assumption by legislation, passed with support from her communist allies through a cowed Lok Sabha, of quasi-dictatorial powers. Misconstruction of the mood of the Indian people led her in 1976 to submit herself to a general election in which she was defeated and lost her seat in the Lok Sabha. The new government, however, did not dare risk public confrontation with her at once, despite the evidence of unconstitutional practice produced by a judicial commission against both her and her son, Sanjit Gandhi. Their own unity and command of the Lok Sabha disintegrated quickly after the death of their leader Moranji Desai in 1979, leaving the way open for Mrs Gandhi to translate her still enormous popular following into a triumphant re-election at the head of a new parliamentary majority in January 1980. With the controversial influence of Sanjit Gandhi removed by his death in an air accident (June 1980) Mrs Gandhi has continued to govern India without any serious challenge to her power. DCW

Gandhi, Mahatma (i.e. 'Great Soul'), ps. of Mohandas Karamchand Gandhi (b. Porbandar, Gujarat, India, 2.10.1869; d. Delhi, 30.1.1948). Leader of the Indian National Congress (1915–48) and father of Indian independence. London-trained barrister who developed a system of passive resistance while in the Transvaal (1907–14) against the Transvaal government's policy of discrimination towards the Indian minority. On his return to India in 1915 he began to adapt the methods of Indian society to political purposes, making himself the leader of a mass movement by becoming a gurulike figure living a life of total poverty and abstinence, dressing only in a loincloth of handwoven cloth and sandals, insisting on the abandonment of western for Indian dress, preaching the boycott of British goods, resorting to Indian village methods of production and 'satyagraha' (nonviolent civil disobedience), replying to his repeated arrests by the British authorities (in 1922, 1930, 1933 and 1942) by hunger strikes. Inevitably, Gandhi's control over the communal violence always latent in Indian society was less than complete and his campaigns of civil disobedience were accompanied by terrorist outrages, riots and loss of life, awakening angry accusations of hypocrisy. When the British sought Congress cooperation in the face of a possible Japanese invasion of India (the Cripps mission, 1942), Gandhi held to his belief that nonviolence could defeat the Japanese, despite their lack of the inhibitions derived from English-speaking public morality. This belief, fortunately for the Indians, was never tested in practice. Gandhi's conviction in 1946 –7 that Indian independence could only be achieved at the cost of partition, and of recognition of Indian Muslim separation in the form of Pakistan, led to his assassination in 1948 by a young Hindu fanatic. To millions worldwide he represented not only an Asiatic revulsion against western urban mechanized civilization based on an idealization of the simple virtues of Indian village communal life, but also the 'true soul' of India. The alternative view is that he delayed the modernization and industrialization of India, and the reduction of environmental destruction through overpopulation, agricultural malpractice and medico-social ignorance, for two more generations. DCW

R. N. Iyer, *The Moral and Political Thought of Mahatma Gandhi* (Oxford, 1973).

Garbo, Greta Louisa Gustafsson (b. Stockholm, Sweden, 18.9.1906; naturalized American citizen, 1951). Swedish/American film actress, brought to Hollywood by her Swedish mentor Mauritz Stiller, who had directed her in *Gösta berlings saga* (*The Atonement of Gösta Berling*, 1924). An enigmatic quality distinguished her from other Hollywood beauties. She was not seductive: more women than men liked her. But in scenes of love she commanded the screen: one felt the presence of passion in *Love* (1927) and *The Flesh and the Devil* (1927). Her voice, faintly husky, assisted in *Anna Christie* (1930) in the transition from silence to sound. Hollywood fostered her aloofness: 'Garbo Talks!' was the cry; it was as if some remote idol had spoken. The atmosphere of reverence accompanied her through the 1930s: *Mata Hari* (1931), *Grand Hotel* (1932), *Queen Christina* (1933), *Camille* (1934). The films were romances with a note of tragedy, but except in *Anna Karenin* (1935) she was never given a role equal to her gifts. At the end of the decade the mood changed: 'Garbo Laughs!' was the slogan for *Ninotchka* (1939). But after a second and less successful comedy she retired, refusing all inducements to return to the cinema, to lead a private life always the object of curiosity, and leaving behind her a dazzling image to which the word deathless seems not inappropriate. DP

A. Walker, *Garbo* (London, 1980).

García Lorca, Federico, see LORCA, FEDERICO GARCÍA.

García Márquez, Gabriel (b. Aracataca, Colombia, 6.3.1928). Colombian novelist; with CORTÁZAR, VARGAS LLOSA and FUENTES, responsible for putting the Spanish-American novel on the international map. Best known for the 'magic realism' of *Cien años de soledad* (Buenos Aires, 1967; tr. G. Rabassa, *One Hundred Years of Solitude*, London, 1970), a reworking of life in tropical Macondo (a mythically enhanced Aracataca), in which realistic and fantastic elements coexist in a lyrical – and highly literary – recreation of the archetypal workings of the rural *mestizo* mind, trapped in a cyclical vision of time. European readers fail to appreciate the high degree of realism (and consequently of relevance to real-life Colombian affairs) in the invention of this world, while Latin Americans dwell on its exploitation of literary echoes and its connections with the fantasies of BORGES or FAULKNER's Yoknapatawpha County. With hindsight, García Márquez's earlier works can all be seen as anticipations of *Cien años*, gradually building up the Macondo environment and atmosphere, but *La hojarasca* (Bogotá, 1955; tr. G. Rabassa, in *Leaf Storm and Other Stories*, London, 1972) and *El coronel no tiene quien le escriba* (Medellín, 1961; tr. J. S. Bernstein, in *No One Writes to the Colonel, and Other Stories*, NY, 1968) are haunting in their own right. Structural and linguistic experimentation has dominated García Márquez's writing since *Cien años*, the outstanding work being the yet more fantastic *El otoño del patriarca* (Barcelona, 1975; tr. G. Rabassa, *The Autumn of the Patriarch*, NY, 1976), the strangest novel of dictatorship since *El Señor Presidente* (1946) by ASTURIAS. García Márquez's last novel prior to his receiving the Nobel prize in 1982 was *Crónica de una muerte anunciada* (Barcelona, 1981; tr. G. Rabassa, *Chronicle of a Death Foretold*, London, 1982). RP-M

D. P. Gallagher, *Modern Latin American Literature* (Oxford, 1973); G. H. McMurray, *Gabriel García Márquez* (NY, 1977).

Garner, Alan (b. Congleton, Ches., UK, 17.10.1934). British writer of novels for young people. Garner's first children's book *The Weirdstone of Brisingamen* (London, 1960) is set in his native Cheshire in the Alderley Edge area. The story depicts two modern children who engage ancient forces of myth and magic in the age-old fight between good and evil. Two following books *The Moon of Gomrath* (London, 1963) and *Elidor* (London, 1965) established Garner as a major writer of children's fantasy/allegory. His most widely appreciated and influential book is *The Owl Service* (London, 1967), winner of the Library Association's Carnegie Medal and the Guardian Award for children's fiction, in which Garner broke new ground in linking the emergence of adolescent sexuality and implicit class tension with the violence of themes embodied in Welsh mythology. The layering of stories and the coexistence of present and past in *Red Shift* (London, 1973) endows this highly complex novel with vision and energy. At a simple level, *The Stone Book* quartet (4 vols, London, 1976–8), being a fictional history of the significance of craftsmanship and of 'belonging' through generations, is striking, and among his reworkings of folklore the finely wrought collection of Celtic stories *The Lad of Gad* (London, 1980) is noteworthy.   JMM

N. Philop, *A Fine Anger: the Work of Alan Garner* (London, 1981).

Garnier, Tony (b. Lyons, Rhône, France, 13.8.1869; d. La Bedoule, 19.1.1948). French architect and urban planner. While a student at the Beaux Arts School of Architecture in Paris, Garnier was awarded the prestigious Prix de Rome but disappointed his teachers by renouncing the study of antique buildings and concentrating instead on the design of an industrial city. The city was to be divided according to function into areas which could evolve independently, ignoring the strict overall symmetry and monumentality characteristic of the Beaux Arts school. The project was eventually exhibited in Paris in 1904 despite disapproval from his professors. The scheme went into considerable detail and included planning of transportation and sewerage systems. Much attention was paid to the careful

zoning of housing at a fairly low density, and this concern for the well-being of the worker was probably influenced by Garnier's contemporary Emile Zola. The buildings themselves were to be constructed of reinforced concrete in a style which owed little to the past, and in this rational treatment of the material Garnier's ideas were close to those of PERRET who had studied with him under Julien Guadet, the professor of architectural theory.

Garnier eventually succeeded in putting many of his theoretical principles into practice when he became city architect of his home town of Lyons and collaborated with the radical mayor Edouard Herriot. Some of the buildings designed under his aegis were the cattle market and abattoirs (1909), the municipal sports centre (1913) and the Etats Unis district housing development (1920).   NW

D. Wiebenson, *Tony Garnier: the Cité Industrielle* (NY, 1969).

Garrod, Archibald Edward (b. London, UK, 25.11.1857; d. London, 28.3.1936). British physician and pioneer of human biochemical genetics. The son of an eminent clinician who himself worked in chemical pathology, Garrod trained in medicine at Oxford and at St Bartholomew's Hospital in London. Apart from a break during WW1, for his services in which he was made KCMG in 1919, his professional career was spent in those two places. Although his interests lay mostly in the practice of clinical medicine, he broke new ground in his early studies of such conditions as alkaptonuria and albinism, and in 1908 summarized his findings in a series of Croonian lectures to the Royal College of Physicians. Entitled *Inborn Errors of Metabolism* (London, 1909), these played a major part in founding human genetics as a science of value to the clinician and were theoretically much in advance of their time. At the turn of the century medicine was largely preoccupied with infectious disease, and Garrod's establishment of a genetic pathology was therefore important. For genetics his demonstration that defects attributable to single genes could be biochemically simple was of the greatest significance.

Garrod served as a director of the medical unit at St Bartholomew's Hospital and later (1920–7) as regius professor of medicine in Oxford.   DRN

Gaudi, Antoni (b. Reus, Tarragona, Spain, 25.6.1852; d. Barcelona, 10.6.1926). Spanish architect who developed a highly original three-dimensional art nouveau style. Before studying architecture in Barcelona Gaudi served an apprenticeship with a blacksmith which later enabled him to design, and sometimes to make, the highly elaborate ironwork which was incorporated into many of his buildings. Emerging as a young architect into an atmosphere of 19c historicism and being highly nationalistic and religious, Gaudi drew much of his early inspiration from the Gothic style. One of his first buildings the Casa Vicens (1883–5) is Gothic in form but owes much to Moorish influences in its decoration. Every available surface is covered in a plethora of multicoloured tiles, a medium which characterizes much of Gaudi's work. His lifelong patron Count Evsebi Güell was a textile manufacturer who gave him access to his library which contained the pattern books of William Morris and the writings of John Ruskin, and Gaudi shared with these men the belief that decorative forms should originate from nature. These ideas were at first expressed as surface decoration but they later took on a much deeper structural significance. In the Güell Park (started 1900), for instance, Gaudi transformed a barren hillside into a series of walkways, grottoes and sinuous retaining walls, in which supporting elements were an expression of his static diagrams, determined by the loads to be carried to earth. His best-known work is the Barcelona church of Sagrada Familia (1884 –1926) which became less recognizably Gothic and more fantastic as its filigree of pierced sculpture progressed. From 1910 until his death Gaudi worked exclusively on this church, eventually living in a nearby small room in order to work on plaster casts of details and models with which to calculate its structural behaviour.   NW

J. J. Sweeney & J. L. Sert, *Antoni Gaudi* (London, 1960).

Gaudier-Brzeska, Henri, *né* Henri Gaudier (b. Saint-Jean-de-Braye, Loiret, France, 4.10.1891; d. Neuville-Saint-Vaast, Pas-de-Calais, 5.6.1915). French sculptor. Gaudier-Brzeska began to make sculpture in 1910. A year later he settled in England and soon after became friendly with HULME and Wyndham LEWIS. Ezra POUND, of whom he made a masterful portrait sculpture, was a consistent supporter of his work. He was briefly associated with FRY's Omega workshops, and exhibited with both the London Group and the vorticists, contributing to the latter's magazine *Blast*. In 1915 he joined the French army and was killed in action. The sculptures he made during his five-year career (many of which are stone carvings based on animal forms) reflect characteristic early modernist concerns, e.g. an interest in African and other primitive art; a sculptural reductionism, in the manner of BRANCUSI; and a preoccupation with the 'dynamic' forms of machines. The critical wisdom used to be that Gaudier-Brzeska had died too young to develop a fully mature style of his own. In recent years, however, his reputation has risen consistently, so that it is now recognized that he successfully combined a 'modernist' style with a mastery of the traditional concerns and techniques of sculpture.   PF

H. S. Ede, *Savage Messiah* (London, 1931); R. Secrétain, *Gaudier-Brzeska* (Paris, 1979).

de Gaulle, Charles André Joseph Marie (b. Lille, Nord, France, 22.11.1890; d. Colombey-les-Deux-Eglises, Haute-Marne, 9.11.1970). President of France. General in the French army; under-minister for war (1940); leader of the French movement in London (1940–3) during the German occupation of France, then of the Committee of National Liberation in Algiers (1943–4); head of the provisional French government (1944). With the liberation of France de Gaulle was elected provisional president (1945), only to resign within 10 weeks. He returned to become head of the 'Government of National Safety' (1958) and president of the French Fifth Republic under a new constitution (1958–65, 1965–9). In French domestic affairs he is to be seen as perhaps the most formidable proponent in modern French history of the somewhat un-French doctrine of a strong elected executive able to manage and dominate an elected parliament. He was often accused of fascist or Napoleonic ambitions by his opponents in France for whom parliamentary absolutism was the only acceptable form of democracy, an accusation convincingly disproved by his abrupt resignations in 1947 and 1969 when he was clearly unable to carry the French people with him. In representing French interests in the world he was an impossible ally and a difficult friend, by reason of his conviction of the continuity of French cultural greatness and its embodiment in himself, especially against the machinations and combinations of the Anglo–American cultural alliance; this he persisted in seeing as a unity, confronting it at one time with his francophone attempt to assert the unity of French-speaking peoples: at another with Franco–German cooperation (in the era of ADENAUER); at another with a kind of cultural pan-Latinism directed towards Italy and the Hispanic-speaking peoples; at other times, notably in December 1944 and in 1965, with attempts to revive the pre-1914 Franco–Russian alliance. De Gaulle viewed the world of the mid-20c through concepts which dated from his pre-1914 adolescence and youth. His military theories, on the reputation of which he had attained office in 1940, involved not only mechanized warfare but the establishment of a long-term elite army, a concept entirely at odds with the French popular tradition of the *levée en masse*. But from 1940 he regarded himself with some justice as the embodiment of the aspirations of the French people, an incarnation of the *volonté générale* of France, past, present and to come. De Gaulle wrote two series of memoirs: *Mémoires de Guerre* (2 vols, Paris, 1954; *War Memoirs*, London, 1955) and *Mémoires d'espoir* (2 vols, Paris, 1970–1; *Memoirs of Hope*: vol. 1, *Renewal, 1958–62*; vol. 2, *Endeavour, 1960–*, London, 1971). DCW

Gause, Georgyi Frantsevitch (b. Moscow, Russia, 27.12.1910). Russian microbiolo-

gist. He graduated with BSc at Moscow University in 1931, and DBiolSc in 1940. Until 1942 he was lecturer, later professor, at the Timiriasev Institute for Biological Research, University of Moscow, where he worked on the structure of populations of micro-organisms in culture. In 1932 he published what has become known as the principle of competitive exclusion, based on experimental work done with micro-organisms in culture. This was the same year in which LOTKA put forward the same principle based on theoretical calculations. Gause used mixed cultures of yeast species in his experiments, and also *Paramecium* cultures. Many of the data published from these experiments and experiments on predation have been used by other ecologists in the formation and testing of stochastic models of the interaction of populations. In 1934 he published *The Struggle for Existence* (Baltimore). In 1942 Gause was appointed deputy, and later director, of the New Antibiotics Research Institute, Moscow. Since that time his work has been concerned with the development and effects of new antibiotics. He was awarded the Stalin prize in 1946. RTi

Gay, Peter (b. Berlin, Germany, 20.6.1923). American historian of ideas. From 1947 to 1969 he taught at Columbia University, moving to Yale in 1969. In his monumental two-volume work *The Enlightenment: an Interpretation* Gay offers a comprehensive synthesis of this major phase of European thought. Rescuing the Enlightenment from both its uncritical admirers and its blind critics, Gay presents it not as a homogeneous body of doctrine but as the network of loosely related and partly overlapping conceptions and aims of the *philosophes*, 'a family of intellectuals united by a single style of thinking'. In the first volume, subtitled *The Rise of Modern Paganism* (London, 1970) and devoted to the education of the philosophes and their construction of their own past, Gay presents their experience as a dialectical struggle to assimilate, and to play off against each other, the two pasts they had inherited, Christian and pagan, and thus to win their independence. In the second volume, subtitled

The Science of Freedom (London, 1970), Gay shows what the philosophes made of the freedom they won, their 'recovery of nerve'. He stresses their rupture with the classical age, and exhibits the ruling model of Newtonian science, purged of Newton's deism, which was to serve them in all realms of knowledge and action: psychology, aesthetics, the social sciences, history, and politics. For all his skill and learning, Gay has not managed to satisfy all scholars that the Enlightenment followed such tidy dialectical schemas; and not all share his optimism that we can 'use the Enlightenment' as a source of practical guidance. Gay's first published work was *The Dilemma of Democratic Socialism: Eduard Bernstein's Challenge to Marx* (NY, 1952), and in addition to two forerunners of his major work on the Enlightenment, *The Party of Humanity* (London, 1964) and *Voltaire's Politics: the Poet as Realist* (Princeton, 1959), he has published two more recent studies of modern German history: *Weimar Culture* (London, 1969), and *Freud, Jews and other Germans* (NY, 1978).   RNH

Geddes, Patrick (b. Ballater, Grampian, UK, 20.10.1854; d. Montpellier, Hérault, France, 17.4.1932). British biologist, social reformer and pioneer in urban and regional planning. Drawing upon his early studies in biology under T. H. Huxley and his reading in sociology (especially the work of Le Play), psychology, philosophy and the French school of human geography, he created a new basis for addressing problems of society and the environment. He showed that by disregarding the traditional boundaries between disciplines, complex urban problems might be better understood. He argued that town planning was a discipline in its own right, different in nature from the bodies of knowledge on which it was based. He introduced into modern planning practice concepts of the city region, of regional planning and of planning method. Among Geddes's most influential publications were *City Development* (Edinburgh, 1904) and *Cities in Evolution* (London, 1915, ⁴1968). The Outlook Tower in Edinburgh, established in 1892, was a permanent exhibition of his planning and other interests, and an expression of his role as an educationalist.   BM

P. Kitchen, *A Most Unsettling Person: an Introduction to the Ideas and Life of Patrick Geddes* (London, 1975).

de Geer, Sten (b. Stockholm, Sweden, 26.4.1886; d. Göteborg, 2.6.1933). Swedish geographer. He lectured at Stockholm University from 1911 to 1928 and then moved to Göteborg. Most of his writing was done during his Stockholm years: after publishing a number of papers on rivers and harbours, in 1919 he issued his famous Atlas showing the distribution of population over the whole of Sweden according to a census of 1917 on the 1:500,000 scale. From 1912 he produced papers on ports and on cities, and in 1918 he published a plan for a new administrative regionalization of Sweden, using watersheds as boundaries wherever possible and recognizing the country's Norrland as marked by heavy winter snow, north of the more favoured, central area with its oak forests and fruit trees, in which Stockholm lies. He was eager to explore new ideas, including the racial geography and the broad concepts of political geography fashionable in the 1920s. In 1926, following an American visit, he wrote a study of the vast developments in favoured areas of the USA, especially from the Atlantic to the Mississippi. De Geer was at once practical and enterprising, simultaneously aware of the value of local study and of broad generalization.   TWF

T. W. Freeman, 'Sten de Geer: a practical geographer', in *The Geographer's Craft* (Manchester, 1967).

Geertz, Clifford (b. San Francisco, Calif., USA, 23.8.1926). American social and cultural anthropologist. His work has been influenced by the approaches of the sociologists Max WEBER and PARSONS and the phenomenologist SCHUTZ. Fieldwork in Java and Bali in the 1950s on the formation of new states and socioeconomic development led to *The Religion of Java* (Glencoe, Ill., 1960), *Peddlers and Princes* (Chicago, 1963) and *Agricultural Involution* (Berkeley, Calif., 1964). A comparative interest in

Islam as well as trading and market forms continued with fieldwork in a Moroccan town (1965–71). In *Islam Observed* (New Haven, 1968) a concern with symbol and metaphor is dominant. He now views society as a text whose many levels the anthropologist interprets as a critic might a novel (see also *Negra: the Theater State in Nineteenth Century Bali*, Princeton, 1980). This interpretive approach, of which he is a leading exponent, produces an anthropology very different from that of, for example, structural-functionalists or MARXists, and is part of the division over the nature of the discipline that has grown stronger since the late 1950s. His writing, which is known for its literary qualities, strives to balance an acute sense of the meanings of social worlds with a conviction that social relations have an observable existence independent of the worldviews of participants and anthropologists alike (see *The Interpretation of Cultures: Selected Essays*, NY, 1973). He has been professor of social science at the Institute for Advanced Study at Princeton since 1970.   MDCG

Gehlen, Arnold (b. Leipzig, Germany [now East Germany], 29.1.1904; d. Aachen, N. Rhine-Westphalia, West Germany, 30.1.1976). German philosopher and sociologist. Gehlen is one of the most influential exponents of philosophical anthropology, which seeks to develop a philosophy of man in biological, social and cultural terms. In his major work *Der Mensch: seine Natur und seine Stellung in der Welt* [Man: his nature and place in the world] (Leipzig, 1940, ⁹1972) he presents a coherent picture, both empirical and philosophical, of man and his powers, and of his peculiar place in the world. Following Herder, Gehlen sees man's distinctive characteristics as being his physical puniness, his biologically unspecialized sense organs, his lack of the full range of powerful instincts that enable other animals to fit neatly into the scheme of things, and his possession of intelligence and imagination whereby he must create for himself what is given by nature to other creatures: namely, the means of his survival – language, myth, social and cultural institutions, tools and practical techniques.

Gehlen rejects metaphysics and ontology, and the traditional philosophical dichotomies between mind and body, theory and practice; and sees truth and values as a collective cultural product embodied in institutions. In his conception of the intimate links between action and theoretical truth he shows the influence of Fichte and of pragmatists like John DEWEY; and in his recognition of a form of intuitive, nonscientific, irrational truth, upon which institutions rest, he continues a German tradition stretching back to Hamann and Jacobi. His pessimism, anti-intellectualism and regressive anti-individualism, and his belief in archaic values enshrined in the authoritarian structures of church, state and law, expounded with great philosophical persuasiveness, make him one of the most serious and disturbing conservative thinkers of our time. Other important works are: *Urmensch und Spätkultur* [Archaic man and advanced culture] (Bonn, 1956); *Die Seele in technischen Zeitalter* [The soul in the age of technology] (Neurvied, 1960); *Moral und Hypermoral* [Morals and hypermorals] (Neurvied, 1965).   RNH

F. Jonas, *Die Institutionenlehre Arnold Gehleus* (Tübingen, 1966).

Gelfand, Izrail Moiseyevich (b. Okna [now Odessa Oblast], Russia, 2.9.1913). Russian mathematician. In the late 1930s he developed the theory of commutative normed rings (Banach algebras) which are of crucial importance in functional analysis and, increasingly, in modern physics. Then he turned his attention, with his collaborators, to the representation theory of locally compact groups, starting with the LORENTZ group (the allowable transformations in special relativity theory). His work in this area unifies the treatment of the classical Lie groups, ubiquitous in physics, with their analogues in algebraic geometry. He also developed integral geometry, which studies the transformation by integrals of functions on a given space in geometric terms. This technique has implications for his work on group representations, as does his third major area of interest, the cohomology of infinite dimensional Lie algebras. Gelfand's principal contributions are thus generalizing and extending classical mathematics by the astute but elegant use of infinite dimensional yet geometric ideas. For more than 20 years he was the director of the Institute of Applied Mathematics of the USSR Academy of Sciences.   JJG

Gell-Mann, Murray (b. New York, USA, 15.9.1929). American physicist educated at Yale University and MIT. His initial work in 1953 led to the introduction of a new label or quantum number, 'strangeness', which in turn yielded a classification scheme for the elementary particles and the interactions they experienced. This classification had a special kind of symmetry which in group theory (the mathematical technique which deals with symmetry operations) is called SU(3) and this led to the prediction of the Ω-particle, spectacularly discovered in 1964. Subsequently, he (and G. Zweig) introduced the idea of fractionally charged particles, the quarks, which formed the basis for the SU(3) symmetry. These quarks are now regarded as the basic ingredient of all hadrons. Gell-Mann's other outstanding contribution came in the introduction of currents (with FEYNMAN) to weak interactions. Subsequently, he was responsible for the development of current algebras. His work has emphasized the importance and practical application of group theory in particle physics. He received the Nobel prize in 1969.   RJC

Genet, Jean (b. Paris, France, 19.12.1910). French novelist and dramatist. Genet's literary career began when this illegitimate son of a French prostitute wrote *Notre-Dame-des-Fleurs* (Paris, 1949; tr. B. Frechtman, *Our Lady of the Flowers*, London, 1964) in Fresnes prison in 1942 on the sheets of brown paper given to French convicts to make up into bags. The novel celebrates crime, betrayal and homosexuality; it was privately printed by Marc Barbézat in 1943. Until the 1960s Genet's novels remained officially banned in Britain and the USA. *Miracle de la Rose* (Paris; tr. B. Frechtman, *Miracle of the Rose*, London, 1965), an account of Genet's

childhood in the reformatory at Mettray and of his adult experiences in Fontevrault prison, followed in 1946. It, too, seeks to glorify crime, but the reader of its luxuriant, rhetorical prose style is frequently brought down to earth by realistic reminders of how uncomfortable prison is and how dirty and stupid prisoners are. In 1947 Genet's play *Les Bonnes* (tr. B. Frechtman, *The Maids*, London, 1957) was produced in Paris by Louis Jouvet. It was followed by *Le Balcon* (tr. B. Frechtman, *The Balcony*, London, 1958), first produced at the Arts Theatre in London in 1957 because of censorship difficulties in France; *Les Nègres* (tr. B. Frechtman, *The Blacks*, London, 1960), produced in Paris in 1958; and by *Les Paravents* (tr. B. Frechtman, *The Screens*, London, 1963), which again met with some censorship problems but was eventually performed at the state-subsidized Odéon-Théâtre de France in 1966.

In 1952 SARTRE analysed and exalted Genet as an existentialist rebel who had failed in his ambition to achieve absolute evil in life but succeeded in realizing it through art. Genet's novels and plays are nihilistic in their total denial of all moral and political values, but fascinating in their imagery and exploitation of avant-garde theatrical devices. Their popular success in the 1960s reflected the greater tolerance which western society had begun to show to criminals and homosexuals, a tolerance which Genet affected to deplore. His most openly autobiographical work *Le Journal du Voleur* (Paris, 1949; tr. B. Frechtman, *The Thief's Journal*, London, 1965) stands comparison with the better picaresque novels of the past, and offers some interesting details about homosexuality.   PMWT

J.-P. Sartre, *Saint-Genet, actor and martyr*, tr. B. Frechtman (London, 1953); R. Coe, *The Vision of Jean Genet* (London, 1968).

Gentile, Giovanni (b. Castelvetrano, Sicily, Italy, 30.5.1875; d. Florence, Tuscany, 15.4.1944). Italian philosopher and educator. As a result of a successful two-pronged attack on the power of the church and the impact of materialistic policies on the education of the young, Gentile seemed eminently suitable for adoption as education spokesman of fascist Italy. A distinguished historian of philosophy, the proponent of pseudo-Hegelian 'actualism' for his theory of the supremacy of the 'ethical state' subsuming the individual, he was also considered the philosopher of Italian fascism. Gentile was prolific in the production of books and papers (e.g. *L'atto del pensare come atto pure* [The act of thinking as pure act], Rome, 1912; *Introduzione alla filosofia* [Introduction to philosophy], Rome, 1933), and held chairs in philosophy in the universities of Palermo, Pisa and Rome. In 1923 he became MUSSOLINI's minister of public instruction and shortly afterwards president of the National Fascist Institute of Culture. The latter office he combined with planning and producing the new *Enciclopedia italiana* [Italian encyclopedia] (35 vols, Milan, 1929–37), the most significant cultural monument of the fascist period of government. While admitting religious formation was a vitally important component of a system of public education, he was opposed to direct church involvement in the organization of education or curriculum content. He became a bitter opponent of the Concordat of 1929 which, he argued, gave the church too much authority in educational provision, and fell from favour as a consequence. For Gentile, education had no objective goal beyond itself, a definition calculated to depress vocational, sectarian and 'progressive' interests. In his search for ways of reconciling the authority of the teacher with the freedom of the child, he tried to moderate unacceptable fascist regimentation. He was assassinated by communist partisans after Mussolini's overthrow. VAMc

H. R. Marraro, *The New Education in Italy* (NY, 1936).

Gény, François (b. Baccarat, Meurthe-et-Moselle, France, 17.12.1861; d. Nancy, Meurthe-et-Moselle, 16.12.1959). French jurist. Starting from the standpoint, expressed in his *Méthode d'interprétation et sources en droit privé positif* [Method of interpretation and sources in positive private law] (Paris, 1899), of challenging the accepted view that the task of the judge and lawyer was interpretation of the French code according to strict logical principles, Gény showed that interpretation required investigation of the realities of social life, and that regard must also be had to custom, authority and tradition developed by decisions and doctrine and free scientific research. In many areas the judge had freedom to choose between different solutions. In his later work *Science et technique en droit privé positif* [Knowledge and technique in positive private law] (4 vols, Paris, 1914–24) he developed a complete legal philosophy. *Science* was knowledge of the social realities which supply law with its social material; *technique* was the lawyer's creative action. Within the field of the social matter, Gény developed a theory of natural law as the basis of any positive law. His work did much to cast new light on the creative role of the judge in the legal process, even in a system of codified law. DMW

B. A. Wortley, 'François Gény' in W. I. Jennings (ed.), *Modern Theories of Law* (Oxford, 1933).

George, Stefan Anton (b. Büdesheim, nr Bingen, Rhineland-Palatinate, Germany, 12.7.1868; d. Locarno, Ticino, Switzerland, 4.12.1933). German poet. George was the son of a vintner; he studied languages, philosophy and art history in Paris, Munich and Berlin, and founded the literary journal *Blätter für die Kunst* (1892). In Paris he met the Mallarmé circle and the symbolists, many of whose works he translated. His works were first published privately. Each book is a complex structure of poems built upon a central theme, stressing mood, expressive clarity and tonal values. The main works are: *Hymnen* [Odes] (Berlin, 1890), *Pilgerfahrten* [Pilgrimages] (Berlin, 1891), *Algabal* (Berlin, 1892), *Die Bücher der Hirten- und Preisgedichte, der Sagen und Sänge und der hängenden Gärten* [The books of eclogues and eulogies, of legends and lays, and of the hanging gardens] (Berlin, 1895), and *Der Siebente Ring* [The seventh ring] (Berlin, 1907) in which he celebrated his love for 'Maximin' (the poet Maximilian Kronberger, who died aged 16) as an apotheosis of spirit (tr. O. Marx & E. Morwitz in *The Works of Stefan George*, Chapel Hill, NC, 1949).

George wrote for a specific readership. He saw the poet as a priest-king whose duty was to guard and pass on the essence of the cultural heritage. He never sought a general public, but addressed himself to his disciples, the initiates of the 'George-Kreis'. He sought to restore language and humanity to essential priority and endowed words with mystical properties, creating his own typography (with the help of Melchior Lechter) to stress their difference from everyday usage. His aestheticism and his belief in *l'art pour l'art* led him and his followers to anticipate a new age of beauty and culture, an 'empire of the spirit'. His works *Der Stern des Bundes* (Berlin, 1914) and *Das Neue Reich* (Berlin, 1926) (tr. O. Marx & E. Morwitz, *The Star of the Covenant* and *The Kingdom Come*, Chapel Hill, NC, 1949), which celebrated this imminent era, were adopted by the Nazi cultural propagandists. George was not a Nazi sympathizer; he refused their offer of the leadership of the new Academy of Arts, would not allow any public celebration of his 65th birthday under the Nazis, and went into voluntary exile in Switzerland (1933). The impression he made on such disciples as RILKE, the literary historian Gundolf and Count von Stauffenberg (who tried to assassinate HITLER on 20.7.1944) may have influenced German thought more than his poetical works.   JHC

E. K. Bennett, *Stefan George* (Cambridge, 1954).

Germer, Lester Halbert (b. Chicago, Ill., USA, 10.10.1896). American physicist who in collaboration with DAVISSON discovered the diffraction of electrons by a crystal of nickel, thus establishing their wave nature. He worked at the Bell Telephone Laboratories and studied thermionics, the erosion of metals and contact physics.   PEH

Gershwin, George (b. New York, USA, 26.9.1898; d. Hollywood, Calif., 11.7.1937). American composer. Gershwin was the most versatile and musically sophisticated of a brilliant genera-

tion of composers writing for the Broadway musical stage in the 1920s and 1930s. He wrote a great number of songs to lyrics by his brother Ira, and he was involved in such successful shows as *Lady be Good* (1924), *Oh, Kay!* (1926) and *Funny Face* (1927). Yet he also craved acceptance as a composer of 'serious' music, and he applied his jazz-tinged style to more ambitious ends in his *Rhapsody in Blue* for piano and orchestra (1924) and his opera *Porgy and Bess* (1935).   PG

I. Gershwin, *Lyrics on Several Occasions* (NY, 1959); R. Payne, *Gershwin* (NY, 1960).

Geyl, Pieter Catharinus Arie (b. Dordrecht, S. Holland, The Netherlands, 15.12.1887; d. Utrecht, 31.12.1966). Dutch historian. Geyl's reputation rests primarily on his *Geschiedenis van de Nederlandsche Stam* [History of the Dutch people] (3 vols, Amsterdam, 1930 –7; partially tr. in *The Revolt of the Netherlands*, London, 1932; *The Netherlands Divided*, London, 1936; *The Netherlands in the Seventeenth Century*, part 2, London, 1964), especially vol. 1, which argued, contrary to the orthodox view of the episode, that it was the whole Netherlands, not just the northern provinces, which rebelled against Philip II, and that the north retained its independence simply because it was in a better geographical position to resist the Spanish forces. Geyl was a 'Great Netherlander' who considered the split between Holland and the Flemish-speaking parts of Belgium a 'disaster' for the 'Netherlands race' (*Nederlandse stam*); he frequently addressed public meetings in favour of reunion. He was also deeply interested in the history of historical writing. His *Napoleon voor en tegen* (Utrecht, 1946; *Napoleon, For and Against*, London, 1949) related changing interpretations of Napoleon's career to the changing preoccupations of the French in general and French historians in particular, concluding that there was no such thing as a correct interpretation and that history is 'an argument without end'. Similar views inform his *Debates with Historians* (London, 1955), which also takes TOYNBEE to task for being oversystematic, and *Encounters in His-*

tory (London, 1963). Few continental historians have been so well known in Britain as Geyl, who lived in London (1914–36) as a journalist and as professor of Dutch history at University College. UPB

Giacometti, Alberto (b. Borgonovo, Graubünden, Switzerland, 10.10.1901; d. Chur, Graubünden, 11.1.1966). Swiss sculptor and painter; son of the Swiss postimpressionist painter Giovanni Giacometti. He settled in Paris in 1922 and studied sculpture for three years under Bourdelle. Between 1925 and 1935 he worked from imagination in a variety of styles, at first mainly cubist, then surrealist. His surrealist sculptures include open cage-like constructions, works with movable parts, a kind of landscape which is also a head lying down, and a woman strangled, with her throat cut. Although he became one of the foremost surrealist sculptors, he was expelled from the surrealist group in 1935, when he began to make sculpture from nature again. There followed a difficult transitional period, when he worked obsessively from a model year after year, making heads which became smaller and smaller until they sometimes disappeared into dust. This came to an end in 1946–7 when he started to make very tall and thin figures, and established his characteristic style. Modelled on slender armatures to be cast in bronze, his late sculptures are mostly upright, standing figures rooted to the base, motionless and frontal, and as hieratic as idols, though he also made a number of portrait busts and a few works which include several figures such as sculptures with two or more figures walking in space. Just as his sculptures have almost no volume, so the paintings of still lifes, landscapes and especially portraits made in his last 18 or so years tend to be in ochres or greys and almost monochromatic. Most of his postwar works were sculpted or painted from his wife, his brother Diego, or from a few other favourite models, who posed for him day after day. Giacometti built up the forms and then destroyed them, over and over again, struggling to capture an impression so complex that it seemed to him ultimately unattainable. REA

R. Hohl, *Alberto Giacometti: Sculpture, Painting, Drawing* (London, 1972).

Giauque, William Francis (b. Niagara Falls, Ont., Canada, 12.5.1895; d. Oakland, Calif., USA, 29.5.1982). American physical chemist. Born of US parents, Giauque studied at the University of California, Berkeley, and remained on the chemistry faculty for the whole of his career. He is best known as the first person (working with D. P. MacDougall) to achieve temperatures less than one degree above the absolute zero by the method which he proposed in 1926 (although DEBYE suggested it independently), which is known as adiabatic demagnetization. The technique is first to align the elementary magnetic ions in certain crystals by a very high magnetic field at as low a temperature as possible (about one degree absolute). The crystal is then thermally isolated and the field removed. The elementary magnets will tend to become misaligned again, but this can only occur at the expense of reducing the ordinary thermal vibration of the atoms, and so the material cools. In his first experiment Giauque used a gadolinium sulphate crystal; whereas this only cooled to about 0.25 degrees above the absolute zero, within a few years other workers using the same technique attained temperatures of only a few thousandths of a degree absolute. This general method of magnetic cooling is still used for reaching the very lowest temperatures. For his pioneer work in this field Giauque was awarded the Nobel prize for chemistry in 1949. Most of Giauque's work has been concerned with low temperature phenomena, in particular the thermodynamic properties of gases and of materials containing magnetic ions. He was the first (working with H. L. Johnston) to discover the rare isotopes of oxygen, those of mass 17 and 18, in atmospheric oxygen. He was also the first to suggest using the electrical resistance of amorphous carbon (e.g. black ink) as a low temperature thermometer. During WW2 Giauque worked on the design of mobile units for the production of liquid oxygen and after 1944 on the design of high field electromagnets. HMR

Gibb, Hamilton Alexander Rosskeen (b. Alexandria, Egypt, 2.1.1895; d. Cherington, Warwicks., UK, 22.10.1971). British orientalist. Laudian professor of Arabic at Oxford (1937–55) and subsequently director of the Center for Middle Eastern Studies at Harvard, Gibb had a great influence on the way in which westerners in the mid-20c and especially the English-speaking world understood Islamic religion and society. In addition to his influence as a teacher, he edited and contributed major articles to the *Encyclopaedia of Islam* (London, 1954). But his best-known work, published jointly with Harold Bowen, was *Islamic Society and the West* (2 vols, London, 1950–7). Gibb never completed the original design of the work: the two substantial volumes dealing with Islamic society as it had developed up to the end of the 18c, when the influence of the West first began to be felt, were not followed by the study of the West's impact to which they were to have been the prolegomena. However, four publications between 1947 and 1963 express a coherent and original view of Islam: *Modern Trends in Islam* (London, 1947); 'The structure of religious thought in Islam' (1948, rep. in *Studies on the Civilization of Islam*, London, 1962); *Mohammedanism: an Historical Survey* (London, 1949); and 'An interpretation of Islamic History' (1953, rep. in *Studies*, 1962). ALCB

Gibbon, Lewis Grassic, ps. of James Leslie Mitchell (b. Grampian, UK, 12.1.1901; d. Welwyn Garden City, Herts., 7.2.1935). Scottish novelist, archaeologist and historical writer. Gibbon grew up in Arbuthnott, the Kincardineshire village he made famous as 'Kinraddie' in *A Scots Quair*, his famous trilogy (*Sunset Song*, London, 1932; *Cloud Howe*, London, 1933; *Grey Granite*, London, 1934). Chris Guthrie, his central character, grows up in rural Scotland but moves (like her creator) from country to small town, then to the city (Aberdeen), experiencing and to some extent representing her nation's anguish as WW1 is replaced by depres-

sion and spiritual poverty. Gibbon was a doctrinaire MARXist and (illogically) also something of a Scottish nationalist – without joining parties of either persuasion. He made his trilogy (televised in 1982–3) a vehicle for his political and cultural views, his distaste for a declining civilization which he analysed in 'diffusionist' terms as the decay of a system which had enslaved originally free, primitive men, systematically degrading them to the depths of the cities in the depression of the 1930s. His own experience in Aberdeen and Glasgow during WW1, in the Middle East in military service, and in Welwyn Garden City as a suburban intellectual, researching his historical books and archaeology in the British Museum and writing furiously at a variety of projects, finds eloquent expression in a flood of books (he wrote 13 in rapid succession). He died just as he was finding popular acclaim. His style (a mixture of English words, Scottish word-order and rhythm, and minimal local vocabulary) does much to emphasize the Scottish atmosphere of his fiction; his fellow-writers admired him greatly, particularly MCDIARMID, with whom he published a trenchant volume of political and literary essays *Scottish Scene* (London, 1934), which remains the best critical work on his own fiction. IC

D. F. Young, *Beyond the Sunset* (Aberdeen, 1973).

Gibbs, Josiah Willard (b. New Haven, Conn., USA, 11.2.1839; d. New Haven, 28.4.1903). American mathematical physicist. One of the founders of thermodynamics and statistical mechanics, Gibbs graduated at Yale (where his father was a professor of sacred literature) in 1858. He later studied at Paris, Berlin and Heidelberg. From 1871 until his death he held the professorship of mathematical physics at Yale – without salary for the first nine years. Among Gibbs's many contributions to science the following were outstanding: (1) He defined the thermodynamic function which he called 'free enthalpy', now more widely known as the Gibbs function. Gibbs demonstrated that the value of this function is a minimum for a system at equilibrium when the temperature and pressure are constant. (2) He enunciated the phase rule, one of the most important achievements of physical science ($P + F = C + 2$): this quantitatively defines the state of equilibrium of a system in terms of the number of phases and components of that system. (3) He underlined the importance of state variables and illustrated the power of entropy-temperature plots. (4) The powerful concept of chemical potential, which enables the condition of equilibrium of a chemical reaction to be formulated in elegantly economical terms, was introduced by him; and he further showed how the potential could be evaluated from experimental data. (5) In statistical mechanics he introduced the seminal concept of the ensemble average. *The Scientific Papers of J. Willard Gibbs* (eds, H. A. Bumstead & R. G. Van Name, NY, 1906, ²1961) continue to provide new insights into thermodynamic phenomena long after his death. An example is his anticipation of the notion of spinodal decomposition, which was 'introduced' and popularized in the metallurgical and mineralogical literature in the mid-1960s.   JMT

Gide, André-Paul-Guillaume (b. Paris, France, 22.11.1869; d. Paris, 19.2.1951). French writer. Gide wrote very good books about his sexual, religious, moral, political and literary problems. In 1893, when convalescing from tuberculosis, he visited Algeria, and, after meeting Oscar Wilde, discovered he was a homosexual. He exalted physical pleasure and freedom from moral constraint in *Les Nourritures terrestres* (Paris, 1897; tr. D. Bussy, *Fruits of the Earth*, London, 1949) when he had – perhaps unwisely – already married his cousin Madeleine Rondeaux in 1895. He called illicit sensuality into question in *L'Immoraliste* (Paris, 1902; tr. D. Bussy, *The Immoralist*, NY, 1930), but was equally critical of his Protestant upbringing, attacking its excessive austerity and hostility to sex in *La Porte étroite* (Paris, 1909; tr. D. Bussy, *Strait is the Gate*, London, 1924), and its tendency towards hypocrisy and self-deception in *La Symphonie pastorale* (Paris, 1919; tr. D. Bussy, *Two Symphonies*, London, 1949). In 1924 he openly defended homosexuality in *Cory-*

don (Paris; tr. F. Beach, NY, 1950) and in 1926 hinted at some of its charms in his most ambitious and self-conscious novel *Les Faux-Monnayeurs* (Paris; tr. D. Bussy, *The Coiners*, London, 1950). He attacked colonialism in *Voyage au Congo* (Paris, 1927; tr. D. Bussy, *Travels in the Congo*, London, 1930) and *Le Retour du Tchad* [Return from Tchad] (Paris, 1928); was attracted by communism to the point of joining the party in 1934, but denounced it in *Retour de l'U.R.S.S.* (Paris, 1936; tr. D. Bussy, *Return from the U.S.S.R.*, NY, 1937).

Self-conscious, introspective and self-critical in all his work, Gide produced his greatest book in his *Journal*, first published in 1939 and continued in *Et nunc manet in te, suivi de Journal intime* (Paris, 1951; tr. J. O'Brien, *The Journals of André Gide*, London, 1947–9) and *Ainsi soit-il, ou les jeux sont faits* (Paris, 1952; tr. J. O'Brien, *So Be It, or, The Chips Are Down*, London, 1960). Gide was a great reader, of English as well as of French literature, and his journals are rich in notations of books as well as of feelings, attitudes, events and personalities. Although, as his *Thésée* (Paris, 1946; tr. J. Russell, *Oedipus and Theseus*, London, 1950) makes clear, he finally died an agnostic, it was after a long struggle in which, as SARTRE wrote, he 'lived out the death agony of God'. Highly influential and successful as a writer, helping to establish the *Nouvelle Revue Française* in 1909 and receiving the Nobel prize for literature in 1947, he also played, in the intellectual debates of his time, the role both of a Socrates and a Montaigne.   PMWT

J. Hytier, *André Gide, romancier* (Paris, 1954); W. Ireland, *André Gide* (Edinburgh, 1963).

Giedion, Sigfried (b. Lengnau, Bern, Switzerland, 14.4.1888; d. Zürich, 9.4.1968). Swiss art historian. After training in engineering, Giedion turned to art history, studying with WÖLFFLIN. Profoundly impressed by Wölfflin's argument for the *Zeitgeist* [spirit of the age] as the underlying explanation for significant changes in style throughout the history of art, Giedion attempted to explain modern architecture in such terms. In *Space, Time and Architecture*

(London, 1941) Giedion set modern architecture both in an historical perspective and in the context of cultural and technological change in the modern epoch. Particularly interested in industrial and engineering advances, and the implications of these for artistic expression, Giedion connected progressive architects' notions about space in architecture to those manifest in EINSTEIN's theories and in cubist painting. He had a dynamic view of history, regarding it as 'an insight into a moving process of life. The historian, the historian of architecture especially, must be in close contact with contemporary conceptions.' He became an active apologist for the modern movement, acting as secretary-general of CIAM (Congrès Internationaux d'Architecture Moderne) from its formation in 1928 until his retirement in 1954. Giedion taught at the Federal Institute of Technology in Zürich, at Harvard and at MIT. Though *Space, Time and Architecture* which emerged from his first period of teaching at Harvard (1938–9) remains his most influential book, a number of important publications followed: *Mechanization Takes Command* (London, 1948), *The Eternal Present: the Beginnings of Art* (London, 1962) and *Architecture and the Phenomena of Transition* (London, 1970), which he completed a day before he died. PAC

Gielgud, Arthur John (b. London, UK, 14.4.1904). British actor and director. Born into a prosperous family with strong theatrical links, Gielgud studied at the Royal Academy of Dramatic Art and received his first professional experience in the theatre with the Old Vic, Nigel Playfair's company and J. B. Fagan's repertory theatre at Oxford. In 1924 Barry Jackson offered him his first starring part in the West End as Romeo in *Romeo and Juliet* and from then on, although success was not instantaneous, he established himself as a juvenile lead. Unlike most other matinée idols, Gielgud was also drawn towards the classical repertoire and in 1929 he joined the Old Vic where his performances, notably as Richard II and Hamlet, became legendary. His verse-speaking was supreme, combining the musical quality of the Victorian actors (without

their affectations) with a quick-silver intelligence. He was also a pioneer of CHEKHOVian acting; and the repertory season which he launched as an actor-manager in 1937 at the Queens Theatre contained what was regarded as the finest Chekhov production, of *Three Sisters*, then seen in the UK. His popularity with the public was reflected in the long runs given to *Richard of Bordeaux* (1932), *Dear Brutus* (1941) and *A Day by the Sea* (1953). After WW2 he joined the Shakespeare Memorial Theatre at Stratford to play Angelo in BROOK's *Measure for Measure*, King Lear, and Benedick in *Much Ado about Nothing*; while his solo recital *The Ages of Man* (1957) proved highly successful on national and international tours. For a time in the early 1960s his style of acting fell out of fashion, but his performance in Alan Bennett's *Forty Years On* (1958), David Storey's *Home* (1970) and PINTER's *No Man's Land* (1975) restored his reputation as one of the greatest living actors. He was knighted in 1953. He traces his career in *An Actor and His Time* (London, 1979). JE

R. Hayman, *Gielgud* (London, 1971).

van Giffen, Albert Egges (b. Noordhorn, Groningen, The Netherlands, 14.3.1884; d. Zwolle, Overijssel, 31.5.1973). Dutch archaeologist. After his initial training as a biologist and several years' experience as a keeper in the State Museum of Antiquities at Leiden he became the first director of the Biologisch-Archaeologisch Instituut at Groningen in 1920, a post from which he was to exert a considerable influence on the archaeology of north-western Europe for several decades. His principal interest lay in the field of environmental archaeology. He regarded the archaeological site as a component of an environment insisting that both aspects should be studied together by a team of appropriate specialists. To improve understanding of complex settlement sites he developed techniques of large-scale area excavation, the value of which he demonstrated at the (terp) site of Ezinge (excavated 1923–34) and the Roman fort at Valkenburg (excavated 1941). He was one of the very few archaeologists of this century to break away from narrow period specializations, believing that the well-balanced archaeologist should be equally proficient in all periods of man's activity and should be in command of all the necessary scientific and historical skills. His teachings are widely followed in the Low Countries today.   BWC

Gilbert, Felix (b. Baden-Baden, Baden-Württemberg, Germany, 21.5.1905; naturalized American citizen, 1943). German/American historian. Educated in Germany, Gilbert published a monograph on the Prussian historian *J. G. Droysen* (Munich, 1931) before emigrating to the USA in 1936. His main intellectual interests lie in the history of historical writing and in the relation between political thought and political action. *To the Farewell Address* (Princeton, 1961) discussed ideas of foreign policy in 18c America. A number of important essays on Florentine political attitudes c.1500 culminated in *Machiavelli and Guicciardini* (Princeton, 1965). Gilbert's work on religious and political attitudes in Venice in the same period is in progress: the major contribution so far is *The Pope, his Banker, and Venice* (Cambridge, Mass., 1980). He has written a history of modern international relations, *The End of The European Era* (London, 1971). Essays on CHABOD, MEINECKE, Hintze, and other historians have been collected in his *History: Choice and Commitment* (Cambridge, Mass., 1977). Equally at home in 16c Italy and 19c Germany, Gilbert combines a wide range with an interest in precisely definable problems. His work draws on two cultural traditions, German historicism and Anglo-American empiricism.   UPB

Gilbreth, Frank Bunker (b. Fairfield, Maine, USA, 7.8.1868; d. Montclair, NY, 14.6.1924) and **Gilbreth, Lillian Evelyn,** *née* Moller (b. Oakland, Calif., USA, 24.5.1878; d. Phoenix, Ariz., 2.1.1972). American contributors to management studies. Frank Gilbreth was the pioneer of motion study and the first to apply the motion picture camera to the analysis of workers' physical movements. He classified human motions, coining the word 'therbligs' (Gilbreth backwards), and developed procedures for estimating standard performance times. His wife collaborated with him in applying the social sciences to industrial management, recognizing the importance of the individual worker as well as emphasizing the need to eliminate work-place inefficiency and to increase productivity. *Motion Study* (NY, 1911) was the first important publication of their research. F. W. TAYLOR's influence can be seen in the *Primer of Scientific Management* (NY, 1912), and further developments of practice in *Applied Motion Study* (NY, 1917).   RIT

Gill, Arthur Eric Rowton (b. Brighton, E. Sussex, UK, 22.2.1882; d. London, 17.11.1940). British stone- and woodcarver, type designer and wood-engraver. After Chichester School of Art (1897–9) he was articled to architect W. D. Caroë (1899). That same year he joined Edward JOHNSTON's first lettering class at London Central School of Arts and Crafts. In 1903 he abandoned architecture to work as a letter-cutter; from 1905 he taught inscriptional lettering and monumental masonry at the Paddington Institute in London. He engraved his first boxwood block (1907) and carved his first stone figure (1909): encouraged by discerning critics – Roger FRY, Harry Kessler, Augustus John – he held successful one-man exhibitions in Chelsea's Chenil Gallery (1911) and at Goupil's Gallery (1914). Between 1913 and 1918 he created 14 stations of the cross bas-reliefs for Westminster cathedral. Later major commissions included work on London Underground's St James's Park HQ (1929); at Broadcasting House (Prospero and Ariel and Deo Omnipotente) (1929 –31); at Palestine Archaeological Museum (1934); at Geneva Palais des Nations (1935–8); and numerous ecclesiastical monuments and war memorials.

Painted shop-fascia lettering for bookseller Douglas Cleverdon so impressed MORISON that he commissioned from Gill for Monotype Corporation a classically based monostroke alphabet akin to Johnston's Underground lettering: Gill Sanserif quickly won widespread approbation. Gill designed 10 other typefaces including Golden Cockerel and Perpetua, with superb titling capitals.

Also a masterly wood-engraver, Gill contributed many illustrations, often incorporating classical letterforms, for books published by – among others – Cranach-Presse, Dent, Golden Cockerel and St Dominic's presses. Greatly influenced by COOMARASWAMY, Johnston, W. R. Lethaby and Thomist writings, Gill wrote books of philosophical and polemical essays including *An Essay on Typography* (London, 1931), *Money and Morals* (London, 1934) and *Work and Leisure* (London, 1935). His *Autobiography* (London, 1940) is an acknowledged classic.   TC

E. R. Gill, *Bibliography of Eric Gill* (London, 1953); M. Yorke, *Eric Gill: Man of Flesh and Spirit* (London, 1981).

Gilliéron, Jules Louis (b. La Neuveville, Bern, Switzerland, 21.12.1854; d. Cergnaux-sur-Gléresse, 26.4.1926). Swiss linguist and dialectologist. From 1883 until his death he taught Romance dialectology at the Ecole Pratique des Hautes Etudes in Paris, where he had been a student. His most important contribution to linguistics was the *Atlas linguistique de la France* [Linguistic atlas of France] (Paris, 1902–9). This consisted of 35 fascicules of between 40 and 100 maps each showing the results of fieldwork undertaken between 1897 and 1901 by Gilliéron's assistant E. Edmont. In all, Edmont was sent to 637 places, and in each locality one informant, sometimes two or three, was interviewed to elicit the local version of 1421 words and phrases designed to discover pronunciation, vocabulary and grammar differences. By questioning mostly middle-aged or elderly people with humble occupations – farmers, gamekeepers, schoolmasters – authentic dialect was ensured. This work was the forerunner of many similar investigations in other countries. Another major contribution by Gilliéron to historical linguistics was his concept of 'therapeutic change'. The 19c had witnessed fierce debate as to whether language changes were governed by rigid 'sound laws'. Gilliéron pointed out that the operation of sound laws would on occasion give rise to collisions between originally different words or to unacceptably eroded forms. As a result languages resort to therapeutic changes which are exceptions to the rigid laws and re-establish distinctions or give greater substance to words.   WSD

Gilson, Etienne Henry (b. Paris, France, 13.6.1884; d. Paris, 20.9.1978). French historian of medieval philosophy. Gilson was professor of the history of medieval philosophy at the Sorbonne from 1921, and at the Collège de France from 1932. After WW2 he spent much of his time at Toronto where he had founded an Institute of Medieval Studies. Gilson's interest in medieval philosophy – which he may be said to have rescued from oblivion – began with his thesis on the nature of freedom in Descartes (1913). His work on the 'sources' of Descartes led him back to the 'scholastic' authors of the Middle Ages. He found them worth reading. He wrote books on Bonaventure, Bernard of Clairvaux, Augustine and Dante. But his main concern was with the historical context of St Thomas Aquinas, whom he rehabilitated as a serious thinker with contemporary relevance. In *The Unity of Philosophical Experience* (NY, 1937) and the Gifford lectures *The Spirit of Medieval Philosophy* (London, 1950), he showed that medieval philosophy was a 'Christian philosophy' not merely in the sense that it was devised by believing Christians and was in harmony with Christian faith, but because it was led to tackle a set of genuine philosophical problems hitherto unconsidered: most notably the problems associated with the idea of 'creation', a notion alien to Greek thought, and with the 'person' on which earlier philosophers had nothing to say. Because his work is historical, Gilson has worn well.   PAH

J. M. Quinn, *The Thomism of Etienne Gilson* (Villanova, 1971); F. C. Copleston, *A History of Philosophy*, ix (London, 1975).

Ginsberg, Allen (b. Newark, NJ, USA, 3.6.1926). American poet. A prolific poet, mystic, social prophet and cultural guru, Ginsberg's long poem in the collection of the same title, *Howl* (San Francisco, 1956), became one of the symbols of the liberation of American culture in the 1950s from an academic formalism and political conservatism.

Influenced by the mysticism and poetics of Blake, and the democratic openness of Walt Whitman, *Howl* celebrated and lamented the casualties of TRUMAN's and Eisenhower's America, and in particular the lives of the bohemians who were identified by John Clellon Holmes as the Beat generation. Ginsberg's subsequent work remained fundamentally true to his libertarian views. *Kaddish and Other Poems* (San Francisco, 1961) contains, in the title poem, a powerfully moving elegy to the poet's mother. EH

E. Mottram, *Allen Ginsberg in the Sixties* (Brighton, 1972); J. Tytell, *Naked Angels: the Lives and Literature of the Beat Generation* (NY, 1976).

Ginsberg, Morris (b. Lithuania, Russia [now Lithuania, USSR], 14.5.1889; naturalized British citizen; d. London, UK, 31.8.1970). British sociologist and moral philosopher, greatly influenced by HOBHOUSE. Trained in the liberal tradition, he was concerned with the broad social and philosophical questions of evolution in relation to man's moral progress, as outlined in *Moral Progress* (London, 1944). He sought to demonstrate how social structure could be related to moral beliefs in society, an interest emanating from his Lithuanian Jewish background and training in Hebrew. He illustrated his arguments from his compendious knowledge of social history and comparative anthropology. The philosophical approach and precision permeated his considerable contribution to social philosophy. From part-time assistant tutor at the London School of Economics he rose to become professor of sociology in 1929. He held this position until his retirement in 1954 when he became emeritus professor. Although recognized as Britain's foremost sociologist in that period, his philosophical approach was rejected by the emerging group of sociologists which included Ralf Dahrendorf and P. S. Cohen. Ginsberg antagonized students at LSE with his dismissive approach to empiricism and quantitative sociology as well as to radical approaches to the discipline. He remained firmly within the sphere of moral philosophy as the basis for social inquiry, a fact illustrated in his final work *On Justice in Society* (London, 1965), by which time the focus of sociological concern had shifted with the massive American development of empirical work. TFC/LMC

R. Fletcher (ed.), *The Science of Society and the Unity of Mankind: a Memorial Volume for Morris Ginsberg* (London, 1974).

Giono, Jean (b. Manosque, Basses-Alpes, France, 30.3.1895; d. Manosque, 8.10.1970). French novelist. Largely self-taught, as a boy Giono enthusiastically read the great books of classical antiquity in translation. Their primitivism and pantheism fused with his own love of nature which had been kindled throughout a childhood spent on the lower mountain slopes of Provence. In the *Trilogie Pan* (3 vols, Paris, 1929–30) which comprises *Colline* (1929; tr. J. Leclerque, *Hill of Destiny*, NY, 1929), *Un des Baymugnes* (1929; tr. J. Leclerque, *Lovers Are Never Losers*, London, 1931) and *Regain* (1930; tr. H. Fluchère & G. Myers, *Harvest*, London, 1939), he evokes a pastoral life which is simple, beautiful, poetic and totally pagan. Giono's love for and communion with nature totally excludes Christianity. His experience at Verdun during WW1 which inspired *Le Grand Troupeau* (Paris, 1931; tr. H. Glass, *To the Slaughterhouse*, London, 1969) made him a convinced pacifist; he was imprisoned for these beliefs for a short while in 1939 by the French government and again in 1945 by the communist resistance, who detected collaborationist tendencies in his pacifism and in his attraction to what he saw as the patriarchal and rustic character of the Vichy regime. His work, which is filled with bold metaphor and sensuous imagery, stands as a protest against modern civilization and the age of the machine. WBS

M. A. Smith, *Jean Giono* (NY, 1966); W. D. Redfern, *The Private World of Jean Giono* (Oxford, 1967).

Giraudoux, Jean (b. Bellac, Haute-Vienne, France, 29.10.1882; d. Paris, 31.1.1944). French dramatist; an ardent champion of literary theatre and of the importance of the text as against the ARTAUDesque theatre of cruelty. After a successful career as a diplomat, novelist and essayist, he turned to playwriting at the instigation of Louis Jouvet for whom he adapted his novel *Siegfried* (1928): the story of a French soldier who raises Germany to its highest pitch of efficiency and power. The play ran for 283 performances and embodied Giraudoux's desire for harmony between the two countries. But his speciality was taking mythological or biblical figures (Judith, Electra, Ondine) out of context in order to explore contemporary preoccupations. He did this most effectively in *La Guerre de Troie n'aura pas lieu* (Paris, 1935; tr. C. Fry, *Tiger at the Gates*, London, 1955) in which Hector, the most passionate proponent of peace, brings about war between Greece and Troy. He turned more and more to a blend of reality and fantasy culminating in *La Folle de Chaillot* [The mad woman of Chaillot] (1945), which shows a madwoman leading impoverished Parisians in a crusade against greedy financiers. Popular in France in the 1930s, his influence since has waned but he remains important as a defender of the word against the encroaching power of *mise en scène*.   MB

Girodias, Maurice, *né* Kahane (b. Paris, France, 12.4.1919). French publisher. His father Jack Kahane, a self-confessed 'booklegger', founded the Obelisk Press in Paris in the 1930s and included among his authors Frank Harris, DURRELL, JOYCE, and, pre-eminently, Henry MILLER. France at this period was famously tolerant of prohibited books – so long as they were not in the French-language. To escape persecution after his father's death in 1939, Maurice changed his Jewish name for that of his French mother, Girodias. Mainly publishing art books during the occupation, in 1945 he started up the Obelisk Press again, with great success – although his first brush with the French law (1946–7) came over French language editions of Miller. In 1953 Girodias founded the Olympia Press. It specialized in outright (but often wittily so) 'dirty books', and avant-garde literary items. Girodias established a profitable liaison with the group of English and American writers centred round the magazine *Merlin* (founded 1952): Alexander Trocchi,

Christopher Logue, Paul Ableman, BECKETT. The Olympia imprint introduced NABOKOV's *Lolita* (1955; Girodias's biggest seller), BURROUGHS's *The Naked Lunch* (1959) and J. P. Donleavy's *The Ginger Man* (1955). This fertile period in the mid-1950s established Girodias's credentials as a major literary patron. With de GAULLE's access to power in 1958, however, a new bourgeois 'puritanism' (as the publisher saw it) led to increasing persecution and Girodias moved his operations to the UK and (especially) the USA from where he still makes powerful statements against censorship. He published the first instalment of his autobiography as *Une Journée sur la terre* (Paris, 1977; *The Frog Prince*, NY, 1980).   JAS

Glaser, Donald Arthur (b. Cleveland, Ohio, USA, 21.9.1926). American physicist, educated at the Case Institute of Technology and the California Institute of Technology. His outstanding contribution to particle physics was in the formulation and development of the bubble chamber technique for particle observation. He realized that particles passing through a superheated liquid (e.g. liquid hydrogen) not only leave observable tracks, but that if collisions occur with the nuclei of the liquid, the resulting events can be observed in great detail. This technique has been exploited for the last 25 years by exposing a variety of bubble chambers to particle beams from accelerators, and has led to many of the discoveries of the 1960s and 1970s which provided the experimental impetus in particle physics. Glaser was awarded a Nobel prize in 1960.   RJC

Glashow, Sheldon Lee (b. New York, USA, 5.12.1932). American physicist. Educated at Cornell and Harvard, Glashow's work has centred on the unification of electromagnetic and weak interactions into a common scheme. He established one of the earliest models which was later amplified, with the addition of new ingredients, by SALAM and WEINBERG into the current unification model for these processes. His extension of these ideas to incorporate the quarks led to the prediction of a fourth quark, the charm quark, and to the particles containing this quark. These particles were discovered between 1974 and 1976 by S. C. C. Ting, B. RICHTER and co-workers. Further applications of these ideas have led to the prediction of more quarks, some already confirmed. The whole spectrum of the quarks and leptons is at present discussed on the basis of Glashow's approach. With Salam and Weinberg, he received a Nobel prize in 1979.   RJC

Glatshteyn, Jacob (b. Lublin, Russian Poland [now Poland], 20.8.1896; d. New York, USA, 19.11.1971). Yiddish poet. Arriving in New York when he was 18, he published his first entry in a local literary journal in October 1914. But only in 1921 did his first volume of poetry appear, *Jacob Glatshteyn* (NY); at once he was placed in the forefront among contemporary Yiddish poets. Glatshteyn became associated with *In-sichistn* [Introspectives] – a group who rebelled against the conservatism of an earlier generation's poetry, stressing the individuality of the poet – and edited their magazine. Over the years he participated regularly in several other journals as columnist, reviewer and literary critic. In 1938, with the onset of Nazism in Europe, Glatshteyn wrote '*A gute Nakht dir, Velt*' [Goodnight to you, world], a poem which is virtually a denial of everything he had stood for, an outcry against the indifference of the world to the Jewish suffering at the hands of the Nazis, a summons to the Jews to return to their own world and their old values. The poem provoked a stir throughout the Yiddish literary world, being variously commented upon as an expression of despair and defeat. From then onwards all Glatshteyn wrote, both in prose and poetry, reflected a revival of that Jewishness in which he had been steeped in his youth. After WW2 he published several volumes of poetry, including *Stralendike Yiddn* [Radiating Jews] (NY, 1946) and *Fun mine gantzer Mih* [Of all my labours] (NY, 1956). JSo

Glueck, Sheldon (b. Warsaw, Russian Poland [now Poland], 15.8.1896; naturalized American citizen, 1920; d. Harvard, Mass., USA, 10.3.1980) and **Glueck,** **Eleanor**, *née* Touroff (b. New York, USA, 12.4.1898; d. Harvard, Mass., 25.9.1972). American criminologists. Taken to the USA with his parents in 1903, Sheldon Glueck studied in American law schools, including Harvard where he subsequently taught. From 1950 he was Roscoe Pound professor of law until his retirement in 1963 when he became professor emeritus of law at Harvard until his death. Between 1925 and 1965 he published a number of books on criminal law in relation to mental disorder, prosecution, police practice, punishment and psychiatry. His contributions to the interface between law and medicine, as well as to the study of the criminal law in action were outstanding. He was US adviser on law governing the Nuremberg war crimes trials. However, he is probably as widely known today for his collaborative work with Eleanor Glueck, which lasted from the time of their marriage in 1922 until her death in 1972, as he is for his outstanding contribution in more strictly legal treatises.

Eleanor Glueck was research associate in criminology at Harvard, working with her husband there for 36 years until her retirement in 1964. 'The Gluecks of Harvard' became an established institution in the pioneering period of American criminology. Together they developed an interdisciplinary approach in searching for answers to controversial issues relating to crime etiology, prediction, prevention, correctional processes, punishment and the individualization of justice. An outstanding feature of the 14 major books they published jointly, in which they surveyed several thousands of cases or criminal careers in great detail, was the attempt to relate the practical concerns of criminal justice to criminological theory and explanation. In this context they became pioneers in the development of prediction studies in criminal behaviour, which they advocated for use by judges as well as in the broader areas of research and policy. Their studies were regarded as both provocative and controversial by their contemporaries. While today there is still much debate as regards many of the issues raised in their prolific output of publications, there is no doubt that they stand in the forefront of 20c pioneers in criminological and criminal justice studies.   FHMcC

Godard, Jean-Luc (b. Paris, France, 3.12.1930). French film director. The most influential film maker of his generation, Jean-Luc Godard began his career as a critic for the specialized Parisian film magazines and then went on to make a number of shorts in the late 1950s. He burst into world prominence with *A Bout de Souffle* (*Breathless*, 1960) and in the next eight years directed 14 further innovative feature films, among them *Vivre sa Vie* (*It's My Life*, 1962), *Pierrot le Fou* (1965) and *Weekend* (1968). Since 1968 Godard has continued an active production career, but most of his work has been made outside the confines of the commercial film industry. After May 1968 he worked first on low-budget 16mm political films – best known of which is *Vent d'Est* (*Wind From the East*, 1969) – and then, from the mid-1970s, on video productions made in Switzerland. His returns to mainstream film production – even if only for the art-house circuit – have been rare in the past decade: *Tout Va Bien* [All is well, 1972] and *Sauve Qui Peut (la Vie)* (*Slow Motion*, 1980).

All Godard's work has a great theoretical interest and there seems little doubt that he will be seen in retrospect as the most significant of all the film makers to emerge from what was known, journalistically, as the New Wave. While his work since 1968 has had comparatively little impact, because the films and video tapes have remained largely unseen, his creative output between 1960 and 1968 was enormously influential, as can be established by comparing his films with those of the equally innovative RESNAIS. The latter's *L'Année dernière à Marienbad* (*Last Year at Marienbad*, 1961) still looks avant-garde, but the revolutionary shooting and cutting style of Godard's 1960s movies has been totally absorbed into the mainstream of world film and television production.   RPA

R. S. Brown (ed.), *Focus on Godard* (Englewood Cliffs, 1972); R. Milne (ed.), *Godard on Godard* (London, 1972).

Gödel, Kurt (b. Brünn, Moravia, Austria-Hungary [now Brno, Czechoslovakia], 28.4.1906; naturalized American citizen, 1948; d. Princeton, NJ, USA, 14.1.1978). Austrian/American mathematician and logician. Gödel worked at the University of Vienna from 1930 to 1940 when he emigrated to the USA. He settled at the Institute for Advanced Studies at Princeton and remained there for the rest of his career. His most important work 'Über formal unentscheidbare Sätze' [On formally indeterminable propositions ...] was published in 1932 (tr. J. van Heijenourt in *From Frege to Gödel*, Cambridge, Mass., 1966). In this he argued, with astonishing ingenuity but in an irresistibly coercive fashion, that in a certain strong and crucial sense mathematics is essentially incomplete. More specifically he proved that for any formal system that contains arithmetic there must be true statements of the system that cannot be proved within it. This completely undermined the 'logistic' project undertaken by FREGE and Bertrand RUSSELL of providing a set of logical axioms from which the whole of pure mathematics (as well as the nonaxiomatic remainder of logic) could be deduced. It also provided a brilliantly fruitful example of the kind of metamathematical inquiry – that is, the strictly formal investigation of formal systems of logic and mathematics – to which logicians have productively applied themselves since the abandonment of the Frege–Russell project.   AQ

E. Nagel & J. H. Newman, *Gödel's Proof* (London, 1959).

Godwin, Harry (b. Rotherham, S. Yorks., UK, 9.5.1901). British botanist. In his final undergraduate year at Cambridge, specializing in botany, he benefited especially from the teaching of Albert Steward and TANSLEY. From them he developed his lifelong interests in palaeobotany and ecology. His first Cambridge appointment was as a demonstrator in the botany school; subsequently he became its professor. With his well-developed background in plant physiology and geology he began the intensive study of successional changes in the local fen vegetation, and the controlling mechanisms of hydroseres. From this developed an understanding of the anthropogenic nature of many types of fen vegetation and the concept of 'deflected succession', and in particular, with his wife's help, an interest in the use of pollen as a diagnostic tool of the earth's history. The framework of the postglacial history of the fens, and later the Somerset levels, was established by their work in the 1930s. Sustained work on pollen analysis dispelled the accepted view that the UK was swept clean of vegetation by the last glaciation, and in 1948 Godwin was able to establish the subdepartment of quaternary research in Cambridge. This attracted specialists in many fields, and in 1953 radiocarbon dating equipment was installed. With its aid dates could be attached to the major postglacial pollen zones, and these zones could at last be synchronized with similar levels on the European mainland. It also became possible to assign dates not only to prehistoric cultures in the UK but also to date the period when the land bridge from Europe was finally broken. This major period of work culminated in the *History of the British Flora* (Cambridge, 1956). BEJ

Goebbels, Joseph Paul (b. Rheydt, N. Rhine-Westphalia, Germany, 29.10.1897; d. Berlin, 1.5.1945). Nazi minister of enlightenment and propaganda (1933–45). The most educated of senior Nazi leaders, with a DPhil from Heidelberg University (1920), he led the Nazi party in Berlin, holding it true to HITLER against the challenge of the Strasser brothers, Otto and Gregor. Goebbels was the most effective orator in the Nazi movement apart from Hitler, and played a major role in the political campaigns (1930–3) which preceded Hitler's capture of power in Germany. Appointed as the first modern minister of propaganda, he controlled and directed the total output of the German media – books, press, radio, theatre and film – silencing or expelling Jews and those whose politics were incompatible with Nazism but riding the other artists with a sure but comparatively loose rein until the outbreak of war. With the turn of the war against Germany from 1943 onwards, Goebbels emerged as the advocate of total mobilization for total war, acquiring special powers as Reich commissioner for total mobilization in August 1944, playing more and more the role of inspiration of continuing German resistance to the Allies as Hitler withdrew almost completely from public appearances. After Hitler's suicide he administered poison to his six children and killed his wife and himself. DCW

R. Manvell, *Doctor Goebbels* (London, 1960).

Goering, Hermann (b. Rosenheim, Bavaria, Germany, 12.1.1893; d. Nuremberg, 15.10.1946). German Nazi politician and ace fighter pilot, Goering held the key post of Prussian prime minister and minister of the interior at the time when the Nazis swept away all barriers to their power in Germany. Acknowledged second to HITLER in the Nazi hierarchy, and Reich air minister (1933–45), Goering built up the Luftwaffe until it was the leading military air force in Europe, though it was never designed to operate as the independent strategic striking force it was sometimes represented as being. Its failure in 1940 in the Battle of Britain marked the beginning of Goering's eclipse and, despite its subsequent triumph over the Allied strategic air offensive at the end of 1943, Goering's enemies in the party saw to it that he did not regain his central position in Hitler's esteem, a task made easier by Goering's preference for ostentatious living, by his vanity and by his addiction to drugs. Before 1939 his origins in the regular imperial officer corps had made him the hope of conservative opponents of Nazism inside Germany, a hope which attracted some attention abroad but did not survive his somewhat equivocal role during the phoney war period, or the Luftwaffe's part in the conquest of the Netherlands and France in 1940. Captured by the Americans in May 1945, he was the senior Nazi brought before the Nuremberg war crimes tribunal, where he gave as spirited a defence of the Nazi record as circumstances allowed and cheated the hangman by swallowing poison on the eve of his execution. DCW

Goffman, Erving (b. Manville, Alta, Canada, 11.6.1922; d. Philadelphia, Pa, USA, 19.11.1982). American sociologist. From 1949 to 1951, while a member of the department of social anthropology at Edinburgh University, he carried out field research on social interaction in the Shetland Islands; and completed a doctorate in 1953 at the University of Chicago, working under E. A. Shils on a study of social stratification. Drawing on these two sources Goffman produced *The Presentation of Self in Everyday Life* (NY, 1959) in which social life is presented as theatre: people are engaged in an elaborate drama as actors in performance. Social activity is seen as essentially projecting a conception of self before others, a dramaturgy which undermines the distinction between appearance and reality. This invitation to the sociological footlights was translated into 10 languages and sold 500,000 copies, a remarkable achievement for an academic text. A fascination for total institutions took Goffman to the National Institute of Mental Health in Bethesda, Maryland, where from 1954 to 1957 he did hospital fieldwork including a year's observation at St Elizabeth's Hospital, Washington. From this work emerged *Asylums* (NY, 1961), which penetrated the world of closed communities that closely direct the lives of inmates to approved purposes. Goffman interpreted the experiences of patients and prisoners rather than presenting the justifications of those who contained them. In 1962 Goffman became professor of sociology at Berkeley, transferring to the University of Pennsylvania in 1968. He wrote a string of books developing the theme of public interactions; these have proved commercially popular in an advertising age, but have been attacked by some academics as a cynical and safe focus upon surface phenomena (e.g. his *Forms of Talk*, Oxford, 1981).

TFC/LMC

Golding, William Gerald (b. St Columb Minor, Cornwall, UK, 19.9.1911). British novelist. Golding's art essentially develops NIETZSCHE's proposition that there is 'an eternal conflict between the theoretic and the tragic worldview'. Son of a rationalist schoolmaster, he read science and English at Oxford, worked in theatre, adult and school teaching, married, and saw naval action in WW2, before publishing *Lord of the Flies* (London, 1954), an exuberant fable about schoolboys reverting to savagery. The four succeeding novels – *The Inheritors* (London, 1955); *Pincher Martin* (London, 1956); *Free Fall* (London, 1959); *The Spire* (London, 1964) – which unite religious drama with science fiction, and fuse analysis of the imagination with incandescent projection of its properties, form the nucleus of his achievement. In each, tragic fable and atavistic material are as much the residue as the source of a quest to reconcile intellectual and intuitive faculties in language of exceptional clarity, sensuousness, violence and ecstasy. Subsequent books mix comedy and social realism more freely with mythological and, in *Darkness Visible* (London, 1979), prophetic subjects, while continuing to display Golding's chameleon capacity to change his linguistic skin in every work. Despite its complexity Golding's art is rooted in popular and primitive experience, while his sense of childhood and theatre, love of words, and obsession with 'the strange, the gruesome and the beautiful' make him the most purely original English novelist of the century.

SJN

M. Kinkead-Weekes & I. Gregor, *William Golding: a Critical Study* (London, 1967); L. Hodson, *Golding* (London, 1969).

Goldmann, Lucien (b. Bucharest, Romania, 20.7.1913; d. Paris, France, 3.10.1970). Romanian writer, one of the leading MARXist literary critics of the 20c. Goldmann left Romania in 1933, in part because of official disapproval of his political activities. After a brief period in Vienna, in 1934 he settled in Paris, which was to be his adopted home until his death.

Strongly influenced by the work of the early LUKÁCS and of PIAGET, with whom he studied, Goldmann developed single-handedly the method of Marxist literary criticism known as 'genetic structuralism'. The method was 'structuralist' in that its aim was to trace correspondence between the structure of a literary work, the form of the author's 'worldvision' and the historical situation of his time. It was 'genetic' in that, unlike certain other forms of structuralism, it concerned itself with the historical and social genesis of works of art, and of the 'mental structures' which informed them. Goldmann's major venture in this field was his strikingly original study of Pascal and Racine *Le dieu caché* (Paris, 1956; tr. P. Thody, *The Hidden God*, London, 1964), in which he traced correspondences between the 'worldvision' of these writers and the 17c religious movement of Jansenism. A 'humanistic' Marxist, Goldmann also published a work of theoretical sociology *Sciences humaines et philosophie* (Paris, 1952; tr. H. White & R. Anchor, *The Human Sciences and Philosophy*, London, 1969) and numerous essays which applied the 'genetic structuralist' method to literature, philosophy and society. Prominent among these writings is a work on Kant, included in *Structures mentales et création culturelle* (Paris, 1970; tr. J. Mans, *The Philosophy of the Enlightenment*, London, 1973). In 1959 Goldmann became director of the Ecole Pratique des Hautes Etudes in Paris, and in his later years produced *Pour une sociologie du roman* (Paris, 1964; tr. A. Sheridan, *Towards a Sociology of the Novel*, London, 1975). TE

Goldschmidt, Victor Moritz (b. Zürich, Switzerland, 27.1.1888; d. Oslo, Norway, 20.3.1947). Swiss geochemist. Justly called the 'father of geochemistry', he was the son of a distinguished physical chemist and moved with his family to Oslo in 1905 when his father was appointed professor of chemistry at the university. After studying geology, mineralogy and chemistry at Oslo, Goldschmidt was appointed full professor and director of the Mineralogical Institute at 26. In 1929 he accepted a similar appointment at Göttingen, Germany. As a Jew, he was forced to resign shortly after the Nazis came to power. He was immediately granted a chair at Oslo but became a refugee when the Germans invaded Norway. He escaped to England, where he spent most of the remainder of his life. Although Goldschmidt did outstanding work in study-

ing rock metamorphism in Norway in his early years, he devoted most of his professional life to an attempt to find the laws underlying the frequency and distribution of the various chemical elements in the earth; his fame rests on this work. His discovery of the fundamental relationship between crystal structure and chemical constitution laid the foundations of crystal chemistry. His most important research is summarized in his treatise *Geochemische Verteilungsgesetze der Elemente* [The geochemical laws of the distribution of the elements] (9 pts, Kristiania, 1923–37). A massive book *Geochemistry* (Oxford, 1954) was published posthumously. AH

Gollancz, Victor (b. London, UK, 9.4.1893; d. London, 8.2.1967). British publisher and writer. Between the foundation of his 'one-man-band' publishing firm in 1928 and his retirement in 1965, Gollancz, an Oxford-educated ex-public schoolmaster, built up an extraordinary reputation. His eye-catching advertisements and the distinctive yellow jackets of his books were the envy of his profession. His most notable achievement was 'to convert people on a big scale to socialism and pacificism' through his Left Book Club. Formed in 1936 with the assistance of John Strachey and LASKI, the club was regarded with suspicion by the then leaders of the Labour party. Within a year it had enrolled over 47,000 members (almost 60,000 by 1939); filled the Albert Hall in London with mass rallies supporting the Spanish republic and campaigning for a Popular Front against fascism; sponsored over 1200 discussion groups throughout the country, and, in the 12 months to spring 1939, published two million books, half a million pamphlets and 15 million leaflets. Gollancz spent £20,000 a year on publicity, on his free magazine *Left News*, and on the organization of the clubs, in addition to his printing and other expenditure. When Clement Attlee formed his 1945 cabinet, it was noted that eight members (which included John Strachey) had been active supporters of the club. The Left Book Club was a most persuasive social movement as well as a book club, and swung the Labour party to open itself to the progressive socialist needs of influential club members. RB

S. Hodges, *Gollancz: the Story of a Publishing House 1928–78* (London, 1978).

Gombrich, Ernst Hans Josef (b. Vienna, Austria-Hungary [now Austria], 30.3.1909; naturalized British citizen, 1947). Austrian/British writer on art. Trained in Vienna by the art historians Julius von Schlosser and RIEGL, Gombrich came to England in 1936 to work in the Warburg Institute, of which he was director from 1959 until 1976. A man of many interests, his reputation rests on several different kinds of book. There is Gombrich the author of that model of lucid popularization, the best-selling *The Story of Art* (London, 1950, [13]1978). There is Gombrich the art-historical scholar, whose penetrating articles on the Italian Renaissance (20 of them collected in his *Norm and Form*, London, 1966, and *Symbolic Images*, London, 1972) are in the manner of WARBURG, whose intellectual biography he has written (*Aby Warburg*, London, 1970), and emphasize the survival or revival of classical formulae in art, literature and ideas. Most original of all, there is Gombrich the psychologist of art, who has fused Warburg's 'formula' with W. Kohler's 'Gestalt', and explored the schemata through which we perceive visual reality; the Gombrich of *Art and Illusion* (London, 1960), *The Sense of Order* (London, 1978), *The Image and the Eye* (Oxford, 1982) and of the essays collected in his *Meditations on a Hobby Horse* (London, 1963). Since his Viennese days Gombrich has been an admirer of POPPER, whose influence can perhaps be traced in Gombrich's uncompromising hostility to vague thinking in general, and to the idea of the 'spirit of the age' in particular (*In Search of Cultural History*, Oxford, 1969). UPB

Gombrowicz, Witold (b. Małoszyce, Russian Poland [now Poland], 4.8.1904; d. Vence, Alpes-Maritimes, France, 24.7.1969). Polish novelist, essayist and dramatist, precursor of the absurd, whose fictional world may owe something to the visionary distortions of Witkiewicz. His first play *Iwona, księżniczka Burgunda* (Warsaw, 1935; tr. K. Griffith-Jones, *Ivona, Princess of Burgundia*, London, 1969) was largely misunderstood at the time, but was enthusiastically acclaimed in the 1960s. Today Gombrowicz is recognized as one of Europe's outstanding writers, while intermittent censorship problems in Poland have made him a cult figure there. Gombrowicz's main existential themes appear full-blown in *Ferdydurke* (Warsaw, 1937; tr. E. Mosbacher, London, 1961): freedom, fear, 'nihility', absurdity, and a highly idiosyncratic complex of pubertal bashfulness that clings to a man throughout adulthood recur in *Pornografia* (Paris, 1960; tr. A. Hamilton, London, 1966) and *Kosmos* (Paris, 1965; tr. E. Mosbacher, *Cosmos*, London, 1966) with obsessive constancy. The parodistic structures of his novels and plays are justified by his cultural philosophy. Naturalism and realism are discarded in the name of 'Pure Form', a concept based on man's immanent longing for shape. Yet Gombrowicz sees that form clashes with the very essence of life, since reality cannot be totally enclosed in form; though, paradoxically, a thought that seeks to define the inadequacy of form thereby becomes form itself. NT

Gomulka, Wladyslaw (b. Białobrzeg, Poland, 6.2.1905; d. Warsaw, 1.9.1982). Polish Communist leader. Trained as a locksmith, Gomulka worked in the oil industry. He joined the youth socialist movement at 16 and the clandestine Polish Communist party in 1926. Involved in strikes as a trade-union leader, he was imprisoned twice in the 1930s, spending the year between (1934–5) at the International Lenin School in Moscow. During WW2 he helped to organize the communist underground resistance and in January 1945 was appointed deputy premier in the communist-dominated Lublin government set up by the Russians. He was given responsibility for the lands taken over by the Poles from the Germans and in December 1945 became secretary-general of the Polish Workers' party. Gomulka led the fight to suppress the Polish peasant party and force the socialists into a merger, on communist terms, with the Workers' party. But he opposed the collectivization of agriculture and the formation of the Cominform in September 1947. This led to his disgrace. On STALIN's orders he was stripped of his offices and finally, in July 1951, arrested and imprisoned. After the death of Stalin and of Bierut who had replaced Gomulka as secretary-general, the latter was rehabilitated (1956). His prosecution by Stalin made him a popular figure, and there was a widespread demand for his return to power. He was restored as secretary-general of the party and held office from 1956 to 1970.

Gomulka curbed the power of the secret police; eased the persecution of the Catholic church; and stopped the collectivization of farms. But people expected more – particularly economic reforms – and in the 1960s his popularity declined rapidly. In March 1968 there was open defiance of the Gomulka regime by intellectuals, and student riots in Warsaw and other cities. In a belated effort to recover the ground he had lost, Gomulka changed Poland's policy towards West Germany and secured the Germans' recognition of the Oder-Neisse frontier in the Polish–West German Treaty of December 1970. Economic reforms were also introduced, but too late and too little to halt the run-down of the Polish economy. Workers' riots at the end of the year led to Gomulka's downfall, as they had led to his earlier reinstatement. He was ousted from office, and replaced by Edward Gierek as secretary-general on 20.12.1970. Gomulka's inability to find a way of reconciling the popular demand for reform with the resistance to change of the communist *apparat* and its Soviet masters epitomizes the postwar history of Poland.   ALCB

N. Bethell, *Gomulka: his Poland, his Communism* (London, 1969).

González, Julio (b. Barcelona, Spain, 21.9.1876; d. Arceuil, nr Paris, France, 27.3.1942). Spanish painter and sculptor. González learned metal welding in his father's workshop. In 1900, after attending evening classes at the Barcelona School of Fine Arts, he moved to Paris, and with his brother Joan he established contact with Spanish artists living there, including PICASSO. The brothers' work at the time, decorative metal groups and heads, derived from their apprenticeship in Barcelona and showed no primitive or cubist influence. After his brother's death in 1908, Julio spent many years in self-imposed isolation, trying without success to paint, and in regular contact only with Picasso and BRANCUSI. In 1927 he gave up painting to become a highly creative sculptor. Adopting the techniques and materials (metal, iron) of his earlier functional and decorative work (only a few pieces were cast in bronze), he brought a totally new conception of the figure to 20c sculpture. He did not treat the figure as mass; instead most of his sculptures were openwork structures in wrought iron giving the figure a fragile, skeletal quality which disembodied it almost to abstraction. His small figures of 1927–30 were semicubist in inspiration, and he also made masks overtly African in derivation. But the tall, stark female figures created after 1931 out of slender rods and uprights of iron or metal, with perfunctory indications of bodily or facial features, were González's major innovations, in which defined empty space (within and around the stick-like limbs) served as form. In 1930 and 1933 he helped Picasso solve technical problems in welded sculpture. By the mid-1930s he had absorbed Picasso's adaptation of antique prototypes for the standing nude, his surrealist distortions (such as a minute knob for a head or a cluster of nails for hair), and figure construction by welding together metal pipes and pieces of sheet metal (e.g. *Maternity*, 1934; *Seated Woman*, 1935; *Woman with a Mirror*, 1936–7). In 1936 –7 he used a more realistic style for a life-sized figure of a peasant woman with a child in her arms (*Montserrat*), symbolizing popular resistance in the Spanish civil war, for the Spanish Pavilion at the 1937 Paris Exhibition. In 1939–40 he made a series of *Hombre-Cactus* [Cactus men], exploring the interaction of real and imaginary forms, with violent distortions.   SOBT

A. C. Ritchie, *Julio González* (NY, 1961); L. Degand, *González* (Amsterdam, 1964).

Goodman, Benjamin David (Benny) (b. Chicago, Ill., USA, 30.5.1909). American jazz clarinetist and bandleader. The white big-band leader who was called the 'King of Swing', Goodman played alongside the leading white musicians of his day (including cornettist BEIDERBECKE) while still a teenager. He was one of the most technically gifted instrumentalists of the era. His early style was influenced by two black clarinetists from New Orleans, Jimmie Noone and Johnny Dodds, and by the white musician Don Murray. After working with Ben Pollack and in studio bands Goodman graduated to leading his own band. Set on originality, he hired the leading Negro arranger Fletcher Henderson. By 1936 Goodman had achieved widespread popularity with ballroom dancers, and his success heralded the 'Swing era', when big bands featuring jazz soloists achieved huge record sales; several of Goodman's sidemen, including trumpeter Harry James and drummer Gene Krupa, became national celebrities. In the late 1930s Goodman boldly tested his public by adding Negro musicians Lionel Hampton and Teddy Wilson to his entourage. Goodman was not an outstanding personality, nor was he a composer or arranger; the winning factors in his success as a bandleader were his facile clarinet playing and dedicated professionalism. For much of his life he courted fame as a performer of classical music, commissioning works from COPLAND, HINDEMITH and others, but it is Goodman's improvisations which will be remembered.   JJC

B. Goodman & J. Kolodin, *The Kingdom of Swing* (NY, 1939); D. H. Coonor & W. H. Hicks, *B. G. On The Record* (NY, 1969).

Goodman, Nelson (b. Somerville, Mass., USA, 7.8.1906). American philosopher. After graduation from Harvard in 1929, Goodman worked as an art dealer for a number of years but returned to Harvard in his mid-30s to write the doctoral dissertation that later developed into *The Structure of Appearance* (Cambridge, Mass., 1951, ²1977). Subsequently he taught at the universities of Pennsylvania and Brandeis before returning to Harvard until his retirement. Goodman is a proclaimed follower of CARNAP, particularly of the early Carnap who aimed to dispel the confusions of everyday thought and speech by recourse to modern formal logic. As far as specific problems are concerned, Goodman has been most influential in propounding his 'new riddle of induction': what right do we have to prefer one of the many conceivable common characteristics of a set of things we have observed to other, less obvious ones, when we generalize about the set as a whole? In *Languages of Art: an Approach to a Theory of Symbols* (Indianapolis, 1968) the idea that art represents reality by resembling it is powerfully and indefatigably criticized.
AQ

Gorky, Arshile, ps. of Vosdanig Manoog Adoian (b. Khorkom Vari, Turkish Armenia, Ottoman Empire [now Turkey], 15.4.1904; naturalized American citizen; d. Sherman, Conn., USA, 21.7.1948). Armenian/American painter. Gorky emigrated to the USA in 1920. He studied and taught art in Boston and in New York, where he settled in 1925. He began to exhibit in 1930 and in 1932 was one of the few Americans, including CALDER, invited to join the Paris *Abstraction-Création* group. His early style (e.g. *The Artist and his Mother*, c.1926–9, in memory of his mother who starved to death in 1918) is characterized by simplified figures rendered in large, flat areas of muted earth tones, a curious blend of Piero della Francesca and CÉZANNE. In the 1930s he drew on sources as varied as Uccello and Ingres, PICASSO and Jóan MIRÓ. He disapproved of politically oriented art, and his contribution to the Federal Arts Projects' 'art-for-the-people' campaign was an abstract mural for Newark airport (*Aviation: Evolution of Forms under Aerodynamic Limitations*, 1935–9) which combined cubist forms and images from aerial photographs with surrealist biomorphic shapes and a somewhat expressionistic surface texture. In the early 1940s Gorky used surrealist psychic improvisation, biomorphic and erotic 'ideograms', expressive colours and gestural textures to recreate memories of an Armenian childhood (e.g. the *Garden in Socchi* series, 1941–3; *The Liver is the Cock's Comb*, 1944). The spontaneous 'improvisation' on which these works was based was said to undergo considerable refinement before being transferred to the canvas in the sinuous black lines and patches of brilliant, 'expressive' colour. It was the expressive vitality of these works which helped to lead the way to abstract expressionism. After a cancer operation in 1946 and a car crash in which he broke his neck, Gorky committed suicide in 1948.   SOBT

J. Levy, *Arshile Gorky* (NY, 1968).

Gorky, Maxim, ps. of Alexey Maximovich Peshkov (b. Nizhni Novgorod [now Gorky], Russia, 28.3.1868; d. Moscow, USSR, 18.6.1936). Russian writer. Born into a family of artisans, he lost his parents at an early age and underwent the deprivations of a poverty-stricken childhood. He followed one profession after another and tramped all over Russia in search of work or as a vagrant. His ordeals are described in such autobiographical works as *Detstvo* [Childhood] (Moscow, 1913), *V lyudiakh* [My apprenticeship] (Moscow, 1969) and *Moi universitety* [My universities] (Moscow, 1923; all three tr. I. Schneider, *Autobiography*, NY, 1953). By the end of the century he had leapt from the obscurity of a provincial journalist to ranking, with Leo TOLSTOY and CHEKHOV, as one of the three most important living Russian short-story writers, novelists and dramatists. The 1890s were a period of new cultural trends in Russia, marking the break-up of the old order and a corresponding shift from the traditional gentry type and populist type of literature to modernism, on the one hand, and, on the other, a renewal of Russian realism of a 'Lower Depths' (title of Gorky's most important and characteristic play) variety, later to issue into the socialist realism, of which Gorky became the declared founder. Unlike Chekhovian resignation, the mood of Gorky's characters is one of self-reliance and a will to live fully and dangerously, combined with a search to tell even the harsh truth. In Tolstoy's assessment, Gorky 'feels himself a stranger, notices everything and reports to a God of his own'. One of Gorky's most impressive achievements was his sketches of Tolstoy, Chekhov, Korolenko, Andreev and others in *Literaturnye portrety* (Moscow, 1924, ²1959; tr. C. Mansfield *et al.*, *Reminiscences*, London, 1949). Most of his fiction shows a world of degraded, afflicted humanity, tramps, prostitutes and revolutionaries or strong, ruthless men, the early capitalist accumulators. The affliction is not Dostoevskyan; the characters are like strongly barbed thistles. They are often rebels or protesters and, in a measure, romantic dreamers. The misery is in the environment. A number of novels (*Mat'*, Moscow, 1907; tr. I. Schneider, *Mother*, NY, 1947; *Delo Artamonovych*, Moscow, 1925; tr. A. Brown, *The Artamonov Business*, NY, 1935; *Zhizn' Klima Samgina*, Moscow, 1927–37; pt 1 tr. B. Guerney, *The Bystander*, NY, 1930; pts 2–4 tr. A. Baksky, *The Magnet, Other Fires, The Specter*, NY, 1931–8) expose emerging capitalist society in Russia and the cultural mentality which Gorky saw as its by-product, and depict forces militating against this.

Gorky supported and subsidized the Bolsheviks, emigrated to Italy (Capri) after the 1905 revolution where he established, with Bogdanov and Lunacharsky, a left-wing Bolshevik faction (*Vperëd*) and tried to dilute MARXism in a 'God-building', quasi-Faustian ideology to advance the coming of a collectivized proletariat. Returning to Russia in 1917, he joined the Bolsheviks in 1919, although initially critical of their seizure of power, and was largely responsible for saving Russian writers and intellectuals from starvation in the immediate postrevolutionary years. During most of the 1920s he lived again in Italy, first opposing the Soviet regime, then advocating it, until 1928 when he returned to the USSR and headed the Writers Union. Belying his pen-name ('the bitter'), Gorky created an image of man with the marks of the soiled underground from which he comes, but also of the features of the future of which he dreams: the question of what man really is meant to Gorky what man can become.   EL

F. Borras, *Maxim Gorki the Writer: an interpretation* (Oxford, 1967); D. Levin, *Stormy Petrel: the Life and Work of Maksim Gorki* (London, 1967).

Gosset, William Sealy (b. Canterbury, Kent, UK, 1876; d. London, 16.10.1937). British statistician, writing as 'Student', who joined the Guinness breweries in 1899 and worked for them in Dublin for three decades, being forced as a result to invent the technique of inference from small samples (1908–17). His first result is now known as the t-test for the population mean; it was the first parametric statistical test not to use the Normal distribution. 'Student' quickly added the t-test for the correlation coefficient from a small sample from a Normal population; and the technique of matched pairs in the design of experiments, in which correlation between two variables is deliberately used to reduce the sampling variation of their difference. These are still the first techniques taught to statisticians. AGPW

L. McMullen & E. S. Pearson, 'William Sealy Gosset', *Biometrika*, 30 (1939), 205–50.

Goudsmit, Samuel Abraham (b. The Hague, S. Holland, The Netherlands, 11.7.1902; naturalized American citizen; d. Reno, Nev., USA, 4.12.1978). Dutch/American theoretical physicist. While students, he and UHLENBECK proposed that an electron should possess an intrinsic spin. They made this suggestion in order to account for the observation that the spectral lines emitted by many atoms were very slightly split into two or more separate lines (the fine structure). They showed that if the electron, besides orbiting the atom, also spun on its axis (like the earth around the sun) it would have the effect of slightly splitting the energy levels for particular orbits, and that this would then necessarily lead to the fine structure of the spectra. Their idea gave rise to some scepticism, but won complete acceptance when in 1928 DIRAC showed that electron spin was a direct consequence of the application of relativity to quantum mechanics.

Goudsmit and Uhlenbeck left the Netherlands in 1927 (there were no jobs for physicists) to take up positions at the University of Michigan. During WW2 Goudsmit was engaged in scientific intelligence with responsibility for investigating German progress on the development of the atom bomb. Apart from his work on spectroscopy, his other main interest was in statistical problems. From 1948 to 1970 he worked at the Brookhaven National Laboratory and from 1951 to 1974 was editor-in-chief of the American Physical Society whose publication the *Physical Review* is one of the world's leading physics journals. In 1958 he founded *Physical Review Letters* for the rapid publication of short scientific papers, and the medium in which many of the most important discoveries in physics are first reported. HMR

Graham, Martha (b. Allegheny, Pa, USA, 11.5.1894). American dancer, teacher and choreographer, and one of the founders of American modern dance, transmitted through her school, choreography and company. Graham rejected formal dance training and evolved a personal means of expression from which she evolved a specifically 'Graham' dance technique. The solar plexus is the mainspring of all movement; the back, rigid in classical ballet, is freer, more flexible and the limbs more extended; the force of gravity is emphasized in falls and floor work; the body does not only extend outwards but also contracts inwards. Her technique creates a body flexible enough to serve choreographic ideas of all kinds, all emotions, yet be capable of growth and development. Her aim in creating ballets was 'to make visible the interior landscape', and in over 150 works she probed into character, motivation and psychological complexities, and explored the myths of Europe and America. *Letter to the World* (1940), *Appalachian Spring* (1944), *Night Journey* (1947), *Diversion of Angels* (1948), *Clytemnestra* (1958) and *Acrobats of God* (1960) reveal her range and mastery of expressive movement. Her foundation of a school and company dedicated to her works and the perpetuation of her style has ensured the continuation of her ideas, which are consequently exerting a formidable influence upon a generation of dancers in the USA (notably Paul Taylor and Merce Cunningham). Companies based upon her style have been founded in London (London Contemporary Dance Company) and Israel (Batsheva Dance Company). She published in 1973 *The Notebooks of Martha Graham* (NY).

SCW

D. McDonagh, *Martha Graham: a Biography* (NY, 1974).

Graham, William Franklin (Billy) (b. Charlotte, NC, USA, 7.11.1918). American evangelist. Graham startled the USA with a simple, direct and dramatic form of preaching which had not been heard since Billy Sunday. It was first heard on a grand scale in Los Angeles in 1949. With the assistance of a professional team of singers and organizers, he filled large halls all over the world. Brought up a strict Presbyterian, he was ordained by the Southern Baptists in 1940. Beginning with the narrow support of fundamentalist Christians, he gradually gathered support from all the major denominations. When he came to England for the Greater London Crusade he was invited only by a small group of fundamentalist Christians, but within a few weeks he had won the respect and support of a much wider platform including the archbishop of Canterbury (Geoffrey Fisher) and the BBC head of religious broadcasting (Francis House). He followed the London crusade with a triumphal progress through Glasgow (1955) and New York (1957). His appeal was simple and uncomplicated, he was charming and in no way aggressive except to sin. He attended assemblies of the World Council of Churches in New Delhi (1961) and Uppsala (1968). His last massive campaign was in Korea in 1973 when American prestige in Asia was at its lowest. He received the Templeton award 'for progress in religion' in 1982. His thoughts are put across in preaching at mass meetings, consultation in committees and in popular radio and TV programmes. His organization is one of the largest electronic churches in the USA. The one book which sums up his appeal is *Peace with God* (NY, 1953).

EHR

Gramsci, Antonio (b. Ales, Sardinia, Italy, 23.1.1891; d. Rome, 27.4.1937). Italian Communist leader and MARXist theoretician. Brought up in poverty in one of the poorest districts of Italy, Gramsci left Sardinia at the age of 20 after winning a scholarship to Turin University. He proved himself a brilliant student, coming under the influence of CROCE's historicist philosophy; but he was early drawn to political activity in the Socialist party. At the end of WW1 he joined with other members of a leftwing group in establishing a paper of their own, *L'Ordine Nuovo* (May 1919). Gramsci was active in developing the role of factory councils in Turin, which was spoken of as the 'Petrograd of the Italian Revolution'. Widespread industrial unrest in 1920 led to the occupation of factories and a general strike, but ended in failure. Gramsci's disgust with reformist socialism led him to take part in a walkout from the Socialist Congress in Livorno (January 1921) and the foundation of a separate Communist party. In May 1922 he was sent to Moscow as the Italian representative on the Third International. His health, always poor, collapsed and he spent much of his time in Russia in a sanatorium. While Gramsci was out of Italy, MUSSOLINI came to power. In May 1924 Gramsci was sent back to Italy to take over the leadership of the Italian Communists in parliament. He followed the Comintern line of a united front against fascism 'from below', seeking an alliance with all workers, whatever their political allegiance, and especially with the peasants. On 8.11.1926 he was arrested by Mussolini's police and spent the rest of his life in prison, the last six years in hospital. He died at the age of 46.

Gramsci's active political career had finished when he was arrested in 1926. As a prisoner, however, he filled more than 30 notebooks (which take up 2350 pages in print) with reflections on politics, philosophy and history. These, together with the letters he wrote to his family, have won him posthumously a reputation as one of the most original political thinkers of the 20c and in the view of many critics the most important European Communist theoretician since LENIN – some would say, since Marx himself (see *Quaderni del Carcere*, ed. V. Garratana, 4 vols, Turin, 1975; tr. Q. Hoare & G. Nowell Smith, *Selections from the Prison Notebooks*, London, 1971; *Lettere del Carcere*, eds S. Caprioglio & E. Fubini, Turin, 1965; tr. L. Lawner, *Letters from Prison*, London, 1975).

Central to Gramsci's thinking was his rejection of the crude version of historical materialism which saw the superstructure of society determined by underlying economic forces; and a reformulation which left room for the influence of ideas on history and the effectiveness of human efforts, whether of an individual or a group, in altering the course of development. This interest in ideas and culture (which, unlike his contemporary LUKÁCS, he combined with the practical experience of a party leader) led him to work out the concept of 'hegemony'. Gramsci developed this concept to explain how a social and economic system can maintain its hold even when it is identified with the rule of one class over others, a 'hegemony' which is not sustained by economic power or physical force alone, but by persuading the other classes to accept the system of beliefs of the ruling class and share their social, moral and cultural values. The same approach, together with his distinction between 'active' and 'passive' revolutions, has suggested ways in which a communist party, like the Italian party after WW2, can expand its influence under a liberal democratic regime and so create the conditions for an eventual capture of power. Gramsci saw the intellectuals playing a central role in the maintenance of a social system (as the priesthood did in the Middle Ages) as well as in preparing the way for an alternative to take its place. On the other hand, while agreeing with Lenin on the need for the Communist party to lead and act in the name of the proletariat, his own practical experience (e.g. with the Turin factory councils in 1919–20) made him conscious of the need to combine this with the participation of the masses in the party's decisions. Marxists seeking to develop an alternative version of socialism to the repressive STALINist–Soviet model for inspiration, have been strongly attracted by Gramsci. Non-Marxists seeking a dialogue with Marxists have been equally strongly attracted by his awareness of the interaction of Marxism with other philosophies, notably the tradition reaching back through Croce to Hegel and Vico.   ALCB

J. Joll, *Gramsci* (London, 1977); M. N. Clark, *Antonio Gramsci and the Revolution that Failed* (London, 1977); A. B. Davidson, *Antonio Gramsci: Towards an Intellectual Biography* (London, 1977).

Granö, Johnnes Gabriel (b. Lapua, Grand Duchy of Finland [now Finland], 13.3.1882; d. Helsinki, 23.2.1956). Finnish geographer. Six years of his childhood (1885–91) were spent in Siberia, though Granö went to school in Oulu and in 1900 to Helsinki University, where he became an assistant in 1903 and a lecturer from 1908 to 1919. In most summers from 1902 to 1916 he visited Siberia, working particularly on glaciation. In 1919 he went to Tartu University, Estonia, and in 1922 became editor of the *Atlas of Finland* (Helsinki, 1879, ⁴1960). He returned to Helsinki in 1923 as professor of geography but moved to Turku University in 1926 and finally back to Helsinki from 1945 until his retirement in 1950. From his initial basic work on physical geography Granö went forward to human experience in his *Reine Geographie* [Pure geography] (Helsinki, 1929). His view was that the surface of the earth consists of a number of different environments bound by the senses of the persons perceiving them. The geographical problem is to place man's 'subjective' environment in a real 'objective' environment. A man of vast and varied experience in the field sciences, Granö is now regarded as an unrecognized pioneer in his emphasis on 'perception'; indeed, as HÄGERSTRAND has commented, he was 50 years before his time.   TWF

O. Granö, 'Granö, Johannes Gabriel', *Geographers: biobibliographical studies*, 3 (1979), 73–84.

Granville-Barker, Harley (b. London, UK, 25.11.1877; d. Paris, France, 31.8.1946). British actor, dramatist, director, manager and theatrical scholar. As an actor of 22 he scored a notable success playing Richard II for the reformer of Shakespearean production, William Poel. Between 1900 and 1907 he acted and directed for the 'Stage Society' which itself sought theatrical reform by introducing an intellectual theatre of social relevance. During this period Granville-Barker also established himself as a successful dramatist with such plays as *The Voysey Inheritance* (1905) and *The Madras House* (1910). Between 1904 and 1907, in partnership with J. E. Vedrenne, he mounted the famous seasons of plays, the majority by modern writers such as G. B. SHAW, Maeterlinck, HAUPTMANN and GALSWORTHY, at the Royal Court Theatre in London. These seasons, though not a financial success, nevertheless placed Granville-Barker indisputably at the centre of the new movement in theatre. In 1912, at the Savoy Theatre, he turned to the 'new Shakespeare', directing *The Winter's Tale* and *Twelfth Night* in a manner which adopted Poel's flowing action and vocal delivery but also introduced highly stylized and colourful sets and costumes by Norman Wilkinson and Charles Ricketts. After 1915 he abandoned the professional theatre for scholarly writing. In this, his finest achievements are his *Prefaces* to Shakespeare's plays (5 series, London, 1927–47) which, uniquely in Shakespearean criticism, located the study of the plays in the realm of stagecraft. The outstanding comprehensiveness, insight and quality of his work make Granville-Barker a leading figure in 20c British theatre. DKP

C. B. Purdom, *Harley Granville-Barker* (London, 1955).

Grass, Günter Wilhelm (b. Danzig, Germany [now Gdansk, Poland], 16.10.1927). German novelist and writer. Grass achieved international fame with his fantastic *Die Blechtrommel* (Berlin, 1959; tr. R. Manheim, *The Tin Drum*, London, 1962), a novel related by a dwarf, Oskar Mazerath, who continually beats a tin drum, gaining power through it as the Pied Piper did with his pipe. Oskar's recollections cover the whole of Grass's lifetime, including the Nazi period, but deal with it in an outrageous, 'Rabelaisian' ironic language which is often barely intelligible, owing

to lack of grammatical sequence. '*Blech*' means not only 'tin' but also (verbal) rubbish. Although the atrocities of Nazism are not omitted, it seems as though Oskar may have been Grass's device for making a first confrontation with events too monstrous to deal with soberly. *Katz und Maus* (Berlin, 1961; tr. R. Manheim, *Cat and Mouse*, NY, 1963), later described as the third part of a 'Danzig trilogy' of which *Die Blechtrommel* is the first, is about a series of baffling events which happen to a man with an enormous Adam's apple. The third volume in the trilogy, *Hundejahre* (Berlin, 1963; tr. R. Manheim, *The Dog Years*, NY, 1965) again deals with the Nazi past in a fantastic way, especially in the third section in which a former stormtrooper goes about West Germany with a dog which used to belong to HITLER, on a campaign of denazification. This again is grotesque and often obscene.

Though Grass has gone on writing in this vein (e.g. *Der Butt*, Berlin, 1977; tr. R. Manheim, *The Flounder*, NY, 1978), and has also written poems and plays, one of which satirizes BRECHT, he took an active part in politics on the side of the Social Democrats and gave support to Willy BRANDT in his election campaigns. Some of his speeches and other political writings are contained in *Uber das Selbstuerständliche* (Berlin, 1965; tr. R. Manheim, *Speak Out!*, London, 1969). This practical concern suggests that it is the artist in him who feels compelled to cope with the unacceptable past by means of ribald fantasy. RDG

A. V. Subiotto, *Günter Grass: the Literature of Politics* (London, 1978); M. Hollington, *Günter Grass: the Writer in a Pluralist Society* (London, 1980).

Graves, Robert Ranke (b. London, UK, 24.7.1895). British poet. Like other young men of his age and class, Graves went straight from public school to fight in WW1. He recorded this and subsequent experience of neurasthenia and recuperation in his autobiography *Goodbye to All That* (London, 1929, ²1957), the title of which signified his renunciation of the social and literary world into which he had been born. Since 1929, except for the periods of the Spanish civil war and WW2, he has made his home in Majorca. Graves has always maintained a careful distinction between his poetry and the novels and other writings which had more popular appeal, such as the historical novels *I, Claudius* (London, 1934) and *Claudius the God* (London, 1934). In his poetry Graves has progressed from a youthful Georgian to become, by turns, a poet of satiric disillusion; a celebrant of polarity, failure and resolution in love; and, finally, a poet whose insights into identity are detached from and rise above ordinary circumstance. He is most commonly thought of as a love poet, a view which his historical and sexual speculations in *The White Goddess: a Historical Grammar of Poetic Myth* (London, 1948, ²1952) did much to underpin and justify. His poetry has been persistently subject to selection and revision, initially in *Poems 1914–1926* (London, 1927), and then in five successive editions of *Collected Poems* (London, 1938–75). Although Graves has presented an *oeuvre* of progressive refinement and polished consistency, this achievement has been possible only because his poetry, for all its emphasis on the integrity of the self and its experience, has employed impersonal means of expression – the archetypal emblem and fable, simple stanzaic forms, and an often conventional diction. ATKC

M. Seymour Smith, *Robert Graves: his Life and Works* (London, 1982).

Gray, Eileen (b. Enniscorthy, Co. Wexford, Ireland, UK [now Irish Republic], 9.8.1879; d. Paris, France, 28.11.1976). Irish designer. Eileen Gray studied at the Slade School of Art, London, and moved to Paris in 1902. She first practised lacquer techniques as a student in Soho, London, and later with Sugawara in Paris. By 1913 she was sufficiently accomplished to exhibit her furniture in the Salon de la Société des Artistes Décorateurs and be patronized by the discriminating collector Jacques Doucet. The decorative scheme she created for Madame Mathieu Levy's flat in rue de Lota in 1919 marked a move away from her earlier work in the emerging French art deco style towards a more architectural form. In 1922 Gray opened a gallery in Paris called 'Jean Désert' which sold her lacquer screens, furniture, lamps, carpets and wall hangings. Her designs, though not appreciated by the French critics, were admired by OUD, and by LE CORBUSIER and Mallet-Stevens, who befriended and influenced her. Encouraged to practise architecture, she designed a house with Jean Badovici at Roquebrune. She made numerous architectural plans and models and executed a few buildings, notably a studio for Badovici in Paris (1930–1) and Tempe a Pailla, Castellar, near Menton (1932–4) for herself. Corbusier's admiration for her work resulted in the inclusion of some of her models for a vacation centre in his pavilion at the Paris Exhibition of 1937. Her last project, while rebuilding war-damaged Tempe a Pailla (1946–9), was for a cultural and social centre; she returned to Paris from the south of France into semiretirement. JMFR

S. Johnson, *Eileen Gray: Designer 1879–1976* (London, 1979).

Green, Henry, ps. of Henry Vincent Yorke (b. Tewkesbury, Glos., UK, 29.10.1905; d. London, 13.12.1973). British novelist. Educated at Eton and Oxford; then joined the family engineering business of which he became managing director. His upbringing and profession gave him access to the life of the factory (*Living*, London, 1929), of high society (*Party Going*, London, 1939; *Nothing*, London, 1950; *Doting*, London, 1952), of servants (*Loving*, London, 1945; *Concluding*, London, 1948), as well as WW2 (*Back*, London, 1946) when he served in the London Auxiliary Fire Service (*Caught*, London, 1943). His uniqueness consists in the objectivity with which he depicted these worlds. This is achieved by the absence of authorial comment, an increasing reliance on finely rendered dialogue, a prose style of such simplicity that it borders on affectation, and by a refusal to pattern his fictions in any obviously thematic way. The absence of moral, social or political perspectives gives his work the immediacy and opaqueness of total acceptance. As a result, the characters cannot be reduced to those simplified patterns favoured by literary critics nor can Green himself be placed easily within any school of thought. For this reason he is likely to remain the favourite of a minority.   DC

E. Stokes, *The Novels of Henry Green* (London, 1959).

Greenberg, Clement (b. New York, USA, 16.1.1909). American art critic who established an international reputation in the 1940s and 1950s for US abstract expressionist artists such as POLLOCK, Arshile GORKY, HOFMANN and KOONING, by means of numerous controversial essays and articles in such journals as the *Nation*, the *Partisan Review*, *Arts Digest* and the *New Leader*. He identified an ever-growing tendency towards nonrepresentational work among contemporary painters, which he saw as symptomatic of a search for the 'absolute': i.e. the creation of something valid solely on its own terms. Greenberg viewed the advent of the 'all-over', decentralized picture, devoid of illusionist space and thus sharing the same space as the spectator, as a threat to the future of the easel painting. His approach is largely formalist although many of his judgements are highly subjective. A large number of his essays were revised and published in an influential anthology, *Art and Culture* (Boston, Mass., 1961). He has written on *Joan Miró* (NY, 1949) and *Hans Hofmann* (London, 1961).   SOBT

Greene, Graham (b. Berkhamstead, Herts., UK, 2.10.1904). British novelist. After a brief career in journalism, Greene published his first novel *The Man Within* in 1929 – a thriller with a historical setting in which the characteristic themes of pursuit, guilt, treachery and failure are already evident. His first popular success was *Stamboul Train* (London, 1932), a thriller with a more topical, and political, flavour. Other works of the same kind, which Greene called 'entertainments', such as *A Gun For Sale* (London, 1936) and *The Confidential Agent* (London, 1939), brought new standards of realism and thoughtfulness to popular genre fiction. Greene was converted to the Roman Catholic church in 1926, but his religious convictions did not become overtly apparent

in his fiction until *Brighton Rock* (London, 1938) in which the moral stereotyping of the conventional thriller is turned upside down by investing the teenage gangster Pinkie with a kind of demonic spirituality. This initiated a sequence of explicitly 'Catholic' novels, *The Power and the Glory* (London, 1940), *The Heart of the Matter* (London, 1948) and *The End of the Affair* (London, 1951) which were as provocative to orthodox Catholics as they were to secular readers, but which established Greene internationally as a major literary figure. In these novels the Catholic protagonist's existential authenticity derives from a sense of sin rather than a state of grace, and the contrast between religious and humanistic values is dramatized in gripping plots of pursuit or sexual intrigue. Greene's work in this phase had much in common with the French Catholic literary tradition of Léon Bloy, PÉGUY, BERNANOS and MAURIAC. In his subsequent work Greene's religious stance has become more equivocal and his subjects more political. *The Quiet American* (London, 1955) was a prophetic critique of US involvement in South East Asia. *The Comedians* (London, 1966) and *The Honorary Consul* (London, 1973) show Greene's sympathy for liberation movements in Central and South America. In these novels, and in *A Burnt-Out Case* (London, 1961), Greene hints obliquely at the possibility of some synthesis of Christianity, MARXism and TEILHARD DE CHARDIN's evolutionary utopianism, but whereas in his middle period he made his own position clear by authorial commentary, he now tends to conceal it behind first-person narrators or dialogue. His most recent works of fiction *Dr Fischer of Geneva; or, the Bomb Party* (London, 1980) and *Monsignor Quixote* (London, 1982) are more like fables than novels, but their import is ambiguous. He has travelled widely, and has lived abroad since WW2; and his work is notable for its vivid and emotionally loaded evocations of various far-flung parts of the world, forming a composite geography which has been dubbed 'Greeneland'. Though chiefly distinguished as a novelist, Greene has also achieved considerable success as a writer of plays, screenplays, essays and travel books. He published an autobiography of his early years, *A Sort of Life*, in 1971 (London) and a sequel *Ways of Escape*, describing the sources of many of his novels, in 1980 (London).   DJL

D. Lodge, 'Graham Greene' in G. Stade (ed.), *Six Contemporary British Novelists* (London, 1976).

Greer, Germaine (b. Melbourne, Victoria, Australia, 21.1.1939). Australian feminist and journalist. Germaine Greer came to the UK in 1964, having graduated from Melbourne and Sydney universities. By 1967 she had completed a PhD at Cambridge, on Shakespeare's early comedies, and was lecturing in Elizabethan and Jacobean drama at the University of Warwick as well as contributing to journals and underground magazines including *Private Eye* and *Screw*, when her agent suggested she write a book about the failure of women's emancipation. Sold by the million and translated into 12 languages, *The Female Eunuch* (London, 1970) became popularly synonymous with 'women's lib'. It was primarily a powerful personal statement, reflecting the flamboyant style of an author whose anarchical position alienated her from both reformist and radical feminists. Greer persuasively demolished the case for the then widely accepted assumption of women's inferiority, ascribing their subordinate status to the effects of the imposed female role which psychologically 'castrates' women. Citing history, literature and popular culture, Greer traced how this oppression developed under patriarchy (through the nuclear family, education, work and capitalism), also enslaving men, as women's self-loathing stimulates male contempt. Greer challenged women to act individually, urging them to reject marriage in favour of communal living. Her second book *The Obstacle Race* (London, 1979) was a more sober and impersonal academic historical study of women painters and their work, from a feminist viewpoint. She still maintains her earlier revolutionary ideals and is cynical about recent advances in women's rights.   MI

Grierson, John (b. Deanston, Tayside, UK, 24.4.1898; d. Bath, Avon, 19.2.1972). British documentary film director. The role of John Grierson in relation to the British documentary movement is somewhat akin to that of REITH to the wider field of British broadcasting. Both men were Scots who saw the public-service potential of a new medium and devoted a lifetime's effort to establishing this against the dominant claims of entertainment. Grierson, who coined the term 'documentary' in a 1926 review of FLAHERTY's *Moana*, made only one film, the silent *Drifters* (1929). Thereafter his role was the formation of a team of committed young documentary film makers – Basil Wright, Edgar Anstey and Arthur Elton among them – and the supervision of production of innumerable documentary films. His major work was accomplished in the period up to 1937, first at the Empire Marketing Board and then at the GPO Film Unit (later to become the Crown Film Unit) – though subsequently he worked in Canada for UNESCO and in Scotland. Grierson's importance lies less in his enthusiasm for the film medium, which he saw as an instrument much like any other, than in his definition of a coherent social aim for it (see F. Hardy, ed., *Grierson on Documentary*, London, 1966). Putting social purpose above aesthetics and instruction above entertainment, he was instrumental in widening the potential application of the film medium.   RPA

J. Beveridge, *John Grierson: Film Master* (NY, 1978); F. Hardy, *John Grierson: a Documentary Biography* (London, 1979).

Griffith, David Wark (b. Crestwood, Ky, USA, 22.1.1875; d. Hollywood, Calif., 23.7.1948). American film director and one of the major contributors to the development of narrative cinema in the period up to 1918. A failed playwright, he turned to the cinema without enthusiasm in 1908 and learned his craft by directing some 400 one-reel (15-minute) films at Biograph. Then in 1915 he produced the three-hour epic *The Birth of a Nation* which, despite its dubious racist content, is generally regarded as the first great masterpiece of world cinema, as well as one of the greatest box office successes of all times. The even more ambitious *Intolerance* (1916) was a commercial failure, but the authentic Griffith touch is still to be found in such works as *Broken Blossoms* (1919) and *Way Down East* (1920). Later, as studio production became more tightly controlled, the man who had once been Hollywood's unquestioned master became first an employee contracted for routine pictures and then an increasingly neglected figure.

The precise nature of Griffith's achievements has been much obscured by the personalized style of film history which has attributed to him virtually every advance in film technique between 1908 and 1916. In fact Griffith was, even at this time, a comparatively backward director in terms of cutting, since his method of continual improvisation (no two takes of a shot were ever the same) prevented him from achieving the smoothness and polish in his editing accomplished by some of his lesser-known contemporaries. Griffith's greatness lay elsewhere: in his towering dramatic command and in the vision which he brought to a despised form of expression from his early theatrical background.   RPA

H. M. Geduld (ed.), *Focus on D. W. Griffith* (Englewood Cliffs, 1971); R. M. Henderson, *D. W. Griffith: his Life and Work* (NY, 1972).

Grignard, François Auguste Victor (b. Cherbourg, Manche, France, 6.5.1871; d. Lyons, Rhône, 13.12.1935). French chemist. Early in his career Grignard came under the influence of P. A. Barbier, head of the department of chemistry in the University of Lyons, who had been investigating the interaction of unsaturated ketones, alkyl iodides, and magnesium (instead of the zinc required by Saytzev's method). Accepting a recommendation from Barbier, Grignard, for his doctoral thesis research, began a study of the reagents and the reactions which now bear his name, and which are still among the most fruitful and widely used in organic synthesis, viz. the interaction, in anhydrous conditions, of alkyl halides with finely divided magnesium in anhydrous ether. This emphasis on the solvent stemmed from an assiduous study of Frankland's work on the inflammable zinc alkyls. Some of the uses of the reagent were reported in a short paper in 1900. Grignard spent much of the rest of his career developing and extending his original discovery. He also studied organic derivatives of aluminium and of mercury, and terpenes. He succeeded Barbier in the chair at Lyons and in his later years was much occupied with his comprehensive *Traité de chimie organique* [Treatise on organic chemistry], the first volumes of which appeared in 1935. Other writers had to complete the work. He shared the Nobel prize for chemistry in 1912 with SABATIER.   NBC

Gris, Juan, ps. of José Victoriano Gonzalez (b. Madrid, Spain, 23.3.1887; d. Boulogne-sur-Seine, Pas-de-Calais, France, 11.5.1927). Spanish painter. He studied art in Madrid before moving to Paris in 1906, where he met PICASSO, APOLLINAIRE and Max Jacob. His early humorous illustrations were influenced by art nouveau. Between 1910 and 1911 he began to adopt the monochrome shifting planes and spatial ambiguities of analytical cubism. Unlike Picasso and BRAQUE, however, he did not pursue cubist reductive experiments to similarly formal conclusions. Gris's premise, from c. 1912 onwards, was the reverse, namely that the artist's starting-point should not be the object, but the abstract elements of painting (shape, colour and texture), arranged and synthesized on the surface so as to suggest objects while retaining their abstract materiality. Above all, Gris wished to emphasize the tangible reality of the picture plane, which he insisted was more important than the objects depicted. He reintroduced colour into cubism (1912), creating decorative and vigorous surface rhythms, often with a diagonal stress. The collage materials he introduced from 1914 onwards (e.g. newspaper, marble- or wood-grained papers) retained their original identities (e.g. *Breakfast*, 1914). From c. 1912 onwards he frequently combined the cubist grid with Renaissance illusionistic space (e.g. *La Place Ravignan, Still Life in front of an Open Window*, 1915). In later years he combined more muted colours and even more simplified forms in austere compositions dominated by an interplay of curves and straight lines.

SOBT

J. T. Soby, *Juan Gris* (NY, 1958); D.-H. Kahnweiler, *Juan Gris: his Life and Work* (NY, 1969).

Gropius, Walter (b. Berlin, Germany, 18.3.1883; naturalized American citizen, 1944; d. Boston, Mass., USA, 5.7.1969). German/American architect. Born into a family of architects, artists and teachers, Gropius played a major role in the development of the theory and practice of 20c architecture and design. The strongest influence on his thought before WW1 was BEHRENS, whose transition from the profession of artist to that of architect and industrial designer, impressed him deeply during the period 1908 to 1910 when he was Behrens's closest assistant and disciple. In partnership with Adolf Meyer, Gropius achieved a memorable landmark in the history of architecture, the Fagus Shoe-Last factory at Alfeld-an-der-Leine, a building which dramatically demonstrated the possibilities of the glass curtain-wall. Novel effects of transparency and light were created by dispensing with solid corners to the building.

Gropius was one of the many who emerged from WW1, having served with distinction at the front, with a passionate desire to re-form European society in such a way as to avoid such nightmares in the future. Although he may be characterized politically as a middle-of-the-road liberal socialist, his postwar attitude was an idealistic, evangelizing one, based in part on the theories of William Morris and John Ruskin, in part on the cultural mission of the German *Werkbund* (in which he had played a prominent part before the war) and in part in sympathy with the adherents of a wide spectrum of political and religious beliefs, which, he thought, could be harnessed in union to forge a new society. This reforming zeal first found expression in his leading participation in extremist groups like the *November-gruppe* and the *Arbeitsrat für Kunst*; he then focused all his energies on the foundation of the Bauhaus (1919), a radical reorganization of the Weimar School of Arts and Crafts. Gropius drew together a brilliant team of avant-garde artists and craftsmen to teach there – Itten, SCHLEMMER, KLEE and KANDINSKY, for example – and created the first academy of art based on principles drawn from 20c art and theory. The Bauhaus was organized to train artists and designers so that they might cooperate, on an international basis if necessary, to create a new environment in which beauty, imagination and economy were instinct in all common artifacts and in a 'total' architecture. The Bauhaus drew upon itself violent criticism from German right-wing extremists, and its life coincided only with that of the Weimar republic. Gropius continued, while director of the Bauhaus, to design buildings of lasting interest and beauty – the Dessau Bauhaus itself (1925) for example. His prevailing interest where housing was concerned was in prefabrication and the development of factory-produced buildings. Gropius was obliged to leave Germany in 1934, and, following a period in partnership with E. Maxwell Fry in England, accepted a post at Harvard University. His later architecture in America was a little dull. An attractive, posthumously executed building in Berlin contains the Bauhaus archive, where a major collection of the documents of his achievements and thought may be studied.

AW

W. Gropius, *The New Architecture and the Bauhaus* (London, 1935); M. Franciscono, *Walter Gropius and the Creation of the Bauhaus in Weimar* (Urbana, 1971).

Grosz, George Ehrenfried (b. Berlin, Germany, 26.7.1893; d. West Berlin, 6.7.1959). German graphic satirist. Grosz's sharp, precise drawings of the soldiery, police, profiteers, tarts and workers of Weimar Germany (particularly Berlin) will always be among the most vivid evidence of the forces that brought HITLER to power. Initially childish and graffiti-like, product of the artist's unbounded loathing of WW1, they reflected the nihilism and simultaneism of Berlin dada, but became less mannered and more pointedly political after the revolutionary defeats of 1919. In 1925 he helped write *Die Kunst ist in Gefahr* [Art in danger], a polemical tract on the uselessness of art except as propaganda, yet at the same time was painting in the 'objective' style of *Neue Sachlichkeit*: an inconsistency which helped soften his line and undermine his self-assurance. Abandoning many of his political convictions, he emigrated in 1933 to a teaching job in New York, where he developed a surreal-academic style and a deeply cynical enthusiasm for the American way of life. This further weakened him as an artist but gives a uniquely ironic flavour to his vivid autobiography (*A Little Yes and a Big No*, NY, 1946). Ironically, too, he died of an accidental fall soon after returning to live in Berlin, where his early work seemed a revelation to the young. An edition of his drawings *Ecce Homo* was published in London in 1967. JWMW

B. Lewis, *George Grosz* (Madison, 1971); H. Hess, *George Grosz* (London, 1974).

Grothendïeck, Alexandre (b. Berlin, Germany, 1928; naturalized French citizen). German/French mathematician. He arrived in France as a refugee in 1941, and for many years refused to take up French nationality out of respect for his Russian father, murdered by the Nazis. His major achievement marks a revolution in algebraic geometry. In collaboration with several other mathematicians, notably BOURBAKI, he unified themes in geometry, number theory, topology and complex analysis. The crucial concept is the scheme, and the étale cohomology of schemes, developed in the 1960s, which proved capable of resolving the important number-theoretic WEIL conjectures. The hardest conjecture was solved affirmatively by Grothendïeck's pupil Pierre Deligne in 1972. Grothendïeck's work also has implications for logic *via* his theory of topoi. He gave a purely algebraic proof of the Riemann–Roch theorem, and an algebraic definition of the fundamental group of a curve. His work is perhaps the most abstract significant development in mathematics since WW2. He was awarded a Fields medal in 1966. Grothendïeck was prominently associated with an antimilitarist move-

ment in the 1960s. He has turned recently to the teaching of mathematics, and since 1978 has been professor at Montpellier University. JJG

R. Hartshorne, *Algebraic Geometry* (NY, 1977).

Grotowski, Jerzy (b. Rzeszów, Poland, 11.8.1933). Polish director and theatre researcher. After studying acting and directing in Cracow and Moscow, working as an assistant director and travelling in Central Asia, Grotowski became artistic director of the municipally subsidized 'Theatre of the Thirteen Rows' in the small Polish town of Opole. There he created a small permanent company, a 'theatre laboratory' dedicated to theatrical research. In 1965, when the company moved to Wročlav (formerly Breslau), it was given the official status of an institute, concerned with 'research into acting method'. Grotowski insisted that the theatre should no longer try to compete, unsuccessfully, with film and television, should reject its reliance upon sets, costume, make-up and technology and become instead a 'poor theatre', exploiting its unique quality – the live communion of actor and audience. The implications of this assertion were explored in productions which were based upon literary classics such as Wyspiański's *Acropolis* (1962) or Marlowe's *Dr Faustus* (1963). The texts were, however, cut and transposed, and their action reset. A new actor-audience configuration was devised for each production and the performances often contained grotesque gesture and vocal incantation, made available to the actor through rigorous training, and producing, in their trance-like 'excess', an atmosphere akin to that of religious ritual. The blasphemous treatment of the text was intended to attack the audience's spiritual complacence by challenging the sanctified national and religious myths which it embodied. Grotowski's systematic research into acting and production became widely influential, particularly with the publication of his book *Towards a Poor Theatre* (Holstebro, Denmark, 1968; London, 1969) and his tours of Europe and America, inspiring, among others, BROOK and the American 'Living Theatre'.

Since 1970 Grotowski has transferred his attention to paratheatrical group activities involving selected members of the public and taking place in the countryside around Wrocław. These combine strenuous outdoor activity, spontaneous creative events and spiritual retreat. It is doubtful whether they will prove as influential as Grotowski's earlier work.

DKP

T. Burzyński & Z. Osiński, *Grotowski's Laboratory* (Warsaw, 1979).

Guderian, Heinz Wilhelm (b. Külm, Germany [now Chelmno, Poland], 17.6.1888; d. Schwangen bei Füssen, Bavaria, West Germany, 15.5.1954). German military strategist and general. Effective as both a theorist and a practitioner of *Blitzkrieg*, Guderian evolved the idea of strategic penetration by tank divisions after studying the work of J. F. C. FULLER and LIDDELL HART. Despite continual discouragement from his superiors, he tested independent tank battalions in manoeuvres in 1932, and three years later was influential in forming three Panzer divisions. His bold and imaginative thinking attracted HITLER's attention, and in May 1938 he was appointed commander of mobile troops, a post from which he put his theories into practice. His book *Achtung! Panzer!* (Berlin, 1937; *Attention! Tanks!*, London, 1937) showed how well he had absorbed the theories of his mentors; the campaigns in Poland, France and Russia (1939–42) demonstrated his mastery of the instrument he had done much to create. He gave his own account of his career in *Erinnerungen eines soldaten* (Heidelberg, 1956; *Panzer Leader*, London, 1952).

JGo

Guevara de la Serna, Ernesto (Che) (b. Rosario, Argentina, 14.6.1928; d. Bolivia, 8.10.1967). Argentinian revolutionary. One of the revolutionary heroes of the 20c, Guevara was born into a middle-class Argentine family of Spanish-Irish descent. Known for his radical views even as a boy, he completed his medical studies in 1953, but as a result of his travels in Latin America and his observation of the poverty of the mass of the people, became convinced that the only way to bring about change was by violent revolution, to which he devoted his life. Che (a nickname derived from his habit of punctuating his speech with the interjection *che*) joined the CASTRO brothers in their campaign (1956–8) to overthrow the Batista government in Cuba, becoming one of Fidel Castro's principal lieutenants. He later used his experience as a successful guerrilla commander to write a highly influential manual on guerrilla strategy and tactics in English as *Guerilla Warfare* (London, 1961). This was followed by *Pasajes de la guerra revolucionaria* (Havana, 1963; *Reminiscences of the Cuban Revolutionary War*, London, 1968). After the conquest of power (January 1959) Guevara became a leading figure in Castro's government, attracting attention in the West by the fire and eloquence of his attacks on imperialism, neocolonialism and US policy in the Third World.

After April 1965 Che Guevara dropped out of Cuban public life and then disappeared altogether. The reason seems to have been a desire to exchange the role of politician and administrator for the more congenial one of revolutionary leader. He was more attracted by the liberation of the Third World, especially his native Latin America, than by making socialism work. He spent some time in Africa with other Cuban guerrilla fighters organizing the LUMUMBA Battalion which took part in the Congo civil war. Then, in autumn 1966, he turned up incognito in Bolivia where he trained and led a guerrilla troop in the Santa Cruz region. His record of this last campaign was published as *Bolivian Diary* (London, 1969). In October 1967 his group was surrounded by troops of the Bolivian army, and he himself was captured and shot.

Che Guevara had already become a legend during his lifetime. The combination of intellectual and revolutionary theorist with man of action and proven guerrilla leader; a middle-class upbringing with the decision to sacrifice a professional career in order to fight for the poor and oppressed; and of an adventurous life with a tragic early death won the admiration of large numbers of young people throughout the world and made him the hero and cult figure of 'the generation of '68', in the years of student rebellion in the West.   ALCB

A. Sinclair, *Che Guevara* (London, 1970).

Guillén, Jorge (b. Valladolid, Spain, 18.1.1893). Spanish poet, ranking with JIMÉNEZ (12 years his senior, and in some respects his master) as one of the outstanding Spanish proponents of 'pure poetry'. Guillén learnt much from Mallarmé and VALÉRY (but more from 17c Góngora), applying this chiefly in poems in traditional Spanish metres. They impress with the brilliance of their intellectual (often recondite, but always striking) metaphors, their startling luminosity, and the – occasionally obtrusive – perfectionism of their formal elegance. His prime concern is with the distillation of pure beauty from objective reality, metaphorically transformed: 'Pure poetry is what is left when all that is unpoetic has been eliminated', and what is left is an intellectual 'canticle' to creation. The bulk of his poetry is indeed collected as *Cántico*, progressively enlarged in successive editions (Madrid, 1928, 1936; Mexico City, 1945; Buenos Aires, 1950; tr. B. Belitt *et al.*, *Cántico: a Selection*, London, 1965; tr. J. Palley, *Affirmations: a Bilingual Anthology 1919 –1966*, Norman, Okla, 1968). *Aire nuestro* [Our air] (Milan, 1968) brought together all his poetry to date. A political exile after the Spanish civil war, Guillén settled in New England, USA.   RP-M

G. R. Lind, *Jorge Guillén's 'Cántico'* (Frankfurt, 1955); I. Ivask & J. Marichal (eds), *Luminous Reality: the Poetry of Jorge Guillén* (Norman, Okla, 1969).

Guillén, Nicolás (b. Camagüey, Cuba, 10.7.1902). Poet laureate of post-revolutionary Cuba, president of the Cuban Writers' Union (UNEAC) and journalist. Guillén is the son of a provincial liberal politician and publisher who was assassinated by conservative troops. A mulatto, he is best known outside Cuba for his contribution to black or Afro-Cuban poetry in *Motivos de son* [Song motifs] (Havana, 1930) and *Sóngoro cosongo* (Havana, 1931), in which traditional Spanish metres such as

the ballad are 'Cubanized', modified by the use of African words, local rhythms such as the *son*, onomatopoeia and popular diction. Equidistant from exclusive *négritude* and superficial folklorism, his poetry gradually developed a wider social concern for the Caribbean in *West Indies Ltd* (Havana, 1934) and the whole of Latin America, adopting an increasingly conscious anti-imperialist stance. Inspired by the Spanish anti-fascist struggle, like VALLEJO and NERUDA, he joined the Communist party in Spain in 1937. Virtually exiled by the dictator Batista from 1953 to 1959, he travelled widely, attending many international congresses. After the triumph of CASTRO's revolution, Guillén returned to Cuba, working indefatigably at home and abroad to promote its culture. In 1981 he was awarded his country's highest honour, the Order of José Martí. His poetry is a major contribution to the creation of a Creole Caribbean identity, uniquely combining political message with popular rhythm and appeal. An English version of *¡Patria o muerte!* (*The Great Zoo and other poems*, translated by R. Márquez), was published in 1972 (London).   SB

Guimard, Hector-Germain (b. Lyons, Rhône, France, 10.3.1867; d. New York, USA, 20.5.1942). French art nouveau architect. Professor at the Ecole des Arts Décoratifs (1894–8) and influenced initially by Horta, he concentrated all his inventive ideas (e.g. the imaginative use of metal, faïence and glass-bricks) on the interior of buildings such as the Castel Berenger (1894–8), a Paris apartment block. His designs for the Paris Métro stations (1899–1904), for which he is best known, are not strictly speaking architecture, but an expression of decorative art nouveau symbols whose abstract dynamic is created by the stylized organic forms of open wrought-iron balustrades and entrance arches.   SOBT

Gunn, Neil Miller (b. Latheron, Highland, UK, 8.11.1891; d. Inverness, 13.1.1973). Scottish novelist, author of 25 novels, some plays and essays, all written in standard English and most depicting the life of the far north-east of Scotland, a region of vanishing culture (particularly the Gaelic world which fascinated Gunn) and under threat from encroaching industrial civilization. After working as an exciseman in Inverness, Gunn embarked on a life of professional authorship, producing a stream of uneven novels, the best of which – *Highland River* (Edinburgh, 1937), *Butcher's Broom* (Edinburgh, 1934), *The Silver Darlings* (London, 1941) – have the status of modern masterpieces in Scotland. Their themes are simple life, the struggle for survival, the historical forces which destroyed Gaelic culture, the poverty of the Highlanders displaced by the Clearances of the 18c. Throughout runs Gunn's mystic interest in 'delight' (a state of high awareness connected with his interest in Zen Buddhism), and his characters frequently experience that sense in pursuit of happiness or merely physical activity: the wisdom of such delight is shown as being destroyed along with the older Gaelic culture of Scotland. Urban life plays little part in Gunn's fiction, but his country settings have a universality which has in part led to a recent critical revaluation and (despite the author's shy personality) an interest in his life. He started no school of followers, and his work remains unique in Scotland.   IC

F. R. Hart & J. B. Pick, *Neil M. Gunn: a Highland Life* (London, 1981).

Gurdjieff, George Ivanovich (b. Alexandropol [now Leninakan], Russia, 13.1.1874; d. Neuilly, Paris, France, 29.10.1949). Russian occult teacher. Although his father was a Greek carpenter and traditional oral storyteller and his mother an Armenian, and he was raised in the southern Caucasus, more precise biographical details of his youth and many of his mature experiences have been cavalierly clouded by Gurdjieff himself. At 16, however, he did abandon his family to seek after secret knowledge among the monasteries and holy men of India, China and Tibet (see *Meetings with Remarkable Men*, London, 1963) – the latter expedition probably financed by the Russian secret service. In 1905 he was practising in the Caucasus as hypnotist, drug healer and instructor in the occult. In 1911 he staked his occult claim to mastership by

taking up residence in Moscow; but his more elaborate plans for establishing a teaching institution were thwarted by WW1 and then the Russian revolution. His lectures and personal presence, however, attracted many followers and in 1915 he successfully lured OUSPENSKY to become his principal spokesman. Only in 1922 was the Institute for the Harmonious Development of Man given physical form, at Fontainebleau, and for the next 14 years it enrolled pupils, including MANSFIELD and A. R. Orage, to its daily regimen of 'intentional suffering' – intense manual labour and question-and-answer sessions with the Master. In 1924 Gurdjieff gave public performances of his skills in New York, and as a consequence cells were established to advance his practices. Following a serious car accident, Gurdjieff delegated his teaching and set about entrusting his knowledge and revelations to paper, especially in the extensive form of *Beelzebub's Tales to His Grandson* (NY, 1950, ²1974). After 1934 he returned to teaching and after WW2 to the further elaboration of his ritual dances.

Gurdjieff's writings, published posthumously, introduced little clarification or consistency into his thought. His ideas are not original, his sources can be readily traced, and the movement he stimulated was obviously part of a reawakening of interest in the occult in the earlier part of this century. Whether charlatan, mystic, scoundrel or 'master', he exercised remarkable authority, charismatically over his disciples and by reputation over much wider American and European circles.   RBW

J. G. Bennett, *Gurdjieff: Making a New World* (London, 1973); J. Webb, *The Harmonious Circle* (London, 1980).

Gurdon, John Bertrand (b. Farnham, Surrey, UK, 2.10.1933). British embryologist and molecular biologist. Gurdon trained as a zoologist at the University of Oxford and worked there until moving to the Medical Research Council laboratory for molecular biology in Cambridge in 1972. He was responsible for providing direct experimental evidence that the nucleus of a mature tissue cell could successfully support the complete development of an animal egg that had been deprived of the services of its own nucleus. This could only mean that the developmental history of the tissue cell providing the nucleus had not been involved in the irrevocable loss of genetic information possessed by the egg nucleus from which it itself was descended. This result removes one whole class of possible hypotheses from the agenda of developmental biology. Gurdon's work until 1974 is reviewed in his *Control of Gene Expression in Animal Development* (Oxford, 1974). DRN

Guston, Philip (b. Montreal, Quebec, Canada, 27.6.1913; d. Woodstock, NY, USA, 7.6.1980). American painter. After studying for three months at the Otis Art Institute, Los Angeles, and travelling to Europe, he entered a period of figurative painting dealing with social themes. The influence of the Mexican mural movement was reinforced by a visit to Mexico in 1934. From 1935 until 1942 he painted murals under the Federal Art Project. During the 1940s Guston's painting began to move towards fantasy under the influence of PICASSO, CHIRICO and Piero della Francesca. In 1948–9 he travelled to Italy and subsequently developed an abstract style related to MONDRIAN's 'plus and minus' compositions in its brushstrokes, using a palette of cream, grey, pink and orange: because of its suggestion of MONET's late work this became known as 'abstract impressionism'. From the mid-1950s the brushwork became more expressive and blocks of colour evoked vague figurative associations. Guston's return to figurative painting in 1968–70 shocked the American art world; the hooded Ku Klux Klan figure returned as a penitent. From 1973 the paintings became more grotesque and overtly autobiographical, employing the style of the 'underground' comics of the 1960s and a thick fleshly facture. Despite his sophisticated art-historical and literary culture, Guston became the main precursor of American 'bad painting' of the late 1970s and early 1980s. MOJN

D. Ashton, *Yes, But ... : a Critical Study of Philip Guston* (NY, 1976); San Francisco Museum of Modern Art, *Philip Guston* (San Francisco, 1980).

Gutiérrez, Gustavo (b. Lima, Peru, 8.6.1928). Peruvian theologian. Despite his Spanish name, Gutiérrez is of Indian origin. He is professor in the departments of theology and social sciences in the University of Lima. He became widely known in the 1970s thanks to his first major book *Teología de la liberación* (Lima, 1971; *A Theology of Liberation*, NY, 1973), which synthesized a number of aspirations that were strongly felt in the Latin American church at that time. It wanted a theology that would not be merely derivative of European theology, but which would speak to the people of Latin America. Since the church felt itself to be oppressed, it would be a committed theology that took the side of the poorest, that translated the Christian concept of 'salvation' into the quasi-political concept of liberation. But Gutiérrez refuses to make such a distinction, which he castigates as 'dualism'. Inevitably he then has to deal with a series of problems, about the level of violence a Christian may accept and about the degree to which MARXist analysis (as distinct from the Marxist worldview) may be used by a theologian. Gutiérrez holds that the military dictatorships of Latin America, with their doctrine of 'national security', represent 'established violence', and so violence may be used to overthrow them. He follows ALTHUSSER in believing that Marxism is 'scientific', and therefore no problem of compatibility with Christian faith can arise. Subsequently a whole school of 'liberation theologians' developed, many of them more extreme than Gutiérrez, the pioneer. PAH

P. Lehmann, *The Transfiguration of Politics* (London, 1974); P. Hebblethwaite, *The Christian-Marxist Dialogue and Beyond* (London, 1977).

H

Haber, Fritz (b. Breslau, Silesia, Germany [now Wročlav, Poland], 9.12.1868; d. Basle, Switzerland, 29.1.1934). German chemist. The son of a dye-stuffs merchant, his early training was in organic chemistry with a view to his entering the family firm. At Karlsruhe, however, he took up the study of physical chemistry, and started to apply it to chemical problems of practical importance. His early studies were of the decomposition of hydrocarbons and in electrochemistry, but his most important work was on the high-pressure synthesis of ammonia from its elements nitrogen and hydrogen. This process, which he developed with Carl BOSCH at the firm of BASF, laid the foundation of the fertilizer and explosives industries. During WW1 he put all his energies into the German war effort, working on explosives, petrol and the poison-gas chlorine. The award to him of the Nobel prize in 1919 led therefore to some criticism from scientists in the Allied countries. In 1920 he became involved in the futile attempt to pay off German war debts by means of gold extracted from sea-water. His last public act was to resign, in 1933, as director of the Kaiser Wilhelm Institute in Berlin in protest against the dismissal of Jewish scientists. He is now rightly remembered as one of the first chemists to bridge fully the gap between pure and theoretical chemistry on the one hand and its industrial applications on the other.   JSR

Habermas, Jürgen (b. Düsseldorf, N. Rhine-Westphalia, Germany, 18.6.1929). German social theorist. The leading representative of the second generation of the Frankfurt school. From 1961 to 1964 Habermas taught philosophy in Heidelberg and in 1964 became professor of philosophy and sociology at Frankfurt. He is currently director of the Max Planck Institute in Starnberg. In his principal works, *Theorie und Praxis* (Berlin, 1963; tr. J. Viertel, *Theory and Practice*, Boston, Mass., 1973) and *Erkenntnis und Interesse* (Frankfurt,

1968; tr. J. J. Schapiro, *Knowledge and Human Interests*, Boston, Mass., 1971), Habermas undertakes a radical antipositivist critique of human knowledge. He argues that, despite their claims, positivism and modern science build upon assumptions which, far from being value-free, are shot through with nontheoretical interests. It is crucial that these interests should be identified and analysed, and that just relations should be restored between theory and practice.

From Holbach and the French Enlightenment to MARX, reason had been a weapon in the battle against myth, superstition and tyranny. Error was synonymous with evil, truth identical with liberation and the human good, and reason and interest, theory and practice were thus intimately linked. With the growth of science and technology, and the rigid bureaucratic organization of industrial society, however, Habermas sees the link taking on a sinister, inhuman form. For reason now acquired a purely instrumental character, and rationality came to consist solely in the efficient marshalling of means in the service of the uncriticized ends of societies founded upon science and social technology. Reason thus lost its emancipative role, and, ceasing to be an organ of discovery or a generator of meaning and value, became a tool of authority and oppression. While claiming to undermine the positivist conception of knowledge as an undistorted transcription of the world as it is, Habermas nevertheless believes that his insight enables him to discover a viewpoint from which practical interest and theoretical contemplation will justly fall together. He conceives a condition in which human communication will be wholly free of domination; where in self-reflection theory and practice, cognition and interest, will legitimately coincide; the depoliticization of life in technological society will be reversed; and the emancipative reason of praxis, which will involve all rational subjects in determining the shape of their lives, will body forth human goals. RNH

T. McCarthy, *The Critical Theory of Jürgen Habermas* (London, 1978).

Hadamard, Jacques (b. Versailles, Yvelines, France, 8.12.1865; d. Paris, 17.10.1963). French mathematician. He first worked on complex function theory, where his theorem on lacunary series is fundamental to the detection of singularities of a function defined by its Taylor series. In 1896 he proved the prime number theorem, first raised by C. F. Gauss and notably discussed by G. F. B. Riemann: the number of prime numbers less than x is asymptotically equal to $x/\log_e x$. This has been called the most important result ever obtained in number theory. It was also proved independently in the same year by de la Vallée Poussin. Hadamard's investigation of geodesics on surfaces of constant negative curvature (1898) initiated a study which continues today and has implications for probability theory, specifically in ergodic theory. It led Hadamard to the idea of well- or ill-posed problems in mathematical physics: a problem is well-posed as a differential equation if insignificant variations in the coefficients produce only insignificant variations in the solution, otherwise it is ill-posed because such behaviour is unlikely to occur in reality. After WW1 Hadamard's interests changed and his short book *On the Psychology of Invention in the Mathematical Field* (Princeton, 1945) provides many fascinating insights into the mathematical mind (notably J. H. POINCARÉ's). Hadamard was an inspiring and influential lecturer at the Collège de France (1909–37), and was elected a member of the French Académie des Sciences in 1912. JJG

Hägerstrand, Stig Torsten Erik (b. Moheda, Sweden, 11.10.1916). Swedish geographer who has made major contributions to two research areas in human geography: spatial diffusion and time-space geography. Hägerstrand studied at Lund under Helge Nelson and was strongly influenced by the mathematical approaches of Edgar Kant. The first introduced him to the meticulous tracking of human migration movements in small areas of rural Sweden, and the second to probabilistic ideas on settlement patterns. The result was his 1953 doctoral thesis *Innovationsförloppet ur Korologisk Synpunkt* (Lund; *Spatial Diffusion as an Innovation Process*, London, 1967) in which the adoption of agricultural innovations by farmers in central Sweden was conceived as a series of diffusion waves whose passage could be mapped, modelled and simulated. The ideas there were elaborated and extended in *Migration in Sweden* (London, 1957). This early work pioneered new methods in cartography and Monte Carlo simulation, which were rapidly taken up by US colleagues in the late 1950s and widely adapted and extended, particularly by computer modelling of diffusion processes. Over more recent decades Hägerstrand has moved from the study of aggregate time-space studies to the detailed dissection of individuals' movements over very short time periods. Hägerstrand and his Lund colleagues have been able to show how an understanding of changes in such trajectories at a microscale allows a clearer understanding of the changes in the aggregate pattern of human population distribution. His work has increasingly drawn him into government advisory work on future population changes at national and European levels. PH

Haggett, Peter (b. Pawlett, Som., UK, 24.1.1933). British geographer. During the early 1960s Haggett was one of the small number responsible for the introduction of advanced quantitative methods to British geography and for the development of human geography as a positivist spatial science. His edited volumes with CHORLEY, *Frontiers in Geographical Teaching* (London, 1965) and *Models in Geography* (London, 1967), were major stimuli; *Locational Analysis in Human Geography* (London, 1965, ²1977) provided an overview of the spatial science approach, introducing much new material from related disciplines; and *Geography: a Modern Synthesis* (London, 1972, ³1980) has popularized the work and integrated it with traditional geographical concerns. Professor at Bristol University since 1966, he has been involved in research on stochastic modelling and the analysis of changing spatial patterns (see A. D. Cliff *et al.*, *Elements of Spatial Structure*, Cambridge, 1975), with special reference to contagious processes (see Cliff *et al.*, *Spatial Diffusion*, Cambridge, 1981). Haggett has made an important contribution to the recent worldwide changes in human geography.   RJJ

Hahn, Otto (b. Frankfurt, Hesse, Germany, 8.3.1879; d. Göttingen, Lower Saxony, West Germany, 28.7.1968). German radiochemist. After studying at Marburg and Munich, Hahn intended to enter the chemical industry. But he spent a short period in the laboratory of Sir William Ramsay at University College London, where he made chemical separations of the products of radioactive decay. This led him to spend some time with RUTHERFORD in Montreal to learn more about radioactivity. For the rest of his active research life (1906–44) he worked in Berlin on the chemistry of radioactive elements and their decay products. In 1907 he was joined by Lise MEITNER, a Viennese physicist, who collaborated with him on many problems until she was forced to leave Germany in 1938.

Hahn's great achievement (for which he received the Nobel prize for chemistry in 1944) was the discovery, with F. STRASSMANN, that when uranium was bombarded with neutrons the products of the reaction contained barium – an element which has only about half the weight of uranium. This suggested that the neutrons were able to split the uranium nucleus in two, a hitherto unthinkable phenomenon. Being chemists, Hahn and Strassmann hesitated to put forward such a revolutionary hypothesis and so Hahn communicated the results to Meitner who was then working in Sweden and whose nephew Otto FRISCH, also a physicist, was visiting her. Meitner and Frisch quickly accepted the great significance of the work; in a letter to *Nature* they called the process 'nuclear fission'. Later, it was established that fission was accompanied by the release of a large amount of energy plus two to three more neutrons. These neutrons could produce further fissions and

so the possibility of a chain reaction accompanied by a large scale production of energy became a possibility. Work on nuclear fission was carried out in Germany during WW2, but the separation of radioactive isotopes suitable for weapons was not achieved and Hahn was never directly involved in military applications. He was extremely upset when the first nuclear bomb was exploded over Hiroshima and he was very active in educating the public and influencing the federal government about the dangers of nuclear warfare. He published his autobiography in 1968, *Mein Leben* (Munich; *My Life*, London, 1970).   HMR

Haile Selassie, *né* Tafari Makonnen (b. Harar, Ethiopia, 23.7.1892; d. Addis Ababa, 27.8.1975). Emperor of Ethiopia. One of the longest reigning monarchs in the world and for more than a generation regarded as the most prestigious head of state in Africa, Haile Selassie was overthrown in the Ethiopian revolution of 1974 and ended his life openly reviled by many of his former subjects. A cousin of the powerful Emperor Menelik, he became one of the regents of Ethiopia in 1916, gradually removed all his rivals and had himself crowned emperor with the throne-name Haile Selassie in 1930. His prime aim – that of every Ethiopian emperor before him – was to consolidate his own power; hence plans for modernization to build up an efficient army and bureaucracy. This process was interrupted by the Italian invasion and conquest (1936–41). His prestige enhanced by his dignified bearing during his exile, Haile Selassie came to enjoy an international status such as no Ethiopian emperor had achieved before. His schemes for modernization involved sending Ethiopians overseas to study and bringing in foreign advisers, thus breaking down the age-old isolation of the country. The emperor's prestige was further enhanced when in 1963 the newly formed Organization of African Unity made its headquarters in Addis Ababa. But Haile Selassie was an autocrat, who proved incapable of devising institutions to meet the growing aspirations of a younger generation of Ethiopians. The 'creeping coup' of 1974 – a combination of army mutinies, strikes and demonstrations – led to his overthrow; he was replaced in due course by an avowedly MARXist–LENINist army officer, Major Mengistu, whose actions were far more sanguinary than those of the old emperor had ever been. RH

L. Mosley, *Haile Selassie, Conquering Lion* (London, 1964).

Haldane, John Burdon Sanderson (b. Oxford, UK, 5.11.1892; d. Bhubeneswar, Orissa, India, 1.12.1964). British geneticist. Haldane, the son of a distinguished physiologist and philosopher of science, became one of the foremost figures of 20c biology. His first experience of experimental science came from acting as assistant to his father. Before WW1 he had started independent experiments on mammalian genetics. During that war he served with distinction in the Black Watch and was wounded. After it he returned to science and at once started publishing a series of studies in which he explored the consequences for evolutionary theory of MENDELian genetics. At the time it was widely believed that Mendelism was not compatible with Darwinian evolution; the work of Haldane and of two contemporaries, R. A. FISHER and S. WRIGHT, demonstrated that this was not so. Haldane's *The Causes of Evolution* (London, 1932) was a landmark in evolutionary theory. Haldane had worked for a while as a biochemist and was one of the first to marry the advances in enzymology to genetics. Perhaps his scientific qualities show best in *New Paths in Genetics* (London, 1941). He had an astounding grasp of a wide range of scientific and other work and an ability to relate apparently disparate problems that proved fruitful in many fields. He was a contributor to human genetics, to human physiology, and even to cosmology. He wrote fiction and verse. In the 1930s Haldane became a communist and his published lectures *The Marxist Philosophy and the Sciences* (London, 1938) provided perhaps the most persuasive presentation of MARXism for scientists then available. His political activities included brilliant scientific journalism for the communist press. His disillusion with communist politics occurred in the late 1940s and early 1950s and was greatly hastened by the discreditable course of Soviet genetics (see LYSENKO). Haldane left the UK for India in 1957 in the hope of helping to establish effective biological work in a country that could not afford much expensive science. He established no coherent school of followers but his influence, though profound on only a small number, was felt more widely than that of almost any other biologist of his day. DRN

R. Clark, *J. B. S.: the Life and Work of J. B. S. Haldane* (London, 1968).

Hale, George Ellery (b. Chicago, Ill., USA, 29.6.1868; d. Pasadena, Calif., 21.2.1938). American astronomer. On graduating in physics at MIT, Hale began research in astronomy with his invention (independently of Deslandres) of the spectroheliograph, a device for photographing the solar disk in the light of a single spectrum line of a particular element; Hale first used it at his private Kenwood observatory in 1892 to photograph clouds of calcium on the sun. He was a man of tremendous energy. While associate professor of astrophysics at Chicago University he founded the Yerkes Observatory in 1897. With his founding of the Mt Wilson Observatory in 1904, with a grant of $150,000 from the Carnegie Institute of Washington, he returned to his first interest of solar physics. Here he erected two solar tower telescopes, one 60 feet high in 1908 and the other 150 feet high in 1912, with which he studied sunspots in great detail. He showed that spots are cooler than the surrounding solar regions, and invariably possess large magnetic fields. In 1908 he expanded the work of the observatory by building a 60-inch telescope, using a disk of glass given to him by his father. In 1917 a local benefactor J. D. Hooker provided the disk for the 100-inch mirror of his next Mt Wilson telescope, which was built with Carnegie funds. Hale's telescope-building culminated with the 200-inch telescope at Palomar Observatory. He had conceived the idea of a very large telescope as early as 1928 and finally obtained funds for it from the Rockefeller Foundation shortly before WW2. It was completed in 1948, 10 years after Hale's death. Ill-health obliged Hale to give up active research during the 1920s. He remained busy in other ways. While at the Yerkes Observatory he started the *Astrophysical Journal*, and in 1904 was a founder of the International Union for Cooperation in Solar Research, which developed into the present International Astronomical Union. He also had a major part in founding both the California Institute of Technology and the Huntington Library, and was first chairman of the US National Research Council. In recognition of his work, the Mt Wilson and Palomar observatories are now called the Hale observatories.   DEB

Halliday, Michael Alexander Kirkwood (b. Leeds, W. Yorks., UK, 13.4.1925). British linguist. He obtained his first degree and MA at the School of Oriental and African Studies, University of London, and lectured for a time on Chinese at Cambridge before moving in 1958 to a post in linguistics at the University of Edinburgh. He was professor of linguistics at University College London from 1965 to 1970, and is now head of the department of linguistics at the University of Sydney, Australia. Like FIRTH, Halliday regards language as a roughly ritualized phenomenon in which each speaker has a finite number of options open to him. He is the originator of 'systemic grammar', which views language as involving a number of systems within which a speaker must make repeated choices among mutually exclusive options. For example, a verb tense system might require a choice between past, present and future, then the selection of future might lead to a further choice between different types of futurity. The whole pattern of systems constitutes a system network, and the grammar of a language can be envisaged as a set of system networks. An early version of this theory is expounded in *The Linguistic Sciences and Language Teaching* (with A. McIntosh & P. Strevens, London, 1964). In recent years Halliday has concentrated on social aspects of language, in particular on specifying and exemplifying the various functions which it serves. He has applied this approach both to child lan-

guage, in *Learning How to Mean* (London, 1975), and to language in general, in *Language as Social Semiotic* (London, 1978). The further development of systemic grammar is being carried out mainly by his ex-colleague Richard Hudson at University College London.   JMA

Halsey, Albert Henry (b. London, UK, 13.4.1923). British sociologist. Director of the department of social and administrative studies at Oxford from 1962, and also professor of social and administrative studies since 1978, Halsey has conducted major studies of the relationships between education, the economy and society (see *Change in British Society*, Oxford, 1978). He has had a profound influence upon educational responses to social disadvantage and to problems of equality and the functions of education in contemporary society. As national director of the Educational Priority Area action-research project (1968–72), he held responsibility for developing and evaluating strategies of positive discrimination in deprived areas, in response to the Plowden Report. While insisting that education can only be a part of a more general and comprehensive movement to overcome poverty and to develop community, he stressed its role in social reform in urban industrial society, educating young people for political and social responsibility, and creating a complementary rather than compensatory education. Halsey has also contributed massively to the debate and research on the links between social class and educational and professional opportunities (see, with A. F. Heath & J. M. Ridge, *Origins and Destinations: Family, Class and Education in Modern Britain*, Oxford, 1980) and has made clear the continuing disproportionate success of the service class, especially while the transition from a tripartite to a comprehensive system of education is incomplete. While not usually identified with the new sociology of the 1970s, with its MARXist perspectives on the curriculum, Halsey has established a social democratic critique of and active involvement in the aims and content of schooling.   RJB

Hamada, Shoji (b. Kanagawa, Japan, 9.12.1894; d. Mashiko City, Tochigi, 5.1.1978). Japanese studio potter. Designated a 'living national treasure' by the Japanese government, he sustained into the modern era the methods and the idea of ceramics as an art traditional in Japanese Teawares. This idea was deeply imbued with Zen Buddhist conceptions of spontaneity and immediate creative action. Yet Hamada was a highly educated ceramic chemist. As a boy he had wished to be a painter in the free Japanese style. But becoming interested in ceramics he entered the Tokyo Industrial College, then worked on glazes at the Kyoto Ceramic Testing Institute. In 1919 he met Bernard LEACH, then working in Tokyo, who became a lifelong friend. Hamada was thus led to combine his chemical skills with the craft tradition of Japanese pottery. In 1920 he left Japan to collaborate in setting up Leach's first kiln at St Ives in Cornwall. Hamada's intention was to gain a perspective upon Japanese traditions. He returned to Japan in 1923 and established his own world-famous kiln at Mashiko. For the rest of his life he continued to visit, work and lecture with Leach. And it was largely through this association that Hamada's enormous influence upon world ceramics was diffused.

Hamada based his art upon natural materials; and he studied the methods of Korean, Chinese and Okinawan potters at first hand. His own pottery was made without any obvious sophistication or elaboration of style or technique, aiming at an unpretentious simplicity which was spiritually profound. He made a wide variety of types: large plates, smaller dishes, bowls, bottles, vases and boxes, each piece individually glazed and painted, using a very wide variety of techniques in familiar as well as totally unfamiliar combinations. His colours often belong to the black-brown-dull green-cream range now so familiar. But he also used a brighter range of reds, greens and blues. All his designs were applied with subtle and inventive brushstrokes. Although his debt to Leach was great, his own work remained profoundly Japanese, and he embodied for the 20c the specifically Japanese idea of the potter as individual creative artist who both forms and decorates his own pieces. PSR

Hamilton, Richard (b. London, UK, 24.2.1922). British painter and printmaker and one of the main pioneers of Pop art. During the early part of his career he worked in a variety of quite different styles, including paintings with a small number of points related to one another by criss-crossed lines, and organized several didactic exhibitions. In 1956 he made the collage *Just what is it makes today's homes so different, so appealing?* (his first and probably *the* first true Pop work to be made anywhere), which reflects his interest in mass commercial culture, advertisements and pin-ups. In spite of this interest in ephemeral, glamorous and gimmicky non-fine-art imagery, his work has remained intellectual and highly complex. It often combines painted areas with photographic images drawn from a wide range of sources, so as to draw attention to process or ambiguity, or to allude to the characteristics of some earlier style such as cubism. Hamilton is an authority on the work of DUCHAMP; in 1965-6 he devoted a year to making a full-scale reconstruction of Duchamp's *Large Glass* (1915-23). REA

Richard Hamilton, exh. cat., Tate Gallery (London, 1970).

Hammarskjöld, Dag (b. Jönköping, Sweden, 29.7.1905; d. nr Ndola, Northern Rhodesia [now Zambia], 18.9.1961). Swedish deputy foreign minister (1951-3); second secretary-general of the United Nations (1953-61). A devout but private Christian, he developed his position in the UN, to which he was re-elected in 1957, into one in which, backed by the middle-ranking powers of the United Nations, he could take a great deal of initiative in mediating between the Western and Soviet blocs, especially in areas of conflict which involved the Third World (Suez 1956, the Congo 1960). In this he pioneered the extension of UN military intervention from the simple stationing of observers to the interposition of substantial emergency forces between the would-be belligerents, a technique first used in the Suez crisis in 1956. By so doing he earned the direct censure of the British and Soviet governments, including Soviet proposals to curtail and divide the secretary-general's powers. Hammarskjöld's death, in an aeroplane crash in Africa in 1961, in circumstances never entirely explained, brought to an end the development of the secretary-general's authority, neither of his successors, U Thant or Kurt Waldheim, being sufficiently sure of their position to follow his example. The device of the emergency force, however, continued to be employed, most notably in the Dutch –Indonesian dispute over West Irian in 1962–3 and in Cyprus after 1964. DCW

Hammett, Louis Plack (b. Wilmington, Del., USA, 7.4.1894). American chemist, distinguished for his contributions to physical organic chemistry. He graduated from Harvard (1916) and from Columbia (1923), and was on the chemistry faculty of Columbia (1920–61) where he now is emeritus professor of chemistry. Through reading the papers of HANTZSCH, WERNER, G. N. LEWIS and BRØNSTED, he was led to work in physical organic chemistry. This term, however, was little used until Hammett wrote *Physical Organic Chemistry* (NY, 1940, ²1970), a book which stimulated much work in the field. Hammett's main original contributions were in two areas. First, in the realm of structure-reactivity relationships he greatly extended the use of linear free energy relationships, introduced by Brønsted in 1924. (Work parallel to Hammett's was done by G. N. Burkhardt in Manchester.) In particular the reactivity of *meta*- or *para*-substituted benzene derivatives was summarized, to a first approximation, through a very simple relation known as the Hammett equation. This has subsequently been modified and extended in application, so that Hammett's ideas are today the basis of the vast field of correlation analysis in organic chemistry. Hammett also pioneered the study and application of concentrated solutions of strong acids through an empirical magnitude, the acidity function, which has become of great value in understanding the behaviour of important organic systems. JSh

Hammett, Samuel Dashiell (b. St Mary's County, Md, USA, 27.5.1894; d. NY, 10.1.1961). American detective-story writer, the most influential pioneer of the hardboiled school of crime fiction which developed out of the pulp magazine *Black Mask* in the early 1920s. Hammett's early experience as a Pinkerton detective enabled him to inject a hitherto unknown realism of milieux and characterization into the crime story. His five novels, *Red Harvest* (NY, 1929), *The Dain Curse* (NY, 1929), *The Maltese Falcon* (NY, 1930), *The Glass Key* (NY, 1931) and *The Thin Man* (NY, 1934), were immediately successful with critics and public. After 1934 Hammett worked fitfully for Hollywood, comic-strips and radio, but published no more fiction. A political radical, Hammett was gaoled in 1951 for refusing to cooperate with Senator MCCARTHY's investigations. Hammett elevated crime fiction from the artificial puzzle mystery to a literary form that seriously explored the corrupt face of American society. He was a strong influence on the work of CHANDLER, as well as on that of current authors such as Ross Macdonald, Roger Simon, Robert Parker and Andrew Bergman. The 1941 classic Huston-Bogart version of *The Maltese Falcon* was an early example of the important *film noir* style. RR

W. F. Nolan, *Dashiell Hammett: a Casebook* (Santa Barbara, 1968); R. Layman, *Shadow Man: the Life of Dashiell Hammett* (NY, 1981).

Hamsun, Knut (b. Lom, Norway, 4.8.1859; d. Grimstad, Aust-Agder, 19.2.1952). Norwegian novelist, dramatist and poet. His earliest (and arguably his greatest) novels – particularly *Sult* (Copenhagen, 1890; *Hunger*, London, 1899, tr. R. Bly, NY, 1970), *Mysterier* (Christiania, 1892; *Mysteries*, London, 1927, tr. G. Bothmer, NY, 1971) and *Pan* (Christiania, 1894; London, 1921, tr. J. W. McFarlane, London, 1956) – established him as a writer confidently in the vanguard of the emergent 'modernist' novel in Europe. They explored with sensitivity and extraordinary penetration the situation of the 'outsider' in a rapidly changing society, and by their attention to 'the unconscious life of the mind' (Hamsun's own policy phrase) anticipated the 'stream of consciousness' novel of the 20c. His best-known (though not his most accomplished) novel is *Markens gróde* (Christiania, 1917; tr. W. Worster, *Growth of the Soil*, London, 1920) which won him the Nobel prize in 1920. Some of his later novels – especially the so-called 'August trilogy': *Landstrykere* (Oslo, 1927; London, 1931, tr. J. W. McFarlane, *Wayfarers*, NY, 1980), *August* (Oslo, 1930; tr. E. Gay-Tift, London, 1931) and *Men livet lever* (Oslo, 1933; tr. E. Gay-Tifft, *The Road Leads On*, London, 1935) – examine the 'wanderer' figure in a society menaced by the spread of industrialism and the growth of commercialism. Some readers are captivated by the sheer fecundity of his narrative inventiveness; others are exasperated by the quasi-fascist values inherent in his works.   JWMcF

A. Gustafson, *Six Scandinavian Novelists* (Princeton, 1940); J. W. McFarlane, *Ibsen and the Temper of Norwegian Literature* (London, 1960).

Handke, Peter (b. Griffen, Carinthia, Austria, 6.12.1942). Austrian novelist and dramatist. Handke has essayed most forms of writing, but it was as an anticonventional playwright that he first came to notice, particularly with *Publikumsbeschimpfung* (Frankfurt, 1966; *Offending the Audience*, London, 1971): four actors circumstantially inform the audience that what they are watching is not a play but simply a stage with four people on it. Subsequent plays were almost equally uncompromising, the best known being *Kaspar* (Frankfurt, 1968; tr. M. Roloff, London, 1972); inspired by the real-life Kaspar Hauser, apparently incarcerated for the first 16 years of his life and therefore, for Handke, an intriguing *tabula rasa* used to demonstrate the WITTGENSTEINian concept that language itself has an implicit value system. Handke's novels too – the first appeared in 1966, his first success in 1970: *Die Angst des Tormanns beim Elfmeter* (Frankfurt, 1970; tr. M. Roloff, *The Goalie's Anxiety at the Penalty Kick*, London, 1977) – show Handke's tendency to strip character and situation to their bare essentials to reveal the mech-

anisms by which personality is formed, actions are taken, novels are written. He is a minimalist who has much in common with ROBBE-GRILLET and the *nouveaux romanciers*, yet his dead-pan, ultraobjective accounts of characters in extreme states of mind moving through everyday yet alien landscapes bring KAFKA to mind, or for that matter CHANDLER, one of Handke's acknowledged heroes. His best books to date are probably *Die linkshändige Frau* (Frankfurt, 1976; tr. R. Manheim, *The Left-handed Woman*, London, 1980), based on a film he wrote and directed about an ordinary woman's bid for independence from her husband, and *Wunschloses Unglück* (Salzburg, 1972; tr. R. Manheim, *Sorrow Beyond Dreams*, London, 1976), a memoir of his mother's life and suicide – not unlike that of his fictional characters. But with three linked novels and a dramatic poem published in 1981 alone, when Handke was still not 40, his writing career is far from complete.

NAJH

Handlin, Oscar (b. New York, USA, 29.9.1915). American historian. Oscar Handlin has done more than any of his contemporaries to humanize and popularize American history by writing about it from the point of view of its less fortunate members. His first book *Boston's Immigrants, 1790–1865: a Study in Acculturation* (Cambridge, Mass., 1941) was a study of the sufferings of the American Irish; he later broadened the theme to produce *The Uprooted: the Epic Story of the Great Migrations that Made the American People* (Boston, Mass., 1951). Handlin concentrated on the sense of alienation, the difficulties in housing, employment and cultural and political assimilation, experienced by the first generations of immigrants. He also gave a painful picture of the cost to that generation of the more complete assimilation of their children into the new culture. In many other works, such as *Adventure in Freedom: Three Hundred Years of Jewish Life in America* (NY, 1954); *The Positive Contribution by Immigrants* (Paris, 1955); *Race and Nationality in American Life* (Boston, Mass., 1957); *The Newcomers: Negroes and Puerto Ricans in a Changing*

Metropolis (Cambridge, Mass., 1960), he emphasized the experience of immigrants and their children, and their contribution to American life. Much of this was severely criticized. Handlin did not know enough about conditions in the areas from which the immigrants came; he generalized from specific and unrepresentative examples; and he relied too heavily and uncritically on foreign-language newspapers. He has done much, however, to make the history of ordinary, often unsuccessful, people legitimate subject-matter for historical investigation. In his two-volume *History of the United States* (NY, 1967–8) he made the history of society, rather than its politics, the subject of general history. Other studies of a rather different genre include *Commonwealth: a Study of the Role of Government in the American Economy: Massachusetts 1774–1861* (NY, 1947) in which he and his wife Mary Flug Handlin were the first to show the 'interventionist' role of government in at least one American state in a period which most people thought belonged to private enterprise, and a much-discussed article, 'Origins of the Southern labor system' (*William and Mary Quarterly*, 3rd series, 7, 1950) in which he argued that race prejudice in America was a result of slavery, rather than one of its causes. JRP

M. A. Jones, 'Oscar Handlin', in M. Cunliffe & R. Winks (eds), *Pastmasters* (NY, 1969).

Hantzsch, Arthur Rudolf (b. Dresden, Germany [now East Germany], 7.3.1857; d. Dresden, 14.3.1935). German physical organic chemist. Hantzsch studied chemistry first at Dresden Polytechnikum, then at the University of Würzburg. He held chairs at Zürich (from 1885), Würzburg (from 1893) and Leipzig (1903–27). His early research was in classical synthetic organic chemistry, especially the synthesis of derivatives of pyridine and of thiazole. He came under the influence of the great pioneer of physical chemistry OSTWALD, and, as a result, himself became a pioneer of the application of the methods of physical chemistry to problems in organic chemistry because of his interests in the relationship between the chemical and physical properties of organic compounds. Hantzsch and WERNER first explained the stereoisomerism of the oximes on the basis of the nonplanar arrangement of the valencies of nitrogen. Hantzsch's later work was much taken up with extending these ideas to the important diazo-compounds. He was often involved in sharp controversy, especially with E. Bamberger. Through his work he was led to develop some of the basic techniques of physical organic chemistry, especially the application of measurements of absorption spectra and of electrical conductivity of solutions. He also worked on the tautomerism of aliphatic nitro-compounds and more generally on 'pseudo-acids' and 'pseudo-bases'. This last work, important in its day, is now subsumed under more general views. NBC

Hardy, Thomas (b. Higher Bockhampton, Dorset, UK, 2.6.1840; d. Dorchester, Dorset, 11.1.1928). British novelist and poet. Hardy's career as a novelist was already finished by 1895, after 20 years in which he had been thought of first as the creator of 'Wessex', and secondly as a tragic ironist. *Tess of the d'Urbervilles* (London, 1891) had been praised; but he was conscious that he had compromised his treatment of sex from fear of prudish criticism; *Jude the Obscure* (London, 1895) he wrote more defiantly, and it became his final gesture. Hardy has been consistently admired: at first, rather condescendingly, as regional novelist, as gloomy ironist, as an amateur of genius whose artificial plots, uneven characterization and awkward style required apologies. Now, the last of the Victorians is seen as the first of the moderns, as a novelist with an exploratory sensibility, with an imagination encompassing realism and symbolism, and a style struggling towards an inclusiveness beyond that of conventional 'good' prose. In 1898 he published his first book of poems, *Wessex Poems*, and a sequence followed up to *Winter Words* (London, 1928) which established him as one of the most fertile poets of the century. As with the novels, the critical history is one of continued respect, developing into a later conviction of major status.

While his volume was large, his range was limited; his tone is compounded of nostalgia, irony, and (though he would reject the term) pessimism. At its best the gravity and honesty of his poetry, and its subtleties of movement, are of a unique kind. His attachment to rigid verse forms, and his eclectic vocabulary, made it easy for critics to see him as a marginal and minor figure. The return to favour of traditional forms, and a slightly xenophobic trend in contemporary English thought, have led to his establishment as a specially English genius, conscious of the movements within his society, and working within native forms. He may be presented as an ancestor of D. H. LAWRENCE, or LARKIN, or set against Henry JAMES as an alternative kind of artist. The appearance of a variorum edition of his poems (ed. J. Gibson, London, 1978) symbolized his status. If his deductions from Darwin and Schopenhauer, his 'evolutionary meliorism' and 'immanent will' seem distinctly of the past, it is a past which the imagination of the present finds increasingly engaging.　BF

F. B. Pinion, *A Hardy Companion* (London, 1968); R. Gittings, *The Older Hardy* (London, 1978).

Harris, Wilson (b. New Amsterdam, British Guiana [now Guyana], 24.3.1921). Guyanese novelist. His professional work as a land surveyor enabled Harris to penetrate remote areas of his native Guyana and to reflect upon the layers of history which have enfolded them. His first published work was a book of poems *Eternity to Season* (Georgetown, 1954) which, perhaps because of his novels' success, subsequently acquired a cult reputation. With *Palace of the Peacock* (London, 1960), the first of the novels forming the 'Guyana Quartet' (1960–3), he established himself as one of the most original and intellectually inquiring of Caribbean writers. The quartet offers a composite portrait of Guyanese history and landscape, incorporates Carib and Amerindian mythology, and analyses not only the effects of colonial conquest on multiracial societies but the psychological impulses which lie behind them. Later novels, all short but several

designed to be read as parts of longer narrative cycles, explore the metaphysical side of man without ever losing touch with the realities of history. Harris's fiction is highly individual in manner and, despite its difficulty, verging sometimes on obscurity, is increasingly regarded as of international stature. Indeed many critics regard Harris as the major Third World novelist of the later 20c. Some of his critical ideas are set out in his essays *Tradition, the Writer and Society* (London, 1967).　ANRN

M. Gilkes, *Wilson Harris and the Caribbean Novel* (London, 1975); H. Maes-Jelinek (ed.), *Explorations: Wilson Harris* (Mundelstrup, Denmark, 1981).

Harrison, Ross Granville (b. Germantown, Pa, USA, 13.1.1870; d. New Haven, Conn., 30.9.1959). American biologist. Harrison invented the technique of tissue culture, by which cells are kept alive for observation outside the body from which they are taken, and was the first to make use of it to answer an important biological question. The techniques of tissue culture are now used for a myriad of purposes in biological and medical practice. But Harrison's influence on 20c biology went far beyond the development of a technique. It sprang from an ability to ask simple, important and answerable questions of complex processes of individual development. His own work, at Johns Hopkins and at Yale, on the development of the nervous system, on the development of the limb and upon the control of growth, stimulated a whole school of American biologists.　DRN

Harrod, Henry Roy Forbes (b. London, UK, 13.2.1900; d. Holt, Norfolk, 9.3.1978). British economist. Educated at Westminster and New College, Oxford, where he read first classics and then history, he spent the rest of his career at Christ Church, Oxford, until retirement. Harrod had a versatile, productive and original intellect. He contributed to economic theory in three main areas: first, to the theory of aggregate demand, where his formulation of the multiplier mechanism for an open economy (see his *International Economics*, Cambridge, 1933, ²1958) partly anticipated KEYNES's analysis of the closed economy in *The General Theory* (1936). Secondly, Harrod contributed to the theory of the firm and imperfectly competitive markets (see *Economic Essays*, London, 1952, ²1972). Thirdly and most famously, he was a pioneer of the modern theory of economic growth, with his one-sector model of a dynamic economy ('An Essay in Dynamic Theory', *Economic Journal*, 1939, later incorporated in *Towards a Dynamic Economics*, London, 1948), in which he sought to analyse the macroeconomic properties of a long-run growth path.

Harrod's other writings included a good deal on international monetary questions (from the later 1950s onwards he advocated a rise in the price of gold); the official *Life of John Maynard Keynes* (London, 1951), with whom Harrod had first studied economics at Cambridge in 1922–3; a biographical essay *The Prof.* (London, 1959), on LINDEMANN; and contributions to philosophy, notably on utilitarianism and on induction. PMO

E. H. Phelps-Brown, 'Sir Roy Harrod: a biographical memoir', *Economic Journal* (1980).

Hart, Herbert Lionel Adolphus (b. Harrogate, N. Yorks., UK, 18.7.1907). British jurist and philosopher. A practising lawyer at the Chancery Bar before WW2, Hart returned to Oxford after 1945 to teach philosophy at a time when Oxford was becoming a major centre of linguistic philosophy. He applied his legal experience and philosophical insights to the study of law when elected professor of jurisprudence at Oxford, a chair he occupied from 1952 to 1968. Hart's standpoint is basically positivist and analytic, with a strong emphasis on linguistic problems. The author of *Causation in the Law* (with A. M. Honoré, Oxford, 1961, ²1983), *Law, Liberty and Morality* (Oxford, 1963) and *Punishment and Responsibility* (Oxford, 1968), Hart's major contribution to legal thinking is *The Concept of Law* (Oxford, 1961). For him, the idea of obligation is at the core of a legal rule. Rules of obligation are supported by social pressure because they are felt to be necessary to maintain

society. Behaviour is regulated by means of primary rules imposing duties, but there are also secondary rules by which primary rules may be identified, which provide powers to change primary rules. Primary rules become a legal system by union with secondary rules. This analysis has generated much comment and criticism, but is the most outstanding modern British contribution to legal thinking. DMW

P. M. S. Hacker & J. Raz (eds), *Law, Morality and Society: Essays in Honour of H. L. A. Hart* (Oxford, 1977); N. MacCormick, *H. L. A. Hart* (London, 1981).

Hartmann, Nicolai (b. Riga, Latvia, Russia [now Latvia, USSR], 20.2.1882; d. Göttingen, Lower Saxony, West Germany, 9.10.1950). German philosopher. After study at St Petersburg, Hartmann went on to Marburg University where he was a pupil of the neo-Kantian philosophers Cohen and Natorp. Professor at Marburg until 1925, then at Cologne University until 1931, he taught at Berlin University until 1945 and his final removal to Göttingen. Hartmann was a copious, somewhat stodgy writer, but unlike most other major figures in German thought since Kant, he was lucid and unspeculatively commonsensical. He had been brought up in the Kantian view that objective reality is a mental construction, given form by the logic that is common to all thinking minds. After much mental travail Hartmann managed to free himself from this ultimately subjectivist notion in a return to something like the realism of Aristotle – his *Die Philosophie des deutschen Idealismus* [The philosophy of German idealism] (2 vols, Berlin, 1923–9) is an expression of this philosophical escape. He distinguished metaphysics as the attempt, in his view impossible to achieve, to give a systematic explanation of the world as a whole through ontology, understood as a study of the basic kinds of things that are actually present to our minds and of the rational aspect of what there is (see 'Neue Wege der Ontologie', 1942; tr. R. C. Kuhn in *New Ways of Ontology*, Chicago, 1953). In a series of large books he distinguished and described various levels of being –

some real, such as matter, life, consciousness and spirit; some ideal, such as mathematical entities and values. At once prominent and respected, but of little political significance, he was left alone by the Nazis, and, untainted by association with them, was acknowledged as the leading national philosopher of Germany in the immediate postwar years.   AQ

W. Stegmueller, *Main Currents in Contemporary German, British, American Philosophy* (Bloomington, 1969).

Hartshorne, Richard (b. Kittaning, Pa, USA, 12.12.1899). American geographer. A Princeton graduate, Hartshorne spent most of his academic career in the Midwest, first at the University of Minnesota (1924–40) and subsequently at Wisconsin (since 1940). His *Nature of Geography* (NY, 1939) is the most complete English-language statement of the basic premises on which geographers work; it has a strong historical emphasis and offers a particularly complete survey of German methodological writing. In *Perspectives on the Nature of Geography* (NY, 1959) Hartshorne presents a briefer restatement and updating of his views. Hartshorne's published work reflects his early interest in philosophy and methodological debate. He also advanced the discussion of problems of political geography, notably those of Central Europe.   PH

Harvey, David (b. Gillingham, Kent, UK, 31.10.1935). British geographer, now at Johns Hopkins University. A Cambridge graduate in the 1950s, Harvey was one of the first British human geographers to embrace the theoretical and quantitative approach being developed in North America. His research was on the statistical modelling of evolving settlement patterns, but his major contribution was his book *Explanation in Geography* (London, 1969), which outlined the positivist conception of science and argued for its adoption by geographers. Soon after publishing this, Harvey perceived that positivism is tied to an ideology of society that precludes major social change. His explorations of other philosophies led to an even more influential book *Social Justice*

and the City (London, 1973), which outlined the limitations of the positivist approach and was the first major presentation, in English, of the case for a MARXist geography. Since then, he has combined research on housing markets and suburbanization with the development of a Marxist science of spatial and environmental relations: *The Limits to Capital* (Oxford, 1982).   RJJ

J. L. Paterson, *David Harvey's Geography* (London, 1982).

Hašek, Jaroslav (b. Prague, Bohemia, Austria-Hungary [now Czechoslovakia], 30.4.1883; d. Lipnice, 3.1.1923). Czech novelist and short-story writer. This locally notorious practical joker's unfinished masterpiece *Osudy dobrého vojáka Švejka za světové války* (Prague, 1923; abridged, London, 1930; tr. C. Parrott, *The Good Soldier Švejk*, London, 1973), a picaresque novel to be ranked with *Don Quixote*, *Simplicissimus* and *Pickwick*, was written and published in parts during 1922–3. Originating in some prewar Švejk stories (included in tr. C. Parrott, *The Red Commissar*, London, 1981), it was based on Hašek's own experiences as a volunteer in the Austrian 91st Regiment on the Galician front in 1915, and features some of his superiors under their real names. That September he deserted to the Russians and joined the Czech Legion, then in 1918 went over to the Bolsheviks, who made him a political commissar in their Fifth Army. Summoned back by the new Czech Communist party at the end of 1920 for an abortive rising, he reluctantly returned to the two years of disillusionment, drink and domestic crises that led up to his death. But he wrote his book.   JWMW

C. Parrott, *The Bad Bohemian* (London, 1978).

Hassel, Odd (b. Oslo, Norway, 17.5.1897; d. Oslo, 15.5.1981). Norwegian physical chemist. Hassel's early education in the physical sciences was in the University of Oslo, and was followed by work at Munich in Professor K. Fajan's laboratory. Thereafter Hassel worked on X-ray crystallography at the Kaiser Wilhelm Institute, Berlin-Dahlem, and gained his doctorate in 1924. He then returned to the University of Oslo where he remained until his retirement in 1964. From 1934 he held the chair of physical chemistry, the first of its kind in Norway. After 1930 his work concentrated primarily on the structure of cyclohexane, its derivatives and related compounds (cf. the work of BARTON). Besides being an X-ray crystallographer, Hassel introduced electron-diffraction techniques and dipole moment measurements into Norway. In the 1950s he entered a new field – the study of the structure of charge-transfer complexes, especially the details of their molecular geometry. His claims to distinction rest notably on his pioneering of physical chemistry, especially structural studies, in Norway. He was awarded the Nobel prize jointly with Derek Barton in 1959.

NBC

Hauptmann, Gerhart (b. Obersalzbrunn, Silesia, Germany [now Szczawno Zdrój, Poland], 15.11.1862; d. Agnetendorf, Silesia [now Jagniatków, Poland], 6.6.1946). German dramatist and novelist. Hauptmann trained as a sculptor in Breslau. He moved to Berlin in 1885, coming into contact with the naturalists Holz, Schlaf and others. During the Nazi period he lived a retired life in Silesia but continued to publish. His early stories were influenced by naturalism, notably *Bahnwärter Thiel* (Berlin, 1888; tr. A. S. Seltzer, *Flagman Thiel*, NY, 1933). His first drama *Vor Sonnenaufgang* (Berlin, 1889; tr. L. Bloomfield, *Before Dawn*, Boston, 1909) was acclaimed as the pinnacle of naturalist drama towards which IBSEN had been striving. His play *Die Weber* (Berlin, 1892; tr. C. R. Mueller, *The Weavers*, San Francisco, 1965) has become synonymous with German naturalism. The 'protagonist' is the mass of Silesian weavers who revolted and were bloodily suppressed in 1844. Unemployment, starvation wages and the loss of human dignity, the resulting tensions and their release in futile violence are studied in detail. Hauptmann used dialect as a means of characterization, writing his original version in the Silesian dialect. The public performance of *Die Weber* was initially banned by the Berlin authorities, and in 1896 the proposal to

award Hauptmann the Schiller prize was vetoed by Kaiser Wilhelm II. Hauptmann gradually moved away from naturalism to neoromanticism, of which *Hanneles Himmelfahrt* (Berlin, 1894; tr. W. Archer, *Hannele*, London, 1894) was, in its 'vision' sequences, anticipatory. Other significant works are: *Der Biberpelz* (Berlin, 1893; tr. L. Lewisohn, *The Beaver Coat*, NY, 1931), *Fuhrmann Henschel* (Berlin, 1899; tr. L. Lewisohn, *Drayman Henschel*, NY, 1913) and *Und Pippa Tanzt* (Berlin, 1906). Hauptmann continued for many years to write verse, plays (40), novels and ambitious epics such as *Till Eulenspiegel* (Berlin, 1928), a mythico-political representation of modern Germany, or the play *Die Finsternisse* [The darkness] (Berlin, 1947) in which he was one of the first German writers to try to come to terms with the persecution of the Jews. Hauptmann was awarded the Nobel prize for literature in 1912.

JHC

K. L. Tank, *Gerhart Hauptmann* (Hamburg, 1959).

Havel, Václav (b. Prague, Czechoslovakia, 5.10.1936). Czech dramatist and leader of the Charter 77 human-rights movement, who started his career as a laboratory technician; after military service (1957–9), while a scene-shifter he studied drama. His first play *Zahradni slavnost* (Prague, 1963; tr. V. Blackwell, *The Garden Party*, London, 1969), the first Czech example of absurdist drama and a satire on the Novotný regime, shows how the emotionless manipulation of language ensures a fine bureaucratic career. *Vyrozuměni* (Prague, 1965; tr. V. Blackwell, *The Memorandum*, London, 1967) continues the theme of bureaucratic jargon, but also introduces Havel's second preoccupation, the interchangeability of social roles; both themes run through his 1970s plays. A staging of his adaptation of Gay's *Beggar's Opera* (*Žebrácká opera*, Trieste, 1976) in a village outside Prague was stopped by the police – and Havel lost his driving licence. Sentenced in 1979 to four and a half years for antistate activities, he was released sick in 1983. RBP

P. I. Trensky, *Czech Drama since World War II* (White Plains, NY, 1978);

M. Goetz-Stankiewicz, *The Silenced Theatre* (Toronto, 1979).

Hawking, Stephen William (b. Oxford, UK, 8.1.1942). British theoretical physicist. His early work concentrated mainly on singularities in space-time and in a series of papers (some in collaboration with R. Penrose and G. F. R. Ellis) he succeeded in showing that any plausible general relativistic cosmology must be singular (see *The Large-scale Structure of Space-Time*, with G. F. R. Ellis, Cambridge, 1973). In our universe, that singularity is the 'big bang', the initial state of indefinitely high density and space-time curvature away from which all stars and galaxies are currently expanding. This view of cosmology is now generally accepted.

The most important part of his later work has been concerned with the general relativistic theory of black holes. He devised a series of ingenious arguments which showed that, if general relativity is correct, the metric of space-time outside any stationary vacuum black hole depends on only three parameters: the total mass, angular momentum and electric charge of the constituent material. When an object has collapsed to form a black hole all other information about it is lost. Hawking also proved a result known as the 'second law of black hole mechanics' by analogy with the second law of thermodynamics: in any classical (i.e. nonquantum) process involving black holes, the sum of the surface areas of all black holes involved cannot be reduced. With B. Carter and BARDEEN he formulated various other laws governing black hole behaviour which also have a formal similarity with the laws of thermodynamics. However, the analogy was considered only in a formal sense since it was then thought that black holes would in fact have zero effective temperature and could never come into equilibrium with a surrounding heat bath. In 1974 Hawking showed that if one applies quantum mechanics to matter fields in the background geometry of a classical black hole metric, one finds a nonzero rate of production of particles with a thermal spectrum. A finite temperature *can* therefore be assigned to a black hole, precisely proportional to the surface gravity in accordance with the earlier analogy. The laws of black hole mechanics can therefore be thought of as truly thermodynamic laws, a conclusion which has major consequences for physics.

Hawking has worked more recently on the problem of trying to find a consistent quantum theory for gravity itself, aiming towards the eventual hope of producing a Grand Unified Theory which would incorporate all particles and interactions. Appointed professor of physics at Cambridge in 1977, his work has been particularly remarkable in view of the severe physical disabilities from which he suffers.   JCM

Hawkins, Coleman Randolph (b. St Joseph, Mo., USA, 21.11.1904; d. New York, 19.5.1969). American pioneer of jazz tenor saxophone playing. Hawkins's superb instrumental technique and knowledge of harmony (combined with his enterprise) made him the first musician to produce jazz on a tenor saxophone. However, his solos on early recordings with Fletcher Henderson (1923) are quite crude and rhythmically uninteresting. After ARMSTRONG had vitalized Henderson's band, Hawkins abandoned ponderous slap-tonguing articulation and became more adventurous rhythmically. By 1925 his only jazz rivals on any saxophone were BECHET on soprano, Frank Trumbauer on C melody, and Adrian Rollini on bass. In the 1930s, during five years in Europe, Hawkins continued to broaden his harmonic vocabulary and developed chordal improvisation that augured the 'modern jazz' of the 1940s. He returned to the USA in 1939 and recorded his masterpiece *Body and Soul*; his bigtoned playing in this ballad and the harmonies he used in his solo inspired saxophonists for generations, his only rival as a mentor being Lester YOUNG. Long after his days as a major innovator were over, Hawkins continued to play magnificently; echoes of his style could be heard years later in the work of Sonny Rollins and COLTRANE.   JJC

A. J. McCarthy, *Coleman Hawkins* (London, 1963).

Hawks, Howard Winchester (b. Goshen, Ind., USA, 30.5.1896; d. Palm Springs, Calif., 26.12.1977). American film director. From his first film *The Road To Glory* (1926) to his last *El Dorado* (1967), via *Scarface* (1932), *Only Angels Have Wings* (1939), *The Big Sleep* (1946), *Red River* (1948) and *Gentlemen Prefer Blondes* (1953), Howard Hawks showed his ability to adapt virtually every conceivable genre, from gangster movie to western, to suit his own purposes. Neither an innovator nor an imitator, he has made some of the best films in already established genres (although it might be argued that his 'screwball' comedies – *Bringing Up Baby* (1938), *His Girl Friday* (1940), *To Have and Have Not* (1944), *Monkey Business* (1952) – constitute a genre unique to Hawks). A storyteller and entertainer *par excellence*, Hawks's direction was functional rather than creative, employing technique to advance the story rather than for its own sake. His films are an exemplification of the Hollywood narrative ideal which seeks to efface all signs of a film's production. As a craftsman of the narrative form Hawks had few peers in his ability to establish and sustain mood and atmosphere, to personalize his films without allowing his directorial hand to intrude to the point of annoying the spectator. Themes of male camaraderie recur in his films but his notion of a male hero is epitomized by the wise-cracking eccentricity of Cary Grant – an actor who was vital to the success of the 'screwball' comedies. Hawks succeeded in moulding actors as typecast as WAYNE to suit his own purpose – *Rio Bravo* (1959) – and during his long career he discovered or brought new life to actors and actresses of the calibre of Montgomery Clift, Rita Hayworth, Jane Russell and Lauren Bacall. Hawks's achievement was to draw memorable performances from his central characters and to present them to the audience in a way that seemed free of a mediating directorial hand.   LJC

R. Wood, *Howard Hawks* (London, 1968).

Haworth, Walter Norman (b. Chorley, Lancs., UK, 19.3.1883; d. Birmingham, W. Mids, 19.3.1950). British organic chemist who made fundamental contributions to the chemistry of carbohydrates and vitamins. As a young man he carried out research on terpenes at Manchester under W. H. Perkin and at Göttingen under Wallach. In 1912 he became a lecturer at St Andrews and under the influence of Purdie and Irvine began his lifework on carbohydrates, at Newcastle from 1920 and at Birmingham from 1925. His first major contribution was the development of methods to determine the size and stereochemistry of the rings present in sugars and their derivatives. He summarized his work in *The Constitution of Sugars* (London, 1929). Once the basic structures of the sugars were known, the way was open for investigations into every aspect of carbohydrate chemistry. Perhaps the most significant was in 1932 when Haworth, in association with E. L. Hurst, determined the structure of, and synthesized, vitamin C, the first vitamin to have its chemical nature elucidated. In 1927 Haworth proposed that cellulose was a long-chain polymer of glucose, an idea which expressed the main structural features of the polysaccharide. In the 1930s he developed methods for studying the finer details of cellulose and other fundamental polysaccharides such as starch and glycogen. He also initiated work on other polysaccharides of biological importance. During WW2 he worked on the chemical aspects of the atom bomb project and initiated a comprehensive series of researches into organofluorine chemistry. He shared the Nobel prize for chemistry with KARRER in 1937.   TGH

Hayek, Friedrich August von (b. Vienna, Austria-Hungary [now Austria], 8.5.1899; naturalized British citizen, 1938). Austrian/British economist and political philosopher whose immensely fertile mind has produced nearly 200 separate works, including major contributions to scientific methodology, psychology and the history of ideas. Hayek's name is virtually synonymous with the cause of libertarianism, the modern successor to the political liberalism of the 19c. His career has encompassed periods as a civil servant and teacher in Vienna (1921–31), Tooke professor of economics at London University (1931–50), professor of social and moral sciences at the University of Chicago (1950–62) and professor at the universities of Freiburg (1962–8) and Salzburg (1968–77). In 1974 he shared the Nobel prize for economics with Gunnar Myrdal, and other honours have been showered on him. His early work, including *The Pure Theory of Capital* (London, 1941), was largely concerned with industrial fluctuations and associated questions. In a second phase of his thought, he concentrated on the problems of individual values in a world of increased economic controls. Works like *The Road to Serfdom* (London, 1944) argue the case for an economic system based on free markets and a political system granting individual freedom within the law. The importance of prices in controlling the functioning of the economy has been a constant theme. *Law, Legislation and Liberty* (3 vols, London, 1973–9) is the major achievement of his later years. PS

Hazard, Paul Gustave Marie Camille (b. Nordpeene, Nord, France, 30.8.1878; d. Paris, 13.4.1944). French pioneer in the history of ideas and the comparative study of literature. He was professor of comparative literature at the University of Lyons from 1911 to 1919, at the Sorbonne from 1919 to 1925, and at the Collège de France from 1925 until his death. In his doctoral dissertation, regarded by some as his most substantial scholarly work, *La Révolution française et les lettres italiennes* [The French revolution and Italian literature] (Paris, 1910), Hazard showed how the French revolution, encouraging national liberation and the growth of a national literature, helped Italy to find her identity and to throw off the chains of French literary models. His most influential work *La Crise de la conscience européenne, 1680–1715* (3 vols, Paris, 1935; *The European Mind 1680–1715*, London, 1953), surveying a whole range of writers, thinkers and intellectual movements, is devoted to that ill-defined zone which separates the 17c and the 18c. Hazard's central thesis is that the 17c, dominated by French neoclassical

models and an ideal of timeless immutable perfection, social hierarchy and authority based on dogmatic theological assumptions (all of which was a search for peace, order and security after the upheavals of the Renaissance and the Reformation), was undermined from within, during the period in question, by a string of critical thinkers such as Spinoza, Malebranche, Leibniz, Fénelon, Locke, Fontenelle, Bayle, who, with their universal criticism of established beliefs and institutions, and the consequent relativism this tended to encourage, had already by about 1680 generated many of the major ideas of the French Enlightenment, and thus begun to pave the way for the French revolution of 1789. 'Reason was no longer balanced wisdom but critical daring.' An immobile civilization founded on the idea of duty to God and to a ruler legitimized by divine right thus gave way to a dynamic secular world of individual rights, freedom of conscience, free criticism of ideas and institutions, faith in empirical science, and a naturalistic, antimetaphysical attitude in general. Though many points of detail have been questioned, and despite the fact that the preceding crisis of the Renaissance (out of which Hazard's modern crisis in no small part arose) is possibly played down, and the serene stability of the classical edifice is doubtless exaggerated, Hazard threw a new and suggestive light on a critical historical phase, and inspired other scholars to follow up his insights and to test his general theses. RNH

Heaney, Seamus Justin (b. Londonderry, Northern Ireland, UK, 13.4.1939). Irish poet. Seamus Heaney's early poems – *Death of a Naturalist* (London, 1966) and *Door into the Dark* (London, 1969) – are largely pastoral and rooted in the poet's own Irish farming background, but they frequently depict a rural life subtly threatened by violence. In his later work this concern develops into a deepening obligation to write directly about the political violence of Northern Ireland, but to do so without seeming to exploit human misery or sacrifice his own aesthetic needs. His achievement has been to accomplish this with little compromise. In *North* (London, 1975), his finest collection, Heaney views Ireland against a wider historical background, depicting it as the victim of successive invasions. Through poems which blend myth, memory, history and anthropology he finds archetypes for the 'intimate tribal revenge' of sectarian killing in contemporary Ireland. Two other collections of poetry are *Wintering Out* (London, 1972) and *Field Work* (London, 1979). His prose writing has been published in *Preoccupations: Selected Prose 1968–1978* (London, 1980). The finest Irish poet since YEATS, Heaney has preferred to stress his affinity with a wider English romantic tradition. He shares with Wordsworth an exalted view of the poetic psyche and a preoccupation with the relationship between imagination and landscape. Heaney's best poetry shows both lyricism and remarkable craftsmanship, as well as a feel for the physicality of language which is distinctively Irish. JAC

Hearn, Lafcadio (b. Leucadia, Ionian Islands, Greece, 27.6.1850; naturalized Japanese citizen; d. Okubo, Japan, 26.9.1904). Irish/Japanese journalist and interpreter of Japan to the West. Of mixed Irish–Greek parentage, he grew up in Dublin and London and emigrated at 19 to the USA, where he was a successful journalist and literary critic. In 1890 he travelled to Japan, married the daughter of a samurai, became a Japanese subject, and was appointed lecturer in English at the Imperial University. His enchantment with the beauty and rustic virtues of old Japan still untainted by the West is expressed in evocative prose in *Glimpses of Unfamiliar Japan* (Boston, Mass., 1894), while *In Ghostly Japan* (Boston, Mass., 1899) and *Kwaidan* (Cambridge, Mass., 1904) reveal his obsession with the supernatural. His last work, *Japan: an Attempt at an Interpretation* (NY, 1904) is a moving account of the traditional culture he saw being sacrificed to aggressive nationalism, bureaucracy and commercialism. He died an embittered recluse, but the idealized accounts he had given earlier of the Japanese, which he now privately repudiated, had been widely read and admired, as much in Japan as in the West, and helped to reinforce the romantic western view of Japan already popularized by Pierre Loti. MS

A. Mordell, *Discoveries: Essays on Lafcadio Hearn* (Tokyo, 1964).

Hearst, William Randolph (b. San Francisco, Calif., USA, 29.4.1863; d. Beverly Hills, Calif., 14.8.1951). American journalist and newspaper tycoon, the subject of one of the finest Hollywood films, *Citizen Kane*. A wealthy Californian, born during the Civil War, Hearst at 24 transformed a debt-ridden San Francisco morning newspaper into a sensational bestseller. His subsequent exploits made him the most controversial figure in American journalism before his 64-year publishing career was ended. When he took over the *San Francisco Examiner*, Hearst was convinced he could out-Pulitzer Pulitzer by ignoring completely the need to be credible. He recruited experienced staff from New York who would give him sensationalism and popular pseudoscientific stories. He redesigned the paper to appeal visually to the new immigrants for whom English was a difficult, second language – and then watched with satisfaction as the circulation soared. The profits were now available for an invasion of New York which he entered in 1895 by buying up cheaply the failing *New York Journal*. The *Journal* rapidly equalled the *World*'s hitherto unsurpassed daily circulation of 600,000. At this point, Hearst is supposed to have cabled to his man in Havana (following the Cuban insurrection): 'You supply the pictures and I'll supply the war.' Hearst's *Journal* worked to create a war atmosphere which, when action came in 1898, was dubbed 'Hearst's War'. It was 35 years before Hearst's special brand of sensationalism became outdated, by which time he was the owner of 26 daily newspapers in 19 cities, 13 magazines, eight radio stations and two motion picture companies. The crash came in 1937 when he was forced to abdicate and watch trustees liquidate a large portion of his empire. Through it all, however, Hearst continued to live in regal style with his mistress Marion Davies, in San Simeon, California –

that monument to 19c American acquisitive capitalism. RB

W. A. Swanberg, *Citizen Hearst* (NY, 1961).

Heartfield, John, ps. of Helmut Herzfeld (b. Berlin, Germany, 19.6.1891; d. East Berlin, 26.4.1968). German graphic designer. Heartfield was the main originator of political photomontage, which he used as a weapon against the civil and military establishment of Weimar Germany and later against the Nazis. A passionate enemy of German militarism, he anglicized his name in 1916 in protest against the wartime slogan, 'Gott strafe England'. Initially a close collaborator of GROSZ, in 1924 he was secretary of the Red group of German artists, also editing the communist satirical magazine *Der Knüppel* and helping to found the ARBKD (Association of Revolutionary Artists) in 1928. His main activity from 1922 on, however, was the design of book jackets and magazine layouts, particularly for the *Arbeiter-Internationale-Zeitung*. He kept this up as an anti-Nazi exile, spending WW2 in England (which he had never visited) before returning to Berlin in 1950 as a staunch but aesthetically unorthodox supporter of the East German regime.
JWMW

W. Herzfelde, *John Heartfield* (Dresden, 1962); E. Siepmann, *Montage: John Heartfield* (W. Berlin, 1977).

Heaviside, Oliver (b. London, UK, 18.5.1850; d. Torquay, Devon, 3.2.1925). British electrical engineer. Heaviside was one of those men of genius who work best alone. By the age of 20 he was using the operator j ($\sqrt{-1}$) as a standard piece of algebra needed to solve ac networks, even though ac did not come into common use for a further 15 years. He coined the words 'inductance', 'impedance' and 'attenuation' now so familiar to all engineers. He went on to deal with the transient behaviour of networks using another operator p which was tantamount to taking a differential, though not precisely so. Soon he had a meaning for $\sqrt{p}$. With such revolutionary concepts it is hardly surprising that his manuscripts submitted for publication were rejected. He received very harsh treatment from his peers and this left him embittered. He declared his main research completed by 1887, and 10 years later took on himself the life of a hermit. He was the first man to suggest that a single telephone line could convey more than one message at a time. He suggested that a conducting layer in the upper atmosphere (now known as the 'Heaviside layer') might act like a conducting sheet while the sea provided another, and that radio propagation was guided and reflected between the two as between transmission lines. This was some years before APPLETON demonstrated the existence of the layer by experiment. Heaviside suggested the use of inductance-loading in telephone lines to reduce acoustic distortion. At 23 he read Maxwell's work extensively and ever after declared himself the apostle of Maxwell. 'I then put Maxwell aside and followed my own way. And I advanced much faster.' During this period he established a symmetry for the whole of electromagnetics. In his main published work *Electromagnetic Theory* (3 vols, London, 1893–1912) he wrote: 'As the universe is boundless one way towards the great, so it is equally boundless the other way towards the small, and important events may arise from what is going on inside atoms and again in the inside of electrons ... From the atom to the electron is a great step. But it is not finality' – this only two years after the discovery of the electron. He had assembled a fourth volume of this work, but it was torn up and scattered by burglars a few days after his death. From partial reconstruction it is clear that it contained a unified field theory to embrace both gravitation and electromagnetism: he called 'twisted nothingness' what EINSTEIN later termed 'curved space'. In 1950 Professor Bjerknes wrote: 'I proposed Heaviside for the Nobel Prize, but alas it was 100 years too early.' ERL

The Heaviside Centenary Volume (London, 1950).

Hebb, Donald Olding (b. Chester, NS, Canada, 22.7.1904). Canadian psychologist. He obtained his doctorate under the supervision of K. S. Lashley at Harvard University in 1936, and subsequently held a number of academic appointments, notably professor of psychology (1947–72) and chancellor (1970 –4) at McGill University. His major contribution to psychology was *The Organization of Behavior* (NY, 1949), in which he made an ambitious attempt to account in neurological terms for many of the phenomena of perception, learning and thinking. Hebb argued in this book that there is spontaneous brain activity which modifies, and interacts with, incoming stimulation. He resurrected the concept of 'attention', which he regarded as an autonomous central process or activity markedly affected by learning. At the neurological level, elemental neural patterns known as 'cell assemblies' were thought to develop as a result of experience, and then combine to form a more complicated neural structure known as a 'phase sequence'. His interest in mental processes led him to reject behaviourism, but he claimed that he made use of the behaviourist method, and he favoured the term 'behaviouristics' to describe his approach. In sum, his theoretical ideas played an important part in the revival of physiological psychology in the 1950s, and in the replacement of simple behaviourist views on learning with more complex and realistic learning theories.   MWE

Heckscher, Eli Filip (b. Stockholm, Sweden, 29.11.1879; d. Stockholm, 26.11.1952). Swedish economic historian who wrote his doctoral thesis on the significance of the railways for Sweden's economic development. He taught at the Stockholm Business School from its foundation in 1909. A *laissez-faire* liberal, much influenced by the ideas of Alfred MARSHALL, Heckscher had a keen interest in current affairs, and wrote regular articles for the Swedish newspapers. As a scholar he was almost incredibly prolific, and a bibliography of his publications up to 1949 runs to 1148 items. In Sweden, he is remembered as the man who established economic history as an independent discipline and wrote the standard *Sveriges ekonomiska historia Fran Gustav Vasa* [Economic history of Sweden since Gustav Vasa] (4 vols, Stockholm, 1935; abridged tr. *The*

Economic History of Sweden, Cambridge, Mass., 1954). Outside Sweden Heckscher is best known as the author of *Merkantilismen* (Stockholm, 1931; *Mercantilism*, 2 vols, London, 1935), a study of economic policy as an agent of unification in Europe before the age of economic liberalism. Although some of its conclusions have been modified by more recent research, it remains a classic. Heckscher is also remembered as one of the first advocates of the use of economic theory by economic historians.
                                                     UPB

A. Gershenkron, 'Eli F. Heckscher', in E. F. Heckscher, *Economic History of Sweden* (Cambridge, Mass., 1954).

Heidegger, Martin (b. Messkirch, Baden-Württemberg, Germany, 26.9.1889; d. Messkirch, West Germany, 26.5.1976). German philosopher. The son of a Catholic sexton, Heidegger entered the Jesuit order as a novice. But by 1915 he was teaching philosophy as a layman at Freiburg-im-Bresgau, returning there in 1928 after a five-year period at Marburg to succeed his old teacher HUSSERL. His doctoral dissertation of 1916 was on Duns Scotus. *Sein und Zeit* (Halle; tr. J. Macquarrie & E. Robinson, *Being and Time*, London, 1962), his most important work, was published in 1927. He displayed some enthusiasm for the Nazi regime following HITLER's seizure of power and was rector of Freiburg University for a while before resigning in 1934. After WW2 Heidegger was prohibited from teaching, and even when the ban was lifted in 1951 he continued his routine of private study. *Sein und Zeit*, designed as the preliminary phase of a general theory of being which Heidegger did not directly pursue, concentrated on the particular kind of existence peculiar to human beings. *Dasein*, as he calls it, is what differentiates men from the inert material surroundings within which they find they have been arbitrarily 'thrown'; it is a condition characterized by anxious awareness of the future, and as containing both the necessity of choice and death, the cessation of being. This gloomy picture of man's place in nature is seen by Heidegger as having practical, ethical consequences. Most people distract their attention from the fact of death and extinction and trivialize their freedom of choice, satisfied to follow a conventional routine. But authentic life is possible if death is resolutely confronted and freedom exercised with a sense of its essentially creative nature. Man, as a temporal being and the former and pursuer of projects, must conceive the world of things around him in terms of its availability for his active purposes. That pragmatist idea consorts a little uneasily with Heidegger's detestation of modern industrial and technological society, notably expressed in his inaugural lecture in which Hitler's achievement of power was welcomed as an opportunity for the German university to speak out for true culture. More repelled, it would seem, by the vulgarity than by the cruelty of Nazism, Heidegger turned in his later thinking to a kind of contemplative quietism. The anxious striving of human existence, the topic of his early, more strictly existentialist philosophy, is replaced by Being itself. The superficial practical busyness of man has the effect of hiding Being from him, although it is always present and we can make ourselves 'open' to it. Like other imaginatively minded thinkers, Heidegger found the obscure and fragmentary writings of the pre-Socratic philosophers to be an agreeably plastic sort of raw material for his speculations which came to be expressed in an increasingly sibylline form. He devoted much attention to elaborate and wayward etymological musings about fundamental items in the Greek philosophical vocabulary. Heidegger's earlier picture of the world, a 20c version of KIERKEGAARD's anguished acknowledgement of the contingent and the irrational, was the most potent and influential presentation of the existentialism that dominated Europe in WW2 and for some years after it. It had an affinity with Karl BARTH's Protestant theology of crisis, traceable to their common Kierkegaardian ancestry.   AQ

G. Steiner, *Heidegger* (London, 1978).

Heifetz, Jascha (b. Vilna, Russia [now Lithuania, USSR], 2.2.1901; naturalized American citizen, 1925). Russian/American violinist, the outstanding figure among 20c virtuosos. Of Russian parent-

age, he was a prodigy who could play Mendelssohn's Concerto at the age of six; after training in St Petersburg he made a sensational debut in Berlin in 1912. He settled in the USA after touring there in 1917. Heifetz possessed an unrivalled mastery of his chosen instrument: his finger dexterity was matched by a powerful yet subtle bowing style, and his tone was vibrantly expressive. All this technical resource was directed towards the interpretation of a wide range of music from Bach and Handel through to SIBELIUS and William Walton (whose Violin Concerto he commissioned). He has played in chamber music with such artists as the cellist Piatigorsky and the pianist Artur Rubinstein, and his work since 1962 as a teacher at the University of Southern California has resulted in the creation there in 1975 of a Heifetz chair of music of which he was the first occupant.   CH

Heimsoeth, Heinz (b. Cologne, N. Rhine-Westphalia, Germany, 12.8.1886; d. Cologne, West Germany, 10.9.1975). German historian of philosophy. Heimsoeth is best known for his *Die sechs grossen Themen der abendländischen Philosophie* [The six great themes of western philosophy] (Berlin, 1922), his writings on German idealism, and for his work as continuator of Windelband's *Lehrbuch der Geschichte der Philosophie* [Textbook of the history of philosophy] (Tübingen, [15]1957). Confining himself for the most part to the philosophy of the modern era, Heimsoeth helped to evolve a novel and highly sophisticated method which avoided both a passive antiquarian reproduction of the classical systems with its minute philological attention to texts, and the Hegelian vice of interpreting earlier systems as steppingstones towards the fully developed ultimate philosophy; he examined the history of philosophy from a '*problemgeschichtlich*' point of view – as a continuous and ever-renewed grappling with fundamental problems or themes. Thinkers like Paracelsus, Bruno, Descartes, Leibniz, Kant, Fichte, Hegel, NIETZSCHE, to whom he devoted illuminating individual studies, are interpreted in the light of their total view of the world, and in relation to the great current of ideas from which they drew and to which they in turn contributed. Perennial philosophical problems and conceptions are seen to evolve, and the works of the past take on significance in the light of the philosophical concerns of the present.   RNH

Heisenberg, Werner (b. Würzburg, Bavaria, Germany, 5.12.1901; d. Munich, West Germany, 1.2.1976). German theoretical physicist who enunciated the uncertainty principle in quantum mechanics. As a young man he worked on the quantum theory with SOMMERFELD in Munich, and then joined BORN at Göttingen where he studied hydrodynamics and the anomalous Zeeman effect. Later he went to Copenhagen to discuss with Niels BOHR the problems of the quantum theory. He sought a way out of the difficulties by concentrating on the observables and formulated the basic ideas of matrix mechanics. He completed the theory with Born and Jordan on his return to Göttingen. Soon afterwards SCHRÖDINGER developed wave mechanics and then showed that it is identical to matrix mechanics. Controversy arose over the interpretation of the wave function and Born suggested the probability interpretation. To make this consistent with observation Heisenberg developed the uncertainty principle which says that the product of the uncertainties of our knowledge of the values of conjugate variables (such as position and momentum, or energy and time) is always greater than PLANCK's constant. Thus the more accurately we know the position of an electron the less we know about its momentum. For his work on the foundations of quantum mechanics, Heisenberg was awarded the Nobel prize in 1933. Subsequently he explained ferromagnetism in terms of the interactions between the electrons and also worked with PAULI on quantum electrodynamics. His contributions to nuclear physics include early work on isospin, nuclear exchange forces, cosmic rays and the theory of the S-matrix. Heisenberg was professor at Leipzig from 1927 to 1941. Although he opposed some aspects of Nazi policy he remained in Germany throughout WW2 and directed the unsuccessful atomic bomb project. After the war Heisenberg helped to rebuild German science, becoming director of the Max-Planck Institute at Göttingen. He also worked on theories of turbulence, superconductivity and elementary particles. Heisenberg wrote several books on the quantum theory and its wider implications, including *Die physikalischen Prinzipien der Quantetherie* (Braunschweig, 1943; *The Physical Principles of the Quantum Theory*, Chicago, 1930), *Physics and Beyond* (NY, 1955) and *Physics and Philosophy* (NY, 1958).   PEH

Heitler, Walter Heinrich (b. Karlsruhe, Baden-Württemberg, Germany, 2.1.1904; d. Zürich, Switzerland, 15.11.1981). German theoretical physicist. Heitler studied at Berlin and Munich universities and was a *Privatdozent* at Göttingen. Leaving Germany when HITLER came to power in 1933, he worked until 1941 at the University of Bristol and then at the Institute for Advanced Studies, Dublin. From 1949 to 1974 he was professor of theoretical physics at the University of Zürich. Although he tackled many problems in theoretical physics he is chiefly known for his work with F. LONDON which explains the mechanism of the valence bonds which bind atoms together into molecules. In particular they were able to show why two hydrogen atoms are bound together into a hydrogen molecule and also why, for hydrogen, only two such atoms can be bound and not three or more. Their theory introduces the concept of 'exchange' – this is the idea that the electron which orbits a hydrogen nucleus can reduce its energy by sharing a more complicated orbit with an electron from another atom. The reduction of energy for both electrons binds the two atoms together as a molecule. Heitler and London's calculations showed that this binding energy was indeed roughly equal to the energy determined experimentally to dissociate a hydrogen molecule into two separate atoms, a conclusion which gave considerable support to their theory. Heitler also wrote more general works on the problems that modern science poses for humanity and of the difficulties which arise if life processes are discussed solely in terms of knowledge gained from the physical sciences (e.g. *Der Mensch und die naturwissenschaftliche Erkenntnis*, Braunschweig, 1961; *Man and Science*, London, 1963).   HMR/WGR

Helgason, Jón (b. Raudsgil, Iceland, 30.6.1899). Icelandic scholar and poet. With S. NORDAL and E. Ó. Sveinsson, Jón Helgason is a refounder of modern Icelandic philological and literary scholarship, but whereas Nordal may be named the W. P. Ker of Icelandic studies, Helgason is their HOUSMAN. He has revitalized textual scholarship, giving it solid philological foundations, and has revived literary studies with deliberately expressed iconoclastic literary judgements designed to force the complacent to question their ideas. As a professor at Copenhagen University he has exerted beneficial influence on an international host of students of medieval Icelandic, not least in applying caustic sanity to bombastic theories. As a poet he has made a powerful impact on 20c Icelandic literature. His slender collection *Úr landsudri* [From the south-east] (Reykjavik, 1939) reveals a Housmanian strain of satire and of black lyricism unique in modern Icelandic literature.
                                        BSB

Hemingway, Ernest (b. Oak Park, Ill., USA, 21.7.1898; d. Ketchum, Idaho, 2.7.1961). American novelist. Behind Hemingway's work lay the whole discipline of prose as understood by the modernist writers who lived as expatriates in Paris after WW1. Hemingway was soon accepted as a peer by Gertrude STEIN, Ford Madox FORD and Ezra POUND. His early work – *Three Stories and Ten Poems* (Paris, 1923) and *In Our Time* (Paris, 1924) – showed his mastery of precise, disciplined descriptive prose and understated dialogue. *The Sun Also Rises* (NY, 1926) did much to popularize the 'lost generation' of expatriates and a chic postwar nihilism. Hemingway's experiences as a Red Cross volunteer on the Italian front in 1918 formed the basis of *A Farewell to Arms* (NY, 1929), a romantic and beautifully written tale of love and war. It was the most popular of all American novels of WW1, and Hemingway found it hard to follow. There were signs of change and deterioration in his personality. He began to sign himself 'Pappy' in his letters, and in the 1930s divided his time between the Florida Keys, where he fished, and Utah, where he hunted. His first, and then his second marriage collapsed; Hemingway turned against old friends, like F. Scott FITZGERALD and DOS PASSOS; and he wrote little of interest other than short stories. Galvanized by the civil war in Spain, he covered the war as a journalist. He found Madrid to be a 'carnival of treachery and rottenness', but refused to criticize the Republican conduct of the war or the policy of the communists. He was the most dutiful of fellow-travellers during the civil war. After the victory of FRANCO and the nationalists in 1939, Hemingway wrote *For Whom the Bell Tolls* (NY, 1940), in which a naive American behaves heroically and the anarchists and communists were mainly to blame for the Republican defeat. His later novels, especially *The Old Man and the Sea* (NY, 1952), were praised, but even the award of the Nobel prize for literature and the Pulitzer prize for fiction in 1952 could not disguise the thinness of his later work. His best writing was 30 years behind him when he committed suicide in 1961.   EH

C. Baker, *Ernest Hemingway* (NY, 1969); S. Donaldson, *By Force of Will: the Life and Art of Ernest Hemingway* (NY, 1977).

Hempel, Carl Gustav (b. Oranienburg, nr Berlin, Germany, 8.1.1905; naturalized American citizen). German/American philosopher of science. Hempel studied physics and mathematics and then turned to philosophy, migrating to the USA and teaching at Yale (1948–55) and latterly at Princeton. He was influenced by REICHENBACH, SCHLICK and CARNAP. Basically a logical positivist, his main contributions are to logic, the philosophy of mathematics and the methodology and philosophy of science. In his *Problems and Changes in the Empiricist Criterion of Meaning* (NY, 1950) Hempel analysed the verifiability theory of meaning, and suggested that a statement is meaningful if translatable into empiricist language. Later he admitted degrees of meaning, and proposed that systems of statements are the ultimate units of significance. He examined the link between observational and theoretical scientific terms in his *Fundamentals of Concept Formation in Empirical Science* (NY, 1952) and replaced the earlier physicalism and operationalism by the notion of the interpretative system, maintaining that it is the theory together with its interpretative system that can be subjected to scientific test. This was followed by more detailed studies of the concept of confirmation. In his *Studies in the Logic of Explanation* (NY, 1948) and *Aspects of Scientific Explanation* (NY, 1965) Hempel analysed scientific explanation, using a model that identified explanation with deduction from a law in the case of experimental data and deduction from a more general law in the case of a law.

PEH

Hendrix, Johnny Allen (Jimi) (b. Seattle, Wash., USA, 27.11.1942; d. London, UK, 18.9.1970). Black American rock guitarist, vocalist and composer. A left-handed player, he used right-handed instruments played upside down and experimented with extreme levels of amplified volume, feedback and fuzztone to achieve new guitar sonorities. He began learning the guitar from the age of 12, and by 1963 was working as a session guitarist. In 1966 he formed a blues band called 'Jimmy James and the Blue Flames'. Influenced by Chas Chandler, formerly of the rock group 'The Animals', he moved to England and formed the 'Jimi Hendrix Experience' with British players Noel Redding (bass) and Mitch Mitchell (drums). Playing soul music and his own compositions, Hendrix led showmanship and destructiveness to new heights in rock music, playing the guitar with his teeth, behind his back and even burning it as the climax of his act. Complementary to this visual psychedelic extravaganza, Hendrix's expanding vocabulary of instrumental techniques and sonorities based on feedback and electronics was virtuosic in its application. His became the measure of rock guitar performance,

influencing players such as Eric Clapton and Pete Townshend and 'heavy metal' bands of the 1970s. His death followed barbiturate intoxication. TEC

C. Welch, *Hendrix: Biography* (NY, 1973).

Henry, Louis (b. Paris, France, 12.2.1911). French historical demographer. Since WW2 Henry has been associated with the Institut National d'Etudes Démographiques. He made his reputation by devising the 'family reconstitution' method of analysing demographic trends via a sample of families studied as exhaustively as the evidence allowed. *Anciennes familles genevoises* [Old Genevan families] (Paris, 1956) applied the method to 19 patrician families of Geneva. Based on genealogies, the most important conclusion of this study was that birth control was practised by the upper classes in the later 17c. *La Population de Crulai* [The population of Crulai] (with E. Gautier, Paris, 1958) applied the same method to a village of about 1000 inhabitants in Normandy between 1674 and 1742. It was based on parish registers, and furnished the model for many later studies in historical demography. Henry has discussed problems of method in *Des Registres paroissiaux à l'histoire de la population* [From parish registers to the history of the population] (with M. Fleury, Paris, 1956) and *Manuel de démographie historique* [Manual of historical demography] (Geneva, 1967). More recently he has turned to the formulation of mathematical models of the process of family building in *Démographie: analyses et modèles* (Paris, 1972; *Population: Analyses and Models*, London, 1976). He has been described as 'one of the two or three most original and influential historical demographers of the century'.

UPB

Henze, Hans Werner (b. Gütersloh, N. Rhine-Westphalia, Germany, 1.7.1926). German composer. At first briefly associated with the avant-garde of STOCKHAUSEN and BOULEZ, Henze has become the leading operatic composer of his generation. The success of his first two operas, *Das Wundertheater* [The wonder theatre] (1949) and *Boulevard*

319

Solitude (1952), enabled him to leave Germany and settle in Italy. At the same time he rejected the doctrinaire serialism he had espoused in his Third Symphony (1951) and instead pursued the eclectic manner of *Boulevard Solitude*, while drawing into his music an Italianate melodic grace and a harmonic lushness redolent of the Mediterranean. Among the first works to show fully the change of style was the opera *König Hirsch* [King Hirsch] (1956), and this new, romantic approach was further developed in two operas to librettos by AUDEN and Kallman: *Elegy for Young Lovers* (1961) and *The Bassarids* (1966), the latter a reworking of Euripides's *Bacchae*. Since completing *The Bassarids* Henze has, at least in his vocal and dramatic works, placed his art at the service of socialist revolution, his committed pieces including the opera *We Come to the River* (1976).   PG

Hepworth, Jocelyn Barbara (b. Wakefield, W. Yorks., UK, 10.1.1903; d. St Ives, Cornwall, 20.5.1975). British sculptor. Barbara Hepworth studied at Leeds and the Royal College of Art in London at the same time as Henry MOORE, and like him was preoccupied for some years with direct carving of stone, marble or wood. She soon began to develop a very stylized and simplified treatment of the human figure, emphasizing the basic underlying forms, a tendency which became increasingly evident after her meeting in 1931 with Ben NICHOLSON, who later became her second husband. Through Nicholson she met ARP, BRANCUSI, MONDRIAN, BRAQUE and other leading artists of the school of Paris, and was closely involved in the international group of constructive artists including Mondrian and GABO who came to London as refugees in the second half of the 1930s. Her own work became completely abstract in 1934, with an emphasis on simple volumetric primary forms such as the ovoid, the sphere and the cylinder. On the outbreak of WW2 she and Nicholson moved to St Ives in Cornwall, where she spent the rest of her life. The influence of the landscape of West Cornwall, with its rugged coastline, wild moorland and ancient stone circles, led to a synthesis of her sense of abstract form and her feeling for, and of being in, the landscape. She tended to carve more deeply into the forms and pierce holes right through them; sometimes produced complex groups of forms; and from 1956 onwards made a number of sculptures in plaster to be cast in bronze. She carried out some of her later works on a much larger scale.   REA

J. P. Hodin, *Barbara Hepworth* (London, 1961); A. M. Hammacher, *Barbara Hepworth* (London, 1968).

Herbert, Zbigniew (b. Lvov, Poland [now Ukraine, USSR], 29.10.1924). Polish poet and dramatist, contemporary of RÓŻEWICZ and like him branded by the experience of war. After WW2 Herbert studied law, economics and philosophy at Torúm and Warsaw universities, and in 1948 he made his poetic debut; but publication was restricted to literary magazines until the more lenient climate of 1956. For the Polish reading public Herbert's name is synonymous with integrity, and like Różewicz he has often been dubbed a moralist. Unlike Różewicz, however, whose quest is restricted to the present, Herbert has not accepted the bankruptcy of prewar values. His poetry presents a constant dialogue and communion with the artefacts of the past, whereby the lost lands of a common civilization may be regained and historic necessity held briefly at bay. History offers a source of compassion, a sense of responsibility for the human conscience, a criterion of self. According to Herbert the poet's supreme moral duty lies in the stringencies of discernment: hence the lucid intellectual structures of his verse, seeking a fragile equilibrium and anchorage-point that will ensure survival. Irony is the hallmark of Herbert's poetry – a touchstone for truth, a foil for self-delusion, a corrective to the energies of imagery. Discomfiting in its ambiguous nonconformity, Herbert's irony invests every poem with a political dimension – the commitment of standing aloof. English translations of his poetry include *Selected Poems* (tr. C. Miłosz & P. Dale Scott, intro. A. Alvarez, London, 1968) and *Selected Poems* (tr. J. Carpenter & B. Carpenter, Oxford, 1977).   NT

Hernández, Miguel (b. Orihuela, Alicante, Spain, 30.10.1910; d. Alicante, 28.3.1942). Spanish poet. A unique phenomenon: the shepherd-poet who became the soldier-poet, voice of the proletariat in arms. In spite of censorship, his death in a nationalist gaol made Hernández a cult figure of the left in FRANCOist Spain. As a poet he served an apprenticeship of classical imitation before emerging with his own voice to create a modern pastoral, an authentic song of a man of the land. He is the poet of love in all its aspects: kinship with nature, brotherhood of man, sexual union. His life's love was the seamstress Josefina Manresa and the trials of a conventional Spanish courtship are recorded in the neobaroque sonnet sequence *El rayo que no cesa* [Lightning without end] (Madrid, 1936). In Madrid in the mid-1930s friendship with ALEIXANDRE and NERUDA changed the course of his life and work – Catholicism gave way to MARXism, individual to collective concerns. During the civil war he was tireless in the Republican propaganda service. His two collections of war poetry *Viento del pueblo* [Wind of the people] (Valencia, 1937) and *El hombre acecha* [Man on the watch] (in *Obras completas*, Buenos Aires, 1960), charting the swing from optimism to pessimism as the Republicans lost ground, are full of passionate conviction if aesthetically uneven. Hernández came to maturity as a poet in prison when he returned to personal considerations of life and death, sustained by love of wife and child. His last collection *Cancionero y romancero de ausencias* (Buenos Aires, 1958; tr. T. C. Jones, *Songbook of Absences*, Washington, 1972) is also his greatest, concentrated emotion being expressed in an often condensed form with moving simplicity. Set to music, Hernández's verses became the protest songs of the last decade of the Franco regime.   PMcD

G. Cleary Nichols, *Miguel Hernández* (Boston, Mass., 1978).

Hertzsprung, Ejnar (b. Frederiksberg, Denmark, 8.10.1873; d. Roskilde, 21.10.1967). Danish astronomer. Hertzsprung graduated from the Polytechnical Institute in Copenhagen in 1898 and spent the next few years as a chemist in St Petersburg. He had always wished to be an astronomer and on his return to Copenhagen he obtained a post at the university observatory. At this time the Harvard observatory was engaged on an extensive survey of the spectra of stars under the direction of E. C. Pickering. The sequence of spectra that was evolved was soon recognized as the consequence of a progression of temperature. Another member of the Harvard team noted that the spectra of some stars show unusually sharp lines. Such spectra were said to have a 'c-characteristic'. In 1905, Hertzsprung found that stars with this characteristic also have very small proper motions (the slow motions across the sky that are due to the motion of the sun and the star itself). He inferred that they are more distant than usual, and therefore intrinsically very bright; in addition, as their colours are little different from usual, the stars have normal temperatures and must be larger than normal. This was the origin of the concept of 'giant' and 'dwarf' stars, now a familiar part of stellar evolution theory. Hertzsprung was also in 1911 an originator of one form of the Hertzsprung–Russell diagram, in which stellar absolute magnitude is commonly plotted against spectral type. His paper was published in an obscure photographic journal and was not known to the astronomical community until H. N. RUSSELL independently proposed a similar diagram in 1913. In 1913, when Hertzsprung was a member of staff at Potsdam observatory, H. S. Leavitt of Harvard discovered a type of variable star in the Small Magellanic Cloud for which the period of the variation in brightness is related to the apparent brightness (and therefore to the intrinsic brightness, since all of the stars are at approximately the same distance). Hertszprung noted the resemblance between these stars and the Cepheid variables, and realized that if this relationship could be calibrated it would be possible to measure the distance of any remote object containing such a variable. The calibration is not straightforward because all Cepheid variables are too distant for a direct measurement of parallax, but Hertzsprung obtained a calibration using a statistical method. He was thus able to determine the distance of the Small Magellanic Cloud. The use of Cepheids for distance measurement is now standard practice. Hertzsprung retired as director of the Leiden observatory, but continued to work on astronomical problems until beyond the age of 90.   DEB

Herzberg, Gerhard (b. Hamburg, Germany, 25.12.1904; naturalized Canadian citizen). German/Canadian physicist. Herzberg became a *Privatdozent* at the Darmstadt Technical University in 1930, but left Germany in 1935 and emigrated to Canada. After obtaining a position in the University of Saskatchewan, he worked from 1945 to 1948 at the Yerkes Observatory, Wisconsin. He then returned to the National Research Council in Ottawa. Herzberg is widely known for his application of spectroscopic techniques to the study of problems in the fields of astrophysics, atomic and molecular physics and physical chemistry. He has had a major impact on the development of spectroscopy, not only through research, but through his four-volume work *Molecular Spectra and Molecular Structure* (4 vols, NY, 1939–79) and his influence as director of the division of physics of the National Research Council of Canada at Ottawa, which he made into a world centre for spectroscopists. Precise work on the energy levels of the hydrogen atoms and molecules H, H_2, H_3 and isotopic variants has provided a fruitful testing ground for quantitative and molecular theory, and Herzberg has often returned to one of these species to find something new. Species of astrophysical importance which he has studied in the laboratory include the interstellar molecules CH and CH^+ and the cometary molecule C_3, a flexible object, which shows little resistance to being bent. In 1971 Herzberg was awarded the Nobel prize in chemistry. In many experiments, the technique of flash photolysis, invented by NORRISH and G. PORTER, was developed and linked to high resolution grating spectroscopy: the spectra of chemically interesting species, for example CH_2, CH_3, NH_2, HCO, HNO, HNCN, were recorded and resolved for the first time. Analysis of the electronic spectra of nonlinear polyatomic molecules presents daunting problems, but Herzberg showed that they could be solved in favourable cases. This work led to the first systematic and detailed account of the electronic spectroscopy of polyatomic molecules. Meanwhile Herzberg's return to old problems has provided new information about such elusive but important species as H_3, H_3^+ and about NH_4.   RFB

Herzl, Theodor (b. Budapest, Austria-Hungary [now Hungary], 2.5.1860; d. Edlach, nr Vienna, Austria-Hungary, 3.7.1904). Austrian journalist, propagandist and founder of the Zionist movement. A citizen of the Austro-Hungarian empire, dismayed at anti-Semitism in Tsarist Russia and in *fin-de-siècle* Paris where he was correspondent for the liberal Viennese *Neue Freie Presse* (1891-4) at the time of the Dreyfus trial; he took up the idea of providing a national status and citizenship for all Jews by creating a Jewish state. In his pamphlet *Der Judenstäat* (Vienna, 1896; *The Jewish State*, London, 1934) he developed the concept of 'auto-emancipation' which had come to the German-speaking world from the Jewish communities in Russia. He convened the first Zionist Congress at Basle (1897) and by tact and diplomacy created a common ground between the great French and German Jewish bankers and philanthropists and the persecuted incipient Jewish nationalists of Tsarist Russia and Poland. This same diplomatic skill, however, failed to win the support of the German emperor or the Ottoman sultan for the Zionist programme of a Jewish 'homeland' to be established in biblical Palestine. He proved equally unsuccessful, when the British authorities offered to discuss the establishment of Jewish settlements either in Egypt (then under British occupation) or in Cyprus or Uganda, in his attempts to persuade his fellow-Zionists to abandon their politicization of the Orthodox Jewish prayer 'next year in Jerusalem' – 'either Israel in Palestine or not at all' was the view of the majority of the Zionists. Herzl's death in 1904 left the Zionist movement divided until the successful emergence, towards the end of WW1, of WEIZMANN restored unity.   DCW

Hess, Harry Hamond (b. New York, USA, 24.5.1906; d. Woods Hole, Mass., 25.8.1969). American geologist. Hess was a brilliant scientist and an able administrator. He was equally good at detailed, meticulous work in his special fields of interest – igneous petrology and mineralogy – and in generating significant ideas in the broader field of global tectonics and mantle composition. He joined the Princeton faculty in 1934 and stayed there for the rest of his academic life. He had a distinguished war record in the US Navy and later, as chairman of the Space Science Board of the National Academy of Sciences, was for a time the principal nongovernmental adviser on the scientific objectives for planetary exploration.

Hess achieved distinction as a mineralogist for his work on the pyroxenes, and as a petrologist for research into the nature and origin of ultramafic rocks. These twin interests are best expressed in his monograph on the Stillwater igneous complex of Montana (*Geol. Soc. Amer. Mem.* 80, 1960). He provided a major stimulus to geological research in the Caribbean, and into the character of the gravity field under submarine trenches in the Pacific. During WW2, as captain of an assault transport, he directed systematic echo-sounding surveys of the Pacific, which resulted in the discovery of striking flat-topped seamounts which he correctly interpreted as subsided islands, and for which he coined the word 'guyot'. Hess's name became intimately linked with Project Mohole, a proposal to drill beneath the ocean into the mantle, which was rejected because of escalating costs, but not before the feasibility of drilling in deep water had been established. The ambitious Deep Sea Drilling Project was a natural successor to Mohole. Hess's surest claim to fame is his hypothesis of seafloor spreading, published in the paper 'History of ocean basins' (*Petrologic Studies*, Geol. Soc. Amer., 1962), in which he argued that new crust is created under mid-ocean ridges and spreads laterally, to descend beneath submarine trenches at tectonically and seismically active ocean margins. This inspiring idea, which offered a driving-force for continental drift, was subsequently confirmed from palaeomagnetic data by Vine and Matthews, and provides the main basis for plate tectonics.
    AH

Hesse, Hermann (b. Calw, Baden-Württemberg, Germany, 2.7.1877; naturalized Swiss citizen, 1923; d. Montagnola, Ticino, Switzerland, 9.8.1962). German/Swiss novelist and poet. Early novels of romantic dreams and idyllic German landscapes brought Hesse a fame which was almost lost in WW1 when (having been rejected for military service) he made continual appeals for peace. His novel *Demian* (Berlin, 1919; tr. W. J. Strachan, London, 1958) had to be published under a pseudonym but was a great success, the central figure, a mystically endowed leader, providing an unusual justification of German soldiers, who were said to have killed their enemies impersonally. In *Siddhartha* (Berlin, 1922; tr. H. Rosner, London, 1954) he wrote in effect a poetic life of Buddha. *Der Steppenwolf* (Berlin, 1927; tr. B. Creighton, London, 1974) was a transference to the contemporary European scene of similarly Buddhistic ideas, this time coloured by the psychology of JUNG, while *Narziss und Goldmund* (Berlin, 1930; tr. G. Dunlop, London, 1959), set in the Middle Ages, repeated a theme common to all these novels, the 'polar', complementary opposition of two contrasting types of men.

During the Weimar republic (1919–33) Hesse stayed aloof from politics. His books continued to be published in Germany during the Nazi regime, and were defended from individual attacks by an official circular in 1937, though he was placed on the Nazi blacklist in 1943. In 1942 he sent to Berlin for publication his *Das Glasperlenspiel* (tr. R. & C. Winston, *The Glass Bead Game*, NY, 1970), a long novel dealing with a game played with beads on an abacus, which symbolically combines all branches of knowledge. It was not accepted, and was published in Zürich (1943). The question throughout the novel is whether it is right to continue the game when political and social life calls out for practical action. The hero decides to abandon the game but dies accidentally as he is making his way towards a life devoted to realizing human rights. In 1946 Hesse received the Nobel prize for literature. He achieved a third triumph in America, in and after the 1960s. Despite the high awards made to him, Hesse's stature as a writer has often been called into question. His thought has been called secondhand, and attention has been drawn to his continual reliance on clichés of expression. He remains, however, one of the bestselling German-speaking writers throughout the world.

RDG

T. J. Ziolkowski (ed.), *Hesse* (NY, 1973); J. Mileck, *Hermann Hesse: Biography and Bibliography* (2 vols, Berkeley, Calif., 1977).

Hettner, Alfred (b. Dresden, Saxony, Germany [now East Germany], 6.8.1859; d. Heidelberg, Baden-Württemberg, Germany, 31.8.1941). German geographer. Trained in geomorphology and climatology, Hettner travelled widely in several continents and developed an influential view of geography as a chorological science, integrating with equal weight the six realms of the physical world – land, water, air, plants, animals and man. At Heidelberg University from 1899 until his death, Hettner published widely and founded his own journal *Geographische Zeitschrift*. His view of geography as the study of the association of phenomena in particular places (regions) – the *länderkundliche schema* outlined how this was done – was introduced to non-German readers in HARTSHORNE's classic *The Nature of Geography* (1939).

RJJ

Alfred Hettner ... Gedenkschrift zum 100. Geburtstag (Heidelberg, 1960); R. E. Dickinson, *The Makers of Modern Geography* (London, 1969).

Hewish, Anthony (b. Fowey, Cornwall, UK, 11.5.1924). British radio astronomer. Hewish played an important part in the pioneering development of radio astronomy and a decisive role in the discovery of pulsars, for which he shared the Nobel prize for physics with RYLE in 1974, the first to be awarded to astronomers. Hewish studied physics at Cambridge and apart from WW2 has spent his life there, attached to the Cavendish Laboratory and the Mullard Observatory; he became professor of radio astronomy in 1971. In addition to assisting Ryle develop the method of aperture synthesis, making it possible for radio telescopes to match the performance of optical telescopes, he became fascinated by the problem of the twinkling or scintillation of radio sources. This effect is caused by the passage of the signal from the distant object through material in the intervening space, especially the earth's upper atmosphere and the neighbourhood around the sun. Using radio scintillation, Hewish built up a detailed picture of the extreme outer regions of the solar atmosphere and studied the solar wind and the fine structure of distant quasars. In 1965 he decided to build a new radio telescope to study radio galaxies and radio events of very short duration. The 18,000 m^2 array was completed in 1967 and Hewish and his student Jocelyn Bell (now Burnell) began to survey the northern sky. By autumn 1967 Bell had picked out an unusual source which they soon discovered was pulsating with high regularity about once a second. No known object in the universe could behave like this except the hypothetical neutron star. Hewish and his colleagues eliminated all other possibilities and in 1968 announced to the astronomical world the discovery of their 'pulsar'. Subsequently many such objects have been discovered and have been confirmed as rotating neutron stars. The discovery opened up new fields in astrophysics and demonstrated the unexpected high scientific return that can come from painstaking and apparently unspectacular science.

MJS

Heyerdahl, Thor (b. Larvik, Vestfold, Norway, 6.10.1914). Norwegian anthropologist. By his epic voyages he made spectacular contributions to the view that identical traits in widely separated cultures may not be coincidences but the result of prehistoric migrations. He noticed that the Polynesian god Tiki closely resembled Virakocha (originally called Kon-Tiki), a legendary pre-Inca god of Peru who escaped a massacre of his people about AD 500 by sailing across the Pacific. The similarity was marked for Heyerdahl by the resemblance between the vast stone statues of Peru and the giant monoliths of Easter Island. By crossing with five companions from Callao in Peru to Raroia in Polynesia on a balsa log raft *Kon-Tiki* in 1947, he set out to prove against prevailing thought that Peruvian Indians could have settled Polynesia. His 1953 archaeological expedition to the Galapagos Islands convinced him that his theories were right. Though many ethnologists disagree, it is now acknowledged that there must have been some prehistoric migrations from South America to Polynesia. Heyerdahl's crossing of the South Atlantic in 1970 in *Ra II*, a boat constructed of papyrus reeds, was undertaken to demonstrate a similar link between ancient Mediterranean civilizations and prehistoric South America. He produced films and books about his expeditions, his best known (*Kon-Tiki Ekspedisjon*, Oslo, 1948; *The Kon-Tiki Expedition*, London, 1950) being translated into 64 languages.　　　EJH

Heyrovský, Jaroslav (b. Prague, Austria-Hungary [now Czechoslovakia], 20.12.1890; d. Prague, 27.3.1967). Czech chemist. Heyrovský's life-work was the discovery and development of polarography, an extremely important electrochemical technique for qualitative and quantitative analysis of inorganic and organic species in solution. He was educated at the Charles University, Prague, and later (1910–14) at University College London, under RAMSAY and Donnan. His interest in electrochemistry developed from the latter, and after WW1 he began the work which led to his invention of the polarographic technique in 1922: the first polarograph was constructed in 1924 (*Rec. Trav. Chim.*, 44 (1925), 496). After this, his whole scientific effort was dedicated to the development of the technique. Important contributions to the field were also made by his fellow countrymen Ilkovič and Vlček. Today, polarography is widely used both for analysis and as a fundamental probe for chemical research into molecular reactivity and stability. In 1926 Heyrovský was appointed as the first professor of physi-

cal chemistry at the Charles University. In 1950 he was appointed director of the new Czechoslovak Polarographic Institute. Nine years later he was awarded the Nobel prize in chemistry – the first Czech national to win a Nobel award. His two most important monographs are *Polarographie* (Vienna, 1941); with R. Kalvoda, *Oszillographische Polarographie mit Wechselstrom* (Berlin, 1960).　　　KRS

Hicks, John Richard (b. Warwick, UK, 8.4.1904). British economist. Educated at Clifton College and Balliol College, Oxford, after spells at the London School of Economics and Cambridge, he was appointed professor of economics at Manchester in 1938. He returned to Oxford in 1946 as a fellow of Nuffield College; in 1952, on appointment as Drummond professor of political economy at Oxford, he moved to All Souls College, where he remained until his retirement in 1971 (though relinquishing the Drummond chair in 1965).

Hicks has made contributions to many areas of economic theory, presenting them in a pellucid, somewhat schoolmasterly English style, with mathematics kept mainly in the background and in appendices. His most important work (for which he was awarded a Nobel prize jointly with ARROW in 1972) has been in general equilibrium theory, where he brought to prominence in the English-speaking world and carried forward the work of WALRAS and PARETO, first in a joint paper (with R. G. D. Allen, in *Economica*, 1934) and then more comprehensively in *Value and Capital* (London, 1939). This work, like KEYNES's *General Theory* (1936), concentrated mainly on the determinants of short-run equilibrium, incorporating plans and expectations referring to the longer term future (so-called 'temporary equilibrium'). In this context, Hicks pioneered the analysis of the stability of multimarket systems.

Among Hicks's other significant contributions are a concept of neutral (and non-neutral) technological change, put forward in his early work on *The Theory of Wages* (London, 1932, ²1963); a clarification of national accounting theory ('The valuation of the social income',

Economica, 1940), distinguishing between national income concepts appropriate to the measurement of production and of economic welfare respectively; an elaboration of Alfred MARSHALL's doctrine of consumer's surplus and its relevance for welfare economics (incorporated in *A Revision of Demand Theory*, Oxford, 1958); and a seminal analysis of the impact of technological change on the terms of trade ('An inaugural lecture', in *Oxford Economic Papers*, n.s. 5, 1953). Much of his later work has been on macroeconomics, particularly economic growth and capital theory (on which he produced two unusually wide-ranging books: *Capital and Growth*, Oxford, 1965, and *Capital and Time*, Oxford, 1973), and also on the relationship between theory and economic history: *A Theory of Economic History* (Oxford, 1969) and *Causality in Economics* (Oxford, 1979).

One of Hicks's best-known pieces is his geometric presentation of some basic features of Keynes's *General Theory*, the so-called IS/LM diagram, which he devised in 1936–7: 'Mr Keynes and the classics' (reprinted in *Critical Essays in Monetary Theory*, Oxford, 1967, and later also incorporated in *A Contribution to the Theory of the Trade Cycle*, Oxford, 1956). PMO

Hieber, Walter (b. Stuttgart, Baden-Württemberg, Germany, 18.12.1895; d. West Germany, 29.11.1976). German chemist. Hieber is the undisputed father of metal carbonyl chemistry, and hence the grandfather of modern organometallic and catalytic chemistry. He was educated at the University of Tübingen, and in 1926 became professor of chemistry at the Chemical Institute at Heidelberg. In 1935 he was appointed as professor of inorganic chemistry at the Technical University of Munich, a position which he held until his retirement in 1964. For many years Hieber had the field of carbonyl chemistry to himself, and laid a solid foundation for later workers (including COTTON, E. O. FISCHER and WILKINSON). He developed practical techniques for working with these compounds and, together with WERNER and STOCK, was responsible for the German dominance in inor-

ganic chemistry, which lasted until the renaissance of the subject in the 1950s. KRS

W. Hieber, *Adv. Organomet. Chem.*, 8 (1979).

Hilbert, David (b. Königsberg, East Prussia, Germany [now Kaliningrad, USSR], 23.1.1862; d. Göttingen, Lower Saxony, Germany, 14.2.1943). German mathematician, educated and first employed at Königsberg, removing to Göttingen in 1895. Hilbert started by effectively terminating the existing theory of invariants. Essentially he did so by solving a more general class of problems and so being led to initiate modern algebraic number theory. Perhaps the most pervasive single concept in modern mathematics is the Hilbert space. It can be regarded as a generalization of ordinary n-dimensional space, in which n is allowed to go to infinity and the concept of distance is preserved by insisting that the sum of the squares of coordinates be a converging sequence. Hilbert was led to this in developing functional analysis; if you wish to give a standardized description of a function that is based on an orthonormal sequence of standard functions (its spectrum) that description will lie in a Hilbert space. This idea has been used in abstract mathematics, in electrical engineering, in quantum physics, and in many other contexts.

Hilbert decisively increased the prestige of the axiomatic method in mathematics. In his *Grundlagen der Geometrie* [Foundations of geometry] (Leipzig, 1899, ⁹1962) his method was to define his subject completely in terms of a finite set of axioms, all mutually consistent and none redundant. He could then use various algebraic models of the resulting structure to prove results without appealing to intuition. For the rest of his life Hilbert propounded the view that all mathematics should be handled on these principles, becoming a network of structures whose existence is strongly independent of the mathematicians who create them. This programme has been shown to be impossible (GÖDEL) and even unthinkable (P. J. Cohen), as well as undesirable (L. E. J. Brouwer). But it has resulted in the normative approach among modern mathematicians; the most influential event in 20c mathematics was Hilbert's proposal of 23 problems, conceived in this spirit (1900). Most have now been solved; each solution was a major event; and many practitioners have been brought up to see mathematics as primarily a discrete set of challenges. AGPW/JCu

H. Weyl, 'David Hilbert and his work', *Bulletin Am. Math. Soc.*, 50 (1944), 612–54.

Hildebrand, Joel Henry (b. Camden, NJ, USA, 16.11.1881). American chemist. Hildebrand's greatest contributions have been to the understanding of the phenomenon of solubility. He recognized (in 1928) that the properties of many mixtures were consistent with the random mixing of the components, even though these might have differing intermolecular forces, and called such mixtures 'regular solutions'. He showed how the regularities could be used to predict the mutual solubility of substances in terms of solubility parameters which reflected the strength of their intermolecular forces. His ideas were presented in a series of books (1924–70), including the classic *Solubility of Non-Electrolytes* (with R. L. Scott, NY, 1950). Some solutions are not 'regular', and the investigation of these using spectroscopic techniques led to his identification (with H. A. Benesi) in 1948 of electron-donor-acceptor (or charge-transfer) complexes. This discovery had a considerable impact on many areas of physical chemistry. On the basis of his investigations into gas solubility, Hildebrand suggested the use of helium–oxygen mixtures, in place of compressed air, for deep diving. Though his original concern was for the avoidance of decompression sickness, such mixtures were found not to induce the narcosis observed in deep dives and virtually all diving to depths greater than 200 feet is now carried out with helium. Hildebrand's *Principles of Chemistry* (NY, 1918; with R. E. Powell, [7]1964) has been used by many generations of students. He was educated at the University of Pennsylvania and, following a year with NERNST and van't HOFF in Berlin in 1906–7, became the first teacher of physical chemistry at that institution. In 1913 G. N. LEWIS invited him to join him in revitalizing the chemistry faculty at the University of California, Berkeley, where he remained on the faculty for some 40 years and continued to be active in research as an emeritus professor. EBS

Hill, Austin Bradford (b. London, UK, 8.7.1897). British medical statistician. Professor of medical statistics at London University, Hill was responsible for introducing into medicine the concept of the controlled clinical trial. Hill showed that when a new treatment became available it was best tested by comparing two groups of patients, otherwise as similar as possible, one group being given the drug and the other a placebo or dummy treatment. He also applied statistical methods to other medical problems and (with Sir Richard Doll) showed the connection between smoking and lung cancer in a large-scale study of British doctors in the 1950s. AJS

Hill, Geoffrey (b. Bromsgrove, Here. & Worcs., UK, 18.6.1932). British poet. Hill, a university lecturer who prefers to avoid publicity, has been called England's only living visionary poet. His first two volumes *For the Unfallen* (London, 1959) and *King Log* (London, 1968) take as their subject the human race's experience of suffering, and struggle powerfully to find meaning in this experience. At the same time Hill constantly questions his own sincerity in pursuing this struggle, and doubts too the fitness of poetry for such a task. 'The whole business of expression', he has said, 'is fraught with the perils of glibness.' Such intense self-mistrust (due to which he writes few poems) has resulted in a tortuously compressed, dialectical poetic style, working obliquely through myth and symbol. *Mercian Hymns* (London, 1971), a compound of myth and history with childhood autobiography, is probably the most accessible work of this notoriously difficult poet. A later volume *Tenebrae* was published in 1978. The serious reader of Hill is forced to re-enact the poet's epistemological struggle and radically to question the ethical purpose of poetry generally.

Such relevant inquiry makes Hill the most indispensable poet of his generation. JAC

Jon Silkin, 'The poetry of Geoffrey Hill', in M. Schmidt & G. Lindop (eds), *British Poetry since 1960* (Oxford, 1972).

Himmler, Heinrich (b. Munich, Bavaria, Germany, 7.10.1900; d. Lüneburg, Lower Saxony, 23.5.1945). Head of the Nazi SS (1929–45), the Gestapo, the secret political police (1934–45), the unified German police forces (1934–45), the *Reichssicherheitshauptamt*, to which the SS, Gestapo and SD (Security Service) were subordinated; and minister of the interior (1943–5). It was under his aegis that the whole Nazi apparatus of repression and genocide, the concentration camps and the extermination camps, functioned, the initiative for these usually lying with his subordinates, especially Heydrich, Kaltenbrunner and Eichmann. A failure both as a schoolmaster and a chicken farmer, Himmler lived off his mistress's income until the Nazis became sufficiently well-financed to provide for him. His weakness and colourlessness, together with the ambitions of his subordinates and the monstrous scale and bureaucratic character of the crimes against humanity wittingly practised by the organizations he headed, combined to make him epitomize the 'banality of evil'. Trusted by HITLER until the penultimate stage of Nazi Germany's collapse (*'treue Heinrich'*), he persuaded himself wrongly that the Western Allies would accept him as head of a German government in an anti-Soviet conspiracy. Arrested by British troops in disguise in May 1945, he committed suicide before he had been completely identified. DCW

Hindemith, Paul (b. Hanau, Hesse, Germany, 16.11.1895; d. Frankfurt, Hesse, West Germany, 28.12.1963). German composer and musical theorist. He was at first something of an *enfant terrible* in his satirical and irreverent compositions such as the orchestral *Kammermusik No 1* [Chamber music] (1922) and the one-act 'play for Burmese marionettes' *Das Nusch-Nuschi* (1920). Gradually, however, other aspects of his personality emerged. He promoted new music,

wrote 'practical music' (the German word is *Gebrauchsmusik*) for amateurs to play and enjoy at home, and acquired a deep belief in music as a major means towards realizing his ideal of the brotherhood of man. Deploring totalitarianism in all its forms, he composed an opera to his own libretto *Mathis der Maler* [Mathis the painter] (1935), in which an artist leads a rebellion against authority – at this time performances of Hindemith's music in Germany were banned by the Nazis. Even so, the ultimate message of *Mathis* is of faith in art rather than in politics. Other 'spiritual' works include the song cycle *Das Marienleben* [The life of Mary] (1923) and the ballet *Nobilissima visione* (1938), inspired respectively by the lives of the Virgin and St Francis of Assisi. His musical language gives prominence to the strong-sounding interval of the fourth but remains tonal; though sometimes dry, the style is marked by high craftsmanship. He was a distinguished teacher in Germany, the USA and finally Switzerland (see his autobiographical account *A Composer's World*, Cambridge, Mass., 1952). CH

Hinshelwood, Cyril Norman (b. London, UK, 19.6.1897; d. London, 9.10.1967). British physical chemist, distinguished for his contributions to chemical kinetics. His interest in the rates and mechanisms of chemical change was aroused by working as an explosives chemist in WW1, before going up to Oxford in 1919. He was fellow and tutor of Trinity College (1921–37), and Dr Lee's professor of chemistry (1937–64). His work on gas reactions, with particular reference to their interpretation in terms of the kinetic theory, led to his best-known book *The Kinetics of Chemical Change in Gaseous Systems* (Oxford, 1926, revised as *The Kinetics of Chemical Change*, Oxford, 1940). Hinshelwood's studies of 'unimolecular' gas reactions laid the foundations for much subsequent work. Another main theme was the study of chain reactions, in which he built upon the work of BODENSTEIN. Related work was done by the Russian SEMENOV, with whom Hinshelwood shared a Nobel prize for chemistry in 1956. The chain reactions studied by Hinshelwood included the hydrogen–oxygen reaction (with particular reference to the phenomena of explosion limits) and the pyrolyses and oxidations of hydrocarbons. At various times he worked on heterogeneous catalysis and on the kinetics of reactions in solution, but from 1936 onwards was increasingly interested in the kinetics of bacterial growth. He saw the bacterial cell as a complex multireaction system, to be dealt with in terms of chemical kinetics. The first decade of his bacterial work led to *The Chemical Kinetics of the Bacterial Cell* (Oxford, 1946), and his final contribution was *Growth, Function, and Regulation in Bacterial Cells* (Oxford, 1966, with A. C. R. Dean). Some of his ideas were much criticized by biologists at the time but have become accepted today. Hinshelwood's experience as a teacher led him to write *The Structure of Physical Chemistry* (Oxford, 1951), a still valuable work. A fine linguist with a good knowledge of the classics, Hinshelwood served as president of the Royal Society at the time of its tercentenary.   JSh

Hiratsuka, Masunori (b. Tokyo, Japan, 19.6.1907; d. Tokyo, 7.3.1981). Japanese educator. Educated at Tokyo Imperial University, Hiratsuka taught in Japan and in the USA before becoming professor of education at Hiroshima Higher Normal School (1939–44). He was professor of education at Kyushu University (1944–63) at a time of huge expansion and massive reorientation in Japan, which he greatly influenced, especially through the Research Institute of Comparative Education and Culture at Kyushu of which he was founder and director. In 1960 he was director of the Department of Education at UNESCO in Paris, but returned to Japan where he became director of the newly established National Institute for Educational Research in Tokyo (1963–78). He strongly supported research (notably, internationally comparative research) with a direct bearing on Japanese educational reform, but also in the rapidly developing Asian context. His influence was unfalteringly liberal, international and moral. He personally conducted research teams working on moral educa-

tion in many countries and across contrasting cultures. Through his encouragement of international and comparative contacts and researches, Hiratsuka contributed greatly to the acceptance of liberal educational ideas in Japan and to the exchange of ideas and experience between Eastern and Western educators. After three early books on biblical studies he wrote *A History of Education in Japan* (Tokyo, 1939), *A History of Modern Education in China* (Tokyo, 1944), *The Future of Japan and Moral Education* (Tokyo, 1959) and *The Future of Japanese Education* (Tokyo, 1962), in addition to editing *An Encyclopedia of World Education* (Tokyo, ²1980) – all in Japanese.   EJK

Hiss, Alger (b. Baltimore, Md, USA, 11.11.1904). Former US State Department official convicted of perjury in January 1950 in denying membership of a communist spy ring in Washington. Hiss graduated from Harvard Law School and rose rapidly in the State Department. He attended the Yalta Conference as an adviser to Franklin D. ROOSEVELT and served as temporary secretary-general of the United Nations at its founding conference in San Francisco. From 1946 to 1949 he was president of the Carnegie Endowment for International Peace. In 1948 the House Committee on Un-American Activities heard testimony from Whittaker Chambers, a self-confessed former courier for a communist spy organization, that Hiss had been a member of the same group in the 1930s. Hiss denied the charges but was found guilty of testifying falsely that he had not passed State Department documents to Chambers in 1938 and had not seen Chambers since 1 January 1937. He served more than three years of a five-year prison sentence before being released.

For charges of treason to be brought against a prominent member of the Eastern Establishment made Hiss's case one of the *causes célèbres* of American political history and bitterly divided American opinion on the question of his guilt or innocence. The House Committee's investigation, in which the future President NIXON first attracted attention, and the trial of Hiss gave impetus to the witch-hunting activities of Senator MCCARTHY who claimed that it provided proof of his charges of communist infiltration of the State Department. Since his release Hiss has sought to establish his innocence by the production of new evidence; but this has not proved conclusive and he has failed to get his case reopened.   ALCB

B. Weinstein, *Perjury* (NY, 1978).

Hitchcock, Alfred Joseph (b. London, UK, 13.8.1899; d. Los Angeles, Calif., USA, 29.4.1980). British film director who made his debut in 1925 and worked primarily in Hollywood from 1940. Although Hitchcock showed himself to be a masterly exponent of sound as early as *Blackmail*, the first British 'talkie', in 1929, his approach to film was largely shaped by the techniques of silent cinema. Virtually all the 50 feature-length films he made during his remarkably successful career are conceived in terms of visual pattern and impact. Hitchcock is an uneven and, in some ways, underexplored film maker. His English output of the 1920s and 1930s contains genuine oddities, like *Rich and Strange* (1932), as well as the overfamiliar *Thirty-Nine Steps* (1935) and *The Lady Vanishes* (1938), but his major work is contained in a single decade of his Hollywood career. There seems little doubt that his future reputation will rest on the series of works extending from *Strangers on a Train* (1951) to *Psycho* (1960) and embracing such masterpieces as *Rear Window* (1954), *Vertigo* (1958) and *North by Northwest* (1959). The French critics, whose claims for the moral profundity of Hitchcock's work led to a major revaluation of his status as a film maker in the late 1950s, pointed to his Catholic beliefs and Jesuit upbringing. But their view of his films as the expression of deeply felt religious anguish is almost as misguided as the earlier dismissal of his Hollywood work, particularly by British critics, as 'mere entertainment'. Hitchcock's themes are those of a more banal, everyday terror – a sense of order and serenity under threat and of values called into question, a suspicion of the dangers of sexual involvement, a nagging fear of the intrusion of the irra-

tional. In this sense his films, with their evident delight in the mechanics of suspense and the possibilities of audience manipulation, are a counterpart to the impulse which led him to conceal his private self behind an instantly recognizable jokey public persona. Hitchcock's lasting importance as a film maker stems neither from his commercial acumen (his career contains sensational flops as well as box-office hits) nor from his supposed moral insight (his interviews reveal a conventionally conservative stance). What is crucial is the fact that the expression of his fundamental concerns uncovers key aspects of the film experience. The way in which we come to adopt the viewpoint of a voyeur in *Rear Window*, identify with a murderer in *Psycho* or share the hero's confusions about his dream woman in *Vertigo* can, if analysed, allow us valuable new understanding of the audience attitudes and emotions involved in film viewing. Thus it is unsurprising that Hitchcock's work, despite his own concern to present it in purely external, mechanistic terms, has in recent years provoked some of the most intense and radical theoretical questioning of the psychology of the film process.   RPA

R. Wood, *Hitchcock's Films* (London, 1965); F. Truffaut, *Hitchcock*, tr. H. G. Scott (London, 1968).

Hitler, Adolf (b. Braunau am Inn, Upper Austria, Austria-Hungary [now Austria], 2.4.1889; d. Berlin, Germany, 30.4.1945). Dictator of Germany. Hitler's political career began after the German defeat in 1918 when he created the National Socialist Workers party. Using a combination of political agitation and mass propaganda directed against 'the system' of the Weimar republic, he exploited the fears and resentments of millions left without work or hope by the depression to win six million votes in the German elections of 1930. Taken into office by a right-wing coalition (30.1.1933), he rapidly disposed of his partners and liquidated all opposition to become in 1934 dictator (*Führer*) of Germany. With enthusiastic support from a majority of the German people he restored the country to a dominant position in

Europe, repudiating the Versailles Treaty, annexing Austria (1938) and occupying Czechoslovakia (1939).

His demands on Poland led to war, and in the first two years (1939–41) the German armed forces under his leadership won an unequalled succession of victories which brought a greater area of Europe under his rule than had been achieved by Napoleon or any other conqueror. Only after he had gratuitously added the USSR and the USA to the British as his opponents was Germany finally beaten; but not until the heart of Germany itself had become a battlefield and the war had lasted nearly six years, claiming more than 25 million lives in Europe alone, was Hitler prepared to acknowledge defeat. He committed suicide, reproaching the German people for failing to live up to his genius.

Hitler's ideas were banal. They are to be found in *Mein Kampf* (2 vols, Munich, 1925–6; London, 1939, tr. R. Manheim, *My Struggle*, Boston, Mass., 1969). 'The struggle for existence', 'survival of the fittest' and 'might is right' were used to provide a pseudobiological justification for the racial supremacy of the 'Aryans' and specifically of the German people as a 'master race' (*Herrenvolk*) with a natural right to living space (*Lebensraum*) at the expense of such inferior races as the Slavs. His originality lay, first, in the literal-mindedness with which he was prepared to put these ideas into effect and, second, in an unrivalled grasp of the means by which this could be done.

The most ruthless example of the first was his campaign to 'eliminate' the Jews from German life, which led to the deliberate extermination of some six million Jewish people. Examples of the second are the use which he made of propaganda (the bigger the lie, the more likely it is to be believed), the manipulation of public opinion, and organized political violence and terrorism. Tactics similar to those which he used to build up his power in Germany were later applied with equal effect in dealing with other nations. Hitler left an indelible mark on the style and institutions of 20c mass politics, including the single-party authoritarian state based on the principle of intolerance.   ALCB

A. Bullock, *Hitler: a Study in Tyranny* (London, ²1964); W. Carr, *Hitler: a Study in Personality and Politics* (London, 1978).

Hjelmslev, Louis Trolle (b. Copenhagen, Denmark, 3.10.1899; d. Copenhagen, 30.5.1965). Danish linguist, the most prominent member of the so-called 'Copenhagen school'. His interest in language began early: as a schoolboy, he won a prize for an essay on compound words in Danish, and as an undergraduate he won the University of Copenhagen's gold medal for a paper on Oscan inscriptions. He was strongly influenced by several years of study abroad, particularly in Paris (1926–7); though he spent most of his life in Copenhagen where from 1937 he was professor of comparative linguistics. He began to develop the linguistic theory and system of analysis known as glossematics in collaboration with Hans Jørgen Uldall. War disrupted this partnership, and Hjelmslev alone produced an exposition of the theoretical principles of glossematics under the title *Omkring Sprogteoriens Grundlaeggelse* (Copenhagen, 1943; tr. F. J. Whitfield, *Prolegomena to a Theory of Language*, Baltimore, 1953, ²1961). There are similarities between his ideas and those of SAUSSURE, though Hjelmslev claimed that he arrived at his theoretical approach independently. He advocated a totally self-contained linguistics, in which formal patterns were all important. They should be described without reference to either semantics (meaning) or phonetics (sounds), the crucial factor being the relationship between the units. In his own words, linguistics should treat language as a 'self-sufficient totality, a structure *sui generis*', and should study 'the relational patterns of language without knowing what the relata are'. It follows that 'linguistic theory cannot be verified ... it can be controlled only by tests to show whether the calculation is self-consistent and exhaustive.'   JMA

Hlinka, Andrej (b. Stará Černová, Slovakia, Austria-Hungary [now Ružomberok, Czechoslovakia], 27.9.1864; d. Ružomberok, 16.8.1938). Slovak nationalist leader and Catholic priest, he created the Slovak People's party (*l'udovó strano*) in 1905 on a campaign for Slovak autonomy within Hapsburg Hungary, transforming it into the *Slovenskà l'udovo strano* in 1918 on the Czech failure to honour what he took to be their wartime pledge of Slovak autonomy in the establishment of the Czechoslovak state; it remained the largest Slovak party in the Czechoslovak state. The party developed definite nationalist, separatist and fascist tendencies, with a uniformed paramilitary organization the Hlinka Guard, especially after his death, on the eve of the coming into brief existence, under HITLER's patronage (1939–44), of the independent state of Slovakia.   DCW

Hobhouse, Leonard Trelawney (b. St Ives, Cornwall, UK, 8.9.1864; d. Alençon, Orne, France, 21.6.1929). British social philosopher. He taught at Oxford until 1897 when he became a leader writer for the *Manchester Guardian*. In 1907 he was appointed as the first professor of sociology at the University of London, a post which he held until his death. Hobhouse made a major contribution both to the discipline of sociology and to liberal political theory, developing a synthesis between the empirical, scientific approach to society which characterized evolutionary theory and the neo-Hegelian view of reality as essentially spiritual. He viewed society as evolving towards harmony and coordination for common ends, not as a result of an inevitable, biological process but of conscious, rational, human direction (*Mind in Evolution*, London, 1901); a fact which he believed capable of empirical demonstration. Rejecting evolution as a struggle for existence in which social reform is self-defeating, he insisted on a positive role for the state in promoting harmony through rational control of the environment (*Social Evolution and Political Theory*, NY, 1911). In bringing together a deep moral commitment to social reform and a scientific understanding of society, Hobhouse made a lasting contribution to a liberal political theory which saw no necessary antithesis between the freedom of the individual and the actions of the state (*Liberalism*, London, 1911).
                                                            RAP

J. A. Hobson & M. Ginsberg, *L. T. Hobhouse: his Life and Work* (London, 1931); S. Collini, *Liberalism and Sociology: L. T. Hobhouse and Political Argument in England 1880–1914* (Cambridge, 1979).

Hobson, John Atkinson (b. Derby, UK, 6.7.1858; d. London, 1.4.1940). British economist. Hobson was a leading new liberal, and an unorthodox economist. After his first book *The Physiology of Industry* (London, 1889), which was fiercely critical of the doctrines of orthodox economics, he was never offered any kind of academic post. He was strongly influenced by Mill and Cobden in his political and theoretical outlook, but he developed an approach to economics which also shared much with VEBLEN and the American institutionalists. His two most important contributions to economic thought were his theories of underconsumption and imperialism. The former, developed in a number of books including *The Evolution of Modern Capitalism* (London, 1894), stated that the uneven distribution of income in capitalist societies created excessive saving, which in turn created excessive investment in productive capacity causing prolonged slumps and unemployment. In his most famous book *Imperialism* (London, 1902), he explained the drive to imperial expansion as a result of the need for capitalists to find outlets for their savings. A policy of redistributing income could therefore be expected to promote both domestic prosperity and international harmony. Both KEYNES and LENIN acknowledged their debts to Hobson and his theories proved highly influential in the British Labour party, helping to make that party receptive to Keynesianism.   AG

P. Clarke, *Liberals and Social Democrats* (Cambridge, 1978).

Ho Chi Minh, *né* Nguyen That Thanh (b. Hoang Tru, French Indo-China [now Vietnam], 19.5.1890; d. Hanoi, North Vietnam, 3.9.1969). Creator of the Vietnamese national liberation movement, and one of the prime leaders of the revolutionary anticolonial movement in Asia after WW2. Nguyen was brought up in rural poverty but spent nearly 10 years in the West and Russia, beginning in London (1915–17) and in Paris (1917–23). He joined the French Communist party in 1920, and at the fifth Congress of the Comintern (Moscow, 1924) first stated his belief in the revolutionary role of the peasants in the struggle against colonialism. He returned to South East Asia as the representative of the Communist International and presided over the foundation of the Indochinese Communist party in 1930.

Ho Chi Minh's opportunity came in 1945 when the Japanese, who had overrun Indo-China and imprisoned and executed all French officials, were themselves driven to surrender to the Western Allies. A guerrilla force formed by his lieutenant Nguyen Giap entered Hanoi where Ho Chi Minh proclaimed Vietnamese independence (Viet Minh) on 2.9.1945. Confronted with the return of the French, Ho Chi Minh resorted to negotiation, but war broke out between them in November 1946. Seven years of fighting followed in which the Viet Minh army used guerrilla tactics to contain the French forces in the cities and then inflicted a decisive defeat on them at Dien Bien Phu in May 1954. Negotiations at Geneva (May–June 1954) left Vietnam divided along the 17th parallel. A separate South Vietnamese state was established with the support of the USA in place of France. War between the North and South was resumed in 1959, with an armed revolt by guerrillas (the Viet Cong) in the South, and led on to the long-drawn-out horror of the Vietnamese war in which the USA became more and more involved as a principal. In 1959 Ho Chi Minh gave up his position as the party's secretary-general and left the active conduct of the war to the collective leadership which he had established.

There was much argument in the West as to whether Ho Chi Minh was a nationalist or a communist. The answer is that he was both and, with TITO, one of the progenitors of the 'national communism' which emerged in the 1960s. He showed great skill in balancing between his two powerful allies, the Russians and the Chinese. His preference was for Moscow but he shared with MAO TSE-TUNG the recognition of the role of the peasantry in the revolutionary struggle. At the time of his death (1969), the Vietnam war had not yet ended in victory for the North and the unification of the whole country under the Hanoi government. But at the end of one of the longest wars of liberation the Vietnamese movement which Ho Chi Minh founded, and for a long time led, was able to claim a unique victory not only over the French but over the USA, the most powerful nation in the world. Ho Chi Minh's *Selected Works* have been published in English by the Vietnamese government (4 vols, Hanoi, 1960–2).   ALCB

J. Lacouture, *Ho Chi Minh* (London, 1968).

Hockney, David (b. Bradford, W. Yorks., UK, 9.7.1937). British painter and printmaker. After art training at Bradford, he studied at the Royal College of Art in London as a contemporary of KITAJ, Peter Philips, Derek Boshier and Allen Jones. His early work, like theirs, is associated with the British Pop art movement, and tends to be mainly autobiographical and illustrative in character, but with a strong element of fantasy and wit. The style is predominantly linear, even calligraphic, and sometimes incorporates written inscriptions or allusions to different kinds of style. About 1964 he began to paint more directly and to show increasing interest in rendering what the eye saw. His paintings have since tended to become more straightforward, with a regard for light, space and volume, and are usually executed either from drawings or from his own photographs (sometimes a combination of the two), including a number of portraits of his friends. He has worked much in California, which has provided the themes for many of his pictures. His paintings, drawings and prints have a strongly individual flavour and often provide an irreverent and amusing commentary on contemporary life (see *David Hockney by David Hockney*, London, 1976).   REA

Hodgkin, Alan Lloyd (b. Banbury, Oxon., UK, 5.2.1914). British biophysicist. An undergraduate at Trinity College, Cambridge, he eventually became a fellow (1936–78) and master in 1978. His academic studies were interrupted by WW2 when he became a scientific officer working on radar for the Air Ministry. After the war he lectured on biophysics at Cambridge and became Foulerton professor (1952–69) and then professor of biophysics (1970–81) in the department of physiology. In 1939, with A. F. HUXLEY, and simultaneously with Curtis and Cole in the USA, he was the first to implant electrodes into squids' giant nerve fibres, originally discovered by J. Z. YOUNG. An intense period of work between 1945 and 1947 provided a description of nerve membrane potential and the changes in potassium ion pulses associated with conduction of nerve impulses. By 1952 he was able to publish a detailed description of the origin of the action potential that has been the basis of the biophysics of the nerve system and which led to the award of the Nobel prize for medicine, with Huxley and ECCLES, in 1963.   CTJ

Hodgkin, Dorothy Crowfoot, *née* Dorothy Crowfoot (b. Cairo, Egypt, 12.5.1910). British crystallographer, her main achievements being the elucidation of the structure of penicillin, vitamin B_{12} and zinc insulin. She was awarded the Nobel prize for chemistry in 1964 and was only the second woman (the first was Florence Nightingale) on whom the Order of Merit was conferred (1965).

Dorothy Crowfoot graduated at Somerville College, Oxford, in 1932 and worked successively with H. M. Powell in Oxford and BERNAL in Cambridge, with whom she began to study biologically interesting molecules. She continued with this on her return to Oxford in 1934. The problems involved in elucidating such structures are enormously greater than those faced by earlier crystallographers (e.g. LAUE and the BRAGGS) working with simple substances like common salt, and only recently have these been overcome, partly by the use of heavy 'marker'

atoms and by the availability of computers of progressively greater power. Dorothy Hodgkin's genius lay in her ability to use her chemical intuition to devise strategies by which, in the days before sophisticated computers, the data analysis could be carried out by the most efficient route, which although long and tedious by present-day standards, still yielded the desired information. The structure of penicillin was arrived at before it had been deduced from chemical work; and that of B_{12}, containing more than 90 atoms, represented at the time a record in crystallographic analysis. Insulin is even more complicated, containing nearly 800 atoms other than those of the associated water molecules. Her work on insulin described in her Bakerian lecture to the Royal Society in 1972 began in the 1930s, and culminated in the establishment by her research group of the structure of zinc insulin in 1972.   DHE

van't Hoff, Jacobus Henricus (b. Rotterdam, S. Holland, The Netherlands, 30.8.1852; d. Berlin, Germany, 1.3.1911). Dutch chemist. Van't Hoff was educated in the Netherlands and in Paris, and spent the rest of his career at the University of Amsterdam. His first, and in many ways most original work was his resolution in 1874 of the problem of chemical isomerism (the existence of more than one distinct substance with the same molecular formula) by proposing that the four bonds around a tetravalent carbon atom were directed towards the corners of a tetrahedron. This idea, which occurred simultaneously to J. A. Le Bell, was ignored, then derided, but finally accepted as the cornerstone of the structural chemistry of aliphatic compounds. From 1884 onwards he devoted himself to physical chemistry, which he can almost be said to have created as a separate discipline. His numerous contributions here include the classification of chemical reactions by order, the thermodynamics of osmotic pressure and of the electromotive force of cells, the effect of temperature on chemical equilibria (the van't Hoff isochore), and an elucidation of the phase relations of double salts which proved to be the key to the exploitation of the salt deposits at Stassfurt in Germany. He was awarded the first Nobel prize for chemistry in 1901. JSR

Hoffmann, Roald (b. Zloczow, Poland, 18.7.1937; naturalized American citizen). Polish/American physical chemist. Professor of chemistry at Cornell University, Hoffmann shared the 1981 Nobel prize for chemistry with FUKUI for their theories concerning the course of chemical reactions. His first major contribution to theoretical chemistry was to extend the range of applicability of simplified quantum mechanical calculations to cover all organic molecules. Together with R. B. WOODWARD he introduced the Woodward–Hoffmann rules which explain why some reagents react easily while other pairs do not do so at all. The basis for the rules lies in the symmetry properties of the molecules concerned, and particularly in the disposition of their electrons. New chemical bonds are formed when the electrons involved form a complete circuit. The rules have great power and a wide range of applicability, to the extent that they are considered by many to be the major theoretical advance in organic chemistry since WW2. WGR

Hofmann, Hans (b. Weissenberg, Bavaria, Germany [now East Germany], 21.3.1880; naturalized American citizen, 1941; d. New York, USA, 17.2.1966). German/American painter whose teaching was an important influence on the development of abstract expressionism in America during the 1940s. He studied in Munich and from 1904 to 1914 lived in Paris where he met PICASSO, BRAQUE, DELAUNAY and MATISSE. In 1915 he founded his own art school in Munich. In 1932 he emigrated to New York where he taught at the Art Students' League and founded an art school in 1934. His teaching emphasized the 'push and pull' of colour and plane on the picture surface; his own practice combined expressionist brushwork, a fauvist sense of brilliant colour and synthetic cubist construction. He held his first one-man exhibition in New York in 1944. His abstract painting is the expression of a response to nature and, in contrast to the careers of most of his American students, enjoyed a magnificent flowering late in his life. MOJN

C. Greenberg, *Hans Hofmann* (London, 1961); The Museum of Modern Art, *Hans Hofmann* (NY, 1963).

Hofmannsthal, Hugo von (b. Vienna, Austria-Hungary [now Austria], 1.2.1874; d. Rodaun, Vienna, 15.7.1929). Austrian dramatist, librettist, novelist, poet and essayist. Hofmannsthal achieved fame at the age of 16 with *fin-de-siècle* poems and playlets, which drew the attention of Stefan GEORGE. From 1906 he wrote libretti for Richard STRAUSS, including *Der Rosenkavalier* (1911) and *Ariadne auf Naxos* (1912). For a time it seemed, from his 'Chandos-letter' (*Ein Brief*, 1902; tr. M. Hottinger & T. and H. Stern, in *Hugo von Hofmannsthal: Selected Prose*, London, 1952), that he was in a situation seen by some as typical of the times, in which words had lost their meaning for him. This was, however, a passing phase. His ambition to write popular works with an appeal also to intellectuals resulted in *Jedermann* (1911; a translation and adaptation of *Everyman*) written for the Salzburg Festival and often performed there. During WW1 he saw Austria-Hungary as a bulwark of European civilization against the East, and wrote of the country's cultural mission. This world vanished in 1919, but defeat induced him to write his masterpiece, the typically Austrian, witty, profound drawing-room comedy *Der Schwierige* (Vienna, 1921; tr. M. Hamburger, *The Difficult Man*, in *Selected Plays*, London, 1963). An unwieldy attempt at defining Austria's role in European history resulted in the complex allegorical play *Der Turm* (Vienna, 1925; tr. M. Hamburger, *The Tower*, in *Selected Plays*, London, 1963). Hofmannsthal was a Catholic of rightwing views in politics, with a great love of tradition, and devotion to the nuances of art. He was greatly admired by ELIOT, whose plays show some of his influence. RDG

H. Hammelmann, *Hugo von Hofmannsthal* (New Haven, 1957).

Hofshteyn, David (b. Korostsh, Russia, 24.6.1889; d. Moscow, USSR, 12.8.1952). Yiddish poet. A student of agriculture and natural sciences at Kiev University, he published five volumes of poetry between 1920 and 1922. He left the USSR in 1923, with a few other Soviet Yiddish writers, and travelled through Europe. For a time he stayed in Palestine, then under the British mandate, writing poetry in Hebrew and contributing to the local Hebrew press. In 1926 he returned to Russia, having established himself as one of the foremost Yiddish poets, the first volume of his collected works appearing in 1923. His poetry is highly personal, yet at the same time imbued with national elements. Frequently he employs biblical quotations as mottoes. Hofshteyn also translated poetry from the European classics (Russian, French and English) into Yiddish. He took an active part in the work of the Jewish Anti-Fascist Committee during WW2 and was arrested, with other Yiddish writers, in 1948 to be executed, on trumped-up charges, four years later. After STALIN's death, with others, he was 'rehabilitated', and his poetry has been translated into Russian and Ukrainian.   JSo

Hofstadter, Richard (b. Buffalo, NY, USA, 6.8.1916; d. New York, 24.10.1970). American historian. The first major American historian to write almost entirely from the viewpoint of the city. He migrated from Buffalo to New York City where he spent nearly all the rest of his life. He was a highly conscious intellectual among professionals; he revelled in ideas and the play of mind on mind, and enjoyed bringing his own attention to bear on the history of collective states of mind, their sources and their consequences. These interests made him in one sense a historian of ideas, and his first book *Social Darwinism in American Thought* (NY, 1944) traced the influence of the idea of the evolutionary struggle for survival as a paradigm for economic development. In *The American Political Tradition and the Men who Made It* (NY, 1948) he inadvertently initiated the 'consensus' theory of American history, which soon assumed far wider proportions and far

greater influence than any he had intended. His own contribution was the suggestion that the 'common climate of American opinion' deserved more attention that it had received; this was an early indication of his long struggle to throw off the profound influence of Charles BEARD and the progressives, with their emphasis on conflict. Hofstadter's extraordinary influence on his contemporaries did not depend on substantive contributions based on sources: he regarded himself more as a 'historical critic', with an acute sense of the immediacy of historical problems that interested him, which nearly always had some source in current political life. But he was also one of the first American historians to adopt the concepts (he was less interested in methodology) of the social sciences into the formulation of historical analysis. In a seminar at Columbia in 1954 he and the political scientist Seymour Martin Lipset developed the concept of status as a social force, and Hofstadter used this insight to reinterpret much of the meaning of the successive reform movements of modern America. *The Age of Reform* (NY, 1955) introduced the idea of status displacement as a motivating force in reform politics. At the same time, obviously reacting to the popular clamour aroused by MCCARTHY, Hofstadter introduced a sceptical view of the populists, in whom he detected indications of xenophobia, anti-Semitism and reaction. The influence of McCarthyism and the attack on academic freedom led to reflections on the standing of intellectuals in a populistic democracy in *Anti-Intellectualism in American Life* (NY, 1963). Hofstadter's interest in ideas and their provenance led him to reflect on his own intellectual antecedents, and resulted in *The Progressive Historians* (NY, 1968), a study of the historical thought and influence of Turner, Beard and Parrington. About the same time, he took the opportunity of the Jefferson Memorial Lectures at Berkeley to examine the idea of legitimate opposition in a democracy – an issue presented by the many forms of 'illegitimate' opposition in the 1960s. *The Idea of a Party System: the Rise of Legitimate Opposition in the United States, 1780–*

1840 (Berkeley, 1969) explained the transition from the older view that opposition to government was potentially seditious, and the significance of this change for the survival of democracy.   JRP

A. M. Schlesinger, Jr, 'Richard Hofstadter', in M. Cunliffe & R. Winka (eds), *Pastmasters: Some Essays on American Historians* (NY, 1969); S. Elkins & E. McKitrick (eds), *The Hofstadter Aegis: a Memorial* (NY, 1974).

Hohfeld, Wesley Newcomb (b. Oakland, Calif., USA, 8.8.1879; d. Alameda, Calif., 21.10.1918). American legal theorist. After Harvard Law School, he began teaching at Stanford University in 1904. In 1913 he published a seminal article in the *Yale Law Journal*, 'Fundamental legal conceptions as applied in judicial reasoning', and Yale offered him a professorship. He remained there until his early death, not a popular teacher but a lasting influence on an elite minority of his students. Throughout his writings Hohfeld criticized the imprecise judicial usage of elementary legal terms, and he formulated a new typology to express and analyse jural relationships (*Fundamental Legal Conceptions as Applied to Judicial Reasoning*, ed. W. W. Cook, Yale, 1919, ²1964). Arranging them as 'jural opposites' and 'jural correlatives', he paired eight legal conceptions to clarify their meanings (e.g. privilege/duty, privilege/no-right, immunity/liability). By this arrangement he meant that each pair of terms (e.g. 'right' and 'duty') are merely two ends of the same relationship: if A owes B money, B has a 'right' to claim from A, A has a 'duty' to pay. The typology was applied by Hohfeld and successive theorists to illuminate complex legal relations. The terminology has been criticized, but the typology has been influential both in jurisprudence and practical law-making.
                                    NJJ

Holmes, Arthur (b. Hebburn-on-Tyne, Tyne & Wear, UK, 14.1.1890; d. London, 20.9.1965). The outstanding British geologist of this century, Holmes entered Imperial College to read physics but the teaching of W. W. Watts and an expedition to Mozambique turned his interest to geology. After WW1 he joined an oil company in Burma, but returned to England when the company collapsed. He took a post teaching geology at Durham University, from which he moved to the Regius chair of geology at Edinburgh.

Fascinated since student days by the phenomenon of radioactivity and the presence of radioactive elements in rocks, Holmes was quick to recognize the fundamental flaw in Kelvin's determination of the age of the earth, based on a simple cooling model, and was the first to establish an absolute geological time-scale based on radioactive decay of uranium in igneous rocks and estimates of rates of sedimentation for the various geological periods. Much of this early work is summarized in his classic *The Age of the Earth* (London, 1927). Holmes's time-scale for the Phanerozoic has required little amendment over the years, although methods have become more sophisticated and the volume of research has increased greatly. Holmes also made contributions to igneous petrology, especially the genesis of East African lavas, and did much to unravel the complex history of Precambrian terrains in Africa. He was from the outset a champion of WEGENER's revolutionary idea of continental drift, at a time when to hold such a view was decidedly heterodox. His idea of convection currents in the earth's mantle as a driving-force for continental drift, put forward in 1929, anticipated the seafloor-spreading hypothesis of HESS, presented over three decades later on the basis of vastly increased oceanographic data. Holmes is best known to generations of geologists for an outstanding introductory textbook, *Principles of Physical Geology* (London, 1944).   AH

Holmes, Oliver Wendell (b. Boston, Mass., USA, 8.3.1841; d. Washington, DC, 6.3.1935). American jurist. Through his judicial decisions (as chief justice, Massachusetts Supreme Court, 1899–1902, and associate justice, United States Supreme Court, 1902–32) and his academic writings (*The Common Law*, Boston, Mass., 1881, and *Collected Legal Papers*, NY, 1920), Holmes is acknowledged as a major influence within American jurisprudence. He was a dominant source of inspiration for those writers usually referred to as 'legal realists', among them LLEWELLYN, John Dewey and Jerome Frank. Holmes's insistence on a practical, as opposed to an abstract approach to law and legal analyses, encapsulated in his declaration that 'the life of the law has not been logic; it has been experience', laid the basis for the realists' later concentration upon the pragmatic and empirical aspects of law and legal procedures. His major theoretical contribution to jurisprudential debate is perhaps his formulation, in a lecture in 1897, of the 'prediction' theory of law: 'The prophecies of what the courts will do in fact, and nothing more pretentious, are what I mean by the law.' The appropriateness of this line of thought remains a matter for debate, but Holmes continues to symbolize a break, especially for US legal thinkers, away from the abstract positivistic analysis of earlier writers (notably John Austin) and towards the development of an understanding of law within its social and economic contexts. A selection from Holmes's writings was edited by Max Lerner: *The Mind and Faith of Justice Holmes* (NY, 1943).

M. D. Howe, *Justice Oliver Wendell Holmes* (2 vols, Cambridge, Mass., 1957–63).

PJH

Holtfreter, Johannes Friedrich Karl (b. Richtenberg, Germany [now East Germany], 9.1.1901; naturalized American citizen). German/American developmental biologist. Modern developmental biology texts still attribute to Holtfreter's work in the 1940s almost all that is known about amphibian gastrulation, the latter being the major developmental event which establishes the body's basic form, the former the animals in which it is most studied. In fact the event had been long observed, for example by WADDINGTON, but it was Holtfreter who took it apart and used dissection, dissociation and recombination of cells and tissue to show how parts of embryos interact. Along with WEISS, he emphasized the cell surface, particularly a hypothesized 'surface coat', as the locale where morphogenesis is organized, a supposition borne out by recent

research. He formulated the hypothesis of chemotaxis (response to gradients of chemical concentration) as the guiding mechanism of cell migration. Together with the role of surface molecules and the mechanical interactions of cells, this is still central in developmental research. Holtfreter has worked at the University of Rochester, New York, since 1947, as emeritus professor of zoology since 1969.

DOM

Hook, Sidney (b. New York, USA, 20.12.1902). American philosopher. Hook is known, intellectually, as the foremost expositor of the ideas of J. DEWEY and MARX, and politically for his leadership of a section of American intellectuals in combating communist and totalitarian influences in intellectual life. As a philosopher, Hook has been concerned primarily with the ways in which values enter into political discourse, rather than with linguistic analysis or the clarification of meanings. As a student of Dewey, Hook has espoused a naturalistic pragmatism in which ideas are seen not as propositions but as guides to action, and knowledge is dependent on experiment and 'reconstructive activity'. It was this standpoint that also led Hook in one of his earliest works to argue that Marx, as against the later revisions by Engels, had an activity theory of knowledge in which the idea of praxis was central. For Hook, philosophy is an empirical discipline, its methods of inquiry contiguous with those of natural and social science. For this reason, Hook has consistently attacked metaphysical absolutes and, in particular, the idea of 'Being' as used by HEIDEGGER in 20c philosophy. Although a consistent opponent of Soviet Marxism, Hook has been a social democrat from 1940 to the present. His major works are *Toward the Understanding of Karl Marx* (NY, 1933); *From Hegel to Marx* (NY, 1936); *John Dewey: an Intellectual Portrait* (NY, 1936); *The Quest for Being* (NY, 1961).

DBe

Hopkins, Frederick Gowland (b. Eastbourne, E. Sussex, UK, 20.6.1861; d. Cambridge, 16.5.1947). British biochemist. Though generally recognized as the father of biochemistry in Britain, Hopkins appears to have entered the field by chance. He first trained as an analytical chemist while studying in the evenings for an external London University BSc. He then read for a medical degree at Guy's Hospital, London, and, when he qualified in 1894 at the age of 33, was appointed to the staff. Four years later he was invited to go to Cambridge as lecturer in chemical physiology. He remained there for the rest of his life, becoming professor of biochemistry in 1914. In spite of initial difficulties, he built up a strong department, which established Cambridge as one of the world's prime centres for biochemical research.

His own researches ranged over a variety of topics from the chemistry of butterfly wing pigments to the mechanisms of cell respiration. Though he considered the latter as his most important concern, others regarded his work on nutrition as the more significant. He discovered the amino acid tryptophan and showed that it is an essential nutrient for animals, thereby establishing for the first time that, in relation to diet, quality must be considered as well as quantity. This important principle was further emphasized by his demonstration that, in addition to carbohydrates, fats, proteins and minerals, animals needed certain accessory food factors, later called vitamins. For this, with C. Eijkman, he was awarded the Nobel prize for medicine. Quantitatively his research output was not particularly impressive and much of his reputation, and certainly the Nobel award, depended on one paper. His greatness lay in the knack he had for singling out crucial areas of study, for example vitamins, and, by a pioneering investigation, highlighting their significance and thereby stimulating further research – by others. He had great faith, which he frequently and effectively aired, that proper application of chemical expertise to biological problems would sweep away the obscurantist ideas that hindered progress and greatly increase understanding of life processes.   GL

J. Needham & E. Baldwin (eds), *Hopkins and Biochemistry* (Cambridge, 1949).

Hopkins, Gerard Manley (b. Stratford, Essex, UK, 28.7.1844; d. Dublin, Ireland, UK [now Irish Republic], 8.6.1889). British poet. Hopkins's poems were not published until 1918, nearly 30 years after his death; and it was another 10 years before they became at all well known. By the 1930s, however, Hopkins was much admired; his technical devices, his unusual diction, his striking juxtapositions of imagery, his colloquial vigour and compressed syntax, all made him seem like a modern poet. More recently there has been a reaction against this judgement, and critics have stressed that in all essentials Hopkins was a Victorian poet, having far more in common with his contemporaries than with the innovators of the 20c. Hopkins is a disconcertingly individual poet, or, as he once said of himself, an 'oddity', who will not fit into convenient literary categories. As a young man at Oxford he was known as a brilliant classicist; he was a devout High Anglican and wrote accomplished but conventional religious poetry. After a spiritual crisis he was converted to Catholicism, and a year or so later entered the Society of Jesus in order to train for the priesthood. At about this time he made an ascetic decision to abandon poetry. In 1875, after several years of Jesuit training, he returned to writing poetry; when his spiritual superior expressed the wish that someone would commemorate in poetry the harrowing shipwreck of the German steamer *Deutschland*, carrying refugees from the anticlerical Falck laws, Hopkins wrote 'The Wreck of the *Deutschland*', his longest and most complex poem. Hopkins was moved by newspaper accounts of the wreck, and by the fate of five Franciscan nuns on board the ship. But in the poem Hopkins also reflects on his own spiritual development and expresses his hopes for the conversion of England. Formally, the poem is startlingly original, an expression of theories about the nature of poetry that Hopkins had been developing during his years of noncomposition. It is influenced by the loose form of the Greek Pindaric ode, by Welsh poetry, and by his desire for a broader vocabulary and less restricted metrical base than the convention of the time permitted.

Though a man of marked individualism and even eccentricity, Hopkins happily embraced the disciplined communal life of the Jesuit order. After 'The Wreck of the *Deutschland*' he went on writing poetry, though never prolifically. Most of his subsequent poems were in the exact, demanding form of the sonnet. In the last years of his short life, Hopkins produced the 'terrible sonnets' which enact a disturbing process of spiritual desolation. These are Hopkins's greatest achievement: an intense, dramatic, dialectical religious poetry, in the tradition of Herbert, whom he admired and loved, and Donne, whom he seems never to have read.   BB

W. H. Gardner, *Gerard Manley Hopkins* (2 vols, London, 1944–9); B. Bergonzi, *Gerard Manley Hopkins* (London, 1977).

Hopkinson, Henry Thomas (Tom) (b. Manchester, UK, 19.4.1905). British journalist. Emerging from Oxford in 1927, he 'barely survived' as a freelance journalist and later as an advertising copywriter, until 1934 when he was appointed assistant editor of *Weekly Illustrated*. For the next four years he experimented, outside working hours, with discarded news pictures, isolating those which were news in themselves from the majority which were simply illustrative of people and places in the news – and developing the idea of a popular weekly picture magazine which would have social as well as political impact. At this point in his life he met Stefan Lorant, 'a visualizer of genius' from Vienna, and an experimental film cameraman fleeing from the Nazis, who had come to London in the hope of starting a picture magazine. 'I discovered that he wanted to do what I wanted to do,' Hopkinson said, 'namely, to show Britain's real face to the people.' *Picture Post* was launched in partnership in 1938. When Lorant moved to other employment shortly afterwards, Hopkinson became the sole editor during the magazine's greatest years (1940–50). His candid 'action' picture stories of WW2 and its aftermath, captured by some of Britain's best photographers,

remained in the minds of many long after the magazine itself had ceased publication. When he was sacked in 1950 because of a difference of opinion with the paper's owner, Sir Edward Hulton, Hopkinson launched himself on a second career as a pioneer in journalism education, first in Africa and latterly in the UK. His autobiography *Of This Our Time* was published in 1982 (London).
                                        RB

Hopper, Edward (b. Nyack, NY, USA, 22.7.1882; d. New York, 15.5.1967). American painter and illustrator. Hopper was one of this century's leading 'realist' painters. His early teachers included Robert Henri, an American portraitist and painter of 'modern life'. But between 1906 and 1910 he made several trips to Europe where he encountered impressionism. On his return to the USA, he made his living as a commercial artist and illustrator. He complained that he disliked drawing people 'grimacing and posturing' and longed only to 'paint sunlight on the side of a house', but this painting style did not mature until the 1920s. Although he remained profoundly suspicious of modernism, he forged a way of working which enabled him vividly to express his preoccupation with loneliness and human isolation. His finest pictures include images of empty streets, figures in automats, a cinema usherette, nudes glimpsed through open windows, or men and women in offices. Perhaps the greatest was *Nighthawks* (1942), which depicts four figures seen through the window of an all-night café. Hopper differed from other painters of the 'American scene' both in the quality of light in his best pictures, and in his insistence on imaginative, painterly reconstruction of an image: he never tried to transcribe a slice of the real, but rather to reinvent it through pictorial means. Although Hopper always had his supporters, and eventually proved able to command high prices, his critical reputation undoubtedly suffered from the dominance of abstract art and the succession of modernist styles. Today, however, he is increasingly acknowledged as among the finest of this century's American artists.
                                        PF

L. Goodrich, *Edward Hopper* (NY, 1971); G. Levin, *Edward Hopper: the Art and the Artist* (NY, 1980).

Horkheimer, Max (b. Stuttgart, Baden-Württemberg, Germany, 14.2.1895; d. Nuremberg, Bavaria, West Germany, 7.7.1973). German social theorist. When the Institut für Sozialforschung was founded at Frankfurt in 1923, Horkheimer was one of the central figures in the first generation of the Frankfurt school and became the institute's director in 1930. When the Nazis came to power the school moved to the USA and Horkheimer moved with it. He returned to Frankfurt in 1950 and took up a professorship at the university.

In a series of influential articles published in the 1930s in the school's journal, *Zeitschrift für Sozialforschung*, collected as *Kritische Theorie* (2 vols, ed. A. Schmidt, Frankfurt, 1968; tr. M. J. O'Connell *et al.*, *Critical Theory: Selected Essays*, NY, 1972), Horkheimer set forth the basic principles applied by the Frankfurt school in their critique of epistemology and industrial civilization, and elucidated their use of the key term 'critical theory'. Horkheimer's basic assumption is that modern civilization is radically diseased, and that only a profound transformation in theory and practice, not piecemeal reform, can cure it. Critical independence of all final doctrines, which are partial and one-sided as such, is called for. This includes MARXism. Horkheimer argues that the idea of an inevitable proletarian revolution which will eradicate alienation and exploitation is mistaken; Marx places too much emphasis on the material forces of history and too little on the role of conscious human thought; and his conception of emancipation is too narrowly economic – hence the interest of the Frankfurt school in psychoanalysis and other forms of emancipation. The theory and analysis of existing society, and indeed science in general, is neither wholly independent of social and economic processes – 'free-floating' as Karl MANNHEIM would have it – nor so inextricably embedded in them as to be their mere by-product, as vulgar Marxism proclaims. Theory is in part a function of social life, but it also enjoys a degree of autonomy: the objects of a theory as well as the concepts involved in the theory itself are largely an uncritically accepted product of a social process of production, and it is the task of 'critical theory' to trace the social genesis of knowledge with a view to human emancipation. Horkheimer thus opposes all forms of empiricism and positivism, claiming that these simply take social phenomena as they find them, thereby endorsing their existence and serving as instruments for their perpetuation. Civilization is threatened by the uncontrolled growth of a technology that derives from empirical sciences that have nothing to say about human values. Horkheimer advocates instead an open-ended conception of reason which he believes is capable of discovering truths which are neither empirical nor analytical, and hence of establishing not only effective means but also true ends. Other major works by Horkheimer are (with ADORNO) *Dialektik der Aufklärung* (Amsterdam, 1947; tr. J. Cumming, *Dialectic of Enlightenment*, NY, 1972) and *Eclipse of Reason* (NY, 1947). The writings of Horkheimer and of the Frankfurt school in general have had an enormous influence – in ways not always intended by its members – on the worldwide movement of student revolt in the past two decades.   RNH

M. Jay, *The Dialectical Imagination* (London, 1973); P. Slater, *Origin and Significance of the Frankfurt School* (London, 1977).

Hörstadius, Sven Otto (b. Stockholm, Sweden, 18.2.1898). Swedish developmental biologist. Educated at the University of Stockholm, he held posts in the department of zoology there until 1942, when he went as professor of zoology to Uppsala University. Hörstadius subjected the ideas of developmental mechanics established by DRIESCH and others to elegant experimental test. He particularly explored the extent to which development is controlled independently of immediate gene action, especially by cytoplasm of eggs and embryos. He found, for example, that cells from opposite ends of the original egg grew into two half-embryos when separated, and did not regulate to form whole embryos despite containing whole copies of the genome. This suggested different cytoplasmic 'determinants' of development across the egg. To test CHILD's hypothesis that this difference is set up by a gradient of some substance, Hörstadius separated cells of sea urchin embryos and recombined those from the far 'animal' and 'vegetal' ends. These fragments, which should re-establish the proposed gradient, did indeed regulate to form whole embryos, important evidence for a developmental hypothesis that is still central. Hörstadius also explored the chemical nature of gradients. His demonstration that gene expression is controlled by the position of a cell within an organism firmly established Driesch's concept of positional information, which has dominated much modern research through the work of WOLPERT and others. Hörstadius chaired the European Council for Bird Preservation from 1960 to 1972; he is an accomplished bird photographer and ornithologist.   DOM

Hoskins, William George (b. Exeter, Devon, UK, 22.5.1908). British historian. A scholar devoted to the historical study of the English landscape and to adult and popular education, Hoskins, more than any other single man, was responsible for establishing local history as a reputable discipline in Britain (he headed the first local history department at Leicester University in 1948) and for the explosion of interest in local history which took place in the 1960s and 1970s. Latterly he added a major television series on 'The Landscapes of England' (1976–8) to the important specialized scholarship and popularization already published, including *Industry, Trade and People in Exeter* (London, 1935), *The Making of the English Landscape* (London, 1955), *The Midland Peasant* (London, 1957), and *Fieldwork in Local History* (London, 1967).   AM

Hotelling, Harold (b. Fulda, Minn., USA, 29.9.1895; d. Chapel Hill, NC, 26.12.1973). American statistician, from 1946 until retirement at the University of North Carolina. In statistics, if the number of variables considered is doubled, the yield of information is less than doubled and the complication of the analysis potentially quadruped; e.g. a bomber may make errors of deflection and of range, which are of different import and correlation, and many tests may be used to select its crew, not all of which add much new information. Hotelling developed (from 1931) economical procedures using many variables simultaneously to measure, assess, and predict performance (his T-test, and 'canonical' correlations and variables), thus initiating much of modern multivariate analysis.   AGPW

Hounsfield, Godfrey Newbold (b. Newark, Notts., UK, 28.8.1919). British inventor. A research scientist at EMI, Hounsfield developed the first computerized axial scanner (CAT scanner). This X-ray apparatus produces far clearer pictures of the brain and of the internal organs than conventional X-ray films. As Hounsfield's scanner rotates around the head, a beam of X-rays passes through from each of hundreds of points around the circle. The X-rays are received by a detector which calculates the proportion of X-rays absorbed by the bone, muscle and other tissue in their path. This information is then used by the computer built into the machine to create a cross-sectional picture of the head. The same process can be repeated at intervals of a fraction of an inch to produce a whole series of cross sections. Modern scanners can be used to examine any part of the body, and with increasing computer sophistication the data can be used to produce sectional pictures of the body in any plane. By comparison with conventional techniques, CAT scanners require a very low dosage of X-rays and without any of the discomfort unavoidable with techniques, such as angiography, which require injection of dyes into the bloodstream.   AJS

Housman, Alfred Edward (b. Fockbury, Here. & Worcs., UK, 26.3.1859; d. Cambridge, 30.4.1936). British poet and classical scholar. A scholar at St John's College, Oxford, Housman failed his finals and worked for a while as a clerk in the Patent Office. Nevertheless in

1892 he became professor of Latin at University College London, and then in 1911 professor at Cambridge, a post he held until his death. He is best known for his poetry; much of his celebrated *A Shropshire Lad* (London, 1896) was written very quickly in the autumn of 1895; *Last Poems* (London), the only subsequent volume to appear in his lifetime, was not published until 1922. His poems are short, often bitter lyrics which combine metrical regularity with an undefined and passionate melancholy – it is this combination of the precise and the indefinite which gives them their distinctive tone. His prose and academic work includes articles notable for their rigorous scholarship and the sarcastic scorn with which their author castigates others' errors, and an edition of the *Astronomica* of Manilius (5 vols, London, 1903–30). Poet and scholar were one in their relish for precision and *le mot juste*.   DD

R. P. Graves, *A. E. Housman: the Scholar-Poet* (London, 1979).

Howard, Ebenezer (b. London, UK, 29.1.1850; d. Welwyn Garden City, Herts., 1.5.1928). British town planner and social reformer. Howard was the initiator of an influential body of ideas and practice in urban planning, now generally called the Garden City movement. A stenographer by occupation, he lived in the USA for some years, and Emerson, Whitman, Bellamy and the economist Alfred MARSHALL were formative influences. Howard's influence stems from one book *To-morrow: a Peaceful Path to Real Reform* (London, 1898), republished later under a new title *Garden Cities of To-morrow* (London, 1902). In this he criticized the social, economic and environmental ills associated with the uncontrolled growth of large cities and the decline of rural populations. He made detailed proposals for the founding and management of 'garden cities' where land uses were controlled in the public interest, each house stood 'in its own ample grounds', all urban land was in public ownership, population size was limited to about 30,000, and the city was surrounded by a belt of agricultural land. The book had immediate impact. The Garden City

Association was founded in 1899, and by 1902 a company had been formed to build the first garden city at Letchworth in Hertfordshire. The second, Welwyn Garden City, was begun in 1920. The Garden City movement quickly attracted interest from abroad, especially from the USA. In the UK the concept won official acceptance, and the postwar towns built under the New Towns Act (1946) were based essentially on garden city ideas. The garden city has been used as the basis for countless urban developments throughout the world, but many of its ideas (e.g. segregation of land uses, limitation of town size, green belts) have been questioned in recent decades.   BM

W. Creese, *The Search for Environment: the Garden City Before and After* (New Haven, 1966).

Hoyle, Fred (b. Bingley, W. Yorks., UK, 24.6.1915). British astrophysicist. Hoyle has been arguably the best-known astronomer of his day, celebrated for his research into the stellar origin of chemical elements, his advocacy of the steady-state model of the universe, and as a popular broadcaster and writer. Educated at Cambridge, he was appointed Plumian professor of astronomy in 1956, and became the founder director of the Institute of Theoretical Astronomy at Cambridge in 1967. Everything Hoyle worked on gave rise to advances in the subject, often his co-workers and students, and his wrong ideas have been as brilliant and fruitful as his right ones. In the 1940s he studied the relationship between the mass and luminosity in stars that gave rise to his interest in stellar chemical composition and in stellar evolution. This latter interest bore fruit in 1955 when he worked with Martin Schwarzschild in determining the evolution of stars a little more massive than the sun. His work on the generation of chemical elements inside stars, through the fusion process, was part of brilliant teamwork with Willy Fowler and Geoffrey and Margaret Burbidge. The process of nuclear synthesis accounted impressively for a wide range of observed data.

Hoyle is best known for his advocacy of the steady-state theory of the universe, which he, BONDI and Tommy Gold built up in the 1950s. The basis for Hoyle's adherence to this cosmological model was as much aesthetic as scientific, and it led to the formulation of the 'perfect cosmological principle', which stated that the universe, on the large scale, not only looks the same in every direction and from any place in the universe but also looked the same throughout all time. As the universe was shown by HUBBLE to be expanding, the perfect cosmological principle led Hoyle and his colleagues to propose that matter, in the form of hydrogen atoms, was being continuously created to fill the space left by the expansion. With Narlikar, Hoyle developed the mathematical framework for this theory although more recent evidence has denied it much credence. He more recently proposed a mass-field theory that avoided some of the difficulties of the earlier theory and took account of more modern evidence, but these ideas have not been widely accepted. In recent years Hoyle has turned away from the astronomical community, resigning from his professorship and other posts in 1973 and concerning himself with public issues, such as the energy crisis (he is an advocate of nuclear power), and carrying out some research into the origin of life in the dust clouds of interstellar space.   MJS

Hrabal, Bohumil (b. Brünn, Moravia, Austria-Hungary [now Brno, Czechoslovakia], 28.3.1914). Czech writer, who is an extraordinary phenomenon for contemporary Czech literature because he writes about life as it is. To do that he uses Czech as it is. He draws on his own broad experience of working as a lawyer, platelayer, train-dispatcher, bank clerk, commercial traveller, steelworker, wastepaper binder, scene-shifter and crowd-scene actor to write earthy stories and novels in colloquial-to-vulgar language. They contain the humour and nonsequiturs one might expect from an ideal intelligent fellow-drinker in one's local. Hrabal's dominant tone is tragifarcical and his method might be called *lumpensurrealismus*, in which the reader becomes intimate with the text rather than with the author or narrator. Hrabal was unable to publish after the

Prague Spring (1968/9), but recanted in 1975. His two most accomplished texts are *Taneční hodiny pro starší a pokročilé* [Dancing classes for the elderly and advanced] (Prague, 1964) and *Obsluhoval jsem anglického krále* [I waited on the king of England] (Cologne, 1977). The first is a one-sentence collage monologue about life, i.e. drink and stunningly beautiful women. The second is an apotheosis of the healthy, animal, loyal, tolerant man, related with humorous, macabre, grotesque and sentimental *joie de vivre*.   RBP

W. E. Harkins & P. I. Trensky, *Czech Literature since 1956* (NY, 1980).

Hubble, Edwin (b. Marshfield, Mo., USA, 20.11.1889; d. San Marino, Calif., 28.9.1953). American astronomer. Hubble was educated at the universities of Chicago and Oxford, where he took a degree in jurisprudence in 1912. On returning to the USA, he started to practise law, but after a year enrolled as a graduate student in astronomy at Chicago. Thereafter, apart from the two world wars, he became a wholly involved astronomer, making outstanding use of the fine instruments at the Mt Wilson and the Palomar observatories – the 60-inch, 100-inch and latterly the 200-inch telescopes. By 1924 he had discovered several Cepheid variable stars in the galaxies M31 and M33, and thus showed that these and similar galaxies are at very great distances from our own galaxy. This work was followed in 1929 by his outstanding discovery of the linear relationship between the speed of recession of galaxies, indicated by the Doppler effect in their spectra, and their distance, known as the Hubble law; the constant of proportionality is the 'Hubble constant'. The Hubble law remains one of the cornerstones of modern cosmology. The extragalactic distance scale has been greatly revised since Hubble's work but the basic principles of all that he did have remained unchanged. The emphasis now is on an extension of his work to try to find a deviation from linearity at large distances in order to derive a model for the universe. Hubble summarized his earlier work in his popular book *The Realm of the Nebula* (Oxford, 1936).   DEB

Hubel, David Hunter (b. Windsor, Ont., Canada, 27.2.1926). American neurophysiologist. Professor of neurobiology at Harvard Medical School since 1968, he was awarded an MD by McGill University in 1951 and, following a period of hospital medicine and army service, moved to Harvard in 1959 where he began collaborative research with Torsten Wiesel on the functional organization of the primary visual cortex (area 17). Wiesel (b. Uppsala, Sweden, 3.6.1924), also since 1968 professor of neurobiology at Harvard Medical School, had gained his MD at the Karolinska Institute, Stockholm, before moving to Harvard in 1959. This work has demonstrated that different stages in the processing of visual information can be identified by examining the differential response characteristics of individual neurones. It has shown that each neurone in area 17 has one of two types of receptive field, 'simple' or 'complex', the former identified with very localized aspects of image processing and the latter concerned with more complex analysis including binocular integration. Recent investigation into the adjacent area 18 has led to the discovery of 'hypercomplex' cells. Developmental aspects of their research have had important implications for clinical ophthalmology, but primarily they have shown that neurophysiological investigation can make an important contribution to the explanation of visual perception. In recognition of this Hubel and Wiesel were awarded the Nobel prize for medicine in 1981.   AJP

Hückel, Erich (b. Berlin-Charlottenburg, Germany, 9.8.1896; d. Marburg, Hesse, West Germany, 16.2.1980). German physicist and theoretical chemist. Hückel contributed to chemistry in two major areas. He was associated with DEBYE in the formulation of the theory of electrolyte solutions, and later developed important quantum mechanical techniques for calculating the electron distribution and bond energies in unsaturated compounds. After graduating at Göttingen, Hückel began his doctoral work under Debye on the X-ray scattering by liquid crystals; he later joined Debye in Zürich and together the details of the Debye–Hückel theory were worked out. A long and severe illness and a period in London separated this first phase from his work on quantum mechanics which began with Niels BOHR in Copenhagen. By considering the symmetry properties of organic molecules, and especially those containing double bonds, Hückel was able to formulate a procedure in which, while single bonds could be described by the overlap of spherically symmetrical electron clouds (σ – bonds), double bonds involved the participation of electron clouds of different symmetry (π – bonds). These, in effect, prevent or inhibit rotation of the two parts of the molecule joined by the double bond. Extension of these ideas to benzene led to a clearer understanding of the aromatic character of benzene derivatives. Hückel's work in this field provided the basis for two widely used techniques in quantum chemical calculations of molecular structure: the valence bond and molecular orbital methods. He published his autobiography *Ein Gelehrtenleben* [A scholar's life] (Weinheim) in 1975.   DHE

von Hügel, Friedrich (b. Florence, Tuscany, Italy, 8.5.1852; naturalized British citizen, 1914; d. London, UK, 27.1.1925). Austrian/British Catholic philosopher of religion, autodidact, eclectic and invalid. Son of a Rhineland father in the service of Austria and a Scottish mother, von Hügel married Lady Margaret Herbert in 1873 and henceforward lived in England. Though he never held an academic post, he earned the justified reputation of being one of the most learned, and wisest, men of his time. His English style always retained an organ-tone stiffness, but with an occasional brilliant phrase. His first book *The Mystical Element in Religion* (London, 1908) shows his grappling with the problem of harmonizing the mystical, rational and institutional elements of Catholicism in a unique and, for him, indispensable synthesis. The storm of the 'modernist crisis' passed him by, though he was in danger of excommunication. He survived – some say thanks to his deviousness, others thanks to his naivety – and in the postwar period acted as a spiritual guide to many, especially Anglicans. His spiritual teaching, found in *Letters to a Niece* (London, 1922), combines a demanding – 'costing' was his term – asceticism with a respect for the way in which grace must 'build on nature'. His remaining work *Essays and Addresses* (London, 1921) shows him again striving to reconcile scholarship and sanctity, nature and grace, ecclesiastical loyalty and the critical temper. He conducted a vast correspondence in French, Italian and German with all the leading 'modernists', and though he judged them with some severity later he remained faithful to the best tradition of 'liberal Catholicism'. The all-inclusive nature of von Hügel's synthesis has led some commentators to confess their bafflement and treat him as an enigma.   PAH

J. P. Whelan, *The Spirituality of Friedrich von Hügel* (London, 1971); L. F. Barmann, *Baron Friedrich von Hügel and the Modernist Crisis in England* (Cambridge, 1972).

Huggins, William (b. London, UK, 7.2.1824; d. London, 12.5.1910). British astronomer. Educated privately, Huggins succeeded to his father's business as a silk mercer and linen draper. However, having always longed for a scientific career, he sold the business in 1854 to devote himself to the study of astronomy. To this end in 1856 he built an observatory for his own use at his new home at Tulse Hill, London. Initially equipped with a 5-inch refractor, two years later he mounted an 8-inch objective by Alvan Clark, later still using a 15-inch telescope. Huggins was fortunate in that in 1859, when he was at an early stage in his work, Kirchhoff had reported on his interpretation of the solar spectrum. Immediately Huggins saw his mission and began the study of stellar spectra. Using newly designed and constructed spectroscopes he mapped the emission lines in the spectra of 26 elements and compared their positions with those of absorption lines in the spectra of bright stars. He found that there were many coincidences between stellar and terrestrial lines, as there are in the solar spectrum, showing that the chemical elements are indeed present in the stars. Huggins's pioneering work in this field was not easy for there were no photographic plates at that time and all observations had to be made visually.

In 1864 Huggins turned his attention to nebulae. It was not known then whether nebulae (for example, the Orion nebula) are clouds of unresolved stars or are wholly new kinds of object. If they are clouds of stars they should show the *absorption* line spectra of stars. On the contrary, Huggins observed that planetary nebulae showed *bright* line spectra, suggesting that they were ' ... enormous masses of luminous gas or vapour'. He could not interpret the spectra that he saw through his spectroscope, and in fact such spectra were not fully explained until the middle of this century. When he returned to the spectra of stars, Huggins sought to find small differences between terrestrial and stellar wavelengths which could be ascribed to the Doppler effect of motion in the line of sight. Visual observations were difficult but he succeeded in 1867 in determining for the first time the speed of a star, finding that Sirius is receding at 29 miles per second. In 1880 he was the first to use a dry photographic plate for astronomical work and adopted it for his work on stellar spectroscopy.   DEB

Hughes, Edward James (Ted) (b. Mytholmroyd, W. Yorks., UK, 17.8.1930). British poet of great power and consistency of purpose: with energy and awe to explore man's relationship with the destructive-creative processes in material nature. *The Hawk in the Rain* (London, 1957) began an attack on complacent protections from natural forces which broke through in *Wodwo* (London, 1967) to confront processes of dissolution in poems controlled by the voice of myth. *Crow* (London, 1970), the first mythic sequence and Hughes's best-known work, systematically tests conceptions against material reality in the process of which basic humanity is tentatively defined. *Cave Birds* (London, 1978) goes further by confronting a complacent hero with the evidence of his own nature which, when it is recognized and accepted, is symbolically married to those same forces at work in the natural world. The tensions in reconciling these inner and outer worlds, and the difficulties in controlling the energies released, are the subject of the comic narrative *Gaudete* (London, 1977). But it is in the farming poems of *Moortown* (London, 1979) that these resolutions and responsibilities are accepted in typically practical and unusually personal terms. Hughes's vigorous poetry of metaphysical seriousness combines humility with wholeness.   TG

K. Sagar, *The Art of Ted Hughes* (Cambridge, ²1978); T. Gifford & N. Roberts, *Ted Hughes: a Critical Study* (London, 1981).

Hughes, Howard (b. Houston, Tex., USA, 24.12.1905; d. nr Houston, 5.4.1976). American businessman. Having inherited a highly profitable oil-well and drilling-bit company from his father, in his early years he made movies, including *Hell's Angels* (1930), *Scarface* (1932) and *The Outlaw* (1941); and was a fine pilot (world airspeed record 352 mph, 1935, and round-the-world flight record, 91 hrs, 1938); and developed very successful businesses (including the original Hughes Tool Company, the Hughes Aircraft Company and major engineering concerns). He had a controlling interest in the Trans World Airlines Company but lost control when he failed to appear to answer antitrust charges. His wealth made him one of America's richest men. In his later years he became a recluse, obsessed with a search for total seclusion. Throughout his life he contributed to the folk mythology of business management. In his early career he personified the folk hero of the successful American businessman; at his death he had become the archetypal antihero, identified with conspiracy and the abuse of power. RIT

Huizinga, Johan (b. Groningen, The Netherlands, 7.12.1872; d. De Steeg, Gelderland, 1.2.1945). Dutch historian. A student-aesthete of the 1890s, enthusiastic for Poe, Verlaine and Huysmans, Huizinga never abandoned the aesthetic approach to history. He was intuitive rather than analytic, a generalist rather than a specialist, who concentrated on the history of culture, trying to identify its changing 'morphology'. He is best known for *Herfsttij der middeleeuwen* (Groningen, 1919; abridged tr. *The Waning of the Middle Ages*, London, 1924) which deals with the culture of the court and the cities of Burgundy in the 14c and 15c, and in particular with the preoccupation with death and decline in the literature of the period. Huizinga's doctoral thesis was concerned with the classical Indian drama, and he wrote on western history from 12c France (essays on Abelard and Alain de Lille) to the contemporary USA (*Mensch en menigte in Amerika*, Haarlem, 1918; *The Individual and the Crowd in America*, NY, 1972). His contributions to Dutch history include *Erasmus* (Haarlem, 1924; NY, 1924), and *Holländische Kultur des siebzehnten Jahrhunderts* (Jena, 1933; *Dutch Civilization in the Seventeenth Century*, London, 1968). *Men and Ideas* (NY, 1959) is a selection of his essays. Huizinga also wrote several pessimistic analyses of the cultural crisis of his time, and a wide-ranging study of the play element in human culture, *Homo Ludens* (Haarlem, 1938; London, 1949). Huizinga was one of the leading Dutch intellectuals of his day. He wrote well for a wide public. He had a strong dislike for the modern technological egalitarian world and an intense nostalgia for the past, aristocratic and bourgeois, which he evoked so skilfully for his readers.   UPB

W. R. H. Koops *et al.* (eds), *Johan Huizinga 1872–1972* (The Hague, 1973).

Hull, Clark Leonard (b. nr Akron, NY, USA, 24.5.1884; d. New Haven, Conn., 10.5.1952). American psychologist. After obtaining a doctorate on concept formation from the University of Wisconsin, he held positions at Harvard and Yale. His other early interests included aptitude testing and hypnosis, but his greatest contributions were in the field of learning. He took the behaviourism of J. B. WATSON, and attempted to extend it. In particular, he disagreed with the early behaviourists in arguing that many complex events intervene between stimulus and response; these events were classified as intervening variables. He claimed that psychology could be turned into an exact science by the use of the hypothetico-deductive method. This method was applied by Hull to conditioning and other simple forms of learning, culminating in his book *Principles of Behavior* (NY, 1943). His theories were also concerned with motivation, and the notion of reinforcement or reward was of crucial significance throughout his theorizing. He endeavoured to construct a highly quantitative general theory of behaviour, but the attempt was overambitious and relatively unsuccessful. While his theoretical approach was remarkably influential at one time, it suffered a rapid decline in popularity in the 1960s. His lasting achievements are: he made the behaviourist approach much more sophisticated and flexible; and he provided a powerful intellectual stimulus for a later generation of American psychologists, including Neal Miller, Kenneth Spence, Hobart Mowrer, John Dollard and Robert Sears.   MWE

Hulme, Thomas Ernest (b. Endon, Staffs., UK, 16.9.1883; d. nr Nieuport, W. Flanders, Belgium, 28.9.1917). British aesthetician and philosopher. Hulme was one of the leading figures in the formation of the imagist movement in modern poetry. He founded the Poets' Club in London in 1908 which attracted F. S. Flint and Ezra POUND to its membership; collectively these three developed a theory of poetry notable for its emphasis on clarity, economy, objectivity and concreteness of detail in poetic language. Hulme wrote a small body of poetry observing these precepts, but his importance lies in his philosophical and aesthetic contributions to the movement. He felt that his age was ripe for a revival of the classical spirit and in his essays he engaged in a concerted attack on romanticism and humanism, both of which he judged to be philosophically untenable and unrealistic: the essay 'Romanticism and classicism' in *Speculations* (London, 1924) is the most cogent statement of his aesthetic vision. The paradox of Hulme's contribution to modern culture is that while he was a moving force in the emergence of a radically distinctive and influential poetics, he was himself a man of deeply conservative sympathies and an articulate spokesman for contemporary militarism.
                    GHC
M. Roberts, *T. E. Hulme* (London, 1938); A. R. Jones, *The Life and Opinions of T. E. Hulme* (London, 1960).

Hume-Rothery, William (b. Worcester Park, Surrey, UK, 15.5.1899; d. Oxford, 27.9.1968). British metallurgist, centrally concerned with the structure and composition of alloys. Hume-Rothery was a key figure in transforming metallurgy from an empirical art to a well-founded science. He graduated in chemistry from Magdalen College, Oxford, in 1922. Postgraduate research under Carpenter at the Royal School of Mines, London University, whetted his metallurgical appetite, and he returned to Oxford to work as a 'metallurgical chemist'. Through careful experimental work, Hume-Rothery and his students found an order in many types of known intermetallic phases (*Phil. Trans. Roy. Soc.*, 233 [1934], 1); the 'Hume-Rothery rules' are now classic guides to alloy composition. Hume-Rothery, who was totally deaf from the age of 18, had an important influence on the development of metallurgy as a recognized science in its own right. He wrote a number of major textbooks (including *The Structure of Metals and Alloys*, London, 1936, [5]1969). In 1957 he became the first professor of the newly founded school of metallurgy at Oxford.   KRS

Humphrey, Hubert Horatio (b. Wallace, S. Dak., USA, 27.5.1911; d. Waverley, Minn., 13.1.1978). Mayor of Minneapolis, Minnesota; Democratic senator for Minnesota (1948–64, 1968–9); unsuccessful candidate for the presidency in 1960 and 1968; majority whip in the Senate (1961–4); vice-president (1965–9). Humphrey was one of the cofounders of the Americans for Democratic Action, which from 1947 to 1965 was the final embodiment of the middle-class intellectual movement for social and political reform in the USA which began with the progressives in the 1890s. As mayor of Minneapolis he made the city a model for reform in city management throughout the USA, capturing the Democratic party organization from the party bosses; and as a leading figure in the ADA, he held the reformist wing of the party together against the pull of the left-wing, break-away, increasingly fellow-travelling 'progressive' party led by Henry Wallace. As a leader of the Minnesota delegation to the 1948 Democratic convention, he insisted on a civil rights clause being inserted in the party platform, driving the states of the 'deep South' to secede from the Democrats and set up an alternative, 'Dixiecrat', party. The Democratic party of the 1950s and 1960s, reformist, democratic, anticommunist, embodying the idea of federal aid and federal leadership, committed to the protection of the civil rights of all minorities, and the successful realization under President L. B. JOHNSON and himself of their social welfare programme was, to a very large extent, the product of Humphrey's political vision and the role he played in defeating both left and right wings of the party in those years. His later career as vice-president and as Democratic candidate for the presidency in 1968 was over-shadowed by the deep divisions in the Democratic party consequent upon the American intervention in Vietnam. DCW

Huntington, Ellsworth (b. Galesburg, Ill., USA, 16.9.1876; d. New Haven, Conn., 17.10.1947). American geographer, one of the most controversial and prolific of his generation. Like TOYNBEE, Huntington was concerned with the complex origins and causes of the world's major civilizations and why they had emerged in particular locations. Although he recognized a triad of causes – climate, heredity, and culture – Huntington laid particular emphasis on climatic factors. He argued that the location of the hearths of particular civilizations could be matched with critical environmental limits, and saw in climatic changes the clues to unexplained shifts in these centres. His work was marked by a wealth of factual detail, often based on his own fieldwork and observations, and a tendency to use such evidence selectively to advance his thesis. He was dubbed an environmental determinist for his advocate-like, rather than judicial, style; his later writing came under increasing criticism. G. J. Martin's *Ellsworth Hunting-*

ton (Hamden, Conn., 1973) suggests that his views were more balanced than his contemporary critics allowed. Born in New England into a Congregational family, Huntington studied at Harvard under William Morris Davis, and later held a post at Yale. As important as his academic contacts were his intensive field periods, first in central Asia and later in all the continents. He was author and coauthor of 57 books and 240 papers. *The Pulse of Asia* (Boston, Mass., 1907), *Civilization and Climate* (Yale, 1915), and *Mainsprings of Civilization* (NY, 1945) were his best-known books, but others – such as *Palestine and its Transformation* (NY, 1911) and *The Climatic Factor as Illustrated in Mid-America* (Washington, 1914) – spelt out the same themes more clearly on a smaller regional canvas. PH

Husaini, Hajj Amin Al- (b. Jerusalem, Palestine, Ottoman Empire [now Israel], 1893; d. Beirut, Lebanon, 4.7.1974). Grand Mufti of Jerusalem. Palestinian political and religious leader, head of one of the two leading political families in the old Turkish Sanjaq of Jerusalem, selected by the British mandate authorities in an attempt to win his loyalty, and appointed as Mufti in 1922. He remained, however, an implacable enemy both of the British mandate and of the Jewish immigrants, seeing in the organization of Arab resistance to them both a religious duty and an opportunity to beat down the rival Nashashibi clan. Weakness and unrealism led him in 1936 to undo the advantages gained after the riots of 1929 in Jerusalem by encouraging an Arab revolt against the British, and to accept aid from fascist Italy. Proscribed by the British in 1937, he went into exile, first to Syria, then to Iraq and, after the British suppression of the 1941 Golden Square revolt in Iraq, he took refuge in Nazi Germany. In January 1949, after the proclamation of the state of Israel, he installed himself in Egyptian-occupied Gaza as head of an 'All-Palestine government', encouraging *fedayeen* raids into Israel. He subsequently fell into disfavour with NASSER who deposed him, leadership of the Palestinians passing to the PLO and to ARAFAT. DCW

Husén, Torsten (b. Lund, Malmöhus, Sweden, 1.3.1916). Swedish international educationalist. A graduate of the University of Lund (1937), Husén's early work was focused on developmental and differential psychology. From this developed his interest in education and soon after WW2 he began research on problems of educational reform in their socioeconomic context. As research professor of education at Stockholm from 1953 to 1971 he contributed actively to Sweden's reassessment of her selective educational system and to the planning and introduction of new provisions based on comprehensive principles. During this period Sweden came to be regarded internationally as a model of educational innovation and in turn much of Husén's research work generated a parallel reputation for its care and accuracy. Husén also worked extensively on comparative and cross-national studies of educational provision and in 1970 he became chairman of the International Institute for Educational Planning, based in Paris. The author of over 40 detailed research reports and studies, including *Problems of Differentiation in Swedish Compulsory Schooling* (Stockholm, 1962), *Social Background and Educational Career* (Paris, 1972) and *Social Influences on Educational Attainment* (Paris, 1972), Husén has more recently published two wide-ranging and provocative analyses of western education and its future, *The Learning Society* (London, 1974) and *The School in Question* (Oxford, 1979). AP

Husserl, Edmund (b. Prossnitz, Moravia, Austria-Hungary [now Prostějov, Czechoslovakia], 8.4.1859; d. Freiburg, Baden-Württemberg, Germany, 21.4.1938). German philosopher. A mathematician before he was a philosopher, Husserl studied at Leipzig and Berlin (where he worked with Karl Weierstrass) before coming under the influence of Franz Brentano in Vienna in 1883. He held posts at Halle from 1887 to 1901, and at Göttingen (where he was a colleague of HILBERT) from 1901 to 1916, when he finally settled as professor at Freiburg – on his retirement in 1928 he was succeeded by his former pupil HEIDEGGER. In 1891 his first book

Philosophie der Arithmetik [The philosophy of arithmetic] (Halle) was ferociously criticized by FREGE. Husserl accepted the criticism and concluded that the proper objects of all the exact disciplines, philosophy as well as logic and mathematics, are essences, abstract entities present to the mind but not themselves states of mind, as he had supposed in common with John Stuart Mill and earlier British empiricists. The notion of philosophy as a pure inspection of consciousness and its immediate objects, free from assumptions and inferences, a development of what Brentano had called 'descriptive psychology', Husserl baptized *phenomenology*. As defined in his *Logische Untersuchungen* (Halle, 1900–1; tr. J. N. Findlay, *Logical Investigations*, 2 vols, London, 1970) it became the explicit method of numerous European philosophers. Where Husserl mainly concerned himself with the mind's intellectual activities and their objects, Scheler and such existentialists as Heidegger and SARTRE applied the phenomenological method to the emotions. In his later work Husserl abandoned the realistic distinction between the mind and its independent objects which he had derived from Brentano and tended towards a view of consciousness as all-embracing, a redirection which was unacceptable to most of his former disciples. An unrelievedly abstract and technical writer, Husserl was the most rigidly professorial of philosophers. His conception of philosophy as a study of meanings is in principle the same as that of analytic philosophers, but their ideas about the nature of the meanings they study are very different from his. Husserl was Jewish by birth but was baptized as a Christian in 1887. AQ

E. Pivcevic, *Husserl and Phenomenology* (London, 1970).

Hutchinson, George Evelyn (b. Cambridge, UK, 30.1.1903; naturalized American citizen). British/American limnologist. Educated at Cambridge, he emigrated to the USA, eventually becoming Stirling professor of zoology at Yale (1965–71). Within the field of limnology, his interests have centred particularly on the history of lakes as revealed in the biological and geochemical remains in their sediments, although he has published in nearly all aspects of freshwater biology. He has been deeply connected with the extensive studies on the limnology of Linsley Pond, Connecticut. Hutchinson has been a stimulating influence for many ecologists, particularly in the USA and Canada, and has drawn on his freshwater studies to write a number of general ecological works. *The Evolutionary Theater and the Ecological Play* (NY, 1965) and 'A homage to Santa Rosalia' (*The American Naturalist*, 153, 1959) are well known to all ecology students of the past 20 years. His single most influential work is *A Treatise on Limnology* (NY, 1957), a complete, authoritative synthesis of the state of the subject to the date of publication. Further volumes have been published at approximately 10-year intervals, but the series is at present incomplete.   RTi

Huxley, Aldous Leonard (b. Godalming, Surrey, UK, 26.7.1894; d. Hollywood, Calif., USA, 22.11.1963). British novelist and writer. A descendant of two famous Victorian families, the scientific Huxleys and the moralistic Arnolds, Huxley was a modern sage with equal commitments to the real and the ideal which he never reconciled. To express his changing ideas of the world he produced novels, essays, scientific speculation and travel books which are representative of the decades in which they were written. His novels of the 1920s, such as *Crome Yellow* (London, 1921), *Antic Hay* (London, 1923) and *Those Barren Leaves* (London, 1925), are with their witty, cynical conversation typical works of the period, exploring ideas in a manner reminiscent of Peacock, and taking as their text the Fulke Greville motto to *Point Counter Point* (London, 1928): 'Oh, wearisome condition of humanity,/Born under one law, to another bound'. Upon this many variations are played. In the 1930s his scientific rationalism alerted him to the dangers of totalitarianism which he expressed in *Brave New World* (London, 1932), his most influential work, where he creates a genetically and psychologically conditioned dystopia of alarming blandness. (A more optimistic version came later with *Island*, London, 1962.) *Ape and Essence* (London, 1948) and *Eyeless in Gaza* (London, 1936) are further expressions of his disgust with humanity from which he turned in the 1940s to a form of mystical idealism, especially in *The Perennial Philosophy* (London, 1945), eventually seeking to escape from the destructive ego and all its works through the controlled use of narcotics (*The Doors of Perception*, London, 1954). Huxley is not a major novelist but made many significant contributions to the literature of ideas.   DC

P. Bowering, *Aldous Huxley: a Study of the Major Novels* (London, 1969); S. Bedford, *Aldous Huxley: a Biography* (London, 1978).

Huxley, Andrew Fielding (b. London, UK, 22.12.1917). British biophysicist. Like A. L. HODGKIN, Huxley studied at Trinity College, Cambridge, eventually becoming a fellow (1941–60). His work was interrupted by WW2 when he worked for the Anti-Aircraft Command (1940–2) and for the Admiralty (1942–5). Then he joined Hodgkin in the highly productive period between 1945 and 1952 that led to the description of the ionic mechanisms by which nerves pass electrical impulses, work that laid the foundation of the modern biophysics of excitable tissue and the award of the 1963 Nobel prize for medicine. Huxley left Cambridge for University College London in 1969 where he is presently a Royal Society research professor. Since the work on nerve conduction mechanisms Huxley has provided important insights into the structure of muscle and on the way in which actin and myosin interact in the muscle contraction process.   CTJ

I

Ibsen, Henrik (b. Skien, Vestfold, Norway, 20.3.1828; d. Christiania [now Oslo], 23.5.1906). Norwegian dramatist and poet. The cultural shock of the impact of Ibsen's dramas on the society of Western Europe in the 1890s had consequences felt far into the 20c and still evident even today. His abandonment of verse as the medium of drama after *Brand* (Copenhagen, 1866; London, 1891, tr. in *The Oxford Ibsen*) and *Peer Gynt* (Copenhagen, 1866; London, 1892, tr. ibid) in order to write prose plays about contemporary problems changed the whole direction of modern drama. The 12 plays he then wrote between 1877 and 1899 – *Samfundets Stótter* (Copenhagen, 1878; *Pillars of Society*, London, 1888, tr. ibid), *Et Dukkehjem* (Copenhagen, 1879; *A Doll's House*, London, 1883, tr. ibid), *Gengangere* (Copenhagen, 1881; *Ghosts*, London, 1888, tr. ibid), *En Folkefiende* (Copenhagen, 1882; London, 1888; tr. *An Enemy of the People*, ibid), *Vildanden* (Copenhagen, 1884; *The Wild Duck*, London, 1890, tr. ibid), *Rosmersholm* (Copenhagen, 1886; London, 1890, tr. ibid), *Fruen fra Havet* (Copenhagen, 1888; *The Lady from the Sea*, London, 1890, tr. ibid), *Hedda Gabler* (Copenhagen, 1890; London, 1891, tr. ibid), *Bygmester Solness* (Copenhagen, 1892; *The Master Builder*, London, 1907, tr. ibid), *Lille Eyolf* (Copenhagen, 1894; *Little Eyolf*, London, 1895, tr. ibid), *John Gabriel Borkman* (Copenhagen, 1896; London, 1897, tr. ibid) and *Naar vi dóde vaagner* (Copenhagen, 1899; *When We Dead Awaken*, London, 1900, tr. ibid) – not only mark a theatrical achievement unparalleled in the history of modern drama but also inaugurated that continuing tradition wherein dramatists like WEDEKIND, G. B. SHAW, Maxim GORKY and BRECHT sought (in the latter's phrase) to give the main problems of the age a dramatic structure. Honesty of vision and courage to proclaim the truth however unexpected or unwelcome it may have been to their contemporaries are the defining qualities of this tradition. Even today the Ibsenist problems still impinge: the place of women in marriage and in society (*Et Dukkehjem*); the conflict across the generation gap (*Bygmester Solness*); the clash between institutionalized authority and individual liberty (*Rosmersholm*); and the menace of pollution in a world of material and commercial values (*En Folkefiende*). Less immediately obvious than this polemic element but, in a more diffuse way, no less significant in the longer term were the results of Ibsen's attention to what he called 'the far more difficult art' of prose. By exploring the potential of 'nonpoetic' dramatic language in ways never before attempted or even suspected, he created a new kind of 'poetry of the theatre'; and his success in conveying subtleties and profundities below the surface of what at first sight seemed little more than the commonplaces of everyday speech opened up new and important possibilities in drama. Other European writers who were themselves exceptionally sensitive to linguistic nuance – among them HOFMANNSTHAL, Henry JAMES, Maeterlinck, JOYCE and RILKE – have commented on this aspect of his genius. Ibsen's works were widely translated into many European languages, pre-eminently German, already during his own lifetime. Collected, translated editions in English are W. Archer (ed.), *The Collected Works of Henrik Ibsen* (12 vols, London, 1906–12) and J. W. McFarlane (ed.), *The Oxford Ibsen* (8 vols, London, 1960–77). JWMcF

M. Meyer, *Henrik Ibsen* (3 vols, London, 1967–71); H. Koht, *The Life of Ibsen* (NY, 1971).

Illich, Ivan (b. Vienna, Austria, 4.9.1926; naturalized American citizen). Austrian/American educational and social theorist. Illich studied theology and philosophy at the Gregorian University in Rome and obtained a PhD in history at the University of Salzburg. He was an assistant pastor in an Irish-Puerto Rican parish in New York (1951–6) and vice-rector to the Catholic University of Puerto Rico (1956–60). He founded the controversial Center for Intercultural Documentation (CIDOC) in Cuernavaca, Mexico, which became in the 1960s a focal point for seminars on institutional 'alternatives'. His book *Deschooling Society* (NY, 1971) attracted sympathetic attention among libertarian educationalists who were starting to doubt the value of compensatory and other urban educational ideas. Later, Illich concentrated on the disabling impact of professional control over medicine: *Limits to Medicine* (London, 1976). The main theme throughout his work has been the 'demystification' through 'deprofessionalization' and 'deinstitutionalization' of 'secrets' associated with religion, education, health – even transport, industrial design and salesmanship. His belief is that people need to be more involved with those decisions and subsequent strategies which affect their lives in a world in which 'the fraud perpetrated by the salesman of schools is less obvious but much more fundamental than the self-satisfied salesmanship of the Coca-Cola or Ford representative because the schoolman hooks his people on a much more demanding drug.' PL

I. Lister (ed.), *Deschooling: a Reader* (Cambridge, 1974); P. Lund, *Ivan Illich and his Antics* (Huddersfield, 1978).

Illyés, Gyula (b. Rácegres, Austria-Hungary [now Hungary], 2.11.1902; d. Budapest, 15.4.1983). Hungarian poet, novelist, dramatist and essayist, the doyen of Hungarian poets. He proclaims a clear social and national message in verse that is modern in style and carefully constructed to display shades and sounds from the contemplative to the passionate, from lyric to narrative and heroic verse. The effect of his early sojourn in France is seen in his use of language, which is as precise as his imagery is eloquent. His prose shares the same characteristics; his autobiographical *Puszták népe* (Budapest, 1936; tr. G. F. Cushing, *People of the Puszta*, Budapest, 1967) is a fine example of totally controlled, passionately committed writing which shocked the nation for whose destiny he shares the same desperate concern as the great romantic poets. Illyés resists political slogans; his concern is for justice and humanity, and he has often risked unpopularity by his independent views. His plays display the same themes, but are written in the traditionally didactic style of the Hungarian theatre, so that their appeal is limited. In his old age he has increasingly taken to writing brief, epigrammatic verse of considerable power. GFC

J. Reményi, *Hungarian Writers and Literature* (New Brunswick, NJ, 1964).

Inge, William Ralph (b. Crayke, N. Yorks., UK, 6.6.1860; d. Brightwell, Berks., 26.2.1954). British churchman. After teaching Greek and Latin at Eton and at Oxford, and brief spells as a parish priest in London and as a professor in Cambridge, Inge was made dean of St Paul's in 1911. The prime minister who secured this appointment (H. H. Asquith) wanted him to 'restore the traditions of scholarship and culture associated with the Deanery in the past' and this Dean Inge did very effectively as a journalist, lecturer and author until his retirement in 1934. He went on writing in his long retirement. Known as 'the gloomy Dean', he attacked the egalitarianism and materialism of the socialists (e.g. in *England*, London, 1924) and lamented the massacre of spiritual values during the two world wars which he witnessed (e.g. in *The End of an Age*, London, 1948). But the religion which he advocated was by no means the mere repetition of orthodoxy; indeed, in theology he was a modernist, fully accepting biblical scholarship. His first book was on *Christian Mysticism* (London, 1899) and, although no mystic, he always had an interest in advanced spiritual experience, as providing a foundation for the religious life when dogmatism had become incredible. He was an expert on the thought of the 3c Neoplatonist Plotinus and, as a Christian Platonist, urged his readers to take refuge in the assurance of direct spiritual intuition at a time when morals seemed to be in chaos (*Christian Ethics and Modern Problems*, London, 1930) and the scientists could hold out no hope of a paradise on earth (*God and the Astronomers*, London, 1933). In a time of many alarming changes, self-disciplined prayer admitted the individual to an eternal world of light and peace.

DLE

A. Fox, *Dean Inge* (London, 1960).

Ingold, Christopher Kelk (b. London, UK, 28.10.1893; d. London, 8.12.1970). British chemist, distinguished for his contributions to the electronic theory of organic chemistry, reaction mechanisms and molecular spectroscopy. He worked under J. F. Thorpe at Imperial College, London; held the chair of organic chemistry at Leeds (1924–30); and was professor of chemistry at University College London (1930–61). The work Ingold published as a lecturer at Imperial College revealed an extraordinary breadth of interest in organic chemistry. In Leeds he worked particularly on the rates and orientation of aromatic substitution. This work led to major contributions to the electronic theory of organic chemistry, parallel to those of R. ROBINSON, with whom he was often in controversy. The ideas and the terminology set out by Ingold (*Chem. Rev.*, 15 [1934], 225) are still widely used today. On succeeding Robinson at UCL in 1930, Ingold was joined by the young Edward D. Hughes from Bangor, thus beginning a collaboration in the study of the kinetics and mechanism of organic reactions, which continued (with only brief interruptions) until Hughes's untimely death in 1963. Their joint work included the detailed investigation of aliphatic nucleophilic substitution and elimination. Other mechanistic studies carried out under Ingold at UCL included further work on electrophilic aromatic substitution, and on prototropy, addition reactions, aromatic rearrangements, electrophilic aliphatic substitution, and substitutions in octahedral inorganic complexes. Ingold's work in molecular spectroscopy largely concerned the detailed investigation and interpretation of the ultraviolet and infrared spectra of benzene and acetylene. His *Structure and Mechanism in Organic Chemistry* (London, 1953, [2]1969) was regarded as authoritative for many years.

JSh

Ingram, Vernon Martin (b. Breslau, Germany [now Wrocław, Poland], 19.5.1924). British biochemist. He worked in England from 1941 to 1958 when he moved to the USA, and in 1961 he was appointed professor of biochemistry at MIT. His early researches were concerned with the structure of proteins but he later turned his attention to the way in which they are formed (*Biosynthesis of Macromolecules*, NY, 1965). Most significant was his demonstration that the abnormal haemoglobin in the blood of individuals suffering from sickle cell anaemia differed from the normal by replacement of a single residue of glutamic acid, in the β peptide chain, by a residue of valine. He thus established for the first time that a typical MENDELian mutation can cause replacement of one amino acid by another in a specific protein (see *Haemoglobin in Genetics and Evolution*, NY, 1965). This had important implications for genetics and molecular biology. But the technique he used was also important. This involved splitting the protein by the action of the proteolytic enzyme trypsin into a mixture of peptides. These were separated by chromatography and electrophoresis on a sheet of filter paper to yield a two-dimensional peptide map – called a 'fingerprint' as the pattern is uniquely characteristic of the protein. This technique makes it possible to discriminate between two very similar proteins and at the same time to pinpoint the structural site at which they differ. It has greatly facilitated the study of other haemoglobinopathies, diseases caused by the presence of an abnormal haemoglobin in the blood, of which some 200 have now been characterized.

GL

Ioffe, Abram Fedorovich (b. Romny, Ukraine, Russia, 17.10.1880; d. Leningrad, USSR, 14.10.1960). Russian physicist. Ioffe, one of the outstanding Soviet physicists of the older generation, started his research with ROENTGEN in Munich, where he received his PhD in 1905. He returned to St Petersburg, where he remained for the rest of his life, devoting himself to the study of many branches of solid state physics. In the early years he investigated the electrical and mechanical properties of non-metals, the plastic deformation of crystals, and the effect of plastic deformation on X-ray diffraction patterns. In the 1930s he started the research for which he is best known – his pioneering work on the physics of semiconducting materials. He studied the effect of impurities on the electrical properties of semiconductors, and he investigated certain metallic alloys which have semiconducting properties. He developed methods for achieving thermoelectric refrigeration, which enables a refrigerator to be made which has neither moving parts nor complicated pipework. He also worked on the principles of rectification, whereby an alternating electric current can be transformed into a direct current. In 1954 he was made director of the Semiconductor Institute of the USSR Academy of Sciences in Leningrad. Ioffe was also responsible for setting up and directing some 16 other scientific institutes in the USSR, including the Leningrad Agrophysical Institute which specializes in the application of physics to agricultural production methods. HMR

Ionesco, Eugène (b. Slatina, Romania, 26.11.1912; naturalized French citizen). Romanian/French dramatist. Ionesco was brought to Paris by his French mother when a year old, but taken back to his father's native Romania when he was 13. He returned to Paris in 1938, and in 1948 tried to learn English by the Assimil method. This addition to his linguistic experience led to the best of all French avant-garde plays *La Cantatrice chauve* (Paris, 1950; tr. D. Watson, *The Bald Prima Donna*, London, 1961), first produced in 1950 and never absent from the Parisian stage since. This intensely amusing mixture of social satire, *Alice in Wonderland*-type logic, verbal delirium and surrealist farce is generally performed as a double bill with *La Leçon* (Paris, 1951; tr. D. Watson, *The Lesson*, London, 1961), a terrifying experiment in the theatre of cruelty and of the absurd. Ionesco's advanced theatrical techniques go hand in hand with rather conservative political views. *Rhinocéros* (Paris, 1960; tr. D. Prouse, *Rhinoceros*, London, 1960) is a violent sat-

ire on all forms of totalitarianism, left as well as right, and Ionesco is equally hostile to the USSR and to SARTRE's theories on commitment. Ionesco's obsession with death is most visible in *Le Roi se meurt* (Paris, 1962; tr. D. Watson, *Exit the King*, London, 1964) while the more spiritual direction of his work, with its insistence upon the human need for love, found expression in the highly successful *La Soif et la faim* (Düsseldorf, 1965; tr. D. Watson, *Hunger and Thirst*, London, 1969). PMWT

R. Coe, *Ionesco* (London, 1971); C. Abastado, *Eugène Ionesco* (Paris, 1971).

Isaacs, Susan Sutherland (b. Bromley Cross, Lancs., UK, 24.5.1885; d. London, 12.10.1948). British educationist, psychologist and teacher. After studying philosophy and psychology at Manchester and Cambridge universities, she became a lecturer in infant school education before starting the work for which she is best known, as principal of the Malting House School in Cambridge from 1924 to 1927. This small, private school for young children of high intelligence was run on experimental lines and owed much to the educational theories of Friedrich Froebel and John DEWEY. It had no fixed curriculum and emphasized finding out rather than direct instruction, emotional expression rather than restrictive discipline. Her subsequent writings, which have had a lasting influence upon the theory and practice of primary education, were based upon her careful observations of Malting House pupils and deal with the intellectual and social growth of young children, notably *Intellectual Growth in Young Children* (London, 1930), *The Children We Teach* (London, 1932) and *Social Development of Young Children* (London, 1933). Some of her conclusions challenged the widely accepted theories of PIAGET concerning the stages of children's intellectual development – a critical trend which did not gain momentum until long after her death. She was appointed head of the newly formed department of child development at the University of London Institute of Education in 1933, where she remained for 10 years, lecturing and writing on the psychology of early childhood. RRStr

D. E. M. Gardner, *Susan Isaacs* (London, 1969).

Isard, Walter (b. Philadelphia, Pa, USA, 19.4.1919). American regional scientist. Trained as an economist, Isard developed research and teaching interests in regional economics and the role of location in economic theory. To further these, he conceived the multidisciplinary subject of regional science, defined as 'the careful and patient study of social problems with regional and spatial dimensions'. In the mid-1950s Isard founded both the department of regional science at the University of Pennsylvania, the leading research and training centre for the subject, and the Regional Science Association, an international learned society with branches and regular meetings in four continents and with several major journals. Isard's contributions to regional science include a trilogy of seminal books – *Location and Space Economy* (Cambridge, Mass., 1956), *Methods of Regional Analysis* (Cambridge, Mass., 1960) and *General Theory* (Cambridge, Mass., 1969), the last two being written by several authors – plus *An Introduction to Regional Science* (Englewood Cliffs, 1975). Not content with launching, establishing and remaining active in this new academic subject, Isard was also involved in the foundation of the Peace Research Society; and at Pennsylvania he held joint appointments in regional science and peace science. RJJ

Isherwood, Christopher William Bradshaw (b. High Lane, Ches., UK, 26.8.1904; naturalized American citizen, 1946). British/American novelist. His career, like that of his lifelong friend AUDEN (with whom he collaborated on three plays and a travel book), falls into English and American periods. Early work is concerned with revolt against his upper-middle-class background, the rise of fascism and imminent war; later work with the Vedantism embraced after settling in California in 1939 and a more frankly treated homosexuality. In crisp ironic prose he has experimented fascinatingly on the frontier between fiction and autobiography. *Goodbye to Berlin* (London, 1939), enormously pop-

ular in several adaptations, is the episodic masterpiece of the early period of compulsive travel and left-wing politics, deftly evoking decadent pre-HITLER Germany through dynamic portraits assembled in a cinematic style by an ironized second self of the author. Isherwood's first spell working on Hollywood filmscripts (1933) inspired *Prater Violet* (NY, 1945), but the best of his later fiction is *A Single Man* (NY, 1964), an elegantly concentrated study of a middle-aged homosexual don. He has since returned to the brilliant autobiographical experiment of *Lions and Shadows: an Education in the Twenties* (London, 1938) with the subtly organized memoirs *Kathleen and Frank* (NY, 1971), *Christopher and his Kind* (NY, 1976) and *My Guru and his Disciple* (NY, 1980). AS

P. Piazza, *Christopher Isherwood: Myth and Anti-myth* (NY, 1978); B. Finney, *Christopher Isherwood: a Critical Biography* (London, 1979).

Issigonis, Alec Arnold Constantine (b. Smyrna, Ottoman Empire [now Izmir, Turkey], 18.11.1906). British automobile engineer. Son of a naturalized Briton, Issigonis was educated in the UK and spent his whole working life in the British motor industry, successively with Rootes Motors, the British Motor Corporation and British Leyland. He was perhaps the last in the line of great British engineer/designers that stretches back to Stephenson and Brunel. In 1959 he designed the Mini, the most successful car ever made in Britain. Seen as a bizarre aberration by some critics at the time, it quickly achieved universal popularity, setting the pace worldwide for small, economical and sophisticated cars. The Mini, not its fuel-hungry, befinned contemporaries from Detroit, was the car of the future. It has subsequently been imitated by every major car manufacturer. Issigonis was also responsible for the almost equally influential Morris Minor in 1948. DS

Ives, Charles Edward (b. Danbury, Conn., USA, 20.10.1874; d. West Riding, Conn., 19.5.1954). American composer. Almost all Ives's music was written before a heart attack in 1918. It abounds in unconventional ideas and audacious experiments. Working in obscurity, he explored atonality, the quotation of other (often popular) music, clashing metres and other devices with imagination. He composed in his spare time while running a successful insurance business, but he had trained with Horatio Parker at Yale, and could produce a professional fugue or symphony.

Ives's taste for musical adventure was stimulated by his father, and showed even during his Yale years, when such conventional works as his First String Quartet (composed 1896, performed 1957) were accompanied by such heterodox efforts as his setting of *Psalm 67* (composed 1898) in two keys throughout. Many of his later innovations were in his songs, ranging from imitations of German *lieder* to powerful, virtually atonal declamations, from serene hymns to boyish skits, from strident epigrams to homely parlour numbers. Often these songs were derived from chamber or orchestral pieces, or were later arranged for different forces.

His scores tend to be crowded with revisions, alternatives and deliberate impossibilities. What mattered, in his terms, was the 'substance' of the music and not its realization, a point of view developed in his *Essays before a Sonata*

(ed. H. Boatwright, London, 1969). This approach was influenced by New England transcendentalism, to which Ives paid homage in his 'Concord' Sonata for piano (composed 1909–15). Other compositions, notably the orchestral *Three Places in New England* (composed 1903–14, performed 1931), evoke the landscape and history of Ives's native region.

In creating such impressions of place and time Ives was willing to draw on existing music, especially marches, hymns and popular songs. Other orchestral works, such as the overture *Browning* (composed 1909, performed 1956), achieve their effects by an original and vigorous use of dissonant harmony, while several pieces for smaller forces, including *The Unanswered Question* for trumpet, four flutes and strings (composed 1908), investigate atonal organization.

Because Ives's music was little known until late in his life, his independence was not generally recognized before many of his techniques had entered the avant-garde stock. His influence has been small, though his achievements mark him out as the first great American composer.   PG

H. & S. Cowell, *Charles Ives and his Music* (NY, ²1969); H. W. Hitchcock, *Ives* (London, 1977).

J

Jackson, John Hughlings (b. Providence Green, Hammerton, N. Yorks., UK, 4.4.1835; d. London, 7.10.1911). British neurologist. A farmer's son of modest education, Jackson earned his way through a medical degree and from 1862 took up appointments at Moorfield's Eye Hospital, London Hospital and the National Hospital for the Paralysed and Epileptic. A cousin's wife's epilepsy (of a form now known as 'Jacksonian') led him to concentrate his research on seizures. Without the assistance of animal experiments or microscopy he formulated the basic principles of epilepsy by clinical observation and autopsy, including the important conclusion that its primary lesion is cerebrally localized. Jackson originated the idea of levels of control within the central nervous system, showed that specific brain areas were responsible for particular limb movements and postulated the now-confirmed hypothesis that seizure is due to 'over-discharge' of neurons. He did much to support the view, favoured today, of localized versus equipotential brain function. A founding editor of the influential journal *Brain* (1878), he is regarded as the founder of British neurology.   DOM

Jaeger, Werner Wilhelm (b. Lobberich, N. Rhine-Westphalia, Germany, 30.7.1888; d. Boston, Mass., USA, 19.10.1961). German classical philologist. Educated at the University of Berlin (1907–11) and taught by WILAMOWITZ-MOELLENDORFF, Hermann Diels, Edouard Norden and others, Jaeger showed an independence from the beginning by orientating himself to the problems of Greek thought and its history. Succeeding to Wilamowitz's chair at Berlin in 1921, he was forced to leave Germany for the USA in 1935, and was appointed professor of classics at Harvard in 1939. Jaeger's early work *Aristoteles. Grundlegung einer Geschichte seiner Entwicklung* (Berlin, 1923; tr. R. Robinson, *Aristotle: Fundamentals of the History of his Development*, Oxford,

1934, ²1948) has dominated Aristotle studies for half a century. The vision of civilizing humanism, originating in early Greek thought, was expressed in his study *Paideia. Die Formung des griechischen Menschen* (3 pts, Berlin, 1934–47; tr. G. Highet, *Paideia: the Ideals of Greek Culture*, 3 vols, Oxford, 1939–44). Jaeger's idealized concept of Greek education has subsequently been modified, but his central theme, the continuity of the Greek concept of man and the fusion of Hellenism and Christianity in Western culture, has exerted a broad influence, particularly in the USA.   KKS

A. M. Fiske, 'Introduction' to W. Jaeger, *Five Essays: with a Bibliography by Herbert Bloch* (Montreal, 1966).

Jaffe, Lionel Francis (b. New York, USA, 28.12.1927). American developmental biologist. Beginning as a student of mathematics, Jaffe completed his undergraduate education in biology and went to the California Institute of Technology where, somewhat in isolation at the institute's marine station, he completed a doctorate on initiation of polarized growth in embryos of the seaweed *Fucus*. His biophysical approach to fundamental developmental processes left him in continued isolation for some years, since most developmentalists, subsequent to the advances in molecular biology in the 1950s and 1960s, took a more biochemical approach. In 1964 Jaffe observed that an electrical voltage forms across *Fucus* eggs while they generate the initial asymmetry basic to further development. He and his collaborators then developed the vibrating probe, the first instrument capable of detecting the pattern of tiny ionic currents in many biological systems. His laboratory has gone on to demonstrate that movements of ions are a hitherto unexpected feature, possibly a control, of many developmental processes from fertilization to regeneration. The combination of a mechanistic, physiological approach with classical developmental thinking has enabled Jaffe and his co-workers to place the electrophysiological study of growth and development on a firm experimental and theoretical basis, promising to expand contemporary understanding of biological regulation in entirely new directions.   DOM

Jahnn, Hans Henny (b. Hamburg, Germany, 17.12.1894; d. Hamburg, West Germany, 29.11.1959). German novelist and dramatist. Early dramas on sexual and religious themes, notably *Pastor Ephraim Magnus* (Berlin, 1919), earned Jahnn a reputation for blasphemy and obscenity which long obscured the achievement of his later novels: *Perrudja* (Berlin, 1929); the trilogy *Fluss ohne Ufer* [River without banks] (*Das Holzschiff*, Munich, 1949, tr. C. Hutter, *The Ship*, NY, 1961; *Die Niederschrift des Gustav Anias Horn* [The notes of Gustav Anias Horn], Munich, 1950; *Epilog* [Epilogue], Frankfurt, 1961); *Die Nacht aus Blei* [The leaden night] (Hamburg, 1956). With the ethical rigour of the expressionist generation and the clinical toughness of the post-FREUDian era, Jahnn explored the spiritual confusions of his age, articulating a deeply tragic but sane and humane vision of life: resolutely anti-Christian, fiercely hostile to technological civilization and rooted in man's biological nature, yet free of the anti-intellectualism, moral relativism and anarchistic vitalism that led many of his contemporaries towards fascism. Jahnn sees man as both a physical being for whom self-fulfilment must lie in acceptance of his natural condition, and a moral being committed to charity and humanity in the face of the amorality of nature. He writes of love and death, ~~~os and male friendship, nature and animal life, science and art, especially music: Jahnn's love of music – he was a music publisher and organ designer of considerable reputation – influenced the 'contrapuntal' form of *Niederschrift*, his *magnum opus* written in exile during the HITLER era, a semi-autobiographical *Bildungsroman* which combines realism, myth, symbolic fantasy and surrealistic invention to trace the spiritual evolution of a fictitious composer amid the confusions and dilemmas of the 20c.   DEJ

Jakobson, Roman Osipovič (b. Moscow, Russia, 11.10.1896; naturalized American citizen; d. Boston, Mass., USA, 18.6.1982). Russian/American linguist, who was one of the founding members of the so-called 'Prague school'. He gained his first degree at Moscow University, where he was influenced by the ideas of the Russian linguist Baudouin de Courtenay. He obtained his doctorate at the University of Prague, and became a close friend of TRUBETZKOY. A professor at Masaryk University in Brno from 1933 to 1939, he was forced to leave Czechoslovakia by the Nazi occupation. After spending some time in Scandinavia, he eventually settled in the USA where he became professor both at Harvard (1949) and at MIT (1957). Jakobson made significant original contributions to a number of areas within linguistics, particularly in phonology (sound patterns). In historical phonology, he was one of the first to realize the interlinked nature of language changes, and in an important paper 'Prinzipien der historischen Phonologie' [Principles of historical phonology] (1931) he set up a schema for describing the realignments which can occur within a sound system as the result of a change. In his book *Kindersprache, Aphasie und allgemeine Lautgesetze* (Uppsala, 1941; tr. A. R. Keiler, *Child Language, Aphasia and Phonological Universals*, The Hague, 1968) he suggested that there might be a universal order of acquisition for speech sounds, a hypothesis which has triggered much subsequent important research. Following on from work done by Trubetzkoy, he continued to develop 'distinctive feature' theory, seeking to isolate those features or components of sound which serve to distinguish one phoneme (sound unit) from another. With Morris Halle he proposed in *Fundamentals of Language* (The Hague, 1956) that 12 binary oppositions (such as that between oral and nasal) might be sufficient to account for the contrasts found in all the languages of the world, a view which has strongly influenced subsequent phonological theory. A prolific and wide-ranging scholar, Jakobson has written several books and nearly 500 articles and reviews, of which a number of important ones are republished in *Selected Writings* (6 vols, The Hague, 1962–82).

JMA

Jamāl al-Dīn, Afghani, see AFGHĀNI (ASADĀBĀDĪ), JAMĀL AL-DĪN.

James, Cyril Lionel Robert (b. Chaguanas, Trinidad [now Trinidad and Tobago], 4.1.1891). West Indian historian and political writer. A highly original political theorist in the 1930s, he has continued to produce books on a wide range of topics but linked always by their scholarly approach and concern for human freedoms. *The Case for West Indian Self-Government* (London, 1933) remains a model today, and in the novel *Minty Alley* (London, 1936) he revealed the imaginative talents that inform much of his work, nowhere more than in *Beyond a Boundary* (London, 1963), a book apparently on cricket but ranging across politics, culture and human relations. It is arguably his finest work, because the most complete reflection of the man. *The Black Jacobins: Toussaint L'Ouverture and the San Domingo Revolution* (London, 1938) is an outstanding study of human aspirations and the colonial mind.

PNQ

James, Henry (b. New York, USA, 15.4.1843; naturalized British citizen, 1915; d. London, UK, 28.2.1916). American/British novelist, short-story writer and literary critic. His father was a well-known Swedenborgian philosopher and one of his brothers, William JAMES, a philosopher and psychologist. Educated in both the USA and Europe, he settled in London in 1876, where he was to spend most of his life. He never married. James's work is seen both as the culmination of the 19c realist tradition of Austen, Balzac, Flaubert and others, and as a decisive move towards the experimental novel of modernism. Similarly he is taken as one of the first writers to bring American literature into a cosmopolitan context, so important for the expatriates who succeeded him.

His writing is usually seen as falling into three broad periods. The first, starting with his second novel *Roderick Hudson* (Boston, Mass., 1876) and *The American* (Boston, Mass., 1877), and containing such masterpieces as *The Europeans* (London, 1878), *Washington Square* (NY, 1881), *The Portrait of a Lady* (London, 1881) and the novella *Daisy Miller* (NY, 1879), is largely concerned with the collision between the American and European cultures and the resulting bewilderment, misunderstandings and tragedies. James's major achievement here lies in remaining unbiased, and exploring both cultures as coherent social and ideological structures with their own moral codes, classes and roles. He refuses to judge, and the reader is prevented from judging the protagonists by standards external to their own context, and it is only within those contexts that discriminations and values can be made.

In the second phase James used similar techniques to explore sexual roles and feminism in America in *The Bostonians* (London, 1886); class conflict and revolution in England in *The Princess Casamassima* (London, 1886); the relationship between acting and social role playing in *The Tragic Muse* (Boston, Mass., 1890); and cultural change and the generational conflict in *The Awkward Age* (London, 1899). By dramatizing the points of view, withdrawing narrative comment and by focusing upon conflict, a heightened sense is achieved of the social materials out of which consciousness and identity are formed, as in the case of the growth of a child in *What Maisie Knew* (London, 1897).

In the final phase James's style becomes more convoluted as it traces all the relationships which define and enmesh his protagonists and which decisions or actions seem to crudify. The great novels of this period (*The Wings of the Dove*, NY, 1902; *The Ambassadors*, London, 1903; and *The Golden Bowl*, NY, 1904), together with their forerunner *The Sacred Fount* (NY, 1901) centre upon secrets, lies and half-truths from which power and value emerge not by revelation, but by reticence or by silent acknowledgement. People are bound by what they share and by what lies unspoken between them. Because these works do not endorse accepted moral codes of self/society, aesthetic/ethical dichotomies, they have always been controversial and often regarded as 'art for art's sake'. James has been treated as an aesthete, as a 'realist' and as a constructor of elaborate and empty verbal games where any 'truth' is unavailable. However, his status will finally rest on his acute vision of the structures of consciousness and identity.

DTC

D. Krook, *The Ordeal of Consciousness in Henry James* (Cambridge, 1962); J. A. Ward, *The Search for Form* (Chapel Hill, NC, 1967).

James, William (b. New York, USA, 11.1.1842; d. Chocura, NH, 26.8.1910). American philosopher and psychologist. James was the oldest of the five children of Henry James, a Swedenborgian theologian, and brother of Henry JAMES the novelist. The family were in Europe from 1855 to 1860, where he experienced erratic schooling in several countries; it returned to the USA in 1860, eventually settling in Cambridge, Massachusetts, which remained James's hometown for life. Decision on a career proved difficult. He began as an art student, then entered the Harvard Medical School in 1863, graduating MD in 1869 after such interruptions as an expedition up the Amazon under the naturalist Louis Agassiz, periods of that ill health and depression which dogged him throughout life, and study in Germany. He joined the Harvard staff as an instructor in anatomy and physiology (1873), subsequently becoming assistant professor of philosophy (1880), professor of philosophy (1885), of psychology (1889), and again of philosophy (1897). He was happily married and had five children. He paid several long visits to Europe, giving the Gifford lectures in Edinburgh in 1901–2: *The Varieties of Religious Experience: a Study in Human Nature* (NY, 1902). *The Principles of Psychology* (2 vols, NY, 1890), which established him as a major thinker, massively sums up the then state of psychology and points forward constructively in two directions, to an objective laboratory psychology, and to a phenomenological study of the stream of consciousness, James's concept of which has been influential in philosophy, psychology and literature. Though James

played an important part in establishing American experimental psychology, his own strength lay in reflective description of normal and abnormal thought, motivation and mental capacity.

James's mature philosophy consists of pragmatism (*Pragmatism*, NY, 1907) and radical empiricism (*Essays in Radical Empiricism*, NY, 1912). The former (influenced by but distinct from that of PEIRCE), often misrepresented as identifying truth with what one happens to like believing, teaches that it is not the role of thought to picture its objects but to promote a fruitful conceptual, behavioural and emotional adjustment to them. The latter teaches that what ultimately exists are innumerable streams of experience which constitute minds in one kind of arrangement and physical things in another. With enthusiastically acclaimed affinities to BERGSON's thought, it points forward to the process philosophy of WHITEHEAD. James was the most effective critic of the absolute idealism of F. H. Bradley and Royce (see *A Pluralistic Universe*, NY, 1909), but allied with them in attacking the psychological atomism of traditional empiricism. His thought always retained the strong moral and personal dimension exhibited in the decision made in his youth to overcome depression by using his free will to believe in free will.

TLSS

R. B. Perry, *The Thought and Character of William James* (Boston, Mass., 1935); B. Kuklick, *The Rise of American Philosophy* (Yale, 1977).

Janáček, Leoš Eugen (b. Hukvaldy, Moravia, Austria-Hungary [now Czechoslovakia], 3.7.1854; d. Ostrava, 12.8.1928). Czech composer. For much of his career he lived in Brno, enjoying only a local reputation. In 1916, when his opera *Její pastorkyňa* (*Jenufa*, 1904) was performed in Prague, he came to much wider attention, and was encouraged to write a rapid succession of major works. These include the boldly scored *Sinfonietta* (1926), the exhilarating *Glagolská mše* (*Glagolitic Mass*, 1927) and two string quartets (1924 and 1928), all of them highly individual, sometimes even quirky, being based on short irregular phrases of modal character. Janáček's greatest achievements came in the operas of his late period: *Výlety páně Broučkovy* (*The Excursions of Mr Brouček*, 1920), *Káťa Kabanová* (*Kaťa Kabanova*, 1921), *Příhody Lišky Bystroušky* (*The Cunning Little Vixen*, 1924), *Věc Makropulos* (*The Makropoulos Case*, 1926) and *Z mrtvého domu* (*From the House of the Dead*, 1930). Widely varied in dramatic tone and setting, these works show his ability to depict characters by means of swift imaginative strokes, to follow the words (usually his own) naturally yet with extreme intensity, and to achieve dramatic effects through a very personal use of the orchestra, involving stark sonorities and rapid developments of motifs. The late operas also reveal his taste for the bizarre and unusual. *Mr Brouček* is a comic fantasy which finds a commonplace man transported to the moon and to the 15c; *The Cunning Little Vixen* is an unpatronizing story of animal life; *The Makropoulos Case* shows the empty fate of a woman who has magically prolonged her existence for 300 years; and *From the House of the Dead* is an austere setting of incidents from Dostoevsky's prison-camp novel. Yet, as *Katya Kabanova* proves, Janáček was moved above all by the inner lives of human beings and by their tragic destinies.   PG

E. Chisholm, *The Operas of Leoš Janáček* (London, 1971); M. Ewans, *Janáček's Tragic Operas* (London, 1977); I. Horsbrugh, *Leoš Janáček* (London, 1982).

Janet, Pierre-Marie-Félix (b. Paris, France, 30.5.1859; d. Paris, 24.2.1947). French psychologist and neurologist. Originally employed as a philosophy teacher, Janet reported a case of hypnosis in 1882 and thereby came to the attention of the Parisian neurologist Jean Charcot who had a particular interest in hypnosis and whose clinics at the Salpêtrière Hospital (the largest mental institution in Paris) attracted students from all over the world. Janet's first academic work under Charcot's supervision dealt with the unconscious mind and led to his being appointed to a position at the Salpêtrière. Incidentally, one of Charcot's other students was a young man called FREUD who shared Janet's interest in the unconscious mind but whose own writings and skills as a self-publicist helped him acquire a much larger audience and greater fame. In the final years of the 19c and the first years of the 20c Janet classified such disorders as amnesia and sleepwalking and consolidated his reputation. One of his important contributions to psychology was his suggestion that hysteria is, like hypnosis, the result of a suggestion being planted in the individual's mind. He explained that patients suffering from different forms of hysteria often had selfish hypocritical parents or came from poor domestic environments. In 1902 Janet was appointed a professor at the Collège de France, a post he held until 1936. His Harvard lectures were published as *The Major Symptoms of Hysteria* (NY, 1907). He worked as a practising physician and wrote and lectured on neuroses, obsessions, anorexia and other syndromes. His major contribution was to link theoretical psychology with modern clinical neurological practices.   VC

Jansky, Karl Guthe (b. Norman, Okla, USA, 22.10.1905; d. Red Bank, NJ, 14.2.1950). American radio engineer and an early pioneer of radio astronomy. He studied physics at Wisconsin University where his father was professor of electrical engineering; in 1928 he joined the Bell Telephone laboratories. Here he was given the task of investigating the directional properties of radio static. He constructed a large directional array working at a wavelength of 14.6m, which could be turned about a vertical axis at the rate of one revolution in 20 minutes. After a year Jansky concluded that the observed maxima in flux are related to sidereal time, and that there is therefore an extraterrestrial component of static. This he located as coming mainly from the direction of the centre of the galaxy. He was puzzled by his inability to detect the sun, and suggested that other celestial bodies might radiate more strongly in the radio region than the sun relatively to their optical radiation. Jansky's study was not pursued by the Bell laboratories, but inspired another pioneer, Grote Reber, to make a 31-ft reflector in 1937 with which he made a radio map of the Milky Way. The topic was not taken up by the astronomical community until after WW2, and then partly through the discovery of solar radio emission by J. S. Hey during WW2. A commonly used unit of radio flux (1 watt $m^{-2}Hz^{-1}$) is named the Jansky. DEB

Jarry, Alfred (b. Laval, Mayenne, France, 8.9.1873; d. Paris, 1.11.1907). French dramatist whose farce *Ubu roi* (1896; tr. B. Wright, London, 1951) is widely regarded as a milestone in the history of the European avant-garde theatre. It is a kind of parody of *Macbeth* in which an avaricious, cowardly and grotesque buffoon Ubu, is egged on by his awful wife to murder the royal family and feather his own nest. He establishes a reign of terror before being defeated by the Tsar and forced into exile. The casual violence of the plot, truculent farcical tone and rapid tempo are combined with a set of highly stylized stage conventions (clowning, masks, fantasticated costumes, cardboard horses' heads, a single painted back-drop) to produce the impression of a crazy never-never land through which the principal character moves like some monstrous puppet. In its frank subversion of authority and savage attack on existing moral and aesthetic values *Ubu roi* opens the way to 20c experimental drama. Jarry's view of the actor as puppet actually prefigures CRAIG's *Übermarionette*. Jarry's other works confirm his mannered style, infantile taste for scatology and antireligious bias. *Gestes et opinions du Docteur Faustroll* [Deeds and views of Dr Faustroll] (Paris, 1911) explains his 'pataphysics' or science of imaginary solutions; it became a favourite text of surrealism. SBJ

R. Shattuck, *The Banquet Years* (London, ²1969); M. M. LaBelle, *Alfred Jarry. Nihilism and the Theater of the Absurd* (NY, 1980).

Jaspers, Karl Theodor (b. Oldenburg, Lower Saxony, Germany, 23.2.1883; d. Basle, Switzerland, 26.2.1969). German philosopher. Jaspers began his intellectual career as a medical student and went on to carry out research in a psy-

chiatric clinic, publishing a textbook on psychopathology in 1913. From 1921 to 1937 he was a professor of philosophy at Heidelberg until dismissed by the Nazis for having a Jewish wife. In 1948 he settled in Basle. His form of existentialism, expounded in his *Philosophie* (3 vols, Berlin, 1932; tr. E. B. Ashton, *Philosophy*, 3 vols, Chicago, 1967–71), is more genial and less anguished than that of HEIDEGGER. It is also less technical in expression, owing little or nothing to the phenomenology of HUSSERL. Jaspers's central idea is that Being, or Pure Being which is in effect God disguised in plain clothes, inevitably escapes our efforts at apprehension. Existence eludes the conceptual intellect and all attempts at inclusive intellectual systematization must fail. At the limit of the intellect's reach we must make a leap; an echo of KIERKEGAARD's hostile reaction to the all-explanatory system of Hegel. AQ

P. A. Schilpp (ed.), *The Philosophy of Karl Jaspers* (NY, 1957).

Jeans, James Hapgood (b. Ormskirk, Lancs., UK, 11.9.1877; d. Dorking, Surrey, 16.9.1946). British physicist, mathematician and astronomer, noted for his contribution to the classical description of radiation, his theory of the origin of the solar system and his popular scientific and philosophical writings. Jeans was educated at Cambridge. His early research was devoted to theoretical physics and he made important contributions to classical physical ideas in the fields of mechanics and the theory of gases, on which he wrote a standard textbook *The Dynamical Theory of Gases* (Cambridge, 1904). He contributed to the classical mathematical description of radiation, which was also developed by RAYLEIGH; the Rayleigh–Jeans formula still finds application for long wavelength radiation although only the quantum mechanical expression is universal. Jeans then turned to stellar dynamics and proposed the theory, detailed mathematically, that the planets of the solar system could have been formed by the tidal interaction of a passing star on the material of the sun. Such an interaction could have pulled out a cigar-shaped bridge of material from the sun to the passing star out of which the planets formed. This theory and the contrasting ideas of Laplace, who postulated the formation of planets from a tenuous nebula surrounding the forming sun, are the two main theories on which cosmogony has since rested. Jeans also worked on the problem of stellar formation and showed that there was a minimum mass of material required for condensation into a star, given the density and temperature of the prestellar gas cloud. Such a minimum mass is now called the Jeans mass. It came as a great surprise when, after publishing his last scientific text *Astronomy and Cosmogony* (Cambridge, 1926), Jeans decided to give up research and turn his gifts as a writer to popularizing science. *The Universe Around Us* (London, 1929) was the first outstanding popular work on astronomy. Jeans followed this up with a number of books (e.g. *The Mysterious Universe*, London, 1930; *The Growth of Physical Science*, London, 1948) and broadcasts that made him the best-known scientist in Britain. His belief that 'the Great Architect now begins to appear as a pure mathematician' underlay his philosophy about which he wrote in *Physics and Philosophy* (London, 1942). MJS

Jeffreys, Harold (b. Harraton, Durham, UK, 22.4.1891). British geophysicist and mathematician. Since entering St John's College to read mathematics, Jeffreys has spent his whole academic life at Cambridge, where he was elected Plumian professor of astronomy in 1946. His book *The Earth: its Origin, History and Physical Constitution* (Cambridge, 1924, [6]1976) presented a consistent account of the earth's internal structure based on much seemingly inconsistent data drawn from different disciplines. His interest in earthquakes then led him to his main area of work, theoretical seismology, and his earthquake travel timetables, first presented in the 1930s and later revised with K. E. Bullen, are still standard in the field. The statistical difficulties in analysing earthquake data led Jeffreys to publish a controversial book *Scientific Inference* (Cambridge, 1931, [3]1973) on the theory of probability. An early advocate of deep boring through the ocean floor, a pro-

gramme begun in the 1950s, he also wrote papers on the shape and constitution of the moon and the planets, and on aero- and hydrodynamics. In mathematics he wrote papers on the asymptotic solution of differential equations and on HEAVISIDE's operator calculus, and with his wife Bertha Swirles Jeffreys a standard volume *Operational Methods of Mathematical Physics* (Cambridge, 1931, [3]1956). A pioneer of geophysics, he remains a vehement critic of the hypothesis of continental drift, arguing that the driving-forces proposed by WEGENER were physically impossible. He rejects plate tectonics, despite the wealth of evidence that has persuaded the majority of geologists to accept its basic tenets. JJG/AH

Jennings, William Ivor (b. Bristol, Avon, UK, 19.5.1903; d. Cambridge, 19.12.1965). British constitutional lawyer and theorist. Educated at Cambridge, and called to the Bar in 1928, he lectured in law at Leeds (1925–9), then joined the London School of Economics where he remained until 1940, establishing his reputation in English law. Along with a number of books on technical areas of law he wrote three works which confirmed him as a leading authority in the field of constitutional law and practice. *Law and the Constitution* (London, 1933) was a major review of the nature and content of the conventions of the constitution which, like DICEY's *Law of the Constitution* (1885), attains the status of an extralegal authoritative source of that constitution. In *Cabinet Government* (London, 1936) and *Parliament* (London, 1937) he traced the development and interrelation of the two bodies, seeing the contest of party as organized, legitimately different opinion as the central feature of British government. Committed to the Commonwealth, he was the first head of the University of Ceylon (1940–56) and was involved in constitution-drafting for Ceylon, Pakistan and Malaysia, later returning to Cambridge as master of Trinity Hall. DCr

Jensen, Georg (b. Raadvad, E. Jutland, Denmark, 31.8.1866; d. Copenhagen, 2.10.1935). Danish silversmith. Jensen's name is associated not only with his work but also with the firm which he founded and which still produces high-quality modern designs in silver and stainless steel. Following his apprenticeship to a goldsmith in Copenhagen, Jensen studied sculpture at the Danish Academy of Fine Arts. Although he abandoned his ambition to be a sculptor when he became a silversmith, he always described himself as an 'orfèvre sculpteur'. In 1904 he opened his first shop in Copenhagen, at first producing reasonably priced silver jewellery embellished with semiprecious stones and his characteristic motifs of flowers and insects. He was joined by the artist Johan Rohde who complemented Jensen's decorative designs with designs of severity using restrained surface decoration. With Harald Neilsen he established the firm's international reputation for well-designed silverware and jewellery. Standards were maintained in the post-WW2 period through the employment of talented young architects, artists and designers such as the sculptor Henning Koppel and the architect Magnus Stephensen. The products of the firm today include innovatory designs as well as revivals of earlier styles.   JMFR

Georg Jensen Silversmithy, 77 Artists 75 Years, exh. cat., Renwick Gallery (Washington, DC, 1980).

Jeremias, Joachim (b. Dresden, Germany [now East Germany], 20.9.1900; d. Tübingen, Baden-Württemberg, West Germany, 6.9.1979). German New Testament scholar. Jeremias was professor in Greifswald from 1929 and from 1935 in Göttingen, where his pastoral concern during the period of Nazism was noteworthy. He concentrated his unrivalled knowledge of the language, history and topography of 1c Palestine on recovering the historical teaching of Jesus, notably in *Die Abendmahlsworte Jesu* (Göttingen, 1935, ⁴1967; tr. N. Perrin, *The Eucharistic Words of Jesus*, London, 1966) and *Die Gleichnisse Jesu* (Göttingen, 1947, ⁸1970; tr. S. H. Hooke, *Parables of Jesus*, London, 1954, ²1963) which developed the work of DODD. Both the historical thrust of his work and the theological importance he attached to this are evident in his *Neutestamentliche*

Theologie (Gütersloh, 1971; tr. J. Bowden, *The Theology of the New Testament*, London, 1971, of which only this first volume appeared: *The Proclamation of Jesus*. This centre of interest placed him outside the mainstream of German theology dominated by BARTH and BULTMANN, but made him especially influential in the UK. His positive conclusions achieved through use of form-critical methods (i.e. the attempt to discern the form taken by a story or teaching in order to make it more easily memorable, or more impressive, as it was passed on in oral tradition) created a bridgehead for this approach in the Anglo-Saxon world at a time when German scepticism was still widely distrusted.   RM

Jespersen, Jens Otto Harry (b. Randers, Jutland, Denmark, 16.7.1860; d. Roskilde, Zealand, 30.4.1943). Danish linguist. As professor of English at the University of Copenhagen (1893–1925), Jespersen was one of the most important Anglists and general linguists in the first decades of this century, and several of his books are now classics in their field, notably *Modern English Grammar* (7 vols, Copenhagen, 1909–49), a major work occupying much of his professional life, *Language* (London, 1922) and *The Philosophy of Grammar* (London, 1924). After an early study of law he devoted himself entirely to his main interest from childhood, language and languages. In his early professional years he was involved with the neogrammarian question and with phonetics, in which he associated himself with Henry Sweet. Subsequently he concentrated on the history and structure of English, on general linguistic theory and on syntactic analysis. While he developed a formal method in syntax which in some respects anticipated present-day transformational practice, his emphasis was on language in actual use and on language teaching. Always concerned with language as a key to international understanding he devised an auxiliary language of his own, Novial, which was highly praised by G. B. SHAW among others.   RHR

N. Haislund, 'Otto Jespersen 1860–1943', *Englische Studien*, 75 (1943), 273–

83; P. Christophersen, 'Otto Jespersen: a retrospect', *Transactions of the Philological Society* (1972), 1–19.

Jiménez, Juan Ramón (b. Moguer, Huelva, Spain, 23.12.1881; d. San Juan de Puerto Rico, 29.5.1958). Spanish poet. Unkind critics have said that Juan Ramón sang continuously whether inspiration breathed or not; but his lyrical inspiration was normally of a very high order. His earliest works belong to *modernismo*, but he discarded these when selecting his successive *Antolojías* [Anthologies] (*Poesía escojida*, Madrid, 1917; *Segunda antolojia poética*, Madrid, 1922; *Antolojia poética*, Buenos Aires, 1944; *Tercera antolojia poética*, Madrid, 1957; selections tr. J. B. Trend in *Fifty Spanish Poems*, Oxford, 1950, and tr. E. Roach, *Three Hundred Poems 1903–1953*, Austin, 1962). The balance of his 'first period' (down to c. 1916) retains a romantic aura of melancholy, with echoes of Heine, Verlaine, Rimbaud. But he will be remembered for his 'second period' (which lasted 40 years), starting with the establishment of his truly personal style in *Eternidades* [Eternities] (Madrid, 1918), with its cult of purity and precision in the pursuit of absolute beauty and its exploration of the essentiality of 'things' in a time-bound world. It combines musicality and lightness with a warmth of feeling lacking in GUILLÉN, and his religious instinct subsumes an element of nature mysticism. But his best loved and most read book undoubtedly remains *Platero y yo* (1914, Madrid, 1917; tr. W. & M. Roberts, *Platero and I*, Oxford, 1958), an endearing and whimsical evocation of his donkey Platero, written in a limpid poetic prose whose apparent simplicity is highly deceptive. He was awarded the Nobel prize for literature in 1956.   RP-M

H. T. Young, *Juan Ramón Jiménez* (NY, 1967); P. Olson, *Circle of Paradox: Time and Essence in the Poetry of Juan Ramón Jiménez* (Baltimore, 1967).

Jinnah, Mohammed Ali (b. Karachi, Sind, India [now Pakistan], 25.12.1876; d. Karachi, 11.9.1948). Founder and first governor-general of Pakistan. A Muslim Indian, he left the Indian Congress party in 1934 as a result of opposition to its domination by its Hindu majority and by M. GANDHI's policy of civil disobedience, in order to found the Muslim League. From 1940 he campaigned for the partition of India and the establishment of a Muslim state, Pakistan, as a separate dominion within the British Commonwealth. He supported Indian participation in WW2 against Germany and Japan, and won almost every seat in the areas with a Muslim majority in the India-wide elections held in 1946. His demands for a 'six-province' Pakistan including the Punjab, Bengal and Assam failed to win British acceptance, and his Muslim League adherents turned to 'direct action'. The resultant riots and mass killings led the British to accept and impose partition. Jinnah achieved his object of a separate Pakistan, but his vision of Pakistan as a modernist and modernizing political state did not long survive his death.

DCW

Johannsen, Wilhelm Ludwig (b. Copenhagen, Denmark, 3.2.1857; d. Copenhagen, 11.11.1927). Danish plant geneticist. The son of an army officer, Johannsen first entered science as an apprentice pharmacist. Qualifying in 1879, he went to the newly created Carlsberg laboratory as an assistant in chemistry two years later. In 1887 he resigned his post in order to free himself for work in applied botany. Although lacking formal training in plant science he visited several European centres, notably Helsinki and Vienna, in furthering his self-education. Before the rediscovery of MENDEL's work he was already deeply interested in the inheritance of quantitative characters and impressed by the approach of GALTON to its study. He was ideally prepared to appreciate the importance of Mendelism and also to analyse the effects of selection on Mendelian populations. In 1903, the year in which he was appointed professor of botany and plant physiology at the Copenhagen Agricultural College, he published an epoch-making paper 'Uber Erblichkeit in Populationen und in reinen Linien' [On heredity in populations and in pure lines] in which the use of so-called pure lines in the analysis of variability was established. He also published, at first in Danish (1905), a text-book of genetics which was of great influence in Europe. A revised edition in German (*Elemente der exakten Erblichkeitslehre* [Elements of the exact science of heredity], Jena, 1909, ³1926) saw the introduction of the key concepts of genotype and phenotype into biology and the coining of the word 'gene'. DRN

John XXIII, *né* Angelo Roncalli (b. Sotto il Monte, Bergamo, Italy, 25.11.1881; d. Vatican City, 3.6.1963). Italian pope. As a young priest, Roncalli was secretary to the progressive bishop of Bergamo, Radini Tedeschi. An army chaplain in WW1, Roncalli then became a Vatican diplomat, serving in Bulgaria (1925–35), Turkey (1935–44) and France (1945–52). He went home to Venice as patriarch and fully expected to end his days there. Surprisingly elected pope in October 1958, it was widely believed he would be simply a caretaker. But in 1959 he announced that he was summoning an ecumenical council: known as the Second Vatican Council, and not completed until three years after his death, yet it bears his imprint. He was concerned with the *aggiornamento* [bringing up to date] of the church. He distinguished between the substance of a doctrine and the way in which it was expressed. This opened up possibilities of dialogue with other Christians and with 'all men of good will'. He ended the Manichaean approach to MARXism by distinguishing between the error (always to be rejected) and the one who errs (always to be esteemed). He embodied this optimism in his final encyclical letter *Pacem in Terris* (1963), which goes far beyond the institutional defence of the church to proclaim the rights of man, whoever they are, wherever they may be. After his death, passages from his diaries appeared as *Il Giornale dell'Anima* (Rome, 1964; tr. D. White, *Journal of a Soul*, London, 1965). Subsequent debate has centred on whether he was a naive holy man who did not foresee the future, or whether, as a cunning old peasant, he knew perfectly well what he was up to. PAH

L. Elliott, *I Will Be Called John* (London, 1974); G. Zizola, *The Utopia of Pope John XXIII* (NY, 1978).

John Paul II, *né* Karol Wojtyła (b. Wadowice, Poland, 20.5.1920). Polish pope. As Poland collapsed in 1939, Wojtyla, son of a widowed army officer, was studying Polish literature at Jagiellonian University in Kraków. He was also an actor of some talent. During the German occupation he worked in a stone quarry – and later published poems about his experiences. Ordained priest in 1946, he wrote a thesis at the Angelicum University in Rome on 'The concept of faith in St John of the Cross'. As he advanced in his ecclesiastical career – bishop, 1958; archbishop of Kraków, 1964; cardinal, 1967 – he continued to work at philosophy, particularly on the system of SCHELER, and remained influenced by phenomenology as a philosophical method. This was evident in his major work *Osoba i czyn* (Lublin, 1969; *The Acting Person*, Dordrecht, 1979). Elected pope on 16.10.1978, he used modern methods to state old truths. In spectacular mass rallies in country after country he sought to define and affirm a clear sense of Catholic identity after the (in his judgement) postconciliar confusion. John Paul is a 'populist'. He appeals to the people over the heads of intellectuals. He dealt severely with the Swiss theologian KÜNG, withdrawing from him the title of 'Catholic theologian'. Yet he asserted human rights, especially in his native Poland. An attempted assassination in May 1981 shocked the world and earned him much sympathy. He made an astonishingly good recovery and resumed his spectacular globe-trotting. PAH

J. Whale (ed.), *The Pope from Poland* (London, 1980); P. Hebblethwaite, *Introducing John Paul II* (London, 1982).

Johns, Jasper (b. Augusta, Ga, USA, 15.5.1930). American painter, sculptor and printmaker. After military service in Japan, he settled in New York in 1949, and in 1954–5 established his mature style with a series of relief-like encaustic paintings of banal images such as targets, maps of the USA, and the US flag (e.g. *Flag*, 1954; *Target with Four*

Faces, 1955) which he referred to as 'preformed, conventional, depersonalized, factual, exterior elements'. He executed these images with a realistic precision which is paradoxically negated by the emphasis on surface texture, thus insisting on the work of art as an object in itself rather than as a reproduction of something else. In his search for impersonal images he painted number charts (e.g. *Number in Color*, 1959) and alphabets. In 1958 he began making realistically painted bronze sculptures of everyday objects like flags, a light bulb, and a coffee can filled with paint brushes; or two beer cans (e.g. *Painted Bronze [Beer Cans]*, 1960). Although these DUCHAMP-inspired immortalizations of the commonplace provided the point of departure for New York Pop art, Johns's hand-painted finish and use of an integral base set his objects apart as 'art', a problem which Roy Lichtenstein and WARHOL sought to overcome with commercial techniques. Johns never fully eradicated the 'artistic' elements in his work, and in 1959 began to emphasize the painterliness of his works with bold, expressive splashes of vivid colour often combined with lettering or numbers (e.g. *The black figure 5*, 1960). In the 1960s he began a long series of nonobjective paintings with objects attached to them (e.g. *According to What*, 1964), confirming his preoccupation with the nature and process of art. This conflict between painterliness and precision continued in his work of the 1970s, especially in his use of a clearly defined linear cross-hatching motif which appears expressive and gestural (e.g. *Weeping Women*, 1975).   SOBT

M. Chrichton, *Jasper Johns*, (exh. cat., Whitney Museum of American Art (NY, 1977).

Johnson, Eyvind (b. Boden, Norrbotten, Sweden, 29.7.1900; d. Stockholm, 25.8.1976). Swedish novelist. Proletarian in his origins, cosmopolitan in his literary affiliations, Johnson represents a Europeanly modernist line within Swedish literature, with PROUST, GIDE and JOYCE as his acknowledged models. His debut as a novelist was in the late 1920s; and between 1925 and 1934 he had published no fewer than eight novels before he made a decisive breakthrough with the first of his four autobiographical 'Novels about Olof': *Nu var det 1914* (Stockholm, 1934; tr. M. Sandbach, *1914*, London, 1970), *Här har du ditt liv!* [Here is your life] (Stockholm, 1935), *Se dig inte om!* [Don't look back] (Stockholm, 1936) and *Slutspel in ungdomen* [Finale in youth] (Stockholm, 1937). These he followed up with his so-called '*Krilon*' trilogy (1941–3) reflecting conditions in Sweden during the early years of WW2. In 1946 he moved into a – for him – new and experimental field with his very Joycean *Strändernas svall* (Stockholm, 1946; tr. M. Michael, *Return to Ithaca*, London, 1952), a modern retelling of the *Odyssey*. *Hans nådes tid* (Stockholm, 1960; *The Days of His Grace*, London, 1965, tr. E. H. Schubert, London, 1968) also discovers modern connotations in the age of Charlemagne. Marvellously inventive, audaciously experimental, he has created a highly personal idiom for himself within the field of the modern Swedish novel. Johnson was awarded the Nobel prize for literature in 1976.   JWMcF

G. Orton, *Eyvind Johnson* (NY, 1972).

Johnson, Harry Gordon (b. Toronto, Ont., Canada, 26.5.1923; d. Geneva, Switzerland, 9.5.1977). Canadian economist. One of the most prolific and energetic economists that has ever lived, Johnson combined an immense output of books, pamphlets, articles and reviews with ceaseless travel to lecture and advise. A graduate of Toronto and Cambridge universities, and fellow of King's College, Cambridge (1949–56), he held chairs at various universities, most notably Manchester (1956–9), Chicago (1959–77) and the London School of Economics (1966–74). His chief strength as an economist lay in his ability to synthesize lucidly diverse views and approaches on particular topics. In his own special field of international trade, however, his work also included many original contributions, such as the concept of an 'optimum tariff'. The collections *International Trade and Economic Growth* (Cambridge, Mass., 1958) and *Aspects of the Theory of Tariffs* (London, 1971) contain many of his best papers on international trade theory. The other main areas of his work were macroeconomics, international monetary theory and questions of science policy, though he is probably best known for such controversial views as that trade and not aid constitutes the best assistance rich countries can give to poor countries, and that 'brain drain' is not detrimental to Third World countries. In later years he was increasingly opposed to interventionist policies. Collections such as *Further Essays in Monetary Economics* (Cambridge, Mass., 1972), *Macroeconomics and Monetary Theory* (London, 1972) and *The Theory of Income Distribution* (London, 1973) contain good examples of his work in all these areas. PS

Johnson, Lyndon Baines (b. Stonewall, Tex., USA, 27.8.1908; d. San Antonio, Tex., 22.1.1973). American politician. Member of the US House of Representatives (1937–48), senator (1948–60) for Texas and leader of the Democratic majority in the Senate (1956–60), vice-president (1961–3), president (1963–8). Born in a poor background in Texas, his rise to political power (and considerable wealth) never purged his mind of his admiration for Franklin ROOSEVELT, his advocacy of federal action to relieve rural and urban poverty, or his feelings of hostility towards and rejection by the private-university-educated upper-middle-class elites of the east and northeast. Generally agreed to be the greatest master of the arts of managing the Senate and the federal government in the 20c, he demonstrated this skill on his succession to the presidency after the assassination of President KENNEDY, by gaining in the 1964 elections the largest majority hitherto achieved by any 20c president and by passing through Congress a programme of civil rights, social welfare and federal aid to education, which successive Democratic administrators had dreamed of, since TRUMAN had launched them in 1948. These very substantial achievements were however offset in the public mind by American involvement in the war in Vietnam and the atmosphere of deceit and wilful misrepresentation at every level which enveloped it, divisions which ran concurrently with outbreaks of urban vio-

lence among those for whom the federal guarantee of civil rights seemed to make no difference to their economic situation or their acceptability to dominant sections of those ethnic groups which lay above them in the social scale. The Vietnamese Tet offensive in February 1968, though a military defeat for its initiators, so destroyed American trust in Johnson, who was known to have been driven by his own obsession with detail into participation in much of the day-to-day conduct of the war, as to cause him to announce that he would not be a candidate for re-election in the presidential elections in November in which his chosen candidate, HUMPHREY, was defeated by NIXON.

DCW

Johnson, Philip Cortelyou (b. Cleveland, Ohio, USA, 8.7.1906). American architect, architectural historian and museum curator. Johnson occupies a unique place in 20c American architecture. As historian and critic he was a leader in the introduction of European modernism into American architecture. As museum curator he was the first director (1930–6) of the innovative department of architecture of the Museum of Modern Art, New York, where he also encouraged the exhibition of modern industrial design. As a practising architect he has designed a small number of extremely influential houses in the Miesian tradition, and more recently a succession of large institutional and commercial buildings.

At university Johnson first studied classics and then history of art; his primary interest was in the history of modern architecture. He arranged the first visits to the USA of both LE CORBUSIER and MIES VAN DER ROHE. In association with an exhibition of modern architecture which he mounted at the Museum of Modern Art he published, with Henry-Russell Hitchcock, an important book *The International Style* (NY, 1932) which analysed the aesthetic characteristics of the new architecture. It is noteworthy that social concerns, which were so much a part of the new architecture in Europe, were not seriously discussed. Johnson returned to study at Harvard in 1940 and qualified as an architect in 1943. Since then he has been in private practice, although from 1946 to 1954 he again acted as director of the department of architecture at the Museum of Modern Art. His architecture is urbane, refined in finishes and details, and composed of elemental masses; as a corpus, his work lacks consistency of direction, and it draws upon a wide range of historical sources, with an emphasis on romantic neoclassicism. By far his most influential building was his own house at New Canaan, Connecticut (1949). Set in a romantic landscape, it is an extremely simple cubic form with walls totally of glass; it quickly became a landmark of the postwar period. He wrote the first book on the work of Mies van der Rohe (*Mies van der Rohe*, NY, 1947, ²1953). His collected writings have recently been published: R. Stern (ed.), *Philip Johnson: Writings* (NY, 1978).   BM

C. Noble, *Philip Johnson* (Tokyo, 1968); N. Miller, *Johnson/Burgee: Architecture* (London, 1980).

Johnson, Uwe (b. Cammin, Pomerania, Germany [now Poland], 20.7.1934). German novelist. Johnson, previously a citizen of the German Democratic Republic, emigrated to West Germany in 1959. Most of his work is concerned with the theme of 'divided Germany'. The experimental *Mutmassungen über Jakob* (Frankfurt, 1960; tr. U. Molinaro, *Speculations about Jacob*, London, 1963) is about the death of a railwayman who is run down by a train where through-traffic crosses between East and West, though this is difficult to discover since the work consists of speculations by unknown persons about an event which is not described until near the end. Jacob may have been killed for political reasons. *Das dritte Buch über Achim* (Frankfurt, 1962; tr. U. Molinaro, *The Third Book about Achim*, London, 1968) is modelled on a real East German champion cyclist who pretends in the book to have been a lifelong communist and conceals his earlier support for HITLER. *Zwei Ansichten* (Frankfurt, 1965; tr. R. & C. Winston, *Two Views*, London, 1967) has a similar theme. The three-volume *Jahrestage. Aus dem Leben der Gesine Crespahl* (Frankfurt, 1970; tr.

L. Vennewitz, *Anniversaries. From the Life of Gesine Crespahl*, London, 1975) reviews German history from 1920 to the 1960s.   RDG

Johnston, Edward (b. San José, Uruguay, 11.2.1872; d. Ditchling, E. Sussex, UK, 26.11.1944). British calligrapher and letter designer. He received no formal education because of chronic ill-health. Youthful interest in letterforms, stimulated by Loftie's *Lessons in the Art of Illumination* (1885), and further encouraged by advice from architects Harry Cowlishaw and W. R. Lethaby, from William Morris's former secretary Sydney Cockerell, and from Mr and Mrs Robert Bridges – who gave him Maund Thompson's *A Handbook of Greek and Latin Palaeography* (1893) and urged him to study half uncials – led to intensive study of medieval manuscripts at the British Museum, and to the Book of Kells. Intuitively recognizing his genius, Lethaby (principal of the London Central School of Arts and Crafts) appointed Johnston the first teacher of lettering (1899): his students included Cobden-Sanderson, GILL, Graily Hewitt, Noel Rooke and Anna Simons. From 1901 until almost his death he also taught at the Royal College of Art. He created masterly calligraphy for the Doves Press and the Cranach-Presse; and for the *Imprint* magazine, which he cofounded with F. E. Jackson, J. H. Mason and Gerard Meynell. Frank Pick commissioned from him in 1915 the celebrated monostroke serifless London Underground alphabet – forerunner of Gill's widely acclaimed Sanserif typeface design – and the familiar bull's-eye symbol. He wrote two notable textbooks: *Writing and Illuminating and Lettering* (London, 1906), which is still in print, and *Manuscript and Inscription Letters* (London, 1909). Through his work and teaching, Johnston has decisively influenced the evolution of printed roman letterforms throughout this century.   TC

Joliot-Curie, Irène (b. Paris, France, 12.9.1897; d. Paris, 17.3.1956) and **Joliot, Jean Frédéric** (b. Paris, France, 19.3.1900; d. Paris, 14.8.1958). French physicists. Working in collaboration with her husband, Irène Joliot-Curie discovered the first chemical evidence for the artificial transmutation of the elements. The daughter of Pierre and Marie CURIE, Irène received her doctorate in 1925. A year later, she married her mother's assistant, Frédéric, and the couple, who became known as the Joliot-Curies, worked closely together and from 1928 onwards jointly signed all their scientific publications. In the early 1930s they performed important experiments which contributed to the discovery of the neutron by CHADWICK and the positron by Anderson. However, their most important work was upon the artificial transmutation of the elements and the synthesis of new radioactive elements. In 1934 they bombarded aluminium, boron and magnesium with alpha particles to give new radioactive isotopes of phosphorus, nitrogen and silicon (*Compt. Rend.*, 198 [1934], 254; *J. de Phys.*, 5 [1934], 153). Today radioisotopes are immensely important in medicine and industry; for the discovery of their artificial synthesis, the Joliot-Curies (only a year later) were awarded the Nobel prize for chemistry. Their later work on the neutron bombardment of uranium was instrumental in the discovery of nuclear fission. An active figure, after WW2, in the development of nuclear reactors and the foundation of the French Atomic Energy Commission, Irène, like her mother, died of leukaemia.   KRS

E. Cotton, *Les Curies* (Paris, 1963); P. Biquard, *Joliot-Curie* (London, 1965).

Jones, Daniel (b. London, UK, 12.9.1881; d. Gerrards Cross, Bucks., 4.12.1967). British phonetician who built up the first university department of phonetics in the UK. After obtaining a degree in mathematics at Cambridge, and subsequently studying law, he began to take a serious interest in language. In 1905–6 he studied phonetics in Paris under Paul Passy, then in 1907 a department of phonetics was established under his direction at University College London, where he eventually became professor in 1921. Jones's approach to phonetics was essentially practical. Following on from the pioneering work of the phonetician Henry Sweet (1845–

1912), Jones continued to develop and refine principles for the phonetic transcription of speech sounds. He invented the system of 'cardinal vowels', a set of reference points which allowed vowels to be precisely and consistently transcribed. His practical outlook is exemplified in his widely used books *An English Pronouncing Dictionary* (London, 1917) and *An Outline of English Phonetics* (Leipzig, 1918), and also in the 1949 edition of *The Principles of the International Phonetics Association* (London), which he prepared. In common with several other linguists of his era, Jones attempted to clarify the nature of 'phonemes', the significant sound units of language. This work culminated in a major book *The Phoneme: its Nature and Use* (Cambridge, 1950).   JMA

Jones, Walter David (b. Brockley, Kent, UK, 1.11.1895; d. Harrow, London, 28.10.1974). British writer and artist. His Welsh father was a printer, his English mother's father a mast and tackle maker in the Pool of London, and he was an art student in London from 1909 to 1921 save for the parenthesis 1915–18 when he served in WW1 as a private in the Royal Welsh Fusiliers. In 1921 he became a Catholic and a member of GILL's craft community at Ditchling, drawn to MARITAIN's theory of art as sacrament and sign. For two years from 1924 he went to North Wales with Gill, and was briefly engaged to Gill's daughter Petra. From this time Jones's flourishing watercolours show a more delicate, free and individual vision than the earlier engravings. His later art, even the inscriptions, was more allusive though still visionary. His prose and verse narrative of WW1 *In Parenthesis* (London, 1937) was acclaimed 'a work of genius' by ELIOT, while his major work *The Anathemata* (London, 1952) was for AUDEN 'very probably the greatest long poem in English in this century'. It is a meditation on the origins of man and of Britain, projected through the events of the Mass. Jones is an ambitious modernist writer, with deep cultural perspectives; with less style than Ezra POUND and less mastery than JOYCE, he has more charm. The second half of his life, lived quietly in rooms in Harrow, produced simpler and more dramatic writings in *The Sleeping Lord* (London, 1974) and *The Roman Quarry* (London, 1981), a posthumous selection. His essays are collected in *Epoch and Artist* (London, 1959) and *The Dying Gaul* (London, 1978).   MJA

D. Blamires, *David Jones: Man and Artist* (London, ²1978); R. Hague, *Dai Greatcoat* (London, 1980).

Joplin, Scott (b. Texarkana, Tex., USA, 24.11.1868; d. New York, 1.4.1917). American pianist and the foremost composer of ragtime (originally called 'ragged time'), the syncopated music which formed the basis of many early jazz compositions. After distinguishing himself in piano-playing contests Joplin wrote down his ragtime compositions, which presented a fusion of Afro-American rhythms and European compositional form. Joplin was not the first composer to have ragtime published, but he was distinctly the most skilful, and his 'Maple Leaf Rag' (1899) displays his fine melodic and rhythmic sense. The racial climate of the time denied Joplin (a black) national fame, but he was respected by young composers of the era, and several, including James Scott, Scott Hayden and the white pianist Joseph Lamb, became his protégés.

Joplin desperately wanted Negro music to gain respect in the USA. To achieve this he composed an extended work *The Guest of Honor* in 1903; he also wrote several marches and waltzes, but 'The Entertainer' (1902) and 'The Cascades' (1904) show that ragtime was his forte. Joplin also wrote *Treemonisha* (an opera in three acts) which was indifferently received at its first performance in 1915; 50 years later it was revived, and accepted with reservations.

Joplin's output of ragtime compositions was sporadic during the last decade of his life, when he was suffering from syphilis, and despondent; even so, his 'Euphonic Sounds' (1909) and 'Magnetic Rag' (1914) are superb. Since Joplin's death, ragtime has enjoyed several revivals in the USA, his works being regularly performed at well-attended festivals.   JJC

H. Janis & R. Blesh, *They All Played Ragtime* (NY, 1950); J. Haskin, *Scott Joplin: the Man Who Made Ragtime* (NY, 1978).

Jouve, Pierre Jean (b. Arras, Pas-de-Calais, France, 11.10.1882; d. Paris, 8.1.1976). French poet and novelist. Jouve's early work was influenced successively by vestiges of symbolism, the *unanisme* of ROMAINS and the pacifism of Romain Rolland. But after a religious crisis he disowned all his previous work and began, with *Noces* [Nuptials] (Paris, 1928) and *Sueur de sang* [Sweat of blood] (Paris, 1933), to work within the tradition of the mystic poets, the influence of St John of the Cross and St Theresa being particularly apparent. His interest in psychoanalysis, to which he was introduced by his second wife, is also apparent in the tension between eroticism and a desire for purity and personal union with the divine presence that characterizes these collections. Jouve adopted a free verse technique, shunning both rhyme and assonance and striving towards a choral effect that reflects his lasting interest in music. In his later work he used more traditional forms but his poetry retained its mystic inspiration, as did novels such as *Le Monde désert* [The deserted world] (Paris, 1927). Exiled in Switzerland during WW2, Jouve was a supporter of the Gaullist cause and the mystic nationalism of his *La Vierge de Paris* [The virgin of Paris] (Fribourg, 1944) has been favourably compared with the work of ELUARD and the other Resistance poets. Jouve was the translator of Góngora, Hölderlin, Shakespeare's *Sonnets* and *Romeo and Juliet*, and the author of essays on Baudelaire, Mozart and BERG. A volume of selected translations has been prepared by K. Bosley: *An Idiom of Night* (London, 1968).   DM

M. Callander, *The Poetry of Pierre Jean Jouve* (Manchester, 1965).

Joyce, James Augustine Aloysius (b. Dublin, Ireland, UK [now Irish Republic], 2.2.1882; d. Zürich, Switzerland, 13.1.1941). Irish novelist. Joyce was educated at Clongowes Wood College, Belvedere College and University College, Dublin. Believing the free development of his spirit and art was threatened in Ireland, he chose voluntary exile and, after an abortive escape to Paris in 1902, left for Europe with Nora Barnacle (whom he later married) in 1904. They lived mainly in Trieste, Zürich (during WW1) and Paris. After the German invasion of France, they moved back to Zürich.

In 1904 Joyce began a collection of related short stories presenting Dublin as a city infected with moral paralysis. Accepted for publication in 1906, *Dubliners* was delayed, by the timidity of printers and publishers, until 1914 (London). Besides publishing a volume of graceful but somewhat conventional lyrics, *Chamber Music* (London, 1907), Joyce had been engaged since 1904 on a long autobiographical novel *Stephen Hero*, the substantial surviving fragments of which were printed posthumously (London, 1944). The materials of this work were rehandled, condensed and drastically reshaped for *A Portrait of the Artist as a Young Man* (NY, 1916) in which Joyce showed the stages by which an embryo artist, Stephen Dedalus, freed himself from the restraints imposed on him by family, race and church. Technical and stylistic innovations which had escaped attention in *Dubliners* were developed in *A Portrait*, and Joyce began to gain recognition as a bold and original writer. However, a play *Exiles* (London, 1918) received little critical notice and was not produced for many years.

From March 1918 onwards chapters of a novel, *Ulysses*, appeared in periodicals despite further difficulties with modest printers and censors. On its publication in Paris in 1922, *Ulysses* was banned in many countries, remaining so in the USA until 1933 and in the UK until 1936, by which time it had earned an international reputation. It is chiefly concerned with the experiences in Dublin on 16.6.1904 of two men – Leopold Bloom, a Jewish advertisement canvasser, who, though often absurd and frequently humiliated, remains, unlike the citizens of *Dubliners*, morally active, resilient and resourceful, and Stephen Dedalus, now bitter, defeated and dispirited. Though the events of the day are among the most commonplace recorded in literature, the brief meeting of the two men is significant for each of

them, and their mental processes are verbalized with unprecedented invention and daring. Though still a controversial novel, *Ulysses* has gradually established itself as one of the major literary achievements of the 20c, perhaps of all time.

Pomes Penyeach (Paris, 1927), more interesting and lively than *Chamber Music*, was overshadowed by the fragments of a new work, provisionally entitled *Work in Progress*, which began to appear from 1924 to the bafflement even of admirers of Joyce's earlier writings. The completed book *Finnegans Wake* (London, 1939) swept aside the limitations of language, space, time and individuality in an attempt to represent, in the mode of a dream, the whole of mankind's history, experience and relationships, personal and social. Since 1939 criticism and scholarship have laboured over *Finnegans Wake*, without as yet unravelling more than some parts and strands of its intricacies of content and manner. Even so, enough has been explored to reveal the grandeur of Joyce's ambition and his prodigious mastery of the resources of language. The critical argument continues as to whether Joyce was an immense talent led astray finally by his own virtuosity into the construction of an incomprehensible folly, or a writer who has dominated the literature of the century with works which have extended not only the frontiers of literature but the limitations of man's understanding of himself. CHP

R. Ellmann, *James Joyce* (NY, 1959, ²1982); C. Peake, *James Joyce: the Citizen and the Artist* (London, 1977).

József, Attila (b. Budapest, Austria-Hungary [now Hungary], 11.4.1905; d.` Balatonszárszó, 3.12.1937). Hungarian poet, who grew up in desperate poverty in the slums of Budapest, yet acquired a good education in Hungary, Austria and France. He early became a MARXist and joined the then illegal Hungarian Communist party, whose slogans appeared for a time in his verse. After conflicts on many issues, he severed his connection with it. His interest in FREUD and his belief that psychoanalytical methods might be applied to the political behaviour of the masses was one of these points of disagreement. The combination of Marx and Freud gives József's poetry a unique flavour. A selection is in *Selected Poems and Texts* (eds, G. Gömöri & J. Atlas, Cheadle Hulme, 1973). Increasing schizophrenia, bouts of depression and treatment led to magnificent poetry and a turning to God in his loneliness and rejection. He committed suicide beneath a train. This background is necessary to understand both the achievement and the uniqueness of his verse, which is self-sufficient, exact in language and evocative in imagery. It is modern, highly intellectual and disciplined writing displaying a humanity and longing for love and harmony that gives added urgency to his social message. Though he uses folk elements and betrays literary fashions of the day, his voice is independent. After WW2 he was presented as a model for young poets, and his influence was far-reaching.   GFC

Juan Carlos I, *né* Alfonso Victor Maria de Borbón y Borbón (b. Rome, Italy, 5.1.1938). King of Spain since 22 November 1975. Although FRANCO outlived the Spanish civil war (1936–9) by 36 years, there were widespread fears that his death would be followed by a renewal of political and social conflict. To provide a guarantee of *continuismo*, Franco in 1969 nominated the grandson of the last king of Spain, Alfonso XIII (abdicated 1931), to succeed him. Juan Carlos, however, had ideas of his own and when Franco died used his position to legitimize a peaceful transition from dictatorship to democracy by unexpectedly assuming the role of a constitutional monarch. Instead of building up a monarchist party, Juan Carlos placed his prestige behind the creation of a democratic constitution (ratified December 1978), and pledged himself to accept whatever government was produced by free elections. His intentions were put to a double test: (1) when a military coup was attempted on 23 February 1981 and the Civil Guard, under Francoist leaders, occupied the Cortes and held members of parliament hostage, the king took an unequivocal stand and rallied the army and the nation to the support of the constitutional regime; (2) when

the ruling union of the Democratic Centre broke up and elections (28 October 1982) were marked by a swing to the left, the king accepted Felipe Gonzalez, the leader of the Spanish Socialist Workers party, as the new prime minister. Many countries are faced with the problem of how to move from the emergency regimes of revolution or dictatorship to a more stable and normal state of affairs. Juan Carlos offers a rare example, successful at least to begin with, of how to use the historic institution of monarchy to make the transition peacefully.   ALCB

Jung, Carl Gustav (b. Kesswil, Thurgau, Switzerland, 26.6.1885; d. Küsnacht, Lucerne, 6.6.1961). Swiss psychiatrist, one of the founding fathers of modern depth-psychology. He qualified in 1900 at the University of Basle, then until 1909 worked under Eugen Bleuler at the Burghölzli, the Zürich insane asylum and psychiatric clinic. In his *Diagnostische Associationsstudien* (Leipzig, 1906–9; *Studies in Word Association*, now in *Collected Works* [CW], vol. 2) he produced experimental proof of 'feeling-toned complexes' – a term he introduced into modern psychology – and, with that, of the existence of the unconscious. FREUD immediately recognized the importance of Jung's discovery. This, together with Jung's work on schizophrenia, led to close collaboration with Freud, lasting until 1913. Jung, however, became increasingly critical of Freud's exclusively sexual definition of libido and incest. Publication of his *Wandlungen und Symbole der Libido* (Leipzig, 1912; *Symbols of Transformation*, CW5) led to a final break. In 1921 he published *Psychologische Typen* (Zürich; *Psychological Types*, CW6), describing the two attitude types of introversion and extraversion, with the subdivision of four functional types. From then onwards he steadily developed his own theories under the name of Analytical Psychology. He saw the psyche as a self-regulating system, presupposing a creative function of the unconscious, and a teleological element in the flow of psychic energy. His experience with patients made him define neurosis as 'the suffering of the soul which has not discovered its meaning'. Meaning can be found through dreams and their symbols in the form of archetypal images, arising from the collective unconscious, a deep layer of the psyche underlying the personal unconscious. Their numinous character compensates the one-sided rationality of the conscious mind. Their understanding leads to growing integration, expressed in the process of individuation, a concept central to Analytical Psychology. Jung's concept of the collective unconscious and of the archetypes led him to explore religious symbolism, both of West and East, myths, historical antecedents such as e.g. alchemy (cf. his *Psychologie und Alchemie*, Zürich, 1944; *Psychology and Alchemy*, CW12) and other borderline phenomena such as ESP. Two of the most important archetypal images are those of anima and animus, the contrasexual images in man's and woman's psyche, thus recognizing the equality of male and female values, of Logos and Eros. Another important archetypal figure is that of the shadow, the inferior part of one's own personality. All those images are projected on to outside people or groups, an important contribution to a better objective understanding of man's interpersonal, social and political activities. A final contribution to psychology is his formulation of the acausal principle of synchronicity, representing a meaningful coincidence of two causally unrelated events – opening up a way to understanding much that is generally considered 'chance' occurrence. His work on the collective unconscious was accompanied and supported by his visits to the Pueblo Indians and the Elgonies of East Africa. Jung's concepts of the libido and the psyche as self-regulating systems, his pioneering work on schizophrenia, his definition of psychological types, and his revolutionary discovery of the collective unconscious with its archetypes, together with the enlargement of the scope of psychology beyond its then accepted frontiers, his insistence on the importance of the search for meaning and his understanding of the interdependence of Logos and Eros make him one of the most germinative thinkers of the 20c. His work has proved of great importance not only for psychology but also for anthropology, religion, art and literature, and history. He died 10 days after finishing his last work 'Approaching the Unconscious', in *Man and his Symbols* (London, 1964). Jung's writings have been translated into English in *The Collected Works of C. G. Jung* (20 vols, eds H. Read, M. Fordham & G. Adler, NY, 1953–79).   GA

J. Jacobi, *The Psychology of C. G. Jung* (London, 1969); G. Adler, *Dynamics of the Self* (London, 1979).

Jünger, Ernst (b. Heidelberg, Baden-Württemberg, Germany, 29.3.1895). German novelist and essayist whose preoccupation with power in its various manifestations has made him a controversial figure. His intellectual honesty and courage, his consistency of purpose and his stylistic brilliance may be acknowledged, but so too must his baleful glorification of war as the supreme test, his lack of feeling and his dangerous irrationalism. His adventurous nature, apparent at 18 when he briefly joined the French Foreign Legion – recounted in *Afrikanische Spiele* (Hamburg, 1936; tr. S. Hood, *African Diversions*, London, 1954) – found satisfaction on the western front in WW1, the formative experience of his life which is recorded and its deeper meaning explored in *In Stahlgewittern* (Hanover, 1920; tr. B. Creighton, *The Storm of Steel*, London, 1929), *Der Kampf als inneres Erlebnis* [The battle as inner experience] (Berlin, 1922), *Das Wäldchen 125* (Berlin, 1925; tr. B. Creighton, *Copse 125*, London, 1930), and *Feuer und Blut* [Fire and blood] (Magdeburg, 1925). He was wounded seven times and awarded Germany's highest war decoration, the *Pour le mérite*. His conception of an authoritarian society dominated by the idea of achievement and revolutionized by technology found expression in *Die totale Mobilmachung* [Total mobilization] (Berlin, 1931) and *Der Arbeiter* [The worker] (Hamburg, 1932). Despite affinities with fascism, he remained aristocratically aloof from the Nazis and his allegorical novel *Auf den Marmorklippen* (Hamburg, 1939: tr. S. Hood, *On the Marble Cliffs*, London, 1947) is clearly anti-Nazi in intention. But, like *Heliopolis* (Tübingen, 1949), *Gläserne Bienen* (Stuttgart, 1957;

tr. L. Bogan & E. Mayer, *The Glass Bees*, NY, 1961) and *Die Zwille* [The sling shot] (Stuttgart, 1973), it demonstrates the failure of Jünger's fiction to breathe life into abstract ideas. He is perhaps at his best in nonfiction (diaries, essays, travel books) where his precise observation of nature – he is a gifted botanist and entomologist – is particularly striking. IW

J. P. Stern, *Ernst Jünger: a Writer of Our Time* (Cambridge, 1953).

K

Kafka, Franz (b. Prague, Bohemia, Austria-Hungary [now Czechoslovakia], 3.7.1883; d. Kierling, nr Vienna, Austria, 3.6.1924). Austrian novelist. Himself slim, sensitive, an intellectual, Kafka was dominated by his well-built, bullet-headed, businesslike father, about whom, he said, all his works were written. This is clearly the case in *Das Urteil* (Leipzig, 1916; tr. E. & W. Muir, *The Judgment*, London, 1949) in which a young man irrationally accepts his father's sentence of death by drowning. The Oedipus situation, only recently at that time announced by FREUD, is less directly portrayed in *Die Verwandlung* (Leipzig, 1915; tr. E. & W. Muir, *The Metamorphosis and Other Stories*, London, 1961) in which an *alter ego* of Kafka wakes up to find he has been transformed into a verminous insect. Verminousness, in part the sense of inferiority towards his father, in part the stigma of being a Jew in a country dominated by non-Jewish German-speakers, and surrounded by Czechs, is Kafka's deepest self-awareness. It appears in a different guise in *In der Strafkolonie* (Leipzig, 1919; *In the Penal Colony*, in *The Metamorphosis*) where an officer on a kind of Devil's Island demonstrates the use of a machine to which prisoners are bound, while a commandment hitherto unknown to them, which may indeed be a sheer absurdity, is tattooed on their bodies shortly before they die. 'Guilt', says the officer, 'is always beyond doubt.' The same is apparently true in Kafka's novel *Der Prozess*, published posthumously (Leipzig, 1925; tr. E. & W. Muir, *The Trial*, London, 1937), in which Josef K. (the initial only is used) wakes up to find he is under arrest on a charge which is never specified. K.'s attempts to confront his accusers, who belong to a court which meets in such places as the attics of houses, grow weaker as he accepts that he has to offer a defence, though he still does not know against what. Finally two men in opera-hats

plunge a knife into his heart. His last words are 'Like a dog'.

Kafka's writings were introduced to the English-speaking world by AUDEN and MUIR, as by an existentialist like KIERKEGAARD or a modern pilgrim like Bunyan's. The analogy with *The Pilgrim's Progress* was probably derived from *Das Schloss* (Berlin, 1926; tr. E. & W. Muir, *The Castle*, London, 1930) in which 'K.' makes vain efforts to enter a castle which seems almost to be a religious symbol, though the novel has also been seen as a satire on Austro-Hungarian bureaucracy. (Kafka himself worked all his life as a civil servant, dealing with workers' accident insurance.) Like all Kafka's novels including the early *Amerika* (Leipzig, 1927; tr. E. & W. Muir, London, 1938) and the fragmentary *Beim Bau der chinesischen Mauer* (Berlin, 1931; tr. E. & W. Muir, *The Great Wall of China*, London, 1960), *Das Schloss* remained unfinished. If differs from Bunyan in the central character's complete uncertainty about the nature and purpose of his efforts, and the oppressive sense of frustration caused by the bureaucratic system.

To understand Kafka it is essential to read his self-lacerating diaries, *Tagebücher, 1910–23* (Frankfurt, 1951; tr. J. Kresh, *The Diaries of Franz Kafka, 1910–23*, 2 vols, London, 1948–9). Only there can the genuine depth of his doubts be experienced, allowing the hideous events of his stories, written with a sure hand and a laconic, even humorous lack of self-pity, to be appreciated as unexaggerated. The claim often made, that Kafka is writing about Everyman, is questionable. That he was writing with superb assurance and great art, above all in *Die Verwandlung*, about his own condition, is beyond doubt.   RDG

R. Gray, *Franz Kafka* (Cambridge, 1973); J. P. Stern (ed.), *The World of Franz Kafka* (London, 1981).

Kahn, Herman (b. Bayonne, NJ, USA, 15.2.1920). American physicist and strategist. 'It was the physicist of the Rand

Corporation, Herman Kahn,' Raymond Aron writes, 'who violated the taboo and obliged statesmen, professional or amateur strategists, and citizens themselves to face what all refuse to consider: what would happen if "it", "the monstrous war", "the impossible war", "the thermonuclear apocalypse" occurred?' This was in his book *On Thermonuclear War* (Princeton) published in 1961, the year in which Kahn joined as cofounder in setting up the Hudson Institute as his research base. In his 1961 study Kahn developed an operational nuclear strategy based on the premise that it was both possible and necessary to 'prevail' in such a war. He suggested that the USA should equip itself with a range of nuclear as well as non-nuclear options, in order to conduct such a war in a rational manner, and argued that appropriate civil defence measures should be taken to allow the USA to cross the so-called 'firebreak'. A later study *On Escalation* (London, 1965) argued (a) that if this threshold between conventional and nuclear war was not seen as a vital distinction, then individually logical and reasonable actions could generate a momentum which could produce nuclear war, and (b) that, after nuclear strikes, de-escalation below that threshold was possible. JGo

Kahn, Louis Isadore (b. Saare, Estonia, Russia, 20.2.1901; naturalized American citizen, 1915; d. New York, USA, 17.3.1974). Russian/American architect. An extraordinarily gifted designer, inspiring teacher and initiator of new directions in architecture, Kahn is one of the most significant architects of the later 20c. Although he only achieved prominence late in his career, from then until his death he designed a succession of remarkable buildings. Some of the terms and phrases he used to express his concepts and the processes of architectural design have become widely quoted: 'silence and light'; 'form and design'; 'searching for what a material wants to be'. Kahn was a leader of the most substantial change of course in architecture since the beginnings of the modern movement – the emergence of an architecture that was less abstract,

richer, more personal and more expressive. Among his many beautiful buildings the most influential is the Richards Medical Research building at the University of Pennsylvania (1957–64), whose tall prismatic towers are a striking expression of Kahn's concept of 'servant and served spaces'. The Government Centre at Dacca, Bangladesh (1962 –74) and the Institute of Management, Ahmedabad, India (1963–74) each exploit elementary forms in brick and concrete, and light, to achieve a haunting, primitive monumentality. BM

R. Giurgola & J. Mehta, *Louis I. Kahn* (Boulder, Colo, 1975); J. Lobell, *Between Silence and Light: Spirit in the Architecture of Louis I. Kahn* (Boulder, Colo, 1979).

Kahn, Reginald Ferdinand (b. London, UK, 10.8.1905). British economist. Never a prolific writer, Kahn is chiefly known for his exceptionally close cooperation with KEYNES, beginning at the time the latter was working on his *Treatise* (1930). He was the chief member of the Cambridge 'circus' of economists, which discussed and criticized Keynes's early drafts of the *General Theory* (1936). The principle of the multiplier propounded in Kahn's article 'The relation of home investment to unemployment' (*Economic Journal*, 41, 2 [1931], 173–98) is his best-known contribution and was devised to obtain an accurate evaluation of the effects of public-works projects. The value of his argument that savings and investment, and not the rate of interest, govern the equilibrium level of output in an economy proved to be an essential link in Keynes's new theory. After Keynes's death in 1947, Kahn remained a leading figure in the Cambridge school of Keynesianism. His major articles were collected in *Selected Essays on Employment and Growth* (London, 1972). PS

Kaiser, Georg (b. Magdeburg, Germany [now East Germany], 25.11.1878; d. Ascona, Ticino, Switzerland, 4.6.1945). German dramatist. Kaiser is primarily seen as the first expressionist playwright, although his output of some 70 plays from 1905 to his death as a penniless exile embraces work in many genres.

His reputation was made by *Von Morgens bis Mitternachts* (1917; tr. A. Dukes, *From Morn to Midnight*, London, 1922), the condensed, spiky, stylized yet anguished *via crucis* of an absconding bank clerk which influenced Elmer Rice's *The Adding Machine* (1923) and J. B. Priestley's *Johnson over Jordan* (1929). His *Gas* trilogy (*Die Koralle*, 1917; *Gas I*, 1918; *Gas II*, 1920) was also widely played, though its utopian-capitalist attitudes now seem as dated as those of LANG's film *Metropolis* (1926). The strength of all Kaiser's work lies in its verbal and structural tightness and its underlying rationality, seen also in the postexpressionist 'people's play' *Nebeneinander* [Side by side] (1923) and the antifascist *Der Soldat Tanaka* [The soldier Tanaka] (1940). WEILL's operas *Der Protagonist* [The protagonist] (1925), *Der Zar lässt sich photographieren* [The Tsar has his picture taken] (1927) and *Der Silbersee* [Silver lake] (1933) are to Kaiser's texts.   JWMW

B. J. Kenworthy, *Georg Kaiser* (Oxford, 1957); E. Schürer, *Georg Kaiser* (NY, 1971).

Kaldor, Nicholas (b. Budapest, Austria-Hungary [now Hungary], 12.5.1908; naturalized British citizen). Hungarian/British economist. A prolific and endlessly inventive theorist whose influence on policy has been unusually direct and successful. Moving to Britain in the late 1920s to be a student, and from 1932–47 a lecturer at the London School of Economics, he rapidly emerged as an important contributor to questions of capital theory, the theory of the firm, monopolistic competition and the theory of taxation. After the publication of KEYNES's *General Theory* (1936) he gradually turned to macroeconomic questions and proceeded to publish outstanding work on trade cycles, economic growth and reform of the international monetary system. This change in his interests was symbolized by his move in 1949 from London to Cambridge as a fellow of King's College and professor of economics (1966–75). He was a tax adviser to a variety of governments and a member of innumerable official commissions and committees both in Britain and abroad. However, it was as special adviser to the chancellor of the exchequer (1964–8 and 1974–6) that he came closest to the policy-making process. His academic work on income distribution was paralleled by his work on taxation policy, particularly his advocacy of *An Expenditure Tax* (London, 1955). From his adviser's post he was instrumental in the detection and plugging of tax loopholes, and the invention of new taxes such as the Selective Employment Tax. His published papers have conveniently appeared as *Collected Economic Essays* (8 vols, London, 1960–79).   PS

Kamerlingh Onnes, Heike (b. Groningen, The Netherlands, 21.9.1853; d. Leiden, S. Holland, 21.2.1926). Dutch physicist. Kamerlingh Onnes studied at Groningen and went to Heidelberg to work under Bunsen and Kirchhoff. He returned to Groningen and obtained his doctoral degree there in 1879. In 1882 he was appointed professor of experimental physics and meteorology at Leiden where he remained until 1923. There he started low-temperature experiments and founded the world-famous cryogenic laboratory. He measured the general thermodynamic properties of liquids and gases under a wide range of conditions of temperature and pressure. He was the first person (on 7.7.1908) to liquify helium (temperature 4.2 degrees above the absolute zero). This opened up a new world of research into the properties of materials at very low temperatures which he fully exploited. In 1911, while studying how the electrical resistance of metals varied as the temperature was reduced, he discovered (in mercury) the phenomenon of superconductivity – the complete disappearance of the electrical resistance of metals at low temperatures (see BARDEEN). Onnes also investigated magnetic properties and demonstrated very convincingly the effect of paramagnetic saturation: i.e. in a very high magnetic field at low temperatures it is possible to line up the elementary atomic magnets in a material so that they are absolutely parallel to one another. His results were in almost precise accord with the theory of LANGEVIN. He was awarded the Nobel prize for physics in 1913.   HMR

K. Mendelsohn, *The Quest for Absolute Zero* (London, 1977).

Kammerer, Paul (b. Vienna, Austria-Hungary [now Austria], 17.8.1880; d. Puchberg, 23.9.1926). Austrian biologist; the most celebrated of those who attempted an experimental demonstration of Lamarckian inheritance. Kammerer was a controversial figure in his lifetime, and has remained so. The results of his experiments on salamanders, toads and sea-squirts were not all relevant to the question of the inheritance of acquired characteristics, but were often startling. With present-day knowledge it is possible to explain some in terms of established genetic principles. Others remain of doubtful significance or value. A museum specimen demonstrating the result of one experiment was shown in 1926 to have been subject to cosmetic treatment, by whom, and for what reason, is unknown, but almost certainly not by Kammerer. He was, however, widely suspected of scientific fraud and shortly afterwards took his life. His theoretical contributions to genetics (as in *The Inheritance of Acquired Characteristics*, NY, 1924) were not impressive and are now only of historical interest.   DRN
A. Koestler, *The Case of the Midwife Toad* (London, 1971).

Kandinsky, Wassily, *né* Vasilii Vasilievich (b. Moscow, Russia, 4.12.1866; naturalized German citizen, 1928; naturalized French citizen, 1939; d. Paris, France, 13.12.1944). Russian/German/French abstract painter. Leader of the pre-1914 Munich wing of German expressionism which took its name from his *Blaue Reiter* almanac, then a member of the Bauhaus staff from 1922 to 1933, Kandinsky was a philosophically well-read artist who used an initially spontaneous but thereafter increasingly rigid vocabulary of signs, shapes and squiggles for the deliberate symbolizing of abstract ideas and intangible states of mind. He was nearly 30 when he gave up an academic career in law to study painting in Munich, working first through a modified *Jugendstil*, sometimes illustrative of Russian legends, towards his fauve-like landscapes of

1908–9. In the 'Improvisations' which developed from these, the Bavarian mountains and bulbous church towers, the symbolic horsemen and saints, began to disintegrate in a frenzied near-abstract explosion, anticipating the abstract expressionism of 40 years later. The first of his theoretical books *Über das Geistige in der Kunst* (Munich; *Concerning the Spiritual in Art*, NY, 1947) appeared in 1911 when he and MARC were planning their almanac, to be named after the horseman and containing contributions by SCHOENBERG and the Russian David Burljuk as well as Kandinsky's play *The Yellow Sound* with its symbolist title and largely nonverbal text. Breaking away from the native Munich artists of the *Neue Künstlervereinigung*, in the winter of 1911–12 they held two shows as a *Blaue Reiter* or 'Blue Horseman' group, centring on Kandinsky, his friend Gabriele Münter, Marc, Macke and Campendonk, and including work by Schoenberg, KLEE and DELAUNAY; later allies included MENDELSOHN and Hugo Ball. Then during WW1 Kandinsky returned to Russia, where he at first worked less intensively, then became involved with TATLIN in the revolutionizing of art administration and museums policy after 1917. Never fully engaged there as an artist, and mistrustful of RODCHENKO's new productivism, in 1921 he was allowed to take up an invitation from GROPIUS to join the Weimar Bauhaus where he taught mural decoration but above all was encouraged to pursue his own work. There he joined with Klee and Feininger in a new group called 'The Blue Four' (his old friend Jawlensky being the fourth), and completed his 'Bauhaus book' *Punkt und Linie zur Fläche* (Munich, 1926; *From Point and Line to Plane*, NY, 1947). Taking German nationality after the Bauhaus moved to Dessau, and always strongly opposed to any politicization of the school, as deputy director he was involved in the replacement of Gropius's MARXist successor, Hannes Meyer, by MIES VAN DER ROHE in 1930, but had to leave the country himself in 1933 when the Nazis closed the school. In Paris, where his pictures became lighter and gayer, suggestive of his friendship with Jóan MIRÓ, he made a new career as a member of the *Cercle et Carré* group, living on his professorial pension and selling to collectors such as Solomon Guggenheim, whose New York museum is now the chief repository of Kandinsky's later work.   JWMW

W. Grohmann, *Wassily Kandinsky: Life and Work* (London, 1958); K. Lankheit (ed.), *The Blaue Reiter Almanac* (London, 1974).

Kapitza, Peter Leonidovitch (b. Kronstadt, Russia, 26.6.1894). Russian physicist. Kapitza has been one of the most outstanding experimental physicists, especially in the period between the wars. His work is remarkable for the very great ingenuity which he displayed in designing experiments and equipment. He was appointed a lecturer at the Petrograd Polytechnical Institute in 1919, but in 1921 he came to Cambridge to work with RUTHERFORD. At first he studied problems in nuclear physics and in his research decided that he needed a powerful magnet to deflect alpha particles. This introduced him to the design of electromagnets which could produce extremely high magnetic fields. The basic principle which he used was to short-circuit the output of a large battery (1924) or, later, a generator through a small coil of wire. In this way he could produce a field of up to half a million gauss for a short time. Even today this performance is very difficult to achieve. These high fields were used in a wide variety of investigations on the properties of materials, the most important being a study of the way in which the electrical resistance of a metal increased in a high magnetic field. Since these magnetic effects usually become larger as the temperature is reduced, he became interested in low-temperature research. He designed novel liquefiers for the production of liquid air, hydrogen and helium, the most outstanding of these being that for helium. This operated by allowing the gas to expand into the cylinder of a small reciprocating engine (which because of the low temperature could not be lubricated with oil) and it enabled liquid helium to be produced without the necessity of first precooling the helium gas with liquid

hydrogen. His design became the prototype for nearly all the helium liquefiers which have been commercially produced. In 1929 Kapitza was elected a fellow of the Royal Society, the first foreigner for 200 years to have been so honoured. His work was so esteemed that in 1933 a special laboratory, the Royal Society Mond Laboratory, was built for him in Cambridge. However, in 1934 he returned to the USSR to visit his family, and he was prevented from returning to the UK. He became director of the Institute for Physical Problems in Moscow where his Cambridge equipment, which was bought by the USSR government, was installed. Here he continued his work, especially on liquid helium, and discovered the phenomenon of superfluidity, the apparent complete loss of viscosity in liquid helium at a temperature of 2.17 degrees above the absolute zero. The school of low-temperature physics which has flourished under his directorship has achieved world renown and in 1978 he was awarded the Nobel prize for physics. Not many details of his work during and after WW2 are available but he has published papers on large-scale electronic devices (magnetrons) and it has been reported that he was involved in the satellite projects.   HMR

D. ter Haar (ed.), *Collected Papers of P. L. Kapitza* (3 vols, Oxford, 1964–7).

Karrer, Paul (b. Moscow, Russia, 21.4.1889; d. Zürich, Switzerland, 18.6.1971). Swiss organic chemist. Karrer studied chemistry at Zürich University under Alfred Werner. In 1912 he joined EHRLICH, the father of chemotherapy, at the Georg Speyer House, Frankfurt. In 1919 he became professor of chemistry and director of the Chemical Institute in the University of Zürich. Karrer's most important research was on plant pigments, especially the coloured hydrocarbons named carotenoids. In 1930 he established the constitutional formula of β-carotene (from the carrot), the chief precursor of vitamin A, i.e. its provitamin. This was the first time the structure of a vitamin or provitamin had been established, and it led to the clarification of the structure of vitamin A itself, and to an acceptance of the material specificity of vitamins, previously doubted. The structures of a range of carotenoids were determined: they had many conjugated double bonds and were composed of isoprene residues (this is applicable to all carotenoids). They were thus recognized as relatives of other important compounds of the plant kingdom, viz. terpenes, camphors, and rubber. Karrer later confirmed SZENT-GYÖRGYI's proposal for the structure of ascorbic acid (vitamin C). He also extended his researches to vitamin E and made important contributions to the study of certain nitrogenous yellow pigments, the flavins, particularly riboflavin (lactoflavin) or vitamin B_2, the phosphate ester of which is the functional group of Warburg's yellow oxidation enzyme. This was the first example of an important idea: the close relationship between vitamins and enzymes (biological catalysts). Most of his work has been in the borderland between chemistry, biochemistry, and physiology (bio-organic chemistry in modern parlance): this borderland has often been a very fruitful field of investigation. Besides over 1000 scientific papers, Karrer published his *Lehrbuch der Organischen Chemie* [Textbook of organic chemistry] (Leipzig, 1930), which passed through 13 editions, and a famous monograph on carotenoids. He received the Nobel prize for chemistry in 1937, jointly with HAWORTH.   NBC

Karsavina, Tamara Platonovna (b. St Petersburg [now Leningrad], Russia, 9.3.1885; d. Beaconsfield, Bucks., UK, 26.5.1978). Russian/British dancer who made her debut with the Imperial Ballet in 1902 and was appointed ballerina in 1909. She was an early associate of the young choreographer FOKINE, sharing his ideals for the revitalization of ballet through the unity of choreography, music and design; and as a leading dancer in Fokine's productions she joined the Russian Ballet formed by DIAGHILEV for its first season in Paris in 1909, and annually thereafter until WW1. She was for Diaghilev not merely an accomplished and beautiful dancer, but a staunch and highly intelligent ally and confidante. Her great roles in this period included those in Fokine's *Les Sylphides, Le Carnaval, The Firebird, Le Spectre de la Rose, Petrushka, Thamar* and *Daphnis and Chloë*, and NIJINSKY was her regular partner. She also took a part in Nijinsky's modern ballet *Jeux*. She continued to dance the classic roles in St Petersburg until the revolution, when she left Russia with her husband, the British diplomat H. J. Bruce, to settle in England. After WW1 she again danced with the Diaghilev company, notably in MASSINE's *Le Tricorne*, and her association with Diaghilev continued until his death in 1929. She lent her prestige and active encouragement to the growing native ballet of her adopted country; and having taught herself English in the 1920s, she published her delightful memoirs *Theatre Street* (London, 1930), a classic of ballet literature.   DAD

R. Buckle, *Diaghilev* (London, 1979); R. Buckle, *In the Wake of Diaghilev* (London, 1982).

Käsemann, Ernst (b. Bochum-Dahlhausen, N. Rhine-Westphalia, Germany, 12.7.1906). German New Testament scholar. A leading pupil of BULTMANN, Käsemann became a pastor and, as an outspoken member of the Confessing church, was briefly imprisoned by the Nazis in 1937. He was professor in Mainz from 1946, in Göttingen from 1951 and in Tübingen from 1959 until retirement in 1971. During the 1950s and 1960s he was attacked by conservative churchmen for his radical criticism, and within scholarly circles was equally controversial. His 1953 lecture on the historical Jesus, reprinted in *Exegetische Versuche und Besinnungen 1* (Göttingen, 1960; *Essays on New Testament Themes*, London, 1964), is reckoned to have sparked off the 'new quest' (see BORNKAMM), and he provoked significant debates on early Christian apocalyptic, and on Pauline and Johannine interpretation, in each case challenging the existentialist theology of his teacher by insisting on the primacy of Christology, the future hope and the cosmic scope of redemption. His masterpiece *An die Römer* (Tübingen, 1973; *Commentary on Romans*, London, 1980) is a monument of theological interpretation, perhaps the greatest since Bultmann's

John (1941). His fierce theological and political passion influenced a generation of pastors, but has left him somewhat isolated in an increasingly conformist church and society. RM

Kastler, Alfred (b. Guebwiller, Alsace, Germany [now France], 3.5.1902). French physicist. Kastler has devoted his life to a detailed study of the spectral lines emitted by atoms. At the Ecole Normale Supérieure he developed a team of extremely able experimenters who have exploited the technique known as 'optical pumping', for which he received the Nobel prize for physics in 1966. Optical pumping is used to study the electrons which orbit an atom. It is of great interest to investigate how the energy of these electrons can be modified by the presence of a magnetic field and also by the magnetism of the atomic nucleus, but these effects are usually so small that, in a gas, they are masked by disturbances due to the motion of the atoms themselves (the Doppler effect). The technique developed by Kastler enables these fine details to be measured with high precision. The method involves exciting or 'pumping' an atomic electron to a higher energy by illuminating it with polarized light of a very precise wavelength (which depends on the atom under investigation). This forces the electron into an orbit which is more distant from the atomic nucleus. The magnetic properties of the electron and of the atomic nucleus can then be probed by detecting how the spectral line emitted by the atom responds to radio waves. Optical pumping enables very precise measurements of atomic properties to be obtained. It has also played an important part in the development of the laser and of atomic clocks, both of which rely for their operation on the pumping of electrons into higher orbits and then using the radiation which is emitted when the electrons fall back to their inner orbits. HMR

Katchalsky, Aharon Katzir- (b. Lodz, Russian Poland [now Poland], 30.9.1914; d. Lod Airport, Israel, 30.5.1972). Israeli biophysicist. When terrorists opened fire at Tel Aviv's airport in May 1972, among the 25 they killed was one of Israel's most distinguished scientists – professor at both the WEIZMANN Institute and Berkeley – who, ironically, had been a conspicuous advocate of Arab-Jewish rapprochement. Katchalsky had emigrated to Palestine in 1925, studied at the Hebrew University, and served in the army in the 1948/9 war. Beginning as a lepidopterist, he switched to protein physical chemistry, helping develop the field of polyelectrolyte research during the 1940s. His major contribution, though, was the use of nonequilibrium thermodynamics to describe irreversible processes in biology, especially transport across membranes (see A. Katchalsky & P. F. Curran, *Nonequilibrium Thermodynamics in Biophysics*, Cambridge, Mass., 1967). He was among the earliest to demonstrate the effectiveness of mathematical modelling and analysis in biology, a development which some view as a coming revolution in the science. Just before his death he had become interested in the modelling of brain and memory function. Described as a 'world citizen', he was a peripatetic teacher and organizer of science, and a popular lecturer who made 'even the most hardened experimentalist believe, for a while, that he understood thermodynamics'. The Katchalsky memorial fellowships and symposia at the Weizmann Institute in Rehovot continue his tradition of scientific internationalism. DOM

Kaunda, Kenneth (b. Lubwe, Northern Rhodesia [now Zambia], 28.4.1924). President of Zambia. One of the most philosophically minded of African leaders, Kaunda began his political career as a local party organizer for the Northern Rhodesian African National Congress, went on to lead a breakaway group of young radicals who formed the United National Independence party, helped bring about the dissolution of the Central African Federation, and led his party to a massive electoral victory, which ensured independence in 1964. As president of Zambia, Kaunda has had to hold together one of the most awkwardly shaped countries in the world, with deep ethnic and social cleavages. From 1965 to 1979 he also had to contend with the immense political and economic difficulties consequent on Rhodesia's UDI. To give his fellow countrymen a unifying political philosophy, Kaunda developed the concept of 'Zambian humanism'. Drawing his inspiration from the 'traditional community', which he saw as a 'mutual aid society', Kaunda stressed the need for a 'man-centred' rather than a 'possession-centred' approach to the problems of government and society (see *Zambia Shall Be Free*, London, 1962, and *Humanism in Zambia*, London, 1969). Critics found his ideas nebulous and contradictory: he did not want to 'create capitalism' in Zambia, but was eager to see 'Zambian business expand and prosper'. He was always moderate and nonracial in his approach to the white-dominated states of southern Africa – an approach expressed in the Lusaka manifesto of 1969.   RH

F. Macpherson, *Kaunda of Zambia* (Lusaka, 1974).

Kautsky, Karl (b. Prague, Austria-Hungary [now Czechoslovakia], 16.10.1854; naturalized Czechoslovak citizen, 1934; d. Amsterdam, The Netherlands, 17.10.1938). German/Czechoslovak MARXist and social democrat. Kautsky studied at the University of Vienna and became the chief exponent of orthodox Marxism in its 'classical' phase. In his first book (published in 1880) he criticized the Malthusian theory of population. In 1883 he founded the periodical *Die Neue Zeit*, which became the most authoritative Marxist journal of its time, and edited it until 1917. During this period the main problems confronting Marxism and socialist controversies about them were ventilated in its columns to become part of the Marxist canon. Before WW1 his prestige as a Marxist theoretician was at its height. He was the coauthor (with E. BERNSTEIN) of the Erfurt programme (1891), the first officially Marxist programme adopted by the German Social Democrats. His political position was at the centre: he criticized both the anarchists and the left wing and the revisionist right wing influenced by Bernstein. Kautsky opposed equally Bernstein's approach to socialism through gradual reform and later the revolutionary strat-

egy of such critics of reformism as Rosa LUXEMBURG. He maintained this position consistently, from the 1901 Congress of the Socialist International in Lübeck, where he led the opposition to revisionism, to his hostile criticism of LENIN and the October revolution, for which he was denounced as a renegade by the Bolsheviks. He again played an important role in the foundation of the Heidelberg programme adopted in 1925 by the German Social Democrats.

Kautsky's writings are concerned with the interpretation of Marxism and include books in which the Marxist method of class analysis is applied to various historical subjects, works such as *Thomas More und sein Utopie* (Tübingen, 1888; *Thomas More and his Utopia*, London, 1927) and *Ursprung des Christentums* (Stuttgart, 1908; *The Foundations of Christianity*, London, 1925). He also wrote extensively on the problems of general theory, his two main works in this respect being *Ethnik und materialistische Geschichtsauffassung* (Stuttgart, 1906; *Ethics and the Materialist Interpretation of History*, Chicago, 1907) and *Die materialistische Geschichtsauffassung* [The materialist interpretation of history] (Stuttgart, 1927). In these he criticized the neo-Kantians who tried to combine Kant's ideas on ethics and Marx's ideas on history, opposing to them his own view which combined Darwin's idea of evolution and the 'orthodox' Marxist approach to history as a natural process, the laws of which were formulated by Marx. According to Kautsky, historical inevitability is part of evolutionary determinism and is thus scientifically ascertainable. Human ethics and human consciousness are simply a function of the 'objective' natural processes in which biology underlies historical evolution. In this respect he differs not only from the neo-Kantians but from the Leninist 'voluntaristic' view of the role of consciousness in political and historical contexts.   LL

I. Kolakowski, *Main Currents in Marxism*, vol. 2 (Oxford, 1978); M. Salvadori, *Kautsky and the Socialist Revolution* (NY, 1979).

Kawabata, Yasunari (b. Osaka, Japan, 14.6.1899; d. Kamakura, 16.4.1972). Japanese novelist, the first Japanese recipient of a Nobel prize for literature (1968). Family deaths deprived Kawabata of a normal childhood, as by the time he was 10 his parents, his elder sister and the grandmother who brought him up had died. Throughout his literary career Kawabata's lifeline seemed to be beauty, which in its purest form was unattainable, and the pathos in this unrealized dream, as expressed in his novels, is often attributed to the circumstances of his childhood. At Tokyo Imperial University, which he entered in 1920, he specialized in literature, first English and then Japanese. Establishing himself as a writer he opposed both the prevailing naturalism, which was confessional and virtually formless, and the rising 'proletarian' school of left-wing writers. Instead he linked himself with a group referred to as the *Shinkankaku-ha* [neoperceptionists] whose leader looked to the European modernist movement for inspiration. Kawabata's own style, however, used the associative techniques of classical Japanese literature and it is this that gives his works their distinctive quality, as in e.g. *Yukiguni* (Tokyo, 1948; tr. E. G. Seidensticker, *Snow Country*, NY, 1965) and *Yama no Oto* (1954; tr. E. D. Seidensticker, *The Sound of the Mountain*, NY, 1970). The action in Kawabata's novels is often *within* rather than between characters, and is hinted at by simple, but pregnant vocabulary rather than being exhaustively described. There is, however, enough of the 20c in his characters to encourage western readers to believe that they can appreciate some of the psychology, and the Nobel citation praised Kawabata as a spiritual bridge between East and West.   BWFP

U. Makoto, *Modern Japanese Writers and the Nature of Literature* (Stanford, Calif., 1976); Y. Hisaaki, *The Search for Authenticity in Modern Japanese Literature* (Cambridge, 1978).

Kazantzakis, Nikos (b. Iraklion, Crete, Ottoman Empire [now Greece], 18.2.1883; d. Freiburg, Baden-Württemberg, West Germany, 26.10.1957). Greek writer. One of the most prolific writers and energetic figures in modern European literature, Kazantzakis came to

Athens from his native Crete in 1906, and while still a student took an active part in the literary life of the Greek capital, writing and producing plays and translating philosophical works including those of NIETZSCHE, BERGSON and William JAMES, which profoundly influenced his later career. He was active in the campaign for the recognition of demotic Greek as the national language. At this time he began an involvement in politics which continued throughout much of his life, despite drastic changes of ideology.

From 1920 Kazantzakis spent much of the next 20 years travelling. The fruits of these years were his lyrical and philosophical credo *Askitiki: Salvatores Dei* (Athens, 1927; tr. K. Friar, *The Saviors of God*, NY, 1960) and his monumental *Odysseia* (Athens, 1938; tr. K. Friar, *The Odyssey: a Modern Sequel*, NY, 1958) at 33,333 lines arguably the longest poem ever written, a work of demonic energy and nihilist despair written in the most extreme form of demotic Greek, incorporating the dialects of many regions. During WW2 Kazantzakis returned to Greece and in 1941 wrote his first serious attempt at a Greek novel: *Vios Kai Politea tou Alexi Zorba* (Athens, 1946; tr. C. Wildmann, *Zorba the Greek*, NY, 1953). During the last 15 years of his life, while living in the south of France, he wrote six more novels – of which the best known is *Christos Xanastavronetai* (Athens, 1954; tr. J. Griffin, *Christ Recrucified*, London, 1954) – in which he dramatized the themes of man's relationship to God and the uncompromising struggle of life against the abyss, which had obsessed him all his life. Kazantzakis continued to write plays and accounts of his far-flung travels and to translate large-scale classics of world literature into Greek, including Homer, Dante and Goethe's *Faust*.   RMB

H. Kazantzakis, *Nikos Kazantzakis: a Biography Based on his Letters* (Oxford, 1969); P. Bien, *Kazantzakis and the Linguistic Revolution in Modern Greek Literature* (Princeton, 1972).

Keaton, Joseph Francis (Buster) (b. Pickway, Kan., USA, 4.10.1895; d. London, UK, 1.2.1966). American film comedian. A creator in cinema, he directed his own feature-length silent comedies, devising brilliant visual gags and bringing a new cohesion to comedy. But he is best known as a player. Called the 'Great Stone Face', he never smiled on the screen. The face was both beautiful and expressive; the combination of melancholy classical features and absurdity of action made him unforgettable. He grew up among a family of vaudeville artists and joined his parents on the stage before he was four years old; his father used him as a projectile and threw him at the back-drop. In 1917 he went into films and appeared in many short comedies: his major works – *Our Hospitality* (1923), *Sherlock Junior* (1924), *The Navigator* (1924), *Seven Chances* (1925), *The General* (1926), *Steamboat Bill Jr* (1928) and *The Cameraman* (1928) – showed a control and a precision of movement never rivalled. In the 1930s he fell on evil times, worked as a gag-writer and appeared in the circus in Paris; but he recovered, remarried (happily) and in subsidiary roles adorned various films: *Sunset Boulevard* (1950), *Limelight* (1952), *A Funny Thing Happened on the Way to the Forum* (1966). In public esteem he has been outdistanced by CHAPLIN; but his is the purer art.   DP

D. Robinson, *Buster Keaton* (London, 1969).

Kelly, George Alexander (b. Perth, Kan., USA, 28.4.1905; d. Waltham, Mass., 13.3.1966). American clinical psychologist. His *magnum opus The Psychology of Personal Constructs* (2 vols, NY, 1955) has revitalized the phenomenological approach to personality appraisal. His early education was biased towards physics and mathematics, and for a time he worked in aviation. The abstract, highly systematic form of his theory owes something to this early experience. He did his PhD in psychology at the State University of Iowa, moved into teaching, and eventually replaced Carl ROGERS as head of the clinical psychology programme at Ohio State University. Personal construct theory owes much to Kelly's work as a psychotherapist. He sees the individual evolving a dynamic set of understandings (con-

structs) of significant aspects of his/her world (elements). He invented a set of techniques, the Repertory Grid, for assessing both the content and the organization of a person's constructs. The Kellyan approach has become popular well beyond its origins in clinical work, and educational and industrial applications have proliferated. In part this is due to the lure of Rep. Grid technique which, through computer analysis, can generate vast amounts of data. His substantive contribution is likely to be more enduring. By emphasizing the active, hypothesis-testing function of personality, Kelly's theory has encouraged a more negotiatory form of interaction between therapist and patient, teacher and learner, and manager and operative. It also allows the possibility of personal growth for *both* members of a pair of interactants.   RRS

Kelsen, Hans (b. Prague, Bohemia, Austria-Hungary [now Czechoslovakia], 11.10.1881; naturalized American citizen; d. Berkeley, Calif., USA, 19.4.1973). Austrian/American jurist, who developed probably the most significant body of legal theory of the 20c. He was professor of law at Vienna, judge of the Supreme Constitutional Court of Austria, and later a teacher in European and American universities. He sought to develop a pure law-theory, free from ethical, political, sociological, historical and other extraneous considerations; these have their importance but not for his general theory of law. This seeks to be general, put forward as a way of showing the pattern and shape of an entire legal order, and positivist in being founded on examination of law laid down, not law as it ought to be. In his view law is a hierarchy of norms or legal propositions, the validity of each of which is derived from a more fundamental proposition which gives it validity. In every legal order there is one ultimate, fundamental proposition, the *Grundnorm*, on which the validity of all others ultimately depends. This may be, for example, that the will of the Queen in Parliament ought to be obeyed, or that the dictates of the Politburo ought to be obeyed. The validity of the *Grundnorm* does not itself depend on any rule of law; it is the fundamental postulate, and it may be changed, for example by revolution. A consequence of his doctrine is that state and law are the same. Severely and powerfully logical, the theory deals with validity and not content and excludes the factors which in truth shape legislation and decisions, for example rightness, expedience. First propounded in *Hauptprobleme der Staatsrechtslehre* [Main problems of public law theory] (Tübingen, 1911), the theory was developed in his *Allgemeine Staatslehre* (Berlin, 1925; revised, *General Theory of Law and State*, Cambridge, Mass., 1945); *Reine Rechtslehre* (Leipzig, 1934, ²1960; *Pure Theory of Law*, Berkeley, 1967). The theory has generated an enormous literature. Kelsen also wrote extensively on international law and the United Nations.   DMW

S. Engel & R. A. Metall (eds), *Law, State and International Legal Order: Essays in Honor of Hans Kelsen* (Knoxville, 1964); California Law Review, *Essays in Honor of Hans Kelsen* (South Hackensack, 1971).

Kendall, Maurice George (b. Kettering, Northants., UK, 6.9.1907). British statistician, with experience in government, shipping, academia, commercial consultancy and the World Fertility Survey. Kendall is the great synthesizer and commentator in modern statistics. Postulating that the differing schools are all addressing themselves to different questions, he has made common a heteroclite form of statistician who follows different systems in different situations. His *The Advanced Theory of Statistics* (3 vols, London, 1961–6; 4th ed. with A. Stuart, London, 1977–9) is the practitioner's Bible. He is also known for redeveloping rank correlation by inventing a new form (Tau) insensitive to the absence of a coherent underlying scale and extending SPEARMAN's work to many observers and several variables (*Rank Correlation Methods*, London, 1948, ³1962).   AGPW

Kendrew, John Cowdrey (b. Oxford, UK, 24.3.1917). British biochemist. By analysing X-ray diffraction patterns of crystals of myoglobin, an oxygen carrying protein isolated from skeletal muscle, he was able to deduce the arrangement in space of practically all the 2600 atoms in the molecule of this protein. This dramatic achievement provided the most compelling evidence that proteins have a stable, definable three-dimensional structure and, by making possible the construction of 'atomic models', gave the scientist, for the first time, a visual image of a protein molecule. For this Kendrew was awarded the Nobel prize for chemistry in 1962, jointly with PERUTZ. It is no exaggeration to say that the work of these two pioneers initiated a new era which has seen an explosive development in our understanding of the nature of proteins and of how they perform their many and various functions in the living cell (see Kendrew, *The Thread of Life*, London, 1966).   GL

Kennan, George Frost (b. Milwaukee, Wis., USA, 16.2.1904). American foreign service officer, ambassador, historian and theorist. He became one of the leading US official authorities on the USSR, serving in Moscow (1933–8 and 1945–6), playing a large part in alerting the American government to the revival of communist anti-American ideology in the USSR in the autumn and winter of 1945, and converting it to the idea of 'containing' the spread of Soviet influence by economic and other action (see his influential article in *Foreign Affairs*, July 1947, 'The Source of Soviet Conduct', attributed to 'X' but soon identified as written by Kennan). By the time the latter appeared he had been appointed head of a new policy planning staff in the state department, although America's 'containment' policy in practice was more obviously military than Kennan would have preferred. In 1952 he returned to academic life where he became one of the most prominent advocates of the 'demythologization' of the American's image of the disinterested nature of US foreign policy and of its analysis on the basis of self-interest rather than ideological content. He published his public recollections as *Memoirs* (2 vols, Boston, Mass., 1969–72).   DCW

Kennedy, John Fitzgerald (b. Brookline, Mass., USA, 29.5.1917; d. Dallas, Tex., 22.11.1963). American politician. US Democratic representative from Massachusetts (1946–52); senator (1952–60); president (1961–3). Roman Catholic scion of notorious Bostonian Irish political dynasty on his mother's side and son of millionaire Democratic power-broker and ambassador to Britain (1938–40), he was groomed for the presidency from the moment his elder brother was killed in action in 1942. A war hero himself, he built up in the 1960s a new-style political machine in which a permanent staff, largely drawn from university-based political scientists, systematized and analysed the processes by which party nomination and presidential election might be achieved despite the comparative and traditional unacceptability to much of American opinion of his father's reputation, his Catholicism and his wealth. In foreign affairs his presidency was marked by a disastrous attempt to overthrow the CASTRO regime in Cuba by subversion, by his defeat of an attempt to blackmail America by the installation of medium-range Soviet nuclear missiles on Cuba in October 1962, by the moderation of his treatment of the Soviet leadership following that defeat (a moderation which led to the first major steps towards a detente between the super powers), and by the total defeat by de GAULLE of his hopes to create a new relationship (the 'Grand Design') between the USA and a European Community enlarged to contain the UK. To this should be added his programme of aid for Latin America, the 'Alliance for Progress', of voluntary assistance to the countries of the Third World through a 'Peace Corps', and his triumphal rallying of German morale by his visit to Germany and West Berlin in June 1963 which dramatized in Central Europe the degree to which his victory in the Cuban missile crisis meant an end to Soviet threats to Berlin. His record of achievement in domestic politics, even on the civil rights issue, was limited to cautiously worded statements of support for civil rights leaders such as KING. He managed nevertheless to create an aura of civilized liberal and cultural leadership during his tenure of the White House which made him (the youngest president in US history) a symbol of hope and renewal. This in turn made his assassination in November 1963, in circumstances which to this day fascinate mystery-mongers and conspiratorially minded historians, seem a turning-point in what was to prove a black and dispiriting decade for American liberalism.   DCW

A. Schlesinger, *The Thousand Days* (NY, 1965).

Kenyatta, Jomo (b. Gatundu, British East Africa [now Kenya], c. 1892; d. Mombasa, 22.8.1978). President of Kenya. The most controversial black African politician of his generation, Kenyatta was sentenced by the British for 'managing' Mau Mau, the most violent and radical nationalist movement in British colonial Africa, and was denounced by a British governor as 'the leader to darkness and death'. Yet as president of independent Kenya, he came to be regarded with esteem and affection by the remaining white settlers, and to be seen by the British as one of their most loyal friends in the Third World. Of mixed Kikuyu and Masai descent, Kenyatta became deeply involved in Kikuyu politics in the 1920s. From 1932 to 1944 he lived in England, returning to Kenya in 1944 to become leader of the newly formed Kenya African Union. A reformer rather than a revolutionary, he was clearly not directly implicated in Mau Mau. By imprisoning him on false charges the British powerfully enhanced his prestige, enabling him to emerge as a truly national leader. At independence he took as his slogan *Harambee* [pull together] and showed remarkable adroitness in maintaining political stability and allowing a considerable measure of political freedom, though radical critics found his regime, avowedly pro-western and capitalist and dominated by the emergent group of Kikuyu entrepreneurs, too little concerned with the needs of the ordinary man. Kenyatta wrote one major work, *Facing Mount Kenya* (London, 1938). A somewhat idealized view of Kikuyu culture and traditions, the book was a powerful assertion

of African values in a society then completely dominated by white settlers. In *Suffering without Bitterness* (Nairobi, 1968), Kenyatta provided his own account of 'the founding of the Kenya nation'.   RH
J. Murray-Brown, *Kenyatta* (London, 1972).

Kerensky, Alexander Feodorovich (b. Simbirsk [now Ulyanovsk], Russia, 22.4.1881; d. New York, USA, 11.6.1970). Kerensky was a Democratic-Socialist member of the Russian Duma (1912–17), and successively minister of justice, minister of war and prime minister in the various provisional governments which held office in Russia between the two revolutions of February (March) and October (November) 1917. When LENIN's Bolshevik party seized power in Petrograd on the second occasion Kerensky escaped into exile, first in France (1919–40), then in Australia (1940–6), and finally in the USA. The one 'strong man' in the provisional governments, he was distinguished for his patriotic refusal to conclude a separate peace with Germany and his (non-MARXist) devotion to parliamentary democracy, falling victim to the antiparliamentarianism of the military right as much as to that of the Bolshevik and social revolutionary left. His memoirs were published as *Russia and History's Turning Point* (NY, 1965).   DCW

Kerouac, Jack (b. Lowell, Mass., USA, 12.3.1922; d. St Petersburg, Fla, 21.10.1969). American novelist. As a novelist, Kerouac was little more than a footnote to Thomas WOLFE. Sociologically, he caught (and invented) a crucial mode of postwar sensibility. He burst upon a society increasingly worried about conformism and a faceless social order with a vision of freedom and restless movement, individualism, and the renewed possibility of self-transcendence through jazz, drugs and sex. The appeal of *On the Road* (NY, 1957) was immediate. His subsequent novels elaborate the myth, dealing with various episodes in his life. Kerouac's prose was energetically sloppy; his exaltation of energy his most endearing quality. Success and fame did not suit Kerouac, and his later novels were mainly dilutions and repetitions.   EH
A. Charters, *Kerouac: a Biography* (NY, 1973); B. Gifford & L. Lee, *Jack's Book: an Oral Biography of Jack Kerouac* (NY, 1978).

Kertész, André (b. Budapest, Austria-Hungary [now Hungary], 2.7.1894; naturalized American citizen). Hungarian/American photographer. Kertész was one of the most prolific and influential of all European photographers in the late 1920s and early 1930s, when he worked for *Vu* magazine and for *Art et Médecine*. During WW1 he served in the Austro-Hungarian army. Wounded in 1915, he began to take photographs during his convalescence and in 1925 moved to Paris to pursue a photographic career. In 1936 he went to New York where he has remained, freelancing until 1949 for such magazines as *Harper's Bazaar* and *Look*, and subsequently working for Condé Nast publications until 1962.

One of the pioneers of modern photojournalism, and a major influence on his friends and successors BRASSAI and CARTIER-BRESSON, Kertész was interested from the outset in the life of people rather than in the unfolding of history. His protagonists are idlers and passers-by rather than statesmen, and he photographs them at revealing moments, demonstrating their anxieties and pleasures, emphasizing their privacy and inner life. This was as evident in *Paris Vu* (Paris, 1936) as in *On Reading* (NY, 1970). Equally, his photographs are rich in jokes; they are the observations of a quick-witted companion rather than of an unrelenting news-gatherer. He promoted liberty and individualism in an era much obsessed by collectivism and the unfolding of history. His photographs can be compared to the films of René Clair and Jean RENOIR. They have something also of the irreverence to be found in HAŠEK's novel *The Good Soldier Švejk*. As western societies have become more regulated and mechanized Kertész's manner, ironic and personal, has become increasingly influential.   IJ
André Kertész: Sixty Years of Photography, 1912–1972 (NY, 1972).

Keynes, John Maynard (b. Cambridge, UK, 5.6.1883; d. West Firle, E. Sussex, 21.4.1946). British economist, and the most influential world figure in economics since Adam Smith, Ricardo and MARX. Himself the son of a Cambridge logician and economist (John Neville Keynes), he read mathematics at King's College, Cambridge; and although making little direct use of mathematics in his subsequent economics, retained a major interest in the subject at least until the completion of his *Treatise on Probability* (London, 1921). His teachers in economics were Alfred MARSHALL and PIGOU. In 1909 he was elected a fellow of King's, which he remained until his death. His first book *Indian Currency and Finance* (London, 1913) received wide professional acclaim. But the work that made him a public figure was *The Economic Consequences of the Peace* (London, 1919). This, the fruit of his participation as a UK treasury official in the peace negotiations after WW1, was essentially a polemical attack on the attitudes and approach of the victorious Allies, especially in the matter of German reparations. A sequel entitled *A Revision of the Treaty* appeared in London in 1922. The two books had little influence on events at the time, but may be seen in retrospect to have encouraged the appeasement policy pursued by the UK government towards Germany in the 1930s.

Keynes's main contributions to economics stemmed from his work on monetary institutions, theory and policy. In *A Tract on Monetary Reform* (London, 1923) he pioneered the case for 'managed money': that is, for giving priority in monetary policy to stability of employment and of the internal price level, rather than to restoration of the pre-1914 gold standard as an end in itself. *A Treatise on Money* (2 vols, London, 1930) was a much more exhaustive but not altogether successful work on the role of money and the price level in economic fluctuations. By far his greatest and most influential work was *The General Theory of Employment, Interest and Money* (London, 1936). Until then, the idea that an unregulated market economy might suffer quasi-permanent unemploy-

ment of resources had no place in the accepted corpus of economic thought; this omission seemed no longer reasonable in the light of British experience after the early 1920s and world experience after 1929. A number of economists grappled with the problem, especially in Cambridge, where R. F. KAHN in particular developed the 'multiplier' model of the impact of public expenditure on employment, and in Sweden, where important elements of *The General Theory* had been foreshadowed by Knut Wicksell and later by LINDAHL, Gunnar Myrdal and Bertil Ohlin. Keynes's work pulled these and other elements together into a unified scheme of analysis based on the new concept of effective or aggregate demand and involving a new pattern of short-run relationships among the markets for labour, consumption goods, capital goods and money. The result was 'the Keynesian revolution': in economic theory, virtually a new branch of the subject, soon christened 'macroeconomics'; and in policy, a transformation of the economic functions of government in industrial market economics. National accounts were drawn up, responsibility accepted for national employment levels and a major role perceived for the government budget as a positive determinant of the business climate. Keynes himself played a large part in the formulation of UK economic strategy during WW2, first through his influential pamphlet on *How to Pay for the War* (London, 1940) and then as an adviser to the chancellor of the exchequer. The possibility that full-employment policies in market economies would lead sooner or later to a persistent problem of wage –price inflation was recognized by Keynes, but his analytical framework could offer no clear-cut solution. The true extent of the dilemma and the policy/strategy and guidelines to be adopted in the face of it have remained matters of controversy among economists.

Keynes's other important achievement during his last years was to help create a new basis for international monetary and economic cooperation after WW2. The climax of these efforts came at the conference of Bretton Woods, New

Hampshire, in 1944, where Keynes led the British delegation and Harry Dexter White the American. The outcome was the establishment of the International Monetary Fund and the International Bank for Reconstruction and Development (the 'World Bank'). The Fund's Articles of Agreement formed a blueprint for global monetary arrangements until August 1971.

Besides his professional accomplishments, Keynes was distinguished as a patron and connoisseur of literature and the arts, and was associated in the 1920s with the Bloomsbury group. PMO
R. F. Harrod, *The Life of John Maynard Keynes* (London, 1951); M. Keynes (ed.), *Essays on John Maynard Keynes* (Cambridge, 1975).

Kharasch, Morris Selig (b. Krzemieniec, Russian Poland [now Kremenets, Ukraine, USSR], 24.8.1895; d. Chicago, Ill., USA, 7.10.1957). American organic chemist. Kharasch emigrated to Chicago at 13 and had his early chemical education in the University of Chicago, to which he returned in 1928 and where he remained until his death. He was one of the founders of the *Journal of Organic Chemistry*, and an editor of *Tetrahedron*. His name is perpetuated by his studies (with F. Mayo) of the influence of peroxides on the addition of hydrogen bromide to alkenes and related compounds. These studies cleared up an extremely confused situation, through Kharasch's understanding of the free-radical mechanism of the peroxide-catalysed addition. These ideas have since been widely applied by Kharasch and others in synthetic and in mechanistic organic chemistry. Kharasch worked (with Frank Westheimer) during WW2 on reaction mechanisms in polymerization, with special reference to wartime synthetic rubber projects. Kharasch had very varied chemical interests: he also studied alkyl mercury compounds, fungicides, and the active principle of ergot, as well as thermochemistry. NBC

Khlebnikov, Velemir Viktor Vladimirovich (b. Tundutovo, Astrakhan, Russia, 9.11.1885; d. Santalovo, Novgorod, USSR, 28.6.1922). Russian poet, the most radical innovator among the postsymbolists. From an obscure provincial background, Khlebnikov studied mathematics at Kazan University (1903–8) and then biology at St Petersburg (expelled 1911); he was in touch with metropolitan literary circles as founder and inspiration of the futurist group from about 1910, but later led a wandering hobo life, especially in his last five years. A genuine visionary, a man 'not of this world', Khlebnikov dreamed of a reformed global order attained through understanding the mathematical keys to human nature and history. He gave no systematic exposition of his ideas, nor could he; they are indivisible from their expression in his lyrics and longer poems, some of which attempt to break through into the supranational, universal language of the new order. Khlebnikov's manner offered a fertile alternative to existing poetic language; although there are considerable differences between individual works, there is persistent experiment with word formation and sound association, and the intellectual frame of reference and imagery depart from familiar areas and range into Slavonic folklore and non-European mythology, the prehistoric and legendary past. He avoids logical sequentiality, making abrupt and frequently grotesque shifts in time-scheme and subject matter, and breaking up metres and rhyme. His mental processes and their expression have sometimes been compared with those of infants and the insane. Mainly ignored by baffled critics and the reading public at large, among poets he has remained a charismatic figure, the spiritual ancestor of successive avant-garde movements. His attitude towards publication was casual; the scattered single works that appeared during his lifetime were collected by devotees between 1920 and 1933, and a further volume of unpublished works appeared in 1940. These editions were brought together and supplied with much additional material by V. Markov as *Sobranie sochinenii* [Collected works] (5 vols, Munich, 1968–71). A selection of his poetry and prose in English translation is to be found in *Snake Train* (ed. G. Kern, Ann Arbor, 1976). GSS

V. Markov, *The Longer Poems of Velemir Khlebnikov* (Berkeley, Calif., 1962).

Khomeini, Ruwalla (b. Khomein, nr Isfahan, Persia [now Iran], 17.5.1900). Known as the Ayatollah Khomeini, fundamentalist religious leader of the Shi'ite Muslims in Iran, arrested in 1963 and exiled by Mohammed Shah Pahlevi for his public and whole-hearted denunciation of the Shah's westernization of Iranian society, especially for the social and political emancipation of women in Iran and the Shah's failure to support the Arab states against Israel. With the collapse of the Shah's government and the Shah's flight into exile in January 1979, the Ayatollah returned from Paris, to become the *de facto* ruler and source of legitimacy in the eyes of the victorious Islamic city mobs and their student leaders and the extremist political parties which sought to capture the government of Iran. Even when a new constitution was introduced in 1980, and a president and Majlis elected, Khomeini, officially recognized as *Veloyat Fagih* [moral supervisor], remained the ultimate source and guarantee of authority in the eyes of the Islamic masses; the extreme antiwestern reaction he embodied remained unchallenged, until the discovery, in the war with Iraq, that isolation from the outside world in a cloud of Shi'ite fundamentalist self-righteousness would not of itself achieve victory began to undermine his authority. DCW

Khorana, Har Ghobind (b. Raipur, Madhya Pradesh, India, 9.1.1922). Indian bio-organic chemist. Khorana's early chemical education was at Punjab University, then at Liverpool University. After further research in Zürich and in Cambridge, he led the organic chemistry section of the British Columbia Research Council in Vancouver from 1952 to 1960, and during this period studied reactions of carbodi-imides, with the aid of which he synthesized coenzyme A and other nucleotide coenzymes. In 1960–70, while codirector of the Institute of Enzyme Research, University of Wisconsin, and holder of chairs in chemistry and the life sciences, he accomplished historic syntheses of complex polynucleotides of known base sequence, thereby helping to clarify important aspects of the genetic code. In recent years he has, with great success, given special attention to the total synthesis of genes, e.g. one from *Escherichia coli* containing 126 nucleotide base-pairs, to regions in genes with special properties, and to various aspects of RNA and DNA chemistry. Since 1970 he has been Alfred P. Sloan professor of biology and chemistry at MIT. In 1968 he was awarded the Nobel prize for physiology and medicine jointly with M. W. Nisenberg and R. W. Holley. NBC

Kierkegaard, Sören Aabye (b. Copenhagen, Denmark, 5.5.1813; d. Copenhagen, 11.11.1855). Danish philosopher and theologian. Kierkegaard was the son of a man of powerful character who had risen by his own exertions from humble beginnings to considerable wealth. At an early stage in his career, overcome by the thought of the obstacles destiny had put in his way, the father had cursed God, a Scandinavian emotional extravagance that was to weigh on him ever afterwards and, as a kind of inheritance of sin, on his son. He died when Kierkegaard was 25. Kierkegaard's university studies coincided with Hegel's death, well before his displacement in the 1840s as the leader of German thought. Kierkegaard found Hegel's system unbearable. To him it was an immense fraud which, by its verbose techniques of reconciliation and rationalization, refused to confront the actual circumstances of man in the world, and in particular the fact of death and the remoteness and inscrutability of God. While Hegel's prose was almost exclusively a colourless and humourless tumult of abstract jargon, Kierkegaard was a gifted and entertaining writer who overcame his imposing adversary as much by mocking wit as by logical refutation. But for all his quaint pseudonyms and resolutely unacademic literary forms there is no question about Kierkegaard's seriousness as a philosopher. Significant in this connection is his relationship with Regine Olsen. At a loose end after leaving the university he got engaged to her, but after a while came to the conclusion that marriage and domestic responsibility were incompatible with the philosophical task to which he felt called. His efforts to extricate himself without an insultingly direct rejection have a certain Dostoevskyan ludicrousness. Kierkegaard's main aim in his conflict with Hegel was the reinstatement of the person. Hegel had denied personal immortality and had treated the human individual as an insubstantial being of secondary importance even in his lifetime, where his true fulfilment, according to Hegel, was to be found in self-annihilating submission to the purposes of social institutions, in particular the state. Hegel had also in effect denied the personality of God which he saw as a poetic myth anticipating in a primitive way the higher philosophical truth embodied in his own doctrine of the Absolute. Hegel had contrasted self-sacrificing service to the state with the individualistic pursuit of self-interested ends in his account of the practical life of man. Kierkegaard interposes his conception of the ethical, at its most familiar in the form of complacent bourgeois respectability, between the aesthetic style of life, a matter of the wayward pursuit of gratification, and the religious life in which mundane ethical rules are transcended. An image of this transcendence, the 'teleological suspension of the ethical', is God's demand that Abraham should sacrifice Isaac, memorably considered in Kierkegaard's early *Frygt og Boeven* (Copenhagen, 1843; tr. R. Payne, *Fear and Trembling*, London, 1939). *Philosophiske Smuler* (Copenhagen, 1844; tr. D. F. Swenson, *Philosophical Fragments*, NY, 1936, ²1962) and *Begrebet angest* (Copenhagen, 1844; tr. W. Lowrie, *The Concept of Dread*, London, 1944, ²1957) argue, against the determination of Hegel, both that Christianity implies the freedom of human agents and that human agents are free; therefore Hegelianism is neither Christian nor true. Kierkegaard's most systematic work *Afsluttende uvidenskabelig Efterskrift* (Copenhagen, 1846; tr. D. F. Swenson & W. Lowrie, *Concluding Unscientific Postscript*, London, 1941, ²1968) attacks the philosophical foundations of Hegel's thought. It argues that actual existence, as we experience it in life, cannot be bureaucratically rationalized in Hegel's way and that men and the world they inhabit cannot be tidily explained. Belief in God is not the solution to a theoretical problem but a free act of faith. In the next few years Kierkegaard devoted himself to an attack, even more calculated to excite public anger than his philosophical writing, on institutional Christianity. Kierkegaard saw the Protestant church as a means of perverting Christ's original message, making it minister to the conventional prejudices of the age. His small local notoriety soon evaporated after his early death at 42 and it was not until BRANDES wrote about him 22 years later that he achieved general recognition. His acceptance as one of the greatest philosophers of the 19c did not come until the present century, first through theologians and then more generally. AQ

E. L. Allen, *Kierkegaard: his Life and Thought* (London, 1935); P. P. Rohde, *Sören Kierkegaard: an Introduction to his Life and Thought* (London, 1963).

King, Martin Luther (b. Atlanta, Ga, USA, 15.1.1929; d. Memphis, Tenn., 4.4.1968). Black American Baptist pastor and leader of the American civil rights nonviolent campaign against segregation in public services, including school and university education, in the American South from his first emergence as leader, in Montgomery, Alabama, of demonstrations against segregation on public buses. A superb orator, of somewhat unconventional private life, winner of the Nobel peace prize in 1964, he headed a movement of considerable political sophistication and tactical skill in which a new generation of black political leaders was to emerge. His assassination in 1968 by a hired assassin was the work of a conspiracy, the members of which have never been identified. DCW

Kinoshita, Junji (b. Tokyo, Japan, 2.8.1914). Japanese dramatist and writer on modern Japanese theatre. Kinoshita specialized in Shakespeare as a student in the late 1930s. His first play, a historical drama, shows the influence of the 'social realism' prevalent among the modern playwrights of the time. During

WW2, however, he sought the 'dramatic' in the folk legends that Japanese audiences all knew. Of his many popular folktale plays, which in the 1950s provoked a new interest in folk art, *Yūzuru* (Tokyo, 1949; tr. A. C. Scott, *Twilight Crane*, NY, 1956) is the most famous. The play was important theatrically in its use of language to set the crane-woman apart from the other characters. In the 1960s Kinoshita turned to recent history for the subjects of his plays. In 1972 he merged his own dialogue with transcripts from the Tokyo war-crime trials in his examination of the problem of war guilt: *Kami to hito to no aida* (Tokyo, 1972; tr. E. J. Gangloff, *Between God and Man*, Tokyo, 1979). He has constantly experimented with forms, seeking a new dramaturgy for a Japanese theatre dominated commercially by a premodern consciousness. Kinoshita is primarily interested in the tragic hero who stands against the flow of history *because* he knows it will overwhelm him. The culmination of his search for such a hero and his many theatrical experiments can be seen in his latest play *Shigosen no Matsuri* [The dirge of the meridian] (Tokyo, 1977). Based on a 12c epic, it portrays, through the losing general, the point in Japanese history where the outcome of a struggle between two families will decide the course of the country's development for the next several centuries. A large chorus out of which and into which the main characters step, several strata of language and the treatment of the cosmic forces which affect the final battle, all made the first production of this play an epochal event in modern Japanese theatre.　　　　BWFP

Kinsey, Alfred Charles (b. Hoboken, NJ, USA, 23.6.1894; d. Bloomington, Ind., 26.8.1956). American sexologist. Kinsey graduated with a PhD in entomology from Harvard in 1920 and studied gall wasps until 1937. When he was 43, Indiana University, where he was teaching, introduced courses in sex education and Kinsey, as a respectable biologist and family man, was chosen to be an instructor. Knowing little about the subject, he first sought information from libraries, discovered that few facts were

available, and conducted his own interviews with such vigour that by his death he and his colleagues had collected around 17,500 sexual case histories. The research continues at the Institute for Sex Research founded by Kinsey at Indiana. The results of Kinsey's investigations were published in two monumental volumes: Kinsey *et al.*, *Sexual Behavior in the Human Male* (Philadelphia, 1948) and Kinsey *et al.*, *Sexual Behavior in the Human Female* (Philadelphia, 1953). These studies were concerned with white American males and females at a particular time in history, but within that limitation they are a very comprehensive documentation of 'who does what, when and with whom' and were a major step towards placing sex research on a respectable scientific footing. Written primarily for the scientific and medical community, they were of such interest to the population as a whole that they became bestsellers. Early readers were fascinated to learn that masturbation was almost endemic among men, many of them continuing the practice after marriage as an additional 'outlet', and that quite a high proportion of women also masturbated occasionally. Even in those relatively intolerant days, they were somewhat surprised to learn that 37 per cent of men had experienced homosexual orgasm at some time since the onset of adolescence, the equivalent figure for women being around 13 per cent. They were either scandalized or vindicated to learn that about half of all married men and about a quarter of all married women committed adultery. Findings of this kind were probably influential in liberalizing attitudes towards sex, even though they cannot be held wholly responsible for the sexual revolution of the 1960s. Also of great interest was the finding that sexual behaviour differed enormously from one individual to another and from one social group to another. Petting, for example, was largely a middle-class phenomenon; the working classes mostly proceeded straight to intercourse with a minimum of foreplay. Criticisms of Kinsey's methodology are that his respondents were all volunteers rather than a random sample, and that the face-to-face interview may have been more inhibiting than an anonymous questionnaire. Nevertheless, the scope of his study remains unrivalled and its validity has generally been supported by subsequent studies, although certain changes in sexual behaviour since the 1940s have been detected. GDW

L. Trilling, 'The Kinsey Report', in *The Liberal Imagination* (NY, 1950).

Kipling, Joseph Rudyard (b. Bombay, Maharashtra, India, 30.12.1865; d. London, UK, 18.1.1936). British short-story writer, poet and journalist. The son of the curator of the Lahore museum, he was sent home to be educated at the United Services College, a minor public school for the sons of service officers, and returned to India in 1882 to work on the staff of the Lahore *Civil and Military Gazette*. The next seven years produced a fine body of writing which quickly established his reputation: *Departmental Ditties* (London, 1886) was followed by several collections of short stories about British India, such as *Plain Tales from the Hills* (London, 1888). By this time the foundations of his subsequent career as a writer and imperialist had been laid. First, as a brilliant reporter he had trained himself to record accurately his exotic world; second, his detachment enabled him to ask questions about his own civilization and what lay beyond it; third, those early years provided him with an answer in the idea of the law which held society together and was best preserved by the loyalty of the in-group, whether of school prefects, Anglo-Indians, the officers' mess, or freemasons. He recorded the expertise and jargon by which these groups expressed their solidarity – in his eyes an absolute virtue which justified the ritualized brutality in many of his stories by which outsiders became insiders or were cast beyond the pale. Returning to London in 1889 ready to defend his ideas against the flabby intellectuals who were betraying the imperial cause, he assumed and retained the role of national bard. His best work is in the two *Jungle Books* (London, 1894 & 1895), the novel *Kim* (London, 1901), his stories *Puck of Pook's Hill* (London,

1906) and *Rewards and Fairies* (London, 1910), and the cryptic, more obscure stories of his last period. Kipling's myth of the law and empire is unsubtle, and only occasionally does his knowingness about life become the inwardness which can reveal complexity of character. Yet the confident simplicity of his ideas enabled him to appropriate for literature large tracts of unclaimed human experience. DC

J. M. S. Tompkins, *The Art of Rudyard Kipling* (London, 1959); A. Wilson, *The Strange Ride of Rudyard Kipling* (London, 1977).

Kirchner, Ernst Ludwig (b. Aschaffenburg, Bavaria, Germany, 6.5.1880; d. Frauenkirch, Graubünden, Switzerland, 15.6.1938). German expressionist painter, sculptor and graphic artist. While studying architecture in Dresden (1901–5) he spent a semester studying art in Munich (1903–4). In 1905 he and three other architecture students, Heckel, Bleyl and SCHMIDT-ROTTLUFF, founded the Brücke artists' community, living and working together, and holding alternate painting and graphics exhibitions. The *Jugendstil* quality of Kirchner's early work soon gave way to the influence of the neoimpressionists, especially Van Gogh and Gauguin. He began to use disquietingly juxtaposed brilliant colours combined with large simplified forms, inspired by the expressive distortions of the primitive sculpture he discovered in the Dresden Ethnographical Museum in 1904. Struck by the expressive directness of German medieval blockbooks, and by the graphic work of Dürer and Rembrandt, he sought to achieve a similar intensity of 'feeling and experience' in his many woodcuts and woodcarvings, characterized by emphatic, often aggressively angular contours. His most frequent theme was the nude: his friends and models informally posed in his exotically decorated studio, or casually disported themselves in the open air. After moving to Berlin in 1911 he recorded his reactions to the city in depictions of cabaret dancers, circus artistes and prostitutes which, especially after the 1912 futurist exhibition at Cassirer's, became more insistently distended, with aggressively jagged contours and more sombre colours (e.g. *Potsdamer Platz*, 1914). Conscripted in 1915, he was soon discharged suffering from tuberculosis. He moved to Switzerland for treatment in 1917. After a series of nervous breakdowns, he settled in Frauenkirch in 1919, where he concentrated on monumental naive-expressionistic alpine scenes characterized by the predominance of garish pastels, many of which he had embroidered or woven into tapestries (e.g. *Up to the Alp*, 1926). From c. 1928, influenced by PICASSO, he developed a more abstract style, incorporating simultaneous viewpoints and large, simplified colour planes to create serenely ornamental and rhythmic surface patterns (e.g. *Lovers*, 1930). His depression grew worse when he was condemned as 'degenerate' by the Nazis in 1937; the following year he committed suicide.   SOBT

W. Grohmann, *Ernst Ludwig Kirchner* (London, 1961); E. Gordon, *Ernst Ludwig Kirchner* (Munich, 1968).

Kirov, Sergey Mironovich (b. Kostrikov, Kirov, Russia, 27.3.1886; d. Leningrad, USSR, 1.12.1934). Russian Communist leader whose assassination marked the start of STALIN's Great Purge. Kirov was trained as a mechanic in Kazan and joined the Bolshevik party at an early age, serving several spells in prison and becoming a party organizer in the Caucasus. In 1922 he was elected to the party's Central Committee, and in 1926 was moved by Stalin to the key post of head of the Leningrad party organization in place of ZINOVYEV. As a supporter of Stalin he was elected to full membership of the Politburo in 1930. He was murdered in 1934 by a young party member Leonid Nikolayev who was accused of being a Zinovyevite terrorist and shot with 13 accomplices. Stalin then claimed to have uncovered a conspiracy to assassinate the entire Soviet leadership, and launched the Great Purge of 1934–8 with the execution of several hundred and the deportation of several thousand Leningraders. Stalin himself has subsequently come under suspicion of responsibility for the death of Kirov as a popular rival who was building up too independent a position. The truth may never become known. Kirov's murder, however, remains a central event in the dark history of the Soviet Union in the 1930s and in Stalin's emergence as dictator.
                                            ALCB

Kissinger, Henry Alfred (b. Fuerth, Hesse, Germany, 27.5.1923; naturalized American citizen, 1943). German/American political scientist and secretary of state. While still a professor at Harvard, Kissinger questioned (in *Nuclear Weapons and Foreign Policy*, NY, 1957) whether the strategy of 'massive retaliation' formulated by DULLES in 1954 would convince any aggressor with a series of limited aims. Relating the technologically possible to the politically desirable, he considered a dual US posture of all-out deterrence and limited nuclear war. For Kissinger, tactical nuclear strikes represented the most effective US strategy against either nuclear powers or powers capable of substituting manpower for technology. In *The Necessity for Choice* (NY, 1960), however, Kissinger drastically revised his earlier views of limited nuclear warfare and urged an increase in conventional war capability, an increase in strategic nuclear weaponry and a North Atlantic Confederation to make deterrence effective in Europe. He also established the arms negotiator's criterion: whether a given measure enhances stability or detracts from it.

Kissinger's use of strategic policies to indicate political choices is demonstrated in his account of his time in office *The White House Years* (NY, 1979). The move from a '$2\frac{1}{2}$' war strategy (the ability to fight a war against a Sino–Soviet monolith and still retain the military capacity to deal with smaller disturbances) to a '$1\frac{1}{2}$' war strategy both harmonized doctrine with capability and signalled to Peking that the US was prepared to differentiate between communist regimes.   JGo

In 1969 Kissinger became special adviser on national security to President NIXON and, in 1973, US secretary of state. The most un-American secretary of state in the 20c, and a recognized 'maverick' in the US academic community, he developed a style of diplomacy that was highly successful on many occasions, most notably the negotiation of the American withdrawal from Vietnam in 1973, the negotiation by 'shuttle diplomacy' between Cairo and Jerusalem of an agreement between Egypt and Israel on the withdrawal of Israeli forces after the 'Yom Kippur' war of 1973, and the reopening of amicable relations between the People's Republic of China and the USA. His success depended, however, on total secrecy of operation and a unified control of the policy-making machinery, two elements which made it in the long run unacceptable to Congress and to the American political elite. His approach to foreign policy emphasized the balance of forces between the USSR and the USA, a balance which he tried to use to negotiate agreements with the USSR aimed as much at the acceptance of limitations on the manner in which each superpower pursued its objectives, as at specific issues of conflict; he sought particularly to persuade both his own fellow countrymen and the Soviet leadership to see and accept the 'linkages' between different areas of conflict. The implied suggestion that the wilful exacerbation of open-ended conflict offended a higher morality than that to which American foreign-policy makers and their critics usually appealed made his diplomacy unacceptable to his fellow countrymen.

DCW

Kitaj, R. B. (b. Chagrin Falls, Ohio, USA, 29.10.1932). American painter. In his painting and polemic Kitaj has tried to demonstrate that fidelity to the modernist tradition does not necessarily imply the abandonment of figuration. As a young man he worked as a seaman on tankers and cargo ships; at the Vienna Academy he mastered figure drawing and anatomical dissection. He came to the UK in 1957 and studied at the Royal College of Art (1960–2), where he formed a close friendship with HOCKNEY. For some time Kitaj's work was associated with British Pop painting, which first came to prominence in 1962. His pictures, however, were stamped by his background in traditional drawing; his admitted 'bibliomania'; and his erudite knowledge of European modernist and socialist culture.

His work achieved its full stature in the 1970s with such large, utopian paintings as *If Not, Not* (1975–6) and *Land of Lakes* (1975–7). In 1976 he organized an exhibition 'The Human Clay', and subsequently became involved in heated public controversies about the role of figuration in contemporary art.   PF

R. B. Kitaj, retro. cat., Hirshhorn Museum (Washington, 1981).

Klee, Paul (b. München-Buchesee, nr Bern, Switzerland, 18.12.1879; d. Muralto, nr Locarno, Ticino, 29.6.1940). Swiss painter and graphic artist. The son of a music teacher, Klee was an accomplished violinist for whom music and art were closely linked throughout his life. In 1900 he studied art under Franz von Stuck in Munich. A tour of Italy (1901–2) revealed the 'architectonic element', which he then sought to fuse with the 'poetic' or expressive element in art. His early work was largely graphic. From 1902 to 1906, living in Bern, he executed a series of fantastic-satirical expressionist etchings (e.g. *Virgin in the Tree*, 1903) combining influences as diverse as Schongauer, Goya, Blake and Beardsley. In 1906 he married the pianist Lily Stumpf and settled in Munich. The febrile, staccato linear rhythms of his etchings up to 1910 bear witness to his interest in MUNCH and ENSOR's graphics. Following his discovery of Van Gogh (1908) and CÉZANNE (1909), he embarked in 1910 on pure watercolours. In 1912 he met KANDINSKY, MARC and the Blue Rider circle, and participated in their second exhibition. In April 1912 he visited Paris where he met DELAUNAY, whose essay on colour dynamism he translated into German. Inspired by orphic cubism, Klee began to use rhythmically organized colour planes to create form, structure and perspective.

A visit to Tunis and Kairouan with Macke and the Swiss artist Moilliet (April 1914) finally convinced him of the expressive power of colour. In 1916 –18 he served in the German army. In 1920 GROPIUS invited him to join the Weimar Bauhaus as form master in charge of the stained glass and book bindery and later of the weaving workshop. He gave theoretical classes on composition. Klee saw artistic activity as a 'simile of creation' in which rational observation and imaginative intuition were fused to give poetico-symbolic expression to the mystery of existence, physical and spiritual. Believing that 'art does not reproduce the visible; rather it makes visible' he considered the process of forming more significant than the final form; the pictorial elements (line, plane, colour and texture) must evoke objects and moods, and express ideas. The dynamism of the artistic process ('only the dead point is timeless') is echoed by the beholder's spatial and temporal experience of the work.

The ambivalence of Klee's naive-hieroglyphic abstractions is reinforced by the addition of witty or bizarre symbolic titles referring to human characteristics or moods. Klee resigned from the Bauhaus in 1931, and taught at the Düsseldorf Academy until his dismissal by the Nazis in 1933, when he returned to Bern. The illness which dominated the last three years of his life led to the creation of more sombre, haunting, mask-like configurations (e.g. *Guardian Angel*, 1939; *Death and Fire*, 1940). Klee's published writings include *Pädagogisches Skizzenbuch* (Weimar, 1925; *Pedagogical Sketchbook*, NY, 1953); *Das bildnerische Denken* (Basle, 1956; *The Thinking Eye*, London, 1961, [2]1969); *Unendliche Naturgeschichte* (Basle, 1970; *The Nature of Nature*, London, 1973).   SOBT

W. Haftmann, *The Mind and Work of Paul Klee* (London, 1954).

Klein, Christian Felix (b. Düsseldorf, N. Rhine-Westphalia, Germany, 25.4.1849; d. Göttingen, Lower Saxony, 22.6.1925). German mathematician and educator. After holding chairs at Erlangen, Munich and Leipzig, Klein was called to Göttingen in 1886 and passed the rest of his career there. In collaboration with F. Althoff, the Prussian minister of culture, he encouraged the postgraduate training of women; many men also took doctorates under his supervision. He was a leader in planning the collected works of the 19c mathematician C. F. Gauss; the *Encyklopädie der mathematischen Wissenschaften mit Einschluss ihrer Anwendungen* [Encyclopedia of mathe-

matical knowledge] (1898–1935), a vast multi-authored project reporting on the state of mathematics of the time; and the International Commission of Mathematics Education, which produced a series of important monographs in the 1900s and 1910s.

Klein's first major contribution to mathematics was his inaugural lecture at Erlangen in 1872, now known as the 'Erlangen programme', in which he proposed to classify the various geometries in terms of the properties of group theory. His work here was important not only for geometry but also for raising in mathematics the status of group theory itself. In concurrent studies he also produced so-called 'projective' models for Euclidean and non-Euclidean geometries. In the 1880s he applied the ideas of group theory to various aspects of differential equations and the theory of functions. Some of this work was produced in competition with J. H. POIN-CARÉ; and the stress under which he was placed seems to have affected his creative powers. Thus, when he came to Göttingen his major mathematical achievements were behind him, and his energies turned more to the educational and public enterprises described above. His papers are collected in *Gesammelte mathematische Abhandlungen* [Collected mathematical papers] (3 vols, Berlin, 1921–3).   IG-G

Klein, Melanie, *née* Reizes (b. Vienna, Austria-Hungary [now Austria], 30.3.1882; naturalized British citizen, 1931; d. London, UK, 24.9.1960). Austrian/British psychoanalyst, who made the most significant contribution to psychoanalytical thought and practice since FREUD. She was first analysed by Sandor Ferenczi in Budapest, having moved there in 1903 after her marriage, and then by Karl Abraham in Berlin. She pioneered the psychoanalysis of children, having devised a technique for adapting Freud's principles to child analysis by using the child's play to achieve understanding of his unconscious. The insight she derived from this greatly influenced her work with adults. In 1926 she moved to London, where her work was already known. She became a member of the British Psychoanalytical Society, taking an active part in the training and scientific programmes.

Klein's work was rooted in that of Freud, whose writings she discovered in 1910, but she extended his approaches in various ways. She elaborated his findings about childhood, tracing them back into earliest infancy. She explored the early object relationships and extended psychoanalytic knowledge about fantasy and the building of the inner world, thereby throwing light on very early mental processes, their derivatives in normal and abnormal development and their manifestations in the psychoanalytical situation. Although her work aroused considerable controversy within, and outside, the British Society, it has deeply influenced the whole development of psychoanalysis. It has opened up the clinical and theoretical understanding not only of normal development and neurosis, but also of psychosis and borderline states; it has also been influential in such fields as aesthetics and sociology. Her publications have been collected in *The Writings of Melanie Klein* (4 vols, London, 1975) and include *The Psycho-Analysis of Children* (London, 1932) and *Narrative of a Child Psycho-Analysis* (London, 1961). BJ

H. Segal, *Klein* (London, 1979).

Klein, Yves (b. Nice, France, 28.4.1928; d. Paris, 6.6.1962). French painter. A self-taught artist and the central figure of the *nouveau réalisme* reaction against abstract painting in the early 1960s. In 1949 he made his first monochrome paintings, applying the pigment to the support with a trowel to create a subtly textured surface which appeared to blend with the wall. He believed in a 'cosmic energy' of colour which led him by 1956 to use almost always a deep ultramarine which he felt was the most cosmic of colours. In 1956 he held an exhibition of floating blue globes and in 1957 began the series of 194 ultramarine blue paintings in which blue was applied with a spray gun. In 1958 he held an exhibition of 'nothingness' in which the bare white walls demonstrated the 'end of easel painting'. He offered the blank walls for sale, but only for pure gold. He developed an interest in

Performance art, e.g. the *Anthropometries* (1958–60), a series of 'ceremonies' during which an audience watched nude models painted blue rolled on to canvases to create impressions of their bodies. In the *Cosmogonies* (1960–2) he experimented with effects created by the intrusion of air, fire and water. He exposed freshly painted blue canvases to the rain, and used a blow lamp on areas of red, yellow and blue pigment to create scorched patches shaped like flames (e.g. *Fire Painting*, 1961–2). SOBT

P. Wember, *Yves Klein* (Cologne, 1969).

Klemperer, Otto (b. Breslau, Germany [now Wročlav, Poland], 14.5.1885; d. Zürich, Switzerland, 6.7.1973). German conductor whose reputation, such is the power of recordings, rests largely on his work with the Philharmonia (later New Philharmonia) Orchestra of London in the 1950s and 1960s. His performances at this time were weighty and slow. Though they could be dull, they were more often grandly impressive: the records he made of Beethoven, in particular, show this. But this late phase had been preceded by others in which Klemperer's style and attitudes were quite different. As conductor of the Cologne Opera (1917–24) he had given the German premières of two operas by JANÁČEK. He had also been chief conductor of the experimental Kroll Opera in Berlin throughout its existence (1927–31), and there he had conducted the stage première of STRAVINSKY's *Oedipus Rex* as well as works by Krenek, HINDEMITH and WEILL. Obliged as a Jew to leave Berlin in 1933, he settled in America, where he conducted the Los Angeles Philharmonic (1933–40) and founded the Pittsburgh Symphony. He also composed two symphonies and published an autobiographical volume, *Minor Recollections* (London, 1964). PG

P. Heyworth, *Conversations with Klemperer* (London, 1973); P. Beavan, *Klemperisms: a Few of Dr Klemperer's Lighter Moments* (London, 1974).

Klíma, Ladislav (b. Domažlice, Bohemia, Austria-Hungary [now Czechoslovakia], 22.8.1878; d. Prague, 19.4.1928). Czech philosopher and novelist inspired mainly by Berkeley, Schopenhauer and NIETZSCHE; an existentialist illusionist. In his life and writings he was an individualist in the strict and the colloquial sense. He was banned in 1895 from all Austrian schools for antistate and antichurch remarks, and then lived off a large inheritance in Bohemia, Switzerland and Austria, drinking and gambling; when the money was gone he lived in a Prague hotel, shining shoes, eating vermin and drinking spirits. The most original of all modern Czech thinkers, he wrote most of his works in his own vivid, lucid, often antigrammatical style before WW1 but published little until the 1920s. In *Svět jako vědomí a nic* [The world as consciousness and nothingness] (Prague, 1904) and *Trakáty a diktáty* [Tracts and diktats] (Prague, 1922) Klíma defined his solipsism: the individual's responsibility is to create his own world within himself through 'total' self-consciousness, 'total' self-awareness and 'total' aiming for the impossible; nothing exists beyond the ego. Klíma's thought is founded on often contradictory extremes, and at their core is his tenet that man's beauty lies in two facts: he need not reproduce and he can kill himself. Klíma's two novels *Utrpení knížete Sternenhocha* [The sufferings of Prince Sternenhoch] (Prague, 1928) and *Slavná Nemesis* [Glorious nemesis] (Prague, 1932) are elegant hotchpotches of wit, violence and caricature, and eloquent manifestations of his philosophy. In them the boundary between life and dream is expunged, and yet *Slavná Nemesis* approaches tragedy.   RBP

Klimt, Gustav (b. Baumgarten, Vienna, Austria-Hungary [now Austria], 14.7.1862; d. Vienna, 6.2.1918). Austrian painter. The son of an engraver, Klimt studied at the Vienna School of Applied Arts. From 1883 to 1892 he and his brother worked for an artist-decorator's firm, painting large realistic historical and allegorical scenes for museums and theatres in Vienna and elsewhere. In 1897 Klimt was a founder-member and president of the Vienna Sezession. He developed a new style characterized by more simplified forms, and influenced by *Jugendstil* decorations and posters, which he used in complex symbolistic compositions (e.g. murals for Vienna University: *Philosophy, Medicine* and *Jurisprudence*, 1899–1907, destroyed 1944). The pessimistic gloom and sensuousness of these works led to violent protests and they were rejected by the university. In 1905 he was commissioned to decorate the dining room of Hofmann's Palais Stoclet in Brussels (executed 1909–11). Influenced by British and Dutch art nouveau (MACKINTOSH and Toorop), Klimt's compositions became far more stylized and sinuous, with all elements except heads treated in a flat, decorative manner with an increasingly geometric emphasis (e.g. *The Kiss*, 1909). This ornamental quality was reinforced by the use of mosaic for the final works. A 'bloodless eroticism' characterizes many works of his later period.   SOBT

Gustav Klimt and Egon Schiele, Guggenheim Museum (NY, 1965); F. Novotny & J. Dobai, *Gustav Klimt* (London, 1968).

Kline, Franz (b. Wilkes-Barre, Pa, USA, 23.5.1910; d. New York, 13.5.1962). American abstract expressionist painter. He studied in Boston and London before settling in New York (1939). Until c. 1950 his style was expressively realistic, his most frequent theme the urban landscape. In 1946, influenced by KOONING, he experimented with a more gestural expressionism (e.g. *Nijinsky [Petrouchka]*, 1948). By 1950, using a Bell-Opticon enlarger to project forms on to the wall, he was magnifying freely drawn, spontaneous brushstrokes into enormous nonobjective forms or ideograms. Restricting himself to black and white, using quick-drying commercial matt and gloss enamel paint and a mixture of house-painter's and conventional brushes, he created monumental configurations of black swirls, diagonals, slabs and girder-like strokes intended to evoke the continuous energy and confusion of urban life (e.g. *Ninth Street*, 1951; *Painting No. 2*, 1954). His forms appeared improvised, but were carefully developed in numerous preparatory sketches; the sense of spontaneity derived from the rapid execution of the final work. The calligraphic quality of these 'black-on-white' designs has often been noted; however, he saw the white not as 'background' but as of equal standing with the black forms, an effect reinforced by the frequent intrusion of the white into or over the black. In the late 1950s he began to use colour again, but did not live long enough to prove that colour could substantially alter or add to his style.   SOBT

J. Gordon, *Franz Kline 1910–1962*, exh. cat., Whitney Museum of American Art (NY, 1968).

Klint, Kaare (b. Copenhagen, Denmark, 15.12.1888; d. Copenhagen, 28.3.1954). Danish furniture designer who was responsible for developing the post-WW2 concept of Danish design which combines a respect for tradition with aesthetic and technical innovation. It was Klint who first looked back to traditional chair types, such as English 18c furniture, reworking them into modern versions which took into account the measurements and proportions of the human body: he was, in fact, one of the most important pioneers in the field of anthropometrics in design. His most notable designs were the Faaberg chair of 1914 and the deck chair and safari chair, both of 1933. Son of the architect P. V. Jensen, Klint was also trained as an architect during the period of Danish neoclassicism. By 1917 he had begun his studies of human measurements and in 1924 he became the head of the department of furniture design at the Royal Academy of Art in Copenhagen. Klint's contribution to international furniture design is less that of a daring aesthetic innovator than of a systematic designer with flair. He worked, from 1927 onwards, with the cabinet-maker Rudolf Rasmussen and passed on his ideas to his pupils, the most famous of whom was Borge Mogensen.   PAS

S. E. Møller (ed.), *Danish Design* (Copenhagen, 1974); R. Andersen (ed.), *Kaare Klint Møbler* (Copenhagen, 1979).

Koch, Heinrich Hermann Robert (b. Clausthal [now Clausthal-Zellerfeld], Lower Saxony, Germany, 11.12.1843; d. Baden-Baden, Baden-Württemberg, 27.5.1910). German bacteriologist. Along with Louis Pasteur and other 19c scientists, Koch demonstrated the role of

micro-organisms in causing many diseases, thus establishing the 'germ theory of disease'. After medical education and military service, Koch established a general medical practice in Wollstein (now Wolsztyn, Poland) where his early work on the life cycle of the anthrax bacillus (causative agent of anthrax) was done. These researches enabled him to obtain an appointment in 1880 as government adviser with the Department of Health in Berlin, and to devote his whole energy to bacteriology and public health. His two most important discoveries soon followed: discovery of the tubercle bacillus (1882: agent of tuberculosis) and the comma bacillus (1883: cholera). These secured his worldwide fame, further enhanced in 1890 by his announcement that 'tuberculin', an extract from the tubercle bacillus, could cure the disease. This claim proved unfounded, but Koch continued to be in great demand to investigate outbreaks of human and animal disease throughout the world. He studied many infectious diseases, including diphtheria, cattle pest, bubonic plague, sleeping sickness and typhoid fever. He was a gifted field epidemiologist, but he made equally important contributions in the laboratory, where he developed many new techniques for growing, staining and identifying pathogenic micro-organisms. 'Koch's postulates', though in essence laid down by earlier workers, established the criteria whereby an organism could be shown to cause a particular disease. In 1891 he became director of a lavishly funded Institute for Infectious Diseases in Berlin. Koch's 1905 Nobel prize was for his work on tuberculosis, the prevention and treatment of which continued to preoccupy him until his death.   WFB

Koechlin, Charles Louis Eugène (b. Paris, France, 27.11.1867; d. Le Canadel, Var, 31.12.1950). French composer and musician. Some musicians are slow to receive the recognition they deserve even though they exercise a strong influence on their generation both as composers and teachers. Such is Charles Koechlin who could unfairly, but not inaccurately at present, be described as a mere catalyst; his treatises on harmony and orchestration are widely used while the majority of his music, in widely diversified forms, remains unperformed. Yet Henri Sauget, one of Koechlin's many distinguished pupils, has aptly written, 'It possesses all the characteristics that should compel recognition: imagination, variety, colour, rhythm, originality, grace, freshness, tenderness, power, nobility and a presence revealing sterling genuineness.'

Koechlin entered the Paris Conservatoire in 1890 and studied with Gedalge and Massenet and with Fauré, who entrusted him with the orchestration of his music for the 1898 London production of *Pelléas et Mélisande*, and on whom Koechlin wrote a monograph (*Gabriel Fauré*, Paris, 1927; London, 1946). Koechlin's own music alternates between extreme simplicity, as in the piano Sonatines, and advanced complexity, as in the orchestral *Le Livre de Jungle* based on KIPLING. His love of the cinema resulted in the 'Seven Stars Symphony' (1933), each movement inspired by a different film star. Justifiably this neglected composer was elected president of the French section of the International Society for Contemporary Music.   JL

H. Sauget, *et al.*, *L'Oeuvre de Charles Koechlin. An Annotated Catalogue* (Paris, 1975).

Koestler, Arthur (b. Budapest, Austria-Hungary [now Hungary], 5.9.1905; naturalized British citizen, 1946; d. London, UK, 3.3.1983). Hungarian/British writer and philosopher. Koestler studied science at Budapest and after a year of working in the Jewish settlements in Palestine became science correspondent for the German Ullstein chain, writing a famous report as a member of the Graf Zeppelin North Pole expedition of 1931. At that time he was an undercover member of the Communist party. He travelled in Russia and Soviet Central Asia in 1932–3, then wrote party propaganda from Paris until he went to Spain, nominally as the *News Chronicle*'s war correspondent. Arrested by the fascists, his British cover saved his life. While in prison he began to move away from both STALINism and communism: his *Ein spanisches Testament* (Zürich, 1938; tr. T. & P. Hewitt, *Spanish Testa-*

ment, London, 1937) is one of the best books to have come out of the Spanish war, certainly a classic study of imprisonment. ORWELL soon hailed him as one of a 'new breed of political writers', meaning people who could write about politics without sacrificing either truth or artistic integrity. His first novel *The Gladiators* (tr. E. Simons, London, 1939) about Spartacus's revolt consolidated his move from communism, though still showed an idealistic socialism. After joining the French Foreign Legion, he escaped from Europe to the UK where, after a brief internment, he served in the Pioneer Corps in WW2. *Darkness at Noon* (tr. D. Hardy, London, 1940) and *Arrival and Departure* (London, 1943) were two extraordinary political novels, perhaps the best analyses of the totalitarian mind ever written: Koestler has some claims to be one of the first to see the awful similarities between Stalinism and Nazism. Although some consider these his best books, he returned to science after the war and began a long series of difficult and profound studies about the biological and psychological nature of man, somewhat losing his old audience without entirely gaining a new scientific one. Most famous was *The Ghost in the Machine* (London, 1967) which argued that a specific flaw in the evolution of the human brain accounted for the 'schizophrenic split' between reason and emotion, sociability and violence. Few modern writers of sense and authority have dared to generalize so widely. The final judgement may be that he was a great popularizer, an absolute prince of higher journalism rather than a truly original thinker or great novelist. But to say 'modern intellectual' is at once to think of Koestler. Recently he produced an anthology of his own writing, *Bricks to Babel* (London, 1981), reducing – he said – 9000 pages to 700. In fact his *oeuvre* is even greater, for he extracted very little from his prolific communist period.   BRC

H. Harris (ed.), *Astride Two Cultures: Arthur Koestler at Seventy* (London, 1975); I. Hamilton, *Koestler: a Life* (London, 1982).

Koht, Halvdan (b. Tromsø, Norway, 7.7.1873; d. Oslo, 12.12.1965). Norwegian historian. Professor at Oslo from 1910 to 1935, Koht was foreign minister of Norway from 1935 to 1940. A prolific writer and an energetic organizer of international projects, Koht is best known for his work on Norwegian history. But he also wrote on American history and was active in other fields. He believed that history was primarily the history of society. He was particularly interested in the relations between social conditions and ideas such as nationalism, socialism and democracy, but rejected determinism. *Norsk bondereising* [Norwegian peasant risings] (Oslo, 1926) is among his most important books; he also wrote on the revolutions of 1776 and 1848. This interest in social forces did not lead him to neglect individuals; he wrote biographies of *Henrik Ibsen* (2 vols, Oslo, 1928–9; NY, 1931), and of Bismarck. Koht's balanced view of the historical process emerges clearly from his *Drivmakter i historia* (Oslo, 1959; *Driving Forces in History*, Cambridge, Mass., 1964).   UPB

Kokoschka, Oskar (b. Pöchlarn, Lower Austria, Austria-Hungary [now Austria], 1.3.1886; naturalized British citizen, 1947; d. Villeneuve, Vaud, Switzerland, 22.2.1980). Austrian/British painter. Loath to be identified with any movement, Kokoschka ranks as a pioneer of expressionism thanks to his raw-nerved early play *Mörder, Hoffnung der frauen* [Murderer, hope of women] (1909), and his drawings and writings in *Der Sturm* throughout 1910. Thereafter his literary output was slight, while the painting which was his lifelong obsession remained mainly impressionist in style and technique; this despite the psychological intensity of his early portraits, the arbitrary perspective of his panoramic landscapes and the symbolism and mythology of his imaginative compositions. Resident in Berlin immediately before WW1 and in Dresden after his discharge due to wounds, he never absorbed the same cubist, futurist and Negro influences as the German expressionists, and from 1924 was largely on the move. Shocked by Nazism in Germany and the suppression of the socialists in Austria, in 1934 he settled in Czechoslovakia, where he painted MASA-

RYK and identified himself increasingly with children's education and welfare. In 1938 he emigrated to England and spent WW2 in London and Cornwall. Yet he remained almost unnoticed there as an artist until he was in his 70s, and even then was never assimilated into the English art scene. Instead he renewed his links with Central Europe, where from 1953 he ran an annual summer course at Salzburg and executed many commissions in West Germany for views of cities and portraits of leading figures. He published his autobiography *My Life* (London) in 1974.   JWMW

E. Hoffmann, *Oskar Kokoschka* (London, 1947).

Kolakowski, Leszek (b. Radom, Poland, 23.10.1927). Polish philosopher. Educated at Lodz, he taught at Warsaw and, as a member of the Communist party, was influential in the development of the liberalization which led to the Polish 'spring' of 1956. From this point he was increasingly critical of communist orthodoxy, becoming a focus of intellectual dissent throughout Eastern Europe. Expelled from the party in 1966 and his chair in 1968, he moved to the West, teaching in North America and in 1970 settling in Oxford, at All Souls College. His writings, originally contributing to the emergence of a MARXist humanism, have shown a progressive move away from Marxism. Stressing the moral responsibility of the individual and rejecting determinism, he has been deeply occupied with traditional problems of metaphysics and ethics. His major work has been a survey of the *Main Currents in Marxism* (3 vols, Oxford, 1978), his defence of which against Marxist critics has shown how far he has come to see Marxism as essentially sterile and inimical to freedom. His most recent work *Religion* (London, 1982), subtitled 'If there is no God ... On God, the devil, sin and other worries of the so-called philosophy of religion', continues his concern with fundamental beliefs which Marxism – and positivism – have set on one side.

DCr

Kolff, Willem Johan (b. Leiden, S. Holland, The Netherlands, 14.2.1911; naturalized American citizen). Dutch/American physician. Educated at the universities of Leiden and Gröningen, he held posts at Leiden (1934–6) and Gröningen (1938–41) before joining the medical department at Kampen. It was here that he developed the world's first artificial kidney; he also produced a blood oxygenator. The kidney was enormous, filling a large room; once built, however, the problems of miniaturization were solvable. In 1950 Kolff emigrated to the USA and was subsequently appointed professor of clinical investigation at the Cleveland Clinic Foundation. In 1960 he moved to the University of Utah as professor of surgery and head of the division of artificial organs. His research interests include kidney transplantation; the application of heart–lung machines; development of an artificial heart for use in patients awaiting a suitable transplant; development of seeing aids for the blind; preservation of organs for transplantation; and further improvements in artificial kidneys and blood oxygenators. In late 1982 the artificial heart he developed was used clinically for the first time. He is the author of over 600 scientific papers.   CR

Kollwitz, Käthe, *née* Schmidt (b. Königsberg, East Prussia, Germany [now Kaliningrad, USSR], 8.7.1867; d. nr Dresden, Germany [now East Germany], 22.4.1945). German graphic artist. Starting in the 1890s Kollwitz's socialist-inspired prints, posters and occasional bronzes, rooted in her own experiences as a doctor's wife in a poor quarter of Berlin, were seen by the German left as moving examples of critical humanitarianism. As such her work was shown in Moscow in 1927–8 and was introduced into China by LU XUN. She is remembered particularly for the nobility of her own features, finely captured in her many self-portraits; the occasionally sentimentalized workers and children of her later years are less compelling.
                                          JWMW
O. Nagel, *Käthe Kollwitz* (London, 1971); R. Hinz (ed.), *Käthe Kollwitz: Graphics, Posters, Drawings* (NY, 1981).

Kolmogorow, Andrey Nikolayevich (b. Tambov, Russia, 25.4.1903). Russian mathematician. Professor at Moscow State University since 1931, Kolmogorov has been immensely influential in all branches of modern probability theory. He is also known for his work in topology, in ring theory, and in functional analysis, where he first came to notice by demonstrating an integrable function having a divergent Fourier series. His most fundamental work in probability theory was his restatement of its foundations as a series of axioms using the language of measure theory; the probability of a random variable falling in a set is expressed as an integral over that set. Not only did this mean that many results in measure theory could be reinterpreted as theorems of probability theory, but, more importantly, it freed the handling of probabilities from questions of interpretation. Since measure theory lies inside pure mathematics, its results apply indifferently in any system in which the axioms of probability in any sense hold (see *Osnovnye Ponyatiya Teorii Veroyatnostey*, Moscow, 1936; *Foundations of the Theory of Probability*, London, 1950). Kolmogorov developed the theory of stochastic processes (whose state at a given stage is a random variable whose distribution depends on knowable factors such as how long it has been going, or some of the past history of the system). Markov had developed a very useful class of processes in which the dependence on past history was minimal; Kolmogorov gave an extremely practical means of finding their distribution functions (his forward and backward equations) by looking at the probabilities of change in very small time intervals to obtain a set of differential equations. These have now been surpassed in elegance, but not at all for practical everyday use in a multitude of situations. He also obtained more general results, such as the law of the iterated logarithm. Related work of his in generalized mechanics relates to the ergodic states of systems; those which are not only possible but always likely to happen. Kolmogorov also worked on the theory of finite automata and produced related work on the theory of randomness. A sequence is taken to be random if the smallest program that will generate it is as long as the series itself.

This is not altogether satisfactory, but it seems that any definitive theory of randomness will have to embody Kolmogorov's work. AGPW/JCu

Koneski, Blaže (b. Nebregovo, nr Prilep, Macedonia, Yugoslavia, 19.12.1921). Macedonian poet and linguist. Macedonian was recognized as an independent literary language only with the establishment of the Yugoslav Republic of Macedonia in 1946. Educated in Kragujevac, Belgrade and Sofia, Koneski played a vital part in creating the standard language. Internationally renowned for his linguistic activities, Koneski is also widely recognized as the finest poet of his generation in Macedonia. He has published several volumes of poems – *Mostot* [The bridge] (Skopje, 1945), *Zemjata i ljubovta* [Land and love] (Skopje, 1948), *Pesni* [Poems] (Skopje, 1953), *Vezilka* [The embroideress] (Skopje, 1955), *Zapisi* [Notes] (Skopje, 1974) – short stories and translations (of Heine and Shakespeare). Like other contemporary East European poets, Koneski has drawn on the rich heritage of the oral tradition, still an immediate source of poetic energy in Macedonia. Koneski's poetry offers a remarkable concentration of qualities of intellect and sensibility, expressed with passionate and resonant simplicity. A selection of his poems has appeared in English: *Blazhe Koneski: Poems* (tr. A. Harvey & A. Pennington, London, 1979). ECH

Kooning, Willem de (b. Rotterdam, S. Holland, The Netherlands, 24.4.1904; naturalized American citizen, 1962). Dutch/American abstract expressionist painter. While apprenticed to a commercial art firm, Kooning attended evening classes at the Rotterdam Academy of Fine Art and Techniques (1916–24). In 1926 he emigrated to the USA where he worked as a commercial artist until 1935, when he took part for a year in the Federal Arts Project. In the 1930s and early 1940s his recurrent themes were haunting images of men and women and simplified organic or bimorphic abstractions with echoes of ARP and Jóan MIRÓ (e.g. *Elegy*, c. 1939), often left incomplete to heighten the expressive content. By c. 1950 Kooning had developed a personal form of abstract expressionism, combining planned and accidental effects, the surface rendered savagely vital by aggressively gestural strokes and slashes of pigment. He has continued since then to alternate between abstractions and the theme of woman, encompassing a wide variety of moods, ranging from aggressive eroticism to rococo sensuousness. In Kooning's work of the 1970s the vestige of a figure lurks in the midst of heavily textured swirls of colour, with white increasingly predominant among the rich colour effects of previous decades. At the same time Kooning began to make bizarrely deformed expressionistic sculptures based on the shadowy figurative allusions of his recent paintings (e.g. *Seated Woman on a Bench*, 1972). SOBT

T. B. Hess, *Willem de Kooning* (NY, 1968).

Köppen, Vladimir Peter (b. St Petersburg [now Leningrad], Russia, 25.9.1846; d. Graz, Styria, Austria, 22.6.1940). Russian/German geographer who developed a system of world climatic regions based on observations of climatic stations and the boundaries of major vegetational belts. In 1874 Köppen moved from St Petersburg to Hamburg to work in the oceanographic office (Deutsche Seewarte). He edited the encyclopedic *Handbuch der Klimatologie* [Handbook of climatology] (1930–), but died before all the volumes were complete. His first classification of world climate was made in 1884 using thermal distinctions alone. Between then and 1936, when his final version was completed, Köppen progressively modified his scheme to incorporate new factors such as the seasonal variations of both temperature and precipitation. Although modified' by later climatologists, notably C. W. Thornthwaite and G. T. Trewartha, the Köppen classification remains that basically in use today. PH

Kornberg, Arthur (b. New York, USA, 3.3.1918). American biochemist. Kornberg's early education was at the City College of New York (BS, 1937) and the University of Rochester, New York (MD, 1941). For over a decade thereafter Kornberg served as a commissioned

405

officer in the US public health service, also being gazetted lieutenant in the US coast guard. He first worked in the nutrition field (1942–5), and from 1947 to 1953 was chief of the enzyme and metabolism section of the National Institutes of Health, Bethesda, Maryland. During this period Kornberg also worked with OCHOA in the NYC College of Medicine (1946), with Carl and Gerty Cori in Washington University School of Medicine (1947) and in Berkeley, California, in 1951 with H. A. Barker (plant biology). After being professor of microbiology in Washington University School of Medicine, St Louis, Missouri (1953–9), Kornberg became professor of biochemistry in Stanford University School of Medicine, a post he still holds. Kornberg's special interests and contributions to thought have lain in the fields of enzyme chemistry, and the synthesis of deoxyribonucleic acid (DNA), an outstanding achievement. Kornberg started with nucleotides from natural sources, but these have been totally synthesized by others, so his synthesis amounts to a total synthesis of DNA. The key step in the synthesis requires a polymerase enzyme, and, in addition, a small amount of natural DNA to act as a 'template', an idea of far-reaching importance. He received the Nobel prize jointly with Ochoa in 1959.

NBC

Korsch, Karl (b. Tostedt, Lower Saxony, Germany, 15.8.1886; d. Belmont, Mass., USA, 21.10.1961). German MARXist theoretician. Korsch studied philosophy and taught at the University of Jena. He was an early, critical communist exponent of Marx (but not through neo-Hegelian spectacles) who tried to extract the philosophical significance of the theory. In *Marxismus und Philosophie* (Leipzig, 1923, ²1930; *Marxism and Philosophy*, London, 1970) he joined LUKÁCS in rejecting dialectical materialism as derived from Engels, with its idea of cognition as a passive reflection of matter as absolute being. Unlike Lukács, he eschewed 'auto-criticism' and was expelled from the party in 1926 for 'ultra-leftism'. He criticized KAUTSKY in *Die materialistische Geschichtsauffassung* [The materialist conception of history]

(Leipzig, 1929). He left Nazi Germany for the USA where he continued his critique of Soviet pseudo-Marxism and wrote and lectured on the philosophy of science and political theory. In *Karl Marx* (London, 1938) he opposed the Hegelian Marx of MARCUSE, ADORNO and other members of the Frankfurt school, tracing the idealist origins of Marx's 'historical materialism' as an early science of society and offering instead a positivist version. From 1950 he lectured in Germany and Switzerland, opposing any monopolistic interpretation of Marxism as inimical to its nature and destructive of a continually renewed theory and revolutionary practice. He became more widely known with the revival of Marxism and the student revolts of the late 1960s.

JCu

Korzybski, Alfred Habdank Skarbek (b. Warsaw, Russian Poland [now Poland], 3.7.1879; naturalized American citizen; d. Sharon, Conn., USA, 1.3.1950). Polish/American founder of General Semantics movement. Educated as an engineer, Korzybski served in Russian military intelligence in WW1, was sent to the USA on a mission and remained there after the Russian revolution. His most influential work is *Science and Sanity* (Lancaster, Pa, 1933) and he was also director of the Institute of General Semantics. He was a highly eclectic and in some respects eccentric thinker who nevertheless had considerable, even popular influence. He linked a wide range of social, psychological, intellectual and even medical ills to 'semantogenic', i.e. linguistic causes, and emphasized the importance of language in the transmission of knowledge from one generation to the next ('time-binding'). He drew on the ideas of PAVLOV and contemporary behaviourism, and on FREUD (the notion of the pathology of symbols) to propose radical language reform as a psychotherapeutic, behavioural cure for society's 'linguistic maladjustment'. He characterized as 'Aristotelian' many of these harmful habits (some enshrined in the canon of western logic) and inveighed against the unthinking acceptance of general terms and linguistic categorizations as providing a clear account of reality, in particular against the conflation of different levels of abstraction. He thought that his philosophy could significantly improve the quality of life of the individual who freed him/herself from the confusions engendered by language. CMH

S. Hayakawa, *Language in Thought and Action* (NY, 1949); A. Rapoport, *Science and the Goals of Man* (NY, 1950).

Kossinna, Gustav (b. Tilsit, Russia, 28.9.1858; d. Berlin, Germany, 20.12.1931). German prehistorian. Kossinna was a leading member of a group of German prehistorians teaching at the University of Berlin in the early years of this century. After studies at Göttingen, Leipzig, Berlin and Strassburg, he settled at Berlin in 1892, becoming professor of German archaeology in 1902. In 1909 he founded the Deutsche Gesellschaft für Vorgeschichte [The German society for prehistory], the influential journal *Mannus*, which he edited, and the monograph series *Mannusbibliothek*. His publications centred on problems of later European prehistory, especially the archaeology of settlement, the origins of the Germanic peoples and their early movements, and the Indo-European problem. His main preoccupation, ethnic identity, led him to stress that archaeological cultures could be identifiable as distinct groups of people or tribes. Several of his ideas on Germanic origins and culture were enthusiastically embraced by Nazi ideologues in the 1920s and 1930s, so that his writing had enormous influence in Central Europe before 1945. His best-known works are *Die Herkunft der Germanen* [The origin of the Germans] (Berlin, 1911), *Die Indogermanen* [The Indo-Europeans] (Leipzig, 1921) and *Ursprung und Verbreitung der Germanen in vor- und frühgeschichtlicher Zeit* [Origin and spread of the Germans in prehistoric and early historic times] (Berlin, 1926, ³1936). MT

Kossoff, Leon (b. London, UK, 7.12.1926). British painter. He attended BOMBERG's drawing classes at the Borough Polytechnic, London, between 1949 and 1953: his art has always been rooted in the pursuit of drawing, which

he practises almost daily. In the late 1950s Kossoff began to mount exhibitions of pictures which combined an expressionist relish in paint substance with a commanding empirical accuracy. In the 1960s, however, his achievement became somewhat obscured from view by the influx of transatlantic, late modernist fashions: he suffered from almost complete critical neglect. Despite this he remained faithful to his vision and produced remarkable series of drawings and paintings, not only from the model but also of various parts of London, e.g. a children's swimming pool in Kilburn, Kilburn Underground station, and Dalston Junction. By the late 1970s a change in the artistic climate led to increasingly widespread recognition, and growing acknowledgement that his achievement was of the very highest, in terms of British, post-WW2 painting. PF

Koyré, Alexandre (b. Taganrog, Russia, 29.8.1892; naturalized French citizen; d. Paris, France, 28.4.1964). Russian/French historian of science and of philosophy. Alexandre Koyré studied at Göttingen under HUSSERL, and in Paris with Léon Brunschwicg and Emile Meyerson. His research in the development of scientific thought was philosophically oriented, in the manner of most 20c French historiography of science. Koyré insisted that the human mind's intellectual activity – religion, philosophy and science – must be viewed as an historically organic unity. This appeared in his work on Jacob Boehme (*La Philosophie de J. Boehme* [The philosophy of J. Boehme], Paris, 1929) and in his *Etudes Galiléennes* (Paris, 1939; *Galileo Studies*, NY, 1978) which stressed the relevance of Galileo's *a priori* mathematical Platonism to the birth of modern physical sciences. On the other hand, in *La Révolution Astronomique. Copernic, Kepler, Borelli* (Paris, 1961; *The Astronomical Revolution*, NY, 1973) Koyré omitted Galileo's astronomical discoveries, which he considered a marginal empirical episode in the development of theoretical astronomy. In his *From the Closed World to the Infinite Universe* (Baltimore, 1957) Koyré maintained that the key factor in the 17c scientific revolution was the breaking down of the hierarchical Aristotelian world, for which philosophers, naturalists and theologians substituted the concept of a geometrically uniform universe. Koyré's work has been highly influential in France, the USA and Italy. Though committed to phenomenology and mathematical Platonism, Koyré combined his philosophical preconceptions with historical scholarship.   PC

Kramers, Hendrik Anthony (b. Rotterdam, S. Holland, The Netherlands, 17.12.1894; d. Leiden, S. Holland, 24.4.1952). Dutch physicist. An outstanding theoretical physicist, Kramers carried out his first research under N. BOHR in Copenhagen and ultimately succeeded EHRENFEST as professor of theoretical physics at the University of Leiden. His work covered a wide range of topics – physiological optics, astrophysics, physical chemistry, the history of science, and relativity – but his outstanding achievements were in the field of atomic physics and quantum mechanics. He developed the theory of the emission and the absorption of light by atoms and molecules and devised a very important approximation method for solving the problem of an electron in a central field of force. He made very significant contributions to the theory of ferromagnetism and antiferromagnetism (see NÉEL) and to the problem of the flow of nonuniform gases. His work on radiation provided an important basis for the theory of quantum electrodynamics (see FEYNMAN). In 1933 he collaborated (with de Haas and Wiersma) in a very important experiment in which, for the first time, temperatures only a few hundredths of a degree above the absolute temperature were attained by the method of adiabatic demagnetization. Kramers was extremely influential in helping to reorganize physical research in the Netherlands after WW2. He was also very active in national and international scientific organizations, and was chairman of the Scientific and Technological Committee of the United Nations Atomic Energy Commission. His *Collected Scientific Papers* were published in Amsterdam in 1956.   HMR

Kraus, Karl (b. Jičín, Bohemia, Austria-Hungary [now Czechoslovakia], 28.4.1874; d. Vienna, Austria, 12.6.1936). Austrian critic and satirist of Jewish origin. His lifework is contained in the periodical *Die Fackel* [The torch] which he founded, and edited in Vienna from 1899 until 1936. From 1912 onwards he was the sole contributor. His one-man crusade was directed against many targets: the corruption of public life in the final years of the Hapsburg empire, the hypocrisy of prevailing attitudes towards sexuality, the insidious influence of propaganda and the press, and the dangers of modern military technology. During WW1 he was the most articulate critic of the militaristic policies of the Central Powers. His most important single work is a documentary drama which reconstructs the folly and cruelty of the war on the basis of contemporary documents, *Die letzten Tage der Menschheit* (Vienna, 1919–22; abridged and tr. A. Gode & S. E. Wright, *The Last Days of Mankind*, NY, 1974). Kraus was also a master of the shorter prose forms of aphorism, satirical gloss and essay. A strong sense of identification with the German language underlies his verbal subtlety and satirical wit (which makes his writings resistant to translation). He argued that an ethically responsive attitude to language could serve as an antidote to the ideological confusion of his day. During the first Austrian republic he campaigned against the resurgence of militarism, and his final work (completed in 1934 but not published until after WW2) is an incisive critique of Nazism *Die Dritte Walpurgisnacht* [The third Walpurgis night] (Munich, 1952). Kraus's writings blend satirical wit with ethical intensity in a manner reminiscent of Swift. His most influential achievement lies in his pioneering critique of propaganda and his prophetic, indeed apocalyptic vision of the consequences for our planet if technology is allowed to run out of control.   EFT

F. Field, *The Last Days of Mankind: Karl Kraus and his Vienna* (London, 1967).

Krebs, Hans Adolf (b. Hildesheim, Lower Saxony, Germany, 25.8.1900; naturalized British citizen, 1939; d. Oxford, UK, 22.11.1981). German/British biochemist distinguished for his studies of intermediary metabolism. Between 1926 and 1930, after medical training in Göttingen, Freiburg, Munich and Berlin and a short period with Peter Rona, Krebs became research assistant to O. H. WARBURG at Berlin-Dahlem. That period had a profound influence on his subsequent development. His first independent work to achieve widespread recognition was the discovery, in 1932 at Freiburg, of the cycle of reactions whereby urea is formed from ammonia and carbon dioxide in the livers of ureotelic organisms. This was the first biosynthetic pathway and metabolic cycle to be described. Dismissed from his post at Freiburg in 1933 following HITLER's rise to power, he joined F. G. HOPKINS in Cambridge. A year later he moved to Sheffield where he founded the department of biochemistry. His formulation in 1937 of the citric acid cycle, the final common pathway for the oxidation of all foodstuffs, led to a Nobel prize in 1953. From 1954 to 1967 he held the chair of biochemistry at Oxford and remained active in research until his death. During his last 25 years he made important contributions to understanding the control of metabolic processes. He published an autobiography in 1952, *Reminiscences and Reflections* (Oxford).

PB

Kripke, Saul (b. Bay Shore, NY, USA, 13.11.1940). American philosopher. Kripke distinguished himself as a youthful prodigy in the field of modal logic, a largely American invention of the early part of this century which suddenly, thanks to him, became of considerable philosophical importance. In his monograph *Naming and Necessity* (1972; Oxford, 1979) he developed philosophical ideas about necessity and possibility, the subject matter of modal logic, which involved the rejection of the widely endorsed assimilation of proper names to 'definite descriptions' (singular terms beginning with the article 'the'). From this barren-looking consideration he derived powerful and interesting conclusions about what is necessarily the case. This brought him into sharp conflict

with the hitherto prevailing assumptions of analytic philosophers. His writings, derived from tape-recorded talks, have a vigorous colloquiality. After some years at Rockefeller University in New York he teaches now at Princeton. AQ

Kristeva, Julia (b. Bulgaria, 24.6.1941; naturalized French citizen). French theorist of language and science. Working from within semiotics, Kristeva developed a critique of western assumptions about language and the sign and in *Semeiotiké: Recherches pour une sémanalyse* [Semeiotiké: studies towards a semanalysis] (Paris, 1969) proposed a *semanalysis* able to grasp the production of meaning and the human subject in language. Detailed examination of the writing practice of Lautréamont and Mallarmé in *La Révolution du langage poétique* [The revolution of poetic language] (Paris, 1974) allowed her to demonstrate this semanalysis and to lay the foundations for a sociology of literature grounded in an attention to language in its social-subjective reality. Subsequently Kristeva has been particularly concerned with the relations between language and the body and has used psychoanalysis to develop an account of the terms and limits of subject identity. This work has involved her in feminist issues, exploring the possible identity of the 'feminine' through reference to the maternal body and pre-oedipal sexuality in *Polylogue* (Paris, 1977; selection tr. T. Gora, A. Jardine & L. S. Roudiez, *Desire in Language*, NY, 1980). A member of the editorial board of the avant-garde review *Tel Quel* since 1970, Kristeva has been, along with BARTHES and DERRIDA, a major figure in contemporary French thought. SH

R. Coward & J. Ellis, *Language and Materialism* (London, 1977); J. Gallop, *Feminism and Psychoanalysis: the Daughter's Seduction* (London, 1982).

Krleža, Miroslav (b. Agram, Croatia, Austria-Hungary [now Zagreb, Yugoslavia], 7.7.1893; d. Zagreb, 29.12.1981). Croatian dramatist, novelist, essayist and poet. Educated in Budapest, Krleža served in the Austrian army during WW1. Thereafter he lived in Zagreb as a professional writer, editor of several magazines and, from 1950, director of the Yugoslav Lexicographical Institute. His wide-ranging interests in European arts, politics and culture are reflected in his many volumes of essays. His creative works are equally prolific: plays, poems, short stories and novels, all marked by a distinctive, vigorous style. From his earliest publications Krleža expressed his MARXist perception of human society in terms of dramatic conflict. He concentrates on recent Croatian history and particularly on what he sees as the decline of the capitalist order. One strand of his work concerns the fate of the Croatian peasant: as victim of WW1 in *Hrvatski bog Mars* [The Croatian god Mars] (Zagreb, 1922), and of history in a volume of poems in the Kajkavian dialect *Balade Petrice Kerempuha* [The ballads of Petrica Kerempuh] (Zagreb, 1936). Krleža is best known abroad for his novel *Povratak Filipa Latinovicza* (Zagreb, 1932; tr. Z. Depolo, *The Return of Philip Latinovicz*, London, 1960) and the cycle of plays about the Glembaj family: *Leda* (Zagreb, 1930), *U agoniji* [Last breath] (Zagreb, 1931) and *Gospoda Glembajevi* [The Glembaj gentlemen] (Zagreb, 1932). Krleža was also outspoken in condemning dogma in the arts. ECH

Kroeber, Alfred Louis (b. Hoboken, NJ, USA, 11.6.1876; d. Paris, France, 5.10.1960). American anthropologist who as a student of BOAS not only extended the analysis of culture – putting forward the Spencer-influenced idea of the superorganic in which the individual is seen as subordinate to culture – but also departed from Boas in claiming that anthropology was history rather than science. Kroeber came to anthropology after having studied literature; he brought with him a notion of the privileged status of linguistic analysis as well as a wide range of interests derived from his German-American liberal bourgeois background (natural history, psychology). He was a prolific scholar (700 published items), working extensively on the California Indians, and followed Boas in becoming a contributor to anthropology in the widest sense. After completing his doctorate on Arapaho decorative art in 1901, he joined the

new department of anthropology at the University of California at Berkeley. By the time of his retirement as its professor in 1946 that department contained the strongest undergraduate anthropology teaching programme in the USA. His book *Anthropology* (NY, 1923) was extremely influential both because it was the only textbook available and because of Kroeber's wide interests. For Kroeber culture was based on an idea of patterns rather than structures, demonstrated for example in his analysis of women's fashions. In his view different cultures may have elements in common, but it is the particular combination which produces distinctive cultures. His theoretical views were rarely made explicit, although in the collection *The Nature of Culture* (Chicago, 1952) his defence of his practice brings out cardinal features. The Boasian list-making tendency was extended by Kroeber to create a way of organizing 'culture groups', a mapping procedure according to which diffused culture traits were described in the manner of natural history (a persistent feature in American anthropology). For Kroeber, culture is above all a creative enterprise whose particular form can only be understood through the reconstruction of historical conjunctures. SLN

Krogh, Schack August Steenberg (b. Grenaa, Randers, Denmark, 13.11.1874; d. Copenhagen, 13.9.1949). Danish comparative physiologist. Krogh trained as a zoologist in Copenhagen, graduating in 1899, and proceeded at once to research on respiratory physiology in frogs. His work was, however, fundamental to problems of great generality in animal and in human physiology, and his own interests were very wide. While he was awarded a Nobel prize in 1920 for his work on gaseous exchange in the lung, work which resolved longstanding controversies about the mechanisms by which gases pass between atmosphere and living tissue, he also made important discoveries on the control of the blood supply to muscles during exercise. Krogh was a pioneer investigator of the relationship between human environment and nutrition in arctic communities. He was appointed professor of zoophysiology in the University of

Copenhagen in 1916. His books *The Anatomy and Physiology of the Capillaries* (New Haven, 1922) and *The Comparative Physiology of Respiratory Mechanisms* (Philadelphia, 1941) are recognized as of classic stature.   DRN

Kropotkin, Peter Alekseevich (b. Moscow, Russia, 21.12.1842; d. Moscow, 8.2.1921). Russian anarchist, geologist and geographer. Born into the Russian nobility, Kropotkin entered the Imperial army in 1862 and served until 1867. Visiting Switzerland in 1872 he became a convinced anarchist, under the influence of Bakunin's teaching. Back in Russia he began active propaganda for the movement, and in 1874 was arrested and imprisoned. Two years later he escaped and fled from Russia, beginning an exile, mainly spent in London, ended only by the revolution of 1917. He saw anarchist communism very much as the next natural stage of social evolution, and part of the wider evolutionary process. In contrast to Darwin's social disciples, he believed that mutuality and cooperation were features of the animal world and already significant forces in society, however masked by coercive government. With MARX he believed that modern productive techniques opened up possibilities of good living conditions for all; capitalism with its wage system must be replaced by communism, but a nonauthoritarian communism. The Soviet state which emerged from the Bolshevik revolution did not have his sympathies. He did not reject the use of force, and supported the Allies against Germany in WW1. His *Mutual Aid: a Factor of Evolution* (London, 1902) is one of the continuing classics of anarchist thought.   DCr

After military service in eastern Siberia Kropotkin developed an interest in the geography of that region and, following studies at St Petersburg University, published studies on glaciology and the physical geography of northern Asia. Although he continued to publish work in physical geography such as *The Desiccation of Asia* (London, 1904) after his flight to England, Kropotkin's anarchist writing was increasingly dominant. His neglected *Fields, Factories, and Workshops* (London, 1898) was seen by GED-

DES as a classic of geographical social criticism, and its concepts of regional interconnections are reflected in Geddes's later writing.   PH

G. Woodcock & I. Avakumovic, *The Anarchist Prince* (London, 1950).

Krupp, Alfried Felix Alwyn von Bohlen und Halbach (b. Essen, N. Rhine-Westphalia, Germany, 13.8.1907; d. Essen, West Germany, 30.7.1967). German industrialist. The Krupp dynasty had been central to German industrial power and business mythology for generations. Friedrich Krupp (1787–1826) founded an iron works in 1812. His son Alfried (1812–87), nicknamed 'the cannon king', sold steel cannon to many nations during Bismarck's second Reich. He was succeeded by his son Friedrich (1854–1902), followed by Friedrich's daughter Bertha (1886–1957) who married Gustav von Bohlen und Halbach. After WW1 Gustav was sentenced to 15 years' imprisonment and a 100 million marks fine. He did not serve the full sentence and the firm was to rise again: it was a scenario to be repeated after WW2. Bertha and Gustav had a son – Alfried – great-grandson of Alfried, the cannon king. Alfried was trained and educated to assume the responsibility for the Krupp empire. His boyhood was strict and austere; private tutors and three technical universities provided an education. He was apprenticed in the company and in 1936 formally entered the Krupp firm as a deputy director. This was the period of the National Socialist party, the rise of HITLER and the German rearmament race to which Krupp, as the major armament manufacturers, were committed. During WW2 they provided armour, guns and ammunition in huge quantities. With Gustav's health failing, Alfried took over the proprietorship of the firm in 1943. He was 36. Krupp factories were repeatedly bombed. Additional workers (men, women and children) were provided from concentration camps and conscripted foreign workers. In 1945 the US forces took Essen and arrested Alfried. He was held in custody for over two years before being brought to trial at Nuremberg for war crimes. His father Gustav was judged too senile to stand trial for events when he was head of Krupp. Alfried was found guilty of plunder and spoliation, and exploitation of slave labour. He was sentenced to 12 years' imprisonment and confiscation of his property, but did not serve the full sentence. In 1951, amidst much controversy, he was released and the confiscation order cancelled. Confiscation of property, it was argued, was unfair; but primarily the balance of world power had shifted, and the Western Allies saw a need for West German industry to be rebuilt. Alfried was paid £25 million compensation for his holdings in German coal and steel companies. He began to reinstate Krupp in Essen. Reinvestment and re-equipment with modern machinery led to the opening of worldwide markets for steel-making equipment, construction machinery, locomotives and heavy plant. Reorganization in 1958 along SLOAN General Motors lines delegated responsibility for day-to-day management to the constituent divisions and companies. In 1960 the order removing the steel companies from Krupp control was rescinded. The Krupp dynasty came to an end in 1967 on Alfried's death.　　　　　　RIT

G. Young, *The Fall and Rise of Alfried Krupp* (London, 1960).

Krushchev, Nikita Sergeyevich (b. Kalinovka, Ukraine, Russia, 17.4.1894; d. Moscow, USSR, 11.9.1971). First secretary, Communist Party of the Soviet Union (1953–64); premier (1958–64). Despite his rise from obscure Ukrainian origins to membership of the CPSU's Praesidium under, and thanks to STALIN, Krushchev was to turn against Stalinism and the cult of personality, denouncing these doctrines at the Twentieth Party Congress in 1956, and surviving the attack of Stalin's former deputy MOLOTOV and the 'antiparty group' in 1958 with the aid of the Soviet army leadership. In domestic politics he allowed a limited degree of latitude (which his successors were later to try to rescind) to Soviet writers and artists, while trying to shift the balance of Soviet industrial policy a little away from its relentless concentration on heavy industry in favour of consumer goods production. In international polit-ics he sought to divide and delude the Western bloc by alternate bouts of peaceful persuasion and violent threats including 'ultimata' over Berlin, the unrestrained testing of nuclear weapons, the encouragement of 'wars of national liberation' and the stationing of medium-range missiles on Cuba to threaten the USA on the one hand, and the acceptance of the partial test ban treaty with the USA in 1963 on the other. The penalty for these kaleidoscopic changes of policy was the alienation of the doctrinally rigid in the Communist bloc, especially the Chinese led by MAO TSE-TUNG, the successive acceptance of Polish national communism under GOMULKA and armed suppression of Hungary in 1956, the loss of control over the Communist parties of Western Europe in the name of polycentrism, and finally his overthrow in 1964 by the other members of the CPSU leadership. The failure of his grandiose attempts to solve Russia's chronic food shortages by wholesale ploughing-up of the 'virgin lands' of Soviet Asia made their task in overthrowing him the more easy. He was succeeded as party secretary by BREZHNEV. Krushchev's memoirs *Krushchev Remembers* were published in English translation in 2 vols (London) in 1972 and 1974.　　DCW

R. Medvedev, *Krushchev* (London, 1982).

Kuenen, Philip Henry (b. Dundee, Tayside, UK, 22.7.1902; d. Groningen, Friesland, The Netherlands, 17.12.1976). Dutch geologist. Born of a Dutch father and a Scottish mother, Kuenen spent most of his life in the Netherlands. He studied at Leiden and became professor of geology at Groningen. Kuenen was one of a group of outstanding Dutch geologists who made a major impact on the science from the 1930s to the 1960s. After his experiences on the Snellius expedition to Indonesia in 1929 he developed an abiding interest in the new subject of oceanography, which he did much to stimulate by his *Marine Geology* (NY, 1950). He will be best remembered, however, as a pioneer in the subdiscipline of sedimentology (a term he coined). He published on subjects as various as the abrasion of sand grains, the origin of beach cusps and the effects of sea-level change on sedimentation. Most important was his recognition from experimental and field observations of the importance of turbidity currents in so-called flysch sedimentation in orogenic belts and his paper with Migliorini (*J. Geol.*, 58 [1950], 91–127) is universally regarded as a classic. AH

Kuhn, Richard (b. Vienna, Austria-Hungary [now Austria], 3.12.1900; d. Heidelberg, Baden-Württemberg, West Germany, 1.8.1967). Austrian organic chemist. Kuhn studied chemistry at Vienna University and later at Munich under WILLSTÄTTER, where he obtained his doctorate for a thesis on the specificity of enzymes. After brief tenure of a chair at the Eidegenössische Technische Hochschule in Zürich, Kuhn took up the post, in 1929, of principal of the institute for chemistry at the newly founded Kaiser Wilhelm Institute (since 1950, Max Planck Institute) for Medical Research in Heidelberg, of which he became the head in 1937. Kuhn's first investigations covered certain theoretical aspects of organic chemistry (stereochemistry, synthesis of polyenes and cumulenes, colour and molecular constitution, the acidity of hydrocarbons) but he is best known for his work in what is now called bio-organic chemistry, to which much of his theoretical work was closely allied. His bio-organic studies included important work on carotenoids (he discovered several new members of this group including γ-carotene), on lactoflavin (riboflavin) or vitamin B_2, and on an important breakdown product of it, viz. lumiflavin. With colleagues he also isolated vitamin B_6, the antidermatitis vitamin (adermin) and determined its constitution. Kuhn was editor of *Liebig's Annalen der Chemie* [Liebig's annals of chemistry] and received the Nobel prize for chemistry in 1938. NBC

Kuhn, Thomas Samuel (b. Cincinnati, Ohio, USA, 18.7.1922). American historian and philosopher of science. Originally an elementary particle physicist, Kuhn is known chiefly for his studies of the development of science, notably in *The Structure of Scientific Revolutions*

(NY, 1962, [2]1969). He divides scientific history into periods of steady development within one set of accepted concepts, called a paradigm, and periods of revolutionary change when the reigning paradigm is replaced by another in a way that he likens to a gestalt switch. In these periods the paradigms compete with each other, a conflict likened to that occurring in Darwinian evolution. The choice of the new paradigm is made by the community of scientists working in that area, a criterion that can remove all objective validity from science unless it is rooted in objective reality. Kuhn denies that science progresses cumulatively, on the ground that successive paradigms are irreconcilable, and yet claims that their periodical replacement constitutes a developing process of increasing sophistication. The concept of paradigm has many meanings, and detailed analysis has identified several types, classified as metaphysical, sociological and construct paradigms. His other books are *The Copernican Revolution* (NY, 1957) and *Sources for the History of Quantum Physics* (NY, 1967). PEH

Kula, Witold (b. Warsaw, Russian Poland [now Poland], 18.4.1916). Polish economic historian. Kula's rise to prominence occurred when he published *Szkice o manufakturach w Polace XVIII wieku* [Studies on manufactures in Poland in the 18c] (2 vols, Warsaw, 1956), 24 case-studies of blast furnaces, mines, cloth factories and other enterprises. His interest in problems of method was revealed by his lively *Rozważania o historii* [Reflections on history] (Warsaw, 1958). His two main concerns were combined in his best-known book *Teoria ekonomiczna ustrojv feudalnego* (Warsaw, 1962; *An Economic Theory of the Feudal System*, London, 1976). In this book, which has given rise to considerable debate, Kula offers a model of typical landed 'enterprise' in early modern Poland, an enterprise operating in a 'non-market milieu', to show that 'the validity of most essential economic propositions is limited in time and place'. This was followed by *Problemy i motody historii gospodarczej* [Problems and methods of economic history] (Warsaw, 1963). *Miary i pudzie* [Measures and men] (Warsaw, 1970) is an important study of the history of weights and measures, treated as a problem in the historical sociology of knowledge. Kula's MARXism in no way inhibits the originality of his thought. If he wrote in a world language he would already have taken his rightful place as one of the leading historians of the later 20c; but in the West his reputation still rests on a small fraction of his work.

UPB

Kun, Béla (b. Szilágycseh, Transylvania, Austria-Hungary [now Czehul Silvaniei, Romania], 20.2.1886; d. USSR, 30.11.1939). Communist leader and head of the Hungarian Soviet Republic of 1919. Mobilized in the Austro-Hungarian army in WW1, Kun was taken prisoner by the Russians in 1916, and joined the Bolsheviks during the Russian revolution. He attracted LENIN's attention and, after receiving training in revolutionary tactics, was sent to Hungary after the collapse of the Central Powers in 1918. Kun started a communist newspaper and founded the Hungarian Communist party on 20.12.1918. He was imprisoned by the Karolyi government but released to join a Communist-Social Democratic coalition. Appointed commissar for foreign affairs, he acquired a dominant position in the government, eliminating the moderates and undertaking to secure Soviet aid. In the meantime he helped to establish a Red Army which reconquered many of the territories lost to Czechoslovakia and Romania. When the Soviet help on which Kun had relied did not arrive, the regime got into increasing difficulties. It lost the support of the peasants by nationalizing the big estates instead of dividing them; the distribution of food broke down; and the army mutinied. The regime collapsed on 1.8.1919 and Kun fled to Vienna and from there to Moscow. On a number of occasions during the 1920s, as one of the leaders of the Third International, Kun attempted to start revolutionary risings in Germany and Austria. He failed to come to terms with STALIN, however; was accused of 'TROTSKYism', and was

eventually liquidated in one of the Stalinist purges before WW2.

ALCB

Küng, Hans (b. Sursee, Lucerne, Switzerland, 19.3.1928). Swiss theologian. After studying for the priesthood in Rome Küng gained his doctorate in Paris with a thesis reconciling Catholic and Protestant views of justification by faith. Published as *Rechtfertigung. Die Lehre Karl Barths und eine katholische Besinnung* (Einsiedeln, 1957; *Justification: the Doctrine of Karl Barth and a Catholic Reflection*, NY, 1964), this quickly established his reputation. He reached a wider public with *Konzil und Wiedervereinigung* (Freiburg, 1960; *The Council and Reunion*, London, 1961), in which he explored the possibilities opened up by the general council Pope JOHN XXIII had surprised everyone by summoning. Appointed a professor at Tübingen in 1960, Küng attended this council (Vatican II, 1962–5) as a consultant theologian. In *Die Kirche* (Freiburg, 1967; *The Church*, London, 1967) he set out the new understanding of the church that Vatican II had made possible. Pope PAUL VI's decision in 1968, against the advice of his own commission, to uphold the condemnation of artificial birth control led Küng to question the doctrine of infallibility. In *Unfehlbar? Eine Anfrage* (Zürich, 1970; *Infallible? An Enquiry*, London, 1971) he suggested that the church remained in the truth despite possible errors of detail. Already the Doctrinal Congregation in Rome had begun proceedings over *Die Kirche*, and in 1975 a formal statement rejected his views on infallibility and two other topics but did not impose any sanctions against him. Meanwhile the bestselling *Christ sein* (Munich, 1974; *On Being a Christian*, NY, 1976) gave rise to an inconclusive dispute with the German bishops, who accused Küng of not sufficiently emphasizing Christ's divine nature. In 1979 he repeated his views on infallibility in a foreword to a controversial history of Vatican I by August Bernhard Hasler. Without any warning the Doctrinal Congregation withdrew Küng's official licence to teach theology. This step, taken just a week before Christmas, coincided with the questioning in Rome of the Flemish theologian SCHILLEBEECKX. The two events caused considerable disquiet both inside and outside the Catholic church. RAN

J. Häring & K.-J. Kuschel, *Hans Küng: his Work and his Way* (London, 1979); R. Nowell, *A Passion for Truth: Hans Küng: a Biography* (London, 1981); L. Scheffczyk, *On being a Christian: the Hans Küng Debate* (Blackrock, Dublin, 1982).

Kurokawa, Kisho (b. Nagoya, Aichi, Japan, 8.4.1934). Japanese architect and town planner. Kurokawa is the most prominent of the younger postwar generation of Japanese architects. Unlike his teachers at Tokyo University, who included TANGE, Kurokawa was determined to develop a specifically Japanese architecture, geared to modern technology, rather than simply import another European style. Both precocious and hyperactive, he attracted international attention in 1960 in the hyperbole surrounding a newly invented architectural school known as metabolism which he helped formulate. The Takara pavilion at the Osaka exposition of 1970 and the Nakagin capsule tower in Tokyo (1972) exemplify the kind of work that Kurokawa built in the name of Metabolism. The idea – described in *Metabolism in Architecture* (London, 1977) – was to emphasize the possibility of change in architecture by separating the building into basic structure and a kit of component parts which could be attached to it as required and, theoretically at least, removed thereafter.

The beginning of Kurokawa's career coincided with the most frenetic period of the Japanese economic boom, which has supported his prolific output (he already has more than 50 major buildings to his credit, as well as the design of half a dozen new towns). Almost uniquely among architects he has emerged as a public figure in his own right, hosting a regular television show.

In recent years Kurokawa has moved away from his earlier obsession with the trappings of flexibility and technological imagery towards a more formal and monumental style, which he explains by referring to traditional Japanese concepts of space. It is a move that mirrors western preoccupations with post-modernism, and has both influenced it and been influenced by it. DS

Kurosawa, Akira (b. Tokyo, Japan, 23.3.1910). Japanese film director whose film *Rashomon* (1950) won the Grand Prix at the Venice Festival in 1951 and opened the gates for the Japanese cinema in Europe. Kurosawa began as a scriptwriter and assistant to director Kajiro Yamamoto in the 1930s, making his first film in 1943. But it was his great series of films in the 1950s and 1960s which established him as one of the world's leading film makers, adept in mixing Eastern and Western styles and with a technical assurance (notably in the use of an extremely mobile camera) which set new standards in filmcraft. Kurosawa has always alternated between examinations of Japan's remote past in his samurai series – *Shichinin no Samurai* (*Seven Samurai*, 1954), *Yojimbo* (1961), *Sanjuro* (1962) – and contemporary subjects, often invested with acute psychological realism and a certain sentimentality – *Nora Inu* (*Stray Dog*, 1949), *Ikuru* (*Living*, 1952), *Ikimono no Kiroku* (*I Live in Fear*, 1955), *Tengoku to Jigoku* (*High and Low*, 1963). Equally distinctive are his personalized adaptations of foreign authors such as his Japanese *Macbeth* (*Kumonosojo*; *Throne of Blood*, 1957) and M. GORKY's *Donzoko* (*Lower Depths*, 1957). Over the years Kurosawa has developed his own repertory company of favourite actors, including Toshiro Mifune and Tatsuya Nakadai, and progressed from black and white into colour and a virtuoso use of the wide screen. A meticulous worker who demands substantial budgets and facilities, he has found it difficult to maintain production over the last 15 years. Only three films appeared in the 1970s: *Dodeskaden* (1970), *Dersu Uzala* (1975), shot in the USSR, and *Kagemusha* (*Shadow Warrior*, 1980), a return to the large-scale historical epic which gained international distribution and gave Kurosawa much needed encouragement for future plans which include a Japanese *King Lear* (*Ran*), being made in 1983. JPG

D. Richie, *The Films of Akira Kurosawa* (Cambridge, 1965); P. Erens, *Akira Kurosawa* (Boston, Mass., 1979).

Kuznets, Simon (b. Kharkov, Russia, 30.4.1901; naturalized American citizen, 1928). Russian/American economist who migrated to the USA as a young man, obtained his doctorate at the University of Columbia and held chairs successively at the universities of Pennsylvania, Johns Hopkins, and, since 1960, Harvard. His research output has been prodigious and as a member of the National Bureau of Economic Research (New York) for more than 30 years he participated actively in a wide range of major research projects. Kuznets is best known internationally, however, for his fundamental research on national income and wealth and on comparative economic growth. It was in recognition of his contribution to national income research and to related studies in comparative long-term growth that he was awarded the Nobel prize for economics in 1971. His own first national income estimates were published by the US Department of Commerce in *National Income 1929–32* (Washington, 1934)

and this was followed by a stream of influential research monographs. His great gift has been the unique mixture of imaginative speculation, technical expertise and meticulous scholarship with which he specifies his research problem, sets up the appropriate analytical framework, clarifies the strategic concepts and then systematically assembles, analyses and interprets a massive, if necessarily incomplete, statistical record. A number of his books are recognized as models of economic method as well as mines of carefully processed statistical information. Among the best known are *National Income and its Composition, 1919–38* (2 vols, NY, 1941), *Capital in the American Economy: its Formation and Financing* (Princeton, 1961) and *Modern Economic Growth, Rates Structure and Spread* (New Haven, 1966). By his many books, articles and conference papers as well as by direct correspondence with innumerable scholars compiling national income and long-term growth estimates in developed and underdeveloped countries, he has been largely responsible for the post-WW2 boom in research in these areas.   PMD

L

Labov, William (b. Passaic, NJ, USA, 4.12.1927). American sociolinguist, who pioneered the systematic study of linguistic variation. After obtaining his BA from Harvard in 1948, he worked as an industrial chemist until 1961, when he went to Columbia University, New York, remaining there for 10 years, first as a graduate student, then as an assistant professor. In 1971 he was appointed to his current post of professor of linguistics and psychology at the University of Pennsylvania. He is regarded by many as the founder of 'sociolinguistics' proper. Adapting sociological survey techniques, he showed that much speech variation, which had previously been regarded as haphazard, could be systematically and predictably correlated with social factors such as class, sex, age and ethnic group. For example, he demonstrated that the presence of postvocalic *r* (as in 'beard') was a prestige feature in New York, and he was able to determine the percentage of *r*-usage in each social class, in a range of speech styles. His work has had important implications for the study of language change, since he demonstrated that speech variation is often an indication that a change is in progress, and has illustrated how changes spread through a community, an occurrence previously regarded as mysterious. Most of his early work was based on New York, and is described in *The Social Stratification of English in New York City* (Washington, 1966) and *Language in the Inner City* (Philadelphia, 1972). Partial summaries of these works are included in a collection of important papers *Sociolinguistic Patterns* (Philadelphia, 1972).   JMA

Labrousse, Camille Ernest (b. Barbezieux, Charente, France, 16.5.1895). French economic historian who established himself with his *Esquisse du mouvement des prix et des revenus en France au 18e siècle* [Outline of the movement of prices and incomes in France in the 18c] (Paris, 1933) and

La Crise de l'économie française à la fin de l'ancien régime [The crisis of the French economy at the end of the ancien regime] (Paris, 1943), two formidably technical books that distinguish between short-, medium- and long-term economic cycles and analyse the mechanism of economic crises under the old regime. These studies are as important for their statistical sophistication and their pioneering quantitative methods as for their implications for the study of the French revolution. Since 1943 Labrousse has published comparatively little, but his influence on the next generation has been very great. Historians of the economy and society of early modern Europe such as Chaunu, Pierre Goubert, Pierre Vilar and LE ROY LADURIE are all in his debt, and it may not be fanciful to attribute the move towards quantitative history in the second edition of BRAUDEL's *Mediterranean* to his influence. Since the 1950s Labrousse has been much concerned with the history of the social structure in general, and that of the bourgeoisie in particular; Adeline Daumard's study of the bourgeoisie of 19c Paris is an example of work which owes much to his inspiration. Closer to MARXism than Braudel, and more deeply committed to rigorous quantitative methods, Labrousse has some claim to be regarded as the *éminence grise* of the Annales school.   UPB

Lacan, Jacques (b. Paris, France, 13.4.1901; d. Paris, 9.9.1981). French psychoanalyst. The founder of a unique and controversial movement in FREUDian psychoanalysis, Lacan first came to prominence with some pioneering articles on Freudian concepts in the 1930s. A practising psychoanalyst, from 1963 he was director of the Ecole Freudienne de Paris. But from 1953 he also conducted a weekly seminar in the University of Paris which exerted a formative influence on a whole generation of French intellectuals. These seminars have been published in France, although his major volume of writings remains *Ecrits* (Paris, 1966; tr. A. Sheridan, London, 1977), which in 900 pages brings together 27 articles and lectures originally published between 1936 and 1966. Lacan's deliberately obscure, hermetic, 'high French' style makes any simple account of his theories almost impossible. But his major enterprise was to reinterpret the writings of Freud in terms of the structural linguistics developed by modern French writers from the work of SAUSSURE, and to some extent JAKOBSON. Rewriting the Freudian unconscious in terms of a 'language' of metaphorical and metonymic devices, he draws suggestive parallels between the infant's entry into language and society itself – which involves an awareness of loss, absence and difference – and Freud's account of the oedipal stage. The child must break with its 'imaginary' relationship to the mother (a relationship of identity and narcissism summarized in the early 'mirror phase' in which the child sees its own body as an 'ideal unity' in a mirror) and take up its place in the 'symbolic order', the network of linguistic and social roles defined by the family (see 'Fonction et champs de la parole et du langage en psychoanalyse', 1956; tr. A. Wilden, *The Language of the Self*, Baltimore, 1973). The repressions entailed in this process involve the opening up of the unconscious and of 'desire', which for Lacan is infinite and insatiable. A fierce opponent of neo-Freudian 'ego-psychology', which he believed tames and dilutes Freud's 'revolutionary' concepts, Lacan was also controversial for his original and, to some, eccentric methods of psychoanalytic practice.   TE

Lack, David Lambert (b. London, UK, 16.7.1910; d. Oxford, 12.3.1973). British ornithologist. Educated at Cambridge, his first post after graduation was as science master at Dartington Hall School. During that time he prepared *The Life of the Robin* (London, 1943), an important early work popularizing scientific natural history. During WW2 he worked for the Ministry of Defence, and this led to an interest in bird navigational problems. On his return to academic life in 1945, Lack was appointed director of the Edward Grey Institute of Field Ornithology at Oxford, a position he held until his death. The author of several influential books, mainly in ecology and ornithology, in *The Natural Regulation of Animal Numbers* (London, 1954) he presented evidence from bird studies to support his view that intrinsic factors dependent on the density of an animal population are more important in controlling numbers and distribution of an animal population than factors independent of population density such as weather. A devout Anglican, Lack also published a somewhat controversial book *Evolutionary Theory and Christian Belief* (London, 1957).   RTi

La Follette, Robert Marion (b. Primrose, Wis., USA, 14.6.1855; d. Washington, DC, 18.6.1925). US congressman (1885–91); governor of Wisconsin (1901–5); US senator (1906–25); Progressive candidate for the US presidency (1908, 1924). The most original and influential figure in the American Progressive movement, his programme as governor of Wisconsin, 'the Wisconsin idea', epitomized the campaign of the Progressive movement to reform American politics. Its separate elements – direct primaries, the equalization of tax burdens as between individual and corporate taxation, the regulation and taxation of the railroad monopoly, on which midwestern farmers were so dependent, government by experts, the mobilization of the popular vote against the party boss system, conservation of natural resources, and antitrust legislation – were adopted by Progressives in other states and at the federal level. That his progressivism was a purely American phenomenon is shown by La Follette's opposition to the arming of US merchant ships in 1917 and his bitter opposition both to the US declaration of war on Germany and to American membership of the League of Nations.   DCW

Lagerkvist, Pär (b. Växjö, Kronoberg, Sweden, 23.5.1891; d. Stockholm, 11.7.1974). Swedish poet, novelist and dramatist. His entire life's work – from the early poems in *Ångest* [Anguish] (1916) and the expressionist plays *Den svåra stunden* [The difficult hour] (1918)

and *Himlens hemlighet* [The secret of heaven] (1919) right up to his heavily allegorical novels of the 1960s – shows a preoccupation with the tension between inhuman evil and human frailty. Although many critics assert that his art never reached a higher peak than in the story of *Bödeln* (Stockholm, 1933; tr. E. Mesterton & D. W. Harding, *The Hangman* in *Guest of Reality*, London, 1936), an allusive account of Nazi Germany and the problem of evil, his international fame had to wait on the publication of his two short novels *Dvärgen* (Stockholm, 1944; tr. A. Dick, *The Dwarf*, London, 1953) and *Barabbas* (Stockholm, 1950; tr. A. Blair, London, 1952). The former, a historical piece set in a Renaissance court, skilfully fuses historical realism with a timeless symbolism; the latter is a wonderfully controlled study of a bewildered and unloved man fumbling his way towards understanding. Lagerkvist's later novels – *Sibyllan* (Stockholm, 1956; tr. N. Walford, *The Sibyl*, London, 1958), *Ahasverus' död* (Stockholm, 1960; tr. N. Walford, *The Death of Ahasuerus*, London, 1960), *Pilgrim på havet* (Stockholm, 1962; tr. N. Walford, *Pilgrim at Sea*, London, 1962) and *Det heliga landet* (Stockholm, 1962; tr. N. Walford, *The Holy Land*, London, 1966) – are not without an element of the portentous.   JWMcF

Lagerlöf, Selma (b. Mårbacka, Värmland, Sweden, 20.11.1858; d. Mårbacka, 16.3.1940). Swedish novelist. Her first book *Gösta Berlings saga* (Stockholm, 1891; tr. P. B. Flach, *The Story of Gösta Berling*, London, 1898), a highly coloured, free-ranging and luxuriantly detailed account of a Värmland rural community through a year of dramatic events, was an immediate success. Her more soberly written, two-volume novel *Jerusalem* (Stockholm, 1901–2; tr. V. S. Howard, London, 1915–18) with its preoccupation with religious problems and its more disciplined narrative structure, was however the work which eventually brought her wider international recognition and contributed to her winning the Nobel prize in 1909. She is nevertheless perhaps best known outside Sweden for her enchanting children's classic *Nils*

Holgerssons underbara resa (Stockholm, 1906–7; tr. V. S. Howard, *The Wonderful Adventures of Nils*, London, 1907), a geography textbook commissioned for use in Swedish schools which describes a small boy's magic flight on gooseback through Sweden.   JWMcF

Laing, Ronald David (b. Glasgow, Strath., UK, 7.10.1927). British psychiatrist. Laing began by arguing that the causes of madness are not biological but due rather to the strains of family life. In his first important book *The Divided Self* (London, 1959) Laing drew on existentialism to describe and explain the behaviour of schizophrenics. What seemed so crazy to those on the 'normal' outside often had a certain sense to it, if only one could put oneself in the position of the schizophrenic. The family may find a person's wish to withdraw intolerable and so call him or her disturbed. Doctors, especially psychiatrists, Laing claimed, were too ready to collude with the family and label 'mad' any individual who behaved oddly. Laing's most thorough book *Sanity, Madness and the Family* (with A. A. Esterson, London, 1964) offered case histories in the light of this approach, showing how communications within the family could become so disrupted that one person might seek refuge in madness. Laing's radical thinking had much appeal in the late 1960s and early 1970s. He helped run Kingsley Hall, a residential treatment hostel where much innovative therapy was attempted. At its best, Laing's work raised profound questions about what society accepts as sane and as insane. This willingness to criticize the system – and, of course, the knotted nuclear family – helped make Laing a radical chic hero. In the 1970s Laing became interested in Zen Buddhism, wrote poems, made an LP and even published transcripts of conversations between himself and his children in *Harpers*, a high-society magazine. None of this endeared him to conventional psychiatrists. Nevertheless, his ideas continue to have some impact on orthodox British psychiatry, as witnessed by the greater attention now paid to the dynamics of a family one of whose members is disturbed.   DMOC

Lakatos, Imre, *né* Lipschitz (b. Debrecen, Hungary, 9.11.1922; d. London, UK, 2.2.1974). Hungarian philosopher of science and mathematics who came to England in November 1956 after the Hungarian uprising. He taught at the London School of Economics from 1960, becoming professor of logic in 1969; he edited the *British Journal for the Philosophy of Science* from 1971. Lakatos achieved fame with a series of articles, in dialogue form, on the nature of creative mathematical reasoning: *Proofs and Refutations* (1963–4; eds J. Worrall & E. Zahar, Cambridge, 1976). Influenced by both Gyorgy Polya and POPPER, he argued that a formalist presentation of mathematics obscures the real nature of living mathematical discovery and invention, which is a quasi-empirical process involving conjectures, the discovery of counterexamples, concept-stretching, and the search for more discriminating proofs. In connection with the empirical sciences he developed his methodology of scientific research programmes (MSRP): the basic units of appraisal are competing programmes, rather than theories, a programme being characterized by a *hard core* of fundamental assumptions and an associated *heuristic* which indicates how the protective belt of subsidiary assumptions should be progressively modified in a content-increasing way that generates novel predictions. MSRP called for a more penetrating kind of historiography for science, involving detailed case-studies to identify the competing research programmes at work and to assess their relative progressiveness. Lakatos and his co-workers carried out a considerable number of such studies.

Brilliant, witty, sometimes outrageous, fierce in controversy, he was an indefatigable letter-writer, supervisor and campaigner for academic values. Much of his work is published in *Philosophical Papers* (2 vols, eds J. Worrall & G. Currie, Cambridge, 1978).   JWNW

Lalique, René Jules (b. Haÿ, Marne, France, 4.5.1860; d. Paris, 5.5.1945). French jeweller, glassmaker, artist, sculptor and designer. Apprenticed at 16 with Parisian jeweller Louis Aucoc, Lalique studied later at the Ecole des Arts Décoratifs in Paris and spent 1879 –80 in London. In his own workshop, opened in 1884 in Paris, he began by designing and making jewellery for Cartier, Boucheron and Aucoc among others. In total break with tradition and the then popular historical revivalism, he made much use of new materials and techniques. His designs of an idealized female face or body with flowing hair, surrounded by graceful floral motifs, inspired and influenced a whole era. Winning great acclaim at the Paris Salon in 1894 and the Paris exhibition of 1900, he created exquisite jewellery for the actress Sarah Bernhardt and made whole collections commissioned by Calouste Gulbenkian as well as for royalty and the aristocracy. Acknowledged as the greatest art nouveau jeweller by 1900, Lalique abandoned jewellery after 1914 to devote his talent to glass as a sculptural medium. His innovative use of demicrystal, in pale and opalescent colours, with which he created superb vases, fountains and sculptural objects, was a crowning success at the 1925 Paris exhibition where an entire pavilion, designed by himself, was devoted to his work. His public commissions for decorative glass panels, lights, illuminated ceilings, etc. included the transatlantic liners *Paris* (1920), *Ile de France* (1927) and *Normandie* (1935). He also made the interior fittings of St Matthew's Church, Jersey (1932).   BC

Lamb, Willis Eugene, Jr (b. Los Angeles, Calif., USA, 12.7.1913). American physicist. Lamb's general interests have been in the physics of atomic and nuclear structure. He received the Nobel prize for physics in 1955 for an extremely careful study of the spectral lines emitted by hydrogen atoms. He showed (with R. C. Retherford, 1947) that two of the possible electron orbits of hydrogen, which according to DIRAC's quantum theory should have had exactly the same energy, were actually very slightly separated in energy. This separation, which is always referred to as the 'Lamb shift', is because the electron is not a point charge; it behaves as if it were a tiny sphere. This has the effect of very slightly changing the energies of the two orbits by different amounts. The measured value of the Lamb shift is very accurately equal to that predicted by quantum electrodynamics (see FEYNMAN). HMR

Lamming, George (b. Barbados, 8.6.1927). West Indian novelist. The most historically minded of West Indian novelists, his classic novel *In the Castle of My Skin* (London, 1953), arguably the foremost single work of literature to have come out of the Caribbean, amalgamates autobiography with fiction. It is a story of growing up in the Barbados and Trinidad of the 1930s and 1940s, a witness to the decline of village life and the emergence of the black middle class. In his other major novels, including *The Emigrants* (London, 1954), *Of Age and Innocence* (London, 1960) and *Natives of My Person* (London, 1972), Lamming uses the motif of the journey to trace the evolving consciousness of the black West Indian from the 16c to modern independence. Lamming has lived for long periods outside the Caribbean, especially in the UK, and has a particular interest in the condition of exiles.
ANRN
M. Morris, 'The poet as novelist: the novels of George Lamming', in *The Islands in Between*, ed. L. James (London, 1968).

Lampedusa, Giuseppe Tomasi di (b. Palermo, Sicily, Italy, 23.12.1896; d. Rome, 23.7.1957). Italian novelist, author of *Il Gattopardo* (Milan, 1958; tr. A. Colquhoun, *The Leopard*, London, 1960), which won the Strega prize in 1959; *Racconti* (Milan, 1961; tr. A. Colquhoun, *Two Stories and a Memory*, London, 1962); and '*Lezioni su Stendhal*' [Essays on Stendhal], published in *Paragone-Letteratura* (1959). *Il Gattopardo*, set in Sicily and covering a 50-year time-span (1860–1910), is ostensibly a historical novel about the demise of the old aristocratic order (incarnated in its protagonist Don Fabrizio, the Leopard of the title) and its replacement by the *nouveau riche* bourgeoisie of the newly united Kingdom of Italy. The novel, appreciated abroad by such diverse figures as ARAGON and FORSTER, was largely misunderstood by Italian critics who, seeing its protagonist in

exclusively autobiographical terms, accused the author of misrepresenting the ideals of the Risorgimento and the subsequent course of Italian history. Consequently they failed singularly to appreciate not only the original, essentially modern symbolic nature of the novel's structure but also the very finely nuanced psychological portrait of Don Fabrizio and the complexity of his relationship to the other characters. TON
O. Ragusa, *Narrative and Drama* (The Hague, 1976).

Landau, Lev Davidovitch (b. Baku, Russia, 22.1.1908; d. Moscow, USSR, 1.4.1968). Russian physicist. One of the most versatile of theoretical physicists, he studied at the universities of Baku and Leningrad before working with N. BOHR in Copenhagen. Shortly after his return to the USSR he went to Kharkov and in 1937 he moved to the Institute for Physical Problems in Moscow where he set up and directed the department of theoretical physics. In 1962 he was involved in a road accident from which he never recovered sufficiently to continue creative work. Landau's outstanding contribution to physics (for which he was awarded the Nobel prize in 1962) was his explanation of the remarkable properties of liquid helium, which had been shown to become a superfluid at very low temperatures; i.e. it was able to flow through exceedingly fine channels with ease, as if it had no viscosity. Landau showed that this could be explained if the behaviour of helium atoms in the liquid was considered as that of a single unified system rather than as independent individual atoms. He suggested that there was a very unusual pattern of 'elementary excitations' of this system (analogous to all the possible vibrations of a plucked violin string). He showed that his proposed special form of the excitations would account for the superfluid phenomenon. It was only many years later that experimental work demonstrated that his explanation was essentially correct. Landau's other research covered such fields as quantum mechanics, magnetism, superconductivity, atomic nuclei and quantum electrodynamics. He was also the coauthor (with E. M. Lifshitz) of the remarkable textbook series *Course of Theoretical Physics* (7 vols, Oxford, 1972–), which has been translated into at least nine languages and remains a standard reference work.　　　HMR

A. Livanova, *Landau: a Great Physicist and Teacher*, tr. J. B. Sykes (Oxford, 1979).

Landowska, Wanda Louise (b. Warsaw, Russian Poland [now Poland], 5.7.1879; naturalized American citizen; d. Lakeville, Conn., USA, 6.8.1959). Polish/American pianist and harpsichordist. She showed an early interest in authentic texts of Bach's keyboard works. In 1900 she moved to Paris and carried out research into 17c and 18c music and its interpretation. Her first public harpsichord recital was in 1903 and in 1909 she published *Musique ancienne* (Paris, 1909; *Music of the Past*, London, 1926). Subsequently she designed her own large two-manual Pleyel harpsichord, taught in Berlin and became the first performer in this century to play the harpsichord continuo in Bach's *St Matthew Passion*. In 1925 Landowska founded the Ecole de Musique Ancienne at St Leu-en-Forêt, near Paris, where she taught and gave recitals. In 1941 she settled in the USA and recorded much harpsichord music for the first time including Bach's complete '48' and *Goldberg Variations*; FALLA and Poulenc wrote concertos specially for her. If her tone-colours now sound overrich there was a vitality and sensibility in her playing which contributed significantly to the revival and understanding of the harpsichord and its repertory.　　　JL

B. Gavoty, *Wanda Landowska* (Geneva, 1956); D. Restout (ed.), *Landowska on Music* (London, 1965).

Landsteiner, Karl (b. Vienna, Austria-Hungary [now Austria], 14.6.1868; naturalized American citizen; d. New York, USA, 26.6.1943). Austrian/American immunologist. After graduating in medicine (Vienna 1891), Landsteiner studied chemistry under HANTZSCH, H. E. FISCHER and Bamberger. In 1898 he returned to Vienna to begin the lifelong studies which were to transform the science of immunology and greatly increase our understanding of the body's mechanisms for protection against disease. From 1909 he was professor of pathological anatomy, but in 1922 he fled the chaos of postwar Vienna and eventually reached the USA to join the Rockefeller Institute in New York. In 1930 Landsteiner was awarded a Nobel prize for his discovery of blood groups. He showed that the clumping of corpuscles sometimes observed on mixing bloods from two different individuals is caused by specific interaction between cell antigens (*agglutinogens*) on the surface of the red corpuscles of one with antibodies (*agglutinins*) in the plasma of the other. From this he worked out the main (A B O) classification and showed that there are also many subsidiary groupings, one of which, Rh, is important in the aetiology of haemolytic disease of the newborn. This work made possible the development of safe methods of blood transfusion. It also provided useful techniques for establishing paternity and for genetic studies on the origins of human populations. Landsteiner explored and defined the various types of immune response and was the first to realize that allergies have an immunochemical basis. Landsteiner's most significant work, however, was directed towards elucidation of the fundamental basis of immunological processes (*The Specificity of Serological Reactions*, Cambridge, Mass., 1945). Of particular significance for the subsequent development of immunology was his demonstration that injection of a protein conjugated with a small molecule, which he called a '*hapten*', can raise antibodies which react specifically with the *hapten*, even though it be a synthetic molecule not encountered in nature. This enabled Landsteiner to define the relationships between antibody and antigen with chemical precision.　　　GL

Lane, Allen, *né* Allen Lane Williams (b. Bristol, Avon, UK, 21.9.1902; d. London, 7.7.1970). British publisher. At 16 he joined the Bodley Head, the publishing firm founded by his uncle John Lane, on condition that he changed his name to Lane. From this apprenticeship Lane would seem to have derived his fanatic devotion to 'fine' books, and his courage in challenging orthodox thinking – whether on matters of morality or publishing practice. On taking over Bodley Head, Lane was joined by his two brothers, and with them he eventually pioneered the experiment in high quality, paperback reprints known as Penguin Books. The first batch of 10 (including works by HEMINGWAY, CHRISTIE, Maurois) came out in 1935. The initial aim was not just to lower price, but to find new outlets and new reading markets, the innovation being developed by Robert de Graff in the USA with Pocket Books founded in 1937. Lane's Penguin Books, however, gravitated more to the 'quality' end of the book trade, and soon after its foundation original titles were generated through the Pelican (nonfiction) imprint. With King Penguins, Penguin 'Specials' and Puffins, Lane quickly penetrated all sectors of general trade publishing. WW2 gave the firm a notable boost so that after 1945 Lane emerged not just as a publisher of cheap books, but as a general educator. Not himself an intellectual, Lane shrewdly harnessed the talents of creative publishers, advisers and general editors. Following the triumphant publication of *Lady Chatterley's Lover* in 1960, Penguin went public in 1961. Despite the firm's continuing success, its hegemony over the British paperback book trade was cut into by new, aggressive publishers who successfully adopted American styles of business. After Lane's death, Penguin was taken over by S. Pearson & Co. for £15 million. JAS

J. E. Morpurgo, *Allen Lane: King Penguin* (London, 1979).

Lang, Fritz (b. Vienna, Austria-Hungary [now Austria], 5.12.1890; naturalized American citizen, 1935; d. Beverly Hills, Calif., USA, 2.8.1976). German/American film director. Lang's work divides into the German period from 1919 to 1933 and the American period from 1936 to 1956. His early training as an architect was reflected in the silent German films, particularly *Der müde Tod* (*Destiny*, 1921) and *Metropolis* (1926). This concern with pictorial design and composition, however, was never seen as an end in itself but was used to convey, often metaphorically,

the oppressive and constricting material circumstances which determine people's lives. In a restrictive political climate Lang resorted to fable and metaphor to express his political concerns. *Dr Mabuse der Spieler* (*Dr Mabuse the Gambler*, 1922) and *Das Testament das Dr Mabuse* (*The Last Will of Dr Mabuse*, 1932), metaphorical portraits of a tyrannical character, were prophetic of historical events. (*Testament* was banned by the Nazis on whom, Lang later claimed, it was an attack.) Lang's first sound film *M* (1931) saw him moving away from the monumental, decorative quality of his silent films towards a greater interest in the psychology and development of character, an interest expanded in the American period (he fled Germany when the Nazis came to power). His first American film *Fury* (1936) continued the investigation into the psychology of mob violence and personal vengeance begun with *M*. *Fury* was the first of a trilogy of films dealing with issues of specifically American social concern. The theme of social criticism – of the environment, laws and conventions – was a consistent preoccupation of Lang's. Where it brought him into conflict with the Nazis in Germany, in America it brought him into conflict with the policy-makers of the Hollywood studio system. After a battle with the producers of *Beyond a Reasonable Doubt* (1956) Lang decided to make no more films in Hollywood, but he had by then completed some classic American movies, including *You Only Live Once* (1937), *The Woman in the Window* (1945) and *The Big Heat* (1953), films which ruthlessly express his bleak and pessimistic worldview. LJC

Lange, Dorothea (b. Hoboken, NJ, USA, 25.5.1895; d. San Francisco, Calif., 11.10.1965). American photographer. Lange was educated in New York. She trained with the photographer Clarence White in 1917–18, and opened a portrait studio in San Francisco in 1919. In 1933 she photographed the first picture of the type for which she became famous, 'White Angel Breadline'. Her first exhibition took place the following year, arranged by Willard Van Dyke in San Francisco. In 1935 she joined the California State Emergency Relief Administration, Division of Rural Rehabilitation, where she photographed to illustrate the reports of Paul Schuster Taylor. Taylor recommended that camps should be officially established and maintained to house migrant agricultural workers. Lange transferred to the Resettlement Administration (later the Farm Security Administration) in 1935 and worked for the agency full-time for the next two years, and intermittently up to 1942. She married Paul S. Taylor in 1935 and together they published one of the most moving and eloquent of photographs and text *An American Exodus* (NY, 1939, ²1969), which championed the rights of the American rural poor. Lange's ear was as good as her eye and the text contains many statements by the people she photographed. Her best-known photograph 'Migrant Mother' was taken in a frozen pea-pickers' camp in Nipomo, California, in 1936 and indicated the level of poverty and distress to which an exemplary American mother had been reduced. It was one of the central photographs in STEICHEN's exhibition 'The Family of Man' two decades later. Lange's later work included *The American Country Woman* (NY, 1967). The compassion of her photographs has been widely celebrated and very rarely emulated.   MH-B

Dorothea Lange: Photographer, intro. G. P. Elliott (NY, 1965).

Langevin, Paul (b. Paris, France, 23.1.1872; d. Paris, 19.12.1946). French physicist. Langevin's research in physics was wide-ranging. His first published work involved studies of the ionization of gases; from the results of later experiments he predicted the properties of the ionosphere which was only investigated experimentally about 20 years later by APPLETON. He also worked on relativity, on the statistics of the interactions of molecules in gases, and on the physics of cloud formation. He is best remembered, however, for his work on the theory of magnetic materials. In the 19c magnetism was thought to be due to microscopic circulating electric currents in certain materials. Langevin reinterpreted these ideas in terms of orbiting electrons (which had recently been

discovered) and he showed that the phenomenon of paramagnetism – the magnetism which is induced in many materials when they are placed in a magnetic field – could be completely accounted for by his theory. He showed that this paramagnetic effect would become stronger at low temperatures because then the atomic vibrations would not upset the electron orbits. His calculations on this accorded well with experimental results obtained by KAMERLINGH ONNES. He also explained the phenomenon of diamagnetism – the ability of materials to repel a magnetic field – with equal success. Yet another side of his versatility was his development during WW1 of an ultrasonic system for the underwater detection of U-boats. He was the first person to use a plate of crystalline quartz to act as an ultrasonic generator – a technique which is widely used today in many branches of industry and technology. He also developed the ultrasonic depth-finder and a method for underwater telephony using ultrasonics. Just before the fall of France in 1940 he was engaged in what was to be his last research, again characteristically in a completely different field: he managed to solve the problem of how to slow down fast neutrons by collisions with atomic nuclei of arbitrary mass – an essential requirement for a nuclear reactor.   HMR

Langley, John Newport (b. Newbury, Berks., UK, 2.12.1852; d. Cambridge, 5.12.1925). British physiologist. He studied at St John's College, Cambridge, and was elected fellow of Trinity College in 1879. After a period as lecturer he became professor of physiology at Cambridge (1903–25). Langley's major interest became glandular secretion. After initially working on the effect of 'jarborandi' on the heart, he found that it had powerful effects upon salivary secretion which he showed to be under sympathetic control. He then went on to show that nicotine blocked nerve impulses at sympathetic ganglia. This research led to extensive studies on the sympathetic nervous system and identification of its specific function (*Autonomic Nervous System*, pt 1, Cambridge, 1921).

Langley had many distinguished students and assistants, notably SHERRINGTON and DALE. He is probably responsible for the success of the *Journal of Physiology*, taking it over from Michael Foster when it was in a financially disastrous state.   CTJ

Langmuir, Irving (b. New York, USA, 31.1.1881; d. Falmouth, Mass., 16.8.1957). American chemist. After graduating from Columbia University in metallurgical engineering in 1903, he pursued research with NERNST in Göttingen. Langmuir was exceptionally versatile, and the first scientist employed by an industrial organization (General Electric Company, 1909–50) to be awarded the Nobel prize (1932). Apart from his classical work in the adsorption of gases at solid (especially catalyst) and liquid surfaces and his derivation of the so-called Langmuir isotherm, he contributed significantly to a variety of fields: chemical reactions at high temperatures and low pressure, atomic structure and valence theory, electrical discharges in gases, thermionic emission in vacuum and atmospheric science. The Langmuir trough, still much used by biophysicists and colloid scientists, and the Langmuir pump, for generating high vacua, bear witness to his inventive flair.
JMT

Lapworth, Arthur (b. Galashiels, Borders, UK, 10.10.1872; d. Manchester, 5.4.1941). British chemist. Lapworth played a fundamental part in developing the present-day electronic theories of organic chemistry. From his research work on naphthalene derivatives and camphor came two of his main interests; the mechanisms of aromatic substitution and of addition to carbonyl groups. In 1909 he went to Manchester University, where he remained for the rest of his academic life, as professor of organic chemistry (1913) and from 1922 as director of the laboratories. His work on camphor led him to study the formation of cyanohydrins. He showed that the reaction was reversible, involved addition of cyanide ion to the carbonyl group, and was catalysed by acid. He also demonstrated that the rate of bromination of ketones is independent of the concentration of bromine and involves enolization as the rate determining step. From this work and that on the addition of hydrogen cyanide to the double bond of conjugated ketones Lapworth developed the modern theory of the classification of reagents in organic chemistry. He first used the terms anionoid and catinoid which in modern nomenclature have become nucleophilic and electrophilic. His analysis of the products of addition to unsaturated ketones and of aromatic substitution led him to the concept of alternating polarities of carbon atoms in conjugated systems (*Memoirs of the Manchester Lit. and Phil. Soc.*, 64, No. 3 [1920], 1), which developed into the modern ideas of inductive and mesomeric effects in organic chemistry.
TGH

Larionov, Mikhail (b. Tiraspol, Russia, 22.5.1881; d. Fontenay-aux-Roses, Seine-et-Marne, France, 10.5.1964). Russian artist, pioneer abstract painter, initiator of Moscow avant-garde exhibitions including 'Donkeys Tail' (1912) and 'Target' (1913). From early study of French postimpressionist art, Larionov developed an original, neoprimitive style typified by *Autumn* (1913) – close to illustrations he made for Russian futurist books. His inventive graphic style and imagery in *Mirskontsa* [Worldbackwards] (Moscow, 1912) and *Pomada* [Pomade] (Moscow, 1913) parallel the handwritten, concrete poetry of A. Kruchenykh and KHLEBNIKOV. This collaboration prompted his creation of progressively abstract painting (rayism or rayonism). His earliest is *Glass* (1912), based on his notion that the eye sees light-rays emanating continuously from objects whereas the brain only makes 'sense' of this information; by reproducing coloured rays on canvas he contrived 'self-sufficient' painting. After 1915 his pseudoscientific theory expounded in *Luchizm* [Rayism] (Moscow, 1913) and supported by linear abstractions such as *Rayonism, Sea Beach* (1914) formed a pragmatic alternative to the mystique of MALEVICH's suprematism, thus contributing to the development of contructivist painting. But he left Russia after being wounded on active service to join DIAGHILEV in 1915, settling in Paris with Goncharova in 1919. His theatrical experiments include neoprimitive designs for *Le Soleil de Nuit* (1916), futurist for *Les Contes Russes* (1917) and modified-constructivist for *Le Renard* (1922), but a career in ballet design was halted by Diaghilev's death in 1929. In later life Larionov ruined his artistic reputation by attempts to antedate his early art in rivalry with KANDINSKY, a fact reflected in all biographies; there have been recent attempts to re-evaluate his true role in exhibitions at the Tate Gallery (*Abstraction: Towards a New Art, Painting 1910–20*, London, 1980, catalogue), and major retrospectives at the Russian Museum, Leningrad (1980) and Tretyakov Gallery, Moscow (1981). SPC

Gontcharova–Larionov, exh. cat., Musée d'Art Moderne (Paris, 1963); W. George, *Larionov* (Paris, 1966).

Larkin, Philip Arthur (b. Coventry, W. Mids, UK, 9.8.1922). British poet. Since the publication of *The Less Deceived* (Hull, 1955), Larkin has been widely regarded in England as the country's most eminent living poet, and accorded a respect which his two subsequent collections of verse *The Whitsun Weddings* (London, 1964) and *High Windows* (London, 1974) have further secured. Dissenting views have deplored a lack of ambition in his work, either on the grounds that the poetry shuns engagement with any form of emotional risk, or that it panders to a 'middle brow' reluctance to take art seriously. Such criticisms, however, tend to confirm the very qualities Larkin's admirers value. His imagination conceives of a postwar, postimperial England of drab surburbia and Welfare-State-sponsored lives in which traditional pieties, either of religion or self-fulfilment, can only be approached with scepticism or, at best, regret. He thus addresses a broad-based intellectual sentiment, emergent in the 1950s and still well ensconced in the national culture, in favour of common sense and empiricism and hostile to any kind of humbug. In Larkin's verse this is put forward less as a mode of realism, for the world he depicts is extensively mediated by a selective sensibility

and calculated rhyming and stanzaic forms, than as a means of reserving judgement. His writing is disdainful of culture as a form of privilege, but the less it allows the self-conceit of being taken in, the more dismayed it seems to be by the spectacle of common life and death. Since coming down from Oxford in 1943, Larkin has pursued a distinguished career in librarianship. ATKC

A. Thwaite (ed.), *Larkin at Sixty* (London, 1982).

Lasker-Schüler, Else (b. Wuppertal-Elberfeld, N. Rhine-Westphalia, Germany, 11.2.1869; d. Jerusalem, Palestine [now Israel], 22.1.1945). German poet, dramatist, short-story writer and essayist. The daughter of a German-Jewish architect, she married and thereby escaped from the provinces to Berlin where round the turn of the century she developed a bohemian lifestyle. She was inspired to write by the 'literary gipsy' Peter Hille and, not unlike him, tried to combine a near-mystical adoration of nature with visions of a biblical utopia. Through her short (second) marriage to Herwarth Walden she became a contributor to *Der Sturm*, one of the major periodicals of German expressionism, a literary style she had helped to inaugurate in her poetry (*Styx*, Berlin, 1902; *Der siebente Tag* [The seventh day], Berlin, 1905; *Meine Wunder* [My miracles], Karlsruhe-Leipzig, 1911; *Hebräische Balladen* [Hebrew ballads], Berlin, 1913). Her first play *Die Wupper* (Berlin, 1909) thematized life in a rich entrepreneurial family surrounded by a proletarian community. She had friends both on the right and the left of the literary-political and artistic spectrum (BENN, MARC, KRAUS, Wieland Herzfelde, HEARTFIELD) who figure in her prose narratives *Der Prinz von Theben* [The Prince of Thebes] (Leipzig, 1914) and in *Der Malik* (Berlin, 1919). In 1933 she emigrated first to Switzerland and then, permanently after 1939, to Palestine. In her plays *Arthur Aronymus und seine Väter* [Arthur Aronymus and his fathers] and the posthumous *IchundIch* [I and I] (1970) she attempted a theatre in which dream, fantasy and realism are mixed. WvdW

H. W. Cohn, *Else Lasker-Schüler: the Broken World* (Cambridge, 1974).

Laski, Harold Joseph (b. Manchester, UK, 30.6.1893; d. London, 24.3.1950). British political scientist who had an important influence on the British left in the 1930s and 1940s. Educated at Oxford, he taught at Harvard (1916–20) and formed a lifelong friendship with Frankfurter, later appointed by F. D. ROOSEVELT to the US Supreme Court. In this period he argued the case for political pluralism, but in his *Grammar of Politics* (London, 1925) moved to the collectivist position in which the state was seen as 'the fundamental instrument of society'. From 1926 to 1950 Laski taught political science at the London School of Economics where his views impressed a future generation of leaders from Africa and Asia. Under the impact of the world depression and the rise of fascism, Laski's fears that the decline of capitalism would lead to the destruction of democracy led him to turn from reformism to MARXism and to argue that socialism was the only available alternative to fascism. These views he developed in *The State in Theory and Practice* (London, 1935), *The Rise of European Liberalism* (London, 1936) and *Parliamentary Government in England* (London, 1938); at the same time he was active as a member of the Labour party's national executive in working for a popular front against fascism, notably in the period of the Spanish civil war (1936–9). His *Reflections on the Revolution of Our Time* (London, 1943) was a bid to influence the postwar settlement; and in 1945 he was chairman of the Labour party in the year of its greatest electoral triumph. Attlee and BEVIN, however, the leaders of the Labour government of 1945–50, had little sympathy with Laski's views. In common with the left-wing group of which the *New Statesman* was the focus, Laski was excluded from power and criticized the Labour government, especially in its foreign policy, for failing to establish a socialist Britain. He continued to teach at the LSE and in 1948 published a long and controversial study of US politics *The American Democracy*. ALCB

K. Martin, *Harold Laski* (London, 1953); B. Zylstra, *From Pluralism to Collectivism: the Development of Harold Laski's Political Thought* (Assen, Netherlands, 1968).

Lasswell, Harold Dwight (b. Donnellson, Ill., USA, 13.2.1902; d. New York, 18.12.1978). American political scientist. He was taught at Chicago by leading figures of the Chicago school, who were transforming the social sciences. Lasswell was to devote himself to the task of making politics an empirically oriented, quantitative discipline, enriched by the other social sciences. Taking the widest possible view of its subject matter, that politics is the study of influence, he saw it as an activity permeating society, in which broad context it has to be studied. The wide sweep of his collaborative writings, with philosophers, lawyers, economists, anthropologists and psychologists, fully exemplify this conviction. His *Politics: Who Gets What, When, How* (NY, 1936) lucidly stated his theory of the way in which the 'values' or 'goods' of income, safety and respect are distributed in societies, and became a classic text of the new behavioural approach to political studies. He was a pioneer in various fields, including communications theory, content analysis and the development of the policy sciences, and few have rivalled his grasp of social knowledge. DCr

A. A. Rogow, *Politics, Personality and Social Science in the Twentieth Century* (London, 1969).

Laue, Max Theodor Felix von (b. Pfaffendorf, Rhineland-Palatinate, Germany, 9.9.1897; d. West Berlin, 24.4.1960). German theoretical physicist who first observed the diffraction of X-rays by crystals, thus establishing their wave nature and providing a powerful tool for the study of crystal structure. His first work was on optics, into which he introduced PLANCK's concept of entropy. An early convert to relativity, he showed that EINSTEIN's formula for the addition of velocities yields Fresnel's expression for the velocity of light in flowing water. At that time the nature of X-rays was unclear, and Laue realized that if they were electromagnetic waves of short wavelength they should be diffracted as light is by a grating. Following his suggestion, Walter Friedrich and Paul Kipping irradiated a crystal of copper sulphate with X-rays and observed a regular pattern of dark spots on a photographic plate behind the crystal. Laue was able to explain this pattern by extending the theory of diffraction to three dimensions, and for this work he was awarded the Nobel prize in 1914. In the hands of the BRAGGS this soon became a powerful technique for determining the structure of crystals.

Laue did not exploit his discovery but continued to work on fundamentals, in particular on a dynamical theory of the interference of X-rays. He was one of the three members of the Prussian Academy to protest against Einstein's expulsion by the Nazis. With equal courage, he successfully opposed the election of Johannes Stark, an opponent of modern physical theories who had become a fervent Nazi. Laue went into retirement during WW2, but afterwards played a leading part in the rebuilding of German science.   PEH

Lauterpacht, Hersch (b. Lemberg, Galicia, Austria-Hungary [now Lvov, Ukraine, USSR], 16.8.1897; naturalized British citizen, 1931; d. London, UK, 8.5.1960). Austrian/British international lawyer and judge of the International Court of Justice. He studied in Vienna, then in 1923 came to England and worked at the London School of Economics until 1938 when he was made professor of international law at Cambridge. His writings made an important contribution to the evolution of modern international law; they reflect his optimism about its development and function. He wrote pioneering works on the use of private law rules and principles in international law, on recognition and on human rights; he produced important studies of the nature of the international judicial function, its place in the settlement of disputes and its role in the development of the law. He edited *Oppenheim*, the standard textbook on international law, the *Annual Digest of Public International Cases* and the *British Yearbook of International Law*. He also had a distinguished career in the practice of international law: he had an active practice at the Bar; he was a member of the International Law Commission; in 1955 he was appointed to the International Court of Justice and he made a substantial contribution to its jurisprudence. He was one of the great international lawyers of this century.   CDG

C. W. Jenks, 'Hersch Lauterpacht: the scholar as prophet', *British Yearbook of International Law*, 1 (1960); G. Fitzmaurice, 'Hersch Lauterpacht: the scholar as judge', *British Yearbook of International Law*, 2 (1961).

Laval, Pierre (b. Châteldon, Puy-de-Dôme, France, 28.6.1883; d. Paris, 15.10.1945). French prime minister (1931 –2); foreign minister (1934–6); prime minister (1935–6); chief minister of the PÉTAIN regime in Vichy (1942–4). Lawyer, mayor (1923–44) and deputy (1914 –27) for Aubervilliers – a working-class constituency north-east of Paris – senator for the Seine (1927–36) and for his native *département* (1936–44), he began as a left-wing quasi-socialist pacifist who narrowly escaped prison for his views in 1918, moving in domestic politics towards the centre and right of French politics but retaining always his opposition to war and his belief that all conflicts could be managed and 'arranged' out of existence. Given French weakness before 1939 and the defeat in 1940 this made him pre-eminently the leader of those, largely from the urban and agricultural rentier classes, the *grande bourgeoisie* and the industrialists, who sought an accommodation with MUSSOLINI in 1935–6, and with Nazi Germany in 1937–44. Convinced that German victories were irreversible, he became the epitome of (and a byword for) collaboration with HITLER's new order in Europe, being prepared to go further than even his supporters could accept. But his reputation for political duplicity made him suspect even to the Nazis, who arrested him in 1944 when he attempted to reconvene the National Assembly as a means of reconciling Vichy France with the invading Western Allies. In October 1945 he was tried by his fellow countrymen on the charge of treason and shot.   DCW

G. Warner, *Pierre Laval and the Eclipse of France* (London, 1968).

Lawrence, David Herbert Richards (b. Eastwood, Notts., UK, 11.9.1885; d. Vence, Alpes-Maritimes, France, 2.3.1930). British writer. The son of a coalminer, Lawrence won a scholarship to Nottingham High School in 1898, and thus symbolized the lasting divide between his working-class upbringing and the middle-class world into which success (first academic, later literary) drew him. A pupil-teacher from 1902, he began to write poetry in 1904 and fiction in 1906, when he also went to Nottingham University College. He worked as a schoolteacher in Croydon between 1908 and 1911, when his first significant publications appeared in the *English Review*; its editor Ford Madox FORD helped him publish *The White Peacock* (NY, 1911), a deeply flawed first novel which nevertheless revealed the conflicts of his intellectual and social experience. He abandoned teaching after a severe illness, and went to Germany and Italy in 1912 with Frieda Weekley (*née* von Richthofen), whom he married in 1914. *Sons and Lovers* (London, 1913) was a major novel which helped free him from the influence of his mother's domination of his early life. His novel *The Rainbow* (London, 1915), charting sexual and social change in a Midlands family between 1840 and 1905, was banned as immoral; its sequel *Women in Love* (written 1916–17; NY, 1920) created a nightmarish account of the individual's divorce from society (but not from relationships) during cultural catastrophe. After poverty and some harassment during WW1, which he strongly opposed, he returned to Italy in 1919. His writing in the early 1920s was characterized by an insistence upon male domination which can be seen in *Aaron's Rod* (NY, 1922) and in his Australian novel *Kangaroo* (London, 1923). During 1922–5 he lived in New Mexico and Mexico, where he wrote *The Plumed Serpent* (London, 1926), a novel describing the revival of an ancient religious consciousness in modern man. He returned to Europe in 1925, and lived in Italy and the south of France. He refused to accept that he was suffering from tuberculosis; fuelled by rage against censorship and by anger stemming from his worsening health, his need to redirect man's consciousness of himself culminated in the passionate moralizing and sexual explicitness of *Lady Chatterley's Lover* (Florence, 1928) and the religio-sexual rebirth created in 'The Escaped Cock' (Paris, 1929). His final works *Apocalypse* (Florence, 1931) and *Last Poems* (Florence, 1932) would stress man's relationship with the cosmos rather than with society. Over 5000 of his letters survive, and must be counted a major work; they provide an incomparable record of his passions, his thinking, and his attractiveness as a fellow human (see *The Letters of D. H. Lawrence*, 7 vols, Cambridge, 1979–). For a writer dying at 44, his output was immense; he was an insistent reviser and rewriter, but 12 novels, 60 stories, travel books, plays, over 900 poems, essays, reviews and paintings demonstrate his compulsion to record the divisions in his nature and his experience: or, as he would have seen it, his desire to recall Western man to a fundamentally religious knowledge of his own nature. JW

E. Nehls (ed.), *D. H. Lawrence: a Composite Biography* (3 vols, Madison, 1957–9); F. Kermode, *Lawrence* (London, 1973).

Lawrence, Ernest Orlando (b. Canton, S. Dak., USA, 8.8.1901; d. Palo Alto, Calif., 27.8.1958). American physicist. Stimulated by a suggestion of EDDINGTON that stars might derive their energy from nuclear reactions, he devised in 1929 the principle of the cyclotron as a means of producing high-energy atomic projectiles to initiate reactors between nuclei. This ingenious device retained charged particles in a region of high magnetic field and accelerated them to very high energies by repeatedly subjecting them to a potential difference of a few kilovolts of radio frequency power. The importance of this technique was acknowledged in 1939 by the award of the Nobel prize for physics. He subsequently used the cyclotron to induce nuclear reactions and to form radioactive isotopes of importance in medicine.

Together with his brother John he made the earliest systematic use of reactors for cancer therapy. He established and directed from 1936 the radiation laboratory of the University of California at Berkeley. In 1961, element 103, which was first detected in his former laboratory, was named Lawrencium (LW) in his honour.   PSF

Lawrence, Thomas Edward (b. Tremadoc, Gwynedd, UK, 15.8.1888; d. Bovington, Dorset, 19.5.1935). British writer and man of action known as 'Lawrence of Arabia'. After Oxford he became an archaeologist, travelling and excavating in Syria until WW1 when he was sent with other British officers to help the Sherif of Mecca in the Arab revolt against the Turks. Through his sympathy with the Bedouin, by his tactical skill in developing guerrilla warfare, and by his own daring exploits he eventually gained a position of great influence. He entered Damascus in 1918 with the leading Arab forces at the conclusion of the campaign. After the war he attempted to escape the legend which had grown around his adventures, joining the RAF as an aircraftsman and living under assumed names. This difficult period of his life is frankly described in *The Mint* (NY, 1936, ²1955). Lawrence's fame is an expression of the traditional British love-affair with the desert and its abstract, ascetic faith; but his continuing reputation rests upon *Seven Pillars of Wisdom* (London, 1926, ²1935), an ambitious, hybrid work in which he seeks to combine a detailed account of the Arab revolt with his own enigmatic spiritual autobiography. The two are uneasily linked by vividly described, exhausting camel journeys which are given both a tactical and psychological significance. Each aspect of the work embodies a contradiction which Lawrence was unable to resolve: thoroughly identified with the Arab cause, he knew as a British agent that this was simply a pawn in a European game; he was also aware that his imitation of an Arab way of life, while undermining his European values, remained, in his own words, 'an affectation'. These contradictions are explored on his journeys through the desert in a style which, at times flowery and arcane, can become direct, exciting and compelling.   DC

R. Graves, *Lawrence and the Arabs* (London, 1927); D. Stewart, *T. E. Lawrence* (London, 1977).

Laxness, Halldór, *né* Gudjónsson (b. Reykjavík, Iceland, 23.4.1902). Icelandic writer. Laxness's works have brought modern Iceland to the attention of the outside world. In his first period, as a young Roman Catholic convert, he produced his first major novel *Vefarinn mikli frá Kasmír* [The great weaver from Kashmir] (Reykjavík, 1927), in which he showed exceptional power as a writer. Changing to a socialistic viewpoint, he produced over the next 20 years the four great novels through which his place as a novelist of international stature is assured. In *Salka Valka* (Reykjavík, 1931–2; tr. F. H. Lyon, London, 1936), *Sjálfstaett Fólk* (Reykjavík, 1934–5; tr. J. A. Thompson, *Independent People*, London, 1945), *Ljós heimsims* (Reykjavík, 1937–40; tr. M. Magnússon, *World Light*, London, 1969) and *Íslandsklukkan* [The bell of Iceland] (Reykjavík, 1943–6), he opened up the microcosm of modern Icelandic society to reveal its bleak poverty and spiritual corruption. The picture is unspoilt by any sentimentality towards the stunted victims; none of the damage done to them by brutal handling is hidden, but the savage indignation roused by the society which bred them leaves no doubt as to where his sympathies lie. Since receiving the Nobel prize in 1955, Laxness has continued publishing novels – the best of which is *Brekkukotsannáll* (Reykjavík, 1957; tr. M. Magnússon, *The Fish Can Sing*, London, 1966) – plays and essays which have shown his unchanged stance as one unafraid to think and speak for himself.   BSB

P. Hallberg, *Halldór Laxness* (NY, 1971).

Lazarsfeld, Paul Felix (b. Vienna, Austria-Hungary [now Austria], 13.2.1901; naturalized American citizen, 1943; d. Paris, France, 30.8.1976). Austrian/American sociologist. A mathematician from a socialist background, Lazarsfeld pioneered empirical social research at Vienna University, where he established a research institute in 1925, the first of its kind (see *Die Arbeitslosen von Marienthal*, Vienna, 1933; *Marienthal. The Sociography of an Unemployed Community*, London, 1972). From 1933 he worked in the USA, building up what became known in 1944 as the Bureau of Applied Social Research at Columbia University, New York, where he became Quetelet professor of social science in 1963. His early consumer and audience research discovered the importance of local 'opinion leaders' in filtering media influences, a finding confirmed in his innovative voting studies, *The People's Choice* (with B. R. Berelson & H. Gaudet, NY, 1948) and *Voting* (with B. R. Berelson & W. N. McPhee, Chicago, 1954). *The Academic Mind* (with W. Thielens & D. RIESMAN, Glencoe, Ill., 1958) showed the dependence of social scientists' views of MCCARTHYism on the 'attitude climate' of their institution. Methods of survey analysis perfected in these and other studies became standard throughout sociology and political science, and Lazarsfeld's fruitful collaboration with R. K. MERTON confirmed the empiricist stamp of American sociology, attacked as excessive by C. Wright MILLS and others. Subsequently he promoted sociological applications of mathematical models (e.g. games theory) and the history of social research. Always an advocate of applied sociology as a tool of social policy, Lazarsfeld stimulated its development in many countries.   JRT

Leach, Bernard Howell (b. Hong Kong, 5.1.1887; d. Hayle, Cornwall, UK, 6.5.1979). British studio potter, and the most influential potter of modern times. The entire ceramic culture of the western world owes its existence and character to his work. He absorbed the ideas and methods of traditional Japanese pottery, revived aspects of English medieval pottery, and during more than 50 years of activity amalgamated the two traditions. By his personal example and teaching, and especially through *A Potter's Book* (London, 1940), he established a new tradition of dedicated studio pottery which moved the art of ceramics out of the sphere of industrial production into the sphere of art.

As an infant, on the death of his mother he was taken by grandparents to Japan for some two years, thus establishing what was to become a lifelong link. Aged 10 he went to school in England. Later he studied etching under Frank Brangwyn, and returned to Japan in 1909 intending to teach etching himself. But he fell profoundly under the influence of living masters of the Japanese 'tea ware' tradition, and began potting himself. After periods in Peking and Korea, where he studied native ceramic traditions, he returned to settle in Britain in 1920, bringing which him the great Japanese potter HAMADA. He established his pottery at St Ives, Cornwall, producing his own wares and training a large number of major potters who came to work with him. He travelled widely, exhibiting, teaching and lecturing, and visited Japan several times. Only in 1972, when his sight began to fail, did he give up potting.

Leach's influence was based upon his own works. His pots reflect his study of Japanese, Korean and Chinese pots – especially Sung wares. He worked predominantly in earth-glaze colours, black to red, and implanted in western ceramics the oriental idea that glaze, decoration and body should be felt as one. He laid much stress upon the calligraphic use of the brush in decoration. His pots thus became works of art in their own right, although they were always usable, and sold as such. Leach found in English medieval wares a non-industrial inspiration which could, like Japanese wares, turn to account the normal hazards of craft manufacture. PSR

M. Rose, *Artist Potters in England* (London, ²1970).

Leach, Edmund Ronald (b. Sidmouth, Devon, UK, 7.11.1910). British social anthropologist. His Cambridge undergraduate education in mathematics and mechanical sciences underpinned a concern for structure and pattern which he has never lost. Five years in China in business (1932–7), fieldwork in Kurdistan in 1938 and six years in the Burma army were the highly unorthodox background for an often deliberately unorthodox anthropologist. *The Political Systems of Highland Burma* (London, 1954) showed a heretical and radical thinker challenging basic presuppositions about what societies are and how we should conceptualize them. Bold and concise, it was a study of social process, structural change and contradiction at a time when equilibrium, function and classification were dominant. *Rethinking Anthropology* (London, 1961) followed, and asserted that the discipline was becoming theoretically moribund because it ignored generalization in favour of too great a concentration on ethnography and comparison, which he dismissed as 'a matter of butterfly hunting'. His interests gradually shifted from kinship and economy to language and communication, but the focus on structure remained. *Genesis as Myth and Other Essays* (London, 1969) continued a long-standing critical conversation with the work of LÉVI-STRAUSS, as does *Social Anthropology* (London, 1982). He held the influential Cambridge posts of professor of social anthropology and provost of King's College between 1966 and 1979. MDCG

Leakey, Louis Seymour Bazett (b. Kabete, British East Africa [now Kenya], 7.8.1903; naturalized Kenyan citizen, 1964; d. London, UK, 1.10.1972). British/Kenyan archaeologist and anthropologist whose academic work has centred on human origins in East Africa. A Cambridge graduate, his fieldwork in East Africa between 1926 and 1935 laid the essential basis for future African Stone Age studies, both archaeological and palaeontological. His early finds were summarized in *Stone Age Cultures of Kenya Colony* (Cambridge, 1931) and *Stone Age Africa* (Oxford, 1936). After WW2 a programme of intensive fieldwork and excavations at Olduvai Gorge brought to light a rich fossil fauna, including early hominids and their associated implements. The discovery and its subsequent detailed publication has been of crucial importance to the study of human origins. A preliminary account was given in *Olduvai Gorge* (Cambridge, 1951) and definitive monographs on various aspects of the finds are included in a series which Leakey edited up to his death and to which he contributed the

major part of the first volume *Olduvai Gorge 1951–1961. A Preliminary Report on the Geology and Fauna* (Cambridge, 1965). His interests and writings were wide, including all aspects of African natural history, primate behaviour and the origins of man (*Adam's Ancestors*, his nonspecialist book first published in 1934, has run through several editions). The International Louis Leakey Memorial Institute of African Prehistory was set up in Nairobi by international subscription to commemorate his work, which has been continued by his wife Mary, his son Richard, and others. BWC

S. Cole, *Leakey's Luck: the Life of L. S. B. Leakey 1903–1972* (London, 1975); G. L. Isaac & E. R. McCown, *Human Origins: Louis Leakey and the East African Evidence* (London, 1976).

Leavis, Frank Raymond (b. Cambridge, UK, 14.7.1895; d. Cambridge, 14.4.1978). British literary critic. Leavis spent his life as a university teacher in Cambridge and published a set of pioneering critical works which trenchantly challenged contemporary literary orthodoxies. These include *Mass Civilization and Minority Culture* (London, 1930), *New Bearings in English Poetry* (London, 1932), *Revaluation* (London, 1936), *The Great Tradition* (London, 1948), *D. H. Lawrence: Novelist* (London, 1955) and (with his wife and co-worker Q. D. Leavis) *Dickens the Novelist* (London, 1970). From 1932 to 1953 he was editor of the literary-critical journal *Scrutiny*, whose rigorous, uncompromising critical programme influenced whole generations of English teachers and students. In what Leavis regarded as an age of cultural decline ('mass' culture, standardization, the loss of traditional values), he insisted on the most disciplined discrimination of the 'quality of life' defined within literary works, and regarded the study of literature as a supremely civilizing pursuit which must be at the centre of any campaign of spiritual renewal. His critical method is marked by its tenaciously close, detailed and sensitive reading of literary texts: along with his fellow-Cambridge critic RICHARDS, he pioneered what became known as 'practical criticism'. Linked to this vigilant scrutiny of the 'words on the page' is a marked moral sense – an insistence that 'great' literature is that which 'makes for Life', but a 'Life' which exists only in its concrete, complex 'realization' in words, rather than in some philosophical theory. As the first and major champion of the novelist D. H. LAWRENCE, Leavis grew increasingly to reject modern society and to return nostalgically to an 'organic' 17c England where 'high' and 'popular' culture were thought to be united. His career was marked by fierce controversy; implacably hostile to the 'literary establishment', he offended many by his abrasive formulations and was granted full recognition by the Cambridge University establishment only late in life. TE

Lebesgue, Henri Léon (b. Beauvais, Oise, France, 28.6.1875; d. Paris, 26.7.1941). French mathematician. Lebesgue studied at the Ecole Normale Supérieure, where he came under the influence of BOREL. This influence continued during his professional career, which he passed at the Collège de France. Taking up Borel's notion of measure, he developed in the 1900s a theory of the integral which was more general in conception and powerful in application than the previous theories (which are associated with the 19c mathematicians Cauchy and Riemann). His relations with Borel suffered later, after some rather trivial priority disputes. Lebesgue applied his new theory to various problems in mathematical analysis, including the relationship between differentiation and integration (the fundamental relationship in the calculus), various properties of trigonometric series (including their relation to 'Fourier series') and the class of functions which could be defined by analytic expressions. These achievements are best seen as a major contribution to a whole generation of French mathematicians including not only Borel but also Denjoy, FRÉCHET and HADAMARD. In later years Lebesgue transferred some of his mathematical interests to other topics, although he did not attain the same level of importance. For example, while his ideas on topology were ingenious, they were outclassed by the achievements of BROUWER. During this period

he also wrote some useful articles on the history and teaching of mathematics. His writings are collected in *Oeuvres scientifiques* [Scientific works] (5 vols, Geneva, 1972–3). IG-G

Le Chatelier, Henry Louis (b. Paris, France, 8.10.1850; d. Miribel-les-Echelles, Isère, 17.9.1936). French chemist and metallurgist. Although he made important contributions to the chemistry of cements, metallurgy and the study of gas reactions, Le Chatelier is best known for the general principle which bears his name. Le Chatelier studied at the Ecole Polytechnique and the Ecole des Mines in Paris (1869–71), where he returned as professor in 1877. His early pioneering work on the chemistry of cements laid a firm basis for much later research, leading him to consider the fundamental laws of chemical equilibrium and, in 1884, to the formulation of the principle named after him, viz. that if a system in stable chemical equilibrium is subjected to a change in external conditions (e.g. temperature or pressure) then the position of equilibrium changes in the direction which tends to annul the external change.

In his later work, largely concerned with high temperature equilibria in gases, with the metallurgy of steel and the properties of alloys, Le Chatelier made full use of, and contributed to, the growing subject of chemical thermodynamics. He developed several methods of measuring high temperatures, introduced the platinum–platinum rhodium thermocouple and invented the inverted stage metallurgical microscope. He laid great stress on the close link between pure and applied science and strongly advocated the introduction of scientific method in the conduct of industry. DHE

Le Corbusier, ps. of Charles-Edouard Jeanneret (b. La Chaux-de-Fonds, Neuchâtel, Switzerland, 6.10.1887; naturalized French citizen, 1930; d. Cap Martin, Alpes-Maritimes, France, 27.8.1966). Swiss/French architect and painter. Trained initially as an engraver and goldsmith, Le Corbusier worked with Josef Hoffmann in Vienna (1905), PERRET in Paris (1908) and BEHRENS in Berlin (1910) before settling in Paris in

1917. In 1918, in reaction to what they saw as the decorative degeneracy of cubism, he and the painter OZENFANT developed purism, based on the architectural equilibrium and functional simplicity of the machine. In 1923 he published *Vers une architecture* (Paris; *Towards a New Architecture*, London, 1927) in which he expounded his revolutionary concept of mass-produced housing based on a ferroconcrete modular skeleton (the 'Dom-ino' system, first formulated 1914–15), which he had already implemented in the Cotrohan house (1921). In the 1920s he published the first of his town-planning projects for futuristic cities focused upon a central complex of identical skyscrapers (e.g. 'Ville Contemporaine', 1922; 'Ville Radieuse', 1935). He also developed a new concept of the private house, based on cubist principles, painted white and raised at least partially on pillars (e.g. the villas at Vaucresson, 1922; Garches, 1927; Poissy, 1929–31). Also innovative was the flow of one room into the next, resulting in a dynamic spaciousness. He subsequently developed the use of stilts for far larger buildings, creating a dramatic effect through the visual-aesthetic surprise of a multistoreyed block raised off the ground (e.g. the Swiss Dormitory in the Paris Cité Universitaire, 1930–2, and the Brazilian Ministry of Education in Rio de Janeiro, 1937–43, with Costa and NIEMEYER). After WW2 Le Corbusier moved abruptly away from functionalism to explore the possibilities of an antirational, expressionistic, emphatically sculptural style, in which the quality of the building material (largely ferroconcrete) is given free play (e.g. the Unité d'Habitation at Marseilles, 1947–52). The culmination of this tendency is found in the roughly textured sculptural mass of the pilgrimage Chapel of Notre Dame du Haut at Ronchamp (1950–4), with the soaring curve of the dark roof floating above the moulded white walls. The impact of this dramatic celebration of concrete led to the development of a new 'brutal' style in architecture. From 1951 to 1956 he was able to realize some of his ideas about town planning in the design and construction of Chandigarh, a new capital for the Punjab, in which the mas-

sively conceived buildings are placed in subtle visual relationships. The brutalism of these buildings was developed even more emphatically in his last works, including the Museum of Modern Art, Tokyo (1957) and the Dominican Friary of La Tourette (1957–60).

Le Corbusier's *Oeuvre complète* (8 vols, Zürich, 1946–70; 6 vols, *Le Corbusier and Pierre Jeanneret: Complete Architectural Works*, London, 1966) has been edited, with the architect's collaboration, by W. Boesiger and (vol. 2) by O. Stonorov: vols 1–3, up to 1938, cover the work of Le Corbusier and his cousin Pierre Jeanneret; vols 4–8, 1938–65, the work of Le Corbusier alone.

SOBT

S. Papadaki (ed.), *Le Corbusier: Architect, Painter, Writer* (NY, 1948).

Lederberg, Joshua (b. Montclair, NJ, USA, 23.5.1925). American geneticist. In 1958 Lederberg was awarded the Nobel prize for medicine, at the age of 33, for the great contributions he had made to the dramatic advances in knowledge of bacterial genetics. In 1946, with TATUM, he obtained the first definite evidence that bacteria can conjugate in a sexual manner. This showed that the mechanisms of heredity in bacteria are basically the same as in other living organisms. It also provided a starting-point for other far-reaching discoveries and in particular facilitated the determination of the order in which the genes specifying particular characteristics are arranged on the chromosome. Later, with N. D. Zinder, he showed that a bacterial virus could act as a vector, transferring small fragments of the bacterial chromosome from one cell to another (transduction) and thus producing recombinant types. Since the proportion of the genome so transferred is small, this provided a method for mapping the fine structure of bacterial genes and opened the way for Yanovsky to demonstrate the structural colinearity of the gene and the peptide chain it specifies. In collaboration with his wife, Lederberg also produced the first firm evidence that mutations can occur spontaneously, thus proving one of the basic assumptions of the theory of evolution.   GL

Lee Kuan Yew (b. Singapore, Straits Settlements [now Singapore], 16.9.1923). Founder of the Singapore Socialist People's Action party (1954), prime minister of the Republic of Singapore since 1959, he is distinguished for the ruthlessness with which he established and maintained what was effectively a Western-orientated, but anticapitalist welfare state throughout the 1960s and 1970s, and for the shipwreck of his hopes of a union of Singapore and Malaysia in 1964–5 on Malay Sinophobia.　　DCW

Lee, Tsung-Dao (b. Shanghai, China, 25.11.1926). Chinese physicist. T. D. Lee, together with C. N. Yang, was awarded the Nobel prize in 1957 for their theoretical work on the principle of parity violation in weak interactions. Detailed studies over many years of the electromagnetic and strong interactions between subatomic particles had shown that they conserved parity, that is, the equations describing them were invariant under inversion of the spatial coordinates (mirror symmetry). It had always been assumed that the same property would hold for the weak interactions, as exemplified by the process of nuclear β-decay. Lee and Yang made a very careful analysis of all the data available up to 1956, and concluded that there was no evidence in favour of such parity conservation. At the same time, they found that they could give a natural explanation of a paradox – called the τ-θ paradox – connected with decay of K-mesons, if parity were not conserved in weak decays. Lee and Yang suggested a number of crucial tests of their hypothesis, which were verified in experiments in the following months. Perhaps the most important result of their work was that physicists no longer considered the so-called conservation 'laws' sacrosanct; each had to be subjected to stringent experimental tests. The other major contribution of Lee and Yang to theoretical physics, in 1960, was also in the field of weak interactions. In particular, they concluded that the light neutral particle, or neutrino, produced in association with an electron in these interactions, was different from the neutrino associated with the muon. This prediction was veri-

fied in experiments in 1961. They also, in the same paper, proposed several other fundamental tests of the nature of the weak interactions. These included the possible existence of a new massive particle, the W-boson, as the quantum or carrier of the weak interaction. Later developments have given estimates for the mass of this particle, and it should be observed at new accelerators within the next few years. Lee and Yang also emphasized the importance of neutral weak currents, the existence of which were finally established in 1973.　　DHP

van der Leeuw, Gerardus (b. The Hague, S. Holland, The Netherlands, 19.3.1890; d. Utrecht, 18.11.1950). Dutch pioneer in the phenomenology of religion. Born into a Dutch Reformed church family and later himself to become influential in its life both as a minister and a leading figure in its involvement with the liturgical reform movement, he studied theology at Leiden, specializing in the history of religion and particularly ancient Egyptian religion. Strongly influenced by his teacher W. B. Kristensen, as professor of history of religion and history of the doctrine of God at the University of Groningen (1918–50) he sought to transform the comparative study of religions from one of detached, descriptive typology, with the systematic cataloguing of religious phenomena, e.g. prayer, sacrifice, saviours, myth, etc., into one of enthusiastic understanding. In his most important work *Phänomenologie der Religion* (Tübingen, 1933; tr. J. E. Turner, *Religion in Essence and Manifestation*, London, 1938) he argues that the phenomenologist can only grasp the essence of religious phenomena in their wholeness if he can admit them into his own inner life, through suspending every possible premature judgement or presupposition concerning questions of truth and falsehood. Thus phenomenology of religion should combine an intense subjectivity (a quality which most later phenomenologists have found difficult to endorse) with value-free examination of religious phenomena, which van der Leeuw paradoxically claims are not mutually exclusive. One important area of religious life where he applied his phenomenological principles was that of reported experiences of religious power in primitive and ancient religious traditions. LPS

Lefebvre, Georges (b. Rijsel, Nord, France, 6.8.1874; d. Boulogne-Billancourt, Paris, 28.8.1959). French historian. Of working-class origin, Lefebvre was something of an outsider and had to wait a long time for academic recognition. He is most widely known for his introduction to the French revolution (*Quatre-vingt-neuf*, Paris, 1939; *The Coming of the French Revolution*, Princeton, 1947), the two volumes of general history *La Revolution française* (2 vols, Paris, 1930; 2 vols, *The French Revolution*, London, 1962–4), and *Napoléon* (Paris, 1935; *Napoleon*, London, ⁶1969). However, his most original contribution to historical research was in studying the French revolution from below. He published articles on problems of food supply in the revolution as early as 1913–14. His doctoral thesis *Les Paysans du Nord pendant la révolution française* [The peasants of the Nord during the French revolution] (Paris–Lille, 1924) argued that there was an autonomous peasant revolution with its own aims which were disappointed by the official revolutionary land settlement. *La Grande Peur de 1789* (Paris, 1932; *The Great Fear of 1789*, London, 1973) studied a rural panic (the spread of a false rumour that the brigands were coming), as an indicator of the attitudes of the peasants at this time. A seminal article published in 1934, 'Foules révolutionnaires' [Revolutionary crowds], discussed the formation of the 'revolutionary mentality' and of its stereotypes of friends and foes, laying down the programme for the research later carried out by Soboul, Rudé and Cobb. His posthumously published *Etudes Orléanaises* [Orléanais studies] (Paris, 1962–3) is a major contribution to the study of social structures in the late 18c. Together with M. BLOCH and FEBVRE, with whom he taught at Strasbourg (1928–35) before moving to the Sorbonne, Lefebvre developed the history of 'mentalities' in France. UPB

R. Cobb, 'Georges Lefebvre', *Past and Present*, 18 (1960), 52–67.

Lefschetz, Solomon (b. Moscow, Russia, 3.9.1884; naturalized American citizen, 1913; d. Princeton, NJ, USA, 5.10.1972). Russian/American mathematician who greatly influenced three generations of American mathematicians. In an autobiographical note, written in 1968, he summarized his work: 'As I see it at last, it was my lot to plant the harpoon of algebraic topology into the body of the whale of algebraic geometry.' His approach was to pioneer the development of topological ideas at a time when algebraic geometry was being developed, notably by O. Zariski, along very algebraic lines. Many of the techniques he invented to deal with algebraic varieties have been applied successfully to complex manifolds; his technique of viewing a variety as made up of all its hyperplane slices is especially fertile. In algebraic topology he proved a very useful fixed-point theorem for transformations of manifolds which has inspired many profitable generalizations (*Algebraic Geometry and Topology*, Princeton, 1957). During WW2 he turned to the stability theory of nonlinear differential equations and dynamical systems, which he redeveloped from a geometrical point of view, though with an eye to engineering applications. Lefschetz was also a brilliant linguist who published articles and books in Russian, French, English and Spanish, and spoke many more languages including Persian. Originally at Kansas University, he spent his later years at Princeton. JJG

Léger, Fernand (b. Argentan, Orne, France, 4.2.1881; d. Gif-sur-Yvette, nr Paris, 17.8.1955). French painter, one of the leading cubists. He studied architecture for several years before turning to painting, and then was strongly influenced by CÉZANNE's preoccupation with forms and volumes. This can be seen, for instance, in his *Nudes in the Forest* (1909–10) in which the figures, trees and landscape are all reduced to simple tubular forms such as disjointed cones, cylinders and cubes. After seeing early cubist paintings by BRAQUE and PICASSO for the first time later in 1910, he began to paint compositions of figures or cityscapes, juxtaposing cubic forms with flat planes tilted in different directions; the space being kept very shallow, with the forms densely packed together and related to the picture plane. By 1913–14 he had evolved a highly personal variant of cubism intended to express the dynamic character of 20c life, using geometric forms and primary colours to evoke movement in space; pictures which, though based on such themes as houses among trees, still life or a seated figure, were sometimes almost completely abstract in treatment. Forms, lines and colours were opposed to one another with the maximum contrast, flat forms against modelled forms, dynamic forms against static ones, neutral colours against contrasting patches of strong vibrant colour.

While serving at the front from 1914 to 1917 during WW1, he was greatly excited by the beauty of machine forms, such as artillery breeches. This influence can be seen in much of his later work, with its emphasis on machine-like forms, strong, simple poster-like contrasts of form and colour, and everyday objects. Even the human figure was often treated like a machine-made object, with tubular forms and a round expressionless face. He was the first painter to interpret industrial civilization in this uncompromising way and to adopt the aesthetic of the machine.

By the mid-1920s his style had become more simplified, with extensive use of flat uniform areas of colour and geometrical shapes combined with enlargements of objects such as playing cards, keys, leaves, pipes and shells; objects with no relationship to one another which were chosen simply for their bold, contrasting forms. This preoccupation with rhythmical contrasts was paralleled by the film *Ballet Mécanique* which he made in 1923–4, showing everyday objects such as shoes, straw hats and bottles set in rhythmical motion. Later on, while a refugee in America (1940–6), he gradually moved away from the machine and returned to man in, for instance, compositions of groups of jugglers, musicians and acrobats. This tendency reached its most realistic form in his *Constructeurs* (1950), a series of large mural-scale paintings of workmen erecting scaffolding, in which

he attempted to create a simple, direct, universally accessible art.   RA

W. Schmalenbach, *Fernand Léger* (NY, 1976).

Lenin, ps. of Vladimir Ilyich Ulyanov (b. Simbirsk [now Ulyanovsk], Russia, 22.4.1870; d. Gorky, USSR, 21.1.1924). Russian revolutionary; founder of the Russian Communist (Bolshevik) party; leader of the Bolshevik revolution of 1917; founder of the Soviet Union and of the Communist International.

By the time Lenin graduated from Kazan University in 1891, he was already a professional revolutionary. In December 1895 he was exiled to Siberia and in 1900 joined other MARXists in exile in producing a clandestine journal *Iskra* [The spark] which circulated in Russia. Lenin's revolutionary vocation rebelled against waiting for the necessary conditions to develop before acting. He sought some way of speeding up the process without abandoning the scientific authority of Marx's analysis which guaranteed the inevitability of success. He found it in his concept of the Party, a totally dedicated group of professional revolutionaries who would not wait for class consciousness to develop amongst the workers spontaneously, but would work unremittingly to foster it from outside, serving as 'the vanguard of the proletariat', constantly making clear to the workers where their true class interests lay. Lenin outlined his proposal in his most famous pamphlet published in March 1902 *Chto delat? (What is to be done?, Collected Works*, vol. 5). At the Second (founding) Congress of the Russian Social Democratic Workers party (held in Brussels and London, summer 1903) he secured a majority – known from the Russian word as Bolsheviks – for reorganizing the party on his model, but only at the cost of alienating the minority ('Mensheviks') who denounced his proposal as setting up a dictatorship 'over' rather than 'of' the proletariat.

The Russian revolution of 1905, however, took both factions by surprise and after two years in Russia Lenin was forced to return to exile and continue his polemics with his fellow revolutionaries. When WW1 broke out he moved to Switzerland and denounced both the

European socialist parties who rallied behind their governments ('social chauvinists') and the pacifists who opposed war as such. He produced his own analysis of the war in *Imperializm, kak noveyshy etap Kapitalizma* (1916; tr. from later retitled ed. as *Imperialism, the Higher Stage of Capitalism, Collected Works*, vol. 22). The conflict, he argued, was the result of the insatiable expansion of imperialism, itself a product of monopoly finance capitalism. Only the overthrow of capitalism everywhere could put an end to imperialism and war.

Lenin's situation was transformed by the overthrow of the Tsarist government (March 1917) in protest against the continuation of the war. Returning to Russia with the connivance of the German army, Lenin at once called for a socialist revolution without further delay. Denounced by other socialists as an opportunist, he only carried the Bolsheviks with difficulty in launching a campaign for peace, land and bread as an immediate programme. Overriding the doubts of his colleagues, he used the Bolshevik-organized workers' militia, the Red Guard, to carry out a coup on 7–8 November 1917, replacing the provisional government with a Council of People's Commissioners of which he was elected chairman. What mattered was to secure power: once that was achieved, everything was possible. Lenin in action showed himself as bold and uncompromising as in his theorizing. His political leadership saved the Soviet government during the civil war of 1920–2 in which the odds (with foreign intervention) were heavily against the Bolshveiks. While giving TROTSKY a free hand in military matters, Lenin won the support of the non-Russian nationalities by proclaiming their right to self-determination (including secession); that of the peasants by handing over the land without compensation. His hopes of revolution spreading throughout Europe failed, but he set up the Third (Communist) International, in March 1919, insisting that those parties who joined must accept its decisions as binding, and proclaimed the right of colonial peoples to independence, an identification of the USSR with national liberation movements of great value for the future. He was ruthless in employing the political police (the Cheka) to root out opposition to the Party's dictatorship and exhausted himself in his efforts to halt the degeneration of the Soviet system into an unwieldy bureaucracy. Taken ill in the spring of 1922 he never recovered his health; during 1923 he suffered several strokes, and died the next year, not yet 54 years old.

No other political leader has ever shown an equal grasp in theory and in practice of what was required to make a revolution. Lenin's writings on the subject, and on imperialism and war, plus the lessons to be drawn from his own experience in 1917 and afterwards are a source for that version of applied Marxism – known as Marxism-Leninism – which has provided the basis for communism as an international revolutionary movement. Lenin, however, could not avoid the consequences, foreseen by LUXEMBURG and other critics, of his seizing power by force and imposing revolution by dictatorship. Once launched on this course, the Party has never been willing to relax its control. The subsequent history of Russia and other Communist states represents a grim commentary on the Marxist claim repeated in Lenin's *Gosudarstvo i revolyutsiya* (Petrograd, 1917; *The State and Revolution, Collected Works*, vol. 25) that dictatorship would eventually wither away into a noncoercive, classless and stateless society.

The fifth edition of Lenin's collected works is *Polnoe Sobranie Sochinenii* (55 vols, Moscow, 1958–65). An English translation of the fourth edition (with notes from the fifth) is *Collected Works* (45 vols, Moscow, 1960–70). The most important of his writings are in *Selected Works* (3 vols, Moscow, n.d.).   ALCB

B. D. Wolfe, *Three Who Made a Revolution* (NY, ⁴1964); A. B. Ulam, *The Bolsheviks* (NY, 1965); A. B. Ulam, *Lenin and the Bolsheviks* (London, 1969); A. Solzhenitsyn, *Lenin in Zürich* (London, 1976).

Lennard-Jones, John Edward (b. Leigh, Gt. Man., UK, 27.10.1894; d. Stoke-on-Trent, Staffs., 1.11.1954). British theoretical chemist. Lennard-Jones was educated at Manchester University, and spent almost all the rest of his career as a physicist at Bristol and as the holder at Cambridge of the first chair in the world with the title of theoretical chemistry. He led the way in the interpretation of the physical properties of gases in terms of the forces between their molecules, using, in the 1920s, the newly developed disciplines of statistical mechanics and kinetic theory. He represented the potential energy of a pair of molecules as the difference between two inverse powers of their separation, one of which represented the repulsive forces at short distances, and the other the attractive forces at large. Such a function is now generally known by his name. His attempt in the 1930s to extend this work to liquids, although influential at the time, was less successful. In 1929 he spent a year at Göttingen studying quantum mechanics, in which field he was responsible (with F. Hund and MULLIKEN) for the concept of molecular orbitals: a description of the electron density within a molecule based on orbitals extending over two or more atomic centres. It has proved a powerful method of approximation in the application of quantum mechanics to problems of valency and spectroscopy. JSR

Leontief, Wassily (b. St Petersburg [now Leningrad], Russia, 5.8.1906; naturalized American citizen). Russian/American economist. Educated at the universities of Leningrad and Berlin, after working at the Economic Research Institute in Kiel from 1927 to 1930 (interrupted in 1929 by a spell as economic adviser to the government of China in Nanking) he came to the USA. In 1931 he was appointed to the economics faculty at Harvard, where he remained until his retirement in 1975. Leontief's celebrated study *The Structure of the American Economy 1919–29* (Cambridge, Mass., 1941, ²1953) was the work which founded input-output analysis, an achievement for which the author was awarded a Nobel prize in 1973. The analysis has an essentially empirical orientation, and can be viewed as a practical application of general equilibrium theory. It is concerned with the inter-

industry structure of an economy; specifically, with the amounts which each 'industry' or sector buys from other industries or sectors (e.g. steel output purchased by vehicle manufacturers as an input into motor cars) in order to end with a series of outputs for sale to final buyers. Besides presenting a summary picture of the structure of the economy, the technique has immense practical application in economic planning. Given a data matrix of interindustry purchases, and given the working assumption of fixed input-output coefficients (i.e. a fixed amount of industry a's products is needed to make one unit of industry b's), it is possible to calculate (by so-called matrix inversion) the total – direct and indirect – requirement of each product needed to produce a given series of final outputs. While full-scale calculations of this sort were so laborious as to be scarcely feasible when Leontief's study first appeared, the development of computers has overcome this difficulty. His other books include *Input-Output Economics* (NY, 1966) and *Essays in Economics* (NY, 1978). PMO

Le Roy Ladurie, Emmanuel Bernard (b. Moutiers-en-Cinglais, Meurthe-et-Moselle, France, 19.7.1929). French historian. A pupil of BRAUDEL, Le Roy Ladurie became widely known after the publication of his doctoral thesis *Les Paysans de Languedoc* (Paris, 1966; abridged, *The Peasants of Languedoc*, Urbana, 1974), concerned with economic and social change from the late 15c to the early 18c, but also with the way in which contemporaries experienced and reacted to these changes. His *Histoire du climat* (Paris, 1967; *Times of Feast, Times of Famine*, NY, 1971) extended the frontiers of history to include climatic change. In the 1970s Le Roy Ladurie continued to work on the agrarian history of early modern France from two points of view. The first might be described as 'ecological': the history, quantitative where the sources permit, of the relationship between population and environment, emphasizing the stability of a particular 'ecosystem', between 1450 and 1750. The second approach might be described as more 'anthropological', and is concerned with customs, rituals and symbols. It is brilliantly exemplified in his study of a riot in a small town in Dauphiné in 1580, *Le Carnaval de Romans* (Paris, 1979; *The Carnival of Romans*, NY, 1979). The two approaches were combined in Le Roy Ladurie's foray into the Middle Ages, *Montaillou village occitan 1294–1324* (Paris, 1975; abridged, *Montaillou: Cathars and Catholics in a French Village*, London, 1978), which headed the nonfiction bestseller lists in France and in English translation. Le Roy Ladurie, in alliance with younger colleagues, has transformed the French historical journal *Annales*, pushing it towards retrospective econometrics and retrospective symbolic anthropology. His views on historical method are explicit in *Le Territoire de l'historien* (Paris, 1973; abridged, *The Territory of the Historian*, Hassocks, 1979). UPB

Leśniewski, Stanisław (b. Serpukhov, Russia, 30.3.1886; d. Warsaw, Poland, 13.5.1939). Polish logician. Together with ŁUKASIEWICZ, he was the leader of the school of logicians which sprang up in Poland after WW1. He held a chair at the University of Warsaw from 1919 until his death. Over the years he developed three general logical systems. 'Protothetic' was a calculus of propositions, based on the 'equivalent calculus' studied by TARSKI. 'Ontology' was a modernized version of traditional logic, corresponding in structure to a theory of classes and relations. 'Mereology' is a study of the part–whole relationship between objects. He did not live to publish complete versions of his systems, and his manuscripts were destroyed during WW2; but his ideas have led to work of high quality since his death, and his reputation is still rising. IG-G

E. Luschei, *The Logical Systems of Leśniewski* (Amsterdam, 1962).

Lever, William Hesketh (b. Bolton, Gt. Man., UK, 19.9.1851; d. London, 7.5.1925). British industrialist. By acquiring in 1884 with his brother James Darcy Lever the lease of a small and unsuccessful soap works in Warrington, Lever laid the foundations of one of the world's largest industrial companies. At that time soap was made from tallow, but the Lever brothers introduced a new formula, using vegetable oil, under the trade name Sunlight. By 1888 the success of their venture enabled them to build a model industrial village in Cheshire, Port Sunlight. Enlightened employers, the company introduced medical care, pensions and a 'sharing in prosperity' – an early form of profit-sharing. In the 20c Lever Bros expanded into a major group of over 200 companies and formed the basis of the multinational corporation Unilever. Lever himself became an MP in 1906, a peer in 1917 and was created Viscount Leverhulme in 1922. RIT

C. H. Wilson, *History of Unilever* (2 vols, London, 1954); W. P. Jolly, *Lord Leverhulme: a Biography* (London, 1976).

Levesque, René (b. New Carlisle, Quebec, Canada, 24.8.1922). Leader of the French Canadian nationalist and anglophobe *Parti Québécois*, and premier of Quebec since 1976, he introduced a programme of linguistic nationalism designed to drive English speakers, whether American or Canadian, out of Quebec, and to force Canadian and American industry in the province to hand over the control to native French-speaking Quebecois. His adroit manipulation of French Quebec resentments against their dominant English-speaking neighbours for a time threatened the union of Federal Canada with the establishment of an independent state of Quebec, a prospect which frightened almost as many Quebecois as Anglo-Canadians, so much so that much of its political effectiveness was destroyed. In May 1980 a referendum in Quebec produced a convincing vote against separatism, 60 per cent of the voters voting 'No', including a narrow majority of French Canadians. But a year later Levesque won a sweeping majority in the Quebec elections. With the issue of separatism shelved – at least for the present – Levesque was able to resume a leading role in the opposition of the provinces to Trudeau's new Canadian constitution, which Quebec alone, in the end, refused to accept (1982). DCW

Lévi-Strauss, Claude (b. Brussels, Belgium, 28.12.1908). French anthropologist. He took his first degree at Paris and was soon afterwards appointed to the University of São Paolo, Brazil. He remained in South America until 1939, spent most of WW2 in the USA and returned to Paris in 1948. He now holds the chair of social anthropology at the Collège de France. Although without doubt one of the greatest anthropologists of our time, he has made his contribution primarily in the philosophical and even speculative areas of the subject. Dense though his ethnographic discussion may be, it rests on a slender foundation of fieldwork and in this respect he stands at the opposite pole to the British and American traditions. Indeed, one of the many reasons for his high status in the contemporary academic world is precisely his antiempiricism together with his largely successful attempt to reinstate a rationalist and intellectualist perspective in the human sciences. He is identified above all as the prime figure in the movement known as structuralism, which has dominated the intellectual worlds of Britain, the USA and Western Europe from the late 1950s until the early 1980s and has only recently begun to show signs of losing its impetus. Lévi-Strauss's wartime sojourn in New York introduced him not only to the structural linguistics of the so-called Prague school but also to the pioneering work in cybernetics and information theory associated especially with SHANNON. Lévi-Strauss combined the new insights of the mathematical theory of communication with the principles of SAUSSUREan linguistics and applied the result to the comparative study of societies and cultures. This was the creative synthesis that made a generalized 'structuralism' possible and he accomplished it single-handed. He has on occasions styled himself a MARXist (at least in part) but in the climate of modern France this is little more than a ritual indicator not so much of what he is as of what he is not (empiricist, existentialist, Catholic, etc.). For all the originality of his approach, his work has always lain in the heartland of traditional social anthropology: kinship, religion and myth. *Les Structures élémentaires de la parenté* (Paris, 1949, ²1967; *The Elementary Structures*

of Kinship, London, 1969) challenged and in many ways subverted former kinds of analysis. Among the principal themes of this lengthy study are the nature/culture dichotomy, the incest prohibition, and the types of marriage exchange. These are woven into a general perspective on human society that elevates a work of close ethnographic analysis into a major anthropological and philosophical classic. Important glosses on this work, as well as important essays on themes more directly related to structural linguistics and communication theory, are to be found in *Anthropologie structurale* (2 vols, Paris, 1958–73; *Structural Anthropology*, London, 1963–77), where the later concern with myth (see below) is also adumbrated. *Le Totémisme aujourd'hui* (Paris, 1962; *Totemism*, London, 1962) was closely followed by *La Pensée sauvage* (Paris, 1962; *The Savage Mind*, London, 1966), and the two together offer an interpretation of the logic of totemic systems and of so-called 'totemism' itself that forms a watershed in modern cognitive and philosophical anthropology. Readers were also inducted into the study of myth, which in recent years has virtually monopolized Lévi-Strauss's attention, yielding the four immense monographs of his *Mythologiques* (Paris, 1964–72; *Introduction to the Science of Mythology*, London, 1970–9). An intellectual autobiography *Tristes tropiques* (Paris, 1955; London, 1973) is a valuable commentary on, as well as exposition of, some of his earlier thinking.   IH

E. Leach, *Lévi-Strauss* (London, 1970).

Lévy-Bruhl, Lucien (b. Paris, France, 19.4.1857; d. Paris, 13.3.1939). French anthropologist and philosopher, somewhat paradoxically associated with a set of views about 'primitive' and 'modern' mentalities which are often and seriously misrepresented and which in any case he largely repudiated in his later years. In *Les Fonctions mentales dans les sociétés inférieures* (Paris, 1910; *How Natives Think*, London, 1926) he outlined a dichotomous view of the two 'mentalities' in terms of which primitive cultures are marked by a 'prelogical' mentality which is blind to the law of contradiction characteristic of modern societies and substitute for it a law of mystical participation (see also *La Mentalité primitive*, Paris, 1922; *Primitive Mentality*, London, 1923, and *L'Âme primitive*, Paris, 1927; *The 'Soul' of the Primitive*, London, 1928). He has been mistakenly supposed to have attributed basic difference of innate psychology to 'primitives'. In fact he was careful to stress the social determination and origin of the collective representations which he saw as dominating their mentality, and he was ready to acknowledge that these prelogical characteristics were limited to certain areas of their experience. In later years, and partly under the impulsion of criticisms by other scholars including DURKHEIM and EVANS-PRITCHARD, he modified the polarity set up in his early and middle monographs, concentrating instead on the affective features of mystical experience, and in the posthumous *Carnets* (Paris, 1949; *The Notebooks on Primitive Mentality*, Oxford, 1975) he moved to a still more radical revision. In recent years an attempt has been made to reinstate some aspects of Lévy-Bruhl's earlier position (in any case by no means wholly discredited), largely by reformulating and recasting them in the light of PIAGET's developmental psychology.　　IH

J. Cazeneuve, *Lucien Lévy-Bruhl* (Oxford, 1972).

Lewin, Kurt (b. Mogilno, Posen, Germany [now Poland], 9.9.1890; naturalized American citizen, 1940; d. Newtonville, Mass., USA, 11.2.1947). German/American psychologist, widely regarded as the father of modern experimental social psychology. Initially prompted by the Gestaltist views of colleagues at the University of Berlin (1921 –33), Lewin developed a highly original and fruitful 'field theory' of human behaviour and launched new areas of psychological research. In 1933 he fled from Nazi Germany to the USA where – at Cornell (1933–5) and then Iowa (1935–44) universities – he began to focus on social processes. Lewin revolutionized social psychology with his demonstrations that complex social phenomena could be investigated using con-

trolled experimental methods. Many specific social psychological theories have their roots in his general theoretical concepts. His ideas that behaviour is a function of the person *and* the environment as he or she perceives it, and that understanding is best achieved by theoretically based experiments (in laboratories and the field), have put their stamp on the whole development of the subject. In 1944 Lewin founded the Research Center for Group Dynamics at MIT, thereby formally establishing the study of groups in social psychology, and also the Commission on Community Interrelations for the American Jewish Congress in New York. The commission used his 'action research' methods in pioneering studies of racial and religious prejudice, and thus exemplified his concern with applying psychology to social problems. Lewin's profound influence on social psychology was exerted through his writings and his wide network of associates and students, many of whom conducted seminal experiments to become leaders in the field themselves.　　MRAT

A. Marrow, *The Practical Theorist* (NY, 1969); L. Festinger (ed.), *Retrospections on Social Psychology* (NY, 1980).

Lewis, Clive Staples (b. Belfast, Ireland [now Northern Ireland], UK, 29.11.1898; d. Oxford, 22.11.1963). British literary scholar, novelist and popular theologian. Lewis was a university teacher all his life, first at Oxford (1925–54) and then from 1954 as professor of medieval and Renaissance literature at Cambridge. After an early period of rationalism he became a convert to Christianity. In a series of books, including *The Problem of Pain* (London, 1940), *Miracles* (London, 1947) and *Mere Christianity* (London, 1952) he showed himself a master of witty and intellectually sustained apologetic as he probed the inconsistencies he detected in the arguments of atheists and agnostics. These publications revealed him as the successor of CHESTERTON, but operating through the continuous dialectic of the university debate rather than single flashes. *The Screwtape Letters* (London, 1942) presents with great skill and humour the tactics of an older devil instructing a younger in the art of tempting an individual soul, and ultimately failing. The science fiction trilogy, beginning with *Out of the Silent Planet* (London, 1938), and the Narnia series, written for children, seek to bring into fiction not only moral choices but spiritual presences and the eternal reality behind appearances. In his scholarly work Lewis was a conscious overthrower and re-establisher; in *The Allegory of Love* (Oxford, 1936) he breathed new life into the lost world of medieval allegory; in *English Literature in the Sixteenth Century* (Oxford, 1954) he took a new and harsh look at critical assumptions about the Renaissance. These academic studies are of a piece with the intensely private love for the serious other world of fairy tale which he attempts to share in his fiction.   RS

C. Walsh, *The Literary Legacy of C. S. Lewis* (London, 1979).

Lewis, Gilbert Newton (b. nr Boston, Mass., USA, 25.10.1875; d. Berkeley, Calif., 24.3.1946). American physical chemist. G. N. Lewis is remembered principally for his contributions to chemical thermodynamics which culminated in the classical book, written with Merle Randall, on *Thermodynamics and the Free Energy of Chemical Substances* (NY, 1923). But he made equally important contributions to the theory of the chemical bond, especially through the concept of pairing of electrons, and to the understanding of the nature of acids and bases. Educated at the universities of Nebraska and Harvard, he spent semesters with OSTWALD at Leipzig and NERNST at Göttingen. After a period with A. A. Noyes at MIT in 1912, he became chairman of the department of chemistry at Berkeley, where he built up one of the leading international schools of chemistry.

Thermodynamics and Lewis's book on *Valency and the Structure of Atoms and Molecules* (NY) both appeared in 1923. In the former the largely mathematical analysis of GIBBS was brought to life by its application to the evaluation of the free energies of over 140 substances. This work laid the foundation of the science of experimental thermodynamics.

In *Valency* Lewis developed his ideas, first published in 1916, on the chemical bond in terms of electron pairs. His views were not readily accepted by physicists at the time but have been largely vindicated by modern quantum theory. His concept of acids and bases was much broader than that based on proton transfer associated with BRØN-STED and T. M. LOWRY. This wider classification – Lewis acids – characterized by substances which can accept a pair of electrons, has been widely accepted and applied in many fields of chemistry. Lewis was also an early participant (1933) in work on 'heavy water'. His final researches were concerned with the colour and fluorescence of chemical substances.   DHE

Lewis, Henry Sinclair (b. Sauk Center, Minn., USA, 7.2.1885; d. Rome, Italy, 10.1.1951). American novelist. With *Main Street* (NY, 1920) Lewis became a famous writer. His subject, life in the small towns of the American Midwest, was viewed with ironic scorn, a hallmark of Lewis's books of the 1920s. *Babbitt* (NY, 1922) contained an even funnier satire of the middle-American businessman. Lewis turned to medicine in *Arrowsmith* (NY, 1925), and to the world of evangelical preachers in *Elmer Gantry* (NY, 1927). With *Dodsworth* (NY, 1929) Lewis transported his businessman, more sympathetically portrayed, to Europe. He received the Nobel prize for literature in 1930, the first American to be so honoured. Lewis's novels of the 1920s constitute an impressive achievement, one perhaps insufficiently appreciated today. His work belongs to a different 1920s than do the novels of JOYCE and KAFKA which appeared contemporaneously. The social and satirical novel as he practised it marks the end of realism as the dominant mode of American fiction. Between Lewis and the early novels of Nathanael West a profound change had taken place in literary culture. At the time of his death, Lewis was half-forgotten.   EH

M. Schorer, *Sinclair Lewis: an American Life* (NY, 1961).

Lewis, John Saunders (b. Wallasey, Mers., UK, 15.10.1893). Welsh writer and political figure who more than any other has left his mark on 20c Wales. Brought up in a Nonconformist minister's family in the Welsh diaspora, he read English at Liverpool University and served in WW1 before making his conscious commitment to Wales under the influence of BARRÈS and Emrys ap Iwan. Conversion to Roman Catholicism confirmed a view of Wales which emphasized the Middle Ages and the Latin tradition. From this position he went on to produce a large and unified body of criticism. *Williams Pantycelyn* (London, 1927) shows the young critic at his most brilliant, while the essays collected in *Meistri'r Canrifoedd* [Masters of the centuries] (ed. R. G. Gruffydd, Cardiff, 1973) and *Meistri a'i Crefft* [Masters and their craft] (ed. Gwyn ap Gwilym, Cardiff, 1980) redefine the Welsh literary tradition within a European context. In 1926 he helped to found the Welsh Nationalist party and was its president to 1939. His political ideas were hierarchic and traditionalist but his Christian humanism abhorred fascism. The preindustrial models of society which he commended held no appeal for the South Wales valleys and under his leadership the party attracted little popular support. In 1936 he took part in direct action against the RAF bombing school at Penyberth, was imprisoned for a year and lost his lectureship at the University College of Swansea. Though he retired from active politics in 1939, the campaigns of the Welsh Language Society in the 1960s and 1970s were inspired by the Penyberth episode and by his radio lecture *Tynged yr Iaith* (Cardiff, 1962; tr. G. A. Williams in *Presenting Saunders Lewis*, Cardiff, 1973). Lewis's withdrawal from politics inaugurated his greatest period as a creative writer. Although he has made important contributions to Welsh poetry and fiction, it is as a dramatist that he has been able to combine a classical sense of society and tradition with his romantic appetite for the living moment. The heroines of his best plays *Siwan* (Llandybie, 1956; tr. Emyr Humphreys in *Presenting Saunders Lewis*, Cardiff, 1973) and *Esther* (Llandybie, 1960) make their commitments without reservation and thus reveal that greatness of which human nature is capable.　　　EMT

A. R. Jones & G. Thomas (eds), *Presenting Saunders Lewis* (Cardiff, 1973); B. Griffiths, *Saunders Lewis* (Cardiff, 1979).

Lewis, Percy Wyndham (b. off Amherst, NS, Canada, 18.11.1882; d. London, UK, 7.3.1957). British painter, novelist and essayist. Lewis's father was American, his mother English. He was educated at Rugby School and the Slade School of Art (1898–1901) and studied painting on the Continent (for the Parisian milieu, see his first novel *Tarr*, London, 1918). He was excited by modernism; *The Theatre Manager* (1909) is perhaps the first English painting influenced by PICASSO's innovations. With *Timon of Athens* (1912) and *The Crowd* (1914–15) Lewis moved further towards abstraction. Reacting against futurism, he became one of the leaders of the vorticist group: *Blast: Review of the Great English Vortex* (1914–15) was the first of three forceful magazines he edited. In WW1 he served with the artillery and in 1918 was seconded as a Canadian war artist and created some of the most memorable images of the war (e.g. *A Battery Shelled*, 1919). His return to a more representational style continued in the portraits of the interwar years (*Edith Sitwell*, 1923; *Eliot*, 1938). His painting *The Surrender of Barcelona* (1936) is a lament for strife-torn Spain. Lacking a studio, he turned to writing. His overambitious *Man of the World* project was split into polemical studies: social and philosophical – *The Art of Being Ruled* (London, 1926), *Time and Western Man* (London, 1927); literary-critical – *The Lion and the Fox* (London, 1927), *Paleface* (London, 1929); satirical – *The Childermass* (London, 1928), *The Apes of God* (London, 1930). Thereafter Lewis's literary criticism, notably of HEMINGWAY and ELIOT in *Men without Art* (London, 1934), is more meritorious than his political pamphleteering. Memories of the western front, neglect of his work by the English Establishment, and his ignorance of German, help to explain his account of the Nazi electoral victory in *Hitler* (London, 1931); after the *Kristallnacht* pogrom in Germany

Lewis, never an ardent supporter of fascism, tried to make amends in the tactlessly entitled *The Jews, are They Human?* (London, 1939). An increasing sense of purgatorial autobiography is evident in the Spanish civil war novel *The Revenge for Love* (London, 1937); in *Self Condemned* (London, 1954), a reflection of his failure to retrieve his fortunes in North America during WW2; and in the metaphysical epic *The Human Age* (London, 1955) which continues *The Childermass* with the more accessible *Monstre Gai* and *Malign Fiesta*. These latter originated in a collaboration with D. G. Bridson for BBC radio drama after Lewis had gone blind.

Though not a sustained thinker, this man 'of *dangerous* vision', the self-declared 'Enemy', remains a challenging social critic who prophesied the loss of empire, politically diseased language, the growth of the media, the cults of youth and the feminine, and exaltation of the time process and the irrational. His art, example and criticism alerted the philistine or insular British to the European avant-garde. Bracing as the earlier literary satires are, the eloquent humanity of the later fiction is more impressive. *The Human Age* is an allegory of *la trahison des clercs* unmatched in modern fantasy.

PLC

W. Michel, *Wyndham Lewis: Paintings and Drawings* (NY, 1971); J. Meyers (ed.), *Wyndham Lewis: a Revaluation* (London, 1980).

Lewis, Thomas (b. Cardiff, S. Glam., UK, 26.12.1881; d. Rickmansworth, Herts., 17.3.1945). British cardiologist and clinical scientist. After preclinical work in his native Cardiff, Lewis went in 1902 to University College Hospital in London, where he remained for the rest of his life. He there pioneered the idea of clinical research as a career, and made fundamental contributions to three separate areas: cardiology, the physiology of the superficial blood vessels of the skin, and the mechanism of pain. His work in cardiology secured him worldwide fame. Using Willem Einthoven's recent 'string galvanometer' (an early version of the electrocardiograph), Lewis clarified much about the nature of the heart-beat and the diagno-

sis of heart disease. During WW1 he studied 'soldier's heart', following many of his patients for years to determine their likelihood of developing further cardiac problems. He summarized his original researches and observations in several books, including *Clinical Disorders of the Heart Beat* (London, 1912, [7]1933) and *Diseases of the Heart* (London, 1933, [2]1942), which were widely used and often translated. His work on skin, culminating in *Blood Vessels of the Human Skin* (London, 1927), elucidated the mechanism of response of the superficial tissues to irritation and injury (the 'triple response of Lewis'). His friend DALE showed what Lewis himself had implied: that much of this response is caused by the release of histamine, an important chemical involved in allergies and other body processes. Lewis's work on pain was stimulated by the intense suffering he experienced from a series of heart attacks which ultimately ended his life. Lewis held that human physiology and disease could be understood fully only when studied in man; hence his championing of the idea of clinical research, of which he was one of the century's greatest practitioners.

WFB

Libby, Willard Frank (b. Grand Valley, Colo, USA, 17.12.1908; d. Los Angeles, Calif., 8.9.1980). American chemist. Libby discovered the concept of radiocarbon dating, invaluable in archaeology, geology and geophysics. He studied at Berkeley, becoming a faculty member in 1933. During WW2 he worked on the Manhattan project. In 1946 he was appointed to a chair at the University of Chicago. In that year he showed that tritium (a radioisotope of hydrogen) was produced by cosmic-ray bombardment of the earth's atmosphere. Korff had already demonstrated that the radioisotope carbon-14 was produced from nitrogen-14 in a similar way, and in 1947 Libby suggested that the amount of atmospheric ^{14}C should be a constant (assuming a constant intensity of cosmic radiation), and that the death of an organism causes the exchange of ^{14}C between itself and the atmosphere to cease. Thus, by measuring the ^{14}C content of a dead biological specimen (e.g.

wood, animal skins, etc.), it should be possible to estimate the time elapsed since its death (as the half-life of ^{14}C is known). Although the accuracy of the technique is such that independent calibration (e.g. by dendrochronology) is needed (probably owing to a variation of the level of cosmic radiation over the millennia), Libby's idea and his subsequent development of the method of radiocarbon dating was described, in the presentation of his 1960 Nobel prize for chemistry, in the following terms: 'Seldom has a single discovery in chemistry had such an impact on the thinking of so many fields of human endeavour.' Libby gave his own account of it in *Radiocarbon Dating* (Chicago, ²1955).

KRS

Liddell Hart, Basil Henry (b. Paris, France, 31.10.1895; d. Marlow, Bucks., UK, 29.1.1970). British military historian and strategist. The formative influence upon Liddell Hart's thinking was the experience of trench warfare in WW1, which generated a humanitarian revulsion at the slaughter that characterized attrition. A recognition that war would remain a tool of diplomacy was the fundamental impetus of most of his interwar thought, with a determination to avoid in any future war the casualties and exhaustion of WW1. The means seemed to lie to hand with the advent of the tank and the aeroplane, offering an avenue to victory without head-on confrontation and its consequent losses. In *Paris, or the Future of War* (London, 1925), Liddell Hart argued that the function of grand strategy was to discover and exploit the enemy's Achilles heel, and suggested that air power would dominate future conflicts since it could paralyse an enemy's 'nerve system'. He put forward his fully articulated theory of war, the 'indirect approach', in *Decisive Wars in History* (London, 1929), arguing that strategy should aim to dislocate an enemy's morale by attacking his mental balance, and consequently affecting his physical capacity to fight. Mechanized warfare provided the means to exploit the elements of movement and surprise and strike at vulnerable points. Liddell Hart's bitter antipathy towards Clause-

witz's ideas, which he supposed to have been largely responsible for the slaughter of WW1, also led to the appearance of *The British Way in Warfare* (London, 1932) which argued erroneously that blockade and peripheral action had been Britain's most effective continental strategy. On the eve of WW2 Liddell Hart swung in favour of the defensive. His earlier ideas, neglected in the UK, had some influence in German and Israeli military circles, chiefly through disciples such as GUDERIAN. His last major contribution to strategic thought *Deterrent or Defence* (London, 1960) suggested that, with a limited number of ground troops, NATO could put up a good defence against a Russian attack. Though basing many of his arguments on a study of the past, Liddell Hart disdained 'the pedantic burrowers in documents'; an intuitive and visionary polemicist, his indirect influence upon the conduct of war was profound, his direct influence less than he was wont to suppose.

JGo

J. Luvaas, *The Education of an Army* (London, 1964); B. Bond, *Liddell Hart: a Study of his Military Thought* (London, 1977).

Ligeti, György Sándor (b. Diciosânmartin [now Tîrnâeni], Transylvania, Romania, 28.5.1923). Hungarian composer. Early works such as the First String Quartet (1954) show Ligeti beginning to emerge from the post-BARTOKian nationalism favoured in Hungary. But it was only after he had moved to the West in 1956 that he could realize his more radical ideas. His first orchestral works *Apparitions* (1960) and *Atmosphères* (1961) opened up a new world of dense textures and ominous, slowly evolving masses, and this style, immediately imitated by many others, also appears in the *Requiem* for soloists, choirs and orchestra (1965). At the same time Ligeti showed himself to have a rare absurdist wit, notably expressed in *Aventures* for three singers and seven players (1963) and later developed to operatic length in *Le grand macabre* (1977, after Ghelderode). In other compositions, such as the Cello Concerto (1966) and the Second String Quarter (1968), the qualities of fast-moving humour and slow meditation are brought together. PG

Lindahl, Erik Robert (b. Stockholm, Sweden, 21.11.1891; d. Uppsala, 7.1.1960). Swedish economist. An outstanding representative of the 'Stockholm school', which included Gunnar Myrdal, Bertil Ohlin and Erik Lundberg, who saw themselves as followers of their countryman Knut Wicksell. They developed Wicksell's monetary theory to take account of conditions of less than full employment, and independently came to many of the same conclusions as KEYNES in his *General Theory* (1936). Lindahl in his *Scope and Means of Monetary Policy* (London, 1929) argued that monetary policy should be devised to minimize the damage to economic equilibrium caused by cyclical fluctuations in income, and this emerged as a dominant theme in his work. His *Studies in the Theory of Money and Capital* (London, 1939) is concerned with the methods by which economic theory can be made to yield an effective economic policy. The interaction between the views of the Stockholm school and those of Keynesian economists has been fruitful in producing a post-Keynesian consensus. PS

Lindemann, Frederick Alexander, Lord Cherwell (b. Baden-Baden, Baden-Württemberg, Germany, 5.4.1886; d. Oxford, UK, 3.7.1957). British physicist, scientific adviser and minister. Lindemann's father, an engineer-scientist, was a naturalized British subject of French-Alsatian origin and his mother was American. He himself went to schools in Scotland and Germany and was a student and colleague of NERNST in Berlin. His best scientific work was done between 1910 and 1924 and showed his liveliness and versatility as a physicist, especially in geophysics. He was one of the most remarkable of the scientists who joined the Royal Aircraft Factory (later Establishment) at Farnborough during WW1; he contributed greatly to understanding the spin of aircraft, partly through his own courageous flying experiments. His two greatest achievements were his work as CHURCHILL's scientific adviser and the re-creation of the moribund Claren-

don Laboratory at Oxford. He went there in 1919 as professor of experimental philosophy and remained, nicknamed 'The Prof', until 1956; he encouraged a broad range of physical research including the famous low-temperature physics work. He played a prominent part in helping scientists to leave Nazi Germany and brought an outstanding group to Oxford. From the early 1930s until the end of his life he was a close friend and adviser of Churchill. He was a minister (paymaster-general) in the wartime government and in Churchill's 1951 government. He advised not only on scientific affairs but on statistical analysis, and headed the prime minister's statistical section. His judgement was sometimes very bad, e.g. in the pre-1939 controversy over radar within government committees which led to a bitter breach with his former friend TIZARD, and in the wartime controversy over the threat from German rockets; sometimes good, e.g. in analysing the size of the German bomber force, the inaccuracy of British bombing or the need for technological education. He was involved with Britain's atomic energy project from 1941 until his death and was largely responsible for the establishment of the Atomic Energy Authority. A friend, G. P. THOMSON, concluded that 'he was better as a critic than as a creator'. MMG

Earl of Birkenhead, *The Prof in Two Worlds* (London, 1961).

Lipchitz, Jacques Chaim Jacob (b. Druskieniki, Grodno, Russia [now Lithuania, USSR], 22.8.1891; naturalized French citizen, 1925; d. Capri, Italy, 28.5.1973). Lithuanian/French sculptor. He was one of the first to apply cubist principles to sculpture; subsequently rejecting what he saw as its restriction to formal issues, he used this experience to develop a new vocabulary with which to express emotional subject matter and a personal response to historical events. Using his preferred medium of bronze, he returned to sculpture the expressive modelling and exploitation of light and shadow of his admired RODIN. Even before his involvement with cubism, Lipchitz's work was stylized, revealing an interest in Egyptian, Scythian and Gothic art.

He had arrived in Paris in 1909 and in 1914 visited Spain with RIVERA. During his cubist period, while he was close to GRIS, he made the stone *Man with Guitar* (1916) where solid is interpenetrated by space. His 'transparent sculpture', open, linear compositions, followed. The work after *Figures* (1926–30), which many consider his masterpiece and which has the quality of a primitive idol, reflected the historical crisis of the time through such themes as the rape of Europa and Prometheus wrestling with the vulture. His extreme distortions of the figure in the work of the 1940s was influenced by PICASSO. During the following decade he made his 'semiautomatics', bronzes modelled by touch alone, and a series of bronzes cast from maquettes incorporating small objects. He emigrated to the USA in 1941, where he exerted a considerable influence, and lived in Italy from 1963. MOJN

R. Goldwater, *Jacques Lipchitz* (London, 1958); A. M. Hammacher, *Jacques Lipchitz and his Sculpture* (London, 1960).

Lipmann, Fritz Albert (b. Königsberg, East Prussia, Germany [now Kaliningrad, USSR], 12.6.1899; naturalized American citizen, 1944). German/American biochemist. In 1927 the Kaiser Wilhelm Institute in Berlin was a world centre for biochemical research, numbering among its staff Otto WARBURG, KREBS and a student of Meyerhof, Fritz Lipmann. After studying creatine-phosphate breakdown during muscle activity, he left in 1931 for a year in the USA, followed by seven years in Copenhagen. He finally settled in the USA in 1941 when he accepted an appointment at Harvard. Meanwhile he studied other biological phosphates, and in 1941 proposed that the high-energy phosphate bond, and its transfer to and from ATP and other molecules, was a 'common currency' of energy transfers in biology. This insight, for which he (with Krebs) received the 1953 Nobel prize for physiology and medicine, opened the way to current understanding of bioenergetics and clarified the relationship between energy use and storage in metabolism. Lipmann has also discovered many important features of molecular metabo-

lism, including acetyl Co-enzyme A. Since 1957 he has been professor of biochemistry at Rockefeller University, New York.   DOM

Lippmann, Walter (b. New York, USA, 23.9.1889; d. New York, 14.12.1974). American journalist who in a 60-year career won a worldwide reputation as a political commentator during the period when the USA emerged as the leading nation of the non-Communist world. Lippmann helped to found the *New Republic* in 1914 and T. Woodrow WILSON is said to have drawn on his ideas for the 14 Points and the concept of the League of Nations. After 10 years with the reformist *World*, his famous column 'Today and Tomorrow' first appeared in the *New York Herald Tribune* in September 1931. In *Public Opinion* (NY, 1922, ²1956), *The Good Society* (NY, 1937, written at the time of F. D. ROOSEVELT's New Deal), *The Cold War* (NY, 1947) and *Essays in Public Philosophy* (NY, 1955), he probed the problems of democratic government, especially those of communication, in a mass society which was becoming a world power.
ALCB

R. Steel, *Walter Lippmann and the American Century* (London, 1981).

Lipscomb, William Nunn (b. Cleveland, Ohio, USA, 9.12.1919). American chemist. Lipscomb is inextricably linked with the field of boron hydride chemistry. He received his doctorate from California Institute of Technology in 1946, and became a faculty member at the University of Minnesota. In 1959 he moved to Harvard. STOCK had performed much early development work on the chemistry of the boron hydrides, and with the advent of the space age these extraordinary and complicated molecules acquired a new importance as potential rocket-fuel additives. By careful low-temperature crystallography, Lipscomb established the structures of a number of these molecules in the 1950s. He also developed bonding pictures to account for their unusual geometries, and brought to bear the science of topology to deduce the number of possible boron hydrides, and to predict their structures, e.g. see *Boron Hydrides* (NY, 1963). For this work, Lipscomb was awarded the 1976 Nobel prize for chemistry.　KRS

Lissitzky, Lazar Markovitch (El Lissitzky) (b. nr Smolensk, Russia, 10.11.1890; d. Moscow, USSR, 30.12.1941). Russian designer. Trained first as an architect at Darmstadt and Riga, a friend of Zadkine and protégé of CHAGALL, from 1917 Lissitzky developed under MALEVICH's influence into a nonfigurative painter and a brilliant and original book and exhibition designer. In 1922 he went to Germany where he was an important linkman between the new Soviet contructivism and the mid-European avant-garde. With EHRENBURG he published the trilingual magazine *Veshch* from Berlin in 1922; with MOHOLY-NAGY he attended the Dada-Constructivist conference at Weimar; with ARP he compiled *Die Kunst-Ismen*, a book on the new ©Isms, in 1925. Throughout that decade he worked equally in Germany and in Russia, where he taught at the Vkutemas school and belonged to the architects' society ASNOVA. In the 1930s he continued his exhibition and publicity work for the Soviet government, but nothing in his later work can compare with his layout for MAYAKOVSKY's poems *Dla Golosa* (1922), his photomontage *The Constructor* (1924), or his abstract room for the Hanover public gallery (1927–8) – all classics of their kind.　JWMW
S. Lissitzky-Küppers, *El Lissitzky* (Greenwich, Conn., 1968).

Littlewood, Joan Maud (b. London, UK, 6.10.1914). British theatre director. Unusually for someone born into a working-class London family, Littlewood won a scholarship to the Royal Academy of Dramatic Arts where she trained as an actress. After acting in repertory in Manchester, she joined Ewan Mac-Coll's Theatre of Action whose manifesto in 1936 outlined a programme for a working-class theatre. With few material resources but with much energy and flair they formed a part-professional, part-amateur theatre company, Theatre Union, which developed a distinctive style, using documentary writing, agit-prop, songs and music hall. After WW2 they formed another company, Theatre

Workshop, which in 1953 took over an old music hall in Stratford, East London. With this base their work expanded rapidly to include rare classics, such as *Arden of Faversham* in 1954, BRECHT and new writers. Littlewood's talent for discovering new dramatists, such as Brendan Behan, and her nurturing of young actors brought the company to the forefront of the new wave of British theatre; and her cheerful, sometimes brash but always vigorous style provided many successes, including *Fings Ain't Wot They Used t'Be* (1959) and *Oh, What a Lovely War* (1963). Unfortunately the commercial success which the company needed for its economic survival also brought problems: the community basis of the theatre was weakened by West End transfers. After a vain attempt to establish a fun palace embracing a mixture of theatre and funfair, Littlewood grew disillusioned and became less active with the Theatre Workshop.　JE
H. Goorney, *The Theatre Workshop Story* (London, 1981).

Llewellyn, Karl Nickerson (b. Seattle, Wash., USA, 22.5.1893; d. Chicago, Ill., 13.2.1962). American jurist and commercial lawyer. After schooling in New York and Germany, Llewellyn studied at Yale University and Law School. Except for a brief period in the German army (1914), two years in commercial practice in New York, and two years as visiting professor in Leipzig, he was a full-time teacher of law at Yale, Columbia and Chicago until his death. Llewellyn was a colourful character, a forceful polemicist and a brilliant, if uneven, teacher and writer – see especially *Bramble Bush* (NY, 1930, ²1951). He is remembered today as a leading member and interpreter of the Realist movement in jurisprudence, especially during the period 1929–40; as a pioneer in legal anthropology (*The Cheyenne Way*, with E. Adamson Hoebel, Norman, 1941); as an outstanding commercial lawyer and the chief reporter of the Uniform Commercial Code; and as a substantial jurist in his own right (*The Common Law Tradition: Deciding Appeals*, Boston, Mass., 1960; *Jurisprudence: Realism in Theory and Practice*, Chicago, 1962).

LLOYD GEORGE

Within an essentially functionalist sociology of law, which owed much to Sumner and Max WEBER, Llewellyn developed a number of original themes that emphasized 'craftsmanship', purposive interpretation and a broad perspective on all legal phenomena, with formal legal rules accorded a central, but a secondary role within 'the institution of law-government'. His prose style was less orthodox than his ideas, many of which have been quite readily assimilated into the mainstream of American legal thought. Since his death Llewellyn's work, especially in commercial law, legal method and legal education, has been developed and promoted by his widow Professor Soia Menstchikoff. WLT

W. Twining, *Karl Llewellyn and the Realist Movement* (London, 1973).

Lloyd George, David (b. Manchester, UK, 17.1.1863; d. Llanystumdwy, Gwynedd, 26.3.1945). British Liberal politician, MP for the Caernarvon Boroughs (1890–1945), president of the Board of Trade (1905–8), chancellor of the exchequer (1908–15), minister of munitions (1915–16), prime minister (1916–22). Though born in Manchester, David Lloyd George grew up in North Wales and was articled to a solicitor in Portmadoc. Entering national politics as Liberal MP for Caernarvon in 1890, he swiftly gained a name as one of the most outspoken of the Welsh radicals – during the South African war (1899–1902) he publicly defended the Boer rights to independence – and when the Liberals won the election of 1905 he became chancellor of the exchequer in Asquith's government. His budgets opened the Liberal assault on the existing structure of social power, and his Old Age Pensions Act of 1908 and National Health Insurance Act of 1911 laid the foundation of what became the Welfare State. His 'People's Budget' of 1909, which included proposals for a surtax on incomes and new taxes on land values, was rejected by the House of Lords, an action which led, after two general elections in 1910, to the Parliament Act of 1911, which largely removed the previous powers of the House of Lords. During this period Lloyd George found himself increasingly

the subject of public comment, first for the comparatively unbridled nature of his private life, and secondly for the allegations of corruption over the award of a public contract to the English Marconi Company. Although Lloyd George continued to be regarded as the representative of the pacifist strain of British radicalism, in 1911 he began to realign himself on the side of Imperial Germany's critics. On the outbreak of WW1 he became a leading advocate of war to the bitter end, and as minister of munitions mobilized British industry in support of General Kitchener's mass armies. In 1916 he took part in the conspiracy to drive the prime minister, Asquith, from office. By so doing, and still more by accepting the premiership in his place, he split the Liberal party irretrievably in two. Lloyd George picked some of the ablest of British business leaders to mobilize all of Britain's resources for war. He succeeded in introducing the convoy system, over the opposition of the Admiralty, and thereby saved Britain from starvation by the U-boat blockade. When he could not change the British army's policy of attrition at the cost of enormous casualties, he came out for the establishment of a limited Supreme Command in France under the French Marshal FOCH. Winning a snap election for the coalition government immediately after the armistice (the 'Khaki election' of November 1918), he was committed to imposing Draconian peace terms on Germany. But by skilful manoeuvring at the Paris Peace Conference he obtained some modification of the terms and from 1919 to 1922 worked to improve the Versailles settlement by his efforts to rehabilitate the European, including the German, economy. These efforts culminated in the Geneva Conference but broke down in face of the German–Soviet rapprochement at Rapallo (April 1922). The same year his attempt, in support of Greece, to contain the revival of Turkish power under ATATÜRK led to a direct confrontation of British and Turkish troops at Chanak. Lloyd George avoided war but gave an opportunity to the Tory party to break away from the coalition and to replace him as prime minister.

In the UK Lloyd George had succeeded in withdrawing British troops from a bitter war in Ireland by the treaty of 1921, which recognized the Irish Free State; but his wartime popularity had been eroded by the postwar depression of British industry. Although 60 at the time of his fall from office, and with an international reputation no other British leader could equal, Lloyd George never again held office. His later history was one of brilliant political inventiveness – e.g. the proposals in the Liberal Yellow Book of 1928, to which KEYNES contributed, and the campaign 'to conquer unemployment' in the 1929 election – but his ideas remained unrealized because of the distrust with which all sections of the political elite regarded him. The Liberal party never recovered from the Lloyd George–Asquith split and Lloyd George's following in Parliament dwindled to a family party of four (1931). He spent the 1930s in writing his controversial *War Memoirs* (6 vols, London, 1933–6) and *The Truth about the Peace Treaties* (2 vols, London, 1938). He was impressed by HITLER when he visited him in 1936, but opposed CHAMBERLAIN's policy of appeasement. He played no part in WW2 and by the time he died, in 1945, had become a purely legendary figure remembered as one of the greatest orators in British history ('the Welsh Wizard') and the architect of victory in WW1; remembered less happily as the great radical leader who preferred power and manipulation to principle, only to condemn himself to the frustration of opposition at the height of his powers.

DCW/ALCB

T. Jones, *Lloyd George* (London, 1951); J. Grigg, *The Young Lloyd George* (London, 1973); J. Grigg, *Lloyd George: the People's Champion, 1902–1911* (London, 1978).

Lockyer, Joseph Norman (b. Rugby, Warwicks., UK, 17.5.1836; d. Salcombe Regis, Devon, 16.8.1920). British astronomer. Lockyer began his working life in 1858 as a clerk in the War Office, making astronomical observations in his spare time from private observatories. His early research work was in solar physics, particularly in studies of the solar spectrum, and he took part in eclipse expeditions to Sicily in 1870 and to India in 1871. In 1866 he suggested that solar prominences might be seen in the absence of a solar eclipse by use of a spectroscope, and on 20 October 1868 made this observation for what he believed was the first time – in fact he was anticipated by Janssen by two months. Although restricted by his professional duties, Lockyer made frequent observations of prominences by his method at weekends and soon observed a bright yellow spectrum line that he attributed to a new element which he called 'helium'. This element was not found in the laboratory until 1895, when it was identified by RAMSAY as a product of radioactivity. In 1873 Lockyer began a programme of laboratory work combined with observations of the solar spectrum at South Kensington in buildings which six years later were officially designated the Solar Physics Observatory. The observatory was linked with the Royal College of Science, where Lockyer was first lecturer and then professor. In the laboratory he showed that the spectrum given by an element in a spark source is different from the spectrum produced by an arc source. As a spark is at a higher temperature than an arc he deduced in his celebrated 'dissociation hypothesis' that some spectrum lines are formed at low temperature and others at high temperature. This concept was an important one in astrophysics, leading HALE for example to recognize from its spectrum alone that a sunspot is cooler than its surroundings. Lockyer applied it to the classification of stellar spectra and to ideas about the way in which stars evolve, although his evolutionary scheme never found favour among his contemporaries and now is of historical interest only. Lockyer retired in 1902, but continued his association with the South Kensington Observatory until it was moved, against his advice and wishes, to Cambridge in 1913. In his disappointment Lockyer, now aged 76, founded in 1912 a new observatory near Sidmouth. The work done there was chiefly concerned with spectral classification. Lockyer founded the journal *Nature*, the first issue appearing on 4 November 1869. He always had an interest in astronomical aspects of archaeology. DEB

T. M. & W. L. Lockyer, *Life and Work of Sir Norman Lockyer* (London, 1928).

Lodge, Oliver Joseph (b. Penkhull, Staffs., UK, 12.6.1851; d. Salisbury, Wilts., 22.8.1940). British physicist and engineer. He studied at the Royal College of Science and at University College London. In 1881 he became professor of physics at Liverpool, and in 1900 was appointed the first principal of the new university at Birmingham. Lodge would have described himself as an 'electrical engineer'. About the turn of the century he was concerned with the setting up of the British electricity supply network (the 'Grid'). He first transmitted dots and dashes by radio at the Royal Institution in 1894 (see *Signalling across Space without Wires*, London, 1897). But he is best remembered for daring to look beyond the limits of 'respectable' science and trying to bring topics now known by the collective name 'extrasensory perception' (ESP) within the framework of accepted science (see *Raymond*, London, 1916). *Past Years: an Autobiography* (London) appeared in 1931. ERL

Loewi, Otto (b. Frankfurt, Hesse, Germany, 3.6.1873; naturalized American citizen, 1946; d. New York, USA, 25.12.1961). German/American biochemist. He studied medicine at Strassburg (1891–6) – only just passing his first medical exam – and then inorganic chemistry with Freund at Frankfurt and physiological chemistry with Hofmeister in Strassburg. His most formative years (1898–1904) were spent as assistant to the pharmacologist Hans Meyer, during which time he also passed a brief period in STARLING's laboratory in London. From 1909 to 1938 he was professor of pharmacology at Graz and after expulsion by the Nazis he took up a similar position in 1940 at the College of Medicine, New York. For Loewi the years in Graz were the most productive. He first worked there on metabolism and control of kidney secretion of substances such as uric acid and glucose, leading to *The Secretion of Urine* (London, 1917). From

these studies Loewi was the first to show that in animals proteins are synthesized from degradation products, i.e. there is a constant rate of turnover. His most important work was of a more pharmacological nature; in 1910 he showed with Fröhlich that cocaine altered the intrinsic sensitivity of sympathetically innervated organs to adrenaline. Then in 1912 he published his famous account of the action of the vagus on the heart as the result of an accumulated substance 'Vagustoff' which possessed the properties of acetylcholine. For this he was subsequently awarded the Nobel prize, with DALE, in 1936. CTJ

Loewy, Raymond Fernand (b. Paris, France, 5.11.1893; naturalized American citizen). French/American industrial designer. Loewy created the profession of industrial design virtually single-handed. He was not the first man to treat product design as a serious pursuit, but he was the first to achieve popular recognition for it. Arriving penniless in the USA after WW1, Loewy worked as a fashion illustrator before setting up his own design studio in 1927. Sheer force of personality and an outrageously flamboyant style allowed him to bully his first clients into believing that they needed him. The immediate commercial success of the products that had received the Loewy treatment convinced most of the major manufacturers that they couldn't do without Loewy, or someone like him. His talent was for turning mere contraptions into stylish and saleable products with a character of their own. The Gestetner duplicator was the first example, which in 1929 he transformed from a cross between a sewing machine and a wheelbarrow into a sleek and streamlined object. Since then he has worked on everything from railway locomotives to the space shuttle. He has, as he is fond of saying himself, done as much as any individual to shape the look of the everyday objects of the 20c. DS

London, Fritz Wolfgang (b. Breslau, Germany [now Wroclav, Poland], 7.3.1900; d. Durham, NC, USA, 30.3.1954), and **London, Heinz** (b. Bonn,

N. Rhine-Westphalia, Germany, 7.11.1907; d. Oxford, UK, 3.8.1970). German/American; German/British physicists. The London brothers established their reputations separately in closely related fields in physics, although the short period of close collaboration between them led to their important theoretical papers on superconductivity. Fritz, who had taken his PhD in philosophy, became interested in theoretical physics at Göttingen and proceeded to work with SCHRÖDINGER at Zürich (1927). Here, with HEITLER, he made his first major contribution: to the quantum theory of the chemical bond. His interest then moved to problems of the dynamics of atomic and molecular interactions. In this field his most important work (1930) was on the van der WAALS forces between nonpolar molecules – 'dispersion or London forces' – the understanding of which was fundamental to the development of theories of gases, liquids and solutions and of the interaction between colloidal particles and macroscopic bodies. Meanwhile, Heinz had become a graduate student at Breslau under Simon working on low temperature physics and, in particular, on superconductivity. With the increasing persecution of Jews, both brothers left Germany (1933–4) and joined Simon in Oxford. There they worked together on their famous papers on superconductivity (1935) which laid the basis of most future work in this field. Heinz continued work on liquid helium first at Oxford and then at Bristol, while Fritz moved to Duke University, North Carolina, and until his early death continued his interest in superconductivity and superfluidity and in the problems posed by the properties of the helium isotope ^{3}He. In the late 1950s Heinz, working at Harwell, returned to cryogenic research: the most important outcome was the invention of the helium dilution refrigerator which has enabled temperatures as low as 0.004K to be attained. DHE

London, Jack, ps. of John Griffith (b. San Francisco, Calif., USA, 12.1.1876; d. Glen Ellen, Calif., 22.11.1916). American novelist. London learned early on that the laws of Darwin and Spencer,

the injunction to eternal struggle, applied to his own life. He was born the illegitimate son of an impoverished spiritualist, and as a young man tramped around the USA, worked as a sailor and labourer and, as he described it, exulted in his strength. The discovery that strength was not enough came when London was exposed to the world of broken and failed men, the 'social pit'. It propelled London towards socialism. The early novels, especially the Alaskan story *The Call of the Wild* (NY, 1903), dramatize Darwinian and Spencerian themes. London's protagonists are often 'blond beasts', heroic and dominating figures who struggle against society and nature. Though he remained a committed propagandist for the cause of socialism, its collectivist dimension was remote from his worldview. His *The Iron Heel* (NY, 1907), which anticipated fascist totalitarianism, was, after Upton Sinclair's *The Jungle* (1906), the most influential piece of socialist propaganda produced in the USA. But London's work was closer to NIETZSCHE than it was to the temperate spirits who dominated the Socialist party in the USA. EH

J. London, *Jack London and his Times: an Unconventional Biography* (NY, 1939); R. Barltrop, *London* (NY, 1977).

Lonergan, Bernard Joseph Francis (b. Buckingham, Quebec, Canada, 17.12.1904). Canadian Roman Catholic theologian and Jesuit. As professor at the Gregorian University, Rome (1953–65), Lonergan moved from a precritical, objective, propositional theology associated with neoscholasticism to an anthropocentric account of reality – from 'the world' which is known, to the 'I' which understands. Personal conversion becomes the experience from which theology begins. Influenced by HUSSERL's phenomenological method, he gives an account of human understanding in which the knowing subject truly understands the objective world only by a conscious self-appropriation of the act of knowing (*Insight: a Study of Human Understanding*, London, 1957). All understanding has a unified structure irrespective of what is understood – using an intentional theory of meaning,

Lonergan has delineated a unified method for all theology (*Method in Theology*, London, 1972). Lonergan's 'transcendental method' aims to elucidate the underlying method of all theology regardless of the content of actual projects of theological understanding. His contribution to Catholic theology has been almost exclusively methodological. He has been widely influential in tearing Catholic theology away from an account of Christian doctrine made up of propositions which express orthodox belief, a development evident in the results of the Second Vatican Council (1962–5).

GT

P. Corcoran (ed.), *Looking at Lonergan's Method* (Dublin, 1975).

Loos, Adolf (b. Brünn, Moravia, Austria-Hungary [now Brno, Czechoslovakia], 10.12.1870; d. Vienna, Austria, 23.8.1933). Austrian architect. He was an important theorist and practitioner in the early phases of the modern movement, an uncompromising advocate of its rejection of ornament. During the three years he spent in the USA (1893–6) he was strongly influenced by the Chicago school, especially by Louis Sullivan. He lived in Vienna from 1897 until his death, except for six years (1922–8) spent in Paris. His most influential work was done between 1897 and 1910. While accepting the rationalism of Otto Wagner, the leading Viennese architect of the time, Loos condemned art nouveau and the Vienna Sezession. Most of Loos's writings were first published as articles in Viennese journals, where he structured his arguments within broad sociopolitical and cultural frameworks. Most famous is 'Ornament und Verbrechen' [Ornament and crime] (1908) in which he argued that while ornament had a place in the past it was degenerate in modern culture. In 'Architektur' [Architecture] (1910) he criticized the modern practice of architecture for lack of craftsmanship and for working in a cultural vacuum. His writings were later republished in two books *Ins Leere Gesprochen* [Spoken into the void] (Innsbruck, ²1932) and *Trotzdem, 1900–1930* [Notwithstanding] (Innsbruck, 1931). His buildings relentlessly expressed his theories. The most influen-

tial was the Steiner house, Vienna (1910). In its use of reinforced concrete, the new material, in its utter lack of ornament and its severe cubic forms, and in its treatment of interior space, it is a landmark in architectural history.

BM

L. Münz & G. Künstler, *Adolf Loos: Pioneer of Modern Architecture* (London, 1966).

Lopez, Robert Sabatino (b. Genoa, Liguria, Italy, 8.10.1910; naturalized American citizen). Italian/American historian. Lopez began by working on the economic history of his native Genoa in the Middle Ages; his publications on the subject include *Studi sull'economia genovese nel medio evo* [Studies on the Genoese economy in the Middle Ages] (Turin, 1936), and *Storia delle colonie genovesi* [History of the Genoese settlements] (Bologna, 1938). After migrating to the USA, his interests broadened to include the history of medieval trade and towns, studied in *The Tenth Century* (NY, 1959), *Naissance de l'Europe* (Paris, 1962; *The Birth of Europe*, London, 1967), and *The Commercial Revolution of the Middle Ages* (Englewood Cliffs, 1971). He has also made a significant contribution to Byzantine studies. Lopez is perhaps most widely known for his controversial views on the relation between economic depression and cultural achievement, expounded in 'Hard times and investment in culture', in W. Ferguson (ed.), *The Renaissance* (NY, 1962), *The Three Ages of the Italian Renaissance* (Charlottesville, 1970), and elsewhere. A sympathizer with the *Annales* movement since the days of Marc BLOCH and FEBVRE, Lopez takes models and quantification more seriously than most medievalists of his generation. His former pupils David Herlihy and Harry Miskimin are among the leading exponents of the quantitative history of the medieval economy. UPB

Lorca, Federico García (b. Fuente Vaqueros, Granada, Spain, 5.6.1898; d. nr Granada, 19.8.1936). Spanish poet and dramatist. His murder by the Nationalists at the start of the Spanish civil war brought sudden international fame, accompanied by an excess of political rhetoric which led a later generation to question his merits; after the inevitable slump, his reputation has recovered (largely with a shift in interest to the less obvious works). He must now be bracketed with MACHADO as one of the two greatest poets Spain has produced this century, and he is certainly Spain's greatest dramatist since the Golden Age. As a poet, his early reputation rested on the *Romancero gitano* (Madrid, 1928; tr. R. Humphries, *The Gypsy Ballads of García Lorca*, Bloomington, 1953), the poems of *Poema del Cante Jondo* (Madrid, 1931), and *Llanto por Ignacio Sánchez Mejías* (Madrid, 1935; tr. A. L. Lloyd, in *Lament for the Death of a Bullfighter, and Other Poems*, London, 1937), all profoundly Andalusian, richly sombre in their mood and imagery, and disquieting in their projection of a part-primitive, part-private world of myth moved by dark and not precisely identifiable forces; but, beneath the flamenco trappings, there is a deeper – perhaps personal – anguish, as well as a superb rhythmical and linguistic sense (the *Llanto* is one of the four best elegies in the Spanish language). Critical interest has since shifted to the tortured, ambiguous and deliberately dissonant surrealist poems of *Poeta en Nueva York* (Mexico City, 1940; tr. B. Belitt, *Poet in New York*, London, 1955), and to the arabesque *casidas* and *gacelas* of *Diván de Tamarit* (NY, 1940). An early major anthology in English is *Poems* (tr. S. Spender & J. L. Gili, London, 1939). As a dramatist, early romantic pieces with social implications such as *Mariana Pineda* (Madrid, 1928; tr. J. Graham-Luján & R. L. O'Connell in *Collected Plays*, London, 1976) and the comic invention of *La zapatera prodigiosa* (first performed 1930, amplified 1935, pub. Buenos Aires, 1938; *The Shoemaker's Prodigious Wife* in *Collected Plays*) established him in the public eye, while his fostering of popular theatre gave him a left-wing reputation which contributed to his death (although his homosexuality also made him a target). His reputation as a playwright rests, however, mainly on the three 'folk tragedies', *Bodas de sangre* (Madrid, 1935; *Blood Wedding*), *Yerma* (Buenos Aires,

1937) and *La casa de Bernarda Alba* (Buenos Aires, 1940; *The House of Bernarda Alba*: all three tr. J. Graham-Luján & R. L. O'Connell, in *III Tragedies*, NY, 1959, incorporated into *Collected Plays*), whose settings recall the *Romancero gitano*, as do the unspecified dark forces (associated with earth, blood, sex, water, fertility/infertility, death, and the moon) which appear to manipulate the characters in *Bodas de sangre* and *Yerma*. Both these plays are richly poetic, with an almost ritualized primitivism (Lorca was highly superstitious, and his dark forces were not mere dramatic ploys). *La casa de Bernarda Alba* is starker: deliberately prosaic, more readily interpretable as social criticism (i.e. of the pressures of convention, the imprisoning effect of mourning customs, the frustration of female sexuality by the need to wait for an acceptable match), but it is so dominated by the title character – who tyrannizes her five daughters – that it emerges as the study of a unique individual rather than a typical woman. Each tragedy has one outstanding female role, those of Yerma and Bernarda having been written for the great tragic actress Margarita Xirgu. Lorca's technical experimentation (which has affinities with innovators as dissimilar as PIRANDELLO and BRECHT) was immensely versatile, and he had a superb sense for stage-effects to reinforce the web of his recurrent imagery.

RP-M

R. C. Allen, *The Symbolic World of Federico García Lorca* (Albuquerque, N. Mex., 1972); M. Adam, *García Lorca: Playwright and Poet* (NY, 1977).

Lorentz, Hendrik Antoon (b. Arnhem, Gelderland, The Netherlands, 18.7.1853; d. Haarlem, N. Holland, 4.2.1928). Dutch physicist. When only 22 Lorentz was appointed professor of theoretical physics at Leiden, where he taught for the rest of his life. His work encompasses the theory of a wide variety of electromagnetic and optical phenomena. He introduced the idea that electricity was due to the motion of individual charged particles. This was the origin of the concept of electrons – though he did not invent the name. He developed a theory of electrical conductivity by assuming that these electrons are deflected by various interactions as they move through a metal, thereby giving rise to electrical resistance. He explained the observation that spectral lines emitted by some atoms are split into three (or more) separate lines when the atoms are in a magnetic field (ZEEMAN effect). This he suggested was due to the fact that the frequency of a vibrating electron would depend on the direction of the vibration relative to the direction of the field. He solved the problem of the dispersion of light – the fact that the velocity of light in a medium depends on its wavelength (this is the reason why a glass prism produces a spectrum from white light), again using the idea of discrete charged particles. His outstanding contribution to physics was his explanation for the fact that it appeared to be impossible to detect the motion of the earth with respect to the 'ether' which was supposed to transmit electromagnetic waves. Lorentz showed that this could be explained if all bodies decreased in length as they moved. His calculation of this 'Lorentz contraction' helped to pave the way for EINSTEIN's special theory of relativity. He was awarded the Nobel prize for physics in 1902.   HMR

Lorenz, Konrad Zacharias (b. Vienna, Austria-Hungary [now Austria], 7.11.1903). Austrian ethologist. Lorenz trained as a medical student at the University of Vienna. He taught at Vienna and Königsberg, specializing in comparative studies of animal behaviour. In 1951 he became head of the research station and in 1961 director of the Max Planck Institute of Behavioural Physiology. Almost all of his concepts arise from his observations on animals under near natural conditions. *Er redete mit dem Vieh, den Vögeln und den Fischer* (Vienna, 1949; *King Solomon's Ring*, London, 1952) and *So kam der Mensch auf den Hund*, 1950; *Man Meets Dog*, London, 1954) are classic popular animal books. Lorenz has studied a wide variety of animals, and his broad viewpoint gave rise to the formulation of the first relatively complete framework for ethology. Lorenz is probably best known for his work on signalling in ducks and imprinting in goslings.

In the 1930s psychologists regarded animal behaviour as wholly modifiable by individual experience – a viewpoint challenged by Lorenz, who, from his comparative approach, was convinced that much of animal behaviour was not flexible, but genetically fixed or innate. He has since been criticized for his emphasis on innate behaviour patterns and most contemporary ethologists believe animal behaviour to be considerably more open to environmental influences than Lorenz would accept. Lorenz has been further criticized for his tendency to extrapolate from animals to man, for example in suggesting that much of human aggressive behaviour is innate (*Das sogenannte Böse*, Vienna, 1963; *On Aggression*, London, 1966). He has recently turned his attention to what he sees as the most fundamental questions facing mankind, in particular overpopulation and environmental deterioration, in *Die acht Todessünder der zivilisierten Menschheit* (Munich, 1972; *Civilized Man's Eight Deadly Sins*, London, 1974). Lorenz has received numerous awards in recognition of his early work, and in 1973 he shared the Nobel prize for medicine with fellow ethologists N. TINBERGEN and K. von FRISCH for work on 'the organization and elicitation of individual and social behaviour patterns'.   PM

W. H. Thorpe, *The Origin and Rise of Ethology* (London, 1979).

Lösch, August (b. Öhringen, Baden-Württemberg, Germany, 6.10.1906; d. Kiel, Schleswig-Holstein, 30.5.1945). German geographer who made major contributions to understanding the spatial structure of economic regions. In *Die räumliche Ordnung der Wirtschaft* (Jena, 1940; *The Economics of Location*, NY, 1945) he takes further the ideas of CHRISTALLER on central-place systems and explores the coexistence of multiple regional systems and the boundary problems arising between them. Although Lösch had written a classic treatise on the relations between economic goods and geographic space, its impact on geography and regional planning was more profound than on economics: the difficulty of incorporating spatial concepts into general equilibrium problems remains. Lösch studied at Freiburg im Breisgau, Kiel and Bonn. He spent three years in the USA during the 1930s as a Rockefeller fellow, writing his major locational work on his return. For most of WW2 Lösch worked at Kiel in an international institute noted for its declared anti-Nazi views. Weakened by privations during the war years, he died from a viral infection at only 39. PH

Lotka, Alfred James (b. Lemberg, Galicia, Austria-Hungary [now Lvov, Ukraine, USSR], 2.3.1880; d. Red Bank, NJ, USA, 5.12.1949). American mathematician. Lotka was born of American parents; he was educated in the UK at Birmingham University, and then at Cornell. For most of his life he worked in New York for the Metropolitan Life Insurance Company. His main work was in the application of mathematical theory to biological situations; he was particularly concerned with evolution and the dynamics of human and animal populations, modelled in terms of birth and death rates, and age distribution. He believed that 'the logistic (curve) expresses what may be regarded as a fundamental law of populations, that a population cannot increase indefinitely in a constantly geometric progression.' His major book *Elements of Physical Biology* (NY, 1925) was reprinted in 1956 as *Elements of Mathematical Biology*. In 1932 Lotka published a paper entitled 'The growth of mixed populations: two species competing for a common food supply'. This was a development of mathematical principles published earlier by Volterra. By presenting a growth law for two competing populations, expressed in terms of interlocking differential equations, Lotka gave a theoretical exposition of the principle of competitive exclusion in the same year that GAUSE offered a description of the principle based on experimental work. RTi

Lovejoy, Arthur Oncken (b. Berlin, Germany, 10.10.1873; d. Baltimore, Md, USA, 30.12.1962). American philosopher and historian of ideas. A critical realist and opponent of pragmatism and various forms of anti-intellectualism, Lovejoy is best known as the virtual originator of the history of ideas in the English-speaking world. As cofounder and first editor of the influential *Journal of the History of Ideas*, and as author of an impressive stream of essays and books which both analysed the scope and methods of the new field of inquiry, and furnished specific studies of major importance, Lovejoy did more than any other person to give intellectual stiffening and respectability to what had too often tended to degenerate into irresponsible if imaginative historical generalization. His method is best exemplified by his two most celebrated books *The Great Chain of Being: a Study of the History of an Idea* (Cambridge, Mass., 1936) and *Essays in the History of Ideas* (Baltimore, 1948). Deploying immense learning in many languages, Lovejoy traces the unspoken assumptions and the implicit ruling ideas of the thought of an individual, a generation, or a period, and subjects them to close logical analysis; he investigated the key use of recurrent words or phrases, an activity he called 'philosophical semantics'; paid due attention to the affective resonances of ideas; and generally showed greater interest in the underlying 'unit ideas' of groups and minor thinkers, as being more typical, than in those of the great intellectual innovators. The overall tendency of his writings was to disintegrate large cultural terms such as romanticism, primitivism, evolutionism, and naturalism, by minutely mapping and prising open the deep logical fissures that run through these apparent monoliths. By opening up this new dimension of systematic conceptual investigation, Lovejoy dug deeper than conventional scholars and cut across the artificial boundaries of subject and nation. RNH

Lovell, Alfred Charles Bernard (b. Oldham Common, Glos., UK, 31.8.1913). British radio astronomer. A pioneer of radio astronomy, Lovell was the first director of Jodrell Bank Experimental Station at Manchester. He pioneered many techniques in radio astronomy. In particular he studied stars that gave out unpredictable but periodic bursts of microwave radiation which he and Fred Whipple later identified as flare stars in the visible spectrum. These were the first ordinary stars apart from the sun to be identified as radio sources. Under Lovell's direction the great steerable parabolic dish of Jodrell Bank's largest radio telescope was completed in 1957; the increase in precision this instrument offered radio astronomers made an important contribution to the development of the subject, making possible the observation of distant radio sources as well as the tracking of space probes, satellites and lunar space flights.   MJS

Lowell, Robert (b. Boston, Mass., USA, 1.3.1917; d. New York, 14.9.1977). American poet. Lowell went from writing a close, symbolic, indeed even an hermetic verse, to the assumption of an Horatian role as the conscience of his generation. He came from a family prominent in New England literary and public life, and had a heightened sense of tradition and the responsibility of the artist to deal seriously with the major ethical issues of the age. His roots in the Puritan past of New England, and his conversion to Roman Catholicism in 1940, came together in his early verse to give him a subject-matter and a symbolism. Leaving Harvard after two years to attend Kenyon College, he came under the influence of TATE and RANSOM, writers who were in the process of leading American literary criticism away from the political emphases of the 1930s towards a more conservative and formalist poetics which praised qualities such as ambiguity and tension, and which sought a poetry of complex syntactic and stanzaic patterns. Tate wrote an introduction to Lowell's first volume *Land of Unlikeness* (Cummington, Mass., 1944), and the movement of critical thought which Tate sponsored, the New Criticism, helped to create the taste by which Lowell's reputation was established.

In the 1950s Lowell transformed his poetry. He abandoned the use of intricate verse metres and stanzas, dropped his religious symbolism, and began to explore his own life and that of his family and friends. He wrote unsparingly about his experiences as a conscientious objector, of his mental breakdown and hospitalization in a sanatorium, and frankly about his wife and his emotional life. When collected as *Life Studies* (NY, 1959), Lowell's new mode was described, perhaps unhelpfully, as 'confessional'. It set the characteristic tone for American poetry throughout the 1960s, during which time Lowell turned towards a more public subject-matter and formal versification in *Near the Ocean* (NY, 1967). During this period he played a prominent part in the opposition then growing in America against the war in Vietnam. Lowell moved to England at the end of the decade, and his verse took an unexpected direction. He began to write what were in effect unrhymed sonnets, hundreds of them, in the form of a verse journal of his life, in which public affairs, historical characters, and other writers figure prominently. Published in numerous volumes before his death, the sonnets were vividly written but lacked a sense of design.   EH
    M. Perloff, *The Poetic Art of Robert Lowell* (Ithaca, NY, 1973); I. Hamilton, *Robert Lowell* (NY, 1982).

Lowie, Robert Heinrich (b. Vienna, Austria-Hungary [now Austria], 12.6.1883; d. Berkeley, Calif., USA, 21.9.1957). American anthropologist. Taken to the USA aged 10, Lowie was a pupil of BOAS and subsequently remained associated with the 'Boasian' school. A prolific writer, his importance derives partly from his publications and partly from his work as a teacher. Most of his working life was spent at the University of California at Berkeley. He taught and wrote during decades which now appear as linking the older anthropology of the late Victorian tradition to the new, fieldwork-based discipline of more recent years. Lowie's own ethnographic research was mainly carried out among the Plains Indians, his studies of the Crow being the principal anthropological source. He displayed a concern with sociological and structural factors that took him well beyond the preoccupation with material culture that marked most Amerindian investigations of the time. Nevertheless, he remained an empiricist in the Boasian tradition, though less committed to its historical particularism. He maintained a consistent interest in cultural evolution and frequently took L. H. Morgan as a critical starting-point for his own studies of social organization, marriage systems and kinship terminology, though this perspective did not exclude awareness of the functionalist approach associated with his British contemporary RADCLIFFE-BROWN. Lowie's influence has been much more pervasive in the USA than in Britain, though most of his major works were published internationally. Certainly his most influential book was *Primitive Society* (NY, 1920), an innovative and programmatic general discussion and the first serious work of its kind since Morgan's *Ancient Society* (1877). KROEBER in a contemporary review, while noting the 'sterile' quality of the insistently idiographic temper of the work, called it 'in every sense modern ... thoroughly American and pragmatic'. Other principal studies include *The History of Ethnological Theory* (NY, 1937), *Social Organization* (NY, 1948) and *Primitive Religion* (NY, 1924). Much of his specialized American research is contained in the posthumous *Selected Papers in Anthropology* (Berkeley, 1960) and in the periodical literature. IH

Löwith, Karl (b. Munich, Bavaria, Germany, 9.1.1897; d. Heidelberg, Baden-Württemberg, West Germany, 24.5.1973). German historian of ideas. His rich and prolific writings sketch a grandiose panoramic view of western civilization's loss of the ancient concept of nature and its replacement by modern historicist philosophies. In his two major works *Von Hegel bis Nietzsche* (Zürich, 1941; tr. D. E. Green, *From Hegel to Nietzsche*, NY, 1946) and *Meaning in History* (Chicago, 1949) he criticizes Christianity for dethroning the Ancients' conception of nature as an eternal, self-subsistent, self-renewing cosmos, in which all things have their place and of which man is but a part, in favour of the Christian notion of a transcendent creator, and of the world as his transitory creation, the sole significance of which is that it provides a setting for man's fate. Modern philosophies of history are criticized as secularizations of this basic vision: the idea of progress expressed by MARX's historical materialism, for example, is really no more than 'Christian eschatology in the language of national economy'. The final phase of the fall from the ancient cosmology, Löwith shows, leads to the various philosophies of historicism and pragmatism, and the attention of men is finally diverted from contemplation of the permanent and the rational to preoccupation with the transient and the trivial. Only in NIETZSCHE's doctrine of eternal recurrence does Löwith detect the possible beginnings of a return to an older cosmology. RNH

Lowry, Clarence Malcolm (b. Liscard, Ches., UK, 28.7.1909; d. Ripe, E. Sussex, 27.6.1957). British novelist, poet and essayist. He was educated at Leys School, Cambridge (1923–7), and St Catherine's College, Cambridge (1929–32). He was an alcoholic, which set a major pattern for his life; but for two short periods, he drank heavily, starting at school. As a 17-year-old schoolboy Lowry sailed as a deckhand on the SS *Pyrrhus* to the Far East, thus establishing a second biographical pattern of travel and residence, in many European countries and the USA. He settled temporarily with his first wife Jan Gabriel in Cuernavaca, Mexico (1936–8). On the break-up of his marriage he lived with his second wife Margerie Bonner in a shack in Dollarton, Vancouver, Canada (1939–54). During this period he made extensive journeys to the USA, Mexico (whence he was deported in 1946), Haiti, England, France and Italy. In 1956 he and his wife settled in Ripe, Sussex, where he died 'by misadventure'. Lowry dramatizes his own life in his works, first as the young seaman Eugene Dana Hilliot in *Ultramarine* (London, 1933), then as Geoffrey Firmin, the alcoholic ex-consul to Mexico in *Under the Volcano* (London, 1947) and as the nameless man who lives in Vancouver Bay in 'The Forest Path to the Spring' (in *Hear Us O Lord from Heaven Thy Dwelling Place*, London, 1961). His peregrinations, heavy drinking, marital problems and the periods he spent in psychiatric hospitals are all relevant background for his novels; the last, for example, forms the basis for *Lunar Caustic* (London, 1958). But the central characters of the novels are placed in a complex structure and framework of literary and artistic reference which create novels of rich 'mythical' density. *Under the Volcano*, widely regarded as his finest work, is replete with literary resonances: COCTEAU's play *La Machine Infernale*, Conrad Aiken (whom Lowry visited in 1929), JOYCE, Shelley, Wordsworth, Dante, Elizabethan drama and poetry, Swedenborg, Aztec myth and the Kabbala, to name but a few. By combining intensely personal self-examination with an intricate pattern of literary and cosmological associations, Lowry produced novels which are among the finest of the postmodernist era. DRic

M. C. Bradbrook, *Malcolm Lowry* (Cambridge, 1974); D. Day, *Malcolm Lowry* (Oxford, 1974).

Lowry, Thomas Martin (b. Bradford, W. Yorks., UK, 26.10.1874; d. Cambridge, 2.11.1936). British chemist. Lowry's major contributions to chemistry centred largely upon his interest in the ability of many chemical substances to rotate the plane of polarized light (optical activity). Trained originally as an organic chemist, he was head of the chemical department at Guy's Hospital Medical School (1913–20) and was appointed in 1920 to the new chair of physical chemistry at Cambridge, where he spent the rest of his life. In the presence of trace amounts of other compounds (catalysts), optically active substances often undergo a change in molecular structure (isomerization) during which they either lose (racemization) or change the magnitude of (mutarotation) their optical activity. In particular, acids and bases are effective catalysts. Studies of the acid-base catalysis of reactions of this kind led Lowry (1923) to an extended definition of acids and bases as, respectively, proton donors and proton acceptors, a concept developed independently by BRØNSTED. The optical rotatory power of molecules also depends on the wavelength of the light employed. This variation of rotatory power with wavelength (optical rotatory dispersion, ORD) had been studied theoretically by Drude

(1907) but experimental data were scarce until Lowry determined the dispersion curves of a large number of compounds and interpreted them in terms of Drude's equations. This work, summarized in his book *Optical Rotatory Power* (London, 1935), foreshadowed the extensive use of ORD during the last 25 years as an important tool in organic chemistry. DHE

Luce, Henry Robinson (b. Tengchow, China, 3.4.1898; d. Phoenix, Ariz., USA, 28.2.1967). American journalist and newspaper publisher. Rising from obscure origins to become one of the most influential and controversial figures in American journalism, Luce built the publishing empire of Time Inc. and became a multimillionaire before he was 35. The son of Presbyterian missionaries, Luce showed an early talent for writing. When he went to Yale he became a managing editor of the student newspaper, the *Yale Daily News*. After working for a year on the *Chicago Daily News*, he moved to the *Baltimore News* where, with his old schoolfriend Briton Hadden, he worked out novel ideas for a 'news magazine'. The two moved to New York and managed to raise $86,000 to launch the first issue of *Time* on 3.3.1923. By 1927 the magazine, which aimed at providing so-called functional information 'for the millions', showed a small profit and thereafter its rise became rapid. Their next step was to plan *Fortune* magazine, aimed at 'big business'. Hadden died before the first issue but Luce carried on successfully. He then evolved the radio documentary feature, *The March of Time*, which presented the news in dramatic form. He followed it in 1935 with an equally successful cinema programme of the same name. Both won international approval. Next came *Life* magazine in 1936, a weekly venture in quality pictorial journalism. Demand for the first issue was so great that the original print order of 446,000 copies soon sold at a premium. (The magazine continued until 1972.) Luce was always identified politically with 'the China Lobby' and Republicanism, and until he retired in 1964 he made sure all his publications toed this line. Perhaps the best explanation of his

success was a friend's: 'He is a dreamer with a very keen sense of double-entry bookkeeping.' RB
D. Halberstam, *The Powers that Be* (NY, 1979).

Luckmann, Thomas (b. Jesenice, Yugoslavia, 14.10.1927; naturalized American citizen). Yugoslav/American sociologist. Raised in Vienna, he studied linguistics, philosophy and sociology in Austria and in the USA, concentrating on sociology and the sociology of religion from 1953. He was strongly influenced by SCHUTZ. Early research into the development of the German churches led to his major publication *Das Problem der Religion in der modernen Gesellschaft* (Freiburg, 1963; revised as *The Invisible Religion: the Problem of Religion in Modern Society*, NY, 1967), followed by his collaboration with Peter BERGER in *The Social Construction of Reality* (NY, 1966). Now professor of sociology and psychology at the University of Constance, West Germany, Luckmann sees personal identity and development as demanding an essentially religious transcendence of biological and social humanity and the *status quo* by means of 'sociologization' within a meaningful structure whose historically intertwined categories are society, individual and religion. Modern industrial society differs from previous forms in that (institutional) norms and values tend to leave the strictly institutional religious sphere, becoming depersonalized as well as desacralized. Religious institutions are privatized. The religiously oriented individual is faced with a number of meaning-systems from which to construct a value-system. Quasi-religious ideologies without social integration compete with the churches for selection. Luckmann virtually denies the possibility of an ultimate secularization of the individual consciousness. Though institutionalized religion may adopt a radically new social form, religion as such persists in the process of irreversible privatization. JCu

Ludendorff, Erich (b. Kruszewnia, Prussian Poland [now Poland], 9.4.1865; d. Munich, Bavaria, Germany, 20.12.1937). An able and conservative product of the German General Staff, Ludendorff worked alongside Paul von Hindenburg in WW1, sharing credit for the victories at Tannenberg and the Masurian Lakes (1914), and serving as first quartermaster-general from 1916 when Hindenburg became chief of the General Staff. He consciously instigated an era of 'total war' based on the active participation of the whole population in the war effort. His aim, enshrined in the Patriotic Auxiliary Service Law of 1916, was an integrated and efficient war effort under the control of a commander who combined the roles of military and political leader, directing foreign and economic policies and controlling propaganda. After recognizing defeat and insisting on an armistice in September 1918, Ludendorff spent the rest of his life maintaining that the German army had never been defeated in the field but 'stabbed in the back by the Home Front'. Associated with HITLER for a time and a National Socialist member of the Reichstag, the eccentricity and confusion of his views left him discredited and isolated by the time of his death. JGo
D. J. Goodspeed, *Ludendorff* (London, 1966).

Lueger, Karl (b. Vienna, Austria-Hungary [now Austria], 24.10.1844; d. Vienna, 10.3.1910). Politician in Hapsburg Austria, leader of the Christian Social party (1888–1910), Burgomeister of Vienna (1897–1910), he largely created the Christian social revolutionary movement in German Austria, as an antiliberal, antisocialist movement based in the cities on the small bourgeois classes threatened by monopoly capitalism on one side and unionism and state socialism on the other, and equally unpopular with the Hapsburg establishment as it was with the Socialist leaders. He used anti-Semitism and anti-Slav feelings as a controlled political weapon rather than as an ideology, a distinction which sometimes escaped those against whom it was directed. HITLER, who lived in Vienna during Lueger's mayoralty, claimed him as his master in the art of mass politics. DCW

Lugard, Frederick John Dealtry (b. Madras, Tamil Nadu, India, 22.1.1858; d. Abinger, Surrey, UK, 11.4.1945). The most influential British colonial administrator in black Africa, Lugard had a varied and adventurous career. After service in the British army in India (1878–87), he went to Nyasaland where he fought Arab slavers (1887–9) and to Uganda where he laid the foundations of the British protectorate (1890–3). Nigeria was the scene of his greatest achievements, first in the service of the Royal Niger Company, then as high commissioner of the newly proclaimed protectorate of Northern Nigeria (1900–6), and finally as governor-general of Nigeria (1912–19), after five years as governor of Hong Kong (1907–12). In Nigeria Lugard was responsible for the conquest of the most powerful Muslim state in tropical Africa, the Caliphate of Sokoto. In Northern Nigeria he worked out a system of administration which he called 'indirect rule', whereby existing African polities were retained as organs of local government, subject to the pressures for reform exerted by British administrators: and he implemented a scheme for the amalgamation of the hitherto separate colonies of Northern and Southern Nigeria, thus making possible the emergence of what is today by far the most populous state in black Africa. Lugard was a prolific writer. His most influential work *The Dual Mandate in British Tropical Africa* (London, 1922) was published after his retirement. The book took its title from Lugard's concept that colonial rule could only be justified if it provided reciprocal advantages for the colonial peoples and for the world at large through the development of hitherto untapped resources. Indirect rule became the gospel of many British colonial administrators in the 1920s. In contrast to more ruthless methods of direct rule applied by Europeans in other parts of Africa, it could be interpreted as a liberal approach to problems of administration; but in practice it tended to favour and consolidate the local power of the most conservative elements in African society, and so came to be vigorously attacked by members of a newly emerging class, the 'western-educated elite', for whose aspirations Lugard had shown scant sympathy.   RH

M. Perham, *Lugard: the Years of Adventure, 1858–1898* (London, 1956); M. Perham, *Lugard: the Years of Authority, 1898–1945* (London, 1960).

Lukács, György Szegedy von (Georg) (b. Budapest, Austria-Hungary [now Hungary], 13.4.1885; d. Budapest, 4.6.1971). Hungarian philosopher and literary theoretician. Lukács, as a MARXist thinker, is one of the most controversial figures in the cultural history of the century. The source of his public repute, which began in the mid-1950s and soared after the Hungarian revolution of 1956, is based on a paradox. Though known primarily as a Marxist writer on aesthetics, his two best books of and on literary criticism, *A lélek és a formák* (Budapest, 1910; *Die Seele und die Formen*, Berlin, 1911; tr. A. Bostock, *Soul and Form*, London, 1971), and *Die Theorie des Romans* (Berlin, 1916, ²1920; tr. A. Bostock, *The Theory of the Novel*, Cambridge, Mass., 1971), were written before he became a communist in 1918, when he was under the influence of SIMMEL and Max WEBER. His major book on Marxism, *Geschichte und Klassenbewusstsein* (Berlin, 1923; *History and Class Consciousness*, London, 1967, ²1971), a collection of essays, yet his only sustained work in sociopolitical theory, was attacked by ZINOVIEV and the leaders of the Russian Communist party, and repudiated by Lukács twice, the second time in abject public confession in Moscow in 1930. When some former French Communists translated the book in 1960, Lukács angrily denounced its unauthorized publication. Only for the English translation did Lukács write a new preface, claiming its 'worth', while indicating some of its 'errors'. The source of Lukács's later appeal outside German-speaking Europe, which came with the renaissance of interest in Marxism among young intellectuals in the 1960s, was that he could be a semi-heretic *within* the Marxist camp; his Hegelian belief in the 'cunning of reason', which he equated with the historic necessity of the triumph of the proletariat, allowed him to pass over the evils of STALINism as an unfortunate stage in the vicissitudes of History. Long before Lukács became a household word among the intelligentsia, an early associate had written of his belief that 'Communist ethics make it the highest duty to accept the necessity of acting wickedly.' This, he said, was 'the greatest sacrifice revolution asked from us'. This defence of the necessary role of terror and deception was depicted by Thomas MANN in *The Magic Mountain*, modelling his Jewish-Jesuit character, Naphta, directly on Lukács. In the concluding pages of *The Theory of the Novel* Lukács had said that we live 'in an age of absolute sinfulness'. For several years, together with a brilliant assembly of Hungarian intellectuals (including K. MANNHEIM and Arnold Hauser), he studied KIERKEGAARD and Dostoevsky. One week before the formation of the Hungarian Communist party he wrote an essay declaring that Bolshevism, because of its use of immoral means, could not produce a moral society. A week later, in an act of conversion, he joined the Communist party. He had become convinced, he wrote, that even the most vile means were necessary to destroy the bourgeois world. After the defeat of the Hungarian Communist uprising in 1919, Lukács went to Germany and then, in 1930, to the USSR where he lived quietly until 1945, editing émigré reviews and writing, returning after WW2 to Hungary. In 1956, when the Communist prime minister Ferenc Nagy proclaimed the independence of Hungary from Russian domination, Lukács joined the short-lived revolutionary government. Nagy was executed. Lukács was briefly interned and then released. He lived quietly in Hungary until his death.

Lukács was a prolific writer, yet apart from an early study (1911) of modern drama, the recently discovered Heidelberg essays on aesthetic culture (1913), *A lélék és a formák* and *Die Theorie des Romans*, his writings on literature are flawed by cautious accommodation to the winds of party doctrine. Thus in *A történelmi-regény* (Budapest, 1954; *Der Historische Roman*, Berlin, 1955; tr. H. & S. Mitchell, *The Historical Novel*, London, 1962), written in the USSR in 1936–7, he used Sir Walter Scott's novels to show the rise of historical consciousness in literature, but ended with a lame chapter on the 'progressive writ-ers' who supported Stalin's 'popular front'. Lukács opposed modernism (he attacked writers such as JOYCE or KAFKA as decadent) and espoused realism. From that point of view, he wrote a number of major studies on writers such as Balzac and Mann. His *Geschicht und Klassenbewusstsein* is of symbolic importance within the history of Marxism. Long before the posthumous publication of Marx's early philosophic writings, Lukács had 'intuited' the Hegelian elements of an 'activity theory' of knowledge in Marx, a point of view adopted by later writers to contrast the early Marx with Engels's scientistic statements of Marxism. In his discussion of 'reification', Lukács was the first to re-introduce the idea of alienation as central to Marx's thought. Using the idea of the class-bound nature of social thought (the theme later developed by Karl Mannheim), Lukács argued that bourgeois thought was a 'false consciousness' since true consciousness resided in the historic identification of the proletariat with universal reason. Within the canon of communist orthodoxy, however, these themes were regarded as being too Hegelian, and as lending themselves to left-wing and syndicalist doctrine. In the end, the career of Lukács as a representative intellectual of his time may be more important than the substance of his many works.   DBe

G. H. R. Parkinson (ed.), *Georg Lukács: the Man, his Work and his Ideas* (London, 1970); G. Lichtheim, *Georg Lukács* (London, 1970).

Łukasiewicz, Jan (b. Lemberg, Galicia, Austria-Hungary [now Lvov, Ukraine, USSR], 21.12.1878; d. Dublin, Irish Republic, 13.11.1956). Polish logician. Łukasiewicz was one of the founders of the remarkable school of logicians which sprang up in Poland after WW1. He made important contributions to modal logic (in which 'is possible' is allowed as a fundamental notion) and many-valued logics (in which truth-values additional to 'true' and 'false' are admitted). He hoped that such logics would become accepted into logic in the same way that non-Euclidean geometries were taken into mathematics in the mid-19c. He also introduced into logic the 'Polish notation' which has found favour in computing for its avoidance of brackets. Łukasiewicz left his chair at the University of Warsaw near the end of WW2. In 1946 he was appointed to the Royal Irish Academy in Dublin, where his continuing studies included an analysis of Aristotle's logic in terms of the recent discoveries in axiomatization and deduction. His book *Aristotle's Syllogistic from the Standpoint of Modern Formal Logic* (Oxford, 1951, ²1957) has inspired a large collection of such studies. Some of his papers are published in *Selected Works* (Amsterdam, 1970).   IG-G

Lumière, Louis (b. Paris, France, 5.10.1864; d. Bandol, Var, 6.6.1948). French film innovator. In December 1895 Louis Lumière was the first person to organize successfully public showings of what he called the 'cinematograph'. By this time he had already established himself as one of Europe's leading manufacturers of photographic equipment and materials and thereby a founder of the world film industry. Lumière's own tiny, 50-second films are mostly 'home movies' or versions of traditional photographic studies. They were initially enormously popular as a novelty and remain the earliest examples of a realistic documentary approach to cinema, but they lost favour with the public after the introduction of the first story films in the early 1900s.   RPA

Lumumba, Patrice (b. Katako Kombe, Kasai, Belgian Congo [now Zaïre], 2.7.1925; d. Katanga, 17.1.1961). Congolese politician. Murdered by his political opponents only seven months after the Congo achieved independence, Lumumba, the country's first prime minister, came to be regarded by many people in the Third World as a symbolic figure, a martyr in the cause of Pan-Africanism and African independence, done to death by the sinister forces of tribalism and neocolonialism. He started his political career as a moderate and, in a work written in 1957, but published posthumously, *Le Congo, terre d'avenir, est-il menacé?* (Brussels, 1962; *Congo My Country*, London, 1962), Lumumba spoke of the need for blacks and whites to work together in harmony. In 1959 he founded the Mouvement National Congolais, the country's first truly national party, which gained enough seats in the May 1960 election to make Lumumba the obvious choice for prime minister. Becoming increasingly radicalized by the difficulties his government faced in the immediate aftermath of independence, Lumumba turned to NKRUMAH for advice and to the USSR for support, thus alienating those Western powers, notably Belgium and the USA, with a special interest in the Congo. A politician of vibrant energy and charismatic powers, Lumumba was also abrasive and unstable. He was removed from power by his former associate MOBUTU, in a military coup in September 1960, when he had been less than three months in office, and subsequently murdered. But the memory of his untimely death and of his radical aspirations haunts his country, now renamed Zaïre, to this day.   RH

J. van Lierde, *La pensée politique de Patrice Lumumba* (Paris, 1963).

Lurçat, Jean Marie (b. Bruyères, Vosges, France, 1.7.1892; d. St Paul de Vence, Alpes-Maritimes, 6.1.1966). French tapestry designer and painter, who contributed to the revival of French tapestry-making in the first half of the 20c. Trained as a painter, Lurçat turned to tapestry design, fascinated both by the technical challenge of '*un art ... doublé d'un artisanat*' and by its architectural potential ('*le propos ... est de chasser ce blanc qui règne à l'origine sur le mur bâti par l'architecte*'). This architectural interest was encouraged by his brother André, the architect, and by the furniture designer turned architect Pierre Chareau, with whom Lurçat collaborated in the 1920s. Lurçat began from first principles, rejecting the idea of tapestry design as the reproduction of easel painting; he deliberately adopted the limitations of *tons comptés*, both for economic and for aesthetic reasons. His earliest designs were mostly executed in needlepoint but, as he mastered the restraints of the medium, he turned increasingly to the specialist weavers of the major *ateliers*. His most significant works date from the late 1930s; in 1939 a state commission allowed him to achieve his ambition of working closely with the Aubusson *artisans*. His book on the craft is *Designing Tapestry* (London, 1950). CAB

P. Hirsch, *Jean Lurçat et la tapisserie* (Paris, 1946).

Luria, Alexander Romanovich (b. Kazan, Russia, 16.7.1902; d. Moscow, USSR, 14.8.1977). Russian psychologist and pioneer of modern neuropsychology. Luria graduated in social sciences from the University of Kazan in 1921 and in medicine from the First Moscow Medical Institute in 1937. From 1924 to 1934 he collaborated with the eminent psychologist VYGOTSKY in investigating the thought, speech and play of children, and in devising educational and therapeutic methods for helping disturbed children. His first major work, published in English, was *The Nature of Human Conflicts* (NY, 1932). After Vygotsky's death in 1934 Luria turned to neuropsychology, concentrating initially on the impairment of speech through brain lesions; his important research in this area was published in *Travmaticheskaia afaziia* (Moscow, 1947; *Traumatic Aphasia*, The Hague, 1970). During WW2 he developed novel methods of restoring the psychological functions of patients suffering from head injuries, and in 1962 he applied these methods in the astonishingly successful rehabilitation of the celebrated Soviet physicist LANDAU, who had sustained severe and seemingly irreversible brain damage in a car crash. Luria's most original and influential research centred on the psychological effects of localized brain tumours; the findings are presented in his monumental *Vysshie korkovye funktsii cheloveka i ikh narusheniia pri local'nykh porazheniiakh mozga* (Moscow, 1962; *Higher Cortical Functions of Man*, NY, 1966). His most widely read book in English is a case-study of a man with virtually unlimited powers of memory, *Malen'kaia knizhka o bol'shoĭ pamiati* (Moscow, 1968; *The Mind of the Mnemonist*, NY, 1968). AMC

Luthuli, Albert John (b. Bulawayo, Northern Rhodesia [now Zimbabwe], 1898; d. Stanger, Natal, South Africa, 21.7.1967). South African political leader. As president-general of the African National Congress from 1952 until his death, Luthuli was the most prominent black South African politician of the 1950s. Strongly influenced by Christian principles, Luthuli became involved in politics at 50 after working as a teacher and local chief. Confined to a rural area through government restrictions throughout most of his presidency of the ANC, he became a powerful symbol of the struggle of black South Africans against apartheid. 'Thirty years of my life', Luthuli said in 1952, 'have been spent in knocking in vain, patiently, moderately and modestly on a closed door.' Choosing the role of a 'middle-man of good will', he remained committed to nonviolence, unaffected by the criticisms of younger, more radical ANC members. In 1960 he was awarded the Nobel Peace prize. (See *Let My People Go*, London, 1962.) RH

Lutyens, Edwin Landseer (b. London, UK, 29.3.1869; d. London, 1.1.1944). British architect. Lutyens might be called a 'reluctant modern'. He disliked modern art. Largely self-taught, he drew inspiration from the past, especially from Roman classicism as interpreted by Sir Christopher Wren (1632–1723). His early career was devoted to designing and renovating country houses and cottages, mostly in Surrey, paying particular attention to the relationship between house and garden: Crooksbury, Farnham (1889); Munstead Wood (1896) for his friend, the gardener-designer Gertrude Jeckyll; Orchards, Godalming (1898). These houses reveal the romantic Lutyens, steeped in the English tradition, combining elements of various styles from Elizabethan to neo-Georgian. He also used elements of the Gothic Revival style: Lindisfarne Castle, Northumbria (1903); Castle Drogo, Devon (1910). His greatest accomplishment was the designing of New Delhi (1912) with its major monuments, including Kingsway, the Jaipur column and the Viceroy's house (completed 1930). Here he combined Indian motifs with a kind of purified European classicism. Other public works include: Hampstead Garden City (1908); Westminster housing scheme, London (1928);

the Midland Bank, Poultry, London (1924); the British Embassy, Washington (1927); Liverpool Roman Catholic cathedral (designed 1929). A member of the Imperial War Graves Commission, Lutyens designed numerous monuments to the dead of WW1. His personal style, characterized by sincerity and a sense of measure, is best seen in the Cenotaph, Whitehall (1919), in which he also used a system of optical correction calculated upon the measurements of the Parthenon. Of these monuments Etaples (France, 1920) is outstanding, and Thiepval (France, 1924), more austere, combines a feeling for Gothic verticality with classical symmetry. Lutyens wrote little about his work, preferring to design. He was imaginative and versatile, but not an innovator. He has been criticized for his lack of explicit sympathy with modern ideas, but his work is unmistakably modern in expression. EK

C. Hussey, *The Life of Sir Edwin Lutyens* (London, 1950); A. S. G. Butler *et al.*, *The Architecture of Sir Edwin Lutyens* (3 vols, London, 1950); R. Gradidge, *Edwin Lutyens, Architect Laureate* (London, 1981).

Luxemburg, Rosa (b. Zamosc, Poland, 5.3.1871; naturalized German citizen, 1898; d. Berlin, Germany, 15.1.1919). Polish/German revolutionary. Of Jewish middle-class origin, after finishing at a Warsaw *Gimnazium*, Luxemburg became a member of a Socialist group and, facing arrest, escaped in 1889 to Switzerland, where she received a doctorate from Zürich University for a thesis on Polish industrial development (*Die industrielle Entwicklung Polens* [The industrial development of Poland], Leipzig, 1898). She became one of the leaders of the Social Democratic Party of the Kingdom of Poland and Lithuania (a precursor of the Polish Communist party), continuing her ties with the SDKPiL even after she settled in Berlin in 1898. Here she acquired German citizenship and became a prominent member of the German Social Democrats. She took an active part in the revisionist controversy as an implacable critic of E. BERNSTEIN, chiefly in the columns of *Die Neue Zeit* and in her speeches at the congresses of the party and of the Socialist International in which she became the leader of the left wing. In her article on social reform and revolution in the *Leipziger Volkszeitung* (1898), reissued as a pamphlet (*Sozialreform oder Revolution*, Leipzig, 1899; *Social Reform or Revolution*, NY, 1937), she summarized all the arguments against the belief in the possibility of reforming capitalism and in favour of revolutionary political action.

When the revolution broke out in 1905 in Russia, Luxemburg returned to Russian Poland, and was arrested in Warsaw. She spent some time in prison in 1906 and returned to Berlin after she was released on bail on health grounds. In Germany she taught at the SD party school and developed ideas about the general strike as a political weapon. She criticized LENIN for his 'opportunism' and 'centralism' which according to her were based on a distrust in the revolutionary potential of the workers' movement. She was also critical of Lenin's acceptance of the idea of national self-determination, but defended him from his Menshevik critics who charged him with 'Blanquism'. In 1912 Luxemburg produced her major theoretical work *Die Akkumulation des Kapitals* (Berlin, 1913; *The Accumulation of Capital*, ed. J. Robinson, London, 1971), in which she tried to prove, on the basis of an analysis of the process of capital reproduction since MARX, that capitalism was doomed and would inevitably collapse on economic grounds.

She was strongly opposed to WW1 and already in 1907 had proposed the thesis that if war broke out, the opportunity should be used to transform it into a Socialist revolution. She was sentenced to a year in prison in 1915 for antiwar speeches; released in 1916, only to be re-arrested four months later. While in prison she wrote the 'Junius pamphlet' about the crisis of social democracy which she attributed to the class collaboration of its reformist leaders in supporting the imperialist war. She argued that the only way out was a socialist revolution, the ideological basis for the creation in 1916 of the Spartacus league. Luxemburg continued to write antiwar tracts from prison (known as *Spartakusbriefe*, or Spartacus letters).

They were distributed illegally by members of the *Spartakusbund* [Spartacus league], which after her release in November 1918 was transformed by her and Karl Liebknecht into the Communist party of Germany. Her pamphlet *Die Russische Revolution* (ed. P. Levi, Berlin, 1922; *The Russian Revolution and Leninism or Marxism*, ed. B. D. Wolfe, Ann Arbor, 1961), which she also wrote in prison, was published only in 1922. In it she welcomed the October revolution as a precursor of world revolution, but strongly criticized Lenin and the Bolsheviks for their national and agrarian policies, and in particular for their dictatorial rule and destruction of freedom. The attempted uprising by the Spartacus league was a failure. Two months later (on the night of 15/16.1.1919) Rosa Luxemburg and Karl Liebknecht were murdered by Freikorps troops. LL

J. P. Nettl, *Rosa Luxemburg* (2 vols, London, 1966).

Lu Xun (Lu Hsün), ps. of Zhou Shuren (Chou Shu-jen) (b. Shaohsing, Chekiang, China, 1881; d. Shanghai, 19.10.1936). Chinese short-story writer, critic and polemicist. After studying in Japan (1901–9), he became a teacher and minor official in the Ministry of Education in Nanjing and Beijing. In 1918, following the Literary Revolution, he published his first short story in the vernacular, 'Diary of a Madman'. Here and in his collected stories, *Nahan* [Call to arms] (Shanghai, 1923), of which the most famous is 'The True Story of Ah Q', he expressed the cruelty, servility and hypocrisy of unawakened China with biting irony and deep compassion for its victims. From 1926 he turned to polemical articles and essays of which he wrote over 600. After holding university posts briefly in Amoy and Canton, he moved in 1927 to Shanghai where he became a founding member of the League of Left-wing Writers and the centre of a circle of radical intellectuals and artists. In the 1930s he was regarded as the spokesman and conscience of Chinese youth, on whom his influence was profound. Although he never joined the Communist party, before his death he saw it as the only hope for China. He strongly influenced MAO TSE-TUNG's thinking, particularly on aesthetics, and has become the object of unqualified adulation by the leaders of the People's Republic of China. For translations of his work see *Silent China: Selected Writings of Lu Xun*, ed. G. Yang (London, 1973). MS

Lynd, Robert Staughton (b. New Albany, Ind., USA, 26.9.1892; d. New York, 1.11.1970) and **Lynd, Helen,** *née* Merrell (b. La Grange, Ill., 17.3.1896; d. Warren, Ohio, 30.1.1982). American sociologists, husband and wife, who produced two classic sociological studies of Muncie, Indiana, published as *Middletown: a Study in Contemporary American Culture* (NY, 1929) and *Middletown in Transition: a Study in Cultural Conflicts* (NY, 1937). Robert Lynd had worked in publishing before being appointed to teach sociology at Columbia University (from 1931). Helen Merrell, whom he married in 1921, taught at Sarah Lawrence College. Their joint work was the first attempt to apply the field methods of social anthropology to a modern western urban community, e.g. in treating the middle class as a tribe. Written in the native American 'muckraking' tradition of social and political commentary, *Middletown* also reflects the influence of MARXism under the impact of the depression. During WW2 Helen Lynd broke new ground with a study in English social history, *England in the Eighteen Eighties: Toward a Social Basis for Freedom* (NY, 1945). ALCB

Lynen, Feodor (b. Munich, Bavaria, Germany, 6.4.1911; d. Munich, West Germany, 6.8.1979). German biochemist. Educated in Munich, Lynen ultimately became professor of biochemistry and director of the Biochemical Institute at Munich University and director of the Max-Planck Institut für Biochemie in 1953. His scientific interests have included the metabolism of cholesterol and of fatty acids, the control of metabolism, and the biochemistry of acetoacetate formation. Like his fellow Nobel laureate of 1964, Konrad BLOCH, Lynen worked on the biosynthesis of cholesterol in humans, i.e. on the complex biochemical mechanism whereby choles-terol is formed from acetate, through the intermediacy of 'activated acetate', a species which he discovered. His work on biosynthesis (and that of Bloch) is conceptually related to that of CORNFORTH. NBC

Lysenko, Trofim Denisovitch (b. Kerlovka, Russia, 17.9.1898; d. Kiev, USSR, 20.11.1976). Russian agronomist. After early research into plant physiol-ogy and development, some of which had legitimate intellectual fruit, Lysenko became a spokesman for highly uncon-ventional theories of inheritance based upon the work of a Russian horticultur-ist I. V. Michurin. His attacks upon MENDELian genetics were extremely fierce and were officially endorsed by the Communist party of the USSR in 1948. There followed a period in which the whole of biology in the USSR, but especially genetics, was ravaged by ideo-logical conflict. Serious scientists were pilloried, laboratories closed or trans-formed into havens of 'Michurinist' biol-ogy, and the teaching and practice of biology perverted. It seems clear that Lysenko himself connived at these abuses and used his position as presi-dent of the Lenin Academy of Agricul-tural Sciences to do so. He was discred-ited after the death of STALIN, and long before his own death, but the damage done to Soviet science was not easily to be repaired. His views are summarized in his *O nasledstvennosti i ee izmenchivosti* (Moscow, 1943; *Heredity and its Variability*, NY, 1946) and in *O polozhenii v biologichesko nauke* (Mos-cow, 1948; *The Situation in Biological Science*, London, 1948). DRN

E. Ashby, *Scientist in Russia* (Harmondsworth, 1947); Z. A. Medvedev, *The Rise and Fall of T. D. Lysenko* (NY, 1969).

M

MacDiarmid, Hugh, ps. of Christopher Murray Grieve (b. Langholm, Dumfries & Gall., UK, 11.8.1892; d. Edinburgh, Lothian, 9.9.1978). Scottish poet, widely regarded as 'the most powerful intellectually and emotionally fertilizing force Scotland has known since the death of Burns'. Son of a rural postman, he returned from WW1 determined to revitalize his own 'small nation'. His achievement as a poet was built on the highly concentrated lyrics in *Sangschaw* (Edinburgh, 1925) and *Penny Wheep* (Edinburgh, 1926) and the sustained inventiveness of *A Drunk Man Looks at the Thistle* (Edinburgh, 1926), which merits a place among the great poems of this century. These were written in Scots, the national language of Scotland prior to its systematic anglicization. MacDiarmid's revival of Scots within the national literary tradition was supported by a lively awareness of modern developments in European poetry, and was consolidated in the better parts of his next three volumes, *To Circumjack Cencrastus* (Edinburgh, 1930), *First Hymn to Lenin* (London, 1931) and *Scots Unbound* (Stirling, 1932). He then turned largely to English, experimenting with scientific and other specialized resources of the vocabulary, and combining nationalist, political and economic propaganda (for social credit in the short term, communism in the long term) with a return to what he saw as the Celtic roots of civilization. The latter was to emerge as a main theme of projects for epic works, only fragments of which achieved publication subsequent to *Stony Limits* (London, 1934), a collection centring on the intellectual austerities of his exile in Shetland, and *Second Hymn to Lenin* (London, 1935). The work of his final period was designed as an epic 'poetry of fact', recording the impact of a world of information on a mind determined to reclaim for poetry the lost territories of the 'prosaic'. Two parts of this never-completed epic were published as *In Memoriam James Joyce* (Glasgow, 1955) and *The Kind of Poetry I Want* (Edinburgh, 1961). A partially *Collected Poems* (NY, 1962), followed by the *Complete Poems* (London, 1978), confirmed the astonishing range of an erratic but invigorating and greatly gifted poet. KB

K. Buthlay, *Hugh MacDiarmid* (Edinburgh, ²1982); E. Morgan, *Hugh MacDiarmid* (Harlow, 1976).

Mach, Ernst (b. Turas, Moravia, Austria-Hungary [now Czechoslovakia], 18.2.1838; d. Haar, nr Munich, Bavaria, Germany, 19.2.1916). Austrian physicist and philosopher. As much a philosopher as a physicist, Mach was an amateur in neither. After a short period at Graz he held the chair of physics at Prague from 1867 to 1895, when he became the first professor of 'inductive philosophy' in Vienna, retiring in 1901. In physics he worked on problems in optics and acoustics, fields calculated to excite philosophical interest in knowledge, and also in the study and recording of rapid motion. His name is preserved in the use of the speed of sound as a unit for the measurement of very high speeds. His enthusiasm for the rationality of the Enlightenment made him hostile to obscurantism in general and to unempirical speculation in science in particular. To preserve its claim to pre-eminent credibility, he believed, science must fully establish its empirical credentials. That meant that all terms in science purporting to refer to what cannot be perceived (such as 'atom', 'force', 'causal connection') must be defined in terms of what really is perceived, which is not physical objects but sensations. Mach's phenomenalist view that all terms not referring to immediate experience are no more than symbolic devices for economy in thought influenced William JAMES and Bertrand RUSSELL and, more directly, philosophers of the Vienna circle such as CARNAP and SCHLICK. Mach was vehemently criticized in LENIN's amateurish effusion *Materialism and Empirio-criticism* (1909). AQ

MACHADO

R. von Mises, *Positivism* (NY, 1968).

Machado, Antonio (b. Seville, Spain, 26.7.1875; d. Collioure, Pyrénées-Orientales, France, 22.2.1939). One of the two greatest Spanish poets of this century (the other being LORCA). Often described as the poet of the 'Generation of 1898', Machado shared its heart-searching preoccupation with Spain's decline and the chances of a return to greatness, as well as its interest in the nature of the Spanish 'soul' as mirrored in Spain's landscape; but he developed a very personal poetry within this context. Born an Andalusian, his family moved to Madrid when he was eight, and he and his brother Manuel (a lesser poet) went to school at the Institución Libre de Enseñanza – the great centre of Spanish liberal thought. His earliest collections were *Soledades* [Solitudes] (Madrid, 1903) and *Soledades, galerías y otros poemas* [Solitudes, galleries and other poems] (Madrid, 1907). Having graduated from Madrid University, he was appointed to teach French in 1907 in Soria, a small Castilian city living largely in the past. There he spent his happiest years, marrying the 16-year-old Leonor (1909), who died in 1912; his identification with the harsh Castilian landscape, coloured first by his happiness and then by his anguished sense of loss, produced the austere poetry of *Campos de Castilla* (Madrid, 1912, amplified 1915; selections tr. W. Barnstone, in *Eighty Poems*, NY, 1959; tr. C. Tomlinson & H. Gifford, *Castilian Ilexes*, London, 1963) by which he is best known, remarkably un-Spanish in its habitual economy and frequent understatement. After Leonor's death, he obtained a transfer to Baeza (back in Andalusia), and the poems added in the 1915 edition include some of his finest, heightened by their double sense of loss (for his teenage wife, and for the Castilian landscape with which she was identified), as well as some succinct philosophical 'parables'. His *Poesías completas* [Complete poems] appeared in Madrid in 1917, subsequent poetry being added in successive editions. He also created two fictitious heteronyms as prose-vehicles for his thought, *Abel Martín* (Madrid, 1931) and *Juan de Mairena* (Madrid, 1936; tr. B. Belitt, *Juan de Mairena: Epigrams, Maxims, Memoranda, and Memoirs of an Apocryphal Professor*, Berkeley, Calif., 1963), equipping each with his own poetry. Identified with the Republican cause in the Spanish civil war, he was ailing when he joined the exodus of refugees over the French border in January 1939, dying the following month. Eclipsed by Lorca during and immediately after the civil war, his reputation has since grown steadily. He remains a potent influence on present-day poetry.   RP-M

N. L. Hutman, *Machado: a Dialogue with Time* (Albuquerque, N. Mex., 1969); A. Terry, *Antonio Machado: Campos de Castilla* (London, 1973).

MacIver, Robert Morrison (b. Stornoway, Western Isles, UK, 17.4.1882; naturalized American citizen; d. New York, USA, 15.6.1970). British/American sociologist and political theorist. Educated at Edinburgh, he first taught at Aberdeen University, moving to Toronto in 1915. From 1927 he was at Columbia University with a chair in political philosophy and sociology. He was president, subsequently chancellor, of the New School for Social Research, New York, in 1963–6. MacIver was very much of a philosopher by training and outlook, and his approach to sociology reflected a fundamental concern to have a sound, clearly articulated theoretical framework, particularly in the light of the empirically oriented approach of American sociology in the 1920s. Of key importance in his thought was the distinction, derived from TÖNNIES, between 'community', or the all-embracing, omnipurpose unit, and 'association', or the limited group with restricted ends. These sociological categories structure his political theory, with its repeated insistence on distinguishing society from the state, which is an association serving limited ends. *The Modern State* (London, 1926) is an analysis and justification of a pluralist, liberal democratic state which ranks high in that tradition.   DCr

Mackinder, Halford John (b. Gainsborough, Lincs., UK, 15.2.1861; d. Parkstone, Dorset, 6.3.1947). British geogra-

470

pher widely known for his heartland thesis of political power-balance introduced in a paper of 1904. From a study of world environmental contrasts in relation to the military logistics prevailing at the time, Mackinder argued that world control implied strategic control of the Eurasian continents. To command Eurasia meant controlling its inner heartland area, while to control the heartland meant controlling the East European plain. By the heartland of Eurasia, Mackinder demarcated an area roughly comparable to that currently occupied by the USSR. Mackinder expanded the original, highly simplified model in *Democratic Ideas and Reality* (London, 1919). His continued insistence on the geopolitical significance of the East European plain has been argued to be one element in shaping German strategic thinking in WW2, as set out by Karl Haushofer. Mackinder's contribution to geography should be seen in a wider context. He worked tirelessly to raise the quality of geography as an academic field in England, first as a reader at Oxford (1887–1905) and subsequently director and first professor of geography at the London School of Economics (1905–25). PH

E. W. Gilbert, *Sir Halford Mackinder, 1861–1947* (London, 1961); B. W. Blouzet, *Sir Halford Mackinder: Some New Perspectives* (London, 1975).

Mackintosh, Charles Rennie (b. Glasgow, Strath., UK, 7.6.1868; d. London, 10.12.1928). British architect and designer. Mackintosh was a central figure of the art nouveau movement in the UK. He criticized his contemporaries who relied on historical styles for their inspiration, striving instead to find a wholly fresh, modern approach to design. He did not, however, reject the past altogether, studying vernacular buildings on his early travels and embodying some of their character in his house designs, notably Hill House, Helensburgh (1902–3). This fusion of traditional Scottish vernacular building with functional architecture is probably best exemplified in his design for the Glasgow School of Art (1898–9). Mackintosh believed that the architect should be an 'art worker' rather than the leader

of a commercial practice, and thought that the lowering of the standard of current work was due to the schism between architecture and fine art. He shared this idea with William Morris, but rejected the medievalism of the Arts and Craft movement. He trained first as an evening student at the Glasgow School of Art and was then articled to the architect John Hutchinson in whose practice he learnt skills later to be of much use to him, including furniture-making and design which took place in a shop in front of the office. His greatest patron was Catherine Cranston, for whom he and his wife, the painter Margaret Macdonald, designed the interiors of several Glasgow tea rooms. Their designs extended beyond spatial originality to include distinctive furniture, light fittings, stencilled wall patterns and tableware. The work impressed members of the Viennese Sezession movement, who invited Mackintosh and his wife to design the interior of a flat for an exhibition in 1900 in Vienna; it was considered sensational by the Austrians, but in his own country he found limited success as an architect. In later life he left Glasgow for the south of England where he turned his energies to watercolour painting, working at Walberswick, Suffolk, and then, after a period at Port Vendres, France, in Chelsea, London. Mackintosh is today recognized as an important figure in the development of modern architecture and is included as one of the leaders in PEVSNER's *Pioneers of the Modern Movement* (1936).
NW

T. Howarth, *Charles Rennie Mackintosh and the Modern Movement* (London, 1952); R. Billcliffe, *Mackintosh Watercolours* (London, 1978).

Maclean, Sorley (b. Isle of Raasay, Inner Hebrides, UK, 26.10.1911). Scottish poet. Through his family background Maclean inherited the powerful influence of Gaelic lore and traditional music, the radical politics of the Land Agitation, and the Nonconformist dissent of the Gaelic Presbyterian Evangelical movement with its rigorous theology and the magniloquence of its extempore sermons and prayers. But it was MARXism which gave him a coherent view of history, enabling him, for instance, to bring together the Highland Clearances and the success of fascism in Spain in the 1930s as related events in the same historical process. A schoolmaster in Scotland throughout his working life, he thrust Gaelic poetry into 'modernity' with *Dàin do Eimhir agus Dàin Eile* [Poems to Eimhir and other poems] (Glasgow, 1943), a collection which finally broke the constraints of that lingering medievalism fostered by the historical circumstances of Gaelic society. Personal emotions mesh with political passions in this powerful sequence of love poems. Here as elsewhere he frequently expresses himself through a dialectical mode in which symbols are pitted against each other. In 1977 he published a selection from his poems written between 1932 and 1972, *Reothairt is Contraigh* [Spring tide and neap tide] (Edinburgh). JMacI

D. MacAmhlaigh (ed.), *Nua-bhàrdachd Ghàidhlig/Modern Scottish Gaelic Poems* [by Sorley Maclean, etc.] (Edinburgh, 1976).

Macmillan, (Maurice) Harold (b. London, UK, 10.2.1894). British member of Parliament (1924–64), cabinet minister (1942–5, 1951–7), prime minister (1957–64). Before 1939 Macmillan was associated with a group of MPs of various parties who looked for an acceptable programme of government-sponsored and -financed industrial and political reform (the *Middle Way* proclaimed in his book of 1934) while opposing CHAMBERLAIN's policy of appeasement. From 1951 to 1957 he was the leader in the cabinet of the pro-European group which evolved the idea of a European Free Trade Area, but too late to forestall or supplant the establishment of the European Common Market. As premier, he presided over the rapid transfer of power to African hands of the British empire in Africa, while attempting firstly to mend the Anglo-American ties so severely damaged at Suez under EDEN, and then, having failed to secure American aid against EEC, to secure British entry into EEC. He saw Britain as 'Athens' guiding and civilizing the power of the USA ('Rome'), perhaps coming closest to this relationship with President

KENNEDY, most notably in the negotiation of the Partial Test Ban Treaty in 1963, but this vision was irreconcilable with that of DE GAULLE. In domestic matters Macmillan practised a mildly interventionist policy which secured a remarkable degree of house construction (1951–4) but led to increasing criticism from the Conservative right, as even the creation of the National Economic Development Council ('Neddy'), in 1961, a cautious experiment in corporativism, failed to solve the basis problems of underinvestment, underproductivity and restrictive practices both among business and labour, or the 'stop–go' alternation in the management of the British economy that this necessitated. Macmillan published four volumes of memoirs: *Winds of Change, 1914–39* (London, 1966); *The Blast of War, 1939 –45* (London, 1967); *Tides of Fortune, 1945–55* (London, 1969); and *Riding the Storm, 1956–9* (London, 1971). DCW

MacNeice, Louis (b. Belfast, Ireland [now Northern Ireland], UK, 12.9.1907; d. London, 3.9.1963). British poet. He was associated with that 1930s radical, left-wing group of writers, modernist in style, which included AUDEN, Stephen Spender, ISHERWOOD and Cecil Day Lewis. MacNeice was educated at Marlborough and Oxford; he lectured at Birmingham in classics under E. R. DODDS, later his executor and editor, and continued a love/hate affair with Ireland all his life. On returning from the USA to his wartime work with the BBC, he began a career in broadcasting as a producer and dramatist which continued for many years. His radio plays include an admired translation of the *Agamemnon* of Aeschylus (London, 1936) and *The Dark Tower* (London, 1947). *Letters from Iceland* (with W. H. Auden, London, 1937) and his verse *Autumn Journal* (London, 1939) convey his disillusionment with contemporary society in the aftermath of the Spanish civil war and the rise of fascism. He was never attracted by communism, however, and the influence of his Church of Ireland upbringing (his father became bishop of Dromore) becomes apparent from 'An Eclogue for Christmas' (1933) onwards; and his respect for human life is clear in 'Prayer Before Birth' (1944). MacNeice was a radical humanist with a Christian background, searching for meaning. Poems like *Autumn Sequel* (London, 1954) and 'On the Four Masters' betray the unease of the Protestant writer in the face of Irish affairs; but his casual, colloquial style has influenced later Northern Irish poets. See *Collected Poems of Louis MacNeice* (ed. E. R. Dodds, London, 1966). KEDH

D. B. Moore, *The Poetry of Louis MacNeice* (Leicester, 1972).

Magritte, René-François-Ghislain (b. Lessines, Hainaut, Belgium, 2.11.1898; d. Brussels, 15.8.1967). Belgian painter. The eldest of three brothers, Magritte spent his childhood in small Belgian towns, the moves dictated by his father's business ventures. When he was 12 his mother drowned herself during the night in the river Sambre without any explanation. In 1913 he met his wife-to-be on a merry-go-round at a fair in Chaileroi, and re-met her by chance at the botanical gardens in Brussels in the early 1920s. Between these encounters he had become a painter. In 1927 the Magrittes moved to a suburb of Paris where he was in daily if not always harmonious contact with BRETON and the French surrealists. In 1930 he returned to Brussels and, with the exception of a few short visits abroad, spent the rest of his life there; a life on the surface as regular and unexceptional as that of a civil servant. His circle was the writers and poets of the Belgian surrealist group.

Magritte started as a 'modernist', influenced mainly by the Italian futurists although tempered by a tender eroticism. A reproduction of CHIRICO's *Love Song* (a classical cast, rubber glove and a ball) reduced him to rare tears and entirely changed his direction. From then on he saw his task as putting reality and its laws to the test, at first by bringing into confrontation certain objects, later by the dialectic resolution of such encounters. An early picture *Les Objects Familiers* (1927) depicts five men in front of whose faces are suspended a shell, a sponge, a jug, a lemon and a bow, whereas in *Le Mouvement Perpetuel* (1935) a strong man is about to lift some dumbbells, one of whose iron balls has replaced his head and carries his features. Magritte explained that this form of visual pun came to him on awakening one night in a room which he knew to contain a bird in a cage and imagining that the bird had been replaced not by, say, a shoe, which would have been a conventional surrealist image, but by a huge egg, thus opening the way to poetic speculation.

Magritte, unlike DALI, never relied on delirium. He thought through his ideas in a perfectly conscious manner. The deadpan execution suspended the spectator's disbelief. Magritte was insistent that no psychological or symbolic aspects were involved. To begin with his technique was limited. Later, through daily application, he became adept. Nevertheless his aim was unaltered; to challenge and evoke the mystery of our world and its laws without recourse to supernatural explanations. The same objects (amongst them the bowler hat, the tuba, harness-bells, fire, stone) and many of the same themes (e.g. night and day, scale, transparency, weight, 'art' itself) recur in his work. There is a hint of the influence of PICASSO in the massive figures he painted towards the end of the 1920s, and two interesting moments of aberration. In 1943, following a directive from the Communist party (of which he was briefly a member) that art should be 'optimistic', he painted for a time in the manner of late Renoir; while in 1948 he produced some fauvist paintings, largely to irritate the French. Otherwise his work was consistently realistic as far as was within his means. He is amongst the greatest creators of poetic images in our time. GM

P. Waldberg, *René Magritte* (London, 1965); S. Gablik, *Magritte* (London, 1973).

Mahler, Gustav (b. Kalischt, Bohemia, Austria-Hungary [now Kaliště, Czechoslovakia], 7.7.1860; d. Vienna, Austria, 18.5.1911). Austrian composer. Often derided during the composer's lifetime and later subjected to neglect, since WW2 Mahler's music has gradually reached a high peak of popularity. Qualities which earlier generations regarded as repulsive or absurd – his intense emotionalism, magniloquence and willingness to sweep rapidly from the sublime to the vulgar, the heroic to the ironic – have endeared him to audiences in an age not responsive to large statements of personal feeling. His ability to encompass doubt, anxiety and contradiction within his work makes him a peculiarly modern artist.

Mahler spent his professional life as a conductor, holding important posts at the Hamburg Opera (1891–7), at the Vienna Court Opera (1897–1907) and ultimately in New York. His composing was largely confined to summer holidays, and his output was small, though consisting almost exclusively of works on a large scale. Chief among these are the nine symphonies – eleven if one counts the unnumbered symphony *Das Lied von der Erde* [Song of the earth] (1911) and the unfinished Tenth, of which a performing version was made by Deryck Cooke (1964). Mahler's other works, most of them orchestral songs, can be considered as satellites of the symphonies, containing ideas which were developed and intertwined in their greater neighbours. Further connections of musical theme and form exist from one symphony to another, so that the *oeuvre* becomes one vast confessional work. The early chapters of that work are contained in the cantata *Das klagende Lied* (completed 1880, performed 1901), the song cycle *Lieder eines fahrenden Gesellen* [Songs of a wayfarer] (composed 1883–5, performed 1896) and the First Symphony (1889). All of these are immediately characteristic in musical style and expressive impulse. Their view of nature as a mirror of feeling is a stock romantic device, but the expression is that of an artist out of joint with his world, and the language is filled with those inconsistencies and dislocations with which Mahler exposed his emotions.

His next group of works, including the Second, Third and Fourth symphonies (1895, 1897, 1901), was nourished by the naive poetry of the early romantic collection *Das Knaben Wunderhorn* [The boy's magic horn]. Music from his settings of these poems filtered into the symphonies, but the flow of sentimental lyricism is accommodated in the Second

and Third within massive dramatic structures calling for solo voices, choirs and large orchestra. The demands of these works are exceeded only by those of the Eighth Symphony (1910), which consists of two immense panels setting the hymn *Veni Creator Spiritus* and the final scene from Goethe's *Faust*. Before this latter work came three purely orchestral symphonies (1904, 1906, 1908) which nevertheless share aspects of tone and musical idea with Mahler's contemporary Rückert songs, notably the cycle *Kindertotenlieder* [Songs on the death of children] (1905). Images of doom and frenzied anxiety become particularly forceful in the Fifth and Sixth Symphonies, the latter having a funeral march finale punctuated by the hammer-blows of fate. In his last works Mahler moved into resignation and farewell, though he still had room for devastating parody. *Das Lied von der Erde*, which in its earlier moments has a vigour only slightly stylized by a chinoiserie suggested by the exotic texts, becomes at last a great song of spiritual departure; the same feeling returns in the slow finale to the Ninth Symphony (1912), where, even more than in its predecessors, the logic of emotion dictates musical form.   PG

A. M. Mahler, *Gustav Mahler: Memories and Letters* (NY, 1946); M. Kennedy, *Mahler* (London, 1974).

Mailer, Norman (b. Long Branch, NJ, USA, 31.1.1923). American novelist. In a long literary career Mailer has published only five novels. His stature as a novelist has been virtually swamped by interest in his nonfiction prose, from political journalism like *The Armies of the Night* (NY, 1968) to biographical fantasies on the life and death of MONROE (*Marilyn*, NY, 1973). He is never less than controversial, and seldom out of the public eye. Yet it is harder now, after some 20 volumes of nonfiction prose over the past two decades, to believe that Mailer will produce a major work of imaginative literature. He published three novels between 1948 and 1955, showing a restless experimental intelligence. *The Naked and the Dead* (NY, 1948), a war novel in the realistic tradition, was followed by a KAFKAn political allegory in *Barbary*

Shore (NY, 1951), and by a novel set in a California resort, *The Deer Park* (NY, 1955). Subsequent novels *An American Dream* (NY, 1965) and *Why Are We in Vietnam?* (NY, 1967) have more the energy of argument than the force of realized life. Mailer's energies have been diverted elsewhere, beginning with *Advertisements for Myself* (NY, 1959), a collection of essays and other prose from the 1940s and 1950s. It is hard not to feel that Mailer is the most spectacular casualty, and the most representative figure, in postwar American literature.

EH

R. Solotaroff, *Down Mailer's Way* (Urbana, 1974); H. Mills, *Mailer: a Biography* (NY, 1982).

Makarenko, Anton Semyonovich (b. Belopol'ye, Ukraine, Russia, 13.3.1888; d. Moscow, USSR, 1.4.1939). Russian educator. Son of a railway painter, Makarenko became director of a teachers' institute at Poltava in 1919. In 1920, after a brush with the authorities, he was put in charge of a colony of delinquents near Kharkhov, renamed the Maxim GORKY colony. There he developed his ideas based upon strict discipline, conformity with the collective, and the shaping of 'the new Soviet man' as a Communist ideal. At that period many Soviet educators were open to 'progressive' ideas as represented by John DEWEY and other North Americans, and Makarenko was severely criticized; but in 1927, with STALIN in power and a repressive reaction in education, Makarenko became director at Kharkhov of a new commune for homeless orphans, at that time an acute problem, and he travelled widely, especially after 1935, lecturing on educational problems. His emphasis on discipline, work and the collective served the apparatus of state control as Stalin envisaged it, rather than earlier communist ideals of morality and culture experienced in 'polytechnical' learning throughout life. Dealing with a captive group, Makarenko's prolific writings contributed little to educational theory and practice for a wider population, especially those trying to link schools with life and work through the 'polytechnical principle' from 1958 onwards.

Thus the experiment soon became little more than a formality.

EJK

Malamud, Bernard (b. New York, USA, 26.4.1914). American novelist. Brought up in the Jewish enclave of Brooklyn and educated in New York, Malamud has absorbed the experience and mores of that subculture into his fiction, often as a metaphor for a wider human condition, although rejecting as reductive the label Jewish-American writer. He has combined teaching with writing, and received several American awards, including a National Book award for *The Magic Barrel* (NY, 1958), and another, together with a Pulitzer prize, for *The Fixer* (NY, 1966). While often comic and highly inventive, he is essentially a humanistic writer who believes that fiction can still be a vehicle for truth; his characteristic themes include an examination of the necessity for moral involvement and the value of suffering, as in *The Assistant* (NY, 1957) and *The Fixer*, and a preoccupation with the process of growth and development, that search for a new direction which involves most of his characters, as in *A New Life* (NY, 1961) or *Dubin's Lives* (NY, 1979). A common motif in his work is that of the prison, often metaphorical or self-inflicted, from which his protagonists must struggle to escape, usually into the recognition and assumption of responsibility. His marriage in 1946 to an Italian provided access to a different cultural background, suggested in *Pictures of Fidelman* (NY, 1969). A leading figure in the liberal humanist tradition, Malamud's hard-won affirmations seek to combat the nihilism which continually threatens his times.

KGM

S. Richman, *Bernard Malamud* (NY, 1966).

Malaparte, Curzio, ps. of Kurt Erich Suckert (b. Prato, Tuscany, Italy, 9.6.1898; d. Rome, 19.7.1957). Italian novelist and journalist. At least in his political involvement and his polemical and scintillating prose style, Malaparte has something in common with D'ANNUNZIO. From 16 until practically the end of his life he took part in military action on several occasions both in

Italy and abroad – fighting on the French, Finnish and Russian fronts – and two of his better-known novels *Kaputt* (Naples, 1944; tr. C. Foligno, London, 1948) and *La pelle* (Rome, 1949; tr. D. Moore, *The Skin*, London, 1952) relate to those experiences. Proudly conscious – perhaps too much so – of his cultural roots and tradition and at the same time in rebellion against them, Malaparte, as a writer and as a soldier-patriot, found the vicissitudes of Europe – and Italy's place in them – focal points of his artistic and journalistic career. A republican till 1921, he joined the Fascist party, but as a result of the publication of his play *Technique du coup d'état* (Paris, 1931; tr. S. Saunders, *Coup d'état: the Technique of Revolution*, NY, 1932), he was accused of antifascist activities and sentenced to five years' imprisonment. At the end of WW2 Malaparte became a liaison officer between the Allies and the Italian army. Before his death he converted from Protestantism to Catholicism.   GS

A. J. De Grand, 'Curzio Malaparte: the illusion of the fascist revolution', *Journal of Contemporary History*, 7 (1972), 73–89.

Malcolm X, ps. of Malcolm Little, alias Hajj Malik El-Shabazz (b. Omaha, Nebr., USA, 19.5.1925; d. New York, 21.2.1965). Extremist US black political leader. Son of a follower of Marcus Garvey and a West Indian mother of mixed race, he abandoned a career as a racketeer while in prison in 1952 on conversion to the 'Nation of Islam', taking the name of Malcolm X, thus rejecting his surname as a relic of Negro slavery. An extremely effective orator, his rejection of the total separation of the Nation of Islam from US society as advocated by Elijah Mohammed in favour of an interracial civil war in America, led to his expulsion from the USA in 1963. Having founded his own Organization of Afro-Americans, he sought and won the support of African and Arab states, embraced orthodox Islam and went on a pilgrimage to Mecca, winning an international reputation. He was assassinated in 1965, alleg-edly by members of the Nation of Islam.   DCW

Mâle, Emile (b. Commentry, Allier, France, 2.6.1862; d. Paris, 6.10.1954). French art historian. An outstanding student, Mâle began teaching while continuing with his research. The publication of his thesis *L'Art religieux du XIIIᵉ siècle en France* (Paris, 1898; *The Gothic Image*, London, 1913) brought him wide acclaim. He continued his medieval studies in a work on the later Middle Ages, and crowned the trilogy with *L'Art religieux du XIIᵉ siècle en France* (Paris, 1922; *Religious Art in France, the XIIth Century*, Princeton, 1978). These works are essentially of the 19c iconological tradition in French art history, but Mâle brought a thoroughness and breadth of reference quite his own. The last work, a pioneering one on a previously unfashionable period, confirmed the eastern sources of Romanesque iconography. Leaving his chair at the Sorbonne to teach in Rome encouraged Mâle to turn to other periods, and he applied his methodology in influential works on baroque and Early Christian cultures.   CF

Malevich, Kazimir (b. nr Kiev, Russia, 23.2.1878; d. Leningrad, USSR, 15.5.1935). Russian pioneer of nonfigurative painting. Strongly influenced by French cubism, particularly LÉGER's work of 1910–12, and stimulated by Russian poetic futurism, Malevich by 1915 had developed the semigeometrical abstract art which he called 'suprematism' and whose extreme examples were the 'White on White' paintings of 1917–18. By 1917 he had shown scores of such works in Petrograd and acquired several disciples. Then, after contributing to the early revolutionary street decorations, Malevich in 1919 went to the State Art Workshops at Vitebsk, where he formed the group called Unovis and soon displaced CHAGALL as the school's director. Here suprematism spread into applied design and three-dimensional models of a quasi-architectural kind, fed by Malevich's extensive theoretical writings (see *Essays on Art*, 2 vols, Copenhagen, 1968). Leaving in 1923 for the Leningrad 'Ginchuk' institute, he found dwindling official support, was criticized for his idealist and anarchist views, and by 1929 had returned to a more representational art. Damned thereafter as 'formalist' (and still counted as such today) his ideas meanwhile took root in the West with his Bauhaus book *Die gegenstandslose Welt* (Munich, 1927; *The Nonobjective World*, Chicago, 1959) and the large retrospective show of his work in Berlin in 1927.   JWMW

T. Andersen, *Malevich* (Amsterdam, 1970); L. Shadova, *Malevich: Suprematism and Revolution in Russian Art, 1910– 30* (London, 1982).

Malherbe, Ernst Gideon (b. Luckhoff, Orange Free State, South Africa, 8.11.1895; d. Salt Rock, Natal, 27.11.1982). South African educator. Harsh memories of the Anglo–Boer war (1899–1902), including scorched earth and the deaths of over 26,000 women and children in concentration camps, helped to dedicate Malherbe to reconciliation and restoration – with education as the prime means. Educated at Stellenbosch University (then Victoria College), Malherbe moved to the University of Cape Town (1924–9) when Sir Fred CLARKE was building up the education department. He had obtained a PhD at Columbia University, New York (1919– 22), with a thesis on *Education in South Africa from 1652* (1922; as vol. I of the same title, with vol. II covering the last 50 formative years, Cape Town, ²1977). This work's scholarship and political commitment to harmony and equality between all South Africans marked him as an educational statesman. He became director of the National Bureau for Educational and Social Research (1929– 39), now the Human Sciences Research Council, which continued outspoken advocacy of educational equality and reform in South Africa. During WW2 Malherbe became director of military intelligence (and thus uncovered many of the ramifications of the diehard Broederbond and Ossewa-Brandwag, still profoundly influential in nationalist politics), and chief of the Army Education Services. From 1945 to 1965 Malherbe was principal and vice-chancellor of the University of Natal, strongly championing its growth, independence and openness to all races. He was a prolific writer and made available otherwise inaccessible material on many aspects of education and life in South Africa. Though he was a loyal Afrikaner, yet a man of international stature, his writings have been embargoed in some Afrikaans universities. EJK

Malinowski, Bronislaw Kaspar (b. Cracow, Galicia, Austria-Hungary [now Kraków, Poland], 7.4.1884; d. New Haven, Conn., USA, 16.5.1942). Polish anthropologist. Born into an academic milieu, Malinowski studied physics and philosophy in Poland, then went to Leipzig, where he was influenced by the folk-psychology of Wundt. Choosing to specialize in anthropology, he proceeded to the London School of Economics, where he completed a thesis on the Australian family, based on secondary sources. In 1914 Malinowski found himself stranded by the outbreak of WW1 in Australia, where he was attending a scientific conference. He remained and carried out field studies, initially in New Guinea and then in the Trobriand Islands. While in the latter, between 1915 and 1918, he developed a method of field research of a qualitatively new kind. Living for an extended period among the people he was studying, speaking their language, participating in their activities (but never attempting to alter their ways), Malinowski invented what is now called 'participant-observation'. It proved particularly valuable for the investigation of exotic customs in context and from the actors' point of view.

In 1922 Malinowski took up a permanent position at the London School of Economics, and in the same year he published the first of his major Trobriand monographs *Argonauts of the Western Pacific*. Between 1922 and 1935 he produced a series of studies of Trobriand culture, each monograph being devoted to a specific aspect of island life: ceremonial exchange, family relations, gardening and magic, etc. All brought out the complex interrelationships between various activities, illustrating a perspective which came to be called 'functionalist'. Malinowski was also concerned with the contrast between the normative expectations about how people should behave and what they actually did, his point being that most people got away with as much as they could, and that consequently the traditional, formal accounts of custom were bound to be misleading. Malinowski propagated a utilitarian theory of culture. Culture provided the means to satisfy basic human needs, and it should be analysed accordingly. This variety of 'functionalism' had little influence, though Malinowski advocated it vigorously in a number of theoretical articles. While his theoretical formulations never provoked great interest, Malinowski's Trobriand studies initiated a new type of ethnographic study, his students producing a series of remarkable monographs on the basis of similar field studies elsewhere. During WW2 Malinowski taught at Yale, and wrote and lectured actively in support of the Allied cause.   AJK

Malraux, André (b. Paris, France, 3.11.1901; d. Paris, 23.11.1975). French novelist, art critic and politician. From the publication of *La Condition humaine* in 1933 (Paris; tr. S. Gilbert, *Man's Fate*, London, 1934) until his proclamation of support for de GAULLE's *Rassemblement du Peuple Français* in 1947, Malraux was widely admired as the model of the left-wing, committed writer. In 1935, in *Le Temps du mépris* (Paris; tr. H. M. Chevalier, *Days of Wrath*, London, 1936) he denounced HITLER's Germany, and in 1936 fought on the Republican side in the Spanish civil war, trying to organize the government airforce into a fighting unit capable of standing up against the German planes provided for FRANCO by Hitler. He himself regarded his novel about the first year of the Spanish civil war, *L'Espoir* (Paris, 1937; tr. S. Gilbert & A. MacDonald, *Man's Hope*, London, 1938), as his best novel, and it is certainly a more orthodox expression of support for communism than *La Condition humaine*, which nowadays reads very much as a denunciation of STALINist opportunism. Malraux fought in the resistance movement, but had already begun his move to the right as a

result of the Hitler–Stalin pact of August 1939. In postwar France he became one of the most active of Cold War warriors, but also developed less obviously political interests in *Les Voix du silence* (Paris, 1951; tr. S. Gilbert, *The Voices of Silence*, London, 1960) and in the three volumes of *La Métamorphose des dieux* (Paris, 1957; tr. S. Gilbert, *The Metamorphosis of the Gods*, London, 1960). Art, he maintained, could not be explained by any FREUDian or MARXist determinism, but was the way in which humanity proved the permanent nature of the human spirit by constantly calling the universe into question. Malraux's limitations as a man of action appeared after de Gaulle's return to power in 1958. He played little part in the events which led to the end of the Algerian war in 1962, but did succeed in reorganizing the Comédie-Française and having all the public monuments in Paris thoroughly cleaned. His work as a novelist often shows more affinities with Pascal, Dostoevsky or NIETZSCHE than with Marx or ORWELL, and his romantic cast of mind is revealed in striking, rhetorical remarks such as the comment that the death of God has already been followed by the death of man.   PMWT

W. M. Frohock, *André Malraux and the Tragic Imagination* (Stanford, Calif., 1952); J. Lacouture, *André Malraux: Une Vie dans le siècle* (Paris, 1973).

Mandela, Nelson Rolihlahia (b. Cape Province [now Transkei], South Africa, 1918). South African political leader. Sentenced to life imprisonment in 1964, Mandela has continued to be regarded inside and outside South Africa as the country's foremost black political leader. Making a name for himself in the Youth League of the African National Congress in the late 1940s, he was a political activist throughout the 1950s and went underground when the party was banned in 1960. Finding that peaceful forms of protest were no longer possible, Mandela reluctantly turned to nonterrorist forms of violence and organized *Umkonto we Sizwe* to carry out sabotage and prepare for guerrilla war. At the Rivonia trial of 1964, Mandela described himself as an 'African patriot' who believed that South Africa 'belonged to all the people who lived in it, not to one group' and aimed to bring about a 'nonracial democracy'.

RH

N. Mandela, *No Easy Walk to Freedom: Speeches and Trial Addresses* (London, 1965).

Mandel'shtam, Osip Emil'evich (b. Warsaw, Russian Poland [now Poland], 15.1.1891; d. nr Vladivostok, USSR, 27.12.1938). Russian poet. Mandel'shtam was born into a middle-class, cultured Jewish family and grew up in St Petersburg, which he immortalized in his poetry. He was educated in a modern anglicized school (Tenishev School), then in Paris (1907–8), Heidelberg (1909–10) and at the University of St Petersburg (1911–16). His first poems appeared in 1910, the same year as he met Gumilev and AKHMATOVA and became one of the founders of the Acmeist movement. His first collection of poetry *Kamén* [The stone] (St Petersburg, 1913) was written between the ages of 17 and 25. His collection *Tristia* (St Petersburg, 1922) is very sophisticated, highly intellectual, full of resonances of Homer, Ovid, Virgil and Dante, and of French and Russian poets, reflecting the Acmeists' 'nostalgic longing for world culture'. Between 1926 and 1930 he wrote no poetry, but continued to publish: two books of prose, *Shum Vremeni* [The noise of time] (Leningrad, 1925) and *Egipetskaya marka* [The Egyptian stamp] (Leningrad, 1928), both closely resembling his poetry; a book of critical essays *O Poezii* [On poetry] (Leningrad, 1928) and a collection called *Stikhotvokniya* [Poems] (Moscow, 1928). As a result of his trip to Armenia (1930) he wrote a cycle of poems *Armenia* (*Novy Mir*, 3, 1931), and an impressionistic prose sketch on the same subject (1932). This was his last published work.

From this point Mandel'shtam disappeared from literature until the 1960s when universal recognition came to him. In reality he lived mostly by translating and the generosity of friends. Although an epigram on STALIN led to his first arrest (1934) and ultimately his death, he did not oppose the political changes in Russia; 'his irony was enough to acknowledge the epic quality' of the revolution. He was doomed to destruction by the very nature of his poetry. He was exiled first to Cherdyn' (the Urals), where he tried to commit suicide, then to Voronezh (1934–7) where he continued to write the poetry now known as *Voronezhkie Tetradi* [The Voronezh notebooks] (Ann Arbor, 1980). The naked existential horror and rapid intensification of his spiritual life were expressed in the cryptic and dense imagery of his last poems. In the middle of 1937 the Mandel'shtams were allowed to return to Moscow. He was rearrested in 1938, sentenced to five years hard labour, and moved from one camp to another until he reached the very edge of Soviet territory – the Far East: 'When Space ended, he hit Time.' Today he looms larger than ever before, partly due to his widow Nadezhda Yakovlevna Mandel'shtam (*née* Khazina) (b. Saratov, 31.10.1899; d. Moscow, 29.12.1980). They met in Kiev in 1919 where she was studying art, and married in 1922. She accompanied him during his two exiles and dedicated her life to his poetry, memorizing it to keep it alive. At 65 she wrote two volumes of memoirs described as 'one of the greatest books of our era' (tr. M. Hayward, *Hope against Hope*, London, 1971; tr. M. Hayward, *Hope Abandoned*, London, 1973). They are not only the most reliable record of the poet's life but a testimony of her time; for Russians, they set a standard of moral and cultural authority. Collections of Mandel'shtam's works are: *Sobranie sochinenii* (3 vols, NY, 1967–9); and translations: *Selected Poems* (tr. D. McDuff, Cambridge, 1973); *50 poems* (tr. B. Meares, NY, 1977); *Poems* (tr. J. Greene, London, 1980); and *Complete Critical Prose and Letters* (tr. J. C. Harris & C. Link, Ann Arbor, 1979).

VP

J. Baines, *Mandel'shtam: the Later Poetry* (Cambridge, 1976); C. Brown, *Mandelstam* (NY, 1975).

Mann, Luis Heinrich (b. Lübeck, Schleswig-Holstein, Germany, 27.3.1871; d. Santa Monica, Calif., USA, 12.3.1950). German novelist and essayist. Heir to an old Lübeck patrician trading family,

Mann repudiated his inheritance and with it the inward-looking culture and authoritarian politics of his national tradition. His major achievements were to open the doors of German literary life to the French intellectual tradition of republicanism and literary *engagement*, and to establish the novel of social criticism as a viable form in Germany. Seeking to bring together literature and politics, he briefly edited the conservative journal *Das zwanzigste Jahrhundert* [The twentieth century] (1895–6). But realizing that social self-knowledge also required a fictional form, he wrote his first three major novels: *Im Schlaraffenland* (Munich, 1900; tr. A. D. B. Clark, *In the Land of Cockaigne*, London, 1929), *Die kleine Stadt* (Leipzig, 1909; tr. W. Ray, *The Little Town*, London, 1930) and *Der Untertan* (Leipzig, 1918; *Man of Straw*, London, 1947), the latter his major satire on the interplay between aggression and submission in Wilhelmine Germany. His concurrent manifesto *Geist und Macht* [Intellect and power] (1910), proclaiming the man of letters as the public conscience of his country, was widely influential.

Mann's French sympathies and pacifist views made him a vocal opponent of WW1. His essay on *Zola* (1915) provoked a painful conflict with his brother Thomas MANN, which has come to be seen as the classic dispute between two fundamental European traditions: liberal utopianism and pessimistic conservatism. Mann achieved his greatest fame under the Weimar republic which he supported almost to the end. He worked for German/French understanding, and in his writing turned to drama and film (*Der blaue Engel/The Blue Angel*, 1930). When the Nazis seized power in 1933 he went into exile in France, in 1936 accepting Czech citizenship from MASARYK. Exile, in which he was reconciled with his brother Thomas, was productive: he wrote numerous antifascist pamphlets and articles; in 1933 he became president of the émigré *Schutzverband deutscher Schriftsteller*; he supported the Popular Front, and from thence moved, with reservations, towards the communists. He also wrote two of his finest novels *Die Jugend des Königs Henri Quatre* (Amsterdam, 1935; tr. E. Sutton,

King Wren, London, 1937) and *Die Vollendung des Königs Henri Quatre* (Amsterdam, 1938; tr. E. Sutton, *Henry IV, King of France*, London, 1938). The German invasion of France compelled him to flight again, this time to the USA by way of Spain, crossing – at 70 – the Pyrenees on foot. His last years in California were spent in straitened circumstances, saddened by the suicide of his wife. The major work of this period was his historical-political autobiography *Ein Zeitalter wird besichtigt* [An age is viewed] (Stockholm, 1945). He died as preparations were being made to welcome him back in honour to the new German Democratic Republic.   JCr

D. Roberts, *Artistic Consciousness and Political Conscience: the Novels of Heinrich Mann* (Bern, 1971); N. Hamilton, *The Brothers Mann: the Lives of Heinrich and Thomas Mann* (New Haven, 1979).

Mann, Thomas (b. Lübeck, Schleswig-Holstein, Germany, 6.6.1875; naturalized American citizen, 1944; d. Kilchberg bei Zürich, Switzerland, 12.8.1955). German novelist. Mann's works are profoundly – and representatively – German, and they are also European classics of the very first rank. His first major novel is *Buddenbrooks* (Berlin, 1900; tr. H. T. Lowe-Porter, NY, 1924). In it he chronicles the decline of a bourgeois family over three generations. The metaphysical design of the novel – whereby 'mind' is seen as the enemy of 'life' – interlocks with the abundantly created realistic panorama of family life to achieve a remarkable comprehension of the changes in bourgeois society in the last half of the 19c. In 1911 he produced *Der Tod in Venedig* (Berlin; tr. H. T. Lowe-Porter, *Death in Venice* in *Three Tales*, London, 1928), a sombre tale which explores the precarious equilibrium of the creative imagination: the perception of chaos invading the disciplined mind seems prophetic, given the date of publication. At the end of WW1 Mann produced a long essay *Betrachtungen eines Unpolitischen* [Reflections of an unpolitical man] (Berlin, 1918) in which he defended the spiritual traditions of his country against what he saw as the facile progressive optimism of

Western Europe. The work is a classic of German 'unpolitical' – i.e. conservative – thought. Yet in the course of the 1920s Mann, in a series of essays and speeches, sought to marshal German culture in defence of the beleaguered Weimar republic and opposed those conservative forces to which he had a few years earlier given such powerful ammunition. In 1924 *Der Zauberberg* (Berlin; tr. H. T. Lowe-Porter, *The Magic Mountain*, NY, 1927) appeared. It is set in a sanatorium in the years 1907 – 14 and is a deeply affectionate, yet ultimately critical, reckoning with German culture, with the legacy of romanticism, Richard Wagner, and NIETZSCHE. Mann was awarded the Nobel prize for literature in 1929. In 1933 he was away from Germany on a lecture tour. Warned by his son Klaus, he did not return, and he finally emigrated to the USA in 1938 having completed the trilogy *Joseph und seine Brüder* (4 vols, 1 – 2, Berlin, 1933–4; 3, Vienna, 1936; 4, Stockholm, 1943; tr. H. T. Lowe-Porter, *Joseph and his Brothers*, 4 vols, London, 1934–44). During WW2 he was seen as the representative of the 'good' Germany, and in countless lectures and broadcasts he denounced Nazi Germany. The novel *Doktor Faustus* (Stockholm, 1947; tr. H. T. Lowe-Porter, *Doctor Faustus*, NY, 1948) was his sombre reckoning with the Third Reich. It explores the 'unpolitical', inward culture of Germany – Protestantism, music, Nietzsche and, of course, the *Faust* legend – in order to define that unnerving spiritual chemistry which meant that the 'nation of poets and thinkers' was peculiarly vulnerable to the seductions of Nazism. In 1952 Mann returned to Europe – but to Switzerland, not to Germany. His fiction is characterized by a (very German) interest in the life of the mind, yet he showed time and time again how mental activity was implicated in the stuff of social and historical experience.   MWS

T. J. Reed, *Thomas Mann: the Uses of Tradition* (Oxford, 1974); E. Heller, *Thomas Mann: the Ironic German* (Cambridge, [2]1981).

Mannheim, Hermann (b. Berlin, Germany, 26.10.1889; naturalized British citizen, 1940; d. London, UK, 20.1.1974). German/British criminologist; the father of modern English criminology. Mannheim studied at the universities of Munich, Freiburg im Breisgau, Strassburg and Königsberg where he read philosophy, economics, sociology and psychology. His thesis was on criminal negligence. In WW1 he served as an artillery officer on the eastern front and later as a judge of courts martial. During the Weimar republic he was a legal adviser and practised in labour law. He was appointed *Privatdozent* in the law faculty of Berlin (1923) and a criminal magistrate. In 1929 he was made professor *extraordinarius* and in 1932 appointed judge in the criminal division of the Supreme Court of Prussia. Fourteen major publications in German had appeared by this time.

In 1933, under HITLER, Mannheim was deprived of academic office and emigrated to the UK. After various minor jobs, including teaching in Pentonville Prison, he joined the staff of the London School of Economics in 1935. His first English-language research was published as *Social Aspects of Crime in England between the Wars* (London, 1940). *Young Offenders* (with Carr-Saunders & Rhodes, London, 1942) was followed by *Juvenile Delinquency in an English Middletown* (London, 1948). *Criminal Justice and Social Reconstruction* (London, 1946) was probably his most influential book. Promoted reader in criminology at London, he retained this first specifically named post in criminology in the UK until retirement in 1955, the year of his pioneering work with Wilkins *Prediction Methods in Relation to Borstal Training*. The two-volume *Comparative Criminology* (London, 1965) was produced during his retirement at the age of 76. Mannheim was closely involved with the Howard League for Penal Reform, and with groups concerned to reform the laws relating to abortion and homosexuality. His signal achievement was the academic development of criminology in the UK. A teacher of prodigious energy, he established a second generation of academic criminologists throughout the English-speaking world.   TPM

Mannheim, Karl (b. Budapest, Austria-Hungary [now Hungary], 27.3.1893; d. London, UK, 9.1.1947). Hungarian sociologist. Mannheim was educated largely at Heidelberg in the 1920s. He became an influential figure in modern sociology with his book *Ideologie und Utopie* (Bonn, 1929; tr. L. Wirth & E. Shils, *Ideology and Utopia*, London, 1936) which promised to open up a major new mode of inquiry, the 'sociology of knowledge'. Mannheim's work coincided with the spreading interest in MARXism among intellectuals in the 1930s, and the thesis of the 'social determination of knowledge' seemed to promise a way of validating Marx's argument that it is 'not the consciousness of men that determines their existence, but their existence which determines their consciousness'. Mannheim's first major essay 'Conservative Thought' (1927; in *Essays on Sociology and Social Psychology*, London, 1953) sought to parallel in political thought what art historians such as RIEGL had done in culture, namely to relate styles of thought, or world-views (*Weltanschauungen*), to specific historical times and social groups, and to show their social function. Thus Mannheim sought to show that the revival of natural-law philosophy in Germany in the early 19c was a response by conservative thinkers to the rise of liberalism. But in *Ideologie und Utopie* Mannheim went further and argued that *all* social thought was related to the class position of social groups, and that the *truth* of a proposition could not be assessed without regard to the social position of the individuals espousing those *Weltanschauungen*; in short, all social thought was ideological, including Marxism itself. But if this were so, if truth is relative to the social group, how is objective knowledge or science possible? Mannheim argued that the intellectual, a free-floating stratum between classes, could achieve disinterested knowledge. Mannheim, however, could not stand up to the philosophical assault which argued that he was confusing the origins of thought with validity and that while one might be able to show why some styles of thought are held by different social groups, the *truth* of a proposition had to rest on independent criteria.

Mannheim was a professor of sociology at Frankfurt from 1926, and after the Nazi takeover taught at the University of London (1933–46) but did not pursue his earlier work. His concerns, as expressed in *Man and Society in an Age of Reconstruction* (London, 1941), were principally with the role of irrationalism in modern society, the destruction of elite standards in culture, and the need for democratic planning. Many of Mannheim's essays, such as those on intellectuals and on generations, have remained influential in sociology, but the promises of a 'sociology of knowledge' have ebbed away, leaving little trace.   DBe

F. W. Rempel, *The Role of Value in Karl Mannheim's Sociology of Knowledge* (The Hague, 1965); G. W. Remmling, *The Sociology of Karl Mannheim* (Atlantic Highlands, NJ, 1975).

Mansbridge, Albert (b. Gloucester, UK, 10.1.1876; d. London, 22.8.1952). British educator. Mansbridge started work as a clerk in a guano firm at the age of 14, eagerly attending evening classes and otherwise educating himself. In 1903 he and his wife founded an association to Promote Higher Education of Working Men, which linked University Extension, the Co-operative movement, for which he now worked, and trade unions. Enthused by Mansbridge's excitement over 'the glory of education', a first branch at Reading in 1904 was followed by plans for others. In 1905 Mansbridge became the first full-time national secretary (at a workman's wage) of the association (now called the Workers' Educational Association), which was seen as distinct from older University Extension: it was more 'popular', more locally based, self-directing and politically committed. In 1908 part-time 'University Tutorial Classes' of a more continuous nature (subsequently three years), with private and public funding – as the 1902 Education Act permitted – began at Longton and Rochdale, and together with shorter and more introductory courses provided a model widely copied, so that in 1919 a World Association for Adult Education was founded. Mansbridge himself resigned his secretaryship in 1916 because of severe illness, but remained influential. Successful campaigning for improvements in elementary and secondary education and freer access to higher education robbed the WEA of its original constituency, so that most of its beneficiaries became 'middle-class' and most of its courses more 'cultural' than politically oriented. But the pioneering work of Mansbridge and his colleagues left its mark not only on the changed character of all universities' extra-mural work after 1945 (including revived University Extension) but on the content and method of many studies within the universities themselves. EJK

Mansfield, Katherine, *née* Beauchamp (b. Wellington, New Zealand, 14.10.1888; d. Fontainebleau, Seine-et-Marne, France, 9.1.1923). New Zealand short-story writer. She left her colonial-Establishment background to write in London, but *In a German Pension* (London, 1911) captures the bitterness and disillusion of her first years in Germany. Her affair with John Middleton Murry, whom she could not marry until 1918, was influential, though distorted by his posthumous editing of her writings. The death of her cherished younger brother Leslie during WW1 determined her 'to make our undiscovered country leap into the eyes of the old world', and her writings now ranged across her New Zealand memories. A tracing of the mysterious 'diversity of life ... Death included' was given urgency by the discovery of tuberculosis (first suspected in 1917). *Bliss and Other Stories* (London, 1920) and *The Garden Party and Other Stories* (London, 1922) foreshadowed a brilliant career; she died after a massive haemorrhage in January 1923. Sometimes misguidedly thought of as an 'English' writer, New Zealand perceptions largely determine the intuitive shifts of understanding that she traces in her work, which often succeeds in conveying fundamental truths through seemingly minor incidents. PNQ

A. Alpers, *The Life of Katherine Mansfield* (NY, 1980).

Mao Tse-tung (Mao Ze-dong) (b. Shaoshan, Hunan, China, 26.12.1893; d. Peking, 9.9.1976). Chinese revolutionary leader and principal architect of the People's Republic of China. After an education in the Chinese classics and history Mao was converted to MARXism during the winter of 1919–20 and in 1923 he became a full-time revolutionary. During a stay in his native village of Shao-shan, local peasant demonstrations (May–June 1925) against the shooting of Chinese by foreign police in Shanghai opened his eyes to the revolutionary potential of the peasantry, neglected both by Chinese intellectuals and by urban Marxists. A Soviet republic was set up in Kiangsi province in November 1931 with Mao as chairman. In October 1934, however, CHIANG KAI-SHEK's Kuomintang troops forced the Red Army, with Mao, to abandon Kiangsi and undertake the famous Long March to N.W. China. When the Chinese Communists renewed their alliance with Chiang Kai-shek to fight the Japanese (September 1937), they followed guerrilla tactics in the countryside and thereby came to control a large area of China. To this period belong some of Mao's best-known writings: *Strategic Problems of China's Revolutionary War* (1936) and *On Protracted War* (1938); *The Chinese Revolution and the Chinese CP* and *On New Democracy* (1940). In 1939 he married his third wife, a film actress, later to be known as Chiang Ch'ing. Mao's successful bid for the leadership of the CCP turned on his handling of relations with the Kuomintang and the 'Sinification' of Marxism, i.e. his insistence (in the Rectification Campaign of 1942) that China should not follow the Russian model blindly. After WW2 STALIN (like the Americans) urged the CCP to collaborate with Chiang Kai-shek and not fight a civil war. Mao ignored his advice, fought, and won it. In 1949 the Communist People's Republic was proclaimed in Peking and Mao, as its chairman, travelled to Moscow to persuade Stalin to sign a treaty and give limited economic aid. For several years China followed the Soviet economic model of centralized planning, priority for heavy industry and collectivization of agriculture.

Little was seen or heard in public of Chairman Mao until 1955, when he took the lead in promoting his own policies.

The first, in spring 1956, was that of 'Letting a hundred flowers bloom', a bid to win the support of the intellectuals and experts by showing that the CCP was willing to listen to criticism. When he found that they called the CP's leadership in question, he turned in disillusionment to the masses and proposed to rely on the ability of the rank and file to develop small labour-intensive enterprises in the framework of the 'people's communes'. This was the policy of 'the Great Leap Forward' (1958) and marked the end of China's reliance on Soviet help and the Soviet model.

The disruption of the economy which followed the Great Leap Forward led to sharp disagreement between Mao and other leaders. Mao, however, turned towards still more radical policies in launching the 'Great Proletarian Cultural Revolution' of 1966–9, deliberately designed to encourage the spontaneous radicalism of the young and the masses against the entrenched party bureaucracy. The result was to plunge Chinese society into chaos; to put a premium on militancy (the Red Guards) at the expense of skill and experience; and to set back China's struggling efforts at modernization by a generation. This extraordinary decision to renew the revolution even at the risk of destroying what it had accomplished was carried out in the name of the man with whom it had so long been identified and was actively linked with the development of a personal cult of Mao ('the Great Helmsman'), and Mao's thought (The Little Red Book).

China was still suffering from the shock of the Cultural Revolution when Mao died in his 83rd year in 1976. It was not until 1980 that the struggle for the succession between the different factions in the leadership resulted in the victory of DENG XIAO-PING and the pragmatists. There is little dispute about the leading role played by Mao in the 1930s and 1940s when he made his most original contribution to Marxism–LENINism and its application to the developing world. He moved the focus of the struggle from the cities to the countryside, and from the urban workers to the peasantry. At the same time he developed a new form of revolutionary activity in the guerrilla warfare which eventually enabled his peasant armies to capture the cities. What remains in dispute is Mao's attempt at revolutionary innovation from the Great Leap Forward of 1958 through the upheavals of the Cultural Revolution and its aftermath. This dispute is at the heart of Chinese politics and until it is settled no evaluation of Mao's place in the history of modern China can be more than tentative.

The Selected Works of Mao Tse-tung, published by the Foreign Language Press in Peking and supplemented by *Selected Readings from the Works of Mao Tse-tung* (1967) provide the best source available in English. Mao's talks and letters (1956–71) were edited by S. R. Schram and published as *Mao Tse-tung Unrehearsed* (Harmondsworth, 1974). ALCB

B. I. Schwartz, *Chinese Communism and the Rise of Mao* (Cambridge, Mass., 1951); S. R. Schram, *Mao Tse-tung* (NY, ²1967); J. P. Harrison, *The Long March to Power* (NY, 1972).

Marc, Franz (b. Munich, Bavaria, Germany, 8.2.1880; d. Verdun, Meuse, France, 4.3.1916). German expressionist painter. He studied theology and philosophy briefly before enrolling at the Munich Academy of Fine Art in 1900. After two visits to Paris (1903 and 1906), he had become deeply impressed by the work of Van Gogh and began to adapt his style to give visual expression to his own pantheistic belief in an inner harmony between man and nature, which he saw manifested in animal forms, especially horses and deer. To heighten the expressive effect he used colour symbolically (e.g. *The Blue Horse*, 1911; *Red Horses*, 1911). In 1910 he met KANDINSKY and joined the New Artists' Association, which they left in 1911 to found the Blue Rider. He contributed three essays to the Blue Rider *Almanach* in which he echoed Kandinsky's belief in the spiritual and mystical element of art. The simplified, curvilinear forms of his earlier works were modified by the impact of his meeting with DELAUNAY and the cubists in Paris (1912), and by the Italian futurist exhibition he saw in Munich later that year. As a result his monumental, simplified forms became increasingly fragmented, and the curvilinear rhythms of the earlier compositions were combined with the geometric structure of the Orphic colour grid, fused in varying degrees with the dynamic force-lines of the futurists to give translucent, crystalline colour effects of a similar degree of intensity to medieval stained-glass windows (e.g. *Animal Destinies*, 1913). By 1914 Marc began to paint nonfigurative dynamic-curvilinear compositions based on the interaction of abstract colour shapes (e.g. *Fighting Forms*, 1914). He was killed in WW1.

SOBT

K. Lankheit, *Franz Marc im Urteil seiner Zeit* (Cologne, 1960).

Marcel, Gabriel Honoré (b. Paris, France, 7.12.1889; d. Paris, 8.10.1973). French Christian philosopher. Red Cross worker in WW1, freelance philosopher thereafter, Catholic convert in 1929, awarded a prize for his plays in 1946 by the Académie Française, he was never easy to pin down. He delivered the 1949 –50 Gifford lectures in Aberdeen *Le Mystère de l'être* (2 vols, Paris, 1951; tr. R. Hague, *The Mystery of Being*, 2 vols, London, 1951) and the 1961 William JAMES lectures at Cambridge, USA, (*The Existentialist Background to Human Dignity*, Cambridge, Mass., 1963). Not accurately described by the label 'Christian existentialist', he reluctantly accepted it in later years as a counter to SARTRE's 'atheist existentialism'. In his *Journal métaphysique* (Paris, 1927; tr. B. Wall, *Metaphysical Journal*, London, 1952) he declares that he would like to be thought of as a neo-Socratic, provided his interrogative attitude were not interpreted as mere scepticism. But Marcel was never a system-builder and preferred to work through what he called 'concrete approaches'. He popularized two ideas which have had a certain vogue. The first is that the human person is more than the 'agglomeration of functions' by which he can be defined: the ticket collector is not merely a ticket collector. The second idea is the distinc-

tion between a 'problem' and a 'mystery'. For Marcel the problem is something outside me, like a crossword puzzle, and it does not really matter whether I solve it or not. On the other hand a mystery involves me personally. In *Etre et avoir* (Paris, 1935; tr. K. Farrar, *Being and Having*, London, 1949) he describes a mystery as 'a problem which encroaches upon its own data'. With this starting-point he finds a wealth of meaning in the analysis of such terms as 'having', 'presence', 'hope', 'love', 'witnessing'. Some readers have been inclined to regard Marcel as the author of highly personal meditations rather than of public-property philosophy, which may account for his influence on some theologians.   PAH

Z. T. Ralston, *Gabriel Marcel's Paradoxical Expression of Mystery* (NY, 1961); K. T. Gallagher, *The Philosophy of Gabriel Marcel* (NY, 1962).

Marconi, Guglielmo (b. Bologna, Emilia-Romagna, Italy, 25.4.1874; d. Rome, 20.7.1937). Italian pioneer of radio telegraphy. In 1894 Marconi learned of Hertz's laboratory experiments in electromagnetic waves, and, with the assistance of A. Righi, conducted early experiments in radio transmission on his father's estate. He developed and enlarged the antennae and in 1895 achieved transmission over 1.5 miles. Unable to interest the Italian government, Marconi moved to England. By 1897 he had achieved transmission over 12 miles and with the help of an Irish cousin lodged a patent and formed the Wireless Telegraph and Signals Co., Ltd. In 1899 he established a wireless station on the Isle of Wight for communication with France and installed transmitters in two boats to send reports to the New York newspapers on the America's Cup yacht race. On 12.12.1901 he transmitted a message by radio across the Atlantic, arousing worldwide interest. In 1909 he shared the Nobel prize for physics with K. F. Brown. In 1919 the Radio Corporation of America (RCA) was formed and acquired his American commercial interests. Marconi next pioneered short-wave transmission using dipole antennae and directional reflectors. In 1927 the Marconi Company's chain of short-wave stations encircled the world. In 1932, still experimenting from his own yacht, he found that microwaves could be received well below the optical horizon, using a phenomenon later known as scatter propagation. RAH

D. Grenston, *Marconi, Father of Radio* (London, 1965); W. P. Jolly, *Marconi* (London, 1972).

Marcuse, Herbert (b. Berlin, Germany, 19.7.1898; naturalized American citizen, 1940; d. Sternberg, East Germany, 29.7.1979). German/American social philosopher. After gaining his doctorate at Freiburg (the university of HUSSERL and HEIDEGGER) in 1922, Marcuse became an associate of the Institut für Sozialforschung in Frankfurt, the centre of the independent MARXism of HORKHEIMER and ADORNO. When HITLER came to power Marcuse fled to Geneva, crossing in 1934 to the USA where the Institut was re-established under the auspices of Columbia University. In 1941 his *Reason and Revolution* (NY, ²1954) argued that Marx is much more Hegelian than was allowed by the official Soviet interpretation, based on that of the dogmatic economic determinists Engels and LENIN. During WW2 Marcuse worked as an intelligence analyst for the US army. When the Institut went back to Europe in the early 1950s he became a university teacher, at Brandeis from 1954 and at San Diego from 1965 where he became the favourite mentor of the student revolutionaries of the ensuing years. Marcuse was the most FREUDian of the 'critical theorists' of the Frankfurt school. He was as committed to the erotic liberation of the unconscious from repression by the conscious mind as he was to the revolutionary liberation of the masses from political and economic domination by the capitalist ruling class. This position was elaborated in his *Eros and Civilization* (Boston, Mass., 1955). His *One-Dimensional Man* (Boston, Mass., 1964) was addressed to the affluent boredom and guilt of the American student population. Its thesis is that capitalism has cunningly anaesthetized the discontent of the oppressed by manipulating the means of communication so as to stimulate trivial, material desires which it is easy to satisfy. The only hope for revolution, he felt, was a marginal elite of unbrainwashed students and radically dispossessed members of the poorest classes. His concept of 'repressive tolerance' was a convenient device for undermining any attempt at compromise between the rebels and the established order. The hostility to Russian communism expressed in *Soviet Marxism* (NY, 1958), on the ground of its oppressively bureaucratized and industrialized nature, has some affinity with the comparably pastoral preferences of his old teacher Heidegger. AQ

A. MacIntyre, *Marcuse* (London, 1970).

Margalef, Lopéz Ramón (b. Barcelona, Spain, 16.5.1919). Spanish ecologist. Margalef is professor in general ecology at the University of Barcelona. He has been concerned with the more complex aspects of ecology, and particularly of community ecology. His research is mostly in the ecology of freshwater animals, and he makes his theoretical points from this basis. He works on methods of assessing the organization of communities of organisms, through such questions as the interactions between diversity and stability in ecosystems, and how these relate to succession from one community to another and to maturity. He challenges the view that in freshwater the natural succession is from unproductive (oligotrophic) communities to productive (eutrophic) communities. His interests also include consideration of the relationships between organisms and community productivity, and the exploitability of present-day ecosystems for human use. In addition to many original papers, he has published a number of books, including *Perspectives in Ecological Theory* (Chicago, 1968). RTi

Marinetti, Emilio Filippo Tommaso (b. Alexandria, Egypt, 22.12.1876; d. Bellagio, Lombardy, Italy, 2.12.1944). Italian writer and futurist. Marinetti moved to Paris in 1893 and studied at the university there, and later at the universities of Pavia and Genoa. His French education and the influence of French symbolist poetry, which he was later to reject while expounding futurism, had a formative influence on his development as a writer and polemical theorist. With a view to revolutionizing the arts, he published the futurist manifestos from 1909 onwards, expounding the tenets of futurism which called upon artists to turn their backs on the past, to celebrate the present in all its forms – including war ('the world's only hygiene') and machinery – and to emancipate themselves from any formal, linguistic or prosodic restraints, using 'words in liberty'. Although Marinetti saw in fascism the possibility of fulfilling futurist aims and principles, he was soon disillusioned, even though the nationalistic side of fascism continued to appeal to him. He fought in WW1 and in the Ethiopian war. In 1929 MUSSOLINI nominated him a member of the Italian Academy. Apart from his manifestos in collaboration with others (*I Manifesti del futurismo* [The futurist manifestos], 4 vols, Milan, 1920), Marinetti's work includes his French poems *La Conquête des étoiles* [The conquest of the stars] (Paris, 1902), *Destruction* (Paris, 1904), *La Ville charnelle* [The sensual city] (Paris, 1908); his satirical tragedy *Le Roi bombance* [The feasting king] (Paris, 1905); and his novels *Mafarka le futuriste* [Mafarka the futurist] (Paris, 1909) and *Gli indomabili* [The untamed] (Piacenza, 1922). GS

J. B. Joll, 'Filippo Tommaso Marinetti: futurism and fascism' in *Intellectuals in Politics* (NY, 1960); J. R. Dashwood, 'Futurism and fascism', *Italian Studies*, 2 (1972).

Maritain, Jacques (b. Paris, France, 18.11.1882; d. nr Bordeaux, Gironde, 28.4.1973). French Catholic philosopher. Converted in 1906, Maritain taught philosophy at the Institut Catholique in Paris from 1914. In the 1920s his *salon* at Meudon was a gathering place for the 'Catholic revival' in art and philosophy: ROUAULT, Henri Ghéon and MOUNIER frequented it. Later he taught at the Toronto Institute of Medieval Studies, at Columbia and at Notre Dame. After a period as French ambassador to the Holy See (1945–8) he went to Princeton, but returned to France to spend his retirement years in Franciscan simplicity near Bordeaux. Maritain was more interested in the contemporary applications of Thomism than in its historical setting. For him it was a form of realism which corrected the subjectivism to which philosophy had succumbed since Descartes. Much of his work was on the theory of knowledge. In *Distinguer pour mieux unir ou les degrés du savoir* (Paris, 1932; tr. G. B. Phelan, *The Degrees of Knowledge*, NY, 1959) he tried to reassert the concept of the hierarchy of sciences derived from Aristotle and Aquinas, while fitting modern physics into his scheme. Theoretical physics has an intermediate position between observational science and pure mathematics. Metaphysics, operatively useless as Maritain admits, nevertheless reveals 'authentic values and their hierarchy'. And he leaves room for theology, a science based on revealed premises. Maritain always insisted that there were other ways of knowing besides the scientific: prereflective knowledge of God, for example, and 'knowledge by conaturality' found in mysticism, poetry and moral experience. Maritain tried to apply these principles to politics and to art, notably in *Humanisme intégral* (Paris, 1936; tr. M. R. Adamson, *True Humanism*, London, 1938) and *Art et scolastique* (Paris, 1927; tr. J. W. Evans, *Art and Scholasticism, and the Fountains of Poetry*, NY, 1962). In his later years he was better received abroad than in France, where he saw younger theologians turning away from Thomism. PAH

A. Timosaitis, *Church and State in Maritain's Thought* (Chicago, 1959); J. W. Evans (ed.), *Jacques Maritain: the Man and his Achievement* (NY, 1965).

Markish, Peretz (b. Polonye, Ukraine, Russia, 17.12.1895; d. Moscow, USSR, 12.8.1952). Yiddish poet. Originally writing in Russian, he turned to Yiddish in 1917. Influenced by the post-WW1 expressionist trends in European poetry, he wrote long narrative poems as well as short lyrics experimenting with innovative language and rhythm. An early long poem was '*Di Kupe*' [The heap] in which he describes the horrors of the anti-Jewish pogroms during the civil war following the Russian revolution of 1917. This poem reads like a biblical lamentation and projects a sense of despair utterly different to the rhetoric encountered in postrevolutionary poetry and which made Markish the subject of heated polemics in contemporary literary periodicals. In 1921, following the example of other writers, he left Russia and spent some time in Paris and Warsaw, where he became associated with '*Di Khalastria*' [The gang], a group of avant-garde Yiddish poets. On his return to the Soviet Union in 1926 Markish took an active part in the literary and cultural life, blending social and national motifs in his poetry but always remaining among his contemporaries the *enfant terrible*. During WW2 he wrote his great epic poem *Milkhome* (2 vols, Moscow, 1948) and *Der Oifshtand in Geto* [The uprising in the Warsaw ghetto] (Moscow, 1947), a kind of prose history of Polish Jews culminating in the Warsaw ghetto uprising of 1943. Markish was arrested in 1949 and executed with a large number of other Jewish writers during the STALINist purges.   JSo

Márquez, Gabriel García, see GARCÍA MÁRQUEZ, GABRIEL.

Marr, David Courtenay (b. Woodford, Essex, UK, 19.1.1945; d. Boston, Mass., USA, 6.12.1980). British psychologist. Educated at Trinity College, Cambridge, he developed a complex mathematical model of the workings of the cerebellum while holding a research fellowship there. In 1973 a visit to the Artificial Intelligence Laboratory at MIT introduced him to the potential of computer modelling in the pursuit of psychological theories. From 1972 to 1976 he was a senior research fellow at King's College, Cambridge, after which he returned to MIT until his untimely death. During this period he developed important new ideas about how the brain builds a representation of the external world from the fragmentary data received from the eye and he was the first to consider how the visual system constructs a representation of objects in three dimensions. Although keen to make use of the techniques of artificial intelligence, he was aware that the development of adequate theories of vision would not be achieved by the relentless pursuit of 'intelligent' computer programs alone, but by their use within the context of a theory that took account of all available knowledge. Marr's unique knowledge of experimental psychology, neurophysiology, mathematics and computing science eminently suited him to his chosen task of explaining vision.   AJP

Marshall, Alfred (b. London, UK, 26.7.1842; d. Cambridge, 13.7.1924). British economist and a dominant figure in British economics from the late 1880s until his death. He read mathematics at St John's College, Cambridge, and was elected to a fellowship in 1865. He turned to economics two years later. In 1877 he moved to Bristol as principal of University College and professor of political economy. He returned to Cambridge and the chair of political economy in 1885, and remained there (retiring from the chair in 1908) for the rest of his life.

Marshall's great work was his *Principles of Economics* (London, 1890, [5]1907). Two other volumes published in his last years, *Industry and Trade* (London, 1919) and *Money, Credit and Commerce* (London, 1923), contain material of historical interest, not least because some of it was written decades earlier, but they do not approach the *Principles* in importance. Drawing partly on the work of J. S. Mill, W. S. Jevons and others, Marshall built a comprehensive analysis of prices and resource allocation along partial-equilibrium lines. In contrast to the general equilibrium theory formulated by WALRAS and PARETO, partial equilibrium looks at the mechanism of supply and demand in a single market that is assumed to be an infinitesimally small but representative fraction of the whole economic system. Marshall's analysis covered markets for factors of production (labour, land, etc.) as well as commodities; and it made pioneering contributions to the study of adjustment processes and stability, notably in formulating the concept of elasticity and in distinguishing among time periods required for different types of adjustment (capital costs and the like being fixed in the short run but variable in the long run). In welfare economics Marshall developed the concept of consumer's rent or surplus which, besides stimulating theoretical debate, has had some practical application in measuring the gains from international trade and from public investment projects.

Marshall also made contributions to monetary economics, including the so-called Cambridge or cash-balance approach to the quantity theory of money (which viewed the value of money as determined, like that of other commodities, by the equilibration of supply and demand); the analysis of credit creation; the purchasing power parity theory of exchange rates (where he anticipated Cassell); and the problem of indexation of contracts to protect economic agents from fluctuations in the value of money. Marshall's expositions of many of these issues were made in his evidence to various official Commissions, published posthumously as *Official Papers of Alfred Marshall* (London, 1926). PMO

J. M. Keynes, 'Alfred Marshall', in *Essays in Biography* (London, 1933); M. Blaug, *Economic Theory in Retrospect* (London, ³1978).

Marshall, George Catlett (b. Uniontown, Pa, USA, 31.12.1880; d. Washington, DC, 16.10.1959). Chief of US Army Staff (1939–45), US intermediary in the Chinese civil war in 1946, US secretary of state (1947–9), secretary of defense (1950–1). With a reputation for unshakeable integrity and relentless dedication to the service of his country, Marshall will forever be historically associated with four sets of events: the expansion of the US army to the position of dominance it enjoyed in 1945 and the concentration on a 'Europe first' strategy involving the direct cross-Channel invasion of Europe; the failure to bring about an agreement between CHIANG KAI-SHEK and the Chinese Communists in 1946; the offer of American aid to a policy of European reconstruction through European cooperation in his speech of 5.6.1947 at Harvard (the Marshall Plan); and the renewed commitment of the USA to a 'Europe first' strategy in American entry into the North Atlantic Treaty Organization in 1949 and the defeat of those who during the Korean War (1950–1) wished to

commit US power to a major land conflict in Asia. DCW

F. C. Pogue, *George C. Marshall*, vol. 1 (NY, 1964); vol. 2 (NY, 1966); vol. 3 (NY, 1983).

Marshall, Thomas Humphrey (b. London, UK, 19.12.1893; d. Cambridge, 29.11.1981). British sociologist. Marshall began his academic career as an historian. He made important contributions to the study of population trends in the period of the Industrial Revolution and afterwards. His interest in sociological questions was initially stimulated by the historical method of such scholars as Seebohm, Vinogradoff and Maitland; and later by his experiences in a prison camp when interned in Germany during WW1. From 1925 to 1956 Marshall was on the staff of the London School of Economics, teaching sociology and eventually becoming head of the department and holder of the Martin White chair. During these years his main concerns were with social stratification and the growth of social policy. In his book *Citizenship and Social Class* (Cambridge, 1950), he analysed the complex relationship that had developed in the UK between the essentially egalitarian rights of citizenship – civil, political and social – and the class inequalities inevitably generated by the operation of the capitalist market economy. He explored the implications of this coexistence of citizenship and class, for both social integration and social conflict, in numerous essays (brought together in *Sociology at the Crossroads*, London, 1963); and an awareness of the basic sociological issues involved distinguishes Marshall's influential introductory text *Social Policy* (London, 1965, ³1970). Marshall's major contribution to the development of sociology in the UK is to have displayed a conception of the subject clearly different from that established by his two predecessors in the Martin White chair, HOBHOUSE and GINSBERG. For them, sociology's closest academic affinities were with anthropology, psychology and philosophy; and their basic orientation was an evolutionary one. For Marshall, sociology is essentially and inescapably an historical discipline in both content and method – although capable of making its own distinctive contributions in conceptual sophistication and in both quantitative and qualitative techniques of inquiry and analysis. In 1973 Marshall published a delightful and informative autobiographical essay 'A British sociological career' (*International Social Science Journal*, 25).　　　　JHG

D. Lockwood, 'For T. H. Marshall', *Sociology*, VII (1974).

Martin, Archer John Porter (b. London, UK, 1.3.1910). British biochemist. Martin's most important appointment has been as head of the physical chemistry division of the National Institute for Medical Research (1952). From his undergraduate days he has been interested in the methodology and theory of the separation of substances which are closely similar chemically, particularly α-amino-acids, the constituent units of proteins. With R. L. M. SYNGE he developed various forms of separation depending on the partition of compounds between two solvents, first by countercurrent methods, but more importantly by column chromatography on cellulose and then, of outstanding importance, by the technique of partition chromatography on paper, or paper chromatography. (The essential feature of chromatography is repeated phase-transfer of solutes.) In paper chromatography the paper provides a stationary phase (water) and various other liquids (usually mixtures) are the second phase. The technique of paper chromatography made possible, among others, the chemical investigation of the structures of three great classes of biological macromolecules: proteins, nucleic acids and carbohydrates. For this work Martin and Synge were jointly awarded the Nobel prize for chemistry in 1952. Later, with A. T. James, Martin developed the method of gas–liquid chromatography, a highly sensitive and potentially precise method of chemical analysis indispensable to every branch of modern chemical science.　　　NBC

Martin, Basil Kingsley (b. London, UK, 28.7.1897; d. Cairo, Egypt, 16.2.1969). British journalist. Under Martin's editorship (1931–65) the *New Statesman*'s circulation rose from c. 15,000 in 1931 to 30,000 in 1939 and to more than 90,000 by 1945. Even before the Spanish civil war, he had proved to be one of the most effective editors of a weekly paper in the history of British journalism. He attracted a large public that was often exasperated by his chip-on-the-shoulder left-wing point of view, but could not resist the readability of his weekly diary of gossip and comment. He also made sure that he was merely the leader of an equally brilliant team of specialist writers. The standard of literary criticism under him was so high that it drew purchasers who loathed the paper's politics. He reflected the views of a generation and supplied it with provocative ideas written by some of the most intelligent commentators of his day. Martin wrote two volumes of autobiography: *Father Figures* (London, 1966) and *Editor* (London, 1967).　　　RB

C. Rolph, *Kingsley Martin* (London, 1973).

Martin du Gard, Roger (b. Neuilly-sur-Seine, Seine, France, 23.3.1881; d. Bellême, Orne, 22.8.1958). French novelist. Born into an old legal family, Martin du Gard studied at the Ecole des Chartes, Paris, qualifying as an archivist and palaeographer in 1908. His stated ambition as a novelist was to write fiction which, thanks to its detailed use of documentary sources, would be able to deal with major political questions rather than with the purely individual concerns of his characters. His first successful novel *Jean Barois* (Paris, 1913; tr. S. Gilbert, London, 1950) traces the conflict between Catholicism and anti-clerical rationalism against the background of a detailed reconstruction of the Dreyfus affair, its curious dialogue form reflecting the author's lasting interest in the theatre. The eight volumes of *Les Thibault* (Paris, 1922–40; tr. S. Gilbert, *The World of the Thibaults*, London, 1939, and *Summer 1914*, London, 1940) represent his greatest achievement and won him the 1937 Nobel prize for literature. Initially conceived as an account of the intertwined destinies of two families, one Catholic and the other Protestant, in its later sections the novel-sequence becomes a vivid panorama of the collapse of

Europe in 1914 and an eloquent plea for peace. An associate of GIDE and the *Nouvelle Revue Française* circle, Martin du Gard was the most reticent of novelists, making almost no public statements as to his beliefs or convictions. His Nobel prize speech and some later pronouncements do, however, reveal his attachment to a TOLSTOYan pacifism and humanitarianism.   DM

D. Boak, *Roger Martin du Gard* (Oxford, 1963); D. Schalk, *Roger Martin du Gard: the Novelist and History* (Ithaca, NY, 1967).

Martinet, André (b. St-Alban-des-Villards, Savoie, France, 12.4.1908). French linguist, noted for his pioneering work on diachronic phonology (sound change). He obtained his first degree at the University of Paris, where he remained until 1945, apart from a brief interlude in Berlin. In 1947 he was appointed head of the linguistics department at Columbia University, New York. In 1955 he returned to his native France, to a chair at the University of Paris, and a post at the Ecole Pratique des Hautes Etudes (1957). His thought has been heavily influenced by TRUBETZKOY and the Prague school; he advocates a 'functional' approach to language in which he stresses the importance of the patterning of the system and the contrasts between linguistic units. He is chiefly known for his work on language change, which he expounded in depth in *Economie des changements phonétiques* [The economy of phonetic changes] (Bern, 1955). He regards linguistic evolution as a perpetual opposition between communicative needs and the tendency to reduce mental and physical effort to a minimum. He suggests that the linguistic system is continually striving for 'economy', a state of equilibrium in which all the relevant factors are optimally balanced against one another. However, true economy can never be achieved because of inevitable disruptive factors, such as the asymmetry of the human vocal organs. A number of Martinet's claims are regarded as controversial, but he was one of the first linguists to stress the importance of internal causality in the interpretation of phonological change. His ideas on language in general are found in a relatively popularized form in *Eléments de linguistique générale* (Paris, 1960; tr. E. Palmer, *Elements of General Linguistics*, London, 1964).   JMA

Martinson, Harry Edmund (b. Jämshög, Blekinge, Sweden, 6.5.1904; d. Stockholm, 11.2.1978). Swedish poet and novelist. In his earliest works – his volume of poems entitled *Nomad* (Stockholm, 1931) and his travel book *Kap Farväl!* (Stockholm, 1933; tr. N. Walford, *Cape Farewell*, London, 1936) – he drew upon his childhood memories and his nomadic youth to advocate a kind of 'primitivism', a belief that individual salvation in the modern bureaucratic world was achieved only by keeping 'on the move'. There followed two autobiographical works – *Nässlorna blomma* (Stockholm, 1935; tr. N. Walford, *Flowering Nettles*, London, 1936) and *Vägen ut* [The way out] (Stockholm, 1936) – which vividly document the harshness and deprivation of his childhood and early life. *Passad* [Trade winds] (Stockholm, 1945) is his most important collection of verse; while *Vägen till Klockrike* (Stockholm, 1948; tr. M. Michael, *The Road*, London, 1955) reverts to the problems of the nomad in the contemporary industrialized world. His international reputation derives largely from his long allegorical and science-fictional poem cycle *Aniara* (Stockholm, 1956; tr. H. MacDiarmid & E. Harley Schubert, London, 1963), especially in its operatic form (1959) with music by K. B. Blomdahl: an account of the reactions of the inhabitants of a giant spaceship set on an irreversible course into endless space. Martinson was one of the chief representatives of the new generation of self-declared 'proletarian writers' in modern Swedish literature. He was awarded the Nobel prize in 1974.   JWMcF

Marx, Karl Heinrich (b. Trier, Rhineland-Palatinate, Germany, 5.5.1818; d. London, UK, 14.3.1883). German social scientist and revolutionary. Born into a Jewish middle-class family, Marx studied law and philosophy at the universities of Bonn and Berlin where he joined the radical followers of Hegel. Barred from his chosen profession of university teaching because of his political views, he turned to journalism and became editor of the liberal *Rheinische Zeitung* in 1842. On the suppression of his paper, Marx emigrated to Paris where he became converted to communism and to the view that the proletariat was the future agent of revolutionary change in society. In 1844 he drafted *Zur Kritik der Nationalökonomie, mit einem Schlusskapitel über die Hegelsche Philosophie* (in Marx-Engels, *Gesamtausgabe*, Berlin, 1932; *Economic and Philosophical Manuscripts of 1844*, Moscow, 1959), which remained unpublished until 1932. They contain a vivid analysis of alienation in capitalist society and present the alternative as a humanistic communism. While in Paris Marx began his lifelong friendship and collaboration with Friedrich Engels. Expelled from Paris, Marx moved to Brussels where he became one of the leaders of the semiclandestine Communist League and (with Engels) set out his materialist conception of history in *Die deutsche Ideologie* (Moscow, 1932; *The German Ideology*, Moscow, 1964). On the eve of the 1848 revolutions, the Communist League commissioned Marx and Engels to produce a *Manifest der Kommunistischen Partei* (London, 1848; *The Communist Manifesto*, London, 1850, [2]1888), still the classic exposition of communism. Marx then returned briefly to Germany where he edited the radical liberal newspaper *Neue Rheinische Zeitung*.

With the subsidence of the revolutions, Marx, his wife and four children, took refuge in London, where he was to live for the rest of his life, and wrote sparkling analyses of the 1848 revolution and its aftermath in France in '*Die Klassenkämpfe in Frankreich 1848 bis 1850*' (1850, Berlin, 1895; *The Class Struggles in France, 1848–50*, NY, 1924, [2]1973) and '*Der achtzehnte Brumaire des Louis Bonaparte*' (1852, Hamburg, 1869; *The Eighteenth Brumaire of Louis Bonaparte*, NY, 1898, [2]1973). But the decades of the 1850s and 1860s were chiefly devoted to the writing of his main work *Das Kapital: Kritik der politischen Oekonomie*, destined, in his own words, 'to lay bare the laws of motion of capitalist society', though Marx also produced

(1857–8) an important rough draft of his total project known as *Grundrisse der Kritik der politischen Oekonomie* (2 vols, Moscow, 1939–41, [2]1953; *Grundrisse* [Outlines], Harmondsworth, 1973). Ill health and Marx's lifelong reluctance to publish meant that only the first volume of *Das Kapital* was published during his lifetime (Hamburg, 1867, [2]1873; *Capital*, London, 1887, [2]1954), the second and third volumes being edited by Engels from Marx's manuscripts (Hamburg, 1885–94; London, 1907–9, [2]1971). *Das Kapital* sought to establish a theoretical definition (based on a labour theory of value) of the exploitation of the working class in capitalist society, denied the long-term viability of capitalism because of the tendency of the rate of profit to fall, and predicted capitalism's supersession by a socialism that would abolish private ownership of the means of production. The state, which under capitalism had been an instrument of class domination, would wither away as the classless society of communism approached.

During the last two decades of his life Marx renewed his involvement in politics. He was one of the leading figures in the First International from its foundation in 1864 until its virtual demise in 1872, following a split with the anarchist followers of Bakunin, and he championed the cause of the Paris Commune of 1871 of which he wrote a spirited defence (*The Civil War in France*, London, 1871). The Commune also supplied Marx with a model of that transitional society between capitalism and communism that he sometimes called the dictatorship of the proletariat. Towards the end of his life Marx's capacity for sustained work deserted him and he was confined mainly to reworking the drafts of *Das Kapital* and preparing further editions of his published works.

Although little known during his lifetime, Marx quickly became famous after his death as the result of the spread of movements which claimed as their doctrine the systematization of Marx's ideas that came to be known as Marxism. With the success of the Bolsheviks in 1917, the enthronement of Marxism as a ruling ideology began. In a very different vein, Marx has enjoyed a considerable reputation as a social scientist being classed along with DURKHEIM and Max WEBER as one of the founding fathers of sociology. Marx's conception of class and his emphasis on the social relations of production as a determining factor have had an abiding influence on the study of history and society. DTM

F. Mehring, *Karl Marx: the Story of His Life* (London, 1934); D. McLellan, *Karl Marx: his Life and Thought* (London, 1973).

Masaryk, Tomáš Garrigue (b. Hodonin, Moravia, Austria-Hungary [now Czechoslovakia], 7.3.1850; d. Lany, 14.9.1937). Professor of philosophy (Czech University of Prague, 1882–1914), member of the Hapsburg Parliament (1891–3, 1907–14), chairman of the Czech National Council, president of Czechoslovakia (1918–35). Alone among Czech nationalist political figures under the Hapsburg empire, Masaryk rejected Pan-Slav sentiments and reliance on Russia to liberate the Czechs, regarding the Russian approach to politics as inherently non-European and irredeemably tyrannical. Instead he turned to Britain and France (to which he escaped in 1916), using his personal contacts to implant in the British cabinet and Foreign Office the conviction that the pre-1914 Austrian empire should be destroyed (*Austria delenda est*) and a union of Hapsburg Czechs and Hungarian-dominated Slovaks created, a union for which he provided the framework by the Pittsburg Agreement (1918) with the leaders of the Slovak minority in the USA (see *The Making of a State: Memories 1914–18*, London, 1928). As president of the new state Masaryk did his best to encourage a reconciliation between the Czechs and the minorities groups, especially the Sudeten Germans, and to maintain Czechoslovak ties with Britain and France. His effectiveness was limited by his conception of the presidency as above politics. But despite the limits he set to the exercise of his role, his influence and example played a substantial part in making Czechoslovakia the one successful democracy in Central and Eastern Europe between the two wars. DCW

R. W. Seton-Watson, *Masaryk in England* (London, 1943); O. A. Funda, *Thomas Garrigue Masaryk* (London, 1978).

Mason, Basil John (b. Docking, Norfolk, UK, 18.8.1923). British meteorologist. Soon after graduating in 1947, Mason brought to cloud physics substantial measures of the disciplines of mathematics and experimental physics. Previously progress in cloud physics had been slow and mainly of a speculative and descriptive nature. He developed a leading school of cloud physics at Imperial College, London, and had a major influence on research in other countries. Between 1948 and 1965, when he became director-general of the Meteorological Office, Mason and his students made many advances in the understanding of the basic physical processes involved in the formation of clouds, rain, snow and hail (see *The Physics of Clouds*, Oxford, 1957, [2]1971), and in the generation of electricity in thunderstorms. This research has had important implications in many fields, including the artificial stimulation of precipitation. Mason also provided a theoretical and quantitative development of ideas for the charging of growing hail pellets in cumulus clouds and this theory of thunderstorm electrification has found widespread acceptance. In recent years Mason has shown great interest in climatic change and has participated in research concerned with the numerical modelling of the global climate. PJM

Massine, Léonide Feodorovitch, *né* Miassin (b. Moscow, Russia, 8.8.1895; naturalized French citizen, 1944; d. Borken, Hesse, West Germany, 15.3.1979). Russian/French dancer and choreographer, chosen when still in his teens by DIAGHILEV to become the leading male dancer and choreographer of the itinerant Ballets Russes in the company's 'middle period' (1914–21). His first role was Joseph in FOKINE's *Legend of Joseph* (1914). Massine's great talent as a dancer was in 'character' roles – he was not a *danseur noble* – such as those he created for himself when Diaghilev encouraged him to become a choreographer, in association with the notable and avant-garde composers and painters then working for the Ballet. One of Massine's early collaborations was with COCTEAU, SATIE and PICASSO on *Parade* (1917); and Leon Bakst designed his *Les Femmes de bonne humeur* in the same year. Two of Massine's enduring successes date from 1919: *Le Tricorne* (designed by Picasso) and *La Boutique fantasque* (designed by DÉRAIN) – both comedy-ballets, Massine's particular forte; and the Miller in *Tricorne* was for years his most famous role. In the 1930s and 1940s Massine worked with many other companies and in many styles, but only a few of his later works survive in repertory (*Le Beau Danube*, *Gaieté Parisienne*, *Mam'zelle Angot*). His period as artistic director and choreographer of Colonel de Basil's Ballet Russe de Monte Carlo saw another important innovation, the 'symphonic ballet'. In *Les Présages* (1933), *Choreartium* (1933) and *Symphonie fantastique* (1936), Massine created ballets to complete symphonies (respectively Tchaikovsky's Fifth, Brahms's Fourth and Berlioz) which caused controversy in musical circles; and though these works are now forgotten, he had opened a new avenue which has been much explored by later choreographers. His autobiography was published as *My Life in Ballet* (London, 1968).   DAD

R. Buckle, *Diaghilev* (London, 1979).

Masson, André (b. Balagny-sur-Thérain, Oise, France, 4.1.1896). French surrealist painter. Masson studied initially in Brussels, moving in 1912 to Paris where he completed his training at the Ecole Nationale des Beaux Arts. At first he was influenced by cubism, but a meeting with the surrealists in 1923 encouraged him to experiment with automatism. It was as a draughtsman, always his strength, that he first used automatism to produce more interesting and convincing results. Later, in 1927, he began to use random areas of glue, coloured sand and a free line produced by squeezing the paint direct from the tube; by these means he realized imagery as spontaneous as that of his drawings. During the 1930s he entered a less automatic domain peopled by insects and monsters engaged in De Sadean metamorphosis, painted in rather harsh and acid colours, but after escaping to the USA during WW2, he returned to a richer and more placid automatism which was to influence the abstract expressionists in general and POLLOCK in particular. Masson's relationship with the early surrealist group terminated after a period of withdrawal, in 1933, but was resumed at the time of the Spanish civil war, an event which provoked a series of brilliant and bitter satirical drawings which are amongst his best work.   GM

M. Leiris & G. Limbour, *André Masson and his Universe* (Geneva, 1947); O. Hahn, *Masson* (NY, 1965).

Matisse, Henri (b. Le Cateau-Cambrésis, Nord, France, 31.12.1869; d. Cimiez, Alpes-Maritimes, 3.11.1954). French painter, sculptor and printmaker renowned as the greatest colourist of the 20c. Matisse studied painting in Paris, mainly at the Ecole des Beaux Arts in the studio of Gustave Moreau, where Marquet and ROUAULT were fellow-pupils. Beginning conservatively, he came under the influence of impressionism only in 1896–7, but by 1899–1900 had begun to use pure colours in a daring and arbitrary way. After working from 1901 to 1904 with a darker palette, making CÉZANNEsque studies of figures and landscapes, he brightened his colours again and began to work in what came to be known as a fauve style, with brilliant colour harmonies of rich luminous reds, pinks, yellows, greens and blues. He was not only the chief originator of this movement, the first radically new art movement of the 20c, but was regarded by the other fauve artists such as DÉRAIN, VLAMINCK and Marquet as the leading figure. From 1906 onwards, he began to work towards a more strongly constructed and monumental style, with flat uniform areas of saturated colour and bold, rhythmical designs. This reached its peak between 1910 and 1916 when he produced some of his greatest large canvases, such as *Music* and *The Dance* (1910), and *The Red Studio* (1911) and *The Moroccans* (1916). In some of the earlier works of this period there are areas of ornamental patterning akin to

Persian miniatures (Matisse made two visits to Morocco in 1911–13), and in the later ones sometimes a tougher, almost cubist linear grid of intersecting planes. The colour areas are enlivened by vivid contrasts and are used to help articulate the space. The themes are often interiors with or without figures, including his own studio with objects standing around. From December 1916 Matisse spent much of his time in the south of France, mainly at Nice, and the Mediterranean light led him to work with higher-keyed, very luminous colours. His style became looser, less stylized and more relaxed. Many of his pictures from then on were executed from female models, including models posed as odalisques, and their rich colours, decorative patterns and sensuous subject-matter give a feeling of calm, hedonism and well-being. From the late 1920s his work tended to become more stylized again, with strongly rhythmical designs and a denser saturation of colour. Confined by ill-health to his bed or a wheelchair in his old age, he gave up easel painting in 1948 and devoted his last years to the design and decoration of the Chapel of the Rosary at Vence (including the design of the stained-glass windows) and the creation of a number of cut-out gouaches, some of monumental proportions. Using sheets of paper hand-coloured with gouache, he cut out shapes with a pair of scissors, and then assistants under his direction fastened the shapes in place. In this way he achieved a late style of great originality. His sculptures, made from 1899 onwards, are mostly stylized figures related to the more three-dimensional phases of his painting, and themselves constitute an *oeuvre* of considerable importance. REA

A. H. Barr, Jr, *Matisse: his Art and his Public* (NY, 1951); J. Guichard-Meili, *Matisse* (London, 1967).

Matta Echaurren, Roberto Sebastián Antonio (b. Santiago, Chile, 11.11.1911). Chilean painter. Since his involvement with surrealism he has developed a personal iconography of semi-abstract and humanoid forms within the vertiginous spaces of paintings, at times huge in size, which combine daring formal experimentation with the exploration of ideas. He studied architecture in Chile and in 1931 left for Paris where he worked for LE CORBUSIER. In 1936 through LORCA he met DALI who introduced him to BRETON. Matta exhibited his first drawings in a surrealist exhibition in 1937 and he began to paint in the following year, exploring automatist techniques. He left for New York in 1939 and stayed there until 1948, exerting a strong influence on Arshile GORKY, and the painters who were to become the New York school. A visit to Mexico with MOTHERWELL in 1941 affected his ideas about the significance of the New World and pre-Hispanic cultures. His continuing interest in FREUD is evinced by his painting *The Vertigo of Eros* (1944). He began to introduce images of humanoid animal-insects; in the monumental painting *Being With* (1946) the semitransparent planes become a machine environment expressing the need for increased social responsibility in an age of technology. His subsequent paintings continue to evoke a cinematic, science-fiction atmosphere. In 1983 he exhibited works based on Shakespeare's *Tempest* using imagery related to primitive and New World cultures. MOJN

W. Rubin, *Matta* (NY, 1957); Arts Council of Great Britain, *Matta 'Coïgitum'* (London, 1977).

Maugham, William Somerset (b. Paris, France, 25.1.1874; d. Cap Ferrat, Alpes-Maritimes, 16.12.1965). British novelist, short-story writer and dramatist. Though qualified as a doctor, Maugham was encouraged by the lively reception of his first novel *Liza of Lambeth* (London, 1897) to pursue a literary career. By 1908 he had published several other novels, a volume of short stories *Orientations* (London, 1899), a travel book about Spain *The Land of the Blessed Virgin* (London, 1905), and established himself as a fashionable playwright of comedies of manners. Though in touch with the experiments of modernist writers, Maugham chose to exploit the formal characteristics of traditional narrative, as is evident from his major novels – the autobiographical *Of Human Bondage* (NY, 1915), *The Moon and Sixpence*

(London, 1919), *Cakes and Ale* (London, 1930), *The Razor's Edge* (NY, 1944) – and his numerous collections of short stories. He commanded a large range of settings and characters, and with that variety he exposed the hypocrisies of respectable society, the disillusioning nature of human relations and the absurdity of life. With Maupassant, an early influence, Maugham shared the qualities of acute observation, fine-edged irony and practised craftsmanship. sc
A. Curtis, *The Pattern of Maugham: a Critical Portrait* (London, 1974).

Mauriac, François (b. Bordeaux, Gironde, France, 11.10.1885; d. Paris, 1.9.1970). French novelist and Catholic pamphleteer. Mauriac's finest and best-known novel *Thérèse Desqueyroux* (Paris, 1927; tr. G. Hopkins, *Thérèse*, London, 1947) contains in their most concentrated form all the themes running through his fiction: the meanness and oppression of French provincial life, the misery produced by sexual incompatibility, the mystery of sin and redemption as seen through the most austere tradition of French Catholicism, and the savage beauty of the countryside to the south of Bordeaux. A more idealized but less convincing picture of family life in the French provinces can be found in the autobiographical *Le Mystère Frontenac* (Paris, 1933; tr. G. Hopkins, *The Frontenac Mystery*, London, 1952), a novel instructive to compare with his magnificent study of the Jocasta complex in *Génitrix* (Paris, 1923; tr. G. Hopkins, London, 1950). Mauriac's political views were sometimes more to the left than conventional orthodoxy normally required, though less violently so than those of the British Catholic novelist Graham GREENE, with whom he is often compared. He did not like FRANCO, sided with the Resistance rather than the Vichy government during the German occupation of France, supported MENDÈS-FRANCE in his successful attempt to end the Indo-Chinese war in 1954, and condemned the use of torture by the French army in Algeria. The development of his political views can be found in *Bloc-notes* [Diary entries] (Paris, 1952–64). Mauriac was awarded the Nobel prize for literature in 1952, and was an ardent supporter of both the return to power of DE GAULLE in 1958 and of his solution to the Algerian problem. PMWT
P. Stratford, *Faith and Fiction: Creative Processes in Greene and Mauriac* (Bloomington, 1964); M. Alyn *et al.*, *Mauriac* (Paris, 1977).

Mauss, Marcel (b. Epinal, Vosges, France, 10.5.1872; d. Paris, 10.2.1950). French anthropologist. Mauss was a nephew of DURKHEIM and in effect a favourite pupil too. He wrote no substantial monograph and undertook virtually no fieldwork. His importance to the English-speaking world rests largely on (a) his collaborative studies on sacrifice (with H. Hubert, *Essai sur la nature et la fonction du sacrifice*, Paris, 1899; *Sacrifice: its Nature and Function*, London, 1964) and on classification (with E. Durkheim, 'De quelques formes primitives de la classification', *Année Sociologique*, VI [1901–3]; tr. & ed. R. Needham, *Primitive Classification*, London, 1963), and (b) the 'Essai sur le don' (*Année Sociologique*, ns, I [1925]; *The Gift*, London, 1954). The essay on classification asserts in strongly 'sociologistic' form the dependence of classificatory systems, including epistemological categories, upon the actual form, structure and distribution of particular human societies. In spite of a largely indefensible reductionism, this study has prompted an entire and still fertile tradition of seeking to relate the interior dimensions of cultural perception and meaning to social structure and organization (cognitive anthropology). It is, however, *The Gift* that has principally established Mauss's fame. Short but dense like all his works, this essay has been more influential as a prompter of ideas than as a closely argued and directed thesis. In it he converted the everyday notions of 'exchange' and 'reciprocity' into part of the fundamental vocabulary of anthropological and sociological discourse. Hard though it may be to 'cash' concepts so general and diffuse, they have nevertheless become part of the capital resources (to adopt EVANS-PRITCHARD's metaphor) of social anthropology. The gift is seen as the nodal feature of a system of total exchange, wherein reciprocity, though formally gratuitous, is in effect obligatory: the gift is never free. The system of 'total prestations' (*prestations totales*), where economic, social, religious, political and kinship-based relationships were all involved with each other, was only to be seen in its empirical actuality in certain 'primitive' or (as he usually put it) 'archaic' societies; but it also served as an analytic base for the study of cultures such as our own in which these aspects of 'prestation' are held apart. At all events, subsequent anthropologists of the French school have been led to extend Mauss's idea into contiguous fields, nowhere more powerfully than in the work of LÉVI-STRAUSS, in particular in his extensive studies of marriage exchange. Mauss was intimately involved in the founding and editing of the mouthpiece of the Durkheim school *Année Sociologique*. He also played a major part in the foundation and direction of the Institut d'Ethnologie in Paris, and by his teaching both there and at the Collège de France contributed immensely to the development and persistence of French, and thus of international, anthropology.   IH

May, Robert McCredie (b. Sydney, N.S. Wales, Australia, 8.1.1936). Australian theoretical ecologist. Educated at Sydney University, he was appointed professor of biology at Princeton in 1972 and since 1975 has held the post of Class of 1877 professor of zoology there. His research interests are particularly concerned with the development of theoretical models in ecology to give insight into the dynamics of single populations or the interactions of populations. He has sought to answer the question whether communities with high diversity and complex interrelationships between the constituent populations are inherently more stable than simpler communities. He concludes that extremely complex communities such as tropical rain forests are dynamically fragile, and more susceptible to perturbation at the hands of man than are the relatively simpler but more stable temperate ecosystems. He finds that naturally occurring single-species communities are often very stable, and considers the destabilization

which may occur in agricultural monocultures to be a result not of their lack of complexity but of their lack of evolutionary pedigree.   RTi

Mayakovsky, Vladimir Vladimirovich (b. Bagdadi, Georgia, Russia, 19.7.1893; d. Moscow, USSR, 14.4.1930). Russian poet. The most politically committed Russian poet, born into the family of an impoverished nobleman. On his father's death, his family moved to Moscow. In 1908 Mayakovsky joined the Bolshevik party. Arrested three times, he began writing verse in prison. He studied at the Moscow School of Painting (1911–14), and met David Burliuk, a painter, who, together with KHLEBNIKOV, had formed in 1910 a group of Russian futurists. Mayakovsky's public career as a poet began in 1912, with the appearance, in a futurist symposium, of *Poshchechina obshchestvennomu vkusu* [A slap in the face of public taste], attacking symbolist art as well as inviting readers ' . . . to throw Pushkin, Dostoevsky, Leo TOLSTOY and all the rest over the board of modernity'. In 1913 he published his first book *Ya* [I] (Moscow), followed by the tragedy *Vladimir Mayakovsky* (Moscow, 1914). In 1915 there appeared the poem *Oblako v shtanakh* [A cloud in trousers, or The 13th apostle], in which intimate confession issues in a public statement: 'Down with your love! Down with your art! Down with your society! Down with your religion!' This was followed by *Fleyta pozvonochnik* [The backbone flute] (Petrograd, 1916), a poem written after Mayakovsky became a third partner in the marriage of Osip and Lilya Brik. The next two poems *Voyna i mir* [War and the universe] (Petrograd, 1917) and *Chelovek* [Man] (Petrograd, 1918) express Mayakovsky's affliction with 'Christ' and 'Utopia'. In 1917 he wrote the first Soviet play *Misteria buff* [Mystery bouffe] (Petrograd, 1918) where myth and biblical elements are projected on modern life. In 1918 appeared *Oda revolnutsii* [Ode to the revolution] and *Levy marsh* [Left march].

From now on Mayakovsky, the '13th apostle', descended from the 'poetic heaven' and worked for the People's Commissariat of Education and for

ROSTA (Russian Telegraph Agency), writing short verse and long poems (*V. I. Lenin*, Leningrad, 1925), and *Khorosho* [Good] (Moscow–Leningrad, 1927), scenarios, essays, giving lectures and recitals throughout the USSR and abroad. Between 1923 and 1928 he edited the controversial journal *LEF* [Left front]. Despite *LEF*'s advocacy of art as a tool of revolution in an anti-aesthetic sense, Mayakovsky's poetry had a deeply lyrical dimension: *Pro eto* [About this] (1923) is a case in point. The plays *Klop* [Bedbug] (1928) and *Banya* [Bathhouse] (1929) attack the new bourgeois spirit, philistinism and bureaucracy.

In 1928 Mayakovsky declared himself 'to the left of *LEF*' and joined his arch-enemies RAPP (Russian Association of Proletarian Writers): 'I consider myself a proletarian poet'. In his last poem *Vo ves' golos* [At the top of my voice] (1930) he speaks of himself as a tribune of the revolution – a self-sacrifice on its altar. In 1930 he took his life – perhaps his last revolutionary act. His creative work has three roots: love, God and revolution; while denying the existence of God, he wished to take his place and assigned to love and revolution the task of solving man's essential problems. The search proved a failure. He also failed to create 'a poetry for all'. He did democratize poetry by introducing ordinary speech, slang and journalese, yet his eccentric metaphors, hyperbole, wild diction and inversions made his work difficult for the uninitiated. But he gave Russian poetic language a wholly new direction and served notice of the very different role for the artist in the coming world. The collected works are: *Sobranie sochinenii* (13 vols, Moscow, 1955–61). For translations see: H. Marshall, *Mayakovsky and his Poetry* (London, 1965); P. Blake (ed.), *The Bedbug and Selected Poetry* (London, 1961). VP

E. D. Brown, *Mayakovsky: a Poet in the Revolution* (Princeton, 1973); H. Briggs, *Vladimir Mayakovsky: a Tragedy* (Oxford, 1979).

Mayo, George Elton (b. Adelaide, S. Australia, Australia, 26.12.1880; d. Guildford, Surrey, UK, 1.9.1949). Australian contributor to management studies. Often identified as the founder of the human relations school, he took management thinking beyond the classical views of scientific management of FAYOL, F. W. TAYLOR and others, with their focus on formality, authority, work measurement, organizational structure, delegation, responsibility and accountability. Mayo was professor of industrial research at the Harvard Graduate School of Business when he undertook the Hawthorne experiment, between 1927 and 1932. Initially a study of the effect of lighting conditions on workers and their performance in the Hawthorne works of the Western Electric Company, Chicago, it led to a recognition of the importance of informal organization, group affiliation and human factors in work. Six female workers, assembling telephone relays, were segregated, and the effect on their performance and morale of different working conditions was observed. First they were involved in the development of a group incentive payment scheme, and working methods with more flexibility: output improved. Then the group reverted to the previous situation, with no incentives and tightly regulated working conditions: output rose further. Mayo deduced that increased productivity was due, not to working conditions, but to improved work satisfaction rooted in a sense of values, group commitment, participation and the interest shown by the researchers. In *The Social Problems of an Industrial Civilization* (London, 1947) Mayo sought to relate his ideas to the wider social context; but essentially he was a social psychologist interested in improving management's ability to manage. RIT

F. J. Roethlisberger & W. J. Dickson, *Management and the Worker* (Cambridge, Mass., 1939).

McCarthy, Joseph (b. Appleton, Wis., USA, 14.11.1908; d. Bethesda, Md, 2.5.1957). Junior Republican senator from Wisconsin (1948–56), his name became synonymous with the wholesale denunciation of US civil servants for treasonable sympathies with communism, beginning with the State Department, which was held responsible for the American failure to sustain the regime of CHIANG KAI-SHEK in China in the period 1946–9. These denunciations, compounded of smears, half-truths and exploitation of the twin concepts of 'guilt by association' and 'there's no smoke without fire', were conducted with an extremely effective use of the US media, especially the comparatively new medium of television, particularly after McCarthy's election as chairman of the Senate Subcommittee on Investigations (1953–5). His downfall came when he attacked the army leadership and then his fellow senators, who censured his conduct in 1954. His success lay in his effective mobilization of grass-roots American anti-intellectualism, nativism and class suspicion in a tradition which went back at least 90 years to the 'Know Nothing' party of the 1860s, the only novelty being that whereas earlier anti-intellectualism and xenophobia tended to be hostile to Catholicism and immigrants from Ireland, Italy and Poland, McCarthy's support tended to come from the Catholic working-class voters as much as from the older Protestant rural Midwest, and to be aimed at the university-trained, upper-middle-class, white Anglo-Saxon Protestant members of the American Establishment as well as at their urban educated Jewish counterparts. DCW

R. H. Rovere, *Senator Joe McCarthy* (NY, 1960).

McDougall, Myres Smith (b. Burton, Miss., USA, 23.11.1906). American international lawyer. He spent almost his whole working career in Yale Law School where he was Sterling professor of international law from 1944 to 1975. He has been largely responsible for initiating a new approach to the study of international law by applying the methods of LASSWELL in the social sciences to its discussion. He uses a new structure for the presentation of his material and new concepts for its analysis. In the books that he has written in collaboration with others and in his many articles he adopts a contextual, policy-oriented view of the international legal system; he does not look at international law as a system of rules but as a process of claim and counterclaim between authoritative decision-makers, postulating as its

overriding goal the dignity of man in an increasingly universal public order. These methods have had a considerable impact and attracted a significant following in the USA, particularly at Yale, but have had less influence in the rest of the world. CDG

W. M. Reisman & B. H. Weston, *Toward World Order and Human Dignity* (NY, 1976).

McGregor, Douglas (b. Detroit, Mich., USA, 16.9.1906; d. Acton, Mass., 13.10.1964). American contributor to the human relations school of management studies pioneered by MAYO. The traditional view of management, advanced by FAYOL and underpinning F. W. TAYLOR's scientific management, recognized management's prerogative to direct and control workers, and assumed that the average employee disliked work; hence managers needed to command, coerce and, if necessary, punish. Moreover the workers would prefer such direction, having little ambition and not wanting responsibility. This McGregor called 'theory X'. His alternative 'theory Y' asserted that physical and mental effort in work was natural; that people would exercise self-direction and control if committed to the objectives; that self-actualization was a great motivator; and that the average person could learn not only to accept but to seek responsibility. The consequences of this alternative theory are set out in *The Human Side of Enterprise* (NY, 1960). RIT

McKay, Henry Donald (b. Orient, S. Dak., USA, 6.12.1899). American sociologist, best known for his collaboration with Clifford SHAW in their monumental 'ecological' analyses of delinquency areas in large cities throughout the USA. The most fruitful years of their collaboration were the 1930s and early 1940s. With a painstaking attention to detail almost unparalleled in the history of criminological research, between 1900 and 1938 they mapped out the distribution of delinquency (and a variety of other social problems) for some 20 American cities: *Social Factors in Juvenile Delinquency* (Washington, 1931) and *Juvenile Delinquency and Urban Areas* (Chicago, 1942). This extraordinary endeavour has been continued by McKay to cover the years up to the mid-1960s. Following in the tradition laid by the 19c cartographers, McKay and other members of the Chicago school developed the 'ecological' approach to the study of social problems, an approach which has been a forerunner to the modern sociological study of crime, and is still widely used in criminological research.   JB

J. Snodgrass, 'Clifford R. Shaw and Henry D. McKay: Chicago criminologists', *British Journal of Criminology*, 16 (1976), 1–19.

McLuhan, Herbert Marshall (b. Edmonton, Alta, Canada, 21.7.1911; d. Toronto, Ont., 31.12.1980). Canadian academic and commentator on communications technology. McLuhan was educated at the universities of Manitoba and Cambridge (UK). Converted to Roman Catholicism in 1937, he thereafter taught only in Catholic institutions – notably, St Michael's College of the University of Toronto, where he was a member of the department of English from 1946 until 1977. He is best known for the studies institutionalized in 1963 as the University of Toronto's Center for Culture and Technology. McLuhan's major books were: *The Mechanical Bride* (NY, 1951); *The Gutenberg Galaxy* (Toronto, 1962); *Understanding Media* (NY, 1964); and *War and Peace in the Global Village* (NY, 1968). He cofounded the journal *Explorations* (1953–9), from which an anthology of essays was published as *Explorations in Communication* (Boston, 1960); and Eugene McNamara edited a selection of McLuhan's literary criticism as *The Interior Landscape* (NY, 1969).

A punning presenter of paradoxes and analogies, McLuhan probed the moral and psychological import of contemporary western means of communication and the status of literary texts within a culture dominated by those means. Assuming a neo-Thomist model of the psyche and developing Harold Innis's work on the political consequences of communications technology, McLuhan held that technology is an extension of the human nervous system and that technological changes, by imperceptibly altering patterns of perception, create new environments of sense and feeling. Electronic communications had, he claimed, created a world of instant awareness to which the categories of perspective space and sequential time were irrelevant and in which a sense of private identity was untenable. Inasmuch as McLuhan's analyses generally ignored the economic determinants of technology, the assurance which denizens of his 'Global Village' took from them was specious, and the authority which communications industries briefly gave them was suspect. Yet McLuhan did create an awareness which made possible further work in communications and cultural studies during the azimuth of his own fame.   MOC

D. Theall, *The Medium is the Rearview Mirror* (Montreal, 1971); J. Fekete, *The Critical Twilight* (London, 1977).

McMillan, Edwin Mattison (b. Redondo Beach, Calif., USA, 18.9.1907). American physicist. McMillan was the first person to prepare a transuranium element. He studied at California Institute of Technology and at Berkeley, where in 1932 he became a faculty member. In 1940, after the discovery by HAHN and Strassmann of nuclear fission, McMillan (with his co-worker Abelson) showed that neutron bombardment of uranium produced not only fission, but a new heavy element which was itself a beta emitter. This new isotope, neptunium-239 (named for the planet one beyond Uranus), was the first element to be discovered beyond element 92, uranium, and was hence the first of the transuranium elements, whose syntheses and chemistry were soon to be developed by SEABORG. For this work, McMillan was awarded, jointly with Seaborg, the 1951 Nobel prize for chemistry. Immediately after WW2, during which he worked on radar, sonar and the Manhattan project, McMillan proposed (independently of Veksler in Russia) the principle of phase-stability which allowed synchrotrons to be developed from cyclotrons, overcoming the problem of relativistic mass increase which had been slowing the particles, causing them to become out of phase with the accelerating pulses. For his work on the synchrotron, a vital and revolutionary research tool for probing the structure of the atom, McMillan (jointly with Veksler) received the Atoms for Peace award in 1963. KRS

G. T. Seaborg, *Man-made Transuranium Elements* (Princeton, 1963).

McMillan, Margaret (b. Westchester, NY, USA, 20.7.1860; d. London, UK, 29.3.1931). British educator. After a childhood in Inverness, Scotland, with her grandparents, Margaret and her sister Rachel (1859–1917) became preoccupied with children's poor health in industrial districts and its effect on their education. Official reports had shown preschool children to be physically and psychologically impaired, for which little medical help was available. As a member of the Bradford School Board (1894 –1902) she campaigned restlessly for health centres for poor children, for school meals and for nursery schools, and was rewarded in 1906 by the Education (Provision of Meals) Act, followed by a 1907 Act for medical inspection. A first school clinic was established in 1908 by Rachel and Margaret, and a first open-air nursery school in 1914. Training of teachers and other personnel was clearly important; and the Deptford (London) centre eventually became the Rachel McMillan Training Centre and Open-air Nursery. Margaret wrote several books, but her active campaigning and example of successful practice were even more influential – both on preschool and on primary education generally. In 1907 MONTESSORI opened her Casa dei Bambini; while in 1910 Norway opened its first school clinics, with the 'Oslo breakfast' playing a significant part. But the McMillan sisters' sense of health, play, rest, and learning as a harmony for small children introduced a more holistic concept. EJK

Mead, George Herbert (b. South Hadley, Mass., USA, 27.2.1863; d. Chicago, Ill., 26.4.1931). American social philosopher and founder of social psychology in the USA. After studying under William JAMES at Harvard, Mead taught at the University of Michigan and, after 1894, at the University of Chicago. With John DEWEY, he founded the 'Chicago school' of pragmatism. He published little but lectured brilliantly; his influence spread largely through students from Chicago's sociology department, the first in the world. His lectures were collected in *Mind, Self and Society* (ed. C. W. Morris, Chicago, 1934). Mead's 'social behaviourism' stressed the differences between human and animal behaviour due to language. Human thinking and human social activity develop as two aspects of human communication. In communicating, we learn to assume the roles of others and monitor our action accordingly. Thereby self-consciousness and individuality develop together with cooperation and social organization; human evolution tends towards maximization of sociability and autonomy. Mead was the first to show the importance of play and games in teaching the child to distinguish between 'Me' (behaviour as perceived by others) and 'I' (behaviour as perceived by oneself) and coordinate them by adopting the impersonal standard of the 'generalized other' (i.e. by social norms). Much of Mead's teaching complemented FREUD's and PIAGET's and is widely accepted in social psychology. In sociology, the symbolic interactionist school regards him as its founder. JRT

M. Natanson, *The Social Dynamics of George H. Mead* (Washington, 1956).

Mead, Margaret (b. Philadelphia, Pa, USA, 16.12.1901; d. New York, 15.11.1978). American anthropologist. The first child of an academic family, Mead was attracted to anthropology by BOAS and Ruth Benedict. Her first study was made in Samoa, in 1925–6, where she investigated the then fashionable topic of adolescence. The transition of Samoan girls into adult women was apparently easy and untraumatic. Contrasting their experience with that of American girls, she wrote her bestselling *Coming of Age in Samoa* (NY, 1928). In the following decade she made a series of ethnographic studies of Pacific cultures, but while publishing important specialist reports she remained concerned to relate her findings to the preoccupations of the general educated public in America. Although dealing with exotic cultures, she addressed problems of childrearing, sex roles and personality which were of immediate relevance to a broad readership. After government-sponsored research during WW2, Mead returned to positions at the American Museum of Natural History, and at Columbia University. She was by now something of a guru. Speaking and writing from a variety of platforms, she propagated her view that while cultural factors are the fundamental determinants of behaviour, they are themselves malleable and capable of improvement. In these years she became the most famous anthropologist in the world. AJK

Meade, James Edward (b. Swanage, Dorset, UK, 23.6.1907). British economist. He studied at Oriel College, Oxford, and Trinity College, Cambridge, then from 1930 to 1937 was fellow and lecturer in economics at Hertford College, Oxford. In 1938–40 Meade worked in the financial section and economic intelligence service of the League of Nations, and then from 1940 to 1947 in the economic section of the British Cabinet Office, ending in 1946–7 as director. While in the Cabinet Office, he was responsible for the compilation of the first set of UK national accounts, an advance facilitated by the conceptual innovations of KEYNES's *General Theory* (1936) as well as by the work of Colin Clark, HICKS and others. From 1947 to 1957 Meade was professor of commerce at the London School of Economics, and from 1957 to 1969 professor of political economy at Cambridge.

Meade is a prolific and meticulous theorist, with more than 20 books to his credit, as well as numerous professional papers. His biggest contributions – which won him a Nobel prize in 1977 jointly with Bertil Ohlin – have been in international economics. His *magnum opus*, *The Theory of International Economic Policy* (2 vols, Oxford, 1951–5) was noteworthy on two counts: first, for its application, at once path-breaking and comprehensive, of Keynesian analysis to macroeconomic policy in an open economy; and secondly, for its exhaustive analysis of tariffs and similar trade controls in a welfare-economic context. Meade's other influential works in this field include *A Geometry of International Trade* (London, 1952) and *The Theory of Customs Unions* (Amsterdam, 1955). He has also made significant contributions to the theory of economic growth – *A Neo-Classical Theory of Economic Growth* (London, 1961) – and to the analysis of measures for reducing inequality without sacrificing efficiency in a market economy – *Efficiency, Equality and the Ownership of Property* (London, 1964), and the report of the Institute for Fiscal Studies Committee (Meade Committee) on the *Structure and Reform of Direct Taxation* (1978). Meade has been a strong advocate of incomes policy, that is, of restraints on collective bargaining, so as to permit full employment to be reconciled with price stability (see in particular *Stagflation*, vol. 1: *Wage Fixing*, London, 1982).

Since 1965 Meade has produced successive volumes of a (mainly non-mathematical) *Principles of Economics*, surveying and restating the corpus of economic theory: *The Stationary Economy* (London, 1965); *The Growing Economy* (London, 1968); *The Controlled Economy* (London, 1971); *The Just Economy* (London, 1976). His *The Intelligent Radical's Guide to Economic Policy* (London, 1975) is written for the general reader and conveys admirably the scope and precision of the author's mind. PMO

Medawar, Peter Brian (b. Rio de Janeiro, Guanabara, Brazil, 28.2.1915). British immunologist. After training as a zoologist at Oxford, Medawar early evinced an interest in some of the problems which were to engage his scientific attention, notably in growth and in ageing. However, the needs of badly burned victims of military action in WW2 turned his attention to the problems of skin grafting between individuals, since in principle a graft may substitute for destroyed tissue, although such grafts are normally destroyed by an immunological response. Medawar later, in collaboration with Billingham and Brent, found a 'laboratory solution' to the problem of graft rejection and this opened up a whole new field of research. For this work he shared the Nobel prize for medicine with F. M.

BURNET in 1960. The new impetus given to transplantation biology at this time is shown, *inter alia*, by the now almost routine grafting of kidneys as a therapeutic measure in man. Medawar has continued to be a working research scientist, but has also attracted admiration for the clarity and wit of his presentation of scientific issues to a wider audience. His Reith lectures on *The Future of Man* (London, 1960) and later collections of essays on scientific and philosophical themes (*The Art of the Soluble*, London, 1967; *The Hope of Progress*, London, 1972) are models of exposition. He is perhaps the outstanding biological exponent of POPPER's scepticism on the role of inductive reasoning in science, and was an early advocate of the belief that in biological interactions at the cellular level responses are elective rather than instructive. A cell, in other words, has information allowing it to perform adequately in a finite number of ways. All that a stimulus can do is cause one performance to be selected from this limited repertoire. On the widest issues of human affairs, Medawar is optimistic. He argues that small-scale advances in removing human misery are always worthwhile, and that millennial aspirations should not stand in the way of 'piecemeal social engineering'.   DRN

Meerwein, Hans Lebrecht (b. Hamburg, Germany, 20.5.1879; d. Marburg, Hesse, West Germany, 24.10.1965). German organic chemist, who was the first to postulate the formation of carbonium ions as reaction intermediates. After a brief period at the Wiesbaden College of Chemistry under H. and W. Fresenius, Meerwein studied at Bonn (1900–3) and at Berlin-Charlottenburg (1903–5). Returning to Bonn, he remained there until 1923, when he accepted the chair of chemistry at Königsberg. From 1928 to 1952 he was head of the Chemical Institute at Marburg. In the latter part of his time at Bonn, he made many studies of rearrangements of molecules related to camphor. The results of this work led him, in 1922, to postulate an intermediate role for cryptoions, later known as carbonium ions. Most organic chemists of that time were not ready for

such a revolutionary idea, which was not generally accepted until the 1930s. Molecular arrangements of this type are now named Wagner–Meerwein rearrangements. Meerwein's other contributions included the extensive exploitation of Lewis acids (e.g. boron trifluoride) as catalysts in organic reactions, the discovery and uses of trialkyloxonium salts, the Meerwein–Ponndorf method of reducing aldehydes and ketones, and the Meerwein reaction (i.e. arylation of various types of compound by diazonium salts). It is said that the great success of these experimental researches was due in no small measure to his ideas on reaction mechanisms and electronic theory, which (until later years) were often well in advance of his time.   JSh

Meinecke, Friedrich (b. Salzwedel, Lower Saxony, Germany, 30.10.1862; d. Berlin-Dahlem, West Berlin, 6.2.1954). German historian. From a family of civil servants, Meinecke studied history under Droysen. He spent 14 years in the Prussian State Archives before entering academic life, and began his career as a historian with studies of Prussia. Meinecke published his first major work when he was 45; *Weltbürgertum und Nationalstaat* (Munich, 1908; *Cosmopolitanism and the National State*, Princeton, 1970), a study of the shift from the cosmopolitan ideals of the Enlightenment to the nationalism of romantics such as Fichte. His second important book *Die Idee der Staatsräson* (Munich, 1924; *Machiavellism*, London, 1957) deals with the development of the idea of 'reason of state' from Machiavelli to Frederick the Great. His third major work *Die Entstehung des Historismus* (Munich, 1936; *Historicism*, London, 1972) is concerned with the ideas of individuality and development in the work of European historians from Vico to Ranke. Meinecke's strength lay in his combination of intellectual with political history, the analysis of literary texts with archival research. His aim was to make a synthesis of cultural and political values, of Goethe and Bismarck. He has sometimes been criticized for his concentration on great men, his neglect of social factors, his belief in the primacy of ideas, and his reverence for the state.

However, he became more critical of the state as he grew older. He was opposed to the Nazi regime and his *Die Deutsche Katastrophe* (Wiesbaden, 1946; *The German Catastrophe*, Cambridge, Mass., 1950) suggests that 'the germs of the later evil' could be found as early as Bismarck.   UPB

F. Gilbert, 'Friedrich Meinecke' in *History: Choice and Commitment* (Cambridge, Mass., 1977).

Meireles, Cecilia (b. Rio de Janeiro, Guanabara, Brazil, 7.9.1901; d. Rio de Janeiro, 9.11.1964). Brazilian poet, acclaimed as the best of her time writing in Portuguese. Orphaned at three, she travelled widely, visiting the Orient which has been a lasting influence on her work. With few themes but using a diversity of forms, she reveals an almost physical sense of association with things, compassion for the fragility of life, and the sad realization that a perfect world has welcomed error – original sin with its burden of guilt – a guilt that finds an outlet in her poetry. She senses the brutality and misused strength of mankind. She seems to demand a kind of life different from the flawed life she experiences. An evergreen quality is evident in her sea poetry *Mar absoluto* [The sea absolute] (Pôrto Alegre, 1945), and she recreates the past in *Romanceiro da inconfidência* [Romance of infidelity] (Rio de Janeiro, 1953), which describes the uprising in Minas Gerais in 1789.
                                          DBr

Meitner, Lise (b. Vienna, Austria-Hungary [now Austria], 7.11.1878; d. Cambridge, UK, 27.10.1968). Austrian physicist. Meitner devoted her life to the physics of radioactivity. She received her doctorate in physics in Vienna in 1905 (only the second woman there to do so) and in 1907 went to work in Berlin at the Kaiser Wilhelm Institute for Chemistry with HAHN. Apart from the period during WW1, she stayed in Berlin until 1938. The German invasion of Austria made her position so insecure that she was helped to escape, first to the Netherlands and then to Sweden. She spent the remainder of her scientific career in Stockholm. In 1960 she retired to Cambridge (UK) where some of her family were living. She is chiefly remembered for her work (with her nephew Otto FRISCH) in interpreting the observations of Hahn and Strassmann that when uranium was bombarded with neutrons, barium was produced. She and Frisch proposed that this was evidence for 'nuclear fission' (a term which they coined). Very soon afterwards Frisch did some experiments in Copenhagen which confirmed their hypothesis. She refused an invitation to take part in the development of the atom bomb and hoped that it would be impossible to make a successful device.   HMR

Méliès, Georges (b. Paris, France, 8.12.1861; d. Paris, 21.1.1938). French film pioneer. He was already working as a conjurer and illusionist with his own theatre in Paris at the time of the first LUMIÈRE showings and he quickly moved over to the new form. In his own work he came to explore a world of theatrical fantasy far removed from the outdoor realism of Lumière. The little films he made at his tiny studio at Montreuil are full of tricks and quirky imaginings and he built up his own world populated by gesticulating devils, amiable monsters and rows of dancing chorus girls. His fantasies helped shape the direction taken by the cinema in the period after the first interest in the novelty of moving pictures had worn off, and his importance far outweighs the limited quantity of his output. But Méliès remained at an artisanal level of production – he was most frequently his own actor, writer and director, producer and distributor – at a time when the cinema was beginning to be industrialized in both France and the USA. By 1912 the vogue for the Méliès style had declined and he eventually died a forgotten and neglected figure. On the surface Méliès is little more than an engaging but quickly superseded pioneer, but his seeming primitiveness should not be allowed to detract from his status as an artist. Looked at with sympathy and historical understanding, his world of the fantastic and the marvellous retains its power to capture and hold our imagination even today.   RPA

P. Hammond, *Marvellous Méliès* (London, 1974); J. Frazer, *Artificially Arranged Scenes* (Boston, Mass., 1979).

Mellaart, James (b. London, UK, 14.11.1925). British archaeologist specializing in Near Eastern studies. His extensive field surveys in Turkey led to the discovery of a number of sites crucial to the question of urban origins. Excavations at Hacilar and Catal Hüyük established a complete and unexpected sequence of urban development beginning in the middle of the seventh millennium (*Catal Hüyük: a Neolithic Town in Anatolia*, London, 1967). His more general studies, including *Earliest Civilizations of the Near East* (London, 1965) and *The Chalcolithic and Early Bronze Ages in the Near East and Anatolia* (London, 1966), are of central interest to the problems of urban origins and cultural transmission between the Near East and Europe. BWC

Melnikov, Konstantin Stepanovic (b. Moscow, Russia, 3.8.1890; d. Moscow, USSR, 28.11.1974). Russian architect. Melnikov was the most individualistic of the group of Soviet architects who came to prominence in the brief flowering of the avant-garde arts which marked the early years following the revolution of 1917. Grouped under the banner of constructivism, Melnikov, along with figures such as Vesnin, TATLIN and LISSITZKY, developed a philosophy that combined elements of cubism and futurism. He believed that architects should involve themselves directly in political activity. His work was not, he claimed, simply in a style which reflected the revolution, but was itself part of the revolution. In the early days there were strong links between the Russian avant-garde and the modernists of Western Europe; LE CORBUSIER, for example, designed several buildings for the Soviet government, and Melnikov produced a pavilion for the Paris exposition of 1925 which created a considerable stir by its extraordinary geometric and spatial qualities. Melnikov tried to develop new building types that would reflect the aspirations of a socialist society in the way that palaces reflected feudalism. He spent much time designing workers' clubs and social centres, the best known of which was the Rusakov club in Moscow, completed in 1927. As the grip of STALINism tightened on the USSR, the avant-garde was purged in favour of an officially approved brand of socialist realism which in architectural terms turned out to be neoclassicism. Melnikov himself was denounced as a 'formalist' in 1936 and prevented from working or communicating with the outside world until the late 1960s. But the power of the few images of his work that did reach the West was such as to make him one of the great architectural might-have-beens of the 20c. DS

Mencken, Henry Louis (b. Baltimore, Md, USA, 12.9.1880; d. Baltimore, 29.1.1956). American journalist and critic. Mencken was a deeply sincere and widely respected 'loner' who devoted most of his considerable literary energies to jeering at democracy from the depths of his older American conservatism. He was hated passionately by many Americans and was almost eclipsed as a 'public voice' during the 1930s when American democracy was at its most triumphant. But before he died, he had the satisfaction of knowing that many more Americans were grateful to him for reminding them of their 18c heritage, of the American language, and of such patricians as Thomas Jefferson and his lifelong desire for a meritocracy. He rarely left Baltimore except to cover a political convention, and worked on all the city's four newspapers at various times between 1899 and 1935, while editing *Smart Set* (1914–23) and the *American Mercury* (1924–33). His ridicule of pretentiousness in the social, literary, political and religious aspirations of the 1920s was gathered in six series of *Prejudices* (NY, 1919–27). As a literary critic, he was a vigorous champion of realism and naturalism in American letters; his voluminous study of *The American Language* (NY, 1919, ⁴1936; Supp. 1, 1945; Supp. 2, 1948) is authoritative. His autobiography was published as *Happy Days* (NY, 1940), *Newspaper Days* (NY, 1941) and *Heathen Days* (NY, 1943). RB

MENDEL

Mendel, Gregor Johann (b. Heinzendorf, Moravia, Austria-Hungary [now Hynčice, Czechoslovakia], 22.7.1822; d. Brünn, Bohemia, Austria-Hungary [now Brno, Czechoslovakia], 1.6.1884). Austrian botanist and founder of genetics. Mendel entered the Augustinian monastery of St Thomas at Brünn in 1841 and was ordained in 1847. He spent the rest of his life at Brünn, except for brief trips abroad, and for two years when he studied at the University of Vienna, where his subjects included physics, zoology and botany. During his career he twice failed examinations which would have qualified him as a teacher (though he seems to have successfully taught physics at Brünn Modern School).

Mendel is now generally recognized as the founder of the study of genetics as an experimental science, on the basis of his work with the humble edible pea (*Pisum sativum*), done in the monastery garden at Brünn. From the results of crosses between pea plants differing in easily recognized characteristics such as flower colour and size (normal or dwarf), Mendel formulated the principles underlying inheritance. He realized that it is not the characters themselves, but the factors determining them, that are inherited. Since, in the second generation of his crosses, plants showing different combinations of parental traits segregated in precise ratios, Mendel concluded, from the number of segregants in different classes, that for any one character the pea plant contains two units of inheritance, and that these units result in crosses according to the laws of probability. Hybrid plants, in which two different units were combined, showed the dominant character, and yielded, as well as hybrid offspring, pure-breeding offspring in which the characters from pure-breeding plants of earlier generations were recovered unchanged (see 'Versuche über Pflanzenhybriden' [Experiments in plant hybridization], *Proceedings of the Natural Science Society of Brünn*, 4 [1865], 3–47). Although there is evidence that Mendel had experience in breeding a range of plants and animals, he did not succeed in following up his revolutionary conclusions. Unfortunately the bota-

nist Nägeli, with whom he corresponded for several years, advised him to work with hawkweed (*Hieracium*), which we know now is unsuitable for genetic studies as it does not always outcross (i.e. it often grows from unfertilized seeds). After 1868 administrative chores consequent upon his appointment as abbot curtailed his genetic investigations; nevertheless he continued to follow progress in biology and in his other field of interest, meteorology.

Mendel's classic paper caused hardly a ripple on the contemporary biological surface: not until 1900, 16 years after his death, was its significance appreciated, following the rediscovery of its main results by Hugo de Vries, Carl Correns and Erich von Tschermak. Therein lies a mystery, which the alleged obscurity of the journal in which Mendel's work first appeared does not account for. There are several citations of the work before 1900; Nägeli, who was familiar with it, was influential in biological circles, and none of the three scientists who rediscovered Mendel's laws seems to have had difficulty in tracking it down. Perhaps the most striking and powerful feature of Mendel's analysis – his use of the number of plants occurring in different classes as a basis for deduction – was too new for biologists to assimilate. It is likely also that the prevailing interest in evolutionary mechanisms led biologists to concentrate their attention on variation which seemed to have an obvious survival value, and characters such as flower colour in peas may have been dismissed as somewhat trivial. But Mendel's place in the pantheon of science is now assured. All subsequent work on genetics has built on his foundations.

APJ

H. Iltis, *Life of Mendel* (NY, 1932); C. Stern & E. R. Sherwood (eds), *The Origin of Genetics: a Mendel Source-book* (San Francisco, 1967).

Mendele, Mocher Seforim, ps. of Shalom Jacob Abramovitch (b. Kapolic, Belorussia, Russia, 20.12.1835; d. Odessa, 8.12.1917). Yiddish and Hebrew writer. Celebrated as the 'grandfather' of both modern Yiddish and modern Hebrew literature, Mendele was a pro-

lific writer and the first to 'translate' contemporary trends in European literature into Yiddish, not by imitation but by drawing on the living sources of his environment. In some of his early and later stories he attacked the narrowness and shortcomings of contemporary Jewish life (see *Dos kleyneme nshele*, Odessa, 1866; tr. G. Stillman, *The Parasite*, NY, 1956), not by preaching but by dramatizing characters and their behaviour. Often he used the poor and dispossessed as his fictional heroes (*Fishke, der kroomer*, Zhitomir, 1869; NY, 1929, tr. G. Stillman, *Fishke the Lame*, NY, 1960), and cripples and beggars appear frequently in his narrative tales. In describing their lives and thoughts Mendele was not aiming to provoke pity or sympathy: by attacking the corrupt practices of the self-appointed leaders of the community, as in his play *Di Takse oder di bande shtot baaley toives* [The tax, or the gang of the town's charity dispensers] (Odessa, 1869), he showed up the evils of society as no Jewish writer had previously done. Mendele employs both satire and humour as in '*Massouous Binjamin ha-slishi*' (1878; tr. M. Spiegel, *The Travels and Adventures of Benjamin the Third*, NY, 1949), and with his acute sense of observation his stories can be studied alike as literature and as documentary of 19c Jewish life in Tsarist Russia. Some of his critics took exception to the emphasis he sometimes laid on the 'negative' aspects of Jewish behaviour; but even they had to admire the mastery and power of the writer who transformed Yiddish from a colloquial idiom to a literary medium. Significantly even Mendele began by writing in Hebrew, but then switched to writing exclusively in Yiddish. Late in life, however, he decided to translate some of his own early Yiddish stories into Hebrew, adapting them to a modern idiom and thereby paving the way for what became modern Hebrew prose.
JSo

Mendelsohn, Eric (b. Allenstein, East Prussia, Germany [now Olsztyn, Poland], 21.3.1887; naturalized British citizen, 1938; naturalized American citizen, 1946; d. San Francisco, Calif., USA, 15.9.1953). German/British/American architect. Trained as an architect in Berlin and Munich, Mendelsohn's powerful and individual imagery was first revealed in an exhibition in Berlin (1919) of sketches made while on army service. Strongly influenced by expressionist theories, he was to crystallize them in the observatory tower at Potsdam (1920) built for further research into EINSTEIN's theories of relativity. This building, designed to symbolize the scientific investigation of the universe, is now regarded as one of the key works in expressionist architecture. In spite of the technical difficulties of translating the idea into reality, Mendelsohn was able to achieve a built form which corresponded closely with the initial sketch. Throughout his life these initial sketches, which he claimed contained the whole organic idea, were unfailingly adhered to during the construction of the building. During the 1920s Mendelsohn moved away from expressionism towards what became the 'international style'. The Schocken department stores at Stuttgart (1926) and Chemnitz (1928), and the Universum Cinema, Berlin (1928), typify this period. In 1933 Mendelsohn left Germany for the UK, joining Serge Chermayeff in practice. From this period a house in Chelsea (1936) and the De La Warr pavilion, Bexhill (1935), are noteworthy. In 1941 he emigrated to the USA. Work from this final period includes the Maimonides Medical Center, San Francisco (1950), and buildings for the Atomic Energy Commission at Berkeley, California (1953). PAC

A. Whittick, *Eric Mendelsohn* (London, 1940).

Mendès-France, Pierre (b. Paris, France, 11.1.1907; d. Paris, 18.10.1982). French prime minister (June 1954–February 1955). He was responsible, first, for the French role in the Geneva South-East Asia Agreements of 20.7.1954 by which French participation in the war against the Viet Minh was ended and the partition of Indo-China into two Vietnamese states, Laos and Cambodia, was formally established; and second for the introduction into the French Assembly for ratification of the European Defence Community Treaty of 1952, where it was rejected on 30.8.1954. He subsequently accepted, as did the Assembly, the alternative Western European Treaty. In domestic politics his coalition of progressive Radicals, reformist Gaullists and Socialists was widely regarded, especially outside France, as heralding the establishment of a stable government and the advent of a new French generation of modern-minded reformists who would break the power of established interests and 'bring France into the twentieth century'. *Mendèsisme*, however, turned out to be short-lived, Mendes's own puritanism (he tried to tackle the widespread curse of alcoholism in France by attacking the small-scale licensed distillers and advocating the consumption of milk rather than wine) demonstrating a certain idealistic disdain for the abiding interests of the common, sensual, French man-in-the-street.   DCW

Menuhin, Yehudi (b. New York, USA, 22.4.1916). American violinist. Menuhin comes from a remarkably talented musical family and won international fame as a violinist while still a boy. His early recordings testify to a strong, well-focused tone of extraordinary expressive range. It was for him that BARTÓK wrote his Sonata for solo violin (1944). In more recent years, problems of technique have detracted from his prodigious musicality, though he has retained public acknowledgement as an apostle of peace and understanding through music. He has helped to make it possible for Russian and Indian musicians to visit the West and has tried to show the absence of musical boundaries by playing with, for example, Indian and jazz musicians. He has encouraged young performers, most notably by founding the Yehudi Menuhin school in 1963 (at Stoke d'Abernon, Surrey, UK) to provide intensive training for musically gifted children. His books include *Theme and Variations* (London, 1972) and *Unfinished Journey* (London, 1977).
                              PG
R. Magidoff, *Yehudi Menuhin* (London, ²1973); R. Daniels, *Conversations with Menuhin* (London, 1979).

Merleau-Ponty, Maurice (b. Rochefort-sur-Mer, Charente-Maritime, France, 14.3.1908; d. Paris, 5.5.1961). French philosopher. A *lycée* teacher until WW2, Merleau-Ponty became a professor at Lyons in 1945, at the Sorbonne in 1949 and was appointed to the Collège de France in 1952. Closest to HUSSERL of the existentialists, he insisted in his *Phénomenologie de la perception* (Paris, 1945; tr. C. Smith, *Phenomenology of Perception*, London, 1962) on the bodily nature of sense perception as a physical interaction between the embodied perceiver and the world he perceives. Each acts on the other: the world by supplying opportunities for agency to the perceiver, the perceiver by endowing his environment with meaning and form. In the early postwar years he was associated with SARTRE as a fellow-traveller of the Communist party, justifying STALIN's rule by terror (see *Humanisme et terreur* [Humanism and terror], Paris, 1947). The Korean War disillusioned Merleau-Ponty who broke with Sartre and moved to a position of comparative political detachment.   AQ

Merton, Robert King (b. Philadelphia, Pa, USA, 5.7.1910). American sociologist. A pupil of PARSONS at Harvard, Merton has taught at Columbia University since 1941, where he was also associate director, with LAZARSFELD, of the Bureau of Applied Social Research. In his work and influence, which have been extensive, Merton has sought to bridge two gaps: between what MILLS called the 'grand theory' of Parsons and the 'abstracted empiricism' of Lazarsfeld, and between general sociology and the specialized fields of social research, to several of which he has made outstanding contributions. *Social Theory and Social Structure* (Glencoe, Ill., 1951, ³1968) remains his major work. Its plea for 'theories of the middle range' and its 'paradigm for functional analysis' were exemplified by influential studies of deviance and anomie, dysfunctions of bureaucracy, relative deprivation and reference groups, role theory, interpersonal influence, sociology of knowledge and historical sociology (see below). Later publications have developed these themes and cover an even wider range. Although the functionalism of the 1950s has been much criticized, respect for the classical quality of Merton's scholarship remains undiminished. The essays collected in *Sociological Ambivalence* (NY, 1976) show how he has modified his approach in a structuralist direction. JRT

Historians of science have been deeply influenced by Merton's doctoral dissertation, first published in 1938, on *Science, Technology and Society in Seventeenth Century England* (NY, ²1970). Although it originally appeared in the rather obscure journal *Osiris* at the invitation of Merton's teacher and mentor SARTON, the work provoked considerable controversy and suggested important innovations, both theoretical and empirical, in the study of science as a social process. His method of collecting biographical data on large numbers of scientists (prosopography) has become a significant technique in the analysis of scientific communities. Theoretically, Merton's work took up the thesis of Max WEBER on the relationship between Protestantism and capitalism by examining the explosion of scientific activity in 17c England as a central part of social and cultural change. Here, in *Social Theory and Social Structure* and in *The Sociology of Science* (Chicago, 1973), a collection of his papers written between 1935 and 1972, he has shown the need for a marriage between history of science and sociology, and has established the sociology of science as a discipline in its own right. LJJ

L. A. Coser (ed.), *The Idea of Social Structure. Essays in Honor of R. K. Merton* (NY, 1975).

Merton, Tom Feverel (Thomas) (b. Prades, Pyrénées-Orientales, France, 31.1.1915; d. Bangkok, Thailand, 10.12.1968). American writer, mystic and monk. A graduate of Columbia University in New York, where he became a Catholic, Merton entered the Cistercians of the Strict Observance (Trappists) at Gethsemani Abbey in Kentucky in 1941. For the rest of his life Merton wrote works of poetry, spirituality, mysticism and theology. His autobiography *The Seven Storey Mountain* (NY, 1948) was an instant success. In the subsequent 20 years before his accidental death while on a visit to Asia, Merton divided his time between his monastic routine of prayer, manual work and solitude, and the growing demands made upon him as a writer and, to some extent, as a public figure. His attachment to asceticism led to his living for a time as a hermit: his concern for the world to an increasing involvement in social issues. This often serious tension in his life helps to explain the popularity of his writings. More than anyone else in the 20c, Merton succeeds in interpreting to the Western mind the meaning of contemplation and the role of the monk. PFL

M. Furlong, *Merton: a Biography* (London, 1980).

Messiaen, Olivier Eugène Prosper Charles (b. Avignon, Vaucluse, France, 10.12.1908). French composer. Messiaen developed very early in his career a distinctive style, based on his own modal system and on a speculative interest in rhythm, and on his wish to expound in music the truths of the Catholic faith. Though these concerns have not been widely shared, he has had a determining influence on the avant-garde through his openness to Asian influences and through his work as a teacher at the Paris Conservatoire, where BOULEZ, STOCKHAUSEN and BARRAQUÉ were all his pupils. The more important of his earlier works are almost all contemplations of religious subjects laid out in several movements. They include compositions for his own instrument, the organ – *L'Ascension* [The ascension] (1934), *La Nativité du Seigneur* [The birth of the saviour] (1935) and *Les corps glorieux* [The bodies in glory] (1939) – which continue the French tradition of sensuous mysticism. But Messiaen was also able to transfer this style to the piano, in *Visions de l'Amen* [Visions of the amen] for two keyboards (1943) and *Vingt regards sur l'Enfant Jésus* [Twenty meditations on the infant Jesus] (1945), and to a chamber group in *Quatuor pour la fin du temps* [Quartet for the end of time] (1941). In subsequent works, including the richly scored *Turangalîla-symphonie* (1949), he approached the theme of human love, which in his marital song-cycle *Poèmes pour Mi* [Poems for Mi] (1937) he had already shown as an image of divine love.

After the massive outpouring of *Turangalîla* he embarked on a short phase of experimentation with serial and numerical procedures. It was the music of this period, and especially the *Mode de valeurs et d'intensités* [Mode of values and intensities] for piano (1949), which excited his younger colleagues and students. His interest in birdsong, accurately transcribed in such works as *Oiseaux exotiques* [Exotic birds] for piano, wind and percussion (1956), led him to a brilliant, highly coloured style exemplified also by later religious works, *Couleurs de la cité céleste* [Colours of the celestial city] for similar forces (1964) and *Et exspecto resurrectionem mortuorum* [And I look for the resurrection of the dead] for large wind ensemble and percussion (1965). His most recent works, including the vast oratoria *La Transfiguration de Notre Seigneur Jésus-Christ* [The transfiguration of our lord Jesus Christ] (1969), draw on techniques from every stage in his development, whose earlier phases are covered in his *Technique de mon langage musical* (Paris, 1944; *Technique of My Musical Language*, Paris, 1950).   PG

R. S. Johnson, *Messiaen* (London, 1975); R. Nichols, *Messiaen* (London, 1975).

Metz, Christian (b. Béziers, Hérault, France, 12.12.1941). French film semiotician. Metz's initial concern was with the nature of cinematic language. Using the systematic understanding of natural language developed by linguistics, he showed the difficulties of any simple idea of cinema as a language and set out the specific terms of cinematic signification (how films produce meanings): *Essais sur la signification au cinéma* (vol. 1, Paris, 1968; tr. M. Taylor, *Film Language: a Semiotics of the Cinema*, NY, 1974; vol. 2, Paris, 1972); *Langage et cinéma* (Paris, 1971; tr. D. J. Umiker-Sebeok, *Language and Cinema*, The Hague, 1974). His later work develops a metapsychology of cinema, examining the structure and mechanisms of the particular relations of viewing that cinema institutes for the spectator (see *Le Signifiant imaginaire*, Paris, 1977; tr. C. Britton, A. Williams, B. Brewster & A. Guzzetti, *Psychoanalysis and Cinema: the*

Imaginary Signifier, London, 1982). Important generally in the field of semiotics (see also *Essais sémiotiques* [Semiotic essays], Paris, 1977), Metz's work has been extremely influential in film studies: it laid the basis for a rigorous approach to questions of signs and meaning in cinema.   SH

Screen Reader 2: Cinema and Semiotics (London, 1981).

Meyerhold, Vsevolod Emilievich, *né* Karl Theodor Kasimir (b. Penza, Russia, 28.1.1874; d. Moscow, USSR, 2.2.1940). Russian theatrical director. He dominated the Russian avant-garde stage from 1914 to the official suppression of what *Pravda* termed his 'alien theatre' in January 1938. Joining the Bolsheviks soon after the revolution, he fought in the Red Army and headed the state theatre organization up to February 1921, before withdrawing to run his own Moscow company at the old Sohn Theatre, known as the Meyerhold Theatre till it closed for rebuilding in 1931. There he staged his best-known productions, from Crommelynck's *Le Cocu magnifique* (1922), with its kinetic-constructivist set and 'biomechanical' acting, to the MAYAKOVSKY and Olyesha plays whose critical approach to Soviet society made him so unpopular with the 'proletarian' polemicists in 1929–30 and the STALINist arts administration later. Originally based on the *commedia dell' arte*, his characteristic methods came to involve abolishing the proscenium, exposing the theatre's back wall, splitting the plot into episodes, structuring dialogue and action like music, making radical adaptations of the classics and carefully picking significant props. Among his collaborators in such innovations were EISENSTEIN and Tretyakov, the artists Popova, Stepanova, RODCHENKO and LISSITZKY, and the composers Shebalin and SHOSTAKOVICH. Ranged thus on the extreme 'left' of the Soviet cultural scene, he was an unperson for some 20 years following his arrest (June 1939) and execution, but exerted a strong influence on those who, like BRECHT in Germany, remained aware of his work.   JWMW

E. Braun, *The Theatre of Meyerhold* (London, 1974); M. Hoover, *Meyerhold:*

the Art of Conscious Theater (Amherst, 1974).

Michels, Robert (b. Cologne, N. Rhine-Westphalia, Germany, 9.1.1876; d. Rome, Italy, 3.5.1936). German sociologist and economist. Michels was born into a worthy German family but spent most of his career teaching outside his native country, at the universities of Turin, Basle and Perugia. An admirer of MOSCA, Michel's most important work was published in 1911: *Zur Soziologie des Parteiwesens in der modernen Demokratie* (Leipzig, ²1925; *Political Parties*, NY, 1949). This is notable as the first attempt to link increasing bureaucratization with the oligarchic tendencies in modern democratic societies. 'The iron law of oligarchy', as he described his main thesis, postulates that as organizations become more complex and bureaucratized, power becomes concentrated in the hands of an elite at the top. The increasing size of organizations and the complexity of the decisions to be made make the participation of the rank and file members impossible; from this follow apathy and alienation, and the increased concentration of the control of communications in a few hands. Michels went on to argue that, once established, the organizational elite made its primary aim the preservation of its power and privileges. If this clashed with the aims of the rank and file, so much the worse for the latter which would always be sacrificed to the former. In this way he explained, from a careful study of the German Socialist party, how the leadership became marked by bureaucratic conservatism, resulting in a decline in radicalism against the original intentions of both the membership and the leaders.

Michels's theory was principally concerned with the bureaucratization of voluntary bodies such as political parties and trade unions. But he argued that if such voluntary organizations ceased to function in a democratic way, and society became dominated by large-scale oligarchic political regimes with a strong common interest in resisting any changes in the *status quo*, the various elites would combine to form an interlocking dominant group. In his later writings Michels came to regard such elitist rule as not only inevitable, but desirable, and did not oppose the rise of fascism in his adopted country of Italy. Subsequent discussion of Michels's thesis has extended it to the state bureaucracy in communist countries (see e.g. DJILAS, *The New Class*, 1957), but has largely refused to accept the inevitability of his pessimistic conclusions in pluralist democratic societies. Michels's *Corso di sociologica politica* has been translated as *First Lectures in Political Sociology* (NY, 1949). ALCB

Mies van der Rohe, Ludwig (b. Aachen, N. Rhine-Westphalia, Germany, 27.3.1886; naturalized American citizen, 1944; d. Chicago, Ill., USA, 17.8.1969). German/American architect and teacher. One of the founders of the modern movement in architecture, his early education was essentially practical: he studied at a trade school and worked on building sites, with experience as a draughtsman and apprentice to a furniture designer before employment in the office of BEHRENS. His personal work after WW1 was influenced by the neoclassical architecture of K. F. Schinkel and the expression of simple construction used by the Dutch architect H. P. Berlage. In 1929 he designed the German pavilion at the Barcelona exhibition – a steel and glass structure in which the space-enclosing partitions were detached from the structural frame. He also designed its furniture in an original and characteristic style which has persisted to the present day. 'Mies' was appointed director of the world-famous Bauhaus in 1930 but closed the school in 1933 as a protest against the Nazis. In 1938 he emigrated to the USA and was appointed director of the school of architecture at the Illinois Institute of Technology. He is said to have based his attitudes to architecture and the teaching of it on St Thomas Aquinas's proposition, 'Reason is the first principle of all human work.' The curriculum at the Illinois school was designed to teach general principles with a strong emphasis on construction, encouraging general rather than specialized solutions, an approach which contrasted with most other contemporary schools of architecture in which the aim was to engender individuality of expression. Mies van der Rohe's own work was based on these principles. His buildings are models of structural clarity and simple geometry. They had enormous influence on his contemporaries and indeed on many present-day architects, who respect his handling of the high-rise skeleton-frame tower block, exemplified in the twin towers on Lake Shore Drive, Chicago (1948–51), and the Seagram building, New York (1954–8). The former is in black-painted steel, aluminium and plate glass; the latter in bronze cladding with bronze-tinted glass. Each building, by using large-scale structural bays, has a considerable degree of flexibility and allows the owners to change spatial arrangements without interfering with the basic structure. A further seminal building is the steel and glass Farnsworth house at Plan, Illinois (1945–50), in which the raised floor seems to hover above the ground, and only plate-glass walls divide the interior from the surrounding landscape. NW

C. P. Johnson, *Mies van der Rohe* (NY, 1947); P. Carter, *Mies van der Rohe at Work* (London, 1974).

Miller, Arthur (b. New York, USA, 17.10.1915). American dramatist. Miller once explained that his ambition was 'to bring to the stage the thickness, awareness, and complexity of the novel'. In an *oeuvre* of modest proportions, Miller has explored the relations of individuals to each other, and to society. His most celebrated play *Death of a Salesman* (NY, 1949) presented personal failure and self-deception in a realistic manner, precisely catching the textures and dreams of lower-middle-class American life. He turned in *The Crucible* (NY, 1953) to the Salem witchcraft trials. The play had a strong contemporary parallel in the attempt to rid America of communist influence. (Miller worked in various proletarian jobs before becoming a professional playwright and in the Federal Theater Project in the 1930s: a natural target for the MCCARTHYites, he declined to 'name names' before the House Un-American Activities Committee in 1956.) In *A View from the Bridge* (NY, 1955), *After the Fall* (NY, 1964)

and *The Price* (NY, 1968) Miller continued his concern with the uncertainties and uneasy conscience of contemporary American life. His later work has met with little success on Broadway: productions include *The Creation of the World and Other Business* (1972), *Up from Paradise* (1974) and *The Archbishop's Ceiling* (1976). EH

D. S. R. Welland, *Miller: a Study of his Plays* (London, 1979).

Miller, Henry (b. New York, USA, 26.12.1891; d. Big Sur, Calif., 7.6.1980). American novelist. The Bad Boy of American letters, Miller did not seriously begin to write until he was 40 and had settled in Paris as an expatriate. There he came under the influence of surrealism, CÉLINE, and a bohemian circle which included DURRELL and Anaïs Nin. Miller's first book *Tropic of Cancer* (Paris, 1931) was quickly followed by other volumes in which he wrote about his early life in New York, his innumerable sexual adventures, and his friends. His books were banned as pornography, and for most of his career were taken less seriously as literature than they deserved. Miller contributed mightily to the cult of self-expression in modern literature, and properly belongs with D. H. LAWRENCE as one of the central writers of the age. His work, and that of Lawrence, helped roll back the boundaries of censorship in the 1950s, when *Lady Chatterley's Lover* and Miller's *Tropic of Cancer* were prosecuted for obscenity in Britain and the USA. Defending himself against one critic, Miller admirably summed up his approach to literature: 'If it [*Sexus*] was no good, it was true; if it was not artistic, it was sincere; if it was in bad taste, it was on the side of life.' In addition to his novels, Miller also wrote travel books and highly idiosyncratic literary criticism. EH

J. Martin, *Always Merry and Bright: the Life of Henry Miller* (Santa Barbara, 1978).

Millett, Katherine Murray (Kate) (b. St Paul, Minn., USA, 14.9.1934). American sculptor and feminist. A graduate in English with a first-class degree from Oxford, Millett was teaching at Columbia University when her involvement in the American civil rights movement of the late 1960s stimulated her awareness of sexual discrimination. When her outspokenness cost her her job, her rebuttal was to meet her antagonists on their own ground by arguing her case in 'mandarin prose'. She extended her PhD thesis beyond literary criticism to demonstrate how patriarchy, using sex as a natural caste system, determines a power structure in which men dominate women. She explained how, between 1830 and 1930, philosophy, literature and the rise of the feminist movement reflected social and technological changes which began to free women from such exploitation. But from 1930 to 1960, feminism was undermined – in Nazi Germany by design, in Soviet Russia by default, and in the USA by a deterioration in the economic and educational status of women. This counter-revolutionary attempt to preserve the patriarchal family, she argued, could be seen in functionalist sociology and FREUDian psychology, but was best demonstrated in the works of D. H. LAWRENCE, who glorified masculinity, Henry MILLER, who expressed the violence of male denigration of women, and MAILER, who brought the counter-revolution to breaking point, explaining yet still imprisoned by the virility cult. Based on this thesis, *Sexual Politics* (NY, 1969) became a cornerstone of the modern feminist movement which, alongside the second sexual revolution, Millett hoped would challenge the separate temperamental categorization of the sexes. *The Prostitution Papers* (NY, 1971) studied prostitutes from a feminist viewpoint, but her subsequent work has been self-exploratory: her autobiography *Flying* (NY, 1974) and a novel *Sita* (NY, 1976), about a lesbian affair. Millett now primarily sees herself as an artist and sculptor.   MI

Mills, Charles Wright (b. Wavo, Tex., USA, 28.8.1916; d. New York, 20.3.1962). American sociologist. Educated at the universities of Texas and Wisconsin, Mills joined the faculty at Columbia University in 1945, where he directed the labour section of the Bureau of Applied Social Research until 1948. *The New Men of Power* (NY, 1948) and *White Collar* (NY, 1951) studied respectively American labour leaders and the 'new middle class'. They combined LAZARSFELD's research methods with ideas derived from MARX, FREUD and Max WEBER through the Frankfurt school, then in exile at Columbia. *Character and Social Structure* (with H. Gerth, NY, 1953) synthesized these ideas with G. H. MEAD's social psychology. In *The Power Elite* (NY, 1956), his best-known book, Mills claimed that postwar America was ruled by an oligarchy of political, military and business chiefs whose hidden monopoly of big decisions pre-empted the democratic process, which had also been corrupted by the mass media. This marked Mills's transition from social researcher to social critic. Increasingly an outsider at Columbia, though a popular lecturer, he attacked the reigning sociologies of Lazarsfeld and PARSONS in *The Sociological Imagination* (NY, 1959) in the name of moral commitment and 'intellectual craftsmanship'. His later works were polemical, protesting against nuclear policy and defending the Cuban revolution. Originally a follower of John DEWEY's social liberalism, at the time of his death Mills was moving closer to Marxism; his work inspired the New Left and 'radical sociology' of the 1960s.
JRT

H. Aptheker, *The World of C. Wright Mills* (NY, 1960).

Milne, Alan Alexander (b. London, UK, 18.1.1882; d. Hartfield, E. Sussex, 31.1.1956). British writer and dramatist. Best known for his books for children which include *Once on a Time* (London, 1917) and *Toad of Toad Hall* (London, 1929), a play based on Kenneth Grahame's *Wind in the Willows* (1908), Milne's fame rests upon the four Christopher Robin books: two of stories, *Winnie-the-Pooh* (London, 1926) and *The House at Pooh Corner* (London, 1928), and two of verse, *When We Were Very Young* (London, 1924) and *Now We Are Six* (London, 1927). Milne's son Christopher was the inspiration and the other famous characters were originally his toys. Illustrator and in a sense cocreator was the artist E. H. Shepherd.

The characteristics of Piglet (small and timid), Eeyore the donkey (gloomy), Kanga (maternal), Tigger (bouncy) are readily identified in a child's world, but it is Pooh, the Bear-of-Very-Little-Brain, a slow-witted, vain and greedy but lovable teddy bear, that is the child's perfect foil. Incidents in the Hundred Acre Wood, a secure, self-contained world, such as playing Pooh-sticks, trying to track a Heffalump, and tracking a Woozle, provide lasting memories and the gentle humour appeals to children and adults alike.   JMM

Milne, Edward Arthur (b. Hull, Humb., UK, 14.2.1896; d. Dublin, Irish Republic, 21.9.1950). British mathematician and astrophysicist. In 1916, while still an undergraduate at Cambridge, he joined the anti-aircraft experimental division of the Ministry of Munitions. After WW1 he returned to Cambridge where he became assistant director of the solar physics observatory in 1920 and. began his work on the theory of stellar atmospheres. At that time little was known about the exact conditions in a stellar atmosphere but within the next 10 years Milne's own work and that which he inspired revolutionized that situation. Outstanding was his study, with R. H. Fowler, of ionization in stellar atmospheres which made it possible to fix a temperature scale to the stellar spectral sequence. In 1925 Milne moved to Oxford, became Rouse-Ball professor of mathematics four years later, and remained at Oxford for the rest of his life. He now turned his attention to the theory of stellar structure and, in particular, to the structures of stars in which some of the material is quantum-mechanically degenerate. The methods which he introduced were valuable but much of his interpretation was mistaken, which brought him into bitter conflict with EDDINGTON.

From 1932 onwards he devoted himself almost entirely to the development of his theory of kinematic relativity, which he regarded as his greatest contribution to science. He accepted EINSTEIN's special theory of relativity but not the general theory, believing that it was possible to derive the laws governing the universe from a small number of general principles. He started by constructing a theory of the universe as a whole and from this deduced results for smaller-scale phenomena – almost precisely the opposite of the procedure adopted by Einstein. With the aid of this theory, Milne worked out new systems of dynamics and electrodynamics as well as a new basis for atomic physics. Kinematic relativity did not win general acceptance and little work has been done on it since his death, but some of his ideas on cosmology, developed during those years, have been of lasting value. Milne's books include: *Relativity, Gravitation and World Structure* (Oxford, 1935) and *Kinematic Relativity* (Oxford, 1948).   JCM

Miłosz, Czesław (b. Szetejnie, Lithuania, Russia [now Lithuania, USSR], 30.6.1911; naturalized American citizen, 1963). Polish/American poet, essayist and translator, professor of Slavic literatures at Berkeley, California, and 1980 Nobel prize-winner for literature. In pre-war Poland Miłosz was a leading figure of the Żagary group, whose catastrophism was a hybrid of SPENGLERian and TOYNBEEan historiosophy. The problems of the intellectual under STALINism are exposed in *Zniewolony umysł* (Paris, 1953; tr. J. Zielonko, *The Captive Mind*, London, 1953), published after Miłosz left Poland for Paris in 1951. Ten years later he settled in the USA. But whatever the gains of adjusting to an American environment, his poetry is steeped in the landscapes of his native Lithuania. Acclaimed as a Catholic poet and as 'the only real pantheist in Polish literature', Miłosz, without denying the strong Christian element in his poetry, is anxious to stress the Manichaean dichotomy that runs through his work. Critics have pointed to the biographical determinants of Miłosz's historicism; but ELIOT, Swedenborg, Simone WEIL, William Blake and his Land of Ulro provide major signposts on the poet's road from pseudo-Hegelianism to gnosis and self-definition. His poetry and essays are closely woven into a canvas of autobiographical confession caught between metaphysics and politics. Miłosz is a complex poet whose epiphanies are rooted in sensual experience, and whose enunciation of moral judgements has willy-nilly made of him the conscience of his nation. Translations of his work have been published as *Native Realm* (tr. C. S. Leach, NY, 1968), *The Issa Valley* (tr. L. Iribarne, Manchester, 1981), and *Emperor of the Earth* (Berkeley, Calif., 1977). NT

Miró, Gabriel (b. Alicante, Spain, 28.7.1879; d. Madrid, 27.5.1930). Spanish novelist and short-story writer. Though never a popular writer because of the complexity of his prose style, Miró is one of the most distinguished Spanish novelists of the first half of this century. Developing from a *fin-de-siècle* decadence in his early work to a restrained modernism, in which he blends traditional and new techniques, his fame today rests principally on three works: *Las cerezas del cementerio* [The cherries in the cemetery] (Barcelona, 1910), *El abuelo del Rey* [The king's grandfather] (Barcelona, 1915), and a two-volume novel *Nuestro Padre San Daniel* and *El obispo leproso* (Madrid, 1921–6; tr. C. Remfry-Kidd, *Our Father San Daniel*, London, 1930). Though conceived on a smaller scale, the latter novel stands comparison with PROUST. Miró sets out to recreate the world of his boyhood in the provincial town of Orihuela, now transformed into the fictional Oleza, and it is in the delicate, subtle and evocative portrayal of a claustrophobic provincial life-style that the work is outstandingly successful. The creation from memory of a lost world is accompanied by a penetrating yet sober depiction of social mores and especially of clerical influence and its asphyxiating effects on provincial society. Although Miró's censure is unmistakable, what stands out in his manner of narration is his Flaubertian *impassibilité*, his complete control over the narrative, the sculptured detail of his prose and his preoccupation with conveying the nature of experience. He is unquestionably the most objective and artistically conscious of the Spanish novelists of his time, and his style has been widely admired. CAL

C. G. Brown, *A Literary History of Spain:* vi, *The Twentieth Century* (London, 1972).

Miró, Jóan (b. Barcelona, Spain, 20.4.1893). Spanish painter and sculptor. At 14 Miró studied under Modesto Urgelli, an imaginative painter much influenced by the 19c Swiss artist Böcklin, also the inspiration of CHIRICO. In 1918 Miró was exposed to cubism and the postimpressionists. In 1919 he visited Paris for the first time and met his fellow countryman PICASSO. Returning to Spain, he began to paint truly original pictures combining direct observation of people and places with a certain cubist formalism. In 1920 he returned to Paris, as he continued to do every winter, spending his summers, until the beginning of the Spanish civil war, either in Barcelona or at the family farm at Montroige: an opportunity to assimilate and distil into his own work the avant-garde ferment of the French capital.

Until 1923 his paintings were dense and precise but, on renting a studio in the same building as MASSON, he came under the influence of the future surrealist group and replaced modified realism by a flattened pictorial plane in which small fantastic creatures, not unlike those invented by Hieronymous Bosch, played out cheerful if mischievous little dramas.

Throughout the 1920s and early 1930s Miró simplified his imagery until it resembled an arbitrary if elegant shorthand on a thinly painted ground usually of one colour. While resisting any pressure to participate in the polemical aspect of surrealism, and never relinquishing an aesthetic bias, his work is the closest to the surrealist ideal of automatism. Playful and erotic, these pictures are amongst the most beautiful of this century.

Intensely disturbed and enraged by the political situation in Europe and especially in Spain, the later 1930s saw Miró deepening his perspective and creating within it solidly modelled creatures, very much more sinister in impact. Yet during WW2, first in France and then in Spain, he created a long series of rather small paintings full of intricate elements – amongst them stars, moons, women and birds in rich and serene colours; a retreat into his own spiritual being. Since 1945 he has continued to work without pause if, at times, with a certain repetitive lack of invention. In the late 1970s, however, at the invitation of a young Spanish theatrical group '*La Claca*', he created a series of costumes and settings for an antifascist fable similar in spirit to JARRY's *Père Ubu*, which had the impact and comic ferocity of his best work in the 1930s: an astonishing achievement for a man in his 80s.   GM

C. Greenberg, *Jóan Miró* (NY, 1948); R. Penrose, *Jóan Miró* (London, 1970).

Mishima, Yukio (b. Tokyo, Japan, 14.1.1925; d. Tokyo, 25.11.1970). Japanese novelist. Mishima is probably the Japanese novelist best known in the West. Many of his novels have been translated and in 1970 his death by ritual self-disembowelment (*seppuku* or *harakiri*) after an extraordinary attempt at *coup d'état* was widely reported. During his career there were major shifts in his attitude towards life and art, but his novels are in general characterized by logically constructed linear plots and a rhetorical beauty of style that make him unique among Japanese writers. Rather weak in constitution himself, Mishima's early heroes were often inadequate physically and unable to relate to the real world. They yearn for the physically strong or the beautiful, and in *Kinkakujii* (Tokyo, 1956; tr. I. Morris, *The Temple of the Golden Pavilion*, NY, 1959) the ideal beauty of the temple, which becomes an obsession for the acolyte hero, has to be destroyed by him at the end. Death and destruction are often strong elements in the visions of these heroes. Mishima changed his own physique in the late 1950s by weightlifting and other sports. His main characters, too, became more robust, and although death is still a major theme, the hero may be in control of his own destiny, as in the novella *Yukoku* (Tokyo, 1961; tr. G. W. Sargent, 'Patriotism' in *Midsummer & Other Stories*, NY, 1966). In the late 1960s Mishima took an active interest in military training, and formed his own private army

the Shield Society. He advocated the traditional concept of the union of learning and martial arts, and openly espoused a Chinese philosophical tradition of the unity of thought and action. Society had degenerated; ideals could compensate for this and death had an absoluteness which transcended it. Mishima made a gesture of defiance to this society when he exhorted a company of the Self Defence Forces to a coup, but he had already rehearsed the preliminaries to his suicide, which he carried out when the soldiers rejected him.   BWFP

J. Nathan, *Mishima: a Biography* (London, 1975).

Mistral, Gabriela, ps. of Lucila Godoy Alcayaga (b. Vicuña, Chile, 7.4.1889; d. New York, USA, 10.1.1957). Chilean poet; the first Latin American to win the Nobel prize for literature (1945). Her three important collections are *Desolación* [Desolation] (NY, 1922; amplified 1923, 1926, 1954), *Tala* (Buenos Aires, 1938), and *Lagar* [Wine press] (Santiago de Chile, 1954; see tr. Langston Hughes, *Selected Poems of Gabriela Mistral*, Bloomington, 1957; fuller selection with same title, tr. D. Dana, Baltimore, 1971). At 18 she fell in love with a railway employee, whose suicide within three years supplied the grief which she was to distil into some of the most effectively melancholy poetry in the Spanish language. Always intense, this treats her unfulfilled love, her frustrated maternal instincts, and a sublimation of these into a universal love for mankind with strong pantheistic overtones. Her best children's poetry is in *Ternura* [Tenderness], whose first edition (Madrid, 1924) was culled from *Desolación*, though 30 new poems were added in the Buenos Aires edition of 1945. As a schoolmistress in southern Chile, she influenced NERUDA in his teens. A woman of great determination, she travelled widely in the Americas and Europe, spending many years in the Chilean consular service; the international recognition which this brought undoubtedly influenced the award of the Nobel prize, which created a sensation in *machista* Latin America.   RP-M

S. C. Rosenbaum, *Modern Women Poets of Spanish America* (NY, 1945); M. C. Taylor, *Gabriela Mistral's Religious Sensibility* (Berkeley, Calif., 1968).

Mitchell, Peter Dennis (b. Mitcham, Surrey, UK, 29.9.1920). British biochemist. Mitchell is a rare example of how one scientist, working alone with unpopular ideas, can effect a revolution. After studying membrane transport with Danielli he began to investigate energy transduction in mitochondria, bacteria and chloroplasts. All these transfer chemical energy in food molecules to an enzyme chain, which hands electrons down to progressively lower energy levels and makes ATP with the energy released. Until then the electron transport – ATP connection – had been a mystery. Unlike ATP formation in fermentation, for example, electron transport is always bound to membranes, which made Mitchell start thinking about the role of spatial organization in the reaction. In 1961 he proposed that electron transport enzymes push hydrogen ions out of the mitochondrion until these build up and start flowing back in, thereby releasing the energy required to push them out and so powering the ATP-making enzymes. The theory was greeted sceptically by biochemists untrained in membranes. Driven from cities by ill health, Mitchell built his own laboratory in an 18c manor Glyn House, and with Jennifer Moyle began amassing evidence for his chemiosmotic theory. By the early 1970s even the most hardened sceptics had to admit that Mitchell had been right. For completely changing the scientific understanding of how fundamental biological processes are organized, Mitchell received the 1978 Nobel prize in chemistry. DOM

Mitchell, Reginald Joseph (b. Talke, Staffs., UK, 20.5.1895; d. Southampton, Hants., 11.6.1937). British aircraft designer. Fascinated by aeroplanes from an early age, he spent the whole of his short working life in British industry. At 24 he had his first success in a government-sponsored competition for the design of a commercial amphibious aircraft. In 1921 he designed the seaplane 'Seal', later called the 'Sea Lion', updated versions of which were used by the RAF into the early 1940s. Britain's first success in the Schneider trophy was in 1922 with a seaplane designed by Mitchell, a Supermarine (privately entered) Sea Lion II at an average speed of 145 mph. In 1924 Mitchell designed the forerunner of the massive Southampton flying boat with retractable undercarriage. The following year he turned again to high-speed machines with the S4, a product of the great Supermarine-Napier combination. This machine held the world speed record at 226 mph. Its immediate successor, the S5, won the Schneider trophy in 1927. In the same year, four Southampton flying boats flew in formation to the Far East, circled Australia and completed a trip of 23,000 miles. In 1929 F/O Waghorn won the Schneider trophy at 328.6 mph in a Supermarine S6. Its later version, the S6A, raised the world record to 407 mph. Britain dominated the flying world through Mitchell's designs. In 1935 he produced the prototype Spitfire K5054 and lived long enough to see its test flight. The part played by the Spitfire in the crucial defeat of the Luftwaffe in the Battle of Britain (1940) is legendary. The name of its creator is often forgotten. ERL

Mitchell, Wesley Clair (b. Rushville, Ill., USA, 5.8.1874; d. Stamford, Conn., 29.10.1948). American economist educated at the University of Chicago in the 1890s when J. L. Laughlin and VEBLEN were teaching a sceptical approach to pure economic theory from very diverse viewpoints. From Veblen, Mitchell acquired the institutionalist vision of economic science which seeks to explain the logic of producers' and consumers' behaviour in relation to an evolving system of economic institutions, and he became the acknowledged leader of the institutionalist school. From Laughlin he acquired the interest which inspired his early researches of which his *History of the Greenbacks, with Special Reference to the Consequences of their Issue: 1862–65* (Chicago, 1903) was the most notable outcome. This interest led directly to the intensive programme of research in business cycles for which he was directly or indirectly responsible, and which was to transform economists' stock of knowledge and quality of ideas in this area and to demonstrate the fruitfulness of an inductive methodology in economic research. Mitchell's method was to begin by detailed observation and measurement (using a variety of currently accepted theories to guide the initial choice of data) and to construct his explanatory theories on the basis of a systematic analysis of the facts observed. His *Business Cycles* (Berkeley, Calif., 1913) was a landmark in American thinking in the area and established Mitchell's reputation internationally as well as nationally. It was not until 1920, however, when he was appointed first director of the National Bureau of Economic Research (which became the world's leading economic research institute and which he helped to found) that his distinctive methodological approach and his own research programme developed the momentum and influence which stemmed from the integrated efforts of a distinguished research team. A stream of important monographs on business cycles came (and is still coming) from the National Bureau, including Mitchell's own massive work on *Business Cycles: the Problem and its Setting* (NY, 1927), a number of books which he coauthored, and his posthumously published research report *What Happens during Business Cycles* (NY, 1951). PMD

A. F. Burns (ed.), *Wesley Clair Mitchell, the Economic Scientist* (NY, 1952).

Mitterrand, François Maurice (b. Jarnac, Charente, France, 26.10.1916). French socialist politician, who served as a minister in 11 short-lived governments under the Fourth Republic. In 1971 he became first secretary of the French Socialist party, with the double objective of creating a left-wing coalition with the Communists and replacing them as the leading party of the left. He was defeated in the presidential election of 1974, but in May 1981 won an outright victory which changed the pattern of French politics since WW2. In the general election that followed (June 1981) the Socialists secured an absolute majority in the Chamber of Deputies even

without their left-wing allies. The Communists, who had dominated the left for so long, polled the lowest percentage of votes since the Popular Front of 1936. Communist ministers took part in the government but were in no position to dictate policy. The bold measures with which Mitterrand began, including the nationalization of industry and the banks, were checked by the economic pressures of the world recession – inflation, rising unemployment, an unfavourable balance of trade. His reaction was to follow moderate rather than radical policies. He showed the same pragmatism in foreign policy where he combined a Gaullist insistence on France's independence with a firm line on maintaining Western strength and vigilance in relation to the Soviet bloc.
ALCB

Mizoguchi, Kenji (b. Tokyo, Japan, 16.5.1898; d. Kyoto, 24.8.1956). Japanese film director with a painterly, poetic style who made a lasting impression on world cinema due to his deep, psychological understanding of his women characters and a stylistic harmony stemming from his often daring use of the sequence-shot (a long take without cuts in which the camera effortlessly weaves through a scene, sometimes stopping for dialogue exchanges and then tracking away to another part of the set and other characters). Like many of his contemporaries, Mizoguchi divided his output (about 90 features) between period and modern subjects. Unhappily most of his silent work is lost (he began directing in 1922), but his 1930s films have recently been revalued, notably *Zangiku Monogatari* (*The Story of Late Chrysanthemums*, 1939), a tragic love story set in the Meiji period with a masterly use of the sequence-shot. *Genroku Chushingura* (*The Loyal 47 Ronin of the Genroku Era*, 1941–2) takes a familiar legend and turns it into an austere ritual by means of formalized acting and some of the most beautiful camera movements in all cinema. His work in the 1950s brought him to a wide European audience, notably the films which defined the oppression and exploitation of women, often in a period setting: *Saikaku Ichidai Onna* (*The Life* *of O-Haru*, 1952), *Ugetsu Monogatari* [Tales of the pale and mysterious moon after the rain, 1953], *Sansho Dayu* (*Sansho the Bailiff*, 1954), *Chikamatsu Monogatari* [Chikamatsu's story, 1954]. Although these films were less rigorously Japanese in their modes of expression than the earlier work, they possessed similar plastic and poetic qualities. His two colour films *Yokihi* (*Princess Yang Kwei-Fei*, 1955) and *Shin-Heike Monogatari* (*New Tales of the Taira Clan*, 1955) make one regret that he did not live to continue experimenting in colour, and, perhaps, wide screen.   JPG

I. Morris, *Mizoguchi Kenji* (Ottawa, 1967).

Mobutu, Sese Seko (b. Lisala, Banzyville, Belgian Congo [now Mobayi, Zaïre], 14.10.1930). President of Zaïre. A close political associate of LUMUMBA, Mobutu, who had been a clerk in the Force Publique, was appointed chief of staff of the Congolese army on independence. In September 1960 he turned on Lumumba and arrested him and other politicians in a military coup. Mobutu assumed supreme power after a second coup in 1965. In his first few years he achieved considerable success in restoring political stability and promoting development. Posing as Lumumba's heir, he founded his own political party, Mouvement Populaire de la Révolution, and propagated his own brand of radicalism ('Mobutuism') which stressed a 'return to African authenticity'. The Congo now became Zaïre, and all names, whether of places or individuals, with European associations were changed. By the late 1970s mounting corruption and spiralling inflation had made Mobutu's regime increasingly unpopular, but Mobutu, a highly astute politician, was able to count on the support of powerful western backers to help him survive.   RH

J. Chome, *L'Ascension de Mobutu* (Brussels, 1974).

Modigliani, Amadeo (b. Livorno, Tuscany, Italy, 12.7.1884; d. Paris, France, 18.1.1920). Italian painter and sculptor. Modigliani received his art training in Italy at Livorno and Venice, though almost all his surviving work dates from after his move to Paris in 1906. For several years (c. 1910–13) he worked mainly as a sculptor, making a remarkable series of stone carvings of very stylized elongated heads under the influence of BRANCUSI and African art, then turned again to painting. His mature paintings were influenced initially by Toulouse-Lautrec and CÉZANNE, but he soon developed a distinctive rhythmical linear stylization. Working with a very limited range of subjects, usually portraits of single figures but occasionally a few voluptuous reclining or seated nudes, he produced over 350 paintings in the space of five years, as well as a large number of pencil drawings. His late works of 1919–20 tended to be increasingly mannered, with very elongated necks and heads, and almond-shaped eyes. His figures are almost always given a dreamy, brooding air and the colours tend to be warm and mellow. Though his work never achieved much recognition in his lifetime, it has since become widely popular and Modigliani himself has become one of the legendary ill-fated artists of Montmartre. Handsome and attractive, he suffered from a tubercular weakness, which was exacerbated by bohemian living and hard drinking.   REA

J. Modigliani, *Modigliani: Man and Myth* (London, 1959).

Moholy-Nagy, László (b. Borsod, Austria-Hungary [now Hungary], 20.7.1895; naturalized American citizen, 1944; d. Chicago, Ill., USA, 24.11.1946). Hungarian/American designer. Head of the Bauhaus basic course from 1923 to 1928, Moholy-Nagy helped introduce the constructivist aesthetic to the West by way of that school. As an activist painter he had left Hungary after KUN's unsuccessful Soviet revolution (1919) and turned, like others of the *Ma* group, to dada and geometrical abstraction before being converted to constructivism under LISSITZKY's influence in Berlin. At the Bauhaus he experimented with textures and materials in three dimensions, ran the metal workshops, began making photographs (and montages and photograms), established the typographical conventions for the Bauhaus books (two of which he wrote), and became fascinated by the effects – static and kinetic – of light, transparency and the mixture of media. Leaving the Bauhaus with GROPIUS, he went into advertising and exhibition design, and made remarkable stage sets for PISCATOR (*The Merchant of Berlin*, 1929) and the Kroll Opera. A year after HITLER's accession to power he abandoned Germany altogether for a brief period of activity in the Netherlands and England, where he photographed Eton and Oxford and devised special effects for the Korda–WELLS film *The Shape of Things to Come*. Then in 1937 he went to Chicago to start the short-lived New Bauhaus, later revived as the Institute of Design. György Kepes and VASARELY are among those who have developed his still fertile techno-aesthetic ideas. JWMW

R. Kostalanetz, *Moholy-Nagy* (NY, 1970); A. Hans, *Moholy-Nagy: Photographs and Photograms* (London, 1980).

Moissan, Henri (b. Paris, France, 28.9.1852; d. Paris, 20.2.1907). French chemist. Moissan's two outstanding achievements were the discovery of elemental fluorine and the development of an electric-arc furnace for high-temperature chemical synthesis. He started his scientific life as a pharmacist's assistant, eventually took a junior post in the Ecole Supérieure de Pharmacie in 1880, and became professor of inorganic chemistry by 1899. In 1884 he tackled one of the then major problems of inorganic chemistry, the isolation of elemental fluorine. This task, which had defeated Davy and Ampère, was completed within two years. Influenced by the work of Frémy and Faraday, Moissan electrolysed cold anhydrous liquid hydrofluoric acid, in the presence of potassium fluoride (to make the solution conducting), and obtained free fluorine (*Compt. Rend.*, 92 [1886], 1543; 93 [1886], 202). In the following years, he systematically investigated the chemistry of this, the most reactive element known, and laid the foundations of modern fluorine chemistry in *Le Fluor et ses Composés* [Fluorine and its compounds] (Paris, 1900). Today, fluorine is prepared on an industrial scale and used for the separation of uranium-235 from

uranium-238 (via uranium hexafluoride) and (on a much smaller scale) for the preparation of a gaseous insulator (sulphur hexafluoride) and perfluoralkanes. In pursuit of synthetic diamonds, Moissan designed and developed an electric-arc furnace, capable of generating temperatures of 3500°C (*Le Four électrique* [The electric furnace], Paris, 1897), which he used to prepare highly pure metal ingots, as well as many novel carbides, borides and silicides (including carborundum). His reports of having made synthetic diamonds are now regarded sceptically. His major published work was *Traité de Chimie Minérale* [Treatise on inorganic chemistry] (5 vols, Paris, 1904–6). In 1906 he was awarded the Nobel prize.
KRS

Molnár, Ferenc (b. Budapest, Austria-Hungary [now Hungary], 12.1.1878; d. New York, USA, 2.4.1952). Hungarian dramatist and novelist, whose reputation outside Hungary depends on a handful of popular plays staged throughout the world. Molnár began his career as a journalist and soon made his name as a keen observer of urban society and its idiosyncrasies. His novel *A Pál-utcai fiúk* (Budapest, 1907; tr. L. Rittenberg, *The Paul Street Boys*, NY, 1927) has become a juvenile classic, filmed and staged many times. His dramas brought him fame, particularly *Liliom* (Budapest, 1909), which achieved even greater popularity in its musical form as *Carousel*; *A testör* (Budapest, 1910; tr. G. I. Colbron & H. Bartsch, *The Guardsman*, NY, 1924); and *Játék a kastélyban* (Great Neck, NY, 1926; tr. WODEHOUSE, *The Play's the Thing*, NY, 1927). Molnár's theatrical sense is unrivalled; his plays demand careful staging and split-second timing to match the witty dialogue. Though his work has been criticized as superficial, the mixture of sentimentality, satire, humour and occasional flashes of deep insight have endeared him to generations of playgoers. He owes little to the Hungarian theatrical tradition, but set new norms for it. GFC

E. M. Basa, *Ferenc Molnár* (Boston, Mass., 1980).

Molotov, Vyacheslav Mikhailovich, *né* Skryabin (b. Kukarka, Vyatka, Russia, 9.3.1890). Member of Soviet Politburo (1921–57), Soviet premier (1930–41), foreign minister (1939–49, 1953–6). Having taken the name 'Molotov' [Hammer] for conspiratorial purposes as a Bolshevik revolutionary from 1905 under Tsarism (he edited *Pravda*, 1912–17), he became right-hand man to STALIN from 1921 until Stalin's death. He is associated with: (1) The Nazi–Soviet Agreement of 23.8.1939 (sometimes known as the Molotov–Ribbentrop pact); (2) his role as the wielder of the Soviet Union's veto in the Foreign Ministers' Council and in the UN Security Council during the first phase (1945–9) of the 'Cold War'; (3) his negotiation of the Austrian State Treaty in 1955; (4) his role in the unsuccessful opposition of the so-called 'anti-party group' to KRUSHCHEV in 1956–7, as a result of which he was stripped of his party offices and employed first as Soviet ambassador to Mongolia (1957–60), and then as Soviet delegate to the International Atomic Energy Authority in Vienna. A hard man, a doctrinaire, a Russian patriot and a Europhobe.   DCW

Moltmann, Jürgen (b. Hamburg, Germany, 8.4.1926). German Lutheran theologian and professor of systematic theology at the University of Tübingen since 1967. As a young prisoner of war, Moltmann conceived the outline of a theological programme which looks in hope to a God who liberates man in the future. Directed by the questions raised by the exiled East German, MARXist-atheist philosopher Ernst BLOCH in *Das Prinzip Hoffnung* (Frankfurt, 1959), Moltmann revived after long neglect the eschatological dimension of Christianity. In *Theologie der Hoffnung* (Munich, 1965; tr. J. W. Leitch, *Theology of Hope*, London, 1967), a profoundly biblical book, Moltmann outlines a God who fulfils his promises, but in novel, unexpected ways which always open up new historical possibilities. Far from being an evasion of historical conflicts, man's hope for the future determines his present commitment to liberating political action.

As a postwar German, Moltmann is particularly sensitive to the phenomenon of Auschwitz and the suffering it represents, and *Der gekreuzigte Gott* (Munich, 1973; tr. R. A. Wilson & J. Bowden, *The Crucified God*, London, 1974) points to the God who identifies with the victims of history by dying on the cross. The dilemma of how one can acquire an identity as a Christian and be involved in liberation struggles is the subject of his account of the church as a messianic community in *Kirche in der Kraft des Geistes* (Munich, 1975; tr. M. Kohl, *The Church in the Power of the Spirit*, London, 1977). Moltmann has instigated a radical shift in the eschatological self-understanding of Christian theology and has attempted to provide a theological justification for a Christian commitment to political action.   GT

C. Morse, *The Logic of Promise in Moltmann's Theology* (Philadelphia, 1979).

Momigliano, Arnaldo Dante (b. Caraglia, Piedmont, Italy, 5.9.1908). Italian classical scholar. Momigliano published two important biographies before he was 30: *L'Opera dell'imperatore Claudio* (Florence, 1932; *Claudius the Emperor and his Achievement*, Oxford, 1934) and *Filippo il Macedone* [Philip of Macedon] (Florence, 1934). He came to England to escape the fascist regime, and was professor of ancient history at University College London (1951–75). For the last 30 years, he has concentrated on the history of classical scholars (Lipsius, Gibbon, Grote, Fustel de Coulanges, ROSTOVTZEFF), or on the reputation of classical authors such as Herodotus or Tacitus in later periods. His articles have been collected into a series *Contributo alla storia degli studi classici* [Contribution to the history of classical studies] (5 vols, Rome, 1955–75). Select articles have appeared in English as *Studies in Historiography* (London, 1966) and *Essays in Ancient and Modern Historiography* (Oxford, 1977). They explore in detail how historians see the past from a point of view conditioned by their own place in the historical process. Momigliano has also found time to go on making his own contributions to classical scholarship, notably in *The*

Development of Greek Biography (Cambridge, Mass., 1971) and *Alien Wisdom* (Cambridge, 1975), which deals with the limits of Hellenization and the way in which the Greeks perceived other cultures. The range of Momigliano's interests suggests that the age of the polymath is not quite over. UPB

Mondlane, Eduardo (b. Gaza district, Portuguese Mozambique [now Mozambique], 1920; d. Dar-es-Salaam, Tanzania, 3.2.1969). Mozambique nationalist leader. Academic in manner and training, pragmatic in his approach to politics, Mondlane was one of the outstanding revolutionary leaders in Africa in the 1960s. Assassinated by a parcel-bomb in a plot probably instigated by the Portuguese, at a time when the success of the liberation struggle in Mozambique seemed far from certain, he is now revered as the father of the modern Mozambique nation. The son of a minor Thonga chief, Mondlane was one of the very few black Mozambicans to study overseas. From Portugal he went to the USA, where he took a doctorate in sociology, worked as a research officer for the UN, and became a university lecturer. Drawn into nationalist politics in 1961, Mondlane played a large part in bringing various nationalist groups together to form Frelimo (Mozambique Liberation Front). In 1964 Frelimo turned to guerrilla warfare and gradually gained control of considerable territory in northern Mozambique. Undoctrinaire in his thinking, and willing to accept aid both from the East and from the West, Mondlane was radicalized by the process of the liberation struggle. 'Liberation', he wrote in his posthumously published *The Struggle for Mozambique* (Harmondsworth, 1969), 'is not simply a matter of expelling the Portuguese: it means reorganizing the life of the country and setting it on the road to sound national development.' He foresaw the danger of a new African privileged group emerging in liberated Mozambique, and spoke of the need for centralized planning to prevent such a development. Mondlane was not a MARXist; but this stress on centralization foreshadows the explicit Marxism–

LENINism of his successor, Samora Machel. RH

Mondrian, Piet (b. Amersfoort, Utrecht, The Netherlands, 7.3.1872; d. New York, USA, 1.2.1944). Dutch painter who was one of the most important pioneers of abstract art. He began his career as a landscape painter in the conservative tradition of the 19c Dutch Hague school, and only began to adopt a more avant-garde style in 1908–9 under the influence of art nouveau, pointillism and fauvism. This change first appeared mainly in a series of pictures of windmills, churches and dunes on the coast of Zeeland, executed in pointillist brush strokes and vivid colours; pictures which sometimes have an almost Van Gogh-like expressionist intensity. In 1912 he moved to Paris, where he was strongly influenced by the analytical cubist paintings of BRAQUE and PICASSO, but decided to carry this style to what seemed to him its logical conclusion of complete abstraction, taking small drawings of trees or the façades of buildings as his starting-point, but simplifying them more and more until almost all traces of the original motifs were eliminated. Back in the Netherlands from 1914 to 1919, he continued this process of progressive simplification, developing stage by stage from cubism to so-called 'plus-and-minus' compositions built out of an intricate harmony of short vertical and horizontal lines (including pictures based on the image of a pier and the sea), to the use in 1917 of completely abstract overlapping rectangular planes of colour, and finally to a flat asymmetrical rectilinear grid. This development, which he pursued with extraordinary logic and consistency, was inspired partly by the writings of the Theosophical movement which he had joined in 1909, and in particular by the Theosophists' emphasis on the cosmic duality of the male, vertical spiritual and the female, horizontal and material principles. In 1917 Mondrian agreed to cooperate with DOESBURG and Bart van der Leck in publishing the periodical *De Stijl*, and he himself contributed theoretical essays setting out the principles of his new style, which he called Neo-Plasticism. He eventually withdrew from the group in 1925 after Doesburg had begun to reintroduce diagonals into his paintings. By degrees he evolved the style by which he is best known: it is based on an asymmetrical grid of heavy black lines on a white ground, enlivened by rectangles of one or more of the three primary colours, red, blue or yellow – that is to say working with a very limited range of simple elements in maximum contrast. After living in Paris again from 1919 to 1938, and in London from 1938 to 1940, he spent the last three years of his life in New York, where he began to work with coloured lines instead of black ones, and sometimes to break up the lines into bars and blocks of contrasting colours analogous to the syncopated rhythms of jazz. This style opened up a number of new possibilities, which he was only beginning to explore at the time of his death.   REA

M. Seuphor, *Piet Mondrian* (NY, 1956); H. L. C. Jaffé, *Mondrian* (London, 1970).

Monet, Claude (b. Paris, France, 14.2.1840; d. Giverny, Eure, 5.12.1926). French painter. Monet's greatest claim to fame is his role as one of the principal creators of the impressionist movement in the late 1860s and in the 1870s. He met Auguste RENOIR and Sisley at the Ecole des Beaux Arts in 1862 and encouraged them to paint in the open air, directly from nature. Working along the Seine at Argenteuil on the outskirts of Paris, sometimes side-by-side with Renoir, he studied light and reflections on water, and heightened his palette so as to convey the brilliance of outdoor light. The name 'impressionism' was even suggested by the title of one of his pictures, *Impression, Sunrise* (1872) and he exhibited in five of the eight impressionist exhibitions held between 1874 and 1886. His acute sensitivity to the changing qualities of the light and atmosphere led him from 1890 onwards to paint series of pictures of the same motif under different conditions of light, working on a number of canvases at the same time and passing from one to another as the conditions of light changed. Beginning with series of such motifs as haystacks, poplars, and the

west front of Rouen cathedral, he devoted most of his later years to studies of his own garden at Giverny where he created a beautiful pond with waterlilies, surrounded by luxuriant vegetation. His interest came to centre above all on the lily-pond itself, looking down on to the water with its patches of water-lilies and reflections of the clouds and sky. From about 1910 his works tended to become much larger than before, and he painted a number of long horizontal mural-like pictures of a decorative but lyrical and mysterious kind in which the water and water-lilies extended right across the canvas; a preoccupation which culminated in the paintings which he executed in the last 10 years of his life for two oval rooms in the Orangerie in the Tuileries Gardens in Paris, where they fill the entire walls so that the visitor is almost completely surrounded by them. These late works are now recognized as among his most original creations, and their huge scale, all-over treatment and sometimes almost abstract shimmering colour surfaces had an important influence on some of the American abstract expressionist painters of the 1940s and 1950s.

REA

C. Toyes *et al.*, *Monet at Giverny* (London, 1975); J. Howe, *Monet* (London, ²1981).

Monnet, Jean (b. Cognac, Charente, France, 9.11.1888; d. Bazoches, Montfort-L'Amoury, Yvelines, 16.3.1979). French international economist, for his generation uncharacteristically dedicated to international collaboration between France, Britain and the USA from his WW1 work in the French Ministry of Commerce, at the Paris Peace Conference and for the League of Nations. In 1939–40 he acted as chairman of an Anglo–French committee on wartime economic collaboration and played a major role in CHURCHILL's offer of Anglo–French union in June 1940. Too Anglophile for DE GAULLE's tastes, with his attachment to the British Supply Council in Washington, he came into his own as head of a French commission to plan the reorganization of French industry in December 1945, evolving the Monnet plan which brought

France above her prewar level of industrial activity in five years. At the same time he established himself as the *éminence grise* of the movement for a Europe united on functionalist lines, inspiring the SCHUMANN plan for the European Coal and Steel Community, organizing support on both sides of the Atlantic for successive moves towards the integration of Europe and serving as first president of the European Coal and Steel Community (1952–5). His vision of European integration was as much technocratic as political, and the political inspiration was more the desire to avoid a repetition of the internecine wars which had nearly destroyed Europe twice in his lifetime by altering the institutional economic and social framework within which inter-European relations in general, and Franco–German relations in particular, were conducted. His ideas remained unacceptable to President de Gaulle, and the Europe that emerged at the end of the 1960s represented the Gaullist much more than Monnet's conception of Europe. His *Mémoires* (Paris, 1977; *Memoirs*, London, 1978) are of greater interest than most political autobiographies. DCW

Monod, Jacques Lucien (b. Paris, France, 9.2.1910; d. Cannes, Alpes-Maritimes, 31.5.1976). French biologist. Trained in Paris as a biologist, where he subsequently taught zoology, he went to the USA in 1936 and then, after serving as a resistance fighter, joined the Institut Pasteur. After a brief period at the Collège de France, he rejoined the Institut as its director. Dubbed the 'architect of molecular biology', Monod's major contributions lay in elucidating the mechanisms of control of gene expression and regulation of metabolic processes, for which he was awarded the Nobel prize for medicine and physiology in 1965. In respect of the former, he anticipated the discovery of messenger-RNA and he formulated the theory that the chromosome is so organized that genes with related functions are clustered together in operons and that expression of such a cluster is under control of a small region at one end of the operon called the 'operator'. This operator is in turn controlled by a 'regulator' gene which codes for a protein 'repressor' that combines specifically with the operator and switches it off. The action of this repressor can be modulated by certain metabolites of low molecular weight, for which it has specific affinity. These new ideas were originally brought together to explain the mechanisms of induction and repression of enzyme synthesis by such metabolites; mechanisms which are of great importance in enabling bacteria to adapt economically to different growth media. The implications of the operon theory, however, spread more widely, revolutionizing thought on gene expression and throwing new light on reproduction of viruses, differentiation and cancer. Monod's other significant contribution was his theory of 'allostery' which explains the regulation of activity of certain enzymes, crucial to the cell's metabolism, to ensure the most economical use of the cell's resources. The activity of these allosteric enzymes is modulated, positively and negatively, by key metabolites quite dissimilar in structure to their substrates. Monod postulated that these effectors must bind at sites on the enzyme different from those occupied by the substrate(s) and bring about their effects by changing the conformation of the enzyme protein so as to vary the activity of the catalytic site. The concept that changes in the conformation of the enzyme molecule played an essential part in the catalytic process had wide implications and fundamentally affected thought about functional proteins in general. As well as being a brilliant scientist, Monod was an active sportsman and musician and also philosopher. In *Le Hazard et la nécessité* (Paris, 1970; *Chance and Necessity*, London, 1971) he expresses the view that the origin of life and the process of evolution are the result of chance. GL

Monroe, Marilyn, *née* Norma Jean Baker (b. Los Angeles, Calif., USA, 1.6.1926; d. Brentwood, Calif., 5.8.1962). American film actress. The illegitimate daughter of a depressive mother, her early life was passed in foster homes. Selected as a model by an army photographer in 1944, she became overnight a forces' pin-up. She won a Twentieth-Century Fox contract in 1946 but her film appearances were restricted to minor roles. Carefully managed publicity and her marriage to the baseball player Joe Di Maggio in 1954 translated her into Fox's outstanding box-office attraction. Any assessment of her screen skills has to be based on a handful of films: *The Seven Year Itch* (1955); *Bus Stop* (1956); *Some Like It Hot* (1959); *The Misfits* (1961). Monroe's private life, signposted by publicity and journalists, was as much a performance as the screen projection. She married Arthur MILLER in 1955, divorced him in 1961, and, after further bouts of acute depression and drug dependence, committed suicide in 1962. America's foremost female sex symbol of the postwar years, Monroe was presented as an ideal of sexual delight and flamboyance. Her photographs, film performances and legend continue to haunt the popular imagination, and even for writers and artists she remains a challenge to their own imaginations.   RBJG

F. L. Guiles, *Norma Jean* (London, 1969); N. Mailer, *Marilyn* (NY, 1973).

Montague, Richard Merett (b. Stockton, Calif., USA, 20.9.1930; d. Los Angeles, Calif., 7.3.1971). American logician and deviser of 'Montague grammar'. He did his first degree and subsequent graduate work at the University of California, Berkeley, where he was particularly influenced by TARSKI. In 1955 he moved to the University of California, Los Angeles, where he remained until his premature death by murder in 1971. His early work was on mathematical logic, but he soon became fascinated with the application of sophisticated logical methods to 'traditional' problems. Montague devised a new logical system for application to natural language. He expounded this in a series of papers, many of which have been republished in *Formal Philosophy: Selected Papers of Richard Montague* (ed. R. H. Thomason, New Haven, 1974). In spite of the technical nature of Montague grammar, it has attracted a large number of adherents, particularly in the form developed since Montague's death by an ex-colleague Barbara Hall Partee of the University of Massachusetts. Partee has shown that, with certain modifications,

Montague grammar is compatible with CHOMSKY's transformational generative grammar, and might therefore constitute the semantic component of the latter.
                                    JMA

B. H. Partee, 'Montague grammar and transformational grammar', *Linguistic Inquiry*, 6 (1975), 203–300.

Montale, Eugenio (b. Genoa, Liguria, Italy, 12.10.1896; d. Milan, Lombardy, 12.9.1981). Italian poet. Writing in the wake of D'Annunzianism, Montale's poetry represents the most creatively decisive reaction against it, and heralds a new era in modern Italian poetry. Self-taught, Montale got his first regular job in 1929 as the director of the Gabinetto Vieusseux Library in Florence from which he was removed in 1938 because of his antifascism. Before coming to Florence in 1927 he had already published his first, and according to some critics, his most original book of poetry *Ossi di seppia* [Cuttlefish] (Turin, 1925). Using the Ligurian seascape and landscape as his 'prey', Montale sets out to probe into his own nature with a view to defining his moral, poetic and existential identity, thereby achieving a 'criticism of life' through a lyricism that is at once personal and impersonal, impressionistic and philosophical.

In *Le occasioni* [Opportunities] (Turin, 1939) Montale evolves a new technique and idiom, laying greater emphasis on personal and autobiographical elements and making use of more allusive and more symbolic language. The tragedy of WW2 looms over some of the best-known lyrics from this volume. In 1948 Montale moved, as a correspondent of *Corriere della sera*, to Milan where he lived until his death. In *La bufera e altro* [The storm and another] (Venice, 1956) the theme of love is presented in the context of political liberation and an atmosphere of spiritual salvation.

In 1963 Montale's wife died. The poet remembered her in a series of poems *Xenia* (in *Satura*, Milan, 1971; tr. G. Singh, Los Angeles, 1970) which, for their controlled poignancy and sophisticated lyricism, have no parallel in Italian poetry and remind one of the poems HARDY wrote after the death of his wife. Besides *Xenia*, there are poems in

Satura which, together with his later verse *Diario del '71 e del '72* (Milan, 1973; tr. G. Singh, in *New Poems*, London, 1976), *Quaderno di Quattro anni* (Milan, 1977; tr. G. Singh, *It Depends: a Poet's Notebook*, NY, 1980) and his last book *Altri Versi* [Other poems] (Milan, 1981) show Montale in a different frame of mind.

Montale also published five books of prose. *Farfalla di Dinard* (Venice, 1956; tr. G. Singh, *The Butterfly of Dinard*, London, 1970) is a book of autobiographical short stories which have a thematic as well as stylistic link with the poetry. The other books – *Auto da fé* (Milan, 1966), *Fuori di Casa* [Houseplants] (Milan, 1969) and *Sulla poesia* [On poetry] (Milan, 1976; selections from the last three books in tr. G. Singh, *Eugenio Montale: Selected Essays*, Manchester, 1978) – reveal him as an original critic and a master of prose, a shrewd observer of the contemporary scene and an immensely gifted thinker.
GS

G. Singh, *Eugenio Montale: a Critical Study of his Poetry, Prose and Criticism* (New Haven, 1973); F. R. Leavis, essay on *Xenia* in *New Poems by Eugenio Montale*, tr. G. Singh (London, 1976).

Monteiro, Domingos Pereira (b. Barqueiros, Trasosmontes, Portugal, 6.9.1903). Portuguese poet and writer. Monteiro's 10 volumes of psychological short stories reveal a brilliant narrative writer of unrivalled readability. Unlike many of his contemporaries he is no regionalist. In a short passage of description or dialogue his skill as a writer enables him to suggest the whole atmosphere of the Amazon forest, a legal squabble, or an exchange between opponents in the Spanish civil war. He gives an importance to feminine psychology that is unusual in Portuguese writing. The influence of Spain and of the Spanish philosophers UNAMUNO and ORTEGA Y GASSET may be seen particularly in the collection *Histórias castelhanas* [Stories from Castile] (Lisbon, 1955), where in the story 'Terra imortal' the death sentence is stoically accepted in all its absurdity. The Spanish obsession with death, manifest in many stories, is seen especially in the

long short stories *Enfermaria, prisão e mortuária* [Infirmary, prison and mortuary] (Lisbon, 1943) which brought him instant recognition.
DBr

A. Ribeiro, *Psicologia e ética na obra de Domingos Monteiro* (Lisbon, 1965).

Montelius, Oscar (b. Stockholm, Sweden, 9.9.1843; d. Stockholm, 4.11.1921). Swedish archaeologist, responsible for systematizing the nomenclature of the Neolithic and Bronze Age periods in Europe. In place of the site names and generalized epochs which had hitherto confused European prehistory, he proposed a simplified chronological scheme of four Neolithic and five Bronze Age periods applicable to the whole of Northern Europe. Each was defined in terms of technology and typology and was given absolute dates. His scheme, first developed in the 1880s, saw final publication in *Les Temps préhistoriques en Suède et dans les autres Pays Scandinaves* [The prehistoric period in Sweden and other Scandinavian countries] (Paris, 1895); *La Civilisation primitive en Italia depuis l'introduction des métaux* [Early civilization in Italy since the introduction of metals] (Stockholm, 1895, ²1904); *Die Chronologie der ältesten Bronzezeit in Nord-Deutschland und Skandinavien* [The chronology of the earliest Bronze Age in northern Germany and Scandinavia] (Brunswick, 1900).
BWC

Montessori, Maria (b. Chiaravalle, Ancona, Italy, 31.8.1870; d. Noordwijk aan Zee, S. Holland, The Netherlands, 6.5.1952). Italian educationist. The first woman to qualify as a doctor of medicine in Italy, graduating from the University of Rome in 1896, she specialized in paediatric and psychiatric work, which led to her interest in the education of mentally handicapped children. As a result of this experience she formulated educational theories of wider application, which have had a lasting influence upon nursery and infant schools. The Montessori method stressed the importance of a 'prepared environment', in which young children were given a wide variety of materials with which they could develop skills at their own pace. These materials were carefully graded, allowing for much repetition, self-correction and self-education. Unlike many other progressive educationists she emphasized the value of work rather than play, and aimed at creating a scientific pedagogy, though this was often expressed in somewhat romantic and mystical terminology. She inspired many devoted supporters in the USA, Britain and on the Continent, who sought to implement her ideas in Montessori schools, societies and associations – a process which has tended to crystallize a doctrine rather than carry forward its original pioneering insights. Her writings included *The Montessori Method* (NY, 1912) and *The Secret of Childhood* (London, 1936).   RRStr

R. C. Orem (ed.), *A Montessori Handbook* (NY, 1966); R. Kramer, *Maria Montessori* (NY, 1976).

Montherlant, Henry Millon de (b. Paris, France, 21.4.1896; d. Paris, 21.9.1972). French novelist and dramatist. The most self-consciously virile of 20c French writers, the aristocratic Henry de Montherlant saw active service as a volunteer between 1916 and 1918, and was seriously wounded. In 1924 he won fame with his refusal to endorse fashionable pacifist attitudes in his *Le Chant funèbre pour les morts de Verdun* [Death chant for the dead of Verdun] and his exaltation of the competitive ethos of modern sport in *Olympiques* [The Olympics]. His masterpiece *Les Célibataires* (Paris, 1934; tr. T. Kilmartin, *The Bachelors*, London, 1960) is nevertheless a very amusing satire of two totally incompetent aristocrats. Irony is less obvious in the four novels composing the series *Les Jeunes Filles* (Paris, 1936–9) and Montherlant's rather unpleasant denigration of women in this book led BEAUVOIR to present him in *Le Deuxième sexe* (1967) as the epitome of the male chauvinist pig. Montherlant was profoundly affected by the humiliation of France in the defeat of 1940, but found some consolation in the success of his plays. *La Reine morte* (Paris, 1942; *The Dead Queen*) and *Le Maître de Santiago* (Paris, 1947; both tr. J. Griffin in *The Master of Santiago, with Other Plays*, London, 1962) combine an Iberian cult of tragic honour with an ostensible and at times ostentatious contempt for the modern world.   PMWT

J. Cruickshank, *Montherlant* (Edinburgh, 1964); P. Ginestier, *Montherlant* (Paris, 1973).

Moore, George Edward (b. London, UK, 4.11.1873; d. Cambridge, 24.10.1958). British philosopher. A student at Cambridge at much the same time as Bertrand RUSSELL, he influenced Russell more than he was influenced by him. Under Moore's leadership they broke away from the prevailing idealistic philosophy which held the universe to be an all-inclusive mind and they defended the independent reality of material objects, minds and their states, and such abstract items as concepts and propositions. After some years of private study in London, Moore returned to Cambridge to teach philosophy until his retirement as professor in 1939. His first publications were in a style of approved idealist murkiness. But in 1903 his conversion was revealed in an essay 'The Refutation of Idealism' (repr. *Philosophical Studies*, London, 1922), directed more against Berkeley than Hegel, and a book *Principia Ethica* (Cambridge, 1903) that were both written with absolute clarity. The former argued against the idea that we really perceive nothing but our own sensations, the latter against the view that moral properties such as goodness can be reduced to properties of any other 'naturalistic kind' such as happiness or evolutionary success. In the book's final chapter he put the faculty of direct moral awareness which it implied to work and claimed to discover that affectionate personal relations and the contemplation of beauty are the only supremely good states of mind. This substantive morality, in a hedonistic form which may have been more than its expounder had bargained for, became the common faith of the Bloomsbury group of British intellectuals in the first decades of the century. Moore's doctrines in ethics were firmly expressed, although in later years he blithely admitted that they might very well be mistaken. On his other main topic, sense perception, he arrived at no settled conclusions except as to the inadequacy of his own first essay on the subject. His philosophical influence was second to none in England between 1910 and the reappearance of WITTGEN-STEIN in the 1930s. He converted a generation to his fundamental assumption that wherever philosophy comes into conflict with common sense it is almost certainly wrong, and many to his immensely painstaking procedure of stating philosophical theses in the plainest possible language. Exemplary in this respect was his gently mocking demolition of the favourite theory of his old idealist teacher McTaggart that time is unreal, as also was his rustic incredulity in the face of the kind of scepticism which maintains that we do not know anything for certain about material things. Philosophy, Moore held, cannot replace or correct the beliefs of common sense. What it should aim to do is to make them wholly explicit by a process of analysis. Just what analysis is, was the topic of many agonized but inconclusive reflections. Nearly all British philosophers of the interwar years show signs of his influence, if only in the problems they felt moved to consider.

AQ

P. A. Schilpp (ed.), *The Philosophy of G. E. Moore* (La Salle, Ill., ²1968); P. Levy, *G. E. Moore and the Cambridge Apostles* (London, 1979).

Moore, Henry (b. Castleford, W. Yorks., UK, 30.7.1898). British sculptor. The son of a coal miner, Moore studied sculpture at Leeds School of Art and the Royal College of Art in London, and was greatly influenced as a young man by the primitive and archaic sculpture in the British Museum, especially black African and pre-Columbian Mexican works. He was attracted mainly by their intensity, unconventional beauty, powerful sense of mass and form, and feeling for the particular character of the materials – the weight and immovability of stone or the organic quality of wood. He concentrated on direct carving and his early sculptures are very massive and slab-like, with little undercutting of the forms and forceful twists in different directions. This can be seen, for example, in his reclining figures of 1929–30, in which the breasts and upraised knees project vigorously upwards like hills;

this association of the human figure with landscape forms has been a recurrent theme of his works. In the 1930s he extended the range of his work under the influence of abstract art and surrealism, including PICASSO's metamorphic paintings of bone-like forms (c. 1929–32). Moore began to make more radical distortions of the human figure and sometimes to carve holes right through his forms, creating interior spaces like caves in rocks – spaces as volumetric and important as the masses surrounding them; or to make two- or four-part reclining figures consisting of several more or less abstract forms grouped together on a base, and suggesting head, legs, pelvis and so on. Though he usually kept some connection with the human figure, he also made a few completely abstract sculptures, including some with open forms threaded with strings.

During the air raids on London (1940 –2) the extraordinary spectacle of hundreds of people sheltering in the Underground inspired his most famous series of drawings, the 'Shelter Sketches'. These studies of people huddled together under blankets or lying in rows along the sides of the tunnels were a timeless expression of human endurance. Their influence can be seen in some of his postwar sculptures of draped figures or family groups. Since WW2 he has worked mainly not with carving but by modelling sculptures to be cast in bronze, which makes possible a wider range of forms. His ideas have usually appeared first as drawings or as small maquettes which he then enlarged to the required scale.

Moore's international reputation has increased steadily. He has become the most famous living sculptor, and has made a number of large sculptures as commissions for public sites, such as the two-piece *Reclining Figure* (1963–5) for the Lincoln Center, New York. Although his works have ranged in style from relatively traditional figure sculptures such as the *Falling Warrior* (1956–7) to completely abstract works, his main theme has remained analogies between the human figure and craggy landscape forms: natural forms such as bones and pebbles, which he collects, have often been the starting-point for these works. REA

R. Melville, *Henry Moore: Sculpture and Drawings, 1921–1969* (London, 1970); D. Finn, *Henry Moore: Sculpture and Environment* (London, 1977).

Moore, Marianne Craig (b. Kirkwood, Mo., USA, 15.11.1887; d. New York, 5.2.1972). American poet. Her poems are meticulous constructs of observation and selection which exclude the personality of their author, and her life demonstrates a discretion which was modest rather than aloof. She began to write at Bryn Mawr College, published her poems in avant-garde magazines in America and Europe, and was from 1925 to 1929 editor of one of the most prestigious of these, the *Dial*. She moved to New York in 1918, living first in Manhattan then, for many years, in Brooklyn, returning to Manhattan some years before her death. William Carlos WILLIAMS and Ezra POUND were early advocates of her work; *Poems* (London, 1921) was published by admirers without her knowledge, and her *Selected Poems* (London, 1935) had an introduction by ELIOT who praised the originality of her language. Her poems employ a fastidious free verse or, more typically, asymmetric stanzas with exactly counted syllabic patterns and unobtrusive rhymes, which accommodate an elaborate prose syntax in which transitions of reference can be extremely rapid. Her writing incorporates quotation from many sources, intending always to establish relations between things with full regard to the fact and detail of their separate identities. Characteristically her work finds moral virtues in the qualities of fitness and appropriateness to context she notices in animals, birds, buildings, machinery and some people; but her best poems are those which make an imaginative wholeness of their context in the miscellany of her perceptions. ATKC

B. Costello, *Marianne Moore: Imaginary Possessions* (Cambridge, Mass., 1981).

Morandi, Giorgio (b. Bologna, Emilia-Romagna, Italy, 20.7.1890; d. Grizzana, 18.6.1964). Italian painter. He has come

to be admired as an exemplar of quiet steadfastness in the pursuit of his art and is regarded as one of the greatest painters of still life since Chardin, who was a considerable influence on his work. Morandi studied in Bologna, and travelled little. He met Carra and CHIRICO in 1919 and exhibited with them in 1921 and 1922. Although influenced by Chirico, Morandi is closer to CÉZANNE in his attitude and his unchanging subject matter. Most of his painting is of simple landscapes and still lifes of bottles, vessels and boxes set up in his studio. His palette is a restricted one, close in tone, with whites, creams, greys and soft rose-pinks; the brushwork is painterly but not expressionistic; and the works are pervaded by the silent mystery of *pittura metafisica*. Chirico wrote of him in 1922, 'He looks at a collection of objects on a table with the same emotions that stirred the heart of the traveller in ancient Greece when he gazed on the woods and valleys and mountains reputed to be the dwelling places of the most beautiful and marvellous deities.' MOJN

Royal Academy of Arts, *Giorgio Morandi* (London, 1970); Des Moines Art Center, *Morandi* (Des Moines, 1981).

Moravia, Alberto, ps. of Alberto Pincherle (b. Rome, Italy, 28.11.1907). Italian novelist, essayist and short-story writer. In early youth Moravia suffered from an illness which he considers a most important factor in his early development. His first novel *Gli indifferenti* (Milan, 1929; tr. A. Davidson, *The Time of Indifference*, London, 1953) is a brilliant analytical condemnation of the cynicism of the Roman bourgeoisie under fascism, and a prototype 'existentialist' novel. After SVEVO's *Senilità* (1898) and *La coscienza di Zeno* (1920), it was the first important novel in the neorealistic tradition. It had an almost dramatic impact – not merely in Italy (see its influence on SARTRE) – and was a stimulus to many contemporary Italian novelists. Among numerous subsequent novels, *Agostino* (Milan, 1944; tr. B. de Zoete, London, 1947); *La romana* (Milan, 1947; tr. L. Holland, *The Woman of Rome*, London, 1949);

La ciociara (Milan, 1957; tr. A. Davidson, *Two Women of Rome*, London, 1958); and *La noia* (Milan, 1960; tr. A. Davidson, *The Empty Canvas*, London, 1961) are the most important. A two-volume collection of his short stories *Racconti romani* appeared in 1954 and 1959 (Milan; tr. A. Davidson, *Roman Tales*, London, 1956). Moravia has travelled widely as a correspondent of *Corriere della Sera*. He is the editor of the important avant-garde cultural periodical *Nuovi argomenti*. His novels have been translated into various languages and his name has often been proposed for a Nobel prize. GS

D. Heiney, *Three Italian Novelists* (Ann Arbor, 1968); E. Montale in *Selected Essays*, tr. G. Singh (Manchester, 1978).

Morgan, John Pierpont (b. Hartford, Conn., USA, 17.4.1837; d. Rome, Italy, 31.3.1913). American financier who created one of the world's most powerful banking-houses by concentrating on financial services to large corporations. He was instrumental in the development of several railroads and some of the largest companies now in existence, such as US Steel, General Electric and International Harvester. RIT

Morgan, Thomas Hunt (b. Lexington, Ky, USA, 25.9.1866; d. Pasadena, Calif., 4.12.1945). American embryologist and geneticist. Morgan studied at the University of Kentucky and took his PhD at Johns Hopkins University, Baltimore. He held three professorships; zoology at Bryn Mawr College (1891–1904), experimental zoology at Columbia University (1904–28), and biology at the California Institute of Technology, Pasadena (1928–45). Although Morgan did significant work in experimental embryology and regeneration, working with a wide range of organisms, he is most generally remembered for his work in genetics, started at Columbia. As the scientific investigation of the principles of heredity gained new impetus from the rediscovery of MENDEL's laws in 1900, Morgan and his team of brilliant research workers at Columbia, especially H. Sturtevant, Calvin Bridges and H. J. Muller, established a sound basis for much of the development of genetics in the following decades. Though initially sceptical of the Mendelian theory, experiments with the fruit fly, *Drosophila melanogaster*, soon convinced Morgan of its general validity. A number of factors, including rapid generation-time and the ease with which large numbers can be bred, make this organism peculiarly suitable for genetic experimentation, and intensive studies followed after 1910. Morgan and his co-workers established the theory proposed by Sutton in 1903 that genes, the units of heredity, are carried on chromosomes. Using the chromosome theory of sex-determination proposed by a colleague and former teacher, E. B. WILSON, Morgan demonstrated the existence of sex linkage in *Drosophila*, and Bridges through his studies of sex-linkage in an abnormal strain obtained convincing evidence for Sutton's theory. Sturtevant analysed genetic crosses to show how the genes are arranged in linear order, and Muller went on to relate genetic 'map length' to the cytological length of the chromosomes (T. H. Morgan, A. H. Sturtevant, H. J. Muller & C. B. Bridges, *The Mechanism of Mendelian Heredity*, NY, 1915). These investigations established genetic mapping as an indispensable tool of analysis and yielded insight into basic genetic mechanisms. The knowledge thus acquired of the genetics of the fruit fly has given it a special status in contemporary research; for example, it is used in population and evolutionary genetics, and also in studies of development, a field that had been of particular interest to Morgan himself. Morgan was awarded the Nobel prize for medicine in 1930. APJ

L. C. Dunn, *A Short History of Genetics* (NY, 1965).

Morgenthau, Hans Joachim (b. Coburg, Bavaria, Germany, 17.2.1904; naturalized American citizen, 1943; d. New York, USA, 19.7.1980). German/American international relations theorist. Educated at German universities and at Geneva, he began his career as a judge in Frankfurt. Leaving Germany in 1932 for Geneva, he did not return after the rise of HITLER but settled in the USA in 1937. From 1943 to 1971 he taught at Chicago, and at the New School for Social Research, New York, from 1974. Morgenthau's high reputation as a pioneer and leading scholar in the field of international relations was achieved in spite of his having to challenge deeply cherished contemporary assumptions. His first major work *Scientific Man versus Power Politics* (NY, 1946) questioned the spreading belief that science can solve all problems, emphasizing against this that politics is the realm of the contingent and the possible. 'International politics, like all politics, is a struggle for power' – this assertion from *Politics among Nations: the Struggle for Power and Peace* (NY, 1948) explains the source of much misunderstanding of his position. Morgenthau in his political realism does not deny the importance of principles, but sees the need for them to be rooted in reality. Far from justifying amorality in international policy, he was calling for a more responsible, because reflective, approach. This led him to be one of the sternest critics of the Vietnam war as an involvement which could not succeed, founded on a too-simplistic crusading spirit against communism. DCr

Mori, Ōgai (b. Tsuwano, Shimane Prefecture, Japan, 19.1.1862; d. Tokyo, 9.7.1922). Japanese novelist, dramatist, literary critic and translator. Mori was born into a medical family and, by concealing his real age, became the youngest graduate of what was later the medical school of Tokyo University. At university he acquired a taste for literature and while his achievements as a doctor were not inconsiderable, it is as a major literary figure that he is best known. During the 1890s, after a four-year stay in Germany as an army physician, he gave great impetus to the romantic movement in modern Japanese literature, and in public debates with Tsubouchi Shōyō helped establish the idea, new to Japan, that drama should be regarded as having value as literature. In the 1900s Mori stood firmly against the rising tide of naturalism in literature and its main product the confessional novel, of which he deeply disapproved. The I- novelists sought an individualistic, ego-centred escape from society; Mori believed that man had a

place in it, if necessary behind a mask, and that there should be a rational relationship between the individual and society. During the 1910s he turned to historical subjects, producing at first a large number of historical novels, of which one of the most famous was *Abe ichizoku* (Tokyo, 1913; tr. D. Dilworth, 'The Abe Family' in *The Incident at Sakai and Other Stories*, Honolulu, 1977). After some critical writing on the theory of the historical novel, he devoted himself to historical research and for the rest of his life his main literary output was not in fiction but in historical narrative and biography. BWFP

J. T. Rimer, *Mori Ōgai* (Boston, Mass., 1975); R. J. Bowring, *Mori Ōgai and the Modernization of Japanese Culture* (Cambridge, Mass., 1979).

Móricz, Zsigmond (b. Tiszacsécse, Austria-Hungary [now Hungary], 2.7.1879; d. Budapest, 4.9.1942). Hungarian novelist, short-story writer and dramatist. The son of an ambitious peasant and a Calvinist minister's daughter, Móricz won instant acclaim with his story *Hét krajcár* [Seven pennies] (Budapest, 1908), a tale of stark poverty which shattered the idyllic pictures of country life commonly depicted in Hungarian literature. This introduced Móricz as a blunt but profoundly sensitive realist. The society he knew – peasants and country gentry – formed the background of his early works, and he did not scruple to reveal the tragic and intimate details of their lives, however sordid. He gradually extended his range from the country to the town, and during his last few years wrote equally effectively of the city slums. Human relationships were an overriding concern: *Légy jó mindhalálig* (Budapest, 1920; tr. L. Körösi, *Be Faithful unto Death*, Budapest, 1962) depicts the innocent schoolboy in the corrupt world of adults. Many of his novels explore the tensions between husband and wife, reflecting his own fragile marriages. Though he was a keen and passionate observer of the contemporary scene, he proved his power as a historical novelist in his trilogy *Erdély* [Transylvania] (Budapest, 1922–35). The vitality and dramatic intensity of his writing have often been imitated, but never excelled by later authors. GFC

J. Reményi, *Hungarian Writers and Literature* (New Brunswick, NJ, 1964).

Morison, Stanley Arthur [Ignatius] (b. Wanstead, Essex, UK, 6.5.1889; d. London, 11.10.1967). British scholar-typographer. He worked on the short-lived, influential periodical the *Imprint* (1913) and thereafter was 'designer of printed matter' for the publishers Burns & Oates (1914), Pelican Press (1919–20) and Cloister Press (1921–2). As typographical adviser to Cambridge University Press (1925–67) and to Monotype Corporation (1923–56), he successfully launched – in collaboration with CUP printer Walter Lewis – many new Monotype book typefaces including Baskerville, Bell, Bembo, Centaur (and Arrighi italic), Ehrhardt, Fournier, Garamond, Goudy Modern, Perpetua (and Felicity italic), Poliphilus (and Blado italic), Romulus and Van Dijck. He also commissioned outstanding display and jobbing faces, among them Albertus and GILL Sanserif. Cofounder, with Oliver Simon, of *The Fleuron* annual (1923–30), he contributed many scholarly essays. For ten years from 1928 he was director for design of GOLLANCZ's newly established imprint and astonished the book trade and the reading public with his gaudy attention-compelling 'yellow jackets'. He completely restyled *The Times* newspaper (1932): his Times New Roman type-family achieved worldwide acclaim for both book and jobbing work. He exerted powerful managerial influence on that newspaper. His editorship of its *Literary Supplement* (1945–7) won it international status. His major publications include *First Principles of Typography* (Cambridge, 1936), *Four Centuries of Fine Printing* (London, 1924), *The History of The Times* (4 vols, London, 1935 –52) and, with Harry Carter, *John Fell, the University Press and the 'Fell' Types* (Oxford, 1967). TC

Morita, Akio (b. Kasugaya, Japan, 26.1.1921). Japanese industrialist who cofounded and directs the Japanese Sony company. Instead of exporting cheaper imitations of western products, which had been the reputation of many Japanese exporters, Sony offered quality products, based on advanced technological concepts at relatively low prices. Transistors, developed for commercial and military use, were applied to consumer products by Sony who brought out the first transistor radio (1955), pocket-sized transistor two-band radio (1957), FM radio (1958), all-transistor television (1959) and a transistorized video tape recorder (1960). It is claimed that the Sony trademark is registered around the world more than any other. Sony's entry into the world markets was via sophisticated but low-key advertising to educate the new consumers without mentioning the company's Japanese origins. By 1963 Sony had become the first Japanese company to offer stock on the United States exchanges and was listed in 1970. Two years later 30 per cent of Sony's stock was American-held.

Morita himself graduated in physics from Osaka Imperial University in 1944 and was commissioned in the Imperial Japanese Navy. After 1945 his appointment to a teaching post at Tokyo University was short-lived since the occupying powers barred former military officers from holding teaching posts. As a result he founded the Tokyo Tsushin Kogyo (Tokyo Telecommunications Company) with the equivalent of $500 capital; this company was to become Sony in 1958. RIT

Morton, Ferdinand Joseph (Jelly Roll), *né* Lemott (b. New Orleans, La, USA, 20.9.1885; d. Los Angeles, Calif., 10.7.1941). American jazz pianist, composer, singer, arranger and bandleader. Morton pioneered a jazz piano style which amalgamated ragtime with improvisation. He was also a brilliant arranger, and a successful composer (some of his works – 'Wolverine Blues', 'King Porter Stomp', 'Buddy Bolden's Blues' – became jazz standards). In the 1920s Morton settled in Chicago (then the main centre for black recording artistes), and organized his own band 'The Red Hot Peppers'; on their 1926 recordings, Morton orchestrated New Orleans style jazz in a way that skilfully retained the verve and excitement of an improvised ensemble. His blending of instrumental voicings within a small band was revolutionary, and he did much to eliminate the crudities and confusion of earlier jazz, his dictum being 'Jazz is to be played sweet, soft, plenty rhythm'. Morton composed many tunes recorded by 'The Red Hot Peppers', including the haunting 'Original Jelly Roll Blues' with a Latin American rhythm he called his 'Spanish Tinge'. After touring with his own big band Morton sank into obscurity during the mid-1930s, but re-emerged in 1938 to make a series of recordings for the Library of Congress in Washington DC, in which he graphically describes the social life of New Orleans at the turn of the century, and plays and sings with great feeling. A revival of interest in his work took him to New York where he resumed a successful career, but by then his health was failing. He moved to California in 1940. JJC

A. Lomax, *Mister Jelly Roll* (NY, 1950); L. Wright, *Mr Jelly Lord* (London, 1980).

Mosca, Gaetano (b. Palermo, Sicily, Italy, 1.4.1858; d. Rome, 8.11.1941). Italian jurist and political scientist. Educated at Palermo University in Sicily, Mosca taught constitutional law there and at Rome and Turin. He became a deputy in 1908, a life senator in 1919, and professor at Rome University in 1923. Mosca's *Teorica* (Turin, 1884; as *Teorica dei governi e governo parlamentare* [Theory of governments and parliamentary government], ²1925) was followed by the work on which his reputation stands, *Elementi di scienza politica* (Turin, 1896, ⁴1939; ed. A. Livingston, *The Ruling Class*, NY, 1939). Pursuing the same vein of thought as PARETO, with whom he disputed the priority for distinguishing between elite and masses, and MICHELS who was a confessed admirer of his work, Mosca turned into a general law the observation that in all societies, from the dawn of civilization to the most advanced, there have always been two classes of people, one the less numerous, which rules; the other, the more numerous, which is ruled. Contrary to theories of majority rule, all societies are governed by minorities, the political class, in

Mosca's terminology. This is so whatever its character – military, religious, plutocratic, bureaucratic – or whatever the myth with which its rule is justified – whether this is the will of God, the will of the people, or the dictatorship of the proletariat.

Mosca's theory was often taken as a justification of fascism, but he himself was a 19c liberal, critical of a democracy based upon universal suffrage but attached to a limited representative form of government and no admirer of MUSSOLINI's, still less of HITLER's dictatorship. The second edition of *Elementi*, published in 1923, left the original text untouched but added a second volume of comment in which Mosca found something to be appraised in 'the democratic tendency' since it brought new blood to the political class 'and so prevents that exhaustion of the aristocracies of birth that is wont to bring on the great social cataclysms.' He did not, however, change his view that societies in the future, as in the past, would continue to be ruled by a governing class and that MARXist preaching of a classless society was the least convincing of all political fictions. ALCB

J. H. Meisel, *The Myth of the Ruling Class: Gaetano Mosca and the Elite* (Ann Arbor, ²1962).

Moseley, Henry Gwyn Jeffreys (b. Weymouth, Dorset, UK, 23.11.1887; d. Gallipoli, Ottoman Empire [now Turkey], 10.8.1915). British physicist. Moseley was the first person to demonstrate that the chemical properties of an element are determined by its atomic number, and not (as previously thought) by its atomic weight. He was appointed lecturer in physics at Manchester, under RUTHERFORD, in 1910. He stayed for three years, and then returned to Oxford. The idea of consecutively numbering the elements in the periodic table, counting hydrogen as 1, was first proposed by Gladstone (1853) and later by Newlands (1864). However, it was not until 1913 that Van den Broek measured the wavelengths of X-rays emitted by an element when bombarded with electrons, and showed that these varied in a regular manner from one element to another. The precise form of this relationship, known as Moseley's law, allowed the explicit determination of the 'atomic number' (a term now introduced by Moseley) of the elements. The importance of this discovery cannot be overstated. It was now possible to 'catalogue' the elements definitively, based on atomic number and not atomic weight, and discover if any were missing. Moseley showed that there were 92 elements up to and including uranium, and that six were not known. Three of these (hafnium, rhenium and francium) have now been discovered; the other three (technetium, promethium and astatine) have been made artificially. A year later, Moseley was dead, killed in action at Gallipoli. KRS

Mössbauer, Rudolf Ludwig (b. Munich, Bavaria, Germany, 31.1.1929). German physicist. In the visible region of the spectrum, gaseous atoms can be stimulated to emit light of a sharp frequency which can then be absorbed by other atoms of the same kind. This is the initial step of the process called resonance fluorescence. The corresponding experiment with the much higher energy γ-rays ordinarily fails because as a γ-ray photon leaves a nucleus, the nucleus recoils, and since energy is conserved, the issuing photon is of too low a frequency to be absorbed by a target nucleus of the same species. If however the recoil energy could be spread over all the particles of a crystal lattice in which the γ-emitting nuclei are embedded, γ-radiation of a very narrow frequency distribution at the transition frequency might be emitted, to be absorbed by target nuclei. Mössbauer, working at the Max Planck Institute in Heidelberg, showed, in a paper published in 1958, that recoil-less γ-emission does indeed occur for some crystals, and moreover that the effect is often strongly dependent on temperature. The low temperature γ-emission is of such sharp frequency in the case of $^{57}Co = {}^{57}Fe + \gamma$ that target nuclei will not absorb unless they are in the same environment as the emitters. However, by a gentle motion, at a rate of the order of 1 cm per second, the absorbing species may be Doppler-shifted into resonance. Thus one may identify, for example, in a cooled solid absorber, ions Fe^{2+}, Fe^{3+} and in general ^{57}Fe nuclei in different structural situations. Somewhat as in the case of nuclear magnetic resonance, the Mössbauer effect gives – in the case of suitable nuclei – information about their properties and electronic surroundings. This is now a subject of many and diverse applications, for example in archaeology, catalysis, solid state science, structure, valency and in the study of biological polymers. Mössbauer was awarded the Nobel prize in physics in 1961. RFB

Motherwell, Robert (b. Aberdeen, Wash., USA, 24.1.1915). American painter who was the intellectual of the New York school. During the early 1940s he made contact with the European surrealists in exile in New York, developing an interest in automatism which he saw as 'a plastic weapon with which to invent new forms'. Influenced by symbolist aesthetics, he came to see abstract form as a pictorial equivalent for states of feeling. He visited Mexico with MATTA in 1941 and in 1943 contributed with POLLOCK and Baziotes to an exhibition of collage. This medium remained an abiding preoccupation; later examples contained material which made conspicuous reference to the culture of Europe. A year later he had his first one-man exhibition and in 1945 became editor of the series 'The Documents of Modern Art' of which *The Dada Painters and Poets: an Anthology* (NY, 1951) influenced neodada and Pop art in the USA. In 1949 he began the series of paintings, many of them mural-scale, *Elegy to the Spanish Republic*, where black vertical bands alternate with ovoid shapes on a white ground, evincing a theme of life and death. During the late 1960s he began his series of 'Opens', colour-field paintings with the outline of three sides of a window. MOJN

F. O'Hara, *Robert Motherwell* (NY, 1965); H. H. Arnason, *Robert Motherwell* (NY, 1977).

Mott, Nevill Francis (b. Leeds, W. Yorks., UK, 30.9.1905). British physicist. Mott is one of Britain's relatively few great theoretical physicists. Apart from his fundamental scientific contributions for over 50 years, he has exerted great influence as departmental head, teacher and author. Both his parents had worked at the Cavendish Laboratory and as far back as he could remember he wanted to do theoretical physics. He read mathematics and, self-educated in physics, worked with RUTHERFORD at Cambridge and Niels BOHR at Copenhagen. In the 1920s he applied the new quantum theory to scattering problems in atomic physics (with H. S. W. Massey, *The Theory of Atomic Collisions*, Oxford, 1933). At Cambridge true physics then meant nuclear physics but, aged 28, Mott went to a chair at Bristol, where his interest in solid-state physics was kindled by the work of his colleagues, and where he stayed for 21 years. Close collaboration between theoreticians and experimentalists made Bristol an international centre for solid-state physics (with H. Jones, *The Theory of the Properties of Metals and Alloys*, Oxford, 1936; and with R. W. Gurney, *Electronic Processes in Ionic Crystals*, Oxford, 1940). War work at the Armaments Research Establishment aroused his interest in plastic deformation of solids which became for him a new field of study after his return to Bristol at the end of WW2. New colleagues he attracted to Bristol also pioneered research into crystal growth and the mechanisms of the photographic process. His general text *Wave Mechanics and its Applications*, with I. N. Sneddon, appeared in 1948 (Oxford).

In 1954 Mott returned to Cambridge (to the Cavendish chair), where his own interests centred on the application of dislocation theory and metal-insulator transitions (often called Mott transitions). Thinking he was unlikely to make further major contributions to physics, he turned increasingly to educational and administrative interests and succeeded CHADWICK as master of Gonville and Caius College in 1959. He resigned early – in 1965 – and returned to solid-state physics and to the developing interest in noncrystalline materials. He applied to them most successfully his talent for examining complex experimental results and interpreting them in terms of simple models (with E. A. Davis, *Electronic Processes in Non-Crystalline Materials*, Oxford, 1971; *Metal-Insulator Transitions*, London, 1974). This work culminated in the award of a Nobel prize in 1977. MMG/MJW

Mounier, Emmanuel (b. Grenoble, Isère, France, 1.4.1905; d. Paris, 22.3.1950). French intellectual, philosopher and editor. Influenced in youth by PÉGUY, he founded a monthly *Esprit*, in order to 'refaire la renaissance', the first one having been botched. His plan was that it should become a laboratory of ideas backed up by study groups dotted all over France – and eventually Belgium and Switzerland. The movement needed a doctrine to mark it off from the totalitarianisms of fascism and communism, as well as from the enfeeblement of the democracies. Mounier's doctrine came to be known as 'personalism', as outlined in books such as *Le Personnalisme* (Paris, 1949; tr. P. Mairet, *Personalism*, Notre Dame, Ind., 1970). Mounier was more important as a midwife and a middleman than as an original thinker, providing a platform for contributors to *Esprit* such as BERDAYEV and Paul-Louis Lansberg, who introduced him to the ideas of Max Scheler on 'sympathy' and 'phenomenology'. The war disturbed all Mounier's categories. Some of his friends were in power at Vichy; for a time he taught at their *école des cadres*. But then he went underground, was arrested by the Vichy police who believed, wrongly, that he was an active member of the Resistance. This mistake saved him in postwar France where he was increasingly seen as a 'Catholic of the Left' and a – discriminating – ally of the Communists. His early death and the keen advocacy of his friends permitted the legends to grow. He was regarded as the 'prophet' who had anticipated the Second Vatican Council (1962 –5). In an obvious sense he had. The commending use of the term 'personalist' (as opposed to 'juridical' or 'essentialist') proved the extent of his influence. PAH

M. Kelly, *Pioneer of the Catholic Revival: the Ideas and Influence of Emmanuel Mounier* (London, 1979); J. Hellman, *Emmanuel Mounier and the New Catholic Left* (Toronto, 1981).

Moynihan, Berkeley George Andrew (b. Malta, 2.10.1865; d. Leeds, W. Yorks., UK, 7.9.1936). British surgeon, and one of the pioneers of surgery of the abdomen; he virtually perfected both the diagnosis and the surgical treatment of duodenal ulcer by partial removal of the stomach. His pre-eminence among surgeons of the early years of the 20c rested on his faultless surgical technique (Moynihan's operative mortality at the turn of the century was as low as that of the average surgeon 30 years later), his careful clinical observation that paved the way to accuracy of diagnosis, and his continuing interest in research. Surgeons from all parts of the world travelled to Leeds to watch Moynihan operate; he showed them that abdominal surgery could be safe and effective long before the introduction of blood transfusion and antibiotics.   AJS

Mrożek, Sławomir (b. Borzęcin, Poland, 26.6.1930). Polish dramatist, short-story writer and cartoonist, whose works have now been translated into most European languages. Mrożek's dramas, like those of RÓŻEWICZ, explore the explosive potential of the absurd, a convention inaugurated in Poland by the precursory work of Witkiewicz and GOMBROWICZ. Any analogies with the world of IONESCO and BECKETT should be explained in terms of affinity, not influence. Mrożek takes as his starting-point some inherent nihilism of bureaucracies, officialdoms and social stereotypes, then leads his parable or fable through a series of strictly controlled incongruities into a realm of bleak and deadpan wryness that often bypasses laughter altogether. His major works explore problems of power and social manipulation, alienation and bourgeois degeneracy; in dramatic terms the climax may pivot on a nonevent or an act of desecration. Critics have been tempted to see Mrożek's plays as metaphors of the political state of Poland. Such are their ambiguities and obliquenesses, however, that they have enjoyed virtually unhampered success throughout the post-STALINist period. In fact, divorced from the shackles of national idiom and bereft of local and temporal reference, Mrożek's dramas expose universal situations in the raw; hence, no doubt, their worldwide appeal. For English translations see: *Słoń* (Kraków, 1957; tr. K. Syrop, *The Elephant*, London, 1962), *Tango* (1965; tr. N. Bethell, London, 1968), *Striptease* (1961; tr. T. Dzieduszycka, NY, 1972) and *Emigranci* (1975; tr. M. & T. Wrona & R. Holman, *Emigrés*, London, 1977). Further plays have been translated by N. Bethell as *Six Plays* (London, 1967).   NT

Mufti of Jerusalem, see HUSAINI, HAJJ AMIN AL-.

Mugabe, Robert Gabriel (b. Kutama Mission, Zwimba, Southern Rhodesia [now Zwimba TTL, Zimbabwe], 21.2.1924). Prime minister of Zimbabwe. One of the most intellectual of contemporary African leaders – the holder of four academic degrees – Mugabe worked as a teacher and entered Rhodesian politics in 1960. In 1963 he broke with Joshua Nkomo, Rhodesia's dominant African nationalist, and became co-founder of the Zimbabwe African National Union. Detained by the Rhodesian authorities in 1964, he was released in 1974 and established himself as leader of ZANU. Forming an alliance (the Patriotic Front) with Nkomo's ZAPU (Zimbabwe African Peoples Union), Mugabe moved to Mozambique which became the base for ZANU guerrilla operations; played a key role in the Lancaster House Conference of 1979; and after ZANU's decisive victory in the February 1980 election became first prime minister of an independent Zimbabwe. Modifying the radical MARXism of the liberation struggle, Mugabe laid special stress on reconciliation between black and white, thus averting a disastrously rapid white exodus, but did not renounce his socialist aspirations and introduced measures in employment, education and health to improve the lot of ordinary black people.   RH
  R. Gray & D. Mitchell, *African Nationalist Leaders in Rhodesia. Who's Who* (Johannesburg, 1978).

Muḥammad ᶜAbduh (b. Shanra, Lower Egypt, 1849; d. Alexandria, Egypt, 11.7.1905). Egyptian Muslim reformer and founder of the modernist school of Islamic revivalism. After early theological studies and a period devoted to Ṣūfī mysticism, in 1872 he came under the influence of Jamāl al-dīn AFGHĀNĪ. Following the latter's expulsion from Egypt in 1879, ᶜAbduh was briefly proscribed, but in 1880 was made editor of the government gazette, through which he promulgated his liberal views. Implication in ᶜUrābī Pāshā's revolt led to his exile in 1882. In Paris in 1884 he collaborated with Afghāni in the publication of the influential journal *Al-ᶜurwa al-wuthqā* [The firm cord], but he eventually took a more moderate line than his mentor, urging education and gradual reform rather than revolution. Returning to Egypt in 1888, he was made chief Mufti in 1899, in which post he effected numerous reforms in Islamic law. He also served on the legislative council and, from 1894, was a member of the supreme council of al-Azhar University, in the curriculum and administration of which he introduced several reforms. His writings include *Risālat al-tawḥīd* [Treatise on the divine unity] (Cairo, 1897), *Al-Islām wa 'l-Naṣrāniyya* [Islam and Christianity] (Cairo, 1902), and an incomplete but influential Qur'ān commentary. His emphases on the rationality of Islam and on its adaptability to modern conditions have been major influences on later reformers.   DMM

E. Kedourie, *Afghāni and ᶜAbduh* (London, 1966); M. H. Kerr, *Islamic Reform: the Political and Legal Theories of Muhammad ᶜAbduh and Rashīd Ridā* (Berkeley, Calif., 1966).

Muir, Edwin (b. Deerness, Orkney, UK, 15.5.1887; d. Cambridge, 3.1.1959). British poet, critic and translator. With his wife Willa he was the first translator into English of KAFKA, BROCH and other German and French writers. His criticism, mainly in essays (the best are collected in *Essays on Literature and Society*, London, 1949, ²1965) and reviews, was, as ELIOT wrote, 'of the best of our time'. His chief prose work, however, was his autobiography (*The Story and the Fable*, London, 1940; extended as *An Autobiography*, London, 1954) in which his Orkney childhood,

his move (over 200 years, he said) to clerking in industrial Glasgow, his loss and recovery of wholeness and faith are recreated in lucid, quietly rhythmical prose; and beneath the personal story is glimpsed the fable of man – Eden, the fall, the journey through the labyrinth of time on ('the way leads on', not back) to enlarged vision. This vision is most fully expressed in his later poetry (*The Labyrinth*, London, 1949; *One Foot in Eden*, London, 1956; *Collected Poems*, London, 1960), a vision in which 'everything, in spite of the practical disorder of life, seems to have its place'. Muir penetrates more profoundly than more fashionable poets into the century's disorders and, modestly and undogmatically, by symbol and myth opens a vision of the larger order.   PHB

P. Butter, *Edwin Muir: Man and Poet* (Edinburgh, 1966); R. Knight, *Edwin Muir* (London, 1980).

Mulliken, Robert Sanderson (b. Newburyport, Mass., USA, 7.6.1896). American chemical physicist who has made a unique contribution ranging from detailed aspects of the theory of the energy states of small molecules to broad generalizations illuminating many problems in chemical binding. Early work was on the isotope effect in the band-spectra of diatomic molecules. Interest in molecular spectroscopy led him to prepare the famous 1930–2 papers in *Reviews of Modern Physics* which still serve as basic texts. Concerned somewhat more with ideas than with experiments, he developed and applied molecular orbital theory (now associated particularly with the names of F. Hund, HERZBERG, LENNARD-JONES and COULSON) to the systematization of electronic energy states. In 1934 he had introduced a new scale of electronegativity of the elements, based upon ionization potential and electron affinity; other original concepts, such as the idea of hyperconjugation and the use of overlap integrals in discussing the strengths of chemical bonds, followed. In 1950 he turned his attention to the structure and spectra of donor-acceptor complexes such as that formed between benzene and iodine: in 1960 he published a paper with the characteristic title 'Some neglected subcases of pre-dissociation in diatomic molecules'. Since 1961 the flow of Mulliken's original work has continued, with papers on new diatomics such as the rare gas dimers, on molecular orbitals and molecular complexes, on Rydberg states, and on many other subjects. There are few aspects of molecular spectroscopy and of valence theory that he has failed to touch with distinction and authority. Professor of physics at the University of Chicago (1931–61), he was awarded the Nobel prize for chemistry in 1966. RFB

Mumford, Lewis (b. Flushing, NY, USA, 19.10.1895). American cultural and social critic. Mumford is a severe critic of contemporary urban technological culture. He rejects the narrow specialization of science and technology, and points to its adverse effects on the quality of life. He argues that the values of western society need to be radically changed to a holistic view of culture, where balance is maintained between a wide spectrum of competing tendencies. An early, and important influence on Mumford was the work of GEDDES, from whom he derived his concepts of the urban region, of an ecological perspective in social issues and of comprehensive regional planning. With others, Mumford founded the Regional Planning Association of America in 1923. To bring about his wider cultural aims, he argued the priority of a more humane environment, the practice of regional planning and the adoption of HOWARD's proposals for garden cities. As a critic and an activist in planning and in architecture he has had a worldwide influence on those professions. Mumford is the author of some 30 books. The four volumes of the *Renewal of Life* series (*Technics and Civilization*, NY, 1934; *The Culture of Cities*, NY, 1938; *The Condition of Man*, NY, 1944; and *The Conduct of Life*, NY, 1951) constitute a major statement of his philosophy. His conviction of the importance of a historical perspective in planning for the future is reflected in another major work *The City in History* (NY, 1961). Mumford's account of his work is given in *My Works and Days: a Personal Chronicle* (NY, 1979). BM

P. D. Goist, 'Seeing things whole: a consideration of Lewis Mumford', *Journal of the American Institute of Planners*, 38, 6 (1972), 379–91.

Munch, Edvard (b. Löten, Hedmark, Norway, 12.12.1863; d. Ekerly, nr Oslo, 23.1.1944). Norwegian painter and graphic artist. Munch's childhood was overshadowed by the early death from tuberculosis of his mother and elder sister. From 1881 to 1884 he studied in Oslo under the realist Christian Krohg. A visit to Paris (1889–90) introduced him to neoimpressionism and symbolism, especially the gloom and fantasy of Redon's prints and Gauguin's expressive line and colour. He resolved to paint the states of mind of 'living people who breathe and feel and suffer and love'. He developed a style by which a scene or experience became a symbolic expression of an emotion. In the 1890s Munch worked on *The Frieze of Life*, an ambitious project (for which he completed 22 canvases) depicting his pessimistic view of the human condition, aspiring to love (*The Kiss*, 1892) but beset by the suffering, both physical (*The Sick Child*, six versions, 1885–1927) and mental (*The Cry*, 1893; *Anxiety*, 1894), which prefigures death (*By the Death Bed*, 1893). The most powerful images in the series are those (influenced by STRINDBERG, whom he met in Berlin in the 1890s) of sexual longing and frustration (e.g. *Puberty*, c. 1893; *Desire*, 1895; *Jealousy*, 1894–5) and of an obsessive fear of female sexuality (e.g. *Ashes*, 1894; *Vampire*, c. 1895). In 1894 he made his first etchings and lithographs; in 1896, in Paris, influenced by Gauguin and Toulouse-Lautrec, he began to make coloured lithographs and woodcuts. His treatment of a single motif (often taken from earlier paintings) in various graphic techniques and colours, altering or heightening the expressive effect, was a major impetus behind the 20c interest in graphics (see KIRCHNER, MATISSE, NOLDE and PICASSO). From 1892 to 1908 Munch lived mainly in Berlin (with visits to Norway, France and Italy), and was a major influence on the young expressionists. After a nervous breakdown in 1908 he settled in Norway. His later works, including landscapes, portraits and everyday scenes, are calmer and less inventive than those of his earlier years.   SOBT

A. Moen, *Edvard Munch: Graphic Art and Paintings* (3 vols, Oslo, 1956–8); W. Timm, *The Graphic Art of Edvard Munch* (London, 1969).

Munrow, David John (b. Birmingham, W. Mids, UK, 12.8.1942; d. Chesham Bois, Bucks., 15.5.1976). British musician and performer of early wind instruments. His remarkable 10-year career influenced considerably the presentation and popularity of early music and determined its transformation from scholarship to living repertoire. One year as a voluntary teacher in Peru stimulated his interest in folk music and original instruments and, after graduating from Cambridge in English, he went to research 17c music at Birmingham University. His large and exotic collection of instruments formed the basis of the lecture tours he began to give with his wife Gillian Reid. While a member of the Royal Shakespeare Company's wind band, he formed his Early Music Consort of London in 1967 which performed in authentic style but with a sound both attractive and new to contemporary listeners – Munrow's own versatility and formidable virtuosity in playing upon a wide variety of instruments was an outstanding feature. He also became widely known as the presenter, from 1971, of 'Pied Piper', the successful BBC radio series, and for his music for BBC TV productions, such as *The Six Wives of Henry VIII* (1970) and *Elizabeth R* (1971). His film music included *La Course en Tête* (1974), *The Devils* (1970), *Zardoz* (1973) and *Henry VIII* (1972). He produced an important reference work *Instruments of the Middle Ages and Renaissance* with discs (Oxford/EMI, 1976).   TEC

Murdoch, Jean Iris (b. Dublin, Ireland, UK [now Irish Republic], 15.7.1919). British novelist and philosopher who from 1948 to 1963 was a fellow and tutor in philosophy at St Anne's College, Oxford. Her first publication was *Sartre: Romantic Rationalist* (Cambridge, 1953). *Under the Net* (London, 1954) marked the beginning of her career as a

prolific novelist: in 25 years she has published 20 novels, as well as plays, poetry and philosophical studies. Her fiction converges with and enlarges on her concern as a philosopher (see *The Sovereignty of Good*, London, 1970) with the relationship between art and morals and the nature of reality, truth, freedom and goodness. In contrast to the egocentric view of existentialism, reality is portrayed in her work as something which the individual can apprehend only by accepting the validity of the existence and experience of others. Individuals gain freedom, essentially, through love: the force that enables them to understand the separateness of other people. Iris Murdoch's novels present society as a rich, ambiguous and complex milieu within which each person shapes his or her own moral identity by responding to random or 'contingent' events and characters. The interaction of personal relationships provides a rich source of comedy, notably in *A Severed Head* (London, 1961). Her comic vision, narrative assurance, mastery of plot and characterization and, perhaps above all, compelling concern with moral issues and recognition of the importance of spiritual experience (for example in *Nuns and Soldiers*, London, 1980) place her work in the tradition of the English social novel and put her in the first rank of modern English writers.   JEEH

A. S. Byatt, *Degrees of Freedom: the Novels of Iris Murdoch* (London, 1965); M. Bradbury, *Possibilities: Essays on the State of the Novel* (Oxford, 1973).

Murdock, George Peter (b. Meriden, Conn., USA, 11.5.1897). American anthropologist best known for his comparative studies of social organization and his contribution to the compiling of cross-cultural surveys. After studying history at Yale and law at Harvard he received his PhD from Yale (1925) and taught there from 1928. From 1960 until his retirement in 1973 he was a professor at the University of Pittsburgh. In his emphasis on social organization and comparative studies Murdock differed from other contemporary American anthropologists (i.e. working in the BOASian tradition). His book *Social Structure* (NY, 1949) exemplified his approach. In this study – based on a sample of 250 cultures – Murdock produced a typology of kinship systems and put forward a theory to account for variation. Murdock's work in Yale's Institute of Human Relations (see *Outline of World Cultures*, New Haven, 1954) was an early instance of multidisciplinary collaboration, and in the use of quantitative techniques foreshadowed what was to become a major methodological shift within anthropology. Murdock is notable not only for his range of ethnographic interests (North and South America, Australia, Africa), but also for his early involvement in applied anthropology, particularly in relation to Oceania.   SLN

Murnau, Friedrich Wilhelm, *né* Friedrich Wilhelm Plumpe (b. Bielefeld, N. Rhine-Westphalia, Germany, 28.12.1888; d. Santa Barbara, Calif., USA, 11.3.1931). German film director. Murnau's reputation and achievement is generally assessed on the strength of just five films: *Nosferatu, eine Symphonie des Gravens* [A symphony of terror, 1922], *Der Letzte Mann* (*The Last Laugh*, 1924), *Faust* (1926), *Sunrise* (1927) and *Tabu* (1931, codirected with FLAHERTY). That he is considered one of the major names of world cinema despite the brevity of his directorial career (he was killed in a car accident) is testimony to the influence of his peculiar blend of expressionism and poetic realism upon the subsequent development of cinematic style. At a time when EISENSTEIN was developing his theories of montage and his German contemporaries were filming expressionist dramas on cramped, artificial sets, Murnau developed a more 'realistic' variant of expressionism by freeing his camera from its restricted and static fixity. The Gothic expressionism of *Nosferatu*, filmed on location, derived from the script and the theme rather than from studio sets. In *Der Letzte Mann*, a city film made in a studio, Murnau succeeded in expressing through camera movement what other directors were expressing through lighting and distortions. Murnau's freewheeling camera broke the bounds of expressionism by suggesting the existence of a reality outside of the frame – in expressionism proper the world stops at the frame's edge. Early in 1927 Murnau was invited to Hollywood and in the same year made *Sunrise*, generally recognized to be one of the last great silent films, as well as a cinematic milestone for the manner in which Murnau's lyrical use of the moving camera presents an imaginative and subjective evocation of the real world. Murnau's pioneering use of the moving camera was one of the cinema's first steps towards developing a form of representation which seemed to be more 'realistic' than the view of the world offered by the static camera.   LJC

L. Eisner, *Murnau* (London, 1973).

Musil, Robert Edler von (b. Klagenfurt, Carinthia, Austria-Hungary [now Austria], 6.11.1880; d. Geneva, Switzerland, 15.4.1942). Austrian novelist. A graduate of an elite military academy, Musil qualified as an engineer at Brünn, but his deep interest in intellectual life drew him to Berlin where he studied philosophy and psychology and wrote his doctoral dissertation on MACH. He was offered a university teaching post but, having already published a novel based on experiences at school (*Die Verwirrungen des Zöglings Törless*, Vienna, 1906; tr. E. Kaiser & E. Wilkins, *Young Törless*, NY, 1964), he decided to devote himself to literature.

Like many others of his generation Musil was strongly influenced by NIETZSCHE's diagnosis of the unease within European civilization and wanted to contribute to a regeneration of culture. But his scientific background set him apart from other creative writers; although his works bear traces of naturalism, aestheticism and expressionism, they are all distinctive products of a mind trained in the techniques of empirical research, determined to take literature beyond all common limits. In *Vereinigungen* (Munich, 1911; tr. E. Wilkins & E. Kaiser in *Tonke and Other Stories*, NY, 1965), for example, Musil developed a unique language of images to transmit to the reader the exact 'feel' of emotions within the psyche of his fictional characters. As an essayist and critic he was acknowledged to be one of the most acute observers of contemporary cultural and social phenomena, writing prose of outstanding precision and beauty. WW1, in which Musil served with distinction, broke some of his ties with Berlin; he moved to Vienna and started to write the work that was to absorb him for the rest of his life. Part novel, part essayistic antinovel, *Der Mann ohne Eigenschaften* (2 vols, Berlin, 1930–3; latest edition, with extensive material from Musil's literary papers, by A. Frisé, Hamburg, 1978; tr. E. Kaiser & E. Wilkins, *The Man without Qualities*, 3 vols, London, 1953–60) is a record of Musil's own existence, sharp-focused in interminable self-analysis, and a portrait of pre-WW1 Viennese high society from the perspective of an irony deepened by the inclusion in the narrative of extensive quotations from well-known contemporaries of all walks of life.

Musil was both neopositivist and mystic: he tried to break the hold of the past by unmasking the hypocrisy in present attitudes and to capture in his writing something of the 'fire' of ecstatic experience from which the spiritual renewal of mankind might come. Though *Der Mann ohne Eigenschaften* was unfinished at his death, it is widely held to be the most brilliant synthesis of the main intellectual, social, political and cultural elements within Austrian and German civilization to have been written in the first half of this century.

JPP

D. S. Luft, *Robert Musil and the Crisis of European Culture, 1880–1942* (Berkeley, Calif., 1980).

Mussadeq, Mohammed (b. Tehran, Persia [now Iran], 1880; d. Tehran, 5.3.1967). Prime minister of Iran (1951–3), having been imposed on the Shah by his own militant following in the Teheran streets in alliance with the major Iranian feudal families anxious at the Shah's reformism. He had been a bitter opponent of the Anglo-Iranian Oil Company since his election to the Majlis in 1942, and was thus an obvious choice for the premiership following the assassination of the Shah's strong-man General Razmara and the nationalization of the company in Iran. Withdrawal of western oil experts and legal action by the company against all

attempts to sell Iranian oil abroad progressively destroyed the Iranian economy and began to move Mussadeq's centre of support steadily towards the Iranian left, the Tudeh party; his assumption of dictatorial powers could not hide the absence of a coherent policy. Despite the continuation of his support in the streets, he steadily alienated or lost the support of the Iranian aristocracy, the modernizing bureaucracy and the army leadership. When the bazaars turned against him, the Shah, with CIA support, instigated an army bazaar coup against him, and dismissed him. His movement, though incoherent as to doctrine and muddled as to aim, was essentially a reaction of injured Iranian pride to Iran's wartime occupation by Britain and Russia and to the youth of the Shah, whose father had so dominated Iranian politics. DCW

Mussolini, Benito (b. Predappio, nr Forli, Emilia-Romagna, Italy, 29.7.1883; d. nr Azzana, Lombardy, 28.4.1945). Prime minister of Italy (1922–43), leader (*Duce*) of the Italian Fascist party (1920–45), head of state of the pro-German rump Republic of Salo (1943–5). Formerly a socialist journalist of working-class origins, he was seduced by French money into supporting Italy's entry into WW1 and, after brief service on the front, moved via editorship of *Il Popolo d'Italia* into the leadership of the Fascist movement. King Victor Emmanuel III was intimidated by fears of a Red revolution and civil war into appointing him prime minister of a coalition government after Fascist strong-arm squads had marched on Rome. By 1928 he had eliminated Italian political parties, made Italy a single constituency voting for 400 members of the Fascist Grand Council, and established, on paper at least, a corporative façade behind which individual Fascist leaders built up their own feudal bailiwicks over Italy's cities. Fascism, as Mussolini practised it, united public works, the politics of theatre and a relentless search for glory abroad (providing the risks were strictly limited), which was expressed in alternating bouts of vainglorious unilateral aggression and in posing as Mussolini the peacemaker.

Anti-German and antagonistic towards HITLER at first, his need to emulate Hitler's triumphs led him into collision with Britain and France. To restrain them he needed Hitler's support in 'an Axis', the image but not the reality of an alliance, for which he sacrificed Austrian independence and Italian ties with Hungary and Poland, and in emulation of whom he introduced anti-Semitism into the fascist lexicon. Italian entry into the war in 1940 was predicated on Britain's collapse following the defeat of France. Britain's survival doomed Italy which lacked the industrial strength to sustain a protracted military effort. Attempts to construct an intellectual content for Mussolini's fascism have always encountered the problem faced by his concentration on the outward appearance of power, backed of course by the ruthless repression of opposition. Mussolini's state was in some sense the political parallel to futurism, with its exposition of action as the only justification for art. Bombast, braggadocio, fustian were imposed on a structure of Italian urban and regional politics, religion and social organization which antedated fascism and was to survive it.

DCW

D. Mack Smith, *Mussolini* (London, 1981).

Muybridge, Eadweard James, ps. of Edward James Muggeridge (b. Kingston upon Thames, London, UK, 9.4.1830; d. Kingston upon Thames, 8.4.1904). British photographer. Muybridge was a pioneer large-plate photographer based in San Francisco and noted for his landscapes from Alaska, central America and the Yosemite Valley. His fame rests on the sequential instantaneous photographs of animal locomotion, developed in 1872–3 and 1878–9 at the behest of Governor Leland Stanford, and at the University of Pennsylvania in 1883–4, resulting in the 781 photogravure plates of *Animal Locomotion* (Philadelphia, 1887). The analysis of movement was presented in the books *Animals in Motion* (London, 1899) and *The Human Figure in Motion* (London, 1901) (both often reprinted, and the inspiration for painters including BACON). Muybridge is justifiably claimed as the father, or at least stepfather, of the motion picture, because of his development of the 'Zoopraxiscope' (1879–80) which projected sequential, instantaneous photographic images. The instrument was successfully demonstrated to learned and popular audiences. Muybridge's Zoopraxographical Hall at the Columbian Exposition in Chicago (1893) was the first commercial motion-picture theatre in the world.

MH-B

R. B. Haas, *Muybridge: Man in Motion* (Berkeley, Calif., 1976).

N

Nabokov, Vladimir Vladimirovich (b. St Petersburg [now Leningrad], Russia, 23.4.1899; naturalized American citizen, 1945; d. Montreux, Vaud, Switzerland, 2.7.1977). Russian/American novelist. Born into a noble Russian family, Nabokov learned English and French as a child and took a degree at Cambridge (UK) after his family had fled the revolution in 1919. His father V. D. Nabokov, a well-known liberal, was the unintended victim of a political assassination in Berlin in 1922, where Nabokov, marrying his lifelong partner Véra in 1925, embarked on the first phase of his career, as the émigré novelist V. Sirin, publishing a series of works in Russian, the best of which is probably *Dar* (Paris, 1937; tr. M. Scammel, *The Gift*, NY, 1963). His work remained intensely pervaded by a sense of loss for his homeland, with exile as one of his persistent themes. With the rise of the Nazis, the Nabokovs moved to France in 1937, and from there to the USA in 1940, where the second phase of his career began with the publication of his first English novel *The Real Life of Sebastian Knight* (NY, 1941). He began teaching, first at Wellesley College, later at Cornell University, became an American citizen and continued a lifelong passion for lepidoptera, in which field he made minor contributions. His writing pursued characteristic themes of loss, exile and longing, at the same time displaying that fascination with illusion, parody, distortion, multiple worlds and language itself, which has led to his recognition both as a major American novelist and a major influence on contemporary fiction. His public reputation blossomed into notoriety with the publication and trial for obscenity of *Lolita* (NY, 1958), a novel more centrally concerned with the potentialities of language than with any prurient interest in the love affair between a middle-aged émigré and the nymphet of the title, told in the form of a highly allusive and symbolic journey across America. The Nabokovs moved to Montreux in 1959, his final stopping place, where he continued to publish, notably *Pale Fire* (NY, 1962) and the family chronicle *Ada* (NY, 1969). A fastidious writer who valued the particular recording of precise detail above generalities, he published his autobiography *Speak Memory* (NY) in 1966. KGM

A. Field, *Nabokov: his Life in Part* (London, 1977).

Nader, Ralph (b. Winsted, Conn., USA, 27.2.1934). American lawyer and campaigner on behalf of consumers. Nader's achievement as one of the most strident supporters of consumers and their rights can be measured in human terms in the number of people spared death and injury in motor-car accidents following the outcry by his book *Unsafe at Any Speed* (NY, 1965). In it he attacked certain US car manufacturers for design and safety shortcomings, being inspired to write the book by his shock at the accident statistics he came across in his legal work. As a result of his findings the US government passed the Traffic Safety Act which imposed far stricter safety standards on US car manufacturers. Nader gave inspiration to a growing consumer movement and expanded his own area of inquiry. He has issued a wide range of reports, on such subjects as the dangers of certain foods and drugs, the hazards of radiation from colour TV sets and, in *Menace of Atomic Energy* (NY, 1979), of nuclear power stations. GHD

Nagel, Ernst (b. Nové Město, Bohemia, Austria-Hungary [now Czechoslovakia], 16.11.1901; naturalized American citizen, 1919). Czech/American philosopher of science. His most important work is concerned with the analysis of scientific method. In *An Introduction to Logic and Scientific Method* (with M. R. Cohen, NY, 1934) and *The Structure of Science* (NY, 1961) he presented a comprehensive account of the nature of scientific explanation, the logic of scientific inquiry and the organization of scientific knowledge from the standpoint of logical empiricism. He also examined the logic of probable inference in *Principles of the Theory of Probability* (Chicago, 1939) and *Gödel's Proof* (with J. R. Newman, NY, 1958). In his 'Logic without ontology' (1944, repr. *Logic Without Metaphysics*, Glencoe, Ill., 1956) he defended a naturalistic interpretation of logic, arguing that logico-mathematical principles must be understood according to their functions in specific contexts. Logical principles are necessary but not sufficient instruments for acquiring knowledge, and all knowledge is subject to revision. Nagel has also written extensively on science and society, scientific values, materialism, determinism and atheism.   PEH

Naipaul, Vidiadhar Surajprasad (b. Chaguanas, Trinidad [now Trinidad and Tobago], 17.8.1932). West Indian novelist. Of Indian parentage, educated at Trinidad and at University College, Oxford, resident in England but a tireless traveller and writer, Naipaul is one of the most important contemporary writers in English because of his consistent refusal to avoid asking questions which, however unwelcome, are basic to civilized existence. *A House for Mr Biswas* (London, 1961) was an epic depiction of rootlessness but eventual fulfilment as seen in the life of one West Indian man. *The Middle Passage* (London, 1962), however, earned Naipaul the lasting hostility of many West Indians, who saw his appraisal of the area's history, culture and possible future as unforgivably harsh. Yet in *An Area of Darkness: an Experience of India* (London, 1964), a self-exploratory account of his search for roots in India, Naipaul is very critical of the British and in his essays can write with formidable insight of the sterility of English life. *The Mimic Men* (London, 1967) adapts these perceptions for creative ends in its depiction of a former Caribbean politician writing his memoirs in London. With his recent novels *In a Free State* (London, 1971) and the remarkable *A Bend in the River* (London, 1979) he confirmed his reputation as a dedicated writer of outstanding

literary and, in the broadest sense, political importance.   PNQ

L. White, *V. S. Naipaul: a Critical Introduction* (London, 1975).

Namier, Lewis Bernstein, *né* Ludwik Bernsztajn vel Niemirowski (b. nr Lukow, Russian Poland [now Poland], 27.6.1888; naturalized British citizen, 1913; d. London, UK, 19.8.1960). Polish/British historian. Namier emigrated to Britain in 1906; studied at Balliol College, Oxford; took British citizenship before WW1 and worked in the Foreign Office on Central European questions during the war. He managed to support himself in business while carrying out research for the best known of his books, *The Structure of Politics at the Accession of George III* (London, 1929) and *England in the Age of the American Revolution* (London, 1930), which criticized interpretations of the political history of the 18c in terms of the struggle between two parties, the Whigs and the Tories, and emphasized the importance of 'connections' rather than programmes and the role of the independent country gentry. These two books, with their structural approach to political history, are a milestone in British historical writing. Following their publication, Namier was appointed professor of history at Manchester (1931–53). Namier was also interested in the political and diplomatic history of the Continent in the 19c and 20c. His most substantial work in this area is *1848: the Revolution of the Intellectuals* (London, 1946). His still valuable essays and reviews are reprinted in *Avenues of History* (London, 1952), *Personalities and Powers* (London, 1955) and *Vanished Supremacies* (London, 1958). Namier has been criticized for taking the ideas and ideals out of history. This criticism is exaggerated, but he did affect a somewhat cynical attitude to human irrationality in general and political irrationality in particular which owes something to FREUD and to PARETO.   UPB

J. Namier, *Lewis Namier: a Biography* (London, 1971).

Namora, Fernando (b. Condeixa, Portugal, 15.4.1919). Portuguese novelist. In this century prose fiction in Portugal was neglected until the 1930s when, under the influence of European and Brazilian writers, Portuguese literature was steered away from historical romanticism and the regional picturesque towards psychological analysis and social motivation in the realist tradition of Eça de Queiroz. Namora, with his 10 novels, short stories and writer's notebooks, was a pioneer in this movement. He trained as a doctor, and his *Retalhos da vida de um médico* [Episodes from a doctor's life] (Lisbon, 1949) won European acclaim. The new interest in social problems was reflected in his campus novel *Fogo na noite escura* [Fire in the dark night] (Coimbra, 1943), the odyssey of a group of university students and their revolt against an effete academicism during WW1. He distinguishes in his novels between town, where a complicated exterior hides provincial detail, and country, which has a simple exterior but masks universals. He uses dialogue to differentiate characters, and has a sense of the significant detail, particularly the unforeseen medical circumstance that attends disease. Death appears not as a peninsular obsession, but rather as an integral part of life, and with disease it figures in *Domingo à tarde* [Sunday afternoon] (Lisbon, 1962), his most mature essay in neorealism. DBr

M. Sacramento, *Fernando Namora: a obra e o homem* (Lisbon, 1968).

Nansen, Fridtjof (b. Store-Frøen, nr Oslo, Norway, 10.10.1861; d. Lysaker, 13.5.1930). Norwegian explorer of the Arctic who used the fame he thereby won to facilitate his entry, first into Norwegian, then into international politics, as leader of relief work in Russia (1920–1), as organizer of the League of Nations refugee work, and inventor of the 'Nansen passport' for the very many stateless persons whom the collapse of the European empires and the revolutions of 1917–22 had left without a country, profession or legal status adequate to enable them to reacquire either. He was awarded the Nobel peace prize in 1922. DCW

Narayan, Rasipuram Krishnaswami (b. Madras, Tamil Nadu, India, 10.10.1906). Indian novelist who has become interna-

tionally acclaimed partly through being championed by the English novelist Graham GREENE and partly through being more widely published outside India than any of his contemporaries. This is to some extent paradoxical, for Narayan is a highly localized writer. His major fiction is always set in Malgudi, an invented town and area based partly on Mysore where Narayan now lives. Although the author of distinguished autobiographical writings (including *My Days*, NY, 1974), he is best known for his short, pithy and highly accurate portrayals of provincial lives in south India. From his first novel *Swami and Friends* (London, 1935) to his latest *The Painter of Signs* (NY, 1976) Narayan has frequently presented the comedy of his culturally divided country where ancient and modern live in confused juxtaposition. In the outstanding *The Guide* (London, 1958) he wrote one of the most amusing but trenchant satires on the Indian propensity for metaphysics. A masterly narrator of short stories who has also written excellent popular versions of the Hindu epics, it is as an observer of human character in elegantly poised English that he has made his major contribution to Indian literature.

ANRN

W. Walsh, *R. K. Narayan* (Harlow, 1971); P. S. Sundaram, *R. K. Narayan* (New Delhi, 1973).

Nash, Paul (b. London, UK, 11.5.1889; d. Boscombe, Wilts., 11.7.1946). British artist, painter and designer, who twice earned himself a reputation as the greatest English war artist. In WW1 Nash's views of the trenches, of the mud, desolation and ruin, created an archetypal image which survives to the present. In WW2 he looked up at the battle in the skies and his art seemed to recoil with shock at seeing almost totally mechanized warfare, while on the ground burnt-out aircraft, bomb craters, jagged trees and rocks represented human despair and pain. Between the wars Nash complained of 'the struggles of a war artist without a war'. In fact his work in peacetime was in itself revolutionary. Nash set out to create a style which would be meaningfully modern yet unmistakably British. Taking the

English romantic landscape tradition as his inspiration, he arrived at a form of visionary surrealism. Surrealism revealed to Nash a peacetime landscape which was just as infertile, as twisted and brooding as it had been in wartime. His work can perhaps be likened to the poetry of ELIOT's *The Waste Land* (1922), where the interwar landscape also becomes a metaphor for the impoverished human spirit.   WJ

A. Causey, *Paul Nash* (Oxford, 1980).

Nasser, Gamal Abdel (b. Alexandria, Egypt, 15.1.1918; d. Cairo, 28.9.1970). Leader of the Egyptian republican and anti-British young officers' movement (1942–52) and first minister of the interior (1952–4), then president of the Egyptian Republic (1954–70), after the military *coup d'état* which overthrew King Farouk in 1952. His grandiloquent vision of Egypt as the dominant figure in three interlocking geographical circles, that of the Arab Middle East, that of Africa and that of the non-European world, was perhaps youthful rhetoric, but his capture of the ambitions of educated Arab youth throughout the Arab-speaking world and his articulation of a century of resentment of European Christian dominance, especially after the successful nationalization of the Suez Canal Company in 1956 and the subsequent Anglo–French failure to overthrow him, made him the acknowledged idol of the Middle East from then until his death – his principal rivals the Husaini dynasty in Iraq and their servant NURI AS-SAÏD being destroyed in the 1958 revolution, and the Saudis being careful never to challenge him directly. He was for long able to avoid confrontation with Israel, hitherto the yardstick of claims to legitimacy among Arab nationalists, by invoking his success against Britain instead. Other Arab governments (e.g. that of Syria in 1958, of Iraq after 1958, of the Yemen, both before and after the military coup of 1962) were anxious to gain his approval to legitimize their position against potential opponents. The Syrian Ba'th leaders attempted union with Egypt, but the union did not long survive the experience of Egyptian intervention into Syrian politics. By intervention in the Yemeni civil war (1962–8) Nasser over-stretched the Egyptian economy badly. His partisans lost out in the power struggle which accompanied the British withdrawal from Aden, and Russian and Arab pressure lured him into shattering defeat at Israel's hands in 1967. No other Arab leader ever approached his personal dominance; but its cost was the subjection of the Egyptian economy to Soviet influence and the long-term exacerbation of inter-Arab conflicts, especially between the governments of Cairo, Damascus and Baghdad.   DCW

Natsume, Sōseki (b. Edo [now Tokyo], Japan, 9.2.1867; d. Tokyo, 9.12.1916). Japanese novelist. After an insecure childhood Natsume proved his considerable intellectual gifts at Tokyo Imperial University, from which he graduated in 1892 having specialized in English literature. He spent three penniless and miserable years in England (1900–3) and in 1903 took up an appointment at his old university, where he lectured on literary theory and English literature. In 1907 he shocked his contemporaries by resigning from his prestigious academic position in order to devote himself to writing fiction. His early works were humorous and satirical and great successes in their time, but it is from the darker post-1910 novels that his lasting fame and significance for modern Japanese literature derive. His major concern in these novels was how the individuality to which many of his generation aspired could be realized in a society where the concept of the individual was still far from being generally understood. Natsume's individualism, as he himself defined it, was distinct from egotism in that it had to be based on respect for other individuals. Decisions made in its name should follow a judgement between right and wrong, without regard to sectional interest, which was still the major referent in Japanese social behaviour. Loneliness, alienation and guilt feelings accompany striving towards individuality. His heroes are often guilt-laden, and as in the case of Sensei in *Kokoro* (Tokyo, 1914; tr. E. McClellan, *Heart*, Chicago, 1957) this may lead to death. During his last years he attempted to transcend these dilemmas by his slogan *sokuten kyoshi* [following heaven and abandoning self]. Many of the problems exposed by Natsume in the complex psychology of his characters are still relevant to Japan and this may well explain his continuing popularity.   BWFP

H. S. Hibbett, 'Natsume Sōseki and the psychological novel', in D. S. Shively (ed.), *Tradition and Modernization in Japanese Culture* (Princeton, 1971); H. Yamanouchi, *The Search for Authenticity in Modern Japanese Literature* (Cambridge, 1978).

Natta, Giulio (b. Imperia, Liguria, Italy, 26.2.1903; d. Bergamo, Lombardy, 1.5.1979). Italian chemist. After studying mathematics at Genoa, Natta graduated in chemical engineering at Milan Polytechnic, remaining there in a teaching post. In 1933 he accepted a chair at Pavia, then posts in Rome and Turin universities before finally becoming director and professor of industrial chemistry at Milan in 1938. He stayed there until 1973 when he retired after a long illness. Following an interest in polymers over a number of years, and being inspired by a lecture given by ZIEGLER, he discovered, in 1954, the stereospecificity of Ziegler catalysts which leads to the formation of stereo-regular polymers. Guided by his wife, a graduate in letters, he introduced the concept of tacticity to describe the new materials, the most important being isotactic polypropylene, currently the fastest growing commodity polymer. In 1963 Natta was awarded the Nobel prize for chemistry, jointly with Ziegler. In addition to a common interest in mountain climbing, Natta shared with Ziegler a facility to combine academic and technological aspects of their studies and a tremendous capacity for hard work, reflected in numerous scientific publications.   RPS

Needham, Joseph (b. London, UK, 9.12.1900). British biochemist and historian. Needham was the son of a Harley Street specialist. He received a conventional boarding-school education and read medicine at Cambridge where he held the post of reader in biochemistry from 1933 to 1966. He has remained at Gonville and Caius College all his life, becoming its master in 1965. He retired in 1976 to devote himself to the completion of his *Science and Civilization in China* (7 vols in 11 or more parts, in progress, Cambridge, 1954–, with many collaborators). This mammoth project, aimed at providing a comprehensive survey of the contribution of China to all fields of science, medicine, philosophy and technology, is widely regarded as one of the major achievements of modern scholarship. Needham formally initiated this project only in 1954, following a successful career as a biochemist. He was one of the many protégés of F. G. HOPKINS. Needham's wife, the well-known biochemist Dorothy Needham, also belonged to this group. Needham's major contribution to biochemistry was the encyclopedic *Chemical Embryology* (3 vols, Cambridge, 1931). He seemed then to be working in one of the most important areas of experimental biology, his work being stimulated by important advances made by SPEMANN in the field of 'organizers'. Retrospectively, however, the research of Needham and other able young scientists attracted into this field appears to be of limited significance. At Cambridge Needham became a lifelong left-wing socialist in politics and an Anglo-Catholic in religion. He has written prolifically on the relations of science, society, and religion in the West, sometimes under the pseudonym 'Henry Holorenshaw'. His interest in Chinese culture was absorbed from Chinese science students in Cambridge during the 1930s. He first visited China in 1942 and became an enthusiastic supporter of the Chinese Communist revolution. Most mutations of Chinese policy have since found in him a keen apologist. CW

Néel, Louis (b. Lyons, Rhône, France, 22.11.1904). French physicist. Néel's most important work has been on the theory of magnetic materials. He started this work at Strasbourg in the laboratory of Pierre Weiss, one of the early workers in this field. In 1940 he moved to Grenoble and there, in addition to his academic research, became the driving force in making Grenoble one of the most important scientific centres in France. The impressive complex of government-supported laboratories around Grenoble is due very largely to his initiative. Néel's great contribution to physics, for which he received the Nobel prize in 1970, was his concept of a special type of magnetic material called an 'antiferromagnet'. In an ordinary ferromagnet, such as iron, the forces between neighbouring elementary magnets are such that they spontaneously line up parallel to one another (e.g. with all their north poles pointing in the same direction). Néel proposed (1936) that there should be other materials in which a spontaneous 'antiparallel' array occurs (i.e. north, south, north, south ...). Two years later experimenters found a compound which seemed to exhibit this transition, but it was not until 1949 when neutron diffraction techniques became available that the details of the actual antiparallel arrangement predicted by Néel could be confirmed. The temperature at which the material becomes antiferromagnetic is now called the Néel point. He also realized that the antiparallel pattern is responsible for the properties of another important class of materials, the ferrites – of which lodestone is the oldest known example. These are of great technological importance and are now used as the basis of many modern electronic devices. HMR

Nehru, Jawaharlal (b. Allahabad, Uttar Pradesh, India, 14.11.1889; d. Delhi, 27.5.1964). Western-educated Indian nationalist leader; president of the Congress party (1929–64) and right-hand man to Mahatma GANDHI; Indian prime minister and foreign minister (1947–64). A high-caste Brahmin, he allied his consciousness of his own status with that of his intellectual ability and his belief in a very English form of parliamentary reformist socialism (reforming from above and seeking justification only in its unquestioning consciousness of its own moral rectitude); and with a very effective sense of the politically practical, and with a determination to assert Indian independence as well as to achieve it. His vision of India as a major Asian power was shown in his policy of neutrality during the Korean War and neutralism thereafter,

as by his signature with CHOU EN-LAI of the Panch Shila and coleadership of the Bandung Conference of 1955. But his advocacy of neutralism went hand in hand with an arrogant pursuit of territorial nationalism which made Kashmir a constant bone of contention with Pakistan, led to the forcible annexation of Portuguese Goa in 1961 and involved him in war with, and humiliating defeat at the hands of, the Chinese over the demarcation of the Indo–Tibetan borders in 1962. In domestic politics his government was a characteristically Indian alliance between local political party feudatories and a centralist Anglophone bureaucracy which, while dealing harshly with non-Indian minorities in Assam and elsewhere, concentrated more on large-scale industrialization than any real reform of the structure of wealth and power in India's villages. Nehru's decision to keep India in the Commonwealth (though as a republic) was perhaps the single most important development in the evolving structure of the Commonwealth since the Statute of Westminster. DCW

M. Brecher, *Nehru: a Political Biography* (London, 1959).

Neill, Alexander Sutherland (b. Forfar, Tayside, UK, 17.10.1883; d. Aldeburgh, Suffolk, 23.9.1973). British teacher, psychologist and educational pioneer. After studying English at Edinburgh University, he taught for a number of years in Scottish state schools, becoming disillusioned with conventional educational practice. In 1921 he became joint founder of a progressive international school in Hellerau, Dresden, which moved three years later to Sonntagberg in Austria. He returned to England in 1924 to set up the progressive school for which he became famous, Summerhill, situated first at Lyme Regis, Dorset, and later at Leiston in Suffolk, where it still operates. Summerhill began as an experimental school, taking about 45 children aged between five and 16. From the start the main principle upon which the school was run was that of freedom, exemplified in such features as optional attendance at lessons, a rule-making school parliament (pupils and teachers having equal voting powers), no sexual prohibitions, and no religious or moral instruction. Neill expounded his educational ideas, which were strongly influenced by FREUD and Homer Lane, in a number of lively and provocative books about his school including *That Dreadful School* (London, 1937), *Summerhill* (London, 1962) and *Talking of Summerhill* (London, 1967). His earlier teaching experiences are described in *A Dominie's Log* (London, 1915), *A Dominie Dismissed* (London, 1916) and other books. Neill's work has aroused both admiration and hostility, and the ensuing debate about the values and dangers of progressivism represents perhaps his greatest contribution to educational theory and practice.   RRStr

M. Rafferty *et al.*, *Summerhill For and Against* (NY, 1970); R. Barrow, *Radical Education* (London, 1978).

Neizvestny, Ernst Iosifovich (b. Sverdlovsk, Urals, USSR, 9.4.1925). Russian artist and sculptor. Neizvestny began to emerge as one of the leading dissident artists in the USSR towards the end of the 1950s. He evolved a style which was neither that of 'official' socialist realism, nor a reflection of the fashionably abstract work then being produced in the West. Because his monumental cubism synthesized elements from both these traditions, he was given his due by neither. Neizvestny's work was publicly insulted by KRUSHCHEV – but when the Russian leader was eventually ousted from power, he chose Neizvestny to carve his tomb. Neizvestny's work became widely known in the West when John BERGER made it the subject of his penetrating analysis *Art and Revolution* (London) in 1969. Following pressure from artists and intellectuals in the West, Neizvestny was able to emigrate from the USSR in 1976, and he now lives in New York. Although his prodigious energy and unbounded sculptural imagination are as much in evidence as ever, the work of the last few years seems to have become infected with an excessive sense of extravagant grandeur.

PF

Németh, László (b. Nagybánya, Austria-Hungary [now Hungary], 18.4.1901; d. Budapest, 3.3.1975). Hungarian essayist, novelist and dramatist. After studying medicine, he turned his independent and original mind to the national and social problems of Hungary after WW1. A modern encyclopedist and polymath, he possessed an intellect almost too versatile to escape the charge of dilettantism. He saw himself as the educator of the nation; between 1932 and 1936 he wrote and edited a journal *Tanú* [Witness] single-handed. His often controversial and complex views stimulated discussion among generations of Hungarian writers and intellectuals, though to foreign observers his vision often seems restricted and his ideas brilliantly perverse. His novels explore human predicaments. His dramas, social and historical, are unashamedly didactic, with action subordinated to dialogue and thought. His numerous literary studies provide new and valuable flashes of insight into Hungarian literature.   GFC

J. Reményi, *Hungarian Writers and Literature* (New Brunswick, NJ, 1964).

Nernst, Hermann Walther (b. Briessen, West Prussia, Germany [now East Germany], 25.6.1864; d. Zibelle, nr Berlin, 18.11.1941). German physical chemist who, more than any other single individual, succeeded in uniting the concepts, and extending the frontiers, of physics and chemistry. His renowned heat theorem, later to become synonymous with the Third Law of Thermodynamics, enabled the equilibrium constants of chemical reactions to be calculated from readily retrievable experimental data (like the latent heats of fusion, melting points, heat capacities, etc.). Nernst's early ambition was to become a poet. But after studying physics in Zürich, Berlin, Graz and Würzburg (1883–7), during which time he came into contact with Helmholtz and BOLTZMANN, he started a remarkably successful career as one of the founders of physical chemistry. Nernst's law (the basis of modern techniques of solvent extraction), relating equilibrium concentrations of a solute distributed between immiscible liquid phases, appeared in 1890–1901, shortly after he had formulated his law of diffusion of electrolytes. He contributed significantly to the understanding of ionic hydration, the idea of buffer solutions, electrochemical cells and solubility products. He devised a novel source of infrared radiation and a special calorimeter which he and his associate LINDEMANN used to determine heat capacities at low temperatures, thereby leading to significant advances in quantum theory. The textbook he published in 1893 (*Theoretische Chemie vom Standpunkte der Avogadroschen Regel und der Thermodynamik* [Theoretical chemistry from the viewpoint of Avogadro's law and thermodynamics], Göttingen) constituted a turning-point in theoretical chemistry. He was awarded the Nobel prize for chemistry in 1920. In 1933, after denouncing the Nazis, he retired to his country home.

JMT

K. Mendelssohn, *The World of Walther Nernst: the Rise and Fall of German Science 1864–1941* (London, 1973).

Neruda, Pablo, *né* Neftalí Ricardo Reyes Basoalto (b. Parral, Chile, 12.7.1904; d. Santiago, 23.9.1973). Chilean poet and winner of the 1971 Nobel prize for literature. Each major Nerudian phase has had a widespread pioneering influence, beginning with the controlled eroticism of *Veinte poemas de amor y una canción desesperada* (Santiago, 1924; tr. W. S. Merwin, *Twenty Love Poems and a Song of Despair*, London, 1969). Its despair was intensified in the death-laden interior monologues of *Residencia en la tierra* (pt I [1925–31] Santiago, 1933; pt II [1931–35] Madrid, 1935; tr. D. D. Walsh, *Residence on Earth*, NY, 1973, which includes the poems of *Tercera residencia*, Buenos Aires, 1947), whose initially bewildering texts discard the syntax of continuous discourse in their attempt to map the corrosive disintegration of his world. A friend of ALBERTI and LORCA, Neruda was consul in Madrid when the Spanish civil war broke out, and full commitment to the Republicans produced the strident public verse of *España en el corazón* [Spain in the heart] (Santiago, 1937; later incorporated into *Tercera residencia*, see above). After a period in Mexico (1940–3), when his continental vision was greatly influenced by the muralists RIVERA and Siqueiros, he entered Chil-

ean politics as a Communist senator; *Alturas de Macchu Picchu* (Caracas, 1946; tr. N. Tarn, *The Heights of Macchu Picchu*, London, 1966), perhaps Neruda's finest poem, uses the symbol of his journey to those ruins to chronicle his spiritual development from 'solitude' to 'solidarity' and his assumption of the role of spokesman of the exploited. This sequence became the second part of his longest work, the epico-lyrical *Canto general* (Mexico City, 1950; parts tr. A. Kerrigan *et al.* in *Selected Poems* [1924–67], London, 1970; and tr. B. Belitt, in *Five Decades: a Selection* [1925–70], NY, 1972), a predominantly tragic survey of what is now 'Latin' America from prehistory to the present day, largely written when Neruda had had to go 'underground' in Chile (1948–9). It perpetuates the stark division of mankind into villains and heroes which had understandably characterized his civil war poems, but it is far more powerful, particularly in the treatment of its overall 'collective' hero: the exploited *pueblo*. Neruda's overtly political period ends with *Odas elementales* (Buenos Aires, 1954) and its sequels (Buenos Aires, 1956 & 1957; tr. C. Lozano, *The Elementary Odes*, NY, 1961, is a selection from all three series): lyrical poems, notable for extreme clarity, the doctrinaire self-effacement of the poet, and their cheerful analysis of the beauty of simple things finding fulfilment through usefulness to mankind. The gentle humour of the *Odas* heightens their charm. The whimsy grows in the conversational poetry of *Estravagario* (Buenos Aires, 1958; tr. A. Reid, *Extravagaria*, London, 1972) which opens an 'autumnal' period with a return to personal concerns; Neruda's best poems about poetry come in *Plenos poderes* (Buenos Aires, 1962; tr. A. Reid, *Fully Empowered*, London, 1975; tr. B. Belitt & A. Reid, *A New Decade* [1958–67], NY, 1969, span this period). Some of Neruda's finest poetry came in the 'winter' of his last six years (marred by illness) whose introspective reinterpretation of experience culminates in the death-conscious meditations of *Jardín de invierno* [Winter garden] (Buenos Aires, 1974) and the serenity of *El mar y las campañas* [The sea and the bells] (Buenos Aires, 1973), on which he was still working when the military coup destroyed his friend ALLENDE and brought about Neruda's sudden collapse and death. His unfinished prose autobiography *Confieso quo he vivido* (Buenos Aires & Barcelona, 1974; tr. H. St Martin, *Memoirs*, NY, 1977) sheds much light on his complex life. RP-M

F. T. Riess, *The Word and the Stone* (Oxford, 1972); R. de Costa, *The Poetry of Pablo Neruda* (Cambridge, Mass., 1979).

Nervi, Pier Luigi (b. Sondrio, Lombardy, Italy, 21.6.1891; d. Rome, 9.1.1979). Italian engineer. Nervi belonged to the great European tradition of architect-engineers. He combined an unerring feel for the formal possibilities inherent in materials and techniques with the capacity to produce detailed, and often innovatory, theories of structures. His principal contribution to modern architecture and engineering was through a series of brilliantly lucid structures which advanced the frontiers of reinforced-concrete construction. He believed that the process of creating form was identical for both the technician and the artist; the design of structures was for him a balance between careful calculation and intuition. Nervi's first important work was the Communal Stadium, Florence (1930–2), followed by aircraft hangars for the Italian Air Force in which he first employed the lattice structures which he was to develop throughout his life. He was particularly concerned to explore the advantages of speed and economy in prefabrication. The exhibition hall, Turin (1948–9), with its great clear span of 240 feet was formed with a corrugated vault composed of thousands of prefabricated concrete units. He continually experimented to find ways of pushing concrete construction techniques to new limits, producing the graceful vaults and domes of the Chianciano Terme (1950–2) and the sports halls for the 1960 Olympic Games in Rome. Nervi transferred the economy and elegance of these clear span structures to multistorey building with the structure for the Pirelli office building, Milan (1958). Nervi was professor of technology and construction in

the faculty of architecture, Rome University, from 1947 to 1961. PAC

A. Huxtable, *Pier Luigi Nervi* (London, 1960).

Neutra, Richard Josef (b. Vienna, Austria-Hungary [now Austria], 8.4.1892; naturalized American citizen, 1929; d. Wuppertal, N. Rhine-Westphalia, West Germany, 16.4.1970). Austrian/American architect. Neutra's work, chiefly in the design of houses, did much to spread the influence of the European modern movement in the USA. He studied at the Technische Hochschule, Vienna, with the pioneer modern architect LOOS. In 1911 he first encountered the new American architecture through the Wasmuth publications of the work of Frank Lloyd WRIGHT. Neutra left Austria in 1919 for Switzerland and then Germany, working with MENDELSOHN in 1921–2. He emigrated to the USA in 1923, working alternately with the Chicago firm of Holabird and Roche and with Wright. In 1926 he established a practice with Rudolph Schindler, another Austrian-born architect with whom he had been a student and who had also worked with Wright. Neutra's personal style developed rapidly in the 1920s. The important and influential Lovell house (1927–9) was a contemporary of key works in Europe (MIES VAN DER ROHE's Barcelona pavilion, and LE CORBUSIER's Villa Stein). Its design brilliantly exploited the dramatic Los Angeles hillside site: constructed in steel frame and concrete, it was conceived as a series of platforms and balconies that straddle and cascade down the precipitous slope. Though the formal elements are recognizably derived from Wright and European modernism, Neutra deployed them with great panache and individualism. Throughout the 1930s he continued to develop a personal idiom, moving further away from European models. The houses of the immediate postwar period are unmistakably American creations. In them Neutra increasingly used natural materials as well as bringing the exotic Californian landscape into view through large window-walls of plate glass. The Kaufmann desert house, Palm Springs (1946–7), and the Tremaine house, Santa Barbara

(1948), epitomize the work of this period which established a pattern for private house building on the West Coast of the USA. Neutra's practice expanded in the 1950s; from then onwards the designs for houses became more rhetorical and repetitive while those for larger buildings never quite demonstrated a comparable sensitivity.

PAC

W. Boesiger, *Richard Neutra, Buildings and Projects* (London, 1964).

Newman, Barnett (b. New York, USA, 29.1.1905; d. New York, 4.7.1970). American painter and sculptor. Newman worked for many years in his father's clothing business and as a part-time art teacher. He painted in his spare time, but c. 1939–40 stopped and destroyed all his early work, with the intention of rethinking the nature of painting. From 1943 he organized exhibitions of primitive art and wrote catalogue forewords for friends such as Adolph Gottlieb and Theodoros Stamos. In 1944–5 he started to make rapid improvisatory drawings with images suggesting plant-and-seed growth and fertilization. His tendency to simplify these led in 1948 to his first painting with a narrow vertical stripe (or 'zip') of colour dividing a uniform field of a contrasting colour. This was a breakthrough for him, and by the end of 1949 he had begun to develop this theme from time to time on a wall-sized scale. His pictures, sometimes in black and white, sometimes in muted or radiant saturated colours, with vertical bands or stripes dividing and animating a contrasting field, were misunderstood at first even by most of the other abstract expressionists, who thought them too simple, but were an inspiration from the late 1950s onwards to many younger painters and sculptors working towards a more reductive form of art. Their simplification was an expression of concentrated energy and richness, and the paintings varied widely in their structure and effects. Newman also made a few metal sculptures, mostly from 1965 onwards, of vertical columns related to his paintings. REA

T. B. Hess, *Barnett Newman* (NY, 1971); H. Rosenberg, *Barnett Newman* (NY, 1978).

Nexø, Martin Andersen (b. Copenhagen, Denmark, 26.6.1869; d. Dresden, East Germany, 1.6.1954). Danish novelist. Although his debut as an author was as early as 1898, it was his first great novel cycle *Pelle Erobreren* (4 vols, Copenhagen, 1906–10; tr. J. Muir & B. Miall, *Pelle the Conqueror*, London, 1913–16) which created his international reputation as a great 'proletarian writer'. A monumental work, it traced the life of a working-class boy through his career as a trade union organizer and strike leader. Nexø's reputation was consolidated by the publication between 1917 and 1921 of his 'Ditte trilogy' (*Ditte Menneskebarn*, Copenhagen) which similarly followed the life of a working-class girl from cradle to grave (*Ditte: Girl Alive!*, London, 1920; tr. A.G. Chater & R. Thirsk, *Ditte: Daughter of Man*, London, 1922; and tr. A. & R. Kenny, *Ditte: Towards the Stars*, London, 1923). A visit to the USSR following the revolution converted him to communism. Four volumes of memoirs published between 1932 and 1939 – two of which have been translated into English (tr. E. Watkins, *Under the Open Sky* and *My Early Years*, NY, 1938) – give a sensitive account of his early life in Copenhagen's slums, his childhood on the island of Bornholm, and his youthful socialist struggles. JWMcF

H. Slochower, *Three Ways of Modern Man* (NY, 1937).

Neyman, Jerzy (b. Bendery, Moldavia, Russia, 16.4.1894; d. Berkeley, Calif., USA, 5.8.1981). Polish statistician. Until 1938, when he emigrated to the USA, he had worked in Poland, though making academic visits to France and England. Between 1928 and 1933, with E. S. PEARSON, he produced the Neyman–Pearson system of hypothesis testing, a set of criteria for maximizing efficiency in the design of tests which is the foundation of modern quality control. Faulty items found in an inspected sample may be ineradicable errors from an acceptable situation, or a signal to close down and reset a machine. The theory looks at the cost and risk of stopping a good machine, then at that of running a bad one, to obtain the best criterion and sample size. Many statistical problems are like this. In 1934 Neyman tackled the problems of using random samples in human populations, drawing on experience with the Polish census – considerations of finance, and of rare but important subgroups, mean that real samples are seldom simple. He proposed a general principle: to take linear combinations of data items and balance them first to eliminate bias and then to minimize variance; this gives rules for deciding how intensively to sample, and where. In 1937 he formulated the 'classical' theory of confidence intervals, rejecting postulated values of an underlying parameter if they would imply that the probability of the actual observations was less than a target value. In the long run, the proportion of occasions on which a true value has been rejected will then be less than the target probability. AGPW

Nezval, Vítězslav (b. Biskoupky, Moravia, Austria-Hungary [now Czechoslovakia], 26.5.1900; d. Prague, 6.4.1958). Czech writer, leader of the prewar avant-garde, who moved through poetism and surrealism to socialist realism. In the 1950s this heavy-drinking bohemian wrote odes to STALIN and doctored his own earlier works – without succeeding in eradicating all their imaginative, colourful, often childlike vigour. His most lasting works are his poems from the 1920s and 1930s, where association, the child's-eye-view and an original use of both modern technological and fairytale poetic vocabulary merge to create imaginative panoramas of life. The most representative of these is the mythicized poetic autobiography *Podivuhodný kouzelník* [The remarkable magician], first published in *Básně noci* [Poems of night] (Prague, 1930). Only after 1945 did Nezval reject that joyous libido, joyous revolution and joyous indulgence in progress which we see in the play *Milenci z kiosku* [Kiosk lovers] (Prague, 1932) and the novel *Valérie a týden divů* [Valérie's week of wonders] (Prague, 1945). A selection of his poems is in *Three Czech Poets* (tr. E. Osers, Harmondsworth, 1971). RBP

A. French, *The Poets of Prague* (London, 1969).

Ngugi, wa Thiong'o/James Ngugi (b. Limuru, Kenya, 5.1.1938). Kenyan novelist. His adolescence coincided with the Mau Mau rebellion of the Kikuyu tribesmen, an experience that has profoundly affected his outlook and his writings. Early novels depicted the values of traditional life and their destruction by the colonizers, though Ngugi was also alert to the destructive factions within village life (see *The River Between*, London, 1965, and *A Grain of Wheat*, London, 1967). Ngugi's political commitment as a writer, together with his determination to achieve educational independence from an English-orientated system, are forcefully expressed in *Homecoming* (London, 1972), a wide-ranging collection of essays. *Petals of Blood* (London, 1977) charted his disillusionment with the Kenya he returned to after a period abroad, exploring the recreation of the colonial system by newly independent Kenyan politicians and speculators. Ngugi was imprisoned by the Kenyan government for a year from December 1977 following the production (in his native language of Gikuyu) of a play critical of the regime; *Detained: a Writer's Prison Diary* (London, 1981) chronicles this experience. PNQ

G. D. Killam, *Introduction to Ngugi* (London, 1980).

Nicholson, Ben (b. Denham, Bucks., UK, 10.8.1894; d. London, 6.2.1982). British painter, son of Sir William Nicholson and nephew of James Pryde, leading British painters of their generation. His early works were mostly lyrical, fluidly brushed-in landscapes and still lifes, though the latter showed an increasing interest in cubism and pictorial structure. In 1931 he met HEPWORTH, who later became his second wife. In the next two or three years Nicholson went several times to Paris, where he visited the studios of BRAQUE, PICASSO, ARP and MONDRIAN, among others, and in 1933 began to produce only abstract work. In 1934 he started to work with precise regular forms such as circles and rectangles, both in his paintings (with immaculate uniform areas of colour) and in a series of white carved low-reliefs which are among his most original creations. He became the chief contact between Britain and the European abstract movement and, partly through his friendships with them, various leading foreign abstract artists such as Mondrian and GABO moved to England briefly, so that for a short period in the late 1930s London was an important centre for the international abstract movement. From 1939 to 1958 Nicholson lived at St Ives in Cornwall, where he once again became the centre of a group of artists, including Peter Lanyon, Patrick Heron and Terry Frost. He began to break away from the Stijl-like severity and purity of his work of the 1930s and to work concurrently in several quite different styles – constructive paintings and reliefs; landscapes; still lifes of an abstracted kind of cubism; and wash drawings made in pencil from nature. The distinctions between these categories gradually disappeared, and elements drawn from different styles were combined in a rhythmical interplay of overlapping linear silhouettes with planes of pure colour and areas of silvery texture. Many of his later works were on the borderline between painting and relief, executed on hardboard, with stony colours and textures and minute changes of level due to scraping with a razor blade or chisel.   REA

J. Russell, *Ben Nicholson: Drawings, Paintings and Reliefs, 1911–1968* (London, 1969).

Niebuhr, Reinhold (b. Wright City, Mo., USA, 21.6.1892; d. New York, 1.6.1971). American theologian, hailed by *Time* magazine as 'the number one theologian of United States Protestantism'. He received his BD from Yale in 1914, and took up the only pastorate of his career in Detroit, remaining there for 13 years. His experience among the workers in Ford factories confronted him with the human cost of dehumanized factory life. His first book *Does Civilization Need Religion?* (NY, 1927) revealed concerns that were to remain with him throughout his life. In 1928 Niebuhr moved to New York as professor of applied Christianity at Union Theological Seminary, remaining there until his retirement in 1960. The important early years in New York saw the publication of *Moral Man and Immoral Society* (NY, 1932), created

out of a deep exasperation with the 'liberal culture of modernity'. Niebuhr particularly questioned the utopian assumptions of kinship with the divine and natural goodness, represented in the Social Gospel movement, and argued fervently for a more sophisticated understanding of the problem of power than had as yet been achieved by either secular or religious moralism. Niebuhr virtually came to abandon his earlier pacifist position and began to engage himself in the development of a political theory; here his interest in MARXism is evident. Although never a doctrinaire Marxist he was attracted to the Marxist analysis of the 'logic' of modern history, and on occasion described himself as a Christian Marxist. As he pondered the relation of politics to ethics, his written reflections became distinctly theological. In *An Interpretation of Christian Ethics* (NY, 1935) he maintained that the normative element in Christian ethical thought is radically perfectionist and transcendent – the *agape*. His simultaneous emphasis on the Calvinist and Lutheran concept of transcendence, combined with a radical reappraisal of that concept, was probably the reason for Niebuhr's being labelled against his liking as 'neo-orthodox'. In 1939 Niebuhr was invited to present the Gifford lectures on *The Nature and Destiny of Man* (2 vols, NY, 1941–3); in book form these are generally regarded as his masterpiece. Throughout his career the central interest was 'the defense and justification of the Christian faith in a secular age'.   LJH

J. R. Bingham, *Courage to Change* (NY, 1961); N. A. Scott (ed.), *The Legacy of Reinhold Niebuhr* (Chicago, 1975).

Niemeyer, Oscar Soares Filho (b. Rio de Janeiro, Guanabara, Brazil, 15.12.1907). Brazilian architect. Brazil's reformist governments of the 1930s and 1940s took to modern architecture eagerly as a conspicuous statement of their commitment to progressive ideas. Niemeyer was the most talented of the group of young Brazilian architects who came to prominence in those years. LE CORBUSIER, who was invited to design the new offices of the Ministry of Education in Brazil, had a profound impact on

Niemeyer and his other collaborators. Niemeyer's fame stems principally from his most flamboyant creation, the new city of Brasilia (1956–63). For two decades it was trumpeted as being among the greatest achievements of modern architecture. Disillusion set in once the extent and the permanence of the surrounding squalid shanty towns became widely publicized. But Niemeyer's best works were not on the city-planning scale of Brasilia. The casino he designed for Pampulha in 1942 was a remarkable blend of Corbusian influences with a richer, more theatrical tradition that has its roots in the native Brazilian baroque style. At Brasilia the complexity of this early work was diluted into the monumental neoclassicism of the government buildings. But for all its drawbacks Brasilia will continue to represent the most powerful single vision of the modern world as it was seen at the mid-point of the 20c.   DS

Nietzsche, Friedrich Wilhelm (b. Röcken, Saxony, Germany [now East Germany], 15.10.1844; d. Weimar, Saxony, 25.8.1900). German philosopher and classical philologist. The son of a pietist parson, he went to grammar school in Schulpforta and subsequently studied classics at Bonn and Leipzig. In 1869 he was given a professorship in classics at Basle. He became one of Wagner's first profound admirers (1868), befriended him but, in 1876, broke away from him. He resigned his professorship in 1879 for health reasons. Rejected by Lou Andreas-Salomé, to whom he had proposed marriage, he withdrew into the existence of a tourist-scholar: Sils-Maria, Sicily, Rapallo, Nice, Leipzig, Turin, where he had a major mental collapse followed by progressive paralysis, probably as a result of a syphilitic infection he contracted as a student. In his first book *Die Geburt der Tragödie aus dem Geiste der Musik* (Leipzig, 1872; tr. F. Golffing, *The Birth of Tragedy out of the Spirit of Music*, NY, 1956), Nietzsche interpreted the relationship of man and world, life and mind as mediated by illusion, myth, religion. In rare moments of Dionysian ecstasy the individual submerges into the species being. Into the senseless turnover that is nature, man's Apolline faculty builds images of the eternal, Platonic ideas, Christian heavens, etc., for solace. With the selective and conceptually delimiting power of language man imposes meanings that suit his taste for survival. Fritz Mauthner and WITTGENSTEIN are strongly influenced by Nietzsche's language theory. Nietzsche's declaration that there is no world beyond this one, that God is dead in *Also sprach Zarathustra* (Chemnitz, 1883; London, 1896, tr. R. J. Hollingdale, *Thus Spoke Zarathustra*, Harmondsworth, 1969) is heralded in *Die fröhliche Wissenschaft* (Chemnitz, 1882; *The Gay Science*, in *The Complete Works of Friedrich Nietzsche*, ed. O. Levy, London, 1909–13) with the observation that religious faith has lost its credibility. With seismographic sensitivity Nietzsche became the prophet and registrar of the historical onset of European nihilism. SARTRE's and CAMUS's thought builds on this analysis. By the creation of the figure of Zarathustra, the teacher of the coming of superman and, contradictorily, of eternal recurrence, Nietzsche believed that in his philosophy he had overcome nihilism. The meaning of history was the appearance, at rare moments, of the exceptional individual. Within the notes which until the appearance of the definitive critical edition of the complete works (*Friedrich Nietzsche, Werke, Kritische Gesamtausgabe*, ed. G. Colli & M. Montinari, Berlin, 1967–) were edited under the title *Der Wille zur Macht* (Leipzig, 1888; London, 1909, tr. W. Kaufmann & R. J. Hollingdale, *The Will to Power*, NY, 1968) Nietzsche dissected Christianity and socialism as faiths of the 'little men', where excuses for weakness paraded as moral principles. In *Zur Genealogie der Moral* (Leipzig, 1887; London, 1910, tr W. Kaufmann, *On the Geneaology of Morals*, NY, 1968) Nietzsche had exposed compassion, charity, faith in God, etc. as virtues of the 'herd'. Nietzsche wanted to prepare the path for the '*Herrenmensch*' [overlord], a new type of man who with his robber instincts was able to manipulate the masses and who was a law unto himself.

Nietzsche's influence has been immense. His adoption by German Nazism could never be complete, because Nietzsche disavowed anti-Semitism, German nationalism and biological racism. St George, Thomas MANN, JÜNGER, GIDE, MALRAUX, YEATS, MUIR, READ were fascinated by him. He also influenced the anthropologists L. Klages, A. Adler, GEHLEN; the post-structuralists FOUCAULT, G. Deleuze, P. Klossowski; and the *nouveaux philosophes* A. Glucksmann, B. H. Lévy.

WvdW

W. Kaufmann, *Nietzsche: Philosopher, Psychologist, Antichrist* (Princeton, 1950); H. W. Reichert & K. Schlechta, *International Nietzsche Bibliography* (Chapel Hill, NC, 1968); R. Hinton Thomas, 'Nietzsche' in *German Politics and Society 1890–1918* (Manchester, 1983).

Nijinsky, Vaslav (b. Kiev, Russia, 12.3.1889; d. London, UK, 8.4.1950). Russian dancer and choreographer, one of the greatest names in ballet. His exceptional virtuosity was evident from childhood, and he danced leading roles early in his career at the Imperial Theatre in St Petersburg. But Nijinsky's genius was to flower in the West, as the star dancer in the new ballets presented by DIAGHILEV's Ballets Russes in Paris and throughout Europe from 1909. His technical accomplishment astounded western audiences for whom male dancing was an art long forgotten, and his remarkable elevation (an apparent ability to hover in the air) has passed into legend. More important was Nijinsky's deep instinct for interpretation in his roles. He revealed his greatest quality not in classical ballets for which he had been trained (though he did dance such parts, including Siegfried in *Swan Lake* and Albrecht in *Giselle*) but in dance-acting roles created for him by FOKINE: the Poet in *Les Sylphides*, Harlequin in *Carnaval*, the exotic golden slave in *Sheherazade*, the nonhuman spirit in *Le Spectre de la Rose*, the pathetic puppet in *Petrushka* (all these in 1909–11). In 1912–13, encouraged by Diaghilev, Nijinsky created his own avant-garde choreography for *L'Après-midi d'un faune* and *Jeux* (both to music of DEBUSSY) and *The Rite of Spring* (to STRAVINSKY's score), which caused a furore: the surviving evidence suggests that Nijinsky demonstrated an innovative choreographic talent, not at the time widely appreciated, which in later years was inherited by his sister Bronislava Nijinska. Nijinsky never returned to Russia after 1911, and mental illness ended his career after 1917. DAD

R. Buckle, *Nijinsky* (London, 1971); B. Nijinska, *Early Memoirs* (NY, 1981).

Nikolais, Alwin (b. Southington, Conn., USA, 25.11.1912). American dancer, choreographer, composer and teacher, who introduced the concept of dance as a total theatrical event in which costumes, props, sounds and lighting assume equal importance with movement. After accompanying silent films and directing marionettes, Nikolais studied dance with American modern dance pioneers, taught and choreographed before being appointed director of the Henry Street Playhouse (1948–70), New York's experimental theatre centre. It was here that he formed his own company and evolved his distinctive theatrical mode, creating *Masks, Props and Mobiles* (1953), the first piece in the new genre. Shortly afterwards he began to compose his own tape scores and to perfect the art of one-man productions, in 1963 becoming the first dance director to use a Moog synthesizer. Nikolais's presentation dehumanizes and androgynizes his dancers so that they evoke primal emotional responses, functioning with great skill and wit in magical, technological environments that extend or obscure their physical images. He has many followers, the most influential being Murray Louis, with whom he now runs a flourishing school and theatre laboratory in New York. By invitation Nikolais founded and directed a dance centre in Angers (1978–81). SAJ

M. Siegel, 'Nik; a documentary study of Alwin Nikolais', *Dance Perspectives*, 48 (1971).

Nixon, Richard Milhous (b. Yorba Linda, Calif., USA, 9.1.1913). US congressman (1946–50), senator for California (1950–2), vice-president (1952–60), president (1968–74). The only US president to resign his office; he did so to avoid impeachment on charges of conniving at illegal practices in the Watergate scandal and consistently misrepresenting the truth to Congress in a jargon so opaque as to become a byword. His name in domestic politics is synonymous with misuse of the presidential powers against political opponents, as it was during his period as senator and vice-president for ruthless and unscrupulous denigration and misrepresentation of those against whom he stood for election. In world politics by contrast he developed a flexibility of policy which, following the advice of KISSINGER, broke the previous rigidity of US policy towards Communist China, exploited disagreement within the Soviet bloc to secure agreements on Berlin (1970), the limitation of strategic arms (SALT I, 1972) and the American withdrawal from Indo-China (1973). The so-called Nixon doctrine committed the USA to supporting the *status quo* in the western Pacific, as a means of reconciling Japan to the reversal of his China policy and the US withdrawal from South East Asia.   DCW

Nizzoli, Marcello (b. Boretto, Emilia-Romagna, Italy, 2.1.1887; d. Milan, Lombardy, 31.7.1969). Italian designer. Nizzoli played a large part in shaping the distinctive character of post-WW2 Italian design along more stylish and sophisticated lines than contemporary German or American models. Olivetti, his major patron, was a firm that believed in using artists to design its products, which were treated as artworks. Adriano Olivetti hired Nizzoli in 1938 initially to design posters, but he turned his hand successively to a whole series of typewriters and business machines. Nizzoli had already made a considerable reputation for himself: he had exhibited in 1914 with the *Nuovo Tendenzia* group; and a series of tapestries he designed after WW1 brought him other commissions for exhibition work, leading eventually to the Gold Medal room at the 1934 Milan aeronautical exhibition. Nizzoli's postwar work for Olivetti embodied the spirit of the Italian economic miracle, the belated industrial revolution that turned Milan into a world design leader.   DS

Nkrumah, Kwame (b. Nkroful, British Gold Coast [now Ghana], 21.9.1909; d. Bucharest, Romania, 27.4.1972). President of Ghana. Widely regarded as the outstanding black political leader of Africa's 'age of revolution' and the most fervent spokesman of Pan-Africanism, Nkrumah ended his life in exile, after being overthrown by a military coup in 1966. By temperament an 'eternal student' with an eclectic appetite for ideas, Nkrumah spent his formative years (1935–47) studying in the USA and Britain, before returning to the Gold Coast in 1947 to become secretary of a newly formed but moderate and conservatively led nationalist party. Endowed with exceptional political flair, Nkrumah soon broke away to form his own political party, the Convention People's party, the first party with a truly mass appeal to emerge in black Africa. Imprisoned by the British as a subversive, Nkrumah was able, after his party's sweeping election victory in 1951, to become the colony's first prime minister. He cooperated harmoniously with the British and secured independence for his country, renamed Ghana, in 1957. But his years in power were marked by increasing internal unrest, to which he responded by dictatorial and repressive measures, and his eventual overthrow was greeted with rejoicing. Despite his ultimate failure, Nkrumah's achievement was monumental. The first black African leader to achieve truly international status, he became a symbolic figure throughout Africa, giving black people everywhere a new pride and confidence in themselves. Without his passionate advocacy of the Pan-Africanist cause, the Organization of African Unity might never have been created in 1963. He propagated his ideas in numerous works. 'Seek ye first the political kingdom' had been his slogan in the 1940s; in the postindependence world of 'neocolonialism' – a concept he did much to popularize – he saw that the 'political kingdom' needed to be accompanied by a greater measure of economic independence. Nkrumah published his *Autobiography* (Edinburgh) in 1957.   RH

B. Davidson, *Black Star* (London, 1973).

Noether, Amalie Emmy (b. Erlangen, Bavaria, Germany, 23.3.1882; d. Bryn Mawr, Pa, USA, 14.4.1935). German mathematician. Daughter of the mathematician Max Noether and sister of the physicist Fritz Noether, Emmy Noether pursued a distinguished career as a mathematician herself. Her lectures at Göttingen, heard by such men as ARTIN and van der Waerden, strongly influenced the development of abstract algebra in 20c mathematics. Her own research work continued the development of the theories of rings and ideals, largely in the style of the 19c German mathematician Richard Dedekind, of whose collected works she was a coeditor in the 1930s. She also contributed to the theory of hypercomplex numbers (a generalization of complex numbers). As a woman, Noether was not able to become a full professor at Göttingen; as a Jewess, she even lost her extraordinary professorship in 1933, and she left for the USA where she obtained a post at Bryn Mawr College. She died there, suddenly, two years later.   IG-G

A. Dick, *Emmy Noether 1882–1935* (Boston, Mass., 1981).

Nolde, Emil Hansen, *né* Emil Hansen (b. Nolde, Schleswig-Holstein, Germany 7.8.1867; d. Seebüll, West Germany, 13.4.1956). German expressionist painter and graphic artist. A trained woodcarver, Nolde was largely self-taught as an artist apart from a brief spell in the Académie Julian (1898–9) and with Adolf Hölzel in Munich, who introduced him to the expressive power of colour. A deeply religious man, he aimed to give expression to his mystic pantheism by intense outbursts of colour, often heightened by grotesque distortion. Many of his paintings are explicitly religious in content (e.g. *Dance round the Golden Calf*, 1910; *Pièta*, 1915), but a visionary religious feeling also pervades the landscapes, still lifes, flower pieces, mysterious primitive figures and mask-like faces which dominate his *oeuvre*. He was invited to join the *Brücke* in 1906 as the only artist of the older generation whom KIRCHNER and Heckel felt to be striving towards an authentic, modern style of expression. But he was essentially a solitary figure and left the group after a year. From 1902 he spent the winters in Berlin, where he was a cofounder of the Sezession (1910), and the summers in his native moorlands of Schleswig-Holstein. His interest in primitive art prompted him to participate in an expedition to New Guinea via Russia and China (1913–14) which resulted in even more richly exotic colour effects and expressively stylized forms (e.g. *Masks and Dahlias*, 1919). It also stimulated his fascination with magic and superstition, which resulted in the hauntingly enigmatic quality of his later work, especially the uncanny visionary heads and figures painted secretly in watercolour at Seebüll after he had been declared 'degenerate' and forbidden to paint by the Nazis (1941–5). The richly textured luminosity of the colours is combined with awkwardly simplified forms to create some of the most intensely powerful images to emerge from German expressionism. He was also a prolific graphic artist, using both woodcut and lithography.   SOBT

W. Haftmann, *Emil Nolde* (London, 1960); W. Haftmann, *Emil Nolde: Forbidden Pictures* (London, 1965).

Nordal, Sigurur (b. Eyjólfsstaðir, Iceland, 14.9.1886; d. Reykjavík, 21.9.1974). Icelandic scholar and poet. Nordal revolutionized the study of medieval Icelandic prose and poetry by treating it as literature, opening up a new vein of research which is still being fruitfully worked. Through his critical writing, his sensitive editions of three major Old Icelandic texts and, most of all, through his influence on and encouragement of younger scholars during his long tenure of his chair in the University of Iceland, he laid the foundations of sound critical scholarship in this field, his work showing a breadth and depth of vision inherited from W. P. Ker, by whom he was greatly influenced. Like Ker, Nordal refused to be tied down to any one period, and his criticism has illuminated both medieval and modern Icelandic literature, while his deeply felt poetry and prose have also exerted a strong influence on younger creative writers.   BSB

Norrish, Ronald George Wreyford (b. Cambridge, UK, 9.11.1897; d. Cambridge, 7.6.1978). British physical chemist. Norrish was a Cambridge man by birth, education and life's work. His early research was in the field of reaction kinetics: he provided experimental evidence for some fundamental ideas in mechanistic organic chemistry, but later concentrated especially on primary photochemical reactions of simple molecules (e.g. aldehydes, ketone, nitrogen dioxide). His work led to a new understanding of photochemical decomposition (photolysis) by ultraviolet and visible light: the principles which emerged remain at the basis of present-day thinking about such reactions. Later, between the two world wars, he studied hydrocarbon combustion, and elucidated the role of formaldehyde as an intermediate in the combustion of the simple paraffinic hydrocarbons, methane and ethane. After 1945, in association with G. PORTER he developed and exploited the method of flash photolysis, in which a powerful flash of light is used to generate radicals, the spectra of these fugitive species being recorded by use of a weaker flash of light released very soon after the first. This made possible the study of reactions having a lifetime of a few millionths of a second. The common term in nearly all the reactions studied in depth by Norrish has been the presence of highly reactive radicals or atoms (odd-electron species) as transient intermediates. He received the Nobel prize in 1967.   NBC

Noske, Gustav (b. Brandenburg, Germany [now East Germany], 9.7.1868; d. Hanover, Lower Saxony, West Germany, 30.11.1946). German socialist leader, minister for the army (1918–20) in the opening days of the Weimar republic, he used the socially stratified and antirevolutionary leadership of the Imperial German army to crush leftwing disorders and Communist risings in Germany, and to contain the threat from the paramilitary forces of the German right, the *Freikorps*, with more effectiveness than his moderate party comrades could stomach, earning the undying enmity of the left. From 1920

to 1933 he was president of the state government of Hanover.   DCW

Nossal, Gustav Joseph Victor (b. Bad Ischl, Salzburg, Austria, 4.6.1931). Australian immunologist. Nossal did all his training in Australia, earning both MD and PhD from the universities of Sydney and Melbourne. His 'one cell, one antibody' concept is central to modern immunology. Nossal injected mice with two kinds of bacteria, knowing it would cause them to make antibodies and so become immune. He then took the mouse antibody-making cells and painstakingly put only one in each of many separate droplets. The droplets also contained both kinds of bacteria. In each droplet, however, only one or the other kind became immobilized, showing that each cell was making only one kind of antibody. This was critical evidence for the modern theory that antibodies are produced in response to infection, not because antibodies are tailored to the foreign molecules, but because the particular cells producing the most appropriate antibodies are stimulated to multiply. Nossal also helped establish the selection hypothesis (see BURNET) by showing that foreign molecules do not enter antibody-making cells, as was required by the 'tailor-made' hypothesis. Nossal is director of the Hall Medical Research Institute, Melbourne.   DOM

Novomeský, Ladislav (b. Budapest, Austria-Hungary [now Hungary], 27.12.1904; d. Bratislava, Czechoslovakia, 4.9.1976). Slovak poet, a lifelong 'communist of the heart', leading member of the prewar avant-garde, resistance worker during the last part of WW2, then chairman of the Slovak Board of Education (1945–50), president of the Slovak Academy (1950–1); in 1951 he was given a five-year prison sentence for 'bourgeois nationalism', was rehabilitated in 1963 and created National Artist in 1964. With *Nedel'a* [Sunday] (Bratislava, 1927) he began as an evocatively melancholic proletarian poet. He reached poetic maturity in labour-camps; in his paean on the October revolution and LENIN – *Vila Tereza* [The villa Tereza] (Bratislava, 1963) – poetry becomes revolution and revolution poetry. His supreme achievement is his reckoning with STALINism and his own imprisonment in *Stamodtial' a iné* [From there and other things] (Bratislava, 1964), bitter poems whose overall message is *Lebensbejahung*: unpleasant memories and grief are as important as pleasant memories and happiness. RBP

Noyes, Elliot Fette (b. Boston, Mass., USA, 12.8.1910; d. New Canaan, Conn., 18.7.1977). American architect and industrial designer. Noyes was a leading member of the generation of Americans who at an impressionable age fell under the spell of exiled European modernists such as GROPIUS and BREUER. He trained as an architect at Harvard, then set up the industrial design collection of the Museum of Modern Art, New York, before establishing his own design practice. Through his work for IBM, Westinghouse and Mobil, Noyes established the criteria for high-minded good taste that characterized the more enlightened US manufacturers in the 1960s. Very much under the influence of his teacher Gropius, Noyes believed that good design was a moral issue. He was dedicated to producing goods that were simple, pure and straightforward. He mocked the more brash and robust products of unselfconscious traditional American design. Noyes was responsible for the complete IBM look, from typography to architecture, enlisting such distinguished talents as EAMES to help him. DS

Nuffield, William Richard Morris (b. Worcester, Here. & Worcs., UK, 10.10.1877; d. Huntercombe, Oxon., 22.8.1963). British motor-car manufacturer. Graduating from the repair of bicycles for Oxford dons, he built the first Morris Oxford car in 1913 and founded Morris Motors Ltd in 1919. He devised successful production methods and popularized inexpensive motoring in Britain (see Henry FORD in the USA). He made a fortune and was the benefactor of Nuffield College, Oxford, and the Institute for Medical Research (Oxford) and the foundation for health, social well-being and education which also bears his name. RIT

Nunn, Thomas Percy (b. Bristol, Avon, UK, 28.12.1870; d. Madeira, Portugal, 12.12.1944). British educator. Educated at Bristol University College, Nunn taught mathematics and science in Halifax and later in London grammar schools and at Shoreditch Technical Institute. From 1905 until his retirement in 1936 he was vice-principal, then director of the London Day Training College, which became the University of London Institute of Education in 1932, and from 1913 he was its professor of education. A brilliant teacher and administrator, and active member of the Aristotelian Society, Nunn is best known for his *Education: its Data and First Principles* (London, 1920), the bible of the 'progressives' in Britain between the wars and later. He held that the cultivation of individuality is the central aim of education, supporting this claim by reference to a 'hormic', or instinct, psychology, predicated on a teleological theory of the evolution of life towards more differentiated and individual forms. Nunn saw education as the handmaiden of nature, fostering the growth of creative individuals, who act as the spearheads of evolutionary advance. A blend of John Stuart Mill's liberalism and social Darwinism, Nunn's theory is now considered problematic in its minimizing of social influences on intellectual development and in its naturalistic justification of its basic value-judgements. JPWh

Nureyev, Rudolf Hametovitch (b. Irkutsk, USSR, 17.3.1938; naturalized Austrian citizen, 1982). Russian/Austrian dancer. Although he began training late in classical ballet, as a soloist with the Kirov Ballet of Leningrad (1958–61) he danced leading roles and was among the most brilliant virtuoso dancers of the younger generation. He sought political asylum in Paris in 1961, and in London in 1962 began an historic partnership with FONTEYN. Nureyev's long career in the West has inspired dancers and audiences alike, and transformed standards of male dancing. His technical accomplishment and the subtlety and excitement of his interpretations have illuminated the traditional classics of the ballet repertory (his Siegfried in *Swan*

Lake and Albrecht in *Giselle* are among his outstanding roles); but he has also danced in works by every important choreographer of this century, in classical, neoclassical and modern idioms. Despite his versatility, it is as a supreme exponent of the classical school in ballet that he has made his international reputation, both with his own performances and through the many imaginative productions which he has mounted with western companies – including *La Bayadère*, *Raymonda*, *Swan Lake*, *The Sleeping Beauty*, *Don Quixote* (of which he also directed a film), *The Nutcracker* and *Romeo and Juliet*. He was appointed director of the Paris Opéra Ballet in 1983.   DAD

A. Bland, *The Nureyev Image* (London, 1976); J. Percival, *Nureyev: Aspects of the Dancer* (London, 1976).

Nuri as-Saïd (b. Baghdad, Mesopotamia, Ottoman Empire [now Iraq], 1888; d. Baghdad, 14.7.1958). Arab officer in the Turkish army, military leader in the Arab revolt (1915–18), military adviser to Prince (later King) Feisal of Iraq (1920–35), repeatedly prime minister of Iraq until his death, Nuri is principally associated with the continuing claims of the Husaini dynasty to the Pan-Arab kingdom they had claimed at the opening of the Arab revolt. Nuri's greatest hopes of this lay in his advocacy from 1942 onwards of the so-called 'Green Crescent' scheme, a union of Iraq, Syria and the Lebanon which would dominate the Middle East. Enmity to President NASSER of Egypt led him to accept proposals for an alliance with Turkey, Iran and Pakistan (with British participation) in the 'Baghdad Pact' of 1955, which made the Husaini dynasty and himself the prime target of radical Arab nationalism; neither he nor his royal master survived the Iraqi army coup of 1958.
                                                      DCW

Nyerere, Julius Kambarage (b. Butiama, Musoma District, Tanganyika [now Tanzania], 3.1922). President of Tanzania. One of the most widely respected leaders in the Third World, Nyerere, president of one of the world's poorest countries, has gained an international reputation for the clarity, originality and humanity of his views on government, society and development, and for his stress on a moral approach to political problems. Trained as a teacher and one of the first Tanganyikan Africans to study overseas, Nyerere became first president of the newly founded Tanganyika African National Union in 1954. Under Nyerere's leadership, TANU developed into one of the best-organized mass parties in colonial Africa, coming to enjoy almost universal support. After independence in 1961, Nyerere, who gained the title *Mwalimu* [teacher] from his people, developed the concept of the democratic one-party state, arranged the union with Zanzibar in 1964, put forward his own version of African socialism, which he termed *Ujamaa* (using this Swahili word meaning 'familyhood' to stress the traditional African values of equality and cooperation), and outlined a policy for political, social and economic development in the Arusha Declaration of 1967. This policy was designed to check the rise of a privileged class, laid special stress on the role of Ujamaa villages based on cooperative principles, and stressed the need for national self-reliance as opposed to excessive dependence on foreign aid. Nyerere's ideas were expressed in many speeches and articles gathered together in *Freedom and Unity* (London, 1967), *Freedom and Socialism* (Dar-es-Salaam, 1969) and *Freedom and Development* (Dar-es-Salaam, 1973). Nyerere's ideas strike some observers as utopian, but despite failures – particularly in economic development – Nyerere has provided his country with a measure of political stability and political freedom rare in postcolonial Africa.   RH

W. E. Smith, *Nyerere of Tanzania* (London, 1973).

O

Oakeshott, Michael Joseph (b. Harpenden, Herts., UK, 11.12.1901). British philosopher. He was educated at Cambridge, where he was university lecturer in history from 1929 to 1949. In 1950 he succeeded LASKI in the chair in political science at the London School of Economics; and retired in 1969. His first book *Experience and its Modes* (Cambridge, 1933) revealed him to be within the English idealist philosophical tradition, to the extent that he denied the realist claim that the knowing mind makes no difference to the thing known. The distinction between subject and object is not one between experience and something else, but is a distinction within experience itself. In political thought he is a sceptic, the main purpose of political activity being to keep the ship of state afloat, rather than to provide wealth and well-being. This theme he elaborated in a collection of essays *Rationalism in Politics* (London, 1962) and also in *On Human Conduct* (Oxford, 1975). AO

W. H. Greenleaf, *Oakeshott's Philosophical Politics* (London, 1966); P. King & B. C. Parekh (eds), *Politics and Experience* (Cambridge, 1968).

O'Brien, Flann, ps. of Brian O'Nolan (b. Strabane, Ireland [now Northern Ireland], UK, 5.10.1911; d. Dublin, Irish Republic, 1.4.1966). Irish novelist, journalist and Gaelic scholar. O'Brien studied Irish, German and philosophy at University College, Dublin. He worked as a civil servant. His most lasting journalism was the column Cruiskeen Lawn, contributed to the *Irish Times* from 1940 under the pseudonym Myles na Gopaleen (collected as *The Best of Myles*, ed. K. O'Nolan, London, 1968), in which he relentlessly castigated the users of all clichés Irish. His novels are *At Swim-Two-Birds* (London, 1939), *The Hard Life* (London, 1961), *The Dalkey Archive* (London, 1964), *The Third Policeman* (London, 1966), and (in Irish) *An Béal Bocht* (Dublin, 1941, ²1964; tr. P. C. Power, *The Poor Mouth*, London,

1973). O'Brien's satire is local, ridiculing the constricting solemnities of Irish life, the Gaelic revival and sentimental Gaelic literature, the tedious provincialism of the Irish church from bleak Christian Brothers to sententious Jesuits, and the plain people of Ireland; he gradually elevates such local idiocies to the level of universal absurdity. His impossibly learned poets Keats and Chapman rival Flaubert's Bouvard and Péchuchet; such characters as his Fr Kurt Fahrt, SJ, and his friend Mr Collopy who tries to interest the Pope in a scheme for women's conveniences, or the inventor de Selby who claims to interrogate the fathers of the church in a cave beneath sea level while perfecting an infernal device, are among the pure comic creations of modern literature. JCu

A. Cronin, *Dead as Doornails* (Dublin, 1974); A. Clissmann, *Flann O'Brien: a Critical Introduction to his Writings* (Dublin, 1975).

O'Casey, Seán, *né* John Casey (b. Dublin, Ireland, UK [now Irish Republic], 30.3.1880; d. Torquay, Devon, UK, 18.9.1964). Irish dramatist. O'Casey's first play was not produced until he was 43; his early life was spent as a labourer. His lifelong socialism brought involvement in socio-republican organizations and his earliest publications were political tracts. An autodidact, he read widely, and was particularly influenced by Shakespeare, Shelley, G. B. SHAW and, later, by the dramatists of the German expressionist theatre. His major tragedies – *The Shadow of a Gunman* (1923), *Juno and the Paycock* (1924) and *The Plough and the Stars* (1926) – all staged at the Abbey Theatre, Dublin, are marked by a poetic naturalism, a combining of comedy and tragedy to provide a dramatic perspective on the struggle for Irish independence and subsequent civil strife. In technique they combine naturalistic, political drama with elements of expressionism and of melodrama. In 1926 O'Casey crossed to London to receive the Hawthornden prize for *Juno*. His disillusionment with Ireland was reinforced by the rejection of his new play *The Silver Tassie* (London, 1928) by Lady Gregory and the directors of the Abbey Theatre. This play, dealing with the horrors of WW1, was produced in 1929 at the Apollo Theatre in London, with a celebrated stage set for the expressionistic Act II designed by Augustus John. O'Casey's later plays – *The Star turns Red* (1940), *Red Roses for Me* (1943), *Purple Dust* (London, 1940), *Cock-a-Doodle Dandy* (1949), *The Bishop's Bonfire* (1955) and *The Drums of Father Ned* (1959) – with their demanding stage requirements and difficult texts, had not much commercial success and are rarely performed. Though he wrote a large amount of journalism, four books of essays and *Autobiographies* (2 vols, London, 1963), his reputation rests primarily on his plays.   EFi

E. O'Casey, *Sean* (London, 1971); C. D. Greaves, *Sean O'Casey: Politics and Art* (London, 1979).

Ochoa, Severo (b. Luarca, Oviedo, Spain, 24.9.1905; naturalized American citizen, 1956). Spanish/American biochemist. Ochoa was educated at Malaga College (BA 1921) and the medical school of the University of Madrid (MD 1929), his interest in biology having been stimulated by study of the work of CAJAL, the great Spanish neurologist. After work with Otto Meyerhof in Heidelberg (1929–31) on muscle physiology and biochemistry, Ochoa returned to Madrid as lecturer in physiology (until 1935), and later head of the physiology division in the Institute for Medical Research. Further work abroad included another period at Heidelberg, a period at the National Institute for Medical Research, London, a period at the Plymouth Marine Biology Laboratory and, from 1939 to 1941, a stay at Oxford working with Sir Rudolph Peters on the biological function of vitamin B$_1$. He then worked with Carl and Gerty Cori at the Washington University School of Medicine, St Louis. In 1942 Ochoa joined the staff of the New York University School of Medicine where he became professor of pharmacology (1946), professor of biochemistry (1954),

and later chairman of that department. Ochoa's research has dealt among other topics with enzymic processes in biological oxidation, synthesis, and energy transfer; the metabolism of carbohydrates and fatty acids; the utilization of carbon dioxide; and the enzymic biosynthesis of ribonucleic acid (RNA), as well as aspects of photosynthesis and the KREBS cycle. More recently he has concentrated on the purification of the enzyme polynucleotide phosphorylase, and the 'priming' action of added RNA in the reaction producing it, and on the genetic code and related messages. He shared the Nobel prize for physiology and medicine with KORNBERG in 1959.

NBC

O'Connor, Frank, ps. of Michael Francis O'Donovan (b. Cork, Munster, Ireland, UK [now Irish Republic], 17.9.1903; d. Dublin, 10.2.1966). Irish short-story writer, novelist and translator. O'Connor grew up in poverty and gives vivid expression to this in his autobiographical books *An Only Child* (NY, 1961) and *My Father's Son* (London, 1968), in experimental novels such as *Dutch Interior* (London, 1940) and in short-story collections from *Guests of the Nation* (London, 1931) to *Collection Two* (London, 1964). The influence of Daniel Corkery (1878–1964) stimulated his interest in republicanism and in the Irish language and he translated many Irish poems, largely collected in *Kings, Lords and Commons* (NY, 1959). Like many others, O'Connor suffered under the literary censorship of the new Irish republic of the 1940s and 1950s and consequently achieved much of his literary reputation in the USA. His short stories capture, often humorously, always perceptively, the shibboleths and the mores of 'a submerged population group' isolated by commitment, oddity or poverty.   EFi

M. Sheehy (ed.), *Michael/Frank: Studies on O'Connor* (Dublin, 1969).

Odets, Clifford (b. Philadelphia, Pa, USA, 18.7.1906; d. Los Angeles, Calif., 14.8.1963). American dramatist, whose work with the Group Theater company in New York after 1931 contributed both to the development of its STANIS-

LAVSKY-derived acting style and to its increasingly radical political orientation. With his first play *Waiting for Lefty* (1935), he was immediately recognized as spokesman for his generation of left-wing intellectuals, and the play's tautly episodic presentation of a developing industrial dispute culminated in a mass meeting with whose decision to 'Strike!' most audiences would vociferously concur. Odets's reputation was affirmed with *Awake and Sing!* (1935), an urban domestic drama of the depression years, and *Golden Boy* (1937), a study of a young violinist driven by poverty into prizefighting, which became the greatest success of his 10-year association with the Group Theater. But he had already been tempted into the profitable Hollywood career whose values he later exposed in *The Big Knife* (1949), and most of his later work for the live theatre utilized 'well-made' formal structures within which the voice of social protest rang with inappropriate stridency. ST

H. Clurman, *The Fervent Years* (NY, 1945); G. Weales, *Clifford Odets, Playwright* (NY, 1971).

O'Faoláin, Seán, ps. of John Whelan (b. Cork, Munster, Ireland, UK [now Irish Republic], 22.2.1900). Irish short-story writer and novelist. O'Faoláin was educated in Cork and later at Harvard. A central concern in his work is the development of the individual personality within an ambiance which is frequently repressive and constricting. His own experiences in academic circles and later as editor (1940–6) of the literary magazine *The Bell* made him a formidable critic of insularity and censorship in Ireland. This is sharply observed in his autobiography *Vive Moi!* (Boston, Mass., 1964), in such novels as *A Nest of Simple Folk* (NY, 1934), *Bird Alone* (London, 1936), *And Again* (London, 1979) and even in his biographies of Hugh O'Neill (*The Great O'Neill*, NY, 1942), Daniel O'Connell (*King of the Beggars*, NY, 1938) and DE VALÉRA (Harmondsworth, 1939). His major contribution to Irish literature has been in the area of the short story, both as writer and as theorist in *The Short Story* (London, 1948). In 10 collections, from *Midsummer Night Madness and Other Stories* (London, 1932) through *The Heat of the Sun, Stories and Tales* (Boston, Mass., 1966) to *Foreign Affairs, and Other Stories* (London, 1976), he develops a technique and tone which is frequently acerbic in depicting the narrow-minded mores of a repressive society; if the later collections are more mellow, they are nonetheless pointedly observed. EFi

M. Harmon, *Seán O'Faoláin: a Critical Introduction* (Notre Dame, Ind., 1967).

O'Flaherty, Liam (b. Inishmore, Aran Islands, Ireland, UK [now Irish Republic], 28.8.1897). Irish novelist and short-story writer. Educated in boarding schools on the mainland, O'Flaherty joined the Irish Guards in 1915 and served on the western front in WW1. Shell-shocked in 1917, he returned to Aran and tentatively began to write. Since then he has worked as a labourer, sailor and teacher in various countries. Among his 15 novels, the most memorable are perhaps *Famine* (London, 1937) and *The Informer* (London, 1925). His best work, concentrating on observation and memory, is in the medium of the short story: *The Short Stories of Liam O'Flaherty* (London, 1937); *Two Lovely Beasts* (London, 1948); *The Stories of Liam O'Flaherty* (NY, 1956); and *The Pedlar's Revenge* (Dublin, 1976). In general simple and uncomplicated, his stories achieve a single, lucid effect; some, such as 'The Cow's Death' or 'His First Flight', grow from his island background and display a keen observation of the natural world, while others, such as 'The Reaping Race', demonstrate a lively awareness of the peasant's response to his environment and to his fellow workers. Stylistically, his use of English is modified by patterns of Gaelic speech to produce a distinctive quality of prose. EFi

Ogden, Charles Kay (b. Fleetwood, Lancs., UK, 1.6.1889; d. London, 20.3.1957). British linguistic psychologist and originator of Basic English. After graduating in classics from Cambridge, Ogden went into publishing, being founder and editor of the *Cambridge Magazine* (1912–23) and editor of

Psyche (1920–31). As a spin-off he was responsible, with F. RAMSEY, for the first English version of WITTGENSTEIN's *Tractatus Logico-Philosophicus*. He collaborated with RICHARDS to produce *The Meaning of Meaning* (London, 1923) which remains essential reading for semantics. In 1927 Ogden founded the Orthological Institute, intended to diffuse knowledge of the simplified variety of English that eventually crystallized as Basic ('British American Scientific International Commercial') English in 1930. This was a very carefully selected subset of standard English, comprising an essential vocabulary of 600 nouns, 150 adjectives and 100 assorted words. The whole vocabulary and a summary of the grammar can be printed on a single sheet of paper. Basic has considerable advantages over artificial languages in being upwards compatible with one of the most widely used natural languages, and having minimal inflexion. By 1939 it was being actively taught in over 30 countries. Despite enthusiastic support by CHURCHILL and F. D. ROOSEVELT, and some British government assistance, Basic failed to live up to its earlier success after WW2, though its influence lives in a diluted form in much contemporary teaching of English to foreigners.   WSD

P. Sargant Florence & J. R. L. Anderson (eds), *C. K. Ogden: a Collective Memoir* (London, 1977).

Oldenburg, Claes (b. Stockholm, Sweden, 28.1.1929; naturalized American citizen, 1953). Swedish/American artist and sculptor. Oldenburg came to the USA in 1936 when his father was appointed Swedish consul in Chicago. In 1956 he settled in New York and in 1957, influenced by the decaying slums of the Lower East Side and by the work of Pop and 'happening' artists such as Allan Kaprow, Jim Dine and George Segal, he rejected abstract expressionism and began to make three-dimensional objects related to the everyday world. This led to the first environmental art exhibition *The Street* (1961), a 'metamorphic mural' with images of buildings, cars, people and other objects made of charred cardboard and wood. A second version of *The Store* (Septem-

ber 1962) contained his first giant objects (e.g. *Giant Ice-Cream Cone*, 1962) and soft sculpture, the latter made of stuffed canvas or vinyl (e.g. *Giant Hamburger*, 1962). By rendering familiar objects in a different material, often denying their function, and by enlarging them, Oldenburg isolated them from everyday contexts. They were revealed as 'fetishes' of materialist culture, mocking the contemporary emphasis on newness and function. In the mid-1960s he began to make three versions of such objects as light-switches, pay-telephones and typewriters: a 'hard' one of painted cardboard or wood; a 'ghost' one of canvas; and a 'soft' one of vinyl. In 1965 Oldenburg produced a series of projects for colossal monuments for public places, e.g. a large half-peeled banana for Times Square (1965), a huge electric fan as a replacement for the Statue of Liberty, and a vast lipstick on a movable tractor (1969, Yale University, one of the few such projects to be realized). In 1967 he organized an earthmoving 'happening' in Grand Central Park, when a gang of paid workers dug a large hole and then filled it in again.
          SOBT

Claes Oldenburg, MOMA exh. cat. (NY, 1969).

Oliphant, Marcus Laurence Elwin (Mark) (b. Adelaide, S. Australia, Australia, 8.10.1901). Australian physicist. Oliphant worked for a jeweller and a public library before earning his way through Adelaide University. RUTHERFORD 'electrified' him during an Australian visit and in 1927 Oliphant followed him to the UK and to Cambridge, becoming 'the son Rutherford never had'. He recorded his memories in *Rutherford: Recollections of the Cambridge Days* (London, 1972). With strong technical as well as scientific talents, he pursued the big machines of nuclear physics – an early accelerator and the high tension laboratory at Cambridge, a proton synchrotron (of which he was an early originator) at Birmingham University after WW2 and a later, unsuccessful, big machine at Canberra. In the 1930s he was part-author of six papers elucidating the reactions of heavy hydrogen and the separation of isotopes of light elements. Oliphant moved to Birmingham in 1937 and in his department the first steps were taken towards the two crucial weapons Germany never had: microwave radar and the atomic bomb, the latter through the memorandum written, with Otto FRISCH, by PEIERLS whom Oliphant had appointed to Birmingham. He himself worked in the USA with his close friend Ernest LAWRENCE on electromagnetic separation of ^{235}U for the Hiroshima bomb. After WW2 he became an opponent of nuclear weapons and an advocate of nuclear power. In 1950 he returned to Australia to direct the Research School of Physical Sciences at the Australian National University, of which he was a cofounder. There he nurtured world status departments in geophysics and astronomy. At the age of 70 he became governor of South Australia for five years, filling the post with great distinction and vigour. MMG

S. Cockburn & D. Ellyard, *Oliphant* (Cammeray, NSW, 1981).

Oliver, Joseph (King) (b. New Orleans, La, USA, 11.5.1885; d. Savannah, Ga, 8.4.1938). American jazz cornetist, bandleader, composer. Mentor of ARMSTRONG, and leader of the famous early 'Creole Jazzband', whose 1923 recordings are usually cited as the first examples of 'classic jazz', since they present polyphonic, rhythmic improvised ensembles. The fame that Oliver had gained in New Orleans greatly increased after he moved to Chicago. He formed his own band, and sent for Armstrong to play second cornet; the empathy between master and pupil was so great that they could improvise simultaneously in harmony. Oliver's speciality was in using a rubber sink-plunger as a trumpet mute; with it he could imitate a rooster crowing, a horse neighing and a growling voice. He skilfully pioneered this technique, which later became a persistent feature of ELLINGTON's arrangements. Oliver continued to tutor and encourage young jazz musicians during the late 1920s, but after failing to establish his band in New York he made a series of ill-fated tours of the Middle West. Eventually he disbanded, and ended his days as a pool-room attendant. JJC

W. Allen & B. Rust, *King Joe Oliver* (London, n.d.).

Olivier, Laurence Kerr (b. Dorking, Surrey, UK, 22.5.1907). British actor and theatre director. The son of an Anglican vicar, he studied at Central School in London and in 1926 joined Barry Jackson's Birmingham Repertory. As an energetic young actor, he quickly came into the reckoning for juvenile leads, receiving his first substantial West End run with COWARD in *Private Lives* (1930). After a brief spell in Hollywood, he returned to the London stage where, in 1935, he alternated the parts of Mercutio and Romeo with GIELGUD. He joined the Old Vic in 1937, playing Hamlet, Henry V, Macbeth and Coriolanus in his first two seasons. His screen successes in *Pride and Prejudice* (1940), *Lady Hamilton* (1941) and *The Demi-Paradise* (1943) drew public popularity; and in 1944 he was appointed codirector of the Old Vic. Olivier's remarkable versatility and power were revealed through outstanding performances, such as Oedipus and Richard III, in two triumphant seasons; and his Shakespearean films, which he also directed, of *Henry V* (1945), *Hamlet* (1948) and *Richard III* (1955), were internationally successful. In 1955 he joined the Shakespeare Memorial Theatre at Stratford to play Titus in BROOK's remarkable *Titus Andronicus*, and in 1957 he showed his sympathy for the new wave of British theatre by playing Archie Rice in OSBORNE's *The Entertainer*. In 1963 he was appointed director of the new National Theatre, then operating at the Old Vic. Among his many roles were his fine Othello and the ageing actor father James Tyrone, in O'NEILL's *Long Day's Journey into Night*; he succeeded in establishing the National Theatre as a major international company. His ill-health (including a recovery from cancer) led to his being replaced in 1973 before the company had moved to its new South Bank building, and since then he has acted mainly in films and television. His autobiography *Confessions of an Actor* (London) was published in 1982. JE

F. Barker, *The Oliviers* (London, 1953); J. Cottrell, *Laurence Olivier* (London, 1975).

Olson, Charles John (b. Worcester, Mass., USA, 27.12.1910; d. New York, 10.1.1970). American poet. Olson made a belated start as a poet in the 1940s, after work in American studies at Wesleyan and Harvard universities, and a brief career in politics with the campaign for F. D. ROOSEVELT's re-election. He resigned from politics to write and study, spent some time in Yucatan investigating the persistence of archaic culture, and was the leading figure at the experimental Black Mountain College in its final years in the early 1950s. After its closure he returned to Gloucester, Massachusetts, his adoptive home town, where he spent the rest of his life, making occasional lengthy forays into the academic world. Gloucester, an early seaport settlement and fishing town, is the focus of his series of *Maximus Poems* (Highlands, NC, 1953, 1956; NY, 1960; London, 1968; NY, 1975), a vector reaching back to Europe and the Mediterranean and forward to the American West. These poems are the lineal descendants of William Carlos WILLIAMS's *Paterson* and Ezra POUND's *Cantos*, but go beyond the static naturalism of the former to envisage a superior civic existence, and behind the cultural threshold of the latter to broach the mythic and prehistoric origins of human culture. Olson's poetry is charged with both large- and small-scale knowledge, and his verse, the theory of which he outlined in his essay 'Projective Verse' (1950), is designed to discharge its meanings through the tense energy of its progression through a field of reference.　　　ATKC

S. Paul, *Olson's Push* (Baton Rouge, 1978).

O'Neill, Eugene Gladstone (b. New York, USA, 16.10.1888; d. Boston, Mass., 27.11.1953). American dramatist. During his lifetime O'Neill was recognized as the only American playwright to have made a permanent contribution to world literature. Although from a theatrical family, O'Neill had almost singlehandedly to invent serious theatre

in America. It was not until he entered the bohemian avant-garde of Greenwich Village, and participated in the Provincetown Players in 1916, that his first play was produced. His first New York production came in 1920 with *Beyond the Horizon*, for which he received a Pulitzer prize. The harsh realism of his early plays, in part based on his experiences as a merchant seaman, was abandoned in a search for richer dramatic structures. In *The Emperor Jones* (1920) and *The Hairy Ape* (1922) he domesticated the experimental forms of expressionism and symbolism. Classical tragedy in the form of Aeschylus' story of the fall of the house of Atreus was used in O'Neill's *Mourning Becomes Electra* (1931). He used masks in *The Great God Brown* and a chorus in *Lazarus Laughed* (both 1926). His final period, in which he wrote *The Iceman Cometh* (1946) and *Long Day's Journey into Night* (1956), was O'Neill's strongest. His preoccupation with the power of illusion, and the intricate, self-destructive passions of an Irish-American family, appear here in fully realized forms. O'Neill's Catholicism, his Irishness, his parents, and a lifelong problem with alcoholism, were often combined in his work with NIETZSCHEan and Darwinian themes, and with a fascination with the tragic forms of classical antiquity.　　　EH

L. Sheaffer, *O'Neill: Son and Playwright* (NY, 1968); C. W. E. Bigsby, *A Critical Introduction to Twentieth-Century American Drama*, i (Cambridge, 1982).

Onsager, Lars (b. Oslo, Norway, 27.10.1903; naturalized American citizen, 1945; d. Miami, Fla, USA, 5.10.1976). Norwegian/American theoretical physicist. Onsager was trained in Norway as a chemical engineer, but equipped himself for tackling more theoretical problems in physics and chemistry by acquiring a formidable knowledge of analysis and other branches of mathematics. His first work was on electrolyte solutions on which he worked with DEBYE in Zürich. But in 1928 he moved to the USA, where he spent the rest of his career, mostly at Yale. His work on electrolytes and his interest in chemical reactions in solution led him to the work on irreversible thermodynamics for which he was awarded the Nobel prize for chemistry in 1968. Classical thermodynamics is concerned only with states of matter at equilibrium and with reversible changes between such states. Although there had been earlier *ad hoc* attempts to bring irreversible processes within its scope, it was not until Onsager's work in 1929–31 that the extension was put on a sound basis. His results are best known in the form of his 'reciprocal relations'. For example, if there is in a solution a gradient of both concentration and temperature then there will be two flows – a flow of matter driven both by the concentration gradient (ordinary diffusion) and by the temperature gradient (thermal diffusion, or Soret effect), and a flow of energy driven by the temperature gradient (thermal conductivity) and by the concentratrion gradient (Dufour effect). Onsager's relations show that the cross-terms, here the Soret and Dufour effects, have, when suitably expressed, the same numerical magnitude. This apparently simple result has wide consequences, some of which have been developed by PRIGOGINE in a more general treatment of irreversible processes. Onsager's other major contribution to theoretical physics was his solution (1942–9) of the two-dimensional Ising problem, a mathematical *tour de force* which was the first exact solution of a nontrivial problem in the statistical mechanics of the equilibrium between different phases of matter.   JSR

Oort, Jan Hendrik (b. Franeker, Friesland, The Netherlands, 28.4.1900). Dutch astronomer. Oort completed his training at Leiden Observatory, where he remained for the rest of his career, becoming director in 1945. He had already done his best-known work before receiving his doctorate. In the mid-1920s it was still debated whether the Milky Way was the whole universe or just one of many galaxies. Oort took the latter view and through his work played a major part in the reassessment of the way we regard the whole universe. He considered a model of our galaxy containing a central nucleus representing 90 per cent of the stars, and a disk spread around that nucleus composed of the remaining stars including the sun. He postulated that the stars in the disk would have circular orbits round the nucleus, like planets around the sun, and worked out what observational effects these stellar motions should display. He then produced the evidence to support his model and thereby demonstrated the rotation of our galaxy, its structure, the position in the sky of the galactic centre and its distance from us. The two equations that describe these basic properties of our galaxy contain the two Oort constants named after him. He also demonstrated that the sun travelled round the galaxy every 230 million years at a speed of 220 kilometres per second and that the mass of the galaxy was about one hundred thousand million times that of the sun. This work was announced in 1925 and remains the basis of modern understanding of galactic dynamics. During the German occupation, Leiden Observatory was closed down and Oort and his colleagues, denied observing facilities, worked on theoretical problems. One of the group, Van der Hulst, predicted the existence of the 21cm radiation produced by neutral hydrogen atoms in cold interstellar gas clouds. Such material was expected to be found mainly in the spiral arms of the galactic disk, and by 1951 Oort and his group had detected this radiation and were beginning to trace out the positions of the spiral arms of our galaxy. Oort and Van der Hulst together demonstrated that the hydrogen gas clouds in the galaxy seem to flow outwards from the centre to the edge of the galactic disk. In 1950 Oort's name became associated with another astronomical phenomenon. He suggested that there were far more comets in the solar system than would ever be observed and that most of these were at vast distances from the sun, contained in a vast 'cloud' surrounding the solar system. Such a cloud is now known as an Oort cloud. Another celebrated piece of work concerned the Crab Nebula. By measuring the expansion rate of the dissipating material from this nebula Oort worked out how long it was since the material had been compact. The dating went back 900 years, thereby confirming that the Crab Nebula was the remnant of the exploding star seen as the AD 1054 supernova. MJS

Oparin, Alexander Ivanovich (b. Uglich, Russia, 2.3.1894; d. Moscow, USSR, 21.4.1980). Russian biochemist. Oparin's principal interest was 'the origin of life', a phrase which he coined and ultimately made respectable. He argued that the quality unique to a living organism is its organization: 'The specific peculiarity of living organisms is only that, in them, there have been collected and integrated an extremely complex combination of a large number of properties and characteristics present in isolation in various dead, inorganic bodies. Life is not characterized by any special properties but by a definite specific combination of these properties.' Life is, therefore, an inevitable outcome of the properties of matter and energy and not the result of a lucky, random combination of chemical substances. He envisaged that the first stage in the genesis of life involved the formation of individual catalysts in a 'primeval soup'. These were then coordinated into chains and cycles and subsequently into protocells and cells, the latter 'guaranteeing, within limits, continual self-preservation and reproduction'. He expounded his views in a series of books (e.g. *Proiskhozhdenie Zhizni*, Moscow, 1924; *Origin of Life*, London, 1936, and *Vozniknoveniye i nachalnoye razvitiye zhizni*, Moscow, 1966; *Genesis and Evolutionary Development of Life*, NY, 1968) and led others to accept that the problem of the origin of life is susceptible to intellectual and experimental investigation. GL

K. Dose, S. W. Fox, G. A. Deborin & T. E. Pavlovskaya (eds), *The Origin of Life and Evolutionary Biochemistry* (NY, 1974).

Oppenheimer, Ernest (b. Friedberg, Bavaria, Germany, 22.5.1880; naturalized British citizen, 1901; d. Johannesburg, Transvaal, South Africa, 25.11.1957). South African mining magnate. In 1917 he founded the Anglo-American Corporation of South Africa with backing from J. P. MORGAN to mine the Witwatersrand goldfield. In 1919 he formed Consolidated Diamond Mines of South West Africa which, with De Beers Consolidated Mines which it acquired, controlled most of the world's diamond supply. He became one of the world's richest men and from this wealth has grown a major, global business corporation. A friend of SMUTS, the Afrikaner soldier and statesman, he became a benefactor of South African education and public welfare and of Commonwealth studies at Oxford University. RIT

Oppenheimer, Julius Robert (b. New York, USA, 22.4.1904; d. Princeton, NJ, 18.2.1967). American physicist. Oppenheimer achieved distinction through personal research, as a teacher, as a director of Los Alamos where the wartime atomic bomb was fabricated, and as an elder statesman of postwar physics. After graduating at Harvard, Oppenheimer went to Europe for four years at the time of the quantum mechanics revolution and developed with BORN at Göttingen a classical part of quantum theory (the 'Born–Oppenheimer method') for handling the electronic, vibrational and rotational degrees of the freedom of molecules. From 1929 to 1942 he divided his time between positions at the University of California at Berkeley and the California Institute of Technology. 'The list of his papers during this period might almost serve as a guide to what was important in physics at that time' (PEIERLS). He was an outstanding teacher. His personal research ceased in 1941. Early in 1942 he took charge of the US work on the design of an atomic weapon. He suggested that this work should be concentrated in a single laboratory: Los Alamos was chosen and he became director. He was an excellent administrator, scientifically and organizationally, and the laboratory was extremely effective. He was a member of the scientific advisory panel which supported the use of the atomic bomb against Japan. After the war he was one of the authors of the 1946 Acheson–Lilienthal Report which proposed the international control of atomic energy, and was chairman of the Advisory Committee of the US Atomic Energy Commission from 1946 to 1952. In 1949 this

Committee recommended that the US should not develop the super- or H-bomb. Meanwhile in 1947 he had become director of the Institute for Advanced Study in Princeton which prospered under him. He talked and wrote much about science and society (e.g. his Reith lectures *Science and the Common Understanding*, London, 1953).

Until the mid-1930s Oppenheimer had had no interest in politics but then became very politically conscious and involved with left-wing groups. In 1940 he married Katherine Harrison who had similarly strong interests. In December 1953 (during the MCCARTHY era) Oppenheimer was told that his security clearance was being withdrawn because his loyalty was in doubt. The Board at the hearings asked for by Oppenheimer found him a 'loyal citizen' but by a two-to-one majority that he was to blame for opposing the H-bomb programme and later lacking enthusiasm for it. The USAEC did not uphold the censure of his H-bomb views but confirmed in a majority verdict withdrawal of his clearance mainly on grounds of 'defects of character'. The case divided the US scientific community for many years. In 1963, as a gesture of reconciliation, Oppenheimer was awarded the Enrico FERMI award by the USAEC.

MMG

P. M. Stern, *The Oppenheimer Case* (NY, 1969); A. Kimball Smith & C. Weiner, *Robert Oppenheimer: Letters and Recollections* (Cambridge, Mass., 1980).

Orozco, José Clemente (b. Ciudad, Mexico, 23.11.1883; d. Mexico City, 7.9.1949). Mexican painter and political cartoonist. With the other two great Mexican muralists RIVERA and David Siqueiros, Orozco wanted to create an heroic new art in postrevolutionary Mexico. But unlike those others he never identified his aims with the programme of any one political party. Orozco never joined the Mexican Communist party which accused him of being a 'bourgeois sceptic'. He also shied away from making monolithic political statements in his art. Of the revolution he wrote: 'I played no part in the revolution, I came to no harm, and I ran no danger at all. To me the revo-

lution was the gayest and most diverting of carnivals.' His murals rely heavily on the native traditions, particularly the neomannerism of Mexican religious art. His figures are nearly always shown suffering, distorted and elongated, flickering with hellfire. Orozco said that this 'cosmic torment' affects us all and he refused to apportion blame for it. In his political cartoons he parodied rich and poor alike, capitalist and communist, Mexican and American. This bitter-sweet humanism endeared him to European writers who compared him frequently to Goya and who found his ambivalence much more palatable than the strident political statements of Rivera and Siqueiros.   WJ

Museum of Modern Art, Oxford, *Orozco* (Oxford, 1980).

Ortega y Gasset, José (b. Madrid, Spain, 9.5.1883; d. Madrid, 18.10.1955). Spanish philosopher, social critic and essayist, one of the most influential Spanish intellectuals of his time. After graduating from Madrid he studied in Germany, returning to become professor of metaphysics at Madrid University (1910–36). He founded several periodicals, including *Revista de occidente* which he directed from 1923 to 1936. A liberal in politics, he opposed Primo de Rivera's dictatorship (1923–30) and sat in the constituent assembly of the republic from 1931 to 1933. Between 1936 and 1945 he lived abroad, unwilling to support either side in the civil war or to hold academic office under FRANCO. In 1948 he founded the Instituto de Humanidades in Madrid.

Philosophically, Ortega moved from neo-Kantianism to a form of existentialism that he expounded unsystematically in a pungent, popular style. He took the individual life, as a finite 'vital project' to be lived under historically given circumstances, as the basic reality. One might live authentically, centred in oneself, or in a state of otherness, a false heteronomy. Culture, encountered as a transmitted reality independent of the individual, sets problems which each generation must resolve, authentically or otherwise; in either case it bequeaths a changed world and a unique problem to its successor. Thus history has a dramatic not a deterministic structure.

Ortega's works – collected in *Obras completas* [Complete works] (6 vols, Madrid, 1946–7) – contain important sociological insights, e.g. on how generations cause social change, or the psychology of extremism. He is best known for *La Rebelión de las masas* (Madrid, 1930; *The Revolt of the Masses*, London, 1932) which echoed warnings of 19c liberals that democracy carried with it the risk of tyranny by the majority. Bolshevism and fascism were symptoms of a usurpation of power by the 'mass man'. A product of rapid population growth and occupational specialization, which had weakened the cultural consensus underpinning modern civilization, the mass man's rising expectations and anomie encouraged violent short cuts to satisfaction, causing instability and cultural decay. Ortega's ideas converged with those of other 'mass society' theorists such as K. MANNHEIM, FROMM and ARENDT.   JRT

J. Ferrater Mora, *Ortega y Gasset: an Outline of his Philosophy* (London, 1956).

Orton, Joe (b. Leicester, UK, 1.1.1933; d. London, 9.8.1967). British dramatist. Once described as 'the Oscar Wilde of Welfare State gentility', Orton was chiefly remarkable for his ability to combine brutally violent action with a mannered verbal polish. His 'bad taste' humour hit a public nerve and won him a large West End audience in the 1960s but his reflex attacks on accepted morality and established authority are too predictable to be really challenging: he became the licensed jester of the carriage trade. His first play to reach the stage was *Entertaining Mr Sloane* (1964) which shows a homosexual businessman and his nymphomaniac sister battling for possession of a young thug. The contrast between the elegantly formal style and the onstage depravity was initially arresting, but Orton's next play, *Loot* (1966), satirizing police corruption, repeated the same device. Obsessed by violence in his work, Orton was battered to death by his male companion Kenneth Halliwell, in their Islington flat in 1967. He left behind an unrevised work *What the Butler Saw* (1969) which, despite an initially

stormy reception, was his most mature play: a perfectly structured farce, set inside a psychiatric clinic, demonstrating the madness of the allegedly sane and the artificiality of conventional sexual normality. Orton's death robbed him of the chance to justify the many hyperbolic claims made on his behalf.   MB

J. Lahr, *Prick Up Your Ears* (London, 1978); C. Bigsby, *Joe Orton* (London, 1982).

Orwell, George, ps. of Eric Arthur Blair (b. Motihari, Bengal, India, 25.6.1903; d. London, UK, 21.1.1950). British novelist and political writer. Son of an official in the Indian civil service, Orwell after education at Eton joined the Burmese police. By 1927, his rejection of his class and profession was complete; returning to Europe he chose to live among the deprived, and completed his rebirth by adopting a new name. *Down and Out in Paris and London* (London, 1933) is remarkably undistorted by his personal compulsions and free from prejudice. His place as a spokesman for socialism who refused to simplify the truth as he saw it was established in *The Road to Wigan Pier* (London, 1937); but *Homage to Catalonia* (London, 1938) is certain to remain the most admired monument to his honesty: his account of the civil war in Spain is idealistic because it presents the Republican cause as necessary and right without disguising its contradictions and ultimate betrayal. The end of WW2 found him a socialist who had little faith in the realizability of socialism by any available political means. Anti-MARXist though he was, he could not dissociate socialism from revolution; nor could he dissociate revolution from tyranny.

Orwell had always written fiction, his first published novel being *Burmese Days* (NY, 1934). As he admitted, he was not really a novelist: 'One has masses of experience which one passionately wants to write about . . . and no way of using them except by disguising them as a novel.' Yet it is by two novels that he is publicly remembered. *Animal Farm* (London, 1945) was primarily an anti-STALINist satire; but its tragic implication that every revolutionary dream will be betrayed gives it the power to disturb readers for whom the evil of Stalinism is simple orthodoxy. Political despair is explicit in *1984* (London, 1949). The book's gloom is often referred to his illness and his growing conviction of the manipulability of the human mind. The book's despair comes not just from the fact that tyranny is universal and that the individual is doomed, but from 'the bottomless selfishness of the human being' (to quote Orwell) dramatized in the notorious 'Do it to Julia'. It is a sad irony that Britain's most admired socialist should have done more by this book to identify collectivism and tyranny in the public mind than any theorist of the right. The flexibility of Orwell's mind can best be seen in the essays and fugitive pieces gathered in *The Collected Essays, Journalism and Letters* (ed. S. Orwell & I. Angus, 4 vols, London, 1968). BF

R. Williams, *Orwell* (London, 1971); B. Crick, *George Orwell* (London, ²1982).

Osborne, John James (b. London, UK, 12.12.1929). British dramatist. His first unaided play *Look Back In Anger* (1956) is generally accepted as the historical starting-point of a new movement in English playwriting. Though traditional in form, it summed up the splenetic frustration of a postwar, bedsit generation who felt stifled by Establishment values. Since then Osborne has continued writing prolifically but, with time, has become less the spokesman for a generation and more an articulate voice in the wilderness attacking the declining quality of British life, trendy populist causes and the corruption of language. Although his theatrical influence has waned, he has created some classic dramatic heroes and written some energetic plays. The most notable are: *The Entertainer* (1957) which uses a decaying and seedy music-hall as a metaphor for post-Suez England; *Inadmissible Evidence* (1964) which charts, with devastating accuracy, the breakdown of a 'menopausal' solicitor; and *A Patriot for Me* (1965) which shows a homosexual officer coming to terms with his nature against the background of the Austro-Hungarian empire. Latterly, Osborne's plays have become poisoned

darts despatched from a private bunker; but he retains an authentic pain, a sharp-toothed irony and a talent for dissent. This impression is borne out by his autobiography covering the years 1929 to 1955 *A Better Class of Person* (London, 1981). MB

S. Trussler, *The Plays of John Osborne* (London, 1969); R. Hayman, *John Osborne* (London, ²1973).

Ostwald, Wilhelm (b. Riga, Russia, 2.9.1883; d. Leipzig, Saxony, Germany [now East Germany], 3.4.1932). German chemist. With van't HOFF and ARRHENIUS he established physical chemistry as an independent intellectual discipline and built up a school at Leipzig University in which were trained many internationally known chemists. In his own research Ostwald developed new methods for measuring the rates of chemical reactions and produced fresh ideas on chemical affinity. He rediscovered catalysis, pointing out that its essence lay 'not in the origination of a reaction but in its acceleration'. In particular he initiated studies of acid catalysis, demonstrating that the catalytic efficiency of an acid was a measure of its strength which, in turn, was determined by its degree of dissociation into hydrogen ions. This was in accord with Arrhenius's new theory of electrolytic dissociation, a theory whose acceptance Ostwald did much to promote. Perhaps his greatest strength lay in his promoting acceptance of such new ideas. To this end he wrote a number of books and founded two scientific journals *Zeitschrift für Physiologische Chemie* (1887), which he edited, and *Annalen der Naturphilosophie* (1902). He was awarded the Nobel prize for chemistry in 1909. In his later years he wrote on philosophy and studied colour theory. GL

E. Farber, *Nobel Prizewinners in Chemistry* (London, 1953).

Otto, Rudolf (b. Peine, Hanover, Germany, 25.9.1869; d. Marburg, Hesse, 6.3.1937). German theologian and pioneer in phenomenology of religion. He taught at Göttingen from 1897, was official professor at Breslau from 1914, and at Marburg from 1917, where he became emeritus professor in 1929. Early influenced by Luther and Schleiermacher, and during his travels from student days impressed by expressions of living religions, he could not reconcile theological ideas with religious experience until he had thoroughly worked through the philosophy of Kant and Fries. The result is his central work *Das Heilige* (Breslau, 1917; tr. J. W. Harvey, *The Idea of the Holy*, London, 1923) in which he established the religious *a priori* in human experience. Developed religions have woven together the rational and the nonrational. Thus the holy includes the good and the beautiful, but its essential moment is the awesome mystery found in all religions from primal to ethical: this Otto named 'the Numinous'. Beyond conception, wholly other, it can only be discussed obliquely by inspection of man's experience or *sensus numinis*. In his wide travels, in Greece, Russia, North Africa, the Near and Far East, he was moved by the depth of religious expression in liturgy, music and art. Later work built on *Das Heilige* and included studies in Hinduism, ethics and plans for an Inter-religious League. But he was not a syncretist, and saw Christianity as religion in its highest form.   RPMi

R. F. Davidson, *Rudolf Otto's Interpretation of Religion* (Princeton, 1947); J. Wach, *Types of Religious Experience* (Chicago, 1951).

Oud, Jacobus Johannes Pieter (b. Purmerend, N. Holland, The Netherlands, 9.2.1890; d. Wassenaar, S. Holland, 5.4.1963). Dutch architect. Oud, together with DOESBURG and MONDRIAN, was a founder member of the *De Stijl* group in 1917. In 1918 he was appointed municipal architect, Rotterdam, where he did much to promote the efforts of CIAM (Congrès Internationaux d'Architecture Moderne) in tackling the enormous problem of rehousing society in postwar Europe. His schemes for Spangen, Rotterdam (1918–19), Hook of Holland (1924–7), the residential district 'De Kiefhoek', Rotterdam (1925–9), and the project for housing 'Blijdorp', Rotterdam (1931), advanced the ideas of modern architects about the mass production of low-cost, working-class housing. Basing his style on *De Stijl* precepts, which can be seen in the early project for a factory at Purmerend (1919), Oud produced a pared-down architecture devoid of ornament which was eloquent in its simplicity. There were, however, many problems in translating the theoretical ideas of *De Stijl* into practical building terms, and following disagreements with Doesburg, Oud resigned from the group in 1921. Oud played a prominent part in the development of modern architecture from the emergence of the 'new objectivity' in the 1920s to the establishment of the 'international style' in the 1930s. A milestone along that route was the 1927 Weissenhof settlement, Stuttgart, planned by MIES VAN DER ROHE with contributions from most progressive European architects including a row of houses by Oud. Oud resigned from his official position in Rotterdam in 1933 and, though he continued as an architect in independent practice, produced no further work of international significance.   PAC

K. Wiekart, *J. J. P. Oud* (Amsterdam, 1965).

Ouspensky, Peter Demianovitch (b. Moscow, Russia, 5.3.1878; d. Virginia Water, Surrey, UK, 2.10.1947). Russian occult philosopher. Born into an intellectual and artistic Moscow family, Ouspensky was obviously stimulated by his father's mathematical interests (Ouspensky's first book was a work of mathematical philosophy *Chetvertoe Izmierenie* [The fourth dimension], St Petersburg, 1909). Expelled from school, his self-education followed his enthusiasms – NIETZSCHE, biology, mathematics and psychology (especially dreams). Not until 1907 did he encounter Theosophy, and that plunged him into researches in an endeavour to justify the existence of a universe beyond the material world through linking mathematical theory with esotericism. In 1908 his studies took him to the Middle East and then, between 1909 and 1911, into mystical experiments devoted to exploring the possibility of an objective magic apart from the experience of subjective mysticism. In 1911–12 he wrote his major book *Klyuch kzaradkam* (St Petersburg, 1912, ²1916; tr. N. Bessaraboff & C.

Bragdon, *Tertium Organum*, NY, 1920, [2]1923) and the studies subsequently collected in *A New Model of the Universe* (tr. R. R. Merston, NY, 1931, [2]1934). His argument was that habitual patterns of thought, especially those created by materialistic science, had impaired thought itself, and that the essential requirement was for the individual to evolve psychologically into a new state of higher consciousness. Ouspensky's successful lecturing brought him to the attention of GURDJIEFF (see *In Search of the Miraculous*, NY, 1949), and from 1915 to 1924 he served as the Master's apostle, propounding his ideas and methods. In 1921 he settled in England and especially after his break with Gurdjieff and the appearance of *Tertium Organum* in English translation his influence rapidly spread through his lectures, classes, publications and the establishment of groups of individuals who were involved in 'the Work', as it was generally called. Although Ouspensky spent WW2 in the USA, he returned to die among his English followers.   RBW

J. Webb, *The Harmonious Circle* (London, 1980).

Owen, Wilfred Edward Salter (b. Oswestry, Salop, UK, 18.3.1893; d. Sambre Canal, Somme, France, 4.11.1918). British poet. Owen's poetic themes and achievement are almost wholly circumscribed by his response to his experiences in WW1 as an officer on the western front. In his youth he was strongly attracted by his mother's religion but, discovering he had no vocation for the church, pursued instead a romantic notion of the poet's calling. In due course natural and religious symbolism played an important role in his interpretation of war. Owen enlisted in 1915, saw heavy fighting early in 1917 and later in the same year was sent to Craiglockhart War Hospital suffering from neurasthenia. There he met Siegfried Sassoon, who did much to confirm Owen's sense of poetic purpose and was chiefly responsible for the posthumous publication of his *Poems* (London, 1920; critical edition, *The Collected Poems of Wilfred Owen*, ed. C. Day Lewis, London, 1963). In the year before his return to France, Owen wrote a series of poems which express directly his loathing of the war, his sense of the comradeship and suffering of the common soldier, and his contempt for a civilian population infected with spurious patriotism and ignorant of conditions at the front. He saw his poetic task as one of warning and truthful witness, in which the essential emotion to be expressed was pity. His poetry is disciplined by careful attention to self-effacing sound patterns, through which it is able to contain a powerfully stated reaction to the horrors of war in which natural bonds are destroyed and soldiers become both Christ-like martyrs and guilt-ridden victims whose agony is the revelation of life's tragic basis. Awarded the Military Cross, Owen was killed a week before the Armistice.   ATKC

H. Owen, *Journey from Obscurity: Wilfred Owen 1893–1918* (3 vols, London, 1963–5); J. Stallworthy, *Wilfred Owen: a Biography* (Oxford, 1974).

Ozenfant, Amédée (b. Saint-Quentin, Aisne, France, 15.4.1886; d. Cannes, Alpes-Maritimes, 4.5.1966). French painter who with LE CORBUSIER formulated the principles of purism. He began to exhibit in Paris in 1908 and was interested in cubism, but he rejected what he saw as cubism's degeneracy towards decorative abstraction and expressed this view in *L'Elan* which he edited from 1915 to 1917. In 1918 he collaborated with Le Corbusier (then known as Charles-Edouard Jeanneret) on a manifesto *Après le cubisme* [After cubism] (Paris) and from 1920 to 1925 they published the review *L'Esprit nouveau*. They asserted the classical principles of order inherent in man, nature and the 20c machine; this they expressed in paintings organized according to the laws of harmonious proportion. A summary of their views was published as *La Peinture moderne* [Modern painting] (Paris, 1925). In 1928 Ozenfant published his best-known book *Bilan des arts modernes et structure d'un nouveau esprit* (Paris, 1928; *Foundations of Modern Art*, London, 1931). In the same year he finished a large mural *The Four Races* at the Musée National d'Art Moderne, Paris. In 1938 he moved to the USA where he founded the Ozenfant School of Fine Arts in New York. He returned to France in 1955.

MOJN

J. Golding, *Ozenfant* (NY, 1973); S. L. Ball, *Ozenfant and Purism: the Evolution of a Style, 1915–1930* (NY, 1982).

Ozu, Yasujiro (b. Tokyo, Japan, 15.12.1903; d. Tokyo, 12.12.1963). Japanese film director who established a worldwide reputation by concentrating on a typically Japanese milieu: lower-middle-class family life and the relations between generations. His skill at universalizing this theme was apparent from his earliest work in the 1920s and 1930s – small-scale comedies and dramas which combined indigenous Japanese formal qualities with influences from his favourite American cinema of the time. He continued making silent films until the mid-1930s; then, with his first sound film *Hitori Musuko* (*The Only Son*, 1936), he fully established the genre which was to make him famous. Ozu's style was spare and undemonstrative – very little camera movement, many close-ups and a fondness for looking at characters from a low camera position on the floor – yet, in collaboration with his regular scriptwriter Kogo Noga, he created dramas, tinged with a dry humour, whose density and interplay of character development are equal to those of the greatest novelists. The film which established his reputation in the West was *Tokyo Monogatari* (*Tokyo Story*, 1953), one of his most complex and moving studies of how children, when grown up, move away from and reject their parents. Although adopting a somewhat conservative view of family life, Ozu often took the side of the younger, modern generation as in *Ochazuke no Aji* (*The Flavour of Green Tea over Rice*, 1952), and directed satirical barbs at the modern company man in *Samma no Aji* (*An Autumn Afternoon*, 1962). He returned to all these themes throughout his career, but he will probably be best remembered for those elegiac studies of parting, where a son or daughter is married off, leaving a parent to face the future alone, as in the beautiful *Banshun* (*Late Spring*, 1949). JPG

D. Richie, *Ozu* (Berkeley, Calif., 1974); J. Gillett & D. Wilson, *Yasujiro Ozu* (London, 1976).

P

Paasikivi, Juho Kusti (b. Tampere, Finland, 27.11.1870; d. Helsinki, 14.12.1956). Finnish statesman. A conservative in politics, a businessman and banker by profession, Paasikivi's guiding principle was the impossibility of a small nation like the Finns hoping to survive in isolation from the power politics of the great powers. In 1938–9 he advocated territorial concessions to Russian demands and, when unsuccessful, worked to end the subsequent Winter War between Finland and the USSR. When a German victory in Europe seemed inevitable (1940–1), he favoured a German alliance; but when it became clear that the Finns had chosen the losing side, he supported a separate peace with Russia. As president in the crucial postwar decade, he convinced the Finns that only by carrying out the Soviet peace terms conscientiously and recognizing the Russians' need to safeguard their security – and particularly that of Leningrad – against a hostile attack through Finnish territory, would it be possible to persuade the Russians in return to leave the Finns free to retain their own distinctive way of life in a western parliamentary democracy, and neither impose communism (as in Eastern Europe) nor absorb them (as they had absorbed the Baltic states). Even more impressive was his success in persuading the Russians to accept Finnish independence on a basis of neutrality which has survived his own death and nearly 40 years of tension between the Soviet Union and the West. ALCB

Pallottino, Massimo (b. Rome, Italy, 9.11.1909). Italian archaeologist. Pallottino joined the Italian Antiquities Service in 1933, and was appointed in 1946 to the new and then unique chair of Etruscology and Italic antiquities at Rome University. There he directed scholarly attention away from traditional funerary concerns to wider issues, notably through his institute's excavation at the Etruscan sanctuary of Pyrgi. *Tarquinia* (Rome, 1937) revealed an outstanding capacity for innovation in the exegesis of archaeological data: the chronological framework he established survives to a degree unique in European archaeology. Pallottino's talent for original synthesis is best seen in his *Etruscologia* (Milan, 1942, ⁶1973; *The Etruscans*, Harmondsworth, 1978). Although his name is universally linked with the archaeology, art, history and language of the Etruscans, Pallottino consistently stressed the broader claims of Italic civilization as a whole, viewed in its Mediterranean setting: the range of his interests and influence emerges afresh from his collected *Saggi di Antichità* [Essays on antiquity] (Rome, 1979). Not least through his membership – frequently presidential and always forceful – of national and supranational committees, Pallottino largely determined the nature of research on pre-Roman Italy until his retirement in 1980. DRid

Pankhurst, Emmeline, *née* Goulden (b. Manchester, UK, 4.7.1858; d. London, 14.6.1928). British pioneer of women's suffrage, leader of the most extreme wing of the movement. She married Richard Pankhurst, a successful London barrister and advocate of women's rights, and was widowed in 1898. With her husband she had founded the Women's Franchise League in 1889; in 1903 her more militant daughter Christabel persuaded her to form the extreme Women's Social and Political Union. Widely recognized as one of the most effective public speakers for the cause, she turned in disillusionment with the Liberals after their 'landslide' electoral victory in 1906 to 'direct action', breaking shop windows, committing arson, breaking up public meetings, chaining herself to railings in public places. Frequently arrested, she went on hunger strike, leading the government of the day by the so-called 'Cat and Mouse' Act to take powers both to force-feed her and to release her and her imitators when the strike showed signs of being effective. After the outbreak of WW1 she played a major part in propaganda devoted to bringing women into war industry and into uniform. The enfranchisement of women in 1918 was her reward; thereafter she emigrated to Canada, returning to Britain to stand as a Conservative party candidate for Whitechapel shortly before her death.   DCW

Pannenberg, Wolfhart (b. Stettin, Germany [now Szczecin, Poland], 2.10.1928). German Lutheran theologian, professor of systematic theology, University of Munich, since 1968. Pannenberg has reacted against his early BARTHian formation in order to substantiate Jewish–Christian assertions about God. *Wissenschaftstheorie und Theologie* (Frankfurt, 1973; tr. F. McDonagh, *Theology and the Philosophy of Science*, London, 1976) locates theology in the matrix of academic sciences as 'the science of God' which offers knowledge about 'the one who determines the whole of reality'. Reality is essentially historical and encompasses the as yet undetermined future, and Pannenberg has been influenced, though not uncritically, by Hegel, especially in his use of 'universal history'. God can be fully known only at the end of history, and we can only know him at all if he chooses to reveal himself in some way. This corresponds with the Old Testament which portrays a God who is revealed and understood by men in historical actions. These events are continually reinterpreted by each generation in an historical tradition which understands the present in terms of its past, pre-eminently in the significance of Jesus of Nazareth for Christian tradition (*Offenbarung als Geschichte*, Gütersloh, 1964; tr. D. Granskou & E. Quinn, *Revelation as History*, London, 1969). The historicity of Jesus' resurrection is crucial, for here Jewish expectations of the end of history as God's judgement, the establishing of justice, and resurrection of the dead are confirmed. Jesus' fate acts as an anticipation (*prolepsis*) of our future (*Grundzüge der Christologie*, Gütersloh, 1964; tr. L. L. Wilkins & D. A. Priebe, *Jesus, God and Man*, London, 1968).

In an as yet fragmentary way, Pannenberg has tried to construct an all-encompassing, primarily historical and eschatological model for doing theology. His more important articles are to be found in *Grundfragen Systematischer Theologie* (Göttingen, 1967; tr. G. H. Kehm, *Basic Questions in Theology*, 2 vols, London, 1970–1).   GT

J. M. Robinson & J. B. Cobb (eds), *Theology as History* (NY, 1967); E. F. Tupper, *The Theology of Wolfhart Pannenberg* (London, 1974).

Panofsky, Erwin (b. Hanover, Lower Saxony, Germany, 30.3.1892; naturalized American citizen; d. Princeton, NJ, USA, 14.3.1968). German/American art historian. Panofsky taught at Hamburg University (1920–33), and moved in the circle of A. WARBURG and CASSIRER. After the Nazis came to power he left Germany and taught at Princeton till his death. Panofsky stood squarely in the German tradition of *Geistesgeschichte*. His *Idea* (Leipzig & Berlin, 1924; Columbia, SC, 1968) was a study of Platonic influences on art theory. His *Studies in Iconology* (NY, 1939) drew the famous distinction between the study of the conventional subject-matter of works of art ('iconography') and the study of their intrinsic meanings ('iconology'). His own iconographical studies of Correggio's *Camera di S. Paolo*, Dürer's *Melencolia*, and so on, are virtuoso performances, even if his interpretations have not always stood the test of time. As for iconology, his essay on the affinities between *Gothic Architecture and Scholasticism* (NY, 1957) is dazzling rather than convincing. Panofsky's most solid contributions to art history were concerned with Northern Europe and Italy in the 15c and 16c: *Albrecht Dürer* (Princeton, 1943); *Early Netherlandish Painting* (Cambridge, Mass., 1953); and *Renaissance and Renascences in Western Art* (Stockholm, 1960). A vivid impression of Panofsky's brilliance and learning is given by the collection of essays *Meaning in the Visual Arts* (NY, 1955).

UPB

J. Bialostocki, 'Erwin Panofsky', *Simiolus*, 4 (1970), 68–89.

Papini, Giovanni (b. Florence, Tuscany, Italy, 9.1.1881; d. Florence, 7.7.1956). Italian writer and essayist. A prolific and polemic writer, Papini joined the futurist movement, edited two influential literary periodicals *Leonardo* and *Lacerba*, and sympathized with the fascist regime. Author of an intellectual autobiography *Un uomo finito* (Florence, 1912; tr. M. P. Agnetti, *A Man – Finished*, London, 1924); in his best-known and much translated books (*Storia di Cristo*, Florence, 1921; tr. M. P. Agnetti, *The Story of Christ*, London, 1923; *Dante vivo*, Florence, 1933; tr. E. H. Broadus & A. Benedetti, London, 1934; and *Vita di Michelangelo nella vita del suo tempo* [The life of Michelangelo in the life of his time], Milan, 1949), Papini brings out the living relevance and validity of his historical characters from a modern layman's point of view. He is also the author of a book of poems *Pane e vino* [Bread and wine] (Florence, 1926) and a collection of drastically critical reviews entitled *Le stroncature* (Florence, 1916; tr. E. H. Wilkin, *Four and Twenty Minds*, NY, 1922) which are for the most part in an anti-CROCEan vein.   GS

Páral, Vladimír (b. Prague, Czechoslovakia, 10.8.1932). Czech novelist, who worked as an industrial chemist in Ústí nad Labem where most of his novels are situated; most of his characters are employees of one particular chemicals plant. He is a prophet of doom and hope, a sarcastic critic of socialist consumerism and a defender of the individual vitalism which can survive under socialism; he is both moralist and joker, both dreamer and vulgarian. Because he avoids political involvement he is the one Czech 1960s experimental writer still publishing in the 1980s. He was among the first signatories of the party manifesto against Charter 77 (28.1.1977). In his first three novels (1964–7), by mathematical use of collage, action duplication and parallelism, he demonstrates empty eroticism and man's alienation from work in Czech consumer society. His two most sophisticated works are *Milenci & vrazi* [Lovers and killers] (Prague, 1969) and *Generální zázrak* [General miracle] (Ústí, 1977). In the first the animal in mankind, i.e. sex and violence, rules, albeit dressed in a motive labelled ambition; everyone is an enemy except when he appears useful to one's ambition; the novel's ideology is based on Vico's barbarianism-civilization cycle. The second is a depressive work depicting a degenerate Czech society. The miracle of the novel's title is true love, but consumer fetishism, even mere money-mindedness, prevents that miracle. Logos and Eros combine to produce further imprisonment rather than liberation. Páral is the MARCUSE of Czech fiction.   RBP

W. E. Harkins & P. I. Trensky, *Czech Literature since 1956* (NY, 1980).

Pareto, Vilfredo (b. Paris, France, 15.7.1848; d. Geneva, Switzerland, 20.8.1923). Italian sociologist, economist (as professor at Lausanne) and engineer (for 20 years of his life). Pareto extended WALRAS's theory of general economic equilibrium and sought to generalize it to the entire range of social phenomena. Pareto took Walras's scheme as his starting-point, but, arguing that economics was only one type of action – namely logical (or rational) action – sought to write, in a *Trattato di sociologia generale* (Rome, 1916; *The Mind and Society: Treatise on General Sociology*, 4 vols, ed. A. Livingstone, London, 1935), a comprehensive scheme to embrace nonlogical actions as well. The heart of Pareto's sociology is a distinction between 'residues' and 'derivations'. Residues are the fundamental sentiments, or expressions of sentiments, ingrained in human nature. Derivations are the intellectual systems of justifications (akin to ideologies) by which people give an appearance of rationality to their beliefs. Pareto set up six classes of residues (e.g. class I: the instinct of combinations; class II: the persistence of aggregates) and four kinds of derivations (e.g. appeal to authority), and set up a conceptual scheme to cross-tabulate the residues and derivations against two types of nonlogical theories: pseudoscientific theories (i.e. those that deviate from logical actions) and 'theories which surpass experience', i.e. reflect ultimate meanings.

The intention of these cross-classifications was to create (as in analytical mechanics) an exhaustive range of types of social actions. The search for equilibria consisted of the empirical verification of the relative proportions of the classes of residues in the different social groups in the population. In exploring the first two classes of residues, Pareto argued that society was always composed of elites and mass, and that the surge to power of new social groups, such as the socialist-led working class, was only a set of 'derivations' that masked a circulation of elites. Few sociologists today accept the elaborate underpinning of Pareto's sociological theories, though the emphasis on elites and the circulation of elites has had a recurrent interest in sociology, alternating with class theories of power. A selection *V. F. D. Pareto: Sociological Writings* was published in London in 1966.   DBe

Pareto's contributions to economics, on the other hand, have come to be recognized in the past half-century as immensely important. In his *Manuale di economia politica* (Rome, 1906; enlarged and improved in the French version, *Manuel d'économie politique*, Paris, 1909; ed. A. S. Schwier & A. N. Page, *Course of Political Economy*, London, 1972) he rejected the treatment of utility as a cardinally measurable quantity whose social maximization involved in principle the comparison of one person's happiness with another's; instead, he treated it as an ordinal concept (i.e. one implying only a ranking by each individual of alternatives available to him) and defined a corresponding social optimum as a condition of society from which it is impossible to make any one individual subjectively better off without simultaneously making at least one other individual worse off. This idea of a 'Pareto optimum' – of which the economic system can in principle generate an infinite number, each with its own distribution of welfare among the individual members – is the fundamental concept of modern welfare economics. Pareto's work led (with subsequent contributions from Barone, PIGOU, Lerner, SAMUELSON and others) to the finding that the conditions for such an optimum will be satisfied by a Walrasian general equilibrium where each consumer is maximizing utility and each producer maximizing profits, all in conditions of perfect competition (i.e. with no single consumer or producer able on his own to influence any market price).

Pareto also made significant contributions to the empirical study of income distribution, enunciating what came to be known as Pareto's Law or the Pareto distribution of incomes. This purported to describe the pattern of inequality of incomes which any society will tend to generate, regardless of its economic system.   PMO

R. Cirillo, *The Economics of Vilfredo Pareto* (London, 1979).

Parker, Charles Christopher (Charlie) (b. Kansas City, Kan., USA, 29.8.1920; d. New York, 12.3.1955). Jazz saxophonist and composer. The alto-saxophonist who was the central figure in the 'modern jazz' or 'bop' movement of the 1940s, and whose influence on jazz improvisation was second only to that of ARMSTRONG. Parker was probably the least eclectic of all jazz musicians, and his entry into the jazz world startled both lay listeners and professional musicians. His innovative use of discordant notes and unexpected rhythms in his improvisations led many to suspect that his methods were haphazard. However, Parker had a natural musical ability which he augmented during his formative years in Kansas City by learning a great deal about harmonic progressions. At first he suffered much verbal abuse at local jam sessions but developed his own style. In New York during the mid-1940s he made a series of small band recordings with fellow musical revolutionary John 'Dizzy' Gillespie; in their solos both used harmonic substitution, whereby chromatic chords replaced those originally specified by the composer. These substitutions created an unexpected sound for the listener, and gave the improviser a wider selection of notes to choose from than hitherto. Trumpeter Miles Davis became one of the thousands of musicians who regarded themselves as disciples of Parker's method. Gradually, aspects of Parker's phrasing and harmonic approach seeped into the commercial big bands, and into the works of popular composers. Even though Parker's personal life was wracked with problems, many of them directly attrib-

579

utable to his long addiction to heroin, his near-faultless technique and fertile imagination were constants in his musical performances.   JJC

I. Gitler, *Jazz Masters of the 1940s* (NY, 1966); R. Russell, *Bird Lives* (London, 1973).

Parsons, Talcott (b. Colorado Springs, Colo, USA, 13.12.1902; d. Munich, Bavaria, West Germany, 8.5.1979). American sociologist. In the quarter of the century after WW2, Talcott Parsons was the dominant figure in sociology, mainly because of his extraordinary effort to create a 'general theory' of social action that would encompass, as a logical system, all the dimensions of human behaviour from individual motivations to macrosocial processes in one grand, conceptual scheme. While such efforts were fairly common in 19c and early 20c social science (e.g. those of August Comte, Herbert Spencer, Lester F. Ward, PARETO and, to a lesser extent, DURKHEIM and Max WEBER), few claimed the range and breadth of Parsons's effort, combining as it did personality theory, general equilibrium theory of economics, cybernetics and anthropological functionalism. Whether this large theoretical synthesis will prove to be a generative source of continuing social inquiry or only a large, sterile morphology of ideal-type concepts built on ideal-type concepts, will remain one of the intriguing questions for social theory for some years to come. Parsons's first major work *The Structure of Social Action* (NY, 1937, ²1968) sought to show how such diverse theorists as A. MARSHALL, Pareto, Durkheim and Weber, could be reinterpreted within a common framework that denied utilitarianism and positivism and stressed the 'voluntaristic' basis of social actions. His next set of works (principally *The Social System*, Glencoe, Ill., 1951) advanced what is called the 'structure-functionalist' approach, in which societies, like a biological organism (though Parsons would repudiate a mechanistic analogy) sought to maintain themselves in a 'homeostatic' way and wherein any element of the system could only be understood (as in the anthropological functionalism of MALINOWSKI) in relation to the whole. Finally, in a further series of works, Parsons sought to establish his 'action theory' whereby all social behaviour could be understood within the framework of the conceptual network he set forth.

Parsons's ambitions can best be understood, perhaps, as an effort to solve the dilemma of the 'fathers' of sociology, Durkheim and Weber. Sociology as a discipline had evolved within an evolutionary or historical framework in which it was assumed (as by MARX) that each epoch was historically distinct, subject to its own 'laws', or (as by Spencer) that there was an evolutionary tendency towards some higher integration. As against this historicism, the 'fathers' of sociology had sought to establish analytical types of social relations (such as TÖNNIES's distinction between *Gemeinschaft* and *Gesellschaft*, or Weber's distinction between traditional and rational behaviour) which would be useful in any social system. Parsons carried this effort further, in a complex and exhaustive way, to establish *logical* types of social relations that could be applied to all social relations, from pair and family groups to large-scale societies. Such an effort risked many intellectual pitfalls. One was the obvious question whether any scheme, no matter how exhaustive, could logically embrace all behaviour without itself becoming so abstract as to make it difficult to find one's way back to the empirical terrain. Another was the tension between an 'intentional' mode of explanation, explicit in his first major work, and the 'functional' explanations of his later work. Parsons sought to eschew that difficulty by stressing the role of values and culture as the 'ends' which integrated all other aspects of behaviour. It was that emphasis on integration that led to the political attack on Parsons, in the 1970s, as 'conservative', and as minimizing the importance of social change. Parsons, in his later work, did seek to include an evolutionary pattern of societal development in his scheme, but that, too, was at an abstract level. Parsons was a voluminous writer, constantly adapting and redefining his system, so that no single work can serve as an adequate introduction.

DBe

F. Bourricaud, *L'Individualisme Institutionnel: Essai sur la sociologie de Talcott Parsons* (Paris, 1977).

Pashukanis, Evgeny Bronislavovich (b. Lithuania, Russia [now Lithuania, USSR], 10.2.1891; d. Moscow, USSR, 2.1937). Russian jurist. During his tenure of a number of judicial and academic offices in Moscow from the early 1920s until 1936 Pashukanis came to exert a powerful influence on Soviet thinking about law. His principal thesis, developed in his *Obshchaia teoriia prava i marksizm: Opyt kritiki osnovnykh iuridicheskikh poniatii* (Moscow, 1924; 'The General Theory of Law and Marxism' in P. Beirne & R. Sharlet, eds, *Pashukanis: Selected Writings on Law and Marxism*, London, 1980) and known as the commodity exchange theory of law, was that law is a social institution peculiar to societies which practise commodity exchange; the corollary of this was that law would cease to exist in a fully socialized economy. It was the claim that law had no place under socialism which brought him into conflict with STALIN, contradicting as it did Stalin's increasing use of legal structures, notably in the New Constitution of 1936. Although he began to realign his theory with Stalin's practice in some later writings, he was denounced and disappeared in 1937. The suppression of his work which followed extinguished his influence in the USSR, although there is some evidence of a partial rehabilitation. Since his death, it is the West where his influence has blossomed, where he has become the most influential Soviet jurist among both MARXist and non-Marxist legal theorists. JAW

E. Kamenka & A. Tay, 'Life and afterlife of a Bolshevik jurist', in *Problems of Communism*, 19, no. 1 (1970).

Pasolini, Pier Paolo (b. Bologna, Emilia-Romagna, Italy, 5.3.1922; d. Ostia, Rome, 2.11.1975). Italian film director. Pasolini was a complex and eclectic artist – poet, novelist, dramatist, critic and theoretician as well as film maker – but it is in the latter role that he made his greatest impact. His film work is complex and ambiguous, making great use of pastiche, metaphor and collage techniques to create a personal style out of elements drawn from reality. Pasolini began his film-making career in the 1960s with *Accatone* (1961) and *Mamma Roma* (1962), two superficially realistic films of Roman proletarian life beneath the surface of which lay a mass of filmic and cultural allusions. The stylistic heterogeneity of Pasolini's work is even more apparent in '*Il Vangelo secundo Matteo*' (*The Gospel According to St Matthew*, 1964) as he strips his subject of its conventional associations of piety and reverence. The conventionalized style applied to this biblical adaptation is given even more striking expression in his versions of two Greek legends, with their eclectically selected elements of landscape and costume, combined with musical and painterly quotations. In the early 1970s he produced his 'trilogy of life' – based on the medieval stories of *The Decameron* (*Il Decamerona*, 1971), *The Canterbury Tales* (*I Racconti di Canterbury*, 1972) and *The Arabian Nights* (1974) – in which his taste for exuberant expression of nudity and sexuality found full scope, before plunging into the bleak world of Sadean ritual humiliation with his last film *Salò* (1975). The murder of Pasolini in 1975 deprived the cinema of one of its most strikingly original and articulate artists.

RPA

O. Stack, *Pasolini on Pasolini* (London, 1969); P. Willemen (ed.), *Pier Paolo Pasolini* (London, 1977).

Pasternak, Boris Leonidovich (b. Moscow, Russia, 10.2.1890; d. Peredelkino, nr Moscow, USSR, 30.5.1960). Russian poet and novelist. Brought up in a cultivated, artistic and intellectual atmosphere (his father was a well-known painter and a friend of Leo TOLSTOY, his mother a pianist), in his poetry Pasternak absorbed visual art and music. He studied music, then philosophy at Moscow (1909–13) and Marburg (1912). In 1911 he joined the futurist group 'Centrifuge'. After the publication of his first volumes of verse *Bliznets v tuchakh* [Twin in clouds] (Moscow, 1914) and *Poverkh bar'erov* [Above the barriers]

(Moscow, 1917) Pasternak's readers were said to include only those 'who could see the grass growing and the blood flowing'. After the publication of *Sestra moia zhizn'* [My sister life] (Moscow, 1917–22) and *Temy i variatsii* [Themes and variations] (Moscow, 1923) 'the complete and total miracle of a poet' revealed itself. He became the poets' poet. In 1925 his book of short stories appeared. Long poems written between 1924 and 1931 ('*Vysokaya bolezn'* [The high malady], '*Devyat'sot pyatyigod*' [Nineteen five], *Lieutenant Shmidt*) reflect the revolution and Soviet reality. Big political events, however, bewildered rather than nourished his imagination. A second book of prose *Okhrannaya gramota* (Leningrad, 1931; tr. A. Brown & L. Pasternak-Slater, *Safe Conduct*, London, 1959) was followed by a new collection of verse *Vtoroe rozhdenie* [The second birth] (Moscow, 1932). He devoted some years to translating English (notably Shakespeare), German and French as well as Armenian and Georgian poets. His own poetry was, at times, criticized for its 'formalism' and 'privacy'. He kept his independence while enjoying some immunity under STALIN, but became the object of acute controversy under KRUSHCHEV in connection with the publication in the West (in Italian, Milan, 1957, and Russian, Ann Arbor, 1958) of his novel *Doctor Zhivago* (written 1945–56; tr. M. Hayward & M. Harari, London, 1958), since it was banned in the USSR. In 1958 he was awarded the Nobel prize which he renounced because of pressure from the Soviet authorities. The novel has been described as a work of genius by some but others consider it far inferior to his poetry which exercised the greatest influence on Russian poets. He developed a syntax of great vigour and complexity. His diffuse rhymes and paradoxical metaphors served his belief that all things are interrelated. His sound associations, apart from their musical effect, give the feeling of 'nature manifesting itself through the defenceless, dreamlike, mediumistic being of the poet'. Even his novel is also about how and why poetry is written. He achieved a synthesis between simplicity and complexity in the poems attributed to Jury Zhivago:

affirmative about the revolution, Dr Zhivago is haunted with regret in the assessment of the damage done to human values and relationships. The novel is episodic with little compelling development, but a truly poetic work. The collected works are *Sochineniya* (3 vols, Michigan, 1961). Translations include: *Fifty Poems* (tr. M. Pasternak-Slater, London, 1963).   VP

D. Davie & A. Livingstone (eds), *Pasternak: Modern Judgments* (London, 1969); H. Gifford, *Pasternak* (London, 1977).

Pathé, Charles (b. Paris, France, 25.12.1863; d. Monte Carlo, Monaco, 26.12.1957). French film pioneer. Charles Pathé was the first man in the 1900s to see the full commercial potential of the cinema. An initiator of the leasing (rather than outright sale) of films, he turned film making from a personal craft into a world industry. Using his enormous commercial talents, Pathé built up a gigantic company which made Paris the centre of world film production and distribution for over a decade. At the height of his power around 1908 he dominated the world cinema to an extent never subsequently equalled, controlling every aspect from the manufacture of stock and equipment, through production to the distribution and exhibition of films worldwide. But already before 1914 his pre-eminence was challenged by American producers, and the outbreak of WW1 led to the dismemberment of the Pathé company for the benefit of shareholders.   RPA

Paul VI, *né* Giovanni Battista Montini (b. Concesio, Brescia, Italy, 26.9.1897; d. Castelgandolfo, Latium, 6.8.1978). Italian pope. The son of a Catholic journalist, he was briefly a Vatican diplomat in Poland, then became a university chaplain in Rome until 1933 when the Fascists insisted on his removal. He then worked in the Vatican, becoming in 1937 under-secretary of state to Cardinal Pacelli, the future PIUS XII. He was a close aide of Pacelli throughout WW2, subsequently defended his attitude to the Jews, and yet was exiled to Milan in 1954. For mysterious reasons, he was made archbishop but not a cardinal.

JOHN XXIII made him a cardinal as soon as he decently could, and at the conclave of 1963 he succeeded John. He inherited the difficult task of steering Vatican II to an harmonious conclusion. His aim – to secure the maximum of unanimity – was greatly put under strain in the postconciliar period when the left accused him of reserving to himself questions such as birth control and clerical celibacy, while the right charged him with wrecking the liturgy, being too keen on ecumenism, and conniving with communists. He will be remembered above all for two encyclicals: *Populorum Progressio* (1967) which recognized the importance of the Third World and prophetically announced that North/South differences would prove more important than East/West differences; and *Humanae Vitae* (1968) which 'banned artificial contraception' and brought him much obloquy as an obscurantist celibate. Paul VI was a man of great warmth and human sympathies, well read and alert rather than original, who failed to put himself across on great public occasions. With old age, his voice sounded increasingly querulous. He wondered whether he should resign. He decided against: such a decision might bind future popes, and, anyway, one cannot resign from 'universal paternity'.

PAH

J. Guitton, *The Pope Speaks* (London, 1968); P. Hebblethwaite, *The Year of Three Popes* (London, 1978).

Pauli, Wolfgang Ernst (b. Vienna, Austria-Hungary [now Austria], 25.4.1900; naturalized American citizen, 1946; d. Zürich, Switzerland, 15.12.1958). Austrian/American physicist. Pauli studied in Germany under the great innovators of quantum mechanics SOMMERFELD (Munich), BORN (Göttingen) and N. BOHR (Copenhagen), but most of his professional career was spent at the Federal Institute of Technology in Zürich where he was professor of theoretical physics. His unusual brilliance was noted even while he was still a young student when he was asked to contribute the article (over 200 pages in length) on relativity for the *Encyclopaedia of Mathematical Science* (1921). This is still accepted as a masterly treatment of the subject (*Theory of Relativity*, Oxford, 1958). His name is indelibly linked with the formulation of the 'exclusion principle' in the theory of atomic structure. Quantum mechanics had already shown that the electrons which surround the central positive nucleus of an atom can only have very special well-defined 'states' or orbits, but it was not clear why, for example, all the electrons could not be in the innermost (lowest energy) orbits. Pauli noted that the widely varying properties of the different species of atoms could be accounted for if the electron arrangement was governed by his exclusion principle – that only *one* electron could be present at any one time in a particular 'state' or orbit. Thus in light atoms, which have few electrons, only the inner, low energy, orbits need be occupied, whereas in heavy atoms many electrons have to fill the outer orbits. However, in order to make his scheme work, Pauli noted that an electron needed an extra attribute (or quantum number) in order that its 'state' could be described. This later came to be known as the 'spin' of the electron (GOUDSMIT). Although the exclusion principle was first used to explain the structure of atoms, its implications are far wider and it was later applied to account for the properties of assemblies of many types of elementary particles, such as the electrons in a metal, and the particles within the nucleus of the atom itself.

Pauli was also the first (c. 1931) to suggest that some features of the decay of radioactive elements seemed to necessitate that a small mass-less, uncharged particle should be emitted at the same time as a beta-particle. This idea was taken up by FERMI who developed the theory in more detail and named the particle the neutrino. Its existence was not established experimentally until 1956. Pauli was awarded the Nobel prize for physics in 1945.

HMR

Pauling, Linus Carl (b. Portland, Oreg., USA, 28.2.1901). American chemist. Pauling entered the California Institute of Technology in 1922, and was excited by the elucidation of mineral structures by X-ray crystallography and by the emergence of quantum mechanics, to which he was later to make outstanding contributions. After a period of study in Europe, mostly with SOMMERFELD in Munich, he returned to Caltech in 1927, and remained there for the next 35 years. Pauling's early studies (1928) of minerals and simple crystalline solids led to the notion that charged atoms (ions) could be regarded as hard spheres and each assigned a definite radius. He worked out a number of simple 'rules' which introduced both an interpretive and predictive framework into inorganic chemistry, and soon became the cardinal principles of mineral chemistry. Through their agency Pauling rationalized and interrelated the structural patterns of the silicate minerals, which had hitherto proved intractable. His paper 'The nature of the chemical bond' (*J. Amer. Chem. Soc.*, 53 [1931], 1367) set out rules relating to the formation of electron-pair (i.e. covalent) bonds between atoms. He showed how quantum mechanics could yield results of broad chemical significance that went well beyond earlier theories of valency. Quantitative reasons were given for the strengths and lengths of chemical bonds and for the shapes, size and magnetic properties of simple molecules consisting of up to a dozen atoms. The concept of 'hybridization of orbitals', vital for the understanding of the directional character of chemical bonding and the well-defined shapes of bonded atomic aggregates, also emerged at this stage. From the observed shapes of amino acids and small peptide molecules, Pauling and COREY formulated a set of structural conditions that any model of a polypeptide chain (that occurs in proteins) must satisfy. He adopted a stereochemical approach to the building of models of polypeptide chains. This led to the description (1950) of the so-called α-helix, the helical structure present in proteins such as myosin and α-keratin. For his research into the nature of the chemical bond and its application to the elucidation of the structure of complex substances he was awarded the Nobel prize for chemistry in 1954. Pauling has made other notable contributions to biology and medicine. With DELBRÜCK he tackled the structure and process of

formation of antibodies and introduced the concept of 'complementary structures in juxtaposition' (the idea contained in the J. D. WATSON–CRICK model of DNA). Probably his most penetrating contribution to medicine was his demonstration of the chemical basis of hereditary disease. Pauling surmised and later confirmed that the haemoglobin molecule in individuals who suffer from sickle-cell anaemia differs in its amino-acid composition from the haemoglobin molecule of a normal person. Of Pauling's numerous texts, *The Nature of the Chemical Bond* (Ithaca, NY, 1939) is widely acclaimed as one of the turning points in modern chemistry. Putting his scientific knowledge and prestige at the service of his political convictions, he has campaigned to promote world peace and to emphasize the genetic dangers of nuclear explosions. He was awarded the Nobel peace prize in 1962.   JMT

Pavelić, Ante (b. Bradina, Bosnia, under Austro-Hungarian occupation [now Yugoslavia], 14.7.1889; d. Madrid, Spain, 28.12.1959). Founder of the (Yugoslav) party for Croatian national rights (1920), member of the Yugoslav parliament (1927–8), he fled to Italy on the establishment of the dictatorship of King Alexander in 1928, and there organized, first with Italian, then with Hungarian aid, the terrorist organization known as the *Ustashe* [Insurgents], which was responsible for the assassination of King Alexander in 1934. On the German conquest of Yugoslavia in 1941, he became head of the puppet government of the Croatian 'independent' state, a regime distinguished, even by the standards of the time, for the ruthlessness with which it persecuted Jews, Serbs, Bosnians and supporters of TITO's partisans. Much sought as a war criminal in 1945, he escaped via Austria and northern Italy to the Argentine, dying 14 years later in Madrid.   DCW

Pavese, Cesare (b. Santo Stefano Belbo, Piedmont, Italy, 9.8.1908; d. Turin, Piedmont, 27.8.1950). Italian poet and novelist. With MORAVIA, Pavese may be regarded as the most significant pioneer of realism in the modern Italian novel.

From the outset of his career he was politically committed like other young writers and intellectuals such as Pajetta, Ginzburg and Lajolo and belonged to the generation of the so-called Turinese resistance. Having obtained his degree on the basis of a controversial thesis on the poetry of Walt Whitman, Pavese started translating American writers, including Melville (*Moby Dick*). He joined his friend Giulio Einaudi in founding the famous publishing firm Casa Editrice Einaudi at Turin. Shortly after this he was arrested, not so much for his antifascism as for possessing politically compromising letters which a friend had entrusted to him. He was condemned to three years' imprisonment during which he wrote his book of poems *Lavorare stanca* (Florence, 1936; tr. W. Arrowsmith, *Hard Labour*, NY, 1977). His three best-known novels are *Paesi tuoi* (Turin, 1941; tr. A. E. Murch, *The Harvesters*, London, 1961), *La bella estate* (Turin, 1949; tr. W. J. Strachan, *The Beautiful Summer*, London, 1960), and *La luna e i falò* (Turin, 1951; tr. L. Sinclair, *The Moon and The Bonfires*, London, 1952). In August 1950 Pavese committed suicide in a hotel. His second book of poems *Verrà la morte e avrà i tuoi occhi* [Death will come and have your eyes] (Turin, 1951), his book of critical essays *La letteratura americana e altri saggi* (Turin, 1951; tr. E. Fussell, *American Literature: Essays and Opinions*, Berkeley, Calif., 1970), and his autobiographical diary *Il mestiere di vivere* (Turin, 1952; tr. A. E. Murch, *The Business of Living. Diary 1935–1950*, London, 1961) were published posthumously.   GS

G. P. Biasin, *The Smile of the Gods: a Thematic Study of Cesare Pavese's Works* (Ithaca, NY, 1968); D. Heiney, *Three Italian Novelists: Moravia, Pavese, Vittorini* (Ann Arbor, 1968).

Pavlov, Ivan Petrovich (b. Ryazan, Russia, 27.9.1849; d. Leningrad, USSR, 27.2.1936). Russian physiologist. He studied medicine at the Medico-Surgical Academy in St Petersburg, where he was asked by S. P. Botkin to establish one of the first European laboratories for work with experimental animals. His first research (1876–88) was concerned with blood pressure and the innervation of the heart. During this time he established a tradition of making repeated measurements on normal, unanaesthetized dogs which was to be very important both in his own later work and in the general development of behavioural studies with animals. He next studied the digestive tract. A fine surgeon, he developed 'Pavlov's pouch', a preparation in which part of the stomach is externalized on the surface of the abdomen with an intact nerve supply, allowing easy access for experiment and observation. His research on the digestive tract was summarized in *Lektsii o rabote glavnykh pishchevaritel'nykh zhelez* (St Petersburg, 1897; *Lectures on the Work of the Digestive Glands*, London, 1902). It earned him in 1904 the first Nobel prize ever given to a physiologist or to a Russian.

But it is his work on conditioned reflexes, begun only in 1897 when he was nearly 50, on which Pavlov's fame rests. This was a natural extension of his research on the digestive tract, since it stemmed from the observation that digestive juices flow in response not only to food, but also to stimuli closely associated with food, even when these stimuli are quite arbitrary (e.g. a technician's white coat, or the beat of a metronome regularly followed by the delivery of food). To study conditioned reflexes, Pavlov developed a further surgical technique, in which part of the salivary glands is externalized on the surface of the cheek. In this way he was able to study the process of learning in a strictly quantitative way, measuring the degree to which a dog forms an association between a 'conditioned stimulus' (e.g. the metronome in the example given above) and food by the number of drops of saliva which the sound of the metronome produces. Pavlov studied conditioned reflexes intensively until his death, summarizing his research in the successive editions of *Dvadtatiletniy opyt ob'yektivnovo izucheniya vysshey nervnoy deyatel'nosti zhivotnykh* [A twenty-year experience of the objective study of the higher nervous activity of animals] (Moscow–Petrograd, 1923, [6]1936) and in *Lektsii o rabote bol'shikh polushariy golovnovo mozga*

[Lectures on the work of the cerebral hemispheres] (Leningrad, 1927). Part of this research was translated into English as *Conditioned Reflexes: an Investigation of the Physiological Activity of the Cerebral Cortex* (Oxford, 1927) and *Lectures on Conditioned Reflexes: Twenty-five Years of Objective Study of the Higher Nervous Activity (Behavior) of Animals*, vols I & II (NY, 1928–41). In these studies Pavlov established a substantial corpus of empirical knowledge in a field which, until then, had been exclusively the province of philosophical speculation. In this way he did much to carry through the materialist programme enunciated by his Russian physiologist predecessor I. M. Sechenov (by whose *Reflexes of the Brain*, 1866, Pavlov was much influenced): to study psychology by physiological methods, and to explain psychological phenomena in terms of physiological reflexes. Pavlov extended this programme in principle even to the field of individual differences and abnormal behaviour. The tradition he started has remained strong both in the Soviet Union and in the West, and it is today undergoing a particularly vigorous development in the study of both learning and personality.

JAG

B. P. Babkin, *Pavlov: a Biography* (Chicago, 1949); J. A. Gray, *Pavlov* (London, 1979).

Pavlova, Anna Pavlovna (b. St Petersburg [now Leningrad], Russia, 31.1.1881; d. The Hague, S. Holland, The Netherlands, 23.1.1931). Russian dancer who took classical ballet for the first time to smaller towns and cities throughout the world, popularizing what had previously been almost a European elitist entertainment. Originally a member of the Imperial Russian Ballet in St Petersburg, guest appearances abroad gave her a taste for independence; by 1913 she had left Russia to form her own company, which was never permitted to be more than a background to her own highly individual performing genius. The choreography and music which formed most of her repertory was often banal, but the content of her programmes was unimportant beside her interpretations, which gave life to the most uninspired material. She did not restrict her performances to the large cities and permanent theatres, believing, with almost religious fervour, that it was her mission to dance whenever and wherever people would come to see her. In an amazing series of tours over 20 years, covering over 350,000 miles and giving nearly 5000 performances, she took ballet to places where it had never been seen before, including towns and settlements in the Near East, Australasia, the Pacific, South America, North America and the Far East. She inspired a whole generation to take up dancing, including Frederick Ashton, Robert Helpmann and Alicia Markova, and even today to the general public her name is synonymous with dancing.

SCW

V. Krasovskaya, *Anna Pavlova* (Leningrad, 1965); K. Money, *Anna Pavlova: her Life and Art* (London, 1983).

Paz, Octavio (b. Mixcoac, Mexico City, Mexico, 31.3.1914). Mexican poet, essayist and polemicist. His first book of poems *Luna silvestre* [Sylvan moon] (Mexico City, 1933) has strong echoes of JIMÉNEZ, and Paz preferred not to include it in the cumulative *Libertad bajo palabra* [On parole] (Mexico City, 1949, expanded 1960, reduced by some 40 poems in 1968; tr. M. Rukeyser *et al.*, *Early Poems, 1935–1955*, Bloomington, 1973), which established him as Latin America's most scintillating poet. Contacts in Spain during the civil war, especially those made at the 1938 Writers' Congress, brought him under the decisive influence of the surrealists, but his quirkily questing mind has since led him into metaphysics, oriental thought, Mexican and other myths, and structural anthropology. These diverse influences intertwine progressively in the successive phases of his poetry, which is always sparkling in its imagery and kaleidoscopic in its changing symmetries. They also spark off deliberately provocative prose works – each a vibrant and ingenious synthesis of other people's views and his own tendentiously polemical responses. His finest prose work remains *El laberinto de la soledad* (Mexico City, 1950; tr. L. Kemp, *The Labyrinth of Solitude*, NY, 1962), a brilliant analysis of Mexican life and its death-laden thought, while *El arco y la lira* (Mexico City, 1956, revised & extended 1967; revised text tr. R. L. C. Simms, *The Bow and the Lyre*, Austin, 1973) is a provocative contribution to the metaphysics of poetry. Other prose available in English includes *Corriente alterna* (Mexico City, 1967; tr. H. R. Lane, *Alternating Current*, NY, 1973), *Conjunciones y disyunciones* (Mexico City, 1969; tr. H. R. Lane, *Conjunctions and Disjunctions*, NY, 1974), and *Los hijos del limo* (Barcelona, 1974; tr. R. Phillips, *Children of the Mire: Modern Poetry from Romanticism to the Avant-Garde*, Cambridge, Mass., 1974). His finest poem is the cyclical *Piedra de sol* (Mexico City, 1957; tr. M. Rukeyser, *Sun Stone*, NY, 1963), whose title symbol is the Aztec calendar-stone; his most complex is *Blanco* (Mexico City, 1967), a scroll with instructions for multiple alternative reading sequences. *Configurations* (tr. G. Aroul *et al.*, London, 1971) is a bilingual selection from *Piedra de sol*, *Blanco*, *Salamandra* (Mexico City, 1962) and *Ladera este* (Mexico City, 1969). The best translations are arguably those by C. Tomlinson: *Selected Poems* (parallel texts, Harmondworth, 1979).

RP-M

R. Phillips, *The Poetic Modes of Octavio Paz* (Oxford, 1972); J. Wilson, *Octavio Paz: a Study of his Poetics* (Cambridge, 1979).

Peake, Mervyn Laurence (b. Kuling, China, 9.7.1911; d. Burcot, Oxon., UK, 17.11.1968). British writer and artist. Peake spent the first 11 years of his life in China; his missionary parents then moved to London. In the prewar period, after training at the Royal Academy schools, he divided his efforts between painting, teaching and writing. Between 1939 and 1945 he wrote *Titus Groan* (London, 1946), the first book in the 'Gormenghast Trilogy'. *Gormenghast* (London, 1950) shows the hero Titus growing up, beginning to perceive that even people close to him are not what they seem; and *Titus Alone* (London, 1959, ²1970) (influenced by a trip in 1945 to Germany, including Belsen) shows Titus, who has left home, in threatening, KAFKAesque surroundings. Of the modern writers of extended fan-

tasy Peake has been the only one (with the possible exception of Doris Lessing) to address problems of style and representation with intelligence and skill. The type of fiction, the type of prose, the type of prose rhythms, these change in ways which correspond to changes in what, for short, can be called Titus's understanding. At the end of *Titus Alone* this understanding is precarious and fragmentary ('modern', in fact), with all the consequences for 'normal' form and unity that entails. Although the trilogy is Peake's outstanding achievement, he also wrote verse and was an accomplished book illustrator.

RBH

M. Gilmore, *A World Away: a Memoir of Mervyn Peake* (London, 1970); J. Batchelor, *Mervyn Peake: a Biographical and Critical Exploration* (London, 1974).

Pearson, Egon Sharpe (b. London, UK, 11.8.1895; d. Midhurst, W. Sussex, 12.6.1980). British statistician. Son of Karl PEARSON, Egon Pearson held the chair of statistics at University College London from 1935 to 1960. He collaborated with NEYMAN in producing the classic series of papers on statistical inference, developing such concepts as the likelihood ratio test of an hypothesis. This states that an hypothesis is not invalidated because it makes observed events improbable; there must be a realistic alternative hypothesis that does better. If a coin is tossed 50 times, and gives 'heads' 50 times, it may still be fair. If we allow that a bias of 53 per cent to heads is physically possible, then that hypothesis is marginally better. Only if we allow for a bias as large as 58 per cent is fairness inconceivable. Unfortunately, the problem of deciding which hypotheses to consider is often intractable.

AGPW

Pearson, Karl (b. London, UK, 27.3.1857; d. Coldharbour, Surrey, 27.4.1936). British statistician. Trained in the law, he turned to mathematics and became professor of applied mathematics at University College London. He was drawn to the study of genetics following GALTON and became Galton professor of eugenics. He clarified Galton's work on correlation, and established the technique of multiple regression. If one quantity, such as the width of a crab, has its relationship to another masked by nuisance variables, or is not to be predicted by one variable alone but by two or three, then all the variables are put into a linear equation, and the relationship expressed by a partial or a multiple correlation. In 1900 Pearson produced the chi-squared 'measure of fit', perhaps the most used of individual statistics. When a fixed number of observations are counted into cells, the deviations from the expected frequencies are not independent. Having found a surplus, a corresponding deficit contains little new information. Pearson's statistic is a balanced summary, and allows an estimate of whether so large a discrepancy could occur by chance alone. The Pearson distributions were designed to allow measured departures from the normal curve in symmetry or in the proportion of height to spread. They have proved to be ubiquitous, especially in showing the effects on derived statistics of the possible choices of samples. Pearson wrote an important treatment of *The Life of Galton* (London, 1914–30).

AGPW

E. S. Pearson, *Karl Pearson* (Cambridge, 1938).

Péguy, Charles (b. Orléans, Loiret, France, 7.1.1873; d. Villesay, Marne, 5.9.1914). French poet, editor and pamphleteer. The son of a joiner who died in 1874 as a result of wounds received during the Franco–Prussian war of 1870 –1, Péguy was brought up by his mother, who went back to her job as a weaver of raffia seats for wooden chairs in order to provide for her family, and by his grandmother, who could neither read nor write but who, as he was later to say, taught him French. He became a socialist, and in 1900 played an active part in founding and editing the *Cahiers de la Quinzaine*, an influential fortnightly review which campaigned vigorously in favour of Alfred Dreyfus, the Jewish officer wrongly accused of selling military secrets to the Germans. However, from 1903 onwards, Péguy became convinced that the campaign for Dreyfus had become a systematic conspiracy against the church, and denounced the transformation of a *mystique* into a *politique*. From 1905 he became increasingly nationalistic, and in 1908 returned to the Catholicism in which he had been educated as a child. This led to the composition of the *Mystère de la charité de Jeanne d'Arc* (Paris, 1910; tr. J. Green, *The Mystery of the Charity of Joan of Arc*, London, 1950) and to an immensely long religious poem *Ève* (Paris, 1914). His intense nationalism, which led him to write that it was only thanks to the 75mm cannon that French was spoken at Rheims, found satisfaction in the outbreak of WW1, and he was killed leading his men to the attack at the first battle of the Marne. His rediscovery of Catholicism made him identify very closely with his peasant ancestors, and he claimed to write (and did so) with the same patient, repetitive effort that his forefathers had ploughed their furrows or his mother had woven her chairs. His religious writings attach great importance to the Incarnation, which he sees as the central doctrine unique to Christianity. He expressed immense distaste for the modern world, for materialism, scientific method and the spirit of 19c capitalism. His enthusiasm for a return to the traditional religious and nationalistic values associated with a predominantly agricultural France was perhaps wrongly interpreted in the 1940s as providing support for the ideology of the Vichy regime. PMWT

Y. Vade, *Péguy et le monde moderne* (Paris, 1965); H. A. Schmidt, *Charles Péguy: the Decline of an Idealist* (New Orleans, La, 1967).

Peierls, Rudolf Ernst (b. Berlin, Germany, 5.6.1907; naturalized British citizen, 1940). German/British theoretical physicist who has contributed extensively to solid-state and nuclear physics. His early work concerned the application of quantum mechanics to a wide range of phenomena. He explained the anomalous Hall effect by suggesting that in some electrical conductors the current flow is due to the drift of positively charged holes instead of negatively charged electrons. He developed the theory of heat conduction in nonmetallic crystals in terms of the propagation of 'phonons' (i.e. quanta of energy associated with atomic vibrations). He proposed a general theory of the diamagnetism of metals and explained the de Haas–Van Alphen effect in bismuth in terms of LANDAU's theory of the quantization of orbits in the magnetic field. His work in nuclear physics included the theory of the neutron–proton system, resonances in nuclear reactions and nuclear rotational states. Working in Birmingham (UK) in 1940, he and Otto FRISCH showed that the critical mass of uranium 235 for a nuclear explosion is small enough for a bomb. This provided the initial impetus for the work on atomic weapons, and thereafter he played a leading part in their development, in New York and at Los Alamos. He has taken an active part in the work of scientists for peace and international understanding, particularly as a member of the Pugwash movement. His books include *The Quantum Theory of Solids* (Oxford, 1955), *The Laws of Nature* (London, 1955) and *Surprises in Theoretical Physics* (Princeton, 1979).   PEH

Peirce, Charles Sanders (b. Cambridge, Mass., USA, 10.9.1839; d. nr Milford, Pa, 19.4.1914). American philosopher and mathematician. He began his career as a scientist, studying mathematics, physics and chemistry. His first work was on photometric research, and on gravity, for the US Coast and Geodetic Survey. He pursued his logic and philosophy privately until 1879, when he was appointed lecturer in logic at Johns Hopkins University. He left in 1884, and in 1887 retired to Pennsylvania. He wrote an immense amount on virtually all aspects of philosophy and logic, but his enduring fame derives from his contribution to the logic of relations, and from his pioneering development of American pragmatism. This latter combined elements of reductive empiricism with a theory which ties the meaning of any concept to the habits and uses which it brings about. Peirce's attempt to reveal the significance of any concept in terms of conditionals relating phenomenal occurrences led him into the usual problems of phenomenalism. Although venerated as the father of modern American empiricism, he himself had scholastic and certainly realistic

leanings. In his later work he attempted to develop the consequences of his belief that the world contains real *continua*, involving unrealized possibilities. This led him to an evolutionary cosmology, in which an ordered world emerges from an undifferentiated continuum of pure feeling. But the speculative aspect of Peirce's philosophy has not had an influence proportional to the importance he gave it. Peirce also worked constantly on the foundations of mathematics and logic, discovering the quantifier independently, six years later than FREGE, and using the work of CANTOR to found his later theories. His *Collected Papers* have been assembled in eight volumes (eds C. Hartshorne, P. Weiss & A. W. Burk, Cambridge, Mass., 1931–5, 1958).   SWB
R. Almeder, *The Philosophy of Charles S. Peirce* (Oxford, 1980).

Penderecki, Krzysztof (b. Debiça, Poland, 23.11.1933). Polish composer and first major musical figure to emerge from the conditions of greater artistic freedom allowed in Poland from 1956. His former BARTÓKian style was replaced by one possessing closer affinities with the contemporary European avant-garde and from 1960 his music found an increasingly wide audience in Europe and the USA. Demanding unconventional performance techniques from mainly conventional musical forces (e.g. string quartet, orchestra, chorus), he exploited and developed new and original sonorities and created a vocabulary of timbral resource involving sound clusters and microtonal densities which suggested inspiration and ideas derived from electronic music. The term 'Polish string music' became identified with sounds and techniques which he pioneered for string ensembles. Although largely new and unfamiliar to listeners, the language of Penderecki's music conveyed a notable directness of expression and tension when employed in the service of dramatic and emotional subjects, including some of great contemporary significance: *Threnody to the Victims of Hiroshima* (1960); *St Luke Passion* (1963 –5); and *Dies Irae* ('Auschwitz Oratorio') (1967). The recipient of many honours and awards, he has also responded to numerous commissions from organizations in Europe and the USA. A former student at the Kraków Conservatory, he was appointed its rector in 1972.   TEC

A. Orga, 'Krzysztof Penderecki', *Music and Musicians* (October 1973).

Penfield, Wilder Graves (b. Spokane, Wash., USA, 26.1.1891; naturalized Canadian citizen, 1934; d. Montreal, Quebec, Canada, 5.3.1976). American/Canadian neurologist and neurosurgeon. An undergraduate at Princeton, he went to Oxford in 1913 as a Rhodes scholar. During breaks in his studies he served as a dresser at a Red Cross military hospital in Paris, and in 1916, while crossing the English Channel, he was wounded during a torpedo attack in which 80 people died. After receiving his MD at Johns Hopkins University where he studied under Sir William Osler, he resumed his studies at Oxford under SHERRINGTON, who inspired him to devote himself to neurosurgery. Lack of funds forced him to return home, and he worked in a variety of distinguished training posts, including spells in Berlin and under CAJAL in Madrid. In 1926 Penfield moved to Montreal where he was to spend the rest of his life. Here he perfected the Berlin technique for the surgical treatment of epilepsy. This required restoring the patient to consciousness after opening the skull (the brain has no pain receptors) and using electrodes over various parts of the brain to locate the epileptic focus, which was then destroyed. In 1931, during an operation, he evoked from a patient vivid and accurate memories of her experiences in childbirth. Similar observations were evoked from other patients, showing that the brain keeps accurate records even though such memories are not normally recalled. That same year the Rockefeller Foundation approved a grant of over $1m for the Montreal Neurological Institute, which opened in 1934 with Penfield as founding director. During the course of over 1000 operations on epileptic patients, Penfield studied the brain scars that result from injury and developed a technique for their removal. He also produced a mass of knowledge about the conscious human brain, including

detailed mapping of areas controlling movements, even down to the controlling areas for small parts of the stomach. He then mapped sensory function in the same way. As a result of his lifetime's work he was able to outline a comprehensive theory dealing with mechanisms of perception, memory, behaviour, consciousness and higher mental processes. By the time he retired Penfield was the author of seven textbooks, as well as numerous scientific papers, essays and articles. Subsequently he wrote two novels, a biography, and three volumes of essays, memoirs and autobiography.   CR

Penrose, Lionel Sharples (b. London, UK, 11.6.1898; d. London, 12.5.1972). British geneticist. After early work as a psychologist, Penrose qualified in medicine and began work on mental deficiency. A massive survey of over 1200 patients in a Colchester institution, and of their relatives, led to a scientifically rigorous approach to the classification and aetiology of mental defect. It also made Penrose the pre-eminent authority on mongolism and aroused his interest in a number of important issues in human genetics. His works *Mental Defect* (London, 1933) and later *The Biology of Mental Defect* (London, 1949) became classics in their field. During a wartime interlude Penrose made a large-scale investigation of the value of shock therapy to patients diagnosed as schizophrenic or as psychotic. The results were sobering in suggesting that although some psychotics might benefit, it was probable that the only effect of treatment was to produce a more rapid improvement in their condition than they would have enjoyed untreated. Subsequently Penrose was appointed GALTON professor of eugenics at University College London (1945–65), during which he made a number of valuable technical contributions. After retiring from his chair he became director of the Kennedy–Galton centre at Harpersbury Hospital, St Albans (1965–72). Penrose succeeded in marrying scientific analysis to humane principles in treating the problems of mental defect and of genetically determined defect of all kinds. His scepticism of the more extravagant claims of positive eugenics and his ambition to cure, or at least alleviate, the condition of the genetically afflicted are now commonplace. He helped to make them so.   DRN

Penzias, Arno (b. Munich, Bavaria, Germany, 26.4.1933; naturalized American citizen, 1937). German/American radio astronomer. Penzias joined the staff of the Bell Telephone Laboratory in 1961. Together with R. WILSON, he was concerned with the Echo communications satellite; the two men were investigating very low levels of residual noise in the signals from their radio receiver when they discovered an unexplained residual noise contribution. With extreme skill they eliminated all known terrestrial sources of possible noise, including pigeons sitting in the receiver, and decided they were actually receiving radiation emanating from the universe at large. Their measurements were made in the 7cm range of radio wavelengths. It was found that the weak signal not only came evenly from the whole sky, indicating the universal origin of the radiation, but that its spectrum corresponded to a black body at 3° absolute temperature. Penzias and Wilson did not have an explanation for their discovery although GAMOW had predicted such a radiation field in 1946. At Princeton, however, Dicke and Peebles had rediscovered Gamow's prediction that the big-bang origin of the universe would result in such a radiation field and Penzias heard of their work by chance, shortly after his discovery. Observation and theory were combined to form what is regarded as the most important cosmological discovery since HUBBLE's work. This 3° radiation field was conclusive evidence for the big-bang theory and counted as fatal evidence for the steady-state theory. Penzias has been director of the Radio Research Laboratory of Bell Laboratories since 1976; he shared the Nobel prize for physics with Wilson in 1978.   MJS

Peretz, Yitzhok Leibush (b. Zamość, Lublin, Russian Poland [now Poland], 18.5.1852; d. Warsaw, 3.4.1915). Yiddish writer. As educator of a whole generation of younger writers who looked upon him as their guide and mentor, Peretz is the father of modern Yiddish literature. Although he began writing in Polish and Hebrew (1876), he published his first Yiddish story in 1888 and thereafter wrote consistently in Yiddish. Poet, dramatist and writer of short stories, Peretz also wrote philosophical essays on literature, history and the function of the writer. For him commitment was all-important; he saw the writer as self-appointed representative of his people. In his poetry Peretz was greatly influenced by German poets, and particularly Heinrich Heine, both in theme and structure. But his major preoccupation was fiction, and where he excelled was in his *Folks-timlikhe geshichten* [Popular folk tales] (18 vols, Warsaw, 1912) in which he transformed living idioms and ideas into highly artistic narratives. In whatever he wrote Peretz retained a simplicity of expression to ensure general accessibility. Outstanding among his works is the poetic drama *Di goldene Keyt* (in *Dramen*, Warsaw, 1910; extracts tr. J. Sonntag, *The Golden Chain*, London, 1953) which deals with the 'eternal Sabbath' that will follow the redemption of the world from evil. When banned from practising as a lawyer, Peretz became an official of the Warsaw Jewish community and spent the last 25 years of his life in that major centre of Jewish literary life. His home became the Mecca of a whole generation of Yiddish writers, whom he inspired and encouraged, including Sholem Asch (1880–1957), David Bergelson (1884–1952), Josef Opatoshu (1887–1954) and David Pinski (1872–1960). Peretz also influenced the Yiddish Art Theatre in its early stages, and a whole group of Jewish painters who emerged in Poland and Russia at the turn of the century, including LISSITZKY and CHAGALL. 'Peretzism', in fact, assumed the significance of a philosophical and aesthetic concept.   JSo

Perón, Juan Domingo (b. Lobos, Buenos Aires, Argentina, 8.10.1895; d. Buenos Aires, 1.7.1974), and **Perón, Eva Duarte de** (b. Los Toldos, 7.5.1919; d. Buenos Aires, 26.7.1952). Husband-and-wife team who together created a military nationalist dictatorship in Argentina, backed by a fascist-style party, the strength of which rested on Eva Perón's ability to organize and inspire the urban working class as a threat to the landed classes who had hitherto exercised power, her natural flair for political organization complementing his ability to personify Argentinian nationalism and hostility to the USA. Perón's overthrow in 1955 by a military junta followed her death, but the Peronista organization and the cult of his wife's memory persisted through the military dictatorship to win free elections in 1973 outright and return Perón to power. On his death nine months later, his second wife ruled for two years, until her manifest incompetence provoked another military coup and the final demise of the Peronista party. DCW

F. Owen, *Peron: his Rise and Fall* (London, 1957).

Perret, Auguste (b. Brussels, Brabant, Belgium, 12.2.1874; d. Paris, France, 25.2.1954). French architect best known for his use of the reinforced-concrete frame as a formal element in architectural design. Perret was educated at the Ecole des Beaux Arts in Paris (1891–5) where he was taught by Julien Guadet, whose important book on the theory of architecture sought to explain the relationship between classical proportion and structure. On graduation he came under the influence of his father, a Parisian building contractor, and in 1905 joined the firm which became Perret Frères. Most architects of this period used concrete as they would masonry, as a massive material. Perret believed that concrete could be used to form prefabricated building elements from which a structural frame and its various infill parts could be put together in a manner hitherto reserved for traditional timber building. His firm built a number of buildings in Paris following this principle – an apartment block in the rue Franklin (1903) and a group of garages in the rue Ponthieu are typical in clearly revealing their concrete frame structure. Later buildings exposed the concrete structure both externally and internally, the surface texture being varied by changing aggregates and shuttering patterns. Two of his larger buildings are

the church of Notre Dame du Raincey in Paris (1922–3) and the railway station at Amiens (1943). He was also responsible after WW2 for rebuilding a large part of Le Havre (1949–56). NW

E. N. Rogers, *Auguste Perret* (Milan, 1955).

Perrin, Jean Baptiste (b. Lille, Nord, France, 30.9.1870; d. New York, USA, 17.4.1942). French physicist. Perrin was educated at the Ecole Normale Supérieure. He became reader (1897) and then professor (1910) of physical chemistry at the University of Paris. In 1940 he escaped from France to the USA. His first experimental research was to confirm that cathode rays were streams of negatively charged particles (electrons) and that they were not some form of radiation like light or X-rays. The work for which he is mainly remembered, however, is his classic determination of the number of molecules which are present in a given volume of a gas. He did this using several independent methods, all of which involved the microscopic observation of the behaviour of extremely fine gamboge particles in water. Due to the opposing action of gravity, which will tend to make the particles sink, and that of diffusion, which will tend to even out the distribution, a stable situation is set up. The concentration of particles then varies with depth in the liquid; by photographing and counting the number of particles at various depths, and by assuming that the thermal energy of a particle is the same as that of a molecule, it is possible to calculate the number of molecules in a unit volume of gas under standard conditions of temperature and pressure. This work, which is a masterpiece of careful experimentation, is described in his book *Les Atomes* (Paris, 1913, [3]1940; *Atoms*, London, 1920, [2]1923). For this work he received the Nobel prize for physics in 1926. Perrin founded many French scientific organizations. He was the creator of the Centre National de la Recherche Scientifique (CNRS), the main government organization for scientific research; he founded the Palais de la Découverte, and was responsible for establishing the institutes of astrophysics and of physicochemical biology, and the Haute-Provence Observatory. HMR

Persson, Sigurd (b. Hålsingborg, Kristianstad, Sweden, 22.11.1914). Swedish jeweller and artist. After an apprenticeship with his father who taught him the traditional techniques and craftsmanship for making ethnic southern Swedish jewellery, he studied under Julius Schneider and Franz Rickert at the Akademie für Angewandte Kunst, Munich (1937–9), and the Konstfackskolan, Stockholm (1942–3). In 1943 he joined with Erik Fleming to make jewellery and train apprentices in his workshop. Since the end of their collaboration in 1945, he has gained international recognition for outstanding work bearing the hallmark of the classic Scandinavian design which dominated contemporary jewellery in the 1940s and 1950s. Unsentimental but sensuous and tactile, his jewellery is bold and geometric in its basic structure, with smooth surfaces of gold or silver supporting diamonds or semiprecious stones. His autobiography was published as *Sigurd Persson Smycken* (Stockholm, 1980). BC

G. Bott, *Schmuck als künstlerische Aussage unserer Zeit* (Königsbach-Pforzheim, 1971).

Perutz, Max Ferdinand (b. Vienna, Austria-Hungary [now Austria], 19.5.1914; naturalized British citizen). Austrian/British molecular biologist. The Nazi takeover of Austria in 1938 prevented Perutz, a graduate student of the chemical crystallographer BERNAL, from returning home from Cambridge, and his nationality enforced his internment in Canada during WW2. But subsequently, he returned to the Cavendish Laboratory at Cambridge to work for W. L. BRAGG, who had pioneered the crystallography (i.e. structural study) of biological molecules: Perutz undertook to solve the three-dimensional structure of haemoglobin, the protein which transports oxygen from lungs to tissues. In fact it took until 1959 to complete the solution, and ironically it was his student KENDREW who first published such a structure the previous year. Even so the techniques used were those developed by Perutz, which remain standard today. For this work Perutz (with Kendrew) received the Nobel prize in chemistry in 1962. His work demonstrates the usefulness of studying molecular structure to understand biological function, an activity continued by Perutz and his laboratory. But Perutz has fostered the 'structural' school of molecular biology in other ways – both J. D. WATSON and CRICK were his protégés – and since 1962 he has been chairman of the important Medical Research Council Laboratory for Molecular Biology at Cambridge. DOM

Pessoa, Fernando António Nogueira (b. Lisbon, Portugal, 13.6.1888; d. Lisbon, 30.11.1935). Portuguese poet, the most important since Camões (1524–80), and one of the outstanding European poets of the 20c. He was descended from New Christians, i.e. Jews forcibly converted to Christianity in the 15c. His father died when Pessoa was five, a loss of lasting influence: there is in his poetry a poignant nostalgia for childhood. In 1895 his mother remarried, and the family moved to Durban, South Africa, where his stepfather was Portuguese consul. From 13 he read widely in English literature and wrote poetry in English. In 1905 he returned to Lisbon with his family, and from 1908 until his death eked out a livelihood as a commercial correspondent in Lisbon. He lived apart, never married: he seems 'to have been born with a vocation for solitude', and it is a constant in his poetry. From infancy he had peopled his loneliness with imaginary figures, a phenomenon that took literary shape in March 1914 with the creation of three heteronyms, poetical figures who would, in their different styles, write the poetry of his multiform genius. They were no mere pseudonyms, but new creations. The first, Alberto Caeiro, is a pagan with simple, acute vision and a rebel against tradition. Ricardo Reis is a monarchist, Jesuit-educated, who writes in the style of Horace. His calm indifference declares: 'We are nothing ... respited cadavers that procreate.' Álvaro de Campos is an extrovert engineer, modelled on Walt Whitman. In the long poem '*Tabacaria*' [The tobacconist's shop], written in 1928, Pessoa/Campos comments from his room opposite, and consoles his loneliness with the thought that the shop, the shop-sign, the tobacconist and 'my verses and their language', will all die with the planet itself.

Pessoa's work was unpublished during his life, except for some English poems and the important *Mensagem* [Message] (Lisbon, 1934) evoking past Portuguese glory with hope for a redemptive future. His poetic works have been collected as *Obras completas* (9 vols, Lisbon, 1942–69). There are a number of prose works on aesthetics and politics. For a selection of his poems in English translation see *Fernando Pessoa: Sixty Portuguese Poems* (tr. F. E. Quintanilha, Cardiff, 1971).   DBr

J. G. Simões, *Vida e obra de Fernando Pessoa* (2 vols, Lisbon, ³1973).

Pétain, Henri Philippe Omer (b. Cauchy à la Tour, Pas-de-Calais, France, 24.4.1856; d. Île d'Yeu, 23.7.1951). Marshal of France (1918–45), minister of war (1934), French ambassador to Spain (1939–40), prime minister (1940), head of state (1940–2). His role as the defender of Verdun in 1915 gave him a prestige which no other French general in WW1 enjoyed, save Marshal FOCH, and which was enhanced by his revival of the morale of the French armies after the mutinies of May 1917 and his success in sustaining that morale through the German offensives of spring 1918. This prestige was enlisted in 1940 to head a new French authoritarian regime, after France's defeat by Germany in a war the initiation of which he regarded as the consequence of French political and moral degeneration. With the German occupation of northern France, the government of France was relocated in Vichy, where, on 10 July 1940, he secured authoritarian powers from the French National Assembly. The ideological direction of this Vichy government was disputed between the French officer class intent on bringing about a moral revival in France, various French fascist leaders and French parliamentary figures such as LAVAL who sought to reconcile France, at as little cost as possible to France's interests and empire, to their expectations of German victory over the UK and the permanent superiority of Nazi Germany over the rest of Europe. With the German occupation of Vichy France in November 1942 Pétain became a German puppet. In 1945 he was tried and sentenced to death, the sentence being commuted to life imprisonment. His political ideas represented the common and long-standing distaste of the Catholic majority of the French officer class for a republic which was in their view corrupt, anticlerical, antimilitarist and neglectful, if not downright hostile, to the army, inefficient in managing the nation's finances and progressively more and more dependent on British policy in Europe, with a parliament so politically divided as to make stable government impossible.   DCW

R. Aron, *The Vichy Regime 1940–44* (London, 1955); G. Blond, *Pétain, 1856–1951* (Paris, 1966).

Peters, Richard Stanley (b. Mussorie, Uttar Pradesh, India, 31.10.1919). British educator. After graduating at Oxford University, Peters taught classics in secondary school before moving to Birkbeck College, London, as lecturer, then reader in philosophy. In 1962 he was appointed professor of the philosophy of education at the University of London Institute of Education from where he has dominated the development of philosophical studies of education far beyond his own institution. During the 1960s – especially after the Robbins Report on *Higher Education* (1963) – when there was a proliferation of courses and new qualifications, Peters's rigorous scholarship and forceful teaching at an advanced level for higher degrees (many taken by lecturers or future lecturers in colleges of education or indeed other university departments) did much to safeguard standards and clarify purposes. Peters also strongly influenced the many lecturers and principals of some 30 colleges of education whose progression towards the provision of new degrees and diplomas (notably the BEd) came under the scrutiny of joint academic boards meeting at the University of London under the aegis of the Institute of Education. His varied publications include monographs on Hobbes and Rousseau and analyses of philosophical and ethical concepts.

EJK

Petipa, Marius (b. Marseilles, Bouches-du-Rhône, France, 11.3.1818; d. Gurzuf, Crimea, Russia, 14.7.1910). French dancer and choreographer who established the supremacy of the Imperial Russian Ballet in St Petersburg, giving the final polish to the technique and form known as classical ballet. His early career as a dancer in Europe has been overshadowed by his work in St Petersburg, where he went in 1862, as *maître de ballet* from 1869 until 1903. Classical ballet technique, which developed under his rule, was a combination of his own French dance schooling, Russian style and technique, and the virtuosity of the Italian school. This he enshrined in a series of ballets, some new versions of contemporary successes, like *Paquita* (1881), *Coppélia* (1884) and *Esmeralda* (1886), and over 50 original works, including *La Bayadère* (1879), *Swan Lake* (part 1895), *Raymonda* (1898) and his masterpiece *The Sleeping Beauty* (1890). The form of the classical ballet which he established was a full evening story ballet, in which narrative was conveyed by passages of mime, interspersed with dances designed to test and show off individual dancers or small groups – the *corps de ballet* being relegated to an almost purely decorative function. By the end of his career his supremacy was being questioned by a new generation, notably FOKINE, but his works are now recognized as fundamental to the repertory of a classically trained company and the touchstone by which classical dancers of today are measured. His memoirs appeared as *Russian Ballet Master: the Memoirs of Marius Petipa* (ed. L. Moore, NY, 1958).

SCW

Petrie, William Matthew Flinders (b. Charlton, Kent, UK, 3.6.1853; d. Jerusalem, Palestine [now Israel], 28.7.1942). British archaeologist specializing in Egyptology, and founder of the British School of Archaeology in Egypt. He carried out extensive surveys and excavations in Egypt, notably at Memphis, Naucratis, the Fayum, the Pyramids of Giza and Meydum, largely under the auspices of the Egypt Exploration Fund

(founded in 1883). His excavations, in their skill, care and speed of publication, were a dramatic advance on the ransacking of Egyptian sites by his predecessors in the field. He developed the technique of sequence dating for predynastic material from the early sites at Nagada, Ballas and Diospolis Parva (discussed in his *Methods and Aims in Archaeology*, London, 1904). From his work at Gurob, Kahun and Tel el-Amarna (Egypt), where he found imported Mycenaean pottery, and a study tour of Greece (1891), he established important synchronisms between the dated Egyptian sequence and the hitherto largely undated prehistoric cultures of the Greek mainland. His excavations at the Palestinian site of Tell el-Hesi (1890) allowed him to define similar synchronisms between the Egyptian and Palestinian sequences.

BWC

Pevsner, Nikolaus Barnhard Leon (b. Leipzig, Saxony, Germany [now East Germany], 30.1.1902; naturalized British citizen). German/British art historian. He studied at the universities of Leipzig, Munich, Berlin and Frankfurt before gaining his doctorate in the history of art in 1924. He then worked as assistant keeper at the Dresden Gallery (1924–8), and from 1929 to 1933 he was a lecturer at Göttingen University, specializing in the history of British art. After emigrating to the UK, he became Slade professor of fine art at Cambridge (1949–55) and later at Oxford (1968–9), and is now emeritus professor of the history of art at the University of London. While in Germany Pevsner published *Leipziger Barock* [Leipzig baroque] (Leipzig, 1928), and *Die italienische Malerei vom Ende der Renaissance bis zum ausgehenden Rokoko* [Italian painting of mannerism and baroque] (Göttingen, 1928–32), considered a standard work on a hitherto neglected period of Italian art. His first English publication *Pioneers of Modern Design* (London, 1936), based on a lecture course held at Göttingen, traces the evolution of 20c functional architecture from the aesthetic re-evaluation generated by William Morris and the Arts and Crafts movement to GROPIUS's radical break with the past in his acceptance of the new materials and forms of the technological age. In *Outline of European Architecture* (London, 1943) Pevsner extends his historical mode of inquiry to encompass the growth of western architecture from the 9c to the 20c, seen as an expression of western civilization. In *The Englishness of English Art* (London, 1957) Pevsner investigates the national characteristics of English art ('cultural geography'), which he sees in terms of polarities or apparently contradictory qualities, e.g. the rational empiricism of Hogarth, Constable or Reynolds in contrast to the cult of the irrational and the fantastic in such diverse instances as Blake, the Decorated style of 1300 and the picturesque. Pevsner's interest in 'cultural geography' has resulted in his monumental project to describe all the *Buildings of England* of historic note, county by county (46 vols, Harmondsworth, 1951–74). Other works include *C. R. Mackintosh* (London, 1950), *High Victorian Design* (London, 1951) and *Sources of Modern Art* (London, 1962).

SOBT

Philips, Anton Frederick (b. Zaltbommel, Gelderland, The Netherlands, 14.3.1874; d. Eindhoven, Brabant, 7.10.1961). Dutch industrialist. Philips's father, a small industrialist, financed the eldest son of the family, Gerard Philips, an electrical engineer, in starting an incandescent lamp factory at Eindhoven in 1891. After working as a stockbroker, Anton joined the family firm in 1895 as salesman and in 1899 became a partner. Sales of light bulbs developed all over Europe. In 1914 the company started systematic scientific research and development, leading to the Philips Laboratories at Eindhoven. In 1922 Anton took over sole responsibility for the firm when Gerard retired, and turned the firm into a worldwide multinational company involved in all aspects of electronics.

RAH

Piaget, Jean (b. Neuchâtel, Switzerland, 9.8.1896; d. Geneva, 16.9.1980). Swiss psychologist, philosopher and biologist. Fascinated as a child by natural history, Piaget studied zoology at the University of Neuchâtel before going to Zürich to study psychology in 1918 and a year later travelling to Paris for further psychological study at the Sorbonne. In 1921 he joined the Institut J.-J. Rousseau in Geneva as its director of studies. His subsequent appointments included professor of the history of scientific thought at the University of Geneva (1929–39); professor of psychology and sociology at the University of Lausanne (1938–51); professor of sociology at Geneva (1939–52); and professor of developmental psychology at the Sorbonne (1952–63). From 1955 he was director of the International Centre for Genetic Epistemology at Geneva. The author of numerous articles and more than 50 books, from which *The Essential Piaget: an Interpretative Reference and Guide* (eds H. E. Gruber & J. J. Vonèche, London, 1977) provides an informative and substantial selection.

Piaget's central interest was in the development of logic, and his main hypothesis was that children are born without the internal mechanisms which allow them to be logical and that they eventually construct these logical mechanisms through their experiences with the world around them. Piaget's account of this interaction with the environment began with the first days of life. It was his view that the child is born with a few built-in reflexes and virtually nothing else. These reflexes produce the experiences which in the first two years of life allow the baby to work out that he is a separate entity, and that the environment around him consists of objects and people. Piaget also thought that during this time the baby discovers the basic spatial and temporal rules of his world. Piaget's observations of very young children were particularly painstaking and still play a central part in research on infancy.

His work on older children is perhaps more controversial. It was with children of four years and older that Piaget pursued most forcefully his hypothesis of an initial lack of logic. Many of his experiments which were designed to demonstrate some surprising gaps in young children's logic are very well known. The most famous is the conservation experiment in which young children apparently treat a perceptual rearrangement of some quantity as a real change in that quantity. Piaget's conclusion that at first children do not understand the principle of invariance of quantity is mirrored by very similar claims made by himself and his colleagues that young children cannot make inferences, that they do not understand the ordinal or cardinal properties of number, that they have no idea about Euclidean coordinates, that they confuse spatial and temporal parameters and that they do not understand the difference between moral rules and arbitrary conventions. At the moment all these negative conclusions about young children are disputed by other psychologists who claim to have shown that the errors detected by Piaget, though interesting, are always a special case: these psychologists argue that young children have the abilities in question but do not always take as complete advantage of them as older people do. The issue is still in doubt, but there is general agreement that Piaget's experiments on children between 4 and 11 years are extremely ingenious and that his interpretations of them are provocative and important.

His work on children between 11 and adulthood is less well known, but makes some important claims. His main idea is that at the beginning of this period children are not able to reflect on their own thought processes; this is said to lead to some severe limitations particularly in scientific reasoning. Much of the experimental work on this period is designed to show that young adolescents are not able to design properly controlled scientific experiments.

Piaget also established a model for the causes of developmental change, and this model applied to the whole of childhood. Development, he argued, is a matter of successive stages. At the beginning of each stage the child is able to interpret what happens to him quite satisfactorily. But later he finds that he often believes two or more contradictory things about the same event. This conflict throws him into disequilibrium, and it is his struggle to regain intellectual equilibrium which eventually leads him to develop new intellectual structures which bring him to the next stage. Then once again he can explain his world to himself satisfactorily, until eventually and inevitably the same process of equilibrium, disequilibrium and a new equilibrium happens all over again. This causal model is difficult to test and has received very little empirical support, but it has had a great influence in educational circles.

Piaget remains by far the most influential figure in developmental psychology of his generation. But the impact of his work and ideas has extended far more widely, particularly in education, biology and philosophy, and this larger influence will undoubtedly grow as his particular achievements are more closely identified and explored. PEB

H. Ginsburg & S. S. Opper (eds), *Piaget's Theory of Intellectual Development: an Introduction* (Englewood Cliffs, 1969); M. A. Boden, *Piaget* (London, 1979).

Picabia, Francis (b. Feydieu, Gironde, France, 22.1.1879; d. Paris, 30.11.1953). French painter, and a major disseminator of dada in Europe and the USA. After studying at the Ecole des Beaux Arts, he painted in an impressionist style (1898–1908). Influenced by Pissarro, in 1910–11 he was influenced briefly by fauvism until he met the cubist group round Gleizes, Villon, etc. He was a founder-member of the *Section d'Or* (1911), painting in an Orphic–cubist style (e.g. *Catch as Catch Can*, 1913). In 1913 he met DUCHAMP at the Armory show in New York, where he returned in 1915 and began his mechanical dada period (1915–21), creating a series of ironically irreverent 'Mechanothropomorphic' fantasies (e.g. *La Parade Amoureuse*, 1917; *Universal Prostitution*, 1916–19). In 1917 he started his satirical journal *391* in Barcelona, at the same time instigating dadaist activities in Barcelona and New York. In 1918 he established links with the Zürich dadaists (ARP, Richter, etc.), and published a volume of poems *La fille née sans mère* [The motherless daughter] (Lausanne, 1918). In 1919–22, in Paris, he continued to produce mechano-dada works, often with comic or aggressive sexual connotations. In 1921 he denounced dada and reverted to representation, painting a series of proto-surrealist scenes. In 1925 he retired to Provence, where from 1927 to 1939 he produced his 'transparencies', i.e. delicate collages of cellophane sheets with colour washes. After his return to Paris (1945) he painted in a nonfigurative style fusing literary and dada reminiscences.   SOBT

M. Saouillet, *Picabia* (Paris, 1964); R. Hunt, *Picabia*, ICA exh. cat. (London, 1964).

Picasso, Pablo Ruiz y (b. Málaga, Spain, 25.10.1881; d. Mougins, Alpes-Maritimes, France, 8.4.1973). Spanish painter, sculptor, printmaker and designer. The most inventive 20c artist, who had a prodigious output and worked in an unprecedented variety of styles. Picasso was the son of a teacher of painting and showed extraordinary talent when young. After working in Barcelona around the turn of the century, he made his first visit to Paris in 1900 and settled there in 1904. From 1901 to 1904 he worked in pervasive blue tones, executing paintings of vagabonds, beggars and prostitutes with a prevailing air of melancholy and pathos, followed by a more serene period of works in pinks, ochres and greys, including a series of pictures of the family life of circus folk. It was only with his *Les Demoiselles d'Avignon*, executed in the winter of 1906–7, that he made his first radical break with tradition, combining the influence of CÉZANNE with that of African masks and breaking up and reassembling the forms in an angular design. His work for the next two years was strongly influenced by African sculpture, with its barbaric vitality and powerful volumes, but by late 1909 he adopted a more detached and Cézannesque approach, working with angular facets and planes in a restricted range of greens, ochres or greys. From 1909 to 1914 he worked in close collaboration with BRAQUE, who had begun to develop along similar lines, and together they created cubism, one of the most revolutionary art movements of the 20c, developing through analytical to synthetic cubism, and initiating the use of collage. Picasso also carried out some of these ideas in three dimensions in a series of sculpture constructions.

Although Picasso continued to make pictures with flat planes of colour in a late cubist idiom up to 1926, he also began in 1915 to work concurrently in a more realistic style, notably in a series of pictures of neoclassical figures made in 1920–4. However, his *Three Dancers*, painted in 1925, marked the beginning of a new period of emotional violence and expressionist distortion, in which the human figure was torn apart and reinvented with an unprecedented freedom to produce highly charged images of a metamorphic and dreamlike character which nevertheless always retained a strong formal design. He was a close friend of the surrealists and his works were often exhibited with theirs. Active as a designer for the ballet from 1917 to 1924, including the design of the sets and costumes for DIAGHILEV's *Parade* in 1917, he later also made a number of important sculptures and a great many prints, including series of etchings to illustrate Ovid's *Metamorphoses* and Buffon's *Histoire Naturelle*.

In 1937 the German bombing of the Basque capital of Guernica during the Spanish civil war inspired him to paint a famous mural *Guernica* as a protest against this great human disaster. He remained in Paris throughout the occupation, in defiance of the Nazis, and painted many pictures expressing the anguish of the time, in which the human figure was subjected to violent distortions. From 1946, he lived mainly in the south of France, where his work became more relaxed and playful. He made many paintings and prints on such themes as nymphs and fauns, and the painter and his model, and also a large number of painted ceramics. Though he continued to work prodigiously in his old age, his later pictures tended to become somewhat repetitive.   REA

A. H. Barr, Jr (ed.), *Picasso: Fifty Years of his Art* (NY, ²1974); W. S. Rubin, *Pablo Picasso: a Retrospective* (NY, 1980).

Piggott, Stuart (b. Petersfield, Hants., UK, 28.5.1910). British archaeologist and prehistorian. Piggott's great contribution to the study of European prehistory lies not only in several outstanding books and monographs on specific subjects, but in his charting of the development of archaeology from its antiquarian origins. His earliest experience of the direction of excavation came at Avebury (Wilts.), as assistant to Alexander Keiller in 1934–8. Military service in Asia during WW2 brought him into contact with the problems of Indian prehistory, an experience from which later stemmed his *Prehistoric India* (Harmondsworth, 1950). Elected to the Abercromby chair of prehistoric archaeology at Edinburgh in 1946, his later fieldwork was conducted in Scotland and England, though his writing constantly reveals his consciousness of Britain as part of Europe. Like his Edinburgh professor CHILDE, he has produced a number of works for the non-specialist reader in which the essence of advanced studies is distilled. These include *British Prehistory* (London, 1949) and *Ancient Europe* (Edinburgh, 1965). His studies in the history of archaeology include several stylish and witty works: *William Stukeley* (Oxford, 1950), *The Druids* (London, 1968) and *Ruins in a Landscape* (Edinburgh, 1976).   MT

Pigou, Arthur Cecil (b. Ryde, Isle of Wight, UK, 18.11.1877; d. Cambridge, 7.3.1959). British economist and disciple of Alfred MARSHALL whom he succeeded as professor of political economy in the University of Cambridge (1908–43). As the leading figure in the Cambridge school of economics, it was he who attracted KEYNES's most withering criticisms when the latter was trying to revolutionize economic theory in the 1930s. Though he had the reputation of being a brilliant lecturer (until ill-health began to blunt his performance in the late 1920s), Pigou's main strength lay in the powerfully logical and lucid quality of his written work. His most original and lasting contributions came in the broad area of welfare economics. The analysis developed in his *Wealth and Welfare* (London, 1912) was elaborated and extended in *Unemployment* (London, 1913); in four successive editions of *The Economics of Welfare* (London, 1920, ⁴1932); in *Industrial Fluctuations* (London, 1927); and in *A Study in Public Finance* (London, 1928). Pigou's objective was to extend and

apply the analytical tools and theories of orthodox Marshallian economics, so that they could prove useful in designing policies to improve social welfare. He was the first economist to examine rigorously, and to suggest fruitful solutions to the basic problems involved in measuring economic welfare, e.g. distinguishing between the private and social costs or benefits of government actions, of defining the national income and of assessing the effects of specific taxes on the redistribution of incomes as between rich and poor. In later years, as he became increasingly involved in defending the classical tradition in economic theory against the attacks of Keynes and his disciples, his writings became more theoretical, e.g. *The Theory of Unemployment* (London, 1933), *The Economics of Stationary States* (London, 1935) and *Employment and Equilibrium* (London, 1941). More recently, the reaction against Keynesian ideas has tended to revive his reputation among economic theorists, and not merely for his contributions to welfare economics.   PMD

D. Collard, 'A. C. Pigou, 1877–1959', in D. P. O'Brien & J. R. Presley (eds), *Pioneers of Modern Economics in Britain* (London, 1981).

Pike, Kenneth Lee (b. Woodstock, Conn., USA, 16.9.1912). American linguist. Pike has made his greatest impact through his written work on phonetics and phonology and his practical skill as a phonetician to become one of the outstanding 20c linguists. His first book *Phonetics* (Ann Arbor, 1943) is a standard work on articulatory phonetics and sets out Pike's theory of syllabification (crests and troughs of stricture). *Intonation of American English* (Ann Arbor, 1946) was one of the first books to bring intonation within the compass of phonemic analysis, and *Phonemics* (Ann Arbor, 1947) was for some time a much used theoretical and methodological textbook on phonemic analysis in phonology. Pike has concentrated on the languages of Central and South America, where he has carried out extensive fieldwork; material from the Mexican Mixteco and Mazateco languages figures prominently in *Tone Languages* (Ann Arbor, 1948). Throughout his life Pike has treated his linguistics as part of his work for Christianity. As founder of the Summer Institute of Linguistics he has organized summer schools and continuing programmes in which young linguists are trained for work in Bible translating and general evangelism. His attempt to envisage linguistics within a more comprehensive view of human life as a whole was set out in *Language in Relation to a Unified Theory of the Structure of Human Behavior* (Glendale, 1954–60), from which he has developed a distinctive version of linguistic theory entitled tagmemics, in which phonology, grammar and semantics are analysed in similar ways, the basic unit of grammar being the tagmeme, the correlation of a grammatical function with a class of grammatical items. Much work on the languages of native America is being done along these lines by Pike's students and colleagues. From 1955 to 1979 Pike was professor of linguistics at the University of Michigan where he completed his *Grammatical Analysis* (with E. G. Pike, Dallas, 1977). RHR

Pilinszky, János (b. Budapest, Hungary, 25.11.1921; d. Budapest, 27.5.1981). Hungarian poet, whose life and work were concentrated on the tragedy of war and human suffering. A Catholic by upbringing, he joined the army in 1944, only to be moved from one prison camp to another in Austria and Germany. His experiences there marked him for life. His poetry is terse, uncompromising, often difficult, and bleak in its message; every word is carefully calculated to express the moral responsibility he felt so acutely. The result is powerful and compelling; rarely has a poet succeeded in disturbing his readers so profoundly. He wrote comparatively little, and with great difficulty. His style is modern and deceptively unstructured; the apparent slightness of his aphorisms disappears on second reading. His influence has been considerable, particularly in a nation whose poets are seen as leaders. But his Christian existentialism carries a universal message; it is not specifically Hungarian or aimed at a particular kind of society. English versions of his work, with essays on it, are in *Selected Poems*

(tr. T. Hughes, Manchester, 1976) and *Crater* (tr. P. Jay, London, 1978). GFC

Pilniak, Boris Andreevich, ps. of B. A. Vogau (b. Mozhaysk, Russia, 29.9.1894; d. 1942). Russian novelist. Pilniak was a 'fellow-travelling' Soviet writer of exceptional if highly erratic gifts. Arrested in 1938, he disappeared after imprisonment and exile. He achieved fame after the publication of *Golyi god* (Moscow, 1922; tr. A. Tulloch, *The Naked Year*, London, 1975), a panoramic non-novel, the subject of which, if any, is revolutionary turmoil. In manner he followed the artistic trend of 'poetic rhythmic prose' initiated by BELY, and exercised considerable influence on Soviet prose in the 1920s. Using many styles, he combined impressionism with dithyrambic, jerky romanticism. Crude, naturalistic descriptions of events, coarse scenes of lovemaking, hymns to animal instincts, coexist incongruously with subtle philosophical meditation and sophisticated or vernacular verbal acrobatics. Pilniak aimed to confuse and shock his readers, and to convey his own inchoate, formless, even mushy experience of life. There are fine moments, especially in his other early work, which includes *Mashiny i volki* [Machine and wolves] (Moscow, 1925) and *Mat' syra-zemlya* (Moscow, 1926; tr. V. Reck & M. Green, *Mother Earth and Other Stories*, London, 1975), but such moments are not easily detectable. His ideological position was both idiosyncratic and eclectic – a blend of NIETZSCHEan humanism, Slavophilism, nationalistic Bolshevism, and anarchism. Such a mixture evoked extreme condemnation from postrevolutionary Russian émigrés, who dubbed Pilniak a prototype of 'cultural disintegration', but also brought him into conflict with the Soviet authorities. The latter circumstances impelled him to produce a more apposite novel: *Volga vpadaet v Kaspiyskoe more* (Moscow, 1931; tr. S. Malamith, *The Volga Flows to the Caspian Sea*, London, 1932) which describes the triumph of man's creative activity in conquering nature and overcoming the old inertia of Russian life. In fact, it was this inertia and everything primitive, rooted in elemental nature, which attracted Pilniak most, even when he dealt with such themes as the Red Army in *Povest'o nepogashennoi lune* [The tale of the unextinguished moon] (Moscow, 1926), a novel inspired by the death of the Red Army Commander-in-Chief Mikhail Frunze. Soviet Russia dazzled him to the extent to which it embodied the sweep and chaos of revolution and repelled him, as the West repelled him, on its way to civilized and industrialized existence. He was interested not in history but in the natural processes of birth, death, survival, sexual passion and general, if uncomfortable, dissolution in organic life. The collected works are: *Sobranie sochineniy* (8 vols, Moscow, 1929–30); *Izbrannye proizvedeniya* (Moscow, 1978).

EL

R. A. Maguire, 'The Pioneers: Pilniak and Ivanov' in *Major Soviet Writers*, ed. E. J. Brown (NY, 1973); V. Reck, *Boris Pilniak: a Soviet Writer in Conflict with the State* (NY, 1975).

Pilsudski, Józef Klemens (b. Zublów, Russian Poland [now Poland], 5.12.1867; d. Warsaw, 12.5.1935). Polish nationalist, leader of a Polish legion which fought for Austria-Hungary against Russia (1914–17), provisional head of the Polish state (1918–21), commander-in-chief of the Polish army (1918–23) and victor over the Bolshevik Red Army at Warsaw in 1920. He led a military coup in 1926, serving as Polish premier (1926–8 and 1930), and minister for war (1926–35), and as the dominant figure in collective military dictatorship until his death. Fiercely nationalist, he saw Poland as a major European power whose independence depended on balancing Germany with Russia, with aid from France. With HITLER's advent into power in Germany in 1933, his conviction that France would not act to suppress his government led him to conclude a 10-year nonaggression pact with Nazi Germany in January 1934. DCW

W. Reddaway, *Marshal Pilsudski* (London, 1939).

Pinatel, Jean (b. Urcuit, Basses-Pyrénées, France, 9.6.1913). French criminologist. After studying in Toulouse and Paris he entered the French public service, first as a magistrate, then as

inspector and later inspector-general of the judicial administration (1941–78), in which capacity he supervised prison administration. As secretary-general of the International Society for Criminology from 1950, and later as its president (1973–8), he was instrumental in developing the organization, which is based in Paris, into a major learned and internationally accredited society in the field of criminology. In recognition of his work he became honorary president of the society on his retirement in 1978. From 1952 to 1973 he taught regularly at the Institute of Criminology, faculty of law, at the Sorbonne. His presidential address to the eighth International Congress of Criminology at Lisbon in 1978 gives a remarkable synthesis of modern thinking in the field of criminology. His most important published works are *La Criminologie* [Criminology] (Paris, 1960, ³1979) and with B. Bouzat, *Traité de droit pénal et de criminologie*, iii *Criminologie* (Paris, 1963, ³1979). JEHW

J. Susini (ed.), *La Criminologie: Bilan et perspectives. Mélanges offerts à Jean Pinatel* (Paris, 1980).

Pincus, Gregory Goodwin (b. Woodbine, NJ, USA, 9.4.1903; d. Boston, Mass., 18.8.1967). American biologist. The son of a lecturer in agriculture, Pincus began in his father's footsteps by graduating at the Cornell School of Agriculture. He then studied genetics and reproductive physiology at Harvard. In 1944 Pincus and Hudson Hoagland established the Worcester Foundation for Experimental Biology and became its codirectors. Using rabbits, Pincus was the first scientist to induce parthenogenesis (virgin birth) in mammals. In 1951 the birth control campaigner Margaret Sanger made Pincus aware of the population explosion and of the effects of uncontrolled fertility on women's lives; this encounter was to influence the rest of Pincus's career. Two years later he and M. C. Chang analysed the antifertility effect of steroid hormones in mammals. Pincus, who was for many years a consultant for G. D. Searle & Sons (pharmaceutical manufacturers), recognized the significance of his laboratory findings and had the courage and persistence to set himself the task of translating these into an effective and socially acceptable method of controlling human fertility. The oral contraceptive pill received its field trials in Puerto Rico and Haiti and, having passed these tests successfully, was adopted internationally. At the time of his death, he and Chang were finishing the development of the morning-after contraceptive pill. His academic career was marked by brilliant research into endocrinology, cancer, cardiovascular problems, ageing and the physiology of reproduction. His principal publications were *The Eggs of Mammals* (NY, 1936) and *The Control of Fertility* (NY, 1965). CR

Pinter, Harold (b. London, UK, 10.10.1930). British dramatist. In his early 20s Pinter began a career as an actor, at the same time publishing occasional poetry in literary journals. He became a dramatist almost by accident, when a friend invited him to write a play for production at Bristol University and *The Room* (one-act, 1957) was completed. His first full-length play *The Birthday Party* (1958) ran for only five nights in London but was vigorously defended by *Sunday Times* critic Harold Hobson and aroused wide interest in a television production (1960). Since then a relatively small number of stage plays has established his international reputation: they include *The Caretaker* (1960), *The Homecoming* (1965), *Landscape* and *Silence* (both one-act, 1969), *Old Times* (1971), *No Man's Land* (1975) and *Other Places* (three one-act plays, 1982), supported by a body of shorter plays and sketches as well as drama for radio and television, much of which has later been presented in the theatre. His screenplays, which display much of his characteristic style, include *The Servant* (1963), *Accident* (1967), *The Go-Between* (1969), *The Proust Screenplay* (London, 1978) and *The French Lieutenant's Woman* (1981). Although he has virtually abandoned his acting career, he continues to direct for the stage. It is the style as much as the content of Pinter's theatre that has attracted much critical attention, and generated some far-fetched theories. From the late 1950s, in a period when social and political commitment was the distinguishing feature of the revitalized English theatre, Pinter has always explored personal rather than public themes. His early plays, sometimes labelled 'comedies of menace', usually show the invasion of some character's haven of security, represented by the room in which the action is set, by an unexplained intruder; later, the threat becomes internalized and Pinter shows similar forces at work within a sexual or family relationship. Pinter's refusal to provide the detailed exposition associated with naturalistic theatre, his insistence that different versions of the past can have equal validity for the present irrespective of their actual truth, and his preference for concluding exchanges of dialogue with pauses or silences rather than verbal resolution, can all become mannerisms, but when his writing is at its best they vividly illuminate the irrational nature of much human action and discourse. His apparently instinctive ability to evoke responses in his audiences at a deep psychological level is matched by an actor's sense of comedy and theatrical timing, and a keen ear for the incongruities and non sequiturs of colloquial speech. MA

M. Esslin, *Pinter: a Study of his Plays* (London, [3]1977).

Pirandello, Luigi (b. Agrigento, Sicily, Italy, 28.6.1867; d. Rome, 10.12.1936). Italian dramatist, novelist and short-story writer. After promising academic beginnings (degrees from Rome and Bonn), a series of family misfortunes spurred him to intense literary activity during the first years of this century; a continuous stream of poems, *novelle* and plays in Sicilian and Italian, as well as essays and critical articles flowed from his pen. The intense depression and eventual insanity of his wife were probably influential in his choice of themes, particularly the enigma of personality, the ambiguity of truth and reality, and the propensity of man to live by his own created myths, both personal and social. Behind his work stand FREUD and EINSTEIN to whose revolutionary theories he gave dramatic shape in a recognizable contemporary context. Only in 1921–2 was he internationally recognized as a dramatist, through his plays

Sei personaggi in cerca d'autore (*Six Characters in Search of an Author*, London, 1923, tr. F. May, London, 1954) and *Enrico IV* (*Henry IV*, London, 1923, tr. F. May, Harmondsworth, 1962). The former has been described rightly as 'the dramatic analogue of *The Waste Land*', for its scope and depth are indeed comparable with those of ELIOT's poem of the same year. *Sei personaggi*, together with *Ciascuno a suo modo* (1924; *Each in His Own Way*, London, 1925, tr. E. Bentley in *Naked Masks*, NY, 1952) and *Questa sera si recita a soggetto* (1930; *Tonight We Improvise*, NY, 1932, tr. M. Abba, NY, 1961) formed what Pirandello himself called his 'trilogy of the theatre in the theatre'; for with these plays he revolutionized modern theatrical techniques, creating a far greater degree of immediacy and involvement than had existed previously. He rejected established conventions because they led to complacency and the reduction of the theatrical experience to mere entertainment instead of serving as a source of instruction. Pirandello's method is a relentless questioning of convention, stripping away layer upon layer of illusion to arrive at the naked truth of the human condition in all its absurdity; for only the recognition of that truth can offer the hope of any real happiness to mankind. The result is pain and suffering, though observed always with infinite compassion.   ADT

G. Giudice, *Pirandello: a Biography* (London, 1975); O. Ragusa, *Luigi Pirandello: an Approach to his Theatre* (Edinburgh, 1980).

Pirenne, Henri (b. Verviers, Liège, Belgium, 23.12.1862; d. Uccle, Brussels, 24.10.1935). Belgian historian. Professor at Ghent (1886–1930) – a French speaker, Pirenne retired when Dutch was made the sole teaching language in Ghent. He wrote 30 books and nearly 300 articles, and became a national figure, commemorated in street names and on stamps, partly for his opposition to the Germans during WW1, and partly for his monumental *Histoire de Belgique* [History of Belgium] (7 vols, Brussels, 1900–32). Historians now remember him best for a series of lively and controversial books and articles on the history of trade, towns and democracy in the Middle Ages, including *Les Anciennes Démocraties des Pays-Bas* (Paris, 1910; *Belgian Democracy, its Early History*, Manchester, 1915); 'The Stages in the Social History of Capitalism', *American Historical Review*, 1913–14; and *Medieval Cities* (first published in English, Princeton, 1925). His last and perhaps best-known book *Mahomet et Charlemagne* (Paris, 1937; *Mohammed and Charlemagne*, London, 1939) was the boldest of all, arguing that the Middle Ages really began not with the barbarian invasions but with the rise of Islam, which cut Christendom off from the Mediterranean and led to a decline in western trade and towns. Pirenne's problem-oriented comparative history attracted M. BLOCH, and in a sense his influence lives on in the French journal *Annales*.   UPB

B. Lyon, *Henri Pirenne* (Ghent, 1974).

Piscator, Erwin Friedrich Max (b. nr Wetzlar, Hesse, Germany, 17.12.1893; d. Starnberg, Bavaria, West Germany, 20.3.1966). German radical theatre director. In Berlin, as organizer of the Proletarian Theatre (1920–1), director (1924–7) for the Volksbühne and head of his own Piscatorbühne (1927–31), Piscator was the chief exponent of that communist-oriented 'Political Theatre' on which he centred his book *Das politische Theater* (Berlin, 1929; tr. H. Rorrison, *The Political Theater*, NY, 1978). This was a form of 'epic theatre', aiming to involve its audience as at a public meeting, and using new stage machinery like lifts and treadmills, together with the projection of documentary material by means of slides or film. Although the '*Totaltheater*' designed for it by GROPIUS was never built, it was already technically and artistically in advance of other avant-garde theatres in Western Europe or Russia, but handicapped by the quality of its scripts and (from 1927 on) the optimism of its financial calculations. Having crashed twice, Piscator in 1931 left to film *The Revolt of the Fishermen* (1934) in Russia, where he stayed until 1936 as head of the International Association of Revolutionary Theatres. He then spent two years in Paris, shelved his communism and from 1939 to 1951 ran a theatre school in New York, where he tried vainly to get a footing on Broadway. Back in West Germany, he had to struggle for 10 years before re-establishing himself as artistic director of the West Berlin Volksbühne in 1962. Here he promoted the new documentary drama of Hochhuth, Kipphardt and Peter Weiss but without achieving the directorial triumphs of the 1920s.   JWMW

M. Ley-Piscator, *The Piscator Experiment* (NY, 1967); J. Willett, *The Theatre of Erwin Piscator* (London, 1978).

Pius XII, *né* Eugenio Pacelli (b. Rome, Italy, 2.3.1876; d. Castelgandolfo, Latium, 9.10.1958). Italian pope. Roman aristocrat and Vatican high-flyer, Pacelli became nuncio to Bavaria in 1917 and witnessed the Communist revolution there. Later he served in Berlin. In 1930 he became cardinal secretary of state and negotiated the Concordat with HITLER in 1933. Inevitably he was elected pope in a one-day conclave in March 1939. WW2 dominated the first phase of his pontificate. The Vatican policy of strict 'impartiality' was often misunderstood as both sides pressed for his acquiescence if not blessing. As a well-known Germanophile and anti-Bolshevik, it sometimes seemed that he gave the Nazi regime too much benefit of the doubt and that his 'silences' on the persecution of the Jews were culpable. His defence was that public denunciation would have made things worse both for Jews and German Catholics. After WW2 he was at first hailed as the 'defender of the city of Rome' because he had saved it from Allied bombardments. Later he was less popular as he interfered in Italian political life in the interests of the Christian Democrats. He turned anticommunism into a system. He was dubbed 'the Pope of the Atlantic Alliance'. He lived too long and talked on too many topics on which he did not know enough. In 1950 he set up a new obstacle to ecumenism by defining the bodily Assumption of Mary as a dogma; and with *Humani Generis* he denounced a vaguely conceived 'new theology' alleged to be found in France. Yet earlier his pontificate had a reforming aspect which gave some hint of things to come: the Holy Week services were reshaped, the eucharist fast was reduced, married convert clergymen were ordained, and at least two of his encyclicals, *Mystici Corporis* (1943, on the church as the mystical body of Christ) and *Mediator Dei* (1947, on worship), both summed up and stimulated theological thinking.   PAH

G. Papini, *The Popes in the Twentieth Century* (London, 1967); J. D. Holmes, *The Papacy in the Modern World* (London, 1981).

Planck, Max Karl Ernst Ludwig (b. Kiel, Schleswig-Holstein, Germany, 23.4.1858; d. Göttingen, Lower Saxony, 4.9.1947). German theoretical physicist who first showed the quantum nature of radiation and together with EINSTEIN founded modern physics. He was deeply interested in fundamental questions of the nature of the universe and impressed by the correspondence between our thought and the external world. During early work on thermodynamics he realized the fundamental character of black-body radiation, since its spectral distribution is independent of the source material. He tried to calculate its energy distribution but could only obtain a formula agreeing with experiment if he assumed that light of frequency v is emitted in discrete quanta of energy hv, where h is Planck's constant of action. He tried without success to fit the quantum of action into the framework of classical mechanics, and this convinced him that a revolutionary new concept had been introduced into atomic physics. For this work he was awarded the Nobel prize in 1918. Einstein later showed that quanta are a feature of all radiation, and found supporting evidence, experimental and theoretical, for the corpuscular nature of light. The concept of quanta is fundamental to modern physics, and underlies the subsequent development of quantum mechanics by SOMMERFELD, Niels BOHR, BORN, DIRAC, HEISENBERG, PAULI and many others. Through the tortuous road leading to his discovery Planck was guided by his belief in the absolute and objective character of scientific truths; he was rewarded by the discovery of a fundamental constant of nature. He continued to develop the quantum theory, and discovered the zero-point energy of oscillators. During his work on the theory of relativity he realized that all matter contains enormous amounts of energy, which might perhaps one day be liberated. He also derived the Fokker–Planck equation for the change in space and time of a distribution of particles subject to small irregular impulses. In later years he wrote extensively on the philosophy of science and on religion, and continued to work on the unification of physical theories. He believed that science is based on the recognition of a reality external to the observer. He wrote on causal laws and the freedom of the will, arguing that there is only an apparent contradiction between them. He assumed that causality is valid in nature, though this cannot be proved, and must be given its appropriate meaning in each field. He professed his belief in an almighty, omniscient and beneficent God, identical in character with the power of physical law. He remained active long after his retirement, and was a firm opponent of Nazism. F. Gaynor has translated and edited *Wisseschaftliche Selbstbiographie* (Leipzig, 1948) as *Max Planck: a Scientific Autobiography and Other Papers* (NY, 1949).   PEH

Plath, Sylvia (b. Boston, Mass., USA, 27.10.1932; d. London, UK, 11.2.1963). American poet. Plath's poems, especially those in her posthumous collection *Ariel* (London, 1965), contributed to a new mood of personal frankness in American poetry in the 1960s. Described, with LOWELL and BERRYMAN, as a 'confessional' poet, Plath wrote freely about her own disturbed feelings. In this she went far beyond the personal dimensions of modern lyric poetry. She explored psychological states and painful emotions which were only to be confronted at great personal cost. Her early poems, written with considerable skill, lacked an urgency of statement. When she met the English poet Ted HUGHES, and after their marriage, she gained access to the inner creative strengths which had previously been suppressed or muffled. In the *Ariel* poems, written in the last two years of her life, Plath worked with a power of invention which was perceived at once to be remarkable. In such poems as 'Daddy' and 'Lady Lazarus' she elaborated a personal symbolism, and strained to breaking-point the capacity of metaphor to structure a lyric poem. The unmistakable note of hysteria and psychological torment led to speculation on the 'murderous' nature of her art. Plath committed suicide at the age of 30, leaving two children. Her *Collected Poems* appeared in 1981 (London), edited by Ted Hughes. In addition to her poems, she wrote short stories, collected in *Johnny Panic and the Bible of Dreams* (London, 1977), and a novel *The Bell Jar* (London, 1963), which first appeared under the pseudonym 'Victoria Lucas'.   EH
C. Newman (ed.), *The Art of Sylvia Plath* (London, 1970); J. Kroll, *Chapters in a Mythology: the Poetry of Sylvia Plath* (NY, 1976).

Plessner, Helmuth (b. Wiesbaden, Hesse, Germany, 4.9.1892). German philosopher. Together with SCHELER, Plessner founded the new discipline of philosophical anthropology in the 1920s. In his *Die Stufen des Organischen und der Mensch* [Man and the stages of the organic] (Berlin, 1928, [3]1975), Plessner examined the relationships of plant, animal, and man to their respective types of environment. In what amounts to a philosophical reinstatement of the ancient concept of nature, of *physis*, and in conscious opposition to such thinkers as the neo-Kantian CASSIRER and the historian of ideas DILTHEY, for whom 'philosophy ends where the bodily dimension begins', Plessner seeks to offer a deeper and more comprehensive account of man; for him, the unity of body and mind is underscored by a derivation of specifically human capacities from man's peculiar place in the natural order, and above all from his relationship to his own body. Unlike the animals, whose life in nature is 'centric', man can distance himself from his body and its movements, and make them an object of reflection for himself; in this sense man adopts an 'eccentric position': he stands both inside and outside himself. Language, institutions, tools, intersubjectivity and all meaningful gestures ultimately stem from this fact. Hence Plessner does not see language as of central importance: language does not explain man's special attributes, his '*Monopole*'; rather, his 'eccentric position' explains language as one among several such '*Monopole*' – a whole range of other, nonverbal forms of human expression, to which Plessner has devoted influential studies, not least *Lachen und Weinen* (Arnheim, 1941, [3]1970; tr. J. Spencer Churchill & M. Grene, *Laughter and Weeping*, Evanston, Ill., 1970). The general effect of Plessner's work is to undermine all forms of anthropocentrism, and to reinstate the ultimate integrity of man and nature. In *Schicksal des deutschen Geistes* [Fate of the German spirit] (Zürich, 1935; republished as *Die verspätete Nation* [The retarded emergence of a nation], Stuttgart, 1959), Plessner provides an acutely perceptive but controversial genealogy of German fascism.   RNH

F. Hammer, *Die exzentrische Position des Menschen* (Bonn, 1967).

Poincaré, Jules Henri (b. Nancy, Meurthe-et-Moselle, France, 29.4.1854; d. Paris, 17.12.1912). French mathematician and philosopher. Perhaps the most brilliant and prolific mathematician of the second half of the 19c, Poincaré made important contributions to virtually all aspects of pure and applied mathematics, and was also influential as a philosopher of mathematics and of science.

Poincaré's chief mathematical interest was differential equations. They led him in the 1880s to important contributions to 'automorphic functions', and later to existence theorems on solutions. Among applications of differential equations, he wrote extensively on the three-body (Sun-Moon-Earth) problem: the 'Poincaré recurrence theorem' is a remarkable result on the recurrence of planetary orbits. He also studied planetary physics, producing important conclusions on possible shapes in which the earth could be in equilibrium. He wrote extensively on heat and thermodynamics, and on probability, where he laid the foundations of ergodic theory. In pure mathematics he introduced a number of notable innovations into topology.

Poincaré's philosophy of science is called 'conventionalism'. For him a scientific theory was a convention, of which one demands 'simplicity' and generality of application; one is not concerned with its truth. This view guided his contributions to the foundations of mechanics in the 1900s, where he saw Newton's laws as 'definitions in disguise' and rather opposed EINSTEIN's theory of relativity, although he enunciated the principle of relativity himself. In the philosophy of mathematics his position was similar to Kant's, and he opposed both the formalism of HILBERT and the logicism of Bertrand RUSSELL. He gathered his philosophical writings into popular books (*La science et l'hypothèse*, Paris, 1903; *La valeur de la science*, Paris, 1905; *Science et méthode*, Paris, 1908; all tr. G. B. Halsted in one volume as *The Foundations of Science*, London, 1913). The English translations of these and of *Dernières Pensées* (Paris, 1913; *Mathematics and Science, Last Essays*, London, 1963) are still in print. In 35 years he produced, on average, a book a year (including editions of his lectures at the Sorbonne) and also about 500 papers. His papers are collected in *Oeuvres* (11 vols, Paris, 1916–54). IG-G

Poincaré, Raymond Nicolas Landry (b. Bar-le-Duc, Meuse, France, 20.8.1860; d. Paris, 15.10.1934). French politician, prime minister (1912–13), president (1913–20), prime minister and foreign minister (1922–4, 1926–9). Radical by party, he was a consistent advocate of strong, not to say nationalistic, government, seeking to strengthen the powers of the presidency while he occupied it, and to reform France's electoral laws to provide for more stable government. As postwar premier he personified French determination to keep Germany weak, rejecting British attempts to rehabilitate German finance, trade and industry, and using the reparations issue eventually to justify French occupation of the Ruhr in 1923. The failure of this policy defeated his cabinet, but he returned in 1926 to head a 'Government of National Union' which stabilized the franc at the cost of rigid financial economies. Patriotic, nationalist, a believer in strong government, suspicious of Britain and of

French Anglophiles, he was, in some sense, a forerunner of the foreign policies practised by DE GAULLE. Poincaré published 10 volumes of memoirs *Au service de la France* [In the service of France] (Paris, 1926–33).   DCW

Poiret, Paul (b. Paris, France, 20.4.1879; d. Paris, 28.4.1944). French couturier, responsible for freeing women from the restrictive corsetry and formal stance, typically Victorian and Edwardian. At 18, apprenticed to an umbrella-maker, he began selling designs to Chéruit and, after working for Doucet and Worth, set up his own business, dressing famous courtesans of the *belle époque*. Poiret always associated with the avant-garde, and was patron to BRANCUSI, André Segonzac, Kees Van Dongen and MATISSE. Prior to DIAGHILEV's Ballets Russes, he introduced vibrant colour and pattern with his orientalist clothes, a strong contrast to the Edwardian faded pastels. He initiated fundamental changes in clothes, and personally influenced interior design by setting up his school and shop, Martine. To facilitate sinuous movement in his supple clothes, he invented the rubber girdle and, in 1907, the brassière. Other radical ventures in which Poiret was successful included inventing and marketing perfume to complement his clothes; setting up publicity brochures illustrated by Paul Iribe and Georges Lepape; engaging a team of young artistic girls, *Les Martineux*, to design wallpapers, fabrics, objects, etc. Although Segonzac stated that Poiret 'was one of the most influential personalities of the early 20c', the designer died in penury.   JWB

Polanyi, Michael (b. Budapest, Austria-Hungary [now Hungary], 12.3.1891; naturalized British citizen; d. Oxford, UK, 22.2.1976). Hungarian/British physical chemist, social scientist and philosopher. Michael Polanyi must be ranked as one of the most versatile scientists of the century. His work embraced the fields of thermodynamics, physical adsorption, X-ray crystallography, fibre science and reaction kinetics; and in his later years his main interests were in social studies and philosophy. Polanyi first qualified in medicine at the University of Budapest

(1913). By then he was already interested in chemistry and had written on thermodynamics and the first of several papers on physical adsorption before the outbreak of WW1. The usefulness of the Polanyi potential theory of adsorption was not fully appreciated for some 40 years; it is now recognized as a fundamental contribution to the subject. In 1920 he joined the Kaiser Wilhelm Institute for Fibre Chemistry in Berlin, where he contributed to the interpretation of the X-ray diffraction patterns of fibres. He moved to HABER's Institute of Physical and Electrochemistry in 1923. His earlier interest in the rates of chemical reactions was now revived and for the next 25 years this was to be his main scientific activity. He originated both experimental and theoretical work and proposed the method of crossed molecular beams for the study of reactions in gases. His work on the 'flames' produced by the reaction of metal vapours, such as sodium, with chlorine-containing substances, contributed to the development of theories of reaction kinetics. In 1933 Polanyi resigned from the Kaiser Wilhelm Institute in protest against the dismissal of Jewish scientists and accepted a new chair of physical chemistry at Manchester. During the 1940s his interests turned towards the problems arising from the conflicts between personal freedom and central planning, especially their impact on scientists. In 1948 he was appointed to a chair of social studies in Manchester and devoted himself not only to studies on the nature of knowledge, skills and discovery (*Personal Knowledge*, London, 1958) but to furthering the cause of personal freedom through the Society for Freedom in Science. From 1958 until his death Polanyi lived and worked in Oxford. There he continued his philosophical writings which were, however, not always received without criticism and suspicion in philosophic circles (*Knowing and Being*, London, 1969; *Scientific Thought and Social Reality*, London, 1974).   DHE

Pollock, Jackson (b. Cody, Wyo., USA, 28.1.1912; d. East Hampton, NY, 11.8.1956). American abstract expressionist painter. Pollock studied at the

Art Students' League under Thomas Hart Benton (1930–3). Between 1938 and 1943 he worked occasionally for the Federal Art Project. He was impressed by David Alfaro Sequeiros's experiments with spray guns and airbrushes. In 1939 and 1941 he underwent JUNGian analysis, using his drawings as therapeutic aids. In 1942 he met MOTHERWELL, HOFMANN and the surrealist MATTA. In 1943 Peggy Guggenheim became his patron. In c. 1940, influenced by the expressive pictorial effects of Benton, postcubist PICASSO, OROZCO and surrealist automatism (MASSON and Matta had moved to New York c. 1940), Pollock began to explore the expressive potential of a primitive gestural imagery, combining aggressive graffiti-like forms with rhythmic calligraphic arabesques and 'activating' the whole surface of the canvas (e.g. The She-Wolf, 1943; The Guardians of the Secret, 1943). In 1947 he began to drip and pour paint arbitrarily on to the canvas spread on the floor, in order to feel more physically involved in the process of painting (hence the term 'action painting'). His automatism was always modified by rhythm and subtle control of lines and drips. The resulting labyrinthine impasto of coloured pigments laced with black and white unify the surface and evoke moods ranging from the dynamic to the oppressive (e.g. Full Fathom Five, 1947; One (Number 31) 1950, 1950), depending on density. In 1950–2 he concentrated on black paintings, using diluted enamel on raw canvas (e.g. Number 14, 1951) to fuse colour and surface. In later works, both black and multicoloured, the traditional figure/ground relationship reasserted itself (e.g. Portrait and a Dream, 1953). Pollock's drip paintings introduced overall painting, with no apparent beginning or end, and the concept of the large-scale wall painting affecting the whole environment. He died in a (perhaps intentional) car crash.   SOBT

F. V. O'Connor, Jackson Pollock (NY, 1967).

Ponge, Francis Jean Gaston Alfred (b. Montpellier, Hérault, France, 27.3.1899). French poet. Although his first prose poems Douze petits écrits [Twelve short pieces] (Paris) were published as early as 1926, it was only after WW2 that Ponge gained public recognition, thanks largely to SARTRE's 1944 essay on his Le Parti pris des choses [The bias of things] (Paris, 1942). The majority of Ponge's prose poems are minutely precise descriptions of everyday objects (an orange, a pigeon, rain) and are characterized by the intellectual rigour of their play on all the meanings of the words used, including archaic and etymological, as they move constantly between a physical description and a lexical definition of the object in an attempt to overcome both its 'otherness' and the instability of language itself. Later texts, such as Le Savon (Paris, 1967; tr. L. Dunlop, Soap, London, 1969), illustrate the creative process by bringing together rough drafts and the finished, object-like poem. Ponge sees his work as having a political import: the purification of language is an equivalent to and a prerequisite for social progress. His overt political concerns are evinced by his early membership of the Socialist party, his trade union militancy during the Popular Front, his participation in the Resistance and his membership of the Communist party from 1937 to 1947. For Sartre, Ponge's work was phenomenological in inspiration; for the theoreticians of the nouveau roman it is a continuation of Mallarmé's work and a direct anticipation of their own interest in the materiality of language.   DM

I. Higgins, Francis Ponge (London, 1979).

Pontoppidan, Henrik (b. Fredericia, Vejle, Denmark, 24.7.1857; d. Ordrup, 21.8.1943). Danish novelist. A prolific writer whose early publications up to 1890 – 13 books in 10 years – can now be seen as a preparation for his main achievement as an author: three great novel cycles, comprising 16 volumes in all (of which only two are available in English). The first cycle – Det forjættede Land [The promised land] (3 vols, Copenhagen, 1891–5; tr. E. Lucas, Emanuel, or Children of the Soil and The Promised Land, London, 1896); and Dommens Dag [Day of judgement] – gives an ironic and hostile account of the prevailing religious orthodoxies. The second cycle Lykke-Per [Lucky Peter] (8 vols, Copenhagen, 1898–1904), which marks the peak of Pontoppidan's achievement as a novelist, is fictionalized cultural history of a high order, introducing and analysing many of the ideas and beliefs of the age. The third, *De Dødes Rige* [The kingdom of the dead] (5 vols, Copenhagen, 1912–16), is again in essence a portrait of an age – the years leading up to WW1 – and is carried along by the cogency of its social comment. Pontoppidan was awarded the Nobel prize for literature in 1917.   JWMcF

Popov, Oleg Konstantinovitch (b. Vyrubovo, nr Moscow, USSR, 31.7.1930). Russian circus clown of international repute. He entered the State Circus School, Moscow, in 1945 and specialized in tightrope walking, but also studied juggling, acrobatics and animal training. He made his debut at Tbilisi, Georgia, in 1949. After working as an assistant to Karandash, he deputized for an injured clown at Saratov and decided to make clowning his career. In 1956 he appeared with the Moscow State Circus in Brussels, Paris and London, and five years later in Cuba, Canada, the USA and Italy. His familiarity with different circus disciplines enabled him to parody other acts on the bill and his frequent appearances in the ring ensured a sympathetic reception for the talented company. Although appreciating tradition he does not portray courageous resignation to inevitable misfortune, as did CHAPLIN, but rather ecstatic surprise at unexpected achievement, reminiscent of Grock. However, it is the character of a mischievous boy, which he created, and his own happy-go-lucky personality that dominate his performance. He has worked in films and musicals, sometimes with his wife Alexandrina Ilynitchna. He was made Artist of Merit in 1957, and awarded the Clown d'Or at the Monte Carlo International Circus Festival in 1981. He has written his autobiography as *Ma Vie de Clown* [My life as a clown] (Paris, 1968).   ADHC

Popper, Karl Raimund (b. Vienna, Austria-Hungary [now Austria], 28.7.1902; naturalized British citizen, 1945). Austrian/British philosopher. The son of a cultivated Viennese lawyer, he secured an education of a broad and varied kind in the disturbed conditions of the city after 1918, writing a dissertation on a topic in psychology and working for some years as a schoolteacher. He was associated with the Vienna circle but was not a member of it, being highly critical of some of the main doctrines of logical positivism. But he shared the interests and problems of the circle and his first book *Logik der Forschung* (Vienna, 1934, ^{6}1976; *The Logic of Scientific Discovery*, London, 1959, ^{2}1968) appeared in a series sponsored by it. In 1937 he left Austria for a teaching post in philosophy in New Zealand and came to the London School of Economics in 1946. Appointed professor of logic and scientific method, he retired in 1969. Popper held that the positivists were wrong to suppose that scientific theory is developed from observation by way of a mechanical routine of inductive generalization. Also mistaken was their attempt to distinguish science from metaphysics, which they regarded as nonsense, by the empirical verifiability of its propositions. Science in his view is a matter of imaginative conjecture, rationally controlled by the resolute pursuit of falsification. A theory 'proves its mettle' by withstanding our determined efforts to refute it. It is falsifiability, the capacity for being falsified, that distinguishes science from nonscience including metaphysics. And nonscience is not always nonsense. It can suggest falsifiable, and thus scientific, hypotheses. Some of it, however, is pseudoscience – in particular MARXism and psychoanalysis, the two great intellectual superstitions of the epoch. A thoroughgoing critique of Marxism is to be found in *The Open Society and its Enemies* (2 vols, London, 1945, ^{5}1966) where Popper uses his theory of scientific knowledge to attack 'historicism', the idea that social science can and should seek out the general laws of historical development. Plato and, too polemically, Hegel are also examined. His criticism of historical prediction is developed in *The Poverty of Historicism* (London, 1957, ^{2}1961). In later work Popper has elaborated an evolutionary view of the growth of knowledge which, he argues, is not something subjective and mental but an objective and self-subsistent product of human activity (*Objective Knowledge: an Evolutionary Approach*, Oxford, 1972, [5]1974). He has also argued for the irreducibility of the mental to the physical, without claiming that the mind can exist independently of the body in *The Self and its Brain* (with J. C. ECCLES, London, 1977). Popper writes with admirable lucidity (see *Unended Quest: an Intellectual Autobiography*, London, [2]1976) and resembles Bertrand RUSSELL in the range of his learning.   AQ

B. Magee, *Popper* (London, 1973).

Porter, Cole (b. Peru, Ind., USA, 9.6.1891; d. Santa Monica, Calif., 15.10.1964). American songwriter. He came from an affluent background and began writing music as a young boy, contributing songs to amateur and university shows in his student years, during which he read law as well as studying music at Harvard. His first Broadway show was a 'patriotic comic opera' *à la* Gilbert and Sullivan called *See America First* (1916). After this failed he went to live in Paris, joined the Foreign Legion and finally married; he and his wife gave fashionable parties on the Riviera, in Paris or Venice and altogether lived the kind of sophisticated life that is implied by such Porter songs as 'You're the Top' and 'I Get a Kick out of You' with their mention of high-life interests from GANDHI and the Mona Lisa to private flying and cocaine. Indeed, in sheer chic he matched his English contemporary COWARD, and after *Gay Divorce* (1932) he was recognized as a major force in the American theatre. Several of his musicals were filmed, including the Shakespeare-based *Kiss Me, Kate* (1948) which some regard as his masterpiece. Musically and in terms of literary elegance he set standards of songwriting that have not been surpassed, while there is genuine passion in such songs as 'Night and Day' and 'Begin the Beguine'.   CH

G. Eells, *The Life that Late He Led* (NY, 1967).

Porter, George (b. Stainforth, S. Yorks., UK, 6.12.1920). British physical chemist.

Porter's work has been concerned with extremely rapid reactions in the gas phase, especially photochemical reactions involving free radicals, and with photochemistry generally. In the late 1940s, in association with NORRISH, he developed a novel technique – flash photolysis, which opened up new realms of physico-chemical investigation of very rapid gaseous reactions. This was an early example of the harnessing of the then adolescent science of electronics to the study of chemical reactions. Porter's subsequent work has been mainly concerned with the application of the flash photolysis method to diverse problems in physics, chemistry and biology. He has also contributed to the study of other techniques, especially radical trapping and matrix stabilization. His contributions to science in general have not been solely in the discovery of new knowledge but in communication between scientists of different disciplines and between scientists and nonscientists. He received the Nobel prize in 1967, jointly with Norrish and EIGEN, for work on ultrarapid reactions.   NBC

Porter, Rodney Robert (b. Newton-le-Willows, Mers., UK, 8.10.1917). British immunochemist. Influenced by the immunologist LANDSTEINER, who linked antibody activity to chemical specifics of antigens, and SANGER, who developed techniques for determining protein structure, Porter investigated the chemical structure of antibodies (i.e. proteins produced to combat infection). Using the protein-cleaving enzyme papain (from papaya) to break up antibodies, he found that they were composed of three distinct regions, two of which were alike and would bind antigens, the chemical targets of antibodies. This explained the ability of antibodies to bind to two sites, thereby connecting and 'clumping' antigens, in terms of chemical structure. In 1963 (with Elizabeth Press) Porter showed that antibodies are composed of four separate peptide molecules linked together. In the 1960s he helped organize the worldwide Antibody Workshops which did much to further molecular immunology. With Edelmann he received the 1972 Nobel prize for physiology and medicine. The structure of antibodies has turned out to provide revolutionary insights into the control and organization of genes. Since 1967 Porter has been Whitley professor of biochemistry at Oxford.   DOM

J. J. Head (ed.), *Chemical Aspects of Immunology* (Burlington, 1976).

Posner, Richard Allen (b. New York, USA, 11.1.1939). American jurist and acknowledged leader of the 'law and economics' movement. Drawing inspiration from Ronald Coase's pioneering work at the University of Chicago, Posner sought to provide an economic rationalization for broad areas of law and legal institutions: *Economic Analysis of Law* (Boston, Mass., 1972, ²1977). Much of the writing was directed to economic analysis as an explanatory tool. Posner attempted to demonstrate, in particular, that the core principles of the judge-made private law (property, contract and tort) contained an implicit economic logic, allocating responsibilities in such a way as to maximize the value of resources to those dealing with them, what he was later to describe as 'wealth-maximization'. This approach, alongside that of Guido Calabresi of Yale, had an enormous impact on legal scholarship in the 1970s: the 'law and economics' movement spread beyond Chicago (where from 1972 to 1980 Posner edited the *Journal of Legal Studies*) to other centres in the USA and then to Canada and Europe. Major controversy surrounded and still surrounds the normative implications of Posner's work, and his latest efforts to argue that wealth-maximization is an appropriate goal of law – *The Economics of Justice* (Cambridge, Mass., 1981) – have done little to dilute the criticism.   AIO

A. Leff, 'Economic analysis of law: some realism about nominalism', *Virginia Law Review*, 60 (1974), 451–82, and 'Changes in the common law: legal and economic perspectives', *Journal of Legal Studies*, 9 (1980), 189–427.

Potter, Helen Beatrix (b. London, UK, 6.7.1866; d. Sawrey, Cumbria, 22.12.1943). British writer and illustrator of children's stories. The first book *The Tale of Peter Rabbit* (London, 1902), and subsequent books published by Frederick Warne in the same small format, contained illustrated tales about rabbits, kittens, mice and other creatures. While the anthropomorphic animal story, often with moral attitudes, was a well-established tradition, Beatrix Potter's particular contribution to the genre was in the quality of her illustrations, drawn from life, and their aptness to the text. Rarely portraying humans, she captured essentially animal characteristics and, latterly, a feeling of the Lakeland landscape. Word and picture were used in an absolutely complementary sense. *The Tailor of Gloucester* (London, 1903) was described by John Masefield as 'a gem of English prose'. Her stories are simple and direct yet her use of language is interesting and uncondescending. The appeal of such animal characters as Mrs Tiggy-Winkle and Jeremy Fisher has made her books lasting nursery favourites in many countries.   JMM

L. Linder, *A History of the Writings of Beatrix Potter, including Unpublished Work* (London, 1971); L. Linder & W. A. Herring (eds), *The Art of Beatrix Potter* (London, ²1972).

Poujade, Pierre (b. Saint-Céré, Lot, France, 1.12.1920). French politician. A small bookseller, from 1954 to 1958 he headed an independent conservative movement in France, *l'Union de Défense des Commerçants et Artisans*, which won 52 seats in the elections of 1956 on a programme of anti-intellectualism, covert anti-Semitism, anti-Socialism and anti-European slogans, basing itself on the protest of France's small shopkeepers, petit bourgeois and self-employed manual workers against high taxation, inflation and central government. The events of 1958, the advent of DE GAULLE and the Fifth Republic, destroyed the basis of the movement, whose leaders faded back into the provincial obscurity from which they had emerged.   DCW

Pound, Ezra Loomis (b. Hailey, Idaho, USA, 30.10.1885; d. Venice, Veneto, Italy, 1.11.1972). American poet. Pound epitomized all that was controversial in modern literature. He, more than any other of the 'Men of 1914' (ELIOT, Wyndham LEWIS, JOYCE), aggressively played the roles of theoretician and publicist for Modernism, a mode of art which was difficult, technically experimental and accepted that the true audience for modern art would be composed mainly of practitioners of the arts and a small group of sympathizing critics.

Pound's early poetry was highly derivative. He had studied Romance languages at the University of Pennsylvania and imitated troubadour poetic forms. His first book of prose *The Spirit of Romance* (London, 1910) offered an enthusiastic account of troubadour and other writing. Pound read the troubadours as the Pre-Raphaelites had, and Dante Gabriel Rossetti's *Early Italian Poets* (1861) was an enduring influence. He learned from Browning, and from YEATS, the use of the *persona* in the dramatic monologue.

From *A Lume Spento* (Venice, 1908) to *Canzoni* (London, 1911) Pound's work remained remote from modernity. He promised to become a new bard of muscular Christianity. But he soon sought a more aggressive tone modelled on classical satire and epigram, which he achieved in *Ripostes* (London, 1912) and *Lustra* (London, 1916). He wanted to replace late-romantic sentiments with a new austerity and precision. At the same time he created the imagist movement (with Richard Aldington and H. D.), pushing the desired brevity and suggestiveness to a new dimension, and began work on the poetic notebooks of the American orientalist FENOLLOSA. Pound's translations based on Fenollosa's notes, collected in *Cathay* (London, 1915), are among the most beautiful of Pound's writings. Their status as translations has been less certain.

Pound's development was complex and rapid, though his best work of the London years, the 'Homage to Sextus Propertius' and 'Hugh Selwyn Mauberley', was virtually unknown until the 1930s. The former poem, closely derived from the Latin, was not a translation but a tribute and an exercise in the manner of the Latin original. 'Hugh Selwyn Mauberley' is the single most brilliant of Pound's shorter pieces. Written in a crisp, emphatic manner, with great use of rhyme and stanza Pound puzzled many readers by his use of a *persona* very much like himself in his earlier, aesthetic period.

Pound settled in Paris after the Armistice, and eventually moved to Italy. His interests ranged over all areas of modern art, from dance to music, painting and sculpture. During the 1930s his interest in social questions grew, as did his appreciation of Mussolini's Fascist regime in Italy. Life in philistine, bourgeois Britain was impossible for someone devoted to art, Pound concluded. Though he never abandoned the humanist notion that the arts had a civilizing mission, he turned against the political culture of humanism, and its democratic expression. He applied to social questions the priorities of art, and was led far along the by-paths of elitism and fascism, in which he saw the promise of a society reorganized along lines which an artist could approve.

Pound began working on a long poem, provisionally entitled 'The Cantos', during WW1. It has as its subject the whole of classical, medieval and modern history and culture. It was to be an epic, but he concentrated on the presentation of what he called 'radiant gists', moments or symbols which were portents or expressions of the age-old struggle of meaning to unfold itself in human affairs. The individual Cantos were published in a series of volumes over some 50 years; it became clear that the design of the poem altered during composition, and that the contingent circumstances of Pound's career, and of modern history, were more significant than any plan. Pound relied heavily on juxtaposition: images, symbols, phrases, characters appear in seemingly fortuitous relation to each other. Some Cantos are more coherent than others – particularly the sequences on the early history of the American republic, and those on China. Many readers have felt that the method of composition was unnecessarily obscure, that there were too many recondite allusions, and that the whole of the poem, left unfinished at Pound's death, could not sustain the meaning imposed on it. The general reader of poetry probably finds the *Cantos* the most forbidding and difficult poem in the English language.

Pound unwisely broadcast over the Italian radio service during WW2, for which he was arrested and sent to Washington (he was still an American citizen) for trial. A psychiatric examination prevented a treason charge. Declared unfit to stand trial, he was sent to a federal mental hospital. He continued to work on his poem in this period, and was awarded the Bollingen prize in 1948 for the *Pisan Cantos*. An award of this distinction, given to an accused traitor, was intensely resented in America. Pound became the focus of a debate whether poetic quality of versification could (or should) be separated from the specific content of the poem, and the author's actions and attitudes. Were, as Pound suggests, the outraged *partizani* who lynched MUSSOLINI no more than 'maggots' eating the 'dead bullock'? Pound's supporters, who included the best poets of the day, preferred to emphasize the many generous services which Pound undertook on behalf of literature, and his great skills as a poet.   EH

N. Stock, *The Life of Ezra Pound* (NY, 1970); H. Kenner, *The Pound Era* (Berkeley, Calif., 1971); E. Homberger (ed.), *Ezra Pound: the Critical Heritage* (London, 1972).

Pound, Roscoe (b. Lincoln, Nebr., USA, 27.10.1870; d. Cambridge, Mass., 1.7.1964). American jurist, leader of those who profess sociological jurisprudence, emphasizing the need to consider the actual working of the legal system in society. He was influenced by EHRLICH. Law was to him social engineering, to secure the maximum of people's wants for the minimum of friction and waste, and involved the balancing of competing interests. He classified the interests protected by law into: (*a*) individual interests: (1) personality, (2) domestic relations, and (3) substance; (*b*) public interests: (1) of the state as a juristic person, (2) of the state as guardian of social interests; (*c*) social interests: (1) in the general security, (2) in the security of social institutions, (3) in general morals, (4) in the conservation of social resources, (5) in general progress, and (6) in individual life. More than anyone else Pound brought home the vital connection between law, its administration, and the life of society, and gave a major impetus to sociolegal studies. His writings are chiefly reprinted series of lectures, such as *Interpretations of Legal History* (Cambridge, Mass., 1922), *Law and Morals* (Chapel Hill, NC, 1924), *Introduction to the Philosophy of Law* (New Haven, 1922, ²1954), *Social Control through Law* (New Haven, 1942) and *Justice According to Law* (New Haven, 1951). His major work, however, is *Jurisprudence* (5 vols, St Paul, Minn., 1959).   DMW

P. Sayre, *Life of Roscoe Pound* (Iowa City, 1948); D. Wigdor, *Roscoe Pound: an Intellectual Portrait* (NY, 1974).

Powell, Anthony Dymoke (b. London, UK, 21.12.1905). British novelist. Powell was educated at Eton and Balliol College, Oxford. His father was a colonel. Part of his WW2 service was in the Intelligence Corps. He has worked as a publisher and journalist. His early novels, beginning with *Afternoon Men* (London, 1931), were from the first compared with those of WAUGH and Aldous HUXLEY, and suffered by the comparison. Whether or not Powell became dissatisfied with novels whose characters were chronically marginal to life, over the decade that followed *What's Become of Waring* (London, 1939) he must have pondered a more fully representative form. His 12-volume sequence *A Dance to the Music of Time*, which began with *A Question of Upbringing* (London, 1951) and ended with *Hearing Secret Harmonies* (London, 1975), set itself a far larger purpose than its predecessors. His typical understatement of that purpose ('considerations of the way in which the upper and middle classes live in England') and his method ('the interrelations of individuals') gives little idea of the work's complexity. The multiplicity of characters, and their constant interchanges of role and partners, observed with ever-polite surprise, offer an image of humanity absurdly subject to the process of time, and multiplying purposes for itself to provide assurance of the reality of the present. The tone of the narrative includes neither anxiety nor scorn; it expresses instead a restrainedly sympathetic acceptance of human absurdity. His autobiography *To Keep the Ball Rolling* (4 vols, London, 1976–82) shows a comparable detachment. BF

J. Tucker, *The Novels of Anthony Powell* (London, 1976); H. Spurling, *A Handbook to Anthony Powell's 'Music of Time'* (London, 1977).

Powell, Cecil Frank (b. Tonbridge, Kent, UK, 6.11.1903; d. nr Milan, Lombardy, Italy, 9.8.1969). British physicist. Powell was awarded the Nobel prize in 1949 for the discovery of a new elementary particle, the pion, through cosmic-ray experiments carried out in 1948. These marked the culmination of his work on the development of special photographic emulsions for the recording of tracks of fast charged particles, which he had commenced in 1938, and had persisted with when other researchers had virtually abandoned the technique as incapable of quantitative results. The pion was the long-awaited quantum or carrier of the strong nuclear field, as predicted by YUKAWA in 1935. Its observation, together with its decay into a muon and neutrino, resolved a mystery in cosmic ray physics. It explained why the abundant cosmic ray particles at sea-level, the noninteracting muons, were produced so copiously: they were the decay products of pions produced by primary cosmic ray nuclei in the stratosphere. The discovery of the pion inaugurated the branch of science called particle physics or high energy physics. It stimulated the building of large accelerators, producing intense and controlled beams required to replace the feeble cosmic radiation and put the subject on a quantitative footing. Powell's research into cosmic rays used small and compact stacks of nuclear photographic films carried into the stratosphere on large plastic balloons, launched in the Mediterranean area in a series of expeditions. It was an ideal experiment for international collaboration, since the recovered film could be distributed to, and analysed in, distant laboratories with the minimum of technical facilities. Powell contributed decisively to the setting up of CERN in 1953, the European accelerator laboratory at Geneva, to which 13 European member-states con-

tribute. He was also one of the founders of the Pugwash movement. DHP

Powys, John Cowper (b. Shirley, Derbys., UK, 8.10.1872; d. Blaenau Ffestiniog, Gwynedd, 17.6.1963). British novelist, poet and essayist. One of a remarkable literary family, Powys spent many years lecturing on literature throughout the USA. But the idiosyncratic criticism and poetry he produced then are interesting chiefly for the light they shed on the novels to which he devoted the latter part of his life. His first major novel *Wolf Solent* (NY, 1929) appeared when he was 57. This and the Wessex books which followed – *A Glastonbury Romance* (NY, 1932), *Weymouth Sands* (NY, 1934; as *Jobber Skald*, London, 1935) and *Maiden Castle* (NY, 1936) – are vivid and often powerful and amusing explorations of the nature of romanticism, written in exile, recalling the mystically charged landscape of his youth. *Owen Glendower* (NY, 1940) and *Porius* (London, 1951) are historical epics; *Porius* is considered by many to be his best work. The problem of sexuality – especially the possibility of diverting erotic desire to spiritual ends – was a constant preoccupation. Powys's later novels grew increasingly fantastic as he dispensed more and more with the particularity of space and time. The best introduction to his thought and writing is the *Autobiography* (London, 1934), a portrait of the mind from inside rather than a record of events. Prolix, sprawling, exclamatory, unwieldy, Powys's novels are nevertheless full of delights for those prepared to put up with their irritations, offering profound insights into the solitary and creative mind. NP

B. Humphrey (ed.), *Essays on John Cowper Powys* (Cardiff, 1972); G. Cavaliero, *John Cowper Powys: Novelist* (Oxford, 1973).

Pratolini, Vasco (b. Florence, Tuscany, Italy, 19.10.1913). Italian novelist. Pratolini came from a working-class background and was brought up in Santa Croce, a working-class quarter of Florence. He experienced poverty, illness and other difficulties in early life which are reflected in his novels. *Il tappeto verde* [The green carpet] (Florence, 1941) is based on his experience as a patient in a sanatorium. His best-known novels *Cronaca familiare* (Florence, 1947; tr. B. Kennedy, *Two Brothers*, NY, 1962) and *Cronache di poveri amanti* (Florence, 1947; *A Tale of Poor Lovers*, London, 1949) are largely autobiographical and also deal with fascism and WW2, and the sufferings they entailed. They show him at his best in drawing female characters and images of Florence. Other novels by Pratolini have a similar sociopolitical background: *Un eroe del nostro tempo* (Milan, 1949; tr. E. Mosbacher, *A Hero of Our Time*, London, 1951), *Metello* (Milan, 1955; tr. R. Rosenthal, Boston, Mass., 1968) and *Lo scialo* [The shawl] (Milan, 1960). Pratolini is one of the major exponents of neorealism in Italian fiction and one of the most humane of Italian writers.　GS

F. Rosengarten, *Vasco Pratolini: the Development of a Social Novelist* (Carbondale, 1965).

Prelog, Vladimir (b. Sarajevo, Bosnia, under Austro-Hungarian occupation [now Yugoslavia], 23.7.1906; naturalized Swiss citizen, 1959). Yugoslav/Swiss organic chemist. Prelog's early education in chemistry took place at the Czech Institute of Technology in Prague (1924 –9). After an enforced period in the fine-chemical industry because of a lack of academic posts, Prelog joined Zagreb University in 1935. After the German occupation of Zagreb in 1941, through the good offices of Richard KUHN and RUŽIČKA, Prelog and his wife escaped to Switzerland, where he started work in the organic chemistry laboratory at the Eidgenössische Technische Hochschule in Zürich, in cooperation with Ružička, whom he succeeded as head of the laboratory in 1957. Prelog's main interests have lain in naturally occurring compounds, from various alkaloids to the antibiotics rifamycin(s) and boromycin. This work generated numerous stereochemical problems (i.e. problems of three-dimensional molecular structure). Prelog has, in consequence, devoted much attention, theoretical and practical, to stereochemistry, especially the concept of both two- and three-dimensional chirality and its biochemical aspects. With R. S. Cahn and INGOLD

he formulated the 'sequence rule' for the unambiguous specification of a particular stereoisomer, a procedure which has superseded some imperfect predecessors. With Hans Gerlich he also discovered a novel type of stereoisomerism, cyclostereoisomerism. Prelog shared the 1975 Nobel prize for chemistry with CORNFORTH.　NBC

Presley, Elvis Aaron (b. East Tupelo, Miss., USA, 8.1.1935; d. Memphis, Tenn., 16.8.1977). American singer. Presley was the outstanding star of early rock-and-roll, the first great idol of postwar popular music. Though not a greatly talented musician, he was able to embody the raw qualities of the new style: its frank sexuality and its youthful vigour. He became the hero of the generation which had come to maturity since WW2 and was looking for something entirely new, alive and their own. Presley made his first recordings in 1953 and began then to make a local reputation. In 1955 he was taken up by a major record company and his music rapidly gained a vast international audience; films followed regularly from 1956. He made no attempt to keep up with the rapid developments in popular music during the 1960s, by which time he had modified his style to become more a night-club singer than a leading figure of juvenile revolt.　PG

J. Hopkins, *Elvis: a Biography* (NY, 1971); A. Hand (ed.), *Elvis Special* (Manchester, 1973).

Prévert, Jacques (b. Neuilly-sur-Seine, Paris, France, 4.2.1900; d. Omonville-la-petite, 11.4.1977). French poet and screenwriter. The enthusiasm which greeted Prévert's *Paroles* (Paris, 1946; tr. L. Ferlinghetti, *Selections from Paroles*, NY, 1958) was unprecedented for a first collection of poetry. The unforced eloquence, playful charm and anarchistic sensibility displayed in this and the books that quickly followed – *Histoires* [Stories] (Paris, 1946), *Spectacle* (Paris, 1951), *La Pluie et le beau temps* [Rain and fine weather] (Paris, 1955) – were welcomed by a public surfeited with the patriotic sententiousness of ARAGON and ELUARD. Before publishing *Paroles*, Prévert had already made two notable careers – as animator of the Popular Front theatre company, the *Groupe d'Octobre*, and as scriptwriter for such film masterpieces of 'poetic realism' as Jean RENOIR's *Le Crime de Monsieur Lange* (1935) and Marcel Carné's *Les Enfants du paradis* (1945). From surrealism he inherited the virtuoso imagemaker's command of surprising juxtapositions, the spirit of vengeful violence against oppressors, and a loathing for literary pretentiousness. His poems are witty and direct and often tell a story. Set to music by Joseph Kosma, many became popular songs. He rejuvenated the commonplace; slang, puns, proverbs, inventories, remarks overheard in the street were all grist to his mill. A poet passionately on the side of humble people, he celebrated the simple joys of the everyday and commiserated with the losses and pains of life – at the risk of sentimentality and self-pastiche.   RSS

W. E. Baker, *Jacques Prévert* (NY, 1967).

Prigogine, Ilya (b. Moscow, Russia, 25.1.1917; naturalized Belgian citizen). Russian/Belgian theoretical chemist. Prigogine was educated at the University of Brussels where he has held a chair of chemistry since 1951. He has built up there since WW2 one of the leading schools of statistical mechanics and thermodynamics. For more than 30 years his own contribution, for which he was awarded the Nobel prize for chemistry in 1977, has been the extension of irreversible thermodynamics, and its application to physical and biological systems. Irreversible thermodynamics, the thermodynamics of systems not at equilibrium, was first developed by ONSAGER, but his treatment was restricted to systems so close to equilibrium that their return to that state was governed by linear laws. Such a restriction excludes most chemical reactions and all biological systems. Prigogine has developed methods for describing systems far from equilibrium which can evolve into stable 'dissipative' states that may show a variety of interesting behaviour, including spatial and temporal oscillations. This work is described in his book with P. Glansdorff, *Thermody-namic Theory of Structure, Stability and Fluctuations* (London, 1971).   JSR

P. T. Landsberg, 'Ilya Prigogine', *Physics Bulletin* (December 1977), 569.

Prokofiev, Sergey Sergeyevich (b. Sontzovka, Ukraine, Russia, 23.4.1891; d. Moscow, USSR, 5.3.1953). Russian composer. Prokofiev's early music shows a bewildering variety of styles, from the grand romantic manner of his First Piano Concerto (1912) to the compact classicism of his First Symphony (1918), and from the barbaric dynamism of his orchestral *Scythian Suite* (1916) to the colourful and parody-ridden fantasy of his opera *Lyubov k tryom apelsinam* (*The Love for Three Oranges*, 1921). During the 1920s he settled down in Paris as a neoclassicist, following the general direction of STRAVINSKY but displaying his own rhythmic vigour and romantic melody; the works of this period include the Second, Third and Fourth symphonies (1925, 1929, 1930). After his return to the USSR in 1933, his music became more mellow, though on occasion he was subjected to official criticism for 'modernism'. He also became a very prolific composer, producing several operas (notably *Voyna i mir/War and Peace*, after Leo TOLSTOY, 1946) and ballets (*Romeo i Dzhuletta/Romeo and Juliet*, 1938; *Zolushka/Cinderella*, 1945), three more symphonies and a host of other works. His death was rather overshadowed by that of STALIN on the same day.   PG

F. Shlifstein (ed.), *Sergey Prokofiev: Autobiography, Articles, Reminiscences* (London, 1960); I. V. Nestyev, *Prokofiev* (Stanford, Calif., 1961).

Proust, Marcel (b. Auteuil, Paris, France, 10.7.1871; d. Paris, 18.11.1922). French novelist. Proust's long, partly autobiographical novel *A la recherche du temps perdu* (8 pts, Paris, 1913–27; tr. C. K. Scott Moncrieff & S. Hudson, *Remembrance of Things Past*, 7 vols, London, 1922–31; tr. T. Kilmartin *et al.*, 3 vols, London, 1981) is one of the most complex in world literature. It is a study of sexual behaviour, with long analyses of male and female homosexuality and of the emotion of jealousy which Proust sees as inseparable from love. It describes the dominance and ultimate fall from power of the old aristocracy and their replacement by a more pushing, vulgar middle class. It depicts the gradual discovery on the part of the narrator, Marcel, of his own artistic vocation, and is, in a way, the very novel which Marcel decides to write in the last volume. It is a discussion of the role and function of art, with the novelist Bergotte, the painter Elstir and the musician Vinteuil confirming Marcel in the view that only art can justify human existence. It offers an account of many overlapping levels in late 19c and early 20c society, from the narrator's own secure, respectable, middle-class background to the raffish world of demi-mondaines such as Odette de Crécy and flamboyant homosexuals like the Baron de Charlus, and from the elegant salons of the Duchesse de Guermantes to the humble and often more attractive world of the family servant Françoise. And, as the title indicates, it is a novel about time.

A chance incident in which a few crumbs of cake (*la petite madeleine*) dipped in tea fill him with almost unspeakable bliss convinces the narrator that the past never dies but remains with us, accessible through the exploitation of involuntary memory by art. It is thus the function of art, for Proust, to recreate our past, and he spent the last 19 years of his life virtually isolated in a fumigated, cork-lined room, writing the novel which would bring his own past to life again. Proust had suffered from asthma from the age of nine, and although this did not prevent him from doing his military service in 1889–90, it did offer a compelling excuse to withdraw from the world of the Paris salons and to write. His homosexuality, coupled with the fact of his being Jewish on his mother's side – at a period in French history characterized by violent anti-Semitism – exacerbated Proust's sense of being an outsider, and much of his novel presents an unbearably gloomy view of human experience. The last seven volumes of *A la recherche du temps perdu* were published posthumously, and his first draft for it *Jean Santeuil* (Paris, 1952; tr. G. Hopkins, London, 1955), like his attack on the biographical approach to literature, *Contre Sainte-Beuve* (Paris, 1952; tr. S. Townsend-Warner, *By Way of Sainte-Beuve*, London, 1958), did not appear until the 1950s. Many of the characters in his novel were based upon real people, but his final creation stands as a wholly autonomous world.　　PMWT

G. Painter, *Marcel Proust* (2 vols, London, 1959–65); J. Bersani (ed.), *Les Critiques de notre temps et Proust* (Paris, 1971).

Prouvost, Jean (b. Roubaix, Nord, France, 24.4.1885; d. Yvoy-le-Marron, Loir-et-Cher, 18.10.1978). French industrialist and publisher. Impressed by the instant success of *Life* magazine in the USA, Prouvost, founder-owner of two Paris newspapers *Paris-Midi* and *Paris-Soir* (1932–9), tried in 1938 to produce a French variant specializing in sporting pictures which, it was hoped, would be novel enough to capture the same sort of market in France. He was not completely successful, however, until 1949, when he added sensational news pictures to his previous formula. Under the title *Paris-Match*, and with himself as president, director-general and chief editor of the enterprise, it immediately broke new ground in pictorial journalism winning international approval and mass sales in France. By employing such photographers as CARTIER-BRESSON and others working for the Magnum picture agency, Prouvost was able to 'scoop' the news-picture market in Europe, the UK and the USA for nearly three decades. His creation has survived profitably, despite intense competition from television, to the present day.　　RB

Puccini, Giacomo Antonio Domenico Michale Secondo Maria (b. Lucca, Tuscany, Italy, 23.12.1858; d. Brussels, Brabant, Belgium, 29.11.1924). Italian composer, and the most important Italian figure in the sphere of opera since Verdi. He was born into a family of (mainly) church musicians at Lucca where he was a choirboy and then (at 14) an organist; a growing creative talent and interest in opera resulted in his startling congregations with themes from Verdi's *Rigoletto* or *La Traviata* which he worked into his improvisations.

Deciding to become an opera composer himself, he entered the Milan Conservatory in 1880. His operatic career was launched with *Le Villi* which, though unsuccessful in the competition for which it was written, won the support of influential people and was produced with success in Milan in 1884. Although his next opera (*Edgar*, 1889) had a cool reception, his reputation was established with the major works that followed: *Manon Lescaut* (1893), *La Bohème* (1896), *Tosca* (1900), *Madama Butterfly* (1904), *La Fanciulla del West* [The girl of the golden West] – which had its première at the New York Metropolitan in 1910 with TOSCANINI conducting and CARUSO as the bandit hero Dick Johnson – *La Rondine* [The swallow] (set in France and produced at Monte Carlo, 1917), the triptych of one-act operas consisting of *Il Tabarro* [The cloak], *Suor Angelica* [Sister Angelica] and *Gianni Schicchi* (1918) and finally *Turandot*, which was not fully orchestrated at his death but was completed by a pupil and first heard in 1926. As the composer of these operas Puccini had become such a national figure that at his funeral MUSSOLINI delivered the oration. Though the critics did not always praise him unreservedly (even *Bohème* was somewhat coolly received by them), the public from the first warmly admired the operas, and that continuing enthusiasm has ensured that they form an essential part of the standard repertory in the world's opera houses. Compared to Verdi's, his style is blander – his leading characters, incidentally, tend to be women rather than men – but it has abundant Italian charm and temperament, and he writes superbly for the voice, as generations of singers have gratefully acknowledged. CH

M. Carner, *Puccini: a Critical Biography* (London, ²1974).

Pudovkin, Vsevolod Ilarionovich (b. Penza, Russia, 28.2.1893; d. Riga, USSR, 30.6.1953). Soviet film director. Pudovkin's studies of science were interrupted by WW1, in which he served at the front, was wounded and captured. On his return to Moscow he became caught up in the contemporary artistic upheaval and in 1922 joined the work-shop in experimental films run by the great Soviet theorist and film maker, Lev Kuleshov. His early films were very varied: the light and inventive *Shakhmatnaya goryachka* (*Chess Fever*, 1925), the instructional film on PAVLOV's experiments *Mekhanikha golovnovo mozgal* (*The Mechanics of the Brain*, 1926) and a classic drama of the 1905 revolution, *Mat* (*Mother*, 1926), adapted from the novel by Maxim GORKY. He made two further brilliant and widely shown silent films, *Konyets Sankt-Peterburga* (*The End of St Petersburg*, 1927), a companion piece to EISENSTEIN's *October*, and *Potomok Chingis-Khan* (*Storm over Asia*, 1928), a study of the awakening of the revolution in Mongolia. Pudovkin's sound films, beginning with *Deserter* (*The Deserter*, 1933), did not have the same impact and he was troubled by ill-health. But he continued teaching film and did recover something of his former status as a major film maker with the historical films – among them *Admiral Nakhimov* (1946) and *Vozvrashchenie Vassiliya Bortnikov* (*The Return of Vassili Bortnikov*, 1953).

Of the three undeniably great figures of Soviet silent cinema – Eisenstein, Pudovkin and DOVZHENKO – it is Pudovkin whose reputation has survived least well. While his major silent films retain their force and authority, there has been no rehabilitation of his sound work. His theoretical writings (see *Film Technique and Film Acting*, London, 1954) now occupy a less prominent place in the current debate on film theory than those of Eisenstein or Kuleshov, but they remain one of the finest source books for a practical understanding of film. Stanley Kubrick is just one of the many contemporary film makers for whom Pudovkin's studies of film technique and acting were a revelation when he first began to learn his craft. RPA

J. Leyda, *Kino* (London, ²1973).

Putnam, Hilary (b. Chicago, Ill., USA, 31.7.1926). American philosopher. Putnam is impressively expert in the physics and mathematics which are seen as the paradigms of knowledge by the kind of analytic philosophy in which he was brought up and still broadly endorses. The publication of his *Philosophical Papers* in 1975 (2 vols, Cambridge, ²1979) showed the range, bulk and imaginative freedom of his work. He has brought his professional familiarity with science to bear on various received ideas held about science by orthodox positiv-ism, showing the often uninformed character of its reverence. In recent years he has contributed in an adventurously abstract fashion to the continuing debate about meaning and truth (see *Meaning the Moral Sciences*, London, 1978). AQ

Q

Qaddafi, Muammar al- (b. Misratah, Tripolitania [now Libya], 1942). Prime minister of Libya since 1970. Officer in the Libyan army of radical Pan-Arab and fundamentalist Islamic views, he led the coup which overthrew King Idris in 1969 and established himself as leader of a socialist state, secured against all but the grossest of mismanagement by the West's need for Libya's enormous oil reserves. Thereafter he was to swing alternately between schemes for cooperation with and union with his Arab neighbours (confederation of Arab republics with Egypt and Syria in 1971, military union with Syria in 1980), none of which got much further than the initial celebrations, and states of near conflict with them, earning himself a unique reputation for political and mental eccentricity, unfair to one whose sole claim to uniqueness was his failure, as the ruler of an Arab state, to develop any feeling of identity with that state to balance the rhetoric of Islamic Pan-Arabism.   DCW

Quasimodo, Salvatore (b. Modica, Sicily, Italy, 20.8.1901; d. Naples, Campania, 14.6.1968). Italian poet. Together with Saba, UNGARETTI and MONTALE, Quasimodo is regarded as one of the most important poets of the post-D'Annunzian generation. In early life he set out to study engineering, but gave it up on account of his father's financial difficulties. He took up many odd jobs before becoming a professor of Italian literature at Conservatorio Giuseppe Verdi in Milan. His first book of poems *Acque e terre* [Waters and lands] (Florence, 1930) was followed by *Erato e Apollion* [Erato and Apollo] (Milan, 1936), *Ed è subito sera* [And suddenly it is evening] (Milan, 1942), *Giorno dopo giorno* [Day after day] (Milan, 1947), *Il falso e vero verde* [The false and true green] (Milan, 1956; see tr. J. Bevan, *Selected Poems*, London, 1965). He also translated classical Greek poetry (*Lirici greci*, Milan, 1940) and several plays by Shakespeare. He wrote literary and critical essays (see *The Poet and the Politician, and Other Essays*, tr. T. G. Bergin & S. Pacifici, Carbondale, 1969). Some of Quasimodo's best poetry is rooted in and inspired by his Sicilian background and a vein of nostalgic melancholy and tenderness runs through his writing – of one living in Italy's industrial capital (Milan), and dreaming of the land of his birth and childhood. Quasimodo was awarded the Nobel prize in 1959.   GS

C. M. Bowra, 'An Italian poet: S. Quasimodo', in *Horizon*, 16 (December 1947), no. 96; E. Montale, in *Eugenio Montale: Selected Essays*, tr. G. Singh (Manchester, 1978).

Queneau, Raymond (b. Le Havre, Seine-Maritime, France, 21.2.1903; d. Paris, 25.10.1976). French poet and novelist. Like PRÉVERT, who also took part in the surrealist movement in the 1920s, Queneau sought to bring back colloquial speech into the language of literature. Like Prévert also, he was not widely recognized until after WW2 when his work became a bridge between the irrational world of BRETON's movement and the philosophical 'absurd' of existentialism. *Si tu t'imagines* [If you think] (Paris, 1951), which assembles most of his poetry, is remarkable for its delight in JOYCEan wordplay and neologisms and for its impertinence towards the niceties of conventional poetic discourse. Language, for Queneau, is not simply a means of expression, but the very subject of his work. He emphasizes its arbitrariness and the freedom of each of us to mint it anew. The humour of linguistic conventions is explored in *Exercices de style* (Paris, 1947; tr. B. Wright, *Exercises in Style*, London, 1958) which consists of 99 different versions of the same insignificant anecdote. His fiction also produced parodies of the novel form – *Le Chiendent* (Paris, 1933; tr. B. Wright, *The Bark Tree*, London, 1968), *Loin de Reuil* (Paris, 1944; tr. H. J. Kaplan, *The Skin of Dreams*, NY, 1948), *Zazie dans le métro* (Paris, 1959; tr. B. Wright, *Zazie*, NY, 1960) – flying in the face of narrative logic with its bizarre coincidences and changes of identity. Played out by picaresque characters from the margins of society in transitory locales and border zones such as fairgrounds, vacant lots, metro stations and suburban cinemas, these superbly crafted tales themselves walk on the edge between comedy and nightmare. In the later years of his life, Queneau collaborated with a number of 'New Wave' film directors and was editor of the prestigious Pléiade encyclopedia. RSS

J. Guicharnaud, *Raymond Queneau* (NY, 1965); V. Mercier, *The New Novel from Queneau to Pinget* (NY, 1971).

Quine, Willard Van Orman (b. Akron, Ohio, USA, 25.6.1908). American philosopher and logician. Quine graduated from Oberlin College in 1930 as a mathematician and arrived at Harvard for his doctoral work, to begin an association only formally ended by his retirement as Edgar Pierce professor of philosophy in 1978. He had some contact with WHITEHEAD in his early work, but more directly influential was a meeting with CARNAP in Prague later in the 1930s. Over the years Quine has produced a number of imaginative and felicitously written treatises on logic of which 'New foundations for mathematical logic' (1937) and *Set Theory and its Logic* (Cambridge, Mass., 1963, ²1969) deserve particular mention. In an early essay he revealed his continuing interest in the philosophy of the subject and first proposed one of the most widely discussed of his ideas: that there is no difference in kind, but only in the degree of our readiness to give them up, between analytic and synthetic truths, which are taken by most empiricist philosophers to report, respectively, relations between concepts and the course of experience. Quine maintains that the notion of *meaning* (as opposed to reference), which is always invoked to explain the distinction, is radically unclear. Another empiricist article of faith is the sharp distinction between science and metaphysics, a distinction that also rests on confidence in the idea of meaning supposedly possessed by the propositions of science but not by those of metaphysics. Quine has revived a basic part of metaphysics in a new logically explicit form, namely ontology: the theory of the main ultimate kinds of thing that exist. He acknowledges an unreflective preference for the doctrine that only material bodies exist, but resists it on the ground that mathematics is necessary for science and makes ineliminable reference to classes or sets, which are abstract, not material. These and related ideas are presented in the form of a systematic philosophy of language in *Word and Object* (Cambridge, Mass., 1960). Quine's influence on American philosophers has grown steadily since the end of WW2 and by 1960 he had converted the ablest younger British philosophers from the hitherto dominant linguistic philosophy of WITTGENSTEIN and AUSTIN. AQ

A. Orenstein, *Willard V. O. Quine* (Boston, Mass., 1977).

Quisling, Vidkun (b. Fyresdal, Norway, 18.7.1887; d. Oslo, 24.10.1945). Norwegian soldier and politician who, after serving as minister of defence (1931–3) in the Agrarian party cabinet, founded the Nasjonal Samling [National Unity] party in imitation of Nazism. In December 1939 he instigated the German attack on Norway of April 1940, betraying Norwegian defence secrets. His reward was to be prime minister of Norway under German occupation (1942–5). His political ideas were racialist and antidemocratic, on the fairly standard model of European fascism, and his name was from 1940 onwards synonymous with treachery and collaboration with the country's enemies. He was executed in 1945. DCW

P. M. Hayes, *Quisling* (London, 1971).

R

Rabi, Isador Isaac (b. Rymanov, Austria-Hungary [now Poland], 29.7.1898). American physicist. Rabi was brought to the USA at the age of one and was educated there. He studied at Cornell and then at Columbia (PhD 1927). He spent the next two years in Europe, including some time in the laboratory of STERN who had developed the technique of molecular beams. In 1929 he joined the faculty at Columbia. From 1940 to 1945 he was associate director of the MIT Radiation Laboratory and when he returned to Columbia after WW2 he spent much of his time in scientific administration and policy-making in national and international organizations. At the 1955 International Conference on the Peaceful Uses of Atomic Energy in Geneva he was the US delegate and the vice-president. Rabi's great scientific achievement (for which he received the Nobel prize for physics in 1944) was to introduce an extra degree of precision into the molecular beam method (Stern). He made the beam pass through a region of electromagnetic radiation (radio waves) combined with a static magnetic field. This field forces the atoms or molecules into a set of different 'states' whose energy depends on how parallel the elementary atomic magnets are to the direction of the field. If the radio waves are now tuned to just the correct frequency, the atoms can be made to flip from one magnetic state to another and this 'resonance', as it is called, can be detected with great precision. The measurements may then be used to calculate the magnetic and mechanical properties of both the molecules and of the atomic nucleus to a high degree of accuracy.   HMR

Rachmaninov, Sergey Vassilievich (b. Semyonovo, Russia, 1.4.1873; d. Beverly Hills, Calif., USA, 28.3.1943). Russian composer, pianist and conductor. He studied music mainly at the Moscow Conservatory, from which he graduated both as a pianist and as a composer. By this time (1892) he had already written his First Piano Concerto and a one-act opera *Aleko*. Clearly he had a bright future. But the failure of his First Symphony in 1897 depressed him so much that he stopped writing altogether, and it was only a course of hypnosis that brought him back to composition with the Second Piano Concerto (1901). By now he had also achieved success as a conductor, mainly of opera, and his career with its three strands continued smoothly until 1917; in this year of the Russian revolution he went with his family to settle in the USA. His career as a pianist continued until a few weeks before his death, and his keyboard style (fortunately preserved in recordings) was both virile and subtle. Though he came to find composition more difficult as a late-romantic in a 'modernistic' age, nevertheless his *Paganini Rhapsody* (1934), Third Symphony (1936) and *Symphonic Dances* (1940) all belong to his last decade. Rachmaninov is the musical heir of Tchaikovsky, rather as (in the sphere of opera) PUCCINI is of Verdi. His piano concertos and solo piano pieces, and perhaps also the Second Symphony (1907), have won immense popularity and attracted many a listener to 'classical' music. However, his full stature cannot be measured without reference to his other music: his three operas may be undramatic, but the choral work *The Bells* (1913) – really a choral symphony – has great atmosphere. His songs may well outlast his more ambitious compositions.   CH

G. Norris, *Rakhmaninov* (London, 1976).

von Rad, Gerhard (b. Nuremberg, Bavaria, Germany, 21.10.1901; d. Heidelberg, Baden-Württemberg, West Germany, 31.10.1971). German Old Testament scholar and theologian. Von Rad was in Leipzig from 1930, in Jena from 1934 (where as a member of the Confessing church he resisted anti-Semitism); he was professor at Göttingen from 1947, and from 1949 at Heidelberg, where he attracted classes of 500 listeners and was the most important influence upon a whole generation of future pastors until his retirement in 1967. After early work on the Hexateuch and a distinguished commentary on *Genesis* (Göttingen, 1953, ⁹1972; tr. J. H. Marks, London, 1972, ²1976), his classic work was *Die Theologie des Alten Testaments* (2 vols, Munich, 1957–60; tr. D. M. G. Stalker, *Old Testament Theology*, London, 1962–5). This forged the history of Israel's confessional statements, which von Rad had earlier helped explicate by form-critical methods into a powerful theological synthesis. (Form criticism is the attempt to discern the form taken by a story or teaching in order to make it more easily memorable, or more impressive, as it was passed on in oral tradition.) His thesis that the creeds of Deuteronomy 26 and Joshua 24 stood at the beginning of the development has not won acceptance, but was influential in directing attention to the religious meaning of the Old Testament and turning the tide against its disparagement by German liberal Protestant scholars such as Harnack. His later work on *Weisheit in Israel* (Neukirchen, 1970; tr. J. D. Martin, *Wisdom in Israel*, London, 1972) explored the significance of this wider cultural phenomenon appearing within the traditions of Israel.   RM

D. G. Spriggs, *Two Old Testament Theologies* (London, 1976); L. Crenshaw, *Gerhard von Rad* (Ware, Tex., 1978).

Radcliffe-Brown, Alfred Reginald (b. Birmingham, W. Mids, UK, 17.1.1881; d. London, 24.10.1955). British anthropologist. Radcliffe-Brown went up to Cambridge University in 1902, where he became RIVERS's first student in anthropology. He made a study of the Andaman Islands in 1906–8, working in the historical and diffusionist manner favoured by Rivers. However, he then fell under the influence of the work of DURKHEIM, and from about 1909 he was the leading British Durkheimian. Working parallel to Durkheim's nephew MAUSS, he developed a Durkheimian approach to primitive society, defining social anthropology as a form of comparative sociology. The ethnologists were concerned mainly with the historical relations between cultures. The new social anthropology was to study the modes of organization and forms of consciousness of contemporary communities, aiming to establish generalizations about human social behaviour by means of systematic comparison.

Radcliffe-Brown's own programmatic writings have not worn well. The constant reiteration of a 'natural science' model, the invocation of organic analogies, the language of function and equilibrium, can be tiresome for the contemporary reader. However, he did define a method of approach which proved to be both practical and fruitful, and some of his particular analyses have still to be superseded. Radcliffe-Brown's fieldwork was soon to seem old-fashioned as the MALINOWSKIan revolution in participant-observation won ground. When he finally published a book on the Andamans (*The Andaman Islanders*, Cambridge, 1922, ²1948), it was very Durkheimian in approach, although the ethnographic materials were largely second-hand. His most important substantive study, of Australian aboriginal kinship systems (*The Social Organization of Australian Tribes*, London, 1931), was based on surveys and formal interviews and drew heavily on previous studies. While not making a significant ethnographic contribution, however, he revolutionized our understanding of the Australian ethnography, and the models which he published in 1930–1 remain fundamental points of reference for Australian anthropology.

Radcliffe-Brown held foundation chairs in social anthropology at the universities of Cape Town, Sydney and Oxford, and also taught in many other centres – notably at the University of Chicago. Wherever he taught he built up a devoted group of students, some of whom were to provide the intellectual leadership in the following generation. Radcliffe-Brown's influence was perhaps at its height during his tenure of the Oxford chair (1937–46). He was later attacked by the Malinowskians for his formalism, by the new structuralists for his positivism, and by his former supporter EVANS-PRITCHARD for his sociological determinism. The programme he developed remains, however, the implicit point of reference for much contemporary work in social anthropology. His later publications include *Structure and Function in Primitive Society* (London, 1931) and *Method in Social Anthropology* (Chicago, 1958).　　　　　AJK

Radek, Karl Berhardovich, *né* Sobelsohn (b. Lemberg, Galicia, Austria-Hungary [now Lvov, USSR], 1885; d. ?1939). Communist propagandist and leader of the Communist International, eliminated during the STALINist purges of the 1930s. Radek joined the Polish Social Democratic party in 1901, took part in the Russian revolution of 1905 and spent a year in prison after its failure. In the years before WW1 he acquired a reputation as a brilliant journalist with a caustic wit, writing for the left-wing papers in Poland and Germany. He met LENIN at the International Socialist conference in Zimmerwald in 1915 and after the Communist seizure of power in Russia in 1917 he joined the Bolshevik party. When the end of WW1 produced a revolutionary situation in Germany, Radek travelled to Berlin as a representative of the Russian party and helped to organize the German Communist party, serving on its Central Committee. After the murder of LUXEMBURG and Karl Liebknecht he was arrested (February 1919). On his release (December 1919), he went back to Moscow and became, with ZINOVYEV, the leading figure in the Praesidium of the (Third) Communist International. In 1923 he returned to Germany to help prepare another attempt at a Communist revolution. The failure of this (autumn 1923) provided an opportunity for Stalin and Radek's other enemies to push him out of office as secretary of the Comintern and a member of the party's Central Committee (May 1924). A strong supporter of TROTSKY, and on the losing side in the struggle for power after Lenin's death, Radek was expelled from the party in 1927 and banished to the Urals. He secured readmission by recanting his views and, tongue in cheek, becoming profuse in his praise of Stalin. In return he was appointed to the editorial board of *Izvestia* and made one of the regime's leading commentators on foreign affairs. In 1935 he was

put on the commission to draft the 1936 Soviet constitution. He had no illusions about the nature of Stalin's regime or what his own fate would be: in September 1936 he was arrested for his part in an alleged Trotskyite conspiracy. In the show trial of January 1937 he played out his role by confessing his guilt to the trumped-up charges and thereby secured a prison sentence instead of execution. He is believed to have died in 1939 either in prison or in a Soviet labour camp.　　　　　ALCB

Radhakrishnan, Sarvepalli (b. Tiruttani, Andhra Pradesh, India, 5.9.1888; d. Madras, Tamil Nadu, 16.4.1975). Indian philosopher. Educated at Madras Christian College, he taught philosophy at the universities of Madras, Mysore and Calcutta, and became vice-chancellor of Andhra University (1931) and of Benares Hindu University (1939); in 1936 he became the first Spalding professor of eastern religions and ethics at Oxford. His lectures and books (for example, *An Idealist View of Life*, London, 1932), including translations of the Upanishads and the *Bhagavadgita*, introduced many British contemporaries to Hindu ideas and demonstrated his mastery of European and Sanskrit literature. Like VIVEKANANDA he considered idealism the culmination of philosophy, and Advaita Vedanta the essence of Hinduism. The highest point of religious experience was the mystic's intuition of his unity with God; the doctrines of the world's religions pointed to this truth. But that did not mean that any doctrine is absolutely true – a mistake which he found in Christianity but not in Hinduism. Rightly understood, he believed, religion was vital for the future of mankind in an unstable world. Combining idealism with liberal humanism, he regarded salvation not as escape from the world but as freedom within it. In keeping with his belief that transcendent knowledge does not absolve men from worldly responsibilities, he devoted his later life to public affairs, becoming ambassador to the USSR (1949–52), vice-president of India (1952–62) and president (1962–7).　　　　　DHK

P. A. Schilpp (ed.), *The Philosophy of Sarvepalli Radhakrishnan* (NY, 1952).

Rádl, Emanuel (b. Pyšely, Bohemia, Austria-Hungary [now Czechoslovakia], 21.12.1873; d. Prague, German Protectorate of Bohemia and Moravia, 12.5.1942). Czech biologist and philosopher. His early interests were the eye and theories of biological development, but even before he became professor of philosophy at the Prague natural sciences faculty (1919) he turned to a Christian antipositivist, antirationalist, antirelativist philosophy. All philosophy must be directly related to the practical life of the individual; for Rádl, concepts like Nirvana are metaphysical suicide, and tolerance is dangerous because it is difficult to distinguish from indifference. His *Západ a Východ* [West and East] (Prague, 1925) is an eloquent, sometimes philistine defence of Western 'method' against Eastern 'mysticism', 'energy' against 'apathy'. For him Soviet communism is as much a product of Eastern mysticism as Tibetan Tantrism. Rádl wrote his most important work *Útěcha z filosofie* [Consolation from philosophy] (Prague, 1946) while he was dying of multiple sclerosis. Its three main ideas are: a God-given immutable moral order exists and has always existed outside man; man either adheres to that moral order or is an anarchist; since Galileo man has become ever less metaphysical (moral) and more materialistic (anarchist); God uses no force and remains an utterly defenceless being who does not interfere with the world.   RBP

Radnóti, Miklós (b. Budapest, Austria-Hungary [now Hungary], 5.5.1909; d. Abda, 8.11.1944). Hungarian poet and essayist, one of the most memorable voices of protest against the inhumanity of fascism during the 1930s. Of Jewish extraction, he became a Catholic under the benevolent influence of Sándor Sik, his literary tutor at Szeged University. Here he joined a group of young radical writers and artists who published one of his early volumes and later played a major role in Hungarian life. Like ADY, ILLYÉS and JÓZSEF, he was attracted to French culture, as shown by his early erotic and rebellious verse and translations. A sense of impending doom, personal and national, began to enter his work prior to WW2. His most remarkable poems the '*Eklogák*' [Eclogues], which were finished in a forced-labour camp in Yugoslavia, use a classical purity of language and form to express the tragedy and hope of his modern world. First published in *Tajtékos ég* [Foamy sky] (Budapest, 1946), '*Eklogák*' are included in *The Complete Poetry* (ed. E. George, Ann Arbor, 1980). Radnóti continued to write poetry until he was shot during a forced march.   GFC

Radzinowicz, Leon (b. Lodz, Russian Poland [now Poland], 15.8.1906; naturalized British citizen, 1947). Polish/British criminologist. Radzinowicz was born into a wealthy medical family, and educated at Lodz and at the Sorbonne, where he studied law. He moved to the faculty of law and economics at Geneva, acquired a wide knowledge of European criminological thought, and in 1927 went to Rome as one of the last students of Enrico Ferri, controversial figure in criminal science and political theory. Radzinowicz returned to Geneva as a *Docent* teaching the positivist criminology of Ferri. In 1932 he became professor at the Free University of Warsaw. Radzinowicz was by this time an outspoken positivist with a capacity for modifying the original doctrine. He produced reports on the Belgian penal system and its experiments in solitary confinement and the use of 'social defence' for habitual criminals. Politically unpopular in Poland, Radzinowicz visited the UK in 1937 to prepare a report on British penal policy. On the outbreak of WW2 in 1939 he settled in Cambridge, where he eventually became a fellow of Trinity College. Although working within the faculty of law, Radzinowicz's wide-ranging criminological interests kept him in contact with scholars in Europe and the USA. His early research and writing in the positivist tradition are less important than his great life work, the *History of English Criminal Law* and its penal policies since the mid-18c (5 vols published to date: London, 1948–).

Radzinowicz's other major achievement was the setting up in 1959 of the Institute of Criminology in Cambridge. The institute not only helped the development of the discipline but confirmed its social and intellectual legitimacy in the eyes of the British 'Establishment'. Its research has been often criticized by the politically radical wing of British criminology, but its official standing has been uniformly high. Radzinowicz, as the first Wolfson professor of criminology, was soon accepted as the leading academic to whom officials turned for advice. He was a member of the Gowers Royal Commission on Capital Punishment (1949–53) and subsequently emerged publicly as an opponent of capital punishment. He was a member of the Royal Commission on the Penal System (which wound itself up before its work was completed in 1967) and, more controversially, chairman of a subcommittee of the Advisory Council on the Penal System that rejected Mountbatten's recommendations for the concentration of dangerous prisoners in a single prison, supporting instead the policy of dispersal which has been the subject of fierce controversy ever since. Radzinowicz's forceful and charismatic personality has left a distinctive mark on British criminology; his outlook maintaining a link with a tradition of universal scholarship.   TPM

Rahner, Karl (b. Freiburg im Breisgau, Baden-Württemberg, Germany, 5.3.1904). German theologian. He became a Jesuit in 1922. Just as he was beginning to make his mark as a theologian the University of Innsbruck, where he was lecturing, was closed down by the Nazis in 1938. He was then in the forefront of the movement known as 'transcendental Thomism': an effort to break out of the narrowness of Roman Catholic theology by marrying the thought of Aquinas with that of Kant. He spent the years 1939–45 in Vienna, engaged in pastoral ministry. The first volume of his *Schriften zur Theologie* (Einsiedeln, 1954; tr. C. Ernst, *Theological Investigations*, London, 1961) inaugurated a series which concluded with the 14th volume (Einsiedeln, 1980; earlier volumes in course of publication in English). These constitute his most substantial work, together with his *Grundkurs des Glaubens* (Freiburg, 1976; tr. W. V. Dych, *Foundations of Christian Faith*, London, 1978), although they are only a

fraction of his immense literary output. During the Second Vatican Council (1962–5), when he was chief adviser to the German-speaking bishops, he established himself as the foremost Roman Catholic theologian of the day. His influence has continued to grow as his students have dispersed his ideas round the world, particularly in Latin America. He invented the notion of 'anonymous Christianity' in an effort to bring out the 'experience of transcendence' which he finds to be latent in humanism. His dogged questioning and openness to modern thought have transformed Roman Catholic theology on a whole range of issues. After holding chairs at Munich and Münster he lives now in retirement in Munich.   FK

Raman, Chandrasekhara Venkata (b. Tiruchirappalli, Tamil Nadu, India, 7.11.1888; d. Bangalore, Karnataka, 21.11.1970). Indian physicist. At Presidency College, Madras, where he received his bachelor degree at the age of 16, Raman showed signs of becoming a great scientist. For 10 years from 1907, however, he was employed as a civil servant in the finance department in Calcutta. In his spare time he cultivated his interest in vibrations and sound, and their relevance to the theory of musical instruments, and worked, at irregular hours, in the laboratory of the Indian Association for the Cultivation of Science. In 1917 he became professor of physics at the University of Calcutta. Within a few years he began to publish work of major importance in optics and acoustics – work which, *inter alia*, offered an explanation for the blueness of the sea and which quantitatively interpreted the vibrational phenomena of the piano, the sitar and the veena. His most renowned contribution came in 1928 when he telegrammed his letter to *Nature* describing 'A New Type of Secondary Radiation'. This was the discovery of the Raman effect which involves the change of wavelength of incident light following absorption by a molecule or radical. The magnitude of the change, and its dependence upon the properties of the absorbing species, constituted a compelling proof for the veracity of the quantum theory which had at that time only recently emerged. Nowadays the Raman effect is used routinely to identify and characterize the structure of molecules and molecular fragments in the solid, liquid and gaseous states. Raman was awarded the Nobel prize for physics in 1929. (He had booked his passage to Stockholm shortly after transmitting his letter to *Nature*.) From 1933 onwards he lived and worked in Bangalore where, in 1934, he founded the Indian Academy of Science, and where, in 1948, he directed the Raman Research Institute. He was a prolific writer – there are more than 500 articles bearing his name – and a key figure in the foundation of Indian science. He, along with TAGORE, M. GANDHI and RADHAKRISHNAN, was conspicuous in the flowering of Indian culture in the first part of the 20c. His scientific curiosity never left him; and his studies of gems and minerals (commenced in 1950), and his analysis of colour and perception and of the physiology of vision were significant, though not universally acclaimed, contributions to natural philosophy.   JMT

Ramos, Graciliano (b. Quebrângulo, Alagoas, Brazil, 27.10.1892; d. Rio de Janeiro, Guanabara, 20.3.1953). Brazilian novelist. Ramos had a bleak childhood with a stern father and a shrewish mother. When his cattle farm was destroyed by drought, his father used his influence to become a judge. The boy's vision of social justice was that it was nonexistent. All this, and life in the backlands with his grandparents, is present in everything he wrote. A lonely child, he read widely and was influenced by Machado de Assis and Eça de Queiroz. During the Getúlio Vargas dictatorship, he was imprisoned as a communist (for his account see *Memórias do cárcere*, 4 vols, Rio de Janeiro, 1953). He became a federal director of education, experience he used in *São Bernardo* (Rio de Janeiro, 1934; tr. R. L. Scott-Buccleuch, London, 1975). *Angústia* (Rio de Janeiro, 1936; tr. L. C. Kaplan, *Anguish*, London, 1946), unique in Brazilian literature, portrays growing sexual anguish, interwoven with jealousy and surviving childhood traumas, and finishes in murder and madness. *Vidas secas* (Rio de Janeiro, 1938; tr. R. E. Dimmick, *Barren Lives*, Austin, 1965), the greatest modern novel in Portuguese, tells of a peasant family and their dog, pitted against the harshness of nature in drought and flood, with unsurpassed descriptions of tropical heat and colour. The work underlines the conflict, threading through all his fiction, between the corrupt littoral and the innocence of the backlands. His writing, though not preaching reform, moves the reader to demand reform.   DBr

F. Ellison, *Brazil's New Novel* (Berkeley, Calif., 1954).

Ramsay, William (b. Glasgow, Strath., UK, 2.10.1852; d. High Wycombe, Bucks., 23.7.1916). British chemist. Uniquely in history, Ramsay discovered a complete and entirely new group of elements, the noble gases. Although trained as an organic chemist under Bunsen and Fittig, he developed an interest in physical chemistry while working with Mills at Anderson College, Glasgow; this continued when he was appointed professor of chemistry at University College, Bristol, in 1880. He discovered an interest in gases, in particular nitrogen oxides. When he moved to the chair of inorganic chemistry at University College London in 1887, he wrote an important book attempting to systematize inorganic chemistry on the basis of Mendeleev's periodic table (*A System of Inorganic Chemistry*, London, 1890). In 1892, RAYLEIGH demonstrated that nitrogen prepared chemically was less dense than that isolated from air. Two years later, he entered into an active collaboration with Ramsay: the former believed that chemically produced nitrogen contained a light gas as a contaminant, the latter that atmospheric nitrogen contained a heavy gas. Ramsay was correct, and in that same year, 1894, Rayleigh announced the discovery of a new element to the British Association. A joint paper was presented to the Royal Society in early 1895 (*Phil. Trans.*, 186 [1895], 187). This new element, argon ('the inactive one') was recognized by Ramsay as the first member to be discovered of a completely new group of elements (now known as the noble, or inert, gases) within Mendeleev's classification; in a scientific investigation over the next decade he isolated every other member of the group. In 1895 he isolated helium (whose existence had been deduced by Frankland and Lockyer from Janssen's observations of the solar spectrum in 1868), and three years later, with the aid of Travers, neon ('the new one'), krypton ('the hidden one') and xenon ('the strange one'). In 1903, with the aid of SODDY, he discovered that helium and 'emanation' (now known as radon) were found during the decay of radium. In 1904, Ramsay was awarded the Nobel prize for chemistry. The monatomic noble gases were believed to be totally inert towards chemical combination until Neil BARTLETT, in 1962, isolated a compound of xenon. Their importance in the development of the theory of chemical bonding cannot be overstated. Argon and helium are, today, gases of immense industrial importance.   KRS

M. W. Travers, *A Life of Sir William Ramsay* (London, 1956).

Ramsey, Frank Plumpton (b. Cambridge, UK, 22.2.1903; d. Cambridge, 19.1.1930). British philosopher, mathematician and economist. Having read mathematics at Trinity College, Cambridge, he became a fellow of King's College. Ramsey was a genius who made outstanding contributions to three quite different disciplines: philosophy, mathematics and economics. In each case the arguments or field of investigation that he opened up came to be extensively developed only some 30 years after his death at the tragically early age of 26. In philosophy, Ramsey's work was concerned largely with the nature of various kinds of knowledge. He wrote a number of important papers, several of them stimulated by Bertrand RUSSELL's and WHITEHEAD's *Principia Mathematica* (1913) or by WITTGENSTEIN's *Tractatus* (1921). In mathematics, he established a pair of related theorems about infinite sets, which gave rise to an extensive new field in mathematics subsequently called 'Ramsey theory'. In economics, Ramsey's two papers each pioneered a branch of theory: optimal taxation or (more broadly) the theory of 'second

best' and optimal savings or accumulation. 'A contribution to the theory of taxation' (1927) considered the question of what tax rates should be applied to different commodities in the raising of a given amount of revenue, if the tax-payers' loss of well-being is to be minimized – the answer being that rates should not be uniform but should vary inversely with the elasticity of demand for a commodity. 'A mathematical theory of saving' (1928) used the calculus of variations to derive a theorem about the proportion of income that a community should save. The proportion is shown, plausibly enough, to vary positively with the scope for increasing society's well-being by higher consumption in the future, and inversely with the value attached to an increment of consumption in the present.   PMO

J. M. Keynes, 'F. P. Ramsey' in *Essays in Biography* (London, 1933); D.H. Mallor (ed.), *F. P. Ramsey: Foundations – Essays in Philosophy, Logic, Mathematics and Economics* (London, 1978).

Randolph, Asa Philip (b. Crescent City, Fla, USA, 15.4.1889; d. New York, 16.5.1979). American black leader, he entered politics as a follower of Eugene Debs, American socialist leader, advocating via the radical black journal, the *Messenger*, the unity of black and white labour and black membership of unions. President and organizer of the Brotherhood of Sleeping Car Porters (principal black union, 1925), and of National Negro Congress, he forced President Franklin ROOSEVELT, by threat of a mass march on Washington, to issue Fair Employment executive orders to railroads. After 1947 he was influential in eroding segregation provisions in the US armed forces.   DCW

Ranganathan, Shiyali Ramamrita (b. Shiyali, Madras, India, 9.8.1892; d. Bangalore, Karnataka, 27.9.1972). Indian librarian. The 20c can show many librarians of outstanding ability but only one of genius. Combining the practical qualities of Melville DEWEY with the intellectual eminence of Henry Evelyn BLISS, Ranganathan made a contribution to the profession that is without parallel. In India he played a major part in the development of a national library system, comparable to Dewey's earlier work in the USA. Beginning as a mathematician, he devoted his total energy to librarianship after appointment as university librarian at Madras in 1924. Prominent in the founding of library associations and schools, in drafting library legislation and in the publication of journals, he worked indefatigably to improve services in the libraries he directed and in teaching librarianship. Later he was active in international work; throughout he was a prolific writer. His thought shows an effective blend of Hindu and Western traditions. His writings provide a unique account of librarianship as a systematic body of knowledge. In *The Five Laws of Library Science* (Madras, 1931, ²1957) he proposed a set of fundamental principles. With constant reference to these he proceeded to expound the more special principles of book selection, classification, cataloguing, reference service and administration. It is a measure of his ability that with all this varied activity he could still be the world's leading thinker in the most demanding subject of classification. *Prolegomena to Library Classification* (Madras, 1937, ³1967), reflecting his work in librarianship as a whole, is the only complete and coherent account in existence of classification theory, to be demonstrated in practice in the *Colon Classification* (Madras, 1933, ⁶1960) which is now widely used in India. Although the scheme itself has not been adopted in other countries, Ranganathan's work has exerted an incalculable influence on classification and indexing in the modern world. DWL

M. A. Gopinath, 'Ranganathan' in *Encyclopedia of Library and Information Science* (33 vols, NY, 1968–81); P.N. Kaula (ed.), *Library Science Today: Ranganathan Festschrift*, i (London, 1965).

Ransom, John Crowe (b. Pulaski, Tenn. USA, 30.4.1888; d. Gambier, Ohio, 3.7.1974). American poet and literary critic. Ransom's first volume *Poems About God* (NY, 1919) shows the influence of FROST; Ransom later repudiated the book. He found his own voice among the Nashville Fugitive group at

Vanderbilt University in the 1920s, associating with Robert Penn Warren, Donald Davidson and Allen TATE among others. Poems published in the *Fugitive Magazine* filled the two volumes *Chills and Fever* (NY, 1924) and *Two Gentlemen in Bonds* (NY, 1927), on which his poetic reputation rests. He constantly revised; the third edition of his *Selected Poems* (NY, 1969) contains 'pairings' of contrasted early and late texts, with Ransom's own commentary. The most striking feature of his poetry is what Graham Hough has called its 'prevailing trickiness of expression', including much archaism. As poetry ceased to flow, Ransom became interested in economic and social problems, defending the values of the old South – for instance, as a contributor in *I'll Take My Stand: the South and its Agrarian Tradition* (NY, 1930). *God Without Thunder* (NY, 1930) argued from a fundamentalist standpoint for the value and place of myth in society; *The World's Body* (NY, 1938) asserted the superiority of art over science; *The New Criticism* (Norfolk, Conn., 1941) examined contemporary practice and outlined Ransom's own critical principles: devotion to text rather than context, and a concern with the relationship between structure and texture in poetry. As a teacher at Vanderbilt University from 1914 to 1937, and later as editor of the *Kenyon Review*, Ransom exercised a great influence on American letters, emphasizing a rigour and austerity which his critical theory defined as 'masculinity'. NP

T. D. Young (ed.), *John Crowe Ransom: Critical Essays and a Bibliography* (Baton Rouge, 1968); M. Williams, *The Poetry of John Crowe Ransom* (New Brunswick, NJ, 1972).

Rao, Raja (b. Hassan, Mysore, India, 21.11.1909). Indian novelist. He has achieved a reputation of great eminence within India on the strength of only three novels, a few short stories and some highly metaphysical novellas. Born into an old Brahmin family, he graduated from Madras University in 1928 and continued his studies in Europe, at Montpellier and the Sorbonne. This intellectual background, and the fact that he has lived much of his life outside India and twice been married to westerners, may explain why his best-known work, the novel *The Serpent and the Rope* (London, 1960), explores the interconnections, both historically and in modern times, between Europe and Asia. Written on an epic scale which Rao does not attempt elsewhere, it is frequently regarded as the most philosophically significant novel in English to have been written in India. His first novel *Kanthapura* (London, 1938) shows the impact of GANDHIan principles upon a traditional community. His other writings are intellectually obscure and little read. Rao has taught Indian philosophy in the USA and France and has exerted as much influence through his teaching as by his writing. In everything he tries to define India as a concept and not just as a country.   ANRN

C. D. Narasimhaiah, *Raja Rao* (New Delhi, 1973).

Rathenau, Walther (b. Berlin, Germany, 29.9.1867; d. Berlin, 24.6.1922). German industrialist, director of the great electrical trust AEG, director of German war economy (1916–18), minister for reconstruction (1921), minister for foreign affairs (1921–2). Both during WW1 and after Imperial Germany's defeat and the emergence of the Weimar republic, Rathenau believed in and preached Germany's ability, through her central geopolitical position in Europe, her industrial wealth and technological inventive ability, to dominate and lead Europe by peaceful penetration rather than conquest. His Jewish origins, his role as foreign minister of the Weimar republic, and his signature of the Treaty of Rapallo (1922) with the Soviet government, made him the inevitable victim of extremist anti-Semitic nationalist assassins.   DCW

H. Graf von Kesseler, *Walther Rathenau: his Life and Work* (London, 1929); J. B. Joll, *Intellectuals in Politics* (London, 1960).

Rattigan, Terence Mervyn (b. London, UK, 10.6.1911; d. Hamilton, Bermuda, 30.11.1977). British dramatist, the leading theatrical craftsman of the years immediately before and after WW2, who early declared his preference for 'plays

of character and narrative over plays of ideas'. His light comedies – notably *French without Tears* (1936), *Love in Idleness* (1944) and *The Sleeping Prince* (1953) – thus worked well enough before their original audiences, but now seem thin and lacking in imaginative life. If his more serious plays were also short on 'ideas', they often compensated through their exact rendering of small corners of English life and manners – middle-class morality in *The Winslow Boy* (1946), the incestuous world of the public school in *The Browning Version* (1948), the niceties of bourgeois adultery in *The Deep Blue Sea* (1952), and the drab routine of the small boarding house in *Separate Tables* (1955). Rattigan's flawed attempts at three-dimensional portraiture – of Lawrence of Arabia in *Ross* (1960), and of Nelson and Emma Hamilton in *A Bequest to the Nation* (1970) – suggested that he had been wise to work mainly within the confines of the increasingly self-doubting world of the wealthier middle classes, in retreat before the encroaching Welfare State, and as resentful as Rattigan himself of the educational advance of the working class dramatized in the new drama of OSBORNE, WESKER and their like.   ST

O. M. Darlow & G. Hodson, *Rattigan: the Man and His Work* (London, 1978).

Rauschenberg, Robert (b. Port Arthur, Tex., USA, 22.10.1925). American assemblage artist who studied in Kansas, Paris (Académie Julian, 1948) and at Black Mountain College (1948–9) under ALBERS. There he met the composer CAGE from whom he derived an interest in the aesthetic potential of the banal. His early works challenge the subjectivity of abstract expressionism (e.g. *White Painting*, 1951, seven plain white panels whose only image was the viewer's shadow). From 1951 he made collages of newsprint, rags and rusty nails (e.g. *Satellite*, 1955), and in 1953 introduced 'combine paintings': i.e. collages with objects attached to or embedded in them (e.g. *Monogram*, 1959, a stuffed ram encased in a car tyre on a collage field articulated with splashes of paint). His aim was to 'fill the gap between art and life'. In 1962 he began to make lithographs and silk screens juxtaposing collage elements with areas of pure paint. In the 1970s he experimented with cardboard, plastic and other fragile materials in reliefs and assemblages. Many of his ideas and images were taken over by younger Pop artists. SOBT

L. Alloway, *Robert Rauschenberg* (NY, 1976).

Ravel, Joseph Maurice (b. Ciboure, Basses-Pyrénées, France, 7.3.1875; d. Paris, 28.12.1937). French composer. Early in his career Ravel was influenced by DEBUSSY, notably in his orchestral song cycle *Schéhérazade* (1903), a dream-picture of the East typical of its period. However, the relationship was reciprocal: Ravel's piano piece *Jeux d'eaux* [Fountains] (1902) anticipates Debussy in its virtuoso pictorialism, and most of his mature music has an exact objective edge quite alien to the Debussyan style. His musical ideas tend to be sharply defined and self-sufficient, and his works to grow more by pointed contrast and varied repetition than by continuous movement. The most extreme case is his orchestral *Boléro* (1928), in which a single melody is obsessively repeated in a crescendo of changing colour, but Ravel's objectivity is also evident in his approach to models taken from elsewhere: the French baroque suite in *Le Tombeau de Couperin* [Couperin's monument] for piano (1919) or orchestra (1920), the Viennese waltz in the ballet *La Valse* [The waltz] (1920), and Spanish folk music in the orchestral *Rapsodie espagnole* [Spanish rhapsody] (1908) and the one-act opera *L'Heure espagnole* [The Spanish hour] (1911). The precision of his orchestration reveals an artist for whom imagination had to be confirmed by calculation. He was able to invest many of his own piano works with perfectly apt orchestral colour, and he did the same for Mussorgsky's *Pictures at an Exhibition* (1922). With such sophisticated resources at his command he also found it possible to evoke a world of infantile fantasy which is both whimsical and knowing, as in *Ma mère l'oye* [Mother goose] for two pianos (1910) or orchestra (1912) and the opera *L'Enfant et les sortilèges* [The child and the spells] (1925, text by COLETTE). PG

A. Orenstein, *Ravel* (NY, 1975); R. Nichols, *Ravel* (London, 1977).

Rawls, John (b. Baltimore, Md, USA, 21.2.1921). American philosopher. Rawls taught at Princeton, Cornell and MIT before going to Harvard, where he has been since 1962. In 1971 the work of many years culminated in the publication of his substantial *A Theory of Justice* (Cambridge, Mass.), the richly detailed development of a simple but powerful initial idea: that the rules of a group are fair to the extent that a person would agree to be bound by them when ignorant of his own possession of characteristics which the rules of the system reward or penalize. Rawls is critical of utilitarians for subordinating individual claims to the overriding demands of the general good. On the other hand he is prepared to endorse inequalities provided that they leave everyone better off. Rawls's mixture of mutually moderating liberalism and egalitarianism impressively demonstrated the applicability of analytic techniques to substantive (rather than methodological) issues in morality. AQ

B. M. Barry, *The Liberal Theory of Justice* (Cambridge, Mass., 1973); N. Daniel (ed.), *Reading Rawls* (NY, 1975).

Rayleigh, John William Strutt, Lord (b. Maldon, Essex, UK, 12.11.1842; d. Witham, Essex, 30.6.1919). British physicist. A peer by inheritance, he began a series of experimental researches at the family seat of Terling Place, Witham, Essex, in 1868. His book *The Theory of Sound* (2 vols, Cambridge, 1877-8) established him as the leading authority on sound, covering as it did every field of contemporary physics. In 1871 he resolved the long-standing problem: why is the sky blue? His solution – still accepted today – invokes the scattering of light by fine particles according to the fourth power of the wavelength, now called Rayleigh scattering. In 1879 Rayleigh succeeded Maxwell as Cavendish professor of experimental physics at Cambridge, where he stayed until 1884. His tenure is marked by the successful introduction of laboratory work in the teaching of elementary physics, an innovation widely copied in England. The range of his interests was continually expanding, notably in the field of radiation and atomic spectra, and his contribution to the theory of black-body radiation is recorded in the Rayleigh–JEANS law. More definitive work was shortly to be done by PLANCK, but Rayleigh never developed any enthusiasm for the new quantum theory – he was, of course, by then in his 60s. In 1895 Rayleigh and RAMSAY discovered a new chemical element, isolating the inert gas argon in what supposedly was pure atmospheric nitrogen. The discovery was a popular one, and Rayleigh was awarded the Nobel prize for physics in 1904 (Ramsay took the chemistry prize in the same year). Rayleigh made contributions also to the organization of British scientific life, serving on numerous committees, and greatly influencing developments in physics despite the revolutions of quantum mechanics and relativity that succeeded him.   JJG

Read, Herbert Edward (b. Kirbymoorside, N. Yorks., UK, 4.12.1893; d. Stonegrave, N. Yorks., 12.6.1968). British poet, critic, editor and writer on modern art. After Leeds University Read served in WW1, during which he cofounded *Art and Letters* (a vehicle for Wyndham LEWIS, ELIOT *et al.*) as well as winning an MC and a DSO. During the 1920s working at the Victoria and Albert Museum, London, he wrote poetry, criticism and learned studies in the applied arts. His career as a cultural protagonist developed during the 1930s when, succeeding FRY, he became editor of the *Burlington Magazine*. He helped organize the Unit 1 exhibition of contemporary British art in 1933 and the surrealist exhibition of 1936, earning an international reputation as a propagandist for modern, especially abstract, art. In a series of books, such as *Art Now* (London, 1933), Read argued his various passions – for 'organic form', anarchism, and the need for art in education. His ideas were of the romantic tradition, from Coleridge's 'Imagination' through to JUNG's theory of the archetype. His championship of Henry MOORE had a

great influence upon Anglo-American taste. After WW2 he cofounded the Institute for Contemporary Arts in London and, as the Grand Old Man, wrote definitive histories of modern art. Read's poetry (*Collected Poems*, London, 1946, ²1966) influenced the 'New Apocalypse' poets of the 1940s and reflects the romantic tenor of his criticism. His outstanding autobiographical writings were brought together in *Annals of Innocence and Experience* (London, 1946).   CF

F. Berry, *Herbert Read* (London, 1953).

Reagan, Ronald Wilson (b. Tampico, Ill., USA, 6.2.1911). Fortieth president of the USA. Beginning as a radio sports announcer in Iowa, Reagan went to Hollywood in 1937 and appeared in more than 50 films over the next 25 years. Twice president of the Screen Actors' Guild and chairman of the Motion Picture Industry Council (1949), he took an active role in MCCARTHY days in investigating communist influences in the movie business. He joined the Republican party in 1962 and served as a popular governor of California (1967–75). An unsuccessful candidate for the presidential nomination in 1968 and 1976, he won it in 1980, defeating a lacklustre Jimmy Carter to become president a few days before his 70th birthday.

A genial and relaxed personality, much at ease at public appearances, Reagan represented right-wing views widely shared by those who feared that the rapid changes of the 1960s and 1970s threatened the dissolution of American society. He won the election on a call for a return to traditional American values of self-reliance, individualism and private enterprise backed up by deflationary policies which would reduce social expenditure, especially on welfare, cut back taxes, reduce government intervention and stimulate economic growth. These old-fashioned policies were renamed 'supply side' economics as distinguished from the management of demand, but whatever chance of success they may ever have had was denied by the combination of a world recession, rising unemployment and a flood of imports, particularly from Asia.

Reagan's chances of balancing the national budget were not improved by the increases he called for in defence spending to bridge the gap which he claimed had opened up between the military capabilities of the USA and the USSR. Relations with the Soviet government became markedly worse (Afghanistan; Poland) followed by a deterioration in relations between the USA and its European allies. By mid-term (when he suffered setbacks in congressional elections) his one success in foreign policy had been to impose a truce on Israel and the other parties in the Lebanese war. Reagan survived an attempted assassination on 30 March 1981. However, his personal popularity could not still growing criticism and disillusionment with his government's failure to break out of the country's economic stagnation or deal with its deepening social problems. ALCB

Reeves, Alec Harley (b. Redhill, Avon, UK, 10.3.1902; d. London, 13.10.1970). British electronics and communications pioneer. Reeves used little mathematics in his work, being a practical engineer with a physical, almost sensuous sympathy for the forces with which he was dealing, and a talent for constructing simple models to help in his work. His best-known invention was Pulse Code Modulation (PCM), made in 1938 while he was working at the Laboratoire Central de Télécommunication in Paris. PCM is the basis of all modern high-frequency telephony, providing for digital representation of analogue quantities. PCM was used to send back information from interplanetary probes. At the British Telecommunications Research Establishment during WW2 Reeves developed the Oboe aircraft navigation system. At Standard Telecommunication Laboratories (STL) after the war he pioneered work on germanium amplifiers, and had developed a two-terminal device when the transistor was invented. In 1957 he started work on optical transmission systems at STL and in 1960 developed his 'equilibrium encoder' for PCM. He took out more than 150 patents. He was also a keen member of the Society for Psychical Research, and

such studies seemed to stimulate his imagination. RAH

Reich, Wilhelm (b. Dobrzynica, Galicia, Austria-Hungary [now Ukraine, USSR], 24.3.1897; naturalized American citizen, 1938; d. Lewisburg, Pa, USA, 3.11.1957). Austrian/American psychoanalyst, and pioneer of sexual freedom. Reich went to Vienna as a WW1 veteran and, within a year, was a member of the Vienna Psychoanalytic Society. In 1927 FREUD refused to analyse him because, supporters of Reich believe, Freud disapproved of his *Die Funktion des Orgasmus* (Leipzig, 1927; *The Function of the Orgasm*, NY, 1942) where Reich stressed the need for sexual fulfilment to achieve personal wholeness. Reich argued that society systematically induced sexual guilt in workers to help keep them oppressed. In 1928 he joined the Austrian Communist party and, in 1930, founded the German Association for Proletarian Sexual Politics which disseminated information on birth control and ran some 'sexual hygiene' clinics. Reich's emphasis on frank sex alarmed conservative psychoanalysts. In 1934 he was edged out of the international psychoanalytic movement and moved to Denmark. From the late 1930s Reich felt he was an isolated prophet, too radical for his time. He moved to the USA where he began to investigate 'orgone energy' on which, he claimed, a person's orgasmic power partly depended. Orgones were cosmic particles, crucial to life, that fell on earth from space. In his laboratory, Organon, Reich claimed to identify and fix these orgones under the microscope. He built 'orgone boxes', which attracted orgones and in which patients could sit. No serious biologist ever found evidence of these particles. Eventually, the Federal Drugs Administration obtained an injunction to stop him selling orgone boxes. Reich refused to appear in court and was jailed for two years for contempt. The temptation has been to dismiss Reich as a crank, but some of his ideas on sexual freedom have turned out to be very powerful. Ten years after his death he was rediscovered by the student radicals of the 1960s who found his combination of revolution and sex a powerful inspiration. The motto 'Make love, not war' is a fitting epitaph since, according to Reich, if we really could make love, we could not make war. A selection from his prolific output was edited by M. B. Higgins as *Wilhelm Reich: Selected Writings* (NY, 1960). DMOC

P. A. Robinson, *The Sexual Radicals* (NY, 1969); C. Ryecroft, *Reich* (London, 1971).

Reichenbach, Hans (b. Hamburg, Germany, 26.9.1891; naturalized American citizen; d. Los Angeles, Calif., USA, 9.4.1953). German/American philosopher. His main achievements lie in his explication of the importance of modern (i.e. EINSTEINian) physics (*Philosophie der Raum-Zeit-Lehre*, Berlin, 1927–8; tr. M. Reichenbach & J. Freund, *The Philosophy of Space and Time*, NY, 1957) and in his contributions to symbolic logic and linguistic philosophy (*Elements of Symbolic Logic*, NY, 1947). In *The Rise of Scientific Philosophy* (Berkeley, Calif., 1951) he explained the chief tendencies and theorems of his fierce empiricism in a popular way. His philosophical project first crystallized in the 'Gesellschaft für empirische Philosophie' in Berlin in the late 1920s. In conjunction with the 'Verein Ernst Mach', Vienna, this society under his and CARNAP's editorship issued the seminal journal *Erkenntnis*, which first appeared in 1930 and, even when Reichenbach had to emigrate in 1933, was kept going in the Netherlands until 1938. It reappeared in 1975 in the USA, in English, but under its original German title. Reichenbach held that, as in everyday life, no certain knowledge was necessary, but only knowledge of probability. He dismissed all nonempirical knowledge as both unscientific and unphilosophical and he therefore rejected Kant's synthetic judgements *a priori*. Logic was for him, as for WITTGENSTEIN and Carnap, an indispensable nomenclature for transposing sentences into formal relational constructs. *Selected Writings 1909–1953* (eds M. Reichenbach & R. S. Cohen) was published in 1978. WvdW

Reichstein, Tadeus (b. Włocławek, Russian Poland [now Poland], 20.7.1897; naturalized Swiss citizen). Polish/Swiss organic chemist. Born in Poland, Reichstein spent his early childhood in Kiev, but was educated first in Jena, then in Zürich, latterly at the Eidgenössische Technische Hochschule (diplomate 1920). He gained his doctorate for work on the flavouring substances of coffee (under STAUDINGER) and continued to work in that field for some years. In 1929 he joined the staff of ETH, becoming assistant to RUŽIČKA in 1931, and associate professor in 1937. In 1938 he became professor of pharmaceutical chemistry in the University of Basle (until 1950) and in 1946 added to his existing duties those of the chair of organic chemistry. He became director of the Institute of Organic Chemistry in Basle in 1960. In 1933, independently of HAWORTH, Reichstein synthesized ascorbic acid (the antiscorbutic vitamin C). He also worked on plant glycosides but, more importantly (1953–4), in collaboration with several workers in other laboratories, he isolated and determined the constitution of aldosterone, an important adrenal cortical hormone. He also collaborated with E. C. Kendall and P. S. Hench (jointly with whom he received the Nobel prize for physiology and medicine in 1950) in work which culminated in the isolation of cortisone and the discovery of its utility in the treatment of rheumatoid arthritis. NBC

Reinhardt, Ad (b. New York, USA, 24.12.1913; d. New York, 30.8.1967). American painter, whose pictures were completely abstract from his student days in the mid-1930s onwards. He began by working in an abstract style derived from the late synthetic cubism of PICASSO and Stuart DAVIS, with interlocking planes of contrasting colours. Then he made a number of works with more broken and complex 'all-over' surfaces built up first of fragmented collages and later covered with active brushwork. From about 1950–1, however, he embarked on a progressive simplification of his colours and of his compositions. Rectilinear all-over 'bricks' of colour gave place to asymmetrical bars on solid grounds, then to symmetry, to fewer and fewer elements, and finally to a simple trisection; at the same time colour contrasts were gradu-

ally eliminated in favour of mono-chrome, first red or blue and finally matt black. Although he was a close friend of the abstract expressionist painters, and took an active part in their discussions in the late 1940s and early 1950s, he maintained a very inde-pendent position. His quest for the absolute of pure painting led him to work from 1960 onwards exclusively on 5ft square canvases symmetrically tri-sected both vertically and horizontally and painted in deep near-blacks, pic-tures in whose mysterious dark surfaces one could just dimly make out, on close inspection, the underlying geometrical structure. Though these works have a strange beauty, it is hard to see what further development would have been possible along these lines had he lived. As a pioneer of reductivist minimal art pursued with rigorous consistency, he has, however, been a source of inspira-tion for many younger painters and sculptors.   REA
L. R. Lippard, *Ad Reinhardt* (NY, 1981).

Reinhardt, Jean Baptiste (Django) (b. Liberchies, Belgium, 23.1.1910; d. Fon-tainebleau, Seine-et-Marne, France, 16.5.1953). Belgian jazz guitarist. In the 1930s he became the first European jazz musician to achieve international recog-nition. Playing an acoustic instrument almost exclusively, he renewed the status of the guitar in the jazz ensemble and made approximately 800 recordings. A French-speaking gypsy, his early life was spent in a caravan near Paris. With lit-tle education he could scarcely write, but he began to play the guitar at 12, displaying exceptional talent in absorb-ing the improvisational basis of tradi-tional gypsy string music. Surviving injuries from a caravan fire in 1928 in which he lost two fingers from his left hand, he devised a substitute fingering technique and continued to perform. He quickly established a reputation as a soloist and virtuosic improviser and made recordings with singer Jean Sablon and the violinist Stephane Grappelly with whom he established an enduring musical relationship. In 1934 Reinhardt and Grappelly formed 'Quintette du Hot Club de France', an all-string

ensemble of violin, guitar, two rhythm guitars and bass which became one of Europe's most original, outstanding and commercially popular jazz groups of the era. It recorded with many visiting American jazz musicians and even broadcast to the USA. After WW2 Reinhardt himself visited the USA and toured with ELLINGTON.   TEC
C. Delaunay, *Django Reinhardt* (Gateshead, ²1981).

Reinhardt, Max, *né* Goldmann (b. Baden, nr Vienna, Austria-Hungary [now Austria], 9.9.1873; d. New York, USA, 30.10.1943). Austrian impresario and theatre director. While never start-lingly original in his theoretical ideas, Reinhardt was so skilled in directing actors and crowds of extras, and so masterly in his handling of modern lighting, the cyclorama and the revolve, that he became the world's best-known theatrical director between about 1911, when he staged his mass spectacle *The Miracle* at Olympia, London, and 1938 when the Anschluss uprooted him from the German-language theatre for good. Long supported on the business side by his brother Edmund, who enabled him normally to work without official sub-sidy, he directed the Deutsches Theater in Berlin from 1905 to 1933; turned a Berlin circus into a 5000-seat theatre in 1919; started the Salzburg Festival with Richard STRAUSS and HOFMANNSTHAL in 1920; staged classic productions of *A Midsummer Night's Dream*, *As You Like It* and other Shakespeare plays; intro-duced STRINDBERG, G. B. SHAW and PIRANDELLO to the German theatre, and developed a long line of outstand-ing actors such as Elisabeth Bergner, Emil Jannings, Werner Krauss, Alex-ander Moissi and Conrad Veidt. One of Reinhardt's legacies was the concept of the director as the presiding intelligence behind the theatrical performance. JWMW
H. Herald, *Max Reinhardt* (Frankfurt, 1953).

Reith, John Charles Walsham (b. Stonehaven, Grampian, UK, 20.7.1889; d. Edinburgh, Lothian, 16.6.1971). Crea-tor of British broadcasting. Reith's earl-iest days were spent in a deeply religious household (his father was moderator of the United Free Church of Scotland); he remained devotional and pious. Educated at Glasgow Academy and the Royal Technical College at Glasgow, he qualified as a locomotive engineer in 1913 and worked briefly as such. War service in France nearly ended his life but, believing he had been saved by a miracle, he was reluctant to resume his former career at the end of the war. 'I believe there is some great work for me to do in this world,' he noted in his diary after hearing a stirring sermon. In 1922 he read an advertisement for a general manager for the newly formed British Broadcasting Company, and was appointed. A man of intellect as well as force of character, he quickly established himself as autocrat of a new realm of human expression mainly in order to ensure that broadcasting in Britain would become a public service not only in performance but in constitution. He was determined that radio should not be integrated into the free market complex in Britain as it had been in the USA. Sneered at by CHURCHILL as 'that Wuthering Height', he was a formidable figure to all in government who had to deal with him. On 1.1.1927 the BBC came into being with Reith, to whom its establishment and form were largely due, as its first director-general. He was soon open to criticism, for he trusted to precept and discipline rather than to more human arts of leadership. But his judgement was usually in tune with a huge if silent majority, even when it included the perpetuation of a 'class' society. In 1938 however his judgement failed him completely. In his opinion, the BBC had reached its maximum size and power. He resigned to become chairman of British Airways. This meant that at a time of national crisis (1939–45) the BBC was without the leader who had formed it and knew it best. The Reith diaries were edited by C. Stuart (London, 1975).   RB

A. Briggs, *The History of Broadcasting in the UK*. i, *The Birth of Broadcasting* (London, 1961), ii, *The Golden Age of Wireless* (London, 1965); A. Boyle, *Only the Wind will Listen: Reith of the BBC* (London, 1972).

Remarque, Erich Maria, ps. of Erich Paul Remark (b. Osnabrück, Lower Saxony, Germany, 22.6.1898; naturalized American citizen, 1947; d. Locarno, Ticino, Switzerland, 25.9.1970). German/American novelist. Born into modest circumstances, he began his career as a sporting journalist. Fame came with his outstandingly successful novel *Im Westen nichts Neues* (Berlin, 1929; tr. A. W. Wheen, *All Quiet on the Western Front*, London, 1929), which touched on a nerve of the time and sparked off a storm of political controversy. It follows the experiences of a class of the 'lost generation' of schoolboys who are forced into premature manhood by their squalid, painful and brutalizing experiences in the trenches of WW1. The young men who return home find in the sequel *Der Weg zurück* (Berlin, 1931; tr. A. W. Wheen, *The Way Back*, Boston, Mass., 1931) that it is impossible to resolve the paradox between the lethal excitement of war and the numbing boredom of ordinary life. Remarque's middle-of-the-road liberalism and internationalism, his streak of sentimentality and pessimistic life view, conflicted with the Nazi concepts of man and society, and found equally little favour with MARXist critics. Remarque wrote nine further novels, notably *Arc de Triomphe* (Zürich, 1946; tr. W. Sorell & D. Lindley, *Arch of Triumph*, NY, 1945), the best of his novels about Germans in exile, but none attained either the sales or the reputation of his WW1 novel, which was made into the classic film by Lewis Milestone (1930). He left Germany at the beginning of the 1930s and made his way to the USA, where he made many friends among Hollywood stars including Paulette Goddard, whom he married in 1958.   RWL

Remizov, Aleksey Mikhailovich (b. Moscow, Russia, 7.7.1877; d. Paris, France, 28.11.1957). Russian writer. Born into a poor merchant family, Remizov gained early experiences in the slum streets of Moscow and on pilgrimages to monasteries and holy places. He became a socialist, was expelled from the university, arrested and exiled to the provinces. In 1904 he moved to St Petersburg and embarked on a prolific and varied literary activity. In 1921 he left Russia, mainly for health reasons, and settled in Paris, where he continued to write. Although largely apolitical, he disapproved of postrevolutionary Russia, but was one of the few émigré writers who greatly influenced Soviet prose. His work is not easily classified. It bears the stamp of Dostoevsky in the gory nightmares of such novels as *Tsarevna Mymra* [Princess Mumra] (Moscow, 1908), *Krestovye Sestry* [Sisters of the cross] (Moscow, 1910), and the remarkable and spooky story of provincial life *Neuyomnyi Buben* [The unhushable tambourine] (Moscow, 1909); of decadent modernism, *Prud* [The pond] (Petersburg, 1907), and the unprintable or privately printed *Tsar' Dodon* (1909); of N. S. Leskov's *skaz* (a spoken, nonliterary narrative form) and folklore, *Skazki russkovo naroda* [Tales of the Russian people] (Berlin, 1923), *Nikoliny pritchi* [Parables of Nicholas] (Paris, 1927); and even semihumorous, hieratic mystery drama *Kozol' Maksimilian* [King Maximilian] (Berlin, 1918). Remizov mimicked folk-legend, tales and apocrypha, with a feeling for the pattern and inflection of 'pure' colloquial Russian (roughly of the 17c) which places him beside BELY as one of the greatest stylists in Russian literature. The 'purity', however, is largely deceptive, for Remizov was at bottom a sophisticated modern, with an admixture of the childlike. The 'Dostoevskyan' strain in his work ingeniously blends the real with the unreal, and uses a complex symbolism in which images belonging to different levels of experience are intertwined or confused. Cases in point are *Rossiya v pis'menakh* [Whirlwind Russia] (Berlin, 1921) and *Ogenennaya Rossiya* [Fiery Russia] (Reval, 1921) which are largely deft exercises in stylistic manner. He had a wonderful calligraphic talent, using weird forms of handwriting, and a passion for books and old manuscripts. Collected works are: *Sobranie sochineniy* (4 vols, Moscow, 1910–12). Among translations are: *The Fifth Pestilence* (tr. H. Brown, London, 1927); *On a Field of Azure* (tr. B. Scott, London, 1946, [2]1975); *The Clock* (tr. J. Cournos, London, 1924); *Stratilov* (tr. J. Cournos, London, 1926). EL

K. Chukovsky, *Psikhologicheskie motivy v tvorchestve Alekseya Remizova* (Moscow, 1914); N. Kobryanskaya, *Aleksey Remizov* (Moscow, 1959).

Renoir, Jean (b. Paris, France, 15.9.1894; d. Beverly Hills, Calif., USA, 12.2.1979). French film director who rose to world fame in the 1930s and, after a spell in Hollywood, returned to France to exercise a powerful influence on the 'New Wave' of 1960s film makers. The son of the painter Auguste RENOIR, he was throughout his life influenced by art, landscapes and personalities. The least arrogant of men, Renoir conceived all his work as a collaborative effort by director, writer, technicians and actors. His early years were filled with uncertainty. He was 30 before he made his first film – deeply influenced by Erich Von Stroheim – and although some of his silent films are in retrospect major works (e.g. *Nana*, 1926), he did not then fully establish his personal style or his link with an audience. The 1930s were for him a period of enormous popular and critical success. As early as 1935 he anticipated the postwar Italian neorealist movement with a story of migrant workers, *Toni*, and the latter half of the decade saw a flood of masterpieces, including such diverse but totally individual works as *Une Partie de campagne* (*A Day in the Country*, 1936), *La Grande Illusion* (*Grand Illusion*, 1937) and *La Règle du jeu* (*The Rules of the Game*, 1939). Although Renoir's years in Hollywood during the 1940s offered nothing to rival these works, after his return to France in the 1950s he was able to produce a series of deeply felt meditations on art and life.

Renoir's importance as a film maker stems from a number of factors: first, the quality of his films, particularly in the 1930s; second, the theoretical importance of his work as it is presented in the writing of the greatest postwar French critic, BAZIN (all Bazin's key concepts – the unique link between film and reality; the essential ambiguity of reality and of those films that reflect it authentically; the significance of the long take – seem to derive from, and find exemplary expression in, Renoir's work); third, throughout his life Renoir influenced personally young film makers of great potential talent at vital moments of their careers: VISCONTI in France in the 1930s, Satyajit Ray in Calcutta in 1950 and, after his return to Paris, TRUFFAUT, Jacques Rivette and many of their New Wave contemporaries. He wrote *Renoir* (Paris, 1962; *Renoir, My Father*, Boston, Mass., 1962) and *Ma vie et mes films* (Paris, 1974; *My Life and my Films*, London, 1974).

RPA

A. Bazin, *Jean Renoir* (London, 1974); R. Durgnat, *Jean Renoir* (London, 1975).

Renoir, Pierre Auguste (b. Limoges, Haute-Vienne, France, 25.2.1841; d. Cagnes-sur-Mer, Alpes-Maritimes, 2.12.1919). French painter. Renoir trained as a porcelain painter and entered the Ecole des Beaux Arts in 1861 where he met MONET, Bazille and Sisley. He lived by decorating fans with copies of French rococo paintings from the Louvre (e.g. by Fragonard and Watteau). His early paintings, often with themes from everyday life, were influenced by Courbet's heavy impasto and dark shadows (e.g. *At the Inn of Mother Anthony*, 1866). In the late 1860s Renoir and Monet began open-air painting together in an improvised, proto-impressionist style using delicate brushwork (e.g. *Skaters in the Bois de Boulogne*, 1868). On the Seine at La Grenouillère (1868–9) and at Argenteuil (early 1870s) he and Monet captured the impression of shimmering light and its reflections by breaking up forms into small dabs and dashes of pure and broken colour. This diffused sunlight was the keynote of the atmospheric Parisian views (e.g. *Pont Neuf*, 1872) of the early 1870s in which he often increased the spontaneity of a scene by sketching from a window high above the street. From the late 1860s he was a member of the circle at the Café Guerbois (Pissarro, Degas, CÉZANNE, etc.). He showed at the first three impressionist exhibitions (1874–7); his work was much criticized for the insubstantiality of his figures' limbs. He experimented with complementary colour and coloured shadows (e.g. *Nude in Sunlight*, 1875–6). His scenes of the ele-

gant and petit-bourgeois worlds at leisure (e.g. *La Loge*, 1874; *Le Moulin de la Galette*, 1876) typify the impressionist depiction of the vitality of modern urban life in feathery brushstrokes of pure and broken colour. From 1877 Renoir had some success at the Salon with society portraits (e.g. *Mme Charpentier and her Children*, 1878) in which soft textures are combined with a perspectival structure, heralding a return to more traditional composition.

A visit to Italy (1881) confirmed his dissatisfaction with the superficiality of impressionism. He rediscovered Ingres, Raphael and French 18c art and tried to reconcile the 'grandeur and simplicity of the old masters' with the impressionist *plein air* approach. *Les Parapluies* marks the transition; begun in 1881–2 in a prismatic, diffused impressionist style, the figures and umbrellas (completed in 1885–6) are more tautly conceived and subdued in colour. In the monumental 'fresco in oils', the *Bathers* (1884–7), spontaneity and iridescence were replaced by contrived poses (from preliminary drawings), incisively defined forms and matt pastel colours. Around 1890 this somewhat harsh linearity gave way to a synthesis of colour, contour and decorative design (e.g. *Young Girls at the Piano*, 1892). Sensuous, warm colours, especially reds and oranges, applied like a transparent haze, were predominant in Renoir's last period (from c. 1895), as in intimate portraits of his wife, children and their nursemaid Gabrielle, who also modelled for the dreamy, voluptuously rounded nudes and seated bathers, some on mythological themes (e.g. *Judgement of Paris*, 1916), of his last years. Crippled by arthritis, Renoir turned to sculpture (c. 1907), adapting themes from previous paintings (e.g. *Venus Victorious*, 1914); after a paralytic stroke in 1910 these works were executed almost entirely by assistants.

SOBT

W. Pach, *Pierre-Auguste Renoir* (NY, 1950); F. Fosca, *Renoir* (London, 1961); J. Renoir, *Renoir, My Father* (Boston, Mass., 1962).

Resnais, Alain (b. Vannes, Morbihan, France, 3.6.1922). French film director. Resnais began his professional career as a documentary film maker. In a series of works culminating in the masterly study of the concentration camps *Nuit et brouillard* (*Night and Fog*, 1955) he developed new ways of combining and counterpointing the basic elements of image, music and text. From 1959 onwards he began to apply these same techniques to the fictional feature film, interweaving past and present, reality and the imaginary in collaboration with such distinguished writers as DURAS (*Hiroshima mon amour*, 1959) and ROBBE-GRILLET (*L'Année dernière à Marienbad*; *Last Year at Marienbad*, 1961). Three further 1960s features showed similar novelty in their formal construction and established Resnais's reputation as one of the most innovative of modernist film makers. Since his return to film making, after a six-year break, with *Stavisky* (1974), this early inventiveness has been replaced by a new classicism and search for formal perfection. Alain Resnais is a complex and contradictory figure: a complete film maker who refuses to write his own scripts, an intellectual with a passion for comic strips, an innovator of enormous subtlety with a profound admiration for the classic Hollywood studio style. His output comprises some of the most imaginative and formally innovative work of modern European cinema and its impact has been worldwide.   RPA

R. Armes, *The Cinema of Alain Resnais* (London, 1968); J. Monaco, *Alain Resnais* (London, 1978).

Reverdy, Pierre (b. Narbonne, Aude, France, 13.9.1889; d. Solesmes, Sarthe, 17.6.1960). French poet. A prominent member of the Parisian avant-garde from 1910, Reverdy was, along with APOLLINAIRE and Max Jacob, one of the founding editors of *Nord-Sud*, a short-lived review illustrated by LÉGER and BRAQUE which provided an important public platform for the cubists and then for the emerging surrealist group in 1917 and 1918. Reverdy's early poetry (subsequently collected in *Plupart du temps* [Most of the time], Paris, 1945) was influenced both by his cubist associates and by the innovations of Mallarmé. With its suppression of punctuation and novel use of typography, it

sought not to reproduce existing reality but to create a specifically poetic reality through the metaphoric juxtaposition of images. A pervasive melancholy haunts these sparse texts, with their extreme verbal sobriety and their deliberate avoidance of all superfluous ornamentation. Although brought up as a free-thinker, Reverdy converted to Catholicism after a serious personal and spiritual crisis, and retired to live in Solesmes in 1926. His later poetry (collected in *Main d'oeuvre* [Labour], Paris, 1949) and prose writings such as *Le Livre de mon bord* [Logbook] (Paris, 1949) develop the religious themes latent in the earlier work and express a deep longing for the transcendental. For the surrealists, Reverdy was, in BRETON's phrase, 'the greatest of living poets' and a direct inspiration for their own work on metaphor and dream imagery. *Selected Poems*, translated by Kenneth Rexroth, was published in 1973 (London).   DM

Reynolds, Osborne (b. Belfast, Ireland [now Northern Ireland], UK, 23.8.1842; d. Watchet, Som., 21.2.1912). British engineer. His main contribution to engineering science was related to the boundary distinguishing the two states in a liquid, that of smooth, laminar flow, and that of turbulent flow. This important discovery led him to evaluate a single dimensionless factor (a number) which determines the onset of turbulence. This number was at once given his name. He was the first to demonstrate cavitation by impact of a fluid and to attribute the accompanying noise to the collapse of vapour bubbles; and to correlate length and time scales in a study of distorted models. The results of his work on fluid flow were far-reaching: a fluid has comparable properties whether it be a liquid or a gas, and many results obtainable in water have their counterparts in air; the theory and practice of aviation were greatly advanced by Reynolds's work: he clarified the way towards the modern boundary-layer theory. Fluid flow is a vital part of the theory of lubrication. In 1883 Reynolds predicted the transatlantic telephone cable. He questioned Newton's laws of motion, suggesting that they might be extended to take account of the 'next order of small quantities' (rates of change of acceleration). He studied astronomy and came to the conclusion that a proportion of the light from the stars must be 'stopped' in interstellar space (brightness is not dependent on distance away). ERL

Rhodes, Cecil John (b. Bishop's Stortford, Herts., UK, 5.7.1853; d. Muizenburg, Cape Colony, South Africa, 26.3.1902). South African politician and industrialist. Execrated or revered as the archetypal late 19c imperialist, Rhodes made a greater impact on the development of southern Africa than any other white man in the region's history. A very young English immigrant to South Africa, he made a fortune on the newly opened Kimberley diamond fields in the 1870s; he developed his imperialist ideas under the influence of Ruskin and Winwood Reade, as an undergraduate at Oxford. His ambitions were grandiose but crude: a fervent believer in the superiority of the 'Anglo-Saxon race', he dreamt of bringing 'the whole uncivilized world' under British rule. His rapidly expanding wealth, based on a monopoly of Kimberley diamonds and a major stake in the goldfields of the Rand, provided him with a secure base for political power. His most spectacular achievement was the establishment of British control over the territories now known as Zimbabwe and Zambia, through the agency of his chartered company the British South African Company. As prime minister of the Cape (1890–6) Rhodes worked to create a South African federation based on an English–Afrikaner alliance under the British flag, but his involvement in the abortive coup against the government of President Kruger in the Transvaal (Jameson's Raid, 1896) discredited him politically and greatly exacerbated the tension that led to the Anglo–Boer war in 1899. His achievements as an economic innovator were more lasting. He introduced new techniques and forms of organization into the rapidly expanding South African mining industry and thus helped to lay the massive economic foundations of South African capitalism. Rhodes's 'native policy' towards black

South Africa was clearly a foretaste of the system of apartheid consolidated by Afrikaner nationalists. RH

J. G. Lockhard & C. M. Wodehouse, *Rhodes* (London, 1963); J. Flint, *Cecil Rhodes* (London, 1976).

Rhys, Jean, *née* Ella Gwendolen Rees Williams (b. Roseau, Dominica, West Indies, 24.8.1890?; d. Cheriton Fitzpaine, Devon, UK, 14.5.1979). West Indian/British novelist and short-story writer, who emigrated to the UK at about 16 and lived a chequered existence in Europe. This is reflected in several penetrating women characters in her fiction. *After Leaving Mr Mackenzie* (London, 1930) and *Voyage in the Dark* (London, 1934) were spare, evocative works, the latter recalling her own voyage to England, and *Good Morning, Midnight* (London, 1939) established her unquestionable power as a writer. With *Wide Sargasso Sea* (London, 1966) – her next novel following her near total disappearance for 20 years – she again drew upon her childhood memories for a finely realized history of Antoinette Cosway, the mad Creole wife in Charlotte Brontë's *Jane Eyre* (1847), Rhys's perfect vehicle for exploring her own complex background, together with her sharp sense of the West Indies and the UK as culturally opposed but historically complementary cultures. The novel encompasses historical, geographical and psychological dimensions to create a work of great originality. *Smile Please* (London, 1979) was an unfinished autobiography which illuminated her personal story with great honesty and simplicity. PNQ

K. E. Roby, *Jean Rhys* (Boston, Mass., 1980).

Richards, Ivor Armstrong (b. Sandbach, Ches., UK, 26.2.1893; d. Cambridge, 7.9.1979). British literary critic and poet. One of the most influential figures in modern literary criticism, Richards has been almost singlehandedly responsible for the introduction of scientific and analytical methods into critical discourse. When invited to lecture in English at Cambridge in 1919 Richards brought to the subject his background in moral science and his extensive, if amateur, interest in psychology: thus began, effectively, the New Criticism which was to dominate Anglo-American criticism for the next 30 years. In *The Principles of Literary Criticism* (London, 1924) Richards drew a distinction between the scientific, or referential, use of language and the emotive use of language; poetry, he argued, is concerned exclusively with the latter and thus exists as a special form of discourse which should be analysed not for its 'truths' but for its linguistic implications and its internal, and self-legitimating, coherence. Careful semantic analysis was the core of Richards's critical method, especially so in *Practical Criticism* (London, 1929), but he added to this a concern with what he saw as the therapeutic function of poetry. In the 1930s and 1940s he became increasingly interested in promulgating the simplified system of English that he had developed with OGDEN known as 'Basic English'. Despite the inconsistencies and eccentricities of his later writings Richards remains one of the greatest critical theorists of the 20c.   GHC

S. E. Hyman, *The Armed Vision* (NY, 1948); J. P. Schiller, *I. A. Richards' Theory of Literature* (New Haven, 1969).

Richardson, Lewis Fry (b. Newcastle-upon-Tyne, Tyne & Wear, UK, 11.10.1881; d. Kilmun, Strath., 30.9.1953). British meteorologist. The possessor of one of the most able, original and versatile minds ever devoted to meteorology, he made fundamental contributions in many fields. In 1910 he published an important paper on the use of finite differences in the solution of the differential equations which arise in physical problems. On joining the Meteorological Office in 1913 he applied and extended these methods to the basic equations of meteorological dynamics and thermodynamics. This work led to the publication in 1922 of his famous book *Weather Prediction by Numerical Process* (Cambridge) which covered the whole field of atmospheric physics and was thus of wider scope than suggested by the title. In 1919 he became very interested in atmospheric turbulence and in the ensuing years published a series of classical papers on the supply of

energy from and to atmospheric eddies. His well-known criterion for 'just no turbulence', called the Richardson number, is a fundamental dimensionless parameter in problems of the turbulent diffusion of the atmosphere. He also produced significant work on the application of tidal theory to the atmosphere, on the convergence of upper winds and on the albedo of the earth's surface. PJM

Richmond, Ian Archibald (b. Rochdale, Lancs., UK, 10.5.1902; d. Oxford, 4.10.1965). British archaeologist. His early interests in Roman Britain soon widened to include Italy, first as a student and later, in 1930–2, as director of the British School at Rome. Among the fruits of this period is his masterly *The City Wall of Imperial Rome* (Oxford, 1930). From 1935 he devoted two decades of intensive work to military sites in northern Britain, including Hadrian's Wall. Later came the excavation of the legionary fortress at Inchtuthil (Perthshire) and of the fort at Hod Hill (Dorset), both milestones in the study of the works of the Roman army. In 1956 he was elected to the newly established chair in the archaeology of the Roman Empire at Oxford and thereafter devoted more time to the study of other Roman provinces. In the field, Richmond relied, to a degree which now seems ambitious, upon his ability to reconstruct plans from small-scale excavations. But his skill in relating archaeological evidence to its historical background was unrivalled. As fieldworker, writer and teacher, his influence has been felt in most parts of the Roman world. MT

Richter, Burton (b. New York, USA, 22.3.1931). American physicist. Educated at MIT, Richter has been, since the 1950s, a proponent of the use of electron–positron annihilations for the study of particle interactions. He has been involved with all the recent e^-e^+ storage rings at Stanford culminating in the SPEAR and PEP accelerators. It was with the SPEAR machine that evidence for the charm quark (see GLASHOW) was first obtained, a new lepton discovered, and the existence of coloured quarks (albeit confined) finally demonstrated. Since then Richter has advocated the construction of ever larger storage rings on the same fundamentally simple grounds: this approach promises to dominate experimental high-energy physics for at least the next decade. In 1976 he received the Nobel prize together with S. C. C. Ting, an independent discoverer of the J/ψ particle (which contains charm quarks). RJC

Rickert, Heinrich (b. Danzig, Germany [now Gdansk, Poland], 25.5.1863; d. Heidelberg, Baden-Württemberg, Germany, 25.7.1936). German philosopher, and one of the founders of neo-Kantianism. In his two major works *Die Grenzen der naturwissenschaftlichen Begriffsbildung* [The limits of natural-scientific conceptualization] (Tübingen, 1896–1902, [5]1929) and *Kulturwissenschaft und Naturwissenschaft* (Tübingen, 1899, [6]1926; tr. G. Reisman, *Science and History*, Princeton, 1962), Rickert argued that Windelband's division of reality into two mutually exclusive spheres, nature and history, was unjustified, since in the last analysis all reality is historical; the various disciplines take their place on a continuum ranging from the network of abstract formulae constructed for practical purposes by the quantitative empirical sciences and strictly corresponding to nothing, to the only truly genuine form of knowledge, that of the unique and particular as it really exists, i.e. history. In opposition to the subjectivism of DILTHEY's *Geisteswissenschaft* [science of mind] he sought to set up a more objective approach to historical studies in the form of a *Kulturwissenschaft* [science of culture]: historical investigation must become an objective science of universal timeless values such as the state, law, art, and religion, as these emerge through the productive life of culture. The relations between the realm of empirical reality and that of timeless objective values are mediated through a third realm of what Rickert terms 'constellations of meaning and value', or *Sinngebilde*, which form the basic material of culture. In spite of certain flaws, his work remains an important philosophic critique of relativism and subjectivism. RNH

Ricoeur, Paul (b. Valence, Drôme, France, 27.2.1913). French philosopher. Ricoeur has written over a dozen books and several hundred articles dealing with a wide range of philosophical questions – the nature of language and interpretation, the role of the subject, the problem of will, history and human action – as part of a continuing debate with contemporary methodologies: structuralism, hermeneutics, phenomenology. Yet all of these inquiries have as their common back-drop Ricoeur's own original project, formed in the 1930s while he was still a student of MARCEL: a philosophy of the will, published in two parts – I. *Le Volontaire et l'involontaire* (Paris, 1950; *Freedom and Nature: the Voluntary and the Involuntary*, Evanston, Ill., 1966); II. *Finitude et culpabilité*, in two books: *L'Homme faillible* (Paris, 1960; *Fallible Man*, Chicago, 1965) and *La Symbolique du mal* (Paris, 1960; *The Symbolism of Evil*, Boston, Mass., 1969). As a prisoner in Germany in WW2, Ricoeur read the writings of JASPERS, HEIDEGGER and HUSSERL. After the war he published a translation of Husserl's *Ideen I*, adding an authoritative commentary, which in turn has been followed by numerous articles on Husserlian phenomenology. A collection of some of these essays has appeared in English as *Husserl: an Analysis of His Phenomenology* (Evanston, Ill., 1967). Taking up the challenge of psychoanalysis and of structuralism within the context of his own reflections on interpretation, Ricoeur has contributed two significant and justly acclaimed works *De l'interprétation: Essai sur Freud* (Paris, 1965; *Freud and Philosophy: an Essay on Interpretation*, New Haven, 1970) and *Le Conflit des interprétations* (Paris, 1969; *The Conflict of Interpretations*, Evanston, Ill., 1974). More recently, his remarkable study on metaphor *La Métaphore vive* (Paris, 1975; *The Rule of Metaphor*, Toronto, 1977) analyses the creation of meaning in language. Aside from his many and varied publications, Ricoeur has influenced philosophical thinking in both the French- and the English-speaking world, primarily as a teacher of philosophy, and in this capacity he has held university positions at

Strasbourg, the Sorbonne, Nanterre, Louvain, Toronto and Chicago.   KMcL

Riding, Laura (b. New York, USA, 16.1.1901). American poet. In the preface to her *Collected Poems* (London, 1938) Laura Riding argued that poetry, by its pure use of language, offered the highest mode of access to truth, so much so that truth and poetry were virtually the same. Subsequently she decided that the formal qualities of poetry inevitably impede its capacity for truth, and thereafter devoted herself to lexicographical inquiries intended to furnish words with clear and unambiguous meanings. Riding's early poetic career involved her, somewhat distantly, with avant-garde literary circles in the USA; in 1925 she came to England at the instigation of GRAVES, and for some years their literary careers were closely associated. They collaborated on two polemical tracts *A Survey of Modernist Poetry* (London, 1927) and *A Pamphlet against Anthologies* (London, 1928), the implicit critical and theoretical principles of which she developed in two works of dazzling argument *Contemporaries and Snobs* (London, 1928), a critique of modishness and pseudotraditionalism in contemporary literature, and *Anarchism is Not Enough* (London, 1928), a discovery of absolute values in the self-existence of the mind. Her belief that there exists a universal truth discoverable through the personal life of the mind gave her poetry an increasingly speculative and abstract quality, in which reality was tested against its negation, while her feminism endorsed the view that women by their domestic separation from the world of action were more attuned to the wholeness of truth than were men. As Laura (Riding) Jackson she made a considered restatement of the revelation of universal truth possible in personal speech in a late prose work *The Telling* (London, 1972) which broke her long public silence.
ATKC

J. P. Wexler, *Laura Riding's Pursuit of Truth* (Athens, Ohio, 1979).

Rie, Lucy (b. Vienna, Austria-Hungary [now Austria], 16.3.1902; naturalized British citizen). Austrian/British studio potter. She began her professional artistic life in Vienna in the 1920s. Her early ceramics were strongly influenced by Japanese lacquer wares. She trained in the Kunstgewerbe Schule, and her wares set out to reconcile the conflicting artistic trends in Vienna: late neoclassicism, *Jugendstil*, Japonism and modernism as geometrical simplification. Although her early work gained substantial recognition, she left Austria for the UK in 1938, where she met and came under the influence of Bernard LEACH. During WW2 she was obliged to earn her living by making fine ceramic buttons for fashionable garments. In 1946 COPER joined her in this work. She held her first solo show as a potter in 1949.

Rie's style developed through meticulous experiment with stoneware and porcelain. Her forms were restrained – bowls, flared bottles and vases – derived from Chinese Sung dynasty and Japanese prototypes. They are not intrinsically utilitarian, but aesthetic objects. She succeeded in unifying warebody and complex slip-glaze surface treatments to produce previously unknown surfaces, going far beyond conventional glaze-on-body application. Delicate mottlings and flashings, and some trickling, run a gamut of restrained colours through black, brown, greys to lavender and even yellow. They appear as functions of the treatment of the pot itself. Each work is unique and inimitable, reached by continually inventive kiln-processing. Her example in this respect has been widely followed.   PSR

M. Rose, *Artist Potters in England* (London, ²1970).

Riegl, Alois (b. Linz, Upper Austria, Austria-Hungary [now Austria], 14.1.1858; d. Vienna, 17.6.1905). Austrian art historian. Riegl studied law and philosophy, and changed to art history at the Vienna Institute of Historical Research. He was appointed keeper of textiles at the Kunstgewerbemuseum in Vienna. In 1877 he became professor of art history at Vienna University. Riegl believed that art history should be universal history and rejected the traditional art-historical distinction between 'fine art' (the representation of man and his actions) and the 'minor' or 'decora-

RIESMAN

tive' arts. *Stilfragen* [Questions of style] (Berlin, 1893) is a history of ornamentation from ancient Egyptian to Arabian art, comparing the constructive principles of geometric and organically derived motifs. Riegl rejected another major art-historical convention: the often arbitrary, prejudicial assessment of the artistic worth of any period of history in accordance with norms attributed to Greek and Renaissance art (cf. *Die Spätrömische Kunstindustrie* [The art industry of the late Roman period], Vienna, 1901, ²1927; and *Die Entstehung der Barockkunst in Rom* [The rise of baroque art in Rome], posth., Vienna, 1907, ²1923). He defined the style of an era in accordance with development from tactile (or haptic) to visual (or optic) perception. Another principle of Riegl's that has been very important in 20c aesthetics is that of *Kunstwollen* or *Stilwollen* (i.e. 'will-to-art' or 'will-to-form'), a specific artist's or period's creative impulse to solve artistic questions. Riegl based his aesthetico-historical judgements on an historical reconstruction of the creative process, and defined it as the trend or style of the artistic forms of a period in the context of contemporary social, religious, scientific and aesthetic thought. SOBT

Riesman, David (b. Philadelphia, Pa, USA, 22.9.1909). American sociologist. After studying at Harvard, Riesman taught and practised law until 1946, when he became professor of sociology at the University of Chicago. Since 1958 he has been professor of social science at Harvard. His principal work *The Lonely Crowd: a Study of the Changing American Character* (with N. Glazer & R. Denney, New Haven, 1950) initiated a major intellectual debate about mid-20c America. Like de Tocqueville a century before, Riesman took America to be the type and trend-setter for modern mass democracy. He suggested that transition from a competitive society of high demographic and economic growth to a stable society of abundance and low fertility caused a change in 'social character'. The 'inner-directed' type described by FREUD, governed by internalized parental authority, gave way to a pliant, conformist 'other-directed' type

that took its cues from the peer group. Riesman's subtle analyses of corresponding changes in politics and popular culture, and of the opportunities for autonomous choice between inner- and other-directed conduct, were continued in *Faces in the Crowd* (with N. Glazer, New Haven, 1952) and *Individualism Reconsidered* (Glencoe, Ill., 1954). His subsequent work has been mostly in the sociology of higher education. JRT

Rietveld, Gerrit Thomas (b. Utrecht, The Netherlands, 24.6.1888; d. Utrecht, 25.6.1964). Dutch architect and cabinet-maker. Rietveld worked as an apprentice in his father's joinery shop from 1899 until 1906, setting up as a cabinet-maker on his own account in 1911 when he also began to study architecture in Utrecht. In 1918, through the agency of the architect Robert van't Hoff, Rietveld joined the *De Stijl* group which had been established the previous year. Immediately he realized the theoretical ideas of the group in a sequence of startlingly inventive designs for furniture. The Red-blue Chair (1918) showed the elements of the chair reduced to bare essentials in an abstract composition of flat planes painted in the primary colours according to *De Stijl* laws. The seat (blue) and the back (red) are separately suspended within an open scaffolding of black-painted wooden battens which abut and overlap, notionally fixing the flux of universal space. Space is not enclosed by the form but passes through it: Rietveld called it 'a fixed image of open spaces'. Subsequent designs for furniture continued to explore this theme (sideboard, 1919; Berlin chair, 1923). The clear separation of wall plane from structure, the deliberate ambiguities in the demarcation of space, which characterize the development of modern architecture in the 1920s, are presaged in Rietveld's designs. But it was in the Schröder house, designed in 1924, that Rietveld demonstrated his ideas with the greatest clarity; and they had an immediate and lasting impact on the development of 20c architecture. Every contemporary architectural magazine of importance published the drawings and photographs of the completed building; the ideas reached progressive architects everywhere. Rietveld had proved that it was possible to conceive of a building that did not box up space; here instead, the volume of the house is extended outwards through a series of overlapping floor, ceiling, wall and balcony planes. The whole is composed as a three-dimensional realization of the ideas pioneered in the paintings of MONDRIAN. Although Rietveld continued to produce buildings throughout the 1930s and again, after a long period with few commissions, in the 1950s up until his death, none of the later buildings, which include the Van Gogh Museum, Amsterdam, achieved the level of innovatory brilliance of the period 1918–25.　PAC

T. M. Brown, *The Work of G. Rietveld, Architect* (Utrecht, 1958).

Rilke, Rainer Maria, *né* René Karl Wilhelm Johann Joseph Maria Rilke (b. Prague, Austria-Hungary [now Czechoslovakia], 4.12.1875; d. Valmont, Vaud, Switzerland, 29.12.1926). Austrian poet. Sent to a military academy at the age of 10, Rilke suffered under a strict regime which contrasted sharply with his indulgent upbringing – his mother treated him virtually as a girl; he was eventually invalided out of the academy. He studied philosophy, literature and art history at Prague and Munich, but left to travel with Lou Andreas-Salomé in Russia, where he felt himself to belong spiritually to the Slavic race. His early poetry tended towards a contrived *fin-de-siècle* sentimentality. He joined an artists' colony in Worpswede in north Germany, where he married Clara Westhoff. He visited RODIN in Paris and began to adapt the artistic techniques of the sculptor, and of the painter CÉZANNE, to his poetry. In his *Neue Gedichte* and *Der neuen Gedichte anderer Teil* (Leipzig, 1907–8; tr. J. B. Leishman, *New Poems*, London, 1964) Rilke penetrated to the very essence of his subject matter. He replaced 'subjective' and 'objective' views with the presence of the 'thing itself', and the poet ceased to exist as a separate factor in the poem. He also adumbrated this complex notion in the melancholic journal-novel *Die Aufzeichnungen des Malte Laurids Brigge* (Leipzig, 1910; tr. J. Lin-

ton, *The Notebooks of M.L.B.*, London, 1930). Rilke's next great project was spread over 10 years, interrupted by WW1. On 11.2.1922 he completed the tenth of the *Duineser Elegien* (Leipzig, 1923; London, 1931; tr. J. B. Leishman & S. Spender, *Duino Elegies*, London, ³1948). A few days later he completed the 55 *Die Sonette an Orpheus* (Leipzig, 1923; tr. J. B. Leishman, *Sonnets to Orpheus*, London, 1936). The cycles complement one another; each sees the poet as the singer of all creation, mystically linked to the original Creator and sharing in the redemption of the world. Rilke's work has been a lasting influence on English poetry; his ability to express abstract ideas in tangible terms impressed AUDEN in particular.　JHC

E. C. Mason, *Rilke, Europe and the English-speaking World* (Cambridge, 1961); E. F. N. Jephcott, *Proust and Rilke* (London, 1972).

Ritter, Gerhard (b. Bad Sooden-Allendorf, Hesse, Germany, 6.4.1888; d. Freiburg, Baden-Württemberg, West Germany, 1.7.1967). German historian whose original field of interest was in the 16c but who was drawn by the events through which he lived into writing about recent German history. Ritter was the last in the tradition of German historians on whom Bismarck's achievement exercised a decisive influence, expressing itself in the belief that politics was the decisive factor in history and power the decisive factor in politics. He combined this, however, as a convinced Lutheran, with the view that 'all political authority rests upon moral bases ... and this erects barriers to the arbitrary actions of even the strongest power'. He argued that this was the true Prussian tradition of statesmanship, the balance of which had been maintained by Bismarck but lost by his successors and destroyed by HITLER. An opponent of Nazism on national and conservative grounds, he wrote a vindication of the German resistance (*Carl Goerdeler und die deutsche Widerstandsbewegung*, Stuttgart, 1956; abridged *The German Resistance*, London, 1958), rejecting the charge that Nazism was the culmination of the German tradition of *Machtpolitik* and militarism. His *Staat-*

skunst und Krieghandwerk (4 vols, Munich, 1954–68; the first three vols, covering 1740–1917, *The Sword and the Sceptre*, Miami, 1969–72) is an historical examination of the problem of the relations between the civil and military powers in Germany, although he did not carry the study beyond 1918. Part of the reason for this was that, while he was writing his book, Fritz FISCHER published diametrically opposed views which Ritter regarded as little short of treason for any German historian. He took the lead in the campaign against Fischer and devoted the last two volumes of his own work and numerous articles to attacking Fischer's views, particularly on the role of Bethmann-Hollweg. It was Ritter's misfortune that the times in which he lived left him, as he felt, no option but to devote his great gifts as an historian to the task of defending Germany's traditions against those who sought to extend condemnation of Nazism to the whole of German history. The polemics in which this involved him should not obscure the fact that his side of the argument needed to be made and that he made it with as much conviction as his critics.

ALCB

Rivera, Diego Maria (b. Guanajuato, Mexico, 8.12.1886; d. Mexico City, 25.11.1957). Mexican painter, a leading artist of the Mexican mural movement, which aimed to create a popular art to express the ideals of the Mexican revolution. Between 1911 and 1921 Rivera lived in Paris as a member of the cubist circle, and visited the Renaissance frescoes in Italy. Returning to Mexico City, he, OROZCO, David Alvaro Siqueiros and others painted murals in the National Preparatory School in 1923, marking the inception of the mural movement. Rivera continued to paint murals in public buildings including the Ministry of Education (1923–9), the Agricultural School at Chapingo (1923–7) and the National Palace (1929–35). In 1927 he visited the USSR and in 1930 went to the USA, painting murals at the San Francisco Stock Exchange and Art Institute and the Detroit Institute of Art (1932). The destruction in 1934 of his mural at the Rockefeller Center, New York, because it included a portrait of LENIN, caused controversy, but he painted a replica, *Man at the Crossroads*, at the Palace of Fine Arts, Mexico City. Rivera's work influenced the American muralists of the Federal Art Project.

MOJN

B. D. Wolfe, *The Fabulous Life of Diego Rivera* (NY, 1963); F. Arquin, *Diego Rivera: the Shaping of an Artist 1889–1921* (Norman, Okla, 1971).

Rivers, William Halse Rivers (b. Luton, nr Chatham, Kent, UK, 12.3.1864; d. Cambridge, 4.6.1922). British anthropologist and psychologist. Rivers received a medical education and lectured in experimental psychology at Cambridge before joining the interdisciplinary Torres Strait expedition under A. C. Haddon in 1898. He was among the first to seek to construct a systematic and (at least by intention) universalistic method of recording and describing kinship relations and structure. Even though many of his assumptions about the fit between kinship terminology and social structure and most of his speculative reconstructions of the history of tribal societies have long been abandoned (see his *History of Melanesian Society*, Cambridge, 1914), his concern for scientific method and for fieldwork as an anthropological tool left a permanent mark on the development of social anthropology in Britain. His monograph on *The Todas* (London, 1906) remains an important ethnographic source. He was a leading figure in the evolution-diffusion controversies of the time, eccentric in many ways though his contribution now seems. His role as a medical psychologist was equally if not more important. During WW1 he treated soldiers invalided out on psychiatric grounds, using many of the insights and techniques (including dream interpretation) advocated by FREUD, whose work he did much to propagate among the educated British public (see his *Instinct and the Unconscious*, Cambridge, 1920, and other works of the same time). He died suddenly and prematurely.

IH

I. Langham, *The Building of British Social Anthropology* (Dordrecht, 1981).

Robbe-Grillet, Alain (b. Brest, Finistère, France, 18.8.1922). French novelist, film maker and literary theoretician. In 1963 Robbe-Grillet provided in *Pour un nouveau roman* (Paris; tr. R. Howard, *For a New Novel*, London, 1966) the brashest and most uncompromising statement of how he thought novels should be written. Psychological analysis, he argued, should be excluded, since this presupposed a belief in the importance of individuals and the reality of private feelings. This might have been possible in the 19c, but was unacceptable today. The telling of a story was also to be eschewed as the relic of the detestable habit of flattering the bourgeois reader. The sympathetic description of the countryside was also out, since this involved 'humanizing' nature through a mistaken belief in the Pathetic Fallacy. Instead, the writer should content himself with the minute, impersonal description of physical objects, an ambition realized in Robbe-Grillet's own novel *La Jalousie* (Paris, 1957; tr. R. Howard, *Jealousy*, London, 1959). Robbe-Grillet also applied some of his theories to the cinema, with *L'Année dernière à Marienbad* in 1960, published as 'ciné-roman' (Paris, 1961; tr. R. Howard, *Last Year at Marienbad*, London, 1962), and *L'Immortelle* in 1963. His later novel *Projet pour une révolution à New York* (Paris, 1970; tr. R. Howard, *Project for a Revolution in New York*, London, 1972) combines formalism and obscurity with a rather insistently sadomasochistic eroticism. He is admired for bringing to the debate about the nature and limitations of fiction associated with JOYCE, BECKETT and NABOKOV a typically Gallic vigour as well as a scientific ambition stemming from his own early training as an agronomist. PMWT

Roberts, Kate (b. Rhosgadfan, Gwynedd, UK, 13.2.1891). Welsh short-story writer and novelist. Her work to 1936 is dominated by the life of the slate-quarrying villages near Caernarfon where she was brought up. A hard life is portrayed from a woman's vantage point and with strongly controlled feeling. Puritanism is treated sympathetically as a force which helps preserve the dignity of the poor, but also with a sense of the human cost of emotional repression. The stoney landscape becomes the outward manifestation of an inner austerity. She turned to writing after the loss of a brother in WW1, an event treated fictionally in *Traed Mewn Cyffion* (Aberystwyth, 1936; tr. I. Walters & J. I. Jones, *Feet in Chains*, Cardiff, 1977). This enacts a resolve to work against the causes of her people's suffering, and may explain her strong involvement with Welsh journalism, publishing and politics over the next decade. Only after her husband's death in 1946 did she return to fiction. Later works focus on the consciousness of women or old people in a small-town milieu in an easier but lonelier, more trivial and more neurotic age. The world of her youth now often appears as an internal standard, the source for a critique of the modern world, but when she returned to her first world in *Te yn y Grug* (Denbigh, 1959; tr. W. Griffith, *Tea in the Heather*, Ruthin, 1968) she produced a small classic of childhood. Kate Roberts's dialogue is often richly dialectal, her narrative spare and understated (see trans., *A Summer Day and Other Stories*, Cardiff, 1946). Her masters in the short story are CHEKHOV and STRINDBERG. EMT

D. Ll. Morgan, *Kate Roberts* (Cardiff, 1974).

Robertson, Dennis Holme (b. Lowestoft, Suffolk, UK, 23.5.1890; d. Cambridge, 21.4.1963). British economist. Educated at Eton and Trinity College, Cambridge, Robertson became a pupil of, collaborator with, but eventual critic of KEYNES. His major works *Money* (Cambridge, 1922) and *Banking Policy and the Price Level* (London, 1926) influenced a generation of economists and laid much of the foundation upon which modern monetary theories have been built. Following a distinguished career at Cambridge, Robertson's growing conflict with Keynes led him in 1938 to accept the Sir Ernest Cassel chair at the London School of Economics. During WW2 he was an economic adviser in the Treasury and renewed his collaboration with Keynes during the Bretton Woods negotiations. He returned to

Cambridge to the chair of political economy in 1944 and remained there until his retirement in 1957. These last years at Cambridge were coloured by his continual struggle against the elements of what was by then established Keynesian orthodoxy. In essence he felt that Keynes had given too much significance to the active correction of disequilibria and too little to the benefits of fiscal and monetary stability. This is set out most clearly in his *Lectures on Economic Principles* (3 vols, London, 1957–9). He was appointed to the Royal Commission on Equal Pay (1944) and the Council on Prices, Productivity and Incomes (1957–9). DMHP

Robinson, Joan Violet (b. Camberley, Surrey, UK, 31.10.1903). British economist of the modern Cambridge school whose original contributions to economics have always been in pure theory but who has remained deeply concerned by the social implications of economic analysis. The combination of sharply incisive intellect, lucid style of exposition and highly developed social conscience has enabled her to exert a powerful influence on students throughout the world. Her first theoretical monograph was *The Economics of Imperfect Competition* (London, 1933) which introduced a new set of concepts and a rigorous new theory of market behaviour into orthodox economic theory. Its virtue was that it showed how to dispense with the traditional assumption of perfect competition which was not only unrealistic, but had been shown by SRAFFA to lead to logically inconsistent results. Later, Robinson participated actively in the KEYNESian revolution in economic ideas, both as a member of the so-called Cambridge 'circus' on which Keynes tried out the early drafts of his new theory of employment and as a writer of texts popularizing and extending the theory, e.g. *Introduction to the Theory of Employment* (London, 1937). Henceforth she stayed at the centre of theoretical controversy as a persistent critic of the static, timeless type of theorizing in which she (and Keynes) had been brought up. She published many influential articles, a sympathetic critique of MARXian theory *An Essay on Marxian*

Economics (London, 1942), which earned her the undeserved reputation of being a Marxist, and another major theoretical monograph *The Accumulation of Capital* (London, 1956); and she collaborated with a young Cambridge colleague, John Eatwell, in writing a highly unorthodox *Introduction to Modern Economics* (London, 1973). Professor of economics at Cambridge from 1965 until retirement in 1971, she maintains a passionate interest in the socioeconomic problems of the real world, particularly the Third World, as is shown in her *Aspects of Development and Underdevelopment* (Cambridge, 1979). PMD

Robinson, John Arthur Thomas (b. Canterbury, Kent, UK, 15.6.1919). British theologian. Best known for his short, explosive book *Honest to God* (London, 1963), Robinson may almost be said to have been two men. One has been a rather conservative, but always lively and stimulating, churchman. The other has been a bold radical (*The Roots of a Radical*, London, 1981). Apart from a spell as bishop of Woolwich (1959–69), he has taught and practised biblical scholarship at Cambridge since 1951. In that capacity he has advocated causes such as the revision of worship in order to make it more corporate (*Liturgy Coming to Life*, London, 1960), and an understanding dialogue between Christianity and Hinduism (*Truth is Two-Eyed*, London, 1979). But his main concerns have been to make the thought of St Paul intelligible and exciting (in a series of books beginning with *In the End God*, London, 1950) and to argue that the New Testament was written at earlier dates than most scholars would accept (*Redating the New Testament*, London, 1976). *Honest to God* made all the more impact because it was written by a scholarly bishop who had been exposed to the almost total indifference of south London to traditional Christianity. Questioning the conventional image of God as a supernatural person, asking whether Jesus need be regarded as God 'dressed up' as a man, and confessing that much in traditional church life, prayer and ethics left him cold, he attracted hostility as the 'atheist bishop' but sympathy from many who found the times as exciting but confusing as he did. In subsequent popular books he tried to be more positive (*The New Reformation?*, London, 1966, and *Exploration into God*, London, 1967), but essentially his significance was negative. He showed that a highly intelligent British theologian, operating away from the world of worship and the Bible, was often more aware of the secular world's questions than of any convincing answers.   DLE

R. McBrien, *The Church in the Thought of Bishop John Robinson* (London, 1966).

Robinson, Robert (b. Chesterfield, Derbys., UK, 13.9.1886; d. Great Missenden, Bucks., 8.2.1975). British chemist. Robinson was one of the dominant organic chemists of the first half of the 20c who helped to lay the foundation of modern organic chemistry. He first studied and then carried out research on the dyewood colouring-matter brazilin at Manchester. From 1912 he held a series of appointments at Sydney, Liverpool (1915–19), St Andrews (1920), Manchester (1922), University College London (1928), culminating in his appointment as Waynflete professor at Oxford from 1930 to 1955. He made fundamental contributions in four major areas: the structure of natural products, many of major biological importance; synthesis; biosynthesis; and mechanistic organic chemistry. For his work on natural products of biological importance, he was awarded a Nobel prize in 1947. It covered alkaloids including morphine, strychnine and tropinone, the plant pigments of the anthocyanin and anthoxanthin group, steroids, and penicillin. Arising out of this work he perceived patterns of biosynthesis, and in a seminal paper in 1917 (*J. Chem. Soc.*, 111 [1971], 876) suggested the importance of the aldol condensation, of carbinolamines in alkaloid biosynthesis and emphasized that the biosynthesis of organic compounds follows recognizable chemical reactions and mechanisms. Robinson developed many new syntheses based on biogenetic ideas, including the syntheses of tropinone in 1917 and of an iridoid in 1958. He did much synthetic work in the steroid field and in

1936 developed the 'Robinson ring extension' which has played a fundamental role in its original and modified forms to the current day. During the 1920s Robinson worked out an electrochemical (electronic) theory of organic reactions. His ideas were undoubtedly stimulated by his intimate contact with LAPWORTH when he was at Manchester. His first general account of his ideas was published in a rather inaccessible form ('Outline of an electrochemical (electronic) theory of the course of organic reactions', *Institute of Chemistry Special Publication*, 1932) but exerted a profound influence in the development of the theory of organic chemistry. He recalled aspects of his scientific life in *Memoirs of a Minor Prophet: Seventy Years of Organic Chemistry*, vol. I (Amsterdam, 1976).   TGH

Rockefeller, John Davison (b. Richford, NY, USA, 8.7.1839; d. Ormond Beach, Fla, 23.5.1937). American oil magnate who began oil refining in 1863 and in 1870 incorporated the Standard Oil Company, which had a near-monopoly of the US market. Antitrust legislation split the corporation, leaving Standard Oil of New Jersey as the largest surviving unit. Rockefeller applied his fortune to medicine, culture and education (including the foundation of the University of Chicago) and other philanthropic ends (including the Rockefeller Foundation). He was succeeded by a dynasty of successful public servants and businessmen.   RIT

Rodchenko, Alexander Mikhailovich (b. St Petersburg [now Leningrad], Russia, 23.11.1891; d. Moscow, USSR, 3.12.1956). Russian constructivist. Between 1921 and 1929 Rodchenko and his wife Varvara Stepanova led the productivist wing of constructivism which dominated Soviet design in those years. Trained originally as a painter, he went over to abstraction in Moscow in 1915, becoming an ally of TATLIN's and would-be rival to MALEVICH. Following his static and hanging constructions of 1920–1, he concentrated on the practical applications of the new aesthetic as argued in meetings of the Inkhuk Institute and in the Production Art manifesto of autumn 1921. He was head of the metalwork department at the Vkhutemas School (1920–30). Making himself an outstanding photographer, he worked for the reviews *LEF* and *Novyi Lef* (1923–8), designed many posters and book jackets, created a model 'workers' club' for the Paris Arts Déco exhibition of 1925 – his one trip abroad – worked on various films and collaborated extensively with MAYAKOVSKY, notably on the sets for his play *The Bedbug* (1929) at the MEYERHOLD Theatre. He was increasingly hampered by accusations of 'formalism', as a result of which his official photographic and publicity work became more conventional. However, in the 1930s he resumed painting in both figurative and abstract modes, though without being able to show his work.   JWMW

D. Elliott (ed.), *Alexander Rodchenko* (Oxford, 1979); G. Karginov, *Rodchenko* (London, 1979).

Rodgers, Richard (b. Long Island, NY, USA, 28.6.1902; d. New York, 30.12.1979). American songwriter. As a child he picked up music mainly on his own, and his liking for musical shows led to contributions to student productions and (with Lorenz Hart) his first published song in 1919. These two men formed a highly successful partnership that only ended with Hart's death in 1943, and during this time Rodgers extended his range musically so that he could compose not only sophisticated songs like 'The Lady is a Tramp' and 'Bewitched, Bothered and Bewildered' but also the orchestral ballet *Slaughter on Tenth Avenue* which was choreographed by BALANCHINE for *On Your Toes* (1936). A new and even more successful partnership now followed, with Oscar Hammerstein II, and their *Oklahoma!* (1943) has been called the first American vernacular opera. Their later super-successes included *Carousel* (1945), *South Pacific* (1949), *The King and I* (1951) and *The Sound of Music* (1959). Most of these shows were filmed and reached worldwide screen audiences. Rodgers's musical style could be irresistibly graceful and lyrical ('Some Enchanted Evening', 'Blue Room') or vivid and dance-like (in big choral num-

bers such as 'There is Nothing Like a Dame' and the *Oklahoma!* title song). His music warmed the hearts of millions during decades of hardship and danger and so contributed much that was positive to our century.   CH

Rodin, Auguste (b. Paris, France, 12.11.1840; d. Meudon, nr Paris, Seine-et-Oise, 17.11.1917). French sculptor. He supported himself for a number of years by working as an ornamental sculptor and at other odd jobs before winning a reputation with the *Age of Bronze* (1875 –6), a naked male figure of a Michelangelesque type so realistic that he was wrongly accused of having cast it from life. In 1880 he was commissioned to make a bronze portal for the Musée des Arts Décoratifs in Paris; this project, known as *The Gates of Hell*, was never completed but included nearly 200 nude figures, many of which were later developed separately on a scale up to or even larger than life. The figures, influenced by both Dante and Baudelaire, were mostly in eloquent movement expressive of a wide range of human emotions, despair and sensuality. Among the major commissions which followed were *The Burghers of Calais* (1886–7), partly influenced by Gothic art, and the monument to *Balzac* (1897), showing the great author enveloped in a robe, with expression concentrated in the head. Nevertheless much of his work aroused violent controversy and the Balzac monument was refused in 1898 by the committee which had commissioned it. Full recognition did not come until after Rodin had organized a large exhibition of his own work in 1900 in a pavilion outside the Paris International Exhibition. From then on he was recognized almost universally as the greatest living sculptor and was in great demand for portrait busts and other commissions. He employed a team of sculptors as assistants to carry out enlargements of his work or make carvings from his plaster models, including Bourdelle and Despiau, and his influence on early 20c sculpture was pervasive. A great many sculptors were influenced by the extremely lifelike character of his work, its expressive light-catching surfaces, its concern with movement and passionate emotion, and by his treatment of sections of the human body, such as torsos and hands, as complete works in themselves. On the other hand many went on to react deliberately against certain aspects of his work: to make their forms more generalized and static; to shun rhetoric and stress the importance of the grouping of forms in relation to architecture; and, perhaps above all, to adopt direct carving of stone or wood so as to emphasize the particular character of the material.   REA

R. Descharnes & J.-F. Chabrun, *Auguste Rodin* (London, 1967); A. E. Elsen, *Rodin* (London, 1974).

Röentgen, Wilhelm Conrad (b. Lennep im Bergischen, N. Rhine-Westphalia, Germany, 27.3.1845; d. Munich, Bavaria, 10.2.1923). German physicist who discovered X-rays. He studied in Zürich and worked in Würzburg, Strassburg and Giessen, finally becoming professor of physics and director of the Physical Institute at Würzburg. He was a meticulous experimentalist who made his own apparatus and preferred to work alone. He detected the compressibility of liquids and solids, and the rotation of the plane of polarization of light by gases. He also worked on the conductivity of heat in crystals, the specific heats of gases, and pyroelectrical and piezoelectrical phenomena. He confirmed Maxwell's prediction that there is a magnetic field in a dielectric whenever the electric field changes. One day in 1895, when experimenting with a Crookes tube, he noticed that some crystals of platinocyanide near the tube were fluorescing. He found that some new rays, which he called X-rays, were emitted from the part of the tube opposite the cathode. In a few weeks of intensive study he established that these rays travel in straight lines, cannot be easily refracted or reflected, are not deviated by a magnet, and can travel up to two metres through the air. He noticed their penetrating power, and was able to photograph some balance weights in a closed box, and the bones in his fingers. He left the medical applications for others to develop. Subsequently, by diffracting them with a crystal, Friedrich and Kipping showed that the X-rays are transverse electromagnetic waves. Röentgen received the first Nobel prize for physics in 1901.   PEH

Roethke, Theodore (b. Saginaw, Mich., USA, 25.5.1908; d. Puget Sound, Wash., 1.8.1963). American poet. Roethke's finely crafted first book of poems *Open House* (NY, 1941) made a strong impression, but his highly individual, romantic voice emerged most clearly in *The Lost Son and Other Poems* (NY, 1949). Of his later collections the most important is *The Far Field* (NY, 1964). His poems explore two main areas of concern; a nature-mysticism deriving as much from Roethke's childhood experience of greenhouses and plant-nurseries as from his reading of Emerson and Thoreau, and an examination of the nature of the self. A tone of tense, anxious questioning alternates with moments of almost hysterical affirmation or yearning. In its use of his own mental breakdowns as a theme his work foreshadows that of the 'confessional' poets of the 1960s and 1970s. Throughout most of his working life he was associated with the University of Washington, where he was first a lecturer (1947–8) and then poet-in-residence (1948–62).   DD

Rogers, Albert Bruce (b. Linnwood, Ind., USA, 14.5.1870; d. New Fairfield, Conn., 18.5.1957). American book designer. A Purdue University graphic arts graduate (1890), he freelanced on *Indianapolis News* and *Modern Art* quarterly before joining Riverside Press, Cambridge, Mass., to design press advertisements and trade books. From 1900 to 1911 he created 60 notable Riverside Press Edition titles, including *The Essays of Montaigne* (1902–4) and *The Compleat Angler* (1909). Thereafter until 1915 he freelanced for various New York printers and publishers. In 1916 he visited England and, with Emery Walker, established the Mall Press, designing *Of the Just Shaping of Letters* (1917) for the Grolier Club. In 1918 the Syndics of the Cambridge University Press commissioned from him a major report on CUP's typography (1919).

Rogers designed three typefaces: Montaigne (1901), Centaur (1915 – cut by Monotype Corporation in 1929) and a poster type for Pelican Press (1918). He was part-time typographical adviser at Rudge's Mount Vernon Press near New York between 1919 and 1928; and, until 1936, for Harvard University Press – though he spent much time from 1928 to 1932 in England, where collaboration with Wilfred Merton and Walker produced T. E. LAWRENCE's translation of Homer's *Odyssey* (1932), which Rogers designed. Before partially retiring to New Fairfield, he designed a superb lectern Bible (1935) for the Oxford University Press; and 14 years later another – the folio World Bible (1949) – for World Publishing Company.   TC

Rogers, Carl Ranson (b. Oak Ridge, Ill., USA, 8.1.1902). American psychologist who pioneered 'client-centred' therapy and helped found the 'human growth' movement. In 1924 he studied at Union Theological Seminary, New York. He switched to psychology and, after completing his PhD at Columbia, worked in a community guidance clinic. His experience led him to argue that therapists 'directed' their patients too much. He began to use the word 'clients' rather than patients to emphasize that therapy is not really like medicine: the client needs help and much attention but is not a sick person who has to hand power over himself to a medical expert. Rogers also felt that the therapist should not impose solutions, so his approach came to be called *nondirective*. A key feature is to sit opposite the client and give him or her total attention, to help create 'positive regard'. Rogers believes that individuals with psychological and psychiatric problems often suffer from a lack of self-esteem. If the therapist can make the client feel worthwhile, much of the battle for cure will be won. Rogers became interested in the idea that everyone (well or 'ill') needs to develop through life and to 'grow' in self-esteem. *On Becoming a Person* (NY, 1961) charted how a person might develop and realize more of his or her potential. Rogers claimed much therapeutic success for his approach. Its real value may turn out to be cultural. His radical ideas helped create a boom in therapy – in the USA, 'growth' was

much in vogue in the 1970s. Rogers also influenced those who question the 'medical model' in psychiatry: if 'patients' are really 'clients', do they need medically qualified psychiatrists who usually deal with them as sick people? Much current critical thinking in psychiatry emphasizes taking power away from psychiatrists and accepting as vital what the 'client' has to offer.   DMOC

Rolling Stones, The. British rock music group formed in 1962/3 including Michael Philip (Mick) Jagger (b. Dartford, Kent, UK, 26.7.1944), Brian Jones (b. Cheltenham, Glos., UK, 28.2.1942; d. Hartfield, E. Sussex, 3.7.1969), Keith Richard (b. Dartford, Kent, UK, 18.12.1943), Charles Robert (Charlie) Watts (b. London, UK, 2.6.1941) and William George (Bill) Wyman (b. London, UK, 24.10.1936). Contemporaries of the BEATLES, they assumed an image of notoriety and defiance to prevailing social conventions and an autonomy which provoked condemnation especially for their attitude to drugs and sex. They became symbolically and influentially associated with a growing youth culture and generational revolt in which heavy rock music became a central force. Their most successful single record ('I Can't Get No Satisfaction', 1965) became widely adopted as principal anthem of the youth movement but equally acknowledged to be one of rock music's most outstanding compositions. Characterized by heavy and intoxicating rhythmic beat, their music, mainly composed by Jagger and Richards, owed much to black music and the blues but was performed with greater aggression and more direct sexuality. Having faced drugs charges and exclusion from the USA (1966–8), they eventually performed free before some 300,000 people at Altamont Speedway, San Francisco (1969), an event which provoked violence, death and intervention by Hell's Angels. Jagger and the Rolling Stones delivered exhibitionism as a principal feature of rock music performance and their success continues undiminished into the 1980s on an international scale.   TEC

P. Gambaccini, *Masters of Rock* (London, 1982).

Rolls, Charles Stewart (b. Monmouth, Gwent, UK, 27.8.1877; d. Bournemouth, Dorset, 12.7.1910). British motor-car and aeroplane enthusiast. Son of Lord Llangattock, educated at Eton and Cambridge, he formed a company in 1902 to promote continental motor cars in the UK before they had become popular. He met Frederick Henry Royce (b. Alwalton, Cambs., UK, 27.3.1863; d. West Wittering, W. Sussex, 22.4.1933), a motor-car designer, in 1904 and together they laid the foundations of the world's most respected motor car: for at that point Royce had designed a car, and Rolls was looking for a vehicle to promote. The Rolls-Royce company was formed in 1906. Royce was the engineer; Rolls the promoter. In 1908 he flew for the first time with Wilbur WRIGHT; in 1910, at the age of 32, he was the first British pilot to die in a flying accident. His name is perpetuated in the Rolls-Royce car, and in the aero-engine company which pioneered the carbon fibres that power many of today's giant jet aircraft. In February 1971, Rolls-Royce Ltd collapsed financially, mainly due to delays and escalating costs on the development of the RB 211 engine, and a receiver was appointed. The government subsequently acquired the assets of the aero-engine, marine and industrial gas turbine divisions of the company while the motor-car company was restructured. RIT

Romains, Jules, ps. (legally adopted in 1953) of Louis-Henri-Jean Farigoule (b. St Julien-Chapteuil, Haute-Loire, France, 26.8.1885; d. Paris, 14.8.1972). French novelist, poet and dramatist. The philosophical basis for Romains's prolific output of novels, poems and plays is provided by the theory of *unanisme* outlined in his early verse collection *La Vie unanime* [The unanimist life] (Paris, 1908). In part a vision of universal brotherhood that has been compared to Whitman, *unanisme* asserts that human groups and communities possess a collective spirit or soul perceptible to the individual through a process of intuition. In aesthetic terms it follows that the novelist or poet is concerned with the development and psychology of the group rather than with its component individuals. *Unanisme* is exemplified by Romains in dramatic form in *Knock ou le triomphe de la médecine* (Paris, 1934; tr. H. GRANVILLE-BARKER, *Dr Knock*, London, 1925), one of the most successful farces of the century, in novels such as *Mort de quelqu'un* (Paris, 1911; tr. D. MacCarthy & S. Waterlow, *Death of a Nobody*, London, 1914), but above all in the 27 volumes of the novel sequence *Les Hommes de bonne volonté* (Paris, 1932–46; tr. W. B. Wells, vols 1–3, G. Hopkins, remainder, *Men of Goodwill*, NY, 1933–46), a vast saga dealing with the evolution of the world between 1908 and 1933. It is generally accepted that the most successful volumes are *Prélude à Verdun* and *Verdun*, in which Romains's skill in the handling of crowd scenes is particularly evident. Romains excelled in the portrayal of collective action and in the depiction of the modern city as a living entity. He spent WW2 in the USA, where he recorded broadcasts on behalf of the Gaulliste movement. He was elected a member of the Académie Française on his return to France in 1946. DM

Romer, Eugeniusz (b. Lemberg, Galicia, Austria-Hungary [now Lvov, Ukraine, USSR], 3.2.1871; d. Kraków, Poland, 28.1.1954). Polish geographer. Romer was from his youth concerned with the restoration of Polish independence. He studied history and geography at the universities of Cracow, Halle and Lwów, after which he went to Vienna and Berlin as a research student in physical geography and climatology. In 1889 he joined the staff of Lwów [Lemberg] University, where he remained until his retirement in 1931. He published papers on physical geography and climate but is best known internationally for his contributions to cartography, notably his atlas *Polski Geograficzno Statystyczny* (Warsaw, 1916), which was a powerful argument for the creation of a new Poland, and his *Polski Atlas Kongresowy* [Congress Atlas of Poland], (Warsaw, 1921). At Lwów he built up a fine department of geography with a cartographical institute, and the physical geography and climatology of Poland remained a lifelong interest. He survived WW2 partly by residing in a friendly monastery, and afterwards was helpful in restoring geography teaching in the Jagellonian University of Kraków. TWF

Roosevelt, Franklin Delano (b. Hyde Park, NY, USA, 30.1.1882; d. Warm Springs, Ga, 12.4.1945). US assistant secretary of the Navy (1913–20), unsuccessful Democratic candidate for the vice-presidency in 1920, governor of New York (1928–32), president (1932–45). The greatest and most misunderstood Democratic president of the USA, his four terms in office are unique in American history. During his presidency America suffered a depression with unemployment and civil strife quite as bad as any in Europe. Roosevelt's first and greatest success was to preserve democracy in America in trials that weakened and destroyed it in Europe, not so much by the programmes of the 'New Deal' which he proclaimed on his inauguration, but by his oratory and personality. His New Deal was in domestic terms a curious mixture of government aid in public works, agricultural support and labour legislation coupled with business protection. It rested, however, on an artificial devaluation of the dollar which isolated the US economy completely from that of Britain and Europe, making payment of war debts and maintenance of the European market for American agricultural products impossible. Roosevelt's presidency saw an enormous strengthening of the federal government's powers vis-à-vis that of the individual states; but despite his creation of a coalition between the ethnic minorities and farmer-labour organizations in the North and Midwest with the conservative racialist agriculturists of the South which was to make the Democratic party dominant for 20 years, Roosevelt never really succeeded in imposing himself on Congress, and his attempt to 'pack' the Supreme Court in 1937, coupled with a new down-turn in the world economy (the 'Roosevelt recession'), lost him much of his popularity. The increasing threat of war in Europe switched his attention towards foreign affairs where his oratory and his

gift for administrative innovation, especially Lend-Lease, were second only to CHURCHILL as the mainstay of morale among the European opponents of Nazi Germany. His vision of postwar security was however essentially one of great power dominance, his scheme for a quadrumvirate of China, Britain, the USA and the USSR (the four policemen) acting to keep the peace in the name of the United Nations, being tempered still further by his knowledge of China's dependence on American aid, Britain's economic weakness and dependence on America for aid and for a share in nuclear power for war and peace, to make winning Soviet cooperation the most important element in his foreign policy in the later years of WW2, especially at the Tehran and Yalta conferences. His unquestioning hostility to colonial empires and to economic spheres of influence bore particularly heavily on Britain, as did his relentless dismissal of and hostility towards the Free French and DE GAULLE. As a political leader, he was both devious in manoeuvre and inspiring in personality (the lion and the fox), and he left very little of his own most intimate papers to enlighten posterity as to his real aims and perceptions. Enough exists however to make it clear that he was as much of a moral and economic imperialist as Woodrow WILSON with an unshakeable belief in the moral superiority of American aims and interests. And though he was worshipped and idolized by many Americans, he was also hated and intrigued against, even in the depths of WW2, to a degree unimaginable in Europe. He died suddenly in office in 1945, being succeeded by TRUMAN. DCW

F. Freidel, *Franklin D. Roosevelt: the Apprenticeship* (Boston, Mass., 1952), *The Ordeal* (Boston, Mass., 1954), *The Triumph* (Boston, Mass., 1956), *Launching the New Deal* (Boston, Mass., 1973); J. Macgregor Burns, *Roosevelt, the Lion and the Fox* (NY, 1956).

Roosevelt, Theodore (b. New York, USA, 27.10.1858; d. Oyster Bay, NY, 6.1.1919). Assistant secretary US Navy (1897–8); governor of New York State (1899–1900); vice-president (1900–1); president of the United States (1901–8);

unsuccessful candidate for the presidency in 1912. A typical member of one of the oldest of New York's moneyed elite families, he was untypical in the degree to which as president he took the USA out of isolationism into an active role in world politics, and in the moderation and intelligent understanding he displayed of the realities of those politics. He chose to play the part of a rough-riding he-man, who made a fetish of physical fitness and 'spoke softly but carried a big stick'. This reputation received confirmation by the unashamed imperialism he displayed in provoking a revolution in Central America in order to secure the lease of the Panama canal zone. This imperialism was the product of intellectual analysis rather than a matter of instinct, being a combination of social Darwinism and a belief in the cultural supremacy of white Anglo-Saxon puritanism with the duty of governing others in the best interest of the whole of humanity and civilization. In the first Moroccan crisis, however, and his settlement of the Russo–Japanese war by the Treaty of Portsmouth (1905), Roosevelt displayed a command of the methods of diplomacy and an appreciation of the limits of American influence in world affairs only occasionally equalled and never outmatched by American statesmen in this century. In domestic affairs he was to display the same inversion of the old tag, *suaviter in modo, fortiter in re*, introducing apparently very far-reaching measures to strengthen federal powers against monopolies and cartels in business, but applying them in practice only to the most flagrant and indefensible cases. When his successor as Republican president, Taft, failed to maintain the momentum of his domestic reforms, Roosevelt challenged him for the nomination as Republican candidate in 1912; failing to receive this, he founded his own 'Bull Moose' party which, with very strong support from progressives, carried the majority of Republican voters, but by dividing the Republican vote, ensured the election of the more conservative Democratic candidate, Woodrow WILSON.   DCW

J. Blum, *The Republican Roosevelt* (Cambridge, Mass., ²1977).

Rosenberg, Harold (b. New York, USA, 2.2.1906; d. New York, 11.7.1978). American art critic. Rosenberg graduated from St Lawrence University in 1927. He is best known as the art critic of the *New Yorker* magazine (since 1966), and as a regular contributor to journals as varied as *Commentary, Encounter, Art in America, Art News* and *Vogue*. He held visiting lectureships at several American universities, such as Berkeley (1962), Princeton (1963), Illinois (1963) and Chicago (1970). His major articles and essays were collected as *The Tradition of the New* (NY, 1959) and *The Anxious Object* (NY, 1964). Rosenberg challenged a traditional art-critical presupposition: that an artist essentially works towards an encounter between a painting and an aesthetically discriminating spectator. In Rosenberg's view the basic concern of post-WW2 art is no longer object-making, but the process of creation and the transformation of materials. In 1952 he coined the phrase 'action painting' to describe the permanent record of this dynamic process; the art-object consists then simply of the 'will to paint' and the 'memory of paintings', in which a spectator is also the vicarious participant. Initially, Rosenberg's concepts of the 'aesthetics of impermanence' and the 'new as value', represented by abstract expressionism and Pop art, were controversial. By 1970 they had become broadly accepted artistic and art-critical conventions in the modern world. His other critical works include *Arshile Gorky* (NY, 1962); *Artworks and Packages* (NY, 1969); *Act and the Actor* (NY, 1971); *The De-Definition of Art* (NY, 1972); *Discovering the Present* (NY, 1973); and *De Kooning* (NY, 1974).
                                                            SOBT

Rosenberg, Isaac (b. Bristol, Avon, UK, 25.11.1890; d. nr Arras, Pas-de-Calais, France, 1.4.1918). British poet. Rosenberg is remembered as one of the soldier poets of WW1; he recreated front-line experience in a few richly expressive poems, and was killed in the last year of the war. But Rosenberg was more than a 'war poet'. By 1914 he had already shown remarkable talents as poet and artist. He grew up in a poor

Jewish home in London's East End and, although lacking in formal education, read widely. Helped by the patronage of some wealthy members of the London Jewish community, he trained at the Slade School of Art. He began writing poetry early, reflecting the influence of Swinburne and Rossetti and the poets of the 1890s, with a further exotic element derived from Hebrew history and legend. He was a skilled craftsman in poetry, draughtsmanship and painting, and by degrees evolved a more experimental, less derivative manner. He brought a painter's eye to his war poetry, and tried to render experience as fully as possible. Unlike other English war poets he did not direct his poetry towards protest or overt pity. This poetry is emotionally powerful though sometimes obscure, and suggests a certain parallel with expressionist painting. If 'Dead Man's Dump' is Rosenberg's most celebrated poem, there are others equally impressive. His poems were first published in a posthumous selection in 1922; a definitive *Collected Works* (ed. I. Parsons, London) finally appeared in 1979.   BB

J. Cohen, *Journey to the Trenches: the Life of Isaac Rosenberg* (London, 1975); J. Liddiard, *Isaac Rosenberg: the Half-Used Life* (London, 1975).

Ross, Ronald (b. Almora, Nepal, India, 13.5.1857; d. Putney, London, UK, 16.9.1932). British physician who demonstrated the transmission of the malaria parasite by mosquitoes. After medical education in London, Ross joined the Indian Medical Service, where he began his researches on malaria. In 1894 Sir Patrick Manson convinced him of the unproved hypothesis that malaria is caused by a parasite transmitted by mosquitoes. Back in India, Ross solved the technical and practical issues, refined Manson's hypothesis, suggested that the *Anopheles* mosquito was the culprit in human malaria, and worked out the cycle of transmission for bird malaria. The Italian G. B. Grassi came to similar conclusions about human malaria in the same year (1898), but Ross received the Nobel prize (1902) alone, despite Grassi's protest. Although Ross returned to England in 1899, he continued to write and travel widely in connection with malaria eradication. In 1926, he became first director of the Ross Institute of Tropical Hygiene in London.   WFB

Rossby, Carl-Gustav (b. Stockholm, Sweden, 28.12.1898; d. Stockholm, 19.8.1957). Swedish meteorologist and oceanographer. For nearly 20 years up to the time of his death, Rossby was regarded as the outstanding figure in synoptic and dynamical meteorology. During that period many of the major developments in meteorology were closely identified with Rossby who often provided the ideas and the leadership necessary for progress. He developed three outstanding university departments of meteorology – at MIT in the 1930s, at Chicago (1941–7), and at Stockholm from 1947. After early work on the dynamics of ocean currents, he began to make fundamental contributions to meteorology, notably in theoretical and synoptic studies of long circumpolar waves and the jet stream, on the application of the vorticity equation to cyclonic development and on a barotropic model atmosphere for use in numerical forecasting. His influence with his contemporaries was a testimony to the fertility of his ideas and to his great personal qualities. His name is perpetuated in meteorology by means of the Rossby diagram in thermodynamics, Rossby waves (the near barotropic waves of the westerlies) and the Rossby number, a ratio of central significance in planetary fluid motions.   PJM

Rossellini, Roberto (b. Rome, Italy, 18.5.1906; d. Rome, 3.6.1977). Italian film director. One of the most controversial personalities in the history of cinema, whose private life at times brought him more attention than his creative work, Rossellini was also one of the most important and significant of all Italian film makers. Though he began by making fascist documentaries, Rossellini was subsequently one of the founders of the Italian neorealist movement of the early postwar years and director of such key films as *Roma Città Aperta* (*Open City*, 1945), *Paisà* (*Paisan*, 1946) and *Germania Anno Zero* (*Germany Year*

Zero, 1947). In the 1950s he made a number of psychological dramas starring his then wife Ingrid Bergman, of which the most influential was *Viaggio in Italia* (*Strangers*, 1953) which opened the way for the early work of FELLINI and ANTONIONI. After a period of work of less importance, Rossellini re-emerged in the late 1960s with a series of huge biographical frescoes on such figures as Socrates, Pascal and Jesus, all shot for television with a distinctly didactic intent. Rossellini's key contribution to the cinema lies in his reaffirmation of the strengths of a realist approach which does not lay claim to some spurious objectivity but which reflects a concerned humanist approach to life and its problems. For Rossellini the cinema's role was to demonstrate the richness of reality and all his stylistic efforts were directed towards the removal of the barriers created by the artifice which normally surrounds fictional film making.

RPA

J. L. Guarner, *Roberto Rossellini* (London, 1970).

Rostovtzeff, Michael Ivanovich (b. Kiev, Russia, 10.11.1870; naturalized American citizen; d. New Haven, Conn., USA, 20.10.1952). Russian/American ancient historian and pioneer of the study of the social and economic history of the ancient world. A Russian liberal, educated at the universities of Kiev and St Petersburg (1888–92), where he also taught and worked on various historico-archaeological projects, Rostovtzeff made his career in the USA after the Bolshevik seizure of power in 1917. As Sterling professor of ancient history and archaeology at Yale (1925–44), he directed the Yale expedition at Dura-Europos (in Syria). His influential and controversial study *Social and Economic History of the Roman Empire* (2 vols, Oxford, 1926, rev. P. M. Fraser, ²1957) advocates the view that the solidarity between the army and the peasantry, combined with inflation and continuous wars, were the causes for the destruction of the bourgeois city life of the empire and therefore of its vital core. An analogous theory was put forward in his massive synthesis *Social and Economic History of the Hellenistic World* (3 vols,

Oxford, 1941), that the urban culture of the Hellenistic bourgeoisie was destroyed by its kings and finally by the Romans through increasing bureaucracy, wars and taxation. Although he emphasized the parallel development of cultural and economic life, Rostovtzeff's work must be seen, rather than in the vulgar MARXist framework, in the tradition of great liberal historiography. KKS

Roth, Henry (b. Tysmenica, Austria-Hungary [now Ukraine, USSR], 8.2.1906). American novelist. A graduate of the City College of New York (1928), Roth was encouraged to write by the poet and critic Eda Lou Walton. His only novel *Call It Sleep* (NY, 1934) appeared to generally enthusiastic reviews, but Roth was unable to complete a second novel. He left New York and his novel was generally forgotten. Returned to print in the 1960s, with the enthusiastic advocacy of Alfred Kazin and Leslie Fiedler, Roth's *Call It Sleep*, like the similarly neglected masterpieces of Herman Melville and FAULKNER, was belatedly accepted as a classic.

Roth drew upon his childhood experiences in New York for his novel, although the story as he tells it is less autobiographical than was at first assumed. The plot describes a crisis in the life of a young Jewish boy, torn between home and the vivid, terrifying life of the streets of Lower Manhattan. His father is a jealous, violent man in the grip of paranoia, and his mother, a loving, gentle soul, cannot help Roth's young hero to adjust to the world outside the family apartment: she does not speak English. Roth has a unique appreciation of the linguistic dilemma of the immigrant family, trapped between a language which they do not command (American English), and one which they do (Yiddish), but which only serves to isolate them. Roth presents their English as a broken, phonetically-transcribed New Yorkese. The Yiddish spoken at home is presented as a clear, standard English. *Call It Sleep* gives us a brilliant approximation of the linguistic chaos within which Americanization took place. EH

B. Lyons, *Henry Roth: the Man and the Work* (NY, 1976).

Roth, Philip (b. Newark, NJ, USA, 19.3.1933). American novelist. Educated at the universities of Bucknell and Chicago, Roth has taught at Chicago and Iowa. He first won acclaim with *Goodbye, Columbus* (Boston, Mass., 1959), a novella and collection of short stories which explored the confrontation of Jewishness, class aspirations and the 1950s crisis of identity. His works to date range from the realism of *Letting Go* (NY, 1962) and *When She Was Good* (NY, 1967) to the borderline between private desires and public normalcy best captured in his most successful novel *Portnoy's Complaint* (NY, 1969) and continued in the later *My Life as a Man* (NY, 1974), *Professor of Desire* (NY, 1978), *The Ghost Writer* (NY, 1979) and *Zuckerman Unbound* (NY, 1981). Fantasy mingles with the realistic in the satire on NIXON's presidency *Our Gang* (NY, 1971), the KAFKAesque nightmare of *The Breast* (NY, 1972), and the mixture of baseball and the American dream of *The Great American Novel* (NY, 1973). In both modes of writing he breaches the boundary between expected behaviour and inner fantasies in order to show how our norms and habits are fictions which attempt to conceal the real pain and uncertainty of living. Sexual desire, exposed to the humiliation of public scrutiny, reveals the comedy of our conventional sexual roles, and the discontinuities out of which we attempt to form identities and careers.   DTC

J. N. McDaniel, *The Fiction of Philip Roth* (Princeton, 1974); S. Pinsker, *The Comedy that 'Hoits'* (Columbia, 1975).

Rothacker, Erich (b. Pforzheim, Baden-Württemberg, Germany, 12.3.1888; d. Bonn, N. Rhine-Westphalia, West Germany, 11.8.1965). German philosopher, one of the leading exponents of philosophical anthropology. In his first major work *Logik und Systematik der Geisteswissenschaften* [Logic of the human sciences] (Munich, 1920) he examined the view that the subject of knowledge is not the timeless universal entity represented by Descartes or Locke, but actual historical individuals whose cognitive equipment is partly created by, and itself constantly modifies, a specific

cultural community. The products of past ages and other cultures come to be viewed not as bizarre distortions of a partially realized, universal human essence, but as authentic expressions of humanity in their own right; the inevitable connection of the humanities, the *Geisteswissenschaften*, with *Weltanschauungen* [worldviews] is shown to be not their weakness but their strength; and the priority of practice and creative life over theory is established. In his influential *Probleme der Kulturanthropologie* [Problems of the anthropology of culture] (Bonn, 1948) and *Philosophische Anthropologie* [Philosophical anthropology] (Bonn, 1966) Rothacker developed his ideas of 'polarity', seeing all cultural phenomena as movements to and from one or another ideal limit or pole; and of *Lebensstil* [style], according to which each culture creates its own distinctive environment, or *Umwelt*, and generates its own unique set of predispositions. Much in Rothacker's writings is strongly reminiscent of Vico and Herder. He advocated an anthropology which would examine all human cultures and historical periods empirically and on their own terms. He seems to have been largely unconcerned by the attendant problems of ethical and cultural relativism.   RNH

Rothko, Mark (b. Dvinsk, Russia [now Daugavpils, Latvia, USSR], 25.9.1903; d. New York, USA, 25.2.1970). American artist. In 1913 Rothko's family left Russia and settled in Portland, Oregon, USA. From 1921 he studied liberal arts at Yale for two years and in 1925 attended briefly at the Art Students' League, New York, before beginning to paint on his own. In 1935 he was cofounder of 'The Ten', a group of expressionist artists. During the 1930s he painted solitary figures in urban settings. In 1938 he began to experiment with automatism, resulting in an abstract biomorphic style similar to Arshile GORKY's (e.g. *Baptismal Scene*, 1945). By 1947 all natural allusions were excluded, leaving thinly washed, sensuous colour forms floating and shifting in space. Rothko's aim was to create universal, timeless symbols expressive of 'man's primitive fears and motivations'. From 1950 he painted on a monumental scale, limiting himself to two or three soft-edged colour rectangles on a canvas. In the late 1950s his bright colours gave way to more sombre tonalities, as in his red-black-maroon murals for a New York restaurant (1958) – now in the Tate Gallery, London. The blurred edges and gestural brushwork give the colour shapes a translucent yet three-dimensional effect, suggesting infinite depths or concentrating attention on the tangibility of surface textures. The huge format is intended to suggest images for contemplation. SOBT

P. Selz, *Rothko* (NY, 1961); D. Waldman, *Mark Rothko* (NY, 1978).

Rouault, Georges (b. Paris, France, 27.5.1871; d. Paris, 13.2.1958). French painter and printmaker; the greatest religious artist of the 20c. For several years in his youth Rouault was apprenticed to a stained-glass artist and afterwards studied painting at the Ecole des Beaux Arts in Paris. From 1892 to 1895 he worked in the studio of Gustave Moreau, becoming Moreau's favourite pupil so that after his death in 1898 Rouault was appointed curator of the Musée Gustave Moreau. Although his early work was strongly influenced by Rembrandt and included a number of biblical subjects such as the Prodigal Son, his importance as a religious artist dates from after 1904, when he became a friend of the Catholic novelist Léon Bloy and was profoundly impressed by Bloy's medieval vision of sin and redemption. The effect of this, paradoxically, was to make him turn away from religious themes for several years and to concentrate on paintings in oil or gouache of prostitutes, clowns and judges in a powerfully expressionist style. Dark in tone and with the forms heavily modelled in slashing brush-strokes, they have an emphasis on the grotesque which many of his contemporaries found deeply shocking. Although he was a friend of MATISSE and Marquet, who had been fellow pupils of his in Moreau's studio, and exhibited with the fauves in 1905, he was never a member of the group and always remained a solitary figure, a recluse and a visionary. Much of his time between 1916 and 1939 was occupied with making prints to illustrate the books which his dealer Ambroise Vollard was planning to publish, including a series of large etchings for *Miserere et Guerre* which is one of the greatest achievements of 20c printmaking. His later paintings tend to be on more traditional religious themes, especially the Passion, and are often executed in a simplified style, with the forms in glowing colours enclosed in heavy black outlines, which seems to owe something to his early experiences with medieval stained glass. However, he seldom achieved the intensity or originality of his early work, and the mood of his later pictures is predominantly one of gentle pathos. REA

L. Venturi, *Rouault: a Biographical and Critical Study* (Lausanne, 1959); P. Courthion, *Georges Rouault* (London, 1962).

Rous, Francis Peyton (b. Baltimore, Md, USA, 5.10.1879; d. New York, 16.2.1970). American pathologist. Despite a disadvantaged childhood and ill health, Rous showed early signs of distinction, winning a scholarship to Johns Hopkins Medical School, where he worked under Sir William Osler, and then studying pathology at Ann Arbor and at Dresden. In 1911 at the Rockefeller Institute in New York he identified an agent that caused cancer, subsequently proving this to be a virus – the Rous Sarcoma Virus (RSV). By studying its resistance to transplanted cells and immunity to viruses, he discovered that much of the existing knowledge on transplantation was based on a fallacy. The importance of his cancer work was disregarded at the time but he was described as 'miraculously unembittered'. At the beginning of WW1 he turned his attention to ways of storing blood and by 1917 had established (with J. W. Turner and O. H. Robertson) the first blood bank near the front line in Belgium. A byproduct of his 1917 technique is still in use today for making suspensions of living cells from tissues. His subsequent discoveries and achievements include the Rous–McMaster biliary fistula; the isolation and characterization of reticuloendothelial cells; outlying acidosis; and the factors that increase the malignancy of cancer cells.

Though honours were showered on him, it was not until 1966 that he received, with C. B. Huggins (a pioneer of cancer treatment), the Nobel prize for medicine for his work on cancer, the most important part of which was done nearly 50 years earlier. In addition to very many scientific publications, his vast range of other writing includes botanical journalism dating from the 1890s to an essay in praise of tactless people in the journal *Perspectives in Biology and Medicine* in 1970.   CR

Rousseau, Henri (b. Laval, Mayenne, France, 21.5.1844; d. Paris, 2.9.1910). French painter. The son of a dealer in tin-ware, Rousseau served for four years in the French army, then in 1871 took a post as a minor inspector in the toll service (*octroi*) of Paris, from which he derives the misleading nickname 'Le Douanier'. He seems to have begun to paint at about 40, and was self-taught. From 1886 he exhibited regularly at the Salon des Indépendants, where his works attracted a great deal of ridicule for their naive and sometimes unintentionally comic character. In 1893 he retired prematurely from the *octroi* at his own request, with the intention of becoming a full-time artist, supplementing his tiny pension by various odd jobs and later by giving painting and music lessons. His work was 'discovered' about 1906–7 by such figures as APOLLINAIRE, Uhde, Vollard, DELAUNAY and PICASSO, who admired and bought his pictures and attended his musical soirées.

The first of the so-called naive painters to achieve recognition, Rousseau retained a childlike innocence and freshness which compensated for his lack of conventional artistic skill, and his uncertain grasp of anatomy and perspective. His work consisted of portraits and figure compositions, small landscapes of Paris and its environs, a few still lifes and a number of exotic jungle scenes with wild animals, almost all of which were executed in the last years of his life and which did much to win him belated recognition. An artist of exceptional imaginative power, he was capable of painting from life, from photographs, from imagination, or from a combination of any of these, and had an instinctive gift for pictorial construction which may have been developed partly through a study of the Italian and northern European primitives in the Louvre, which he is known to have visited regularly. His recognition opened the way to an interest in the work of other naive painters and to an appreciation of the category of naive art produced by untutored and unsophisticated artists. But of these Rousseau remains the greatest.   REA

R. Alley, *Portrait of a Primitive: the Art of Henri Rousseau* (Oxford, 1978); Y. le Pichon, *The World of Henri Rousseau* (Oxford, 1982).

Rowntree, Benjamin Seebohm (b. York, UK, 7.7.1871; d. High Wycombe, Bucks., 7.10.1954). British contributor to management studies. He joined the family cocoa and chocolate firm, Rowntree & Co. Ltd, in 1889 and made various managerial innovations, including a company pension plan in 1906, the five-day week in 1919 and employee profit-sharing in 1923. In *The Human Factor in Business: Experiments in Industrial Democracy* (London, 1921), he advocated joint consultation between management and workers. A works council, the disclosure of management information to employees and the payment of a full-time shop steward were pioneering developments in the Rowntree company. He studied industrial welfare and his *Poverty: a Study of Town Life* (London, 1901) became influential. In 1919 he founded a series of Oxford management conferences which became a forum for the exchange of views on management. Rowntree believed that community service was the basic purpose of involvement in industry and that the industry from which people earned their living should provide the means to a life worth living.   RIT

Roy, Manabendra Nath, *né* Narendranath Bhattacharya (b. Arbelia, India, 6.2.1887; d. Dehra Dūn, 25.1.1954). The most prominent Asian communist figure outside China in the interwar years, he first moved into the communist orbit in 1917 in Mexico, where he was living in exile after a period as leader of the extremist revolutionary wing of the Indian independence movement in Bengal. In 1919 he moved to Moscow, winning LENIN's friendship and a prominent place in the executive of the Comintern, the Third International, as the embodiment of Lenin's hopes of destroying the colonial bases of western capitalist strength. Although he was both an effective organizer and speaker his absence from India incapacitated him from seriously threatening the domination of the Indian nationalist leadership by Mahatma GANDHI, and his own consciousness of his Asian origins drove him to break with the Comintern in 1929 and to make himself both in and out of British prisons the principal voice for an indigenous Asian communism, a position he did not abandon until the achievement of Indian independence in 1947.   DCW

Royce, Frederic Henry, see under ROLLS, CHARLES STEWART.

Różewicz, Tadeusz (b. Radomsko, Poland, 9.10.1921). Polish poet and dramatist whose plays, like those of MROŻEK, or GOMBROWICZ and Witkiewicz before him, have made a striking contribution to the repertoire of the absurd. The cataclysm of war and the total collapse of moral sanctions and civilization leave no room for conventional poesy. For Różewicz, who claims not to know what poetry is, man was killed in Auschwitz, poetry is dead – and yet the need persists; so Różewicz calls himself 'a poet who has been'. Post-Auschwitz poetry precludes 'beautiful' verse, and postulates the need to relearn speech, to name everything anew, to reconstruct man and recreate an ethical standard. This would seem to stipulate the creation of facts, not lyrics; and Różewicz's theory of poetic deed is perhaps to be connected with some primordial concept of catharsis. Minimalization disclaimers apart, Różewicz is the master of unvoiced devices that convey his meaning through the vibrations of the subtext, and the creator of a new versification system in Polish prosody that makes no concessions to rhyme or alliteration. His quest for salvation in the banal values of the great anonymous

herd and his restricted lyrical register make Różewicz one of the most representative voices of his epoch. A selection of his work in English is *Conversations with the Prince and Other Poems* (tr. A. Czerniawski, London, 1982).   NT

Rulfo, Juan (b. Apulco, Jalisco, Mexico, 16.5.1918). Mexican novelist and short-story writer. His childhood was marked by orphanhood and violence: his father was killed in the religious strife of the late 1920s and his mother died six years later. His native Jalisco, ravaged by erosion and war, provides the background and atmosphere of his fiction. Rulfo's nonliterary career has been in relatively obscure posts in commerce, the bureaucracy (migration and indigenist agencies) and television. His central position in Latin American literature is based on two brief works: the stories of *El llano en llamas* (Mexico City, 1953; tr. G. D. Schade, *The Burning Plains and Other Stories*, Austin, 1967) and a novel, *Pedro Páramo* (Mexico City, 1955; tr. L. Kemp, NY, 1959). These works sum up the so-called 'novel of the Mexican revolution' and the traditions of regionalism, but go far beyond them in depth, ambiguity and literary quality. The presence of death and guilt, the problematic father-son relationships and a haunting vision of paradise become hell, often presented from a disorientated and tragically limited narrative point of view, cause these enigmatic creations almost unanimously to be considered as very close to the fundamentals of the Mexican psyche.   SB

Russell, Bertrand Arthur William (b. Trelleck, Gwent, UK, 18.5.1872; d. Penrhyndeudraeth, Gwynedd, 2.2.1970). British philosopher. Russell's parents died when he was very young and he was brought up, until he went to Cambridge in 1890 at 18, by his grandmother, the intelligent, independent-minded but puritanical widow of Lord John Russell, the Liberal prime minister. His first contact with people of his own age was at an army crammer's where he was prepared for a scholarship to Trinity College, Cambridge. He flourished in the brilliant undergraduate society of Cambridge, then at its most glittering.

He was soon elected to a fellowship, shortly after marrying Alys Pearsall Smith. A visit to Germany led to his first book *German Social Democracy* (London, 1896). A year later his fellowship dissertation came out: *Essay on the Foundations of Geometry* (Cambridge, 1897). The more or less idealist view of that book, the academic orthodoxy of the time, was undermined in the next few years by two things: the influence of G. E. MOORE, and his own conviction that idealism could not account for mathematical truth. In perhaps his greatest work *The Principles of Mathematics* (Cambridge, 1903) he arrived independently at the view of FREGE that mathematics is a continuation of logic and that its subject-matter is a system of Platonic essences that exist in a realm outside both mind and matter. For the next few years, in collaboration with WHITEHEAD, he worked to turn the discursive prose of the *Principles* into the fully developed and symbolically expressed formal system of *Principia Mathematica* (3 vols, Cambridge, 1910–13). He was held up exasperatingly by the discovery that a contradiction followed from what seemed intuitively evident assumptions about the nature of classes or sets, something that was to have as much influence on philosophy in general (by calling for attention to the meaningless as well as the true and the false) as on mathematical logic, where it initiated inquiries that overthrew in the end his and Frege's idea of the relation of mathematics and logic. In the next few years Russell left his wife to become the lover of Ottoline Morrell; met WITTGENSTEIN who was to disturb his philosophical self-confidence and, for a time, to superannuate him in philosophical influence; wrote his brilliantly concise and original introductory book *The Problems of Philosophy* (London, 1912) and so embarked on 10 years of important work in epistemology, in which were published *Mysticism and Logic* (London, 1918) and *Analysis of Mind* (London, 1921). Russell was a member of a famous English political family; he succeeded to the title of 3rd Earl Russell but refused to use it. His interest in politics dominated his life in WW1 in the course of which he was

fined in 1916 and imprisoned in 1918 for vehement conduct in the cause of pacifism. Expelled from Trinity, he did not accept reinstatement after the war but married Dora Black as his second wife and spent the years until the end of the 1930s as a professional writer and lecturer and, for a considerable period, as head of a progressive school. The outbreak of WW2 found him, with his third wife Patricia Spence, in the USA. There he was debarred from teaching in New York because of the libertarian ideas about sexual morality, education and war he had been expounding in popular fashion in the preceding years. But damages received for a later wrongful dismissal enabled him to survive until the success of his *History of Western Philosophy* (London, 1945) solved all financial problems for the rest of his long life. Returning to England in glory after the war (he was made OM in 1949 and won the Nobel prize for literature in 1950) he was disappointed by the lukewarm reception of his last professionally ambitious philosophical work *Human Knowledge* (London, 1948). From 1954 and the Bikini H-bomb tests his main preoccupation was the danger of nuclear war. In 1960 he led the militants of the Committee of 100 out of the main body of the CND and in 1961 was imprisoned with his fourth and final wife Edith Finch for taking part in a sit-down demonstration in Whitehall. His last years were spent in North Wales. He retained his lucidity and his powers to amuse and to infuriate to the end.   AQ

A. J. Ayer, *Russell* (London, 1972); R. W. Clark, *The Life of Bertrand Russell* (London, 1975).

Russell, Henry Norris (b. Oyster Bay, NY, USA, 25.11.1877; d. Princeton, NJ, 18.2.1957). American astronomer. Russell graduated from Princeton University *insigne cum laude* and spent three years in England at the Cavendish Laboratory, Cambridge and at the university observatory, where he worked with Hinks determining stellar parallaxes. He spent almost all his subsequent career at Princeton. Russell was intimately concerned with the results of observation. He was the part-originator, with HERTZ-

SPRUNG, of the celebrated Hertzsprung–Russell diagram (the HR diagram), which is the basis of present studies of stellar evolution. In this diagram, stellar absolute magnitude (i.e. stellar brightness at a standard distance) is plotted against spectral type, varying from hot B-type stars to cool M-type stars. Russell first presented this form of the diagram at the meeting of the Royal Astronomical Society in London on 13.6.1913, and then in a classic paper, 'The spectrum-luminosity diagram' (*Popular Astronomy*, 22 [1914], 285). The particular form of it given by Russell referred to Population I stars only (i.e. young stars in the solar neighbourhood) and shows the characteristic 'main sequence' and 'giant branch' together with one white dwarf star (the faint component of the double star o2 Eridani). However, Russell failed to recognize the true anomaly of this star, thinking that its position on the diagram might be faulty through an inaccurate spectral classification. In common with other theorists, Russell used the HR diagram as a basis for discussion of stellar evolution, suggesting in his early days that in addition to the release of gravitational energy through contraction, energy could also be generated by 'dwarf stuff' in main sequence stars and 'giant stuff' in giant stars. Such speculation was premature and a true picture could emerge only after EDDINGTON's work on the internal structure of stars and modern knowledge of nuclear reactions. In 1929 Russell was the first astronomer to make a comprehensive analysis of the solar spectrum in order to determine the relative abundances of the elements. He showed that the sun is made chiefly of hydrogen; in spite of the approximations of the analysis, his values are in surprisingly good agreement with modern ones. At a time when good astronomy books were scarce, Russell was senior author of a popular textbook, *Astronomy* (with R. S. Dugan & J. Q. Stewart, 2 vols, Boston, Mass., 1926–7).

DEB

Rutherford, Ernest (b. Brightwater, New Zealand, 30.8.1871; d. Cambridge, UK, 19.10.1937). British physicist. Rutherford's scientific career began in New Zealand in 1893 when he devised a sensitive magnetic detector of radio waves. He continued work on this for a short time at Cambridge where he had become, in 1895, one of J. J. THOMSON's first two research students. The discovery of X-rays in 1895, radioactivity in 1896 and the electron in 1897 changed completely Rutherford's line of research and he spent the rest of his life exploring the structure of the atom. Although his scientific record is one of almost unbroken progress it was marked by three high peaks of achievement. The first came in 1902 when he was Macdonald research professor in physics at McGill University, Montreal. With the collaboration of SODDY, a young Oxford graduate attached to the chemistry department at McGill, Rutherford showed that the complex sequences of radioactive transformations could be explained if radioactivity were the spontaneous breaking up of atoms of one kind to form atoms of another, emitting ionizing radiations in the process. This revolutionary idea was not at first generally accepted but its validity soon became abundantly clear. For this work and for his proof that the alpha-rays from radioactive substances were atomic fragments and not, as was widely held, a form of X-ray, Rutherford received the 1908 Nobel prize for chemistry. His second, even higher, peak of achievement came in 1911 during his 12 years as professor of physics in Manchester. In a classic series of experiments carried out with the assistance of Geiger and Marsden, Rutherford proved that, in contrast to the existing view, the atom consists of a minute, positively charged and extremely dense central core or nucleus, the very light, negatively charged electrons occupying the rest of the enormously bigger, largely empty, atom. It would be difficult to exaggerate the influence of the discovery of the atomic nucleus on the whole field of physics. Rutherford's third great achievement occurred near the end of his time at Manchester, between 1917 and 1919, when his wartime work on submarine detection had reached fruition. Working largely on his own, he obtained clear evidence that the nucleus of the nitrogen atom may, on rare occasions, be split when nitrogen is bombarded by helium nuclei, the products of this nuclear reaction being oxygen and hydrogen nuclei. The artificial transmutation of matter had been detected for the first time.

In the autumn of 1919 Rutherford succeeded J. J. Thomson as Cavendish professor in Cambridge. After confirming and extending his work on artificial disintegration he directed the efforts of the laboratory towards improvements in experimental techniques. Until this time the apparatus devised by Rutherford and his school had combined great ingenuity with extreme simplicity. These devices were, by now, reaching the limits of their usefulness and new, more powerful means of detecting and counting particles were needed as well as more copious streams of bombarding projectiles than were available from radioactive sources. Major rewards for this policy came in 1932. In that year CHADWICK, whom Rutherford had brought with him from Manchester, discovered the neutron (a particle whose existence had been predicted by Rutherford in 1920), which soon came to be recognized as a fundamental constituent of matter. In the same year COCKCROFT and Walton, actively encouraged by Rutherford, succeeded in bringing about the first nuclear disintegration by artificially accelerated hydrogen nuclei. These achievements marked the start of an era of tremendous expansion in nuclear physics, the subject which had its origin in Rutherford's Manchester research.

Rutherford was a big man in every way, a prodigious worker, genial and ebullient by nature, unquenchable in spirit. As an experimenter Rutherford must be placed in the same class as Faraday; as a leader with a genius both for choosing the most penetrating lines of attack and for inspiring his men, he was in a class of his own. Very many of his scientific articles have been brought together in *The Collected Papers of Lord Rutherford of Nelson* (3 vols, London, 1962–5). WTD

A. S. Eve, *Rutherford* (Cambridge, 1939); N. Feather, *Lord Rutherford* (London, ²1973).

Ružička, Leopold (b. Vukovar, Croatia, Austria-Hungary [now Yugoslavia], 18.9.1887; naturalized Swiss citizen, 1916; d. Zürich, Switzerland, 26.9.1976). Croat/Swiss chemist. Ružička in a personal account describes himself as a bio-organic chemist. At school he had a classical training and originally intended to be a priest, but finally he decided that his life-work would be the organic chemistry of natural products. He studied chemistry at Karlsruhe under STAUDINGER and began research on the pyrethrins (alicyclic natural insecticides). In 1912 he moved to the Eidgenössische Technische Hochschule, Zürich, with Staudinger. Apart from two years (1926 –8) at Utrecht he spent his working life at the ETH, where he became professor of organic chemistry (1928). He was awarded a Nobel prize jointly with BUTENANDT in 1939.

Ružička contributed to the major areas of natural product chemistry. In 1921 he started work on the synthesis of sesquiterpene perfumes and on the structures of the important odours, civetone, muscone, jasmone and irone. From this work he proved the existence for the first time of carbon rings with more than 8 atoms and opened the way to a study of large (13–24 atoms) and medium (9–12 atoms) sized carboxylic rings. About 1920 he also began work on the higher (di- and tri-) terpenes and developed the technique of sulphur dehydrogenation to convert terpenes to aromatic compounds and so elucidate their ring systems. Ultimately he determined many triterpene structures including β-amyrin and lanosterol. His analysis of terpenoid structures led him first to the isoprene rule, which stated that terpenoids were composed of the 5-carbon unit of isoprene, and subsequently to the biogenetic isoprene rule. This has had an enormous impact on natural product chemistry and explains how many natural compounds, including many of biochemical significance, such as the steroids and the carotenoids, are all formed from one precursor, isopentenyl pyrophosphate. Ružička worked directly on the steroids and significantly contributed to the chemistry of the male sex hormones androsterone and testosterone, deducing the structure of and synthesizing the latter before it had been isolated. The royalties on his testosterone patents made Růžička a wealthy man. He used much of his wealth to collect 17c Dutch and Flemish paintings which were subsequently presented to the Museum of Art, Zürich.

TGH

Ryle, Gilbert (b. Brighton, E. Sussex, UK, 19.8.1900; d. Oxford, 6.10.1976). British philosopher. The son of a doctor, Ryle gained three first-class honours degrees at Queen's College, Oxford. He taught at Christ Church, Oxford, from 1924 until WW2. He soon came to notice for his forceful articles on philosophical logic and philosophical method, which unequivocally limited philosophy to the dispelling of linguistically engendered confusions. Returning to Oxford after the war as professor of metaphysical philosophy, he argued at length in *The Concept of Mind* (London, 1949) that the traditional dualist view of mind and body as wholly distinct and puzzlingly related things was just such a confusion. As senior professor Ryle made Oxford the philosophical centre of the English-speaking world for the first two postwar decades. In *Dilemmas* (Cambridge, 1954) he argued that the apparent conflicts between scientific findings and our everyday convictions are not fundamental and that the two can be consistently accommodated to each other. His *Collected Papers* (2 vols, London, 1971) display the full range of his interests, particularly in the history of philosophy which he treated, without anachronism, as of live philosophical interest. *Plato's Progress* (Cambridge, 1966) is an adventurous and idiosyncratic body of speculations about the intended meaning and use of Plato's writings and about their date and authenticity. The main concern of his final years was the topic of thinking, perhaps the most 'mental' of the things we do with our minds and thus most encouraging to dualists. His writings on the topic were collected as *On Thinking* (Oxford, 1979).

AQ

O. P. Wood & G. Pitcher (eds), *Ryle: a Collection of Critical Essays* (NY, 1970); W. Lyons, *Gilbert Ryle* (Brighton, 1980).

Ryle, Martin (b. Brighton, E. Sussex, UK, 27.9.1918). British astronomer. Ryle graduated from Oxford in 1939 and joined the Telecommunications Research Establishment (TRE), Malvern, where he worked on the development of radar. In 1945 he moved to the Cavendish Laboratory, Cambridge, working with J. A. Ratcliffe's radio group (he later formed an independent radio-astronomy group). Ratcliffe advised him to study radio emission from the sun, following some work of J. S. Hey during WW2. Hey had noticed while investigating a particularly striking instance of noise jamming of radar signals that the interference apparently came from the sun, and associated it with the presence of a large sunspot. By using two separated aerials as an interferometer, Ryle was able to show, as he had suggested, that the radio emission came from an area of the sun close to the visible area of the sunspot. This was the first of a succession of interferometers of increasing resolution, culminating in Ryle's celebrated technique of aperture synthesis, which proved extraordinarily powerful when applied to the discovery and investigation of discrete nonsolar sources. A 180-acre site outside Cambridge was the beginning of the Mullard Radio Astronomy Observatory: the first fully operational aperture synthesis interferometer was built on it. This instrument was used to produce a well-known catalogue, designated 4C, of about 5000 radio sources. It was followed in succession by the 'One Mile Radio Telescope' and the 'Three Mile Telescope'.

Ryle's contributions to radio astronomy rest as much on the work done with his instruments as with their development. He showed that positional accuracy is not the prerogative of the optical astronomer, but radio interferometric techniques can give a much increased accuracy. In general, ordinary stars are not radio sources, but the few radio stars that have been observed can be used to tie together the optical and radio grids. Much radio astronomy is concerned with the most distant objects in the universe and is therefore well suited to cosmological studies. Ryle and his colleagues used their data to make an important statistical test of current cosmological models, in which they counted the number of radio sources that can be detected down to particular limits of signal strength. They found an excess of faint sources over the number expected and concluded that the universe is not in a steady state. Using his largest interferometers, Ryle was able to examine the larger and closer radio sources with an extraordinarily high resolution. These studies often showed the presence of a double structure, the origin of which is still studied by theoreticians. Ryle has been professor of radio-astronomy at Cambridge since 1959, and became the twelfth astronomer royal in 1972. He shared a Nobel prize with A. Hewish in 1974. DEB

S

Saarinen, Eero (b. Kirkkonummi, Finland, 20.8.1910; naturalized American citizen, 1940; d. Birmingham, Ala, USA, 1.9.1961). Finnish/American architect. In the course of his short career, Saarinen not only designed a series of major buildings, but also charted a course for the generation of architects who succeeded him, finally moving beyond the narrow definitions of modernism that had been laid down in the 1920s. Saarinen's father Eliel was himself a distinguished architect who worked in a romantic, historical style, and who emigrated to the USA in 1923. Eero went into partnership with him in 1936, but although his presence increasingly made itself felt, it was only after his father's death in 1950 that Saarinen could express himself fully. The first major building produced under his own name was General Motors' technical centre at Warren, Ohio (completed in 1955). It was a complete break with his father's style, an austere exercise in architectural abstraction. But in his subsequent buildings, Saarinen moved towards a synthesis between modernism and the more traditional architectural qualities espoused by his father.

Saarinen's terminal for TWA at Kennedy Airport, New York (completed in 1962 after his death), was remarkable not simply for its sweeping and dramatic lines, but for the way in which it suggests flight: it looks like a bird, with wings, a body, claws and even a beak. Saarinen's buildings were personal. Each arose from the particular circumstances of the commission and its context, rather than as examples of a universal solution to a particular type. The results were of variable quality. Sometimes, as with the US Embassy in London (completed 1960), which attempts to reflect the architecture of a traditional London square, they were not altogether resolved. Saarinen's reputation is now on the rise again with the success of the younger architects who trained under him, and who have pioneered postmodernism.   DS

Sabatier, Paul (b. Carcassonne, Aude, France, 5.11.1854; d. Toulouse, Haute-Garonne, 14.8.1941). French chemist. As a young man he studied at the Ecole Normale Supérieure; and was influenced in his early career by Berthelot, whose laboratory he entered in 1878. Although Sabatier's work was principally experimental and devoted to the chemical 'manipulation' of solid catalysts so as to secure the rapid build-up of certain products and the suppression of others, he was amongst the first to identify and define the phenomenon of chemisorption, which refers to the preferential uptake of chemical species at a solid surface. OSTWALD and others were of the erroneous opinion that gaseous reactants, upon impinging on solid catalysts, were *ab*sorbed in micropores not *ad*sorbed at exterior surfaces. Sabatier's work was, and still is, of great practical importance: hydrogenation reactions are, for example, a vital part of the modern chemical industry. And Sabatier's idea that catalysts function by generating a surface intermediate compound which is sequentially broken down and reformed is still a valuable framework for discussion in elucidating the behaviour of new catalysts. Sabatier was professor of chemistry at Toulouse University from 1882, and in 1912 was awarded the Nobel prize, with François GRIGNARD.
                               JMT

Sabin, Albert Bruce (b. Bialystok, Grodno, Russia [now Poland], 26.8.1906). American microbiologist. An émigré with his family to the USA, Sabin made his first major contribution to medicine shortly after graduating from New York University in 1931: the isolation of virus B, which is inherent in monkeys and is a cause of human death. By 1939 he was associate professor of paediatrics at New York University and already firmly interested in polio, noting in 1941 that the onset of paralysis generally came within 24 hours of strenuous exercise. During WW2 Sabin served in the US Army Medical

Corps, where he developed a vaccine against dengue fever, a deadly and contagious viral haemorrhagic disease; successfully vaccinated against Japanese encephalitis 65,000 soldiers serving in Okinawa; isolated a protozoan parasite called toxoplasma, describing the symptoms and producing a method of diagnosis – though the disease is normally mild, if caught during pregnancy it can cause brain damage and blindness to the unborn child. After WW2 Sabin returned to Cincinnati where he classified the 100 or so strains of polio virus into three types (a discovery made also by other scientists), and then, in 1956, two years after SALK, he produced a live-virus polio vaccine, to be taken orally, which largely replaced the Salk vaccine. In 1959 Sabin identified the Echo 9 virus, which was epidemic in Milwaukee and caused an illness like intestinal flu; and he later studied the effect of the virus on pregnant women and the unborn child. In 1970 he became president of the Weizmann Institute of Science and since 1974 has been distinguished research professor of biomedicine at the Medical University of South Carolina. CR

Sachs, Julius von (b. Breslau, Silesia, Germany [now Wročlav, Poland], 2.10.1832; d. Würzburg, Bavaria, Germany, 29.5.1897). German botanist. After working for the outstanding physiologist J. E. Purkinje in Prague, Sachs went on to become eventually professor of botany at Freiburg (1867) and then at Würzburg (from 1868). He contributed to every area of botany but figured especially in the early development of plant physiology. He elaborated techniques of microchemistry, detailed the morphology and physiology of germination, and, reviving a technique conceived in 1699 and now known as hydroponics, he grew plants in water with known additives and established their basic nutritional requirements. His observation of starch grains in chloroplasts, but only in illuminated areas of leaves, established the synthetic aspect of photosynthesis. He also studied growth periodicity (and is perhaps the father of the sigmoid growth curve), helio- and geotropism, meristem mor-

phology and transpiration. His study of the daily folding and opening of mimosa leaves was the first demonstration of an endogenous circadian oscillator in biology. His *Geschichte der Botanik von 16 Jahrhundert bis 1860* (Munich, 1875; *History of Botany, 1530– 1860*, Oxford, 1906) is unique for its time in tracing the development of ideas in botanic research, and his various texts, many of which were long the definitive works in plant physiology, influenced the shift in England and the USA from pure systematics to a more functional study of plants. DOM

Sadat, Mohammed Anwar el- (b. Talah Monufiya, Nile Delta, Egypt, 25.12.1918; d. Nasr City, nr Cairo, 6.10.1981). Revolutionary Egyptian officer, associate of Colonel NASSER, general secretary of the National Union party (1957–61), speaker of the Parliamentary Assembly (1960–1, 1964–9), vice-president (1969), he succeeded Nasser as president on his predecessor's death in 1970. At first continuing Nasser's policy of bidding for leadership of the Arab world with Soviet support, he played the major part in the Syrian– Egyptian attack on Israel in November 1973. The successful Israeli defeat of this attack, the near-disaster which only US intervention prevented from overtaking the Egyptian Third Army, and the unsympathetic attitude taken both by the Soviets and by his fellow-Arab countries towards the immense debts Egypt had incurred in the six years of war and near-war between 1967 and 1973, led Sadat to break with the USSR, expel all Soviet advisers, repudiate his debts to the USSR, and turn towards the USA. KISSINGER, by assiduous 'shuttle' diplomacy between Cairo and Tel Aviv, was able to negotiate a disengagement of Egyptian and Israeli forces, and an Israeli withdrawal. It took the ill-advised attempt by President Carter to bring the USSR into the discussion of a Middle Eastern settlement to drive Sadat into a dramatic flight to Israel and the prolonged negotiations which led, with renewed American mediation, to the signature of the Israeli –Egyptian peace treaty of March 1979. Sadat's initiative involved him and his people in a partial repudiation of their earlier Pan-Arabism in favour of a full-blooded celebration of Egyptian ('Pharaonic') nationalism, looking to a record of civilization much older than anything the Arabs as such could claim. He was assassinated by Muslim extremists at a military parade in Cairo. DCW

Sadler, Michael Ernest (b. Barnsley, W. Yorks., UK, 3.7.1861; d. Oxford, 14.10.1943). British educator. The son of a doctor, Sadler was renowned for his encouragement of the less fortunate. After graduating at Oxford in 1885 he became secretary to the Oxford Delegacy for University Extension Lectures, and in 1891 lectured in Philadelphia. He served on the Bryce Commission on secondary education (1894), and in 1895 was appointed to 'the most delectable task in the world' as director of special inquiries and reports to what was later the Board of Education. Already convinced that Britain lagged behind in educational research and comparative inquiries, Sadler produced 11 large volumes on education in Europe, the British empire and the USA. He also investigated nine British local authorities and made recommendations for reorganization following the Education Act of 1902 which established secondary education. After a disagreement, Sadler became part-time professor at the University of Manchester (1903–11), then vice-chancellor of the University of Leeds (1911–23). He was master of University College, Oxford, from 1923 to 1934. Sadler was convinced that 'the things outside the schools matter even more than the things inside the schools, and govern and interpret the things inside', especially in relation to the then neglected education of the majority, and to prospects for young workers. On this aspect and others he admired German initiatives; elsewhere he spoke of British education's indebtedness to American experiments. In 1938 he was greatly concerned with the Spens Report which might have blended technical and preprofessional with 'genuine' secondary education; he also wrote pioneer papers on the education of women, and on the teaching of the social sciences. EJK

Saint-Exupéry, Marie-Antoine-Roger de (b. Lyons, Rhône, France, 29.6.1900; d. off Corsica, 31.7.1944). French novelist and aviator. Trained as a pilot in 1921, Saint-Exupéry was one of the great figures of the heroic period of commercial aviation, celebrated for his exploits in flying mail-planes on the Toulouse–Casablanca and the France–Dakar–Latin America routes. As a director of Aeropost Argentina from 1929 to 1931, he was responsible for pioneering the dangerous trans-Andean routes. Mentioned in official dispatches for his daring mission over Arras in 1940 (the basis for his novel *Pilote de Guerre*, NY, 1942; tr. L. Galantière, *Flight to Arras*, NY, 1942), he spent much of WW2 in the USA, broadcasting on behalf of the Free French. He later served as a volunteer pilot with the Free French forces and was lost without trace off Corsica after a reconnaissance mission over Annecy and Grenoble. His professional experience provided the thematic basis for novels such as *Vol de Nuit* (Paris, 1931; tr. S. Gilbert, *Night Flight*, London, 1931) and *Terre des hommes* (Paris, 1939; tr. L. Galantière, *Wind, Sand and Stars*, NY, 1939). Remarkable for their restrained accounts of heroism, his novels celebrate the values of fraternity and solidarity in a manner that has led to their comparison with the early fiction of MALRAUX and with the existentialism of SARTRE. In a completely different vein his *Le Petit prince* (NY, 1943; tr. K. Woods, *The Little Prince*, NY, 1943) has become one of the best loved of modern children's novels and has also proved to have considerable appeal for his adult readers. Saint-Exupéry was posthumously honoured by being made Commandeur de la Légion d'honneur. DM

Saint-John Perse, ps. of Marie-René-Auguste Alexis Saint-Léger Léger (b. Saint-Léger des Feuilles, Guadeloupe, 31.3.1887; d. Paris, France, 20.9.1975). French poet and diplomat. The poet Alexis Saint-Léger Léger was a high-ranking French diplomatist who took the pen name of Saint-John Perse in 1924 in order to keep the two sides of his personality separate. His first poems *Eloges* (Paris, 1911; tr. L. Varèse,

Praises, NY, 1924) celebrate the beauty of his childhood in the tropical paradise of the French West Indies. His best-known poem *Anabase* (Paris, 1924; tr. T. S. ELIOT, *Anabasis*, London, 1930) is, as Eliot said in his preface, 'a series of images of migration, of conquest of vast spaces in Asiatic wastes, of destruction and foundation of cities and civilizations of many races or epochs of the ancient East'. His hostility to Germany and to the Munich agreements of 1938 led him, in 1940, to be deprived of his French citizenship by the Vichy government and he spent the war years in exile in the USA. This led to the publication of the poems *Exil* (Buenos Aires, 1942; tr. D. Devlin, *Exile*, NY, 1944) and *Pluies* (Buenos Aires, 1942; tr. D. Devlin, *Rains*, NY, 1944). He was restored to French citizenship after WW2, and awarded the Nobel prize for literature in 1960. His poetry is characterized by a predominance of the logic of the imagination over that of surface reason, by an intense awareness of verbal rhythms, and by an exotic but always technically accurate language. Like that of CLAUDEL, it eschews the use of rhyme, and requires careful reading to bring out the initially sometimes obscure meaning. A bilingual edition of his poetry with translations by W. H. AUDEN and others is *Collected Poems* (Princeton, 1971).   PMWT

R. Caillois, *Poétique de Saint-John Perse* (Paris, 1954).

Sakharov, Andrei Dmitrievich (b. Moscow, USSR, 21.5.1921). Russian theoretical physicist who helped to develop the Soviet hydrogen bomb, and political dissident who has criticized the lack of democracy and legality in the Soviet Union. In 1948 he joined a new group to carry out research on thermonuclear weapons. He thought this was vital for world peace, and was attracted by the immensity of the task. In practice his contribution was crucial; he also worked on controlled fusion reactions. In 1953 he was made a full member of the Academy of Sciences. Sakharov's political activities grew out of his work. After 1958 he tried to halt nuclear weapons tests, and pressed for the Partial Test Ban Treaty (1963). In 1968 he wrote an

essay calling for genuine Soviet–American cooperation and a convergence of the two systems, *Razmyshleniya o progresse, mirnom sosushchestvovanii i intellektualnoi svobode* (Frankfurt; *Progress, Coexistence and Intellectual Freedom*, London). When this was published in the West, he was barred from secret work. His research now extended to gravitation and cosmology. After 1970 he became more active in defending human rights, and in 1975 received the Nobel Peace prize. In January 1980 he was banished to Gorky, where he lives under police surveillance. A man of immense intellectual achievement and moral courage, he maintains his faith in the power of reason and the human spirit (see *Trevoga i Nadezhda*, NY, 1978; *Alarm and Hope*, NY, 1978).   DH

Salam, Abdus (b. Jhang, India [now Pakistan], 29.1.1926). Pakistani theoretical physicist. Educated in Lahore and Cambridge, UK, Salam has held the chair of theoretical physics at Imperial College, London, since 1957. Since 1964 he has combined this with the directorship of the International Centre for Theoretical Physics at Trieste. Salam's work has centred on the unification of the weak and electromagnetic forces in nature (see GLASHOW). In 1967 he was independently responsible (at the same time as WEINBERG) for the successful model based on symmetry of the type $SU(2) \times U(1)$ which gives such unification. These theories implied the existence of a new weak interaction, the natural current, which was confirmed in the early 1970s in bubble-chamber experiments with neutrino beams. Salam has always favoured group-theory techniques (group theory is the mathematical tool which is used to study symmetry operations) in particle physics and is currently engaged in attempts to unify the strong and gravitational interactions together with the weak and electromagnetic. He received a Nobel prize in 1979 with Glashow and Weinberg.   RJC

Salazar, António de Oliveira (b. Vimieiro, Alto Alentejo, Portugal, 28.4.1889; d. Lisbon, 27.7.1970). Minister of finance in Portugal (1928–32), prime minister, leader of the only permitted political party, the Portuguese National Union, and virtual dictator until incapacitated by a stroke in 1968. His domination over political life in Portugal, backed by his use of an efficient and ruthless political police, made his country into a quasi-fascist state based on a corporative Catholic philosophy, without freedom or shadow of political disorder, without economic discontent or significant growth, and without the style or the cult of personality normally associated with fascist governments. Under his dictatorship quiet and unspectacular progress (save in the sphere of spectacular public works so characteristic of fascism) was registered but at a rate of development which kept Portugal itself well behind the rest of Europe, and made the Portuguese colonies in Africa natural breeding grounds for self-professed MARXist independence movements which exhausted all Portuguese efforts to suppress or contain them and made possible the restoration of democracy to Portugal by military coup in 1974. DCW

Salinas, Pedro (b. Madrid, Spain, 27.11.1891; d. Boston, Mass., USA, 4.12.1951). Spanish poet. A member of the postsymbolist 1927 generation, Salinas typically combined the professions of poet, critic and academic and made a major contribution to the dissemination of Hispanic culture in universities at home and abroad. His collected verse is a discourse on the nature of reality, taking the reader through the looking glass of appearances and emphasizing poetry as imaginative re-creation. The major subjects of this contemplative poetry of difficult simplicity and fine romantic irony are nature, woman and self. His most famous collections *La Voz a ti debida* [The voice owed to you] (Madrid, 1933) and *Razón de amor* (Madrid, 1936; tr. E. L. Turnbull, *Truth of Two and Other Poems*, Baltimore, 1940) reveal the synthesizing genius of the generation. Together these works form one of the great modern love cycles, a witty updating of the courtly love tradition with BERGSONian overtones in the subtle and lucid analysis of shifting perceptions and emotions, of consciousness in flux. Taken as the epitome of prewar 'pure' poetry, Salinas has unjustly been accused of excessive intellectualism and dehumanization. The experience of civil war, exile, WW2 and the atomic bomb broadened Salinas's poetic concerns and his postwar work is a sustained defence of liberal humanism and ecology. PMcD
J. Crispin, *Pedro Salinas* (NY, 1974).

Salinger, Jerome David (b. New York, USA, 1.1.1919). American novelist. J. D. Salinger attended a number of colleges without taking a degree, and saw active service in WW2 (1942–5). The success of *The Catcher in the Rye* (Boston, Mass., 1951) should intrigue the social historian as much as the literary critic. Holden Caulfield was taken as a contemporary Huck Finn, and readers' identification with him was for a time almost universal. A novel which replaced Huck's hope with self-pity and proclaimed the agony of leaving childhood and entering the 'phony' adult world seemed to express a whole culture's uncertainty. The demotic narrative style has charm, but the hero's sensitivity is not handled with sufficient irony. A similar distrust of life marks *Nine Stories* (Boston, Mass., 1953, published as *For Esmé, with Love and Squalor*, London, 1953), in which Salinger began the fragmentary 'saga' of the Glass family, carried on in a handful of long-short stories (*Franny and Zooey*, Boston, Mass., 1961; *Raise High the Roof-Beam, Carpenters; and Seymour: an Introduction*, Boston, Mass., 1963; and in the *New Yorker*, 1965: 'Hapworth, 16, 1924'). These stories are explicitly religious, but in an eclectically mystical mode. They try to go beyond a simple rejection of the conventional world and to establish a bond between the spiritually superior and their ordinary fellows. It is difficult to share Salinger's affection for his weakly dramatized family of extravagantly beautiful minds, yet the attempt to present spiritual love directly in fiction is a brave one. Unfortunately, Salinger seems to have lost interest in the Glass family, and in writing fiction. BF

Modern Fiction Studies, XII, 3 (Autumn 1966) (J. D. Salinger Special Number).

Salk, Jonas Edward (b. New York, USA, 28.10.1914). American virologist. Having graduated in science (1934) and in medicine (1939), Salk went to the University of Michigan School of Public Health in 1943, and then, in 1947, to the University of Pittsburgh as research professor of bacteriology. But between 1942 and 1947 he had worked also for the US army, developing a flu vaccine – necessary experience for his later achievement. Infantile paralysis (poliomyelitis) loomed large in the American consciousness, and President Franklin D. ROOSEVELT – himself paralysed by the disease from the age of 21 – had inaugurated the 'March of Dimes', a fund that financed research into the disease. In 1949 the American microbiologist John Enders and his colleagues at Harvard developed a technique for growing polio virus in the laboratory. This meant, at last, a plentiful supply of virus for research purposes. Salk, with his co-workers at Pittsburgh, was able to combine Enders's technique with his own experience of vaccine production, so that in 1952 he produced a vaccine made with killed virus. After preliminary testing, massive field trials were launched in 1954 and some early Salk vaccine batches were found to be dangerous, leading to a few early disasters. Because of the March of Dimes, vaccine research was in progress at several centres, and a few years later SABIN produced a different vaccine, this type made out of a live virus that had had its virulence bred out of it. This new vaccine had three advantages: it could be produced in large quantities, it could be given by mouth and, because it replaced the 'wild' level of virus with a harmless virus, it meant that even nonvaccinated members of a population were substantially protected. Since its main disadvantage was that it required refrigeration – a problem in tropical countries but not in the West – most of the world went over to Sabin vaccine; the only significant exceptions were Scandinavia and the Netherlands, where vaccination of the population can be nearly 100 per cent because almost nobody has any conscientious objections. However, Salk vaccine is likely to re-establish itself in the fight to eradi-cate poliomyelitis worldwide; it does not need refrigeration, and it is clearly better to eliminate a virus altogether than to replace it with a milder strain, however harmless. Polio vaccine development was Salk's outstanding scientific achievement. But the Nobel prize was awarded, rightly, to John Enders. Salk remained at Pittsburgh until 1963 when he moved, as founding director, to the Salk Institute for Biological Studies in San Diego. In 1970 he married Françoise Gilot, former mistress of PICASSO. Although he retired in 1975, Salk is still active at the institute.   CR

Samuelson, Paul Anthony (b. Gary, Ind., USA, 15.5.1915). American economist. Educated at Chicago and Harvard universities, Samuelson has been professor of economics at MIT since 1940. He won a Nobel prize for economics in 1970. He has a unique status within the economics profession in the second half of the 20c. He has neither aspired to nor achieved an ideological influence like that of FRIEDMAN; and his utterances on issues of public policy are seldom profound or far-reaching. While he was by no means the first to make extensive use of mathematics in economic analysis, his achievement lies in having set new standards for economic theory as a rigorous, quasi-scientific discipline. He has done for economics what HEIFETZ did for the violin. The flavour of Samuelson's accomplishment can best be grasped by scanning not so much the two treatises of which he is author and coauthor respectively (see below), but the many dozens of theoretical articles brought together (with other pieces) in his *Collected Scientific Papers* (4 vols, Cambridge, Mass., 1978). Two characteristics of these papers stand out: their range, and the number of occasions on which the author has transformed previously loose or inconclusive theoretical findings into clear-cut and decisive results. Numerous topics in demand and utility theory, capital theory, public expenditure, international trade, business cycle theory, financial market theory and welfare economics have benefited from this treatment.

As for treatises, *Foundations of Economic Analysis* (NY, 1947, ²1961) provided a comprehensive restatement of general equilibrium theory and made notable advances in the analysis of market stability. *Linear Programming and Economic Analysis* (with R. Dorfman and SOLOW, NY, 1958) applied to economic theory the mathematical discoveries of linear programming due to G. B. Dantzig and others, and also related these to LEONTIEF's input-out analysis and VON NEUMANN's growth model.

Along with his logical and mathematical facility, Samuelson has a pungent style of writing. His *Economics* (NY, 1948, ¹¹1980) has been a worldwide, bestselling introductory textbook in successive editions and more than 20 languages since it was first published. PMO

Sandage, Allan Rex (b. Iowa City, USA, 18.6.1926). American astronomer. His early work, with Martin SCHWARZ-SCHILD, was concerned with the stage of stellar evolution when a star expands and cools to become a red giant. Sandage also studied groups of stars: the spherical globular clusters of old, well-evolved stars and younger stars in open clusters. Sandage has always been fascinated with observational cosmology; his early experience of working with HUBBLE was important. In 1953 he and Hubble distinguished the brightest stars in galaxies as irregularly varying stars now called Hubble–Sandage variables. Their potential use as 'standard candles', to determine intergalactic distance scales, was not feasible because of their irregularity, and much of Sandage's work was concerned with establishing such distance scales in the universe and in attempting to produce the best possible value for the Hubble constant (the number that describes how fast the universe is expanding). His identification of bright objects in distant galaxies as regions of excited hydrogen gas and not bright stars, as Hubble had believed, led to Sandage's estimate that the universe was 13 thousand million years old. His interpretation of other difficult observational data has led him to propose a small positive value for the deceleration parameter, a number describing the rate at which universal expansion is slowing down. In 1960 Sandage discovered a star-like object in the position of the

radio source 3C 48 and later other optical identifications of quasi-stellar sources, better known as quasars, believed to be the most distant objects in the universe. He was also involved in the first identification of a galactic X-ray source. MJS

Sander, August (b. Herdorf an der Sieg, N. Rhine-Westphalia, Germany, 17.11.1876; d. Cologne, West Germany, 20.4.1964). German photographer. Sander's reputation as one of the greatest of all European photographers began to develop only in the 1950s. He studied painting in Dresden, worked as a portrait photographer in Linz, Austria, until 1909 and then moved to Cologne. Around 1910 he began to think of a large-scale ethnographic project 'Man of the Twentieth Century'. Not until 1927 was the scheme actually announced, and in fact it was never fully realized. In 1929 he published 60 of his portraits in *Antlitz der Zeit* (*Face of Our Time*, 1936), which was intended as an introduction to his major project. In 1934 the German authorities seized all available copies of the book, and ordered that the plates should be destroyed. Sander's work was unacceptable in Nazi Germany because in its arrangement it implied that such leaders of civilization as the composer HINDEMITH and the architect Otto Poelzig had evolved from ancestors in folk society. Sander's leaders of modern culture look remarkably self-possessed; in comparison the rest appear archaic, their postures and costumes determined by traditional usages. The encyclopedic scope of Sander's project belonged to the 19c rather than to the 20c; the plain, naturalistic manner of his portraiture also followed earlier examples, although he is usually classified as a New Objectivist, and associated with such artists as DIX. IJ

G. Sander, *August Sander: Photographer Extraordinary* (London, 1973).

Sanger, Frederick (b. Rendcombe, Glos., UK, 13.8.1918). British biochemist. The only person yet to receive two Nobel prizes in the same category (chemistry), Sanger received the first award in 1958 for work begun as a graduate student at Cambridge. Pioneering the experimental procedures, which have since become standard, as he went along, Sanger solved the two-dimensional structure of a protein, insulin (i.e. the order in which amino-acid molecules are strung together to form the larger macromolecule). The research confirmed the peptide theory of protein structure, and also changed attitudes to biological research by showing that at least some complex biological phenomena may be studied by reducing them to their component, chemical parts, thereby helping launch the field of molecular biology. Sanger then extended the art of sequencing to other macromolecules, first developing the 'fingerprinting' technique of separating RNA, the genetic messenger molecule, into its components to help determine its structure. This contributed substantially to the 'breaking' of the genetic code. Subsequently Sanger developed means of sequencing DNA, the genes themselves, for which he shared his second Nobel prize in 1980. This work is essential to understanding how genes are controlled, and also lays the groundwork for modern genetic engineering. Sanger has carried out his research at Cambridge continuously since his postgraduate years. DOM

Santayana, George (b. Madrid, Spain, 16.12.1863; d. Rome, Italy, 26.9.1952). American philosopher. Child of a Spanish father and an American mother, Santayana was brought to the USA when very young, receiving a proper Bostonian education that wound up at Harvard. It never managed to Americanize him, for he always kept his distance from the culture of the USA, observed its youthful crudity with a measure of genial contempt and after 23 years as a professor at Harvard departed for good for Europe in 1912 as soon as he could afford to do so. He spent the years of WW1 in England, for the most part in Oxford, and in 1924 settled in Rome for the remaining years of his life, from WW2 onwards as the permanent guest of a community of nuns. Santayana was never purely a philosopher. He wrote poems, an excellent bestselling novel *The Last Puritan* (London, 1935) and a great deal of admirable literary criticism. These writings were informed by his philosophy just as his philosophy was never exclusively technical but involved with the rest of culture. If he was, as some would disparagingly say, a literary philosopher, he was at any rate a fine stylist and a profoundly civilized thinker. His general outlook is naturalistic. He regarded the transcendental claims of religion and of the German idealistic philosophy which supplied the 19c with a diluted alternative to theistic supernaturalism as infantile superstitions. Human beings are natural objects, rooted in a world of material things. But if neither in fact nor as a possibility purely spiritual beings, men can pursue ideals and sustain civilization. Santayana despised idealism and Germany, its spiritual home, but was devoted to Christianity as an institution, in particular Catholic Christianity, so long as the doctrines were only credited as expressions of a noncredulous cosmic piety. Santayana was generally sceptical about knowledge, holding that belief in the external world rests on an act of 'animal faith'. *Scepticism and Animal Faith* (London, 1923) conveys better than any other volume the essence of his philosophy. His political conservatism also has a sceptical foundation. Santayana left no school, but like Montaigne he is likely to be read long after his more arduous and pedantic contemporaries are forgotten. Santayana's earlier philosophical position was set out in the four volumes of *The Life of Reason* (London, 1905–6); the later philosophy of *Scepticism and Animal Faith* was developed in another four-volume work *Realms of Being* (London, 1928–40). AQ

T. Sprigge, *Santayana, an Examination of his Philosophy* (London, 1974).

Sapir, Edward (b. Lauenberg, Schleswig-Holstein, Germany, 26.1.1881; d. New Haven, Conn., USA, 4.2.1939). American linguist. After emigrating to the USA with his parents at the age of five, he graduated from Columbia University in 1904. His early work was on Germanic languages, but as a young graduate student he was inspired by the anthropologist BOAS to work on American Indian languages, in which he rapidly made a reputation as an expert. He spent 15 years based on Ottawa, during which he produced works of major importance on Nootka and other Canadian Indian languages. In 1925 he moved to the University of Chicago, and then in 1931 became professor in anthropology and linguistics at Yale, where he remained until his death. As a scholar he was equally respected by linguists and anthropologists, and wrote numerous articles and monographs relevant to both fields on an extraordinarily wide range of topics. His one book *Language* (NY, 1921) was intended for a general audience and is both clear and stimulating – though it contains several ideas which he later changed or developed more fully. In that book, and elsewhere, he expressed his conviction that language was primarily a social phenomenon which must be dealt with within its cultural context. He repeatedly stressed the interdependence of language and culture: on the one hand speech must be studied within its social setting, and on the other language is a guide to 'social reality', since 'the real world is to a large extent unconsciously built up on the language habits of the group'. He emphasized the interplay of elements within language, and considered the formal organization of linguistic units to be more important than their physical reality. He regarded physical description as a mere mechanical preliminary to the discovery of underlying patterns and relations which were likely to have 'psychological reality' in the minds of the speakers. After his death a selection from his work was published as *Selected Writings in Language, Culture and Personality* (ed. D. G. Mandelbaum, Berkeley, Calif., 1949).   JMA

Sargent, John (b. London, UK, 27.12.1888; d. London, 16.2.1972). British educator. After graduating at Oxford Sargent taught in schools and was an inspector before becoming director of education at Southend-on-Sea (1927) and then for Essex (1931). In 1938 he went to Delhi as educational commissioner, a post which enabled him to influence educational progress and planning throughout the subcontinent, mainly because of his firm links with M. GANDHI. The latter's scheme of basic

education for villages, and for the spread of low-level schooling as a first necessity, was blended with Sargent's sponsorship for centres of excellence and for the development of modern and technological education. Plans jointly drawn up before independence in 1947 (unofficially known as 'the Sargent Plan') carefully mapped out developmental stages over the next 40 years. Though criticized at the time as too slow-moving, they are still far from being fulfilled, and their main lines have proved to be soundly based. They have helped the new republic to establish practical priorities, and their recommendations have been widely influential in other developing countries. In 1953 Sargent became warden of Missenden Abbey Adult Education College, but maintained ties with India as an examiner of (mainly Indian) higher degree students of London University, who still quote his *Society, Schools and Progress in India* (Oxford, 1968). His professional contribution to Indian educational development was greatly enhanced by the respect for Indian initiatives which he invariably displayed.   EJK

Sarnoff, David (b. Uzlian, Minsk, Russia, 27.2.1891; d. New York, USA, 12.12.1971). American communications entrepreneur. Sarnoff, a largely self-taught Jewish immigrant from Russia, was perhaps the key figure in the shaping of the modern broadcast and communications system in the USA, where he was taken by his family in 1900. First at American Marconi and then at RCA (of which he was chairman for 20 years from 1949 until his retirement), Sarnoff was involved with the whole history of 20c communication systems from marine telegraphy, through radio to television. Although he tended to surround himself with flattering publicity (such as the myth that he picked up messages from the sinking *Titanic*), his achievements were real. He was not an engineer and never held a single patent, but he had a crucial flair for foreseeing and shaping the application of the new electronic technology, starting with his famous pioneering definition of the new social phenomenon of broadcasting as early as 1916.   RPA

C. Dreher, *Sarnoff: an American Success* (NY, 1977).

Sarton, George Alfred Léon (b. Ghent, E. Flanders, Belgium, 31.8.1884; naturalized American citizen, 1924; d. Cambridge, Mass., USA, 22.3.1956). Belgian/American historian of science, Sarton was exiled to the USA in 1915. Educated in philosophy and the natural sciences, he embarked in his 20s on a single-minded mission to make the history of science into an articulate discipline, believing that this would provide a history of human thought and a better understanding of the nature of man. He succeeded in building the discipline's infrastructure: already in 1912 he had founded *Isis*, still the major journal in the subject; in the USA he created a learned society and established the subject's identity and its claim to a place in universities. All this was intended to be preliminary to achieving the 'new humanism', a holistic and all-embracing synthesis based on appreciation of science in history. He began an ambitious *Introduction to the History of Science* (3 vols, Baltimore, 1927–48), which only reached the third volume and the year 1400; it has been called an 'inspired dictionary'. As a propagandist for an idealized view of science, he launched his subject on a path which diverged from mainstream analytical history. Sarton's legacy, in addition to the subject's professional identity, lay primarily in his bibliographies, documentation and fact-finding (15 books, over 300 articles and notes, and 79 critical bibliographies). His working life was financed by the Carnegie Institution and spent at Harvard.   MMG

Memorial issue of *Isis*, 49 (1957).

Sartre, Jean-Paul (b. Paris, France, 21.6.1905; d. Paris, 15.4.1980). French philosopher, novelist, dramatist and critic. The best-known French thinker of the early postwar years, Sartre was the most Parisian of philosophers even though he was the nephew of Albert SCHWEITZER, the Alsatian theologian, and drew most of his inspiration from German sources. He graduated from the Ecole Normale Supérieure in 1929 and between 1931 and 1945 served as a *lycée*

teacher, apart from a period as soldier and prisoner of war in 1940. Le Havre, one of the places where he taught, appears, lightly disguised, in his first and best novel *La Nausée* (Paris, 1938; London, 1948, tr. R. Baldick, *Nausea*, Harmondsworth, 1965). Between 1936 and 1940 he published three monographs on the imagination and the emotions in the phenomenological style of HUSSERL, and then in 1943 his chief philosophical work *L'Etre et le néant* (Paris; tr. H. E. Barnes, *Being and Nothingness*, NY, 1956) was published. By the end of WW2 Sartre had emerged as the leading figure in French existentialism and, as often happens to French philosophers (Voltaire and BERGSON, for example), had become the acknowledged general intellectual authority of the period. Editor of an influential review *Les Temps Modernes*, novelist, dramatist, metaphysical literary critic and political ideologist, he preserved his ascendancy until the 1960s and the replacement of his style of thought by structuralism. Politically indifferent until WW2, according to Simone de BEAUVOIR, he was politicized by his experiences of the resistance movement and soon declared himself as a not uncritical but always immovably loyal ally of the Communist party. In his last philosophical work proper, *Critique de la raison dialectique* (Paris, 1960; tr. A. M. Sheridan-Smith, *Critique of Dialectical Reason*, London, 1976), the attempt to reconcile the unmitigated individualism of his original existentialist position with MARXian collectivism is rendered impenetrably obscure by the incompatibility of the two things he is trying to bring together. That original position is novel only in being a French transcription of the ideas of HEIDEGGER. The latter's *Dasein* is Sartre's *le pour-soi*, both being the characteristic style of existence of the human individual, an emptiness or 'negativity' that has to be given content by free, indeed arbitrary, acts of choice. Where *Dasein* is revealed to Germans by anxiety, dread and the fear of annihilation, the *pour-soi* of the French becomes aware of its nature by way of boredom and disgust, fed by such things as the waiterish activity of waiters in cafés (Sartre's usual habitat).

Man, Sartre says, brings nothingness into the world with him, a melodramatic way of saying that he can conceive of himself and the world as being different from what they are. Acting by choice and not instinct, he is free, and is at any moment a system of projects directed towards the future. Recognition of the existence of other human individuals arouses shame and guilt. In sexual love, even more than in other human relationships, the goal is possession and domination of the other. This glum conviction is not easy to square with the philanthropic notion of 'working-class solidarity' that is the recurring theme of Marxist uplift. AQ

A. Manser, *Sartre: a Philosophic Study* (London, ²1967).

Sartre's novels and plays are inseparable from his philosophical and political writings but are never subordinate to them. The *Chemins de la liberté* [Roads to freedom] trilogy (*L'Age de raison*, Paris, 1945; tr. E. Sutton, *The Age of Reason*, London, 1947; *Le Sursis*, Paris, 1945; tr. E. Sutton, *The Reprieve*, London, 1947; *La Mort dans l'âme*, Paris, 1949; tr. G. Hopkins, *Iron in the Soul*, London, 1950) reflects the politicizing effect of his captivity in WW2 and begins to move away from the individualism of *La Nausée* and *L'Etre et le néant* to the contention that the freedom to which man is condemned can only be realized in political commitment and action. A similar evolution towards an overtly political stance can be seen in the sequence of plays from *Les Mouches* (Paris, 1943; tr. S. Gilbert, *The Flies*, London, 1946) to *Les Séquestres d'Altona* (Paris, 1959; tr. S. & G. Leeson, *Loser Wins*, London, 1960) which are so many demonstrations that man chooses his actions but does so in a situation that is not of his choosing or making. A dialectic between choice and situation governs all of Sartre's literary criticism, from *Qu'est-ce que la littérature?* (Paris, 1947; tr. B. Frechtman, *What is Literature?*, London, 1950) to *L'Idiot de la famille* (vols 1 & 2, Paris, 1971, vol. 3, Paris, 1972; tr. C. Gosman, *The Family Idiot*, vol. 1, Chicago, 1981), a massive but unfinished study of Flaubert which combines the 'existentialist psychoanalysis' of *Saint Genet, comédien et martyr* (Paris, 1952; tr. B. Frechtman, *Saint Genet, Actor and Martyr*, London, 1964) with the theoretical innovations of *Critique de la raison dialectique* in an attempt to reach a total understanding of a single individual. Sartre consistently refused all official honours, including the Nobel prize for literature which was offered him after the appearance of the autobiographical *Les Mots* (Paris, 1963; tr. B. Frechtman, *The Words*, NY, 1964). DM

R. Aronson, *Jean-Paul Sartre: Philosophy in the World* (London, 1980).

Satie, Erik Alfred Leslie (b. Honfleur, Calvados, France, 17.5.1866; d. Paris, 1.7.1925). French composer. Satie's modest but highly original talent is evident from such early compositions as the three *Gymnopédies* for piano (1888), which evoke the ancient world by means of pure simplicity and monotonous repetition. During the next decade he worked as a café pianist and involved himself with various aesthetic-mystical sects, but in 1898 he retired to an industrial suburb of Paris where he lived in self-imposed poverty for the rest of his life. He began to compose works with bizarre titles, like the *Trois morceaux en forme de poire* [Three pieces in the form of a pear] for two pianos (1903, in fact a set of six pieces), still childlike in their simplicity and utterly unassuming. In 1911, thanks to the efforts of DEBUSSY and RAVEL, he came to wider attention, and his unambitious, mocking stance endeared him to younger contemporary artists: he was 'discovered' by COCTEAU, who ensured that his influence spread to Poulenc and others. His nonchalant neglect of conventional musical values, such as complexity, variety and expressive force, also brought him a posthumous admirer in CAGE. PG

R. Myers, *Erik Satie* (London, 1948); P. D. Templier, *Erik Satie* (London, 1969).

Sauer, Carl Ortwin (b. Warrenton, Mo., USA, 24.12.1889; d. Berkeley, Calif., 18.7.1975). American geographer, regarded as the most prominent US cultural geographer of his generation. A native of the Missouri Ozarks and a

University of Chicago graduate, Sauer was for over 50 years on the Berkeley faculty and built up a distinguished graduate school at the University of California. His research ranged widely in space and time and was marked by a deep concern with the use of the environment in a humane way, and a belief that rural peoples over the centuries had learnt much that contemporary society must not forget. In *Agricultural Origins and Dispersals* (NY, 1952), Sauer presented a synthesis of archaeological knowledge and speculation to argue for new locations where the domestication of plants and animals had already begun. His earliest regional writing was on the Middle West and his reports on the Upper Illinois Valley (1916), the Ozark Highlands (1920) and the Kentucky Pennyroyal (1927) are classics. After moving to California he became fascinated with Baja California and the American Southwest, and began a longstanding research interest in Spanish America, particularly Mexico and the Caribbean, which led to major reports published in the Ibero-Americana series which he founded in 1932 with the anthropologist KROEBER. Sauer made occasional methodological statements on the nature of geography (e.g. the influential *Morphology of Landscape*, Berkeley, Calif., 1925) but he would seem to have regarded them as interruptions to his substantive field studies. In his productive retirement years he published three major books, *The Early Spanish Main* (Berkeley, Calif., 1966), *Northern Mists* (Berkeley, Calif., 1968) and *Sixteenth Century North America: the Land and the People as Seen by the Europeans* (Berkeley, Calif., 1971), each exploring transatlantic contacts and images. He died with a fourth volume on 17c views of the North American environment almost complete.   PH

Saussure, Ferdinand de (b. Geneva, Switzerland, 26.11.1857; d. nr Geneva, 22.2.1913). Swiss linguist, widely regarded as the 'father of modern linguistics'. He is also the inspiration behind the 'structuralist' movement in the social sciences and literary criticism. Born and brought up in Geneva, he studied Indo-European languages at the universities of Leipzig and Berlin. At the age of 21, he published his famous *Mémoire sur le système primitif des voyelles dans les langues indo-européennes* [Memoir on the primitive system of vowels in Indo-European languages] (Leipzig, 1878) which has been called 'the most splendid work of comparative philology ever written'. After several years teaching in Paris, he returned to his native Geneva as a professor in 1891 and remained there until his death. His most famous work *Cours de linguistique générale* (Paris, 1915; tr. W. Baskin, *Course in General Linguistics*, NY, 1959) is a synthesis of several years' lecture notes compiled and published posthumously by his students. It contains, in a somewhat disorganized form, his most important ideas. To him language is a system of signs. A linguistic sign is arbitrary in two senses: first, there is no intrinsic link between the *signifier* (word) and the *signified* (meaning); second, linguistic signs cut up the fabric of the world arbitrarily – they are not merely labels applied to autonomous entities. It follows that any language unit can be defined only in relation to the other units within the system, in terms of its syntagmatic (co-occurrence) relationships and paradigmatic (substitution) relationships with other units. Saussure stressed the dichotomy between *form* (the organization within a system) and *substance* (the physical medium in which the system is realized), regarding form as more important. The interdependence of linguistic units and the distinction between form and substance can be likened to a game of chess: it is the role of each chessman in the system which matters, not the physical substance out of which it is made. As long as each chessman is readily distinguishable from every other one, the game can be played satisfactorily. This emphasis on different roles, irrespective of substance, led to Saussure's well-known dictum that 'in language, there are only differences'. The notion that every item in a system both defines and is defined by all the other items is the essence of structuralism, and is the facet of his thought which has had the most profound effect on later generations. In addition, he made a number of influential methodological distinctions, in particular that between *langue* and *parole* (the communal language system, versus individual manifestations of the system), and *synchronic* and *diachronic* linguistics (the study of a language at a single point in time, which he considered to be primary, versus the study of language change). He also made a number of programmatic statements about the need for developing a general science of signs – suggestions which were belatedly, but intensively followed up by proponents of semiology such as LÉVI-STRAUSS and BARTHES.   JMA

E. F. K. Koerner, *Ferdinand de Saussure: the Origin and Development of his Linguistic Thought in Western Studies of Language* (Braunschweig, 1973); J. Culler, *Saussure* (London, 1976).

Schapiro, Meyer (b. Shavly, Kovno, Russia [now Siauliai, Lithuania, USSR], 23.9.1904). American art historian. Schapiro studied at Columbia University, where he lectured in the department of art history and archaeology from 1929 onwards. From 1965 to 1973 he was professor of the history of art at Columbia. In the 1930s he adopted a MARXist standpoint as in 'Nature of abstract art' (*Marxist Quarterly*, I, 1937), where he discussed postfuturism and 'mechanical abstract' art of the first half of the 20c as an abstract rather than as a causally perceptive apprehension of industrial process. Later he adopted a more eclectic approach when relating the formal and symbolic qualities of works of art to the general sociocultural context. Schapiro's interests are exceptionally catholic and range from 'Romanesque art' (*Selected Papers*, vol. 1, NY, 1977) and 'Late antique, early Christian and medieval art' (*Selected Papers*, vol. 3, London, 1980) to 'Modern art: 19th and 20th centuries' (*Selected Papers*, vol. 2, NY, 1978). He has also written monographs on *Van Gogh* (NY, 1950) and *Cézanne* (NY, 1952).   SOBT

Scharoun, Hans (b. Bremen, Germany, 20.9.1893; d. West Berlin, 25.11.1972). German architect. Scharoun was one of the few figures of stature among the pioneering architects of the 1930s who did not emigrate to the USA during the Nazi period. Not that he was a collaborator – he built nothing larger than a private house between 1933 and 1945. But perhaps because his work contained the highly emotive approach of the expressionists as much as the rationalism of the international style, he was more acceptable to the likes of Albert Speer than were GROPIUS or BREUER. Scharoun trained at the Berlin Polytechnic, and in the years after WW1 joined the avant-garde Ring group. In 1927 he designed part of the Weissenhof estate in Stuttgart at the invitation of MIES VAN DER ROHE, and later he planned the Siemenstadt area outside Berlin. But it was only after WW2 that Scharoun's career began to flourish. His design for the Berlin Philharmonic concert hall (completed 1963) is one of the most dramatic examples of architectural expressionism. It has an astonishing, even alarmingly haphazard, look: restless outlines, and a complicated interplay of interior spaces that recalls the fiery watercolours he painted in his youth. His powerful design for the Staatsbibliothek on a neighbouring site was completed after his death.   DS

Scheler, Max (b. Munich, Bavaria, Germany, 22.8.1874; d. Frankfurt, Hesse, 19.5.1928). German philosopher and sociologist. Scheler studied and taught at Jena and Munich, where he absorbed the phenomenological approach of HUSSERL's disciples. He freelanced from 1910 to 1919 and briefly became a Roman Catholic; thereafter he was professor of philosophy and sociology at Cologne. He combined phenomenology with irrationalism and transcendental idealism, believing that emotions as well as reason can reveal eternal values. His philosophical influence was greatest in Weimar Germany and in France after 1945. Scheler's sociology has outlived his philosophy. Broaching a phenomenology of social sentiments, in *Über Ressentiment und moralisches Werturteil* (Leipzig, 1912; tr. L. Coser, *Ressentiment*, NY, 1961) he agreed with NIETZSCHE that resentment characterized modern culture, but as the result of bourgeois society, not of Christianity. *Die Wissensformen und die Gesellschaft* (Leipzig,

1926; tr. M. S. Frings & K. W. Stikkers, *Problems of a Sociology of Knowledge*, London, 1980) combined sociology of knowledge with philosophical idealism. 'Real factors' determine the historical emergence of 'ideal factors', but not their value. Thus religion is not displaced by scientific truth, as positivism asserts; rather, social change has promoted one truth at the expense of the other. Religious values ranked highest for Scheler, who attacked liberalism and humanitarianism in the name of an aristocratic, hierarchical worldview.   JRT

J. R. Staude, *Max Scheler, an Intellectual Portrait* (NY, 1967).

Schelling, Thomas Cromble (b. Oakland, Calif., USA, 14.4.1921). American strategist. One of a group of strategic analysts working at the US RAND Corporation, Schelling applied game theory to deterrence on the basis of the belief that the break between nuclear and conventional weapons was one of the rare natural distinctions which made it possible to limit war by tacit bargaining. In *The Strategy of Conflict* (Cambridge, Mass., 1960) he put forward the 'theory of interdependent decision': an opponent constrains his adversary through his expectations of the consequences of his own actions. The essence of these tactics is some voluntary but irreversible sacrifice of freedom of choice, resting on the paradox that the power to contain an adversary may depend on the power to bind oneself: that in bargaining weakness is often strength. He suggested that if all-out nuclear attack were prevented by mutual confidence in the certain power of the nuclear deterrent, the stability of that confidence would increase with the number of retaliatory weapons each side possessed – the so-called 'stable-balance' concept. 'Coercive diplomacy' in the nuclear age was the subject of Schelling's *Arms and Influence* (New Haven, 1966). Since the nature of military force has made it increasingly difficult to employ it to secure political objectives, a state must know how to use it to persuade an opponent to concede the issue from fear of the consequences of continued resistance. 'Manipulation of risk' exploits the fact that matters may get out of hand to derive effective results from threats which, if implemented, would prove disastrous for the instigator. For Schelling nuclear planning is planning for a war of 'nerve, of demonstration and of bargaining', not target destruction for local tactical purposes.   JGo

Schiele, Egon (b. Tulin an der Donau, Lower Austria, Austria-Hungary [now Austria], 12.6.1890; d. Vienna, 31.10.1918). Austrian painter. Initially under the influence of KLIMT and the highly decorative style of Viennese art nouveau, Schiele, whose talent emerged while he was still at school, developed a kind of art akin to expressionism and related to that of KOKOSCHKA. Like him, Schiele reached maturity around 1910. Although he painted landscapes and many symbolic figure compositions which expressed a pessimistic view of life, Schiele's chief medium was the coloured drawing and his chief subjects were the self-portrait and the female nude. The fierce eroticism of both verges often on pornography. Schiele's interest in the portrait reflects a concern for the human personality current in Vienna at the time and his obsession with death and decay was shared by many contemporary writers and philosophers in Austria, convinced as they were, not merely of the imminent collapse of the Hapsburg empire but of all European civilization. Schiele died young, a victim of the influenza epidemic that raged throughout the world in 1918. He had not realized his great potential, although he had produced thousands of drawings and scores of paintings of irresistible power and had already emerged as the leader of Viennese modernism in the visual arts.   FPW

F. Whitford, *Egon Schiele* (London, 1981).

Schillebeeckx, Edward (b. Antwerp, Belgium, 12.11.1914). Belgian/Dutch theologian. Flemish by birth he joined the Dominican Order in 1934 and taught in Louvain before moving to Nijmegen in 1957 as professor of theology at the Catholic University. The Roman Catholic church in the Netherlands was the first to put into effect the reforms sanctioned by the Second Vatican Council (1962–5), and he soon became known as the chief theological adviser to the Dutch bishops. Immensely learned, his first books showed his fidelity to Thomism. He became convinced that the doctrine of Christ needed to be entirely rethought on the basis of the results of modern biblical criticism. *Jezus, het verhaal van een levende* (Bloemendaal, 1974; tr. H. Hoskins, *Jesus*, London, 1979), the first volume of a projected trilogy, was suspected of heresy but, after interviewing the author, the Congregation for the Doctrine of the Faith in Rome expressed its satisfaction with the explanations which he gave on the points at issue. The second volume *Gerechtigheid en liefde* (Bloemendaal, 1977; tr. J. Bowden, *Christ*, London, 1980) has not aroused the same controversy. In many shorter essays, however, he tirelessly champions the ideas of those who would like to see further reforms in the Roman Catholic church.   FK

Schlemmer, Oskar (b. Stuttgart, Baden-Württemberg, Germany, 4.9.1888; d. Baden-Baden, 13.4.1943). German artist, theatre researcher, designer and dancer. Schlemmer entered the Bauhaus in Weimar in 1921 as head of the sculpture workshop, the work of which he gradually broadened into the field of theatre research. He viewed the art of the stage as essentially an interplay of space, light, form and colour which obeyed its own laws and which need not rely on the written word, the imitation of nature or even the human actor. In his research he did, however, often introduce the human figure into an abstract stage-space, analysing the effect in mechanical and geometric terms and producing 'dances' such as the *Triadischen Ballett* [Triadic ballet] (Zürich, 1922), performed by masked and padded human figures. Schlemmer also designed sets for the traditional theatre. He described his theories and experiments, which have influenced both modern theatre and dance, in the book *Die Bühne im Bauhaus* (with L. MOHOLY-NAGY, Munich, 1925; *The Theater of the Bauhaus*, Middletown, Conn., 1961). DKP

Schlesinger, Arthur Meier (b. Columbus, Ohio, USA, 15.10.1917). American historian. More than any of his contemporaries, Schlesinger exemplifies the American belief in the immediate relevance of the dialogue between past and present. His work has always been guided by the aim of constructing a history of American liberal politics and political ideas, which the historian in his own time could defend. In *The Age of Jackson* (Boston, Mass., 1945) the Jacksonians appear as an alliance between new democratic forces rising in the West, and an upsurge of democratic sentiment in the East based on the demands of a new working class. Schlesinger implied a historical anticipation of the alliance between labour and agriculture against the self-interested forces of business, which had emerged under Franklin ROOSEVELT in the New Deal. He pursued the theme in his three-volume history *The Age of Roosevelt: the Crisis of the Old Order* (Boston, Mass., 1957), *The Coming of the New Deal* (Boston, Mass., 1959), and *The Politics of Upheaval* (Boston, Mass., 1960), politically committed history, deeply researched and written with a verve that was sure to reach a wide public. Schlesinger's search for America's liberal past led to an attempt to construct a liberal philosophy, worked out in *The Vital Center* (Boston, Mass., 1949), which expressed his antipathy to totalitarianism of both left and right, and a preference for democratic social reform undertaken by a government big enough to restrain the powers of business. Schlesinger's involvement with public life became more explicit when he accepted a post on President KENNEDY's White House staff. After Kennedy's assassination, Schlesinger returned to university life by accepting the Schweitzer chair at the City University of New York. He capitalized on his recent experience to write *A Thousand Days: John F. Kennedy in the White House* (Boston, Mass., 1965) with which he moved from the role of the historian to that of the participant. Some of his revelations raised questions about the proprieties to be observed in writing contemporary history. But Schlesinger was not to be deflected from his commitment to the political life of his own time. The Vietnam war produced *The Bitter Heritage: Vietnam and American Democracy, 1941 –1966* (Boston, Mass., 1967). The abuse of presidential power (that was to culminate in NIXON's disgrace) was traced by Schlesinger in *The Imperial Presidency* (Boston, Mass., 1973). Schlesinger has been keenly aware of the problems of the committed historian. It cannot be said that he has freed himself from a certain predictability. But within the general framework there is always a wealth of detail and incident. He is also concerned with the influence of ideas in shaping public policy, and many of his works reflect this interest.   JRP

M. Cunliffe, 'Arthur M. Schlesinger, Jr' in M. Cunliffe & R. Winks (eds), *Pastmasters: Some Essays on American Historians* (NY, 1969).

Schlick, Moritz (b. Berlin, Germany, 14.4.1882; d. Vienna, Austria, 22.6.1936). German philosopher. Schlick's first university studies were in physics, PLANCK being one of his teachers. He taught at Rostock from 1911 until his move in 1922 to MACH's chair of 'inductive philosophy' at Vienna. There he became the leading initiator of the Vienna circle of logical positivists and remained its head until his murder by a student on the steps of the university library in 1936. Schlick began as a philosopher of science but soon broadened his scope. His *Allgemeine Erkenntnislehre* (Berlin, 1918; tr. A. E. Blumberg, *General Theory of Knowledge*, NY, 1974) is a lucidly and agreeably written treatise which expounds an empiricism much like that of Hume: all knowledge of fact comes from sense experience, all necessary truth is formal or definitional in nature, causality is regular sequence. Soon after Schlick came to Vienna he fell under the spell of WITTGENSTEIN's newly published *Tractatus* (1921). He came to agree with Wittgenstein that, in the latter's words, 'philosophy is not a theory but an activity', namely that of the clarification of meaning. In the spirit of Mach he adopted a phenomenalist account of human knowledge of the external world, holding that it provided everything for which realism could meaningfully ask.

In a more unregenerately metaphysical vein he argued that different observers can communicate only the shareable form, not the ineluctably private content, of their experience.   AQ

V. Kraft, *The Vienna Circle: the Origin of Neo-positivism* (NY, 1953).

Schmidt, Bernhard Voldemar (b. Neissar Island, Estonia, Russia [now Estonia, USSR], 30.3.1879; d. Hamburg, Germany, 1.12.1935). German optician. Schmidt was an imaginative and skilful optician who devised the coma-free optical system called the 'Schmidt telescope' (or camera). After becoming successively a telegraph operator, a photographic retoucher and a worker at an electrical instrument manufacturer's, he took an engineering course and started to make small astronomical mirrors in a private workshop. His work was of fine quality in spite of the loss of his right arm while working with explosives in his youth. In 1926 he joined the Hamburg Observatory in a voluntary capacity, where he was encouraged to undertake the construction of optical equipment, at a time when optical telescopes, refractors or reflectors, could give good star images only over a small region close to the optical axis; further from the axis the images rapidly developed radial, comet-like tails, called comae. In 1929 Schmidt designed and constructed a radically new optical system consisting of a spherical mirror and a correcting plate at its centre of curvature: the classical Schmidt system which is coma-free with good definition over a large field. The system has revolutionized many aspects of astronomical work; it can photograph a large area of the sky at one time, and has important applications in all branches of physics where a fast widefield camera is needed. Many examples of the Schmidt camera now exist, one of the latest being the 48-in UK Schmidt erected recently in Australia.   DEB

A. A. Wachmann, 'From the life of Bernhard Schmidt', *Sky and Telescope*, 15, 4 (1955).

Schmidt, Maarten (b. Groningen, The Netherlands, 28.12.1929; naturalized American citizen). Dutch/American astronomer. Schmidt first photographed the spectrum of a quasar (quasi-stellar object) and correctly interpreted the spectrum as highly red-shifted, indicating that these objects are at enormous distances from our own galaxy. He began his astronomical training at Leiden but emigrated to the USA in 1956 to work at Mt Wilson Observatory and teach at the California Institute of Technology. In 1960 he obtained the spectrum of the optical component of an unusual double radio source, named 3C 273, believed to be a nearby star. He and his collaborator Jesse Greenstein could not understand the spectrum of this object as the spectral lines did not correspond to those normally found in stellar spectra. By 1963 Schmidt realized that he could make sense of the spectrum if the lines had been shifted from much shorter wavelengths. Such a red-shift could be due to the object having a high relative velocity away from the earth or to extreme gravitational effects. Schmidt showed that the gravitational argument could be decisively ruled out and that quasars had recessional velocities a significant fraction of the speed of light, and comparable to or in excess of those of distant galaxies. Because of their relative brightness, this implied that at such distances these objects must be enormously powerful sources of energy and quite unlike any other known objects in the universe. Since 1978 Maarten Schmidt has been director of the Hale Observatory.   MJS

Schmidt-Rottluff, Karl, né Karl Schmidt (b. Rottluff, nr Chemnitz, Saxony, Germany [now East Germany], 1.12.1884; d. West Berlin, 10.8.1976). German expressionist artist. The last survivor of the *Brücke* group. Like his friends KIRCHNER and Heckel, he started painting as a German fauve largely stimulated by NIETZSCHE, then after 1910 began reflecting the new angularity of cubism and the forms and features of African and Pacific art. Like them he was less impressive as a painter than as a graphic artist, producing many splendid woodcuts as well as illustrations and other designs. After 1933 the Nazis treated his work as 'degenerate', and in 1941 forbade him to paint. Following their defeat he joined the staff of the West Berlin Hochschule für Bildende Kunst.   JWMW

W. Grohmann, *Karl Schmidt-Rottluff* (Stuttgart, 1956).

Schnabel, Artur (b. Lipnik, Austria-Hungary [now Lipniki, Poland], 14.4.1882; naturalized American citizen, 1944; d. Axenstein, Schwyz, Switzerland, 15.8.1951). Austrian/American pianist. Schnabel studied the piano in Vienna with Theodor Leschetizky, a great teacher who numbered Paderewski among his pupils. Unlike most pianists of his time, however, Schnabel concentrated not on the virtuoso repertory but on the sonatas and other solo works of Beethoven, Schubert and Brahms. To this music he brought a perfect technique allied to an unusual awareness of musical structure and shaping, so that his performances, though not at all coldly analytical, seemed rather to rediscover the composer's intentions than to add expressive superfluities. His insight was that of a creative artist: he was the composer of three symphonies, a piano concerto and various other works, influenced to some degree by his friend SCHOENBERG, whose music he admired but never played in public. Like Schoenberg, he was driven from Germany by the Nazis and settled in the USA. He made many recordings, which have proved a rewarding study to later pianists unable to benefit from his teaching at first hand. He also published several books, including *Reflections on Music* (Manchester, 1933), *Music and the Line of Most Resistance* (Princeton, 1942) and *My Life and Music* (London, 1961).   PG

C. Saerchinger, *Artur Schnabel* (London, 1957); K. Wolff, *The Teaching of Artur Schnabel* (London, 1972).

Schneider, David Murray (b. New York, USA, 11.11.1918). American anthropologist best known for his contributions to kinship analysis and symbolic anthropology. A student at Cornell and Harvard, he taught at the London School of Economics, at Harvard and at Berkeley before becoming professor at Chicago in 1960. His book (with George Homans) *Marriage, Authority and Final Causes: a Study of Unilateral Cross-Cousin Marriage* (Glencoe, Ill., 1955), a critique of

LÉVI-STRAUSS's *The Elementary Structures of Kinship* (Paris, 1949), prompted a harsh and polemical reply from Rodney Needham (*Structure and Sentiment*, Chicago, 1962) the effect of which was lessened by Lévi-Strauss's rejection of Needham's defence. What was at issue was the problem of whether the structures of societies with positive marriage rules and the structures of societies with preferential marriage rules are of the same order. While the debate has focused largely on kinship and marriage, the underlying issues involve the character of model-building in social anthropology as a whole and bear directly on the positivistic orientation of British social anthropology (see Schneider in M. Banton, ed., *The Relevance of Models for Social Anthropology*, London, 1965). In recent years Schneider, along with V. TURNER and GEERTZ, has been credited with formulating a new approach to the study of culture through emphasizing the symbolic dimension. Schneider's brief *American Kinship: a Cultural Account* (Englewood Cliffs, 1968) reveals a mentalist approach linked to but quite different from structuralism.   SLN

Schnitzler, Arthur (b. Vienna, Austria-Hungary [now Austria], 15.5.1862; d. Vienna, 21.10.1931). Austrian writer. Schnitzler is the chronicler *par excellence* of the Austrian bourgeoisie between 1890 and 1914. Often he has been identified with the world which he recreates in such psychological detail. But this is to overlook the considerable critical astringency of which he is capable. In *Der Weg ins Freie* (Berlin, 1908; tr. H. Samuel, *The Road to the Open*, NY, 1923) and *Professor Bernhardi* (Berlin, 1912; tr. H. Landstone, London, 1927) he offers a remarkable portrait of the uncertainties that plagued the Jews in the anti-Semitic climate of Vienna in the first decade of this century. *Anatol* (Berlin, 1893; tr. H. GRANVILLE BARKER, London, 1911), *Der einsame Weg* (Berlin, 1904; tr. H. Björkman, *The Lonely Way*, Boston, 1904) and *Das weite Land* (Berlin, 1911; tr. T. STOPPARD, *Undiscovered Country*, London, 1979) capture the strange mixture of hedonism and self-deprecating irony, of cynicism and self-righteousness that bedevilled the

sexual mores of the time. And *Leutnant Gustl* (Berlin, 1901; tr. R.L. Simon, *None but the Brave*, NY, 1926) and *Reigen* (Vienna, 1903; tr. F. & J. Marcus, *Merry-Go-Round*, London, 1953) created public scandals: the former because of its hilariously unflattering – yet never simply caricatured – depiction of the attitudes of a young army officer; the latter because it shows, in ten short scenes, a series of sexual encounters between figures from all levels of Viennese society. The critical perspective – above all in respect of linguistic evasion and half-truth – is devastating. But Schnitzler feared – and the 1920 Berlin performance of *Reigen* was to prove him right – that the play could be easily (or wilfully) misunderstood. Schnitzler and FREUD lived and worked in the same city, and the similarity of their outlook has often been remarked. But Schnitzler anchored the sexual attitudes which he uncovered in a precisely observed social setting. He was a master of the techniques of inward narration: *Leutnant Gustl* is the first great interior monologue in European literature.   MWS

M. Swales, *Arthur Schnitzler* (Oxford, 1971).

Schoenberg, Arnold Franz Walter, *né* Schönberg (b. Vienna, Austria-Hungary [now Austria], 13.9.1874; d. Los Angeles, Calif., USA, 13.7.1951). Austrian composer. The inventor of the musical method (some would say language) known as serial composition, Schoenberg remains the most controversial figure in modern music. He was largely self-taught: a respectable though unremarkable String Quartet in D Major (1897) shows the influence of Brahms and Dvořák. However, the musicians who had played the quartet refused to perform his string sextet *Verklärte Nacht* [Transfigured night] (1899) and the audience actually protested when some of his new songs were presented in 1900. For Schoenberg was already moving away from the traditional major–minor key system which until this time had been universally accepted as fundamental to music. He found himself rather like the first atheist in a society of hitherto unquestioning believers. From now onwards, as he himself remarked, 'the scandal never ceased' and every step in his development provoked opposition.

Nevertheless Schoenberg pursued his lonely path with courage. In 1900–1 he sketched out his vast choral-orchestral *Gurrelieder* [Songs of Gurra] (finally completed 1911), the instrumentation of which includes 10 horns and a set of iron chains; in 1901 he also married. Influential people began to notice his music, too. Richard STRAUSS helped to start him on a career as a teacher (his future pupils were to include BERG and WEBERN) and MAHLER also gave him support – without, however, being fully convinced by this new style of music. A publishing contract with Universal Edition from 1909 helped him to reach an international audience, though public response remained largely hostile. Increasingly, he wrote atonally (i.e. without the use of keys) in such pieces as the Second String Quartet (1908), the operatic *Erwartung* [Expectation] (1909) and *Pierrot lunaire* (1912) for voice and five instruments. After 1920 he began to write music in which his by now nontonal methods had evolved into the serial technique, in which a certain order of the 12 notes within an octave was chosen as the basis for each piece. His serial works include the Wind Quintet (1924), the orchestral Variations (1928), the Third and Fourth String Quartets (1927 and 1936) and the Violin Concerto (1936). However, in such later pieces as the *Ode to Napoleon* (1942) for reciter, piano and strings and the Piano Concerto of the same year he re-established a certain contact with tonality; and his Variations for band (1943) are in a straightforward G minor. In fact he was much less doctrinaire about his 'system' than some of his supporters and regarded himself as an artist with a vocation and not a mere intellectual explorer. His unfinished opera *Moses und Aron* (1932), to his own libretto, reveals his deep religious sense. Compelled to leave Germany in 1933, he emigrated to the USA where he spent his remaining years. He was respected there as a teacher but at first neglected as a composer, although that did not stop him from working on further scores. However, from about 1948 he saw the growing acceptance of his music. Its influence on other (mainly young) composers was strong indeed in the decade following 1955; but today we seem rather to be witnessing a slower and more natural integration of his discoveries into a broader-based musical language. Schoenberg's critical and theoretical writings include *Style and Idea* (NY, 1950, ²1975) and *Harmonielehre* (Vienna, 1911, ²1921; *Theory of Harmony*, NY, 1948). CH

C. Rosen, *Schoenberg* (NY, 1975); M. Macdonald, *Schoenberg* (London, 1976).

Scholem, Gerhart Gershom (b. Berlin, Germany, 5.12.1897; d. Jerusalem, Israel, 20.2.1982). German/Israeli historian of ideas. Scholem was born into an assimilated Jewish family. He studied mathematics, physics and Semitic philology at Berlin, Jena and Bern universities. As an adolescent he became interested in Zionism, and through reading the historian Heinrich Graetz and BUBER, in the Kabbala. He learned Hebrew and found that the history of the Kabbala and its sources was almost completely ignored by scholars if not by cranks; for his doctorate at Munich he investigated the origins of the Kabbala, using the university's great collection of Hebrew manuscripts. He collected Kabbalistic manuscripts and books, sought out Hebrew scholars with anything to say on the subject and abandoned phenomenology, taught at Munich by HUSSERL's disciple Pfänder, for Semitics. Encouraged by Buber, the private scholar Robert Eisler, the Aby WARBURG circle in Hamburg and others Scholem became an expert on the Kabbala. He finished his dissertation in 1923 and emigrated to Israel. He was soon appointed to research into the Kabbala at the new Hebrew University (inaugurated in 1925) and was professor of Jewish mysticism from 1933 to 1963. Scholem saw mysticism as amorphous and the mystic as one who conserves and develops the tradition in which he lives, rediscovering the ancient sources and communicating to others his unique 'illuminations' and their transposition into the theology and symbols of his education and guides. Scholem rejected the theory that different religious mysticisms rest on wholly different bases. His historical analyses of various experiences of the divine, their expressions and communication within Jewish tradition, and the resulting conflicts, are major contributions to the history of religions. His important works include *Die jüdische Mystik in ihren Hauptströmungen* (Zürich, 1957; *Major Trends in Jewish Mysticism*, NY, 1954), *Jewish Gnosticism, Merkabah Mysticism, and Talmudic Tradition* (NY, 1960) and *Zur Kabbala und ihrer Symbolik* (Zürich, 1960; *On the Kabbalah and its Symbolism*, NY, 1965). His memoir of his friendship with BENJAMIN, their surviving correspondence, and his account of his education and departure for Eretz Yisrael are major sources for the study of 20c German Jewish intellectual life: *Walter Benjamin: Die Geschichte einer Freundschaft* (Frankfurt, 1975); *Walter Benjamin – Gershom Scholem Briefwechsel, 1933–1940* (Frankfurt, 1980); *Von Berlin nach Jerusalem* (Frankfurt, 1977; *From Berlin to Jerusalem: Memories of my Youth*, NY, 1980). JCu

Schönberg, Arnold, see SCHOENBERG, ARNOLD.

Schottky, Walter Hans (b. Zürich, Switzerland, 23.7.1886; d. Pretzfeld, Bavaria, West Germany, 4.3.1976). German physicist. Schottky was professor of theoretical physics at the University of Rostock from 1923 to 1927, but he spent the remainder of his life in industrial research, working for the Siemens company. Although his doctoral work (1912, under PLANCK) was on special relativity, he devoted most of his career to electronics and to solid-state physics; many effects and devices are named after him. In 1915 he invented the screened-grid valve and in 1918 discovered the superheterodyne principle which is used in radio and television receivers to this day. He worked on the emission of electrons from metallic and oxide cathodes and determined how this could be influenced by the application of an electric field. He was one of the pioneers in studying and explaining the properties of semiconductors and he was one of the earliest researchers (1929) to conceive the idea that a 'hole' could carry charge in a semiconductor – he called this a 'defect electron'. He also contributed to our understanding of the theory of crystal rectifiers and of imperfections in crystals. HMR

Schrödinger, Erwin (b. Vienna, Austria-Hungary [now Austria], 12.8.1887; d. Vienna, 4.1.1961). Austrian theoretical physicist who discovered the wave equation that describes the motion of atomic and nuclear particles at nonrelativistic energies. As a young man, Schrödinger worked on statistical mechanics, magnetism and EINSTEIN's theory of relativity. After hearing of de BROGLIE's ideas on the wave nature of matter he tried to find a quantum mechanical differential equation whose solutions are the de Broglie waves. In his search he was guided by the relation, originally developed by Hamilton, between the wave and geometrical theories of optics. The analogy between the variational formulations of optics and mechanics, together with de Broglie's formula for the wavelength of an electron, gave him the equation he sought, which is named after him. The solutions of this equation for bound electrons give the allowed energy states, and hence the spectroscopic frequencies of atoms, and for free electrons they describe scattering phenomena. Subsequently he showed that his wave mechanics is mathematically identical to the matrix mechanics of BORN and HEISENBERG. Since the Schrödinger equation is easier to handle mathematically, physicists prefer to use wave mechanics. Schrödinger interpreted the absolute square of the wave function as the charge density, but later on Born proposed the probability interpretation. For his work on wave mechanics Schrödinger was awarded the Nobel prize in 1933, jointly with DIRAC. Exiled from Austria during WW2, he took refuge in Dublin where he continued his scientific work and wrote some books notable for their philosophical subtlety: *What is Life?* (Cambridge, 1945), *Space–Time Structure* (Cambridge, 1950), *Science and Humanism* (Cambridge, 1954), *Expanding Universes* (Cambridge, 1956) and *Mind and Matter* (Cambridge, 1958). PEH

Schumacher, Ernst (b. Bonn, N. Rhine-Westphalia, Germany, 16.8.1911; d. Switzerland, 4.9.1977). German economist and conservationist. It was only after a long and distinguished career as an economic adviser, first to the Control Commission in Germany (1946–50), and then to the UK National Coal Board (1950–70), that Schumacher wrote the book whose title was to become a catchphrase to the conservation movement, *Small is Beautiful* (London, 1973). The thesis of the book was not entirely new: he argued that societies should stop seeking economic growth through industries which were energy- and capital-intensive but which marred the environment and ignored the sensibilities and aspirations of the people who worked in them and whose lot they were intended to better. But he was the first to set down the argument with such a sense of compassion and conviction that he was taken seriously by governments as well as by the disenchanted individual. His alternative proposition was to harness the talents of workers and deploy them in small groups – he was not necessarily against doing this in large firms. He asked, too, that rich men's answers should not be applied to poor men's problems, that developing countries should not be weighed down with debt repayments to advanced nations who had loaned money to pay for ill-advised growth. His philosophy bore fruit in the workings of the Intermediate Technology Development Group, which promoted small-scale enterprises in developing countries, and of which he was chairman.   GHD

Schuman, Robert (b. Luxembourg, 29.6.1886; d. Metz, Moselle, France, 4.9.1963). French conservative parliamentarian under the Third Republic (1919–40), MRP deputy (1944–62), prime minister (1947–8), foreign minister (1948–53). His birth in Luxembourg, his conservatism and his conversion towards Catholic liberalism make him almost the archetype of the first generation of 'Europeans'. He was the architect of the approach to European integration which practises functionalism while preaching federalism and which established the main European institu-tions in the years 1949–57. The European Coal and Steel Community founded in 1952 has its origins in the so-called 'Schuman plan', proposals made by him in May 1950 and pushed to completion against British opposition with American support; his was the political drive, but the proposals themselves were the work of MONNET. DCW

Schumpeter, Joseph Alois (b. Triesch, Moravia, Austria-Hungary [now Czechoslovakia], 8.2.1883; naturalized American citizen; d. Taconic, Conn., USA, 8.1.1950). Austrian/American economist who migrated to the USA in 1932. Apart from a short period in business and politics following WW1 (he became minister of finance in Austria's first Republican government in 1919), Schumpeter committed himself to rigorous academic research and teaching. He was educated at the University of Vienna, then a leading centre for economics, and became successively professor at Graz (1911), Bonn (1925) und Harvard (1932). The first of his 17 books *Das Wesen and Hauptinhalt der theoretischen Nationalökonomie* [The being and essence of the theoreticians of the national economy] (Leipzig, 1908) was a scholarly monograph on economic methodology; the last, a monumental *History of Economic Analysis* (NY, 1954), almost complete when he died, was edited by his wife Elizabeth Boody, herself a distinguished economic historian. Schumpeter's major contribution lay in his theory of economic development originally outlined in *Theorie der wirtschaftlichen Entwicklung* (Leipzig, 1912; *The Theory of Economic Development*, Cambridge, Mass., 1951). It broke with all previous theories of capitalist economic development by explaining economic growth and its fluctuations as part of a coherent dynamic process in which economic forces were the strategic variables. For Schumpeter innovation by the profit-maximizing capitalist entrepreneur was the key to productivity growth: the clustering of innovations initiated by the imaginative few explained recurrent booms in economic activity; and overproduction caused by the rush of less gifted entrepreneurs to imitate successful innovations explained the downturns in prices, profits and investment associated with slumps. In the 1920s and 1930s Schumpeter elaborated and gave empirical content to this system of ideas. His *Business Cycles* (2 vols, NY, 1939) applied a unique mixture of theoretical, historical, quantitative and comparative techniques of analysis to explain growth and fluctuations in the USA, Germany and UK from the late 18c to the 20c. In *Capitalism, Socialism and Democracy* (NY, 1942) he brought in sociological and political ideas to analyse the impact of recent changes in the structure of business organization on the nature of the economic development process for the mixed capitalist economy.   PMD

S. E. Harris (ed.), *Schumpeter: Social Scientist* (Cambridge, Mass., 1951).

Schutz, Alfred (b. Vienna, Austria-Hungary [now Austria], 13.4.1899; naturalized American citizen; d. New York, USA, 20.5.1959). Austrian/American social philosopher. Schutz worked as a private scholar while following a banking career in Vienna and, after 1939, in New York, until appointed professor at the New School of Social Research there in 1952. In *Der sinnhafte Aufbau der sozialen Welt* (Vienna, 1932; tr. G. Walsh & F. Lehnert, *The Phenomenology of the Social World*, London, 1967) he used HUSSERL's phenomenology to provide a philosophical basis for Max WEBER's 'interpretative (*verstehende*) sociology', in opposition to the positivism and behaviourism of the Vienna circle. In the USA, influenced by G. H. MEAD, he reversed his Husserlian view that the individual is prior to society and founded a distinct phenomenological sociology (see his *Collected Papers*, 3 vols, The Hague, 1962–6). Because of the dominance of positivism in American sociology until the 1960s, he was acclaimed only posthumously. Schutz's main ideas – that social science must begin by describing the commonsense assumptions with which people construct and interpret their social existence, and that the sociologist is a part of whatever he investigates – converged with the later views of WITTGENSTEIN. Together they have also influenced ethno-

methodology and the critical theory of HABERMAS.   JRT

H. R. Wagner (ed.), *Alfred Schutz on Phenomenology and Social Relations* (Chicago, 1970).

Schwarzschild, Karl (b. Frankfurt, Hesse, Germany, 9.10.1873; d. Potsdam [now East Germany], 11.5.1916). German astronomer. Schwarzschild is best remembered for work he did not live to see appreciated: his contribution to the study of black holes, following his work on EINSTEIN's general theory of relativity. At an early age Schwarzschild displayed a remarkable aptitude for mathematics, publishing two papers on the mathematical deduction of double star orbits from only three observations. Alongside mathematics, astronomy was his great love and the subject he chose for a profession. In 1909 he became director of the Astrophysical Observatory at Potsdam, where he remained until his early death in 1916.

Of the three main contributions Schwarzschild made to astronomy, the first was in measuring the apparent magnitudes or brightnesses of stars, photographically calibrating photographic exposures in order to place star magnitudes on to an absolute scale. This work involved painstaking observational surveys of thousands of stars. Then Schwarzschild examined the motions of stars with respect to the sun and developed a mathematical model to simplify the apparent chaos of those motions. Perhaps more important in hindsight was his work on heat flow and thermodynamics in the solar interior, leading to his theory of radiative equilibrium, published in 1906: he showed that in any element of the solar material as much radiation must be absorbed by the material as is radiated, thereby being in equilibrium and demonstrating that transfer of energy through the mass of the sun is carried out by radiation. During military service in WW1, Schwarzschild contracted a disease that proved fatal. In his last few months he studied Einstein's newly published general theory of relativity. He had already worked on some of the physical consequences of special relativity and his contribution to general relativity lay in his formulation of the concept that a massive body must have a radius greater than some critical radius in order for light to be able to leave that body. If the mass is compressed to within that critical radius then the object cannot be seen, it is a black hole. In recent years, when black holes have been studied intensively, that critical radius has been named the Schwarzschild radius.   MJS

Schwarzschild, Martin (b. Potsdam, Germany [now East Germany], 31.5.1912; naturalized American citizen, 1938). German/American astronomer. The son of Karl SCHWARZSCHILD, Martin emigrated to the USA from Nazi Germany in 1937 and in 1947 became Higgins professor of astronomy at Princeton. Working with SANDAGE, by 1952 Schwarzschild had developed the key concept about what happens to a star when it has exhausted the main supply of hydrogen fuel in its hot central core, where hydrogen is fused into helium. Using the latest results from nuclear research, the two developed models showing that after hydrogen burning in the core a shell of burning hydrogen surrounding the core continues to fuel the star while the core itself collapses gravitationally, thereby releasing more energy. At this stage the star rapidly expands and cools to become a red giant star. This work was a key to further understanding of stellar evolution. Schwarzschild continued his development of the work with HOYLE and later with Härm, showing that the helium in the core would ignite suddenly in what is called the helium flash. His *The Structure and Evolution of the Stars* (Princeton, 1958) remains the classic text on this subject. Schwarzschild then returned to a problem he had been interested in earlier in his career, that of convection and turbulence in the outer envelope of a star. He was especially interested in the observable effects in the sun due to turbulence, the phenomenon of granulation in the sun's surface layers. To study this transient result of underlying motions he pioneered high-altitude unmanned balloon observations which were later extended for other astronomical work. His lively and inquiring approach to the subject led Schwarzschild into studies of galaxies and their evolution and many other aspects of astronomy.   MJS

Schweitzer, Albert (b. Kaysersberg, Alsace, Germany [now France], 14.1.1875; d. Lambaréné, French Equatorial Africa [now Gabon Republic], 4.9.1965). German theologian, physician, musician and moralist whom many would rank among the most inspiring figures of the 20c. While a lecturer at Strassburg University he published *Das Messianitäts- und Leidensgeheimnis* (Tübingen, 1901; tr. W. Lowrie, *The Mystery of the Kingdom of God*, London, 1925), in which he first presented the thesis that the teaching of Jesus was dominated by contemporary Jewish apocalyptic ideas about the imminence of the end of the world. This theory was restated in his best-known book *Von Reimarus zu Wrede* (Tübingen, 1906; tr. W. Montgomery, *The Quest of the Historical Jesus*, London, 1910), which drew the conclusion that when seen in true historical perspective Jesus is an enigma to the modern mind. Schweitzer's subsequent theological work was principally devoted to the study of St Paul – *Die Mystik des Apostels Paulus* (Tübingen, 1930; tr. W. Montgomery, *The Mysticism of Paul the Apostle*, London, 1931) – though long before the appearance of this book he had given up academic teaching in order to train as a medical missionary. Taking his medical doctorate in 1913, he settled at Lambarene in French Equatorial Africa, which was to remain the scene of his life's achievement. Nevertheless he frequently travelled abroad to lecture and to give organ recitals, being an accomplished performer. He had a deep knowledge of the music of J. S. Bach, exemplified in his *J. S. Bach, le musicien-poète* (Paris, 1905; tr. E. Newman, 2 vols, London, 1911, ²1938), a musicological classic, if somewhat romantically mystical in its interpretation of the composer. His later theological views were markedly liberal – theistic with a strong humanitarianism popularized in the slogan 'Reverence for life' (see *Strassburger Predigten*, Munich, 1960; tr. R. H. Fuller, *Reverence for Life*, London, 1970). Schweitzer was awarded the Nobel Peace prize in 1952.

He wrote an autobiographical account *Aus meinem Leben und Denken* (Leipzig, 1931; tr. C. T. Campion, *My Life and Thought*, London, 1933). BMGR

O. Kraus, *Albert Schweitzer: his Work and his Philosophy* (London, 1944); G. McKnight, *Verdict on Schweitzer* (London, 1964).

Schweizer, Eduard (b. Basle, Switzerland, 18.4.1913). Swiss New Testament scholar. After studying at the universities of Marburg, Basle and Zürich and after a period as a minister in the Swiss Reformed church (1936–46), Schweizer held chairs at the University of Mainz (1946–9) and at the University of Zürich (1949–78). Many of his most important articles examined New Testament words and phrases against their Hellenistic and Jewish background, but his primary concern has always been the theological ideas of the New Testament writers. His articles in the *Theologisches Wörterbuch zum Neuen Testament* (Stuttgart, 1959–73; tr. G. Bromiley, *Theological Dictionary of the New Testament*, Grand Rapids, Mich., 1968–74) have had a considerable influence on subsequent scholarly discussion. His published writings – for example, *Gemeinde und Gemeindeordnung im Neuen Testament* (Zürich, 1959; tr. F. Clarke, *Church Order in the New Testament*, London, 1961); and *Jesus Christus* (Münich, 1968; tr. D. E. Green, *Jesus*, London, 1971) – are all marked by a concern to take the New Testament seriously as a set of 1c documents and to study them as thoroughly and as critically as possible before attempting to make their main theological ideas intelligible to modern man. Schweizer stresses the importance of the religious experience of the Spirit in the early Christian communities. He has studiously avoided close association with any one school of interpretation, but it is possible to trace in his writings the influence of his teachers, Emil Brunner, BULTMANN and Karl BARTH, the three most influential modern theologians. His influence on theological thought has probably been even greater in the English-speaking world than in Switzerland or Germany. GNS

Schwitters, Kurt (b. Hanover, Lower Saxony, Germany, 20.6.1887; d. Kendal, Cumbria, UK, 8.1.1948). German artist, poet and sculptor. In 1919 he founded the first dada group in Hanover. But unlike most dadaists Schwitters's ambition was not to create artistic anarchy; he wanted to build a new art out of the rubble of the old. He became the first great master of collage, making art out of society's waste – used bus tickets, cigarette packets, stamps and envelopes. By using recycled materials Schwitters ensured that his collages would appear completely different from the prewar collages made by PICASSO and the cubists, which were primarily aesthetic experiments. Schwitters invented the word '*Merz*' to describe his collages – he found the word by chance while using the letterhead of the Kommerz-und-Privatsbank. Neither the irony of its origins nor its meaning in spoken French were lost on him. Unlike most dada artists he never went on to become a surrealist, for his interests lay neither in the exploration of the psyche nor in the making of protest art. In fact he often revealed himself throughout his career to be more traditionalist than nihilist, for example, in painting academic landscapes and portraits. In the *Merz* collages he searched for and found a highly original and profound pictorial beauty. In the early 1920s, contemporaneously with his best collages, Schwitters also began similar experiments with language. His '*Sonate in Urlaute*', a pioneering sound-collage, was recited at the Bauhaus in 1924. Also at this time he made his first *Merzbau*. Using more of society's waste he turned his house into a piece of sculpture by building caves, secret grottoes and tunnels in the rooms and corridors. The Nazis declared his work degenerate in 1937 and he was forced to flee, first to Norway and then, in 1940, to the UK where he lived and died in almost total obscurity. WJ

Sciascia, Leonardo (b. Recalmuto, Sicily, Italy, 8.1.1921). Italian novelist and essayist. A highly individual writer belonging to an illustrious tradition of *meridionalisti*, focusing on the social, cultural and ultimately political problems of the Italian South. His characteristic mode is the investigation, sometimes factual as in *L'affaire Moro* [The Moro affair] (1978), sometimes 'fictional' (*Il giorno della civetta*, Turin, 1961; tr. A. Colquhoun, *Mafia Vendetta*, London, 1963; *A ciascuno il suo*, Turin, 1966; tr. A. Foulke, *A Man's Blessing*, London, 1969; *Il contesto*, Turin, 1971; tr. A. Foulke, *Equal Danger*, London, 1974), but always rooted in the fertile soil of public corruption. This central concern, suggested initially by the Mafia-dominated life of the South, Sciascia has long recognized as an insidious, all-pervading malady at the heart of any society which is organized primarily for the production of wealth and power for the few. Writing very much in the tradition of Voltaire and the Enlightenment, Sciascia employs a searing irony, a biting wit in his continual exposures of criminality masquerading as legality, in his dogged refusal to compromise his rationalistic humanity with any form of equivocation or ambiguity. In his writing, the defeat of an individual whose culture is also a social vision, not merely a form of self-indulgence, always represents the defeat of what is best in man; yet in Sciascia's life and work it is that which persists to challenge a formidable, impersonal, machine-like corruption which in the last analysis is the system, the state. ADT

G. W. Slowey, 'Sciascia's *Il giorno della civetta*', *Journal of the Association of Teachers of Italian*, 27 (Spring 1979), 50–9; G. Jackson, *Sciascia: a Thematic and Structural Study, 1956–76* (Ravenna, 1981).

Scott, Charles Prestwich (b. Bath, Avon, UK, 26.10.1846; d. Manchester, 1.1.1932). British journalist. Scott's greatest achievement was to turn a provincial daily newspaper into a national, even a world, force for liberalism without alienating his largely provincial 'bourgeois' audience. The *Manchester Guardian*, described by Brendan Bracken, CHURCHILL's wartime minister of information, as 'the greatest viewspaper in the world', was founded as a weekly in 1821 and did not become a daily until 1855. Only when Scott had been appointed editor in 1872, at the age of 25, did the quality of his editorials on Liberal politics win the paper much attention outside its home city. First, Scott increased the recruitment of authoritative 'specialist' writers from the new local university in order to appeal to enlightened opinion everywhere as well as to that of the new 'foreigners' of Manchester – the German, Greek, Armenian and Jewish refugees who had brought cultured tastes as well as business acumen to their new home. Second, he divided the editorship to leave himself free to pursue Liberal party leaders and formulate policy, while C. E. Montague, his chief assistant, remained in Manchester to supply the day-to-day needs of the paper. Scott became as important to LLOYD GEORGE as Stead had been to Gladstone, while 'the Guardian school of writers' was nurturing such names as J. L. Hammond, Kingsley MARTIN and Malcolm Muggeridge, as well as Howard Spring and Neville Cardus. Scott cared passionately for the ends for which he fought – among them Irish freedom, women's suffrage, Zionism and opposition to the Boer war, 'the best thing the MG has done in my time' (Scott to Lloyd George, 8.4.1930). Throughout his career he firmly disdained any form of journalism which might be thought manipulative rather than persuasively informative ('Comment is free: facts are sacred'). RB

J. L. Hammond, *C. P. Scott* (London, 1934); D. Ayerst, *Guardian: Biography of a Newspaper* (London, 1971).

Scriabin, Alexandr Nikolayevich (b. Moscow, Russia, 6.1.1872; d. Moscow, 27.4.1915). Russian composer. Scriabin began his career as a composer-pianist, following in the footsteps of Chopin and Liszt. The great bulk of his output is piano music, and it is on this that his reputation rests. It includes 10 piano sonatas (1892–1913), an early concerto, and many preludes and other short pieces still widely played today. From 1903 his style became more individual; by 1907, when he composed his orchestral *Le poème de l'extase* [Poem of ecstasy], it was thoroughly eccentric, drawing on complex harmonies and bounding, wayward developments, all at the service of mystical notions derived from theosophy. His later works, includ-

691

ing *Prometheus* for orchestra with chorus and the projection of colours on to a screen (1911), were preparatory exercises for a final 'Mystery' of which only sketches were ever written. This was to unite all the arts and, with the composer himself as messiah, lead the human race on to a new spiritual plane.

PG

H. Macdonald, *Skryabin* (London, 1978).

Seaborg, Glenn Theodore (b. Ishpeming, Mich., USA, 19.4.1912). American chemist. Seaborg played a vital role in the discovery of nine of the 14 actinide elements. He was an undergraduate at UCLA and studied for his doctorate under G. N. LEWIS at Berkeley. In 1937 he became Lewis's assistant for two years, and in 1939 began work upon the radiochemical identification of radio-isotopes of common elements produced in E. O. LAWRENCE's cyclotron. In 1940, in collaboration with E. M. MCMILLAN, Kennedy and Wall, Seaborg prepared a new isotope of neptunium (Np^{238}) by bombarding uranium-238 with deuterons (isotopes of hydrogen). This decayed to give an isotope of a new element, plutonium-238 (named for the planet two beyond Uranus), of atomic number 94. The high fissionable plutonium-239 was identified in 1941 as a decay product of neptunium-239: this discovery culminated in the destruction of Hiroshima and Nagasaki. Many more man-made transuranium elements were to be identified, isolated and studied by Seaborg and his group (elements 95–102, inclusive) in the following two decades. In 1944 Seaborg recognized that the 14 elements from actinium (No. 89) onwards to element 102 (not then known) formed a new series of transition metals within the periodic table, electronically similar to the lanthanides. He christened them the actinides. In 1951, jointly with McMillan, Seaborg was awarded the Nobel prize for chemistry for his work on the transuranium elements (see *Man-made Transuranium Elements*, Princeton, 1963). From 1961 to 1971 he was chairman of the United States Atomic Energy Commission, whence he returned to a chair at Berkeley.

KRS

Seeckt, Hans von (b. Schleswig, Schleswig-Holstein, Germany, 22.4.1866; d. Berlin, 27.12.1936). German soldier. As chief of army command (1920–6), it fell to Seeckt to preserve the continuity of the German army after its defeat in 1918 and under the terms of the Versailles settlement, which restricted the Reichswehr to 100,000 men. His aims were a well-disciplined army, faithful to Prussian traditions and loyal to himself. He achieved them by prohibiting soldiers from engaging in any political activity – he described parliament as 'the cancer of our time' – and by controlling the selection of officers to produce an elite corps with high educational attainments, 95 per cent of which came from the same restricted aristocratic and military backgrounds as had the Imperial officer corps. He vigorously pursued covert rearmament, using paramilitary units to supplement the army and after 1922 cooperating with Russia in experimenting with tanks, gas and paratroops – all forbidden to Germany under the Versailles settlement. Seeckt's own political ambitions may have encouraged him to base the Reichswehr on obedience alone and not on any ideals of the state; he refused in 1920 and in 1923 to choose between the Weimar republic and its enemies on the right, and probably sought the presidency, which went to Hindenburg in 1925. He has often been blamed for leaving the army unduly vulnerable to HITLER's manipulations, though this underrates the careful calculations made in 1933 by some at least of Hitler's future generals.

JGo/DCW

J. W. Wheeler-Bennett, *The Nemesis of Power: the German Army in Politics, 1918–45* (London, ²1964); F. L. Carsten, *Reichswehr and Politics, 1918–1933* (Oxford, 1966).

Seferis, George, ps. of Georgios Seferiades (b. Smyrna, Ottoman Empire [now Izmir, Turkey], 13.3.1900; d. Athens, Greece, 20.9.1971). Greek poet, critic and diplomat. Born in the cosmopolitan city of Smyrna, Seferis left his homeland in 1914, shortly before the massacres of 1922–3 in which the Christian minority was expelled from Turkey to be exchanged with the Muslim minority of

Greece. Seferis took up residence in Athens, and between 1918 and 1924 studied law and literature in Paris. In 1926 he embarked on the diplomatic career that took him to England, Albania, South Africa, Egypt and Turkey, culminating in his appointment as Greek ambassador in London (1957–62).

Seferis began writing poetry in the 1920s, and his first collection, influenced by French symbolism, appeared in Athens in 1931. A decisive influence after that was the poetry and ideas of T. S. ELIOT, whose work he translated into Greek. In adapting Eliot's ideas on myth and tradition, in particular, to his personal experiences as a Greek and to the Greek tradition, he created a poetic voice whose impact among Greek speakers has surpassed even that of Eliot in the English-speaking world. Taut and often deeply pessimistic, his poetry frequently however affirms a faith in the power of 'myth' or 'miracle' to illuminate and enrich modern life and restore its forgotten links with past tradition. His collected poetry, written between 1924 and 1966, was published as *Poiemata* [Poems] (Athens, 1940, ²1950, ³1960, ⁸1972), and in English translations as *Collected Poems 1924–1955* (tr. E. Keeley & P. Sherrard, Princeton, 1967, London, ²1969, ³1982) and *Three Secret Poems* (tr. W. Kaiser, Cambridge, Mass., 1969). His critical work, among the most perceptive and humanistic of all modern Greek criticism, has been collected as *Dokimes* [Essays] (2 vols, Cairo, 1944, Athens, ²1974; selection tr. R. Warner, *On the Greek Style*, London, 1967).

In 1969 Seferis was one of the first Greek men of letters to speak out against the dictatorship of the 'Colonels' (1967–74) and in his last years was subjected to official vilification and harassment. He was awarded the Nobel prize for literature in 1963.　RMB

Seghers, Anna, ps. of Netty Radvanyi, *née* Netty Reiling (b. Mainz, Rhineland-Palatinate, Germany, 19.11.1900; d. East Berlin, 1.6.1983). German novelist and short-story writer whose major themes are social injustice and the political upheavals of the modern age. In 1928 she joined the Communist party and was awarded the Kleist prize for her first book *Der Aufstand der Fischer von St Barbara* (Potsdam, 1928; tr. M. Goldsmith, *The Revolt of the Fishermen*, London, 1929) – filmed by PISCATOR (USSR, 1934) – the story of a fishermen's strike which is brutally crushed. Between 1933 and 1947 she lived in exile, first in Paris and then in Mexico, gaining international acclaim for her masterpiece about antifascist resistance in prewar Germany *Das siebte Kreuz* (Mexico, 1942; tr. J. A. Galston, *The Seventh Cross*, Boston, Mass., 1942) – which was filmed by Fred Zinnemann (Hollywood, 1944) and won the Büchner prize in 1947 – and for *Transit* (Konstanz, 1948; tr. J. A. Galston, *Transit Visa*, Boston, Mass., 1944), a powerful novel based on her own experiences of the desperate plight of German émigrés in Marseilles. After 1947 she became a key figure in East German literature and served as president of the writers' union (1952–78), but her stature has not been adequately recognized in the West.　IW

Segovia, Andrés (b. Linares, Granada, Spain, 21.2.1893). Spanish guitarist. As a result of the success of a recital at the age of 15 Segovia was encouraged to make his career as a soloist, something much rarer then than it is today. His fame quickly spread and he continued into his 80s to give recitals in many parts of the world. He did more perhaps than any other player to bring about the present-day popularity of the classical guitar. To widen his repertory he effectively arranged compositions originally intended for other instruments by, for example, Bach, Mendelssohn and Schumann. More importantly he encouraged contemporary composers to write music specially for him, including Rodrigo, FALLA, Tansman and Villa-Lobos. Segovia always gave encouragement to young players of promise and a number of pupils have achieved international reputations, among them Alirio Diaz and John Williams.　JL

B. Gavoty, *Segovia* (Geneva, 1955); G. Clinton (ed.), *Andrés Segovia* (London, 1978).

Sékou Touré, Ahmed (b. Fatanah, French Guinea [now Republic of Guinea], 9.1.1922). President of Guinea. One of the most enduring of radical leaders in the Third World, Sékou Touré built up a power base for himself in the local trade union movement and went on to found the *Parti Démocratique Guinéen*. In 1958 Guinea, under Sékou Touré's leadership, was the only French colony to reject General DE GAULLE's offer of autonomy within the French community in favour of immediate independence. Guinea's capacity to survive the immense difficulties produced by a precipitate French withdrawal encouraged all the other French colonies in Africa to ask for independence in 1960. To have expedited the French decolonization of Africa was Sékou Touré's greatest achievement. His later record is less impressive: his regime, threatened by frequent but abortive coups, has shown itself so repressive that over one million Guineans have left the country. The record of economic development compares unfavourably with other ex-French colonies, despite the country's considerable resources, and Sékou Touré, though prolific in his publications, has little attraction as an ideologue in Third World circles.   RH

L. Adamolekun, *Sékou Touré's Guinea* (London, 1976).

Sellin, Johan Thorsten (b. Örnsköldsvik, Vaster Norrland, Sweden, 26.10.1896; naturalized American citizen). Swedish/American criminologist. A prolific and versatile pioneer in a number of key areas of the subject. His outstanding work has included the relevance of 'culture conflict' to criminality – *Culture Conflict and Crime* (NY, 1938); crime levels in times of economic depression; the deterrent efficacy of the death penalty; the devising of a sensitive index of crime; and defining the characteristics of those officially identified as delinquents: *The Measurement of Delinquency* (with M. E. Wolfgang, NY, 1964) and *Delinquency in a Birth Cohort* (with M. E. Wolfgang & R. M. Figlio, Chicago, 1972). This diversity of interests which has characterized Sellin's career has been matched by no superficiality of treatment of the questions he has examined. In each area, Sellin's contribution has provided a starting-point for subsequent analysis and debate.   JB

Semenov, Nikolai Nikolayevich (b. Saratov, Russia, 15.4.1896). Russian physicist and physical chemist, distinguished for his contributions to chemical kinetics and other fields. He graduated in the faculty of physics and mathematics at St Petersburg in 1917. After a brief period at Tomsk, he returned to Leningrad to work in the institute which, in 1931, became the Institute of Chemical Physics of the USSR Academy of Sciences. Semenov was appointed its first director, an office which he still holds. His earliest work was on elementary processes involving ions, electrons and electrical phenomena in gases and solids, and on molecular phenomena in the condensation of vapours and molecular beams. His worldwide fame rests on his contributions to chemical kinetics, particularly in the realm of chain reactions. He has investigated extensively the phenomena of explosion limits, connected with branched radical chains, and many other features of flames, combustion and detonation. Much of his work was parallel to that of HINSHELWOOD, with whom he shared a Nobel prize for chemistry in 1956. His best-known books are *Tsepnye Reaktsii* (Leningrad, 1934; *Chemical Kinetics and Chain Reactions*, Oxford, 1935) and *O Nekotorykh Problemakh khimicheskoy Kinetiki i Reaktsionnoy Sposobnosti* (Moscow, 1954; *Some Problems of Chemical Kinetics and Reactivity*, London, 1958).   JSh

Sena, Jorge de (b. Lisbon, Portugal, 2.11.1919; d. Calif., USA, 4.6.1978). Portuguese writer. Trained as a civil engineer, Sena has a claim to be considered a 20c polymath, whose prolific output ranges over poetry, drama, novel, short story, criticism, and translation of European and American classics. In 1959 he visited Brazil for a congress, and stayed to teach in Brazilian universities until 1965 when he moved to the University of Wisconsin, to the chair of Portuguese and Brazilian literature. From 1970 he was professor of Portuguese and comparative literature in the University of California. His love of polemic is evident in his early poems, particularly in *Coroa da terra* [Crown of earth] (Lisbon, 1946), where he condemns the misery and wastage of the human condition. His translations of the English poems of PESSOA improve on the originals. He has much to suggest about the meaning and autonomy of music as shown in *Arte de música* [The art of music] (Lisbon, 1968), a meditation on the works of Bach, Handel, Beethoven and Mozart. He is perhaps best known as a critic, and has contributed much to Camonian scholarship. Some of his best writing has appeared in his prefaces. He gives short shrift to critics in Portugal, and regards himself as a 'Lusitanian world citizen'. His most beautifully told narrative is his reconstruction of the last days in Lisbon of the poet Camões: *Super flumina Babylonis* [Beside the waters of Babylon] (Lisbon, 1966). DBr

O. Lopes, '*Modo de Ler*', *Crítica e Interpretação Literária*, 2 (Oporto, 1969).

Sendak, Maurice Bernard (b. Brooklyn, NY, USA, 10.6.1928). American children's picture-book author and illustrator. Sendak's reputation, despite early success as an illustrator, rests largely upon *Where the Wild Things Are* (NY, 1963) which epitomizes in many ways certain modern characteristics in books for young children. Max, the hero, dreams of wild monsters, becomes their king and submerges himself in wildness until he decides to 'Stop' when all the Wild Things obey and he is welcomed home. The content reflects Sendak's understanding of children's psychological needs: the need to transgress and to attain self-control; the subconscious fear of rejection and need for acceptance. Recognition of negative aspects of childhood, of the value of play, avoidance of the literal and of cliché and the use of powerfully allusive imagery mark all Sendak's work. His talent is versatile and innovatory ranging from the relatively conventional nonsense verse contained in the four little books collected as *The Nutshell Library* (4 vols, NY, 1962) to the haunting fantasy *Outside, Over There* (NY, 1981), a fable constructed upon fear of losing family and sibling jealousy. Sendak's spare but deft use of words and rhythm is as striking as the visual experience. JMM

S. Lanes, *The Art of Maurice Sendak* (NY, 1981).

Senghor, Léopold Sédar (b. Joal, Senegal, 9.10.1906). Senegalese statesman and poet. A student in Paris, he met CÉSAIRE and elaborated with him the concept of '*négritude*' – the assertion of the specificity of francophone Negro literature. *Chants d'ombre* [Songs of darkness] (Paris, 1945) is a good example of the rhapsodic tone adopted by Senghor to celebrate his native land and of how he constantly fuses the self and the external world in a protean torrent of epithets. *Hosties noires* [Black hosts] (Paris, 1948) multiplies the borrowings from African languages. *Anthologie de la nouvelle poésie nègre et malgache* (Paris, 1948; extracts tr. J. Reed & C. Wake in *Selected Poems*, NY, 1964) has a preface by SARTRE, announcing black francophone poetry to be the most powerful revolutionary verse currently being written. *Nocturnes* (Paris, 1961; tr. J. Reed & C. Wake, London, 1961) is a form of incantation in which African words infiltrate the French text. As always in Senghor, the reading involves a double process: the text may be read as an untendentious narrative, but also as an assertion of a difference (i.e. as a transparent text through which we see the richness and the limitations of western culture). His reputation is now firmly established as the creator of *Les Fondements de 'africanité', 'négritude' et 'arabité'* (Paris, 1967; tr. M. Cook, *The Foundations of 'africanité', or 'négritude' and 'arabité'*, Paris, 1971). Feeling the need to obey neither his Christian upbringing nor the French humanist tradition, Senghor argues unequivocally for the inalienable imperatives of '*négritude*'. Since 1960 he has been president of the republic of Senegal. DGL

Sérgio, António (b. Damão, Goa [now India], 3.9.1883; d. Lisbon, Portugal, 24.1.1968). Portuguese thinker and essayist. The greatest Portuguese thinker of the 20c, Sérgio was the teacher of a whole generation. A relentless polemicist, he attacked the myths that had engulfed the hearts and minds of his country. His eight volumes of collected essays (*Ensaios*, Lisbon, 1920–58) are unique in the history of Portuguese thought and letters. He became a republican after 1910, having resigned a naval commission, and set out on his lifelong mission to reform the Portuguese mentality through attention to clear and creative thinking. His whole work has been characterized as an exercise in the Socratic method. Sérgio saw, proclaimed and discussed the basis of this reform as a problem of education. This implied disciplined training for teachers and students, and an emphasis on self-government in school and university which, he believed, should lead to training in democracy and social cooperation. Sérgio joined the leading liberal review *Seara nova* [New harvest], founded in 1921, and in his search for the roots of the present he wrote the excellent *Breve interpretação da história de Portugal* [A sketch of the history of Portugal] (Lisbon, 1923, ²1972). He was minister of education in 1923, and imprisoned several times and exiled under SALAZAR's regime.   DBr

G. Moser: 'The campaign of "Seara nova" and its impact on Portuguese literature, 1921–1961', *Luso-Brazilian Review*, 2, 1 (1965), 15–42.

Servan-Schreiber, Jean-Jacques (b. Nancy, Meurthe-et-Moselle, France, 13.2.1924). French journalist and writer. Son of a leading French journalist and resistance leader, Servan-Schreiber became a fighter-pilot with the US Air Force in North Africa when his family fled there in 1943. His declared 'love affair' with the American way of life did not prevent him from working with distinction as diplomatic editor of *Le Monde* from 1948 to 1951. When he left daily journalism in 1953 to found the first French weekly news magazine *L'Express*, his great admiration of the news values and the compartmentalized lay-out of *Time* magazine was at once apparent. *L'Express*, which he sold to Sir James Goldsmith in 1977, was an immediate success but his interests turned more towards politics. He was secretary-general of the Social Radical party from 1969 to 1971, president from 1971 to 1975 and from 1977 to the pre-

sent. He was elected deputy for Nancy to the National Assembly from 1970 to 1978 but without a post in the government. He was made head of the new government computer research institute when it was launched in March 1982. His books include *Lieutenant en Algérie* (Paris, 1957; *Lieutenant in Africa*, London, 1958) and *Le Défi americain* (Paris, 1968; *The American Challenge*, Harmondsworth, 1968) – this last book being a warning against the Americanization of France and Europe.   RB

Seton-Watson, Robert (b. London, UK, 20.8.1879; d. Skye, Inner Hebrides, 25.7.1951). British historian, who as a young man took up the cause of the subject nationalities of the Hapsburg empire and acquired an unrivalled knowledge of their history and languages. During WW1 he worked to secure the break-up of the empire, the creation of independent states for the South Slav and the Czech and Slovak peoples, the incorporation of Transylvania into Romania and the absorption of the nine German-speaking provinces of Austria into Germany. He acted as liaison between the exiled Slav leaders and British political leaders (see his *Masaryk in England*, London, 1943); and at his own expense founded (1916) the weekly *New Europe* in which he wrote critically of the opportunities wasted by British and Allied policy. He took a leading part in the Rome Congress of Oppressed Austrian Nationalities and had the satisfaction of seeing his friends create the independent states of Yugoslavia and Czechoslovakia and incorporate Transylvania in Romania. After WW1 Seton-Watson helped to found the School of Slavonic Studies at London University and the *Slavonic Review*. In 1922 he was appointed the first holder of the MASARYK chair of Central European history in London. His most substantial work as a historian was *Disraeli, Gladstone and the Eastern Question* (London, 1935). He was a Liberal in the Gladstonian tradition, with the same strong commitment as Gladstone to the principle of nationality and the rights of small nations. His unimpressive appearance and diffident manner gave little idea of the moral courage of which he was capable and which he displayed in his outspoken criticism of CHAMBERLAIN's policy of appeasement and the Munich Agreement (see his *Britain and the Dictators*, London, 1938). He lived to see Munich annulled and Czechoslovakia liberated, but died deeply distressed by the Prague coup of 1948 and the enforced communization of Eastern Europe. (*The Making of New Europe*, London, 1980, is based on Seton-Watson's papers and written by his two sons Hugh and Christopher, both of whom followed their father's example and became historians of modern Europe.) ALCB

Shahn, Ben (b. Kovno, Russia [now Kaunas, Lithuania, USSR], 12.9.1898; d. New York, USA, 14.3.1969). American painter and graphic artist who was a leading social realist during the depression years. He was brought to the USA in 1906, was apprenticed to a lithographer, and attended university until 1922 when he enrolled at the National Academy of Design. During the 1920s he travelled in Europe and Africa; he was attracted by postimpressionist painting, particularly by DUFY. He was employed as a photographer under the Federal Art Project and in 1931-2 painted the works for which he is best known, 23 paintings entitled *The Passion of Sacco and Vanzetti* about the imprisonment, trial and execution of two alleged anarchists. After working as an assistant to RIVERA, Shahn painted a number of murals during the later 1930s. When, after WW2, he returned to easel painting, book illustration and poster design, his social commitment remained. A collection of his writings *The Shape of Content* (Cambridge, Mass.) was published in 1957. MOJN

J. T. Soby, *Ben Shahn: his Graphic Art* (NY, 1957); J. D. Morse (ed.), *Ben Shahn* (NY, 1972).

Shalyapin, Fyodor Ivanovich, see CHALIAPIN, FYODOR IVANOVICH.

Shankar, Ravi (b. Benares [now Varanasi], Uttar Pradesh, India, 7.4.1920). Indian sitar player and the most influential exponent of Indian classical music and culture in the West. As a child he developed skills as dancer and then instrumentalist through membership (1930-8) of a touring troupe of Indian dancers and musicians led by his elder brother Uday, by whom he was guided in the absence of a conventional formal education. An early interest in western music developed during extended periods of residence in Paris and tours of Europe and the USA. He became a disciple of Ustad Allauddin Khan and in the mid-1940s began his own performing career. From 1949 to 1956 he was director of music for External Services, All-India Radio, and director of the AIR instrumental ensemble into which he introduced western instruments. A close relationship with the violinist MENUHIN began in 1951 and mutual respect for each other's music and culture led to collaborative musical ventures including joint performances in 1966 and 1967. His own concertos for sitar and orchestra (1971 and 1976) and his appearance at Woodstock Pop Festival (1969) are further examples of Shankar's quest for musical meeting points between East and West and of the increased intercultural popularity of the sitar brought about by his performances. He has described aspects of his own background and musical development in *My Music, My Life* (NY, 1968). TEC

Shannon, Claude Elwood (b. Gaylord, Mich., USA, 30.4.1916). American pioneer of mathematical communication theory, Shannon was educated at the University of Michigan, and after academic research joined the Bell Telephone laboratories. In 1948 he published a classic paper 'The mathematical theory of communication' in the *Bell System Technical Journal*. Shannon was seeking to give a coherent treatment of all forms of information transmission systems, whatever their physical nature. His paper used such terms as information, redundancy and message, which are now commonplace. Developed further in a series of papers, Shannon's work is fundamental to all modern communication systems. In 1949 he published with WEAVER *The Mathematical Theory of Communication* (Urbana). RAH

Shapley, Harlow (b. Nashville, Tenn., USA, 2.11.1885; d. Boulder, Colo, 20.10.1972). American astronomer. After two years as a crime reporter on Kansas and Missouri newspapers, Shapley studied astronomy at the University of Missouri. After four years he became a graduate student at Princeton University where he worked on eclipsing binary stars under H. N. RUSSELL. His first position was at the Mt Wilson Observatory where he used the new large telescopes, studied variable stars, and proposed that the cyclic changes in brightness of Cepheid variable stars are due to their pulsation. He was the first to suggest that the globular clusters are associated physically with the galaxy and distributed symmetrically about its centre. This led him to the idea that the sun occupies a position far from the centre of the galaxy. At this time there was great uncertainty about the distance scale of the universe, and in particular there was controversy over the role of the spiral nebulae: were they small close neighbours of the galaxy, or large objects at very great distances? In 1920 the National Academy of Sciences organized the 'Great Debate' on this question. Shapley maintained that the spiral nebulae were close, partly because a distinguished positional astronomer, van Maanen, had claimed to have measured the rotation of several of them directly on photographs. Shapley was opposed by Heber Curtiss of Lick Observatory who was of the opinion that these nebulae were at great distances. The controversy was not settled until 1924 when HUBBLE published his first observations of Cepheid variable stars in the spiral nebulae, M31 and M33, showing that Curtiss was right. In 1921 Shapley became director of Harvard College Observatory, where he remained until he retired in 1952. In later life he took an active interest in national and international affairs, and was even publicly denounced by MCCARTHY. Shapley replied: ' . . . I have only to say that the Senator succeeded in telling six lies in four sentences, which is probably the indoor record for mendacity.' He was one of the initiators of UNESCO. (For his own account of his work, see *Through Rugged Ways to the Stars*, NY, 1969.) DEB

Shaw, Clifford Robe (b. Luray, Ind., USA, 13.8.1895; d. Chicago, 1.8.1957). American sociologist of the University of Chicago whose work represents a landmark in the attempt by criminologists to understand the relationship between levels of crime, delinquency and other forms of social pathology on the one hand, and the physical and social characteristics of neighbourhoods on the other. Shaw's ethnographic studies and, more important, his patient mapping of delinquency data for a large number of American cities over many years provided new insights into the 'ecological' patterning of delinquency. Some indication of the importance of the work that Shaw and his associates (in particular MCKAY) carried out between the late 1920s and early 1940s at the University of Chicago (see *Social Factors in Juvenile Delinquency*, with H. D. McKay, Washington, 1931, and *Juvenile Delinquency and Urban Areas*, with H. D. McKay, Chicago, 1942) is given by the fact that it remains to this day influential in the development of criminological theory. He helped to lay the foundations of the environmental approach to crime causation, and sociological concepts such as 'anomie', 'delinquent subcultures' and 'opportunity structures' can be traced back to Shaw's early work. The early delinquency prevention programmes in the USA (most notably the Chicago Area Project, which became the prototype for the programmes of the KENNEDY-JOHNSON era) were in no small part his brain-child, and this creation reflected Shaw's extraordinary energy and organizational ability. JB

J. Snodgrass, 'Clifford R. Shaw and Henry D. McKay: Chicago criminologists', *British Journal of Criminology*, 16 (1976), 1–19.

Shaw, George Bernard (b. Dublin, Ireland, UK [now Irish Republic], 26.7.1856; d. Ayot St Lawrence, Herts., UK, 2.11.1950). Irish dramatist and critic. Shaw was educated in Dublin, leaving school at 15 to work as a clerk. In 1876 Shaw moved to London where he began his career as a journalist, becoming art critic for the *World* (1885–8), music critic for the *Star* (1888–90), and later theatre critic for the *Saturday Review* (1895–8), where, in trenchant criticisms, he learned the qualities of good dramatic writing which he was later to embody in his own plays (see also *The Quintessence of Ibsenism*, London, 1891; *The Perfect Wagnerite*, London, 1898). Following an encounter in 1882 with Henry George, the American political economist, and encouraged by reading MARX, Shaw became a convinced socialist and in 1884 joined the Fabian Society, which was committed to evolutionary rather than revolutionary change from capitalism to socialism (see *The Intelligent Woman's Guide to Socialism and Capitalism*, London, 1928; *Everybody's Political What's What*, London, 1944). Both Shaw's dramatic awareness and his political and ideological convictions are evident in such plays as *John Bull's Other Island* (London, 1907), *Major Barbara* (London, 1905), *Man and Superman* (London, 1903), *The Doctor's Dilemma* (London, 1906) and *St Joan* (London, 1924). Shaw's first major recognition as a dramatist came when, between 1904 and 1907, the Royal Court Theatre, London, decided to stage seasons of intellectual plays, among them 11 by Shaw including a revival of *Candida* (London, 1894). Shaw continued to write through two world wars until his death in 1950, and, while there is some modification of viewpoint at times – as in the disillusionment so pervasive in *Heartbreak House* (London, 1919) – the central concerns of his work remain constant. His is a theatre of ideas, heavily didactic in spite of the wit of the dialogue. Many of the plays are dramatized essays on the subject of individual responsibility or integrity when opposed to the conformist demands of a society severely limited in its imaginative scope: Peter Keegan, the unfrocked priest in *John Bull's Other Island*, speaks out for social justice rather than the illusions of utopia or progressive materialism; Joan of Arc asserts her individual freedom of spirit against the insidious power of ecclesiastical orthodoxy. Theatrically unadventurous, Shaw's plays are relatively static;

vigorous stage business or dramatic action would hinder the clash of ideas which provides the seminal conflict in Shaw's dramatic aesthetic. Collected editions are: *Works* (36 vols, London, 1930–50); *The Complete Plays* (London, 1934); *The Complete Prefaces* (London, 1934).   EFi

R. J. Kaufmann (ed.), *GBS: a Collection of Critical Essays* (London, 1965); M. Holroyd (ed.), *The Genius of Shaw* (London, 1979).

Shepard, Sam, *né* Samuel Shepard Rogers (b. Fort Sheridan, Ill., USA, 5.11.1943). American dramatist who caught the first wave of the off-Broadway revolution and rode it farther than any of his contemporaries. Shepard is not a city playwright but a midwestern wanderer who has driven the backroads of the land, tramped its wilderness, scored on its main streets. He alone among his peers has a romantic feeling for the American landscape. Shepard himself is a protean figure. The weird dreamlike terrains of his plays sparkle with the insights of a man who has inhabited many worlds – those of musician, actor, horse breeder, screenwriter, waiter, and even, in his latest incarnation in Terence Malick's *Days of Heaven* (1978), movie star.

Hoboes, thieves, rock'n'rollers, Martians, cowboys, moguls, madmen – Shepard's heroes range as widely as his interests. His plays are dreamscapes of the American wasteland where the past and the present coexist. Shepard has described his most recent plays as 'painting in space'. But the best of his early work (*Chicago, Icarus's Mother, Red Cross,* 1966; *La Tourista,* 1967) and the plays of the early 1970s (*Operation Sidewinder,* 1970; *Tooth of Crime,* 1972) show off his visual as well as verbal panache. Shepard likens the structure of recent plays like *Angel City* (1976) to jazz, a pretension which rationalizes his characters' frequent solos which wreak havoc on conventional narrative lines. When the combination of word hocuspocus and physical transformation works (as it does in *Chicago, Tooth of Crime, Operation Sidewinder* and in *Little Ocean,* 1974), Shepard's sensory blitz can be stunning. In 1979 Shepard's more accessible *Buried Child* won the Pulitzer prize for drama.   JLahr

Sherrington, Charles Scott (b. London, UK, 27.12.1857; d. Eastbourne, E. Sussex, 4.3.1952). British neurophysiologist. He took his medical degree at Cambridge in 1885 at which time he presented his first scientific paper, with LANGLEY, on the dog brain. Already Sherrington was an accomplished poet, being commended by Longfellow. Sherrington studied briefly with Götz in Strassburg on the effect of removing parts of the brain of the dog, and, before settling down to what became his lifelong work, he spent a short but clearly lively period in Spain investigating inoculation against cholera in cattle. In 1887 Sherrington took up a post at St Thomas's Hospital. Although he concentrated largely on the effects of brain pathology, he also became interested in other areas such as scar tissue formation. It was this work at St Thomas's that formed the scientific basis of modern neurology, through Sherrington's study of the effects of brain or spinal injuries on patients. In 1895 he became professor of physiology at Liverpool University, thereby initiating his more detailed work on spinal reflexes, the control of muscles and the relationship between the voluntary and involuntary nervous system, culminating in the classic *The Integrative Action of the Nervous System* (London, 1906). In this he postulated that neural reflexes must use more than one neurone; so he proposed a synapse and a neurotransmitter substance to connect the two nerve cells. In 1913 Sherrington became the Waynflete professor of physiology at Oxford, a post that he held until retirement in 1935. Of the students with whom he worked during this period, three (ECCLES, FLOREY and Granit) subsequently received the Nobel prize and many others became distinguished scientists. At Oxford he continued his neurophysiological studies, developing modern techniques for recording nerve activity and outlining the nature of communication between nerves and between nerves and muscles. Despite his prolific contribution to the neurosciences (he published 320 papers), the Nobel

prize in 1932, jointly awarded with ADRIAN, came virtually at the end of a highly distinguished career. He delivered the Gifford lectures in 1937–8 and these, published as *Man on his Nature* (Cambridge, 1940), provided another classic statement, this time of his philosophy.   CTJ

J. C. Eccles & W. G. Gibson, *Sherrington, his Life and Thought* (Berlin, 1979).

Shklovsky, Viktor Borisovich (b. St Petersburg [now Leningrad], Russia, 24.1.1893). Russian writer, literary theorist and critic. As leader of the Russian formalists (*OPOYAZ* – Society for the Study of Poetic Language) and member of the futurists and Serapion Brothers, he exerted a strong influence on the development of early Soviet prose literature and on the formal tendency in literary criticism which later developed into structuralism. His first theoretical work *Voskreshenie slova* (St Petersburg, 1914; tr. R. Sherwood, *The Resurrection of the Word*, in S. Bann & J. Bowlt, eds, *Russian Formalism*, Edinburgh, 1973) distinguished between true 'perception' of innovative art and mere 'recognition' of outmoded art forms, and promoted the futurists' new 'devices'. Formalist collections of 1916–19 developed Shklovsky's theory of the distinctiveness of 'practical' and 'poetic' languages and stressed the 'estrangement' of the art 'object'. In his major work *O teorii prozy* [On the theory of prose] (Moscow – Leningrad, 1925) Shklovsky again emphasized that the formal structure of literature (its arrangement of 'devices') rather than content determines its aesthetic effect. He illustrated theories like 'estrangement' in practice by creating his own literary genre in a series of semi-autobiographical works. By 1930 Shklovsky had partially recanted his theories under pressure from MARXist critics and he later worked on studies of the classics, cinema and further volumes of memoirs.   RJS

V. Erlich, *Russian Formalism* (The Hague, ²1965); R. Sheldon, 'The formalist poetics of Viktor Shklovsky', in *Russian Literature Triquarterly*, 2 (Winter 1972).

Shlonsky, Abraham (b. Kriukov, Ukraine, Russia, 6.3.1900; d. Tel Aviv, Israel, 18.5.1973). Hebrew poet, editor, critic and translator. Until 1921 he lived in Russia, and the influence of Russian poetry, particularly of Pushkin, BLOK, MAYAKOVSKY, and the events of the Russian revolution and the civil war, remained paramount throughout his life. From 1921 until his death he lived in Palestine-Israel, where his sympathies were linked to the left. An exceptional mastery of the Hebrew language led him to radical innovations both in style and in coining new words in a revived and expanding language. A militant critic of old classical literary forms, he became the principal pioneer of avant-garde expressionism in Hebrew literature. For this purpose his literary journals *Ketuvim*, *Turim* and *Orlogin* became the great and formidable iconoclasts, trying to destroy the literary worlds of BIALIK, TCHERNICHOWSKY, Shimoni and others. His poetry, collected in *Kol Shirei* (3 vols, Tel Aviv, 1960–8), has a vibrant, strident note, searching for revolutionary solutions. His translations of Pushkin, Blok, BRECHT, Manger, Leivick, Shakespeare, Mayakovsky, Gogol and others are masterpieces in their own right. Shlonsky remained a rebel to the end of his days, becoming active against war and advocating peace with the Arabs.

CA

Shockley, William Bradford (b. London, UK, 13.2.1910). American physicist. Shockley's parents were American and he was brought up in California. He graduated from the California Institute of Technology, obtained his PhD (1936) at MIT, then joined Bell Telephone laboratories. During WW2 he was director of research of the US Navy antisubmarine warfare operations group and after the war became director of solid state research and later of transistor physics research at Bell. His research interests have included ferromagnetic domains and the plastic properties of metals. His most outstanding contributions have been in the field of semiconductor physics and especially towards the invention of the junction transistor. In 1956 (with BARDEEN and W. H. Brattain) he was awarded the Nobel prize for physics for detailed studies of the properties of semiconductors and the development of the transistor. In the early 1970s he caused considerable controversy over his contention that human intelligence was mainly the result of heredity, claiming as evidence the tendency of blacks to score on average 15 points below whites in intelligence tests.

HMR

Shoghi Effendi Rabbani (b. Haifa, Palestine, Ottoman Empire [now Israel], 1.3.1897; d. London, UK, 4.11.1957). Iranian head of the Bahā'ī religion from 1921 to 1957, he was responsible for transforming it into a worldwide movement. His grandfather ᶜAbbās Effendi ᶜAbd al-Bahā' (Bahā'ī leader 1892–1921) appointed him first 'Guardian' in his will. ᶜAbbās had already followed a policy of preaching Baha'ism as a 'progressive' religion in the West. His grandson, educated at the American College in Beirut and (briefly) Oxford, carried this policy further by concentrating on the small western Bahā'ī communities, abandoning or minimizing various Oriental doctrines and practices, and creating a western-style administration. His own writings in English and Persian (mostly encyclical letters) and his translations of scripture into English reinterpreted Baha'ism as a new 'world faith' suited to the needs of the modern age. From 1937 he conducted a series of international missionary 'Plans' by which Baha'ism was spread widely. A new religious community was effectively created under the control of a highly developed hierarchical system. Shoghi Effendi married in 1937, but there were no children. Since he had by then expelled all his male relations from the religion, the hereditary Guardianship was deemed to have ended on his death, leadership of the movement passing, in 1963, to an international elected body.

DMM

R. Rabbani, *The Priceless Pearl* (London, 1969).

Sholem Aleichem, ps. of Sholem Yakov Rabinovitch (b. Freislav, Ukraine, Russia, 18.2.1859; d. New York, USA, 13.5.1916). Yiddish writer. Unrivalled as the greatest humorist in Yiddish literature, like MENDELE he gave voice to the speech of ordinary people, extracting from it the finest subtleties of phrase and structure. At 21 he became a rabbi, but after two years devoted himself entirely to writing. He moved to Kiev, spending a substantial inheritance speculatively and in encouraging young writers. In 1905 he left Russia and settled in Switzerland, though lecturing extensively in Europe and in the USA. He emigrated to America in 1914 and when he died tens of thousands of New York Jews followed the hearse of the 'Jewish Mark Twain'. As distinct from Mendele, as a writer he does not sit in judgement; he simply identifies with the victims, speaking their language, dreaming their dreams and sharing their hopes. His international popularity is the more surprising given that his humour rests entirely on Jewish characters and to a large extent on their language and the way they use it. His unique folklore style is the prime reason why so few good translations of his books are available. One of Sholem Aleichem's most famous creations is Tevye the milkman who conquered the international stage as *Fiddler on the Roof* (1965). A simple villager, beset by domestic and political problems, he would like to understand this world but cannot; instead, he creates another, an imaginary world where he is at home and from which no one can remove him. Providing his own answers to his many questions, Tevye's humour is as irresistible as it is deadly serious. Outstanding among Sholem Aleichem's books are *Stempeniu* (1888; tr. H. Bermann, London, 1914); *The Old Country* (tr. J. & F. Butwin, NY, 1946); and *Inside Kasrilevke* (tr. I. Goldstick, Montreal, 1949). Sholem Aleichem was the first to write in Yiddish for children, and adaptations of his work were significant in the founding of the Yiddish Art Theater in New York.   JSo

Sholem Yakov Rabinovitch, see SHOLEM ALEICHEM.

Sholokhov, Mikhail Aleksandrovich (b. Kruzhilino na Donu, Russia, 24.5.1905). Russian novelist. Born and brought up in the Don Cossack region, he was full of ardour at the thought of witnessing the dawn of great events and so joined the Communist party and was active in the civil war. After an interval of work as a manual labourer he returned to his native village and since then has spent hardly any time away from it. Apart from his literary fame and extensive honours, including the Nobel prize for literature (1965), he combines the reputation of outspokenness and fervent, patriotic loyalty to the Soviet order, and of independence of mind and anti-intellectualism. His first writings, begun in 1924, were stories of the Don Cossacks (*Donskiye rasskazy*, Moscow, 1925; tr. H. C. Stevens, *Tales from the Don*, London, 1961) and the subject came to dominate the greater part of his other work. The tales revealed a writer of great natural talent, with an almost breathtaking narrative and visual gift. His real fame came with the publication of *Tikhiy Don* (4 vols, Moscow, 1928–40; tr. S. Garry, *And Quiet Flows the Don*, London, 1934, and *The Don Flows Home to the Sea*, London, 1940) which took 12 years to complete. It is a Cossack counterpart to Leo TOLSTOY's *War and Peace* (1863–9), in structure, design and portrayal of character, though not in psychological and intellectual depth. Its four parts offer a panorama of Cossack life on the eve of WW1, during the war and especially during the revolution. The novel conveys a sense of the vast expanse of Russia in her natural and historical excessiveness and tumult, and Sholokhov's gallery of portraits grows naturally into and out of the landscape. He does not conceal the horrors of a society out of joint, or the complexity of human situations, but describes his world with an open-eyed acceptance which goes some way towards cleansing it. Written in a language whose exuberance and, at times, crudeness are distinctly Sholokhov's, these verbal idiosyncrasies became even more pronounced in his subsequent work, where he tends to use or misuse them for mere spicy flavour and comic effect. This is evident in his second big novel *Podnyataya tselina* (2 vols, Moscow, 1932–60; tr. S. Garry, *The Virgin Soil Upturned*, London, 1935, and tr. H. C. Stevens, *Harvest on the Don*, London, 1960), the second volume of which came out 27 years after the first. It is concerned with collectivization among the Cossacks. The novel's documentary value is greater than the artistic, although the story is told with Sholokhov's customary naturalistic frankness. His last important work deals with WW2: *Oni srazhalis' za rodinu* [They fought for their country] (1943–6); but it is episodic, somewhat repetitive and lacks cohesion. There is irony in the fact that Sholokhov, who himself complained that it is intolerable to turn into a national monument while still alive, has become the quintessential establishment figure in Soviet literature.

EL

D. H. Stewart, *M. Sholokhov: a Critical Introduction* (Ann Arbor, 1967); R. Medvedev, *Problems in the Literary Biography of M. Sholokhov* (Cambridge, 1971).

Shostakovich, Dmitri Dmitrievich (b. St Petersburg [now Leningrad], Russia, 25.9.1906; d. Moscow, USSR, 9.8.1975). Russian composer. Shostakovich's early works, which include his First Symphony (1925) and his Gogol opera *Nos* [The nose] (1927), reveal a caustic wit, a disrespect for tradition and a keen awareness of what was happening in Western Europe. In his next two symphonies (1927 and 1929) he aimed to glorify the young revolutionary society, but then his Fourth Symphony (composed 1936), influenced by MAHLER, took him into a world of personal feeling which provided the expressive substance for most of his later symphonies, concertos and string quartets. However, he decided to hold the Fourth Symphony in reserve, for by now the doctrine of socialist realism had been promulgated and one of its first victims had been his opera *Ledi Makbet Mtsenskovo u yezda* [The Lady Macbeth of the Mtsensk district] (1932). Berated for his failure to be optimistic in spirit and popular in tone, he produced 'a Soviet artist's practical creative reply to just criticism' in his Fifth Symphony (1937), but there was no great change in style. Instead Shostakovich gave vent to his feelings in chamber music, complying with expectations in his Seventh Symphony, the 'Leningrad' (1941), and withholding his less acceptable scores. STALIN's death enabled him to return to large-scale symphonic expression in his

Tenth Symphony (1953), but he continued to suffer official harassment, especially after the appearance of his Thirteenth Symphony (1962), with its YEVTUSHENKO text remarking on Russian anti-Semitism. His later works, including the Fourteenth and Fifteenth symphonies (1970 and 1972), are bleakly obsessed with mortality. In 1979 S. Volkov edited and published *Testimony: the Memoirs of Shostakovich* (NY).   PG

I. Martynov, *Dmitri Shostakovich* (NY, 1947); N. Kay, *Shostakovich* (London, 1971); H. Ottaway, *Shostakovich's Symphonies* (London, 1979).

Sibelius, Jean, *né* Johan Julius Christian (b. Hämeenlinna, Häme, Finland, 8.12.1865; d. Järvenpää, Lappi, 20.9.1957). Finnish composer. His long life does not imply quite so long a career: his first major works (the *Kullervo* symphony and the tone poem *En saga*) date from 1892, and after 1925 (the year of the tone poem *Tapiola* and his incidental music to Shakespeare's *Tempest*) he entered into virtual retirement. He is most celebrated for his orchestral tone poems, the seven symphonies and the Violin Concerto (1903), and it is on these that his reputation rests. This reputation is perhaps highest in the English-speaking countries and of course in Scandinavia (some English critics have considered his symphonies to be in the same class as Beethoven's), but elsewhere he is a less central figure. His stated symphonic ideal was 'style and severity of form, together with the profound logic that creates an inner connection between all the musical ideas', and this aim is well realized in the symphonies, culminating in the one-movement Seventh (1924) which, for all its relative brevity, has an epic breadth of style. That same quality is also a feature of those works inspired by Finnish legend such as *En saga*, *The Swan of Tuonela* (1893), the striking *Luonnotar* for voice and orchestra (1910) and *Tapiola*, that unique evocation of the northern forests. Sibelius has not been a notably influential figure, but is to be valued both as a powerful symphonist and a visionary poet of northern nature.

CH

R. Layton, *Sibelius* (London, ²1978).

Sickert, Walter Richard (b. Munich, Bavaria, Germany, 31.5.1860; d. Bathampton, Avon, UK, 22.1.1942). British painter and etcher. Sickert's father was a Danish artist and his mother half-English, half-Irish; they settled in England when he was six. He spent three years as an actor before beginning to study art, first briefly at the Slade School, then as an assistant to Whistler. Whistler and Degas, both of whom became his friends, were the two great influences on his early style. His experience of the stage was reflected both in his liking for music-hall subjects and his tendency to relate figures to one another and to their settings in a way that suggests some dramatic or psychological relationship. After spending the years 1899 to 1905 abroad, mainly in Dieppe, but partly in Paris and Venice, he returned to London, where his studio in Fitzroy Street became the meeting place for various younger artists such as Harold Gilman, Spencer Gore and Robert Bevan, with whom he formed the Camden Town group. His subjects tended to be drawn from that rather seedy quarter of London, often low-life scenes, such as nudes lying on untidy beds, but with an interest in effects of interior light and painted with a low-toned muted richness of colour. Although he was opposed to the innovations of postimpressionism, his later work gradually became brighter in colour and included a number of pictures painted from photographs or adapted from Victorian black-and-white illustrations. A striking personality, influential as a teacher and cosmopolitan in outlook, he played a major role in the assimilation of late 19c French art in Britain.   REA

W. Baron, *Sickert* (London, 1973).

Sidgwick, Nevil Vincent (b. Oxford, UK, 8.5.1873; d. Oxford, 15.3.1952). British chemist. Sidgwick made outstanding contributions to our understanding of the chemical bond, particularly for transition metal complexes. At Oxford he gained first-class honours in natural science (1895) and in classics (1897). He worked for a short time with OSTWALD in Leipzig, and returned to a fellowship at Lincoln College in 1901. In 1910 he wrote the first of his three classic textbooks *The Organic Chemistry of Nitrogen* (Oxford, [2]1947). It was more than a decade before, under the influence of the concepts of RUTHERFORD, Niels BOHR, G. N. LEWIS and WERNER, he produced his electronic theory of valency. He showed that Lewis's concept of electron sharing within organic compounds could be extended to transition metal complexes. In particular, he introduced the important concept of the coordinate bond, in which two electrons are donated as a pair from one atom to another (*The Electronic Theory of Valency*, Oxford, 1927). His research thereafter was concerned with producing the evidence to support his theories. In 1935 he was awarded the title of professor. His magnum opus was *The Chemical Elements and their Compounds* (Oxford, 1950). This and his second edition of *The Organic Chemistry of Nitrogen* are still standard reference works.
                                                    KRS

Sigerist, Henry Ernest (b. Paris, France, 7.4.1891; d. Pura, nr Lugano, Ticino, Switzerland, 17.3.1957). Swiss medical historian and reformer. Sigerist studied and practised medicine in Zürich, also developing a keen interest in medical history and oriental languages. In 1925 he succeeded Karl Sudhoff as professor of the history of medicine and director of the Institute for the History of Medicine at Leipzig, then the only major centre for this subject in Europe. In 1932 he transferred to the recently founded institute at the Johns Hopkins Medical School, Baltimore, USA, modelled on Leipzig. As a committed socialist, Sigerist was a controversial appointment to both posts, but his growing distinction as a student of medieval medicine and his remarkable versatility as a linguist and thinker in the social sciences for a time overcame prejudice. At Baltimore Sigerist attracted a wide following. He was a charismatic figure on the American immigrant left. His work aroused national publicity, and he increasingly wrote in a popular vein, rather than as a scholar. His unpopularity within the medical profession was provoked by his persistent advocacy of socialized medicine. Such actions as support for Russia against Finland drew adverse publicity. He tactfully retired to Europe in 1947 to work on his *History of Medicine* (2 vols, NY, 1951–61). This drastically incomplete work, the published part of which deals only with primitive and Oriental medicine, is nevertheless a tribute to Sigerist's breadth of scholarship, insight as a social scientist, and lightness of touch as a writer. It is the model for all future histories of medicine. Among Sigerist's other 50 books and some 500 articles the greatest impact was made by his *Einführung in die Medizin* (Leipzig, 1931; *Man and Medicine*, NY, 1932), an historical introduction to modern medicine for medical students; *Civilization and Disease* (Ithaca, NY, 1943), an outline of medicine as a social science; and *Socialized Medicine in the Soviet Union* (NY, 1937; also issued in the UK by the Left Book Club), an unveiled defence of Soviet social policy, written with the polemical charm which was Sigerist's strength and weakness. CW

Sikorski, Igor Ivanovich (b. Kiev, Russia, 25.5.1889; naturalized American citizen, 1928; d. Easton, Conn., USA, 26.10.1972). Russian/American aircraft pioneer. At the age of 12, inspired by his mother's interest in the inventions of Leonardo da Vinci, Sikorski made a working, rubber-powered toy helicopter. In 1908 he made a tour of Western Europe and became aware of recent work in heavier-than-air powered flight. His early attempts using petrol engines failed, but he built some successful fixed-wing planes. In 1919 he emigrated to the USA, and after teaching for some years he founded the Sikorski Corporation with Russian friends; the company was later incorporated in United Aircraft. In 1939 he returned to helicopters, and now, having an efficient team of engineers, soon built a working helicopter. He was always his own test-pilot for the first flight of any new machine. RAH

Sillanpää, Frans Eemil (b. Hämeenkyrö, Finland, 16.9.1888; d. Helsinki, 3.6.1964). Finnish novelist. Sillanpää's work expresses the deep-rooted characteristics of the Finnish people by concentrating on the instinctual life of its humblest representatives. His studies in biology at the University of Helsinki provided him with a lasting philosophical framework (derived also from Ernst Haeckel and OSTWALD). This pantheistic outlook was present in his first novel *Elämä ja aurinko* [The living sun] (Helsinki, 1916) and was developed further in his later work for which he received the Nobel prize for literature in 1939. His characters are frequently social misfits, isolated and exceptional individuals, as in *Hurskas kurjuus* (Helsinki, 1919; tr. A. Matson, *Meek Heritage*, London, 1938) where the political issues of the civil war (1918–19) are perhaps secondary to the analysis of an individual peasant psyche experiencing them; and as in *Nuorena nukkunut* (Helsinki, 1931; tr. A. Matson, *The Maid Silja*, London, 1933) where the brief full summer in the experience of the young peasant girl symbolizes the comparative brevity of her life. Sillanpää's main thesis, that man is part of nature, is expressed through lyrical, personal narrative in *Ihmiset suviyössä* (Helsinki, 1934; tr. A. Blair, *People in the Summer Night*, London, 1966). He spent his last 20 years repeating this message, for instance in numerous broadcasts on Finnish radio. KKS

J. Ahokas, *A History of Finnish Literature* (Bloomington, 1973).

Silone, Ignazio, ps. of Secondo Tranquilli (b. Pescina dei Marsi, Abruzze e Molise, Italy, 1.5.1900; d. Geneva, Switzerland, 22.8.1978). Italian novelist and political activist. Silone lost his parents in 1915 during the earthquake at Marsica. This tragedy and the social and political problems of Italy in the aftermath of WW1 aroused a passion for social justice which made him join the Socialist party in 1918, the Communist party in 1921, and work as an editor or collaborator for many political newspapers and periodicals. In 1926, with fascism in full swing, Silone was arrested and expelled from Italy. He took refuge in Spain and France from where he was subsequently driven out to take shelter eventually in Switzerland in 1930. A year later he abandoned the Communist party. In 1944 he returned to Italy and resumed his political activities as a

Christian Socialist. His first novel *Fontamara* (Zürich, 1930; tr. G. David & E. Mosbacher, London, 1934) was originally published in German and subsequently in Italian and English. Other novels by Silone are: *Bread and Wine* (tr. G. David & E. Mosbacher, London, 1926; Italian ed. *Pane e vino*, Zürich, 1937); *Il semo sotto la neve* (Zürich, 1941; tr. F. Frenaye, *The Seed Beneath the Snow*, London, 1943); *Una manciata di more* (Milan, 1952; tr. D. Silone, *A Handful of Blackberries*, London, 1954); *Il segreto di Luca* (Milan, 1956; tr. D. Silone, *The Secret of Luca*, London, 1959); *La volpe e le camilie* (Milan, 1960; tr. E. Mosbacher, *The Fox and the Camellias*, London, 1961) and *L'avventura di un povero cristiano* (Milan, 1968; tr. W. Weaver, *The Story of an Humble Christian*, NY, 1971). Silone also wrote a play *Ed egli si nascose* (Zürich, 1944; tr. D. Laracy, *And He Did Hide Himself*, London, 1946), and a book of essays in the form of a novel, *La scuola dei dittatori* (Zürich, 1938; tr. G. David & E. Mosbacher, *The School for Dictators*, London, 1939). Underlying all his work and determining its ethos is Silone's characteristic synthesis of socialism and Christianity, political realism and ethical idealism, the forces of society and the forces of history. While trying to achieve this synthesis he exploded the myth of communism as a panacea for social ills and injustices and as a means to achieve a new social order. GS

R. W. B. Lewis, *The Picaresque Saint* (Philadelphia, 1959); M. Foot, 'The new Machiavelli', in *Debts of Honour* (London, 1980).

Simenon, Georges (b. Liège, Belgium, 13.2.1903). Belgian novelist. Simenon began his career as a junior reporter on the *Gazette de Liège* at the age of 16 before moving to Paris in 1922. He published an estimated 150 popular novels under a wide variety of pseudonyms before creating his most famous character Maigret in 1933 (*M. Gallet décédé*, Paris, 1933; tr. N. Ryan, *Maigret Stonewalled*, London, 1959). He has subsequently published over 200 novels, some 100 of which deal with the cases of Commissaire Maigret. Although classics of detective fiction, the Maigret novels

rely less upon the deductive principles of 'scientific' detection than upon a psychological analysis of the criminal and upon Maigret's subjective understanding of his motives. All of Simenon's novels are characterized by their remarkable feel for atmosphere and by their frequently melancholy evocation of Paris and provincial towns. The Maigret novels have been translated into more than 40 languages and many have been filmed and adapted for television. Simenon is a member of the Académie Royale de Belgique and of the American Academy of Art and Letters. DM

Simmel, Georg (b. Berlin, Germany, 1.3.1858; d. Strassburg, Alsace, Germany [now France], 26.9.1918). German sociologist whose reputation has waxed and waned, and waxed again at different times (Simmel was translated by the Chicago sociologists Park and Burgess in 1921, long before Max WEBER became known in the English-speaking world, but was then neglected for almost 30 years). He is a prime illustration of the difficulties which beset the individual who (to use BERLIN's distinction) was by nature a talented fox, but wanted (and ultimately failed) to be a hedgehog. Simmel was a brilliant stylist and essayist, especially in the field of culture, but he sought to create a major 'system' of sociology. He distinguished history from sociology on the ground that the former dealt with the varied contents of human experience whereas sociology, in order to have a distinctive subject matter, would deal only with the 'forms' of interaction, just as geometry was a formal analytical technique independent of any specific spatial content. This aspect of Simmel's work appealed to the Chicago school, since they wanted to specify the formal social processes in social change: competition, conflict, accommodation and assimilation. In Germany, Leopold von Wiese sought to extend Simmel's 'formal sociology' into a systematic theory. The sterility of these efforts led to Simmel's long obscurity. The 'resurrection' of Simmel came with the translation of his brilliant essays – on money, on the stranger, on the aesthetic significance of the face, on ruins ('ruins are man's link to nature'), and his essays on the dyad and the triad which were used in the study of small groups and coalition strategies. Simmel always saw the duality of every phenomenon. Money, he pointed out, made relations between individuals impersonal, but by freeing individuals from benefices and payment in kind permitted the development of individual choices. Such dualities, he felt, were a permanent aspect of human experience, and he argued that alienation, thus, would be a perennial condition of human life – a statement that led LUKÁCS to accuse him of cynicism and of interpreting as eternal a condition characteristic only of capitalism. For almost all his life, Simmel was a private scholar, sustained by a small family inheritance, since his Jewish origins kept him from a university chair until 1914, when he was named a professor at Strassburg, a post he held until his death four years later. *Die Philosophie des Geldes* (Leipzig, 1907; *The Philosophy of Money*, NY, 1978) is Simmel's outstanding work. Other major works are *Einleitung in die Moralwissenschaft* [Introduction to moral philosophy] (Leipzig, 1892–3), *Soziologie* [Sociology] (Leipzig, 1908), *Lebensanschauung: Vier metaphysische Kapitel* [Life-views: four metaphysical chapters] (Berlin, 1918). Two useful collections are those by K. H. Wolff, *The Sociology of Georg Simmel* (NY, 1950) and by D. N. Levine, *Georg Simmel on Individuality and Social Forms* (NY, 1971).   DBe

L. A. Coser (ed.), *Georg Simmel* (Englewood Cliffs, 1965); D. P. Frisby, *Sociological Impressionism: a Reassessment of Georg Simmel's Social Theory* (London, 1981).

Simon, Herbert Alexander (b. Milwaukee, Wis., USA, 15.6.1916). American economist and social scientist. He studied at Chicago University and, after holding various posts at Chicago, Berkeley and the Illinois Institute of Technology, he was appointed in 1949 to a chair of administration at Carnegie-Mellon University, Pittsburgh, where he has remained. In 1965 he became R. K. Mellon professor of computer sciences and psychology. He was awarded the Nobel prize for economics in 1978.

Simon's work has been concerned mainly with producers' behaviour, and specifically with the organizational and psychological foundations of decision-making in the modern corporation. Starting from an interest in administrative science (see *Administrative Behavior*, NY, 1947, ³1976, and *Public Administration*, NY, 1950), Simon played a leading role during the 1950s in developing the 'behavioural' theory of the firm, which challenged simple profit-maximizing assumptions and stressed the complex internal structure of the large corporation, the multiplicity of its goals and subgoals and the need for 'satisficing' rather than 'maximizing' models of decision-making (see *Models of Man*, NY, 1957, and *Organizations*, with J. G. March, NY, 1958). By a natural progression Simon then turned his attention to the problems of information-processing in large organizations, bearing in mind that information itself and the human capacity to exploit it in rational calculation are both limited. Thus, he has investigated the use of computer models in simulating human problem-solving (e.g. chess playing) and other cognitive processes, and in supplying 'decision support systems' for corporate policy-makers (see *The Shape of Automation*, NY, 1960, ²1965; *The Sciences of the Artificial*, Cambridge, Mass., 1969; *Human Problem Solving*, with A. Newell, Englewood Cliffs, 1972; *Models of Discovery*, New Haven, 1977; *Models of Thought*, Boston, Mass., 1979).   PMO

Simpson, George Gaylord (b. Chicago, Ill., USA, 16.6.1902). American palaeontologist. Widely considered to be the greatest palaeontologist of this century, Simpson went to Yale University as an undergraduate and subsequently became professor first at Columbia, then at Harvard. Simpson's special interest has always been fossil mammals, and his most important taxonomic work is *Principles of Classification and a Classification of Mammals* (Amer. Mus. Nat. Hist. Bulletin, NY, 1945). His wider fame rests on two outstanding books *Tempo and Mode in Evolution* (NY, 1944) and *The Major Features of Evolution* (NY, 1953), in which he evaluates the contribution of the fossil record to the mid-20c neo-Darwinian synthesis which followed the great discoveries in genetics some years earlier. Terms that Simpson coined, such as 'quantum evolution' and 'adaptive zone', have since become common currency. His important work on ancient biogeography bears up well, and he has been a highly successful popularizer of science, notably in *The Meaning of Evolution* (Yale, 1949). AH

Sinatra, Francis Herbert (Frank) (b. Hoboken, NJ, USA, 12.12.1915). American popular singer, also a screen actor. As his name suggests, Sinatra had Italian parents from whom he inherited his musicality. During WW2 he was a popular radio singer and an idol of 'bobby-soxer' teenage girls, with a romantic yet lively personality that earned him the name 'Swoonatra'. Inevitably he was signed up for the screen, like his fellow-crooner CROSBY, and though not especially handsome he proved very successful with such films as *Anchors Aweigh* (1945), in which he played a sailor on leave, and *High Society* (1956), in which he costarred with Crosby and ARMSTRONG. More unexpected was his success as a serious screen actor in a number of films beginning with *From Here to Eternity* (1953) and continuing to include such films as the British thriller *The Naked Runner* (1967) in which Sinatra played an 'unsuspecting pawn of British intelligence'. 'Ol' Blue-eyes' still occasionally sings, most recently in Polish for an American propaganda film (1982) commenting on political events in that country. His voice could be lightly romantic in a song such as 'Nancy', or dramatic and compelling as in 'My Way' – this latter song seeming especially to suit a personality containing a hint of menace as well as of warmth. One of the great durable names of show business, he is regarded with both awe and affection. CH

A. Shaw, *Sinatra: Twentieth-century Romantic* (NY, 1968).

Singer, Isaac Bashevis (b. Radzymin, Poland, 14.7.1904; naturalized American citizen, 1943). Polish/American novelist. Son of a Hasidic rabbi, he grew up in Warsaw and was given an orthodox religious education. In 1935 he emigrated to the USA. Writing in Yiddish, many stories were published under the penname 'Isaac Bashevis', and much journalism as by 'Warshofsky', but initial book publication takes the form of English translations. In 1978 he was awarded the Nobel prize for literature. His command of Yiddish idiom is compared to that of SHOLEM ALEICHEM and the quality of his style is said to defy translation. His devotion to a dying language and to subject matter based on imaginative recollections of Polish Jewry delayed his recognition among English-speaking critics. BELLOW's translation of 'Gimpel the Fool' (*Partisan Review*, 1953) was instrumental in establishing his reputation. Singer uses traditional story-forms: family history, *Bildungsroman*, portrait of a society as in *The Family Moskat* (tr. A. H. Gross, NY, 1950), *The Manor* (tr. E. Gottlieb & J. Singer, NY, 1967), *Shosha* (NY, 1978). He is traditional in a very different way in his use of folk motifs and supernatural fantasy. His novels are precisely realistic in social and natural detail but show man in the presence of powers he cannot understand, within a physical world that shadows an esoteric spiritual truth. *Satan in Goray* (tr. J. Sloan, NY, 1955), his first novel – originally published in Yiddish (Warsaw, 1935) – and *The Family Moskat*, his first novel to be published in English translation, set a pattern for his work: religious tradition, terrifying moral collapse and final ambiguous vision. His short stories, of which the title story of *Gimpel the Fool and Other Stories* (tr. S. Bellow *et al.*, NY, 1957) is a supreme example, present the spiritual dramas of individuals at the edge of rationality. Gimpel makes the quintessential Singer remark: ' . . . the world is entirely an imaginary world, but it is only once removed from the true world'. His *Collected Stories* were published in New York in 1981. BF

I. Malin (ed.), *Critical Views of Isaac Bashevis Singer* (NY, 1969).

Skinner, Burrhus Frederic (b. Susquehanna, Pa, USA, 20.3.1904). American psychologist. He obtained a doctorate from Harvard University in 1931 for research on reflex behaviour, and returned to Harvard in 1948, where he remained until retirement in 1975. In 1968 he received the National Medal of Science award – only the second psychologist to be so honoured. Skinner's approach to psychology has always been that of radical behaviourism, and his goals have been to predict and control behaviour without speculating about internal processes or states. His basic position was expressed in *The Behavior of Organisms* (NY, 1938), and involves shaping behaviour by reinforcing or rewarding any changes in the desired direction and extinguishing any undesired changes by means of nonreinforcement. His views developed as a result of research on simple learning in rats and pigeons, but subsequently he has addressed several major problems. In his novel *Walden Two* (NY, 1948), an entire society is controlled by his operant techniques, and in *Verbal Behavior* (NY, 1957) he attempted to account for human language and its development in conditioning terms. Skinnerian conditioning techniques have also been applied in the clinical field – where Skinner's first contribution dates back to 1953 with his interest in shaping the behaviour of chronic psychotic patients – and in education: as early as the 1930s he devised one of the first teaching machines and was involved in the development of programmed learning. Skinner has been extremely influential, and undoubtedly has developed a powerful technology that can be used successfully in clinical and educational practice. However, controlling behaviour is not the same as understanding it, and the Skinnerian approach has been criticized for failing to explain cognitive functioning and complex learning. This is especially the case with his work on language, where a simple conditioning approach seems quite inappropriate.

MWE

Sloan, Alfred Pritchard (b. New Haven, Conn., USA, 23.5.1875; d. New York, 7.2.1966). American business manager and contributor to management studies. In *My Years with General Motors* (NY, 1965) he described the creation of a vast, modern corporation. From 1923 to 1946 he was president, then chairman, of General Motors, which was on the brink of ruin when he took over the management. The company's founder William C. Durant had been a dominant individual but, in complete contrast to Henry FORD, ran a large business by treating each of the 25 constituent companies, including Cadillac, Buick, Olds and Oakland (later Pontiac), as uncoordinated, independent businesses. Sloan developed an organizational structure, management style and control system which combined central policy formulation and coordination with managerial decentralization. He set each division a return on investment as a criterion for its efficiency and contribution to the whole. Common accounting standards were created. The General Motors organization, with decentralized, divisional product manufacturing and marketing coordinated by central policy and authority with staff services, became a model for large business organizations.

RIT

P. F. Drucker, *Concept of the Corporation* (NY, ²1972).

Smith, Bernard William (b. Sydney, N. S. Wales, Australia, 3.10.1916). Australian art historian. For many years professor of fine art at Sydney University, Smith has never been content to treat 'fine art' as a merely academic subject, and through his many publications his influence has been considerable internationally, upon geographers, historians and anthropologists. His original study *Place, Taste and Tradition* (Sydney, 1945) was informed by MARXist thinking in its exploration of the ways in which Australia's art was determined by local and historical influences, while in *European Vision and the South Pacific 1768–1850: a Study in the History of Art and Ideas* (Oxford, 1960) he pursued these ways of thinking in more detail and produced a book of outstanding importance. *The Spectre of Truganini* (Sydney, 1981), the text of his 1980 Boyer lectures for the Australian Broadcasting Commission, considered the effects of the aboriginal presence upon Australian culture.

PNQ

Smith, Bessie (b. Chattanooga, Tenn., USA, 15.4.1894; d. Clarksdale, Miss., 27.9.1937). Black American blues and jazz singer. Known as 'Empress of the Blues', from her style evolved the jazz singing of ARMSTRONG, Billie Holiday and others. Born in conditions of extreme poverty, she rose to become the highest paid and most successful Negro entertainer of her time. Her career began in 1912 with 'Ma' Rainey's Rabbitt Foot Minstrels. She toured extensively with travelling shows during the 1920s and appeared in the film *St Louis Blues* (1929). 'Down Hearted Blues' (1923) with pianist Clarence Williams was the first of nearly 200 recordings she made in the following decade. It sold over two million copies in the Negro ('Race') market and successive recordings contributed substantially to her fame and prestige. Other notable jazz instrumentalists were involved, including James P. Johnson, Fletcher Henderson, Louis Armstrong, Charlie Green, Joe Smith, Tommy Ladnier and, later, Benny GOODMAN and Jack Teagarden. She possessed a large and powerful voice with a wide expressive range combined with an outstanding technique and ability to create enormous emotional intensity and expression. Her career was severely affected by her alcoholism and by the effects of the Depression upon commercial musical life. She died following a motor accident.   TEC

C. Albertson, *Bessie, Empress of the Blues* (London, 1975).

Smith, David Roland (b. Decatur, Ind., USA, 9.3.1906; d. Albany, NY, 23.5.1965). American sculptor and painter. Smith is widely regarded as the finest and most original American sculptor of this century. A man of prodigious and sometimes destructive energies, Smith began his adult life as a painter, but by the early 1930s his pictures regularly spilled over into the third dimension. He continued to experiment with sculptural objects and in 1932 was deeply impressed by reproductions of welded sculpture by PICASSO and GONZALEZ. In 1934 he set up a studio in Terminal Iron Works, a machinist's shop in Brooklyn. Following trips to Europe and the Soviet Union, Smith became involved in the Federal Art Project: in 1937 he began work on *Medals for Dishonor*, a series of antiwar medallions. But in the 1940s he began to draw freely in space with rods and wires: these works owed something to surrealist imagery, and were also often related to the abstract expressionism which was then emerging in American painting. In the 1950s Smith seemed to return more to the recognizable model of the human figure; at least his work was increasingly totemic in structure. In the 1960s, however, the organic and anthropomorphic references began to disappear – especially in the *Cubi* series which involved the arrangement of geometric volumes of stainless steel. These literally mechanical sculptures lacked the expressive force of the best of his earlier work. Smith's emotional life was in some chaos at this time, and he died prematurely following a car accident. PF

G. McCoy, *David Smith* (London, 1973).

Smith, Florence Margaret (Stevie) (b. Hull, Humb., UK, 20.9.1902; d. London, 7.3.1971). British poet and novelist. A prolific and highly popular poet, Stevie Smith combined her literary career with 30 years' work as a publisher's secretary and a spinsterish life in an unfashionable outer London suburb. She started in fiction with her eccentric and original *Novel on Yellow Paper* (London, 1936), a witty anatomy of the bizarre, bathetic and seemingly inconsequential aspects of human behaviour. Her poetry pursues similar themes, borrowing widely from fable, riddle, nursery rhyme and ballad forms; childishly simple in style, but subtle and immensely varied in tone. Eccentricity and a mocking humour are its chief characteristics. Her principal publications in this period were *A Good Time Was Had By All* (London, 1937), *Tender Only to One* (London, 1938), *Mother, What Is Man?* (London, 1942) and *Harold's Leap* (London, 1950). From *Not Waving But Drowning* (London, 1957), her finest collection, followed by *The Best Beast* (NY, 1969) and *Scorpion* (London, 1972), her poetry deepens in seriousness: loneliness, death and a puzzled attitude towards religion are constant preoccupations. Her enthusiasm for radio and live performance (she sometimes sang her poems set to music) brought her a wide audience, enabling her to escape the obscurity of much postwar poetry. JAC

K. Dick, *Ivy and Stevie: Conversations and Reflections* (London, 1971).

Smith, Ian Douglas (b. Selukwe, Southern Rhodesia [now Zimbabwe], 8.4.1919). Prime minister of Rhodesia. As leader of the right-wing Rhodesian Front, Smith was largely responsible for his country's Unilateral Declaration of Independence in 1965. Enjoying immense popularity among Rhodesia's 250,000 whites, who saw epitomized in him the simplicity and rugged independence that had enabled a small white minority to create a prosperous state in country previously given over to African 'barbarism', Smith dominated Rhodesian politics for a decade and a half, exasperating all British negotiators who tried to bring the Rhodesian 'rebellion' to an end by peaceful means. Smith's obduracy provoked a violent response from the country's black nationalists, leading to a guerrilla war (1972–9) which cost over 20,000 lives, before the Rhodesian government eventually accepted the principle of African majority rule. After the transformation of Rhodesia into the independent African state of Zimbabwe Smith remained active in his country's politics as leader of the Republican Front, representing the interests of those whites who chose to remain. RH

P. Joyce, *Anatomy of a Rebel: Smith of Rhodesia* (Salisbury, 1974).

Smuts, Jan Christiaan (b. Riebeck West, Cape Colony [now South Africa], 24.5.1870; d. Irene, Transvaal, 11.9.1950). South African prime minister, soldier and philosopher. The outstanding African political leader of the first half of the 20c, Smuts achieved eminence in his own country and internationally. Born in the British colony of the Cape, Smuts completed his education at Cambridge and became state-attorney of the South African Republic. During the Anglo–Boer war he proved an outstanding guerrilla commander. After the war he was an ardent advo-

cate of conciliation between Boer and Briton and played a major part in drawing up the constitution of the Union of South Africa (1910). Active in South African politics for the rest of his life, he was leader of the South African, later the United party and served as prime minister twice (1919–24 and 1939–48). During WW1, after service in German South-West and East Africa, he joined the Imperial War cabinet. More than any other individual, he was responsible for putting forward the concept that the British empire should evolve into a 'commonwealth' of free and equal members. He also played a formative role in establishing the League of Nations.

Regarded with immense esteem in international circles, Smuts's position in his own country was less happy. He failed to grasp the strength of Afrikaner nationalism. Many Afrikaners regarded him as *slim* [tricky] and deeply resented his part in bringing South Africa into WW2 on the British side. White workers hated him for his ruthless suppression of the 'Rand revolt' of 1922. Black South Africans found he had little to offer them: though more moderate and more pragmatic on the 'native question' than Afrikaner Nationalists, he accepted most forms of segregation and found no part for blacks in national politics. But he was a fervent South African patriot: he was a South African expansionist who would have liked to absorb both South West Africa (Namibia) and Rhodesia (Zimbabwe) in the Union. Smuts also achieved distinction as a botanist and as a philosopher. In *Holism and Evolution* (London, 1926) he argued that wholeness ('holism') was a fundamental factor in the universe, that 'wholes' possessed a 'self-realizing power' and that 'holistic evolution' implied 'a cosmic process of individuation', extending from the inorganic to the highest order of human personality. RH

W. K. Hancock, *Smuts*, vol. 1: *The Sanguine Years: 1870–1919* (Cambridge, 1962); vol. 2: *The Fields of Force* (Cambridge, 1968).

Soddy, Frederick (b. Eastbourne, E. Sussex, UK, 2.9.1877; d. Brighton, E. Sussex, 22.9.1956). British radiochemist.

Soddy worked with RUTHERFORD (1900 -2) at McGill University, Montreal, then continued his studies with RAMSAY (1903) at University College London. During these years he worked on problems concerning the radioactive decay of radium, showing that it was a phenomenon involving atomic disintegration and the formation of the element helium – the first unambiguous example of the generation of one element from another. In 1904 he was appointed lecturer in physical chemistry and radioactivity at Glasgow University, a post which he held until he became professor of physical chemistry at the University of Aberdeen in 1914. Soddy formulated his most important ideas in Scotland. The concept that elements with identical chemical properties may have different radioactive properties was suggested independently by Strömholm and Svedberg in 1909, and in 1910 by Soddy, but it was Soddy alone (*Nature*, 92 [1913], 399) who suggested the term isotopes ('equal place') for atoms of the same element (i.e. of the same place in the periodic table) with different atomic weight (and hence different radioactive properties). Soddy was also the first to formulate the 'displacement law', that loss of an α-particle causes the change of an element into the element of lower mass next-but-one in the periodic table (*Chemistry of the Radio-Elements*, London, 1911). After his appointment (1919) as the Dr Lee's professor of chemistry at Oxford (a position he held until 1937), Soddy abandoned active research in chemistry, devoting much of his time to economic and social theory, and to unusual geometric problems and mechanical devices. An interest in metallurgy revealed itself in his encouragement of HUME-ROTHERY, and in 1920 he proposed the value of isotopes for the determination of geological age. In 1906 Soddy had spoken of the possibility of being able to unlock the great store of the internal energy of uranium; in 1949, he was to write of himself (*The Story of Atomic Energy*, Nova Atlantis, 1949) as the sole surviving participator in the discoveries and ideas which in 1945 culminated in the large-scale release of atomic energy at the end of

WW2. He was awarded the Nobel prize in 1921.   KRS

Söderblom, Nathan (b. Trönö, Hälsingland, Sweden, 15.1.1866; d. Uppsala, 12.7.1931). Swedish theologian and churchman. Söderblom was professor for the history of religions in Uppsala from 1901, and from 1912 concurrently in Leipzig. He was largely responsible for introducing the modern study of religion in Sweden. He wrote on mysticism, and antedated OTTO in emphasizing the holy (see his article on holiness in *Encyclopedia of Religion and Ethics*, ed. J. Hastings, Edinburgh, 1913, and *Das Werden des Gottesglaubens* [The origin of belief in God], Leipzig, 1916). In Edinburgh he delivered the Gifford lectures of 1931, published as *The Living God* (Oxford, 1933). In 1914 he became archbishop of Uppsala and was the leading figure in the ecumenical movement, notably at the Stockholm conference of 1925. His practical church work included renewing the liturgy, writing devotional books and composing hymns. In 1930 he was awarded the Nobel Peace prize.   RM

H. G. G. Herklots, *Nathan Söderblom, Apostle of Christianity* (London, 1948); B. Sundkler, *Nathan Söderblom: his Life and Work* (Uppsala, 1968).

Sologub, Fyodor, ps. of Fyodor Kuzmich Teternikov (b. St Petersburg [now Leningrad], Russia, 17.2.1863; d. Leningrad, USSR, 5.12.1927). Russian novelist, dramatist and poet, who came to be known as an 'archetypal decadent' and 'the Russian Verlaine'. A man of almost pathological complexity and morbid disposition, he was subject to extreme pessimism, but his verse, and to a lesser extent his prose, are measured and calm in manner and quietly demonic in spirit. Born in St Petersburg, he lived for many years in provincial backwaters, doing teaching and minor school administrative jobs. Only after the publication of his novel *Melkiy Bes* (Berlin, 1905–7; tr. J. Cournos & R. Aldington, *The Little Demon*, London, 1916), at which he had worked for more than 10 years, was he able to leave school teaching and become a professional writer. He was basically apolitical, but, with many other contemporary Russian writers, he sided with the 1905 revolution, although in 1917 he remained politically aloof. He evolved, and was predisposed towards, a deeply dualistic, Manichean view of life in which the Platonic ideas of the good and the beautiful are counterposed to, but also intermingle with, a perverse sensualism based on the notion of an evil world of diversity and desire and a quasi-FREUDian correlation of sex and death. The view has all the signs of an indictment of the ugliness and vulgarity of Sologub's social environment, and is a way of escaping from it. *Melkiy Bes*, which made Sologub famous, is a complex and compelling rendering of his Manichean philosophy against the background of social squalor and the devious experiences of a paranoid provincial school teacher attracted by an innocent but libidinous young beauty. An earlier novel *Tyazhelye sny* (St Petersburg–Moscow, 1896; tr. V. W. Smith, *Bad Dreams*, Ann Arbor, 1978) as well as some short stories and the later prose works *Tvorimaya legenda* (3 vols, Moscow, 1908–12; tr. J. Cournos, *The Created Legend*, London, 1916–21) are variations on the dualistic theme, although tending to aesthetic sentimentalism. The same must be said of Sologub's hieratic plays, which are far inferior to his novels and are virtually unstageable. Unlike the prose, Sologub's verse is simple, lucid, precise and marked by understatement, even at its most symbolist and occult. Both prose and poetry are distinguished by a subtle, if rather morbid, sense of humour, but Sologub is said never to have been seen laughing during the whole of his life. EL

F. D. Reeve, *The Russian Novel* (London, 1966).

Solow, Robert Merton (b. New York, USA, 28.8.1924). American economist. One of the newer generation of leaders of the economics profession, whose wide-ranging interests and originality have been recognized by many honours, including the presidency of the American Economic Association (1980). A graduate of Harvard and Chicago, Solow has taught at MIT since 1949, where his name has been closely associ-

ated with that of SAMUELSON. He has been a pioneer of the use of mathematical models in economics, and was joint author with Samuelson and Robert Dorfman of *Linear Programming and Economic Analysis* (NY, 1958), a book which taught linear production theory to a whole generation of young economists. His work on growth theory, particularly his neoclassical growth model and his path-breaking work on calculating the sources of US growth, aroused widespread interest. Other major fields of interest have been macroeconomic theory and the theory of capital and interest as represented by *Capital Theory and the Rate of Return* (Chicago, 1964) and *Growth Theory: an Exposition* (NY, 1970). PS

Solzhenitsyn, Aleksandr Isaevich Kislovodsk (b. Kislovodsk, USSR, 11.12.1918). Russian prose writer, and Nobel prize winner (1970), who is often compared with Leo TOLSTOY and Dostoevsky. He graduated in mathematics and physics at Rostov University (1936–9), and during WW2 he served at the front as an officer. In 1945 he was arrested for criticizing STALIN in a letter to a friend. He spent the next eight years in labour camps. Released in 1953, he remained in exile for three more years. He dates the beginning of his serious writings from the late 1940s. He contracted cancer and spent several months in Tashkent. Between 1955 and 1958 he wrote his major novel *V kruge pervom* (NY, 1968; tr. T. P. Whitney, *The First Circle*, London, 1968) about political prisoners in the Soviet inferno. Released from exile (1956), he settled in Riazan' as a teacher of physics and mathematics. In 1960 he submitted a short story *Odin den' Ivana Denisovicha* (1962; tr. M. Hayward & R. Hingley, *One Day in the Life of Ivan Denisovich*, London, 1963) to the editor of *Novy Mir*, a leading Soviet literary journal. The history of the story's publication is described in *Bodalsia telionok s dubom* (Paris, 1975; tr. H. Willetts, *The Oak and the Calf*, London, 1980). KRUSHCHEV authorized the publication to make use of it in his cautious attempt to demythologize Stalin. In 1963 Solzhenitsyn published three further stories: the idea of *Matrionin dvor* (1963; tr. H. Willetts, *Matryona's House*, 1963) is expressed in its original title *The village cannot stand without a righteous man*; the others were *Sluchay na Stantsii Krechetovka* (1963; tr. M. Glenny, *The Incident at Krechetovka Station*, 1963) and *Dlia pol'zy dela* (1963; tr. D. Floyd & M. Hayward, *For the Good of the Cause*, London, 1963). He became a celebrity at home and abroad. He gave up teaching, joined the Union of Soviet Writers and began to collect material for the documentary work *Arkhipelag Gulaga* (3 vols, Paris, 1973–5; tr. T. P. Whitney, *The Gulag Archipelago*, 3 vols, London, 1974–8), an artistic investigation of the entire system of Soviet oppression since 1918. Both *V kruge pervom* and *Rakovy korpus* (London, 1968; tr. N. Bethell & D. Burg, *Cancer Ward*, London, 1968) were rejected. But his determination to inform the world of the magnitude of the crimes committed by the Soviet Communist party led to his initiation of an open campaign from 1966 onwards. The publication of *V kruge pervom* and *Rakovy korpus* abroad in 1968 was followed by his expulsion from the writers' union. A series of violent attacks on him in the Soviet press only contributed to his popularity and authority. He continued to write *August Chetyrnadtsatovo* (Paris, 1974; tr. M. Glenny, *August 1914*, London, 1972), a first 'knot' of his main work – a history of the Russian revolution. In 1973 the KGB seized a copy of *Arkhipelag Gulaga*, thus prompting Solzhenitsyn to publish it immediately in the West. The publication abroad of this work, which Solzhenitsyn himself saw as a potentially lethal weapon against the Soviet regime, led to his arrest and deportation from Russia in 1974. Settling first in Zürich with his second wife and children, his attacks began to be aimed as much at the West as at the USSR, because he believes that the revolution betrayed Russia's special Christian mission, while the West connives in this betrayal by maintaining relations with the Soviet Union. The strong emotional need in Solzhenitsyn to return to his Slavophil origins reflects a widespread trend within the Soviet intelligentsia. It is a form of spiritual and cultural national-

ism, a search for true national identity observable in all Solzhenitsyn's writings. His early works show an extraordinary economy of means and are devoid of his later shrill notes and strident moralizing. Unlike Tolstoy, he does not always succeed in integrating a whole philosophy of life into one work. Unlike Dostoevsky, who makes his antagonists almost more convincing than his protagonists, he often allows his own ideas to proceed uncontradicted. His political statements have become increasingly narrow-minded and have had, if anything, a damaging effect on the quality of his creative imagination. *Lenin v Zurikhe* (Paris, 1975; tr. H. T. Willetts, *Lenin in Zurich*, London, 1975) is a sad example of his artistic failure. The role of Tolstoy has been assigned to Solzhenitsyn more by fate and by history than by his talent. He seems now to have abandoned literature in order to write the 'political and spiritual history of Russia since the beginning of the century'. He published many of his 'knots' in émigré periodicals. His work has undoubtedly a value which reaches beyond literature, but many regret his attempts to act as a 'second government' and his consequent desertion of his artistic homeland in Russian literature. Since 1976 he has lived in the USA.   VP

K. Fever (ed.), *Solzhenitsyn: a Collection of Critical Essays* (Englewood Cliffs, 1976); F. Barker, *Solzhenitsyn: Poetics and Form* (London, 1977).

Sommerfeld, Arnold (b. Königsberg, Prussia [now Kaliningrad, USSR], 5.12.1868; d. Munich, Bavaria, West Germany, 26.4.1951). German theoretical physicist who pioneered the analysis of atomic spectra using the quantum theory. He studied at Göttingen under Felix Klein and developed a method of using the theory of functions of a complex variable to solve boundary-value problems. He applied this to the propagation of electromagnetic waves along wires and to the diffraction of electrons by a wedge-shaped slit. He also collaborated with Klein on a treatise on the theory of tops. As professor at Munich, Sommerfeld directed experimental work on electrons and founded a school of theoretical physicists who applied the new ideas of EINSTEIN and PLANCK to atomic problems. He used the theory of relativity to calculate the angular distribution of *Bremsstrahlung*, or continous radiation, and applied N. BOHR's atomic theory to the splitting of spectral lines in a magnetic field (the ZEEMAN effect). His *Atombau und Spektrallinien* (Braunschweig, 1919; *Atomic Structure and Spectral Lines*, London, 1923) went through many editions. He analysed many X-ray, atomic and molecular spectra in terms of energy levels, quantum numbers and selection rules, and used quantum mechanics to calculate the energies and rates of atomic transitions. Later work was devoted to the application of quantum mechanics and FERMI statistics to the motion of electrons in metals. Sommerfeld's pupils included DEBYE, PAULI, HEISENBERG, HEITLER and BETHE. Repelled by the anti-Semitism of the Nazis, he went into retirement and wrote a six-volume treatise on theoretical physics. PEH

Sorel, Georges-Eugène (b. Cherbourg, Manche, France, 28.11.1847; d. Boulogne-sur-Seine, Paris, 28.8.1922). French social philosopher. Despite abrupt and apparently erratic changes of political allegiance – from MARXism and revolutionary syndicalism to the mystical nationalism of BARRÈS and the royalism of the supporters of *Action Française* – all his writings are informed by the central moral vision of a full creative life in a ·society of free producers. This is evident in his most famous work *Réflexions sur la violence* (Paris, 1908; tr. T. E. HULME, *Reflections on Violence*, NY, 1914), which contains his two most celebrated notions, those of 'violence' and 'myth'.

Raised in straitened circumstances, at 18 Sorel was admitted to the Ecole Polytechnique, and in 1870 he began his professional career as an engineer for the government department of bridges and roads. Only in 1892 did he retire from government employment to devote himself to the pursuit of his ideas. Influenced by the writings of Vico, Marx and Proudhon, CROCE, BERGSON, NIETZSCHE and William JAMES, Sorel rejected two of the main pillars of western social and political thought: the

Greek doctrine of salvation by knowledge, and the Judaeo-Christian doctrine of historical theodicy. Natural science cannot provide models of the innermost essence of 'natural nature' which in itself is inscrutable, chaotic and subject to entropy; at best science tells us about 'artificial nature' which is that part of it upon which man, by his scientific theories, has been able to impose some kind of precarious order. Perhaps, according to Sorel, the most dehumanizing tendency of modern times is the attempt to treat all human problems as soluble by technoscientific methods; to construct a 'social physics' which will enable men to organize society 'rationally' and to predict the future; and to convert the free choices made by individuals into rational decisions computed by experts. Sorel was equally opposed to the belief that the historical process was governed by inexorable laws which guarantee the ultimate realization of a rational utopia where all values would be realized. Only the conscious and unremitting pursuit of freely chosen moral goals, relentless energy and will, can inaugurate a society of creative producers. Sorel hated democracy, parliaments, compromise, 'reasonable' solutions of any kind, and preached the doctrine of the 'social myth' – this was not a rational plan of action or a scientific prediction, nor yet a utopia, but an energizing vision which inspires and galvanizes the masses into action. An example of this is Sorel's myth of the 'general strike'. It is unlikely that Sorel foresaw such an event actually taking place, but the belief in it could be – and indeed has proved to be – a potent force in persuading the working classes of their collective capacity for epic action. 'The goal is nothing; the movement is everything.'

Sorel rejects the classical view that men seek primarily happiness, and asserts the supreme value of untrammelled exercise of the will for its own sake: the imposition of a freely generated human stamp or pattern upon the resistant material of nature; self-realization and self-expression, individual and collective, through spontaneous creative work. Hence Sorel's aversion to hedonism and materialist values, and his willingness to countenance – indeed extol – violence under certain circumstances as the reassertion of basic human dignity. His writings were read by political leaders as far apart from each other as LENIN and MUSSOLINI (both of whom he admired), and he has exerted an enormous influence on the rebellious youth movements of the mid-20c.   RNH

I. Berlin, *Against the Current* (London, 1979); J. Stanley, *The Sociology of Virtue* (Berkeley, Calif., 1982).

Sorokin, Pitirim Alexandrovich (b. Turya, Russia, 21.1.1889; naturalized American citizen, 1930; d. Winchester, Mass., USA, 10.2.1968). Russian/American sociologist. Educated at the Psychoneurological Institute and the University of St Petersburg, he was active in Russian revolutionary politics. After a varied career as factory hand, journalist and tutor he became personal secretary to KERENSKY and cabinet minister in the 1917 Russian government. Sentenced to death by both the Tsarists and the Bolsheviks and having accepted the position of professor of sociology at the University of Leningrad in 1919, he was banished in 1922 for anti-Bolshevik teaching. Once in the USA he taught at the University of Minnesota between 1924 and 1930 before being appointed as the first professor of sociology at Harvard where he established the department and served as chairman until 1955. Sorokin had an encyclopedic knowledge of history which he assiduously applied in his sociological research to provide a masterful analysis of social change at the macrolevel, particularly in *Social and Cultural Dynamics* (4 vols, NY, 1937–41). He was a pioneer of sociological research and under his leadership Harvard developed as a major centre for social science research in the USA. His contribution to sociology included his major works on social mobility and on *Contemporary Sociological Theories* (NY, 1928) through which he played a significant role in introducing the European intellectual tradition into the USA. He developed much of the framework of rural sociology and of small-group research, but his greatest impact was felt through his sophisticated methodological critique of

pseudoscientific sociology. Sorokin centred his students' attention on the development of technically complex social theory. It was from this school that the work of PARSONS emerged.   TFC/LMC

Soulages, Pierre (b. Rodez, Aveyron, France, 24.12.1919). French painter. He is one of the most important of the group of abstract artists of the school of Paris who came to prominence after WW2. His large, sombre paintings in which blacks and browns predominate express for many a pessimistic vision, but he himself avers that he is interested only in the qualities proper to painting: relationship of forms, colour, rhythm and material. He studied at the Ecole des Beaux Arts, Montpelier, and after WW2 moved to Paris where he had his first one-man show in 1949. The broad, dark strokes of oil paint on a glowing ground may relate to the prehistoric and Romanesque art of his childhood environment. He designed sets for Graham GREENE's play *Héloïse et Abélard*, performed in Paris in 1949, and for the ballet *Geste pour un génie* [Gesture for a spirit] in 1952.   MOJN

J. J. Sweeney, *Soulages* (London, 1972).

Soyinka, Akinwande Oluwole (Wole) (b. Abeokuta, Nigeria, 13.7.1934). Nigerian dramatist, who has also excelled as a novelist (*The Interpreters*, London, 1965; *Season of Anomy*, London, 1973), as a poet (including *Idanre and Other Poems*, London, 1967, and *Ogun Abibiman*, London, 1976) and as an essayist (*Myth, Literature and the African World*, Cambridge, 1976). Soyinka himself comes from a Yoruba tradition but he has always insisted that the writer should be judged aesthetically and not nationalistically. He thus sees himself as part of world literature and not as an advocate of black or African sensibilities. His own education was at the universities of Ibadan and Leeds, and in the early 1950s he was associated with the Royal Court Theatre in London where his first major play was staged. These early plays are deft comic satires with village settings. Later work for the theatre, often evolved with university actors, has become more experimental both intellectually and in terms of stagecraft, as in *Madmen and Specialists* (1970). That he has lost none of his capacity for simple narrative is shown in *Aké* (London, 1981), his autobiography of childhood. During the Nigerian civil war Soyinka was held in detention for nine months; *The Man Died: Prison Memoirs* (London, 1972) is the embittered account of his ordeal. Soyinka has never espoused fashionable causes and as a result has sometimes been the target of severe criticism. But no writer has made a more diverse or challenging contribution to Anglophone African literature.

ANRN

E. D. Jones, *The Writing of Wole Soyinka* (London, 1973); J. Gibbs, *Critical Perspectives on Wole Soyinka* (Washington, 1980).

Spark, Muriel Sarah, *née* Camberg (b. Edinburgh, Lothian, UK, 1.2.1918). British novelist. Her first novel *The Comforters* (London, 1957), about a young woman recently converted to Catholicism who struggles against the will of the novelist who has created her, evidently reflected Muriel Spark's own religious experience and self-consciousness about the business of writing fiction. It set the pattern for a long and brilliant sequence of novels in which a poised, intrusive and always surprising authorial manner ruthlessly measures human folly and wickedness against the standards of eternity, and at the same time plays dazzling and disconcerting games with the conventions of narrative. Among her early books, *The Prime of Miss Jean Brodie* (London, 1961) and *The Girls of Slender Means* (London, 1963) are particularly enjoyable for their wit and evocation of period, while the later novellas *The Driver's Seat* (London, 1970) and *Not to Disturb* (London, 1971) are perhaps her most boldly experimental works. Muriel Spark has lived in Rome for some years, and writes often about the international rich, both exposing and relishing their amoral behaviour. DJL

P. Kemp, *Muriel Spark* (London, 1974).

Spearman, Charles Edward (b. London, UK, 10.9.1863; d. London, 17.9.1945). British statistician and psychologist interested in human intelligence. He studied extensively in Germany, initially under Wilhelm Wundt, and then from 1911 to 1931 he occupied a chair at University College London. His first influential article 'General intelligence objectively determined and measured' was published in Germany in 1904. If a general factor of (say) intelligence exists (g-factor), then individuals' performances on otherwise unrelated tests will be correlated. In factor analysis, arithmetical manipulation of observed correlations gives a picture of a postulated underlying factor. If this picture persists through several independent experiments one accepts the postulate. A. E. Maxwell, R. B. Catell, K. G. Jöreskog and others have developed procedures to do the arithmetic for, say, 600 variables and 15 factors, without labour or much risk of error. Since repetition remains difficult, users often announce results on the strength of one experiment, which is unsound. Spearman also produced his 'footrule', a correlation of ranks, which is both useful and uncontentious. His *The Abilities of Man: Their Nature and Measurement* (London, 1927) is an intelligible account of his two-factor (general and special-ability) theory of intelligence and his sometimes far-fetched deductions from it. AGPW

Spemann, Hans (b. Stuttgart, Baden-Württemberg, Germany, 27.6.1869; d. Freiburg im Breisgau, Baden-Württemberg, 12.9.1941). German embryologist. Spemann was perhaps the most influential developmental biologist of the first half of the 20c. From a series of beautiful experimental investigations of the early embryonic development of amphibians (newts and frogs) he was able to show that interactions between sheets of embryonic cells were responsible for some of the decisions committing particular groups of cells, and their descendants, to develop into the tissues and organs which they became in the adult. Thus, he early showed that those surface cells of the head which were destined to form the lens of the eye would, in some species, only do so if they suffered contact with the future retina which underlay them. Furthermore, surface cells which were *not* destined to form a lens could be induced to do so if they experienced the appropriate contact. This phenomenon is known as embryonic induction.

Spemann later, with his colleague Hilde Mangold, demonstrated that the whole of the central nervous system of amphibian animals was formed under the influence of an inductive stimulus from contiguous cells. The central nervous system is anatomically of extreme complexity and it was tempting to suppose that only the most complicated of stimuli could induce it. However, Spemann himself, and many others since, showed that the cells being induced were largely responsible for the details of their response to induction. His earlier designation of the inducer of the nervous system as the 'organization centre' of the embryo reflected the importance of its role and its apparent ability to create a quasi-normal embryo out of willing cells whatever the insults they had endured.

Spemann's work was recognized by a Nobel prize in 1935 and in the same year his researches were admirably recounted in his Silliman lectures, to be published as *Embryonic Development and Induction* (New Haven, 1938). As is often the case, he was more cautious than many of his enthusiastic followers. Today the nature of inductive stimuli remains an object of investigation, but is not thought to hold the secret of development.   DRN

O. Mangold, *Hans Spemann, ein Meister der Entwicklungsphysiologie, sein Leben und sein Werk* (Stuttgart, 1953).

Spencer, Stanley (b. Cookham-on-Thames, Berks., UK, 30.6.1891; d. Taplow, Bucks., 14.12.1959). British figure and landscape painter. Spencer studied at the Slade School in London (1909–12), and from the very beginning of his career showed a gift for visionary painting of an idiosyncratic kind. The three recurrent themes running through his work have been: the village of Cookham where he was born and where he spent the greater part of his life; his preoccupation with religion reflected not only in his frequent use of biblical subjects, but in a mystical belief that even everyday acts, such as the sewing on of

a button, were religious acts and a part of perfection; and a concern with sex, both overt and as an element in religion. Many of his pictures of biblical themes were depicted as happening in the setting of Cookham, with himself and his neighbours taking part (for instance, his *Resurrection*, 1923–7, in the Tate Gallery, London, shows people rising from their graves in the churchyard at Cookham), and miraculous events and everyday domestic ones are shown taking place side by side. His experiences as a Red Cross orderly and soldier in WW1 led to his commission to decorate the memorial chapel of Burghclere, near Newbury, with mural paintings, culminating on the east wall in a huge *Resurrection of the Soldiers*; the most impressive and original cycle of mural paintings (1926–32) produced by any British artist in this century. However, in addition to the imaginative figure compositions which he regarded as his prime interest, he always continued to paint a number of landscapes and portraits which are painstakingly detailed and accurate in their realism. His paintings, often intense and dramatic, with a strong sense about them that something important is happening, tend to avoid conventional beauty and emphasize the grotesque. This was in part a reflection of his own eccentric and complex personality. John Rothenstein has edited *Stanley Spencer the Man: Correspondence and Reminiscences* (London, 1979).   REA

M. Collis, *Stanley Spencer: a Biography* (London, 1962); D. Robinson, *Stanley Spencer: Visions from a Berkshire Village* (London, 1979).

Spengler, Oswald (b. Blankenburg, Brandenburg, Germany [now East Germany], 28.5.1880; d. Munich, Bavaria, Germany, 8.5.1936). German philosopher of history. A former gymnasium teacher, Spengler was in his late 30s, living as a private scholar in Munich, when he published the book on which his reputation rests, *Der Untergang des Abendlande* (2 vols, Munich, 1918–22, ²1923; tr. C. F. Atkinson, *The Decline of the West*, NY, 1926–8). Conceived before WW1 and finished in 1917, the exigencies of wartime delayed its appearance until

1918, thereby ensuring that it made an unprecedented impact on a generation which had just been through the experience of war and, for German-speaking peoples, defeat. In this dark, rhapsodic work, with its scattered arresting insights, Spengler sought to initiate a 'Copernican revolution' in historiography: dispassionate scrutiny reveals history to be devoid of any fixed point of reference or unifying meaning. Spengler's new discipline of 'cultural morphology' uncovers the existence of eight (or more) cultures – the Egyptian, the Chinese, the Ancient Semitic, the Indian, the Magian, the Apollonian or Greco-Roman, the Faustian or Western – which mysteriously spring into being, grow, flower and decline. The total outlook of each – its activities and artefacts in all their finest ramifications – is informed by its own distinctive 'soul' or 'style' and each is conceived as being insulated by a cultural envelope utterly impermeable to the products of other cultures. Using biological analogies (especially that of a seed), Spengler maintains that each of these self-contained historical units has an identical life-cycle lasting some one thousand years. If we know at which point we stand in our own cultural cycle, we can predict in broad outline what the future holds for us: Faustian culture, according to Spengler, was moving from its autumn period into winter. As with all schematic historical constructions, Spengler's distorts and suppresses the facts; and his extreme cultural relativism seems to preclude genuine understanding of the past. Spengler wrote a further book *Der Mensch und die Technik* (Munich, 1931; tr. C. T. Atkinson, *Man and Technics*, London, 1932). This attracted some attention but he never won an academic appointment and his attempts to establish himself as a political commentator were unsuccessful. His political ideas had some affinity with those of the National Socialists but his hopes of influencing them came to nothing and he died in isolation. His impact was immense but brief. Who, apart from scholars, reads him today? It is said that KISSINGER gave *The Decline of the West* to President NIXON as a bedside book.

RNH

H. S. Hughes, *Oswald Spengler: a Critical Estimate* (NY, 1952); W. Dray, *Perspectives on History* (London, 1980).

Sperry, Roger Wolcott (b. Hartford, Conn., USA, 20.8.1913). American neurologist. While studying for his PhD in zoology under WEISS at the University of Chicago, he challenged the conventional genetic view of neuronal specificity and proposed instead his theory of chemo-affinity. In a series of elegant experiments he demonstrated that interneuronal connections are critically determined by chemical gradients rather than by specific genetic information; a concept that is still central to modern developmental neurobiology. From Chicago Sperry moved to Harvard where he again reacted against conventional wisdom by rejecting LASHLEY's theory of cortical equipotentiality and the law of mass action. In 1954 Sperry was appointed to his current post of professor of psychobiology at the California Institute of Technology. Here he began a long series of experiments on cerebral commissurotomy in animals. Contrary to earlier work in this field Sperry demonstrated quite striking disconnection effects, thus confirming his earlier intuitions that discrete pathways in the brain carried specific types of information. This work led to Sperry's celebrated research on human commissurotomized or 'split-brain' patients for which he was awarded the Nobel prize for physiology and medicine in 1981. This work has demonstrated, often quite spectacularly, the importance of cerebral commissures to the interhemispheric integration of perceptual and motor function and has revealed the specialization of the right hemisphere for nonverbal processes and the dominance of the left hemisphere for language processing. In addition Sperry has explored the implications of this work for theories of consciousness.

AJP

Spock, Benjamin McLane (b. New Haven, Conn., USA, 2.5.1903). American paediatrician. Spock studied at Yale and Columbia universities and practised as a paediatrician from 1933. From 1944 to 1946 he served in the US Navy. Then in 1946 he published *The Commonsense*

Book of Baby and Child Care (NY) which was made widely available as an inexpensive paperback. This book was extremely important for two reasons. First, it was probably the only book on child care which did not advocate a traditional 'hardline' approach. Spock suggested a relaxed and gentle approach which influenced millions of parents in the years which followed. During the Vietnam war he was accused by President NIXON of corrupting the youth of America by his permissive attitude towards children. Second, it was the forerunner of a whole host of 'popular' medical books by qualified authors, intended to explain things to lay readers in a simple and readable way. Spock's book has already sold over 28 million copies and has had a tremendous influence on authors and publishers of medical books.   VC

Springer, Axel Caesar (b. Hamburg-Altona, Germany, 2.5.1912). German newspaper proprietor. A suburban printer and book publisher in 1945, Springer, with help from the British Control Commission, rose rapidly to great prosperity in the confusion of postwar Germany. He is now the most powerful newspaper proprietor in Europe. He has no real counterpart. He has created an extraordinary and most complex press organization, which controls 40 per cent of all editions of West German daily newspapers, more than 80 per cent of regional newspapers, 90 per cent of Sunday newspapers and around 50 per cent of weekly periodicals. He publishes two-thirds of the newspapers bought in the largest city of the Federal Republic, Hamburg, and in West Berlin. He could create an unrivalled nationwide political platform. Springer, however, disclaims all such thoughts. His editors assert their autonomy, he says. The Springer press, however, has 'Springer' views about most big issues from foreign policy to nuclear power stations. Like Springer himself, it is consistently right of centre. Its collective viewpoint seems to be based on a belief that vast daily sales (largely to industrial workers and their families) means mass approval of what the Springer press has to offer. Springer's career shows how a consumer society in Europe's richest industrial nation can accord a political mandate to commercially successful mass journalism.   RB

H. Dieter-Müller, *Press Power: a Study of Axel Springer* (London, 1969).

Sraffa, Piero (b. Turin, Piedmont, Italy, 5.8.1898; naturalized British citizen). Italian/British economist (and protégé of KEYNES) whose article on 'The laws of return under competitive conditions' (*Economic Journal*, 1926) demonstrated with unprecedented clarity the logical inconsistency at the heart of orthodox economic theory. Sraffa showed that the assumption of perfect competition which underlay the accepted theories of production and exchange was not only unrealistic but theoretically indefensible. The effect was to turn the attention of leading economic theorists to developing models of imperfectly competitive or monopolistic market situations and eventually to lay the basis for the modern theory of the firm. In 1927 Sraffa, who was finding it increasingly difficult to pursue his research in Italy under a fascist dictatorship, migrated to a lectureship in the University of Cambridge. There he embarked in the 1930s on what was to be his life's work, a definitive edition of the collected writings of Ricardo: *The Works and Correspondence of David Ricardo* (11 vols, Cambridge, 1951–73). In this monumental work of scholarship, a major contribution to the history of economic thought, he was assisted by his colleague at Trinity College, Maurice Dobb. Sraffa's last published work – he is now emeritus reader in economics at Cambridge – a spin-off from his research on Ricardo, was another path-breaking essay in pure theory: *The Production of Commodities by Means of Commodities* (Cambridge, 1960). It presents an elegant solution to a theoretical puzzle which had baffled Ricardo, but its chief interest lies in the fact that it contains an implicit critique of modern theory and that it set off a lively economic controversy on alternative economic models.   PMD

de Staël, Nicolas (b. St Petersburg [now Leningrad], Russia, 5.1.1914; naturalized French citizen, 1948; d. Antibes, Alpes-

Maritimes, France, 16.3.1955). French painter of Russian origin. De Staël was born into an aristocratic, military family. He was exiled to Poland in 1919 and in 1922, after his parents' deaths, moved to Brussels where he was educated and studied at the Académie des Beaux Arts (1932–3). He travelled in Europe and North Africa until 1938, when he settled in Paris. He joined the French Foreign Legion on the outbreak of WW2, but after demobilization he started painting synthetic cubist works in 1942. By 1944 he was back in Paris, a friend of BRAQUE and an abstract painter. He took his own life in 1955. De Staël's compositions changed gradually from earthy to extremely adventurous colour combinations on a large scale. Their lively effect contrasts with the rigorous, usually vertical, underlying structure of blocks and patches of colour (e.g. *Untitled*, 1951). Between 1952 and 1955 he struggled to keep his works predominantly abstract while still affirming their origin in objects and events: at times merely evoking a landscape or seascape; at times directly representing, e.g. components of a still life, football players or jazz musicians. From the late 1940s onwards he won a considerable Anglo-American reputation, aided in the 1950s not only by the immediate vitality of his work but by the figurative elements which made them generally amenable. JGr

G. Duthuit, *Nicolas de Staël* (NY, 1950); D. Cooper, *Nicolas de Staël* (London, 1961).

Stalin, Joseph, ps. of Joseph Vissarionovich Dzhugashvili (b. Gori, Georgia, Russia, 21.12.1879; d. Moscow, USSR, 5.4.1953). Russian revolutionary and for 25 years undisputed ruler of the USSR. Educated at the Tiflis Orthodox Seminary, Stalin joined the political underground movement in 1900, and was arrested seven times between 1902 and 1913. From 1913 to 1917 he was exiled to Siberia but returned to Petrograd on the outbreak of the revolution in 1917 and played an important role in the Bolshevik seizure of power (November 1917). In the new government he held two posts, commissar for nationalities and commissar for state control, which gave him power over the growing state bureaucracy. His reputation was that of a hard worker and this secured him the key post of secretary-general of the party's Central Committee in 1922, a post which he held until his death. Stalin was, as TROTSKY scornfully called him, the bureaucrat of revolution; he could not match the brilliance of the intellectuals of the party, Trotsky, ZINOVYEV and BUKHARIN; but their underestimation of his intelligence and political skill was to cost all three of them their lives.

After LENIN's death (1924) Stalin outmanoeuvred his rivals, and from 1928 to his death in 1953 exercised greater personal power, for a longer period, than any other figure in history. He withdrew the concessions to capitalism Lenin had made in his New Economic policy; put no further reliance on hopes of worldwide revolution to solve Soviet Russia's problems and under the slogan of 'Socialism in one country' launched the country into a second revolution, pursued with a ruthless disregard for the cost in human suffering. In a succession of five-year plans, he carried out a crash process of industrialization which lifted the USSR from a backward country to one of the leading industrial nations. The collectivization of agriculture was less successful and in the campaigns to break peasant resistance the number of those who perished was of the order of 10 million. Just as Russia was recovering from these upheavals, Stalin launched a new campaign aimed at eliminating anyone from the party and state bureaucracy, and eventually the army, who was even suspected of independence, and at cowing the remainder into subservience. A series of show trials, in which leaders publicly 'confessed' to fabricated charges and were then executed or imprisoned, was the façade for a purge which assumed monstrous proportions and again involved millions of people.

When HITLER attacked the USSR in 1941 Stalin appointed himself C-in-C and after initial disasters rallied the Russian people to throw back the invading armies. The advance of the Soviet armies in their turn enabled him to create a new Soviet empire in Eastern

Europe where a hundred million people found themselves living under nominally independent regimes which in fact were subject to control from Moscow. The final years of Stalin's dictatorship were described by his successor KRUSHCHEV as a nightmare in which no one felt safe, and the whole country lived under a pall of fear.

There is little agreement within the Communist world or outside it on how to judge Stalin's extraordinary career, his personality, his motivation or his talents. It can be claimed, on Stalin's behalf, that he was the chief architect of the Soviet Union of which Lenin was the creator; that his industrialization of Russia, which survived the devastation of WW2 and has proved capable of producing a nuclear armament the equal of the USA, is the turning-point in modern Russian history. The creation of this military-industrial complex brought meagre benefits for the mass of the Russian people, but under his leadership the USSR defeated Hitler's Germany and embarked on the postwar expansion which has made it the only rival of the USA as a super-power, while the bureaucratic state which he created has survived his death by at least 30 years. Against this has to be set the appalling and unequalled price in human deaths, suffering and fear exacted by his methods; the systematic use of terror to extinguish human rights, freedom and creativity; the pathological suspicion, deceit and cruelty which he not only displayed himself but made the basis of the Soviet system and left as a *damnosa haereditas* from which his successors have proved unable to free themselves.

It is unlikely that in this century at least there will be any agreement on where to strike the balance between Stalin's achievements and (in KENNAN's phrase) 'a criminality without limits'. But it can hardly be contested that no other man who has ever lived, even Hitler, had a greater or more brutal impact on so many individual lives.

Stalin's career gives his writings an interest which they could not claim on purely intellectual grounds. The most important are to be found in *Voprosy leninizma* (Moscow, 1926, [11]1939; *Leninism*, London, 1940 or *Problems of Lenin-*

ism, London, 1953). This collection includes *Theory and Practice of Leninism* and *Foundations of Leninism*.   ALCB

A. B. Ulam, *Stalin: the Man and his Era* (NY, 1973); R. C. Tucker, *Stalin as Revolutionary 1879–1929: a Study in History and Personality* (NY, 1973); R. Hingley, *Joseph Stalin, Man and Legend* (London, 1974).

Stamp, Lawrence Dudley (b. London, UK, 9.3.1898; d. Mexico City, Mexico, 8.8.1966). British geographer who developed the concept of land-utilization surveys and applied it first in the UK and then at an international level. During the interwar years Stamp established the Land Utilization Survey of Britain which mapped the whole of the surface area of the country at a scale of 1:63,360 (1933–9) and published a county-by-county series of monographs (1936–9). The results of the survey were drawn together in Stamp's *Land of Britain: its Use and Misuse* (London, 1948); they formed an important documentary source for land-use planning in the postwar period. A prolific writer, Stamp produced over 30 books, including standard regional texts on Asia and the British Isles. He served on a number of royal commissions (1941–2 and 1955–8) and played a prominent part in establishing geography as an applied field, of particular value in relation to physical-planning problems. He entered King's College, London as an undergraduate at the age of 15 and held his first professorship only 10 years later. The tempo he set then continued throughout his life; he was an indefatigable traveller, field researcher and organizer, and in the last phase of his life he devoted much time to expanding and restructuring the work of the International Geographical Union.   PH

Stanislavsky, Konstantin Sergeyevich, *né* Alexeyev (b. Moscow, Russia, 18.1.1863; d. Moscow, USSR, 8.8.1938). Russian theatre director and cofounder of the Moscow Art Theatre. Son of a wealthy factory owner, Stanislavsky was an amateur actor before turning to directing at a time when the art of the director was still in its infancy. He formed the Society of Art and Literature in 1888 and

10 years later, with Vladimir Nemirovich-Danchenko, the Moscow Art Theatre. Although the company made a considerable impact on the barren theatrical scene in Russia at the turn of the century, and has since become one of the best-known companies in the world, Stanislavsky's earliest work with it was characterized by a fanatical over-attention to detail which provoked CHEKHOV, whose major plays he first produced, to a mixture of admiration and dismay. Stanislavsky is best known for the 'System' of actor-training which he formulated in a series of books, *Rabota aktera nad soboy* (Moscow, 1926; *An Actor Prepares*, NY, 1936), and *Building a Character* (NY, 1950) and *Creating a Role* (NY, 1961), the latter two edited from his notes after his death. Here, and in his autobiography *Moya zhizn' v iskusstve* (Berlin, 1924; *My Life in Art*, Boston, Mass., 1926) and in *Stanislavsky Produces Othello* (London, 1948), details of his working life and his approach to acting are carefully described. Never intended either as a formula for transforming a bad actor into a good one or as a defence of naturalistic acting to the exclusion of all other approaches, the System has not always been well understood. In America STRASBERG, working with Group Theater, and later The Actors' Studio of New York, placed more emphasis on limited aspects of the training at the expense of the whole. For Stanislavsky the System developed only slowly over his entire working life, during which, as director, actor and teacher at the Moscow Art Theatre, he constantly experimented in style and form, and freely acknowledged the mistakes of his earliest work. The System was his means of helping actors, himself included, to channel the power of inspiration at the root of all great acting. He advocated a technique which concentrated on the inner elements of character rather than on the externals, using a series of exercises and improvisations to create the whole life of a character whose stage-life is confined by the text. The central elements of the System are still widely used in drama schools, and Stanislavsky is one of the three main theorists, with MEYERHOLD and BRECHT, of the art of acting in the 20c.

JMW

D. Magarshack, *Stanislavsky: a Life* (London, 1950).

Stanley, Wendell Meredith (b. Ridgeville, Ind., USA, 16.8.1904; d. Salamanca, Spain, 15.6.1971). American biochemist and virologist. After graduating from Illinois University, he carried out chemical research under Adams in the USA and under WIELAND in Munich before joining the newly established Rockefeller Plant Pathology Unit at Princeton University in 1931 to work on tobacco virus. By 1935 he had isolated the virus in crystalline form. At first he thought it was a simple protein but by 1938 he had come round to the view that it contained some 5 per cent ribonucleic acid. The impact of this demonstration that a virus, possessing at least some of the attributes of a living organism and particularly the power of self-reproduction, could be isolated by methods appropriate to a protein and could be crystallized like an ordinary chemical was enormous, and may even be claimed to mark the birth of molecular genetics. It opened up the possibility that the nature of self-production might some day be understood in chemical terms. In 1946 Stanley's work brought him a Nobel prize and in 1948 he moved to Berkeley as professor of molecular biology and of biochemistry.

GL

Stapledon, William Olaf (b. Ches., UK, 10.5.1886; d. Caldy, Ches., 6.9.1950). British novelist and philosopher, a follower of WELLS who outstripped his master in visionary projection. Stapledon read history at Balliol College, Oxford, and became an extramural lecturer for Liverpool University. He was the author of philosophical and autobiographical works as well as of the science fiction for which he is remembered. *Odd John* (London, 1935) and *Sirius* (London, 1944) are novels in which the protagonists are, respectively, a superman and a superdog. *Last and First Men* (London, 1930) and *Star Maker* (London, 1937) are fictional histories of the cosmos: *Last and First Men* pursues human evolution for millennia beyond *homo sapiens*, while *Star Maker* shows a symbiotic 'community of worlds' coming to understand the true meaning of creation. In their mental exploration of the outermost horizons of time and space, and in their icy detachment from most human concerns, these two books are unsurpassed. They may be described as an attempt to render mystical insights worthy of Dante or Blake in the scientific and sociological language of the present day.　　PP

C. C. Smith, 'Olaf Stapledon's dispassionate objectivity', in T. D. Clareson (ed.), *Voices for the Future* (Bowling Green, Ohio, 1976); P. A. McCarthy, *Olaf Stapledon* (NY, 1982).

Starling, Ernest Henry (b. London, UK, 17.5.1866; d. Kingston, Jamaica, 2.5.1927). British physiologist. One of the outstanding exemplars of the heroic period of British physiology, Starling spent his whole working life in the University of London, at Guy's Hospital Medical School as a student and lecturer in physiology, and, from 1899, as Jodrell professor of physiology at University College London. Many of his researches focused on two areas: endocrinology and cardiovascular physiology. With his lifelong friend and collaborator Sir William Maddock Bayliss, Starling identified and established the role of secretin, a digestive hormone. Starling coined the word 'hormone' in 1905 to describe secretin and other substances produced in one part of the body but active elsewhere, and his lectures on hormones helped to establish endocrinology as a special area of scientific knowledge. His work on the heart and blood vessels was even more wide ranging, for he elucidated many of the main parameters relating heart function, blood pressure and blood flow, particularly at the capillary level. He had an unusual capacity to synthesize disparate evidence and data into more general physiological hypotheses, such as 'Starling's law of the heart' or 'Starling's equilibrium'. These generalizations have in their major features stood the test of time and form the basis of modern exercise physiology. His *Principles of Human Physiology* (London, 1912, ⁴1926) remained a standard source for many years. Starling

also had strong views on the importance of science and scientific education for national life.　　WFB

Staudinger, Hermann (b. Worms, Rhineland-Palatinate, Germany, 23.3.1881; d. Freiburg, Baden-Württemberg, West Germany, 8.9.1965). German organic and macromolecular chemist. It was in Strassburg under Johannes Thiele that Staudinger made his first major contribution to organic chemistry, the discovery of the highly reactive ketenes, which formed the subject of a famous monograph *Die Ketene* [The Ketenes] (Stuttgart, 1912). In 1912, after a period in Karlsruhe, he succeeded Willstätter at the Technical University in Zürich and remained there for 14 years before migrating to Freiburg in 1926. In Karlsruhe, Staudinger achieved a simple synthesis of the hydrocarbon, isoprene, the constituent monomer of the natural high polymeric hydrocarbon, rubber, as well as the synthesis of polyoxymethylenes. This work led to Staudinger's major contribution, the long-chain-molecule theory of the structure of polymers. He first advanced this theory in 1920, but there was much opposition from the proponents of the 'aggregate-of-small-molecules' theory. Unable to obtain the equipment necessary to use the newly developed Svedberg ultracentrifuge method for molecular weight measurements, Staudinger developed the solution viscosity method into a reliable and accepted method of measuring the molecular weights of macromolecules, and used it to support his theory. The long-chain-molecule theory is now a well-established part of chemical thought. As early as 1926, Staudinger appreciated the importance of macromolecules to biology, and in his *Makromolekare Chemie und Biologie* [Macromolecular chemistry and biology] (Basle, 1947) he visualized the molecular biology of the future. His pioneer work on macromolecular chemistry constitutes a major foundation for modern molecular biology. Recognition of his work as a whole came belatedly with the award of a Nobel prize in 1953.　　NBC

Stead, Christina Ellen (b. Sydney, N.S. Wales, Australia, 17.7.1902; d. Sydney,

31.3.1983). Australian novelist. Regarded as Australia's 'lost' novelist, she remained unpublished in her native Australia until 1965 and little regarded by Australian critics until she became the first recipient of the Patrick White award in 1974. This neglect was partly a consequence of her living abroad, principally in Europe and the USA from the mid-1920s to 1968, and partly because one of her novels *Letty Fox: Her Luck* (NY, 1946) was long banned in Australia because its heroine was considered depraved. Also her settings are often international. Her first novel *Seven Poor Men of Sydney* (London, 1934) is one of her few wholly Australian works in theme and setting, reconstructing in the proletarian characters some of her feeling about being a misfit in her own country. Her best-known novel *House of All Nations* (London, 1938) is a massive but loosely constructed book which analyses the working methods of a financier and the empire he controls. Equally important is *The Man Who Loved Children* (NY, 1940) which looks at the influence of heredity and environment upon personality and talent. Stead's is a socialist but undoctrinaire view of the world, concerned with female lives without being didactically feminist. Her work may now be regarded as the authentic voice of mid-century Australian alienation. ANRN

R. G. Geering, *Christina Stead* (Melbourne, 1969).

Steichen, Edward (b. Luxembourg, 27.3.1879; d. West Redding, Conn., USA, 25.3.1973). American photographer. Brought up in the USA, Steichen studied painting in Paris between 1900 and 1902. But he had begun to take photographs in the late 1890s and continued to do so after his years in Paris. Closely associated with STIEGLITZ, his pictures were published in the latter's influential magazine *Camera Work*. In 1902 Steichen became a member of the Photo-Secession, an avant-garde organization established by Stieglitz. Steichen went back to Paris in 1906, where he gathered material by RODIN, MATISSE and CÉZANNE which Stieglitz exhibited at his New York gallery at 291 Fifth Avenue. In 1911 he began to work as a fashion photographer, and remained a commercial photographer until 1938. From 1947 he directed the department of photography at the Museum of Modern Art, New York, for which he organized 'The Family of Man' exhibition (1955), a vast display of 'human-interest' photography which subsequently toured the world. Steichen's primary importance lies in his early work as a symbolist photographer. His pre-1914 photographs refer to spirit in humanity and to harmony in nature. Like many of his contemporaries he believed artists to be seers, in touch with the laws of nature. In later life Steichen was also an activist and organizer, who did much to provide American photography with a strong institutional basis. IJ

D. Longwell, *Steichen: the Master Prints, 1895–1914, the Symbolist Period* (NY, 1978).

Stein, Mark Aurel (b. Budapest, Austria-Hungary [now Hungary], 26.11.1882; naturalized British citizen, 1904; d. Kabul, Afghanistan, 6.3.1943). Hungarian/British explorer and archaeologist who provided the basis of modern knowledge of the geography, history and cultures of Central Asia. As a result of more than 15 journeys on foot and horseback (two of which alone totalled nearly 25,000 miles) through some of the highest and most isolated mountains and deserts in the world, he established for the first time the extent of the intercourse between Indian, Iranian, Hellenistic and Chinese civilizations and the overland lines of communication between China and the West during the many centuries before these were finally replaced by the sea route. In his first three journeys (between 1900 and 1916) he crossed the Hindukush and Pamirs, and explored Chinese Turkestan. His most famous discovery was the 'Cave of the Thousand Buddhas' at Ch'ien-fo-tung, from which he brought back a great cache of documents in several languages and works of art which had been walled up since the 11c. Following the discovery of the prehistoric Indus civilization, Stein undertook a series of journeys to trace its vestiges westward to the Tigris. Other expeditions established the line of Alexander's route and of

Marco Polo's journeys. At the age of 80, he was exploring the gorges of the Indus climbing a succession of passes 14 – 15,000 feet high. Stein added greatly to geographical knowledge of Central Asia by carrying out accurate surveys on his journeys, in one region alone (that of the northern Nan-Shan ranges) covering nearly 50,000 square miles. His archaeological finds (from two of his expeditions he brought back nearly 400 cases of material) have occupied scholars for many years, in addition to his own numerous publications. He was a gifted linguist as well as an archaeologist and geographer and the vast mass of manuscript material which he recovered, for example in Sanskrit, Chinese and Tibetan as well as in hitherto unknown languages (such as Sogdian, Saka-Khotani), were of great importance for linguistic studies. ALCB

Stein, Gertrude (b. Allegheny, Pa, USA, 3.2.1874; d. Paris, France, 27.7.1946). American prose writer. An expatriate from 1902, she was a focus for the avant-garde, and for the American love-affair with France. Her early writing, of which *Three Lives* (Norfolk, Conn., 1909) is a good example, stresses subjective expression, and depends on obtrusive verbal devices – especially repetition. *Tender Buttons* (NY, 1914) develops the tendencies of the earlier work to the limits of intelligibility. Like much of her work, it can be described as experimental rather than exploratory. *Four Saints in Three Acts* (written 1927, produced 1934), an opera with music by Virgil Thompson, illustrates her conception of a play as like landscape 'not moving, but always in relation'. She wrote much literary theory (as in *Composition as Exploration*, London, 1926). Art, she argued, must seize 'the complete actual present', and the American English language must learn 'to encompass a continent'. Her own work can hardly be said to have gone beyond the first aim. *The Autobiography of Alice B. Toklas* (NY, 1933) is the obvious place to begin the reading of Stein, with its ironic narrative method and its provocative portraits of her acquaintances and friends. BF

J. R. Mellow, *Charmed Circle: Gertrude Stein and Company* (NY, 1974).

Stein, Peter (b. Berlin, Germany, 1.10.1937). German theatre and film director, noted for his original treatment of European classics and his clarified use of BRECHTian techniques. Stein had no formal theatre training, but after working as a *dramaturg* at the Munich Kammerspiele he directed BOND's *Saved* (1967) in a trenchant, colloquial version which created an immediate impact. He was drawn towards a MARXist–LENINist stance and created a furore with his production of Peter Weiss's *Vietnam Discourse* (1968), where the commentator collected money in aid of the Vietcong. He was sacked from the Kammerspiele, but his reputation as a left-wing director was enhanced by his production of Brecht's *The Jungle of the Cities* (1968) and his Brechtian 'appropriations' of classic plays, such as Goethe's *Tasso* and Kleist's *The Prince of Homburg*. His target was bourgeois individualism, expressed in an epic production of IBSEN's *Peer Gynt* (1971). In 1970 Stein established a theatre collective to run the Schaubühne am Halleschen Ufer in West Berlin, with pilot experiments to bring theatre to the working classes. Stein abandoned the agitprop style of his early years; but initiated historical examinations into the background of European classics, including a Shakespearean collage in 1976. His production of *The Oresteia* (1980) took nine hours to perform but was described as 'the haunting measure for any production in this decade'. JE

C. D. Innes, *Erwin Piscator's Political Theatre: the Development of Modern German Drama* (Cambridge, 1972); M. Patterson, *Peter Stein* (London, 1981).

Steinbeck, John Ernst (b. Salinas, Calif., USA, 27.2.1902; d. New York, 20.12.1968). American novelist. His anti-intellectualism and responsiveness to unconscious 'natural' forces were intensified by the influence of the biologist E. P. Ricketts from whom he derived his concept of 'is thinking', of the primacy of '*what* or *how* instead of why'. This led not to a fiction of detached observation, but to a more purposeful use of the characteristic mixture of naturalism and vitalism that marked his work from the start as in *To A God Unknown* (NY, 1933). This is most clearly illustrated by his use of biological images, especially of the struggle for survival and of the group as organism. *The Grapes of Wrath* (NY, 1939) is his most successful work in its combination of social realism and epic. The Oklahoma migrants of this story are both victims of economic circumstance and heroic images of man. Much of his work depends on the reduction of character and action to their simplest elements: *Of Mice and Men* (NY, 1937) and *The Pearl* (NY, 1947) are representative. He was awarded the Nobel prize for literature in 1962. BF

E. W. Tedlock & C. V. Wicker (eds), *Steinbeck and his Critics* (Albuquerque, N. Mex., 1957).

Steiner, George (b. Paris, France, 23.4.1929). American literary critic. Steiner was educated at the universities of Paris, Harvard, Chicago and Oxford. He is extraordinary fellow of Churchill College, Cambridge, and professor of English and comparative literature at the University of Geneva. After two ambitious works of literary criticism *Tolstoy or Dostoyevsky* (London, 1958) and *The Death of Tragedy* (London, 1960) Steiner achieved considerable impact in the UK and the USA with a number of provocative essays (collected in *Language and Silence*, London, 1967, and *Extraterritorial*, NY, 1971) analysing a 'crisis' in human culture arising from the pressures of totalitarian politics, illiteracy and modishness upon humanity's central capacity, language itself. His major work *After Babel* (Oxford, 1975) focused on the problems of literary translation (a concern reflecting his own trilingual background), argued for the necessary contribution of a rich poetics and of a grasp of the historicity of language to an adequate linguistics, and suggested the deep demand for privacy, territoriality and shared secrecy as the basis of both the origin and the variety of human languages. These themes are further explored in essays collected as *On Difficulty* (Oxford, 1978), and one

major influence in this field is analysed in an excellent study *Heidegger* (London, 1978). Steiner's vivid rhetorical style and polymathic range are best exemplified in *In Bluebeard's Castle* (London, 1971). BS

Steiner, Rudolf (b. Kraljevec, Croatia, Austria-Hungary [now Yugoslavia], 27.2.1861; d. Dornach, nr Basle, Switzerland, 30.3.1925). Austrian founder of Anthroposophy. The son of a Catholic stationmaster, he studied natural sciences at Vienna University and from 1889 to 1897 worked on Goethe's scientific writings for the Weimar edition. From 1897 he was assistant editor of a literary journal, worked for a short time in workers' education and became general-secretary of the German section of the Theosophical Society. In 1912 he left to found the Anthroposophical Society with its headquarters at Dornach, where the Johannistempel (later renamed the Goetheaneum) was built in 1913 in Steiner's version of late art nouveau. Anthroposophy was an educational as much as a religio-scientific theory, which moved from a simplified Hegelian monism to a vague, eclectic ideology indebted to Egyptian religion, and to gnostic and Buddhist ideas. The spiritual in people has to be educated to perceive the spiritual in the universe, from which they are separated by materialism; the world consists of a hierarchy of emanations between matter and spirit; evolution is the gradual incarnation of (created) spirit. Christ helped people to win freedom from material blindness; in the 20c he made another appearance in the etheric element. Steiner's theory has influenced a number of writers and artists (e.g. KANDINSKY in his apocalypses). Its most significant effects have been the Steiner schools in various countries, which have stressed creativity as a means to spiritual insight, especially in teaching the maladjusted. Steiner's autobiography *Mein Lebensgang* (Dornach, 1924; *Autobiography*, NY, 1928) and his collections of lectures (e.g. *Die Philosophie der Freiheit*, 1894; *Philosophy of Freedom*, London, 1916) describe his way and theory. A 300-volume edition of his works is planned. JCu

A. P. Shepherd, *A Scientist of the Invisible* (London, 1954); A. C. Harward (ed.), *The Faithful Thinker* (NY, 1961).

Stern, Otto (b. Sohrau, Upper Silesia, Germany [now Zory, Poland], 17.2.1888; naturalized American citizen; d. Berkeley, Calif., USA, 20.8.1969). German/American physicist. Stern was professor of physical chemistry at Hamburg. He left Germany in 1933 and accepted an appointment at the Carnegie Institute of Technology where he remained until his retirement in 1945. His most outstanding achievement was the development of the technique of molecular beams. If a substance is heated in a small oven and the atoms or molecules which evaporate are allowed to escape through a small hole in the oven wall into a long evacuated tube, they travel down the tube as a fine beam of molecules which can be condensed into a small patch on a plate at the far end of the tube. One of the most important early applications of this technique (with W. Gerlach in 1920) was to make such a beam of silver atoms pass through a region where there was an inhomogeneous magnetic field. Two separate distinct patches of silver were deposited at the detector at the end. This gave strong confirmation (a) to the idea that an atom acted as an elementary magnet, and (b) to the prediction of quantum theory that such an elementary magnet can only line up in two (or in a very limited number) directions in a magnetic field. Classical theory predicted a complete range of directions and a correspondingly smeared distribution at the detector. Stern exploited the molecular-beam technique in several other classic experiments. By diffracting the beam from a crystal surface he was able to demonstrate the wave nature of particles in a very direct manner. In 1933 he used the method to measure the magnetic moment of the proton (the nucleus of the hydrogen atom). This aroused great interest because its value was found to be two and a half times greater than theory predicted and it showed that it is by no means the simple particle that hitherto had been supposed. Stern was awarded a Nobel prize for physics in 1943; further exploitation of the molecu-

lar-beam method has led to other Nobel prize awards – notably those to RABI and to LAMB. HMR

Stevens, Wallace (b. Reading, Pa, USA, 2.10.1879; d. Hartford, Conn., 2.8.1955). American poet. A deliberately conservative man, who followed in his father's footsteps in politics, religion and chosen profession, Stevens was a resolutely modern poet, sceptical and relativist to the core. On leaving Harvard in 1900, where his studies were mainly literary and he contributed poems to the *Monthly* and the *Advocate*, he went to New York to try his hand at journalism for a year before enrolling in law school. Called to the Bar in 1904, he worked in various legal and commercial offices, and in 1917 moved to Hartford to work for an insurance company (he became vice-president in 1934) until his death. By the time he left New York he had become associated with a number of poets including William Carlos WILLIAMS, and had begun to publish in small avant-garde magazines, such as *Poetry* and *Others*, the poems collected in his first book *Harmonium* (NY, 1923). Its sales were poor, and for some time Stevens wrote little. In the 1930s his writing became more prolific and after his second book *Ideas of Order* (NY, 1935) he published a new collection every few years, culminating with *Collected Poems* (NY, 1954). His essays on poetry were collected in *The Necessary Angel* (NY, 1951). Stevens's poems start from the nonavailability of traditional belief and pursue the possibility of value and quality in a secular world. Persistently he observes a distinction between the notion of the world as it is and human knowledge of it, interrogating the nature of order in the world, whether discovered in it or imposed by the mind, and the character of human relation to the world through the imagination. His poetry is speculative and meditative, an internal debate rather than a monologue, and a vein of verbal wit and fantasy is one of its immediate attractions. His earlier work, which betrays most dissatisfaction with the texture of American life, is compressed and emblematic, and often employs an ornate diction to emphasize the fictional status of its objects. His later poetry is looser in structure, the debate more systematic and potentially didactic: the mortality of the spirit seen as the occasion for a fully human life rather than a pretext for tragic feeling. ATKC

F. Kermode, *Wallace Stevens* (Edinburgh, 1960).

Stieglitz, Alfred (b. Hoboken, NJ, USA, 1.1.1864; d. New York, 13.7.1946). American photographer. Stieglitz was educated in New York and at the Berlin Polytechnic Institute and the University of Berlin (1882–90) where he studied photographic science. In 1897 he founded and edited *Camera Notes* (to 1902). He held his first retrospective exhibition at the Camera Club, New York. The artistic significance of his early urban realist photographs was recognized by DREISER. In 1902 he founded *Camera Work* and the Photo-Secession movement. *Camera Work* featured the work of Photo-Secession photographers printed exquisitely in photogravure, but also pictures by artists whom Stieglitz exhibited (1905–17) in the Little Galleries of the Photo-Secession, otherwise known as '291'; *Camera Work* also published the prose of Gertrude STEIN for the first time. *Camera Work* concluded publication in 1917 with a double issue devoted to STRAND. In 1917 Stieglitz began his series of photographs of Georgia O'Keeffe; they married in 1924. He began his series of small pictures of clouds, later called the *Equivalents* series, in 1923. Stieglitz provided the stimulation and focus of the American avant-garde in painting, photography and literature. By his own work and his support of other photographers Stieglitz gained fine art status for photography in American culture. His influence was celebrated in a volume of essays, edited by Waldo Frank and others, and published in 1934 under the title *America and Alfred Stieglitz* (NY, ²1975). Aesthetically his photographic prints are almost in a class of their own. His concept of the photograph as an 'equivalent' (to interior states of mind and feeling) has been widely influential. MH-B

S. Greenough & J. Hamilton (eds), *Alfred Stieglitz: Photographs and Writings* (Washington, 1982).

Stimson, Henry Lewis (b. New York, USA, 21.9.1867; d. Huntingdon, NY, 20.10.1950). US secretary of war under Taft (1911–13), Franklin ROOSEVELT (1940–5) and TRUMAN (1945) and secretary of state under Hoover (1929–33), governor-general of the Philippines (1927–9). As secretary of state and secretary of war to Roosevelt and Truman, Stimson was perhaps second only to KISSINGER as a genuine realist in the conduct of American foreign policy in this century. A lawyer by training, he believed most firmly in the rule of law as the restraint on power, and in most cases exhibited a clear-sightedness about the ideals and aims of other nations as well as of his own fellow countrymen which epitomized the best virtues of the East Coast elitist background in which he was raised. He is, however, most unfortunately remembered by American historians for his one real lapse from realism and pragmatism, the so-called Stimson doctrine, by which in January 1932 he made it US policy not to recognize any changes in the Far East brought about by the use of force. This doctrine, though somewhat reminiscent of Canute's courtiers, was intended to restrain Japan by enlisting the supposedly irresistible force of a putative 'world opinion'; for long Stimson was inclined to blame British pusillanimity for its failure. As secretary of war in 1944–5 he was instrumental in securing the American initiative which led to the Nuremberg War Crimes trials. He was also one of the most formidable critics of Soviet actions in Europe among President Truman's advisers, urging the proper diplomatic use of America's monopoly of nuclear weapons to limit the single-mindedness with which the Soviet leadership pursued their myopic conception of security on their western frontier. His advice, given shortly before his death, against American intervention in South East Asia could, if followed, have saved his country from ignominious defeat two decades later. DCW

Stock, Alfred (b. Danzig, Germany [now Gdansk, Poland], 16.7.1876; d. Aachen, N. Rhine-Westphalia, Germany, 12.8.1946). German chemist. Stock's contribution to chemistry lies not only in the superlative experimental work which he performed, in particular, on boron and silicon hydrides, but in the high-vacuum techniques he developed to make this work possible. Educated in the University of Berlin, Stock undertook postgraduate research in Emil FISCHER's institute. He received his doctorate in 1899 and worked for a year under MOISSAN in Paris, returning to a post at Berlin. For nine years he worked upon the hydrides, nitrides and sulphides of phosphorus, arsenic and antimony. In 1909 Stock embarked on his classic study of the boron hydrides (a field which was later to produce a Nobel prize for LIPSCOMB) and silicon hydrides. The experimental difficulties of handling these very reactive, volatile, unstable, explosive materials cannot be overemphasized, but Stock developed vacuum techniques which permitted their chemistry and unique bonding features to be established. His work on silicon established the foundations of the modern silicone industry; he developed a technique for the electrolytic preparation of beryllium, which became the basis for its commerical production; and devised a technique of chemical nomenclature which has been universally adopted by inorganic chemists. During this period Stock, through prolonged exposure to mercury vapour, developed chronic mercury poisoning; from 1924 he devoted the remainder of his life to investigating and combating the pathological effects of mercury.   KRS

E. Wiberg, *Chem. Ber.*, 83 (1950), 19.

Stockhausen, Karlheinz (b. Burg Mödrath, nr Cologne, N. Rhine-Westphalia, Germany, 22.8.1928). German composer. Stockhausen has been at the forefront of musical thought since 1951, when he reacted to the experience of MESSIAEN's *Mode de valeurs et d'intensités* (1949) by composing *Kreuzspiel* [Crossplay] for six players, one of the first scores to apply SCHOENBERG's serialism to scales of rhythmic and dynamic values. The next year he went to Paris to study with Messiaen, and there began his work in electronic music. His subsequent compositions, including *Kontra-Punkte* [Counterpoint] for 10 players (1953) and two electronic *Studien* [Studies] (1954) created with artificial sounds, continued the search for a perfect musical order in which every component – pitch, duration, intensity and tone-colour – was to be organized according to the same laws. From this point his conceptions broadened. His next electronic work *Gesang der Jünglinge* [Song of the young men] (1956) joins vocal sounds with the studio-synthesized material in what is a full union of music and language. Here too, and in *Gruppen* [Groups] for three orchestras (1958), Stockhausen adds space to the composer's means: the latter work has the separated orchestras pursuing independent paths or else throwing sounds from one to another. An extraordinarily complex score, *Gruppen* is made up of 'groups', each of which is a schematic amplification of a single sound.

Stockhausen's instrumental music benefited from the acoustic studies made necessary by his electronic work. In *Kontakte* [Contacts] for piano, percussion and tape (1960) he brought the two media together, requiring the players to imitate electronic sounds. In *Momente* [Moments] for soprano, chorus and instruments (1962) he concerned himself, in studio manner, with the composition of tone-colours from the assembled resources, while in *Mixtur* [Mixture] (1965) the sounds of an orchestra are transformed by electronic equipment.

Stockhausen increasingly found ways of mediating between polar extremes, and his pursuit of unity in diversity led him to integrate recordings from around the world in two tape pieces, *Telemusik* (1966) and *Hymnen* [Anthems] (1967). His urge to combine live with electronic music led him to form his own ensemble of musicians using conventional and electronic instruments. His experience with this group encouraged him to allow the performer considerable freedom, especially in *Aus den sieben Tagen* [From the seven days] (1968), a set of prose poems intended to stimulate the musician's intuition. This phase in

Stockhausen's output was also prompted by mystical ideas, in particular by a view of music as a means of spiritual communion and enlightenment. Such considerations remain important in the later works, beginning with *Mantra* for two pianos and electronics (1970), in which Stockhausen has returned to the complete notation of his ideas, these works usually being based on one or more haunting melodies. Sometimes, as in *Mantra* or *Inori* [Adorations] for dancer and orchestra (1974), the result is a massive and obsessive musical development. Other works, such as *Musik im Bauch* [Music in the belly] for six percussionists (1975), are more concerned with the ritual demonstration of the physical and psychical powers of music.

The enormous influence of Stockhausen's compositions and writings, the latter collected in four volumes (*Texte* [Texts], Cologne, 1963–78), has not been hindered by his charismatic appearance as lecturer, conductor or performer at festivals all over the world.

PG

K. H. Wörner, *Stockhausen: Life and Work* (London, 1973); R. Maconie, *The Works of Karlheinz Stockhausen* (London, 1976).

Stokes, Adrian Durham (b. London, UK, 27.10.1902; d. London, 15.12.1972). British painter, poet and writer on art. Stokes's aesthetic education began with a trip to Italy in 1922. Here he met Ezra POUND who encouraged him in his writing of *The Quattro Cento* (London, 1932) and *The Stones of Rimini* (London, 1934). These early works set out the central preoccupations of his career – the dichotomy of the 'carved' and the 'modelled' in artistic production, and the nature of art as an expression of the inner life of the maker. During psychoanalysis with Melanie KLEIN, Stokes integrated her notions of infantile 'position' (aggressive, the ego's inability to cope with 'otherness') with modelling, and the 'depressive position' (reparative, respecting 'otherness') with carving. Ever fascinated with the idea of unity in a work of art, Stokes attributed it to a balance of these two tendencies. A poet (a selection is in *Penguin Modern Poets*

23, Harmondsworth, 1973) and a painter, as well as the author of some 20 books on art, dance and the philosophy of perception, it was Stokes's achievement to assimilate psychoanalytical language into the study of the formal and material qualities of art objects (see *The Image in Form: Selected Writings*, ed. R. Wollheim, Harmondsworth, 1972). *The Critical Writings of Adrian Stokes* were brought together in 1978 (3 vols, London).

CF

Stopes, Marie Charlotte Carmichael (b. Edinburgh, Lothian, UK, 15.10.1880; d. Dorking, Surrey, 2.10.1958). British birth control advocate. In 1904 Marie Stopes was awarded a doctorate in botany at the University of Munich. In 1921 she and her second husband, Humphrey Verdon Roe, founded their first birth control clinic in the Holloway district of London. Through practical work in her clinic and through talking and writing on the subject she helped to lead the fight for the dissemination of advice on the subject of birth control. Marie Stopes is said to have acquired her passionate, personal interest in the subject of birth control after the failure of her own first marriage which was annulled in 1916. Before she made it possible for people to talk openly about the subject of contraception, opposition from the church and the medical profession had ensured that scientific progress in this discipline had been slow. It is difficult to overestimate the importance of the role she played in European society. Without her lead the population explosion which followed the improvement in living standards throughout Europe would have been much more damaging.

VC

Stoppard, Tom (b. Zlin, Czechoslovakia, 3.7.1937). British dramatist, whose earliest performed play *Rosencrantz and Guildenstern Are Dead* was first seen in a student production in autumn 1966, and six months later was brought into the National Theatre. Stoppard has continued to be the most commercial 'non-commercial' dramatist of his generation, using extreme verbal dexterity to juggle with ideas and conventions – theatrical in *Rosencrantz*, philosophical in *Jumpers*

(1972), political in *Travesties* (1974) – and pressing parody into service as a vehicle for semiserious dialectic. Stoppard has distinguished such full-length works from his self-defined 'nuts-and-bolts comedies', which use similar techniques to construct intellectual cross-word-puzzles – sometimes, as in *After Magritte* (1970), backwards, with the opening tableau a solution to which the rest of the play unravels the clues; sometimes, as in *The Real Inspector Hound* (1968), turning his own fascination with theatrical levels of illusion to frankly farcical effect. Stoppard's political concerns, notably in the field of human rights, have adapted less readily to his theatrical skills, though *Night and Day* (1978), on the theme of press 'freedom', gave him his first success in the commercial sector. He continues to squat cheerfully on a fence of his own construction between 'serious' and boulevard theatre, observing and utilizing both.   ST

C. W. E. Bigsby, *Tom Stoppard* (Harlow, 1976); R. Hayman, *Stoppard* (London, 1977).

Stow, Randolph (b. Geraldton, W. Australia, Australia, 28.11.1935). Australian poet and novelist, who for many years has lived quietly in east Suffolk, UK, although all his writing – with the exception of *Girl Green as Elderflower* (London, 1980) which reflects his English locality – draws with great sensitivity and complexity upon his boyhood landscape of Australia and upon time spent in the Trobriand Islands off New Guinea. In both poetry and prose he is strongly influenced by a powerful awareness of the individual self and an ever-present alertness to time and history. These potentially conflicting drives are resolved in the rendering of personal worlds which convey a strong sense of specific, local settings, set against a wider acceptance of impermanence and decay. In poetry Stow's skills are well represented by *A Counterfeit Silence: Selected Poems* (London, 1969), and this range is complemented in semiautobiographical terms by *The Merry-Go-Round in the Sea* (London, 1965), where the innocence of childhood is broken by awareness of war against the Japanese to the north. *Visitants* (London, 1979) is a prose work, innovative in form and cross-cultural in range, which explores existential issues against a background of island cargo cults and of previous visitants to the South Seas.   PNQ

R. Willbanks, *Randolph Stow* (Boston, Mass., 1978).

Strachey, Christopher (b. London, UK, 16.11.1916; d. Oxford, 18.5.1975). British computer pioneer. After education at Gresham's School and King's College, Cambridge, he worked at Standard Telephones and Cables. During WW2 he gained experience with a digital differential analyser. After the war, while teaching mathematics as a schoolmaster, he wrote a program for the National Physical Laboratory's pilot ACE (Automatic Computing Engine) and a simulation program for the Manchester University Mark 1, far larger than any previous program. He joined the National Research and Development Corporation in 1951 where he was responsible for the overall design of the Ferranti Pegasus computer. He always stressed the primacy of convenience of use of computers over engineering convenience and developed the concepts both of multiprogramming and time-sharing. Seconded to Canada he programmed most of a simulation for the St Lawrence Survey, another *tour de force* in computation which advanced the opening of the Great Lakes to shipping by several years. While working as a private consultant he employed staff to study the *theory* of programming, claiming that his was the first group in the world to work on the subject. In 1962 he was elected to a senior research fellowship at Churchill College, Cambridge, and took responsibility for design of the high-level language CPL (often known as Christopher's Programming Language) and its compiler for the new Atlas computer. Particularly important was its later development BCPL (Basic Computer Programming Language). In 1965, after a year as visiting lecturer at MIT, he moved to Oxford and set up the Programming Research Group; he was elected to a chair in 1971. As a result of his work on CPL he had become even more concerned with the need for a comprehensive theory of programming language semantics, and he worked on this at Oxford. Strachey was a member of a notable literary family (a nephew of Lytton STRACHEY) and showed great facility in handling words as well as mathematical concepts.   RAH

A. Hyman, *Computing: Dictionary of Terms, Concepts and Ideas* (London, 1976).

Strachey, Giles Lytton (b. London, UK, 1.3.1880; d. nr Hungerford, Berks., 21.1.1932). British biographer and essayist. Strachey was the waspish central figure of the Bloomsbury group. 'We are as remarkable as the Johnson set', he announced; the truth of the statement was marred by his awareness of it. *Eminent Victorians* (London, 1918) made his name. These brief, elegant, lively debunkings of Victorian worthies were both refreshing and shocking after the solidly reverent two-volume tomes they replaced. Their entertainment value has lasted, though their conclusions have been challenged and their novelistic technique now seems slightly deceitful in its impish assumption that the biographer can enter and withdraw at will from the mind of his subject. In *Queen Victoria* (London, 1921) Strachey kept his mockery under control and demonstrated a more secure scholarship; in *Elizabeth and Essex* (London, 1928) he pioneered the psychoanalytic biography. In his insistence that the biographer interprets facts rather than simply relates them, and that he must be an artist to do so, Strachey effected a fundamental change in 20c biographical practice; but his own legacy is small, and written in a prose which dangerously skirts cliché.   NP

C. R. Sanders, *Lytton Strachey: his Mind and Art* (New Haven, 1957); M. Holroyd, *Lytton Strachey: a Critical Biography* (2 vols, London, 1967–8).

Strand, Paul (b. New York, USA, 16.10.1890; d. Orgeval, Yvelines, France, 31.3.1976). American photographer. Strand attended the Ethical Culture High School where Lewis Hine taught a photography course. He responded to the influence of the avant-garde exhibitions arranged by STIEGLITZ and to the Armory Show. His first exhibition was held at Stieglitz's Gallery '291' in 1916. The portfolio of his work published in the last double issue of *Camera Work* in 1917 broke through 'pictorialist' style and represented for Stieglitz the arrival of the photographic medium in the 20c. The realist *Blind Woman* and the abstract *White Fence, Port Kent* (both 1916) are crucial photographs. Strand went on to make films: the experimental *Mannahatta* with Charles Sheeler in 1921; *Redes* [The wave] for the Mexican government in 1934; worked as a cameraman on *The Plow that Broke the Plains* directed by Pare Lorentz (1935); coedited *Heart of Spain* (1938–40) and filmed and codirected *Native Land* with Leo Hurwitz (1942). His work is informed by left-wing views deeply held and trenchantly expressed. In 1940 he published 20 hand gravures under the title *Photographs of Mexico* (NY, [2]1967). After WW2 he worked on a notable series of books, commencing with *Time in New England* (with Nancy Newhall, NY, 1946); *Le France de Profil* (Lausanne, 1950); *Un Paese* (Turin, 1955); *Tir a'Mhurain, Outer Hebrides* (Dresden, 1962); *Living Egypt* (London, 1969); *Ghana – an African Portrait* (London, 1975). These books remain exemplary in the substance of the photographic observation and the quality of printing. Strand was one of the greatest printers among photographers ever known and a corpus of his work was printed for museum collections shortly before his death. His work, radical and humanist, unites piercing social observation to the highest aesthetic achievement. Exhibitions of his work were widely seen in the 1970s.   MH-B

C. Tomkins, *Paul Strand: Sixty Years of Photographs* (NY, 1976).

Strasberg, Lee, *né* Israel Strassberg (b. Budzanow, Galicia, Austria-Hungary [now USSR], 17.11.1901; d. New York, USA, 17.2.1982). American theatre director and teacher of acting. Strasberg grew up in New York from the age of seven, and first studied acting with STANISLAVSKY's former pupil Richard Boleslavsky. When the Group Theater split off from Theater Guild in the early 1930s, he formed with Cheryl Crawford and Harold Clurman a triumvirate who ran the company until its demise in 1941. During this time he based his rehearsal methods on his understanding of Stanislavsky's System, with particular emphasis on the use of 'affective' or 'emotional memory'. The Method, as it came to be known, was given more prominence in his years as head of the Actors' Studio of New York which he founded in 1948, and which included among its pupils DEAN, Paul Newman and BRANDO. Though his success as a director of plays was limited, Strasberg's influence on American acting, in particular screen acting, was greater than that of any other theatre practitioner of his time.   JMW

Strauss, Levi (b. Bavaria, Germany, 1829; d. San Francisco, Calif., USA, 1902). German/American clothing manufacturer. At the age of 14 Strauss emigrated to the USA. Two older brothers, already engaged in the dry goods business in New York, encouraged him to trade in California selling goods and canvases to the gold prospectors. Realizing that the most needed commodity was 'tough pants', he set about making tarpaulin and canvas trousers known as 'waist-high overalls' using indigo dyed cloth. The famous copper rivets were derived from a trouser-maker, Jacob Davis, whom Strauss utilized and who used harness-makers' rivets to strengthen pockets and points of strain in prospectors' trousers. It was during the 1860s that Strauss decided to use a tough sailcloth from Nîmes in France (*serge de Nîmes*, now called denim), and to adapt the trousers themselves from those worn by Genoese sailors (known as Genes, and hence the name 'jeans'). Until WW2 Levi jeans had been exclusively cowboy and workers' wear, and even during the war their availability was restricted to defence workers. But being hardwearing, comfortable and cheap, the garment became the most sought-after commodity when back in general production. The 1960s saw the explosion of the blue jean-Levi phenomenon; jeans becoming the most universal fashion garment ever, with the style spreading to jackets, skirts and shorts. What had been originally inexpensive, hardwearing workgear has now become the most imitated of items, and increasingly expensive as leisure and casual wear. But the fundamental item of clothing – trousers in heavy weight denim – has remained basically unaltered in style for over 127 years, a unique achievement.   JWB

Strauss, Richard Georg (b. Munich, Bavaria, Germany, 11.6.1864; d. Garmisch-Partenkirchen, Bavaria, West Germany, 8.9.1949). German composer. Strauss began his career as a follower of Brahms but then switched his allegiance to Wagner and Liszt, who were the predominant influences on his tone poems composed between 1887 and 1898. These works, which include *Till Eulenspiegel* (1895) and *Also sprach Zarathustra* [Thus spake Zarathustra] (1896), ask for a large orchestra and abound in strong illustrative effects. In the operas which followed, *Salome* (1905, after Wilde) and *Elektra* (1909), Strauss developed his style almost to the point of atonality and used extreme dissonance to convey highly charged emotion. But instead of imitating SCHOENBERG's contemporary departures, Strauss moved into a world of elegant comedy in his next opera, *Der Rosenkavalier* [The cavalier of the rose] (1911), which, like *Elektra*, has a sophisticated text by HOFMANNSTHAL. The collaboration between poet and composer, charted in *The Correspondence between Richard Strauss and Hugo von Hofmannsthal* (ed. E. Sackville-West, London, 1961), continued in *Ariadne auf Naxos* (1912), *Die Frau ohne Schatten* [The woman without a shadow] (1919), *Die ägyptische Helena* [Helen of Egypt] (1928) and *Arabella* (1933). Strauss's style changed little during this period, for he was able to supply the needs of symbolist melodrama or bourgeois comedy from his rich store of lyrical romanticism. With his last opera *Capriccio* (1942), however, his music became more refined and his exuberance was turned into nostalgia, the predominant mood of his *Vier letzte Lieder* (*Four Last Songs*) for soprano and orchestra (1950).   PG

W. Mann, *Richard Strauss: a Critical Study of his Operas* (London, 1964); N. Del Mar, *Richard Strauss: a Critical*

Commentary on his Life and Works (3 vols, London, 1963–72).

Stravinsky, Igor Fyodorovich (b. Oranienbaum [now Lomonosov], Russia, 17.6.1882; naturalized French citizen, 1934; naturalized American citizen, 1945; d. New York, USA, 6.4.1971). Russian/French/American composer. The most widely influential 20c composer, Stravinsky gave western music a new conception of rhythm, a new approach to form and a new critical attitude to tradition. His rhythmic innovations came quite suddenly in *Vesna svyashchennaya* (*The Rite of Spring*, 1913), composed like the earlier *Zhar'-ptitsa* (*Firebird*, 1910) and *Petrushka* (1911) for DIAGHILEV's Russian Ballet. In evoking scenes of pagan ritual in ancient Russia the *Rite* uses violent syncopation, rapid changes of metre and barbaric repetition to create angular and propulsive rhythms which are the music's main motivating force. Continuous development is largely abandoned; instead the structure is one of separate blocks, with sharp cuts from one kind of material to another.

The massive dynamism of the *Rite*, which is scored for a very large orchestra, was never to be repeated, though its rhythmic and formal ideas were developed in the smaller, more intricate works of the next few years. During this period Stravinsky remained in Western Europe, where his work for Diaghilev had secured his reputation as a leader of the avant-garde. However, he continued to be absorbed in Russian folk tales and ritual, portraying with ceremonial precision a village wedding in his ballet *Svadebka* (*The Wedding*, begun 1914, produced 1923), in which his rhythmic ingenuity and his block structures are starkly revealed by the monochrome colouring of voices, percussion ensemble and four pianos.

By the time *The Wedding* was staged Stravinsky had already set off in a new direction. His very individual arrangements of music attributed to Pergolesi, made for the ballet *Pulcinella* (1920), had led him to reconsider the music of the past: the Russian manner gave way to neoclassicism. He borrowed forms,

musical ideas and styles from music throughout the western tradition but always made them his own. For instance, his opera-oratorio *Oedipus Rex* (1927) looks back to Handel in its general shaping and its monumental choruses, while the arias have something of Verdi's passion and the orchestral music is occasionally tinged with popular music of the period.

By adopting such masks Stravinsky was able to distance himself from his work and so to achieve a concentration on artifice and order: this was the guiding aim of his neoclassicism, as stated in his *Chroniques de ma vie* (2 vols, Paris, 1935–6; *Chronicle of My Life*, London, 1936, ²1975), and more fully in his *Poétique musicale* (Cambridge, Mass., 1942; *Poetics of Music*, Cambridge, Mass., 1947). Yet there is certainly also an element of satire, even of destructiveness, in the wit with which he used Bach in his Violin Concerto (1931), or Mozart in his opera *The Rake's Progress* (1951), or jazz in a variety of smaller pieces.

After *The Rake's Progress* Stravinsky purified his style by examining both the more distant past (from Machaut to Gabrieli) and the music of WEBERN. Like such younger contemporaries as BOULEZ and STOCKHAUSEN he found in Webern's discipline a new model of order on which he could base his own language: the master of neoclassicism became a disciple of serialism, hitherto regarded as its diametrical opposite. The compositions of this period include several sacred cantatas, among them the *Canticum sacrum* (1956) and the *Requiem Canticles* (1966). Living in Los Angeles, where he had moved from Paris in 1940, Stravinsky also contributed to several conversation-books with Robert Craft: *Conversations with Igor Stravinsky* (London, 1959), *Memories and Commentaries* (London, 1960), *Expositions and Developments* (London, 1962) and *Themes and Conclusions* (London, 1972).   PG

V. Stravinsky & R. Craft, *Stravinsky in Pictures and Documents* (NY, 1978); E. W. White, *Stravinsky: the Composer and his Works* (London, ²1979); R. Craft, (ed.), *Stravinsky: Selected Correspondence*, vol. 1 (NY, 1982).

Strawson, Peter Frederick (b. London, UK, 23.11.1919). British philosopher. After WW2 service and brief tenure of a post in Wales, Strawson became a fellow of University College, Oxford, in 1948. In 1950 articles on Bertrand RUSSELL's philosophical logic and on the concept of truth attracted immediate attention. His attack on the formalistic distortions of the actual use of language perpetrated by logicians was systematically developed in his *Introduction to Logical Theory* (London, 1952), an important contribution to the linguistic philosophy dominant at the time. His *Individuals* (London, 1959) carried forward his original interest in names, and his counter-Russellian thesis of their indispensability for discourse, but in a pioneering and comprehensive way, as a 'descriptive metaphysics'. Kant, whom he saw as a fellow-practitioner of that discipline, was the subject of a powerful and imaginative study *The Bounds of Sense* (London, 1966). In 1968 Strawson succeeded G. RYLE as professor of metaphysical philosophy in Oxford.   AQ

Z. van Straaten (ed.), *Philosophical Subjects* (Oxford, 1980).

Stresemann, Gustav (b. Berlin, Germany, 10.5.1878; d. Berlin, 3.10.1929). Deputy in the German Reichstag (1906–29), leader of the National Liberal party (1917–29) and of the Volkspartei (1919–29), chancellor (1923) and foreign minister (1923–9). A patriot and a nationalist who conceived the establishment of German hegemony in Central and Eastern Europe with substantial gains at the expense of France and Belgium in the West in 1917, Stresemann's sense of realism led him in 1923 to advocate German recovery through a fulfilment of all those parts of the Versailles Treaty of which he could not secure the reform or abandonment as a reward for German good behaviour, hoping to see the recovery of German power by economic and diplomatic means. He was thus the architect of the limited but loudly celebrated rapprochement with France which resulted in the downwards revision of German reparation payments in 1924, the signature of the Treaty of Locarno in 1925, the admission of Germany to the League of Nations in 1926

and the evacuation by British and French troops of the Rhineland in 1928–9. At the same time he supported the clandestine links between the Reichswehr and the Red Army, and signed a nonaggression treaty with the USSR (1926). In his later years Stresemann was in some sense a European, in that he supported early moves towards the development of transnational institutions such as the Bank of International Settlements (1928) and fathered the development of German–French industrial cartels; but he hardly deserved the adulation or the Nobel Peace prize awarded to him.   DCW

H. A. Turner, *Stresemann and the Politics of the Weimar Republic* (Princeton, 1963).

Strindberg, Johan August (b. Stockholm, Sweden, 22.1.1849; d. Stockholm, 14.5.1912). Swedish dramatist, novelist and critic. Strindberg was – in O'NEILL's phrases – 'the precursor of all modernity in our present theatre ... the most modern of the moderns'. The range and variety of his authorship was astounding; in the realm of drama he wrote historical plays, realistic tragedy, plays of dream and fairy tale, one-acters and what he himself defined as 'chamber plays', in styles which were variously naturalistic, neoromantic, symbolic and expressionistic; in addition he was a novelist of notable achievement, an essayist, critic, historian and a prolific letter writer. The two greatest achievements of his earlier career were *Mäster Olof* (written 1872, Stockholm, 1881; NY, 1914, tr. W. Johnson in *The Vasa Trilogy*, Seattle, 1959), a work which opened up a new epoch in Swedish drama, and the novel *Röda rummet* (Stockholm, 1879; *The Red Room*, London, 1913, tr. E. Sprigge, London, 1967), a brilliant and biting satire on the life and customs of contemporary Stockholm. From then until his nervous crisis of 1895–7, the so-called 'Inferno crisis', his writing was greatly varied in genre – short stories, drama, history, critical essays – though it was for the most part in keeping with naturalist doctrine. The two volumes of short stories *Giftas* (Stockholm, 1884–6; London, 1913, tr. M. Sandbach, *Getting Married*,

London, 1972), the dramas *Fadren* (Helsingborg, 1887; *The Father*, London, 1899, tr. M. Meyer, London, 1964) and *Fröken Julie* (Stockholm, 1888; Philadelphia, 1912, tr. M. Meyer, *Miss Julie*, London, 1964), and the novel *Hemsöborna* (Stockholm, 1887; tr. E. H. Schubert, *The People of Hemsö*, London, 1959) are the key works of the period. Ultimately, however, it is the 'post-Inferno' work in the field of drama that provides the most impressive evidence of Strindberg's audacious experimentalism; these were years when he was moved by a new complexity of intent, though the striking diversity of styles here in evidence never failed to receive the stamp of his own highly personal and unifying vision. He 'rediscovered' the fascinations of historical drama, finding in it a genre unexpectedly amenable to his new and mystic conceptions of God and Man; he redeployed his talent for naturalistic drama in *Brott och brott* (Stockholm, 1899; NY, 1912, tr. E. Sprigge, *Crime and Crime*, NY, 1960), *Påsk* (Stockholm, 1900; *Easter*, Cincinnati, 1912, tr. E. Sprigge, London, 1963), and (supremely) in *Dödsdansen* (Stockholm, 1901; NY, 1912, tr. M. Meyer, *The Dance of Death*, London, 1975). It was, however, particularly with the emergent expressionism of *Till Damaskus* I–III (Stockholm, 1898–1904; Boston, Mass., 1913; tr. W. Johnson, *To Damascus*, Seattle, 1979) and *Stora landsvägen* (Stockholm, 1908; NY, 1945, tr. A. Paulson, *The Great Highway*, NY, 1965), the neoromanticism of *Kronbruden* (Stockholm, 1902; tr. E. Björkman, *The Bridal Crown*, NY, 1915) and *Svanehvit* (Stockholm, 1902; tr. E. Björkman, *Swanwhite*, NY, 1915), together with the incipient surrealism of *Ett drömspel* (Stockholm, 1902; NY, 1912, tr. M. Meyer, *A Dream Play*, London, 1975) and of *Spöksonaten* (Stockholm, 1907; NY, 1916, tr. M. Meyer, *The Ghost Sonata*, London, 1964) that Strindberg contributed most influentially to the European drama of the 1920s. His plays have been widely translated into English, and versions by many different hands exist.   JWMcF

M. Lamm, *August Strindberg* (NY, 1971).

Sukarno, Achmed (b. Surabaja, Java, Dutch East Indies [now Indonesia], 6.6.1901; d. Djakarta, 21.6.1970). President of Indonesia (1950–68), former member of the Indonesian nationalist movement (1927), collaborated with Japan during the period of Japanese occupation (1942–5), foremost in the Indonesian nationalist conflict with the returning Dutch colonial authority (1946–9). An Indonesian Muslim trained as an engineer in Dutch schools, Sukarno was typical of many successful Third World nationalist leaders in that, having no chance of advancement in the native society of his country, he posed towards outsiders as a leader of that society while at the same time taking advantage of its disruption and disintegration under colonial rule and still more under the collapse of colonialist authority to turn native forms of protest and rebellion to his own advantage. Through his adaptation of the traditional role of populist Muslim rebel leader against the native sultans and their oppressions, he made himself into a charismatic popular leader who alleviated the distress caused by the breakdown of traditional institutions and concealed his own inability to create new forms of social organization by providing his audiences with theatrical oratory directed against a continuous succession of enemies, external and internal. A megalomaniac, both in his vision of an Indo-Malay empire stretching from Malaya to Australia, and in his domestic policies, he disguised his authoritarianism under the double-speak of 'guided democracy' and his powerlessness against external enemies under the slogan of 'confrontation' which, by playing on the American fears of communism and the UN's rhetoric of anticolonialism, succeeded in forcibly suppressing the Christian independence movement in Amboina, and the Muslim fundamentalist rebels in Sumatra and the Celebes, and in translating the unwilling people of Dutch Papua New Guinea ('West Irian') from Dutch to Indonesian rule in 1963, but failed to browbeat the British and Malaysians in 1963–5. A military coup in 1966 massacred his communist allies, confined him to his palace and eventually removed him from office. But the Indonesian economy was to take much longer to recover from the appalling costs with which his tyranny and megalomania had burdened it.   DCW

Sun Yat-Sen (b. Hsiang-shan, Kwantung, China, 12.11.1866; d. Peking, 12.3.1925). Founder and leader of the Chinese Nationalist movement, the Kuomintang, and briefly president of the 'United Provinces of China' in 1913, after the overthrow of the Manchu dynasty in the revolution of 1912. Sun Yat-Sen was typical of westernizing revolutionary leaders in Oriental societies in that he was born into a lowly position in a rigidly structured society (the son of a peasant) and achieved his advancement and education entirely outside his society, becoming a Christian, and American citizen (in Hawaii), a doctor (trained in the British colony of Hong Kong), and rising to prominence among the Chinese colonies in exile, in the USA and in Canada, where the racialism of the society in which they found themselves made unity the only chance of survival. Sun Yat-Sen became the ideologue of the nationalist movement in exile, basing his ideology on 'Three Principles', nationalism, democracy and socialism (1898), founding successive propaganda organizations of which the Kuomintang (founded 1891) was the most successful. His death in 1925 from cancer made him the martyr-saint of Chinese nationalism, disputed between the Kuomintang and the Chinese Communist party who sought to capture his aura in the person of his widow, made a vice-chairman of the Chinese People's Republic in 1950. DCW
    H. V. Schiffrin, *Sun Yat-Sen and the Origins of the Chinese Revolution* (NY, 1968).

Sutherland, Earl (b. Burlingame, Kan., USA, 19.11.1915; d. Miami, Fla, 9.3.1974). American biochemist. In 1957 Sutherland, then professor of pharmacology at Western Reserve University School of Medicine, Cleveland, and his co-workers were trying to find out how the hormones glucagon and adrenalin release blood sugar from storage in the liver. When hormone was added to liver extract a hitherto unknown molecule was produced, an ATP derivative christened cyclic AMP. It emerged that both hormones increased the production of cyclic AMP, which in turn carried out the glucose release work inside the cell. On the basis of this, Sutherland proposed the 'second-messenger' hypothesis: that the action of one or several hormones is to increase or decrease a single molecular species inside the cell, which coordinates the various components of hormone response. Conceiving of hormone action as a molecular rather than a whole-cell process was a major conceptual advance. Cyclic AMP now has whole journals devoted to its involvement in an amazing variety of biological controls, from slime moulds to humans, while numerous other second-messenger interactions, and second messengers as diverse as cyclic GMP and calcium ions, have been discovered throughout biology. From 1963 Sutherland was professor of physiology at Vanderbilt University School of Medicine.   DOM

Sutherland, Edwin Hardin (b. Gibbon, Nebr., USA, 13.8.1883; d. Bloomington, Ind., 11.10.1950). American criminologist and sociologist. Probably the most influential theorist and teacher of his generation, he established a school at the University of Indiana that achieved pre-eminence after the demise of the famous Chicago school of the 1920s. His *Principles of Criminology* (Chicago, 1934, [7]1966) achieved immense popularity and contained his first formulation of the theory of differential association. Sutherland was the major instigator of studies of business crimes, especially corporate crimes, and is generally associated with the concept of 'white collar' crime extensively explored by some of his most distinguished pupils, notably CRESSEY and Clinard. Rejecting psychoanalytic explanations of crime and analyses in terms of personal pathology, Sutherland attempted a criminological theory predicated upon principles of social rationality. His influence spread throughout the English-speaking world and his textbook has been continuously in print for 50 years. A prolific writer of papers, many have been collected in *The Sutherland Papers* (eds A. Cohen, A.

Lindesmith & K. Schuessler, Bloomington, 1956). TPM

Sutherland, Graham Vivian (b. London,
UK, 24.8.1903; d. London, 17.2.1980).
British painter and printmaker. Sutherland began as an etcher of pastoral
landscape subjects in the tradition of
the 19c artist Samuel Palmer, but gave
up etching c. 1930 and began to experiment with painting. He did not make
his first mature paintings until about
1935 when the landscape of Pembrokeshire in Wales gave him the idea of representing nature indirectly by paraphras-
ing what he saw; isolating forms such as
tree roots or boulders which stimulated
his imagination, and giving them the
character of mysterious presences, powerful images heightened by strongly
emotive colour. Most of these works
were first carried out as small
watercolour studies, which he afterwards
used as the basis for oil paintings. During the years 1941–5 he was employed
as an official war artist to make paintings of bomb damage and iron foun-
dries, to which he gave an intensely dramatic character. From 1947 he spent
much of his time in the south of
France, especially at Villefranche and
Menton, which led to his adopting
higher-keyed colour and introducing
Mediterranean motifs such as vine per-
golas and palm palisades, as well as
standing forms based on the principles
of organic growth (sometimes a fusion
of animal and plant forms) to suggest
the presence of a human figure by a
substitution. After 1967, however, he
returned to Pembrokeshire themes.

Although primarily a highly original
painter of landscape forms and a powerful and inventive colourist, he also
painted a number of portraits from 1949
onwards, in which he tackled the human
figure directly, such as those of Somerset MAUGHAM, Lord BEAVERBROOK
and Sir Winston CHURCHILL, and
became one of the outstanding portrait
painters of his generation. His interest
in religious themes culminated in the
design of a vast tapestry of *Christ in
Glory in the Tetramorph* for Coventry
cathedral. REA
D. Cooper, *The Work of Graham
Sutherland* (London, 1961); J. T. Hayes,

The Art of Graham Sutherland (London,
1980).

Suzuki, Daisetsu Teitaro (b. Kanazawa,
Japan, 18.12.1870; d. Tokyo, 12.7.1966).
Japanese religious philosopher. That the
West has come to an awareness of Zen
Buddhism is almost entirely due to the
labours of this Japanese scholar.
Although never a monk, Suzuki studied
Zen under Soyen Shaku who persuaded
him to take as his mission the bringing
of Eastern thought to the West. His life
came to exemplify a wish for mutual
understanding (he even married an
American). He went, in 1897, to Chicago to assist Paul Carus with the Buddhist publications of the newly formed
Open Court Publishing Co. He stayed
10 years in the West where his influential writings appeared regularly. In 1924
he founded the *Eastern Buddhist* magazine which became a major vehicle for
dissemination. The same year he was
appointed professor of religious philosophy at Otani University, Kyoto. In 1936
he participated in the World Congress
of Faiths in London. Widowed in 1939,
he spent WW2 renewing contact with
Zen in Kamakura, but in 1949 went to
Hawaii for the East–West Philosophers
Conference and took up teaching
appointments at Claremont College and
Columbia University. By 1950 an internationally known figure, Suzuki became
a member of the Japanese Academy and
was decorated with the Cultural Medal
by the emperor. At 88, living in Japan
he was able to witness the worldwide
diffusion of interest in Zen, due to his
innumerable articles, 100 books in Japanese and nearly 30 in English, among
them *Studies in the Lankavatara Sutra*
(London, 1930) and *Zen and Japanese
Culture* (London, 1959). JIS

Svevo, Italo, ps. of Ettore Schmitz (b.
Trieste, Austria-Hungary [now Venezia
Giulia, Italy], 19.12.1861; d. Motta di
Livenza, Veneto, 13.9.1928). Italian novelist. Born into a middle-class Jewish
family of German descent, Svevo was
privately educated in Germany until the
age of 17 when he returned to Trieste
and took up a job as a bank clerk after
his father had run into financial difficulties – an event recounted in his first

novel *Una vita* (Trieste, 1893; tr. A. Colquhoun, *A Life*, London, 1963), published at his own expense. His second novel *Senilità* came out in 1898 (Trieste; tr. B. de Zoete, *As a Man Grows Older*, London, 1949). Between these two publications Svevo married Livia Veneziani whose parents had a business of which Svevo took over the management after the death of his father-in-law. In 1907 Svevo met JOYCE who was living in Trieste and teaching English; the two men became close friends. It was to Joyce that Svevo owed his recognition in France as an important writer. Discouraged by a complete lack of critical interest in his first two novels – MONTALE was the first Italian writer to recognize Svevo's importance as a novelist and write about him in *L'Esame* (1925) – Svevo stopped writing. After a silence of some 25 years he brought out what is generally considered to be his most significant work, *La coscienza di Zeno* (Bologna, 1923; tr. B. de Zoete, *The Confessions of Zeno*, London, 1930). This largely autobiographical novel initiated a new phase in Svevo's writing, introducing a humorous and ironical tone which colours all his subsequent works and in particular the short stories and plays, *La novella del buon vecchio e della bella fanciulla ed altri scritti* (Milan, 1929; tr. L. Collins-Morley, *The Wise Old Man and the Pretty Girl, and Other Stories*, London, 1930), and *Corto viaggio sentimentale e altri racconti inediti* [Short sentimental journey and other unpublished stories] (Milan, 1949). Along with PROUST and Joyce, Svevo is generally regarded as one of the most important European exponents of the 'stream of consciousness' technique and *La Coscienza di Zeno* as the best example of Svevo's use of that technique. In this novel the use of interior monologue is effectively used to recount the memories which bob up to the surface of the writer's consciousness and find expression in his amused analysis of his own personality. Trieste has a symbolical significance in Svevo's works, comparable to that of Dublin in Joyce's *Ulysses*. GS

P. N. Furbank, *Italo Svevo: the Man and the Writer* (London, 1966); E. Montale, 'Italo Svevo' in *Eugenio Montale: Selected Essays*, tr. G. Singh (Manchester, 1978).

Svoboda, Josef (b. Caslav, Czechoslovakia, 10.5.1920). Czech designer. He trained as an interior designer, and at the School of Applied Arts in Prague, graduating in 1948. He was appointed in 1951 as chief designer to the National Theatre in Prague. He there instituted a regime of technical experiment, based on a concern with the nature of space in stage design, and the total integration of the design function into the production process. Characteristically Svoboda's designs are heavily atmospheric, reminiscent of the 'rhythmic space' exercises of APPIA, with whom he shares an interest in the application of musical concepts to spatial organization. In 1966 he created a triumphant design for *The Storm* (Ostrovsky) for the National Theatre at the Old Vic, London. This production demonstrated his use of the technique of simultaneous projection, one among his many technical innovations.   RC

Syme, Ronald (b. Eltham, N. Island, New Zealand, 11.3.1903). British historian of ancient Rome, whose studies have opened numerous innovatory paths. Educated in New Zealand and at Oriel College, Oxford, Syme served at the British Legation at Belgrade and Ankara (1940–2) before his appointment as professor of classical philology at the University of Istanbul (1942–5) and then as Camden professor of ancient history at Oxford (1949–70). His first book was *The Roman Revolution* (Oxford, 1939); but published at the outbreak of WW2, it was another 10 years before it received the attention it deserved. Syme interpreted the transformation of the Roman republic into an empire as the consolidation of a new elite around Augustus following a fierce struggle between political factions at the top. The historical method of prosopography (i.e. investigating the common background characteristics of a group of historical actors by means of a collective study of their lives) was Syme's innovation. Subsequently his scholarly work has concentrated on three areas: Tacitus, Balkan studies and the *Historia*

Augusta. His achievement with this latter collection of imperial biographies has been to demonstrate its genesis and historical inauthenticity (mainly in *Ammianus and the Historia Augusta*, Oxford, 1968, and in *Emperors and Biography: Studies in the Historia Augusta*, Oxford, 1971). His grasp of the language and concepts used in Roman society, combined with his sense of style, has made him the foremost scholar of Roman historiography (see *Tacitus*, 2 vols, Oxford, 1958). KKS

Synge, John Millington (b. Dublin, Ireland, UK [now Irish Republic], 16.4.1871; d. Dublin, Ireland, UK, 24.3.1909). Irish dramatist. Synge's early education was largely by private tuition; he went to Trinity College, Dublin, from 1889 to 1892. In 1898, on the advice of YEATS, he visited the Aran Islands. This journey changed the direction and quality of his writing. There he found language vital and resonant from interaction with Gaelic, and a rural people whose innate dignity and strength could provide him with material for tragedy and comedy alike; a blend of beauty and brutality described in *The Aran Islands* (London, 1907). The fruits of the visit to Aran are evident from his plays: *In the Shadow of the Glen* (Dublin, 1903); *Riders to the Sea* (Dublin, 1904); *The Playboy of the Western World* (Dublin, 1907); *Deidre of the Sorrows* (Dublin, 1910). Synge was an individualistic writer, celebrating, in language 'as fully flavoured as a nut or an apple', the 'fiery and magnificent, and tender' qualities of the popular imagination which he found in the west of Ireland. His dramatic characters are rooted in the earth but are constantly 'shying clods against the visage of the stars'. EFi

D. Greene & E. M. Stephens, *J. M. Synge* (London, 1959).

Synge, Richard Laurence Millington (b. Liverpool, Mers., UK, 28.10.1914). British biochemist. After graduating from Cambridge in 1936, Synge stayed to research with N. W. Pirie (1936–9) and at the Wool Industries Research Association in Leeds (1939–41). He joined the staff of the latter in 1941, then that of the Lister Institute of Preventive Medicine in London (1943) and in 1948 became head of the department of protein chemistry at the Rowett Research Institute, Bucksburn, Aberdeen. Synge shared the Nobel prize for chemistry in 1952 with A. J. P. MARTIN for work on partition chromatography. He has also investigated analytical problems concerning large peptides, especially peptide antibiotics, and since 1948 he has worked on the digestion of proteins by ruminants and on intermediates in protein metabolism. He maintains a wide-ranging interest in physical techniques of separation of complex molecules (e.g. electrokinetic ultrafiltration). NBC

Szasz, Thomas Stephen (b. Budapest, Hungary, 15.4.1920; naturalized American citizen, 1944). Hungarian/American psychoanalyst who has pioneered the antipsychiatry movement. In 'The myth of mental illness' (*American Journal of Psychiatry*, 1960), Szasz argued that since psychiatrists could not agree on a diagnosis for schizophrenia, neither on its causes, nor on the course the so-called illness would take, schizophrenia, the queen of mental illnesses, must be a bogus malady. And psychiatrists were bogus doctors: they believed they were in the medical business, but were actually agents of social control. In a powerful analogy, Szasz compared modern lunatics to 17c witches who were so labelled to ostracize them as people of whom society did not approve. Szasz accuses psychiatrists of being too ready to fulfil this role, both in the West and in the Soviet Union. He has condemned fiercely Russian psychiatrists who label dissidents as mad. Szasz does not deny that people have problems in life. But these are not diseases. As a psychiatrist, Szasz is happy to treat people who come to him of their own free will. But free will is essential. Unlike most criticisms of psychiatry, Szasz's writings have a right-wing flavour. If mental illness is a myth, it follows not simply that psychiatrists should have less power but that 'diminished responsibility' on account of insanity cannot be used as a defence in criminal actions. However disturbed people seem, they are responsible for their actions. Szasz has been enormously influential in drawing attention to the political and social power of psychiatrists. Thousands of people a year are detained in hospitals against their will on the grounds that they are psychiatrically ill. Szasz's powerful analysis gave an intellectual foundation to those who criticized that system. Among his books are *The Myth of Mental Illness* (NY, 1961), *The Manufacture of Madness* (NY, 1970) and *The Myth of Psychotherapy* (NY, 1978).　　　DMOC

Szent-Györgyi, Albert (b. Budapest, Austria-Hungary [now Hungary], 16.9.1893; naturalized American citizen, 1955). Hungarian/American biochemist. He fled from the Bolshevik revolution in 1919 and eventually settled in the Netherlands where he held appointments at Leiden and Groningen universities. There he discovered the catalytic role of fumaric and succinic acids in cellular respiration, an observation of critical importance for later understanding of cellular energy metabolism. Extending his studies to plant tissues, he discovered a reducing agent, hexuronic acid, which he subsequently isolated at Cambridge, in the laboratory of Gowland HOPKINS. He identified hexuronic acid with vitamin C and renamed it ascorbic acid. For these two discoveries he was awarded a Nobel prize in 1937. On returning to Hungary he became interested in the biochemistry of muscle and, with Straub, discovered the protein actin and showed that threads of a complex of actin and myosin contracted when treated with ATP – thus mimicking the contraction of muscle *in vivo* (*Chemistry of Muscular Contraction*, Cambridge, Mass., 1951). After exciting, but difficult, experiences during WW2 and its aftermath, he emigrated to the USA. GL

Szilard, Leo (b. Budapest, Austria-Hungary [now Hungary], 11.2.1898; naturalized American citizen, 1943; d. La Jolla, Calif., USA, 30.5.1964). Hungarian/American physicist and biologist. Szilard was a most creative, versatile and practical scientist, and politically far-sighted. After studying electrical engineering and serving in the Austro-Hungarian army in WW1 he took up physics in Berlin. There he worked with EINSTEIN and LAUE and in 1929 wrote a paper which, 35 years later, became a cornerstone of modern information theory. A refugee in England, he turned to nuclear physics, seeking the element which would yield a nuclear chain reaction and lead to atomic power and bombs.

Early in 1939 after the discovery of uranium fission Szilard, now in the USA, persuaded FERMI to join the research which led to the first controlled nuclear chain reaction in December 1942 at Chicago. At Szilard's instigation Einstein had written to F. D. ROOSEVELT in August 1939 about the possibility of atomic bombs. In July 1945 Szilard organized a petition of atomic scientists arguing that atomic bombs should not be used against Japan. After WW2 he turned to biology, both experimental (fundamental studies of bacterial mutations and biochemical mechanisms) and theoretical (problems of ageing and memory). His scientific papers were published as *The Collected Works of Leo Szilard* (eds B. Feld & G. Szilard, Cambridge, Mass., 1972), and aspects of his scientific life in *Leo Szilard: his Version of the Facts* (eds S. Weart & G. Szilard, Cambridge, Mass., 1978).　　　MMG

T

Tagore, Rabindranath (b. Calcutta, W. Bengal, India, 6.5.1861; d. Calcutta, 7.8.1941). Indian writer who sprang to the fashionable attention of western readers in 1913 when he won the Nobel prize for literature for his collection of poems *Gitanjali: Song Offerings* (London, 1912). These poems in English were based on his Bengali originals written since the mid-1890s although they are substantially different in conception. In his native Bengal his patrician background and total commitment to Bengali culture made him a figure of veneration throughout his life, and today he is still regarded by his countrymen as the greatest Bengali of all time: certainly none can match him in the breadth of his talents, for he was an outstanding poet, storyteller, playwright, composer and philosopher, as well as being the founder of Santiniketan University where a programme to encourage rural values was enshrined in a workable educational system. He championed the traditional dances of India, he was a painter of note, and he gave to the Bengali language a cultural status which it had not enjoyed previously in printed form. Though not inclined to take an active part in politics, he lent a prominent voice to early 20c expressions of nationalism and in 1919 renounced his knighthood in protest at British policy in the Punjab. His most important works were written in Bengali but he translated many of his own poems into English, forming new collections – for example, *The Gardener* (London, 1913) – which do not exist in the same form in his mother tongue. Though little read in the West today, Tagore's influence over M. GANDHI and the makers of modern India was enormous, extending equally into the society of intellectuals and peasants.   ANRN

H. Banerjee, *Rabindranath Tagore* (New Delhi, 1971); B. C. Chakravorty, *Rabindranath Tagore: his Mind and Art* (New Delhi, 1971).

Takhtajan, Armen Leontovich (b. Shusha, Russia, 10.6.1910). Russian botanist. Educated at Tbilisi University, he is currently professor emeritus at the Komarov Botanical Institute, Leningrad. The world's leading exponent of neo-Darwinian evolutionary systematics of the flowering plants, he is also a distinguished biogeographer. Between 1942 and 1980 he developed major new hypotheses on the origin and diversification of the angiosperms. Many of his ideas have been, at least tentatively, widely accepted. Takhtajan's outstanding contribution to botany is based on a comprehensive knowledge of the world's flora and an encyclopedic but critical and scholarly evaluation of a an international literature. The latter covers such diverse and recently developed fields as comparative phytochemistry, serology, DNA hybridization and amino acid sequences of proteins, the ultrastructure of the pollen grain and conducting system, as well as more traditional areas of study. With the almost universal acceptance of the theory of continental drift in recent years, evolutionary studies are increasingly focused on the differentiation of floras and faunas in response to changing positions of the land masses. As this subject develops, Takhtajan's major works are likely to provide a conceptual framework for years to come.

FW

Tange, Kenzo (b. Imabari, Japan, 4.9.1913). Japanese architect and town planner. Tange was the first 20c Japanese architect to establish a worldwide reputation. Like many Japanese of his generation he was deeply influenced by the designs of LE CORBUSIER. Tange's Peace Centre, completed in 1955 and built on the site of the epicentre of the first atomic bomb, dropped on Hiroshima, set a pattern for an evolving hybrid of European and Japanese architecture. The centre has an exposed concrete structure in Corbusian style, but its details have a precision and delicacy that suggest traditional Japanese timber

743

architecture. The most important example of the style was Tange's town hall at Kagawa (1958), a *tour de force* in the sensitive use of concrete and glass, and much imitated by American and European architects. Later in his career Tange moved towards a more pronounced interest in town planning. He set up an influential planning and research institute at Tokyo University, working also on the design of the Tokyo Olympic stadium. At this stage he came up with a mercifully unrealized plan to build a new town on stilts over Tokyo bay. Tange's influence came increasingly to be felt outside Japan while the younger generation was attempting to develop a more specifically Japanese architecture. Since the early 1970s Tange has been engaged on a wide range of ambitious planning projects in Europe and the Middle East.   DS

Tansley, Arthur George (b. London, UK, 15.8.1871; d. Grantchester, Cambs., 25.11.1955). British botanist. Tansley received his first botanical stimulus as a schoolboy and wrote his first papers (in the school magazine) on the general principles of classification. At Cambridge he read botany, zoology, physiology and geology (1890), before journeying through Ceylon, the Malay Peninsula and Egypt (1900–1) to extend his knowledge of world vegetation patterns. Fluent in German, he read the great German textbooks of the period and, impressed both by the superiority of continental texts and their relative dearth in the UK, founded the *New Phytologist* in 1902. This journal carefully nurtured the infant growth of British plant ecology and initiated the reformation of the teaching of plant sciences. Under his inspired leadership a surge of interest was aroused in British ecology, and studies were undertaken from moorland to marine habitats. Due mainly to this stimulus the British Ecological Society came into existence in 1913. In the 1920s Tansley wrote two of his most influential books: *Practical Plant Ecology* (London, 1923) and, with T. F. Chipp, *Aims and Methods in the Study of Vegetation* (London, 1926). Elected Sherardian professor of botany in Oxford in 1927, he completed *The British Islands*

and their Vegetation (Cambridge, 1939) shortly after his retirement. His strong influence continued to be felt in the Wildlife Conservation Committee of the 1940s which contributed much to the later formed Nature Conservancy (1949). He was knighted in 1950, an acknowledgement of his immense achievements in the analysis, recording and conservation of Britain's wild heritage.   BEJ

Tàpies, Antoni (b. Barcelona, Spain, 13.12.1923). Spanish painter best known for paintings with a thick sand and plaster texture in earth colours and incorporating common materials which often resemble eroded village walls, palimpsests of marks and graffiti. While his work is related to informal art and *arte povera*, his use of humble materials has a moral and contemplative purpose. He is a self-taught artist for whom the Spanish civil war was a formative experience, and he subsequently developed an interest in the culture of the Far East. From 1948 to 1951 he was a founding member of the Barcelona surrealist group *Dau al Set*; during this period he experimented with collage. He then spent a year in Paris where he met PICASSO and in 1953 he visited New York. It was during that year that his characteristic style of painting emerged. In 1957 he helped found the *El Paso* group which promoted abstract, informalist art in Spain. His later work includes assemblages using furniture. Tàpies's use of material is never purely formal but seeks to create a mysterious, tragic and at times humorous poetry of the object.   MOJN

Solomon R. Guggenheim Museum, *Antoni Tàpies* (NY, 1962); R. Penrose, *Tàpies* (NY, 1977).

Tappan, Paul Wilbur (b. Danbury, Conn., USA, 25.12.1911; d. Oakland, Calif., 9.7.1964). American criminologist. As a sociologist with legal training he was unique among American criminologists. After graduate work at the University of Wisconsin, he taught at several universities including Berkeley, New York and Harvard. The main emphasis of his work in penology lay in condemning the overreach of the criminal justice system and the way in which it ignored human rights in pursuit of the 'treatment' ideology. He first developed this thesis in his brilliant study *Delinquent Girls in Court* (NY, 1947), in which he anticipated some of the current concerns about the 'treatment' model in regard to the goals of the penal system. As a criminologist he will be remembered primarily for his questioning of Edwin SUTHERLAND's concept of 'white collar' crime. Internationally his main contributions came as consultant and American representative at various conferences between 1955 and 1960. Also consultant to the New Jersey Commission on the *Habitual Sexual Offender* (NJ, 1950) and chairman of the US Board of Parole (1953–4), his outstanding American service to the law was as associate reporter (1952–62) with Herbert Wechsler on the drafting of the American Law Institute's model penal code. Here he was mainly responsible for the sentencing provisions. His critique of the California code led to proposals for recasting sentence and parole provisions in a more acceptable fashion. Despite all these involvements he managed to produce a major textbook *Crime, Justice and Corrections* (NY, 1960), a sequel to his *Juvenile Delinquency* (NY, 1949).   JEHW

Tarski, Alfred (b. Warsaw, Russian Poland [now Poland], 14.1.1902). Polish logician and mathematician, a brilliant member of the distinguished group of logicians working in Poland in the interwar years. Excluded, because Jewish, from a faculty university post, Tarski taught concurrently in a high school and at Warsaw university until 1939. Since 1942 he has been based at the University of California at Berkeley. Productive over a wide range of logical and mathematical topics, he made pioneering studies of the 'equivalential calculus' and refined considerations of the notions of the consistency and completeness of formal logical theories. A most notable achievement was his monograph of 1933 ['The concept of truth in formalized languages'] (tr. J. H. Woodger in *Logic, Semantics, Metamathematics*, Oxford, 1956). This has been the starting-point for all logically serious discussions of the subject ever since. In it

Tarski rehabilitates the classical correspondence theory of truth in contemporary logical guise. Since WW2 Tarski has continued to work on a wide variety of logical and mathematical topics, usually of a rather specific and technical kind. More generally his work has served to legitimate semantic discourse about the relations between language and the world, explicitly proscribed by WITTGENSTEIN although practised by him. QUINE's critique of the analytic-synthetic distinction was foreshadowed by Tarski, and he also had much influence on CARNAP and POPPER.   AQ/IG-G

K. Popper, *Objective Knowledge* (Oxford, ⁵1974).

Tata, Jamsetji Nasarwanji (b. Naosari, Baroda, India, 3.3.1839; d. Bad Nauheim, Hesse, Germany, 19.5.1904). Indian businessman whose success in developing cotton mills, and in property investment, enabled him to endow educational and welfare projects. He provided a cornerstone for India's economic development by promoting the modern steel industry. His elder son Sir Doraliji Tata (1859–1932) was involved in the discovery of rich iron ore at Orissa and, with a younger son Sir Ratanji Tata (1871–1918), a company was started which, together with associated large, heavy engineering works, became a major contributor to India's industrialization.   RIT

F. R. Harris, *J. N. Tata* (London, 1958).

Tate, John Orley Allen (b. Winchester, Ky, USA, 19.11.1899; d. Nashville, Tenn., 9.2.1979). American literary critic and poet. Tate studied at Vanderbilt University, Tennessee, where he became friends with RANSOM and Robert Penn Warren; the three were involved in the emergence of a distinctive modern Southern literary and intellectual movement, stressing the values of a traditional, agrarian society and upholding the centrality of art to society. The movement, known as the Fugitive group, was responsible for the controversial symposium *I'll Take My Stand* (NY, 1930) which addressed itself to the dangers of liberalism, socialism and naive trust in the values of scientific and technological progress. Tate's poetry, much of it very distinguished, is noted for its classical severity and restraint; his criticism follows a similarly antiromantic bias, seeing romanticism itself as the result of a misguided conflict between rationalism and the claims of the poetic imagination. Influenced by ELIOT, Tate praised the Metaphysical poets and sought to encourage the use of similar modes of irony, allusion and ambiguity in modern poetry. His criticism, ultimately more influential than his poetry, has been collected in *Essays of Four Decades* (Chicago, 1969). His one novel *The Fathers* (NY, 1938) deals with the decline of Southern society in the post-Civil War period. *Collected Poems: 1919 –1976* (NY, 1977) contains all of Tate's major poems.   GHC

G. Hemphill, *Allen Tate* (Minneapolis, 1964); F. Bishop, *Allen Tate* (NY, 1967).

Tatlin, Vladimir Evgrafovich (b. Kharkov, Russia, 16.12.1885; d. Novodevichi, USSR, 31.5.1953). Russian artist, best known in the West for his models for a proposed *Monument to the Third International* ('Tatlin's Tower'), exhibited in Petrograd and Moscow (1920), and in Paris (1925). After a European tour (1913) including, he said, visiting PICASSO's Paris studio, he invented *Painterly reliefs* (1914) then *Corner, counter reliefs* (1915), mostly destroyed but known from photographs and recent reconstructions. Using wood, metal, glass, etc., Tatlin constructed these sculptures which alluded to the world about them in a nonrepresentational way, the *Corner, counter reliefs* having additional struts of wire or rope, stretching across the corner of the room or out into the space in front of the wall, fulfilling in an original way prescriptions for futurist sculpture advanced by the Italian BOCCIONI (manifesto, 1913). An enthusiastic supporter of the Bolshevik revolution in 1917, he was commissioned to design a *Monument to the Third International* in 1919. He made wooden models of a tower (reconstruction, Stockholm, 1967–8) planned as a gigantic slanted, metal scaffolding, 400m high, to contain suspended glass halls: a cylinder for legislative assemblies, a pyramid for executive

committee meetings, a hemisphere as an information centre; all three were to rotate mechanically – each year, month and day, respectively. Never built, it was the most ambitious of a number of utopian projects planned by artists for the new Soviet society (see LISSITZKY's horizontal skyscraper designs, *Sky-hook*, 1924) which were unrealizable for technical and economic reasons. The pragmatic aspect of these works and his dubious connection with a productivist manifesto (1920) has resulted in his reputation as a leading constructivist overshadowing a truer assessment of him as an idealist. This emerges in his designs for *Zangezi*, staged at his exhibition in Petrograd (1923); he said he saw in Khlebnikov's play a fusion of the poet's study of language and the 'laws of time' into a 'super-new form'. Likewise he made a man-powered glider (exhibited in 1932) entitled *Letatlin*, punning on his own name and the Russian verb 'to fly'. Rarely can an artist's legendary reputation have rested on so few surviving works, though many original paintings, drawings, book illustrations and stage designs from his early and post-1930 traditional periods were exhibited in Moscow in 1977. His practical designs for clothes, stoves, etc. from the early revolutionary years have commanded affection for this, in reality, aloof artist, while his cult of materials in abstract, linear constructions has inspired many subsequent constructivist artists.   SPC

Vladimir Tatlin, exh. cat., Museum of Modern Art (Stockholm, 1968); *V. E. Tatlin*, exh. cat., Sovetskii khudozhnik (Moscow, 1977); J. Milner, *Vladimir Tatlin and the Russian Avant-garde* (London, 1983).

Tatum, Edward Lawrie (b. Boulder, Colo, USA, 14.12.1909; d. New York, 5.11.1947). American biochemical geneticist. Tatum studied at the University of Wisconsin and in 1937 joined BEADLE at Stanford where they collaborated in an investigation into biochemical mechanisms of gene action. Initially they worked on eye-colour pigments in the fruit fly *Drosophila melanogaster*, but then decided that the fungus *Neurospora crassa* would be more suitable for experiments on gene action. They were quickly successful in obtaining nutritionally demanding mutants of *N. crassa* which enabled them to formulate the one-gene one-enzyme hypothesis (Beadle & Tatum, 'Genetic control of biochemical reactions in *Neurospora*', *Proc. Nat. Acad. Sci.*, 27 [1941], 499–506). Their data laid the foundations for subsequent analyses of biochemical pathways, as well as of gene action, while the techniques they developed were used not only in experimental biology but also in industry. Tatum later cooperated with LEDERBERG in experiments which resulted in the discovery of genetic recombination in the bacterium *Escherichia coli*, another landmark of enormous significance in the development of genetics and molecular biology (Lederberg & Tatum, 'Gene recombination in *Escherichia*', *Nature*, 158 [1946], 558). In 1958 Tatum received, with Beadle and Lederberg, the Nobel prize for medicine.   APJ

J. Lederberg, 'Edward Lawrie Tatum', *Ann. Review Genetics*, 13 (1979), 1–5.

Tawney, Richard Henry (b. Calcutta, W. Bengal, India, 30.11.1880; d. London, UK, 16.1.1962). British economic historian, social critic and reformer. After leaving Oxford, Tawney became active in the Workers' Educational Association. He found it stimulating to combine teaching cotton-workers, potters and miners with writing his first major work of scholarship *The Agrarian Problem in the 16th Century* (London, 1912). After serving in WW1, he moved as professor to the London School of Economics (1931–49) where he played a major role in developing economic history as a separate discipline. Tawney was a great teacher, and in 1926 was one of the founders of the Economic History Society, serving as joint editor of its *Review* which set high standards of scholarship for the subject. The same year he published his classic study *Religion and the Rise of Capitalism* (London, 1926), a book in which his mastery of the English language as well as his learning were used to penetrate the economic morality and practice of what came to be known as 'Tawney's century', England between 1558 and 1640. He followed this by editing, with Eileen

Power, three volumes of *Tudor Economic Documents* (London, 1927) and explored the claims of Harrington (1611–71) to be the first English writer to find the cause of political upheaval in social change. A lengthy article which Tawney contributed to the *Economic History Review* on 'The rise of the gentry 1558–1640' gave rise after WW2 to one of the most celebrated historical controversies of the century, and he rounded off his academic career by publishing a masterly study of an early capitalist politician Lionel Cranfield (*Business and Politics under James I*, London, 1958).

Tawney valued history as a means of exploring, in concrete form, the perennial questions of the relationship between economics, politics and morality, and it was consistent with this view that he should take an active part in promoting social reform. His greatest influence was in providing the Labour party with a social philosophy which owed nothing to MARXism. A convinced Christian, Tawney made morality the basis of his socialism, arguing that a good society could be built only by good men. In *The Acquisitive Society* (London, 1921) he based his criticism of capitalism on the grounds that its encouragement of acquisitive behaviour corrupted both rich and poor. In a second, widely read book *Equality* (London, 1931), Tawney looked critically at the UK class structure, urging the extension of social services and more progressive taxation to reduce the gross inequalities which it perpetuated. Tawney's religious beliefs were a stumbling block to many socialists, but his argument that the acquisitive spirit was the great enemy in personal as well as social life made a deep appeal to many in the Labour party and was reinforced by the simplicity of his own life.   ALCB

R. Terrill, *R. H. Tawney and his Times* (Cambridge, Mass., 1973).

Taylor, Frederick Winslow (b. Philadelphia, Pa, USA, 20.3.1856; d. Philadelphia, 21.3.1915). American management studies theorist and practitioner. Though well educated, Taylor began his working life as an apprentice machinist (1875–8); he was a shop-floor worker in the Midvale Steel Works (1878) and worked his way up to chief engineer by 1890. He became a consultant in engineering and management, but from 1901 devoted himself to furthering scientific management. Management was seldom thought of as a specific function before Taylor's new thinking aimed at maximizing prosperity for employer and employee. He believed that systematic study of the way work was done would lead to increased efficiency and, thus, greater prosperity. In *The Principles and Methods of Scientific Management* (NY, 1911) he amalgamated various ideas, such as time-study and the payment of premium bonuses, into a set of principles for facilitating workers' and managers' cooperation by scientific quantification of work. Some of those claiming to adopt his methods did not adopt the social responsibility inherent in his principles. A committee of Congress criticized Taylor in 1912. He retorted that scientific management was neither a set of efficiency devices nor a set of cost-accounting tools but a revolution in thinking for workers and management.

RIT

Taylor, Geoffrey Ingram (b. London, UK, 7.3.1886; d. Cambridge, 27.6.1975). British physicist and applied mathematician. One of the most prolific and wide-ranging scientists of the century, Taylor was educated at Cambridge, where, apart from work at the Royal Aircraft Establishment, Farnborough, during WW1, he spent his professional life and where he was appointed Yarrow research professor in 1923. He was the classical physicist *par excellence* and was outstanding for a very wide variety of studies, especially in the mechanics of fluids and solids. Of particular importance was his work on turbulent motion in fluids. This he applied to problems in meteorology and oceanography and even to the mechanics of swimming of small creatures. During WW2 he made important contributions to the knowledge of shock waves in explosions. He was one of the first people to make a systematic study of the plastic deformation of crystalline materials and he invented (1934) the concept of a 'dislocation'. This is a form of atomic misarrangement in a crystal which, if present, enables the

crystal to deform at a stress maybe 1000 times less than that of an ideally perfect crystal. More recent work has shown that, unless very carefully prepared, all crystals contain large numbers of these dislocations and it is the way in which they move and interact which controls their strength and the way they deform.

HMR

Taylor, Hugh Stott (b. St Helens, Mers., UK, 6.2.1890; d. Princeton, NJ, USA, 17.4.1974). British chemist. After graduating in chemistry at Liverpool University, Taylor worked with ARRHENIUS in Stockholm and BODENSTEIN in Hanover. From 1914 to his death, except during WW1 when he returned to the UK (to work on ways of synthesizing ammonia), he remained at Princeton. He made two significant contributions to theories of catalysis. First he recognized that only a relatively small fraction of the surface of a solid catalyst is effective: the idea of 'active sites' was introduced by him in this context in 1925. At such sites two or more reactant species could be adsorbed, a notion which extended earlier views formulated by LANGMUIR and SABATIER. His second contribution was to identify the existence of 'activated adsorption', which rationally explained the observation that the extent of adsorption sometimes increases with increasing temperature, a fact which seemed to run counter to LE CHATELIER's principle. He was quick to recognize the significance of UREY's discovery of deuterium (an isotope of hydrogen) in 1932. By judicious use of H_2 and D_2, Taylor greatly elucidated the mechanistic details of many important chemical reactions.

JMT

Taylor, Thomas Griffith (b. London, UK, 1.12.1880; naturalized Australian citizen; d. London, 5.11.1963). British/Australian geographer who made vigorous contributions to the debate over environmental determinism. Taylor's 'stop-go' hypothesis suggested that while the basic environmental resources of an area and its relative location determined the basic direction of economic development, the other classic factors of labour and capital determined the rate of development. Taylor emigrated to Australia with his parents while in his early teens. After graduating from Sydney University he specialized in glaciology and worked at Cambridge and in the Antarctic (with the Scott expedition) before returning to Sydney as its first geography professor in 1920. His views on the unfavourable climatic conditions over much of arid and tropical Australia brought him into public conflict with the Australian government intent on increasing migration, and he left Australia in 1928 for North America. Here he founded Canada's first geography department (Toronto), returning to retirement in Australia in 1951. Taylor's strongly held and vigorously argued ideas permeate his many books. His ideas on the Australian environment were set out in *Climatic Control of Australian Production* (Melbourne, 1915) and continued through a number of publications to *Australia: a Study of Warm Environments and their Effect on British Settlement* (London, 1941). His experiences of Canada were reflected in a parallel volume on *Canada: a Study of Cool, Continental Environments and their Effect on British and French Settlement* (London, 1947). On a still broader canvas the links between environment and political and economic organization were set out in *Environment and Nation* (London, 1936) and *Urban Geography* (London, 1949). Taylor's account of his own explorations is given in his autobiographical *Journeyman Taylor* (London, 1958). PH

Tchernichowsky, Saul Gutmanovich (b. Mikhailovka, Crimea, Russia, 20.8.1875; d. Jerusalem, Palestine [now Israel], 14.10.1943). Hebrew poet, essayist and translator. Tchernichowsky studied medicine and languages in Heidelberg. His poetry reflects national revival and rebellion against the accepted norms of the Jewish religion, combined with admiration for the heroic Jewish past and for the beauty of Greek poetry and drama. On Jewish issues he was an extreme nationalist, admiring strength, beauty and fighting. His language is both classical and innovative: he coined many new Hebrew words from his vast medical and linguistic knowledge. He wrote a remarkable series of poems on

the landscapes of the Crimea and the Ukraine, and, under the influence of Greek and Russian poetry, another series of lyrical-erotic poems notable for their bold language and imagery. He also wrote a long epic poem on the Jews in medieval Germany [Baruch of Mainz], published a monograph on the Italian Hebrew poet *Immanuel von Rom* (Berlin, 1925) on whom he modelled himself, and translated into brilliant Hebrew works by Anacreon, Sophocles, Homer, Longfellow, Goethe, Shakespeare and others. His works were collected in 10 volumes (Jerusalem, 1930), and a selection in English as *Tchernichowsky and his Poetry* (tr. L. Snowman, London, 1930). CA

M. Ribalow, *The Flowering of Modern Hebrew Literature* (NY, 1959); E. Silberschlag, *Saul Tchernichowsky* (NY, 1968).

Teague, Walter Dorwin (b. Decatur, Ind., USA, 18.12.1883; d. Annandale, NJ, 5.12.1960). American industrial designer who earned himself the title 'the dean of industrial design' through his pioneering work in the 1920s and 1930s. Teague came to New York in 1907 and studied lithography at the Art Students' League, and it was as a graphic designer that he first earned a reputation; his renowned 'Teague borders' were exhibited at the Metropolitan Museum of Art in the 1920s. In 1926 he turned his office at 210 Madison Avenue into a specialized industrial design office and his first commission came in the following year from Eastman Kodak to restyle the Baby Brownie camera. Like his contemporaries Norman Bel Geddes, LOEWY and Henry Dreyfuss, Teague became one of the names used as publicity for the products with which they were associated. He worked on a number of consumer products, the most notable being his Marmon V.8 automobile of 1932, but most of his operations were devoted to interiors and exhibition displays. He worked for many years for Ford, contributing to their pavilion at the Century of Progress exhibition in Chicago (1933–4) and more substantially at the New York World's Fair (1939) where he designed the complete Ford building along with others for

United Steel and the Du Pont company. Teague's work was neither innovatory nor radical and he avoided the excesses of streamlining and styling for which, for example, Bel Geddes is known. He succeeded, nonetheless, in representing the new professional, the 'industrial designer', by establishing modes of office practice and by becoming, in 1944, the first president of the American Society of Industrial Designers. W. D. Teague Associates is still one of the more substantial New York industrial design offices. In 1940 he published *Design This Day: the Technique of Order in the Machine Age* (NY). PAS

J. L. Meikle, *Twentieth-century Limited: Industrial Design in America 1925–1939* (Philadelphia, 1979).

Teilhard de Chardin, Pierre (b. nr Clermont-Ferrand, Puy-de-Dôme, France, 1.5.1881; d. New York, USA, 10.4.1955). French Jesuit priest, palaeontologist, mystic and – from the mid-1950s – cult figure. In China for most of his working life (1923–46), he spent his last years in New York (1951–5), partly because his Jesuit superiors would not allow him to take up a professional post in Paris, partly because he preferred 'Anglo-Saxons'. He had also been forbidden to publish except on scientific matters. The result was that there was an air of clandestinity about the manuscripts which circulated in the 1950s containing hints of his bold and visionary synthesis of science and Christian faith. For Teilhard, evolution was not just a theory about the origin of living species: it involved understanding the world as 'cosmogenesis', a dynamic and upward-moving process in which all distinctions between matter and spirit were dissolved. Everything in the world is interrelated. Where his elder BERGSON saw evolution as increasingly divergent, Teilhard saw it as increasingly convergent. The world is heading, he believed, towards the 'omega point' where love will be all in all. For him, Christ was at the very heart of the process of 'cosmogenesis', its immanent force and its eventual goal. In man evolution is consciously endorsed; Christian faith announces what the goal of the process is – but it does so not from the outside but rather by extrapolation from already visible trends. For Christians this implied a new approach to matter, work and progress. His speculative books had to wait for posthumous publication. The best known are *Le Milieu divin* (written 1926, Paris, 1957; tr. B. Wall, London, 1960) and *Le Phénomène humain* (completed 1942, Paris, 1955; tr. B. Wall, *The Phenomenon of Man*, London, 1959). Teilhard has been criticized both by scientists and theologians. But his optimistic synthesis of Christianity and evolution has appealed to many. The difficulty in appraising his work lies in deciding to what literary genre it belongs: it is an original amalgam of science, theology and poetry. PAH

C. E. Raven, *Teilhard de Chardin: Scientist and Seer* (London, 1962); B. Towers, *Teilhard de Chardin* (London, 1968).

Teller, Edward (b. Budapest, Austria-Hungary [now Hungary], 15.1.1908; naturalized American citizen, 1941). Hungarian/American physicist. One of the brilliant Hungarian Jews who emigrated in the interwar period to Germany and then to the USA, where he arrived in 1935. Trained in chemical engineering and physical chemistry, he had become a distinguished and original theoretical physicist. However, he is best known for his influence and attitudes on nuclear affairs. In WW2 he worked at Los Alamos, not on fission bombs but on the future hydrogen bomb, and henceforth saw nuclear energy as a solution to the major problems of war and peace (e.g. *Energy from Heaven and Earth*, San Francisco, 1979). In 1951 he devised with S. Ulam a configuration which would ensure that a relatively small fission explosion could ignite an arbitrarily large amount of thermonuclear fuel; consequently he is known as the 'father of the H-bomb'. Passionately anticommunist, he accepted – even welcomed – the nuclear arms race as the best method of containing the USSR and ensuring world peace (*The Legacy of Hiroshima*, NY, 1962). His evidence at the US Atomic Energy Commission security hearings in 1954, which accused J. R. OPPENHEIMER of obstructing the progress of the H-bomb, reflected and caused deep and bitter rifts in the US scientific community. More recently Teller has exercised a cautious influence on nuclear-reactor safety criteria. MMG

H. York, *The Advisors: Oppenheimer, Teller and the Superbomb* (San Francisco, 1976).

Temple, William (b. Exeter, Devon, UK, 15.10.1881; d. Westgate-on-Sea, Kent, 26.9.1944). British churchman. The son of Frederick Temple, archbishop of Canterbury (1896–1902), he was himself archbishop of Canterbury from 1942 to 1944 – the only instance of a son succeeding his father in the Anglican Communion's senior bishopric. After periods as a fellow of Queen's College, Oxford, as a headmaster, and as a London rector and canon, he became bishop of Manchester (1921) and archbishop of York (1929). He was an influential advocate of a large measure of self-government for a church which had previously been under the detailed control of the state. But his leadership was national and international rather than denominational. As president of the Workers' Educational Association, as a creative adviser to the BBC, as chairman of a large and well-prepared conference on 'Politics, Economics and Citizenship' (1924), and as a prominent figure in the creation of the World Council of Churches, he caused so many people to admire and trust him that he was able to negotiate an end to the religious disputes which had bedevilled the state's school system (as part of the R. A. Butler Education Act, 1944). Much in demand as a preacher and lecturer, his approach was conservatively Christian but never narrow-minded or deliberately irrational. It may be seen applied to the philosophy of religion in *Nature, Man and God* (London, 1934); to the interpretation of the church's creeds in *Doctrine in the Church of England* (London, 1938, the report of a commission at work under his chairmanship since 1925); and to the reconstruction of society in *Christianity and Social Order* (London, 1942). A Christian socialist, he articulated an idealism which prepared for the electoral victory of the British Labour party in 1945. His key teaching was that the loving purpose of God had been revealed in the event of Jesus Christ's life. DLE

F. A. Iremonger, *William Temple* (London, 1948).

Tesla, Nikola (b. Smiljan, Croatia, Austria-Hungary [now Yugoslavia], 9.7.1856; naturalized American citizen, 1891; d. New York, USA, 7.1.1943). Yugoslav/American electrical engineer. There are probably more legends about Tesla than about any other experimenter in electrical science. A claim was made by himself and by others who reputedly witnessed the event that he was able to light some 200 50-watt lamps at 26 miles from a generator by using the earth alone as transmitting medium. In engineering his most important work was the invention of the induction motor in 1888. Since Faraday's experiments in 1831, direct current motors and generators had been developed commercially to a high standard of efficiency and effectiveness. Their one weakness was that of requiring heavy currents to be fed to the rotating member through rubbing contacts – carbon or copper brushes passing over a succession of metal strips mounted cylindrically on the shaft. Tesla set himself the task, in the 1870s, of developing a brushless motor that would be fed from *alternating* current, which is easier to generate than direct current; he predicted that such a machine would dominate the world of electric drives. He constructed his first induction motor in 1883 in after-work hours, and in 1884 emigrated to the USA where he sold the patent rights for his system to the Westinghouse Company in Pittsburgh. His dedication to the induction motor was more than justified. After a fierce commercial struggle with Edison's direct current system, the Tesla-Westinghouse ac system won out. Today over 95 per cent of the power of electric drives in the world consists of induction motors. Russians acclaim Dobrowolsky as its inventor; it is almost certain that he invented it quite separately from Tesla, at about the same time, but it is doubtful whether, like Tesla, he saw it as dominating the engineering world. Tesla brought his motor to commercial success within a very short time. ERL

J. J. O'Neill, *Prodigal Genius: the Life of Nikola Tesla* (NY, 1944); I. Hunt & W. Draper, *Lightning in his Hand: the Life Story of Nikola Tesla* (NY, 1964).

Tesnière, Lucien (b. Mont-Saint-Aignan, Seine-Maritime, France, 13.5.1893; d. Paris, 6.12.1954). French linguist. A distinguished scholar working as a specialist in Russian and other Slavic languages, and involved in dialectology, literary studies and language teaching, he remains best known for his general linguistic writings. He contributed a substantial appendix (183 pages) on the statistics of the languages of Europe (numbers of speakers, etc.) in Antoine Meillet's *Les langues dans l'Europe nouvelle* [Languages in modern Europe] (Paris, 1928), but his most important book, published posthumously, was *Eléments de syntaxe structurale* [Elements of structural syntax] (Paris, 1959), on which he had been working since the 1930s. It can now be seen that he was anticipating some of the salient features of transformational grammar and of other systems of linguistic description in active development today, more particularly in the priority he accorded to syntax, in his formalization of syntactic transformations ('translations' in his terminology), and in his prime concern for internal structural order and its relations with the overt linear order of actual sentences.   RHR

R. H. Robins, 'Syntactic analysis', *Archivum linguisticum*, 13 (1961), 78–89; M. G. Worthington, 'A precursor of the transformational approach to descriptive syntax: Lucien Tesnière', *Romance Philology*, 21 (1967–8), 303–17.

Thatcher, Margaret Hilda, *née* Roberts (b. Grantham, Notts., UK, 13.10.1925). British Conservative minister of education and science (1970–4), leader of the Conservative party in place of Edward Heath, prime minister (1979–), the first woman in British history to hold that position. Her defeat of Heath was taken to herald the advent to power of a new activist Toryism, which would cut government expenditure and intervention in business and industry, bring down inflation by control of the money supply, defend British interests in world affairs more actively, increase defence expenditure, reduce the corporate power of the trade unions, and move away from the consensus politics of the 1950s. The alliance of forces within the Tory party on which her power vested comprised a curious union between disaffected elements from the traditional establishment, industrial entrepreneurs and the lower bourgeoisie (from whose ranks she herself sprang) antagonized by the growth of corporate power both in business and in the unions. Its doctrines were equally a mixture of 19c Manchester school economics, Chicago school monetarism, a puritanical disapproval of public expenditure *per se* and an anticommunism reminiscent of the height of the Cold War. The introduction of 'Thatcherite' politics coincided with a major world recession at a time when the earnings from North Sea oil were inflating the value of sterling – circumstances rather different from those in which and for which those policies had originally been evolved – without affecting the determination with which they were applied. At a time when support for her policies was faltering, her firmness in the unexpected crisis over the Falkland Islands (1982) and Britain's success in the first war to be fought with a woman as prime minister greatly increased both her popularity and her confidence.   DCW

Thom, René Frédéric (b. Montbéliard, Doubs, France, 2.9.1923). French mathematician. In the 1950s he developed a powerful geometric theory of differentiable manifolds, called cobordism theory, for which he was awarded the Fields medal in 1958. This is a deep cohomology theory, i.e. it turns important geometric problems into algebraic ones to seek solutions. A major consequent success of the theory was J. Milnor's surprising discovery in 1956 that spheres of dimension 7 or more can possess inequivalent differentiable structures; another was S. Smale's affirmative solution of the J. H. POINCARÉ conjecture in dimensions greater than 5. During the 1960s Thom developed catastrophe theory which he (and Arnold in Moscow) used to illuminate singularities of differentiable mappings. Since then the theory has found many applications, some in biology as Thom hoped, though none as yet of the power he would wish, and some much more controversial from which he has disassociated himself. He has taught at Grenoble, Strasbourg and, since 1963, at L'Institut des Hautes Etudes Scientifiques at Bures-sur-Yvette where he is professor of mathematics.

JJG

Thomas, Dylan Marlais (b. Swansea, W. Glam., UK, 27.10.1914; d. New York, USA, 9.11.1953). British poet. His precocious yet fully fledged talent brought him early success which developed into something more akin to notoriety as a composite public myth emerged in which both the irregularities of his personal life and the obscurity of his poetry played a part. He came to London in the year of publication of his first book *18 Poems* (London, 1934), and thereafter his life was divided between Wales and London, and Wales and America, as he earned a living by broadcasting, scriptwriting, and finally touring the American reading circuit. His major themes are sex, death and time, and their interconnection in the continuity between individual life and natural processes. His poetry articulates these themes through its emphasis on a distinctive authorial voice addressing its own childhood and adolescent experience. Thomas's fictional and dramatic writing (*Portrait of the Artist as a Young Dog*, London, 1940; *Under Milk Wood*, London, 1954) puts these themes in a communal context, whereas his poetry assumes the completeness of individual experience within the universal terms which inform his vision of it. By accepting and celebrating the limits of individual experience Thomas's poetry disengages from social discourse, asserting in its place a language which, while highly figurative, requires to be read literally (as he maintained) rather than expressively. His *Collected Poems* (London, 1952) sold 30,000 copies in the first year, but the myth which enveloped him in his own lifetime has tended posthumously to overshadow his genuine popularity with generally unfavourable critical judgement. [ATKC]

C. Fitzgibbon, *The Life of Dylan Thomas* (London, 1965).

Thomas, Philip Edward (b. London, UK, 3.3.1878; d. Arras, Pas-de-Calais, France, 9.4.1917). British poet. Edward Thomas felt that his literary intentions, which placed him in the rural tradition of English prose writing, were thwarted by his financial dependence on literary journalism and commissioned work. In books such as *Beautiful Wales* (London, 1905) and *The South Country* (London, 1909) he was able to reconcile such conflicting motives, but his predicament reflects something of his sense of the vulnerability of rural life and values in the face of urban encroachment and the mass anonymity of city and suburban life. Thomas found in the English countryside, its people, animals and landscape, emblems of continuity with an ancient, valuable past and touchstones of identity and feeling in himself as solitary onlooker and witness. The poems he began to write late in 1914, many of which drew on episodes from his prose writings, owe something to his friendship with FROST. Yet in their subject matter they represent a fresh emphasis on his relationship to the rural life he observed, and in their direct and understated language they confirm Thomas's theoretical convictions as a critic of modern verse. His personal anxieties and his feeling for the English countryside and its people were powerfully unified by WW1, which extended his sense of the precarious situation of the world to which his imagination was attached. He enlisted in 1915, and was killed in action before the publication of his *Poems* (London, 1917). The definitive edition of the poetry is *The Collected Poems of Edward Thomas* (ed. R. G. Thomas, Oxford, 1978). ATKC

W. Cooke, *Edward Thomas: a Critical Biography* (London, 1970).

Thomas, Ronald Stuart (b. Cardiff, S. Glam., UK, 29.3.1913). Welsh poet. Ordained into the church in Wales in 1936, he has spent a lifetime in Welsh rural parishes, notably at Manafon in upland Powys from 1942 to 1954, a period during which he also learned Welsh. The poems of these years, mostly

collected in *Song at the Year's Turning* (London, 1955), reflect a townsman's encounter with nature, a cultured priest's encounter with the peasantry, and the confrontation of rural Wales with its romantic image. The result is on the one hand a self-questioning and self-revealing poetry, on the other a redefined mythology of Wales, not Dylan THOMAS's 'childhood land' but a bare, bitter, broken place which yet holds truths denied to the affluent society. Themes of religious quest already evident in volumes such as *Not that He Brought Flowers* (London, 1968) become dominant in *Laboratories of the Spirit* (London, 1975) and *Frequencies* (London, 1978). R. S. Thomas's God is defined through need and absence, and inhabits an inner not an outer space. Stylistically his poetry is built on the austere and sometimes bitter cadence. He rejects much of the intellectual riches of western civilization but relents in a moment's vision of an illuminated field. In his lifetime R. S. Thomas has moved, geographically and spiritually, further into Welsh-speaking Wales, and much of his prose writing is in Welsh.
EMT

Poetry Wales (Spring 1972), a special R. S. Thomas number; W. Moelwyn Merchant, *R. S. Thomas* (Cardiff, 1979).

Thompson, Edward Palmer (b. Oxford, UK, 3.2.1924). British historian. Britain's leading *engagé* and MARXist historian in the postwar era, and a major figure in the 'New Left' in the late 1950s, he achieved an immediate reputation with *The Making of the English Working Class* (London, 1963). In this Thompson gave class an historical specificity located in the Industrial Revolution: he was thus breaking with that routine Marxism which insists that *all* societies are class societies, while offering the most satisfactory analysis of class yet presented by any British historian. He treats class not as a 'structure' or a 'category', but as an 'historical phenomenon' which appears 'when some men, as a result of common experiences (inherited or shared), feel and articulate the identity of their interests as between themselves, and as against other men whose interests are different from (and

usually opposed to) theirs'. By launching the Centre for the Study of Social History at the University of Warwick, Thompson originated a whole new approach to the study 'from below' of the hidden complexities of earlier British society, particularly in the realm of 'crime' and law enforcement, seen at its best in his own *Whigs and Hunters: the Origin of the Black Act* (London, 1975), which with patience, skill and flair recreated the world of the foresters of Windsor and East Hampshire in 1723. Thompson has emerged as the leading spokesman for a pragmatic and humane Marxism against the highly theoretical combination of Marxism and structuralism of such continental figures as ALTHUSSER. Most recently he has returned to direct political activism in the cause of nuclear disarmament. AM

Thompson, John Eric Sidney (b. London, UK, 31.12.1898; d. Cambridge, 9.9.1975). British archaeologist and authority on Maya civilization. As a member of the field staff of the Field Museum of Natural History in Chicago (1926–35) he carried out an extensive programme of fieldwork in Belize (then British Honduras) on Mayan sites at Lubaantun, Busilha, the Cayo district and San José. In 1936 he joined the Carnegie Institution of Washington, thereafter devoting his efforts to the decipherment of Mayan hieroglyphs (*Maya Hieroglyphic Writing*, Washington, 1950; and *A Catalogue of Maya Hieroglyphs*, Norman, Okla, 1962) and to the study of Maya ethnography. BWC

Thomson, George Paget (b. Cambridge, UK, 3.5.1892; d. Cambridge, 10.9.1975). British physicist. The son of J. J. THOMSON, G.P. (as he was always called) lived through the most exciting years of atomic and nuclear research at Cambridge. As a young man he played an important role with LINDEMANN and TIZARD in the development of aircraft, and wrote a treatise on *Applied Aerodynamics* (London, 1918). He began his research in atomic physics by studying positive rays, a field pioneered by his father. He then realized that the apparatus could be modified easily to see whether the electron has any wavelike behaviour. He passed a beam of electrons through a thin metallic foil and observed a series of concentric rings on a photographic plate behind the foil. These he attributed to the diffraction of the electrons by the tiny crystals comprising the foil, thus confirming experimentally DE BROGLIE's ideas on their wave nature. For this work he was awarded a Nobel prize in 1937, jointly with DAVISSON. He showed that the radii of the rings are related to the energy of the electrons and to the spacing of the crystal planes, so making electron diffraction a powerful technique for the study of crystal structure. These researches are described in his *Wave Mechanics of the Free Electron* (London, 1930) and *Theory and Practice of Electron Diffraction* (with W. Cochrane, London, 1939). He then turned to nuclear physics and made some early experiments with slow neutrons. He saw that his results on the neutrons emitted in uranium fission might have important military applications, and alerted the government. In further experiments he showed that it is not possible to attain a chain reaction with uranium oxide. In 1940 he formed and steered the Maud Committee to assess the military potentialities of uranium fission. This committee coordinated the work that established the practicability of an atomic bomb, using uranium 235 separated by the gaseous diffusion of uranium hexafluoride. The project was subsequently transferred to the USA. After WW2 G.P. directed a group that discovered some of the unstable subnuclear particles in cosmic radiation and investigated the associated nuclear disintegrations. He also pioneered the study of nuclear fusion, with its still unrealized prospect of almost unlimited power. G.P. had great physical insight and an instinctive knowledge of the order-of-magnitude of physical quantities. He displayed these gifts on a wider scale in his books on *The Atom* (London, 1930) and *The Foreseeable Future* (London, 1957). PEH

Thomson, Joseph John (b. Cheetham Hill, nr Manchester, UK, 18.12.1856; d. Cambridge, 30.8.1940). British physicist. Thomson was trained in the Cambridge tradition of mathematical physics, and his early work was on Kelvin's theory of the vortex atom and Maxwell's electromagnetic theory. As Cavendish professor (1884–1919) he began experimental work on the electrical discharges in gases. He showed that the cathode rays are streams of charged particles, and by simultaneously deflecting them by electric and magnetic fields found that they have a mass to charge ratio about a thousand times less than that of the hydrogen ion, irrespective of the material of the cathode or the gas in the tube. This suggested that all atoms contained very light particles. They were called electrons; for this discovery Thomson was awarded a Nobel prize in 1906. He then tackled the problem of the arrangement of the electrons in the atom and proposed the Thomson model, in which the positive and negative charges are evenly spread throughout the atomic volume. This was subsequently superseded by RUTHERFORD's model in which the electrons surround the central, massive, positively charged nucleus. He also studied the positive rays in an electrical discharge and by combining electric and magnetic deflection was able to separate ions of different masses, including the isotopes of neon. Although he was personally clumsy, Thomson had a genius for designing experiments and telling his assistants how to get them to work. He established the reputation of the Cavendish Laboratory, where he was succeeded by Rutherford. PEH

Thorpe, William Homan (b. Hastings, E. Sussex, UK, 1.4.1902). British ethologist. A pioneer in the exploitation of sound recording and its analysis for the study of bird song, his work on the chaffinch has served as a model for many later studies. He founded the Ornithological Field Station at Cambridge in 1950 (later to become the Sub-department of Animal Behaviour), and served as its director until his retirement in 1969. Thorpe is particularly interested in the adaptive influence of individual experience on behaviour (see *Learning and Instinct in Animals*, London, 1963). He also believes that biologists should consider human nature as falling within their field of study, and in *Animal*

Nature and Human Nature (London, 1974) he attempts to integrate scientific fact with theological thought. He pursued this further in *Purpose in a World of Chance: a Biologist's View* (Oxford, 1978). The author of numerous scientific papers, he traced the development of his particular area of zoology in *The Origin and Rise of Ethology* (London, 1979), making, however, only limited reference to his own contribution.   PM

Thurber, James Grover (b. Columbus, Ohio, USA, 8.12.1894; d. New York, 2.11.1961). American humorist. A cosmopolitan who never forgot his provincial background, Thurber was born into a respectable family with a local reputation for wit and imagination. His career began on the Columbus *Dispatch*, and he worked as a journalist in France and New York before joining the *New Yorker* in 1927. A consummate stylist and compulsive reviser, he contributed a flow of memorable comic pieces which pivot around a central preoccupation with the problems of his bewildered misfits in a confusing and inexplicable world, collected in books like *My Life and Hard Times* (NY, 1933). Finely attuned to the absurdities and disjunctions of his times, he created a series of almost archetypal characters comically at odds with their world, epitomized in Walter Mitty (1939), while injecting into these creations a rich vein of fantasy and intimations of a darker underside. His drawings, which he always deprecated, are marvellous comic reductions, often defying logical explanation, and he enjoyed regular exhibitions until his lapse into blindness, the legacy of a childhood accident, around 1941. He continued to dictate prose, increasingly obsessed with fantasy, the role of the creative imagination and a JOYCEan preoccupation with language itself (as in *Lanterns and Lances*, NY, 1961) and fulfilled a lifelong ambition by acting in a New York dramatization of *The Thurber Carnival* (NY, 1945) in 1960.   KGM

C. Holmes, *The Clocks of Columbus* (NY, 1972); B. Bernstein, *James Thurber* (NY, 1975).

Tiffany, Louis Comfort (b. New York, USA, 18.2.1848; d. New York,

17.1.1933). American designer, and leading exponent of the art nouveau style, most noted for his work in iridescent and stained glass. Eldest son of Charles L. Tiffany who founded the great New York jewellery firm of Tiffany & Co., he began his career as a painter in the impressionist style, influenced by European and Near Eastern art. While exhibiting at the Philadelphia Centennial Exhibition in 1876 he became interested in the applied arts, started work in stained glass and studied glassmaking techniques at the Heidt factory, Brooklyn. In 1879 he formed the firm of Louis C. Tiffany, Associated Artists, which was dedicated to the radical reform of American interior decoration and whose wealthy clients included the White House, which he redecorated in 1883–4. In 1878 he established his own glassworks in New York, and in 1885 formed the Tiffany Glass Co. which specialized in windows, screens and lighting fixtures. Probably impressed with Emile Gallé's glass at the 1889 Paris Exhibition, in 1892 he reorganized his firm as the Tiffany Glass & Decorating Co. and in the following year was designing a completely new style of vessel glass at Corona, Long Island, working notably with Arthur J. Nash, an English glassblower. His 'favrile' glass was an instant success, being entirely furnace-made with an iridescent finish (patented 1880).   RHV

R. Koch, *Louis C. Tiffany: Rebel in Glass* (NY, ²1966).

Tillich, Paul Johannes (b. Starzeddel, Brandenburg, Germany [now East Germany], 20.8.1886; naturalized American citizen, 1940; d. Chicago, Ill., USA, 22.10.1965). German/American philosopher and theologian. The origins of Tillich's distinctive form of Christian existentialism lie in a reaction to 19c German culture Protestantism. However, unlike the influential school of dialectical theology in pre-HITLER Germany, whose major representative was Karl BARTH, Tillich proposed a reconciliation of religion and secular society. The political implications of his position forced his departure from Germany when Hitler came to power, and he emigrated to the USA, where he taught at

Union Theological Seminary in New York, at Harvard and at the Chicago Divinity School. Tillich's influence on theology and the academic study of religion in the USA was and continues to be enormous. His views, developed above all in *Systematic Theology* (3 vols, Chicago, 1951–63), involved a marriage of existentialist philosophy with the ontological tradition in Christian thought. The ontological, Augustinian tradition provided him with a theoretical basis for the claim that full humanity necessarily involved some reference to God or 'ultimate concern'. Existentialism enabled him to articulate 'the courage to be' in the face of the tragic side of life. Aside from theology narrowly considered, Tillich's writings include major studies of religion and culture, depth-psychology and social and political issues. PFL

J. L. Adams, *Paul Tillich's Philosophy of Culture, Science and Religion* (NY, 1965); W. & M. Pauch, *Paul Tillich: his Life and Thought* (London, 1977).

Tinbergen, Jan (b. The Hague, S. Holland, The Netherlands, 12.4.1905). Dutch economist. Elder brother of Nikolaas TINBERGEN the zoologist, he originally studied physics at Leiden University. Then in 1929 he joined the Central Bureau of Statistics in The Hague, where he remained, apart from a two-year spell (1936–8) with the League of Nations secretariat in Geneva, until 1945. From 1945 to 1955 he directed the Netherlands Central Planning Bureau. He also held the chair of development planning at Rotterdam University for 40 years (1933–73). In 1969 Tinbergen was awarded, jointly with Ragnar FRISCH, the first Nobel prize for economics for his pioneering work on econometrics, that is, the quantitative estimation of economic relationships by the application of formal statistical techniques to economic data. His major contributions in this field appeared in the 1930s (*An Economic Approach to Business Cycle Problems*, Paris, 1937; *Business Cycles in the USA, 1919–32*, Geneva, 1939; later he added *Business Cycles in the UK, 1870–1914*, Amsterdam, 1951). He also argued the merits of econometric studies in a celebrated

debate with KEYNES, who was sceptical. Tinbergen's other major work has been in the theory of economic policy and planning. In *On the Theory of Economic Policy* (Amsterdam, 1952) he propounded, contemporaneously with MEADE, the analysis of economic policy by means of a system of simultaneous equations, using predetermined policy targets as the dependent variables and policy instruments as the independent variables. His later publications include *Economic Policy: Principles and Design* (Amsterdam, 1965), *Shaping the World Economy* (NY, 1962) and *Utuecklingsplanering* (Stockholm, 1967; *Development Planning*, London, 1968). PMO

Tinbergen, Nikolaas (b. The Hague, S. Holland, The Netherlands, 15.4.1907). Dutch ethologist. Tinbergen began his scientific career as an undergraduate student in the Zoological Laboratory at Leiden, where he subsequently obtained a PhD for his work on the orientation behaviour of the digger wasp, and then became a member of the teaching staff. During the German occupation, Tinbergen was arrested in September 1942 and confined in a hostage camp until the liberation of Holland in 1945. After WW2 he returned to Leiden, but in 1947 he moved to Oxford as a lecturer in zoology. Oxford later awarded him a personal chair in zoology, a position which he occupied until his retirement in 1974. Described as 'a Grand Master of Ethology', his pioneering work on the biological study of animal behaviour under natural or near-natural conditions has exerted an important influence on the development of research and ideas in this field. His classic studies on the courtship behaviour of sticklebacks and social patterns in gulls reflect his concentration on the study of the evolution and adaptive significance of behaviour through observation and experiment. This analytical approach to a hitherto largely descriptive area of zoology is set out in his book *The Study of Instinct* (Oxford, 1951), and more recently in *The Animal in its World. Explorations of an Ethologist, 1932–1972* (2 vols, London, 1972–3). In association with his wife, he has applied the observational methods of ethology to a study of autism in children ('Early childhood autism – an ethological approach', *Zeitschrift für Tierpsychologie*, supp. 10, 1972). In 1973 Tinbergen shared the Nobel prize for medicine with fellow ethologists LORENZ and K. von FRISCH for his work on the 'organization and elicitation of individual and social behaviour patterns'. Tinbergen has written over 70 scientific papers and several books, full details of which are given in a selection of essays presented to him on his retirement (*Function and Evolution in Behaviour. Essays in Honour of Niko Tinbergen*, eds G. Baerends, C. Beer & A. Manning, Oxford, 1975). PM

W. H. Thorpe, *The Origins and Rise of Ethology* (London, 1979).

Tippett, Michael Kemp (b. London, UK, 2.1.1905). British composer. Tippett is unusual among composers in having addressed himself in most of his larger works to contemporary social, ethical and psychological problems. The first of these public statements was the oratorio *A Child of our Time* (1941), which characteristically takes an archetypal form, the Bach passion, and brings it up to date by replacing the chorales with Negro spirituals. Concerned with the morality of violent action against an inhuman regime, the work is also about the need for the individual to recognize within himself 'the shadow and the light'. This is again fundamental in the opera *The Midsummer Marriage* (1952), where a young couple are made to face themselves before they can face each other. Tippett's second opera *King Priam* (1961) takes a myth of destiny and reinterprets it as a drama of decision-making; *The Knot Garden* (1970) is about the healing through self-knowledge and sympathy of a breaking marriage; and *The Ice Break* (1977) concerns itself with broader issues of division, between nations, races and generations. The rest of Tippett's relatively small output includes four symphonies, four string quartets and various vocal compositions, all with the bounding sprung rhythms and enriched tonal harmony which mark his largest works. He is also the author of a volume of essays, *Moving into Aquarius* (London, 1958, ²1974). PG

I. Kemp (ed.), *Michael Tippett: a Symposium on his Sixtieth Birthday* (London, 1965); E. W. White, *The Operas of Michael Tippett* (London, 1979).

Titmuss, Richard (b. Beds., UK, 16.10.1907; d. London, 6.4.1973). British sociologist. Titmuss had little formal education, leaving school when he was 15. After writing *Problems of Social Policy* (London, 1950), the official history of social policy during WW2, he was offered the chair of social administration at the London School of Economics. There he was not only very influential in the development of social work training but became one of the leading intellectual advocates of the need to maintain and extend collective welfare provision, as well as an adviser on welfare policy to the Labour party and to the governments of Tanzania and Mauritius. In his major books *Essays on the Welfare State* (London, 1958), *Income Distribution and Social Change* (London, 1962) and *The Gift Relationship* (London, 1970) he developed arguments in favour of universal welfare benefits showing in detail where and why the market failed. He believed that the aim of social policy should not be simply to provide a safety net for the dependent and disadvantaged but should foster those relationships which could give every individual a sense of belonging to a community by encouraging behaviour motivated more by altruism than by self-interest. AG

D. A. Reisman, *Richard Titmuss* (London, 1977).

Tito, ps. of Josip Broz (b. Kumrovec, Croatia, Austria-Hungary [now Yugoslavia], 7.5.1892; d. Ljubljana, Slovenia, 4.5.1980). Communist leader of the Yugoslav partisans' resistance movement in WW2 and creator of postwar socialist Yugoslavia. A metalworker by trade, Tito was captured by the Russians in WW1 and became a communist. He served five years in a Yugoslav prison (1929–34) and after a period in Moscow became secretary-general of the Yugoslav Communist party. When HITLER attacked the USSR, Tito organized a partisan resistance movement which in

1943 numbered over 250,000. Seven major German offensives were launched against the partisans, with more than 10 German and 6 Italian and quisling divisions taking part in 1943, and with heavy wartime losses of more than 11 per cent of the Yugoslav population. The partisan movement took over the government of Yugoslavia at the end of WW2, setting up a Communist regime which quarrelled with the West over Trieste and with STALIN over Tito's determination to preserve Yugoslav independence. The breach with the USSR became public in June 1948 when Yugoslavia was expelled from the Cominform and Stalin used all pressure short of war to overthrow Tito's regime. Tito's rebellion established Yugoslavia's right to pursue its own road to socialism and not to be bound to the Soviet model. Tito, as president, inaugurated a federal constitution which recognized the five major Yugoslav nationalities as sovereign republics and carried through the decentralization of many economic decisions to workers' councils in the factories. Abroad he was a pioneer, with NEHRU and NASSER, of the policy of nonalignment, grouping together states which sought to remain neutral between the USA and the USSR and to end colonialism. In 1968 he denounced the Russian invasion of Czechoslovakia and prepared for possible conflict with the USSR after his death by strengthening the Yugoslav defences and creating a collective leadership to succeed him. When he died in 1980 he had vindicated his stand for independence against the USSR by giving the republic he had created 30 years of stable leadership.

ALCB

P. Auty, *Tito* (London, 1970); F. W. D. Deakin, *The Embattled Mountain* (London, 1971); D. Wilson, *Tito's Yugoslavia* (Cambridge, 1979).

Tizard, Henry Thomas (b. Gillingham, Kent, UK, 23.8.1885; d. Fareham, Hants., 9.10.1959). British chemist and scientific administrator. Bad eyesight prevented Tizard from following his father (an eminent hydrographer) into the Royal Navy. Well taught in mathematics, he read chemistry at Oxford and briefly worked with NERNST in Berlin,

where he met LINDEMANN; their lives were to converge and cross at many subsequent points. In WW1 Tizard qualified as a pilot and was deeply involved in experimental flying for the Royal Flying Corps and in important research in the new science of aeronautics, especially in fuel for aircraft engines – commitments which continued after the war. For 10 years from 1933 he was chairman of the Aeronautical Research Committee. A year after returning to Oxford in 1919 to teach chemistry, he abandoned science as a personal activity and turned his whole mind and energies to science as a national asset and to its application to the needs of industry and defence. He joined the Department of Scientific and Industrial Research, becoming its secretary in 1927. From 1929 to 1942 he was rector of Imperial College which he saw as the first of the technological universities vital to Britain's future. In 1935 he became chairman of the Air Ministry's Committee for the Scientific Survey of Air Defence which played a key role in ensuring that radar was fully operational for the defence of Britain in 1939: Tizard's administrative capacity and his dual experience in science and in the Flying Corps were crucially important. This committee was the occasion for the well-known quarrel between Tizard and Lindemann which had the unfortunate result that Tizard's services were underused in WW2. His greatest wartime achievement was his mission to the neutral USA in September 1940 which aimed at 'bringing American scientists into the war before their Government'. Its task was, by offering British weapon secrets, to enable the US armed forces to reach the highest level of technical efficiency. Tizard led the mission he had urged for months against opposition; it was an outstanding personal and national success. Tizard had become president of Magdalen College, Oxford, in 1942. In 1946 he left to become chairman of the Labour government's Defence Research Policy Committee and its parallel for civil science, the Advisory Council on Scientific Policy. In contrast to Lindemann, he was deeply sceptical about the value of Britain's atomic deterrent and about atomic power.   MMG

R. Clark, *Tizard* (London, 1965).

Tobin, James (b. Champaign, Ill., USA, 5.3.1918). American economist. A Harvard graduate who, since 1957, has held the Sterling chair of economics at Yale. Tobin has directed a long series of papers at the clarification and extension of KEYNES's macroeconomic models, particularly in relation to fiscal and monetary policies. He was a member of President KENNEDY's Council of Economic Advisers (1961–2) and has been a stern critic of 'monetarism' in all its varieties. Money to Tobin is only one part of a 'continuous spectrum of assets' each of which can be substituted for others. The work for which he is chiefly recognized is in portfolio selection theory. Here he overturned the usual orthodoxy that investors seek the biggest return on their investment, arguing that private and institutional investors balance their holdings in accordance with both the mean and the variance of expected returns. Following this approach, he went on to measure the effects of monetary policies, interest rates and inflation on investment decisions. His general outlook is that of an undogmatic Keynesian, faithful to the spirit, but not necessarily the letter, of Keynes. The value of his work was recognized by the award of the Nobel prize for economics in 1981. Many of his essays have been collected in *National Economic Policy* (New Haven, 1966) and *Essays in Economics* (2 vols, Amsterdam, 1971–5).   PS

Todd, Alexander Robertus (b. Glasgow, Strath., UK, 2.10.1907). British organic chemist. After reading chemistry at Glasgow University and carrying out postgraduate work at Frankfurt, Todd joined Robert ROBINSON's school in Oxford and while working for a DPhil synthesized the flower pigments (anthocyanins) of the rose, the mallow, the pelargonium, the cornflower and the primula. Synthetic methodology was to be the central theme of Todd's massive contribution to organic chemistry. A new challenge arose in 1934: research on vitamin B_1, or thiamine the antiberi-

beri vitamin, in Barger's laboratory in Edinburgh. In collaboration with F. Bergel an expeditious total synthesis of crystalline thiamine was achieved and subsequently used in large-scale production. Subsequently Todd and his associates have worked on a series of major bio-organic problems: vitamin E, other members of the vitamin B group, especially the structurally formidable antipernicious anaemia vitamin B_{12} or cyanocobalamin, co-enzymes, nucleosides, nucleotides and nucleic acids, and on aphid pigments. Two successes of these later years should be mentioned: the synthesis of adenosine triphosphate (the ubiquitous biochemical energy mediator); and flavin-adenine dinucleotide, an essential biological redox catalyst. These were the fruits not only of encyclopedic knowledge and an intuition for organic chemical reactions, allied to an unerring sense of the practical usefulness of various procedures of the organic chemical laboratory, but also of an immense drive, enthusiasm, and capacity for organization and leadership. Todd received a Nobel prize in 1957 and was president of the Royal Society from 1975 to 1980.   NBC

Todorov, Tzvetan (b. Sofia, Bulgaria, 1.3.1939; naturalized French citizen). Bulgarian/French literary theorist, philosopher of language, historian of ideas, who has lived in France since 1963. Todorov is best known for his outstanding contributions to the structuralist study of literature, particularly of prose: *Grammaire du Décaméron* [Grammar of the *Decameron*] (The Hague, 1969), *Introduction à la littérature fantastique* (Paris, 1970; tr. R. Howard, *The Fantastic: a Structural Approach to a Literary Genre*, Cleveland, 1973), *Poétique de la prose* (Paris, 1971; tr. R. Howard, *The Poetics of Prose*, Ithaca, NY, 1977). More recently, in moving beyond structuralism to a revived hermeneutic tradition, he has written on philosophical and cultural questions of symbolization, interpretation, and the discovery of 'the other': *Théories du symbole* (Paris, 1977; tr. C. Porter, *Theories of the Symbol*, Ithaca, NY, 1982), *Symbolisme et interprétation* [Symbolism and interpretation] (Paris, 1978), *La Conquête de*

l'Amérique: la question de l'autre [The conquest of America: the question of the other] (Paris, 1982). Todorov has introduced Russian literary theorists to western readers: the Russian Formalists, in *Théorie de la littérature* [Theory of literature] (Paris, 1965), Bakhtin, in *Mikhaïl Bakhtine: Le Principe dialogique* (Paris, 1981). He is coauthor, with O. Ducrot, of *Dictionnaire encyclopédique des sciences du langage* (Paris, 1979; *Encyclopedic Dictionary of the Sciences of Language*, Baltimore, 1979). In these books, as in his many essays, Todorov reveals wide scholarship and historical grasp as well as theoretical originality.
AMS

J. Culler, *Structuralist Poetics* (London, 1975); T. Hawkes, *Structuralism and Semiotics* (London, 1977).

Tolkien, John Ronald Reuel (b. Bloemfontein, Orange Free State, South Africa, 3.1.1892; d. Bournemouth, Dorset, UK, 2.9.1973). British fantasy writer. Tolkien's exceptional gifts as a philologist were recognized in his election to Oxford chairs of Anglo-Saxon (1925) and English language and literature (1945). His reputation, however, rests upon the unique fictions his scholarship inspired rather than upon his comparatively few academic publications. For Tolkien, as his lecture *Beowulf: the Monsters and the Critics* (London, 1936) demonstrates, early European texts were not merely linguistic documents from an otherwise irrelevant past. His sympathy for their imaginative ethos informs both his defence of romance against the charge of 'escapism' in fantasy's most compelling apologia, his 1939 paper 'On Fairy-Stories' (in *Tree and Leaf*, London, 1964) and his own fictional world of Middle-Earth (i.e. Old English *Middangeard*, the world). Its mythical history, and from 1917 Tolkien's lifelong obsession, *The Silmarillion* (London, 1977) was never completed, but in an offshoot from it, *The Hobbit* (London, 1937), he created a new race, the hobbits, as authentic as the dwarves, elves and dragons to whom he restored their original mystery and power. With the encouragement of the Inklings, an informal group of Oxford men who shared Tolkien's Christian commitment, his dislike of modern life and his distaste for modernism in the arts, the sequel to *The Hobbit*, *The Lord of the Rings* (3 vols, London, 1954–5), developed into a quest romance whose imaginative scope, narrative control and moral seriousness won an unprecedented readership and ensured fantasy recognition as a significant and influential genre of modern fiction.
NHK

H. Carpenter, *J. R. R. Tolkien: a Biography* (London, 1977); H. Carpenter, *The Inklings* (London, 1978).

Toller, Ernst (b. Samotschin, Posen, Germany [now Szamocin, Poland], 1.12.1893; d. New York, USA, 22.5.1939). German dramatist. Toller studied law in Grenoble and enlisted in 1914. He had a mental breakdown because of war experiences and was invalided out in 1916. He became a utopian pacifist and revolutionary, increasingly sceptical about the possibility of combining respect for the individual with revolutionary action. He continued his studies at Munich and Heidelberg universities. He played a major part in the first Munich soviet of April 1919 and for his activities was sentenced to five years' imprisonment for treason; it was during this period that his best-known plays were published. He used expressionist techniques (tableaux or 'Stationen', dream sequences and abstract figures) to express the relationship between the individual and the crowd in *Die Wandlung* (Potsdam, 1920; tr. E. Crankshaw, *Transfiguration*, in *Ernst Toller: Seven Plays*, London, 1935), *Masse-Mensch* (Leipzig, 1920; *Masses and Men* in *Seven Plays*), and *Die Maschinenstürmer* (Leipzig, 1922; *The Machine Wreckers* in *Seven Plays*), and anticipated the rise of National Socialism in *Der entfesselte Wotan* [Odin unchained] (Potsdam, 1924). After *Hinkemann* (Potsdam, 1924; in *Seven Plays*) in which a crippled soldier returns to find himself rejected by post-war society, Toller's vision became increasingly despondent. Communist critics chided him for his bourgeois idealism, while bourgeois critics found his pathos excessive. In 1927 PISCATOR produced *Hoppla, wir leben!* [Hoppla, such is life!] (Potsdam, 1927), a satirical calendar of the materialism and chauvinism of the Weimar republic. Toller's later works include an autobiography *Eine Jugend in Deutschland* (Amsterdam, 1933; tr. E. Crankshaw, *I Was a German*, London, 1934) and *Pastor Hall* (tr. S. Spender, London, 1939). Toller was forced into exile in Switzerland in 1933, then to France and the UK, finally emigrating to the USA in 1936. He tried unsuccessfully to establish himself as a writer in Hollywood, and committed suicide in New York in 1939, just after HITLER had invaded Czechoslovakia. KF

R. Beckley, 'Ernst Toller', in *German Men of Letters*, vol. III (London, 1968); S. Lamb, 'Ernst Toller and the Weimar Republic' in K. Bullivant (ed.), *Culture and Society in the Weimar Republic* (Manchester, 1977).

Tolstoy, Aleksey Nikolayevich (b. Nikolayevsk [now Pugachyov], Samara, Russia, 10.1.1882; d. Moscow, USSR, 23.2.1945). Russian novelist and dramatist. He had the misfortune of gaining recognition in spite of, and indirectly because of, belonging to the same family as Leo TOLSTOY (his mother was a Turgenev). He became a White émigré after the revolution, but returned to the USSR in 1923 and by the mid-1930s had become a prominent Soviet writer. His significance is due to his considerable artistic gifts and to his being a talented example of the reconciliation between the intelligentsia and the Soviet order; next to Maxim GORKY and SHOLOKHOV he was acclaimed as a socialist realist. His early work is anecdotal in character, with vivid, even sparkling and satirical descriptions of the disintegration of Russia's upper classes. But such propensities were brought under increasing control in his mature work, as can be seen in the exquisite autobiographical tale *Detstvo Nikity* (Berlin–Moscow, 1919–22; tr. V. Dutt, *Nikita's Childhood*, London, 1945). After 1923 he began to write largely for entertainment, with a marginal social aim, as in the WELLSian novel *Aelita* (Berlin–Moscow, 1924) about an expedition to Mars to establish communism there. Although highly inventive, these novels, like his plays on similar adventure themes, are unremarkable as literature. Quite different are his two major works, a trilogy *Khozhdeniye po mukam* (1919–41; tr. I. C. T. Litvinova, *The Road to Calvary*, London, 1953), which he finished on the day HITLER invaded the USSR, and *Pyotr Pervyy* (Moscow, 1925–45; tr. T. Shebunina, *Peter I*, London, 1956), an unfinished masterpiece of historical recreation. Tolstoy's picture of the middle-class intelligentsia on the eve of the October revolution in the trilogy is one of the most incisive portrayals of this period in Russian cultural and intellectual history, the main ideological thread being the transition from a closed world of private concern and pursuits to an eventual understanding of and sharing in Russia's historical and political destiny. But Tolstoy's talent is shown best in the magnificently drawn incidents of the revolution and civil war, even though the descriptions verge at times on the sensational. Tolstoy is remarkable when he deals with concrete facts and people rather than with abstract themes, ideas or ideologies. EL

L. M. Polyak, *Aleksey Tolstoy – Khudozhnik* (Moscow, 1964).

Tolstoy, Lev Nikolayevich (Leo) (b. Yasnaya Polyana, Russia, 9.9.1828; d. Astapovo, 20.11.1910). Russian writer. One of the greatest world-authors of prose fiction and a significant dramatist, Tolstoy intended most of his writing – fiction as well as essays – to bring about social reform. An opponent of all political, social and religious institutions, he believed that any change had to begin with the individual and that only by living in the right way could any person hope to achieve fulfilment for himself and, therefore, for others. He reduced Christian thought to a few basic precepts, centrally 'The Kingdom of God is within you'. His fictional characters are drawn chiefly from the classes Tolstoy knew best: the aristocracy and peasantry, not the middle classes. Non-Russians tend to be ridiculed, as do foreign customs grafted on to 'Russian' life – whether English agricultural methods or French society manners. All classes of people in his works achieve a full life by avoiding the foreign, the societal, the bureaucratic and the artificial, and by embracing the domestic, the familial, the spontaneous and the natural. Moscow is shown as a city where family life can prosper better than in the capital of St Petersburg; but it is in the country, working in a natural setting, that Tolstoy's people attain their truest lives. In his novels and short stories, marriage is the greatest human challenge. His own large family was a testing ground for his theories, more liberal on paper than in practice. His wife, *née* Sofiya Andreyevna Bers (1844–1919), shared his desire for children and assumed responsibility for them. The diaries they both kept show their different expectations. The question of sexual relations becomes increasingly important in Tolstoy's later fiction. It is a darkening view but, in 20c terms, an increasingly relevant one. Women's role is initially seen as complementary to men's in family life: women have different tasks and duties. But, beginning with *Anna Karenina* (Moscow, 1876–7; NY, 1886, tr. R. Edmonds, Harmondsworth, 1954) and especially clearly in a later work like the story *Kreitserova Sonata* (Berlin, 1890; London, 1890, tr. L. & A. Maude, *Kreutzer Sonata*, London, 1924), Tolstoy demonstrates that unless there is shared understanding translated into the sharing of household tasks and child-rearing, men and women will poison life for each other. Sex as lust or procreation is understandable to Tolstoy (although he condemns the former); sex as romantic interaction between a husband who has had sexual experience from early youth and a wife who is 'pure' is a travesty and an injustice. Tolstoy sees this situation as one of men's making, but his women react to it with disastrous rapidity. Beginning with the standard 19c view that women were naturally spiritual or that peasants were naturally better than the aristocracy (as in *Voina i mir*, Moscow, 1868; *War and Peace*, London, 1886, tr. R. Edmonds, Harmondsworth, 1957), Tolstoy moved closer to anarchism. 'Tolstoyanism' overtook him as in his later years he himself involuntarily became an institution. The proceeds of his last novel *Voskresenie* (St Petersburg, 1899; tr. L. Maude, *Resurrection*, London, 1899–1900) helped persecuted religious minorities like the Dukhobors.

His influence on such reformers as M. GANDHI has given even wider scope to Tolstoyan ideas.   BH

J. Bayley, *Tolstoy and the Novel* (London, 1966); H. Gifford (ed.), *Leo Tolstoy: a Critical Anthology* (Harmondsworth, 1971).

Tönnies, Ferdinand (b. Eiderstedt, Schleswig-Holstein, Germany, 26.7.1855; d. Kiel, Schleswig-Holstein, 9.4.1936). German social theorist and philosopher. He received his doctorate in classical philology from Tübingen University in 1877, and in 1881 was appointed lecturer at the University of Kiel where he remained until ousted by the Nazis in 1933. An academic leader for half a century, his most influential work was his study of the rise of modernity, capitalism and the modern state. Utilizing two ideal, typical concepts of *Gemeinschaft* [community] and *Gesellschaft* [translated as society], he synthesized the work of Hobbes (on whom he was an international authority: *Thomas Hobbes: Leben and Lehre* [Thomas Hobbes's life and doctrine], Stuttgart, 1896, ³1925; and see his edition of Hobbes's *The Elements of Law*, Cambridge, 1928), MARX, Maine and Gierke into a major developmental theory of sociology: *Gemeinschaft und Gesellschaft* (Leipzig, 1887; *Community and Society*, Michigan, 1957). In this work he outlined a shift from social relationships embodying natural will and governed by folkways, mores and religion to a situation of rational will embodied in laws and contract. His contribution was to articulate theoretically the main themes of the transition from medievalism to modernity and the growth of individualism, impersonality and the emergence of the Hobbesian concept of society. Like Marx he offered an economic interpretation of history, although he suggested that trade was the major driving force and initiator of capitalism. Acutely aware of the social maladjustments caused by rationalism and individualism, he was a strong supporter of the labour movement in its struggle with emergent German capitalism. Tönnies was a founder member and president of the German Sociological Society and the Society for Social Reform. By preaching the need for a scientific sociology which linked pure and applied theory to empirical inductive research, he brought a new level of statistical and methodological consciousness to the emerging discipline of sociology.

TFC/LMC

Torga, Miguel, ps. of Adolfo Correia da Rocha (b. São Martinho de Anta, Trásosmontes, Portugal, 12.8.1907). Portuguese poet and writer. The son of poor parents, his birthplace and the people living there have been the major influence on his work: 40 volumes of poetry, drama and travel, which includes 12 volumes of diary, a commentary on Portuguese society over the last 40 years, and several collections of short stories, acclaimed as some of the finest in the language. A vigorous critic of SALAZAR, Torga did his stint in prison, and saw some of his works banned. For a boy in his situation there were only two choices: the seminary or Brazil. He fled the seminary and embarked for Brazil in 1919, to eke out menial tasks on a coffee estate. By saving his earnings he returned home and took up medical studies in Coimbra where he still practises. He rejected his childhood Catholicism but kept the imagery. He is conscious of the social vocation of the healer and its nearness to that of the poet and the priest, symbolized in the short story *Libertação* [Liberation] (Coimbra, 1944). He joined the *Presença* movement which sought a renewal in the arts, but left in 1931 to go his own way. His short stories owe much to clinical observation, helped by his daily experience in the consulting room. As with his poetry, they are the fruit of his 'uncontaminated vision' that invests a lyrical innocence in what he writes. His love of Portugal is clear in the many journeys recorded in the diaries: *Diário* (10 vols, Coimbra, 1941–63), and also in his epiphanies of the great figures of the past in his *Poemas ibéricos* [Iberian poems] (Coimbra, 1952). Hope and despair alternate in his work, but a fundamental optimism leads him to proclaim his faith as a poet in *Orfeu rebelde* [Orpheus in revolt] (Coimbra, 1958). A selection of his stories is published as *Farrusco the Blackbird* (tr. D. Brass, London, 1950).

DBr

J. de Melo, *Miguel Torga, Obra e o homem* (Lisbon, 1960); D. Brass, 'The art and poetry of Miguel Torga', in *Sillages*, 2 (Poitiers, 1973), 67–93.

Toscanini, Arturo (b. Parma, Emilia-Romagna, Italy, 25.3.1867; d. New York, USA, 16.1.1957). Italian conductor. With FURTWÄNGLER, he was one of the first conductors to gain a wide audience through records: some of his performances, notably those of the Verdi *Requiem* and of Beethoven's Seventh Symphony, are 'gramophone classics'. In an age when great liberties could be taken in the name of interpretation, Toscanini was remarkable for his faithfulness to the score and for his dynamic precision of rhythm and texture. He made his name first as a conductor of opera, and was responsible for the premières of Leoncavallo's *I Pagliacci* (1892), PUCCINI's *La Bohème* (1897) and other works. In later years he gained equal renown for his concert performances, but he refused to appear in fascist Italy or Nazi Germany and so moved to New York, where in 1937 the NBC Symphony Orchestra was created for him.

PG

P. C. Hughes, *The Toscanini Legacy* (London, 1959).

Tournier, Michel (b. Paris, France, 19.12.1924). French novelist. Tournier studied philosophy in Paris and in Germany and subsequently worked in broadcasting, in publishing and as a translator before receiving the Grand Prix du Roman Français de l'Académie Française for his first novel *Vendredi ou les limbes du pacifique* (Paris, 1967; tr. R. Manheim, *Friday and Robinson: Life on Speranza Island*, London, 1972). His second novel *Le Roi des Aulnes* (Paris, 1970; tr. B. Bray, *The Erl King*, London, 1972) won the Prix Goncourt. Both novels are reworkings of existing myths or stories, *Vendredi* being an exploration of the Robinson Crusoe theme and *Le Roi des Aulnes* of the St Christopher and the Erl King myths against the background of East Prussia during the Third Reich. Tournier's interest in the creation and exploration of myths has continued with *Les Météores* (Paris, 1975; tr. A. Carter, *Gemini*,

London, 1981), a baroque treatment of the spiritual and sexual implications of twinship, and with *Gaspard, Melchior et Balthazar* (Paris, 1980; tr. R. Manheim, *The Four Wise Men*, London, 1982), a very free and inventive reworking of the legend of the Magi, extended to include the Russian myth of a fourth king who did not reach Bethlehem in time for the Nativity. Constantly moving from the lightest of fantasy to the grotesque and the sinister, Tournier's fiction represents a move away from the formal experiments of the *nouveau roman* towards a more classic form of storytelling based upon the weaving together of realist elements and a flamboyant use of the exotic and the fantastic. Erotic themes figure prominently in all of his novels, which joyfully celebrate anal and oral sexuality as well as homosexuality. DM

Toynbee, Arnold Joseph (b. London, UK, 14.4.1889; d. London, 22.10.1975). British historian. Toynbee is known to the world for his massive *A Study of History* (London: vols I–III, 1934; vols IV–VI, 1939; vols VII–X, 1954), the most ambitious attempt to date to present the recurring patterns of universal history. The abbreviated version of the first six volumes *A Study of History* (London, 1946) was a bestseller.

Toynbee's special expertise lay in Greek history and literature and from 1919 to 1924 he was the first incumbent of the chair of Byzantine and modern Greek language, literature and history at London University. For 30 years thereafter he was director of studies at the Royal Institute of International Affairs in London, and throughout the interwar years he was responsible for the year-by-year *Survey of International Affairs* published by the institute, models for the writing of contemporary history.

The first six volumes of *A Study of History* are pervaded by a deep pessimism; but the four published after WW2 are marked by a messianic revivalism. Toynbee identified 21 civilizations which, he claimed, have passed through similar stages of growth, breakdown (including a 'time of troubles') and eventual dissolution, the final phase in each case being characterized by the formation of a 'universal state'. Certain

'laws' are advanced to account for certain critical developments, for example, the famous 'challenge and response' theory. Briefly stated, the regular pattern of social disintegration is a schism of the disintegrating society into a recalcitrant proletariat and a less and less effective dominant minority. The process of disintegration does not proceed evenly, it jolts along in alternating spasms of rout, rally, and rout. In the last rally but one, the dominant minority succeeds in temporarily arresting the society's lethal self-laceration by imposing on it the peace of a universal state. Within the framework of the dominant minority's universal state the proletariat creates a universal church, and after the next rout, in which the disintegrating civilization finally dissolves, the universal church may live on to become the chrysalis from which a new civilization eventually emerges. *A Study of History* was received much less favourably by professional historians, who, among other things, were able to point to many errors in detail, than by the reading public at large. There could, however, be no gainsaying the scale of the achievement. Toynbee had sought to bring unity and meaning to historical studies when they were beset by relativism, nominalism and rank nationalism. Most significantly of all perhaps for the subsequent course of historical study, Toynbee had cleared the path towards comparative history and had broken with the tradition of exclusively western-orientated history. AM

M. F. Ashley-Montague (ed.), *Toynbee and History* (London, 1956).

Trakl, Georg (b. Salzburg, Austria-Hungary [now Austria], 3.2.1887; d. Cracow, Galicia, Austria-Hungary [now Poland], 3.11.1914). Austrian poet. Trakl studied pharmacy in Vienna and became a drug addict. In 1914 his artistically gifted sister committed suicide and he lost the only person he could relate to. In the same year he was conscripted into the Austrian medical corps. Horrified at the suffering of WW1, he attempted suicide, was moved to Cracow for observation, and died of a cocaine overdose. Trakl never found a place in his society. He could never keep a job and saw himself as the outsider whose values nobody shared. His sense of displacement is expressed in his poems *Gedichte* (Leipzig, 1913; tr. L. Getsi, *Poems*, Athens, Ohio, 1973) and *Sebastian im Traum* [Dream of Sebastian] (Leipzig, 1914), which centre on themes of imminent disaster, decay, death and dissolution, as well as the colours and symbols of autumn, and which range from a structured impressionist style (influenced by French symbolism) in the earlier to an hallucinatory expressionism in the later pieces, with their free verse and irrational associations of ideas. Trakl's dissolution of syntax and return to Hölderlin's free rhythms made him a formative influence on expressionist poetry and the German lyric since 1945.   JHC

M. Hamburger, *Decline: Twelve Poems by Georg Trakl* (St Ives, 1952); C. Saas, *Georg Trakl* (Stuttgart, 1974).

Trilling, Lionel (b. New York, USA, 4.7.1905; d. New York, 5.11.1975). American literary critic. Generally regarded as one of the outstanding modern American critics, Trilling has, through his writing and his teaching, exerted a profound influence on the study of literature in the USA. Educated at Columbia University in New York, he joined the English faculty there in 1931. His first book was, appropriately, the critical biography *Matthew Arnold* (NY, 1939), for he shared with Arnold a deep concern for the social and cultural context of literature and a belief in the moral function of criticism. These values were, to some extent, restated in his second book *E. M. Forster* (NY, 1943), but they were to receive their fullest articulation in the collection of essays *The Liberal Imagination* (NY, 1950). Here Trilling addressed himself directly to the relationship between literary ideas and social thought and sought a place for literary criticism at the very centre of liberal culture. Though influential as a critic, Trilling founded no school. But it was his interest in FREUD that dominated the later phases of his career and among his most eloquent essays are those that analyse the complex relationships between the mechanisms of the mind and the mechanisms of art, most notably 'Art and neurosis' in *The Lib-*

eral Imagination and 'The authentic unconscious' in *Sincerity and Authenticity* (NY, 1972). Other essays by Trilling are collected in *The Opposing Self* (NY, 1955), *A Gathering of Fugitives* (Boston, Mass., 1956) and *Beyond Culture* (NY, 1965). His one novel *The Middle of the Journey* (NY, 1947) is a subtle analysis of the effects of communism on a group of American intellectuals.   GHC

L. Fraiberg, *Psychoanalysis and American Literary Criticism* (Detroit, 1960).

Troeltsch, Ernst (b. Augsburg, Bavaria, Germany, 17.2.1865; d. Berlin, 1.2.1923). German theologian, philosopher and historian of ideas; leading theoretician of liberal Protestant theology. As a dissatisfied student of A. Ritschl in Göttingen and as lecturer there, he had contact with the 'history of religion school' which emerged around 1890, and was subsequently dubbed the systematician of that movement. His early writings focused on the scientific study of religion and the relation of faith, history and philosophy; e.g. *Die Absolutheit des Christentums und der Religionsgeschichte* (Tübingen, 1902; *The Absoluteness of Christianity and the History of Religions*, London, 1972). After two years in Bonn he was appointed professor of systematic theology in Heidelberg (1894–1914). During this period he shared a house with Max WEBER and wrote *Die Soziallehren der christlichen Kirchen und Gruppen* (Tübingen, 1908–11; *The Social Teachings of the Christian Churches*, London, 1931), which pioneered the use of sociological methods in history and theology, and introduced the church-sect-mysticism typology. In 1914 he accepted a personal chair in philosophy at Berlin and concentrated on questions of modern culture. He never completed his 'cultural synthesis', but *Der Historismus und seine Probleme* [Historical relativism and its problems] (Tübingen, 1922) was a first step, taking up his 'old problem of absoluteness on a much broader scale and tending towards a totality of cultural values, not just one's religious position'. This broadening out of his theological concerns to embrace the whole (European) social and cultural scene was a consistent following-through of the programme of Schleiermacher three generations earlier. Troeltsch maintained connections with England despite WW1: his posthumous *Christian Thought* (London, 1923) contains lectures written for English audiences, and a selection of his work in English was published as *Ernst Troeltsch: Writings on Theology and Religion* (eds R. Morgan & M. Pye, London, 1977). It is a measure of the public and political esteem enjoyed by Troeltsch after WW1 that he was mentioned as a possible president for the new republic.   RM

J. P. Clayton (ed.), *Ernst Troeltsch and the Future of Theology* (Cambridge, 1976).

Trotsky, Leon, ps. of Lev Davidovich Bronstein (b. Yanovka, Ukraine, Russia, 7.11.1879; d. Coyoacán, nr Mexico City, Mexico, 20.8.1940). Russian revolutionary leader. Trotsky first came to prominence in the 1905 revolution as the spokesman of the St Petersburg soviet; he was imprisoned in 1906 and exiled to Siberia from where he escaped to settle in Vienna, earning his living as a journalist. While in prison, Trotsky had worked out his own way of reconciling MARXist theory to Russian conditions by the concept of 'permanent revolution'. Trotsky argued from his experience in 1905 that the Russian bourgeoisie was too weak to carry through the coming revolution which would have to be taken over by the proletariat and would not therefore stop at the bourgeois stage but would immediately be followed by a socialist revolution. As soon as this took place the proletariat would be deserted by the peasantry, who would join the mass of small owners in opposing it. Since the proletariat in Russia was a minority, it would not be able to maintain itself in power unless it could rely on help from a socialist revolution in the West. But this could be expected because the revolution in Russia would touch off a conflagration in the rest of Europe.

Trotsky greeted the outbreak of the 1917 revolution in Russia as the beginning of the permanent revolution he had predicted. As chairman of the Petrograd soviet he worked with LENIN to overthrow the Provisional government, and was named as commissar for foreign affairs. His job was to make peace with the Germans and he conducted the negotiations at Brest-Litovsk. He was then made commissar for war and given the formidable task of creating the Red Army. The role he played in winning the civil war clearly established him as second only to Lenin. His rapid advancement made powerful enemies for him. Trotsky was a charismatic orator and a brilliant debater, but during Lenin's illness (1922–4) he allowed himself to be outmanoeuvered by STALIN whose intellectual mediocrity he despised but whose shrewdness and gift for political manipulation he underestimated. In January 1928 he was exiled to Alma Ata and a year later banished from the USSR. He moved in turn from Turkey to France, then Norway before finding asylum in Mexico (1936). From exile Trotsky continued to attack the 'degeneration' of the Soviet regime under Stalin's leadership. In 1933 he took steps to set up a Fourth International composed of parties which accepted his leadership, but these never attracted much support. His most effective weapon against Stalin was his polemical power as a writer. He poured out a stream of articles, pamphlets and books of which the best known are *Moya Zhizn'* (Berlin, 1930; *My Life*, London, 1930); his celebrated *Istoriya russkoy revolyutsii* (2 vols, Berlin, 1931–3; *The History of the Russian Revolution*, 3 vols, London, 1932–3); and his final indictment of Stalinism, *The Revolution Betrayed* (London, 1937). He was assassinated, presumably by Stalin's agents, in 1940. By then the official history of the Russian Communist party had been rewritten to minimize and denigrate his role.

Trotsky's courage and determination in continuing his single-handed campaign against Stalin are unquestionable. Equally unquestionable are his commanding personality and intellectual powers. But his intellectual arrogance and inability to accommodate himself to other people prevented him being an effective political leader. Trotsky was dogmatic in his refusal to consider the possibility that the features he denounced in Stalinism were inherent in the methods used to force through the revolutionary settlement in Russia. He regarded the dictatorship which he and Lenin had established as justified because (he claimed) it was exercised in the interests of the proletariat, and so was quite different from Stalin's dictatorship, which he condemned not because it was undemocratic but because it acted only in its own interests.   ALCB

B. D. Wolfe, *Three Who Made a Revolution* (NY, 1948); I. Deutscher, *The Prophet Armed: Trotsky 1879–1921; The Prophet Unarmed: Trotsky 1921–1929; The Prophet Outcast: Trotsky, 1929–1940* (3 vols, London, 1954–63); L. Kolakowski, *Main Currents in Marxism*, iii, *The Breakdown* (Oxford, 1978).

Trubetzkoy, Nikolai Sergey'evic (b. Moscow, Russia, 16.4.1890; d. Vienna, Austria, 25.6.1938). Russian linguist, the father of the so-called Prague school of linguistics. The son of a Russian prince, he studied linguistics at Moscow University. After taking his doctorate at Leipzig in 1915, he returned to teach at Moscow. His work was partially interrupted by WW1, but in 1922 he became professor of Slavic philology at the University of Vienna, where he remained until his death. Strongly influenced by SAUSSURE, he was more interested in overall structure than in individual details, and tried to set up principles for dealing with the phonology (sound system) of any language. He expounded these in his book *Grundzüge der Phonologie* (Prague, 1939; tr. C. Baltaxe, *Principles of Phonology*, Berkeley, Calif., 1969), which was regarded as a major statement of their beliefs by the linguistic circle of Prague, a society of scholars founded by Trubetzkoy's great friend JAKOBSON. Trubetzkoy claimed that phonemes (phonological units) were abstract concepts, not physical entities. For example, there could be 20 different types of [t] in a language, yet they might all be treated as a single sound by speakers of the language. Phonemes could be identified by their contrastive function: if two contrasting sounds caused a difference in meaning (as in *bat* versus *pat*), then they must be regarded as separate phonemes. For this reason, Trubetzkoy's views are sometimes labelled 'functionalist'. Trubetzkoy set up an elaborate classification scheme showing the relationship of each phoneme to every other phoneme, indicating the extent to which any had properties which it shared with others. He thus paved the way for 'distinctive feature' theory, which was developed more fully by Jakobson.   JMA

J. Vachek, *The Linguistic School of Prague* (Bloomington, 1966).

Truffaut, François (b. Paris, France, 6.2.1932). French film director. Truffaut's cinematic career began with a moving account of his own troubled childhood *Les Quatre Cents Coups* (*The 400 Blows*, 1959), and this autobiographical thread has persisted as he followed his alter ego Antoine Doinel through four further films up to *L'Amour en Fuite* (*Love on the Run*, 1978). Throughout his work Truffaut keeps to a classically orthodox narrative technique but, as befits a man whose twin idols are Jean RENOIR and HITCHCOCK (See *Les Films de ma vie*, Paris, 1975; *The Films in My Life*, London, 1980), his subject matter is totally eclectic, including comedy (*Jules et Jim*, 1961), science fiction (*Fahrenheit 451*, 1966), the Hitchcockian thriller *La Sirène du Mississippi* (*Mississippi Mermaid*, 1969) and the film-within-a-film (*La Nuit Américaine/Day for Night*, 1973). If the tone of his early work is irrepressibly lighthearted – as in the unforgettable *Tirez sur le Pianiste* (*Shoot the Piano Player*) of 1962 – his later work shows a more sombre tone and increasing preoccupation with death: *L'Histoire d'Adèle H* (*The Story of Adele H*, 1975) and *La Chambre Verte* (*The Green Room*, 1978). But his enormous popular success with his tale of occupied Paris, *Le Dernier Métro* (*The Last Metro*, 1980), made clear that through all the shifts and changes of his career he has not in any way lost his contact with the mass audience. There is a reticence at the heart of Truffaut's work (shown most clearly in the Antoine Doinel series and in *L'Enfant Sauvage/The Wild Child*, 1970), but few film makers of the past 20 years have shown such a delight and sureness of touch in the art of storytelling.   RPA

D. Allen, *François Truffaut* (London, 1974); A. Insdorff, *François Truffaut* (London, 1981).

Truman, Harry S. (b. Lamar, Mo., USA, 8.5.1884; d. Kansas City, Mo., 26.12.1972). US senator (1936–44), vice-president (1945), president (1945–53). In domestic politics Truman's accession to the presidency on F. D. ROOSEVELT's death in office marked the beginning of the break-up of that alliance between conservative Southern opinion, the more adaptable part of big industrial leadership, the trade unions, the larger ethnic groups, and progressive intellectuals which had made it possible for his predecessor Franklin Roosevelt to win four presidential elections in a row. Progressives (and their ultra-left allies) 'bolted' the party to run Henry Wallace as a separate candidate in 1948; at the same time the increasing strength of the more moderate Americans for Democratic Action led by HUMPHREY with their programme of dismantlement of all legislation inhibiting the civil rights of black Americans, drove conservative Southerners also to 'bolt' the party to establish their own States' Rights party, the 'Dixiecrats'. Despite these breaks in the Democratic coalition Truman won the 1948 election by a very narrow margin on a reform programme, the 'Fair Deal', of increased social welfare and public health expenditure, which he lacked the congressional strength to carry through into law. In foreign affairs Truman adopted from the beginning a less conciliatory attitude towards the USSR than Roosevelt had practised, moving steadily, as perhaps befitted the man who had authorized the use of atomic weapons against Japan, towards a reversal of traditional American noninterventionism in the affairs of other continents than their own. The turning-point was the enunciation of the Truman doctrine in March 1947 pledging American support for 'free people who are resisting attempted subjugation by armed minorities and by outside pressures' (aimed at Greece and Turkey), which was successively followed by the G. C. MARSHALL plan, resistance to the Soviet blockade of Berlin, the conclusion in 1949 of the North Atlantic Treaty Alliance, and the rallying of the United Nations behind American resistance to the North Korean attempt to unify the two Koreas by force in 1950, and to the subsequent Chinese intervention to save the North Koreans from the results of their consequent defeat. Truman wrote subsequently his own *Memoirs* (2 vols, NY, 1955–6). DCW

A. Steinberg, *The Man from Missouri* (NY, 1962); C. Phillips, *The Truman Presidency* (NY, 1966).

Tschichold, Jan (b. Leipzig, Saxony, Germany [now East Germany], 2.4.1902; naturalized Swiss citizen, 1942; d. Locarno, Ticino, Switzerland, 11.8.1974). German/Swiss book designer and calligrapher. Deeply influenced in youth by JOHNSTON's *Writing and Illuminating and Lettering* (1906), he studied calligraphy, etching, wood engraving and bookbinding at Arts and Crafts schools in Leipzig and Dresden (1919–21) before beginning to teach calligraphy at Leipzig under Tiemann. Between 1921 and 1925 he designed hundreds of calligraphic advertisements for trade fairs, worked briefly at Poeschel & Wittig and freelanced for various publishers. The Weimar Bauhaus exhibition (1923) profoundly impressed him. After 1926 he taught calligraphy and typography at the German Master Printers' School, Munich. Escaping from Nazi Germany to Basle in 1933, he resumed freelance designing (now for Swiss publishers). In 1947 LANE appointed him Penguin Books' chief designer with complete responsibility for all printed matter; he formulated detailed, precise rules for styling everything, thereby effecting noteworthy improvements in composing rooms throughout Britain. Returning to Switzerland in 1949 to practise as typographical consultant for various German and Swiss publishers, he joined the pharmaceutical company Hoffman–La Roche in 1955 to design their entire output of printed matter. He designed numerous successful typefaces, including Sabon, Saskia and Transito. His publications include *Die Neue Typographie* [The new typography] (Berlin, 1928), *Typographische Gestaltung* (Basle, 1935; *Asymmetric Typography*, London, 1967), *Schatzkammer der Schreibkunst* [The treasury of the art of writing] (Basle, 1945), *Die Proportionen des Buches* [The proportions of the book] (Stuttgart, 1955), *Des Buches und der Typographie* [Of the book and typography] (Basle, 1975).   TC

Tshombe, Moise Kapenda (b. Mushoshi, Belgian Congo [now Zaïre], 11.1919; d. Algiers, Algeria, 29.6.1969). Congolese politician. In the early 1960s Tshombe was the most execrated politician in black Africa. In 1960 he led the secession of the province of Katanga (now Shaba) and so threatened the newly independent ex-Belgian Congo with collapse. He was deeply implicated in the murder of LUMUMBA, and he had no hesitation in making use of white mercenaries against his political opponents in 1960–1 and again in 1964–5 when he became prime minister of the Congo. A shrewd, flexible politician, he was certainly not the European stooge his opponents accused him of being; he used Europeans for his own ends. He spent his last two years in detention in Algiers, to which he had been taken after being hijacked on a flight from Spain, where he had lived in exile after being overthrown by MOBUTU in 1965.
                                                    RH
I. D. Colvin, *The Rise and Fall of Moise Tshombe* (London, 1968).

Tsubouchi, Shōyō (b. Minokamo City, Gifu Prefecture, Japan, 22.6.1859; d. Atami, 28.2.1935). Japanese novelist, dramatist, scholar and educationalist; Japan's first translator of Shakespeare. Tsubouchi played an active role in encouraging the development of the modern novel and the modern theatre in Japan. Born into a middle-status *samurai* family and a member of the intellectual elite by the early 1880s, he shocked his contemporaries by publishing a novel and a treatise on fiction in 1885. This was to give literature a dignity which it had long lost in Japan. Tsubouchi urged psychological realism in the novel as opposed to the situational structure and facile didacticism that had become the norm. In 1890 he founded the literature department of what is now Waseda University and the next year published *Waseda Bungaku*

[Waseda literature], soon to become one of the most influential literary journals. In the 1890s Tsubouchi was urging priority for characterization in historical drama and writing historical plays himself for the *kabuki* theatre. He started a movement for the creation of a new dance drama in the early years of this century. The performance of *Hamlet* in Japanese in 1911 by a company of student actors under Tsubouchi's leadership is regarded as a pioneering step in the establishment of modern theatre in Japan. In 1915 Tsubouchi resigned from Waseda University and retired to the sea coast to devote himself to writing and translating. His first translation of a Shakespeare play (*Julius Caesar*) appeared in 1884 and he had completed the corpus by 1928. The early translations reflected Tsubouchi's concern to preserve as much as possible of the classical theatre tradition and many owe much to *kabuki* diction and style. He was overtaken by events, however, and there is much more contemporary, colloquial Japanese in the later pieces. BWFP

M. G. Ryan, *The Development of Realism in the Fiction of Tsubouchi Shōyō* (Seattle, 1975).

Tsvetayeva, Marina Ivanovna (b. Moscow, Russia, 26.9.1892; d. Yelabuga, Khabarovsk, USSR, 31.8.1941). Russian poet, essayist and critic. Brought up in a highly cultured Moscow family, privately educated, and having made several extended visits to Western Europe, Tsvetayeva married early, survived the revolutions and civil war alone with her daughter in Moscow (another daughter died), then in 1922 followed her husband, a former White officer, into emigration. They lived first in Prague, then moved to Paris in 1925; Tsvetayeva returned with her young son to Moscow, again following her husband, in 1939. Evacuated after the outbreak of WW2, with husband and daughter arrested, and unable to find work of any kind, she took her own life. She was not published in the USSR until 20 years after her death; there is still no adequate edition of her work. Though not as completely alienated from Russian and émigré literary circles as is sometimes thought, she was never connected with any literary movement; her work is closest to that of MAYAKOVSKY and PASTERNAK among her contemporaries. She was a prolific lyric poet; the greatest mature collection is *Posle Rossii* [After Russia] (Paris, 1928), a book published three years after completion and ignored by contemporaries. She frequently combined her lyrics into cycles and showed a persistent leaning towards major forms: romantic dramas in verse (1918–20), dramas on classical themes in the later 1920s, and longer poems, 10 of which were written between 1920 and 1930. Among the latter are her masterpieces, the lyrical *Poema gory* [Poem of the mountain] (Paris, 1926) and *Poema kontsa* [Poem of the end] (Prague, 1926), both contained in *Selected Poems* (tr. E. Feinstein, Oxford, 1981), and the satirical *Krysolov* [The rat-catcher] (Prague, 1925–6). Her criticism and mainly autobiographical prose, to which she turned increasingly in the 1930s, is as strikingly original as her verse. Tsvetayeva was a writer of strong and simple fundamental ideas, all essentially romantic: the isolation and sanctity of the creative artist; the injustice and inhumanity of bourgeois society; the moral superiority of the individual over the mass; the impossibility of reciprocated sexual love; the sordid inadequacy of material reality. More personal is her passionate commitment to lost causes. Tsvetayeva's greatness stems primarily from her tempestuous, vituperative style, something previously unknown in women's poetry; she violently juxtaposes contrasting lexical registers and is prodigiously inventive in metre and rhythm, and in the orchestration of sound.   GSS

S. Karlinsky, *Marina Cvetaeva: her Life and Art* (Berkeley, Calif., 1966).

Tukey, John Wilder (b. New Bedford, Mass., USA, 16.6.1915). American statistician, of Princeton and of Bell Telephone laboratories. In the 1950s he developed the jack-knife technique, sacrificing precision to universality. With a few well-defined exceptions, any statistic, especially one whose sampling behaviour is little-known, can be treated to produce an improved estimate together with a variance estimate and viable confidence intervals. In the 1960s Tukey produced the system of exploratory data analysis by which most types of data can be reduced to a smoothed form, and exceptional or erroneous items identified. This suggests hypotheses for testing, and is most useful if different sections of the data need differing models (see his *Exploratory Data Analysis*, NY, 1977).   AGPW

Turing, Alan Mathison (b. London, UK, 23.6.1912; d. Wilmslow, Ches., 7.6.1954). British mathematician and pioneer in computer theory. Turing graduated from King's College, Cambrige, where he was elected to a fellowship in 1935. In 1937, working at Princeton, he published a paper 'On computable numbers, with an application to the *Entscheidungsproblem*', and developed the concept of a theoretical computer, the Turing Machine. This concept, which he is believed to have derived from the string of operation cards used to determine the sequence of operations in BABBAGE's analytical engines, is fundamental to the modern theory of computability. In 1938 Turing returned to the UK, and during WW2 he worked on code-cracking at Bletchley Park. In 1945 he joined the National Physical Laboratory at Teddington to work on the construction, design and use of a large automatic computer to which he gave the name of ACE (Automatic Computing Engine). In 1948 he accepted a readership at Manchester University and became assistant director of MADAM (Manchester Automatic Digital Machine), the computer with the largest memory capacity in the world at that time. His efforts in the construction of such early computers and the development of early programming techniques were of major importance. Turing was much interested in the question of whether machines can think. One of his suggestions was that machine thought would more closely resemble human thought if a random element could be introduced, such as a roulette wheel. He proposed as a criterion of a machine's intelligence the question of whether anyone can tell if his or her queries are being answered by a machine or a person at the far end of a data-link. Such criteria ignore the physical – particularly the quantum-mechanical – basis of living systems, and are philosophically profoundly unsatisfying. However, from a mathematical point of view, Turing's criterion has proved valuable. In 1952 Turing published the first part of his study of morphogenesis, a theoretical attempt to show how a uniform and symmetrical structure could develop into an asymmetric structure with a definite pattern as a result of diffusion. He died, however, before his work could be finished.   RAH

S. Turing, *Alan M. Turing* (Cambridge, 1959).

Turner, Frederick Jackson (b. Portage, Wis., USA, 14.11.1861; d. San Marino, Calif., 14.3.1932). American historian. Turner taught at Wisconsin University from 1889 to 1910 and then for a further 14 years at Harvard. He had one important idea: that the frontier of free land had exercised a definitive influence on American life. National character, the independence of the individual and above all American democracy were attributed to the liberating force of the West – wherever it may geographically have been situated at any particular period. The extraordinary force of this idea, one of the dominating influences on the interpretation of American history during the first half of the 20c, may be attributed to three factors: its simplicity; it satisfied a national desire for single, all-purpose explanations; its Americanism – which was very important to Turner himself – it made the great Mississippi valley rather than Europe, or even the East Coast, the source of truly American values; and its timing: the original paper on this theme was delivered in 1893, just when the frontier was coming to an end – and when an economic crisis shook the country. It appeared in book form with a collection of his later frontier essays as *The Frontier in American History* (NY, 1920).

Turner's message was also a prophetic warning. This historic source of American democracy had ceased to exist, and giant corporations were taking over the economy. The nation must re-examine its values if it wanted them to survive. In some ways Turner was more an epic writer than a historian. He had little interest in institutional history, and did not really grasp the importance of showing how frontier conditions were transmitted into democratic institutions. Despite these weaknesses, his vision had an important element of truth.   JRP

R. Hofstadter, *The Progressive Historians* (NY, 1968).

Turner, Victor Witter (b. Glasgow, Strath., UK, 28.5.1920; naturalized American citizen). British/American social anthropologist. His work and influence have displayed three interlinked but distinct phases. In the first he was a leading associate of Max Gluckman. His meticulous fieldwork among the Ndembu of Zambia formed the basis of *Schism and Continuity in an African Society* (Manchester, 1957), the classic Manchester school study of social structure in conflict and of social process as it works through the lives of individual village people. The second phase was grounded in the same fieldwork but focused in a series of detailed studies (e.g. *The Forest of Symbols*, Ithaca, NY, 1967) on the complexities of ritual symbolism, developing techniques for its decoding. In contrast to LÉVI-STRAUSS, he has stressed the multivocality of symbols and the grounding of meaning in experience. In the third phase, coming to fruition after he moved to the USA in 1964, he has sought to transcend both the social-structural and single-society frameworks of his earlier work. From Arnold van Gennep's theory of rites of passage he has, by stressing the liminal stage, developed a conception of social life as movement between structured interaction and 'communitas', a direct, unstructured experience of others: *The Ritual Process* (Chicago, 1969). His wide-ranging subsequent investigations of communitas have focused particularly on pilgrimage.   SRC

Tutuola, Amos (b. Abeokuta, Nigeria, 6.1920). Nigerian fantasist. Tutuola is a Yoruba storyteller whose *The Palm-Wine Drinkard and his Dead Palm-Wine Tapster in the Dead's Town* (London, 1952) did much to draw the richness of Nigeria's folk traditions to the attention of western readers and to establish the credentials of postwar African literature in English. Although a work of almost surrealistic fantasy and ingenuity, *The Palm-Wine Drinkard* has become the focus of much debate within Africa because of its idiosyncratic and semi-educated prose style. Later novels by Tutuola have been written in much the same vein, including *My Life in the Bush of Ghosts* (London, 1954) and *The Witch-Herbalist of the Remote Town* (London, 1981). Tutuola taps Yoruba mythology to great effect but his imagination prevents his books from being merely derivative. His lack of artifice – largely a consequence of his own minimal formal education, and his varied experience as coppersmith, government messenger and storekeeper – allows him to blend modern and traditional terms without the anachronisms jarring. Tutuola's is an inimitable voice in contemporary African literature.   ANRN

B. Lindfors, *Critical Perspectives on Amos Tutuola* (Washington, 1978).

Tzara, Tristan, ps. of Samuel Rosenstock (b. Moineşti, Romania, 16.4.1896; naturalized French citizen, 1945; d. Paris, France, 24.12.1963). Romanian/French poet and essayist whose name is indelibly associated with dadaism. In fact, he is the only poet to leave substantial work from both the dada and surrealist epochs. In 1916, with Hugo Ball and Richard Huelsenbeck, he founded the dada movement at the Cabaret Voltaire in Zürich. In the face of a European civilization madly bent on self-destruction, Tzara flung the truculent negations of his dada manifestoes – *Sept manifestes Dada* (Paris, 1924; tr. B. Wright, *Seven Dada Manifestos*, London, 1971). He urged that the art of poetry be reduced to the random assembly of words clipped from newspapers; he scattered the war-torn Continent with iconoclastic reviews (*Dada*, 1917–21); and baited audiences with noisy and deliberately pointless theatre performances. He was 'awaited like a Messiah' in Paris where he took dada in 1920 for its most tumultuous manifestations. The disintegration of Paris dada in 1922 coincided with the birth of surrealism. Seven years later, Tzara was reconciled with his former rival BRETON, and it was in the ranks of surrealism that he wrote his poetic masterpiece *L'Homme approximatif* (Paris, 1931; tr. M. A. Caws, *Approximate Man*, Detroit, 1973). Here he moves to a more structured, dialectical interplay between the themes of night and day, dream and reality, movement and fixity, flawed 'approximation' and integral fullness. In 1935 he accompanied ARAGON and ELUARD into the French Communist party, and later into the Resistance. His poetry thereafter – *La Face intérieure* [The interior face] (Paris, 1953); *A haute flamme* [In a high flame] (Paris, 1955) – is much more sustained, serene and epic in style, gaining in accessibility what it loses in bite.

RSS

M. A. Caws, *The Poetry of Dada and Surrealism* (Princeton, 1970); E. Peterson, *Tristan Tzara* (Rutgers, NY, 1971).

U

Uhlenbeck, George Eugene (b. Batavia, Java, Dutch East Indies [now Indonesia], 6.12.1900; naturalized American citizen). Dutch/American physicist. Uhlenbeck is a theoretical physicist who emigrated to the USA in 1927. His research has been concerned with the theory of atomic structure and quantum mechanics, statistical mechanics, the kinetic theory of matter, and nuclear physics. He is best known because of the proposal which he made, jointly with his friend GOUDSMIT, that the electron possesses an intrinsic spin. HMR

Unamuno, Miguel de (b. Bilbao, Vizcaya, Spain, 29.9.1864; d. Salamanca, 31.12.1936). Spanish thinker, novelist and poet. Virtually all his work is coloured by his obsessive longing to find some assurance of a personal afterlife, explored most directly in *Del sentimiento trágico de la vida* (Madrid, 1913; tr. J. E. C. Flitch, *The Tragic Sense of Life in Men and Peoples*, London, 1921), but also present in two other book-length studies *La agonía del cristianismo* (first pub. in French as *L'agonie du christianisme*, Paris, 1925; tr. P. Loving, *The Agony of Christianity*, NY, 1928; first Spanish publication, Madrid, 1931, in the more propitious atmosphere of the Republic), and the early *Vida de Don Quijote y Sancho* (Madrid, 1905; tr. H. P. Earle, *The Life of Don Quixote and Sancho*, London, 1927). This is the most stimulating commentary on *Don Quixote* ever written, but it tells us more about Unamuno (through the 'significance' he reads into the text) than it does about the book's intended 'meaning' or how Golden Age readers saw it. The same is true of the essays on Spain in *En torno al casticismo* [The Spanish tradition] (Barcelona, 1902), which influenced all subsequent Spanish interpreters of Spain's life and culture; Unamuno's notion of *intrahistoria* – the patterned and unifying sedimentation of past small happenings and daily life – which he deemed more insightful than traditional history's divisive chronicle of

major events, foreshadowed modern social history, but remained at the intuitive level. His major achievement as a poet was *El Cristo de Velázquez* (Madrid, 1920; tr. E. L. Turnbull, *The Christ of Velazquez*, Baltimore, 1951), meditations on Velazquez's *Crucifixion*, but the highly poetic content fails to coalesce (despite its intricate imagery). His last poems have a more incisive approach (bilingual edition, tr. E. Mas-López, *The Last Poems of Miguel de Unamuno*, Madison, 1974). Today, Unamuno is chiefly respected for two of his collections of long short-stories *Tres novelas ejemplares y un prólogo* (Madrid, 1920; tr. A. Flores, *Three Exemplary Novels*, NY, 1956) and *San Manuel Bueno, mártir, y tres historias más* (Madrid, 1933; tr. F. de Segovia & J. Pérez, *San Manuel Bueno, mártir*, London, 1957; and for two of his five novels *Niebla* (Madrid, 1914; tr. W. Fite, *Mist*, NY, 1929) and *Abel Sánchez* (Madrid, 1917) – a modern exploration of the Cain-and-Abel theme. *Niebla*, in many ways an existentialist novel *avant la lettre*, adds a new twist to Unamuno's fundamental quest for immortality by using a confrontation between the hero Augusto Pérez and his creator Unamuno as a 'model' for exploring the relationship between Unamuno and God. RP-M

P. Ilie, *Unamuno: an Existentialist View of Self and Society* (Madison, 1967); F. Wyers, *Miguel de Unamuno: the Contrary Self* (London, 1976).

Undset, Sigrid (b. Kalundborg, Zeeland, Denmark, 20.5.1882; d. Oslo, Norway, 10.6.1949). Norwegian novelist. Her earliest novels, of which *Jenny* (Christiania, 1911; tr. W. Emme, London, 1930) is the most significant, are largely concerned with the problems of the role of women in contemporary society. Her undisputed masterpiece is the trilogy *Kristin Lavransdatter* (Christiania, 1920–2; tr. C. Archer & J. S. Scott, London, 1930): set in 14c Norway with a wealth of colourful historical detail, it follows the career of Kristin from girlhood to old age in her search for self-fulfilment and for a faith capable of sustaining her. Shortly after completing this novel, Sigrid Undset was received into the Roman Catholic church; and all her subsequent work is strongly marked by this conversion. The four-volume novel series *Olav Audunssøn* (Oslo, 1925–7; tr. A. G. Chater, *The Master of Hestviken*, London, 1928–30), the action of which is set in the late 13c, is, however, less successful than the earlier historical trilogy. Most of her later novels – for example, *Gymnadenia* (Oslo, 1929; tr. A. G. Chater, *The Wild Orchid*, London, 1931), *Den brændende busk* (Oslo, 1930; tr. A. G. Chater, *The Burning Bush*, London, 1932) and *Den trofaste hustru* (Oslo, 1936, tr. A. G. Chater, *The Faithful Wife*, London, 1937) – have a contemporary setting and show a deep preoccupation with moral and religious problems. JWMcF

A. Gustafson, *Six Scandinavian Novelists* (Princeton, 1940); A. H. Winsnes, *Sigrid Undset: a Study in Christian Realism* (London, 1953).

Ungaretti, Giuseppe (b. Alexandria, Egypt, 10.2.1888; d. Milan, Lombardy, Italy, 1.6.1970). Italian poet, who came to Paris in 1914 and started writing verse under the influence of the French avant-garde. His first book of poems *Il porto sepolto* [The sunken harbour] (Udine, 1916), which appeared in a limited edition, and was later included in *L'Allegria di naufragi* [The happiness of the shipwrecks] (Florence, 1919), marks a decisive break from the poetic conventions of Carducci, Pascoli and D'ANNUNZIO. Whatever influences Ungaretti may have undergone – for instance, Petrarch and Leopardi on the one hand, and French contemporary poetry and futurism on the other – he transcended in his own 'hermetic' poetry, which is written in a new succinct and quintessential way which has a certain affinity with imagism. But the moral maturity, technical mastery and artistic control behind his verbal economy and evocative subtlety brought into Italian poetry what Ezra POUND calls 'Sophoclean hardness'. In *Sentimento del tempo* [Feeling of the time] (Florence, 1933), while maintaining the formal and

technical brilliance of *L'Allegria*, Ungaretti's poetry acquired a new spiritual depth as he dealt with the themes of memory, a personal universe in which time and space are outside of chronological time, and a religious crisis which centres upon the poet's awareness of an unbridgeable gulf between God and man. *Il dolore* [The grief] (Milan, 1947) is Ungaretti's most personal book of poems, concerned with the death of his brother and of his son. Ungaretti wrote three further volumes of poetry: *La terra promessa* [The promised land] (Milan, 1950), *Un grido e paesaggi* [A cry and landscapes] (Milan, 1952) and *Il taccuino del vecchio* [The notebooks of the old man] (Milan, 1960; tr. A. Mandelbaum, *Selected Poems of Giuseppe Ungaretti*, Ithaca, NY, 1975). He also translated poems by SAINT-JOHN PERSE, Góngora, Blake, ESENIN, Paulhan, Mallarmé, Ezra Pound and 40 sonnets by Shakespeare. GS

G. Singh, 'The Poetry of Giuseppe Ungaretti', *Italian Studies*, 28 (1973); J. Jones, *Giuseppe Ungaretti: Poet and Critic* (Edinburgh, 1977).

Updike, John (b. Shillington, Pa, USA, 18.3.1932). American novelist. Updike studied at Harvard and at the Ruskin School, Oxford. *The Poorhouse Fair* (NY, 1959), like the novels that followed it, made death a central theme, and, like many of them, it underpinned its narrative with mythological supports. Sex joined death in *Rabbit, Run* (NY, 1960), its hero finding in the former his one escape from the terror of the latter. The 'Rabbit' sequence, up to *Rabbit is Rich* (NY, 1981), observes a world of mere consumption that ironically implies man's need for spiritual purpose. *Couples* (NY, 1968) and, on a smaller scale, *Marry Me* (NY, 1976) explored through a tangle of adulteries the terror of bourgeois man in a universe not made for the comfort of commuters. Updike's irrepressible mythmaking, at its most overt in *The Centaur* (NY, 1968), has given ironic depths to his work, but at the expense of an occasionally wilful formalism; while his distinctive blend of the real and the fabulous, the erotic and the spiritual, and his elegant *New Yorker* style, by turns witty, precise, and metaphorically evocative, but always self-conscious, have left some readers uncertain how seriously to take him. At least he must be allowed the considerable achievement of domesticating within a subtly observed conventional society the angsts of a specifically 20c spirituality. BF

D. Thorburn & H. Eiland (eds), *John Updike: a Collection of Critical Views* (NY, 1979).

Urey, Harold Clayton (b. Walkerton, Ind., USA, 29.4.1893; d. La Jolla, Calif., 5.1.1981). American chemist, distinguished for his investigations of the separation and properties of isotopes (he discovered deuterium) and of atomic and molecular structure, and in cosmochemistry. Urey taught in rural schools (1911–14), and graduated BS from Montana (1917) and PhD from the University of California (1923). He was associate in chemistry of Johns Hopkins University (1923–9), on the chemistry faculty of Columbia University (1929–45), at the Institute for Nuclear Studies in Chicago (1945–58), and professor of chemistry at large in the University of California (1958–70). Urey's earliest researches were mainly on atomic and molecular spectra and structure; hence the book *Atoms, Molecules, and Quanta* (with A. E. Ruark, NY, 1930). He made his name in 1932 as the first (in collaboration with F. G. Brickwedde and G. M. Murphy) to isolate deuterium, the heavy isotope of hydrogen. For this work he received the Nobel prize in 1934. Thereafter he made many studies of the separation of isotopes, the effect of isotopy on physical and chemical properties, isotopic exchange reactions, etc. He was prominent in the WW2 atomic energy project. Later he turned to chemical problems of the origin of the earth, meteorites, the moon, and solar system, writing *The Planets* (New Haven, 1952), *Some Cosmochemical Problems* (Philadelphia, 1963) and numerous papers. JSh

Utrillo, Maurice (b. Paris, France, 26.12.1883; d. Le Vésinet, Landes, 5.11.1955). French painter. The illegitimate son of the painter Suzanne Valadon, he began to drink heavily while still a boy and was encouraged to paint by his mother as a distraction. Working mainly from picture postcards, he painted Montmartre and provincial churches, and is famous above all for his pictures of the streets of the Montmartre area in Paris. At his best, during the years 1910–14 approximately (often known as his 'white period' because of its emphasis on white walls, greys, blues, browns and blacks), he made many subtle modifications to the picture postcards he was working from, simplifying and purifying the forms, stressing the textural contrasts and creating a feeling of melancholy and loneliness. His later pictures became increasingly looser and more slipshod in execution, but were also more colourful and contained more figures. REA

P. Petrides (ed.), *Maurice Utrillo: l'oeuvre complet* (2 vols, Paris, 1959–62).

Utzon, Jørn (b. Copenhagen, Denmark, 9.4.1918). Danish architect. Having studied with the influential critic and historian S. E. Rasmussen at the Royal Academy of Fine Arts in Copenhagen, Utzon worked for short but formative periods with Gunnar Asplund in Denmark, AALTO in Finland, and Frank Lloyd WRIGHT in the USA. His mature style reflects these experiences. He brings together a careful, often traditionally Danish, attitude to materials with a feeling for an organic relationship between buildings and landscape from Wright, the rigorous discipline of Asplund and the creative expressionism of Aalto. These characteristics can be seen in the courtyard housing near Helsingør and Fredensborg. Both these schemes show the houses hugging the contours of an undulating landscape, grouped together to create enclosure and frame views. Utzon established his claim to be considered as one of the most original architects of the century with his winning scheme for the design of Sydney Opera House in 1956. That monument, with its billowing sail-like parabolic concrete shells on the peninsula jutting out into the harbour, is fixed in the imagination of people throughout the world. Utzon will be remembered as its designer long after the problems with construction (brilliantly solved by Ove Arup) have been forgotten.   PAC

T. Faber, *New Danish Architecture* (London, 1968).

Uvarov, Boris (b. Uralsk, Russia, 5.11.1888; naturalized British citizen, 1943; d. London, UK, 18.3.1970). Russian/British entomologist who made major contributions to the knowledge and prevention of locust plagues. He graduated in 1910 at St Petersburg University, worked in the Caucasus, and in 1920 joined the Imperial Bureau of Entomology in London. He is best known for his theory of solitary and gregarious locust phases and formation of swarms in restricted outbreak areas, published as an article in 1921. From the 1930s he organized or inspired field and biogeographical investigations on three major locust species in Africa and South West Asia; these received international support and eventually led to international cooperation in the supervision of outbreak areas of two of the species and the surveying and control on a regional basis of the third. Between 1945 and his retirement in 1959 he was the first director of the Anti-Locust Research Centre in London, which under him assumed a leading role in research on locusts. His own numerous publications on *Acridoidea* dealt with their taxonomy, biogeography and ecology, with emphasis on the effects of climate on their fluctuations: his last contribution was a comprehensive handbook *Grasshoppers and Locusts* (2 vols, Cambridge, 1966 & London, 1977). zw

Anti-Locust Research Centre, *In Memoriam Sir Boris Uvarov KCMG, FRS, 1888–1970* (London, 1970).

V

Valentino, Rodolpho Alfonzo Raffaelo Pierre Filibert Guglielmi (Rudolph) (b. Castellaneta, Apulia, Italy, 6.5.1895; naturalized American citizen; d. New York, USA, 23.8.1926). American silent film actor, Valentino created a myth; the ultimate in sex symbols, he was known as 'The Great Lover'. Tastes in fantasy sex change; with female emancipation the lure of masculine domination lost its force. But the dark Latin looks and the air of sexual condescension won susceptible women's hearts. With sound it would have been difficult to speak some of Valentino's lines ('I am he that loves you'), but he was fortunate in a period which still clung to the idea of the omnipotent male. An age, too, of ballroom dancing in which the male partner commanded. Valentino began as an exhibition dancer; his first film success *The Four Horsemen of the Apocalypse* (1921) showed him at the start as an insolent exponent of the tango. It was later, in *The Sheik* (1921), *Blood and Sand* (1922), *Monsieur Beaucaire* (1924), *The Eagle* (1925) and *Son of the Sheik* (1926), that he developed the romantic command which brought mourners in thousands to watch his hearse driven through New York. Valentino married first a Mexican dancer who locked him out on their wedding night, and second a dominating and probably lesbian production designer Natacha Rambova; divorce followed, though not so quickly.

DP

A. Walker, *Rudolph Valentino* (London, 1976).

Valéry, Paul Ambroise (b. Sète, Hérault, France, 30.10.1871; d. Paris, 20.7.1945). French poet and essayist, with two major intellectual preoccupations: the workings of the human mind, especially his own; and the creation of 'pure' poetry. He exploited the first mainly in his prose works, treating the exclusive pursuit of abstract ideas with attractive irony in *La Soirée avec Monsieur Teste* (Paris, 1896; tr. M. Gould, *An Evening with Monsieur Teste*, London, 1936), and

discussing in fascinating detail the relationship between doing and thinking about what one is doing in *Eupalinos ou l'architecte* (Paris, 1923; tr. W. McCausland Stewart, *Eupalinos; or the Architect*, Oxford, 1932). He was much influenced in his quest for poetic purity by Stéphane Mallarmé (1842–96), and maintained that prose differed from poetry in being solely an instrument for the communication of facts or ideas. Unlike poetry, in which form was all important, prose thus perished in the telling. Poetry alone, in which the expression of ideas or emotions played only the minutest role, could rescue language from eternal flux. There is consequently some irony in the fact that Valéry's best and best-known poem '*Le Cimetière marin*' (in *Charmes*, Paris, 1922; tr. C. Day Lewis, *The Graveyard by the Sea*, London, 1946) is a complex and eloquent philosophical statement of the pagan as opposed to the Christian concept of death. Valéry was elected to the Académie Française in 1925, and became a kind of official man of letters, invited to express views on all varieties of men, manners and events. He did so with great elegance, publishing *Regards sur le monde actuel* in 1933 (tr. F. Scarfe, *Reflections on the World Today*, London, 1951) and carrying literary criticism to its highest level since Sainte-Beuve in *Variété* (Paris, 1922–4) and *Tel Quel* (Paris, 1941–3). In spite of long periods when he had to earn his living at the Havas news agency, he rose at 4.30 every morning to watch his mind working, writing down his observations on its treatment of mathematics, science, literature and psychology in his *Cahiers* [Notebooks] (Paris, 1957–61).

PMWT

N. Suckling, *Paul Valéry and the Civilized Mind* (Oxford, 1954); J. Robinson, *Analyse de l'esprit dans les Cahiers de Valéry* (Paris, 1963).

Valle-Inclán, Ramón Maria del (b. Villanueva de Arosa, Pontevedra, Spain, 28.10.1866; d. Santiago de Compostela,

Corunna, 5.1.1936). Spanish novelist and dramatist. The only modern Spanish dramatist of European stature (apart from the much younger LORCA), he began with plays such as *Aguila de blasón* [The heraldic eagle] (Barcelona, 1907) and *Romance de lobos* (Madrid, 1908; tr. C. B. Lander, *Wolves! Wolves! A Play of Savagery in Three Acts*, Birmingham, 1957), an original and violent reworking of the Don Juan myth set in feudal Galicia. After a series of farces such as *La marquesa Rosalinda* [The marquise Rosalind] (Madrid, 1913) on the theme of marital infidelity and *Farsa y licencia de la reina castiza* [Farce and licence of the pure and noble queen] (Madrid, 1922) on the subject of Queen Isabel II's promiscuous habits, he developed an entirely new and highly personal kind of drama which he entitled '*esperpento*'. This consists of an expressionistic and grotesque deformation and satire of various aspects of traditional Spanish life and strongly prefigures the theatre of the absurd of BECKETT and IONESCO. The best of these plays are *Luces de Bohemia* (Madrid, 1924; tr. G. Gillespie & A. Zahareas, *Bohemian Lights*, Edinburgh, 1976) and *Los cuernos de don Friolera* [The horns of Don Friolera] (Madrid, 1925). But Valle-Inclán's contribution to the novel is equally important. Starting with the decadent *Sonatas* (Madrid, 1902–4; tr. M. H. Broun & T. Walsh, *The Pleasant Memoirs of the Marqués de Bradomín: Four Sonatas*, NY, 1924), which relate in a deliberately refined and exotic style the amorous adventures of a Galician aristocrat, he moved on to more solid topics with a trilogy on the Carlist war. His outstanding fictional achievements, however, were *Tirano Banderas* (Madrid, 1926; tr. M. Pavitt, *The Tyrant. A Novel of Warm Lands*, NY, 1929), a structurally and stylistically brilliant narrative on South American politics, and the unfinished cycle of novels *El ruedo ibérico* [The Iberian road] (2 vols, Madrid, 1927 & 1928) on Spanish political life in the later 19c.   CAL

A. Zahareas (ed.), *Ramón del Valle-Inclán: an Appraisal of his Life and Works* (NY, 1968); V. Smith, *Ramón del Valle-Inclán* (NY, 1973).

Vallejo, César (b. Santiago de Chuco, Peru, 16.3.1892; d. Paris, France, 15.4.1938). Peruvian poet, and one of the two most influential Latin American poets this century (the other being NERUDA). Only two books of Vallejo's poetry were published during his lifetime, both before he left for France in June 1923: *Los heraldos negros* [The black heralds] (Lima, 1918; tr. R. Bly *et al.*, represented in *Twenty Poems of César Vallejo*, Madison, 1963; and in *Neruda and Vallejo: Selected Poems*, Boston, Mass., 1971; both collections also include poems from *Trilce* and the posthumous works); and *Trilce* (Lima, 1922; tr. C. Tomlinson & H. Gifford, *Ten Versions from 'Trilce'*, Cerrillos, N. Mex., 1970). The posthumous poetry, published as *Poemas humanos* [Human poems] (Paris, 1937), is seen by its translator and most recent editor C. Eshleman as having been intended to form three books, *Nómina de huesos* [Payroll of bones] (1923–36), *Sermón de la barbarie* [Sermon on barbarism] (1936 –7), and the Spanish civil war cycle *España, aparta de mí este cáliz* [Spain, take this cup from me] (1937–8) (see *The Complete Posthumous Poetry*, C. Eshleman & J. Rubia Barcia, bilingual edition, Berkeley, Calif., 1978). *Los heraldos negros* is a late *modernista* work, but already displays Vallejo's willingness to create new words to match his moods, as well as his ability to switch registers within a poem. *Trilce* goes further, shattering all conventions in its effort to capture rapid sensations, occasionally veiling their source so hermetically that one can only respond to inchoate and disparate resonances (at their densest, these poems are by far the toughest in the Spanish language); many were written during a three-month imprisonment on trumped-up charges. Soured and haunted by the experience, Vallejo left Peru for ever two years later. *Nómina de huesos* shows an increasing social involvement, and in the late 1920s Vallejo became a communist (but the poems argue no doctrine and preach no solution, though they 'identify' with suffering humanity). He visited Russia, publishing a broadly eulogistic travelogue on his return: *Rusia en 1931* (Madrid, 1931). In the same year he

779

published the better of his two didactic novels (*El tungsteno* [Tungsten], Madrid, 1931), a bitter protest against mining conditions in the Andes, marred by an oversimple socialist realism and by weak characterization. *Sermón de la barbarie*, written under the emotional impact of the Spanish civil war but with the inward depth of personal dilemmas, contains some of the finest posthumous poems. *España, aparta de mí este cáliz*, though one of the best poetic works to come directly out of the civil war, is shallower: linguistically simple (to reach a wider audience), dividing the world into heroes and villains in a way which his other poetry shows he knew to be untrue, and indulging in resonant public platform rhetoric. It is the poetry from *Trilce* to *Sermón de la barbarie* which has proved most influential, not by prompting close imitations (as happened with Neruda) but by inciting younger poets to have the courage to be true to personal experience and create fresh styles to capture it.   RP-M

J. Higgins, Introduction to *César Vallejo: an Anthology of his Poetry* (Oxford, 1970); J. Franco, *César Vallejo: the Dialectics of Poetry and Silence* (Cambridge, 1976).

Vandenberg, Arthur Hendrick (b. Grand Rapids, USA, 22.3.1884; d. Grand Rapids, Mich., 18.4.1951). US senator (Republican) for Michigan (1928–51), he abandoned his prewar isolationist stance to become, at President TRUMAN's urging, the leading Republican embodiment of bipartisanship in US foreign policy, acting as US delegate to the initial meeting of the UNO in 1945, and playing a major part in obtaining congressional support for the Truman doctrine and the MARSHALL Plan in 1947, for US membership of NATO in 1949, and for US participation in the limited war in Korea in 1950. *The Private Papers of Senator Vandenberg* were edited by his son Arthur H. Vandenberg Jr (Boston, Mass., 1952).   DCW

Vansittart, Robert Gilbert (b. Farnham, Surrey, UK, 25.6.1881; d. Denham, Bucks., 14.2.1957). British diplomat and pamphleteer. Permanent under-secretary in the Foreign Office (1930–8) and chief diplomatic adviser (1938–40), Vansittart enjoyed during his life the slightly unjustified reputation of being an outspoken opponent of the policy of appeasement associated with CHAMBERLAIN. In practice he advocated the postponement of a confrontation with Germany until rearmament made Britain strong enough to curb and inhibit HITLER. He had no compunction on grounds of *Realpolitik* to the appeasement of Italy and Japan. A bad judge of men and a writer of forbiddingly prolix style, he was anti-German on culturist-racialist grounds, as became clear in the violent controversy he engaged in, after he had published *Black Record* in 1941, a pamphlet which argued a historical continuity between the harassment of the classical Roman empire by the Teutonic tribes and Nazism, and advocated a peace settlement of draconian severity. Subsequently he transferred his hatred of Germany into an equally violent stand against STALINist Russia.   DCW

Van Vleck, John Hasbrouck (b. Middletown, Conn., USA, 13.3.1899; d. Cambridge, Mass., 27.10.1980). American physicist. A pioneer of quantum mechanics, Van Vleck is one of the few in that field whose training was almost entirely completed within the USA. He initiated some of the most significant advances in the theory of magnetism, particularly of magnetic crystals, and his book *The Theory of Electric and Magnetic Susceptibilities* (Oxford, 1932) is still a standard text. His most important work was the development of the theory of those processes in which the electron orbits of magnetic atoms (or ions) in crystals are affected by the presence of the surrounding nonmagnetic ions, and the profound way in which these nonmagnetic ions can influence the magnetic properties. He also developed the theory of interactions between the magnetic ions themselves and showed how this is influenced by the thermal motion of the ions, which is always present. All this work has been subsequently confirmed to a very high degree of precision by many detailed experimental investigations. He was awarded the Nobel prize for physics in 1977.   HMR

Varèse, Edgard Victor Achille Charles (b. Paris, France, 22.12.1883; naturalized American citizen, 1927; d. New York, USA, 8.11.1965). French/American composer who emigrated to the USA in 1915; almost all his earlier music was lost or destroyed. His output effectively began with *Amériques* (1926), scored for an enormous orchestra and celebrating not only a new homeland but a new world of the imagination. Although influenced by DEBUSSY, STRAVINSKY and SCHOENBERG, the work is original in its evolving form, rhythmic complexity, elaborate percussion writing and massive eruptions of sound. It opened the way to the urban poetry of most of Varèse's later works which include *Hyperprism* for a small orchestra of wind and percussion (1923) and *Ionisation* for 13 percussionists (1933). Varèse was also attracted to the primitive and magical aspects expressed in his *Ecuatorial* (1934), which sets a Maya imprecation for bass voice and small orchestra. He composed little for the next 15 years. With the arrival of electronic resources, for which he had long been pressing, he set to work in earnest once more, producing *Déserts* for orchestra and tape (1954) and the *Poème électronique* (1958), one of the few masterpieces of electronic music.   PG

L. Varèse, *Varèse: a Looking-Glass Diary*, vol. 1: 1883–1928 (NY, 1972); F. Ouellette, *Edgard Varèse* (London, 1973).

Vargas Llosa, Mario (b. Arequipa, Peru, 28.3.1936). Peruvian novelist. One of the creators of the new Latin American novel, and responsible (along with CORTÁZAR, GARCÍA MÁRQUEZ and FUENTES) for putting this on the international map. Paradoxically, his desire to capture a reality which is often repulsive has led him away from stark realism into radical (and often confusing) manipulations of time, space, and identity, designed to achieve the effect of a revelation when the puzzles are finally solved, as in his first full-length novel *La ciudad y los perros* (Barcelona, 1963; tr. L. Kemp, *The Time of the Hero*, NY, 1966). This is set in a paramilitary school in Lima at which Vargas Llosa had studied, and which he turns into a

microcosm of Peru. *La casa verde* (Barcelona, 1966; tr. G. Rabassa, *The Green House*, NY, 1968) – another exposé – alternates between a whorehouse in coastal Peru and the exploitation of primitive tribes in the Amazon jungles: its technical experiments are more successful than those in *La ciudad*. His most complex novel *Conversación en la Catedral* (Barcelona, 1969; tr. G. Rabassa, *Conversation in the Cathedral*, NY, 1975) is also his finest, and one of the subtlest treatments of the dictatorship theme. After pausing to write a book about a friend and fellow-novelist (*García Márquez: Historia de un deicidio* [García Márquez: the history of a deicide], Barcelona, 1971), Vargas Llosa produced a disconcertingly different novel *Pantaleón y las visitadoras* (Barcelona, 1973; tr. G. Kolovakos & R. Christ, *Captain Pantoja and the Special Service*, London, 1978), a richly comic treatment of Pantoja's methodical plan to supply prostitutes for the army's use, hilariously documented by the printing of operation orders, communiqués, messages and letters. *La tía Julia y el escribidor* [Aunt Julia and the scribbler] (Barcelona, 1977) applies this talent for comic invention to the life of a scriptwriter of soap-operas whose insanity brings chaos to the scripts and confusion to the public, but this fantastic story alternates with instalments of a realistic narrative rooted in the author's early years of married life in Lima in the 1950s (his favourite period). *La guerra del fin del mondo* [The war of the end of the world] (Barcelona, 1981), a complex novel set in 19c Brazil, marks a switch to the seemingly realistic depiction of historical events narrated in an 'open' style.   RP-M

L. A. Diez, *Mario Vargas Llosa's Pursuit of the Total Novel* (Cuernavaca, 1970); C. Rossmann & A. W. Friedman (eds), *Mario Vargas Llosa: a Collection of Critical Essays* (Austin, 1978).

Vasarely, Victor (b. Pecs, Austria-Hungary [now Hungary], 9.4.1908; naturalized French citizen, 1959). Hungarian/French painter who was one of the principal originators and exponents of op art, geometrical abstraction which aims to stimulate particular perceptual effects. This approach enjoyed a vogue during the 1960s, a period of optimistic belief in technology and behaviourism, when Vasarely's reputation was at its highest; his critical standing has since declined. He arrived at his characteristic method through constructivism: MOHOLY-NAGY was one of his teachers in Budapest in 1929, the year before he went to Paris. He began by working as a graphic artist and it was under the influence of August Herbin that he started to paint geometrical abstractions in the late 1940s. He was a leading member of the *Groupe de Recherche d'Art Visuel* (GRAV), formed in 1960, which emphasized a scientific approach and viewer-participation. Vasarely has been a prolific writer of manifestoes. In 1970 he opened his own 'didactic' museum in Gordes, Vaucluse, France.

MOJN

M. Compton, *Optical and Kinetic Art* (London, 1967); V. Spies, *Victor Vasarely* (NY, 1971).

Vaughan Williams, Ralph (b. Down Ampney, Glos., UK, 12.10.1872; d. London, 26.8.1958). British composer. The main influences on Vaughan Williams were English folksong and early English church music. His total output, ranging from operas and symphonies to simple songs, is full of contrasts – the tranquillity of the *Tallis Fantasia* and much of the Fifth Symphony or *Flos Campi* with the sharper, more dissonant Fourth and Sixth symphonies and the fury of the satanic sections of *Job*. Vaughan Williams's background was comfortably middle class; his mother belonged to the Wedgwood and Darwin families, his father was a country parson. It was in 1903, after the Royal College of Music and Cambridge University, that he began to collect folksongs. A year later he was appointed editor of *The English Hymnal*; the *Sea Symphony* was begun in 1905. In 1908, to widen his experience, he went to Paris for three months and worked with RAVEL who was three years his junior but already established and 'exactly the man I was looking for'. Soon followed the important song cycle 'On Wenlock Edge', the vocal lines still owing much to folksong, the atmosphere of the piano

and string quartet accompaniment showing that study with Ravel had not been wasted. Vaughan Williams brought to English music renewed individuality, depth of vision and broad humanity. JL

M. Kennedy, *The Works of Ralph Vaughan Williams* (London, 1964); U. Vaughan Williams, *R. V. W.: a Biography* (London, 1964).

Vavilov, Nikolai Ivanovich (b. Moscow, Russia, 26.11.1885; d. Saratov, USSR, 26.1.1943). Russian botanist. He was educated privately at a local commercial school (a career in commerce was planned by his father) and at the Timiriazev Academy in Moscow. Between 1913 and 1914 he worked with W. BATESON at the newly established John Innes Horticultural Institute. His pioneering work there investigated the genetically based resistance of cereals to fungal diseases. He returned to Russia in 1914, and immediately began the work for which he is best known, the origin of cultivated plants. A series of well-planned, but physically daunting expeditions took him to Persia, Abyssinia, Afghanistan, China, Central and South America. The Abyssinian expedition was financially backed by no less than LENIN himself. His vigour, enterprise and originality were building his reputation at a remarkable rate and by 1921 he was president of the Lenin Academy of Agricultural Sciences and director of the Institute of Applied Botany. In a few short years Vavilov was able to establish no fewer than 400 research institutes with a total staff of 20,000 by 1934. His journal the *Bulletin of Applied Botany, Genetics, and Plant Breeding* became a leading international publication. 26,000 varieties of wheat were cultivated at his experimental station in Leningrad; sadly all these collections were eaten during the siege. But from this prodigious labour emerged a new synthesis of the origin of cultivated plants, the first great advance in this field since de Candolle, and the basis for all future work. *Inter alia* it led to the foundation of the British Empire Potato Collection on which much potato breeding is based. But the clouds of political orthodoxy began to gather about him. He lost the notorious battle with the LYSENKOists in 1939, he was soon removed from all his executive positions and disappeared into the concentration camps. He was condemned to death for spying for England in a five-minute trial in July 1941. Many of his staff were executed or imprisoned and he may never have known of his election as a foreign member of the Royal Society in 1942. The man who had done more than any other to feed Russia died of starvation in a labour camp in 1943.

BEJ

Veblen, Thorstein Bunde (b. Manitowoc Co., Wis., USA, 30.7.1857; d. nr Menlo Park, Calif., 3.8.1929). American economist and social critic. Perhaps the best-known iconoclast in American social thought, Thorstein Veblen came to public attention in 1899 with the publication of *The Theory of the Leisure Class* (NY) – his only book to achieve popularity in his lifetime – an unsparing attack on business civilization and its values. What gave it currency was Veblen's talent for the colourful phrase, such as 'conspicuous consumption' or 'captains of industry', which sought, in the ironic mode that was his style, to deride the efforts of the new 'pecuniary classes' to gain prestige. Within that first book, however, were the seeds of a sociological economics that Veblen developed only fitfully in the next 25 years. This was the idea (which can be found to some extent in Adam Smith's *Theory of Moral Sentiments*, 1759, and in Rousseau's *Discourse on Inequality*, 1755) that the prime motivation for economic development is not gain in wealth in a narrow sense, but social status. This centrality of status, and its correlate, the role of envy, still remains a largely unexplored field in the history of social thought. Veblen himself was the quintessential 'outsider' and 'marginal man'. Of Norse parentage, he grew up in a lonely existence on a Minnesota farm. English was his second language and, because of his idiosyncratic ways, he never found a permanent position in American academic life. The theme which ran like a thread through all his writings was the inherent tension between 'business' as profit-seeking, and the 'instinct for workmanship', or the useful production

of goods and services. This led Veblen to some path-breaking studies (e.g. *The Theory of Business Enterprise*, NY, 1904) on the way that profit-seeking creates irrational behaviour, such as the emphasis on marketing and advertising, and to his guarded belief (in *The Engineers and the Price System*, NY, 1921) that a syndicalist revolution, led by engineers, could use technology for the maximum production of needed goods.

Veblen has often been hailed as a radical, because of his sardonic attacks on business values, and as a reactionary (by ADORNO) because of his populist derision of culture. Though he never created a 'school', or had direct followers, Veblen's influence on American social thought derives from his repudiation of classical economics. What ultimately provides direction for an economy, Veblen insisted, is not the price mechanisms but the value system of the culture in which the economy is embedded. That emphasis, called 'institutional economics', has returned in recent years, principally in the work of GALBRAITH and Robert Heilbronner, because of the difficulties of standard economic theory in providing effective management of economic policy. Veblen's other very important work was *Imperial Germany and the Industrial Revolution* (NY, 1915), a classic study of how the industrial 'late-comer' is able to use the advantages of newer technology to gain competitive advantage.

DBe

J. Dorfman, *Thorstein Veblen and his America* (NY, 1934).

van de Velde, Henry Clemens (b. Antwerp, Belgium, 3.4.1863; d. Zürich, Switzerland, 25.10.1957). Belgian painter, designer and architect. Velde is a pivotal figure in the history of the early modern movement. He transmitted British Arts and Crafts ideas to the Continent; he was one of the few art nouveau designers to see that mechanized production was not incompatible with artistic individualism; his teaching practice at Weimar anticipated that of the Bauhaus (and he recommended GROPIUS's appointment); his work influenced expressionist architecture, although he distanced himself from expressionism. Above all, his name is associated with the 1914 Congress of the Deutscher Werkbund in Cologne. There he was a leading contributor to the debate on *Typisierung* initiated by Muthesius, defending artistic values and advocating a gradual evolution towards norms of design in opposition to the economic utilitarianism of Muthesius's demand for immediate, concerted efforts to create standard types. And his Cologne exhibition theatre was one of the first modern designs to exploit the potential of the tripartite stage.

In some ways van de Velde's life is a paradigm of his generation. Trained as a painter, he was influenced by Morris's ideas and became convinced of the social value of forging links between the fine and applied arts and architecture. From the 1890s onwards the variety of his output (typography, textiles, wallpaper, ceramics, furniture, architecture) provided a practical demonstration of his beliefs. He gained a reputation in France (designing rooms for Bing's *L'Art Nouveau* and the interior of Meier-Graefe's *Maison Moderne*) and in Germany. He designed the interior of the Folkwang Museum, Hagen, for K.-E. Osthaus and in 1902 moved to Weimar as artistic adviser to the Grand-Duke of Saxe-Weimar, with a brief to 'raise the artistic level of the craft products and craftsmen of the state' which culminated in the creation of the Weimar School of Arts and Crafts, built to van de Velde's designs. He became director of the school and actively encouraged cooperation with local craftsmen and industries. In 1914 rising German nationalism forced his resignation and he later left Germany. His buildings of the 1920s and 1930s (e.g. Villa Wolfers, Kröller-Muller Museum) show his mastery of the new rationalist architectural language. His *Geschichte meines Lebens* [Story of my life] (Munich, 1962) appeared posthumously.

CAB

K.-H. Hüter, *Henry van de Velde* (Berlin, 1965).

Vening Meinesz, Felix Andries (b. Scheveningen, S. Holland, The Netherlands, 30.7.1887; d. Amersfoort, Utrecht, 10.8.1966). Dutch geophysicist. Vening Meinesz studied civil engineering at the Technical University of Delft, where he became professor of geophysics. Early in his career he accepted an invitation to undertake a gravity survey of the Netherlands. From this came his interest in geodesy, to which he was to make highly significant contributions, notably by pioneering a method of studying gravity at sea, using a pendulum technique aboard a submarine. His greatest discovery was a belt of negative anomalies beneath the deep submarine trenches associated with island arcs. This he interpreted as due to a compressive down-buckling of the crust, which formed an important basis for the later interpretation, in plate-tectonic theory, that these regions are *subduction zones* where oceanic crust descends beneath the continental margins. His most important work is summarized in his five-volume *Gravity Expeditions at Sea* (Delft, 1932–60). Although not a supporter of continental drift, he believed in convection currents in the mantle and developed an elegant model before the notion became fashionable.

AH

Venizélos, Eleuthérios (b. Mourniés, Crete, Ottoman Empire [now Greece], 23.8.1864; d. Paris, France, 18.3.1936). Cretan leader of the Greek nationalist movement against Ottoman rule, prime minister of Greece (1910–16), leader of national government against the Greek monarchy (1916–17), prime minister (1917–20, 1924, 1928–32 and again for seven months in 1933). He lived in exile in Paris after the abortive antimonarchist rising and civil war in 1935. Liberal republican, believer in the Greek *Megala Idée* of reviving the Greek empire of classical and pre-Ottoman days, he was also markedly Anglophil and Francophil, wishing to bring Greece into WW1 on the side of the Allies against Germany and Turkey. His ambitions led him and his country into military invasion of Turkey in 1920, with British encouragement, but they were not strong enough against the revived Turkish nationalist forces led by ATATÜRK, the end being ignominious defeat and flight, the sack, with massacre, of the largely Greek-inhabited city of Smyrna and a wholesale exchange of populations as part of the peace settlement. Thereafter, the basis of his electoral strength in the island and frontier provinces of Greece more recently freed of Ottoman rule lost much of its *raison d'être*. His legacy was a Greece still divided between monarchist, authoritarian centralism and various forms of urban, rural and island protest.   DCW

Ventris, Michael George Francis (b. Wheathampstead, Herts., UK, 22.7.1922; d. Hatfield, Herts., 6.9.1956). Professional architect but noted for his achievements in deciphering the Mycenaean script known as Linear B. Working for more than 10 years Ventris eventually broke the script in June 1952, publishing his preliminary findings jointly with his collaborator John Chadwick under the title 'Evidence for Greek dialect in the Mycenaean archives' in *Journal of Hellenic Studies*, LXXIII (1953). The definitive publication, again jointly with Chadwick, showed it to be an archaic form of Greek and appeared as *Documents in Mycenaean Greek* (Cambridge, 1956). He was killed in a car accident at the age of 34.   BWC

J. Chadwick, *The Decipherment of Linear B* (Cambridge, 1958).

Venturi, Franco (b. Rome, Italy, 16.5.1914). Italian historian. Son of the art historian Lionello Venturi, he followed his father, who refused to swear loyalty to the Fascist regime, into exile in France, where he wrote his first book *La jeunesse de Diderot* [Diderot's youth] (Paris, 1939). He fought in the Spanish civil war and was an active member of the Resistance in his native Piedmont before returning to historical research. His appointment as cultural attaché to the Italian embassy in Moscow gave him access to archives for his major work *Il Populismo Russo* (Turin, 1952; *Roots of Revolution*, London, 1960), a study of Herzen, Bakunin and others seen as 'a page of the history of the European socialist movement'. Since then he has taught in Turin and confined himself, more or less, to the history of the Enlightenment, especially in Italy. His second major work *Settecento Riformatore* [18c reformers] (vol. 1: *Da Muratori a Beccaria* [From Muratori to

Beccaria], Turin, 1969; vol. 2: *La Chiesa e la Repubblica* [The church and the republic], Turin, 1970; vol. 3: *La Prima Crisi dell'Antico Regime* [The first crisis of the ancien regime], Turin, 1979) is still unfinished. His Trevelyan lectures *Utopia and Reform in the Enlightenment* (Cambridge, 1971) and his selected essays *Italy and the Enlightenment* (London, 1972) give a fair idea of his approach.

Venturi has always focused on the political history of ideas, the study of the functions of ideas in actual political situations, as opposed to more philosophical or sociological approaches, which he finds respectively too abstract and too reductionist. One of the first to react against CROCE, yet no MARXist, a socialist but not a utopian, Venturi is somewhat isolated in contemporary Italy.   UPB

Venturi, Robert (b. Philadelphia, Pa, USA, 25.6.1925). American architect and writer on architectural theory whose work has done much to influence the development of architecture in its struggle to outgrow the purist approach of the early modern movement. His first book *Complexity and Contradiction in Architecture* (NY, 1966) was claimed by the American historian Vincent Scully to be the most influential writing on contemporary architectural thought and action since LE CORBUSIER's *Vers une architecture* (1923). Venturi drew attention to the many long-lasting qualities of architecture which the earlier, narrow-based functionalism ignored, pointing out, for example, the dichotomy which the requirements of the practical programme set up between plan form and elevational treatment. His later book *Learning from Las Vegas* (Cambridge, Mass., 1972), written with his wife Denise Scott Brown, and Steven Izenour, analyses the nature of the American suburbs, where a distinction is made between one type of building which announces its function externally through its imagery, the so-called 'duck', and the other basic type, a simple practical structure which conveys its use-pattern through the medium of conventional applied archetypal shapes – the 'decorated shed'. The result of this writ-

VERTOV

ten work, together with the buildings of his practice, done in collaboration with his wife and his partner John Rauch, have caused many young architects to look anew at the buildings which make up the environment and to incorporate 'pop' features into their designs without necessarily reverting to simple-minded historicism. NW

D. Dunster (ed.), *Venturi and Rauch: the Public Buildings* (London, 1978).

Vertov, Dziga, ps. of Denis Arkadyevich Kaufman (b. Bialystok, Grodno, Russia [now Poland], 2.1.1896; d. Moscow, USSR, 12.2.1954). Russian director and theoretician of documentary films. Vertov entered the Soviet cinema during the postrevolutionary civil war, touring the country in a propaganda train and making newsreels and his first feature-length compilation film *Godovshchina revolyutsii* [The anniversary of the revolution] (1919). In August 1922 Vertov and his Cine-eye (*Kinoglaz*) group published their call to action: *My. Variant manifesta* (Moscow, 1922; *We. Variant of a Manifesto* in *The Film Factory: Soviet Cinema in documents, 1917–36,* eds R. Taylor & I. Christie, London, 1983). They asserted that 'the future of cinema art lies in a rejection of its present', which was 'leprous', and extolled the virtues of the machine, and particularly the camera, in creating new Soviet man and new Soviet reality. Their second manifesto *Kinoki. Perevorot* (Moscow, 1923; *The Cine-eyes. A Revolution* in *The Film Factory,* op. cit.) claimed: 'I am the Cine-eye. I am the mechanical eye. I, the machine, show you the world as only I can see it.' Vertov's ideas on the construction of new reality through dynamic editing (*montage*) were tested in the series of *Kinopravda* (Cine-truth) newsreels (1922–4) and in a series of feature-length documentaries, *Shagai, Sovet! (Forward, Soviet,* 1926), *Shestaia chast' mira (A Sixth Part of the World,* 1926), *Odinnadtsatyi (The Eleventh Year,* 1928), and *Chelovek skinoapparatom (The Man with the Movie Camera,* 1929). Vertov experimented next with editing sound both in harmony with and in counterpoint to edited images: *Simfoniia Donbassa (The Symphony of the Donbass,* known also as *Enthusiasm,* 1930), *Tri*

pesni o Lenine (Three Songs of Lenin, 1934) and *Kolybel'naya (Lullaby,* 1937). Vertov fell from favour in the 1930s as his films were inaccessible to mass audiences but he remains perhaps the most important theoretician of documentary cinema. RTay

Verwoerd, Hendrik Frensch (b. Amsterdam, The Netherlands, 8.9.1901; d. Cape Town, South Africa, 6.9.1966). South African prime minister. The son of Dutch missionaries, Verwoerd became the most powerful Afrikaner politician of his generation, the theoretician and architect of *apartheid.* He followed a familiar Afrikaner career pattern, moving from academic life (at Stellenbosch University) to journalism (editor of *Die Transvaaler,* 1937–48) and finally to politics as leader of the National party in the Senate and minister for native affairs (1950–9), prime minister (1958–66). During the war he made no secret of his anti-British, pro-German sentiments; in 1961 he achieved the ambition long cherished by many Afrikaners of making South Africa a republic and subsequently withdrawing from the Commonwealth. His most substantial achievement was to provide the legislative framework for the system of 'separate development' (*apartheid*). Rejecting the crude old Boer notion of the permanent inferiority of the 'kaffir', he believed that every 'race' must be allowed to develop its own potentialities in its own environment. Hence the establishment of a system of Bantu education and the provision for an entirely self-governing Bantu 'homelands' based on the old 'native reserves'. Hence, too, his determination to apply draconian measures to repress black political movements based on urban areas which he regarded as forming part of 'white South Africa'. Aloof but unassuming, Verwoerd was a reassuring leader for many white South Africans. Dictatorial towards his colleagues, he was dogmatic to the point of fanaticism in his views. He was assassinated by a mentally deranged white man in the chamber of the South African parliament. A. N. Pelzer has edited *Verwoerd Speaks: Speeches, 1948–66* (Johannesburg, 1966). RH

A. Hepple-Jones, *Verwoerd* (London, 1967).

Verzijl, Jan Hendrik Willem (b. Utrecht, The Netherlands, 31.8.1888). Dutch international lawyer. He was educated at the University of Utrecht where he became a professor in 1919. He also held chairs at Amsterdam and Leiden. He undertook some work for the Dutch government in the practice of international law but his main importance and his reputation today rest on his academic work; he is the outstanding figure in international law in the Netherlands. Few living writers on international law have greater authority and experience than Verzijl. He has produced an immense number of articles on almost every aspect of international law, written in many different languages. His major works are the *Jurisprudence of the World Court* (Leiden, 1965), an important commentary on the work of the court, and the monumental, still unfinished, *International Law in Historical Perspective* (10 vols, Leiden, 1968–). His wide-ranging knowledge of legal and political history makes this very different from the usual type of textbook, and the size of the task that he began when already over 70 demonstrates his dedication to his subject. CDG

Vian, Boris (b. Ville-d'Avray, Seine-et-Oise, France, 10.3.1920; d. Paris, 23.6.1959). French novelist and musician. One of the most charismatic figures in the bohemian world of postwar Paris, Vian first won public acclaim as a jazz trumpeter and soon enjoyed the reputation of being the 'prince' of the cellar clubs of St-Germain-des-Prés. An accomplished musician, he was also an influential critic and his articles in *Jazz Hot* did much to establish a French audience for modern jazz. He achieved literary notoriety with *J'Irai cracher sur vos tombes* (Paris, 1947; tr. B. Vian, *I Will Spit on your Tombs*, Paris, 1947), a novel allegedly translated from the American and published under the pseudonym 'Vernon Sullivan', which provoked a scandal because of its treatment of sexual and racial themes. After an obscenity trial in 1947, the novel was banned in 1949. The scandal largely overshadowed the merits of the novels published by Vian under his own name, the best being *L'Ecume des jours* (Paris, 1947; tr. J. Sturrock, *Mood Indigo*, NY, 1968) and *L'Automne à Pékin* [Autumn in Peking] (Paris, 1947). Although virtually ignored on publication, these later established a cult reputation and now enjoy very widespread popularity, largely because of their combination of extraordinary verbal inventiveness, humour and their highly poetic sense of pathos. Vian's songs and poems display a similar fascination with word play and are further typified by their subversive humour and antimilitarist sentiments. Vian was the translator of works by CHANDLER, Peter Cheyney and A.E. Van Vogt. DM

Vicens Vives, Jaime (b. Gerona, Spain, 6.6.1910; d. Lyons, Rhône, France, 27.6.1960). Spanish historian. Vicens Vives drew attention to himself with his doctoral thesis on Ferdinand the Catholic and the city of Barcelona. A patriotic Catalan, involved in the civil war on the Republican side, he was excluded from university teaching until 1947, and had to live by his pen. After his appointment as professor at Saragossa and later Barcelona, he was able to channel his abundant energy into the establishment of economic and social history in Spain, a history more or less on the model of FEBVRE, Marc BLOCH and BRAUDEL. His *Historia de los remensas* [History of the 'remensas'] (Barcelona, 1945) dealt with serfdom and social conflict in 15c Spain. His *Approximación a la historia de España* (Barcelona, 1952; *Approaches to the History of Spain*, Berkeley, Calif., 1970) emphasized geopolitical factors in Spanish history, more especially the contrast and conflicts between the inward-looking centre and the outward-looking periphery. He also edited a five-volume economic and social history of Spain and Spanish America, and produced a *Manual de Historia Económica de España* (Barcelona, 1959; *Economic History of Spain*, Princeton, 1969). His missionary activities in favour of economic and social history did not lead him to neglect the political dimension; in addition to his thesis, he published two studies of Ferdinand the Catholic.

Singlehanded and in less favourable circumstances than his French colleagues, Vicens Vives's achievement was not on the scale of that of Bloch and Febvre, and his 'school' was relatively small. But no Spanish historian this century has done so much to make his colleagues more outward-looking.   UPB

Vidal de la Blache, Paul (b. Pézenas, Hérault, France, 21.1.1845; d. Tamaris-sur-Mer, Var, 5.4.1918). French geographer. At first an historian and classical scholar, following his graduation at the Ecole Normale Supérieure he spent three years in Athens. He became a university teacher at Nancy in 1872 and moved to Paris in 1877. In Nancy he developed the knowledge that he used in his last work *France de l'Est* [The east of France] (Paris, 1917, ³1919), but his most famous book is the *Tableau de la géographie de la France* [Portrait of the geography of France] (Paris, 1903). As a man of his time, he was eager to give a worldview of human geography, best seen in his *Atlas Vidal-Lablache* (Paris, 1894, ⁶1951) which covers the whole of human history in its physical setting. After his death a number of his papers on human geography were collected together by de Martonne in *Principes de géographie humaine* (Paris, 1921; *Principles of Human Geography*, Chicago, 1926). He was a classic example of a geographer concerned at one and the same time with the whole world and his immediate environment.   TWF

T. W. Freeman, 'Vidal de la Blache', in *The Geographer's Craft* (Manchester, 1967).

Vigo, Jean (b. Paris, France, 24.4.1905; d. Paris, 5.10.1934). French film director. Dying at the tragically early age of 29, Vigo was able to complete less than three hours of film in all. Yet he ranks as a major figure in the French cinema. Vigo had already made a silent documentary study of the Riviera *A Propos de Nice* (1929), and a short documentary on the swimmer Jean Taris, when he began work on the 47-minute *Zéro de Conduite* (*Zero for Conduct*, 1933). Here, in his portrait of a repressive school system countered by a schoolboy revolt, he was able to draw on his own school

background and attitudes inherited from his father, a noted anarchist murdered in prison. The film leavens its precise observation with humour and caricature, but was authentic and powerful enough to be banned for a dozen years. In the feature-length *L'Atalante* (1934) Vigo turned to adult relationships, showing the loves, quarrels and misunderstandings of a young bargee and his wife. Again Vigo was able to achieve a unique poetry out of a synthesis of realistic detail and fantastic exaggeration (the figure of the mate, played by Michel Simon). Vigo died soon after the opening of *L'Atalante*, which was for a time mutilated by its distributors and dubbed with an irrelevant popular song. But his voice persists into the present, and he remains an example to all who struggle for an independent cinema, as the tributes in such films as TRUFFAUT's *Les Quatre Cent Coups* (1959) and Lindsay Anderson's *If ...* (1968) testify.   RPA

P. E. S. Gomes, *Jean Vigo* (London, 1972); J. M. Smith, *Jean Vigo* (London, 1972).

Vilar, Jean (b. Sète, Hérault, France, 25.3.1912; d. Sète, 28.5.1971). French actor, theatre director and manager. After studying with Charles Dullin, and codirecting a provincial touring company during WW2, he inaugurated in 1947 the annual theatre festival at Avignon with which he remained associated for over 20 years. In 1951 he became director of the Théâtre National Populaire, which he revitalized by the formation of a quasi-permanent company and his progressive ideas on organization, artistic policy and relations with the public. Adapting COPEAU's notion of the 'bare platform' to the vast stage of the 3000-seat auditorium in the Palais de Chaillot, he jettisoned the divisive elements of curtain and footlights and curtailed sets in favour of imaginative lighting and costume, which benefit the moving actor. His repertoire was impressively catholic but attracted criticism for allegedly reflecting left-wing sympathies and a bias towards contemporary relevance. Audiences, however, remained loyal, sustained by low seat-prices, young people's matinées, post-performance discussions and other 'demystifying' innovations as well as by the excitingly high standard of direction and acting (see *De la tradition théâtrale* [On theatre tradition], Paris, 1955, ²1963). Vilar resigned in 1963 to oversee the expansion of the Avignon festival into an international event, but his work at the TNP has served as a model and inspiration for other state-subsidized theatres in Paris and the provinces. DHR

C. Roy, *Jean Vilar* (Paris, 1968).

Visconti, Luchino (b. Milan, Lombardy, Italy, 2.11.1906; d. Rome, 17.3.1976). Italian film director. As Duke of Modrone and descendant of the aristocratic rulers of Milan, breeder of racehorses and outstanding producer of opera at La Scala, Visconti is an unlikely member of the Italian neorealist movement. Yet after a spell in France working with Jean RENOIR, Visconti emerged as a committed MARXist, and his first two films *Ossessione* (*Obsession*, 1942) and *La Terra Trema* (*The Earth Trembles*, 1948) are both outstanding works of neorealist inspiration, showing a clear sympathy for the poor and underprivileged and a keen sense of the political realities of the mid-1940s. *La Terra Trema* in particular is a work of outstanding power, which takes its text from a Verga novel but is acted by untrained fishermen and spoken in Sicilian dialect. It is clear, however, that the choice of a neorealist approach owes as much to the spirit of the time as to Visconti's deeper aspirations (he followed the austere *La Terra Trema* with a production of Shakespeare's *As You Like It* with sets by DALI). In retrospect one can see that the films derive as much from Visconti's sense of character and dramatic structure as from their surface realism, and subsequently he was to develop a vein of realism more openly related to the traditions of the 19c novel. Films like *Senso* (*The Wanton Contessa*, 1954), *Il Gattopardo* (*The Leopard*, 1963), *Morte a Venezia* (*Death in Venice*, 1970) and *L'Innocente* (*The Innocent*, 1975) use colour, spectacle and star players to create a sumptuously realized period reconstruction, but the characters are always placed in relation to the social forces and upheavals of

their time. Thus Visconti, for all his taste for opulence and operatic effect, remains one of the cinema's true realists. RPA

G. Nowell-Smith, *Luchino Visconti* (London, 1967); M. Stirling, *A Screen of Time* (London, 1979).

Vittorini, Elio (b. Syracuse, Sicily, Italy, 23.7.1908; d. Milan, Lombardy, 12.2.1966). Italian novelist and journalist. Although his formal education was minimal, he taught himself English and worked as a newspaper editor and translator of English and American novelists during the 1930s. He became an active antifascist during the period of the Spanish civil war and from then on was involved in the production of communist underground newspapers, becoming chief editor of *L'Unità* by 1945. He founded and directed *Il Politecnico* (1945–7), which aimed at fostering a new, popular-based morality of commitment and tolerance, eschewing the cultural elitism which had hitherto characterized Italy. He worked for 'a culture which protects from suffering, which fights it and eradicates it', rather than the traditional one of 'consolation'. As editor of *Il Menabò* (1959–66) and of important, innovatory series of texts for the publishers Bompiani, Einaudi and Mondadori, Vittorini continued to promote the works of foreign and new Italian writers in the postwar period, advocating a literature which reflected life in a technologically advanced society and rejecting all nostalgia for Italy's agrarian past as false and anachronistic. His own, essentially lyrical novels, especially *Conversazione in Sicilia* (Milan, 1941; tr. W. David, *Conversation in Sicily*, Harmondsworth, 1961) and *Uomini e no* [Men and not men] (Milan, 1945), true to his cultural ideals, aimed at the creation of authentic contemporary myths, endeavouring to seek out ways of setting 'the offended world' to rights. ADT

S. Pacifici, *A Guide to Contemporary Italian Narrative* (NY, 1962); D. Heiney, *Three Italian writers: Moravia, Pavese, Vittorini* (Ann Arbor, 1968).

Vivekananda, Swami, ps. of Narendranath Datta (b. Calcutta, W. Bengal, India, 12.1.1863; d. Calcutta, 4.7.1902).

Indian spiritual leader. Like many English-educated Hindus he had joined the Brahmo Samaj, a modern theistic movement, but from 1884 he followed the traditional Hindu saint Ramakrishna (1836–86), after whose death he became a *sannyasi* [monk]. His lecture tours in the USA and UK (1893–6, 1899–1900) impressed many, not only on account of his rhetoric and showmanship, but also because of his evident familiarity with Hinduism and the ease with which he presented it in western terms. His western success won him admirers throughout India among those who knew English, the language in which he mainly taught. In 1897 he organized the Ramakrishna Mission, staffed by *sannyasis* and devoted to charitable work in India and worldwide teaching. The true Hinduism, he held, was Advaita Vedanta which regards all phenomena as imperfect manifestations of one reality. Enlisting western idealism and evolutionary ideas in its support, he did much to restore Advaita to its present prestige among modern Hindus after a period in which it had been largely rejected as hampering progress; he presented it as the most rational and scientific creed, and a cure both for India's backwardness and for western materialism. His ideas influenced Aurobindo Ghose, Aldous HUXLEY, ISHERWOOD, RADHAKRISHNAN and Romain Rolland. *The Complete Works of Swami Vivekananda* (8 vols, Calcutta) were published between 1972 and 1978, following the appearance of several less complete editions.   DHK

Vlaminck, Maurice (b. Paris, France, 4.4.1876; d. Rueil-la-Gadelière, Eur-et-Loire, 11.10.1958). French fauve painter, of Flemish stock. Virtually self-taught, Vlaminck was also a professional racing cyclist, and played the violin in a theatre to earn a living. In 1899–1900 he met DERAIN with whom he formed the Ecole de Chatou. Rejecting an academic or intellectual approach to art, Vlaminck wished to express his feelings in paint without reference to the art of the past. After the 1901 Van Gogh retrospective, where Derain introduced him to MATISSE, he adopted Van Gogh's gestural brushstrokes and bright palette. To heighten impact, he used more strident colour combinations than Van Gogh, especially red, orange, pink and yellows, straight from the tube (e.g. *Circus*, 1906). Vlaminck took part in the 1905 Salon d'Automne where he, Derain, Matisse and others were dubbed 'fauve' or 'wild' by the critic Louis Vauxcelles. After a superficial interest in CÉZANNE (e.g. *Flood at Ivry*, 1908) and cubism (*Self-Portrait*, 1910), his disregard for structure led him (c. 1915) to an idiosyncratic expressionist realism using acute perspectives, gestural brushwork and sombre colours to depict rural scenes reminiscent of 17c Dutch landscapes (e.g. *Winter Landscape*, 1935).
                                    SOBT

P. Selz, *Vlaminck* (NY, 1963); P. Cabanne, *Vlaminck* (Paris, 1966).

Von Neumann, Johann (b. Budapest, Austria-Hungary [now Hungary], 3.12.1903; naturalized American citizen, 1937; d. Washington, DC, USA, 8.2.1957). Hungarian/American mathematician. Von Neumann was an infant prodigy who went on to qualify in chemistry at Berlin University, in chemical engineering at the Technische Hochschule in Zürich, and in mathematics at Budapest University. His definition of ordinal numbers, published at the age of 20, has been universally adopted. Von Neumann matured rapidly as a mathematician, working at the universities of Berlin (1926–9) and Hamburg (1929–30), and then moving to Princeton (1931), first to the university, then to the Institute for Advanced Study (1933) where he spent the rest of his life. Up to WW2 the bulk of Von Neumann's work (150 papers in all) was in pure mathematics. In 1932 he published a formulation and proof of the ergodic hypothesis of statistical mathematics and a book on quantum mechanics, *Mathematische Grundlagen der Quentenmechanik* [The mathematical bases of quantum mechanics], which is still a standard text. In the late 1930s, in collaboration with F. J. Murray, he published an important work on 'rings of operators' (since called Von Neumann algebras) which proved to be of value in quantum theory. During WW2 Von Neumann worked on the theory of the atomic bomb, and this directed his attention to problems of computation. In computer theory he did pioneering work on logical design; the problems of securing reliable answers from a machine with unreliable components; the function of memory; matching imitation of randomness; and the problem of constructing automata capable of reproducing their own kind. There is doubt about the origin of the concept of a stored-program computer, but no doubt that Von Neumann produced its classical formulation. RAH

Bulletin of the American Mathematical Society, 64 (May 1958) was devoted to Von Neumann's life and work.

In economics Von Neumann became universally known for two path-breaking contributions, both mathematical and conceptual. One was his multi-sector model of economic growth, an English version of which appeared in the *Review of Economic Studies* (1945–6). This was concerned with the formal properties of efficient growth paths, i.e. paths which maximize the economy's rate of growth over some very long period. In Von Neumann's economic system commodities are used wholly as inputs into given technological processes to produce increased quantities of the same commodities. Even with these highly abstract assumptions the delineation of possible growth paths and the exhaustive analysis of their properties was a major intellectual achievement. The mathematical basis of Von Neumann's model – a set of linear simultaneous equations – is the same as that used in input-output analysis (see LEONTIEF), activity analysis and linear programming. His other legacy in economics is the theory of games, which he and Oskar Morgenstern created in their monumental *Theory of Games and Economic Behavior* (NY, 1944). This studies the problems of rational behaviour in situations of interdependent decision-making, i.e. where one's own course of action depends, or should depend, on what one's competitor or colleague is likely to do (and vice versa). Concepts (such as 'zero-sum' and 'prisoner's dilemma') devised by game theorists have gradually found their way into

ordinary (or at least semiordinary) discourse. PMO

R. D. Luce & H. Raiffa, *Games and Decisions* (NY, 1957); J. Vanek, *Maximal Economic Growth* (Ithaca, NY, 1968).

Vorster, Balthazar Johannes (b. Jamestown, Cape Province, South Africa, 13.12.1915). South African prime minister. Succeeding the assassinated VERWOERD as prime minister in 1966, Vorster dominated the South African scene in an almost Bismarckian manner for a decade. Regarded as an extreme right-winger – he had been detained during WW2 on account of his pro-Nazi views – he proved an extremely tough minister of justice (1961–7) and was responsible for many stringent measures designed to remove or silence South African dissidents. As prime minister, he acted more pragmatically in the field of foreign affairs and was the architect of the policy of 'dialogue' and 'detente' with black African states, a policy largely contradicted by the South African intervention in Angola in 1975. In internal affairs his premiership was marked by no significant changes in the structure of *apartheid*. The granting of independence to the black 'homelands', beginning with the Transkei in 1976, was a logical development of the policy laid down by Verwoerd. In 1978 Vorster was elected state president on retirement from the premiership, but was later forced to resign, when he was seen to be implicated in the 'Muldergate' scandal. His *Selected Speeches* (Bloemfontein, 1973) have been edited by O. Geyser. RH

Vossler, Karl (b. Hohenheim, nr Stuttgart, Baden-Württemberg, Germany, 6.9.1872; d. Munich, Bavaria, West Germany, 18.5.1949). German linguist and Romance scholar. He held chairs at Heidelberg (1902), Würzburg (1909) and Munich (1911). His deep and continually broadening love of Romance culture, especially Italian, is reflected in the wide range of his publications on literature (works on Dante, Racine, La Fontaine, Lope de Vega) and linguistic topics. An ambitious theorist rather than a practical philologist, he sought to explain literary and linguistic developments from a general, cultural perspective, rejecting materialist accounts. His work in linguistics (see *Positivismus und Idealismus in der Sprachforschung* [Positivism and idealism in linguistic research], Heidelberg, 1904, and *Geist und Kultur in der Sprache*, Heidelberg, 1925; *The Spirit of Language in Civilization*, London, 1932) shows a consequent rejection of deterministic explanations of sound change (neogrammarian 'sound laws'), and an emphasis on aesthetic and stylistic factors in the origination and diffusion of change under the influence of the Italian linguist CROCE. Thus Vossler, within a historical perspective, stressed the creative and conscious individual (especially the great writer) in the development of language and culture, and has been criticized for overemphasizing the literary element. His individualism should be set against his evocation of progressing and evolving national and human culture. He belongs to the Humboldtian, idealist tradition in linguistics, one antithetical to the scientific aspirations of American structuralism. He was retired early by the Nazis, but reinstated at the age of 73. CMH

I. Iordan-Orr, *An Introduction to Romance Linguistics* (rev. R. Posner, Oxford, 1970).

Voulkos, Peter (b. Bozeman, Mont., USA, 29.1.1924). American studio potter. Originally trained as a painter at Montana State University and graduating in 1949, he then turned to ceramics, and studied at the California College of Arts and Crafts. Thus he was placed firmly in the centre of that artistic movement known as action painting or abstract expressionism, adapting its approach and methods to ceramics. He regards his work as sculpture in clay; and he employs assistants to throw basic shapes which he then manipulates. Much of his work is very large. He applies a theory of continuous active exploration of, and search for, what may be done with each individual piece of clay. He believes that the arrival of any conscious understanding of what the potter is doing marks the end of the creative act. His large platters he treats almost as canvases, scattering the surfaces with blobs and pellets of clay, streaks and scratches. Voulkos has taught throughout his working life, and in 1958 he became a member of the faculty at Berkeley, an appointment which enabled him to achieve widespread dissemination of his ideas. From the mid-1950s onwards Voulkos rejected all previous standards of fine craftsmanship, just as many contemporary painters seemed to be doing, in order to achieve what he regarded as autonomous, authentic work, embodying life to the full. PSR

Vuillard, Jean Edouard (b. Cuiseaux, Saône-et-Loire, France, 11.11.1868; d. La Baule, Morbihan, 21.6.1940). French painter. He was one of the *Nabis*, a symbolist group influenced by Gauguin which included BONNARD, Maurice Denis and Sérusier; they banded together while at the Académie Julian in 1889 and continued to exhibit as a group throughout the 1890s. Prior to this Vuillard studied at the Ecole des Beaux Arts under Gérôme. From 1891 he frequented intellectual and literary circles, including Mallarmé's famous Tuesday evenings. He was closely associated with *La Revue Blanche* for which he made lithographs. Together with that of Bonnard, his painting has been dubbed 'intimist' for its subject matter, drawn from the tranquil everyday life of middle-class homes and the settings of drawing rooms, kitchens and local parks and gardens. Although often linked with Bonnard's, Vuillard's style differs substantially in its greater tonality, more restricted palette and the emphasis on patterning. He also produced graphic work, designed stage sets and painted decorative panels; Japanese prints were an influence on much of his art. While his painting was adventurous in colour and pattern in the 1890s and achieved a certain stability in the 1900s, it became more conventional formally in the 1930s but with some surprising innovations in subject matter, such as a hospital operating theatre and factory interiors. MOJN

A. C. Richie, *Edouard Vuillard* (NY, 1954); J. Russell, *Vuillard* (London, 1971).

Vygotsky, Lev Semyonovich (b. Orsha, Russia, 17.11.1896; d. Moscow, USSR, 11.6.1934). Russian psychologist whose theories of cognitive development, in particular his view of the relationship between language and thinking, have strongly influenced both MARXist and western psychology. Although his main life's work was concentrated into the 10 years between 1924, when he moved to the Institute of Psychology at Moscow, and his death, many of his insights have only recently become accessible to western readers in translation. As a whole, his work is extraordinarily varied and unorthodox. Although he worked within the assumptions of dialectical materialism, he rejected the fashionable reflexology of his experimental precursors. His best-known work *Myshlenie i rech* (Moscow, 1934; *Thought and Language*, Cambridge, Mass., 1962) was briefly suppressed as being against the STALINist-approved approach to psychology; today, however, his contributions are given an honoured place in his homeland. His openness to intuition, his undogmatic approach to experimental methodology, and the ease with which he moved back and forth between pure and applied fields, help to explain the richness of his output. Overall, he emphasizes the role of cultural and social factors in the development of cognition. Society provides symbolic tools which shape thinking, and language is the most important of these. His views on language and the internalization of action have influenced the development of PIAGET's theory and that of BRUNER. In the educational field, he put forward the concept of the 'zone of proximal development' – the gap between the child's present performance and the competence that can be developed through instruction – which looks ahead to current concerns about finding the learning experience for a child which best matches the stage he or she has reached. His block materials for studying the development of concept formation have been widely used in clinical psychology as a diagnostic instrument and have significantly advanced research into the nature of thought disorder in psychopathology. Many of his concerns are represented in the work of his distinguished disciple LURIA.   RRS

W

van der Waals, Johannes Dederik (b. Leiden, S. Holland, The Netherlands, 23.11.1837; d. Amsterdam, 8.3.1923). Dutch physicist. Van der Waals came late to a scientific career but his first published work, his doctoral dissertation at Leiden (1873) was, as J. C. Maxwell said, to put him immediately among the foremost scientists of his age. There are three simple states of matter: solids, liquids and gases, the first of which is always a distinct phase, but the latter two of which can be changed one into the other by suitable changes of pressure and temperature. These facts were first stated clearly by Thomas Andrews of Belfast in 1869, and it was his work that van der Waals sought to interpret. His tools, newly created by Maxwell and BOLTZMANN, were the rudiments of kinetic theory and statistical mechanics. Van der Waals contributed nothing to the formal development of these subjects but proved to be a master at devising suitable approximations, with sound physical bases, by which they could be applied to real physical problems. The mastery was shown in his dissertation *Over de Continuiteit van Gas- en Vlœistoftœstand* (*On the Continuity of the Gas and Liquid States* in *Physical Memoirs*, 1 [1890], 333). It led him to a simple equation between the pressure, volume and temperature of a fluid, which is still known by his name, while the treatment on which he relied is known now as a mean-field approximation. With perhaps less justification his name is also often attached to the attractive forces between molecules. His skill in approximation was later shown in his theory of fluid mixtures and, more strikingly, in a theory of surface tension which introduced the key idea that the free energy of an inhomogeneous system depended not only on its density but on the gradient of the density. Van der Waals's work was unaccountably neglected in the 50 years after 1914, but is now widely discussed. His career was spent at the University of Amsterdam

(1877–1907); he was awarded the Nobel prize for physics in 1910.   JSR

Wach, Joachim (b. Chemnitz, Saxony, Germany [now East Germany], 25.1.1898; naturalized American citizen; d. Orselina, Switzerland, 27.8.1955). German/American student of comparative religion. He conceived *Religionswissenschaft* [the science of religion] to have three areas of interest, hermeneutics (the theory of understanding), the study of religious experience and the sociology of religion. In an attempt to integrate these areas and isolate the universal features of religion, Wach argued that any religious experience tends to find expression in three fields of human activity, theoretical (theology, cosmology, anthropology), practical (cults) and sociological (religious fellowship and community). Wach insisted (*Sociology of Religion*, Chicago, 1944) on the corporate nature of religion and on the value of sociological investigation of the relation between empirical religion and society, reflecting Max WEBER's theories, but he refused to see religious life as an epiphenomenon of social structure, preferring – echoing the influence of OTTO – to understand the integration of individuals within the religious community on the basis of shared, profoundly impressive religious experiences. He also argued, rather controversially, that hermeneutics for *Religionswissenschaft*, in order to grasp intuitively the qualitative differences between religious traditions and to understand the meaning of each as a living totality, requires religious instinct and subjectivity. Among his most important works are *Types of Religious Experience* (Chicago, 1951) and *The Comparative Study of Religions* (NY, 1958).   LPS

Waddington, Conrad Hall (b. Evesham, Here. & Worcs., UK, 8.11.1905; d. Edinburgh, Lothian, 26.9.1975). British geneticist. Having trained as a geologist, Waddington turned to genetics and developmental biology at a time of great activity in both fields. His early work in Cambridge extended that of the SPE-MANN school in demonstrating embryonic induction of the central nervous system in birds. He was later, in Edinburgh, to be a prolific contributor to both genetics and embryology, and above all to the theoretical understanding of their problems. He produced convincing experimental evidence that the action of selection upon a genetically heterogeneous population may mimic the inheritance of acquired characteristics. His evolutionary thinking was forcefully presented in his *The Strategy of the Genes* (London, 1957). Throughout his career he was much concerned with the interactions between science and the arts, perhaps notably the visual arts, and between biology and philosophy. This found expression in *The Scientific Attitude* (Harmondsworth, 1941) and *The Ethical Animal* (London, 1961).

DRN

Wagenfeld, Wilhelm (b. Bremen, Germany, 15.4.1900). German industrial designer. Wagenfeld was one of the leading designers of his generation. Trained first as a silversmith, he later studied at the Weimar Bauhaus producing, in collaboration with K. J. Jucker, that classic of early Bauhaus design, the metal and glass table-lamp (1923–4) which was singled out by GROPIUS and MOHOLY-NAGY as a prototype for mass-production. (Wagenfeld himself was more sceptical: 'These designs ... were, in fact, extremely costly craft designs.') As he established closer links with industry, Wagenfeld became increasingly critical of Bauhaus attitudes to industrial production and, more significantly, those of the *Deutscher Werkbund* (of which he was a member from 1925). He did not move to the Dessau Bauhaus but remained in Weimar working first as assistant and from 1929 as director of the metal workshop of the Bauhochschule. From the late 1920s onwards he received numerous commissions from leading manufacturers. In 1935 he was appointed artistic director of the Lausitzer Glaswerke, with a brief to improve design quality at all levels. Wagenfeld designed a wide range of articles for commercial and domestic use, including heat-resistant glassware, porcelain, light fittings and door furniture. The most memorable of his designs combine Bauhaus formal ideals with a mastery of the material and of the production process (e.g. the glass tea-service, c. 1932; the 'Kubus' range of modular, stacking kitchen containers in pressed glass, c. 1938). Since WW2 Wagenfeld has published *Wesen und Gestalt der Dinge um uns* [The nature and shape of the things around us] (Potsdam, 1948) and has continued to work as a teacher, designer and design consultant, establishing the Werkstatt Wagenfeld in Stuttgart in 1954 for research and development in industrial design.

CAB

Wilhelm Wagenfeld: vom Bauhaus in der Industrie, exh. cat. (Cologne, 1973).

Wagner, Wieland Adolf Gottfried (b. Bayreuth, Bavaria, Germany, 5.1.1917; d. Munich, West Germany, 17.10.1966). German operatic producer and scenic designer; grandson of Richard Wagner. His career as stage designer began with the 1937 *Parsifal* at Bayreuth, and in the early 1940s he designed and produced opera at Nuremberg and Altenburg. In 1951 he and his brother Wolfgang as codirectors revived the Bayreuth Festival. For the next 15 years he was much in demand at other houses, especially at Stuttgart, as well as at Bayreuth (where he produced all the works of his grandfather from *Der fliegende Holländer* [1843] to *Parsifal* [1882] at least once). His repertory was restricted – apart from Wagner, it consisted of *Fidelio*, *Carmen*, *Aida* and *Otello*, *Salome* and *Elektra*, *Wozzeck* and *Lulu*, Gluck's *Orfeo* and two works by Orff – but the intensity and rigour of his artistic approach exerted an influence that transcended his own sphere of activity, and lives on many years after his untimely death. His particular achievement in the early postwar years at Bayreuth was to make a virtue out of necessity by pruning back the luxuriant realistic detail of the typical older Wagner production, replacing literal adherence to stage directions with a new emphasis on simplicity of sets and basic action, imposition of new visual images, and powerful and expressive use of lighting (influenced by APPIA and his theories of 'active light' and 'living space'). If at times his productions were criticized for quirkishness, they were never dull or derivative. The finest of them, especially perhaps the 1951 Bayreuth *Parsifal*, set new standards of directness, epic breadth and depth of psychological penetration.   PJB

V. Gollancz, *The King at Bayreuth* (London, 1966); G. Skelton, *Wieland Wagner: the Positive Sceptic* (London, 1971).

Wajda, Andrzej (b. Suwałki, Poland, 6.3.1927). Polish film director. A product of the Łodz film school, Wajda began his career with a series of films on Poland's recent past. His war trilogy – *Pokolenie* (*A Generation*, 1955), *Kanał* (1957) and *Popiół i diament* (*Ashes and Diamonds*, 1958) – attempts to come to terms with the national experience and the three films show an increasing complexity and use of bitter irony as the director moves away from the prevalent notions of socialist realism and the positive hero. If Wajda's work in its beginnings has links with Italian neorealism, a new richness of style and symbolic imagery is shown by his fourth film *Lotna* (1959), a sumptuously coloured tale of Polish cavalry pitted against German tanks at the outbreak of war in 1939. Wajda continued producing prolifically throughout the 1960s and 1970s, but his touch was uneven and only rarely does most of this work – much of it made in coproduction with French, British and German companies – approach the qualities of his first trilogy. Three films, however, stand out for their unique and progressive insight into film-making under a Communist regime. *Wszystko na sprzedaż* (*Everything for Sale*, 1968) is a complex self-examination, provoked by the death of his friend, the actor Zbigniew Cybulski. Subtly interweaving fact and fiction, it remains a remarkable portrait, though couched in personal, not political, terms. *Człowiek z marmuru* (*Man of Marble*, 1977) continues this probing of the nature of film-making, but now some of the political pressures and constraints are more apparent in the story of a young film maker prevented from stating the truth about the STALINist era. With the temporary success of the Solidarity Union, however, Wajda was able to make *Człowiek z żelaza* (*Man of Iron*, 1981) which brings the earlier film up to date and presents a powerful (and now poignant) celebration of the coming of a new political order.   RPA

B. Michałek, *The Cinema of Andrzej Wajda* (London, 1973).

Walcott, Derek (b. Castries, St Lucia, Windward Islands, 23.1.1930). West Indian poet and dramatist, who has lived most of his life in Trinidad, the country which forms the human setting for Walcott's exploration of the history and landscape of the Caribbean. All of his writing displays a concerned complexity that owes much to modern British and American writers. *In A Green Night: Poems 1948–60* (London, 1962) shows a richness which establishes the relevance of the local West Indian setting without any striving for 'universality'. Walcott's extensive scholarship is always securely located in the specific, and in *Another Life* (London, 1973) the result is poetry impressive both in range and humanity. His plays, well represented by *The Dream on Monkey Mountain and Other Plays* (NY, 1971), owe much to folk and Creole patterns in their imagination and humour. Resonant with both historical awareness and everyday perceptions, Walcott's deeply personal voice has established the significance of the Caribbean experience with passion, dignity and wit.   PNQ

E. Baugh, *Derek Walcott* (London, 1978).

Wałęsa, Lech (b. Popowo, Mazowsze, Poland, 29.9.1943). Polish trade union leader. A leader in the 1980 strike in the Lenin shipyards in Gdansk which marked the beginning of the most serious crisis in the Soviet group of Communist states since the suppression of the Prague Spring in 1968. Lech Wałęsa was elected chairman of the committee which negotiated the charter of 30 August 1980 in which the Polish government conceded the right for workers to form independent trade unions with the rights to strike and to freedom of expression. He was then made chairman of the national confederation of all such unions, Solidarność [Solidarity]. Although neither Wałęsa nor the Polish government wished to force a political confrontation, it was impossible to avoid one, not least because of the hostile reaction of the Soviet Union and other East European regimes to recognition of Solidarity, a rival grassroots alternative to the Communist party as an authentic representative of the Polish working classes. In an effort to master the crisis and avoid open Soviet intervention, the minister of defence, General Jaruzelski, took over as prime minister in February 1981 and attempted to reach agreement with Solidarity. Nothing, however, could stop Solidarity (which by the time of its first congress in September 1981 numbered 9½ million members) putting forward demands for a democratic electoral system and a share of state power. Wałęsa himself was a moderate, criticized by the more radical members of the trade union movement, and a devout Catholic who kept in close touch with the Polish primate, Archbishop Glemp. The combination, however, of the natural gifts of the working-class leader (frequently described as charismatic but not demagogic) with his insistence on staying close to the workers he represented and his personal integrity enabled him to represent, as no one else in postwar Polish history, the aspirations of a frustrated nation still unreconciled to the imposition of an authoritarian Soviet regime. When Jaruzelski broke off negotiations and imposed martial law in December 1981, Lech Wałęsa was arrested and held in isolation for a year. On his release in December 1982, however, he showed no signs of having changed his views, and Poland was no nearer a resolution to the underlying conflicts which had now extended from the disastrous economic situation to a crisis of confidence in the regime. ALCB

Waley, Arthur David, *né* Schloss (b. Tunbridge Wells, Kent, UK, 19.8.1889; d. London, 27.6.1966). British orientalist and translator of Chinese and Japanese literature. He joined the British Museum in 1913; to catalogue the oriental paintings he taught himself Chinese and Japanese, and by 1918 had published his first volume of translations, *A Hundred and Seventy Chinese Poems* (London), followed by *More Translations from the Chinese* (London, 1919), *The Nō Plays of Japan* (London, 1921), *An Introduction to the Study of Chinese Painting* (London, 1923), and four more volumes of Chinese poetry. These are noted for their closeness to the spirit of the originals and for his use of 'sprung rhythm'. Although inspired partly by G. M. HOPKINS and Ezra POUND, Waley's original style influenced a generation of British poets.

He wrote biographies of Chinese poets: Po Chü-i (London, 1949), Li Po (London, 1950), and Yüan Mei (London, 1956), and books on Chinese Buddhism, of which the most popular was *Monkey* (London, 1942), a translation of a 16c Chinese novel. *The Way and its Power* (London, 1934), *The Analects of Confucius* (London, 1938), and *Three Ways of Thought in Ancient China* (London, 1939) made the main schools of early Chinese philosophy accessible to the general reader. To many his greatest achievement was his translation of the 11c *Genji Monogatari* (*The Tale of Genji*, 6 vols, London, 1925–33), a very long and subtle Japanese novel. Though retranslated by western scholars with the benefit of recent Japanese research, *Genji* in Waley's version remains unique for its scholarship and style.

A close friend of FRY, WOOLF and Lytton STRACHEY, Waley was too dedicated to his own intellectual world to join the Bloomsbury group. Although master of the most difficult texts, he never learned to speak Chinese or Japanese and never visited the Far East, perhaps because, as the Chinese philosopher Chuang Tzu said, in Waley's own translation, 'He whose sightseeing is inward can in himself find all he needs. Such is the highest form of travelling.'

MS

I. Morris (ed.), *Madly Singing in the Mountains: an Appreciation and Anthology of Arthur Waley* (London, 1970).

Walker, Miles (b. Carlisle, Cumbria, UK, 13.8.1868; d. Gloucester, 22.1.1941). British electrical engineer. Walker began his career with a degree in law in 1890. A chance meeting with a day student at Finsbury Technical College convinced him that his love of machines should be professionally pursued. He soon had patents on an electrical surface contact (pick-up) system for electric traction and for the joining of adjacent track rails. As with many famous inventors some of his ideas never succeeded. He found industry restricting and transferred to academic life in 1912 as professor in the faculty of technology at Manchester University, and embarked on a book on electrical machine design. The scope of his book increased many times and the resulting work (*Specification and Design of Dynamo-electric Machinery*, London, 1920) laid out complete design-sheets and formulae for all known types of machine down to the smallest detail. These sheets became accepted in design offices throughout the world. Modern design-sheets have hardly changed from Walker's originals.   ERL

Wallas, Graham (b. Sunderland, Tyne & Wear, UK, 31.5.1858; d. London, 9.8.1932). British political scientist. An early member of the Fabian Society and first professor of political science at the London School of Economics. Although he was one of the contributors to *Fabian Essays in Socialism* (London, 1888), he later resigned from the Fabian executive and in 1904 left the society altogether because he disagreed with its increasing antiliberal bias. He always regarded socialism as the fulfilment of liberalism, not as its antithesis. His two most influential books were *Human Nature in Politics* (London, 1908), in which he criticized the view that political action was based on rational calculation, emphasizing instead nonrational factors like accident, prejudice and custom; and *The Great Society* (London, 1914) which recognized the obstacles which the growing centralization and impersonality of modern industrial societies placed in the way of individual self-fulfilment. Yet Wallas still asserted the possibility of a rational reconstruction of society to make more general the conditions for human happiness.   AG

P. Clarke, *Liberals and Social Democrats* (Cambridge, 1978).

Wallis, Barnes Neville (b. Ripley, Derbys., UK, 26.9.1887; d. Leatherhead, Surrey, 30.10.1979). British engineer and inventor. As a young man Wallis worked on building torpedo-boats, destroyers and a battleship. His most important work was concerned with the air. Whilst the government were building the R101, Barnes Wallis designed and supervised the building of a rival airship, the R100, using private money. Not only did he complete the work earlier, but the R100 was built out of only 11 basic parts. It had 50 per cent more lift than the R101 and was faster and easier to handle. Wallis relied on petrol aero-engines; the R101 had heavier diesel engines. The R101 crashed on a test flight whilst Wallis's vessel crossed the Atlantic. But the failure of its rival led to the dismantling of R100. This episode was to become almost a pattern for the rest of his life. Barnes Wallis was the man whose ideas were rejected, only to be proved right in the years ahead, by which time it was often too late to salvage anything. His connection with the Vickers Company, begun with airships, was continued with the design of an aircraft named the Wellesley, whose bodywork was of woven metal. The Air Ministry rejected the design, but Vickers continued with it, and from this work was born the Wellington bomber that played such an important part in the early years of WW2.

As early as 1939 Wallis began thinking how to shorten the war. He argued that since it took 150 tons of water to make one ton of steel, the main target should be the bombing of the great dams in the Ruhr, so as to deprive Germany of her armaments factories. But his first attempt, the 'earthquake' bombs, was unsuccessful and government scientists did not take kindly to his second idea – the 'bouncing bomb'. But he won his battle with the Establishment; in 1943 the Möhne and Eder dams were breached by bouncing bombs. His most revolutionary idea was an aircraft that could change the shape of its wings whilst in flight, the variable geometry or 'swing-wing' aeroplane. The Swallow was the first tail-less aircraft and he had hoped to develop it into a plane that could cover 10,000 miles non-stop at a height of over 50 miles and a speed of 14,000 miles per hour. But again government preferred to spend its money on other projects and he never lived to see his final dream realized. ERL

L. E. Morpurgo, *Barnes Wallis: a Biography* (London, 1972).

Walras, Marie-Esprit Léon (b. Evreux, Eure, France, 16.12.1834; d. Clarens, Vaud, Switzerland, 3.1.1910). French economist, one of the originators of the 'marginal revolution' in economic thought in the last three decades of the 19c. Walras had no formal training in economics and so was unable to pursue a career as an economist in France; however, he was appointed in 1871 to the new chair of political economy in what eventually became the University of Lausanne. There he embarked on a reconstruction of economics in three parts – the first in pure theory, the second in applied economics (dealing with what we should now call industrial economics) and the third in social economics, i.e. mainly questions of public finance. In the event the first leg of this enterprise took up most of his life's work. He published two collections of essays *Etudes d'économie sociale* [Studies in social economy] (Lausanne, 1896) and *Etudes d'économie appliquée* [Studies in applied economy] (Lausanne, 1898) on the second and third legs, but his *Eléments d'économie pure* (2 vols, Lausanne, 1874–7; *Elements of Pure Economics*, London, 1953) was a systematic treatise which he improved and extended through several subsequent editions and which became a classic in mathematical economics. Walras carried the new technique of marginal analysis to its logical-mathematical conclusion by applying it to markets in general. He showed how to formulate an interdependent system of equations relating to prices and quantities in all markets for the economy as a whole. However, his outstandingly original contribution to modern economic theory was to develop a model of general equilibrium, defining the conditions under which the market mechanism maximizes, benefits and minimizes costs for the economy generally. Because its application calls for a high level of mathematical expertise, Walras's model

only recently became a source of inspiration for the now fast-developing specialization of mathematical economics.

PMD

J. R. Hicks, 'Leon Walras', *Econometrica* (1934); M. Morishima, *Walras' Economics* (Cambridge, 1977).

Walser, Robert (b. Biel, Bern, Switzerland, 15.4.1878; d. Herisau, Appenzell, 25.12.1956). Swiss writer. He came from a family of artists and academics. For much of his life he was a bohemian traveller, spending long periods in Zürich and Berlin, which had a number of notable bohemian coffee-houses. In the short story *Der Spaziergang* (Frauenfeld, 1917; tr. J. C. Middleton, *The Walk and Other Stories*, London, 1957) he made the uncertainty of his lifestyle the subject of self-ironizing comment. On the suggestion of Bruno Cassirer, a distinguished Berlin publisher, and Christian Morgenstern, a satirical writer, Walser began writing novels. These appeared in quick succession: *Geschwister Tanner* [The brothers and sisters Tanner] (Berlin, 1907); *Der Gehülfe* [The draughtsman] (Berlin, 1908), *Jakob von Gunten. Ein Tagebuch* [Jacob of Gunten: a diary] (Berlin, 1909). It is above all this third novel which continues to exercise fascination, not least because of its 'Institute Benjamenta' with its complex interior architecture, a possible forerunner of KAFKA's vision in *The Castle*. Walser was a master of impressionist short stories, capturing moods, the detail of objects, and pathetic fallacies. From 1929 onwards Walser had to live in a sanatorium because of mental ill health. His admirers included Kafka and MUSIL, whom he influenced stylistically.

WvdW

G. C. Avery, *Inquiry and Testament: a Study of the Novels and Short Prose of Robert Walser* (Philadelphia, 1968).

Waltari, Mika (b. Helsinki, Finland, 19.9.1908; d. Helsinki, 26.8.1979). Finnish novelist. Waltari's international fame rests on his numerous large-scale historical novels which explore the recurrent themes of disillusionment and the fate of humanist values in a materialist world. He began as one of the leading writers of the so-called 'Firebearers', the 1920s literary movement, fully expressing its new urban experience as well as the youthful exuberance of the jazz-loving generation in his first novel *Suuri illusioni* [The grand illusion] (Porvoo, 1928). Immensely productive and master of various literary genres, Waltari finally turned to the historical novel in the 1940s. His novel *Sinuhe, egyptiläinen* (Porvoo, 1945; tr. N. Walford, *Sinuhe the Egyptian*, London, 1949), set in Egypt at the time of the pharaoh Ekhanaton, can be called 'the grand disillusion': its theme illustrates, in a fundamental way, the disillusionment and resignation of the Finnish bourgeoisie when nearly all its basic values collapsed through the turmoil of WW2. The conflict between idealism and realism provides the central theme of Waltari's later historical novels, most of them set in the classical Mediterranean world, such as *Turms, Kuolematon* (Porvoo, 1955; tr. E. Ramsden, *The Etruscan*, London, 1957) and *Ihmiskunnan viholliset* (Porvoo, 1964; tr. J. Tate, *The Roman*, London, 1966). His work has been translated into more than 30 languages. KKS

Walter, Bruno, *né* Bruno Walter Schlesinger (b. Berlin, Germany, 15.9.1876; naturalized French citizen; naturalized American citizen, 1946; d. Beverly Hills, Calif., USA, 17.2.1962). German/French/American conductor who began his career in minor German cities and then in 1901 was called to the Vienna Court Opera by MAHLER. After Mahler's death he conducted the first performances of *Das Lied von der Erde* (1911; *The Song of the Earth*) and the Ninth Symphony (1912), and retained a lifelong affection for Mahler's music; he published a monograph *Gustav Mahler* (Vienna, 1936; London, 1937). His performances were noted for an unsentimental sweetness of expression; this made him a valuable interpreter of Brahms and other late romantic music, though he was also admired in Beethoven and in opera. As a Jew he was obliged to leave Germany in 1933; he settled eventually in the USA but continued to appear internationally in his 70s. He wrote *Theme and Variations*

(NY, 1946) and *Von der Musik und vom Musizieren* (Frankfurt, 1957; *Of Music and Music-making*, London, 1961). PG

Wang Ching-wei, *né* Wang Chao-ming (b. Canton, China, 4.5.1885; d. Nogaya, Japan, 10.11.1944). Chinese nationalist politician, close associate of SUN YAT-SEN, rival for the leadership of the Kuomintang with CHIANG KAI-SHEK. Influenced in early career by anarchist doctrines, he turned against the Chinese Communists in 1927, on nationalist and antiwestern rather than ideological grounds. As leader of the Executive Yuan (1932–6), he ran the domestic government of China for Chiang, but his antiwestern feelings and his consciousness of Japanese military superiority made him the principal advocate of Sino-Japanese cooperation, especially after Chiang's 1936 agreement with the Chinese Communists, and a target for extremist assassins. In 1939 he was expelled from the Kuomintang, and moved over to the Japanese side, attracted by Pan-Asian propaganda. He headed the Chinese collaborationist government in Nanking (1940–4). DCW

Warburg, Aby (b. Hamburg, Germany, 13.6.1866; d. Hamburg, 26.10.1929). German cultural historian. Warburg was a banker's son and his private means enabled him to avoid an academic career and to build up a magnificent library. He was particularly interested in the survival and transformations of the classical tradition. He liked to work on precise and even narrow problems but to place them in a wider context. His 1893 essay on Botticelli's *Birth of Venus* and *Primavera* begins with classical influences on the representations of floating hair and draperies, then discusses pictorial schemata in more general terms. Warburg admired NIETZSCHE and saw the classical tradition in Dionysian (and demonic) as well as in Apollonian terms, noting for example the survival of the ancient gods as astral demons. He had little time for narrow specialists; to avoid the 'frontier police' between disciplines, he organized his library not into 'art history', 'literature', etc., but into 'images', 'ideas' and 'action'. A distinguished group of intellectuals, including CASSIRER, PANOFSKY and Saxl, gathered around Warburg and his Hamburg library in the 1920s. After Warburg's nervous breakdown the library was turned into a research institute and after HITLER's rise to power the Warburg Institute was moved to London. It is Warburg's best memorial, together with 40 essays, collected into the *Gesammelte Schriften* [Collected writings] (Leipzig, 1932).   UPB

E. H. Gombrich, *Aby Warburg: an Intellectual Biography* (London, 1970).

Warburg, Otto Heinrich (b. Freiburg, Baden-Württemberg, Germany, 8.10.1883; d. West Berlin, 1.8.1970). German biochemist and cell physiologist. In 1914 Warburg was made a member of the Kaiser Wilhelm Gesellschaft and given a laboratory at Dahlem, Berlin, where he worked, except for interruptions caused by two world wars, until he died. His researches, described in five books and some 500 papers, had a seminal effect on the development of biochemistry. Warburg was a brilliant experimenter and devised techniques, particularly of manometry and spectrophotometry, which have been the mainstays of many biochemical laboratories over a span of 60 years. He used these to greatest effect in the investigation of oxidative processes occurring in living cells. He isolated and characterized many of the enzymes and their coenzymes, thus laying much of the foundation on which rests present understanding of the cell's energy metabolism. The methods he devised for the isolation of the enzymes have found widespread industrial application and the techniques he developed for their assay are still widely used, especially in clinical diagnosis. His contribution to this field of study was monumental and justified the award of two Nobel prizes (1931 and 1944); by HITLER's decree he was unable to receive the second. In his researches on cancer and photosynthesis he also showed brilliant originality and made many important discoveries. But his intolerance of criticism and obsession with his own theories estranged him from the mainstream of thought in these areas and, towards the end of his life,

he was clinging to views almost universally rejected by other scientists.   GL

H. A. Krebs, *Otto Warburg: Cell Physiologist, Biochemist and Eccentric* (Oxford, 1981).

Ward, Barbara Mary (b. York, UK, 23.5.1914; d. Lodsworth, W. Sussex, 31.5.1981). British conservationist, economist and writer. One of the most intelligent and articulate apostles of the burgeoning movements for environmental protection and the conservation of diminishing natural resources, the need for which she outlined to a wide public in her two books *Spaceship Earth* (London, 1966) and *Only One Planet* (with R. Dubos, London, 1972). Her wide interests and concerns included urban planning and renewal, and she and her husband Robert Jackson worked in India and Pakistan as advisers on development planning. She pursued a brilliant career as a journalist, helping to establish the respected international voice of the *Economist*, for which she became a foreign editor; and from 1963 to 1973 she was Schweitzer professor of international economic development at Columbia University. She was a devout Roman Catholic throughout her life.   GHD

Warhol, Andy, *né* Andrew Warhola (b. Forest City, Pa, USA, 8.8.1927). American artist and film maker. Born of Czech immigrants, he studied art at the Carnegie Institute of Technology and worked as an advertising draughtsman and illustrator in New York before achieving celebrity in the early 1960s. His apparent devotion to eliminating individuality in art conspired to elevate his reputation as illustrator, printmaker, impresario and a nominal leader of the 'Pop art' movement. He has avoided serious interpretations of his art which is deliberately founded upon artificial contrivances. His silk-screen prints frequently depict figures who have infected the popular imagination: Jacqueline Kennedy, PRESLEY, Elizabeth Taylor. They also often show mundane subjects such as soup cans. In 1963 he began making films, and since then his New York 'factory' has produced more than 80 films: *Chelsea Girls* (1967) and others exploit randomness and are offered as an assault upon all accepted aesthetic values. Warhol offered some comments on himself in *From A to B and Back Again* (NY, 1975).   RBJG

Washburn, Sherwood Larned (b. Cambridge, Mass., USA, 26.11.1911). American physical anthropologist, who pioneered the study of primate behaviour and ecology under natural conditions. Washburn obtained his undergraduate and graduate training at Harvard, and after holding appointments at Columbia and Chicago took up the chair of anthropology at Berkeley from which he retired in 1979. Washburn's early researches were devoted to primate anatomy. He was particularly concerned with functional approaches as a means of improving interpretation of the fossil record of human evolution. He showed how behavioural evolution and the acquisition of culture directed morphological evolution, particularly in the brain. With I. DeVore he undertook one of the first ethological and ecological studies of baboons in the natural habitat, and developed a school of primate field studies. Washburn chose baboons for investigation because they inhabit savanna environments similar to those occupied by early hominids, and highlight, through contrast, a number of issues in human evolution. For example, he noted the evolutionary problem of infant care in a species in which the offspring are born immature, because of constraints imposed by the anatomical requirements of bipedalism, and develop slowly because of the value of a long learning period. The type of sexual behaviour found in baboons in which oestrus females abandon offspring to consort with dominant males would be quite incompatible with human infant survival. Washburn argued that the origin of the human female menstrual cycle in which the female is more or less sexually receptive to the male was a means of ensuring a constancy of protection and food supply for herself and her offspring.   GA-H

Watson, James Dewey (b. Chicago, Ill., USA, 6.4.1928). American molecular biologist. Watson trained as a zoologist

and made his entry into research as a biochemist. He only found his true métier when he joined CRICK at the Cavendish Laboratory in Cambridge in 1952. The story of their collaboration is told in colourful terms in *The Double Helix* (London, 1968). From it came the most important revolution in 20c biology. Watson, Crick and WILKINS discovered the structure of deoxyribonucleic acid (DNA) and found it to be beautifully appropriate for the storage and transmission of genetic information. They shared a Nobel prize for this work in 1962. Watson continued, after his return to the USA, to play an important part in molecular biology. His *The Molecular Biology of the Gene* (NY, 1965) was an authoritative description of the state of this branch of science, of which he was one of the founders. DRN

Watson, John Broadus (b. Greenville, SC, USA, 9.1.1878; d. Westport, Conn., 25.9.1958). American psychologist who founded behaviourism. Watson spent the first 14 years of his career studying animal behaviour and especially how animals learn (see his field studies with Lashley on bird navigation). In 1912, in a series of lectures at Columbia University, Watson argued that human beings should be studied as objectively as animals. Psychology should do away with introspection and concentrate on analysing behaviour. He argued that experiments showed that emotions and feelings were a consequence of conditioning rather than contemplation (see *Psychology from the Standpoint of a Behaviorist*, Philadelphia, 1919). Only by studying what could be externally observed could psychology become properly scientific. Watson was deeply hostile to religion. He expected to be criticized since most contemporary psychologists believed human beings, possessing souls, were utterly different from beasts.

Watson also argued that human beings are very plastic, capable of being conditioned – or of self-conditioning – to behave in any desired way. One extension of this idea was that neurotic behaviour was not due to any inherent instability but rather to inappropriate learning. Watson showed in 1920 that he could condition a child, little Albert, into being afraid of a rat he had previously liked. Then, by exposing Albert gradually to the rat, Watson could cure the phobia.

Watson not only preached the study of behaviour but also wanted psychology to explore all aspects of human life – in the factory, even in the bedroom. Unfortunately Watson himself was hounded out of Johns Hopkins in 1920 after a divorce scandal and later married a student. Bitter about his dismissal, he immediately went to work for the advertising agency John Walter Thomson where he used his psychological theories to condition people to want all manner of new goods and brands. Watson's influence on psychology in this century was decisive. He succeeded in turning American psychology away from introspection and towards scientific experiments. Unfortunately, his successors have made this scientific psychology far narrower than Watson would have wished. DMOC

D. Cohen, *John Watson: a Biography* (London, 1979).

Watson, Thomas John (b. Campbell, NY, USA, 17.2.1874; d. New York, 19.6.1956). American industrialist. Thomas Watson was born into a Scottish family which had moved to the USA. In 1895 he joined the National Cash Register Co. run by the buccaneering John Henry Patterson, pioneer of high pressure sales methods. Patterson, a fellow Scot and a competent engineer, had developed a paternalistic style of management and demanded complete loyalty and dedication to the company amounting to a quasi-religious fervour. In all these matters Watson studied, and later excelled, Patterson. The ruthless methods used to eliminate competition led to an antitrust prosecution and Watson and others from NCR were in 1913 convicted and sentenced to a year in gaol; which was later set aside. Then the unpredictable Patterson sacked Watson.

Watson became manager of the profitless Computer-Tabulator-Recording Co. which in 1923 changed its name to IBM (International Business Machines). He had a share in the profits which in the 1930s was to make him the most highly paid executive in the USA. IBM was dominated by his personality. He introduced Patterson's methods in a more benevolent form. Engineering was firstrate, organization superb, and the salesmen worked under pressure which has become legendary. The Watson slogan THINK appeared everywhere in the organization. There was a company style of dress, company songs, and a great deal of razzamatazz at sales conventions over which Watson presided. Drinking at work was forbidden and smoking discouraged. IBM spread round the world. Watson became a philanthropist on a princely scale. His son, Thomas J. Watson Jr, became president of IBM in 1952 and chief executive in 1956. IBM has mastered modern electronic technology and dominates the world market in computers in a manner which has no comparison in any other industry. RAH

T. G. & M. R. Belden, *The Lengthening Shadow* (NY, 1961); W. Rodgers, *Think* (NY, 1970).

Watts, Alan Wilson (b. Chislehurst, London, UK, 6.1.1915; naturalized American citizen; d. Mill Valley, Calif., USA, 16.11.1973). American philosopher, comparative religionist, theologian, student of mysticism, even Californian guru, Watts is best regarded as a polymath who taught liberation. We in the West are in a state of confusion, he argued, adrift without landmarks in a universe which more and more resembles the Buddhist principle of the 'Great Void'. We seek solace in satisfying our egos. What is required is change of consciousness, of how we feel our existence. In reality, was his conclusion, we and everything around us are interrelated, and are necessary components of a unified process. Based in California – he was for a time the dean of the American Academy of Asian Studies in San Francisco – Watts wrote extensively (with particular public success in *The Way of Zen*, NY, 1957, and *Psychotherapy East and West*, NY, 1961), lectured widely, was a research fellow at the Bollingen Foundation (1951 and 1962) and at Harvard (1962–4), participated in various societies, and had connections with the Esalen Institute. His message – neither looking deeply into the self as

803

FREUD did, nor looking into society and politics in the fashion of MARCUSE – helped formulate the Human Potential movement. Watts's emphasis on the contemplation of knowing and being has meant, however, that his influence has recently waned in the face of the more dynamic orientations. Rarely intending to be a strict scholar, his achievement was subtly to delineate the consciousness-expansion movement of the 1960s.

PLFH

Waugh, Evelyn Arthur St John (b. London, UK, 28.10.1903; d. Combe Florey, Som., 10.4.1966). British novelist. Son of man-of-letters Arthur Waugh and younger brother of popular novelist Alec Waugh, Evelyn was educated at Lancing and Oxford. His first two novels *Decline and Fall* (London, 1928) and *Vile Bodies* (London, 1930) were brilliantly funny satirical farces with an underlying note of despair. They established Waugh as the literary voice of the generation that came of age after WW1, especially in the world of high society in which he preferred to move. The breakup of his first marriage after only a year appeared to precipitate his conversion to Roman Catholicism in 1930, and some of the pain and disillusionment of this marital experience can be traced in *A Handful of Dust* (London, 1934), his most serious work up to that date and, some critics think, his best. Extensive travels in the interwar years produced several travel books and two hilarious novels about Africa, *Black Mischief* (London, 1932) and *Scoop* (London, 1938). In the 1930s Waugh adopted an unfashionable political stance, sympathetic to MUSSOLINI and FRANCO, but when WW2 began he was one of the very few established English writers to seek – and find – active service. His trilogy *Men at Arms* (London, 1952), *Officers and Gentlemen* (London, 1955) and *Unconditional Surrender* (London, 1961) charts the hero's gradual disillusionment with the notion of the war as a 'crusade'. Collectively entitled *Sword of Honour*, the trilogy is widely regarded as the most distinguished work of fiction about the war by an English writer. Waugh was a romantic High Tory with an anarchistic streak, who enjoyed affronting egalitarian opinion in postwar Britain. His novel *Brideshead Revisited* (London, 1945) was notable for its elegiac celebration of the English Roman Catholic aristocracy and its scorn for 'the century of the common man'. It dismayed many admirers of his earlier work but brought him popular success, especially in the USA, and caused him to be linked, in criticism, with other 'Catholic novelists' such as GREENE and MAURIAC. Other postwar novels included *The Loved One* (London, 1948), a satire on modern American burial rites, and *The Ordeal of Gilbert Pinfold* (London, 1957), a remarkably clear-eyed self-portrait. Waugh emphatically dissociated himself from the experiments of literary modernism; he regarded himself as a craftsman, producing books which were well made, classically lucid, and entertaining as well as instructive. Nevertheless his obsession with the theme of decline is characteristically modern and his contribution to the tradition of the English comic novel was original. His works have worn as well as those of any English writer of his generation. DJL

C. Sykes, *Evelyn Waugh* (London, 1975).

Wayne, John (Duke), *né* Marion Michael Morrison (b. Winterset, Iowa, USA, 26.5.1907; d. Los Angeles, Calif., 11.6.1979). American film actor. Raised in California, where he became a football star, his friendship with film director John FORD led to his playing bit parts from 1928. *The Big Trail* (1930) was his first break, but it was as Ringo Kid in Ford's *Stagecoach* (1939) that Wayne's image and reputation were formed. Frequently starring in Ford's films, Wayne became one of Hollywood's biggest box-office attractions. By the end of 40 years on the screen, he had appeared in some 250 films, including such western classics as *Fort Apache* (1948), *She Wore a Yellow Ribbon* (1949), *Rio Grande* (1950) and *The Man Who Shot Liberty Valance* (1962). Off-screen Wayne was as ultra-patriotic as on it; during the MCCARTHY era he helped to found the Motion Picture Alliance for the Preservation of American Ideals, and later the Vietnam war became something of a personal crusade. As the most celebrated star of the American western, he contributed powerfully to the popular mythology of the American West and to the simplification of the American ideal of male heroism, a combination, in the film parts he played, of virility, sentimentality and apparent sincerity.   RBJG

Weaver, Warren (b. Reedsberg, Wis., USA, 17.7.1894; d. New Milford, Conn., 28.11.1978). American mathematician noted for his contribution to communication theory. Building very much upon the work of SHANNON, he analysed the problem of communication into three parts. The first is the technical problem, the province of information theorists like Shannon; to what degree can one expect the original signal to survive the process of sending intact, and how is it likely to mutate? The second is the semantic problem, one amenable to linguistics; given the signal, perhaps muted, will it be understood as the sender intended (for instance, words may be clear and still convey nothing)? The third is the effectiveness problem, one mainly of social psychology; does the signal, as understood, affect the receivers' conduct as intended (for instance, is it remembered)? Limiting results at the technical level have implications at the second and third. (See his book written with C. E. Shannon, *The Mathematical Theory of Communication,* Urbana, 1949.)   AGPW/JCu

Webb, Martha Beatrice, *née* Potter (b. Gloucester, UK, 22.1.1858; d. Passfield Corner, Hants., 30.4.1943), and **Webb, Sidney James** (b. London, UK, 13.7.1859; d. Passfield Corner, Hants., 13.10.1947). British social inquirers and political activists. Beatrice and Sidney Webb constituted the most prolific 'partnership' in British history this century. They were socialists before they met, believing in the intimate connection between social inquiry and political action. In social inquiry and research, they created labour history as a separate study with *The History of Trade Unionism* (London, 1894) and *Industrial Democracy* (London, 1897); laid the modern basis for the Welfare State in the minority report of the Poor Law Commission (1905–9); and undertook the most extensive *History of English Local Government* (7 vols, London, 1903 –30). In education and publicity they produced a stream of pamphlets for the Fabian Society; founded the London School of Economics (1895); and established the *New Statesman* (1913) as an organ of socialist propaganda. As political activists, having attempted to permeate the upper reaches of society and government, they made themselves 'clerks to labour' in the early 1910s, which resulted in Sidney writing the Labour party's policy document of 1918, *Labour and the New Social Order,* committing the Labour party to establishing a 'national minimum of civilized life' and to the common ownership of the means of production. Sidney Webb, as Lord Passfield, served in the Labour governments of 1924 and 1929–31. In later life the Webbs became attracted and committed to the socialist experiments of the USSR, from which resulted *Soviet Communism: a New Civilisation?* (London, 1935). The publication of the complete text of Beatrice Webb's *Diaries* (vol. 1: *My Apprenticeship,* eds N. & J. Mackenzie, London, 1982) revealed an unsuspected gift of psychological perception which, together with her powers of social observation, make them classics of their kind.   AO

A. M. McBriar, *Fabian Socialism and English Politics 1884–1918* (Cambridge, 1962); M. I. Cole, 'Beatrice and Sidney Webb', in J. M. Bellamy & J. Saville (eds), *Dictionary of Labour Biography,* ii (London, 1974).

Weber, Joseph (b. Paterson, NJ, USA, 17.5.1919). American physicist, who made the controversial claim that he had detected gravitational waves, possibly coming from the centre of our galaxy. Professor of physics at the University of Maryland since 1958, Weber has had a long interest in the experimental testing of the theory of general relativity. This theory predicts that when a massive object is accelerated it will radiate a gravitational wave analogous to electromagnetic radiation and travelling at the speed of light. Unfortunately the predicted strength of gravitational waves is extremely small, even from accelerations of gigantic masses such as from a collapsing galaxy. Despite the weakness of the expected signal, Weber began building his detector in 1957. By 1969 he claimed the detection of some simultaneous events which he attributed to gravitational waves, and in subsequent months he observed about 200 such events. Some of the data suggested the waves were coming from the direction of the centre of the Milky Way galactic system. However, despite strenuous efforts from several teams around the world to duplicate and improve on Weber's technique, no gravitational waves have been detected by any other group and the whole matter remains very ambiguous. Nevertheless Weber has pioneered and stimulated a new area of experimental physics.   MJS

Weber, Karl Emil Maximilian (Max) (b. Erfurt, Germany [now East Germany], 21.4.1864; d. Munich, Bavaria, 14.6.1920). German sociologist. Weber, along with DURKHEIM, is considered one of the 'fathers' of modern sociology. Given the protean scope of his knowledge, and the extent of his interests and influence, he is the single major figure in 20c social thought who can be compared, in intellectual range, with MARX. Weber was appointed professor of political economy at Freiburg in 1894 and at Heidelberg in 1897. He suffered a nervous breakdown between 1898 and 1903 and did not teach again until after WW1. An inheritance left to him in 1907 enabled him to continue his work as a private scholar. Three themes run through Weber's work: the nature of domination (*Herrschaft*); the character of rationality; and the intertwined relation of ideas to material interests in the processes of social change, specifically the relation of religious ideas to economic activities. Weber's political sociology focuses on the persistent role of domination in social life. He distinguished between three types of authority: traditional, in which the ways of the past and the authority of the elders hold sway; charismatic, wherein the personal voice of an individual, rooted in some magical or religious basis, is the source of authority; and the legal-rational, where norms and laws are the basis of

rule. In using these typologies, Weber sought to cut across the traditional distinctions found in political theory (e.g. the monarchy, aristocracy, democracy classification of Aristotle – or the revision of those modes by Montesquieu), to set forth an analytical scheme. Weber also thought, implicitly, that social change occurred most often when a charismatic figure could arise who, through his personal authority, would break the bonds of the traditional order. Once the revolutionary ardour ebbed, there would come the 'routinization of charisma', just as the Catholic church became an organized body to promulgate the teachings of Jesus. The charismatic individual is akin to Hegel's 'world-historical figures' who by breaking the cake of custom transform historical periods. While Weber may have derived the idea from Hegel, however, he would reject the suggestion that these individuals, unwittingly, served the 'cunning of reason'. The crucial factor in politics, argued Weber, was not classes but bureaucracies. Weber distinguished between three kinds – the patriarchal, the patrimonial and the legal-rational – and these 'modes of domination' can be looked at as 'axial structures' shaping a social order as much as Marx's 'modes of production'. However, since Weber took bureaucracy not property as the 'key' to social structure, for him capitalism and socialism were not two antithetical systems but two kinds of bureaucratic modes of organization. The concept of rationality was Weber's key to the understanding of modern economic activities and all other activities moulded on the model of economics. For him, capitalism was defined not by acquisitiveness or profit-seeking, since these can be found in older societies as well, but in the rational organization of production and of marketing, the detailed cost-accounting and assessment of efficiency which modern rational procedures could provide.

Weber's interest in religion arose from a double source. One was the question why capitalism had developed in the West, rather than in other culture areas, such as Asia, where there were large resources and educated classes. The other was the question of status positions of different social classes. He proposed the 'Protestant ethic' as a relevant answer to both, by arguing that, unlike Catholicism (which had demeaned economic activities and had held the profit-seeker in low social esteem), Protestantism regarded all work as a justified 'calling' and, by treating all men in an individualistic and impersonal way, paved the way for rational modes which allowed capitalist enterprises to flourish. Weber went on to write books on the religion of China, of India and ancient Judaism, exploring the relation between these religions and the different kinds of social structures within those cultures.

Weber's methodological essays have been important in creating a style of sociology that is distinct from utilitarianism or positivism on one side, or historicism and idealism on the other. Against positivism, Weber insisted that the meanings individuals attach to their activities are essential to the understanding of those actions and that these meanings are embodied in the norms governing social structures. Against the historicism of writers such as DILTHEY, Weber argued that one could establish causal-functional, or general explanations, by the use of the comparative method and the 'ideal type'. This neo-Kantianism has become for many sociologists an epistemological ground to avoid the determinism and materialism of Marxism. The two men who, in vastly different ways, responded to Weber's thought were PARSONS, who first translated Weber's *Die protestantische Ethik und der 'Geist' des Kapitalismus* (1905, Tübingen, 1922) into English as *Protestant Ethic and the Spirit of Capitalism* (London, 1930), and then sought to formalize Weber's sociology of action in a more extensive scheme, and the Hungarian philosopher LUKÁCS, who began his intellectual work within the Weber circle, but rejected him on his conversion to Marxism.

At Heidelberg Weber exercised a wide personal influence over a large selection of German intellectual life. His credo, making fidelity to knowledge the basis of scholarly activities, and his warnings not to confuse politics with science, are contained in two poignant lectures given towards the end of his life, 'Science as a

vocation' and 'Politics as a vocation' (translated in *From Max Weber*, NY, 1946). The latter essay contains Weber's discussion of the 'ethics of responsibility' and the 'ethics of conscience', one of the most compelling discussions of the risks of violence in political life.

Weber's major work, unfinished at his death, is *Wirtschaft und Gesellschaft* (ed. J. Winckelmann, 2 vols, Tübingen, 1922, ⁴1956; 3 vols, *Economy and Society*, NY, 1968) which contains his major discussions on types of economic activities, his classifications of power and bureaucracy, and his sociology of religion. A representative collection of essays can be found in *From Max Weber* (eds H. H. Gerth & C. Wright Mills, NY, 1946). His most accessible work is the *Wirtschaftsgeschichte* (Munich, 1924; *General Economic History*, London, 1961), which was reconstructed by students from a set of lectures given by Weber shortly before his death.   DBe

R. Bendix, *Max Weber: an Intellectual Portrait* (London, 1960).

Webern, Anton Friedrich Wilhelm von (b. Vienna, Austria-Hungary [now Austria], 3.12.1883; d. Mittersill, Salzburg, 15.9.1945). Austrian composer. With BERG one of the earliest pupils of SCHOENBERG, whom he immediately followed in atonality. Unlike his teacher, he made no return to tonal composition. Schoenberg's later invention of serialism enabled Webern to develop a highly organized style and to produce small and intricate pieces which he saw as images of the perfect divine order in nature. Webern's concision is evident from his earliest tonal works, and his contemporary atonal compositions (1908 –14) are often very short: the extreme point is reached in the last of his *Three Little Pieces* for cello and piano (1914), an adagio movement in only 20 notes. There was no time or need for anything but the statement of a few musical ideas, and no room for further development in this style. For the next decade Webern concentrated on songs, where the text could provide a form. His finest work of this period is the set of *Six Trakl Songs* for voice, two clarinets and two strings (1924), where the vocal melody, fragile or stark, is set off by the variegated sounds of a small ensemble.

The adoption of serialism at first brought little change to Webern's style, but in his Symphony (1929) he realized the potential of the new technique for creating densely patterned music. Of the two short movements the first is a double canon in sonata form and the second a palindromic set of variations.

In the poet Hildegarde Jone, Webern found a kindred spirit, and it was her verse that he set exclusively in the vocal compositions that followed the Symphony. The most important of these – Webern's largest works – are the two cantatas (1946 and 1950). The formal complexity of these tightly structured works rivals that of the late Renaissance masters he admired. Webern's essential simplicity, naivety and sentimentality are revealed in his *Briefe an Hildegarde Jone und Josef Humplik* (Vienna, 1959; *Letters to Hildegarde Jone and Josef Humplik*, Bryn Mawr, Pa, 1967) and his *Der Weg zur neuen Musik* (Vienna, 1960; *The Path to the New Music*, Bryn Mawr, Pa, 1963); they are not hidden in his music which is nevertheless rigorously constructed and rhetorically novel.

PG

W. Kolneder, *Anton Webern* (London, 1968); H. Moldenhauer, *Anton von Webern: a Chronicle of his Life and Work* (London, 1978).

Wedekind, Frank (b. Hanover, Lower Saxony, Germany, 24.7.1864; d. Munich, Bavaria, 9.3.1918). German dramatist. In addition to his plays Wedekind enjoyed a considerable reputation for his performances with the Munich cabaret *Die elf Scharfrichter* at the turn of the century. He wrote and performed his own poems and his individual blend of satire and social comment was also published in the journal *Simplicissimus*. A scathing account in verse of Kaiser Wilhelm II's notions of piety earned Wedekind a prison sentence for *lèse majesté*. Wedekind was also master of the short prose narrative with a sting in the tail. As a dramatist Wedekind may be seen as a direct forerunner of expressionism. He challenged the naturalist domination of the German stage and his plays baffled contemporary actors, so much so

that the author was obliged to play his own roles in his own individualistic way. Wedekind's language ranges from hyperbole to banality without warning, he employs grotesque and parody, and foreshortens his characters to caricatures in a circus of inadequate individuals seeking to sustain an inflated and untenable image of their own self-importance. Into an essentially male-dominated world Wedekind introduced the 'womanly woman' who, by her nature and instincts, presented a destructive and overwhelming challenge. As 'emancipator of the flesh' Wedekind sought to highlight the sexual undertow to social activity, and his expressionistic stylization of sexuality as the dominant mode occasioned great offence. Early plays such as *Frühlings Erwachen* (1891; tr. F. Fawcett & S. Spender, *Spring's Awakening* in *Five Tragedies of Sex*, London, 1952) placed the innocent adolescent at the mercy of his or her instincts on the one hand and of a grotesquely caricatured adult authority on the other; the two Lulu plays *Erdgeist* (1895; tr. F. Fawcett & S. Spender, *Earth Spirit*, in op. cit.) and *Die Büchse der Pandora* (1902; tr. F. Fawcett & S. Spender, *Pandora's Box*, in op. cit.) developed the theme of rampant female sexuality and its inevitable destruction in a bourgeois environment. Both plays ran into difficulties with the censor and the latter play was not performed until 1905. BERG witnessed this performance in Vienna. Wedekind's most popular and successful play satirizes the bourgeois world through its hero, a confidence trickster: *Der Marquis von Keith* (1901; tr. C. R. Mueller in *Masterpieces of the Modern German Theatre*, NY, 1967). Wedekind combines brilliant use of language and epigrammatic style in allowing the confidence trickster to outwit himself.

ADB

A. Best, *Frank Wedekind* (London, 1975).

Wegener, Alfred Lothar (b. Berlin, Germany, 1.11.1880; d. Greenland, Denmark, 11.1930). German meteorologist and geophysicist. Wegener is a romantic figure in the annals of science. A geological 'outsider', he put forward the revolutionary hypothesis of continental drift at the beginning of this century. He suffered intense criticism in consequence from the pillars of orthodoxy in geophysics and geology, only to be triumphantly vindicated long after his death with the general acceptance of the theory of plate tectonics, which has transformed the whole character of geology. Wegener took his doctorate in astronomy. From early days he had cherished an ambition to explore in Greenland, and had become fascinated by the comparatively new science of meteorology. He was selected as meteorologist to a Danish expedition to northeast Greenland. A second expedition to Greenland in 1912 included the longest crossing of the ice cap ever undertaken. After WW1 Wegener succeeded his father-in-law Köppen as director of the meteorological research department of the Marine Observatory at Hamburg. In 1924 he moved to Graz University, but died while making a third expedition to Greenland in 1930, probably from overexertion.

Though Wegener achieved distinction as a meteorologist and as an Arctic explorer, his fame rests on his continental-drift hypothesis, first presented publicly in 1912 in a lecture before the German Geological Association in Frankfurt. His great book *Die Entstehung der Kontinente und Ozeane* (Braunschweig, 1915; *The Origin of Continents and Oceans*, London, 1924) sets out the hypothesis and its supporting evidence in full. Wegener was less impressed by the so-called jigsaw fit of the continents bordering the Atlantic than by evidence from fossils of free migration of terrestrial organisms between these continents in the Mesozoic era. Since geophysical evidence appeared to preclude the former existence of transoceanic land bridges which had subsequently sunk without trace, the only logical alternative was that the continents had drifted apart. Supporting evidence was drawn from the close geological matches between the continents, from palaeoclimatology, in which field Wegener was a pioneer, and from other fields of geophysics. Wegener had difficulty in finding a driving force sufficiently strong to move continents thousands of kilometres, but tentatively favoured a combina-

tion of tidal and *Pohlflucht* [flight from the poles] forces. For all the criticism, the continental-drift hypothesis found a small number of staunch supporters, most notably ARGAND, A. HOLMES and the South African geologist Alexander du Toit. Retrospectively, with much new evidence especially from oceanography and rock magnetism, the soundness of most of Wegener's arguments has come to be appreciated in spite of earlier opposition to so revolutionary a concept.   AH

Weil, André (b. Paris, France, 6.5.1906). French mathematician, who has worked in India, France, Brazil, Chicago; and latterly at Princeton University. The father of modern algebraic geometry, both through his own discoveries and by means of the associated Weil conjectures that have fuelled further research over a period of 30 years. In conventional geometry shapes are represented by equations which characterize the coordinates of the points that make them up. The coordinates must be quantities such that equations are meaningful; originally they were always real numbers, which meant that the equations were not always solvable. By the 19c the basic field was the complex numbers in which all polynomials can be solved, but this gives a rich structure in which rather too much may be going on. Weil introduced geometries over finite fields, so that the mathematician may choose an appropriate basis for his particular problem. A particular class of such problems will be restrictions of problems not yet solved for the general case, such as the Riemann hypothesis. Other problems may feed back into number theory as results about the distribution and density of classes of numbers. Weil could take a collection of rationals and look at the compact subsets of the product space of all their completions. He developed the theory of integration on topological groups, and could make statements about such number-based structures in terms of volumes.   AGPW

Weil, Simone (b. Paris, France, 3.2.1909; d. Ashford, Kent, UK, 24.8.1943). French philosopher and religious apologist. Her Jewish intellectual family background, her agnostic upbringing and her brilliant studies at the best schools including the *khâgne*, a preparatory class normally reserved for boys, and the Ecole Normale Supérieure (1928–31), pointed to a distinguished academic career. Taught by Alain (ps. of Emile Chartier) in literature, philosophy and logic (from 1925), she began to develop a distinctive philosophy of her own which basically belongs to the Platonist and Stoic frameworks – though systematization of her philosophy proves difficult as her thought was expressed not in discursive language but in essays and commentaries. Although she published little, and only in Alain's *Libres propos*, in French syndicalist papers and later in the *Cahiers du Sud*, the impact of her thinking has grown rapidly since WW2 (largely thanks to Gallimard's editor CAMUS). Rejecting her intellectual birthright she set out on a course of ultimate commitment, by taking part in the Spanish civil war (1936), by becoming a manual labourer, by joining the Resistance, and finally by refusing to eat while the victims of WW2 suffered. Yet she retained a position of total noncommitment as regards religious or political institutions. Her religious thinking (mainly in *La Pesanteur et la grâce*, Paris, 1949; tr. E. Craufurd, *Gravity and Grace*, London, 1952; and *Attente de Dieu*, Paris, 1950; tr. E. Craufurd, *Waiting on God*, London, 1951) is essentially in the mystic tradition, but rather than choosing the Kabbala she turned to the gnostic elements in Catholicism, determinedly staying outside the church. In her political thinking (mainly in *Oppression et liberté*, Paris, 1955; tr. A. F. Willis & J. Petrie, *Oppression and Liberty*, London, 1958; *Ecrits historiques et politiques*, Paris, 1960; extracts tr. R. Rees, *Selected Essays 1934–43*, London, 1962) she is concerned with the nature and possibility of individual freedom in various political and social systems, finally opting for liberalism rather than socialism. Through her studies of Greek epic and tragedy, combined with her knowledge of modern industrial society, she developed a concept of the human person, integrating work and whole being, which is the least explored and perhaps

the most interesting aspect of her thought (see *L'Enracinement*, Paris, 1949; tr. A. F. Willis, *The Need for Roots*, London, 1952). Even in its unfinished form Weil's thought indicates an original thinker. It reinterprets a vast body of material both ancient and modern, and it might have developed, particularly, into an important philosophy of culture.   KKS

S. Pétrement, *Simone Weil: a Life*, tr. R. Rosenthal (Oxford, 1977); P. Winch, Introduction to *Simone Weil: Lectures on Philosophy*, tr. H. Price (Cambridge, 1978).

Weill, Kurt (b. Dessau, Germany [now East Germany], 2.3.1900; naturalized American citizen, 1943; d. New York, USA, 3.4.1950). German/American composer whose earlier works, including his first opera *Der Protagonist* [The protagonist] (1926, text by KAISER), are in a dark and bitter expressionist style which owes something to his teacher BUSONI and something to SCHOENBERG. This style was considerably modified when he became BRECHT's musical collaborator in 1927. He evolved a cabaret-like manner, using popular clichés and an acid tonality to stress the corruption of capitalist society which Brecht was exposing in such works as *Die Dreigroschenoper* (1928; *The Threepenny Opera*) and *Aufstieg und Fall der Stadt Mahagonny* (1930; *Rise and Fall of the City of Mahagonny*). In 1933 he was obliged to leave Germany; in 1935 he settled permanently in the USA. There he concerned himself almost exclusively with the Broadway musical theatre, for which he composed *Johnny Johnson* (1936), *Knickerbocker Holiday* (1938), *Lost in the Stars* (1949) and other scores.   PG

Weinberg, Steven (b. New York, USA, 3.5.1933). American physicist. Educated at Cornell and Princeton universities, Weinberg's major contribution to physics is in his 1967 model for the unification of the weak and electromagnetic interactions (see GLASHOW). This model, developed independently by SALAM, led to the prediction of a new interaction, the weak neutral current, the existence of which was confirmed in the early 1970s. This was the first step in unifying forces into a single interaction, a step which has been followed by many physicists in more recent years and gives the promise of unifying all the forces of nature. Not only has Weinberg been one of the founders of this movement but, like Salam, is one of its major exponents today. Together with Glashow and Salam he received a Nobel prize in 1979. Weinberg is also the author of a stimulating cosmological investigation *The First Three Minutes* (NY, 1977). RJC

Weiss, Paul Alfred (b. Vienna, Austria-Hungary [now Austria], 21.5.1898; naturalized American citizen). Austrian/American developmental biologist. Educated at the University of Vienna, he took up his first American appointment (at Yale) in 1930 and from 1933 to 1954 he was professor of zoology at the University of Chicago. After periods at the Rockefeller Institute, New York, and the University of Texas, he has been professor emeritus at Rockefeller University since 1966. Weiss helped bring the study of morphogenesis (i.e. the generation of form during embryonic development) from descriptive to mechanistic analysis. He demonstrated the reversibility of differentiation in chick skin and amphibian eyes, and studied the interaction of cells as they sort themselves out into differentiated tissues. Applying A. Curtis's sponge experiments to higher organisms, Weiss dissociated cells, placed them in culture and watched them migrate, touching, clasping or avoiding each other, to establish spatial relationships similar to those in the organism. He focused attention on the cell surface as a locus of developmental control, and with A. Tyler proposed an early theory of cell adhesion in terms of antibody – antigen-like interactions of cell surface molecules. Weiss extended such ideas to the theory of contact guidance whereby cells find their way, while migrating through embryos, by varying adhesion to surfaces. These ideas continue to inform current morphogenetic research and especially recent interest in extracellular material. DOM

Weizmann, Chaim (b. Motol, Grodno, Russia, 27.11.1874; naturalized British citizen, 1910; d. Rehovot, Israel, 9.11.1952). Zionist leader, distinguished scientist, president of Jewish Agency for Palestine and of the World Zionist organization (1921–31, 1935–46), president of Israel (1948–52). Educated in Germany, he acquired British citizenship while reader in biochemistry at Manchester University. His friendship with SCOTT, the editor of the influential liberal newspaper the *Manchester Guardian*, and his position as director of the Admiralty Laboratories (1916–19), gave him the entrée to Liberal political circles and Liberal sympathizers in government and opened the way for his tireless proselytization of Britain's political decision-makers, which was to result in November 1917 in the BALFOUR Declaration pledging British support for a 'National Home' in Palestine for the Jewish people. The realization of this pledge in the Allied victory, the development of the 'National Home' and the amelioration of the subsequent conflicts between Jewish settlers, the more Arab nationalist elements among the Palestinian Arabs and the British mandatory government called for the continuous exercise of the same skill as leader of the Zionist movement and as diplomatist vis-à-vis the British government; but his position was undermined as the Arab revolt of 1936 both shifted the centre of the problem from London to Palestine and threatened the British, obsessed as they were by the spectre of a European war for which they were far from ready, with a major military distraction in the eastern Mediterranean. In 1939 the failure of the Round Table conference in the face of intransigence from the Jewish and Arab Palestinians alike and the consequent British attempt to promulgate a compromise settlement – which, if successfully implemented, would have made any further growth of the Jewish 'National Home' dependent on Arab approval – made any further role for him impossible save as a figurehead for a Jewish state whose final establishment owed more to force than persuasive diplomacy, at least as Weizmann practised it. Weizmann's autobiography was published in 1949: *Trial and Error* (London). His *Letters and Papers* are being published under the general editorship of Meyer Weisgal (vol. 1, London, 1968).　　　DCW

M. Weisgal & J. Carmichael, *Chaim Weizmann* (NY, 1962); B. Litvinov, *Weizmann: Last of the Patriarchs* (London, 1976).

Wellek, René (b. Vienna, Austria-Hungary [now Austria], 22.8.1903; naturalized American citizen, 1946). Austrian/American literary theorist and critic. Educated at the University of Prague, Wellek emigrated to the USA in 1939 where he taught English, Slavic and comparative literature at various universities, including Iowa (1939–46) and Yale (1946–52). He occupied the Sterling professorship in comparative literature from 1952 to 1972. His influential central conviction that the study of literature should be 'intrinsic' or 'specifically literary' is expounded in *Theory of Literature* (NY, 1949). Though written in collaboration with Austin Warren, 13 of the 19 chapters are by Wellek, and the book bears his peculiar intellectual stamp with its debts to Roman Ingarden and the literary theory of the Prague school, and its essentially Kantian view of aesthetic experience as 'purposiveness without purpose', consisting in disinterested contemplation of objects intrinsically pleasant and interesting. Wellek's book is a densely argued and convincing plea for the autonomy of literature and art, treating the literary work as a complex many-layered whole, embodying a 'system of norms', and as a creation which must be described, analysed, and evaluated as an aesthetic structure in its own right, not reduced to historical, social, biographical or psychological causes, or identified with the responses of the reader. Wellek's own criticism, however, often lacks any sense of vivid response to individual works of literature. Four of the five projected volumes of his monumental *A History of Modern Criticism 1750–1950* (Yale, 1955–66) have been published to date.　　　RNH

Welles, George Orson (b. Kenosha, Wis., USA, 6.5.1915). American film director and actor, chiefly celebrated for his first film *Citizen Kane* (1941) which he wrote (in collaboration with Herman J. Mankiewicz), acted in, produced and directed at the age of 24. His experience as a stage actor and director at the Gate Theatre, Dublin, in 1931 and as the founder of the Mercury Theatre, producing the radio adaptation of WELLS's *The War of the Worlds* on Hallowe'en in 1938 which created national panic, singularly well equipped Welles to create such a controversial masterpiece for the cinema. The central role of Kane, generally based upon the life and times of the newspaper magnate HEARST, was acted by Welles himself who gave the character a combination of charm, bravado, megalomania and humour. Welles's skills as actor were deftly supported by the cinematic devices he used as director. The story is told from no less than five, though not always consistent, points of view. Such inconsistencies as there are Welles apparently overcame by parodying penny-dreadful journalism and using albeit quasi-psychological mystery to which the film's first line 'Rosebud' is presented as a key. Welles engineered theatrically lit compositions. A single source of light frequently disguises the absence of elaborate film studio sets. Sounds of crowds convince us of their presence though we do not see them. Welles's mastery of cinematic illusion has rarely been surpassed to so much effect. Among his subsequent films are *The Magnificent Ambersons* (1942), *The Stranger* (1946), *Macbeth* (1948), *Othello* (1952), *Touch of Evil* (1958), *The Trial* (1962), *Chimes at Midnight* (1966) and *The Immortal Story* (1968). All demonstrate different aspects of his abilities but none match the achievement and influence of *Citizen Kane*.　　　RBJG

A. Bazin, *Orson Welles* (Paris, [2]1958); P. Kael, *The Citizen Kane Book* (NY, 1971).

Wells, Herbert George (b. Bromley, London, UK, 21.9.1866; d. London, 13.8.1946). British novelist, journalist, scientific visionary and encyclopedist. Wells came from an impoverished lower-middle-class background, and was apprenticed in a drapery store at 14. He studied biology under T. H. Huxley at the Normal School of Science (now Imperial College), London – a scientific training which set him apart from his literary contemporaries. *The Time Machine* (London, 1895), *The War of the Worlds* (London, 1898) and other early works are now recognized as pioneering masterpieces of science fiction. Wells explores time and space and creates alien societies in order to give body to the new cosmogony arising out of Darwin's evolutionary theory and the laws of thermodynamics. After 1900 he diversified his energy into a number of fields. A series of social novels culminating in *Tono-Bungay* (London, 1909) and *The History of Mr Polly* (London, 1910) reveals his powers of observation and sociological generalization, his sympathy for the 'little man' and his irrepressible humour. His impatience with the literary establishment was vented in a famous quarrel with Henry JAMES. He briefly joined the Fabian Society, engaging in polemic with such fellow-members as George Bernard SHAW and the WEBBS (whom he depicted in *The New Machiavelli*, London, 1911). With *A Modern Utopia* (London, 1905) and subsequent works he became one of this century's few wholehearted utopian writers. Though a persistent critic of the League of Nations, he championed the idea of world unification, which he saw as the only alternative to devastating conflict. He foresaw many of the world's present discontents: his fictional warnings of future wars include *The World Set Free* (London, 1913) in which he predicted the atomic bomb. He was the moving spirit behind the Sankey declaration of the Rights of Man, a precursor of the United Nations Charter.

Wells portrays man as a biological species with a precarious hold on its environment. He saw himself as a 'human ecologist', and once described modern life as a 'race between education and catastrophe'. He was a lifelong educator whose progressive and rationalistic view of human civilization is expounded in *The Outline of History* (London, 1920, abridged as *A Short History of the World*, London, 1922); also in his *Experiment in Autobiography* (London, 1934). His thought now seems an influential, though somewhat dated, synthesis of evolutionism, pragmatism and various strands of socialism. His literary gifts are most fully embodied in the fiction he wrote before 1910. These works, especially his 'scientific romances' with their preoccupation with man's place in an inhospitable but ultimately conquerable universe, have profoundly affected the modern imagination.   PP

B. Bergonzi (ed.), *H. G. Wells: a Collection of Critical Essays* (Englewood Cliffs, 1976); N. & J. Mackenzie, *The Time Traveller: the Life of H. G. Wells* (London, 1973).

Wendt, Albert (b. Apia, Samoa [now Western Samoa], 27.10.1938). Samoan novelist and poet. Educated in Samoa and at Victoria University, Wellington, New Zealand, he now teaches at the University of the South Pacific in Suva. His aim is to present an 'honest view' (his words) of the mixed inheritance of the South Seas, an area burdened with European stereotypical depiction. The fine poetry collection *Inside Us the Dead* (Auckland, 1976) and the richly detailed family-saga novel *Leaves of the Banyan Tree* (Auckland, 1978) advance his declared aim, as complex artistic works and as deeply felt personal testaments. He acknowledges the influence of both CAMUS and FAULKNER upon his writing, but his work is sharply original in content and local in commitment, skilfully balancing the diverse pressures to produce a unique insight into a world of great cultural and political importance.

PNQ

Went, Fritz Warmolt (b. Utrecht, The Netherlands, 18.5.1903; naturalized American citizen, 1942). Dutch/American botanist. The son of Utrecht University's professor of botany, he lived with his parents in the Botanic Gardens. Educated at Utrecht University, where he then taught until 1927, his first research was on the growth response of oat coleoptiles to light, which led later to the discovery of polar auxin transport (see the important text, with J. V. Thimann, *Phytohormones*, NY, 1937). Following a period in Java, he moved to the USA as assistant professor of plant physiology at the California Institute of Technology, where the first air-conditioned greenhouses were built under his direction. From his work on environmental control he developed the economically important discovery that tomatoes are diurnally thermoperiodic, which subsequently led to the building of the Pasadena phytotron in 1948. Later Went served as director of the Missouri Botanical Garden and as professor of botany at Washington University; currently he is emeritus research professor at the Desert Research Institute of Nevada. It was while living downwind from Los Angeles that he turned his attention to air pollution. In collaboration with A. J. Haagensmit he elucidated the phytotoxic component of smog; not SO_2, as was previously thought, but an olefin-ozone mixture. The blue haze over mountains, he showed, was aromatic substances given off by plants. He calculated that there must be 0.32×10^9 tons of such particulate matter in the atmosphere at any one time, and from this number derived the controversial but stimulating idea that much of the world's coal and oil resources might have derived from this aerosol. As a research botanist Went has studied almost all facets of the plant sciences, from cell physiology through taxonomy and field ecology to the economic basis of life.   BEJ

Weöres, Sándor (b. Szombathely, Austria-Hungary [now Hungary], 22.6.1913). Hungarian poet and dramatist, whose lyric virtuosity far exceeds that of any of his contemporaries. He writes everything from children's verse – he himself began to compose verse in infancy – to immense metaphysical and cosmic myths, frequently dark and sombre in tone. He has been influenced by such varied and exotic sources as ancient Chinese poetry, Gilgamesh, Negro mythology and Polynesian legends, but also acknowledges his debts to a poet such as William Blake. He is a prolific translator. Complex in thought and sometimes obscure, he has exercised a strong intellectual influence on his contemporaries. His versatility is further shown in the remarkable volume *Psyche* (Budapest, 1972), purporting to be the work of an early 19c poetess, and in his anthology of hidden treasures of Hungarian verse *Három veréb hat szemmel* [Three sparrows with six eyes] (Budapest, 1977). A collection of his poetry in

English is in *Sandor Weöres and Ferenc Juhász: Selected Poems* (tr. E. Morgan, London, 1970).   GFC

Werfel, Franz (b. Prague, Bohemia, Austria-Hungary [now Czechoslovakia], 10.9.1890; d. Beverly Hills, Calif., USA, 26.8.1945). Austrian novelist and poet. A German-speaking Jew, like KAFKA, Werfel was much influenced by his native Prague. He saw military service in WW1, but his outspoken pacifism led to a charge of treason. He settled in Vienna in 1917, and met Alma Mahler, whom he married in 1929. He left Austria at the Anschluss and settled finally in California. Werfel never forgot his Jewish background but was deeply conscious of the Austrian tradition; in later years he was strongly drawn to Catholicism. *Der Weltfreund* [The universal friend] (Leipzig, 1911) established Werfel as a lyric poet of stature. *Einander. Oden, Lieder, Gestalten* [Each other. Odes, songs, forms] (Leipzig, 1915) secured his position as a leading German expressionist. Werfel sought to praise a new humanity and spiritual brotherhood; his poems from the trenches published in *Der Gerichttag* [The Day of Judgement] (Leipzig, 1919) all but despair of mankind, but summon up a deeply felt belief in man's capacity to sustain true spiritual values. Werfel wrote a number of plays but is chiefly remembered for his prose fiction. *Der Abituriententag. Die Geschichte einer Jugendschuld* (Vienna, 1928; tr. W. Chambers, *Class Reunion*, NY, 1929), *Barbara; oder die Frömmigkeit* (Vienna, 1929; tr. G. Dunlop, *The Hidden Child*, London, 1931), *Das Lied von Bernadette* (Stockholm, 1941; tr. L. Lewisohn, *The Song of Bernadette*, NY, 1942) all bear witness to his conviction that individual spiritual values will ultimately triumph. In his preface to *Bernadette* he signalled his intention to 'magnify the divine mystery and the holiness of mankind'. Werfel's work is grounded in a faith that transcends religions, a mystical energy that is expressed as *Frömmigkeit*, [piety]. The capacity of the individual to express his/her inalienable individuality through dedication and self-sacrifice is the ultimate confirmation of human values. His suspicion of 'civilization' emerges in his 'Utopian' novel *Stern der Ungeborenen, Ein Reiseroman* (Stockholm, 1946; tr. G. O. Arlt, *Star of the Unborn*, NY, 1946). ADB

L. B. Foltin (ed.), *Franz Werfel, 1890 –1945* (Pittsburgh, 1961); W. H. Fox, 'Franz Werfel', in A. Natan (ed.), *German Men of Letters*, III (London, 1964).

Werner, Alfred (b. Mulhouse, Alsace, France, 12.12.1866; naturalized Swiss citizen, 1895; d. Zürich, Switzerland, 15.11.1919). German/Swiss chemist universally recognized as the father of modern coordination chemistry. It was in 1891 (the year after he achieved his doctorate) that he first put forward his ideas upon bonding which were eventually to revolutionize inorganic chemistry. Two years later these were developed, with especial reference to transition metal compounds. Werner argued that the factor determining the structure of coordination compounds was not the primary valency (oxidation state) of the metal (or other central atom), but its coordination number (i.e. the number of ions, atoms, radicals or molecules directly bonded to the metal, now known collectively as ligands). The ligands were postulated to be arranged in simple, spatially geometric patterns, with the octahedron as the commonest arrangement, corresponding to size-coordination. A corollary of this theory was that some coordination complexes should exist as optically active isomers. For the next 20 years Werner (professor at Zürich University from 1895) and his co-workers published over 150 papers concerning the preparation, characterization and stereochemical configuration of numerous complexes. It was not until 1911, however, with his successful isolation of the first optically active transition metal complex, that his theories were generally accepted. Two years later he was awarded the Nobel prize. (See *The Selected Papers of A. Werner*, ed. G. B. Kauffman, NY, 1968.) KRS

Wesker, Arnold (b. London, UK, 24.5.1932). British dramatist. A pioneer of the revival of English social drama and an advocate of human brotherhood and the dissemination of culture. Brought up in a family of Jewish communist immigrants, he turned his experience to good account in the 'Wesker Trilogy' (*Chicken Soup with Barley*, 1958, *Roots*, 1959, and *I'm Talking about Jerusalem*, 1960) which traces the gradual political disillusionment of the Khan family between 1936 and 1959. Of the three plays, *Roots* has been singled out for its study of a Norfolk peasant girl's discovery of her capacity to articulate ideas and feelings. Wesker achieved commercial success with *Chips with Everything* (1962), an expressionistic study of the English class system's capacity to absorb rebellion. The relative failure of his cultural missionary work with an organization called Centre 42 seemed to blunt his political idealism and he turned to more private themes. *The Wedding Feast* (1974), an adaptation of a Dostoevsky story to an English setting, showed that he could still powerfully convey domestic ritual and class tyranny. *Caritas* (1981), produced by the National Theatre, London, was also impressive, a one-act study of a 14c religious anchoress. Although a leading figure in the postwar British theatrical revival, Wesker is currently more honoured abroad than in his native land. MB

G. Leeming & S. Trussler, *The Plays of Arnold Wesker* (London, 1971).

West, Rebecca, ps. of Cicely Isabel Andrews, *née* Fairfield (b. County Kerry, Ireland, UK [now Irish Republic], 25.12.1892; d. London, UK, 15.3.1983). British journalist, novelist and critic. Taking her pen name from IBSEN's *Rosmersholm* (1886), Rebecca West joined the staff of the *Freewoman* in 1911 and the *Clarion* in the following year, quickly establishing herself as a major feminist voice. Acerbic, witty, incisive, her early work (ed. J. Marcus, *The Young Rebecca: Selected Essays by Rebecca West 1911–17*, London, 1981) brought her to the attention of WELLS, by whom she bore a son, the novelist Anthony West. Wells's name for her, 'Panther', aptly summarizes the lean ferocity of her prose. Her first novel *The Return of the Soldier* (London, 1918), about an amnesiac shell-shock victim, introduced a recurrent theme: the contrast between women's creative nurturing instincts and men's destructive ones. As a novelist Rebecca West has demonstrated psychological insight and a mastery of English prose – the novellas in *The Harsh Voice* (London, 1935) are as good as STEAD – but her best work is nonfictional. Her masterpiece is her Yugoslav travelogue *Black Lamb, Grey Falcon* (2 vols, NY, 1941), which is about many things, but most bitterly about 'the infiltration of peace with the depravity of war'. Like her compelling study of *The Meaning of Treason* (NY, 1947, [2]1982) it rests securely on techniques learned in journalism: immediate, vivid description; lucid, assured summarizing; the assumption of intelligence but not of particular knowledge in the reader; arresting and memorable phraseology. Her phrase-making ability is her most striking asset: her writing is full of sentences which stay in the mind, such as, 'All men should have a drop of treason in their veins, if the nations are not to go soft like so many sleepy pears.' What gives the phrase-making point, and saves it from the ephemerality of journalism, is the organizing intelligence behind it: the lines which stick are the crucial ones, which are meant to. *Rebecca West: a Celebration* (NY, 1977) selects from a lifetime's work.   NP

G. E. Hutchinson, *A Preliminary List of the Writings of Rebecca West: 1912–1951* (New Haven, 1957); P. Wolfe, *Rebecca West: Artist and Thinker* (Carbondale, 1971).

Weston, Edward Henry (b. Highland Park, Ill., USA, 24.3.1886; d. Carmel, Calif., 1.1.1958). American photographer. Weston set up his first portrait studio in Tropico (now Glendale), California, in 1911. His pictorialist photographs, using a soft-focus lens and derived from Whistler and others, won him prizes during WW1. His emergence as a classic modern master of the 8×10 plate camera dates from 1922, immediately before he met STIEGLITZ, STRAND and Charles Sheeler. His style developed during two visits to Mexico City with Tina Modotti in 1923–5 and 1926. After the mid-1920s he abandoned matte-platinum papers in favour of glossy commercial papers which enhanced the 'magic realism' of his

sharply focused subjects. These included portraits of the painters of the Mexican mural renaissance, nudes, landscapes and still life, notably shells and vegetables. He lived in Carmel from 1929 when nearby Point Lobos became a key subject. With Edward STEICHEN he organized the American section of the '*Film und Foto*' exhibition in Stuttgart, 1929. His methods inspired the formation of the *f*.64 group in 1932. In 1937 he became the first photographer to receive a Guggenheim fellowship (renewed 1938) and photographed in California, Arizona, New Mexico and Nevada. He received a major exhibition at the Museum of Modern Art, New York, in 1946 and became an intense influence on the photographic medium. He was incapacitated for many years by Parkinson's disease.   MH-B

B. Maddow, *Edward Weston: Fifty Years* (Millerton, 1973).

Weyl, Hermann (b. Elmshorn, Schleswig-Holstein, Germany, 9.11.1885; naturalized American citizen; d. Zürich, Switzerland, 8.12.1955). German/American mathematician, especially noted for the establishment of symmetry as an essential tool in applied mathematics and mathematical physics. He worked at the universities of Zürich (1913–30), Göttingen (1930–3) and Princeton (1933–55). The configuration space in which the results of possible observations lie will not in general have a well-known geometrical structure; or, especially in cases where the space has very many dimensions, a known structure may be present but unrecognized. One way of characterizing the space is to look at the group of symmetries; that is, of transformations of the space into itself. By analogy, it is useful to describe angular momentum in terms of invariance under rotation, i.e. by symmetry in the momentum space associated with the configuration space; and linear momentum by similar reference to linear displacement. In this way concepts originally defined in Euclidean space may again be recognized in the configuration spaces of quantum physics or general relativity (see *Symmetry*, Princeton, 1952). Mathematically speaking, this work of Weyl's appears as the development of the necessary apparatus by, for instance, studying the global properties of Lie groups (extending results of CARTAN) and finding forms (Weyl chambers, the maximal Torus, etc.) to express these structures in a tractable manner. These results can also be regarded as geometry, and Weyl had earlier (pre-1920) been noted as a geometrician. His *Die Idee der Riemannschen Fläche* [The idea of the Riemann surface] (1913) gave a complete description of the 1-dimension complex Riemannian manifold; this object resembles a 2-dimensional Euclidean space in its degree of complexity. Later he developed the programme of uniquely embedding any compact 2-dimensional Riemannian manifold in Euclidean 3-space, thus providing a standard method of visualizing novel structures within a well-known space. Weyl's earliest work was on spectral theory and analytic number theory. Here he proved classic results about the equidistribution of sequences of real numbers modulo 1.

AGPW

Wharton, Edith Newbold, *née* Jones (b. New York, USA, 24.1.1862; d. Saint-Brice-sous-Forêt, Seine-et-Oise, France, 11.8.1937). American novelist. Born into, and married within, the old social aristocracy of New York, it was her intimate but critical understanding of this exclusive society and the *nouveau riche* class which infiltrated and supplanted it which provided much of the material for her fiction. Her marriage was unhappy (her husband's mental illness led to divorce in 1913), and from 1907 she lived in France as a permanent expatriate. She began to write and publish stories in the 1890s, possibly for therapeutic reasons; financial independence allowed her to write for the satisfaction of her own critical standards. Like Henry JAMES, her mentor more by virtue of his literary conscience than by any influence of style, she wrote about a narrow social world. However, if her characters lack the fine depth of consciousness of James's they are more firmly placed in their social setting, and her plots are clear in outline and governed by an exact and ironic authorial tone. Her novels of New York society –

The House of Mirth (NY, 1905), *The Custom of the Country* (NY, 1913) and *The Age of Innocence* (NY, 1920) – link two sorts of conflict, between personal independence and social convention, and between genteel wealth and the brash fortunes accumulated in the expanding West. They suggest that social energy will always have the edge over a social decorum which comprises and suppresses its moral sense. In *Ethan Frome* (NY, 1911) and *Summer* (NY, 1917) she turned her attention to rural and small-town Massachusetts to portray other types of social and moral confinement.

ATKC

R. W. B. Lewis, *Edith Wharton: a Biography* (NY, 1975).

Wheeler, John Archibald (b. Jacksonville, Fla, USA, 9.7.1911). American physicist. He obtained his PhD in physics at Johns Hopkins University in 1933 and then, after working for a year in New York with Gregory Breit and for another year in Copenhagen with Niels BOHR, took a teaching post at the University of North Carolina. In 1938 he moved to Princeton where he became professor in 1947. With Bohr, he worked on the mechanism of nuclear fission and in the years 1942–5 he collaborated on developing methods for controlling nuclear reactors and other devices, as part of the Manhattan project. With FEYNMAN at Princeton he analysed the loss of energy by an accelerating charge and showed how it can be interpreted in terms of back reaction by distant absorbing particles. He introduced the concepts of the scattering matrix and resonating group structure and, with D. L. Hill, put forward the collective model of the atomic nucleus. With F. G. Werner and others he used the liquid drop model to investigate the properties of possible superheavy nuclei. Between 1950 and 1953 Wheeler again devoted himself to weapons research, first with TELLER and others at Los Alamos, working on the principles of the hydrogen bomb, and then as director of Project Matterhorn at Princeton, working out a detailed design for this and other devices.

After the completion of this project in 1953, Wheeler turned his attention to

EINSTEIN's general theory of relativity, his particular interest being in its view of the relation between particles and the gravitational field. It was then common to consider particles as fundamental objects and fields as being mathematical constructs which were merely convenient for working out particle interactions. But Wheeler and Feynman had shown that this view runs into difficulties when considered within the context of quantum electrodynamics. Einstein's view was that particles rather than being 'immersed' in space-time were themselves essentially geometrical objects. Wheeler introduced the idea that space-time could be considered as multiple connected with 'wormholes' linking positive and negative electric charges. When quantum theory is combined with general relativity, space-time is considered as constantly fluctuating between one geometry and another with a certain probability that it will be in any one state with its associated wormhole configuration. Wheeler has also been a pioneer of the modern study of continued gravitational collapse; it was he who first introduced the term 'black hole'. An important contribution to this subject was his systematic analysis (with B. K. Harrison, K. S. Thorne and M. Wakano) of the possible equilibrium configurations for objects composed of cold material. His other publications include *Geometrodynamics* (NY, 1962), *Gravitation Theory and Gravitational Collapse* (Chicago, 1965, with B. K. Harrison, K. S. Thorne and M. Wakano), *Spacetime Physics* (San Francisco, 1966, with E. F. Taylor) and *Gravitation* (San Francisco, 1972, with C. W. Misner and K. S. Thorne). JCM

Wheeler, Robert Eric Mortimer (b. Edinburgh, Lothian, UK, 10.9.1890; d. London, 22.7.1976). British archaeologist. As keeper of archaeology at the National Museum of Wales (1920–6) he gave fresh impetus to the discipline of archaeological excavation realizing that if the subject were to develop, rigorous new techniques would have to be evolved for the extraction of primary data from the soil and for its proper study and publication. His early excavations at Segontium (1921–2), Brecon

Gaer (1924–5), Caerleon (1926) and Lydney (1928–9) demonstrate the emergence of an entirely new style of excavation which French archaeologists today still call 'Le système Wheeler'. He was to perfect his technique still further when as a director of the London Museum and lecturer at the Institute of Archaeology of London University he undertook the more extensive explorations in the pre-Roman and Roman town of Verulamium (1930–4) and the Iron Age hill-fort of Maiden Castle (1934–7). Following a period as director-general of archaeology in India (1944–7), imposing his standard of technical excellence on the subcontinent, and carrying further the study of the Indus civilization, he returned to London to the chair of archaeology of the Roman provinces. His published excavation reports are the greatest monument to the revolution in excavation technique which he brought about and the handbook *Archaeology from the Earth* (Oxford, 1954) succinctly summarizes his objectives and procedures. From 1949 to 1968 he served as secretary of the British Academy and played a major role in the reforms which created the modern academy. BWC

Whinfield, John Rex (b. Sutton, Surrey, UK, 16.2.1901; d. Dorking, Surrey, 6.7.1966). British chemist, inventor of polyester fibre and film. After Cambridge, Whinfield worked for a year with Cross, a pioneer of the viscose rayon process, before joining Calico Printers in 1923. It was here, with the experimental support of Dickson, that he prepared the first polyester fibre in 1941, thereby exploiting a gap in the massive work of CAROTHERS. Whinfield was characteristically phlegmatic in his appraisal of his discovery, but it launched him on a lifelong association with the development of 'Terylene' fibre, first with the Ministry of Supply during WW2 and later with Imperial Chemical Industries as a director of the fibres division. RPS

Whipple, George Hoyt (b. Ashland, NH, USA, 28.8.1878; d. Rochester, NY, 12.2.1976). American pathologist, best known for his work on disorders of the blood and of the gastrointestinal tract. Whipple became interested in medical research as a student at the Johns Hopkins University medical school, where he remained on the staff until 1914, working on bile pigments and blood coagulation. He also first described a rare disorder (now known as Whipple's disease) of the intestines. At the University of California (1914–22) he systematically showed the dietary importance of liver, kidney and meat in stimulating the bone marrow to produce red blood cells in experimentally produced anaemia in dogs. This information was turned to clinical use by two Harvard physicians, George Minot and William Murphy, who revolutionized the treatment of pernicious anaemia with liver and other foodstuffs. The role of vitamin B12 in pernicious anaemia was subsequently elucidated, but Whipple, Minot and Murphy shared the 1934 Nobel prize for their researches. Whipple went to the University of Rochester School of Medicine in 1922, where he continued his researches on bile, blood proteins and blood clotting, including classic work on thalassemia, a genetic bleeding disorder found in people of Mediterranean extraction. As a trustee of the Rockefeller Foundation (1927–43) and in other powerful positions, Whipple also played a crucial role in American medical research.   WFB

G. W. Corner, *George Hoyt Whipple and his Friends* (Philadelphia, 1963).

White, Patrick Victor Martindale (b. London, UK, 28.5.1912). Australian novelist. Born (in Knightsbridge) during one of his parents' visits to England, White was educated at schools in Australia before being 'ironed out' at Cheltenham College (which he hated) and going on to read modern languages at King's College, Cambridge, where his enduring interest in European literature and culture began. He returned to Australia in 1946, together with Manoly Lascaris (with whom he has lived ever since) and *The Aunt's Story* (London, 1948), a favourite among his own novels which captures both the spirit of this time and the essential qualities of White's writing. Scathing satire in social observation, a strong sense of 'the coun-

try of the mind' in his settings and a relentless exploration of spiritual quest are foremost among these; the basic loneliness of life is redeemed by moments of vision and shared understanding. The Nobel prize for literature (awarded in 1973) confirmed the international reputation of his writings, thereby achieving a status for Australian writing from which many other authors have benefited. Novels such as *Voss* (London, 1957) and *The Eye of the Storm* (London, 1973) are outstanding for their creation of central characters unforgettable in their pride – and discovery of humility. White's autobiography *Flaws in the Glass* (London, 1981) proved that he applied the same relentless scrutiny to his own failings.   PNQ

G. A. Wilkes (ed.), *Ten Essays on Patrick White* (North Ryde, NSW, 1970).

Whitehead, Alfred North (b. Ramsgate, Kent, UK, 15.2.1861; d. Cambridge, Mass., USA, 30.12.1947). British philosopher. The son of a clergyman, Whitehead went to Trinity College, Cambridge, in 1880 as a scholar in mathematics. He was elected to a fellowship in 1884. Early work on algebra from a comprehensive point of view prepared him for the collaboration with his great pupil Bertrand RUSSELL on *Principia Mathematica* (3 vols, Cambridge, 1910–13) in which the derivation of all mathematical concepts and assumptions from those of logic is attempted in a rigorously deductive fashion. The book revolutionized logic and had a profound influence on philosophy, particularly in the English-speaking world. Whitehead moved to London in 1910, becoming professor of applied mathematics at Imperial College in 1914. A projected fourth volume of *Principia*, on geometry, which was Whitehead's responsibility, was never written: instead he produced an important series of books between 1919 and 1922 in which, in the manner of the *Principia*, such exact notions of geometry as point and line (and their temporal correlates such as instant) are defined in terms of the comparatively vague and unideal items spread out in time and space that we actually come upon in experience. In 1924, at the advanced age of 62, Whitehead started a new and notable career as professor of philosophy at Harvard, where he remained active until his death 23 years later, although formally leaving his chair in 1937. The main fruits of this metaphysical phase of Whitehead's work are his magisterial presentation of his own disbelief in the ultimate reality of the mathematically tidy Nature of Newtonian physics through the medium of a discursive history of science: *Science and the Modern World* (NY, 1925) and the much less digestible *Process and Reality* (Cambridge, 1929) in which his 'philosophy of organism' receives its official exposition. A widely learned and amusing man, Whitehead has had more influence, apart from his share in *Principia*, through occasional brilliant *aperçus* than through his system proper which remains the preserve of devotees.

AQ

I. Leclerc (ed.), *The Relevance of Whitehead* (London, 1961).

Whittle, Frank (b. Coventry, W. Mids, UK, 1.6.1907). British aeronautical engineer. His 1927 student thesis at the RAF College, Cranwell, proposed a new form of aircraft engine. This burned cheaper oil fuel so that expanding gases pressed against the turbine blades which, drawing in air from the front of the engine and compressing it, then forced it out at the back. He patented the idea in 1930 but had no funds to exploit it. The Air Ministry reluctantly agreed to support him in 1939, just before the outbreak of war. The first test flight of the new engine was in 1941, but development was too late to play a significant part in the war. Subsequently the jet engine was developed to provide the power for all today's commercial planes and so change the nature of air transport.

RIT

Whorf, Benjamin Lee (b. Winthrop, Mass., USA, 24.4.1897; d. Wethersfield, Conn., 26.7.1941). American linguist known chiefly for his pronouncements on the relationship between language and thought. Born and brought up in a suburb of Boston, he studied chemical engineering at MIT and then became a fire prevention officer, a career which he maintained until his death, turning down offers of academic posts, and working on linguistics in his spare time. Whorf's interest in linguistics began in his mid-20s, when he worked extensively on Maya writing. After meeting the linguist SAPIR and enrolling as the latter's student, Whorf's linguistic work gained depth and direction. Influenced by Sapir, who believed that a person's language shaped his worldview, and also by his own study of the superficially strange Hopi language, Whorf formulated his 'linguistic relativity principle' (also known as the 'Sapir–Whorf hypothesis'), that 'users of markedly different grammars ... arrive at somewhat different views of the world.' This view was expressed in a number of popularizing articles, the best known being 'The relation of habitual thought and behavior to language' (1939), in which he claims that speakers of a Standard Average European (SAE) language envisage concepts of time, space and matter differently from Hopi speakers. For a selection from his work, see J. B. Carroll (ed.), *Language, Thought and Reality: Selected Writings of Benjamin Lee Whorf* (NY, 1956). JMA

Wieland, Heinrich Otto (b. Pforzheim, Baden-Württemberg, Germany, 4.6.1877; d. Starnberg, Bavaria, West Germany, 5.8.1957). German organic chemist. After study at the universities of Munich, Berlin and Stuttgart, Wieland received his doctorate (1901) under Thiele in Munich. He returned to Munich in 1925 to succeed WILLSTÄTTER and occupied the chair of chemistry there for 27 years. Wieland's work ranged widely over organic chemistry and bio-organic chemistry. In its first phase he concentrated on nitrogenous organic compounds, notably the products of interaction of nitrogen oxides with alkenes and with aromatics, and stable organic nitrogen radicals (e.g. diphenyl nitrogen). In his later years Wieland's work was almost entirely in the field of naturally occurring compounds: on alkaloids, including morphine, strychnine, and lobelic alkaloids; on the poisonous cyclopeptides from 'death-cap' mushrooms; on butterfly-wing pigments (i.e. the biologically important pterins); and above all, for some 20 years on bile acids, of major importance in the digestion of fats. This last work was of great general importance in clarifying the structure of the steroids. Wieland also devoted a substantial part of his life's work to biological oxidations: he recognized the universal significance of dehydrogenation in that context and so helped to unite organic chemistry and biochemistry. Possessed of an encyclopedic knowledge of chemistry as a whole, he was for 20 years editor of *Liebig's Annalen der Chemie* [Liebig's annals of chemistry]. He was awarded a Nobel prize in 1927 jointly with WINDAUS.   NBC

Wiener, Norbert (b. Columbia, Mo., USA, 26.11.1894; d. Stockholm, Sweden, 18.3.1964). American mathematician. An infant prodigy, Wiener suffered in his youth from excessively intensive instruction. He took his doctorate at the age of 19 with an (unpublished) comparison between mathematical logic as developed by Bertrand RUSSELL, and algebraic logic in the tradition of the German mathematician Schröder. Over the next few years he oscillated between mathematics, philosophy and engineering. However, in 1919 he obtained a post in the mathematics department of MIT, where he passed his entire career as a mathematician. Wiener was a colourful character, and one of the world's great bad lecturers; although he became famous as a popularizer of various mathematical and social topics, his research papers are often difficult to follow, exhibiting the same propensity for disorder that attended his lectures. His most successful writings as such are his autobiographical books, in which he frankly describes the difficulties which prodigyhood had brought him.

Wiener's mathematical research covered a wide, and rather unusual, collection of topics. In mathematical analysis he studied integral equations (of which a particular kind has been named after him) and harmonic analysis (including Fourier transforms). His interests in applications included potential theory; ergodic theory and statistical mechanics, with especial reference to Brownian motion; and a scattering of topics in

quantum mechanics and relativity theory. An especial interest was cybernetics, a general theory of communication and information processing, in which various techniques of analysis, found by him and others, played useful roles. His researches led to a book *Cybernetics* (NY, 1948), followed by popular studies of the ethical, social and even religious implications of cybernetics in *The Human Use of Human Beings* (Boston, Mass., 1950) and *God and Golem Inc.* (Cambridge, Mass., 1964). Publication of his *Collected Works* is in progress (Cambridge, Mass., 1976–).   IG-G/RAH

Wigglesworth, Vincent Brian (b. Kirkham, Lancs., UK, 17.4.1899). British insect physiologist. Wigglesworth studied medicine but, influenced by Hopwood, did his first research in biochemistry on an insect. He taught at the London School of Tropical Medicine, researching basic physiology to obtain an understanding of processes in medical entomology. His *Principles of Insect Physiology* (London, 1939) established the new subject. In 1945 he formed a small team called the Unit of Insect Physiology in Cambridge University, which investigated basic mechanisms related to agricultural pests, and he later became the Quick professor of biology. He attracted a remarkable procession of students and visiting workers who extended the subject and established it in research centres throughout the world. His outstanding discoveries are on the hormones controlling insect development but he contributed to every facet of their physiology. However in the Royal Society's Croonian lecture of 1948 he advocated insects as an ideal medium for studying pure physiology. In consequence, the subject has become increasingly an academic one, of great interest but mostly divorced from its original purpose of forming a foundation for understanding and solving applied problems.   JWLB

J. Beament, 'Wigglesworth's contribution to insect biology', in M. Locke & D. S. Smith (eds), *Insect Biology in the Future* (NY, 1980).

Wigner, Eugene Paul (b. Budapest, Austria-Hungary [now Hungary], 17.11.1902; naturalized American citizen, 1937).

Hungarian/American physicist. Wigner, who went to the USA in 1933, is a theoretical physicist whose interests have covered a very wide field, including the theory of the atomic nucleus, the design of nuclear reactors and the theory of metallic cohesion. His unique contribution is to have exploited to the full the concept of symmetry in physical theories. For example, one could calculate a certain property relating to the surface of a simple cube. This might be an expression involving a, b and c, the lengths of the three edges of the cube which meet at one point. Then this expression must clearly be unchanged if we substitute a for b, b for c, and c for a, wherever they occur, since the three edges are identical. More generally, the laws of physics cannot be different for directions or motions to the left than for those to the right, nor should results for negative times differ from those for positive times. Wigner showed that the application of these general principles (using a branch of mathematics known as group theory) is a powerful tool in predicting basic physical behaviour. For this he was awarded the Nobel prize for physics in 1963. HMR

Wilamowitz-Moellendorff, Ulrich Friedrich Richard von (b. Markowitz, Prussia, Germany [now Markowice, Poznań, Poland], 22.12.1848; d. Berlin, Germany, 25.9.1931). German classical philologist. Wilamowitz was perhaps the last classical scholar to have had a universal grasp of his discipline; equipped with a firm and innovatory methodological awareness and with an ability to incorporate the results of new scholarship into his own work, he was profound and pioneering in almost every branch of Greek studies. His philological contributions include textual criticism, literary history and criticism, epigraphy, biography, religious history and prosody. Professor at Greifswald (1876–83) and at Göttingen (1883–97), he was appointed professor of ancient philology at the University of Berlin (1897–1921), playing a central role in the great publications of the Berlin Academy of Sciences. Wilamowitz translated the Greek tragedians into German, and his commentaries on the dramas brought about a revaluation of Euripides; similarly his editions of Callimachus (Berlin, 1882), of the Bucolic poets (Berlin, 1905) and of Pindar (Berlin, 1922) have led to a significant reassessment of these authors, and his Homeric contributions are important in the tradition of literary criticism of Homer. The subjective nature of Wilamowitz's studies is undeniable, and his biography of Plato (2 vols, Berlin, 1919) is unmistakably autobiographical. His controversy with NIETZSCHE over the latter's *Birth of Tragedy* (1872) bears all the marks of a deep antagonism even though fought by Wilamowitz in the interests of scholarship. He published his memoirs as *Erinnerungen 1848–1914* (Leipzig, 1928; *My Recollections, 1848–1914*, London, 1930). KKS

H. Lloyd-Jones, Introduction to U. v. Wilamowitz-Moellendorff, *History of Classical Scholarship*, tr. A. Harris (London, 1982).

Wilder, Thornton Niven (b. Madison, Wis., USA, 17.4.1897; d. New Haven, Conn., 7.12.1975). American dramatist and novelist, equally prolific and successful in both forms, whose novel *The Bridge of San Luis Rey* (NY, 1927) and plays *Our Town* (1938) and *The Skin of Our Teeth* (1942) were all awarded Pulitzer prizes. Although his essentially optimistic, outgoing writing was most closely in tune with the American mood of the pre-depression years, Wilder continued to celebrate the variety and value of human life when a more sombre spirit prevailed. A fluidity of chronological sequence, a conscious manipulation of the mechanics of construction, and a combination of these non-naturalistic elements with a sense of experiential adventure characterized his work; and the eventual commercial success of *The Matchmaker* (1954, though originally staged as *The Merchant of Yonkers* in 1938), as of its musical version *Hello, Dolly!* (1965), typically revealed both his consummate control of stagecraft and his affirmatory (if arguably lightweight) view of life. ST

R. Burbank, *Thornton Wilder* (NY, 1961); D. Haberman, *The Plays of Thornton Wilder* (Middletown, 1967).

Wilkins, Maurice Hugh Frederick (b. Pongaroa, N. Island, New Zealand, 15.12.1916). British biophysicist. Like many scientists who graduated on the eve of WW2, Wilkins's first jobs were military – for the Ministry of Home Security in 1938, and at the University of California at Berkeley on the Manhattan project (which produced the atomic bomb) in 1944. His significant scientific contribution, however, was to the crystallographic study of DNA, which he and FRANKLIN worked on in London, while J. D. WATSON and CRICK were modelling the molecular structure in Cambridge. Wilkins's contribution to the discovery of the double helix was perhaps as much in forming a link between the London and Cambridge groups as it was in actual experimental work. He shared the 1962 Nobel prize in physiology and medicine with Watson and Crick. He also developed the electron-trap theory of luminescence and phosphorescence, worked out light microscopy, particularly interference, techniques for cytochemical research, and has done structural studies of nerve membrane. He has worked at King's College, London, since 1946. In 1969 he was president of the British Society for Social Responsibility in Science. DOM

Wilkinson, Geoffrey (b. Todmorden, W. Yorks., UK, 14.7.1921). British chemist. Wilkinson is best known for his outstanding synthetic abilities in the field of organometallic chemistry. He was educated at Imperial College, London (1939–42), where he returned in 1956 as professor of inorganic chemistry. In the interim, he worked on atomic research with the National Research Council of Canada (1943–6), and with SEABORG in Berkeley as a nuclear chemist (1946–50). After a short spell at MIT (working on metal carbonyl complexes) he was appointed to Harvard in 1951. In 1952, Wilkinson (in collaboration with Rosenblum, Whiting and R. B. WOODWARD) published a paper which is now a milestone in organometallic chemistry (*J. Am. Chem. Soc.*, 74 [1952], 2125): he correctly deduced that ferrocene (a molecule discovered independently by both Pauson and Miller) was a so-called 'sandwich compound'. Since then, he

has been in the vanguard of the renaissance of inorganic chemistry, writing with COTTON the definitive textbook (*Advanced Inorganic Chemistry*, NY, ⁴1980), developing catalysts of commercial importance, and (through his elegant synthetic work) gaining insight into their mechanistic functions. In 1973, jointly with E. O. FISCHER, he was awarded the Nobel prize for chemistry.
KRS

G. Wilkinson, *J. Organomet. Chem.*, 100 (1975), 273.

Williams, Frederic Calland (b. Stockport, Ches., UK, 26.6.1911; d. Manchester, 11.8.1977). British electrical engineer. Williams is best known for his work on radar at the Telecommunications Research Establishment, and for inventing an electronic memory system (1949) which led to the building of the world's first commercial digital computer, the Ferranti Mk I (1951). Working under the direction of Sir Robert Watson-Watt at TRE, he invented the Plan Position Indicator and the radar homing device known as 'H₂S'. In 1946 he became professor of electrical engineering at Manchester and spent some 10 years on the development of computers using electronic valves, particularly the use of the vacuum pentode. In the mid-1950s he turned his attention to heavy electrical machinery and had immediate success in inventing a brushless variable speed induction motor with a spherical rotor. The machine was never exploited commercially but in the process of analysing it he laid the groundwork for the design of all the arch motors and linear motors to follow.
ERL

Williams, Raymond Henry (b. Pandy, Gwent, UK, 31.8.1921). British sociologist of culture, literary critic and novelist. An undergraduate at Trinity College, Cambridge, after WW2 service he became an adult education tutor in Oxford. In 1961 he returned to Cambridge as a lecturer in English, and in 1974 was appointed professor of drama. Williams made an immediate impact with his first two major books *Culture and Society* (London, 1958) and *The Long Revolution* (London, 1961), as ideologically committed to the reassessment of English literary tradition as to the analysis of contemporary cultural forms. In his subsequent work, though apparently diverse – on drama, film, novels, the Press, language, television and political theory – Williams has pursued in detail ideas and arguments identified in those earlier books. Everything he has written (including his own novels) has been stamped by a quest for what Williams calls 'cultural materialism', and affirms a radical concern for the processes of communication and for the relationship between communication forms and social institutions. A committed socialist, he rejects traditional MARXist analyses of culture, emphasizing that 'cultural practices are forms of material production' (see *Culture*, London, 1981). But he remains probably the most influential figure in the current revival of Marxism as a basis for political and literary thinking (see *Marxism and Literature*, Oxford, 1977), and formative in the development of communication and cultural studies. An autobiographical account of his intellectual and political development is presented in *Politics and Letters* (London, 1979). PF

J. P. Ward, *Raymond Williams* (Cardiff, 1981).

Williams, Thomas Lanier (Tennessee) (b. Columbus, Miss., USA, 26.3.1911; d. New York, 25.4.1983). American dramatist. His first stage success came in 1945 with *The Glass Menagerie*, which included the recurrent, semiautobiographical archetypes of a domineering elderly mother, crippled daughter and artistic, rebellious son. Williams achieved a more notorious fame for the claustrophobic sexuality of *A Streetcar Named Desire* (1947) and *Cat on a Hot Tin Roof* (1955), but he continued to expose the pain of loneliness and of imminent mortality, combining a parable-like universality with a sure sense of the specific in speech patterns and locale. While he has only rarely chosen the form of dramatic allegory, as in *Camino Real* (1953), most of his prolific work utilizes symbolism (often eponymous) but not with invariable success, sometimes mixing realistic and archetypal characters, as in *The Rose Tattoo*

(1951) and *The Milk Train Doesn't Stop Here Anymore* (1962), and in others making plot subservient to drifting personal encounters, as in *The Night of the Iguana* (1961) and *Small Craft Warnings* (1972). Williams's more recent work has suffered as much from the fact that personalized exposure of pain is out of fashion as from any diminution of energy – an energy to some extent recharged by his successful confrontation with his own dependencies, and his ability openly to declare the homosexuality necessarily understated in his earlier plays. ST

B. Nelson, *Tennessee Williams: the Man and his Work* (NY, 1961); J. L. Tharpe (ed.), *Tennessee Williams: a Tribute* (Jackson, Miss., 1977).

Williams, William Carlos (b. Rutherford, NJ, USA, 17.9.1883; d. Rutherford, 4.3.1963). American poet. His career can be seen as complementary to that of Ezra POUND, his lifelong friend and rival from their days at the University of Pennsylvania. Both were preoccupied with the prospects for an American culture, but whereas Pound took his vantage point in Europe, Williams insisted on the importance of working through contact with indigenous materials and forms. For many years he combined work as a doctor in general practice with a steady output of poetry, experimental prose, novels, short stories, essays and plays. The idea of the new was central to his work: unprecedented thoughts and feelings responsive to a new urban and technological world, but related to the cyclical renewals and destructions of natural forces. He found traditional cultural forms unsuited to his purposes, and looked for precedents in modern painting and photography, the design of machinery, and the disrupted fluency of local speech. Public recognition came late, and until his mid-50s his poetry was issued in small editions by expatriate or coterie publishers. This work was gathered in two volumes of *Collected Later Poems* (NY, 1950) and *Collected Earlier Poems* (NY, 1951). *Paterson* (5 books, NY, 1946–58), his most ambitious poem and the fulfilment of a lifetime's intention, examines the New Jersey industrial town in terms of the history of its site and the correspondence of urban and human topographies, threading together documentary sources and lyric and dramatic verse in writing which establishes its authority outside the author's point of view. His last poems, collected in *Pictures from Breughel* (NY, 1962), perform a nonegotistical recapitulation of his life and experience. ATKC

R. Whittemore, *William Carlos Williams, Poet from Jersey* (Boston, Mass., 1975).

Willstätter, Richard Martin (b. Karlsruhe, Baden, Germany, 13.8.1872; naturalized Swiss citizen; d. Locarno, Ticino, Switzerland, 3.8.1942). German/Swiss organic chemist. In 1890 Willstätter entered the University of Munich where he came under the influence of Adolf von Baeyer, eventually succeeding him in 1916. He retired prematurely in 1924, as a gesture against increasing anti-Semitism in Germany. In 1938, with the aid of his pupil A. Stoll, he emigrated to Switzerland to escape from the Gestapo. Willstätter worked with Einhorn on the structure of cocaine (1894) and later continued to work on tropine alkaloids. By 1898 he had brilliantly shown that earlier formulae were wrong and that the alkaloids were seven-membered-ring bicyclic compounds. Thence he was led to the preparation of cyclo-octatetrene in 1913, work impugned at one stage but later vindicated by J. W. von Reppe's large-scale synthesis. Willstätter also worked on quinones, quinone imines, related dyes, and on the theory of the oxidation of aromatic amines (with HABER). His work reached a peak in 1905–14 with his studies on chlorophyll and on anthocyanins. He laid the foundations for the later elucidation of the complete structure of chlorophyll by Hans FISCHER. His work in this field led to an interest in enzymes, in adsorbents, and in photosynthesis, the first topic occupying much of his later years. He received the Nobel prize in 1915. NBC

Wilson, Alan Geoffrey (b. Bradford, W. Yorks., UK, 8.1.1939). British geographer who has made significant contributions to mathematical models of human spatial interaction. Using models originally developed in statistical mechanics, Wilson built up an alternative to the gravity models widely used in the 1950s in urban and regional planning to forecast flows of traffic, freight and migration. His entropy-maximizing models allowed more accurate estimates of flows, while removing the need for a formal dependence on physical analogies. The Wilson model has been extended to a wide number of planning situations, and theoretical links have been established to both linear programming models and catastrophe theory. Many of Wilson's contributions are summarized in *Entropy in Urban and Regional Modelling* (London, 1970), *Urban and Regional Models* (London, 1974) and *Catastrophe Theory and Bifurcation* (London, 1981). A Cambridge mathematics graduate, Wilson worked in nuclear physics and in the mathematics advisory unit of the Ministry of Transport before moving to the chair of geography at Leeds. PH

Wilson, Charles Thomson Rees (b. nr Glencorse, Lothian, UK, 14.2.1869; d. Carlops, nr Glencorse, 15.11.1959). British physicist and inventor of a unique scientific device, the cloud-chamber, which has been of incalculable value in the development of atomic physics. By causing vapour to condense on the electric charges which charged atomic and subatomic particles, travelling at speed through a moist gas, liberate in their collisions with atoms, the cloud-chamber makes the tracks of those particles visible. In 1894, during a vacation spent at the observatory on Ben Nevis, Wilson's interest was aroused by the optical effects produced by the sun, shining through cloud and mist. He tried to reproduce these effects on a small scale at the Cavendish Laboratory in Cambridge and made the crucial observation of the part played by electrically charged particles, ions, in the condensation process. The discovery of X-rays in 1895 and radioactivity in 1896 provided Wilson with convenient sources of ionizing particles. The intellectual excitement generated in the laboratory by these discoveries, followed in 1897 by J. J. THOMSON's discovery of the electron, provided the stimulus which led Wilson to his novel idea and eventually to its successful realization. The simple elegance of Wilson's experimental arrangement does not immediately reveal the vision behind its conception or the patience and consummate practical skill needed to construct and operate it. In 1911 Wilson published the first pictures of the tracks of electrons and atomic nuclei. These and subsequent photographs revealed new atomic phenomena – as well as others hitherto studied indirectly – with such clarity that individual events could be examined in detail. Although his chief claim to fame rests on the cloud-chamber, Wilson made important studies in cosmic-ray and atmospheric physics. He submitted his last paper, on thunderstorms, at 87. In 1927 Wilson shared with A. H. COMPTON the Nobel prize in physics for his photographs of the interaction of X-rays with electrons. BLACKETT wrote: 'Of the great scientists of his age, he was perhaps the most gentle and serene, and the most indifferent to prestige and honours.' WTD

Wilson, Edmund (b. Red Bank, NJ, USA, 8.5.1895; d. New York, 12.6.1972). American literary critic. There is no school of 'Wilsonian' critics, nor a systematic or coherent aesthetic position or practical technique to be drawn from his work. Yet Wilson is, by common consent, the greatest of American critics. In the dedication to *Axel's Castle* (NY, 1931) Wilson described criticism as 'a history of man's ideas and imaginings in the setting of the conditions which have shaped them'. His extended volumes of critical and historical investigation, including *To the Finland Station* (NY, 1940) on the roots of revolutionary MARXism, and *Patriotic Gore* (NY, 1962) on the literature of the American Civil War, suggest the range of his interests. Wilson was for years a regular reviewer of books, and the volumes, such as *The Shores of Light* (NY, 1952), which collect his reviews, constitute an unparalleled account of modern letters. His particular strength as a critic lay in his gusto: for more than 50 years he wrote about literature high and low with evident pleasure; scarcely anything he wrote is dispensable. To V. S. Pritchett, Wilson was 'an American Johnson'. TRILLING wrote of Wilson that 'one got from him a whiff of Lessing at Hamburg, of Sainte-Beuve'. Wilson's *Letters on Literature and Politics*, edited by his widow Elena, were published in 1977 (NY). EH

S. Paul, *Edmund Wilson* (Urbana, 1965); J. Wain (ed.), *An Edmund Wilson Celebration* (Oxford, 1978).

Wilson, Edmund Beecher (b. Geneva, Ill., USA, 19.10.1856; d. New York, 3.3.1939). American biologist. Wilson graduated from Yale in 1878 and then worked in several American universities, including Johns Hopkins and Bryn Mawr, before settling in Columbia University in 1891. His early research interests were embryological and he was responsible for beautiful accounts of the development of a number of invertebrate animals, and for experimental investigations of developmental processes. Much of his work was carried out in Europe, notably at the zoological station at Naples. At Columbia, Wilson helped in the foundation of modern cytogenetics which followed the rediscovery of MENDEL's work in 1900. Between 1905 and 1912 he himself published a series of important papers on the behaviour of chromosomes during spermatogenesis, and was one of the first to establish the chromosomal determination of sex. Perhaps more important, as head of the department of zoology at Columbia he encouraged the work of T. H. MORGAN and his colleagues on the genetics of *Drosophila*. Wilson was one of the great founding fathers of American experimental biology. His book *The Cell in Development and Inheritance* (NY, 1896, [3]1925) was a celebration of the new biology and a stimulus to its further growth. In the first edition he suggested that the recently discovered nucleic acids were candidates for the position of *the* hereditary material. Nearly half a century later his insight was vindicated. DRN

Wilson, Edward Osborne (b. Birmingham, Ala, USA, 10.6.1929). American biologist. Educated at the universities of Alabama and Harvard, he joined the

Harvard faculty in 1956 and is now professor of zoology. His main interests lie in behavioural and evolutionary biology, and he has carried out some brilliant research on social insects (see *The Insect Societies*, Cambridge, Mass., 1971). However, he is most widely known for his book *Sociobiology: the New Synthesis* (Cambridge, Mass., 1975), in which he founded a new discipline concerned with the systematic study of the biological basis of all social behaviour. Focused mainly on animal societies, this account has stimulated a great deal of further research. But Wilson sees sociobiology as working towards a unified science in which the same parameters and quantitative theories are used to analyse all forms of social behaviour in man and the other animals. The basic issue is the extent to which human social behaviour is genetically determined. Wilson has been viciously attacked by a Harvard group for allegedly concealing a political message in his writings, based on his supposed views that human social behaviour is genetically fixed. Wilson clearly does not hold such views but in dealing with issues such as religion, culture and ethics, he was undoubtedly treading dangerous ground, and the controversy, which has generated much heat, does at least highlight the susceptibility of sociobiology to distortion for political ends.

PM

Wilson, John Tuzo (b. Ottawa, Ont., Canada, 24.10.1908). Canadian geophysicist and geologist. Tuzo Wilson was for many years professor of geophysics at Toronto. Like most of his contemporaries in geophysics, he was a staunch opponent of continental drift, and was best known for his ideas on continental accretion through time. He was, however, among the first to realize the significance of the new oceanographic research and quickly abandoned his earlier stabilist views. The paper in which he coined the now indispensable term 'transform fault' (*Nature*, 207 [1965], 343 – 7) is considered a classic, and contains the germ of the revolutionary new concept of plate tectonics, developed quantitatively shortly afterwards by W. J. Morgan, D. P. McKenzie and Y. Le Pichon. Wilson continued to produce

fruitful and insightful ideas well into middle age; two of these warrant special mention: the notion of so-called hot spots in the mantle as agents controlling the volcanicity of oceanic islands, and the recognition that the Lower Palaeozoic rocks on the two sides of the North Atlantic contain evidence of the closing of an ancient ocean, subsequently termed Iapetus. The more general idea which he outlined of a cycle of successive opening and closing of oceans, thereby creating orogenic belts, is known as the Wilson cycle.　　AH

Wilson, Robert Woodrow (b. Houston, Tex., USA, 10.1.1936). American radio astronomer. Wilson, together with PENZIAS, discovered the universal microwave three-degree background radiation that remains from the 'big-bang' origin of the universe. Wilson was working as a member of the technical staff at the Bell Telephone laboratories when he and Penzias made their discovery, for which they were awarded the 1978 Nobel prize for physics.　　MJS

Wilson, Thomas Woodrow (b. Staunton, Va, USA, 28.12.1856; d. Washington, DC, 23.2.1924). Professor of government at Princeton University (1890–2), president of Princeton University (1902–10), Democratic governor of New Jersey (1911–12), president of the United States (1913–21). Though widely portrayed as a progressive reformer, Wilson was by temperament and conviction a conservative who did not believe (as did Theodore ROOSEVELT and his Progressive supporters) that American institutions needed radical reform but rather that they needed applying. As a politician he had the sense to recognize his own lack of technical skill and to rely on the advice and employ the capacity of backstage manoeuvring of others, most notably his *éminence grise*, Colonel Edward House. The other side of Wilson's belief in the superiority of Anglo-Saxon political institutions lay in his conviction that they should be imposed on others, even by force if necessary, making him towards Mexico, in the revolutionary years 1913–16, a kind of moral imperialist.

With the outbreak of war in Europe in 1914, Wilson embarked on a policy of legalistic neutrality. After failing to secure a mediated peace, he campaigned in 1916 on a noninterventionist platform, only to see his second inauguration in March 1917 surrounded by circumstances, such as German unrestricted U-boat warfare and the attempt to incite Mexico to war against the USA, which made a declaration of war a month later inevitable. Wilson, however, insisted that the USA fought not as an ally but as an 'Associated Power' and refused to take cognizance of any agreements between his allies on the nature of the postwar settlements. His peace programmes, as spelled out in his Fourteen Points, involved the destruction of the three great multinational empires (Germany, Austria-Hungary, the Ottoman Empire) in favour of the establishment of national states, disarmament, open diplomacy, arbitration in place of war as a means of resolving national disputes and the establishment of a league of states backed by world opinion as a means of enforcing adherence to these procedures. On this basis he forced an armistice with Germany on Britain and France.

Wilson's moral imperialism, however, had nothing to work on. The ideas he sponsored were widespread but more popular with intellectual radicals than with the electorate of Britain and France. His appearance at the Paris conference did not so much give him a platform from which to appeal to the peoples of Europe as expose his weakness as a negotiator confronted with the parliamentary skills (and majorities) of LLOYD GEORGE and CLEMENCEAU. He was forced into a series of politically damaging compromises to secure inclusion of the charter of the League of Nations in the Peace Treaty, and then failed to secure American ratification by the Senate. His health broke down entirely, and his last 14 months in office offered a tragic contrast to the hubris with which he had arrived in Europe to make peace. DCW

A. S. Link, *Woodrow Wilson: a Brief Biography* (Cleveland, Ohio, 1963).

Windaus, Adolf Otto Reinhold (b. Berlin, Germany, 25.12.1876; d. Göttingen, Lower Saxony, West Germany, 9.6.1959). German chemist. As a student of medicine Windaus attended Emil FISCHER's lectures in the University of Berlin in 1895. The physiological applications of Fischer's work greatly impressed him and provided the beginnings of his approach to chemical research and thought. In 1897 he came under the influence of Heinrich Kiliani at Freiburg, who suggested the study of the chemistry of the glycosides of digitalis (cardiac glycosides), and then that of cholesterol. Most of the rest of Windaus's research was devoted to the chemistry of steroids, first the centrally important sterol, cholesterol, and later ergosterol and its irradiation products, as part of a series of investigations on the antirachitic vitamin complex, vitamin D, especially vitamin D_2 or calciferol. Later work has shown the great importance of both digitalis (in therapy) and cholesterol in cardiovascular disease. Windaus's influence on junior colleagues led to Adolf Butenandt's studies of steroidal sex hormones and Walther Hückel's study of the stereochemistry of condensed ring systems of the type found in steroids. A minor but important feature of Windaus's early work was the study of imidazole derivatives, particularly the α-amino-acid histidine, and the related biogenic amine histamine, which Windaus discovered. The latter is now known to be implicated in allergic conditions (e.g. hay fever). Windaus also isolated vitamin B_1 (thiamine) from yeast showing it to be a thiazole and not an imidazole derivative, and worked on the structure determination of colchicine. He received the Nobel prize in 1928. NBC

Winnicott, Donald Woods (b. Plymouth, Devon, UK, 7.4.1896; d. London, 25.1.1971). British paediatrician, child psychiatrist and psychoanalyst. After completing his medical training at St Bartholomew's Hospital, London, he was appointed assistant physician at Paddington Green Children's Hospital in 1923 and worked there for the next 40 years. During the 1920s he was drawn to psychoanalysis, particularly to

Anna Freud's and Melanie KLEIN's new theories of child analysis. He was analysed by James Strachey and by Joan Rivière, and began practising as a psychoanalyst in the mid-1930s. Although he founded no new school, Winnicott's influence on psychoanalytic theory and on child care and education was considerable. His most important technical innovation was the Squiggle Game designed for therapeutic consultations with children: the therapist draws a random scribble and invites the child to make it into a meaningful drawing by adding marks on the basis of what he or she 'sees' in it, and then to produce a new scribble for the therapist to complete; the drawings serve as points of departure for therapeutic interchanges. Winnicott's researches with the Squiggle Game were reported posthumously in *Therapeutic Consultations in Child Psychiatry* (London, 1971). His other books include *The Child, the Family and the Outside World* (London, 1964), *Maturational Processes and the Facilitating Environment* (London, 1965) and *Playing and Reality* (London, 1971).

AMC

Winograd, Terry Allen (b. Takoma Park, Md, USA, 24.2.1946). American computer scientist and psychologist. He graduated in linguistics from University College London, and then studied for a PhD (1970) in applied mathematics at MIT. Since 1972 he has been a research consultant for Rank-Xerox and since 1974 has held a professorial post in computer science and linguistics at Stanford University. Winograd is one of the leading advocates of the use of artificial intelligence in the development of psychological theories. His particular concern has been the development of computer programs that model the brain's ability to comprehend natural language. In *Understanding Natural Language* (NY, 1972) Winograd described an innovative program which was the first to take account of the relationship between language, thought and action. Since then he has been concerned with computer models of semantic and syntactic aspects of comprehension and with examining the implications of the procedural/declarative distinction (i.e.

'knowing how' versus 'knowing that') for theories of knowledge representation.

AJP

Winters, Yvor (b. Chicago, Ill., USA, 17.10.1900; d. Palo Alto, Calif., 25.1.1968). American literary critic and poet. While, broadly speaking, a practitioner of the New Criticism, Winters's critical writings are notable for their insistence on the primacy of evaluation and the belief that poetry should consist of rational, paraphrasable statements about human affairs which are subject to objective analysis; beyond this, Winters argues that all good poetry is morally edifying and that, fundamentally, all legitimate critical activity is of a moral nature. His detractors point to the extreme idiosyncrasy, even ridiculousness, of his judgements (Robert Bridges a better poet than ELIOT, WHARTON superior to Jane Austen and Henry JAMES), but a number of his essays have the status of critical classics and his work, as a whole, has been enormously influential, both as a corrective to accepted literary judgements and as a restatement of the moralist position. *In Defense of Reason* (Chicago, 1947) is a collection of his most important writings on American literature, and *The Function of Criticism* (Denver, 1957), with its Arnoldian title, collects together essays of both a critical and theoretical nature. Winters was awarded the Bollingen prize for poetry in 1960: his verse is noted for its meditative qualities, its metrical formality, and its Californian settings (*Collected Poems*, Denver, 1952, ²1960).

GHC

S. E. Hyman, *The Armed Vision* (NY, 1948); J. Casey, *The Language of Criticism* (London, 1966).

Wittfogel, Karl August (b. Woltersdorf, Germany [now East Germany], 6.9.1896; naturalized American citizen, 1941). German/American sociologist. He was associated with the Frankfurt Institute for Social Research but never became one of its leading members. Active in the Communist party, he was imprisoned briefly after HITLER came to power in 1933, afterwards settling in the USA where he became increasingly hostile to Soviet communism. His early research concerned China and the reasons for the apparently static character of Asiatic society which appeared to contradict unilinear schemes of historical development. His major work is *Oriental Despotism* (New Haven, 1955), subtitled 'A comparative study of power', in which he attempts to demonstrate that there exists not one but two paths of historical development, one leading to Western pluralism, the other to Eastern totalitarianism. He traces the bureaucratic collectivism of the USSR and China to the earlier development of bureaucratic collectivist regimes, made necessary by the need for large-scale schemes of irrigation in arid regions. His wider thesis has been strongly contested particularly because of his practice of generalizing the findings from his studies of Asiatic societies to explain widely dissimilar cultures and social systems.   AG

V. Melotti, *Marx and the Third World* (London, 1977); G. L. Ulmen, *Science and Society* (NY, 1978).

Wittgenstein, Ludwig Josef Johann (b. Vienna, Austria-Hungary [now Austria], 26.4.1889; naturalized British citizen, 1938; d. Cambridge, UK, 29.4.1951). Austrian/British philosopher. Wittgenstein was the son of an Austrian industrial magnate and was raised in a rich and cultivated home. In 1911 he came to England, studying aeronautical engineering until he moved to Cambridge to pursue a philosophical interest in mathematics. FREGE, to whom he had written, advised him to seek out Bertrand RUSSELL and the contact was fruitful. Russell generously admitted that he was soon learning as much from Wittgenstein as he was teaching him. Wittgenstein served in WW1 in the Austrian army and was taken prisoner on the Italian front in 1918. From here he sent his first work *Tractatus Logico-Philosophicus* to Russell and it was published in journal form in 1921 (London, in German and English, 1922; tr. D. F. Pears & B. F. H. Guinness, London, 1961). Partly inspired by religious writings of Leo TOLSTOY he had found during the war in a ruined village in Galicia, Wittgenstein dedicated himself in 1919 to a life of simple asceticism. He gave his money away to his relations and abandoned philosophy. In the following years he worked as an elementary schoolteacher in the Austrian countryside (until that ended in disaster), an amateur architect and a convent gardener. In the late 1920s SCHLICK and other members of the Vienna circle sought him out to discuss the ideas of his *Tractatus* and he decided to return to philosophy, moving back to Cambridge in 1929. There he was the centre of a small, intensely loyal cult. In 1939 he succeeded G. E. MOORE as professor of mental philosophy and logic, but he was absent on menial war work soon afterwards and resigned altogether in 1947. Four years later he died after a period of severe illness. For a long time he had meditated suicide, fearing that he shared the pronounced strain of insanity in his family (two of his brothers killed themselves). Soon after his death the main outlines of his later views were published in his *Philosophical Investigations* (tr. G. E. M. Anscombe, Oxford, 1953, ²1958). These ideas had been broadly familiar since the mid-1930s through the writings of disciples and the clandestine circulation of lecture notes. Since then there has been a continuous flow of posthumous publications. Wittgenstein's early philosophy is propounded in the *Tractatus* as a series of aphorisms or gnomic sayings, almost unsupported by argument. It starts from the question of how language, and therefore the kind of complex thinking that human beings alone are capable of, is possible. The answer is that language must, if it is to have a definite meaning, contain propositions that are pictures of the facts of which the world is composed. The facts, it follows, must be of the kind that allow themselves to be depicted. Most, if not all, of the propositions we actually assert or consider are not of this elementary pictorial nature, but they must be equivalent to collections of such simple elements, united by the formal notions treated in the logic of Frege and Russell. Only simple propositions and logically articulated collections of them can be true, or false, of the world. The necessary truths of logic and mathematics are disguised tautologies, verbal truisms in which two ways of saying the same thing are connected. Judgements of value are not propositions at all. Traditional metaphysical philosophy is senseless and so, Wittgenstein surprisingly declares, are his own assertions in the *Tractatus*, although, he implies, in an altogether less contemptible way. A selection of these ideas, with the more startlingly implausible items such as the picture theory of meaning left out, constituted the main theses of the logical positivism of Schlick and CARNAP. For a time, it appears, Wittgenstein looked kindly on their reinterpretation of his thoughts in the spirit of Hume and MACH. His later writings, whose style is rambling and inconsequential, reject most of what is said or implied in the *Tractatus*, apart from its claim that 'philosophy is not a theory but an activity'. But whereas in the early work that activity was 'the logical clarification of thoughts', by the *Investigations* it is the removal of philosophical puzzlement, typically as it arises from an inconsistency between logically defensible theses, often of a sceptical nature, and the basic convictions or assumptions of common sense. Relief is to be sought in a therapeutic technique of 'reminders' which reveal the source of the philosophical paradox in a misunderstanding of common language. Wittgenstein rejects his earlier conception of language as a calculus, with identifiable simple elements, coming to see it as a complex collection of communicative instruments of different kinds which must be considered within the total context of communication. In another image he describes language as an assemblage of 'language-games', as various in their nature as ordinary games (hopscotch, polo, chess and so on). Particularly influential has been his anti-Cartesian theory about the language we use to report and discuss our own and other people's mental states. This vocabulary does not get its meaning by correlation with private experiences since as a public means of communication it must be governed by publicly applicable rules. Wittgenstein left a number of devoted disciples behind him. His later work had some general influence on the 'linguistic philosophy' prevalent in Britain and the USA between 1945 and 1960. AQ

A. Kenny, *Wittgenstein* (London, 1973); W. W. Bartley III, *Wittgenstein* (NY, 1973).

Wittig, Georg (b. Berlin, Germany, 16.6.1897). German organic chemist. Wittig has devoted most of his research to the borderland between inorganic and organic chemistry, with fruitful results. He has pioneered the study of the organometallic chemistry of main-group elements, in both its mechanistic and synthetic aspects. His name is perpetuated in the Wittig rearrangement, the Wittig reaction and the Wittig hydrocarbon. His major contributions include the preparation and use of organolithium reagents; the discovery of didehydrobenzene (benzyne) and related compounds through metal-halogen exchange reactions, with extension to strained cycloalkynes; the discovery of the mechanism of rearrangement of ammonium ylides, and numerous other items, but above all the discovery of phosphorus ylides and in 1953, their reactions with carbonyl compounds to give alkenes (the Wittig reaction). This reaction, of great range and flexibility, has been applied on the industrial scale in the synthesis of vitamin A_1 acetate, as well as in hosts of laboratory-scale syntheses. Wittig received the Nobel prize in 1979. NBC

Wodehouse, Pelham Grenville (b. Guildford, Surrey, UK, 15.10.1881; naturalized American citizen, 1955; d. New York, USA, 14.2.1975). British/American novelist. After a brief and disastrous sally into banking, Wodehouse (Plum to his friends) rapidly established himself in journalism and in the realm of boys' fiction. This led to his uniquely funny and impeccably plotted novels and stories – over 100 in all – featuring the unforgettable Ukridge, Psmith, Emsworth, Mr Mulliner, Bertie Wooster and the inimitable Jeeves. Wodehouse also had great success in theatre during the 1920s and 1930s, collaborating with, for example, Cole PORTER, GERSHWIN and Irving Berlin in smash hit musicals such as *Oh, Kay!* (1926) and his own *A Damsel in Distress* (1928), his best-known lyric being Jerome Kern's 'Bill'. Interned by the Germans during WW2, his broadcasts from Berlin were much criticized, but he was later officially cleared of all intimations of collusion. Knighted only weeks before his death, Wodehouse remains widely read and internationally adored, and may now be seen without qualification to be one of the finest writers of the century.   JC

R. Usborne, *Wodehouse at Work* (London, ²1976); J. Connolly, *P. G. Wodehouse: an Illustrated Biography* (London, ²1981).

Wohlstetter, Albert (b. New York, USA, 19.12.1913). American strategist. A former member of the American RAND corporation and the University of Chicago faculty, and now director of research for Pan Heuristics, Los Angeles, Wohlstetter has exercised a decisive influence on the development of strategic thought since WW2, developing concepts such as the distinction between 'first-strike' and 'second-strike' capability, and 'fail-safe', as well as contributing to debates about how to harden missile sites and the avoidance of nuclear accidents. Wohlstetter established the conceptual framework of deterrence in an article entitled 'The delicate balance of terror' (*Foreign Affairs*, 1959). He defined deterrence as the capacity to survive an enemy attack and subsequently inflict reprisals. A credible capacity to inflict reprisals presupposed the ability to survive a nuclear attack, and then to penetrate and destroy an enemy's deterrent weapons system; its susceptibility to control after an enemy attack, and its budgetary acceptability in peacetime. Wohlstetter also emphasized the inextricable connection between strategic doctrine and choice of weapons, and demonstrated that a deterrence strategy was a matter of comparative risks and was thus aimed at a rational enemy. 'Fail-safe' procedures, in turn, were aimed at reducing the chances of accident without correspondingly increasing vulnerability to a rational surprise attack. In 'Nuclear sharing: NATO and the N + 1 country' (*Foreign Affairs*, 1961) he challenged the view put forward by KISSINGER, urging that NATO countries should not acquire

or develop a joint nuclear force but should rely on the US nuclear guarantee as the most credible and responsible deterrent. Wohlstetter's basic argument effectively did away with any ideas of definitive technological stability in a nuclear age, and his work provided the main intellectual impetus behind the enlarging, diversifying, dispersing and hardening of the US nuclear deterrent in the 1960s.   JGo

R. Aron, *The Great Debate* (NY, 1963).

Wolfe, Thomas Clayton (b. Asheville, NC, USA, 3.10.1900; d. Baltimore, Md, 15.9.1938). American novelist. A bestselling novelist in his own lifetime, Wolfe's postwar reputation has settled at a more modest level. His critics have sometimes pointed out that Wolfe was without craft or discipline. The books poured out, Wolfe once explained, as though produced by 'intemperate excess, an almost insane hunger to devour the entire body of human experience'. The first draft of *Look Homeward, Angel* (NY, 1929) was said to contain anything from a quarter to half a million words, the manuscript filling up suitcases. 'It is a book made out of my life, and it represents my vision of life to my 20th year', Wolfe wrote to Maxwell Perkins. The story of Wolfe's relations with Perkins, and the prodigious work which they both put into the manuscript, is no less flattering to the novelist than to his editor. In the novels which followed, from *Of Time and the River* (NY, 1935) to *The Web and the Rock* (NY, 1939) and *You Can't Go Home Again* (NY, 1940), Wolfe told the story of his life in vast detail and with lyric intensity. As a stylist, he was extravagantly romantic, and showed little development from first to last. After graduating from the University of North Carolina in 1920, Wolfe studied at Harvard, and taught for some years at New York University. He travelled in Europe and lived in London. But the autobiographical nature of his art kept his attention firmly fixed on his home and his early years. He wrote of little else.   EH

A. Turnbull, *Thomas Wolfe* (NY, 1968); A. Scott Berg, *Max Perkins* (NY, 1979).

Wolfe, Tom, ps. of Thomas Kennerly, Jr (b. Richmond, Va, USA, 2.3.1931). American journalist. Wolfe, an innovative writer of nonfiction in English, emerged in the mid-1960s when the radical character of events in America persuaded young writers, mostly working journalists, to try to revitalize newspaper and magazine journalism in the face of television's misleading *total* immediacy (i.e. the so-called 'narcotizing dysfunction'). The titles of his works indicate his style, which is a mixture of comic strip, jet set and academic jargon. His works include *The Kandy-Kolored Tangerine-Flake Streamline Baby* (NY, 1965), *The Electric Kool-Aid Acid Test* (NY, 1968), *Radical Chic and Mau-Mauing the Flak Catchers* (NY, 1970) and *The Right Stuff* (NY, 1975). They are all original studies of contemporary American culture, especially the drug, rock and car culture of California, and are written with honesty and clarity. It was not just the flashy colours or the punctuation or the hip talk that made Wolfe so outstanding an innovator. His is a way of reporting at least one side of the truth, as vividly as possible, particularly for those who care, have the talent for writing and have realized the impossibility of absolute objectivity. It is *private* reporting which aims to establish direct contact between event and reporter and reader. It is a difficult technique which can easily slip into exaggerated self-consciousness. But its creative possibilities may ultimately bring about the end of 'formula' journalism. His own anthology of this new writing form is *The New Journalism* (NY, 1973). RB

Wölfflin, Heinrich (b. Winterthur, Zürich, Switzerland, 21.6.1864; d. Zürich, 19.7.1945). Swiss art historian. In *Renaissance und Barock* (Basle, 1888; *Renaissance and Baroque*, London, 1964) Wölfflin attempted to formulate objective criteria for a history of styles, combining the 'emphatic' notions of von Hildebrande with a system of stylistic analysis. *Die Klassische Kunst* (Basle, 1898; *Classic Art*, London, 1952) and *Kunstgeschichtliche Grundbegriffe* (Munich, 1915; *Principles of Art History*, London, 1932) continued and broadened the attempt into a general thesis where

five polarities were devised (e.g. linearity *v.* tonality, closed *v.* open form) to demonstrate all stylistic transformations. A charismatic teacher, Wölfflin pioneered the use of twin projectors in lecturing, thus emphasizing his methodology. His externalizaton of style into a period or national spirit to which artists subconsciously conformed, and which operated almost independently of other history, has become unfashionable – but his techniques of formal analysis, conscientiously 'scientific', remain of immense value. CF

Wolpert, Lewis (b. Johannesburg, Transvaal, South Africa, 19.10.1929). British developmental biologist. Wolpert, like many who unsettled biology during the 1960s, started professionally in the physical sciences, working as an engineer in South Africa and with the Israel Water Planning Department. Subsequently he became a lecturer in zoology at King's College, London. Wolpert revived the more holistic approach to developing organisms which had been left virtually untouched since the work of DRIESCH, at a time when most biologists were caught up in molecules and reductionism. That both the theory and practice of biological pattern formation is today a flourishing research area is largely due to his efforts. Wolpert's own innovatory ideas have included the 'French flag' model, a way of expressing the possible role of gradients of signalling substances during development of organisms. His work has extended from the formation of birds' wings to the regeneration of the invertebrate *Hydra*. DOM

Wood, Henry Joseph (b. London, UK, 3.3.1869; d. Hitchin, Herts., 19.8.1944). British conductor. Although as a child he showed exceptional talent as an organist, Wood was 20 before he had his first experience as a conductor – with a touring opera company. In 1895 Robert Newman put him in charge of the Promenade concerts at London's Queen's Hall, a connection he was to retain until his death and which remains his lasting memorial. He was a strict disciplinarian and did much to combat the pernicious deputy system which enabled one orchestral player to attend at rehearsal and another at the performance. Over the years, in addition to the standard repertory, Wood introduced hundreds of new works by British and foreign composers. During the Promenade season of 1902, for example, he conducted the first English performance of SIBELIUS's First Symphony and in 1912 the world première of SCHOEN-BERG's *Five Orchestral Pieces*. Knighted in 1911, *My Life of Music* (London, 1938) is his autobiography.   JL

Woodward, Comer Vann (b. Vanndale, Ark., USA, 13.11.1908). The leading modern historian of the American South, Woodward has always seen the interpretation of the past to the present as a problem with political dimensions. When he began to write, the literature and traditions of the South were steeped in sentimental legends, supported by archaic racial attitudes, and Southern history was written almost entirely from the point of view of white supremacy. Woodward did far more than any other historian, and probably more than any other writer, to transform the record of the era following Reconstruction. His brilliant biography *Tom Watson, Agrarian Rebel* (NY, 1938) argued that a possibility had once existed of racial cooperation among poor farmers against their economic and political oppressors. *Reunion and Reaction* (Boston, Mass., 1951), with its revisionist account of the Compromise of 1877 (over the disputed presidential election of 1876) revealed a secret deal between Northern businesses and those Southern white politicians who called themselves 'Redeemers', and who thereby regained control over Southern political, social and economic life. In the same year came his *Origins of the New South* (Baton Rouge, 1951). This proved to be one of the most significant works of history written in that period. Woodward traced the record of white-dominated 'Redeemer' administrations, revealed their vicissitudes and corruptions, and explained the disfranchisement of the Negro in the 1890s in the light, no longer of 'corrupt' black voting practices, but of the politics of the populist revolt against the domination of big planters and big business. This work opened the way for disillusioned and realistic studies of Southern politics and society, transforming the subject.

The Strange Career of Jim Crow (NY, 1955), coming in the midst of the intense political controversy over school desegregation, suddenly made its author famous. Woodward here demonstrated that the 'Jim Crow' laws which barred Negroes from participating in political life and which segregated them throughout Southern society dated only from the 1890s and later. He produced evidence of considerable racial mixture before that period. The effect on the Southern segregationist assertions that segregation dated 'from time immemorial' was shattering. But Woodward's argument suffered from its too direct political application. He was taken as meaning that mental and moral segregation were equally recent, and that a relatively free, mixed society had previously been the norm. His precautions against this simplification of his views were lost in the excitement aroused by his main thesis. Other historians, equally committed to racial equality, showed that such equality as was attained in the South after Abolition had at best been fragile and for most places and times had not existed. Woodward's revisions of the book (NY, [2]1957, [3]1966) took account of these views and it remains a leading work of reinterpretation, but perhaps also a warning against the hazards of writing historical revision as direct political statement. Most recently he has edited, in *Mary Chestnut's Civil War* (New Haven, 1981), the famous *Diary from Dixie*, showing how and when it came to be written.

Woodward began his academic career in Georgia, moved in 1946 to the Johns Hopkins University, and in 1961 became Sterling professor of American history at Yale. Woodward has always been a deeply Southern historian, who felt white racism as an offence against the best of which the South is capable. In a famous essay 'The irony of Southern history' (1952) he observed that the South had stood aside from the victorious 'mainstream' of American history because it had suffered defeat – and by implication, that the nation might have something to learn by listening to the experience. In this and other essays published as *The Burden of Southern History* (Baton Rouge, 1960, ²1968) he has induced the South to become more self-critically aware of its place in history, and the world to become far more subtly aware of the South.   JRP

D. Potter, 'C. Vann Woodward' in M. Cunliffe & R. Winks (eds), *Pastmasters* (NY, 1969); M. O'Brien, 'C. Vann Woodward and the burden of Southern liberalism', *American Historical Review* (1973).

Woodward, Robert Burns (b. Boston, Mass., USA, 10.4.1917; d. Boston, Mass., 8.7.1979). American chemist. Woodward was an organic chemist who dominated the subject from the late 1940s until his death. He was admitted to MIT when 16, and at 20 had been awarded his PhD. After a brief appointment at the University of Illinois in 1937, Woodward moved to Harvard, remaining there until his death. He made fundamental contributions to organic chemistry covering structural elucidation, total synthesis, biosynthesis and reaction mechanisms. His work was based on meticulous attention to detail, a powerful logical and highly analytical approach, a profound understanding of the electronic and stereochemical behaviour of molecules and a prodigious memory. He was able to communicate his knowledge and enthusiasm with wit, lucidity, and a magnificent command of the English language. In his work on structural elucidation Woodward demonstrated the significance of using physical methods, illustrated by his rules for correlating ultraviolet spectra with structure. He worked on antibiotics (penicillin, 1945; terramycin, 1952), alkaloids (strychnine, 1948; cevine, 1954), macrolides (magnamycin, 1956; oleandomycin, 1960), fish poisons (tetrodotoxin, 1964) and organometallic compounds (ferrocene, 1952). He also contributed significant ideas to an understanding of the biosynthesis of natural products. He synthesized many fundamentally important compounds of great complexity, including quinine (1944), cholesterol and cortisone (1951), lysergic acid (1954), strychnine (1954), reserpine (1956), chlorophyll (1960), and colchicine (1963). The culminating achievement was the synthesis, in collaboration with Professor A. Eschenmoser (ETH, Zürich) of vitamin B_{12}. For his work on synthesis he was awarded the Nobel prize in 1965. During his work on vitamin B_{12} he was initially puzzled by stereochemical results opposite to those he expected. He realized that he was dealing with a fundamental question and, in 1965, in collaboration with R. HOFFMANN, he recognized the role of conservation of orbital symmetry in the determination of the stereospecificity of concerted reactions. The generality of these ideas (*Angewandte Chemie*, 8 [1970], 71) represents one of the fundamental advances in organic chemistry.   TGH

H. Wasserman, 'Profile and scientific contributions of Professor R. B. Woodward', *Hetereocycles*, 7 (1977), 1; D. Dolphin, 'Robert Burns Woodward, three score years and then?', ibid, p. 29.

Wooldridge, Sidney William (b. London, UK, 16.11.1900; d. London, 25.4.1963). British geographer. Trained as a geologist (DSc London, 1927), most of Wooldridge's work was in geomorphology. His research focused on the physical landscape of the London basin, on which he published the influential *Structure, Surface and Drainage in South-East England* (with D. L. Linton, London, 1939, ²1955). From 1929 he taught geography in the University of London, holding chairs at Birkbeck (1944–7) and King's (1947–63). He argued strongly that geography is a synthetic discipline bridging the physical and human sciences and characterized by its use of the regional method: see *The Geographer as Scientist* (London, 1956) and *The Spirit and Purpose of Geography* (with W. G. East, London, 1951, ²1958). His regional geography focused on the identification of physiographic units, description of which asked questions about their origins (hence his work in geomorphology) and about their relationship to human activity (illustrated by his neoenvironmentalist studies of Anglo-Saxon settlement patterns). As is clear from his campaigning for the unity of geography as the study of land surfaces, Wooldridge was also an enthusiastic proponent for, and exponent of, field teaching.   RJJ

Woolf, Adeline Virginia, *née* Stephen (b. London, UK, 25.1.1882; d. Rodmell, W. Sussex, 28.3.1941). British novelist and critic, daughter of biographer Sir Leslie Stephen, and member of the Bloomsbury group, a coterie which fostered the values of Cambridge liberal humanism in the early 20c. She radically revised literary conventions in order to capture 'reality' with greater immediacy. Her perceptive and tough-minded critical essays (e.g. *The Common Reader*, 2 vols, London, 1925–32; *The Death of the Moth*, London, 1942; *The Moment*, London, 1947) show her awareness of this task. In defining her shifting, elusive reality, she attacked the 'materialists' BENNETT, WELLS and GALSWORTHY for their naively detailed rendering of the surface of life which ignored the crucial interaction of the mind and the external world. Such interaction occurs at intense but brief moments of illumination when the mind holds together the facts and their symbolic significance. She aimed to combine poetic intensity with careful observation of contemporary manners. In *Mrs Dalloway* (London, 1925), her first major novel, she depicts vividly and satirically a day in the life of her upperclass heroine, creating by means of interior monologue, flashback and imagery, a pattern of meaning centring on Mrs Dalloway's emotional frigidity; this is counterpointed with the tragic nightmares of the shell-shocked Septimus whose suicide – his act of self-sacrifice – merges with her own thoughts at the end of the novel in a private moment of redemption. *To the Lighthouse* (London, 1927) explores further the nature of reality through the discrepancy between Mr Ramsay's meticulous adherence to fact and his wife's creative imaginativeness which is transcended briefly at the end of the first part of the novel and then subjected to the erosion of time and death in a central poetic meditation. This too is overcome in the painfully achieved vision of the painter Lily at the end of the novel where life's emotional and moral complexity takes on the impersonality of an aesthetic design. An increasing emphasis on image, symbol and myth accentuates the stylized pattern of Woolf's fiction which culminates in *The Waves* (London,

1931), where descriptive prose poems alternate with the soliloquies of the six main characters to represent in the temporal worlds of the novel the timeless rhythm of life. The wave in motion is unchanging. Though the range of experience depicted is narrow, Woolf's novels have a firm structure of ideas and values often ignored by adulators of Bloomsbury and its ethos. Her personal life has been extensively documented in her *Letters* (eds N. Nicolson & J. Trautman, 6 vols, London, 1975–80) and *Diary* (ed. A. O. Bell, 5 vols, London, 1977–83). DC

Q. Bell, *Virginia Woolf* (2 vols, London, 1972); A. McLaurin, *Virginia Woolf: the Echoes Enslaved* (London, 1973).

Wright, Frank Lloyd (b. Richland Center, Wis., USA, 8.6.1867; d. Phoenix, Ariz., 9.4.1959). American architect, and one of the most significant figures in 20c architecture. His career in practice, extending over 74 years from 1885 to 1959, was exceptionally long and prolific. Philosophically he was akin to Emerson and Thoreau; he sought an architecture which was close to nature and which reflected American values.

Some of Wright's earliest work was the most influential. In a series of houses built before 1910 he enunciated the idea of the 'Prairie House', close to the soil of which it was a part, and with strong horizontal emphases in its low overhanging roofs and its bands of windows. The interior space was transformed from the rigidly compartmented spaces of conventional houses to flowing interpenetrating spaces. These were the forerunners of modern houses in many countries. Two other buildings of this period stand out: the Larkin office building, Buffalo, New York (1903), for its spatial organization and for the highly articulated cubic forms of its exterior, and Unity church, Oak Park, Illinois (1904) for its wholly innovative use of reinforced concrete as an architectural material. In 1910 Wright's work was published in Germany in what has become known as the first Wasmuth Portfolio: *Ausgeführte Bauten und Entwürfe von Frank Lloyd Wright* [Buildings and designs of Frank Lloyd

Wright] (Berlin). The drawings had an immediate and profound impact on European architecture.

Wright argued for an 'organic' architecture. His interpretation of this concept defies simple definition, but it entails being natural, being free from externally imposed influences, a building being at one with its surroundings, and its interior and exterior space being unified. Like many masters of 20c architecture, Wright proposed a new form for an ideal city – which he called Broadacre City (1934). He condemned the congestion of traditional cities and advocated a dispersed pattern of living dependent on the automobile, where time replaced distance as a measure of accessibility. Wright's American agrarian ideals were given further expression in the founding, in rural settings, of Taliesin, Wisconsin (1911) and Taliesin West in the Arizona desert (1938). These centres were home, studio and workplace, schools for aspiring young architects, and places of pilgrimage.

Wright's work is interspersed with a succession of buildings which attracted international acclaim: the Imperial Hotel, Tokyo (1916), Falling Water, Bear Run, Pennsylvania (1935), the Johnson administration building (1936) and Research Tower (1944), Racine, Wisconsin, the Unitarian church, Shorewood Hills (1947), the Price Tower, Bartlesville, Oklahoma (1955), the Guggenheim Museum, New York City (1956), and the Marin County Civic Center, San Raphael, California (1957). In addition, Wright wrote some 20 books and numerous articles – on his own work, his life and philosophy, and on architecture in general. *An Autobiography*, first published (NY) in 1932, was revised in 1943 and 1962. *An Organic Architecture* (NY, 1939) and *An American Architecture* (NY, 1955) were followed by *A Testament* (NY, 1957). BM

E. Kaufmann & B. Raeburn (eds), *Frank Lloyd Wright: Writings and Buildings* (NY, 1960); R. C. Twombley, *Frank Lloyd Wright: his Life and Architecture* (NY, 1979).

Wright, Judith (b. nr Armidale, N.S. Wales, Australia, 31.5.1915). Australian poet. Raised on her family's sheep sta-

tion, she went to Sydney University and then spent a year in Europe. Most of her poetry has been written in the mountains of southern Queensland. Although celebrated as the first important modern poet in Australia to express the female experience, Wright is primarily one of the founders of a wholly Australian voice in literature. Much preoccupied with time ('The Moving Image' of her first collection, Melbourne, 1946, of that title) and with the antiquity of Australia, out of which man has shaped his discordant modern society, several of her early poems such as 'Bullocky' and 'Woman to Man' have become standard English-language anthology pieces. Her poetry from the 1950s became more metaphysical as she faced up to both her personal feelings about love and sexuality and the implications of life in an atomic age. In Australia she enjoys a high reputation as a literary critic, particularly as a champion of early Australian poets, but her pervasive influence and outstanding achievement is as a lyricist (see *Collected Poems, 1942–1970*, Sydney, 1970). ANRN

A. K. Thomson (ed.), *Critical Essays on Judith Wright* (Sydney, 1968); A.D. Hope, *Judith Wright* (Sydney, 1976).

Wright, Orville (b. Dayton, Ohio, USA, 19.8.1871; d. Dayton, 30.1.1948) and **Wilbur** (b. Melville, Ind., USA, 16.4.1867; d. Dayton, Ohio, 30.5.1912). American aeroplane pioneers. As a youth Orville was interested in printing machinery and started the West Side Press. Wilbur, his brother, joined him. Next they started making and repairing bicycles. They noted the gliding experiments of Otto Lilienthal, and thought technology ripe for manned flight in powered heavier-than-air machines for engines were becoming lighter and there was some understanding of aerodynamics. The Wright brothers had not only read and corresponded with pioneers of gliding but had made observations of bird flight, and more particularly considered the problem of control. They made a six-foot wind tunnel in which they experimented with monoplanes, biplanes and triplanes with many different sizes and contours of wings. In 1905 'Flyer III' stayed airborne for more than 30 minutes and was able to fly in figures-of-eight. Controlled, powered flight had been achieved and news of the achievement spread abroad. Wilbur Wright made a public exhibition flight at Le Mans, France, on 6.8.1908, and the following year the brothers secured a US army contract for the world's first military aeroplane.   RAH

Wright, Sewall (b. Melrose, Mass., USA, 21.12.1889). American geneticist and mathematician, who introduced stochastic processes to models of population structure and evolution, and devised the methods of path coefficients for analysing inheritance that is quantitative in nature. Wright took his doctorate at Harvard and held various posts in genetics mainly in the universities of Chicago (1926–54) and Wisconsin (1955 –60). With R. A. FISHER and HALDANE he was the founder of the mathematical theories of population genetics. Wright showed that when populations were small, chance could play an important part in changing the frequency of genes in populations, which is the essence of the evolutionary process. The phenomenon is known as 'genetic drift' or the 'Wright effect'. The extent, however, to which drift contributes to long-term evolution depends upon whether alternative genes affect reproduction and survival and are thus subject to natural selection or whether they are neutral. There is still substantial controversy on this point; while some genes are clearly adaptive many others appear to behave as though they were neutral. The population structure of man, throughout most of human prehistory, has been ide-ally suited for drift effects with small population size and geographical isolation, but it still remains problematic how important drift has been in human evolution. Wright's major book is *Evolution and the Genetics of Populations* (4 vols, Chicago, 1968–78).   GAH

Wynne-Edwards, Veno Copner (b. Leeds, W. Yorks., UK, 4.7.1906). British biologist. Educated at Oxford, he became an assistant professor in zoology at McGill University, Montreal, in 1930, from where he carried out pioneering work on the distribution of seabirds at sea. He returned to the UK and the chair of natural history at Aberdeen University which he held from 1946 to 1974. In 1962 he published his famous book *Animal Dispersion in Relation to Social Behaviour* (London) in which he put forward the hypothesis of population homeostasis: that is, that animal populations control their numbers by social and hormonal mechanisms, which have evolved to impose restraints for the common good on the reproductive output of individuals, thereby preventing overexploitation of resources. In 1956 he set up the Grouse Research Unit, now based at Banchory, Scotland, in order to test his ideas. His book was extremely influential, and provided tremendous stimulus to research workers in ethology and ecology. Criticisms of his hypothesis, notably by LACK and J. Maynard Smith, have been based largely on its dependence on group selection for the evolution of altruistic traits. The issue is by no means closed, and new models and field evidence are constantly being put forward.   PM

Y

Yalow, Rosalyn Sussman (b. New York, USA, 19.7.1921). American biochemist. Raised in the poor South Bronx area, Yalow was the first physics major at Hunter College for women and then the only female physics graduate student at the University of Illinois (1942–5). Job applications were sometimes returned with the observation, 'Unfortunately, Dr Yalow is both Jewish and female.' Despite such drawbacks, she joined the radioisotope unit of the New York Veterans' Administration Hospital in 1947 when radioisotope applications in medicine were just beginning, and addressed the problem of hormone measurement. Endocrinology was blocked in the 1950s because inability to measure tiny, fluctuating amounts of hormones in blood meant equal inability to effectively study hormone physiology. With S. Berson, Yalow combined antibodies possessing high affinity for insulin with radioactive insulin and the serum to be tested. Nonradioactive insulin in the serum displaces some radioactive insulin from antibody binding, and its presence can be determined by measuring this displaced radioactivity, down to exceptionally small amounts. Radioimmunoassay has since provided important new insights about diabetes and similar conditions; has led to faster, more accurate diagnosis and drug monitoring; and has opened up new fields of study in the biological regulator molecules, unthinkable without the precision and sensitivity of the assay. Yalow has become something of a model for the increasing number of women entering science and shared the 1977 Nobel prize in physiology and medicine. Since 1972 she has been senior medical investigator at the Veterans' Administration Hospital. DOM

Yang, Chen Ning, see LEE, TSUNG-DAO.

Yates, Frances Amelia (b. London, UK, 28.11.1899; d. Claygate, Surrey, 29.9.1981). British cultural historian, and reader in the history of the Renaissance at the WARBURG Institute, London. Her first book was *John Florio* (London, 1934). Her major contributions to cultural history appeared after WW2. They include *The French Academies of the Sixteenth Century* (London, 1947); *The Valois Tapestries* (London, 1959), a sort of iconographical detective story; *Giordano Bruno and the Hermetic Tradition* (London, 1964); *The Art of Memory* (London, 1966); *The Rosicrucian Enlightenment* (London, 1972), and a number of important essays, some of them collected in her *Astraea* (London, 1975). She concentrated on England, France and Italy in the 16c, with forays into other areas and other periods. Associated with the Warburg Institute for nearly 40 years, she acknowledged a considerable intellectual debt to its former director Fritz Saxl. Her concern with the occult (*The Occult Philosophy in the Elizabethan Age*, London, 1980), with court festivals, with iconography, with the imperial idea and with the classical heritage, places her firmly within the Warburg tradition. Her deep interest in Shakespeare found expression in *Shakespeare's Last Plays* (London, 1975). In some ways a sturdy empiricist, who denied having any method, and claimed to be concerned simply with the texts, her approach was essentially intuitive when it came to interpreting those texts and relating them to one another. Her greatest strength lay in the combination of a concern for the documents with an almost visionary historical imagination. UPB

Yeats, William Butler (b. Dublin, Ireland, UK [now Irish Republic], 13.6.1865; d. Roquebrune, Alpes-Maritimes, France, 28.1.1939). Irish poet. Yeats enjoyed many honours in his lifetime, including the Nobel prize for literature in 1923. Since his death his life and works have been the object of virtually uninterrupted critical attention. He remains among the three or four masters of modern literature. Born into a Protestant Irish family, he grew up in Dublin and in London, only to return to Ireland in his late adolescence, entranced by its myths, legends and folkways. His literary career began in London, where with Ernest Rhys he founded the Rhymers' Club. His first poems were marked by a fascination with the occult and Celtic myth, and by a delicate precision of style. Returning to Dublin in 1896, his feelings for Ireland deepened to the point where he could be described as a Fenian. In collaboration with Lady Gregory, Yeats threw himself into the creation of an Irish literary theatre, and was at the centre of the Irish literary revival. After the turn of the century, Yeats's verse became harsher as he sought a more ironic and epigrammatical style. His agonized relationship with Maud Gonne, a fiery Irish patriot, transformed his preoccupation with mysticism into a broader social awareness. Ezra POUND detected a new note in Yeats with 'No Second Troy' in *The Green Helmet and Other Poems* (London, 1910), and with the appearance of *Responsibilities* (London, 1914). Yeats's attention now turned to politics and civic matters, the waking world of affairs, as opposed to the dream-world of myth and aesthetic reverie. He never lost his conviction that such things had an important place in the nourishment of art, and remained a conservative in his belief in a landed aristocracy as the true preservers of tradition. Yeats never came to terms with a modernizing industrial world. His great strength as a poet lay in his power of symbolic expression. He seized upon myths, and invented his own, in pursuit of a view of man's nature and of human history. The sources for his thought are comically eclectic, and the description of the pattern of his myth in *A Vision* (London, 1925) is one of the strangest books of the century. But such things had their uses for the poet, as was made clear in *The Tower* (London, 1928) and *The Winding Stair* (NY, 1929). Here Yeats transformed the idiosyncratic nature of his philosophy into art. The tragic violence of Irish history gave a particular energy to his verse, but his finest poems look to classical myth and history for parallels and structure. In 'Sailing to Byzantium' he contrasts the 'monuments of unageing intellect', the

perfections of art, with the 'sensual music' of youth, whose world is far behind him. Old age gave Yeats a hunger for life which was a new departure. In 'Among School Children' he came closest to embodying his view of humankind in a questioning openness before the unresolved antinomies of life and thought.   EH

J. Hone, *W. B. Yeats 1865–1939* (London, 1943); H. Bloom, *Yeats* (NY, 1970).

Yevtushenko, Yevgeny Aleksandrovich (b. Zima, nr Irkutsk, USSR, 18.7.1933). Soviet poet who belongs to the tradition of 'civic', socially committed poetry; his great ambition was to become the spokesman for his whole generation. He was educated at the Moscow Literary Institute (1951–4). His first collection of poems *Razvedchiki gryadushchevo* [Prospectors of the future] (Moscow, 1952) revealed the influence of MAYAKOVSKY, without his strength and conviction. Among later volumes *Stikhi raznykh let* [Poems of various years] (Moscow, 1959) and *Vzmakh ruki* [A wave of the hand] (Moscow, 1962) show his interest in the key issues of the day. He achieved enormous popularity during the early days of the KRUSHCHEV 'thaw' as the representative voice of a vast army of young people. His courageous denunciations of STALINism *Nasledniki Stalina* [Heirs of Stalin] in *Pravda* (October 1962) made his name famous throughout the world. But he failed to justify these hopes of his generation just as the period itself failed to realize them. He in fact never touched upon the 'forbidden themes'. Even in his famous poem 'Babi Yar' (1961), he condemned a Nazi crime, not a Soviet one. Perhaps the more personal and lyrical side of his talent is more likely to survive than are his 'sensational' poems, since his 'civic protest' often degenerates into rhetoric. There is almost an excess of clarity in his verse, an absence of suggestiveness and mystery. As a pre-eminently public poet he appeals mainly to the 'simple people', and tends to simplify his poetic language and imagery. Even in his best poems *Stantsiya Zima* [Zima junction] (Moscow, 1956) he shuns complex metaphors and experimental versification. His collection *Ottsovsky Slukh* (Moscow, 1978; tr. A. Boyars & S. Franklin, *The Face Behind the Face*, London, 1979) appeared to show that he succeeded where Mayakovsky had failed in creating 'poetry for all': his poems have become comprehensible for everybody, and have therefore ceased to be poetry. He has persistently emphasized the many faces of his 'self' and the versatility of his poetry, but the more he changed the more obviously his poetry stayed the same. He himself is under no illusions: quite recently he virtually abandoned poetry for prose and published *Talant est' chudo nesluchainoe* [Talent is a miracle coming not by chance] (Moscow, 1980) and *Tochka opory* [Fulcrum] (Moscow, 1981). For English translations see *Selected Poetry* (intro. R. Milner-Gulland, London, 1964); *Selected Poems* (tr. P. Levi & R. Milner-Gulland, London, 1962).   VP

G. Reavey, *The Poetry of Y. Yevtushenko* (London, 1966); A. Sinyavsky, 'In defence of Pyramid', in *For Freedom of Imagination* (NY, 1971).

Young, John Zachary (b. Bristol, Avon, UK, 18.3.1907). British neurologist. Young trained in the Oxford school of zoology but his research, although based first there (1931–45) and later at University College London, where he was professor of anatomy (1945–74), was carried out largely at the Zoological Station in Naples and the Marine Biological Laboratory in Portsmouth. His research on the nerve fibres, nerves and nervous systems of animals has been of great importance to modern neurology. His early work on giant nerve fibres in squids paved the way for crucial experiments upon which our understanding of the conduction of nerve impulses rests. His analysis of brain and behaviour in the octopus made that animal classical material for the synthesis of structure and higher function in the nervous system. His work can be approached through *The Memory System of the Brain* (Oxford, 1966) and *The Anatomy of the Nervous System of Octopus vulgaris* (Oxford, 1971). Young's wider interests are reflected in his Reith lectures on *Doubt and Certainty in Science* (Oxford, 1951) and in a series of masterly texts, *The Life of Vertebrates* (Oxford, 1951), *The Life of Mammals* (Oxford, 1957), and *An Introduction to the Study of Man* (Oxford, 1971).   DRN

Young, Lester Willis (b. Woodville, Miss., USA, 27.8.1909; d. New York, 15.3.1959). American tenor-saxophonist of the 'swing era' who influenced many jazz musicians in the 1940s and 1950s. After playing in King OLIVER's band, Young joined Count BASIE. His playing attracted wide interest and in 1934 he joined Fletcher Henderson's band (replacing HAWKINS). Henderson urged Young to adjust his style because his light tone and minimal vibrato were so unlike Hawkins's work, but he refused to compromise, and later rejoined Basie. Young's recording debut in 1936 was widely acclaimed. His saxophone playing was quite novel and he improvised totally new phrases: his consecutive recordings of the same tune reveal his unusual powers of variation. Young excelled at accompanying vocalists, and his backings to singer Billie Holiday are perfect; his rare excursions on clarinet are almost as original as his saxophone playing. The *joie de vivre* of Young's playing in the 1930s rarely appears in recordings from later decades (his service in the US army in WW2 proved lastingly traumatic). His work greatly influenced many tenor-saxophonists (e.g. Stan Getz and Zoot Sims) and echoes of his playing can also be heard in the alto-saxophone styles of Lee Konitz and Paul Desmond.   JJC

Yukawa, Hideki (b. Tokyo, Japan, 23.1.1907; d. Kyoto, 8.9.1981). Japanese physicist educated at Osaka University. In 1935 he proposed that the force between nucleons (protons and neutrons) was of a new type, the strong interaction, and that to account for its short range a new particle, the meson, was required. This particle, the π meson (or pion), was found in 1947 and recognized as the mediator of the strong interaction. Today all forces, strong, electromagnetic, weak and gravitational, are regarded as having mediating particles associated with them. This idea, together with FEYNMAN's description of the processes, forms the basis for modern views of particle interactions. Yukawa was awarded a Nobel prize in 1949. **RJC**

Z

Zamenhof, Ludwik Lejzer (b. Białystok, Grodno, Russia [now Poland], 15.12.1859; d. Warsaw, 14.4.1917). Polish philologist and creator of Esperanto. Born to Jewish parents in an area ruled by Russians but peopled by speakers of Polish and German, Zamenhof became convinced at a very young age that a common language would remove the causes of national and race hatreds. After qualifying as an oculist, he devoted his time to developing his original idea, and in 1887 published *Lingvo Internacia* (Warsaw; *Dr Esperanto's International Tongue*, Warsaw, 1888) setting out the grammar, pronunciation and some 900 roots of words for a *'lingvo internacia'*. This language, now known as Esperanto ['hoping one'], is a synthesis of elements from various European languages, and remains the most popular artificial language, having more than 100,000 speakers. Since 1887 its vocabulary has been greatly expanded, and over 10,000 books and numerous periodicals have appeared in it. Although fairly easy for speakers of most European languages, some features of its grammar, pronunciation and script make it less than ideal as a true world language. Given its date and place of origin, Esperanto was a great step forward in artificial languages; given its failings, its greater popularity than more elegant successors such as Ido or Novial is surprising.   WSD

Zamyatin, Yevgeniy Ivanovich (b. Lebedyan', Tambov, Russia, 1.2.1884; d. Paris, France, 10.3.1937). Russian short-story writer, novelist, dramatist and critic. A naval engineer, Zamyatin made his literary debut in 1908 as a follower of Leskov and REMIZOV, combining the 'ornamental' prose of these writers with irony and satire reminiscent of Gogol and Saltykov-Shchedrin. The setting for his early work is provided by the stagnant backwater of provincial Russia: *Uyezdnoye* [District tales] (London, 1913). A temporary stay in the UK during WW1 prompted scathing stories

about English life *Ostrovityane* [The islanders] (Petrograd, 1918). By nature a nonconformist, Zamyatin became a Bolshevik before the revolution, but left the party soon after it. He exercised considerable influence among younger Soviet writers, especially the 'fellow-travelling' group of the 'Serapion Brothers' which included Zoshchenko, Fedin, Kaverin and Tikhonov. He also supported the 'formalist' school of literary criticism temporarily led by SHKLOVSKY and Zhirmunsky. During the 1920s Zamyatin's opposition to the Soviet regime became more pronounced and he joined the 'inner emigration': those intellectuals, writers and poets (such as the high-priest of the 'decadents', SOLOGUB) who remained in Russia but stood aloof from the postrevolutionary order, or actively opposed it. Hostility to the revolution is expressed in such stories as *Peshchera* [The cave] (London, 1923) and, even more, in *Vzroslym detyam skazky* [Tales for adult children] published in Russia in the early 1920s. A gift for description and a controlled but whimsical scepticism is blended with a preference for gruesome episodes. He fought against any threat to his independence. He resigned from the Writers' Union and asked STALIN to allow him to emigrate. The request was granted in 1932. Zamyatin lived and died in Paris in extreme misanthropy, embittered by the follies of the émigré environment. His most important fictional work is the utopian-anti-utopian novel about a mechanized, regimented future, *My* (tr. G. Zilboorg, *We*, NY, 1925; first Russian edition, NY, 1953), which was only partly published in Russia and discredited him for good with the Soviet authorities. It represents a cruel satire on the standardizing tendencies in Russian life as Zamyatin saw it at the time and is a schematic, fanciful compound of Dostoevsky's Grand Inquisitor, Shigalev (in *The Possessed*), and 'The Man from the Underworld', who jeers at a planned future. The novel was a prototype for Aldous HUXLEY's *Brave New World* and

ORWELL's *1984*. Zamyatin was a highly talented social journalist, with a remarkable picturesque narrative skill, but hardly an artist and quite innocent of psychological insight. Apart from anticipating Huxley and Orwell, his importance lies in his literary criticism, which is sharp and stimulating. M. Ginsburg has translated *The Dragon: Fifteen Stories by Yevgeny Zamyatin* (NY, 1966) and has edited and translated *A Soviet Heretic: Essays by Yevgeny Zamyatin* (Chicago, 1970).   EL

Zavattini, Cesare (b. Luzzara, Emilia-Romagna, Italy, 20.9.1902). Italian screen writer. A former journalist and writer of children's stories – one of which eventually became *Miracolo a Milano* (*Miracle in Milan*, 1950) – Zavattini wrote or coscripted about 100 films in all, from the 1930s through to the 1970s. His outstanding work is that undertaken with DE SICA in the early postwar years and including such key neorealist films as *Sciusca* (*Shoeshine*, 1946), *Ladri di Bicicletta* (*Bicycle Thieves*, 1948) and *Umberto D* (1951). The collaboration between the two men was remarkably close and it is reasonable to regard Zavattini as coauthor in a full sense of the word. All his work of this period is rooted in a moral impulse related to the necessity of making people see the life around them, which for Italians had been buried for years by MUSSOLINI's rhetoric. For Zavattini the cinema's greatest strength lay in its 'original and innate capacity for showing things that we believe worth showing, as they happen day by day' (see *Sequences From a Cinematic Life*, Englewood Cliffs, 1969). Though he did not contribute to the theoretical basis of the neorealist movement in the early 1940s, he remained its most tenacious defender in the 1950s. He and De Sica resumed conventional commercial film making – built around colour, exciting stories and acted performances by star players – but Zavattini continued to advocate an austere cinema for which neorealism would be only the first stage. His ideal was a film which would show a man's life as it is revealed in a simple incident (an example he gave was buying a pair of shoes), in real time, without contrivance or acting. The technical implications of this – refusal of conventional division of roles, professional actors and fictionalized stories – form a striking anticipation and justification of early 1960s *cinéma-vérité* filming.   RPA

Zeeman, Pieter (b. Zonnemaire, Zeeland, The Netherlands, 25.5.1865; d. Amsterdam, 9.10.1943). Dutch physicist. The discovery of the effect which bears his name was announced in 1896, following theoretical prediction, and he shared with H. A. LORENTZ, who gave a classical interpretation of the observations, the second Nobel prize for physics (1902). The energy levels of atoms and molecules respond to applied magnetic fields and the effects, although small, may be observed in their optical spectra. The interaction between an applied magnetic field and the magnetic moment arising either from the orbital motion of an unpaired electron in an atom or ion or from its intrinsic moment leads to the separation of energy levels and to changes in the characteristics of polarization of the radiation according as one observes parallel or perpendicular to the direction of the magnetic field. Some simple atomic cases can be interpreted in terms of classical theory, but more general treatments require quantum mechanical theory, which recognizes that the magnetogyric ratio for electron spin should be about twice that for the orbital motion of electrons. The Zeeman effect is of crucial importance in the characterization of the energy states of open-shell atoms and ions, for the splitting and characteristics of polarization enable the inner quantum numbers for both upper and lower states to be determined. It would be impossible to analyse the spectra of transition metals without observations of the Zeeman effect. Electron spin resonance and nuclear magnetic resonance exemplify the Zeeman effects of unpaired electrons and of nuclei, while recent experiments include those in which a selected transition of a (gaseous) paramagnetic radical is shifted into resonance with a nearby fixed laser frequency by applications of a magnetic field. Zeeman's discovery, which links electricity, magnetism and the spatial orientation of elementary magnets in a field, has proved to be of major significance both in physics and in chemistry. RFB

Zhdanov, Andrey Aleksandrovich (b. Russia, 1896; d. Moscow, USSR, 31.8.1948). One of STALIN's chief lieutenants in the dictatorship which was established over the Soviet Union. Zhdanov first came into prominence during the purges (1936–8) when Stalin eliminated the surviving Old Bolsheviks and replaced them with men who owed everything to his favour. Zhdanov succeeded KIROV in the key post of party boss of Leningrad (1937–45), becoming a full member of the Politburo in 1939. Much relied upon by Stalin in party affairs, in 1946 he replaced Malenkov as the dictator's right-hand man, a position which he held until his death from heart disease in 1948. Zhdanov is best remembered for *Zhdanovschchina* ['the Zhdanov time'] when he implemented with brutal methods Stalin's policy of rooting out alien western influences in Russian cultural and scientific life. The policy was endorsed by the Central Committee of the Communist party in a resolution drafted by Zhdanov and adopted on 14 August 1946. This was directed against two literary magazines castigated for publishing work by the satirist Zoshchenko and the poet AKHMATOVA. The two writers were expelled from the Union of Soviet Writers which was itself reorganized. From literature Zhdanov (who was an intelligent and well-read man, see his *Essays on Literature, Philosophy and Music*, London, 1950) broadened his attack to philosophy, the theatre, films, music (e.g. SHOSTAKOVICH) and science, demanding that all trace of western influence, or cosmopolitanism, should be eradicated. The campaign continued until Stalin's death in 1953, acquiring anti-Semitic overtones. ALCB

Ziegler, Karl (b. Helsa, nr Kassel, Hesse, Germany, 26.11.1898; d. Mülheim, N. Rhine-Westphalia, West Germany, 11.12.1973). German chemist. After graduating in chemistry at Marburg, Ziegler lectured at Frankfurt before going on to Heidelberg for 10 years. He left in 1936 on being offered, despite his antipathy to the political climate, the chair in chemistry at Halle. In 1943 he accepted the directorship of the Kaiser-Wilhelm Coal Research Institute at Mulheim where, being given a free hand, he was able to combine his brilliance as a chemist with his shrewd awareness of the technical potential of scientific discovery. His earlier work on trivalent carbon and many-membered rings was complemented by a special interest in organometallic compounds which, in 1953, led, in particular, to a low-pressure polymerization process for polyethylene, a commodity plastic. For this, in 1963, he was awarded the Nobel prize, jointly with NATTA, who had extended the use of Ziegler catalysts to stereospecific polymerization. RPS

Zinovyev, Grigory Yevseyevich, ps. of O. G. Radomylsky (b. Yelizavetgrad [now Kirovograd], Ukraine, Russia, 11.9.1883; d. Moscow, USSR, 25.8.1936). Russian revolutionary and Communist leader. Zinovyev joined the Russian Soviet Democratic Workers party in 1901, and took LENIN's side in the split (1903) between the Bolshevik and Menshevik factions. After taking part in the 1905 revolution, he went into exile in Western Europe in 1908, becoming one of Lenin's closest collaborators and returning to Russia with him in April 1917. He opposed Lenin's proposal to seize power, but became one of the new regime's outstanding orators, a full member of the Politburo and chairman of the Communist International established in 1919, the last an office which made his name well known throughout the world. When Lenin became ill, Zinovyev formed a coalition with Kamenev and STALIN to prevent TROTSKY succeeding him. But when this had been accomplished, Stalin turned against his two allies (1925). Neither Zinovyev's control over the Leningrad party organization, nor his position in the Comintern, nor the alliance he formed with Trotsky in 1926, prevented Stalin from forcing him out of the Politburo and the Comintern and in 1927 out of the Communist party. Subsequently readmitted and twice expelled again, he was arrested in 1935, tried secretly for 'moral complicity' in the assassination of KIROV and condemned to 10 years' imprisonment. The following year he was retried in the first of the big purge trials staged by Stalin, found guilty on a fabricated charge of conspiracy, and executed.   ALCB

Zweig, Stefan (b. Vienna, Austria-Hungary [now Austria], 28.11.1881; naturalized British citizen, 1938; d. Petropolis, nr Rio de Janeiro, Brazil, 23.2.1942). Austrian/British essayist, biographer, dramatist, novelist and translator. He came from a family of wealthy industrialists and, for the rest of his life, retained a remarkable, Eurocentric cosmopolitanism as a result of his bourgeois education and extensive travel in Central and Western Europe, India, Africa, North and Central America and Russia. He studied modern languages and philosophy at the universities of Vienna and Berlin, which, together with his considerable talent for empathy, accounts for his skills as a translator of Baudelaire, Verhaeren, Rolland, Suarès, Barbusse and PIRANDELLO. During WW1 he worked in the archives of the Austrian War Office, then moved to Zürich in 1917–18 when his pacifist convictions became clear. These are evident in his much-performed play at that time *Jeremias* (1917; tr. E. & C. Paul, *Jeremiah: a Drama in Nine Scenes*, NY, 1922). Between 1919 and 1934 Zweig lived mainly in Salzburg. When German Nazism became oppressive he moved to England. After a triumphant lecture tour in South America he settled in Petropolis, only to find that his feelings of loneliness and isolation became overwhelming. Weighed down by the thought that Europe, even in the event of an Allied victory, would be permanently scarred by the atrocities of fascism he took his own life. Zweig was an extraordinarily prolific writer, capable of a subtle musicality of style, as his work as a librettist for Richard STRAUSS in the early 1930s shows. His prose excels in psychologically sensitive portrayals of character, whether fictional or factual. His admiration for and friendship with FREUD clearly left its mark on him. His most important works are the collection of essays *Die Baumeister der Welt. Versuch einer Typologie des Geistes*, vol. 1,

Drei Meister. Balzac, Dickens, Dostojewski; vol. 2, *Der Kampf mit den Dämonen. Hölderlin, Kleist, Nietzsche*; vol. 3, *Drei Dichter ihres Lebens. Casanova, Stendhal, Tolstoi* (Leipzig, 1920–8; tr. E. & C. Paul, *Master Builders: an Attempt at the Typology of the Spirit*, London, 1930); *Sternstunden der Menschheit* (Leipzig, 1927; tr. E. & C. Paul, *The Tide of Fortune*, London, 1940), a small volume of five historical miniatures; and *Die Welt von Gestern*, (London, 1942; tr. *The World of Yesterday. An Autobiography*, London, 1943). Most of the rest of his work is available in English translation.   WvdW

R. J. Klawitter, *Stefan Zweig: a Bibliography* (Chapel Hill, NC, 1965); D. A. Prater, *European of Yesterday: a Biography of Stefan Zweig* (Oxford, 1972).

Zwicky, Fritz (b. Varna, Bulgaria, 14.2.1898; d. Pasadena, Calif., USA, 8.2.1974). Swiss astronomer. Zwicky was of Swiss parentage, and although he worked in the USA for most of his life he retained his Swiss nationality. Educated at Zürich University, he went as a theoretical physicist to the California Institute of Technology in 1927, becoming successively assistant and associate professor of theoretical physics, and then professor of astrophysics until his retirement in 1968. Astronomy was only one of his many interests and activities. He was an engineer and a philosopher, and was guided in his astronomical research by his philosophical views. These are expressed in his *Morphological Astronomy* (NY, 1957) which is an expression of his 1948 Halley lecture at Oxford. An example of his insight is his prediction in 1934 of the existence of neutron stars, which were discovered many years later by radio astronomers as pulsars. He was one of the first few astronomers to realize the potentialities of the newly invented Schmidt camera, and between 1936 and 1940 developed an 18-in instrument which he set up on Palomar Mountain. In spite of its small size this proved very successful. With it Zwicky discovered 18 supernovae in galaxies, determining their light curves and even obtaining the spectra of some of them. His discoveries of these rather rare phenomena represent a significant fraction of all of the supernovae presently known. In his later years Zwicky contributed much to the study of galaxies, particularly clusters of galaxies, multiple galaxies and the bridges of matter that sometimes connect their components. His six-volume catalogue of galaxies is a classical work in this field.

DEB

Classified Index

Césaire, A.
Char, R.
Claudel, P.
Cocteau, J.
Colette, S. G.
Drieu La Rochelle, P.
Duras, M.
Eluard, P.
Genet, J.
Gide, A.-P.-G.
Giono, J.
Giraudoux, J.
Ionesco, E.
Jarry, A.
Jouve, P. J.
Malraux, A.
Martin du Gard, R.
Mauriac, F.
Montherlant, H. M. de
Péguy, C.
Ponge, F. J. G. A.
Prévert, J.
Proust, M.
Queneau, R.
Reverdy, P.
Robbe-Grillet, A.
Romains, J.
Saint-Exupéry, M.-A.-R. de
Saint-John Perse
Simenon, G.
Tournier, M.
Tzara, T.
Valéry, P. A.
Vian, B.

ITALIAN
Buzzati, D.
Calvino, I.
Campana, D.
D'Annunzio, G.
Fo, D.
Gadda, C. E.
Lampedusa, G. T. di
Malaparte, C.
Marinetti, E. F. T.
Montale, E.
Moravia, A.
Papini, G.
Pavese, C.
Pirandello, L.
Pratolini, V.
Quasimodo, S.
Sciascia, L.
Silone, I.
Svevo, I.
Ungaretti, G.
Vittorini, E.

SPANISH (inc. South American)
Alberti, R.
Aleixandre, V.
Arrabal, F.
Asturias, M. A.
Azorin
Baroja y Nessi, P.
Borges, J. L.
Cardenal, E.
Carpentier, A.
Cela, C. J.
Cernuda, L.
Cortázar, J.
Fuentes, C.
García Márquez, G.
Guillén, J.
Guillén, N.
Hernández, M.
Jiménez, J. R.
Lorca, F. G.
Machado, A.
Miró, G.
Mistral, G.
Neruda, P.
Paz, O.
Rulfo, J.
Salinas, P.
Unamuno, M. de
Valle-Inclán, R. M. del
Vallejo, C.
Vargas Llosa, M.

PORTUGUESE (inc. Brazilian)
Amado, J.
Cabral, J. de M. N.
Castro, J. M. F. de
Cortesão, J. Z.
Meireles, C.
Monteiro, D. P.
Namora, F.
Pessoa, F. A. N.
Ramos, G.
Sena, J. de
Sérgio, A.
Torga, M.

RUSSIAN
Akhmatova, A. A.
Babel', I. E.
Bely, A.
Blok, A. A.
Brodsky, I.
Bulgakov, M. A.
Bunin, I. A.
Chekhov, A. P.
Ehrenburg, I. G.
Esenin, S. A.

Balthus
Beckmann, M.
Bertoia, H.
Beuys, J.
Boccioni, U.
Bomberg, D.
Bonnard, P.
Brancusi, C.
Braque, G.
Calder, A.
Cézanne, P.
Chagall, M.
Chirico, G. de
Dali, S.
Davis, S.
Delaunay, R.
Derain, A.
Dix, O.
Doesburg, T. van
Dubuffet, J.-P.-A.
Duchamp, M.
Dufy, R.
Ensor, J. S.
Epstein, J.
Ernst, M.
Gabo, N.
Gaudier-Brzeska, H.
Giacometti, A.
González, J.
Gorky, A.
Gris, J.
Grosz, G. E.
Guston, P.
Hamilton, R.
Hepworth, J. B.
Hockney, D.
Hofmann, H.
Hopper, E.
Johns, J.
Kandinsky, W.
Kirchner, E. L.
Kitaj, R. B.
Klee, P.
Klein, Y.
Klimt, G.
Kline, F.
Kokoschka, O.
Kooning, W. de
Kossoff, L.
Larionov, M.
Léger, F.
Lipchitz, J. C. J.
Magritte, R.-F.-G.
Malevich, K.
Marc, F.
Masson, A.
Matisse, H.

Matta Echaurren, R. S. A.
Miró, J.
Modigliani, A.
Mondrian, P.
Monet, C.
Moore, H.
Morandi, G.
Motherwell, R.
Munch, E.
Nash, P.
Neizvestny, E. I.
Newman, B.
Nicholson, B.
Nolde, E. H.
Oldenburg, C.
Orozco, J. C.
Ozenfant, A.
Picabia, F.
Picasso, P. R. y
Pollock, J.
Rauschenberg, R.
Reinhardt, A.
Renoir, P. A.
Rivera, D. M.
Rodchenko, A. M.
Rodin, A.
Rothko, M.
Rouault, G.
Rousseau, H.
Schiele, E.
Schlemmer, O.
Schmidt-Rottluff, K.
Schwitters, K.
Shahn, B.
Sickert, W. R.
Smith, D. R.
Soulages, P.
Spencer, S.
de Staël, N.
Stokes, A. D.
Sutherland, G. V.
Tàpies, A.
Tatlin, V. E.
Utrillo, M.
Vasarely, V.
Vlaminck, M.
Vuillard, J. E.
Warhol, A.

DECORATIVE AND INDUSTRIAL ARTS
(inc. pottery, design, fashion,
typography)
Carder, F.
Chanel, G.
Coper, H.
Daley, W.
Dior, C.

THE HUMANITIES

HISTORY

CLASSIFIED INDEX

Ramsey, F. P.
Tarski, A.
Thom, R. F.
Tukey, J. W.
Von Neumann, J.
Weil, A.
Weyl, H.

PHYSICAL SCIENCES

PHYSICS
Appleton, E. V.
Auger, P. V.
Bardeen, J.
Bernal, J. D.
Bethe, H. A.
Blackett, P. M. S.
Bloch, F.
Bohr, A. N.
Bohr, N. H. D.
Boltzmann, L. E.
Born, M.
Bragg, W. H.
Bragg, W. L.
Bridgman, P. W.
de Broglie, L. V. P. R.
Chadwick, J.
Cockcroft, J. D.
Compton, A. H.
Cowley, J. M.
Curie, M. and P.
Davisson, C. J.
Debye, P. J. W.
Dirac, P. A. M.
Duhem, P. M. M.
Ehrenfest, P.
Einstein, A.
Fermi, E.
Feynman, R. P.
Frisch, O. R.
Gabor, D.
Gell-Mann, M.
Germer, L. H.
Gibbs, J. W.
Glaser, D. A.
Glashow, S. L.
Goudsmit, S. A.
Hawking, S. W.
Heisenberg, W.
Heitler, W. H.
Herzberg, G.
Hodgkin, D. C.
Hückel, E.
Ioffe, A. F.
Jeans, J. H.
Joliot-Curie, I. and J. F.
Kamerlingh Onnes, H.

Kapitza, P. L.
Kastler, A.
Kramers, H. A.
Lamb, W. E. Jr
Landau, L. D.
Langevin, P.
Laue, Max T. F. von
Lawrence, E. O.
Lee, T.-D.
Lindemann, F. A.
Lodge, O. J.
London, F. W. and H.
Lorentz, H. A.
Mach, E.
Marconi, G.
McMillan, E. M.
Meitner, L.
Moseley, H. G. J.
Mössbauer, R. L.
Mott, N. F.
Néel, L.
Oliphant, M. L. E.
Onsager, L.
Oppenheimer, J. R.
Pauli, W. E.
Peierls, R. E.
Perrin, J. B.
Planck, M. K. E. L.
Powell, C. F.
Rabi, I. I.
Raman, C. V.
Rayleigh, J. W. S
Richter, B.
Röentgen, W. C.
Rutherford, E.
Sakharov, A. D.
Salam, A.
Schottky, W. H.
Schrödinger, E.
Shockley, W. B.
Sommerfeld, A.
Stern, O.
Szilard, L.
Taylor, G. I.
Teller, E.
Thomson, G. P.
Thomson, J. J.
Uhlenbeck, G. E.
Van Vleck, J. H.
van der Waals, J. D.
Weber, J.
Weinberg, S.
Wheeler, J. A.
Wigner, E. P.
Wilson, C. T. R.
Yukawa, H.
Zeeman, P.